THE NEW

Child
Health
Encyclopedia

Emergency Telephone Numbers

DOCTOR

_____

POISON CONTROL CENTER

_____

HOSPITAL

_____

DRUGGIST

_____

FIRE DEPARTMENT

_____

POLICE

_____

AMBULANCE

_____

For information on first aid and emergency action see Part III, pages 117–144.

Emergencies

Boston Children's Hospital

THE NEW

Child Health Encyclopedia

The Complete Guide for Parents

Frederick H. Lovejoy, Jr., M.D.
Medical Editor

David Estridge
Executive Editor

A DELTA BOOK/MERLOYD LAWRENCE

A DELTA BOOK/MERLOYD LAWRENCE
Published by
Dell Publishing Co., Inc.
1 Dag Hammarskjold Plaza
New York, New York 10017

For information address: Delacorte Press/Merloyd Lawrence, New York, New York.
Delta ® TM 755118, Dell Publishing Co., Inc.

November 1987
10 9 8 7 6 5 4 3 2 1

A hardcover edition of this book is available from Delacorte Press,
  1 Dag Hammarskjold Plaza, New York, New York 10017.

Library of Congress Cataloging in Publication Data

The new child health encyclopedia.
  "A Merloyd Lawrence book."
  Includes index.
    1. Pediatrics—Popular works. 2. Children—Health and hygiene. I. Lovejoy, Frederick H. II. Estridge, David. III. Children's Hospital (Boston, Mass.)
RJ61.N389 1987   618.92   87-6809
ISBN 0-385-29541-3 (Delacorte)
ISBN 0-385-29597-9 (Delta pbk.)

*Dedicated to the memory
and spirit of Colleen M. Maxwell*

MEDICAL CONSULTANTS

MILTON H. ALPER, M.D.
Anesthesiologist-in-Chief

SUSANA R. ALVAREZ, M.D.
Formerly Medical Director, Martha Eliot Health Center

DONNA M. AMBROSINO, M.D.
Assistant in Medicine (Infectious Diseases)

CONSTANTINE S. ANAST, M.D.
Director of Laboratories (Endocrinology)

MARY ELLEN AVERY, M.D.
Formerly Physician-in-Chief

IRVING W. BAILIT, M.D.
Associate in Medicine (Immunology)

SUSAN S. BAKER, M.D., Ph.D.
Formerly Assistant in Medicine (Gastroenterology and Nutrition)

CHARLES F. BARLOW, M.D.
Neurologist-in-Chief

PATRICIA BARTOSHESKY
Formerly Seat Belt Coordinator, Highway Safety Bureau, Commonwealth of
Massachusetts

ANTHONY S. BASHIR, Ph.D.
Speech Pathologist (Hearing and Speech)

JONATHAN BATES, M.D.
Formerly Senior Associate in Medicine (Ambulatory Medicine)

STUART B. BAUER, M.D.
Assistant in Surgery (Urology)

WILLIAM R. BEARDSLEE, M.D.
Associate in Psychiatry

DIANA J. S. BEARDSLEY, M.D.
Formerly Assistant in Medicine (Hematology and Oncology)

WILLIAM BERENBERG, M.D.
Chief, Services to Handicapped Children

DONALD M. BERWICK, M.D.
Assistant in Medicine

WILLIAM G. BITHONEY, M.D.
Assistant in Medicine (Ambulatory Medicine)

PRESTON R. BLACK, M.D.
Assistant in Surgery

YVES R. BOREL, M.D.
Senior Associate in Medicine (Immunology)

T. BERRY BRAZELTON, M.D.
Chief, Child Development Unit

PHILIP BREITFELD, M.D.
Assistant in Medicine (Hematology and Oncology)

JAN L. BRESLOW, M.D.
Formerly Chief, Division of Metabolism

MICHAEL J. BRESNAN, M.D. (deceased)
Formerly Associate Chief of Neurology

ELIZABETH R. BROWN, M.D.
Formerly Associate in Medicine (Newborn Medicine)

JANE C. BURNS, M.D.
Assistant in Medicine (Infectious Diseases)

LLOYD M. CAIRNS, M.D.
Formerly Research Fellow in Medicine (Immunology)

THRASSOS CALLIGAS, M.D.
Fellow in Psychiatry

ALDO R. CASTANEDA, M.D.
Surgeon-in-Chief; Cardiovascular Surgeon-in-Chief

CLAIRE CHAFEE-BAHAMON
Formerly Coordinator, Planning and Evaluation, Massachusetts Poison Control
System

WILLIAM D. COCHRAN, M.D.
Senior Associate in Medicine (Newborn Medicine)

STEVEN D. COLAN, M.D.
Assistant in Cardiology

FRANCIS SESSIONS COLE, M.D.
Formerly Assistant in Medicine (Newborn Medicine)

ARNOLD H. COLODNEY, M.D.
Senior Associate in Surgery (Urology)

HARVEY R. COLTEN, M.D.
Formerly Chief, Division of Cell Biology (Cystic Fibrosis)

JOHN C. COOLIDGE, M.D.
Senior Associate in Psychiatry

JOHN F. CRIGLER, JR., M.D.
Chief, Division of Endocrinology

ALLEN C. CROCKER, M.D.
Chief, Developmental Evaluation Clinic

ROBERT K. CRONE, M.D.
Senior Associate in Anesthesia and in Medicine

CONSTANCE M. CROWLEY, R.N., P.N.P.
Nursing Program Director

CHESTER C. d'AUTREMONT, M.D.
Senior Associate in Psychiatry

DAVID RAY DeMASO, M.D.
Assistant in Psychiatry and Cardiology

HOWARD DUBOWITZ, M.D.
Formerly Assistant in Medicine (Ambulatory)

JAMES M. EASOM, PHARM.D.
Formerly Assistant Director, Massachusetts Poison Control System

JOHN B. EMANS, M.D.
Assistant in Orthopaedic Surgery

S. JEAN EMANS, M.D.
Associate Chief, Division of Adolescent and Young Adult Medicine

MICHAEL F. EPSTEIN, M.D.
Chief, Division of Newborn Medicine

ANGELO J. ERAKLIS, M.D.
Senior Associate in Surgery

RICHARD A. FERBER, M.D.
Assistant in Medicine and in Neurology

JOHN H. FISHER, M.D.
Senior Associate in Surgery

GARY R. FLEISHER, M.D.
Chief, Division of Emergency Medicine

ALEJANDRO F. FLORES, M.D.
Assistant in Medicine (Gastroenterology and Nutrition)

JUDAH M. FOLKMAN, M.D.
Director, Surgical Laboratories

ELLEN M. FRIEDMAN, M.D.
Assistant in Otolaryngology

H. HARRIS FUNKENSTEIN, M.D.
Director, Learning Disabilities, Department of Neurology

DONALD C. FYLER, M.D.
Associate Chief, Department of Cardiology

MARK C. GEBHARDT, M.D.
Assistant in Orthopaedic Surgery

RAIF S. GEHA, M.D.
Chief, Division of Immunology

DONALD A. GOLDMANN, M.D.
Senior Associate in Medicine (Infectious Diseases)

DONALD P. GOLDSTEIN, M.D.
Chief, Division of Gynecology

ALLEN M. GOORIN, M.D.
Assistant in Medicine (Hematology and Oncology)

JOHN W. GRAEF, M.D.
Associate in Medicine (Pharmacology and Toxicology)

RICHARD J. GRAND, M.D.
Formerly Chief, Division of Gastroenterology and Nutrition

PAUL P. GRIFFIN, M.D.
Formerly Orthopaedic Surgeon-in-Chief

RICHARD H. GROSS, M.D.
Associate in Orthopaedic Surgery

WARREN E. GRUPE, M.D.
Formerly Chief, Division of Nephrology

JOHN E. HALL, M.D.
Orthopaedic Surgeon-in-Chief

WILLIAM E. HARMON, M.D.
Chief, Division of Nephrology

GORDON P. HARPER, M.D.
Director of Inpatient Services, Department of Psychiatry

GERALD HASS, M.B., B.S.
Senior Associate in Medicine (Ambulatory Medicine)

PAMELA HAWLEY, M.S.
Genetics Associate

GERALD B. HEALY, M.D.
Otolaryngologist-in-Chief

W. HARDY HENDREN, M.D.
Chief, Department of Surgery

ROBERTA R. HENRY, R.D.
Director, Nutrition and Food Service

ALICE S. HUANG, Ph.D.
Director of Laboratories (Infectious Diseases)

JULIE R. INGELFINGER, M.D.
Associate in Medicine (Nephrology)

LEONARD B. KABAN, D.M.D., M.D.
Associate in Oral Surgery

AUBREY J. KATZ, M.D.
Associate in Medicine (Gastroenterology and Nutrition)

JOHN F. KEANE, M.D.
Senior Associate in Cardiology

SHERWIN V. KEVY, M.D.
Senior Associate in Medicine (Hematology and Oncology)

JOHN A. KIRKPATRICK, M.D.
Radiologist-in-Chief

PAULA KLANE, R.N.
Formerly Head Nurse, Emergency Room

BRUCE R. KORF, M.D.
Assistant in Neurology

CYNTHIA KRETSCHMAR, M.D.
Formerly Assistant in Medicine (Hematology and Oncology)

RUTH C. LAMBERT, R.N.
Clinical Director of Nursing

ANNE M. LANG, J.D.
Associate Director (Human Resources)

PETER LANG, M.D.
Associate in Cardiology

SAMUEL A. LATT, M.D., Ph.D.
Chief, Division of Genetics

DONALD Y. M. LEUNG, M.D., Ph.D.
Assistant in Medicine (Immunology)

RAPHAEL H. LEVEY, M.D.
Associate in Surgery

MELVIN D. LEVINE, M.D.
Formerly Chief, Division of Ambulatory Medicine

HARVEY L. LEVY, M.D.
Senior Associate in Medicine (Genetics)

CESARE T. LOMBROSO, M.D.
Senior Associate in Neurology

FREDERICK H. LOVEJOY, JR., M.D.
Associate Physician-in-Chief

SAMUEL E. LUX, M.D.
Chief, Division of Hematology and Oncology

FREDERICK MANDELL, M.D.
Senior Associate in Medicine

BRUCE J. MASEK, Ph.D.
Associate in Psychology

ROBERT P. MASLAND, JR., M.D.
Chief, Division of Adolescent and Young Adult Medicine

TREVOR J. McGILL, M.D.
Associate Otolaryngologist-in-Chief

KENNETH McINTOSH, M.D.
Clinical Chief, Division of Infectious Diseases

FRANCIS JOHN McLAUGHLIN, M.D.
Assistant in Medicine (Pulmonary Medicine)

LYLE J. MICHELI, M.D.
Associate in Orthopaedic Surgery

MICHAEL B. MILLIS, M.D.
Assistant in Orthopaedic Surgery

ALLEN A. MITCHELL, M.D.
Assistant in Medicine (Pharmacology and Toxicology)

JUDITH SURVEYER MITIGUY, R.N., M.S.
Coordinator of Preadmission Preparation Programs

JOHN MODLIN, M.D.
Formerly Assistant in Medicine (Infectious Diseases)

JOHN B. MULLIKEN, M.D.
Associate in Surgery (Plastic Surgery)

MARIETTE MURPHY, M.D.
Assistant in Medicine (Family Development Study)

JOSEPH E. MURRAY, M.D.
Senior Associate in Surgery (Plastic Surgery)

ALEXANDER S. NADAS, M.D.
Cardiologist-in-Chief, Emeritus

DAVID G. NATHAN, M.D.
Physician-in-Chief

HOWARD L. NEEDLEMAN, D.M.D.
Associate Dentist-in-Chief

ELI H. NEWBERGER, M.D.
Chief, Family Development Study

JANE W. NEWBURGER, M.D.
Associate in Cardiology

WILLIAM I. NORWOOD, M.D.
Formerly Senior Associate in Cardiovascular Surgery

EDWARD O'ROURKE, M.D.
Assistant in Medicine (Infectious Diseases)

JUDITH S. PALFREY, M.D.
Chief, Division of Ambulatory Medicine

DOROTHY A. PATTON, R.N.
Head Nurse, Clinical Research Center

JULIAN L. PEARLMAN, M.D.
Senior Associate in Medicine

ROBERT A. PETERSEN, M.D.
Senior Associate in Ophthalmology

EUGENE U. PIAZZA, M.D.
Associate in Psychiatry

ORAH S. PLATT, M.D.
Associate in Medicine (Hematology and Oncology)

CHARLES POPPER, M.D.
Formerly Assistant in Psychiatry

ALVIN F. POUSSAINT, M.D.
Senior Associate in Psychiatry

LEONARD A. RAPPAPORT, M.D.
Assistant in Medicine (Ambulatory Medicine)

JOEL M. RAPPEPORT, M.D.
Associate in Medicine (Hematology and Oncology)

ALAN B. RETIK, M.D.
Chief, Division of Urology

ARTHUR R. RHODES, M.D.
Formerly Chief, Division of Dermatology

JULIUS B. RICHMOND, M.D.
Director of Child Health Policy

RICHARD M. ROBB, M.D.
Ophthalmologist-in-Chief

FRED S. ROSEN, M.D.
Scientific Director, Cystic Fibrosis Center

ROBERT K. ROSENTHAL, M.D.
Associate in Orthopaedic Surgery

STEPHEN E. SALLAN, M.D.
Senior Associate in Medicine (Hematology and Oncology)

FRANK J. SANTOPIETRO, D.P.M.
Podiatrist, Division of Sports Medicine

SAMUEL R. SCHUSTER, M.D.
Senior Associate in Surgery

ROBERT C. SHAMBERGER, M.D.
Assistant in Surgery

JOHN SHILLITO, JR., M.D.
Associate Chief in Neurosurgery

BARRY T. S. SMITH, M.D.
Formerly Chief, Division of Newborn Medicine

CAROLYN SMITH, R.N.
Coordinator, Myelodysplasia Program

NORMAN P. SPACK, M.D.
Associate in Medicine (Adolescent and Young Adult Medicine)

ANN R. STARK, M.D.
Senior Associate in Medicine (Newborn Medicine)

LUDWIK S. SZYMANSKI, M.D.
Associate in Psychiatry

H. WILLIAM TAEUSCH, JR., M.D.
Formerly Chief, Division of Newborn Medicine

RITA L. TEELE, M.D.
Radiologist

ARTHUR W. TROTT, M.D.
Formerly Senior Associate in Orthopaedic Surgery

CAROLYN S. TURNER, Ph.D.
Clinical Supervisor, Child Development Unit

FRANK J. TWAROG, M.D.
Associate in Medicine (Immunology)

JOSEPH UPTON, M.D.
Assistant in Surgery (Plastic Surgery)

JOSEPH P. VACANTI, M.D.
Assistant in Surgery

PATRICIO F. VIVES, M.D.
Associate in Medicine (Ambulatory Medicine)

W. ALLAN WALKER, M.D.
Chief, Division of Gastroenterology and Nutrition

STANLEY WALZER, M.D.
Psychiatrist-in-Chief

HOWARD J. WEINSTEIN, M.D.
Associate in Medicine (Hematology and Oncology)

W. KEASLEY WELCH, M.D.
Formerly Neurosurgeon-in-Chief

HARLAND S. WINTER, M.D.
Associate in Medicine (Gastroenterology and Nutrition)

PAUL H. WISE, M.D., M.P.H.
Assistant in Medicine (Ambulatory Medicine)

MARY ELLEN WOHL, M.D.
Chief, Division of Pulmonary Medicine

JOSEPH I. WOLFSDORF, M.D.
Associate in Medicine (Endocrinology)

JOHN W. WOOD, M.D.
Formerly Senior Associate in Medicine (Genetics)

REGINA M. YANDO, Ph.D.
Formerly Chief, Division of Psychology

ALEXANDER ZISS, M.B.A.
Associate Director

Contents

Introduction

Since 1869 the mission of The Children's Hospital in Boston has been to provide the highest quality health care for children. The largest pediatric medical center in the nation, Boston Children's Hospital is an acknowledged leader in the treatment and prevention of every imaginable pediatric health problem—from those arising in the first minutes of life to those occurring during adolescence and early adulthood. Children's also engages in research that has helped to identify and cure innumerable diseases which once limited the length and quality of the lives of so many of our children. Moreover, as the primary pediatric teaching hospital of the Harvard Medical School, Children's has helped to train more pediatricians than any other teaching hospital in America.

As a pioneer and leader in pediatric health care, Children's Hospital recognizes a special, continuing obligation to share as widely as possible our experience in caring for healthy and sick children. By making health information in nontechnical language readily available to all who spend important parts of their lives with children, we hope to boost self-confidence in their substantial capacity to protect and improve child health. We believe that quality health care is every child's right and can be a reality wherever our readers live—in the inner city, a suburban town, or a small farming community.

Indeed, we are fortunate to live in an era when the growth of medical knowledge is accelerating and lifesaving medical technology keeps expanding. Simultaneously, a concerned public increasingly desires authoritative information about health care. Those who have a stake in the future of children, especially parents, relatives, teachers, and friends, want the most recent medical information—whether it be about caring for a growing baby, treating colds and flu effectively, learning about breakthroughs in surgery, or dealing with active teenagers.

We believe that the *New Child Health Encyclopedia* represents a major advance in helping satisfy this need for accurate information and reliable guidance. Well-informed parents become essential partners with physicians and nurses in caring for their child's health. This is especially important in the vital area of preventive medicine. Good health is no accident.

This book is divided into four parts:

Part One, "Keeping Children Healthy," provides a perspective from which parents can promote sound health practices from infancy through young adulthood. Knowledgeable parents come to understand their child as a unique, growing individual rather than focusing narrowly on a particular problem or symptom.

Part Two, "Finding Health Care for Children," describes how parents can take advantage of our health care system to enhance their child's health.

Part Three, "Emergencies," is a guide that shows how to handle the most common—and often the most serious—problems stemming from accidents or the sudden beginning or complication of an illness.

Part Four, "Diseases and Symptoms," provides a comprehensive guide to the entire spectrum of problems, common and rare, physical and emotional, that can affect children. Our aim throughout the researching and writing of these 289 entries has been to give parents a focused view of what they need to know to deal with illness in the home or, if need be, what to expect of health professionals when a child requires medical care.

The first three parts are designed to be read by every parent. Most of the entries in Part Four such as *Measles, Diabetes,* and *Sprains,* are intended to be read as needed. Others, such as *Colds, Fever, Drug Abuse,* and *Genetic Disorders Overview,* have much to offer the parent, or other reader who cares for children, as background for promoting and maintaining good health.

Professional writers from the Health Information Department have researched, composed, and edited all the material in this book. Members of the staff of Boston Children's Hospital have generously served as expert medical consultants for each entry as well as for all the other information. Our common aim is to help parents and other caregivers promote child health.

The working partnership between an informed public and the pediatric medical community is one that can only be enhanced by the publication of *New Child Health Encyclopedia.* And as our readers become increasingly familiar with the information presented here, we know that they will want to make good health and regular health care for all children a priority. In turn, the health and health care of children nationwide should be strengthened.

Frederick H. Lovejoy, Jr., M.D.
Associate Physician-in-Chief
Boston Children's Hospital

Part I
Keeping Children Healthy

1 | "Is My Child Normal?"

NOTE: Italicized words in the text refer to specific entries in Part IV.

Every child is "special." A subtle interplay between "nature," or genetic makeup, and "nurture," or environmental influences, makes each child a unique human being. At the same time, all children follow a generally similar path, a similar series of landmarks in growth and development. Information about these developments can be both exciting and comforting to new parents. It must be used carefully, however, because all babies differ in some respects from any theoretical ideal "average." A healthy child may exceed standards of growth and development in some areas and fall below standards in others. It is sensible, therefore, for new parents to worry less about what is "normal" and concentrate instead on noticing their own child's strengths and weaknesses. By encouraging children to cultivate strengths, parents are likely to help them compensate for—even overcome—weaknesses.

Rather than seeking rigid standards, it is more realistic and reassuring for parents to think about a "normal range" within which to consider a child's progress at any age or stage of development. Awareness of this "normal range" will make most parents feel more relaxed as they see that what their child is achieving or displaying falls within the range of what is normal for children of the same age. The few parents whose child's growth or behavior falls significantly outside this range are then alerted to seek help.

Growth can be defined broadly as the process of becoming physically larger and more mature; development as the process of becoming more complex, physically and mentally. Such a distinction is probably more descriptive than measurable, because growth and development are very much intertwined. Charts and graphs cannot be relied upon exclusively to show the level of growth and development of a child. In fact, as the child gets older and more complex, unique characteristics become more obvious and "average" figures become less helpful.

We hope the following general observations will help parents understand and enjoy the remarkable unfolding of mind and body in their own child. (See also chart on pp. 8–11.)

THE NEWBORN PERIOD

A baby does not enter the world a "blank slate"—without a history or predispositions. For many months the fetus has been growing and developing at a rate never to be equaled after birth. Toward the end of pregnancy the fetus has begun to sleep, wake up, and practice motor movements such as kicking. Hearing and sight have also developed, and the fetus is known to respond to sounds and bright lights.

During labor and delivery the baby is propelled from a comfortable, well-insulated resting place into a strange and startling environment. This process is usually so stimulating that the baby is quite alert immediately afterward. For a short time newborns are in a quiet, wide-eyed mood, ideal for the first encounter with their parents.

At birth the baby must make extraordinary adjustments. As newborns start to breathe on their own, they are likely to grunt and cough. Some babies appear blue briefly after being cut off from the mother's oxygen supply. It is also common for an infant to stop breathing for short periods of time, even up to 20 seconds. In some babies, muscle tone may be poor. Normally these conditions disappear within minutes as the newborn rapidly adjusts to the external world. (See discussion of newborn checkup in Chapter 6, "Going to the Doctor.")

An hour or so after birth, an infant is likely to fall asleep. As the baby slumbers, arms and legs may twitch. Upon awakening after another hour or so, the infant is likely to be more active than before and display a great range of exciting behavior: grasping and startling reflexes, crying, the "rooting" (nursing) reflex, stepping motions when held over a table or bed, and the turning of the head to follow sights and sounds.

BABYHOOD: FIRST YEAR

Although the development of parents' love for a child (also called bonding, or attachment) can begin very shortly after birth and progress during the first few weeks of life, it often takes weeks or months for parents and baby to adjust to one another. Dialogue between adult and infant develops gradually.

At first, just figuring out what it is that a new baby wants can be intricate. A baby's communication signals are quite subtle, but they are present and available for adults—especially parents—to tune in to. The early weeks of life could be considered a time of attuning as parents learn to read their baby's cues: eyes widening and brightening, looking away, or glazing over; face softening as the baby grows alert to visual stimuli and focuses on a face, a voice, or an object; skin turning pale or rosy; yawning; hiccuping; spitting up; or even having a bowel movement when excited or overstimulated by what is going on in the immediate vicinity.

Parents need to be alert and patient during the first few months as their baby slowly begins to form familial bonds. An infant coos and babbles spontaneously, as well as displaying other behavior, such as rounding the lips or opening and closing the hands.

Although some babies smile right from birth, most babies do not become responsive until the age of 2 or 3 months. By about the fourth month many babies are cooing reciprocally with parents. Imitation of parents' vocalizing usually occurs about the age of 6 or 7 months. Over the first 6 months an infant gradually realizes that the parents are special caregivers.

Throughout infancy, babies cry frequently—and loudly. Crying is one of the many ways babies have of expressing themselves. Paying attention to crying and comforting the baby does not "spoil" the child. In fact, attention and comfort are vitally important reinforcing bonds between parent and child, encouraging later communication and fostering the emergence of self-esteem and trust.

Sometimes periodic crying late in the day can concern parents by its timing (often the hectic supper time) and by the inconsolability of the infant (see *colic*). The crying period may be the result of digestive adjustments to feeding or simply may be a discharge of accumulated excitement to the nervous system. If a baby is dry, recently fed, burped, and still cries, there may be a need to release pent-up energy. When a crying episode is exhausted, the child often falls deeply asleep.

Attending to a baby's needs may seem to require endless energy and patience. At the same time, the rewards of watching the baby's development can be limitless. During the first year of life, a baby is growing and developing—and, thereby, learning—at a phenomenally rapid rate. Babies make significant advances during this time. For example:

- controlling of attention
- sharpening of vision and hearing
- movement control
- eating and growing
- early communication skills

THE TODDLER: ONE TO THREE

When children begin to walk, or toddle, their newfound mastery of their world gives them enormous fuel for exploration. Nothing seems too difficult for a toddler to try—usually over and over again! Parents spend untold energy and time in pursuit of the adventurous toddler.

The most important tasks in children's first years have to do with establishing attachment to their parents, and then learning how to separate from them, and then beginning to find and model their own personalities, their individual identities.

"Separation anxiety," the need to be near Mommy or Daddy and the corresponding fear of strangers, marks the emergence of strong individual preferences. Parents should try to keep in mind the positive side of a child's seemingly negative reaction during the last half of the first year to virtually anyone other than a family member. These reactions show a rapidly growing ability to see differences, to compare, and to realize that Mommy and Daddy are different from others.

This awareness, in turn, seems to strengthen attachments to parents and perhaps to other family members. Then, as the child moves out into the world and begins to walk and explore, self-awareness and self-assertion blossom. The child learns the power of "I am!" For example, a toddler who wants to feed herself is practicing and testing her abilities in order to grow in personal independence. Another, learning to walk, strives until he masters this extraordinarily complex and useful skill. Once the skill is achieved, he beams with delight and pride in this remarkable capability.

Children are born with an internal motivation to strive and master both themselves and their environment. Parents should accept with pleasure and enthusiasm their roles as facilitators of their child's growth and striving toward increasing independence. The central mission of the toddler is the struggle toward increasing autonomy, or self-actualization. This astonishingly creative struggle need not be turned into a struggle between the outward-bound child and a controlling or overprotective parent.

Toddlers are also sometimes portrayed as being "negative," hard to please, and willful. What actually is happening is that toddlers want to choose for themselves. When toddlers are asked "What do you want?" the answer almost always will be "Nothing" or "Everything," since their experience is so limited. But given a specific set of attractive alternatives—Rice Krispies or granola, toast or blueberry muffins—they will choose what they like best after a period of seemingly random trial-and-error learning.

The toddler needs to be respected as a separate person, as well as being given warm parental attention and care. Granted such consideration children rapidly acquire strengths and growing self-sufficiency.

THE PRESCHOOL PERIOD: TWO AND A HALF TO FIVE

As charming and adorable as children in the preschool period can be, they are likely to be equally as frustrating and overwhelming at times. The preschooler must integrate the rapid development of skills—talking ability, for example—with an increasing number of developmental challenges—such as learning to treat other children gently. Because the behavior provoked by this ongoing conflict can be either pleasurable or reprehensible to an observer, it sometimes is difficult to remain objective and to tell whether a preschooler's actions are appropriate or signs of trouble.

Throughout these years there is growing mastery of physical skills. Some 1-year-olds have begun to walk; some 2-year-olds have mastered walking, running, and climbing and can walk up and down stairs one at a time. By age 2½ to 4, many children have become toilet-trained (which means they have mastered much more than just a "physical skill"). By age 3, many children can balance on one foot, walk upstairs one foot after the other, and pedal a tricycle. And by age 4, many children can hop on one foot, throw a ball overhand, and manage scissors with some degree of skill. How quickly children master these skills—and how good their motor skills are—is highly dependent not only on innate capabilities but also on gentle parental help and encouragement.

The acquisition of language skills usually parallels that of motor development. Around the age of 2 or so, most children know how to say several dozen words, to begin to form sentences two or three words long, to point correctly to some body parts, and to express the negative. During the next year a child's vocabulary size expands greatly, and by the third year a child is likely to have a vocabulary of several hundred words, to use short sentences with ease, and to process information to ask questions. Parents should understand that a child of this age makes many errors in speaking. Children are exploring language just as they explore the physical world, and a parent who becomes anxious or corrects too much will only inhibit them. By 6 or 7, generally, many speaking errors disappear and a child speaks more fluently and more grammatically. Increasing ease in speaking prompts children to tell complex—often long-winded—stories to whoever will listen.

Story ideas come from a child's growing imagination as he or she tries to make sense of the world. Most preschool children have little understanding of what adults think of as logical. They have their own reality, which is not what seems objectively real or true to adults. A 3-year-old child may believe, for example, that little characters actually live in a television set. He or she may insist that this is the case since the characters appear on the screen when the TV is turned on. As a child reaches age 4, however, capacities for reasoning and logic start to develop. Children slowly comprehend the meaning of symbols, which explains why they become capable of "playing house" and similar games with few real props or none. "Representational play" usually starts about the middle of the second year and expands and elaborates the child's growing comprehension of the world.

Preschool children tend to be fascinated by larger-than-life imaginary characters such as superheroes and monsters. These serve to help children work out their fears of aggression and aggressive feelings along with the conflicts between the desire to be powerful and the reciprocal desire to be safe and protected. Imaginary figures can serve to enrich children's fantasy lives and enable them to adjust to the rules of the adult world. For example, a 4-year-old boy may accurately play-act the "father" and speak to an imaginary "mother" in imitation of his own parents.

As children become increasingly aware of the way the world works, and their similarities to and differences from others, they are likely to begin playing more with other children. While this play is full of pleasures, the more children interact with others, the more opportunities they have to become frustrated by or angry with others' desires. Negative feelings sometimes explode in the form of temper tantrums, which can be triggered by seemingly neutral events. Although tantrums tend to begin during the toddler period and persist throughout the next year or so, not every child has them and every child copes with anger and frustration somewhat differently.

Parents can help a child accept these feelings by acknowledging the anger or sadness but still putting limits on striking out and hurting others or oneself. The way a child deals with these feelings may or may not match the parents' style. When temperaments differ radically, parents experience considerable frustration before learning to accommodate and respond to a child's way of coping. If they can stay cool and set an example, they can be enormously influential. They can help increase the child's options by demonstrating ways of dealing constructively with hurt feelings and anger.

Parents have an easier time when they accept that confrontations with their preschooler are inevitable. They can consider temper tantrums and other outbursts as "normal" and remember that preschoolers will need time to learn to control their impulses and recognize what the rules are. Trying to reinforce positive behavior and overlooking annoying acts tends to be more helpful than punishing a child for outbursts. When punishment must be given, it should be reasoned and humane. Children—even preschoolers—need to have limits set fairly to know what is expected of them and why.

Regardless of reassurance from other parents, physicians, or experts, some parents suspect that their child's rambunctiousness and rebelliousness are excessive or "abnormal." Such parents need not assume that they are simply incapable of handling a preschooler, but should consult a pediatrician. (See Chapter 3, "Promoting Mental Health," and Chapter 6, "Going to the Doctor.")

THE SCHOOL YEARS: FIVE TO TWELVE

While physical development slows between ages 5 and 12, other kinds of growth proceed rapidly. School-aged children learn to balance their needs and desires with the requirements that society and their own physical, moral, social, mental, and emotional development impose on them. Developmental tasks are set both by the individual from within and by those around. Such tasks include the following:

- attaining and maintaining a sense of self-esteem, either by being adept or knowledgeable in a certain area or by compensating through boasting, aggressiveness, or other behavioral ploys. The search for solid self-esteem and a positive self-image inevitably involves some frustration and pain. The desires of two children to attain self-esteem and a positive self-image often clash and result in one child's demeaning the other in order to gain a feeling of supremacy. In many cases, certain children—often those whose shortcomings in particular skills are more obvious than those of the others—are used as scapegoats. They may be selected last in gym class and labeled "weirdo," "nerd," or simply "slow." At various times, insecurities lead all children to fear that they are unpopular, and they may pick on other children more than usual or agonize to parents that "nobody likes me."
- finding acceptance among peers, avoiding the taint of being "unpopular," even at the expense of individuality.

INFANT-CHILD DEVELOPMENT

Approximate Age* (Years)	Self-Regulation; Self-Awareness; Self-Care	Social-Emotional Behavior	Communication	Response to Objects; Play	Fine-Motor Skills; Eye-Hand Coordination	Cognition	Body Mastery
1/12, 1	Internal balance among systems develops (homeostasis). Can sleep several hours, be alert and responsive for extended periods.	Looks at faces; follows faces with eyes.	Is startled at loud noises. Vocalizes distress (cries). Quiets, alerts to sounds, voices.	Looks at objects and follows briefly.	Hands fisted.	Looks, follows, responds to faces, voices, objects, and sounds.	Movements are mostly undirected. Raises head slightly when lying on stomach.
		Smiles responsively to faces and voices.		Turns head toward sound and searches with eyes.	Hands partially opened.		
						Repeats arm movements to keep toy activated.	
	Sucks on fist when reflexes bring hand to mouth.		Begins random vocalizing of vowellike sounds. Looks at speaker and responds by smiling.	Follows an object from side to side and up and down.	Grasps toy placed in hand.		Holds head erect when held upright.
1/4	Gazes at own hand.	Distinguishes mother from others; responds more to her.	"Special" cry for hunger. Shows vocal signs of pleasure.	Looks directly at toy, waves arms, and moves body.		Looks for object at point of disappearance.	Raises head high and looks around when lying on stomach.
					Clasps hands together.		Rolls from front to back.
	Clasps and plays with hands.	Feelings for and responses to people (especially primary caregivers) develop into strong attachments.	Vocalizes syllables, babbles, laughs.	Growing interest in objects and toys.		Secures partially hidden object.	
	Comforts self by sucking thumb, pacifier.		Uses sounds like ga, da, muh, oh, oo.	Begins to reach.	Grasps objects near hand.	Plays with and examines objects.	
			Vocalizes in response; may imitate familiar sounds.	Brings both hands toward a toy and grasps it. Shakes, bangs, waves, and bats objects.		Repeats behavior for adult attention.	
1/2	Plays with own feet.	Behavioral responses reflect widening range of feelings.	Expresses anger or displeasure with vocalizations other than crying.	Transfers toy from one hand to another.	Transfers toy from one hand to another.	Anticipates and reacts to games.	Rolls from back to front (4–8 mo)
3/4	Discovers genitals.	Begins to differentiate familiar people from strangers. Develops shyness.	Vocalizes to, and in response to, others.	Holds two toys at once, one in each hand.		Vocalizes sounds similar to those heard.	Sits alone (5–9 mo).
	Feeds self cracker or cookie.		Uses several different syllables with some wordlike, then phraselike, utterances.	Mouths, rotates, drops objects and toys.			
		Some "stranger anxiety" emerges with clinging to primary caregivers.		Examines and explores toys; pushes, pulls to get desired toy.		Uncovers hidden toy. More complex object play.	Early stepping movements (5–11 mo).
	Takes bottle without help.			Bangs two toys together at mid-line.			
			Croons to music at times.	Reverses object (e.g., bottle) to functional side.		Follows trajectory of fallen toy.	Pulls to standing position.
			Appears to understand some simple words (up, bye-bye).	Slides, crumples, swings, and tears paper.		Imitates sounds and gestures.	
				Grasps small objects with thumb and index finger (pincer grasp).			

INFANT-CHILD DEVELOPMENT

Approximate Age (Years)	Self-Regulation; Self-Awareness; Self-Care	Social-Emotional Behavior	Communication	Response to Objects; Play	Cognition	Body Mastery
1	Holds spoon and uses fingers to feed self bits of food.	Autonomy emerges in self-feeding and more independent play as baby is more mobile.	Plays speech-gesture games (pat-a-cake, peekaboo). Responds to "No," shakes head.	Plays pat-a-cake, peekaboo, etc. Drops objects into container.	Uses locomotion to secure toy, explore, seek caregiver.	Scoots, crawls to move around. Sits down, walks with help (7–12 mo).
		Checks often with caregivers.	Jargon begins; voices many consonants, syllable combinations.	Uses hammer, spoon to bang; makes sounds (such as playing a xylophone).	Touches adult hand to prompt activity with toy.	Stands alone (9–16 mo).
			Has a few consistent words.	Takes covers, lids off containers. Puts one object inside another.	Looks at pictures, helps turn pages.	
1¼	Cooperates in dressing (puts foot into shoe, arm into shirt).	Hugs, carries doll, bear, favorite toy.	Follows simple directions.	Finds toy hidden by screen, furniture, door.		Walks a few steps (9–17 mo).
		Hugs family members.	Recognizes and identifies many objects, pictures, some body parts.	Imitates scribbling with crayon.		Climbs up stairs on hands and knees.
	Partially feeds self with fingers and spoon.	Likes to "help" others.	Consistently uses some true words along with gestures.	Puts small objects into container.		Starts and stops walking with improving control.
	Shows pleasure in mastery (walking, climbing, throwing).	Is often negativistic, wanting independence, but also is loving, seeking affection and attention.	Understands simple questions.	Builds with blocks. Imitates tower of 2 or more blocks.		Throws a ball.
				Puts lids on containers (sets them on).		Walks backwards (pulling a toy).
	Identifies own body parts (eye, nose, hair, mouth).		Repeats words heard in conversation.	Puts pegs in pegboard when shown how.		Walks upstairs, then downstairs with help (13–20 mo).
1½		Puckers and gives kiss.	Gradual increase in words and decrease in gestures.	Likes to play with parents' possessions (pots, pans, hats, shoes, tools, cosmetics).		Climbs onto furniture.
			Demonstrates understanding of verb forms ("Come here," "Sit down"), personal pronouns ("Give it to me"). Combines 2 words.	"Pretend" play begins with feeding doll, putting doll to bed, etc.		
				Scribbles spontaneously. Imitates crayon stroke.		
				Explores cabinets, drawers, boxes.		
				Attempts to activate toy after demonstration.		

INFANT-CHILD DEVELOPMENT

Approximate Age (Years)	Self Regulation; Self-Awareness; Self-Care	Social-Emotional Behavior	Communication	Response to Objects; Play	Body Mastery
2	Removes garments; unsnaps front, side. Manages cup; uses spoon to "scoop" food.	Emerging autonomy and independence may escalate into temper tantrums. Imitates adult activities (housekeeping, using tools).	Names, labels objects and pictures (dog, ball).	Builds tower of 5 or more blocks. Uses cup with little spilling. Searches for causal mechanism to activate wind-up toy.	Seats self on small chair. Squats and returns to standing.
2½	Refers to self by name. Assists in dressing. Shows pride in what he/she can do. Refers to self by pronoun (me, I).	Likes to please parents, but also demonstrates more and more autonomy by doing things "by self" (shows opposing extremes). Plays interactive games (hide and seek), playing out some fears and trying out new behaviors.	Imitates sounds during play (animals, cars, trucks). Initiates some 2-word sentences ("Eat cookie," "Go bye-bye"). Vocabulary expands daily. Uses plurals, personal pronouns, 3-word sentences.	Handles spoon well. Symbolic play—uses one object as another (stick for spoon). Attempts circular stroke with crayon when shown how. Turns pages of a book. Holds crayon with fingers and thumb.	Kicks ball. Jumps, both feet. Runs. Can walk on tiptoe. Walks up and down stairs alone, may hold rail.
3	Has partial or complete bladder and bowel control. Identifies 6 or more body parts.	Relates selectively to family members as individuals. Can be cooperative.	Asks for help. Knows colors. Repeats numbers, jingles, phrases.	Uses means to obtain an end; foresight and some planning in play. Demonstrates short-term and long-term memory of events, places, sequences.	Jumps from step to ground. Jumps a few inches.
3½	Puts on simple garment. Knows full name and gender. Feeds self skillfully. Buttons, unbuttons large front buttons.	Has some relationships with others outside family. Gradually becomes less negativistic, more vulnerable. Begins to play with other children. Separates from parent fairly easily.	Relates simple experience. Talks about use of objects. Understands meaning of 2 or 3 of anything. Relates more complex events.	Draws vertical and horizontal lines following demonstration. Pretend play is more elaborate. Handles small toys skillfully. Builds with blocks and Legos, strings beads, uses pegboards, puzzles, clay, paint. Can copy circle, cross.	Alternates feet going downstairs. Rides tricycle using pedals. Hops a few steps on one foot. Can broad jump 12 inches or more.

Approximate Age (Years)	Self-Regulation; Self-Awareness; Self-Care	Social-Emotional Behavior	Communication	Response to Objects; Play	Body Mastery
4	Washes face and hands; combs hair; goes to toilet with occasional help.	Shows interest in sex differences.	Compares sizes, shapes; describes characteristics.	Sorts by color, simple shapes.	Can stand on one foot several seconds.
	Dresses and undresses self with some help.	Is strong-willed, but can be reasoned with.	Names 3 or more colors.	Can use scissors to cut.	Skips on one foot.
		Likes to show off.	Asks questions in correct form.	Can paint and shape clay into crude, sometimes recognizable shapes.	Catches big ball.
	Knows front and back of most clothing.	Some new fears emerge.	Can follow 2- and 3-step instructions.	Can draw a face, person with 2 or more parts.	
	Concerned with issues of power and protection of self.	Issues of power and protection are demonstrated in play and maybe at bedtime.			
5	Sorts toys and possessions; separates from others.	Can begin to share some things.		Begins to understand simple rules, procedures, sequences.	Can throw and catch bean bag
	Takes small trips in neighborhood independently.	Plays cooperatively much of the time.		Copies a square, triangle.	Can walk up and down stairs carrying object.
	Shows fairly accurate view of own abilities.	Can make and honor a simple bargain.	Can learn and repeat address and telephone number.	Understands and follows simple rules of games.	Throws ball overhand with good force and direction.
	Dresses & undresses with little help.	Has set of values, sense of fairness.	Can tell simple stories.	Draws a person with head, body, arms, legs.	Gallops; begins skipping, alternating feet.
	Zips and buttons.	Can be gentle, friendly, sensitive to feelings of others.	Can describe common objects.	Colors, cuts, pastes imitated models creatively.	Bounces ball.
	Does simple tasks independently.	Wants acceptance and attention from peers and adults.	Can answer phone, take simple messages.	Prints some letters and numbers.	Can learn to skate.
	Usually laces and ties shoes.			Ties shoelace and bows after much practice.	Rides bicycle.
6	Growing capacity for self-regulation of behavior (e.g., activity, aggression).	Can usually delay gratification and wait his/her turn.		Can demonstrate understanding of some basic quantitative, directional, time concepts.	

*This chart represents "typical" ages at which behaviors can be observed to emerge. There is a *range* of ages during which most infants and children develop skills and understandings.

- finding adult role models, including teachers, coaches, entertainers.
- learning to reconcile different value systems, including the one at school and the one at home, and beginning to understand that compromise and relativism are not signs of weakness.
- carving a niche in the family, by performing in ways that bring praise from parents—and respect or sometimes jealousy from siblings.
- exploring independence by testing limits; during the later school years, attempts to achieve independence may include smoking, using foul language, and breaking minor—or sometimes, major—rules.
- becoming aware of and comfortable with one's own body, sometimes through "playing doctor," looking at or touching the bodies of peers (usually of the same sex), or masturbating.
- coping with phobias, such as fear of failing and fear of losing physical or mental control.
- handling strong urges, such as hunger at inconvenient times, desiring sensual contact with others, and needing praise and attention.
- developing a sense of right and wrong.

While these complex tasks are being pursued, the cognitive skills of the school-age child become more refined. Examples:

- maintaining attention and persisting at a boring task for the sake of long-term goals.
- perceiving cause-and-effect connections (comprehending, for example, that television characters do not "live" in the TV set).
- developing both the short-term and long-term memory.
- interpreting complex situations and deriving useful generalizations from them for future use.
- continuing to learn to speak, an accomplishment which involves both cognitive and physical skills and rivals learning to walk in its certainty to give a child a huge boost in self-confidence.
- reading, writing, and using numbers.

The more highly developed a child's skills in these categories, the more he or she is likely to fulfill self-defined goals. If a child has significant difficulty in more than one of these areas or cannot compensate for weaknesses in one area through strengths in others, he or she risks failing to achieve a positive self-image.

Parents should be sensitive to the possibility that children who seem unusually aggressive, poor at school work, or socially unpopular are not being lazy or defiant. They simply may be ill equipped, either innately or because of external circumstances, to meet society's expectations, and they need an increased amount of support from parents, family, and perhaps professionals. It is especially important for parents to offer encouragement and support for every child throughout the school years. Any concern should be discussed with a teacher, physician, or counselor.

While schools serve an indispensable educational and socializing function for children, many traditional American primary and secondary schools emphasize and reward conformity and uniformity. The special strengths, gifts, and proclivities of individual children tend to be either overlooked or given scant encouragement. Parents can balance the work of the schools by encouraging these gifts and by taking an active role in the schooling of their children. They can supplement children's learning opportunities outside of school, and also attempt to influence school policies and curricula.

ADOLESCENCE

For every child, progressing from childhood to adulthood involves major physical, emotional, and social changes—and the adjustment to them. Among the most obvious examples are development of body characteristics, sexual feelings, and career plans. For some children, the metamorphosis from childhood to adulthood happens fairly quickly—during the teenage years. For others, however, the transition is somewhat slower, and adolescence persists into the early 20s or beyond. In general, the end of adolescence can be defined as the time when a person assumes an individual identity and attains the ability to cope independently with internal and external problems.

If adolescence ends at adulthood, when does it begin? Distinctions between adolescence and puberty often are not clear. Puberty is best described as the period during which the body takes on adult characteristics and adolescence as the time during which a person grows and develops psychologically, emotionally, and socially. For most children, puberty begins roughly during the period between ages 8 and 13 for girls and 9 and 14 for boys. Adolescence begins roughly about two years after the onset of puberty as a result of the emotional effects of the physical changes of puberty combined with externally imposed social changes (such as advancing from elementary school to junior high).

It can be extremely difficult for girls and boys who mature either very early or very late. Severe problems of self-esteem and social adjustment can be averted if early or late blooming is dealt with directly. Even if parents are available and supportive, young people who are either "ahead" or "behind" schedule suffer emotionally from being either the first or last to mature. This all-too-common pain should not be minimized or ignored by parents and relatives; children need their continuing love and confidence.

The rapidity with which puberty can transform a child often startles parents. Within a short time—sometimes just a year or two—a child may grow six or seven inches taller, develop an adult physique, and begin to speak with a significantly lower voice.

For most girls, these changes begin to take place between the ages of 8 and 13, when the very first signs of breast development—breast buds—emerge, the activity of sweat glands increases, and pubic hair begins to grow. Within the next several years, body development accelerates, height spurts occur, and menstruation begins. Some girls attain their adult physique before the age of 13; others do not do so until age 18.

Most boys begin puberty about a year or two later than most girls. The first signs of puberty among boys are usually the darkening of the scrotum and the lengthening of the penis. Over the next two to six years (usually between ages 12 and 18), a boy's genitals continue to enlarge, pubic hair develops, and height increases. During puberty, both boys and girls tend to develop deeper voices and more body hair. The hormonal changes that produce these effects also tend to promote side effects such as oily skin and hair, *acne,* and excessive perspiration.

In general, adolescents tend to pass through the following stages:

EARLY ADOLESCENCE: TEN TO THIRTEEN

The major emotional task of a child during early adolescence is to begin to establish an identity separate from his or her parents. Because friends are also going through this process, most young adolescents turn to one another for support and advice. These early peer groups, or "cliques," usually are divided by sex, since the first awkward stirrings of sexual attraction between boys and girls tend to preclude friendships between the sexes. Some children also develop sudden "crushes" on adult role models of both sexes.

Logically, a young adolescent cannot stake out an individual identity until he or she recognizes his or her family identity. In coming to grips with parental values and viewpoints, children necessarily test at least some of them. Sometimes this testing takes the form of open rebellion. Usually, however, it takes more subtle forms, such as contradiction or secretiveness. Many children feel ambivalent about this process: at the same time that they are testing their individuality and independence, they desire the support and comfort of their families. These contradictory feelings are difficult to discuss and reconcile. For parents to dismiss the process as "just testing," is, therefore, an oversimplification of the identity-finding process through which a child is struggling.

Similarly, teasing a young adolescent about bodily changes can provoke painful feelings of inadequacy. Children at this age are acutely aware of everything about their bodies, especially the negative features, such as fat, perspiration and odor, unwanted hair, and acne (even a single pimple!). In addition, nearly all children are dissatisfied with their own levels of development; they believe they are either too physically immature or too well developed. Many children fear that they will never develop or that they will develop too slowly or quickly, and that their peers are progressing at a much more satisfactory rate.

In an effort to deal with fears and worries about physical development, both boys and girls experiment with different "looks"—using especially clothing and hair styles. This preoccupation with physical appearance is natural, but it contributes to the mistaken belief that everyone is looking at the child's body. Even well-meant support from a parent (encouraging a child to be an individual in physical appearance, for example) can backfire: the child is trying to mold an identity precisely by imitating the style of peers. In fact, any gratuitous comments at all about a child's image are likely to provoke resentment from the young adolescent.

MIDDLE ADOLESCENCE: FOURTEEN TO SIXTEEN

A child's preoccupation during middle adolescence is with establishing a sexual identity. This process includes dealing with sexual feelings as well as with continuing self-doubts about body image. Parents may be surprised that child development specialists place a great deal of emphasis on this process, and may not realize how critical handling normal sexual feelings is for a teenager, and how difficult it can be. In general, society refuses to acknowledge the strength of adolescent sexual feelings and thereby further confuses the young adolescent who is attempting to deal with them.

To complicate the scenario, the dating game among midadolescents provides a poor system for selecting caring companions. Certain boys and girls often are viewed as eminently desirable dates, while others are shunned. This pattern in most cases precludes the possibility that caring relationships will develop. Yet, simultaneously, strong sexual feelings—and, undoubtedly, in some instances, feelings of love —may preoccupy an adolescent.

Sexual feelings sometimes manifest themselves in ways other than dating or explicit sexual behavior. It is common, for example, for teenagers to behave aggressively. Parents may find it helpful and constructive to initiate open, honest, adult discussion of what is going on in their children's "private lives" as a way of underlining their own concern and caring. Openly referring to their own adolescent struggles may bring parents much closer to children who are striving to become responsible adults. It may be helpful, as well, to consult programs and books on "parent effectiveness" and similar approaches to open communication between parents and adolescents.

Of course, sexuality is not the only area in which teenagers must reconcile internal desires with external restrictions. Midadolescents are continually striving to develop a self-image in the face of the pressures from groups (such as teammates) or individuals (such as siblings). Teenagers are asked to conform to the standards of peers, parents, teachers, and other authority figures and must gradually sort out their own values while this is going on.

LATE ADOLESCENCE: SEVENTEEN AND BEYOND

The boundary between late adolescence and early adulthood is a subjective one. It may be defined as the period when a person develops individuality and a personal value system as practical guides for coping with internal and external conflicts. In any society, children become adults when they are accepted as independent, responsible individuals by other adults—especially those who formerly were protectors and caretakers.

As high school ends and work or higher education begins, daughters and sons usually start the transition to independent living. The process of separation is a delicate, often difficult one for children and parents. Nearly adult children want and need to assert their independence, yet feel the tug of many ties to their parents and home. Parents, simultaneously, are eager for their children to move successfully into this next stage of independence, yet naturally feel protective of them and their choices. Both parents and children need to be aware of their own ambivalences as they inevitably move apart. One positive way of keeping in perspective the sensitive feelings which constantly come to the surface is for children and parents to recall that they feel strongly because they care deeply about each other.

For many young adults, getting out of high school—no matter how pleasant the experience was—is somewhat of a relief. Restrictions are relaxed, and pressures from peers and from parents and other adults begin to subside. For some teenagers, this newfound freedom means experimentation; many young adults have their first intimate sexual experiences during this period. For other teenagers the freedom is primarily that of expressing individual opinions. As a group, young adults may be the most thoughtfully principled members of society, even if some live out their principles inconsistently.

Because late adolescents have usually learned to withstand peer groups' opinions, body-image problems tend to decrease and social relationships tend to be more caring and less self-serving. Many young adults fall in love. In the past, falling in love during the late teens or early 20s often led to marriage. Today, with more sexual freedom, growing concern for making women's opportunities equal to those of men, and the economic reality that most women work, falling in love during late adolescence is less often a prelude to marriage.

For many modern couples delaying marriage does not mean delaying intimate relationships. Many young adults live together—for many motives, including interest in experimenting with compatability, testing the strength of feelings, or delaying more permanent alliances until they are financially feasible. At this stage, most parents can do little to prevent their child from following such a path, even though they may disapprove. They are wise to withhold advice unless asked. However, parents who have set an example and not interfered too much are sometimes surprised to find that their formerly rebellious midadolescent begins to seek advice occasionally during young adulthood.

On the other hand, some young adults do not often consult their parents. In adjusting to newly found individuality, certain late adolescents may adopt a rigid value system. An issue may be viewed as unambiguous, and conflicting opinions on the subject dismissed or labeled outrageously wrong. Others' feelings may be met with righteous indignation. This outlook can have the paradoxical effect of reducing a person's individuality and creativity. In most cases, however, fairness and moderation gradually begin to pervade young adults' outlooks, especially if they are exposed to a variety of other opinions. School and college experiences can either reinforce or temper the rigidity of late adolescence.

In general, what can most effectively modify rigid opinions is a sense of direction. For some young adults, finding the right work in life becomes a major developmental crisis. Just as midadolescents tend to interpret their lives sexually, so young adults tend to define themselves in terms of career goals. Whether to pursue an academic or a vocational route is usually the first major decision—and it is rarely an easy one. If parents or other counselors usurp the decision, such as forcing an adolescent to go to a certain college or to take a particular job, his or her developing sense of autonomy can be undermined. Mutual respect in exchanging opinions and ideas can be the key to finding the best path.

2 Promoting Physical Health

Most children can be healthy and grow physically strong if they get proper physical care, nutrition, and exercise. Since the center of a child's world is the home, parents can promote health by furnishing three basic necessities:

- They can teach children to care for their bodies.
- They can provide a sensible, nutritious diet.
- They can encourage children to get adequate rest and exercise suitable for their age and physical development.

CARE OF THE BODY

A healthy body is clean, clothed as much as the environment requires, and realistically protected from bacteria, viruses, damaging chemicals, and other threats to health. Because the body itself has many natural protective mechanisms, basic care essentially means enhancing these strengths.

INFANT AND BABY

Bathing

The number of baths a baby needs depends on the condition of the skin, the weather, and the baby's activities. For example, an infant who has dry skin and sleeps for much of the day may need a full bath only once or twice a week. On the other hand, a baby whose skin is moist and who seems uncomfortable in hot weather may enjoy a full bath or sponge bath every day.

In most cases bathing an infant more than once a day is not necessary as long as the face, hands, and diaper area stay relatively clean. Some physicians and nurses recommend giving babies sponge baths during the first few weeks or months of life, especially until the umbilical cord stump heals.

Baths should be given in a warm room and on a surface that is at a height comfortable for the person giving the bath, such as on the kitchen counter. A changing table or an adult's lap can also be used. Safety and comfort in handling the baby are essential for tub baths.

Have at hand mild soap, mild shampoo (usually needed just once or twice a week), at least two washcloths, a soft towel, cotton balls, and clothing. Lotions and powders are unnecessary for the baby's health and comfort. (If powder containing talc is used, great care should be taken not to let the baby breathe the dust, which can irritate the respiratory tract. Some parents prefer cornstarch powder.)

For a sponge bath, the bathing surface should be covered with a thick towel; for added safety an infant's bath board can be used. The water temperature should be comfortably warm—about 100° F (37.8° C), approximately the same temperature as the baby's body. The baby can be held slightly elevated on the towel with the support of the bather's hand under the head. The other hand can be used to wash the baby, starting at the top. If the hair is to be washed, the scalp should be massaged gently with shampoo. Hair should be rinsed thoroughly with a wash-cloth; usually, two or three rinses are necessary to remove all soap. Many babies develop *cradle cap,* a scaly scalp condition, which can be readily treated at home.

A baby's face can be rinsed lightly with a washcloth; the rest of the body can be lightly soaped by hand or with a washcloth. (If the baby's skin is dry, soap can be omitted except on the days that the baby's scalp is shampooed.) The baby's body should be rinsed two or three times with a fresh, wet washcloth. The bather should pay special attention to the creases in the baby's skin, which should be gently blotted dry.

After the unbilical cord stump has healed, an infant may enjoy a bath. Parents can try the tub or switch to sponging if the baby seems frightened. Once a baby begins to like the tub, parents should be prepared for exuberant kicking and splash-ing and may want to wear old clothes or an apron during the bath.

For a tub bath, a baby bathtub or a similar tub—a clean plastic dishpan will do—should be filled with about two to three inches of comfortably warm water. The baby's body should be immersed slowly in the water, with one of the bather's hands supporting the baby's head. The other hand should be free to wash the baby.

Between baths, parents should keep an eye on the baby's face and hands, rinsing them periodically with a damp washcloth to keep them clean. With each diaper change, the baby's bottom should be wiped clean with a sponge or cloth. The skin always should be patted completely dry before dressing the baby.

By the time a baby is 6 months old or so, the family bathtub can be used. To get a baby used to the large tub, parents can place a small tub within the dry bathtub for a week or so.

An infant never should be left alone in the bath for a moment, even if the telephone or doorbell rings. A baby can slip under the water, bump the hot water tap, or become terrified at being suddenly alone. If the person giving the bath must leave the room for any compelling reason, the baby should be taken out of the tub, wrapped quickly in a towel, and carried along.

Eye, Ear, Nose, and Nail Care

The general rule of thumb about keeping a baby clean is not to worry about anything inside the baby's body. Almost any foreign material that gets into a body orifice will work itself out naturally with the help of mucus or other body fluid. An exception to this general rule may be a rare foreign object that lodges in the nostril (see *nose, injury to and foreign objects in*) or other orifice. Cotton swabs can be used to gently clean the outside orifices, but never the inside.

To clean a baby's eyes, parents can dip a cotton ball in comfortably warm water and carefully wipe the eye from the inner corner to the outer corner. The outside of the ears can be cleaned the same way or with a damp washcloth. Parents need not worry about wax within the ears; any excess will eventually work itself out. The nose also should be cleaned only on the outside with a moist cotton ball or wash-cloth.

A baby's fingernails and toenails should be trimmed regularly to avoid self-inflicted scratches. Parents should cut the nails straight across with blunt baby scissors or a clipper. The best time to trim nails is while the baby sleeps; if the baby is awake, one parent can hold the baby while the other clips the nails.

Caring for a Newborn's Navel

The stump of the umbilical cord, which is attached to the navel, usually falls off after one to three weeks, sometimes leaving a slight wound. Until this wound heals, it should be kept dry and clean. Covering the wound with a bandage is not necessary. Many physicians and nurses advise giving a newborn sponge baths rather than tub baths until the navel has healed.

If the navel and surrounding area become red, infection may be present and a physician should be consulted. Physicians sometimes recommend swabbing the navel with rubbing alcohol on a sterile cotton ball to speed drying of the stump and to prevent infection.

Circumcision

Circumcision involves surgical removal of the tiny sheath of skin (foreskin) that covers the end of the penis. Circumcision may be chosen for religious or cultural reasons.

For many years the great majority of boys in the United States were circumcised for reasons of hygiene, but now health professionals generally agree that uncircumcised boys do not have any special hygienic problems. A policy statement from the American Academy of Pediatrics concludes, "there is no medical indication for routine circumcision of the newborn." Circumcision has not been shown to prevent venereal disease, cancer, or other serious health problems, and contrary to folk wisdom, circumcision does not prevent either masturbation or premature ejaculation. The decision to circumcise is solely a matter of parental discretion. If parents do opt for circumcision, they should have the procedure performed within a week of their son's birth, and no earlier than the first 12 to 24 hours of life.

At birth, the foreskin is fused with the head of the penis. Removing the foreskin (circumcision) leaves an open wound, which should be protected to prevent it from sticking to the baby's diaper. The head of the penis can be swabbed with petroleum jelly and wrapped loosely in sterile gauze. While healing, the penis should not be washed. A physician should be consulted if parents have questions; healing usually requires about three days. Parents should watch for bleeding and signs of redness or swelling, and make sure of a full urinary stream.

When circumcision is not performed, smegma, a substance composed mainly of cells naturally shed from the skin of the penis, may accumulate under the foreskin of mature males if proper hygiene is not practiced. In rare instances, later in life, smegma can allow germs to multiply and mild infection or irritation can develop.

For the uncircumcised baby, parents should not try to retract the foreskin of the penis for cleaning because it is virtually impossible to pull the foreskin back before about 18 months to 3 years of age for most boys without causing pain. (The foreskin becomes increasingly retractible as boys grow older.) Cleaning under the foreskin is not necessary for hygienic purposes until the foreskin is retractible. Until then, the foreskin of an uncircumcised penis should be left alone. Later, parents can gently retract the foreskin during bathing in warm water to wash the penis.

Labial Adhesions

Adhesions are very thin bands of fibrous or scarlike tissue which form between two surfaces normally separate from each other. Occasionally, adhesions partially fuse the labia minora, or inner lips, of a young girl's external genitals. This condition, though abnormal, is common and correctable. If parents notice such a condition, a physician should be consulted.

Mild cases of labial adhesions correct themselves (the labia separate naturally) when a girl reaches puberty and her ovaries begin to produce the hormone estrogen. More extensive adhesions may not separate without treatment. In any case, forceful separation of the labia is not an acceptable method of treatment; it does not prevent recurrences and is painful and upsetting for a child. Good hygiene is an important part of treatment and may prevent the formation of labial adhesions.

Diapering

There is no foolproof way of keeping both a baby's bottom and bedding dry and comfortable. Parents may have to experiment to determine whether to use cloth diapers, disposable diapers, or a combination of both. Disposable diapers sometimes trap wetness, prevent the circulation of air, and thereby promote the development of *diaper rash.* For the same reasons, some babies get sore bottoms from wearing plastic pants over cloth diapers. On the other hand, disposable diapers are often more convenient. If an infant gets diaper rash from wearing paper diapers, cloth diapers may be substituted.

If neither disposable diapers nor plastic pants are used, a piece of cotton-covered vinyl can be placed over the regular sheet in the crib to prevent soiling of the bedclothes. Another option is to use cloth diapers and disposable diaper liners, which slow the soiling of diapers.

A newborn baby needs to be changed frequently, unless *diarrhea* increases the frequency. The goal always is to change diapers whenever they become wet or soiled.

A baby should be diapered on a wide, flat surface, preferably a changing table. (It sometimes helps to give older babies a toy to prevent them from becoming bored and kicking during the changing.) Stool and urine can be wiped from the baby's bottom with a clean part of the soiled diaper or a clean, damp cloth. The skin of the diaper area can then be rinsed thoroughly with a damp, comfortably warm washcloth or disposable wipe. It is important to dry the baby's bottom carefully. When holding a baby's ankles, a finger can be kept between them to prevent grinding one ankle against the other. Cloth diapers should be fastened only with diaper pins that have heads protected by plastic coverings. Parents should be very careful when securing the pins.

A baby should not be left alone for a second while being changed or while still on the changing surface. A baby can roll over and off the table in a twinkling. Remember this maxim: "Always keep at least one hand on the baby during diapering."

Clothing

Because they lose heat easily, newborn babies need to be kept warm. They should be bathed and dressed in rooms that may be too warm for older children and adults —at least 80° F (26.7° C). In addition to a diaper, a baby should wear a cotton undershirt. How much clothing a baby wears depends on the surrounding air temperature. A sleeping suit or baby bag and a blanket are recommended if the home is less than 70° F (21.3° C). On a summer day, a diaper alone may be sufficient. If an infant is too hot, restlessness, irritability, and sweating are common symptoms. Blue lips, cool skin (especially nose and fingers), and crying are symptoms of chilling.

An infant's wardrobe usually consists of sleeping clothes. As the baby grows, daytime clothes can be added. A rule of thumb is that a baby wears one more layer of clothing than does an adult. In general, parents can gauge whether the baby is dressed too warmly by checking for sweating and the skin temperature of arms, legs, and neck, and looking for an especially rosy color in the cheeks.

Shoes and socks are not needed until a baby starts to walk. Booties or socks are fine if the floors are cold or when the baby goes outside. Some physicians recommend that no shoes be worn while a baby is learning to walk, providing walking surfaces are clean and safe. When shoes are selected, they should be soft, flexible sneakers or well-fitted, new leather shoes with flexible soles.

Teething

Teeth begin to form before birth; after birth, the teeth continue to develop and begin to move through the overlying bone and gums. Several months before teeth actually appear (erupt), an infant usually starts chewing motions and salivating. The teething process usually begins when a child is approximately 6 months old, and the primary set is usually complete by the third birthday. (See *teething* for a full discussion, including problems and discomfort.)

Tooth cleaning is necessary even though a baby's molars have not come through. Parents should wipe an infant's teeth with a clean cloth or tissue. As a child grows older, parents should begin to brush and eventually supervise the child's toothbrushing and flossing.

Fluoride can protect children's teeth from cavities (caries). Children whose families live in communities with fluoridated water supplies receive fluoride protection in their drinking water. For children who do not get fluoridated water, fluoride supplements should be given in fluid or pill form or as part of a children's multivitamin as a physician prescribes. Dentists recommend that children take a fluoride supplement until about the age of 12 or until all permanent teeth have come in.

YOUNG CHILD

Young children tend to be naturally curious about their bodies and many enjoy learning how to care for themselves. This is the age to start teaching. By the age of 2 or 3 a child is likely to be able to help with bathing, dressing, and toothbrushing. Children's enthusiasm about such activities can be heightened if parents turn routines into games: they can compose bathtub songs with their child, have the child guess which piece of clothing goes on next, and brush their own teeth when their child begins to brush.

Bathing

Toddlers usually love bath time; water play is fun. Some toddlers make efforts to wash themselves, usually managing to clean a bit of the face, arms, hands, and legs.

By age 4 or 5 most children can do part of the bath. As long as the bathroom is safe (free of sharp objects, household cleaners, and small electrical appliances), the bath not slippery (lined with a nonslip bath mat or nonslip stickers), and the water comfortably warm, children can begin to bathe themselves. Children under 8 years old should not be left unsupervised in a bathtub. Even a well-coordinated, responsible child can accidentally turn on the hot water tap or slip under the water without ever calling for help. Always begin a bath by turning on the cold water first, then adding hot.

Clothing

By the age of 2 some children are able to undress themselves, although few are able to put clothes on without help. A full-length mirror in the bedroom can show children the relationship of clothing to body parts. If possible, a child's wardrobe should be chosen with activity in mind.

By the time a child is a toddler, well-fitting, durable shoes are needed. A good shoe has a flexible sole, a firm arch support, and a strap or tie to hold the heel in place and prevent the foot from slipping forward. Since a child's feet grow quickly, shoes are a big expense for a family, but it is essential that they fit correctly.

A young child's bones are softer than an adult's, and poorly fitting shoes can cause foot bones to "set" in a position that later may cause functional or cosmetic problems for the child. Unlike clothing, shoes should not be handed down from one child to the next; even if they are the correct size, the older child's feet usually have molded them in a way that makes a perfect—or even comfortable—fit for the younger one impossible.

Tooth Care

Toothbrushing should begin after a child's primary molars come in (around age 1½ or 2 years). Initially, parents can do the brushing, although toddlers often want to do it themselves. To encourage a child's initiative, parents can coach a young child as he or she brushes and then touch up any missed places. When the children become proficient at brushing alone (often at about the same time as they learn how to tie shoes), parents can simply check the teeth when they are done. It is a good idea to praise a child's efforts—no matter how effective—as a way of encouraging good, lifelong toothbrushing habits.

Unless an unusual tooth or gum problem appears earlier, a child should first visit the dentist after all the primary teeth have come in—usually between 2½ and 3 years of age. Annual visits for checkups and topical fluoride treatments to the teeth are advisable.

It is best for children to brush teeth after meals and at bedtime. The combination of the use of fluoride toothpaste, topical fluoride applications to a child's teeth in a dentist's office, and fluoride in the water source (or fluoride supplements) is effective in minimizing tooth decay.

Parents should begin flossing their children's teeth around the age of 4 years. A child's dentist or dental hygienist can recommend what type of floss to use and can teach parents and child proper flossing techniques.

By the time a child is about 6, primary ("baby") teeth begin to be replaced by permanent ones. Primary teeth are usually lost in about the same order as they came in: incisors, first molars, canines, second molars. Permanent teeth are usually in by the time a child reaches puberty. ("Wisdom teeth"—those that sometimes erupt behind the second molars—rarely come in before adolescence.)

Diet is an important part of dental care for children. Although sweets need not be forbidden, it is best to monitor intake of foods that contain added sugar, including sweetened cereals. Many dentists believe that the type and consistency of sweets are just as important as the amount consumed. Sweets eaten as part of a meal—flavored gelatin—for instance—may be less likely to cause decay than those eaten as snacks, such as candy bars. And sticky sweets—caramels and dried fruits, for example—may be more harmful than those that do not adhere to the surface of the teeth.

Toilet Training

Toilet training is a process that requires considerable sensitivity and patience. It is a learning experience for parents as well as for children.

Children differ greatly with regard to when they learn to use the toilet. Some children, especially those with the helpful model of an older brother or sister, achieve daytime bladder and bowel control by the end of the second year. Others do not reach those milestones until after their third or even fourth birthdays.

When a toddler reaches the age of about 18 months, parents may want to start looking for evidence that the child is ready to use the toilet. Until roughly that age, children usually have involuntary bowel movements shortly after every meal. By the middle or end of the second year or so, children are likely to begin to recognize when a bowel movement is coming—an ability that is essential before they can learn to use the toilet. Some children, by making distinctive faces or noises, may indicate that they feel a bowel movement starting. Sometimes children go into a corner or other "hiding place" to have a bowel movement. Other signs of a child's readiness include staying dry longer than usual; showing an interest in urine and feces; complaining about dirty diapers; and displaying curiosity about the toilet practices of parents or older siblings.

When a child seems ready to learn how to use the toilet, parents should start with some preliminary lessons. They can point out stools to the child, show how stools are flushed down the toilet, and talk with the child about how he or she is soon going to use the bathroom "just the way grownups do." Parents also should make it clear that going to the toilet is to be the child's achievement, not the parents'. Children who come to view using the toilet as a goal are more eager to learn. Conversely, when children feel pressured to please parents by using the toilet, they may feel undue anxiety.

During preliminary discussions about toilet training, it is a good idea for parents to familiarize their child with a potty. A free-standing potty is preferable to one that fits into a regular toilet because it is easier for the child to use and can be used anywhere.

By the time a child is about 2 it may be possible to start training efforts. Parents should keep in mind that, given even a minimum of gentle help, children finally train themselves on their own timetable. (For reasons that are not entirely clear, boys tend to learn toilet techniques more slowly than girls.)

It may be helpful to place the child on the potty at times when it is likely that he or she will have a bowel movement. Parents may want to quietly encourage their child to stay on the potty for perhaps five minutes and to talk about what he or she is doing. If the child does not want to stay for even that long, no parental pressure or criticism should follow. By giving a bowel movement a special name, the parent provides a verbal cue that in time becomes part of the child's way of announcing the start of the movement. If the child does go, parents should offer enthusiastic praise. If the child does not have a bowel movement or urinate within that time (which is the rule rather than the exception for quite a while), parents should praise the child for trying and say that there will be more chances to try the potty later.

Parents should not make going to the toilet a source of frustration or a power struggle. However frustrated they may sometimes feel, parents should try to remember that a child may suffer unnecessarily—or even learn more slowly—if he or she fears parental disapproval for failure to "perform."

Once a child learns to use the toilet, parents should teach the child proper wiping and washing habits. Girls should always wipe from front to back to avoid getting stool and potentially infectious organisms in the vagina and urethra. A boy also should wipe from front to back after having a bowel movement. During the first months of toilet use, parents must help children to wipe themselves in order to ensure removal of stool or urine. After wiping, the child should be shown soap-and-water handwashing—a habit to be practiced every time the toilet is used.

In the early stages of training, parents should not switch from diapers to training pants. Switching at a time when a child is just beginning to learn to use the toilet may cause anxiety. Sometimes children who are making progress start telling their parents that they do not like diapers, thereby alerting parents to make the switch.

There are certain types of bowel problems that can arise in connection with toilet training. Some children have *constipation* or loose bowel movements. Others may display signs of deliberately withholding stools. One way to deal with this latter tendency may be to encourage the child to look at feces briefly and then flush the toilet. Sometimes young children consider feces to be parts of their own bodies, and they may be reluctant to part with them. Having children inspect their stool each time and then allowing them to flush the toilet can satisfy their curiosity and reduce anxiety. Generally, however, if a child develops bowel problems during toilet training, the best move may be to ease up on training efforts and ask the physician or nurse for advice.

Children who are learning to use the toilet commonly have periodic lapses of control. Such lapses sometimes occur long after the completion of the toilet-training process. Lapses often are provoked by stressful situations, such as the arrival of a new baby, the illness of a family member, or going to daycare for the first time. In all cases, parents should be sympathetic and understanding. If accidents persist, consultation with a physician may be helpful.

Achieving consistent nighttime control typically occurs from a few months to a year or more after a child has learned to use the toilet. The child who is relatively late in achieving daytime control may be well into his or her fifth year before staying dry regularly through the night. If a child does not seem to be making progress by this age, the cause is likely to be slow development of bladder control—and not emotional troubles or defiance (see *bed-wetting*). Parents should ask their child's pediatrician for advice about dealing with bed-wetting.

ADOLESCENT

Adolescents are capable of and interested in taking care of their own bodies. Diplomatic and understanding advice and encouragement are needed from parents.

Body Odor and Bad Breath

Adolescents perspire more than younger children because of the development of special glands under the arms. These glands produce a substance that interacts with bacteria often present even on clean, healthy skin. This combination can cause body odor. Nervousness, stress, and physical exercise or exertion can lead to wetness, in addition to odor.

For some teenagers it seems that no matter how much they wash, heavy perspiration and odor persist. Deodorants (designed to mask odor) and antiperspirants (designed to mask odor and prevent wetness) can be of some help. In addition, wearing loosely woven, natural-fiber clothing helps wetness evaporate.

Bad breath most often results from poor dental hygiene; it can be a sign of infection, deficient nutrition, or poor health. Perhaps because their parents tend to be careful about brushing children's teeth, young children usually do not get bad breath. Some older children get bad breath if they become lax about care of teeth and gums. Although parents should encourage their children to brush their teeth, constant nagging usually is counterproductive. When teenagers realize that having bad breath can be a social barrier, they may be more likely to take teeth and gum care seriously.

Skin and Hair Care

The hormonal changes of adolescence usually increase production of the oil glands in the skin of the face, scalp, neck, chest, and back. Many teenagers have problems with oily skin or hair or with mild to severe *acne.* Oily skin and mild acne sometimes can be controlled by washing two or three times a day with a mild, nonperfumed soap or with a special soap for oily skin. Oil-based makeup should be avoided; even water- or alcohol-based makeup can aggravate mild acne. The hair should be washed at least twice a week and should be kept off the face, if possible. Over-the-counter acne preparations, especially those containing benzoyl peroxide, may be effective. Exposure to the sun or a sunlamp for short periods of time may help. (Sunlamp treatment should be supervised by a physician.)

Although moderate to severe acne may improve with consistently good hygiene, medical treatment is likely to be necessary for healing. For more information, see *acne.*

Menstrual Hygiene

During menstrual periods most women use tampons or pads or a combination of both.

Physicians have found that the improper use of tampons with high-absorbency material increases the chance of developing *toxic shock syndrome,* a serious bacterial disease. Research indicates that the highest risk of developing this disease occurs when a woman leaves a tampon in place for more than seven hours, especially if menstrual flow is not heavy. Tampons no longer contain possibly hazardous absorbent material. Manufacturers recommend that women change a tampon once every four hours (unless flow is heavy enough to require more frequent changing), use the smallest-sized tampon possible, and wear pads at night.

In general, tampons may be used as soon as a young woman starts menstruating. Some physicians recommend waiting until periods become regular (usually about a year after periods start), but using tampons earlier is not harmful.

Using tampons allows a young woman to continue her usual activities virtually uninterrupted. The same range of activities is possible with pads, although a young woman cannot swim while wearing one and she may worry that the pad is visible through thin or porous clothing. Modern improvements in pads have, however, produced a much smaller, more absorbent form.

As long as attention is paid to genital hygiene, including taking a daily bath or shower, menstrual odor should not become a problem. Feminine sprays and douches can irritate the genital area and, potentially, be predisposing for the development of a vaginal infection (see *vaginitis and vaginal discharge*). If odor or heavy, persistent discharge develops despite consistently good hygiene, a physician should be consulted.

Physical Self-examinations

Young men and women who have reached puberty should begin a routine monthly habit of self-examination for signs of cancer. This practice is recommended by the American Cancer Society. If a young person detects a rare early sign of cancer and reports it promptly to a physician, the physical and emotional "savings" to the individual and the family can be incalculable (see *cancer*).

Breast Self-examination for Females Breast cancer is the most common cause of cancer deaths among women in the United States. At present, one of every 12 women in the United States develops breast cancer at some time in her life. Although breast cancer is unusual among women under 20 years old, beginning breast self-examination early in life and making it a habit is strongly recommended. Fortunately, the great majority of lumps or masses in the breasts of women under 20 years old are harmless fluid-filled cysts or solid tumors (see *breast development and disorders*).

FIG. 1. BREAST SELF-EXAMINATION

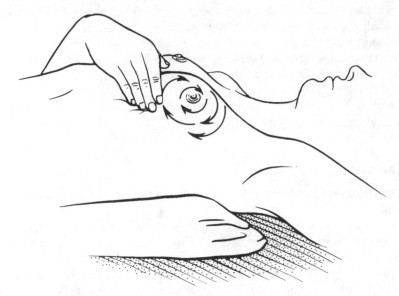

1A. A woman should use a circular, massaging motion with one hand over each breast.

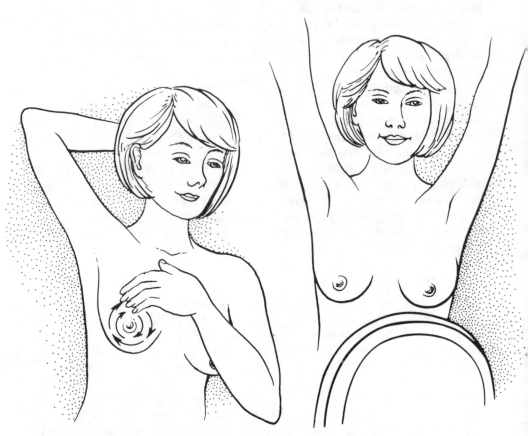

1B. The circular, massaging motion should also be used while standing, preferably in the shower, using soap and water.

1C. By raising the arms and looking at her breasts in a mirror, a woman can note even slight changes, such as dimples or pulling of the nipple.

Breast self-examination is simple and takes about five minutes. The best time for a self-exam is one week after the end of a menstrual period. While lying down and then standing, a young woman can use both eyes and hands to detect swelling, thickened areas, or lumps.

First, while lying down, a woman uses a circular, massaging motion with one hand over each breast (see Fig. 1A). The pressure applied should be firm and probing to locate any lumps deep within the breast tissue. This should be repeated while standing. If done during a shower, the thoroughness can be increased by using soap and water to maximize the pliability of the skin (see Fig. 1B).

Using a mirror (as in Fig. 1C) can be especially helpful. By raising the arms over the head and looking for variations from the normal alignment and symmetry of the breasts, a woman can note even slight changes. The most common, visually evident changes are either a dimple in the skin or a pulling in of the nipple. Any discharge (clear or bloody) from a nipple should also be reported to a physician. About 75 percent of all breast cancers occur under the nipple areola region or in the upper, outer portion of the breast.

Testicle and Breast Self-examination for Males Although cancer of the testes is very rare among males of any age, it is worth checking in order to catch it early. It is often a rapidly developing tumor and in some cases can cause sterility (see *genito-urinary tumors*). Young men should examine their testicles once a month while taking a shower. Each testicle should be felt individually with the tips of the fingers for the presence of a lump of any size. Also, if either testicle feels tender or sore or if the examination is painful in any way, a physician should be consulted. Any abnormal discharge from the penis should also be reported to a physician. (See Fig. 2.)

FIG. 2. TESTICLE SELF-EXAMINATION

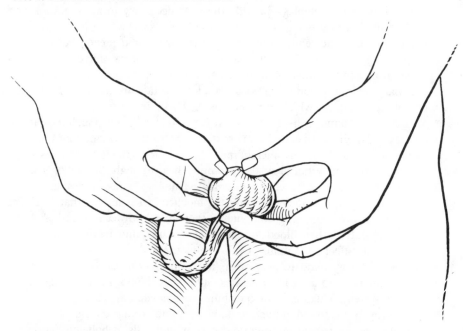

Each testicle should be felt individually with the tips of the fingers for the presence of a lump, soreness, or tenderness.

Breast cancer is very rare among men of any age (its incidence is about 1 percent of that among women). Nevertheless, while showering, men should routinely feel each nipple briefly once a month to check for the presence of a lump of any size. Even if a suspected lump feels tiny, it should be reported to a physician.

Occasionally a young man's nipples may become tender or enlarged. If such a condition persists for more than two weeks, it should be reported to a physician. This is not a symptom of cancer but warrants medical attention (see *gynecomastia*).

NUTRITION

Nutrition is the foundation of a child's health. Good nutrition, which supplies the body with energy for physical activity, is essential for growth and helps fight illness. Although approximately 40 percent of Americans are significantly overweight (at least 20 percent heavier than the recommended weight for height and build), poor nutrition and lack of a balanced diet are still problems for many people.

Good nutrition depends on the intake of nutrients—substances that are extracted from foods during digestion and are needed to supply energy, to maintain and build the body's cells, and to regulate body processes. About 50 nutrients are needed daily to ensure proper growth and body function. If a child's diet supplies the recommended daily amounts of the 10 most important nutrients, the remaining 40 nutrients are usually supplied, as well.

The following list briefly describes the 10 most important nutrients:

- <u>Protein</u> is found in meat, poultry, soy products, fish, dried beans and peas, eggs, cheese, milk, and milk products. It is an essential building block for new cells, including those in muscles, blood, and bones. Protein also helps keep existing cells healthy.
- <u>Carbohydrate</u> is found in cereals, potatoes, beans, corn, bread, and sugars. It is a source of energy. Unrefined carbohydrates—such as whole grains and fresh fruits and vegetables—provide the fiber necessary to aid digestion and the elimination of wastes.
- <u>Fat</u> is found in shortening, oils, butter, margarine, and meats. Fat provides more energy per unit of weight than either protein or carbohydrate. It is an essential part of the walls of every cell and provides the body with fatty acids necessary for many body functions. In addition, fats are associated with the fat-soluble vitamins, which are vitamins A, D, E, and K.
- <u>Vitamin A</u> is found in liver, carrots, sweet potatoes, greens (such as spinach and collards), margarine, and some butter. It helps the formation and maintenance of skin and mucous membrane cells and strengthens the body's resistance to infection. Vitamin A also promotes healthy night and color vision.
- <u>Vitamin C</u> is found in broccoli, citrus fruits, mangos, strawberries, and other fruits and vegetables. It is necessary for biochemical reactions that form the structure of the cementing compounds that hold body cells together; these compounds strengthen blood vessels, heal wounds, and increase the body's resistance to infection. Vitamin C also helps the body use iron.
- <u>Thiamin (B1)</u> is found in lean meat, nuts, and fortified cereal products. It enables the body to use carbohydrates and assists the normal functions of the nervous system. Thiamin also contributes to a normal appetite.
- <u>Riboflavin (B2)</u> is found in liver, milk, yogurt, and cottage cheese. It helps the body use energy as well as generate energy within cells. Riboflavin helps produce healthy skin and eye tissues, and helps keep vision clear.
- <u>Niacin</u> is found in liver, meat, poultry, fish, peanuts, and fortified cereal prod-

ucts. It contributes to the body's use of energy and carbohydrates and the production of fat cells. It also aids digestion and promotes a normal appetite.

- Calcium is found in milk and milk products (including cheeses and yogurt) fish, and greens (including kale, collard, and mustard greens). It combines with other minerals and protein to give structure and strength to bones and teeth. Calcium is essential for blood clotting and normal muscle and nerve function.
- Iron is found in liver, red meat, dried beans and peas, enriched farina and prune juice, among other foods. Iron is an essential component of hemoglobin, the red substance in blood that carries oxygen to and carbon dioxide from the cells. It is needed to prevent nutritional anemia and resulting fatigue.

These 10 nutrients, as well as the remaining 40, are found in foods of the four food groups:

- Milk—including milk products—supplies calcium, riboflavin, and protein.
- Meats, eggs, and legumes—including fish, poultry, beans and peas, soy extenders, and nuts—supply protein, niacin, iron, and thiamin.
- Fruits and vegetables supply vitamins A and C, as well as fiber.
- Grain—including foods made from grains (such as breads, pasta, rice, cereals, and corn products)—supplies carbohydrate, thiamin, iron, and niacin, as well as fiber.

Healthy young children who generally eat a balanced diet do not require daily vitamin supplements.

FROM BIRTH TO ONE YEAR

The first food for a newborn who is being breast-fed is a thick, yellowish liquid called colostrum. This substance is produced by the mother's breasts before birth and for two or three days afterward. It is a unique compound of water, sugar, protein, fat-soluble vitamins, and minerals which in many respects is much more nourishing than ordinary milk or synthetic formula. Colostrum contains several kinds of important chemical factors: some that can confer immunity on the infant from certain infections and allergies, others that promote growth.

After the first few days of life, when the mother's breast milk normally comes in, an infant's body gets all required nutrients from breast-feeding. It is important to remember that breast milk also contains growth factors, offers immunity, and may be less likely to cause allergic reactions than prepared formulas. Parents, however, may choose to formula-feed rather than breast-feed infants. Normal growth and development occur whether an infant is breast- or formula-fed. Formula can be purchased already prepared (requiring refrigeration after opening) or as concentrate or powder that can be prepared as needed.

Once babies begin drinking milk, they generally consume about 3 ounces for each pound of weight within a 24-hour period. Unmodified cow's milk should not be given to children less than 6 months old; the protein concentration is high and infants may not be able to excrete products of protein metabolism without becoming dehydrated. In addition, it may damage the gastrointestinal tract, resulting in chronic, microscopic blood loss.

Whenever an infant receives milk from a bottle, whether formula or breast milk, any feeding equipment (bottles, rubber nipples, and nipple covers) must be carefully cleaned and handled. Bottles and accessories can be cleaned effectively and conveniently in a dishwasher. Books on both breast- and formula-feeding may be helpful. (See sources of information at end of chapter.) Breast-feeding information and counseling is available from local chapters of the La Leche League and the Nursing Mothers Council.

Introduction to Solids

Solid foods are usually introduced into an infant's diet at 4 to 6 months of age. Initially, solids should constitute only a small part of a baby's diet: milk continues to be the major food.

It makes no difference which solid foods (vegetables, fruit, or cereal, for example) are introduced first as long as only one new food is added at a time. This practice enables a parent to identify more readily a food to which a child might be allergic. Solids typically chosen first for infants include iron-fortified rice cereal, strained or pureed fruits (such as peaches or apples), or strained or pureed vegetables (such as carrots or peas), which babies sometimes prefer because of their distinctive flavors. Citrus fruits, wheat products, nuts, and chocolate may prove allergenic for some children.

Some parents may prefer preparing their own cooked fruits and vegetables at home for their babies, using food mills and blenders. Most commercially prepared baby foods now contain no additives. Any parent thinking of straining commercially canned fruits and vegetables for a child to eat should read nutrition information on the labels of containers to check for additives. Fruits and vegetables commercially canned for adults may have high salt content or other undesirable additives.

An infant often shows the most interest in solids at lunchtime. For snacks, at around 8 months, the baby may prefer something to chew on, such as a cracker or a slice of zwieback. Finger foods, such as small pieces of toast or slices of banana, should be introduced, and children should be encouraged to pick up foods, regardless of the mess, as a step toward self-feeding.

When babies voluntarily reduce their intake of milk or formula, the need for solid foods increases. Because a 6-month-old needs about 800 or 900 calories daily, an infant who continues to drink four 8-ounce servings of milk (575 calories) needs a little over 200 calories in solid foods (the equivalent, for example, of one ounce of minced chicken, plus 3/4 cup of rice cereal or a cup of applesauce). As long as the baby continues to drink milk, the daily protein requirement will be met, regardless of how many solids are eaten.

All babies, of course, do not like the same things. A baby should be encouraged to eat whichever foods are appealing. It is best in the early months to avoid mixtures of food until it is clear what a baby can handle. Families who follow diets that do not contain the basic foods mentioned earlier, because of nutritional or religious preferences, should always discuss the nutritional needs of their child with their physician or nurse.

Baby foods are packaged commercially or can be prepared at home from the foods served for family meals. Babies should not have foods that are spicy, salty, or seedy, or contain caffeine or alcohol.

Parents buying baby foods should read labels to make sure that they contain minimal or no added salt and sugar. Because of public concern about food additives, many baby food manufacturers have voluntarily eliminated salt and sugar. Many preservatives have also been eliminated, and commercial baby foods must therefore be refrigerated after opening. When preparing baby food at home, the food should be strained through a sieve or pureed in a food processor, blender, or food mill until nearly smooth. Neither salt nor sugar should be added.

Transition to Cow's Milk

When babies are 6 to 12 months of age, a transition from breast milk or formula to pasteurized or sterilized whole cow's milk can begin. Switching to cow's milk should be discussed with the physician or nurse, especially if a baby has experienced reactions to other foods. Babies should not be given skim or low-fat milk during the first two years because more than 40 percent of skim or low-fat milk calories are protein. As mentioned before, the immature infant cannot excrete products of protein metabolism when they are so concentrated without losing excessive water. Moreover, skim or low-fat milk is lacking in certain essential fats and the fat-soluble vitamins (A, D, E, and K). Infants who are given skim or low-fat milk can suffer deficiencies of these nutrients.

SECOND YEAR

After the first year, which is marked by extremely rapid growth, a child's growth, weight gain, and appetite normally begin to slow down. Ideally, a 1-to-2-year-old child's daily diet might include all of the recommendations listed below. Realistically, if a child at this age receives most or all of these foods over a two-to-three-day period, he or she will usually be well fed and healthy. In other words, parents should not become overly concerned if any one day's intake fails to include more than a third or so of the following ideal recommendations.

- Three servings from the milk group. One serving equals 1 cup milk, 1 cup yogurt, 1½ ounces of cheese, 1 cup pudding, 1¾ cups ice cream, or 2 cups cottage cheese.
- Two servings from the meats, eggs, and legumes group. One serving equals 2 ounces cooked lean meat, fish, or poultry; 2 eggs; 2 ounces cheese; ½ cup cottage cheese; 1 cup dried beans or peas; or 4 tablespoons peanut butter. (Parents should remember that raw fruits and vegetables, nuts, hot dogs, and large portions of peanut butter can be serious choking hazards for children less than 3 years old.)
- Four servings from the fruit-vegetable group. One serving equals ½ cup cooked fruits or vegetables, ½ cup fruit or vegetable juice, 1 cup raw vegetables or fruits, or a piece of fruit, such as a medium-sized banana or apple.
- Four servings from the grain group. One serving equals 1 slice bread, 1 cup ready-to-eat cereal, or ½ cup cooked cereal, pasta, or grits.

A good, nutritious menu for a 1-year-old might consist of a breakfast of juice, an egg, a slice of toast, and milk; a lunch of cereal, a serving of fruit, and milk; and a dinner of meat, poultry, or fish, a cooked or easily digested vegetable, a serving of potatoes or rice, a slice of bread, a serving of fruit, and milk.

A 1-year-old usually eats many of the foods the family eats. A wide variety of foods may be cut into safe, small pieces or cubes so that the child can pick them up easily.

Even if a child is eating solid foods, parents often have another nutritional concern—snacking. A child's growing body naturally requires additional "fuel" during the day. As long as snacks are nutritious, are not sugar-laden, and do not take the place of foods eaten at regular meals, snacking should present no difficulties for young children. Good snack foods include fresh fruit, fruit juices, frozen juice pops, partially cooked carrots, small chunks of cheese, and crackers and peanut butter.

A nutritional concern that usually arises around age 2 is how to manage a child's intake of sweets. Excess weight gain, tooth decay, and poor nutrition can occur because of eating too many sweets. Although children's intake of sweets should be restricted, an occasional cookie or other dessert usually is harmless to sound health.

It is wise to avoid sweets that are sticky, such as taffy or caramels, or those that a child tends to keep in the mouth for some time, such as a lollipop. Certain nutritious foods, particularly dried fruits, also cling to the teeth and can cause tooth decay. Sweets that can be eaten quickly are usually best. Toothbrushing immediately after children eat sweets is one way to protect teeth.

Eating should be a pleasing, satisfying experience shared with family and friends. Food never should be given as a reward or withheld as punishment.

PRESCHOOL CHILD

The general nutritional requirements for a 1-year-old apply to children of the 2-to-5 age group as well, except that the portions would be larger. Breakfast might be cereal with milk, toast, and fruit followed by a lunch of a sandwich, soup, fruit, and milk. Dinner might consist of meat, poultry, fish, or a dairy product; one raw and one cooked vegetable; potato or bread; fruit; and milk. Young children can be given dessert, but not more than two or three times a week. By the time a child is 2 or 3, he or she should be able to eat what the rest of the family eats.

At age 2, many children who have been eating well and gaining weight steadily begin to show less interest in eating and at mealtimes cannot be tempted either by old favorites or special new recipes. Such a loss of appetite in an otherwise healthy child is not unusual. In most cases, in a matter of several weeks or two to three months, the familiar appetite and zest for eating return in full force. Parents need to become accustomed to variations in children's appetites and food interests as the children grow. Frequent nutritious snacks are helpful. It is also important to remember that after the first year children's food intake decreases naturally. If children are growing and gaining weight, parents do not have to worry about food intake.

Between ages 2 and 5, appetite generally increases because the growing body rapidly uses fuel. As long as a child eats three balanced meals and drinks three 6-ounce glasses of milk daily, nutrition should be adequate. If it appears that what a child likes is providing adequate nutrients, it does not make sense to force novel or distasteful foods. Of course, a child should be encouraged periodically to try different types of foods and tastes.

As is true of younger children, most children between 2 and 5 years old cannot last from meal to meal without a snack. If a child complains of hunger, a nutritious snack should be offered. Offering a selection of snacks allows the child to choose what seems most enjoyable.

By now, children are spending more time with other children and are exposed to varied eating habits. In most cases this exposure gives rise to the question of eating sweets. Children will want to know why a playmate can have candy when it is forbidden for them. It is worth explaining to children in appropriate language the health reasons for limiting sweets.

If sweets are not ordinarily kept in the house but are purchased only when a special event occurs, children may not feel that they are being deprived of "treats."

Generally, children between the ages of 2 and 5 become slimmer as they grow taller. If a child seems overweight by comparison with other children of the same age, a physician or registered dietitian should be consulted about diet modification. Any systematic attempt to reduce a young child's food intake must involve the entire family in a positive, nonpunitive team effort. A child should never be put on a weight loss diet of any kind without medical supervision. Nutritional deficiencies caused by dieting can be harmful to a child's health and interfere with normal growth (see *weight problems*).

SCHOOL YEARS

From about 5 years of age onward, children usually eat the same foods, in varying quantities, as do other family members. To ensure adequate nutrition, a balanced diet is important. Daily intake should average from 1,700 to 2,700 calories, depending on weight and level of activity (see chart). Guidelines are available in child nutrition books or from the Office of the Surgeon General, a branch of the U.S. Department of Health and Human Services. (Bookstores in the Federal Buildings of many cities often carry Health and Human Services publications.)

As children near adolescence, their rapidly growing bodies prepare for the adolescent growth spurt. The basic nutritional requirements of an adolescent are similar to those of a child, except that an adolescent usually eats larger portions and more often. In general, an adolescent should consume about 2,700 to 2,900 calories per day (see chart). However, parents may be startled to discover that adolescents often consume much more than 2,900 calories during growth spurts or when in training for sports or engaging in other strenuous activities.

The teenage years can be a period when young people are least interested in eating well, and when snacks and fast foods such as hot dogs, french fries, and sugar-laden carbonated beverages become favorites. It is worth noting that the nutritional content, especially the protein portion, of some fast foods may be satisfactory. On the other hand, the salt and fat content of fast foods that are fried can be quite high. Parents should continue to encourage teenagers, in a good-natured way, to eat well, taking into consideration the enormous peer pressures accompanying the multiple, difficult changes of adolescence.

When anyone participates in vigorous physical activities, dietary needs increase accordingly. Vigorous activity means increased burning of stored calories. As a result, a child's appetite increases. This additional need for food should not be met by the tempting fats and carbohydrates in so-called "junk food," but instead should be filled by supplementary foods. To ensure that they consume adequate nutrients and calories, teenagers should never follow fad diets when participating in vigorous physical activities, when trying to lose weight—or at any other time, either. A physician or registered dietitian should be consulted if active teenagers have questions about what and when to eat, or seem to be overweight or underweight.

				Mean Heights and Weights and Recommended Daily Energy Intake	
Category	Age (years)	Weight (pounds)	Height (inches)	Energy Needs (calories, with range)	
Infants	0–1/2	13	24	lb × 230 (95–145)	
	1/2–1	20	28	lb × 210 (80–135)	
Children	1–3	29	35	1300	(900–1800)
	4–6	44	44	1700	(1300–2300)
	7–10	62	52	2400	(1650–3300)
Males	11–14	99	62	2700	(2000–3700)
	15–18	145	69	2800	(2100–3900)
	19–22	154	70	2900	(2500–3300)
Females	11–14	101	62	2200	(1500–3000)
	15–18	120	64	2100	(1200–3000)
	19–22	120	64	2100	(1700–2500)

For more complete information on feeding children from birth through adolescence, see *Parents' Guide to Nutrition,* by Boston Children's Hospital with Susan Baker, M.D., Ph.D., and Roberta R. Henry, R.D. (A Merloyd Lawrence Book, Reading, Massachusetts: Addison-Wesley, 1986).

SLEEP

Everyone needs sleep to replenish the body's energy and allow complex physiological processes to be completed, especially brain processes. Children particularly need sleep to restore the supply of energy consumed by their growing bodies. The amount of sleep varies according to age, physical and emotional health, physical activity, and nutrition. Obviously, newborns and young children require more sleep than do older children.

For reasons that are only partially understood, each night every individual, regardless of age, requires a period of rapid-eye-movement (REM) sleep. REM sleep, during which dreams occur, usually accounts for half the sleeping time of infants and about one quarter of the sleeping time of children over 2. Sleep cycles begin with a period of deep sleep, followed by a period of light sleep, and then a period of REM sleep. This cycle occurs about five times in eight hours of sleep, with each REM period lasting about 10 to 20 minutes.

NEWBORN BABY

Newborns sleep about 18 hours a day and, once asleep, generally do not awaken until they move their bowels, feel hungry or cold, or experience some other physical discomfort. Noises, such as traffic, barking dogs, music, or human voices usually do not wake sleeping newborns.

FIRST SIX MONTHS

Until about 3 months of age, sleeping patterns may coincide with feeding times— an infant falls asleep after breakfast, wakes when hungry, is fed, and then falls back to sleep until hungry again. As parents of infants can verify, irregular sleep patterns are the rule rather than the exception.

By 6 weeks of age, many infants have one period a day of extended sleep, between 4 to 6 hours, and stay awake for an extended period during the day, usually in the afternoon.

Between 3 and 6 months of age, a baby's sleeping patterns gradually become less dependent upon the body's immediate needs. By 6 months, an infant's sleeping and eating patterns are less closely linked, and begin to follow a pattern cued by parents and other members of the household. Rather than drifting off to sleep right after feeding, the infant begins to stay awake longer during the day and may take several naps.

Most infants do not sleep through the night until they weigh 10 or 12 pounds. Many infants awaken at night for reasons related to their eating. For example, the sleep pattern of a breast-fed baby is usually different from that of a formula-fed baby.

SIX MONTHS TO ONE YEAR

An infant of 6 to 12 months requires about 13 hours of sleep out of 24, but this may vary from 9 to 18 hours. A typical sleeping pattern includes a 10- to 12-hour night and two naps of varying lengths. Even if an infant does not seem sleepy in the afternoon, he or she needs to be encouraged to take a nap. The child often plays quietly, resting at the same time.

Often, parents' fondest hope is that a baby will sleep through the night. However, sleeping through the night is highly variable, and all babies wake several times during the night as they move about in their sleep. If they are not disturbed, they drop right back to sleep. To assure a child's safety and hygiene, parents should respond to cries. For example, a diaper pin could work itself loose, a blanket could become twisted around the body, or a child who is wet may simply need a change. Children are reassured, as well, to find that parents respond to their cries.

If an infant has been sleeping through the night regularly only to begin waking again, it may be because of an illness or a change of routine or environment. Causes of occasional night waking can include the stimulation of a busy day, a bad dream, or teething.

By 9 months a baby generally is kept awake or awakened by external noises, the comings and goings of others, or even temperature changes.

The sleeping patterns of a 6- to 12-month-old begin to follow the routine of the household. Parents can be faced with the recurring problem of getting a baby to sleep. Parents can no longer assume that if a baby is tired he or she will go to sleep. Activity in the home can prompt a baby to stay awake to see what is going on. An overtired child may not be able to relax enough to fall asleep. Another cause of nighttime waking may be a child's fear of being separated from the parents. (For a full discussion of separation fears, see *phobias.*) In addition, infants may begin to have sleep terrors and nightmares. (For discussion of these problems, see *sleep disorders.*)

Children should not be allowed to take a bottle to bed. In addition to the danger of choking on part of the bottle, a strong possibility exists of rapid decay of teeth because sugar-laden liquid can easily pool in the mouth. If infants are sleeping through the night and suddenly begin waking, they should be given water only if other soothing measures have failed. Giving juice or milk tends to reinforce the waking habit and provides the child with additional energy to stay awake.

TODDLER

Children from 1 to 2½ usually continue to require about 13 hours of sleep each night. Sleep patterns still follow the household schedule, although variations should be expected occasionally. For example, at this age children often lie down for naps whether or not they are really sleepy, simply because they have become used to lying down and closing their eyes at a certain time each day. A 1-year-old usually sleeps through an 11- or 12-hour night and takes two daytime naps.

By 15 to 18 months of age, a child's sleep needs change again. He or she is not sufficiently tired to take two naps a day, but one nap often is not quite enough. These children generally cannot make it through to afternoon naptime without a morning nap and cannot stay awake until bedtime with just the sleep of the morning nap. A period of fussiness often results.

Other factors that awaken children at this age include a change in the child's sleep pattern, a change in the parents' schedule, and teething. Children also may wake up frightened during the night, usually because of some form of nightmare or night terror (see *sleep disorders*).

Another nighttime problem can be a child's getting up and walking. Unlike sleepwalking (see *sleep disorders*), this walking occurs while the child is wide awake. Because climbing out of a crib and walking around alone in the dark can be dangerous, parents should try to explain that the nighttime is for sleeping, not exploring.

PRESCHOOL CHILD

Until ages 4 to 6, most young children sleep 12 hours a day (including nap time), although sleep duration varies from 10 to 14 hours in 24. In fact, a preschooler's sleep patterns may vary daily according to the day's activities, health, *growing pains,* and other factors. At some time during this period, children usually stop napping.

If involved in activity, a preschooler may ignore fatigue and the body's need for sleep. The child may then become overtired, which often is indicated by crankiness, fussiness, irritability, loss of appetite, or drowsiness.

Preschoolers may also awaken at night. They usually fall asleep again if they are not crying or afraid and no physical cause is apparent. A preschooler may have nightmares or night terrors (see *sleep disorders*). Among children of this age, night terrors are much less common than nightmares. Preschoolers may mutter or speak clearly in their sleep.

SCHOOL YEARS

Between 5 years of age and the beginning of adolescence, children need approximately 8 to 10 hours of sleep. Sleeping habits of this age group are influenced by daytime activities and the child's physiological and psychological needs.

Adolescents need approximately 7 or 8 hours of sleep a night. Adolescents' sleeping habits are influenced by their daytime activities and by their physiological and psychological needs. Insomnia may become a problem for some adolescents (see *sleep disorders*). Adolescents generally have strong preferences about when and how long they sleep.

EXERCISE

Regular exercise is good for everyone. Research indicates that people who exercise regularly are healthier and live longer than those who do not. Exercise is particularly useful in strengthening the heart and lungs, as well as keeping the body fit.

Children generally require little coaxing to exercise. Most children eagerly play outdoors or inside, and they generally get enough daily exercise because of their incessant activity. A few hours of riding a tricycle or roller-skating, for example, easily fulfills a child's exercise requirement.

Even children with health problems, such as *asthma* or a *heart murmur,* need to exercise. A physician can give advice about the types of activities best suited for such children and how long they should exercise. Parents may need to encourage children with health problems to exercise. When a child is disabled or otherwise limited in movement, a physician or physical therapist can recommend exercises adapted to the needs of the child.

INFANCY AND THE PRESCHOOL YEARS

A child's lifelong program of exercise begins during infancy. Most babies love to grab and shake objects and can be encouraged to kick their feet. Parents can further motivate their infants to engage in movement games. For example, cooing and laughing with a baby while he or she pushes with the feet back against the parent's hands encourages leg movement and strength. Moving a baby's arms in and out or up and down while singing songs usually brings squeals of delight and exercises the limbs. Holding the baby upright with feet on the floor, or in a horizontal position with hands touching the floor, and encouraging the child to push off the floor is both a game and an exercise.

Some children as young as 6 months enjoy swimming movements. These movements can strengthen leg and arm muscles and increase the working capacity of hearts and lungs. Parents should keep in mind, however, that young children are almost certain to forget the swimming movements shortly after the lessons cease.

Recreational swim activities for infants and their parents are offered by youth clubs, the Red Cross, and the Y.

After infancy, young children generally do not need coaxing to play. To make playtime enjoyable, safe, and physically beneficial, children can be given toys that stimulate movement, such as balls, wagons, or wheeled toys that can be pushed across the floor. Children can be encouraged to play games that involve movement, such as hide-and-seek and ring-around-a-rosy. Young children enjoy climbing on playground jungle gyms, swinging on swings, or riding tricycles.

As children near school age, their physical skills increase. Usually, 4- or 5-year-olds are capable of participating in more physically demanding activities. Children can take part in activities that develop advanced motor skills as well as overall strength and coordination, such as simple gymnastics or games that require kicking, throwing, and catching.

ELEMENTARY SCHOOL YEARS

A child in elementary school usually exercises regularly—in a physical education class, by playing games at recess, or through participation in extracurricular activities. By taking part in these activities, a school-aged child usually gets plenty of exercise.

At home, school-aged children often like joining other family members in their daily exercise routines. For example, a young child may join a parent as he or she stretches and does calisthenics before breakfast. Or an 8-year-old may want to jog along on a short morning run. Along with group bicycle rides or swimming lessons, such activity not only motivates the child to exercise but may encourage other family members to exercise longer.

In addition to school exercise programs and family exercising, a young child may want to join in a particular physical activity. If a child expresses a desire to play soccer or take a dance class, he or she should be encouraged to do so. Of course, if the strength or coordination required exceeds a child's ability, alternative activities should be suggested. Children can enroll in swimming, soccer, tennis, gymnastics, skating, or dance classes offered by their schools or community centers.

JUNIOR AND SENIOR HIGH YEARS

As children near the teenage years, their physical abilities increase. The capabilities and potential of an athletic child begin to become apparent. Junior and senior high school students usually pick favorite spots and begin to develop and polish their abilities.

If a child cannot decide which activity best suits his or her capabilities and desires, parents may want to offer suggestions, but a child should not be pushed into a sport. A child's physical makeup should be considered. Children also should feel comfortable with physical activities and should participate in those physical activities that they find enjoyable, physically and emotionally. The sense of achievement and satisfaction in being successful is essential for all growing children.

Equipment and Clothing

Protective equipment is indispensable in sports that involve body contact or fast moving objects, and should include recommended body pads, protective face masks, goggles or glasses, helmets, or gloves (see *eye injuries* and Chapter 4, "Accident Prevention"). All equipment should be checked carefully for wear. Even if children run only once a week, their shoes should fit properly and provide adequate support for growing feet.

Children can quickly become overheated or very cold when exercising vigorously. Proper dress can help reduce problems such as heat stroke, heat fatigue, hypothermia, or frostbite (see *exposure to temperature extremes*).

Types of Exercise

There are several categories of exercise. Of key importance is aerobic exercise—activities that increase the body's demand for oxygen and make the heart pump blood faster. Increased blood flow strengthens the heart and improves the overall capacity of the cardiovascular system. Aerobic exercise also strengthens muscles, tendons, and ligaments and improves body flexibility. It involves moving quickly and includes such activities as soccer, swimming, running, cycling, basketball, cross-country skiing, and dance. For maximum benefit to the heart, blood vessels, and lungs, these activities should be performed three times a week for at least 30 minutes.

Another category of exercise consists of activities that increase muscle strength. These activities include calisthenics (such as sit-ups, push-ups, squat-thrusts, leg lifts, and chin-ups), isometrics, and weight-training. Isometric exercises are those that work the muscles without moving the body—for example, by forcing bent arms to hold the body at a fixed distance from a wall. Weight-training (the use of free weights such as barbells and dumbbells and fixed weights such as weight machines and pulley machines) must be carefully supervised because of the high risk of injury if excessive weights or repetitions are attempted.

A third category of body development encompasses disciplines that increase the flexibility of muscles, tendons, and ligaments, such as dance, hatha yoga, and certain calisthenics. They include all types of stretching and are extremely valuable because they help keep the body limber and thereby reduce the chances of injury during physical activity. They can be applied to all moving parts of the body, and are essential preparations for any vigorous sport. They can be learned from physical education instructors, in special classes, or, in some cases, from books.

Conditioning

Conditioning is essential before exercising to ensure that the body is strong enough to meet the physical demands made of it and to reduce the risk of injury. Conditioning focuses on strengthening muscles (especially the heart) and other body parts, thereby increasing the body's tolerance of stress.

No one should exercise vigorously when tired: fatigue often leads to injury. (For information on specific injuries, see *ankle injuries; arm injuries; dislocation of joints; fractures; knee injuries; sprains*.)

A child should begin any new physical activity slowly to allow the body time to adjust. For example, a child should begin a running program by no more than a few minutes of relaxed jogging. A child can add another minute or two to exercise time at each outing. Eventually, such conditioning leads to the ability to exercise for long periods of time, which is particularly important for endurance sports such as cross-country skiing or running.

In addition to conditioning the heart and lungs, a child should stretch muscles, ligaments, and tendons before vigorous exercise, as suggested above. No matter what the sport, conditioning is essential to reduce the risk of injury and increase performance.

SEX EDUCATION

OFFERING INFORMATION

Regardless of whether parents offer information and guidance, by their own example they teach their children attitudes about sex and sexual conduct. Children

FIG. 3. FEMALE AND MALE REPRODUCTIVE SYSTEMS

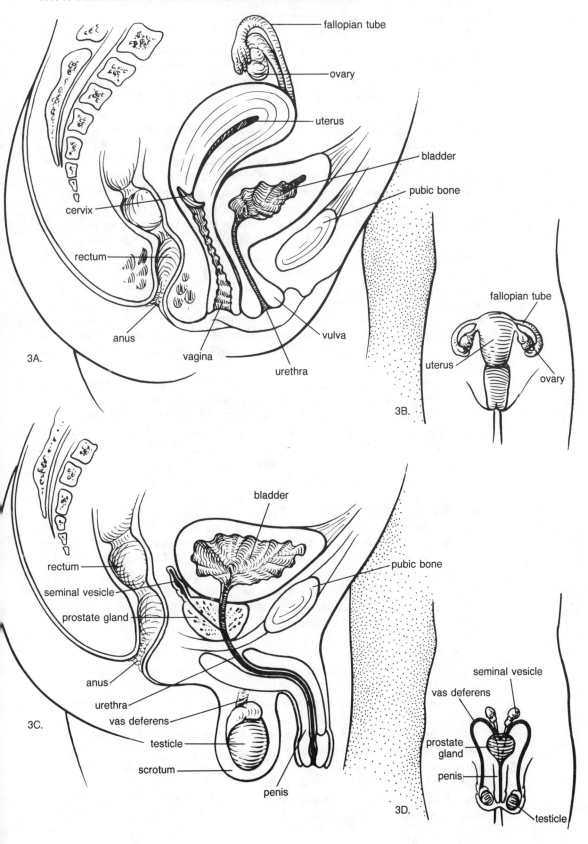

observe their parents' gestures of affection (or lack of them) and their reactions to sexual references (or portrayals) on television.

It is best for children and easiest for parents if sex education begins as soon as children are old enough to make general observations about matters related to sex: their bodies and body functions, the difference between boys and girls, how women look when they are pregnant. The amount and complexity of detail parents need to provide in their answers should correspond to the amount of detail expressed in the questions. For instance, when a 3-year-old asks "Where do babies come from?" parents need not begin a discussion of eggs, sperm, and intercourse. All a child may want to know at that point is "How does a baby get out of the mother?" not necessarily "How does a baby get into the mother?" In fact, a young child is likely to become confused by, and tune out, information that is too complex.

For young children, information almost always needs to be repeated and concrete explanations given before they really understand. Parents can gauge their child's understanding of sex and reproduction by asking their child, for instance, to tell them how babies are born. They may find out that the child has misunderstood a fundamental detail. Often, once a child understands an elusive but crucial fact, he or she is suddenly filled with questions.

Simply providing a sex education book and telling children to "feel free to ask" is not enough; children often feel too embarrassed or uninformed to ask any questions. Parents should never assume that children who do not ask questions about sex are not interested. From time to time—when a baby is born, for instance— parents should ask children questions or volunteer information easily and naturally.

Good books about sex education can be helpful for children. Preschool children enjoy having books read to them. For young children, parents might want to provide simple books about where babies come from. Adolescents who feel uncomfortable talking with their parents about sex might pick up and read books that their parents make available on family bookshelves. Parents who feel comfortable doing so can say that they would be glad to talk after a child has read a sex information book. (See Fig. 3 for details of the female and male reproductive systems.)

WHERE TO FIND INFORMATION

Public libraries and Planned Parenthood chapters usually are well-stocked sources of information and guidance about sex and reproduction. Parents can ask the reference librarian for assistance; the phone number of the local Planned Parenthood chapter is listed in the white pages of the telephone directory. Programs offered by clinics, schools, churches, or synagogues can provide a variety of information about sex and reproduction. For specific problems a physician, psychotherapist, or counselor should be consulted.

MASTURBATION

Masturbation is the stimulation of the genitals for sensual pleasure. Children need to know about masturbation. Almost all children at certain developmental stages masturbate. This is a normal part of physical, psychological, and even social growth.

All young babies explore their bodies as self-awareness develops. Through routine care such as bathing and diaper-changing, all babies discover the pleasant sensations of touch. During times of separation, such as bedtime, it is natural for babies to soothe themselves by attempting to recreate these pleasant sensations. One of the most universal methods of self-comforting is masturbation; others are rocking (see *head-banging)* and *thumb-sucking.* As babies grow and become interested in people and things beyond themselves, early childhood habits such as masturbation tend to be replaced by other activities. Among children going through puberty as well as older adolescents, stimulation of genitals serves as a normal way to release sexual tension, gratify sexual fantasies, explore sexual capacities and responses, and even control sexual drives.

Masturbation is universal and, when practiced in private and in moderation, is not in any way unusual or harmful.

MYTHS AND MISINFORMATION

In addition to paving the way to responsible relationships and dispelling fears, providing accurate information about sex is the most effective way to prevent teenage pregnancy and sexually transmitted diseases.

Many American teenagers believe that pregnancy can be avoided by urinating, douching, or bathing immediately after having intercourse; by taking a birth control pill before intercourse; by having sexual intercourse during a menstrual period (not a guarantee); or by having the male withdraw before ejaculating.

Anyone who knows the facts will not be deceived by these half-truths and myths, but knowing the facts is crucial. Obviously, when young men and women know exactly what causes pregnancy, they are better prepared to prevent it. Adolescents need to learn about birth control methods and how to use them *before* deciding if or when to have sexual intercourse.

Parents should be reassured that sex education is not a license to practice. Research shows that teenagers who receive accurate sex education are less likely to have casual, thoughtless sex than are those teens whose only means of learning about sex is through experience or street talk. In addition, having access to reliable sex information can be remarkably beneficial to an adolescent's feelings of self-esteem and sense of adequacy.

Adolescents are frequently embarrassed to admit to peers, parents, or even medical professionals that they have questions about sex. Even adolescents who are not embarrassed to ask questions rarely take the initiative to seek out information from knowledgeable people. If information is not readily available, adolescents are unlikely to seek it out.

RESULTS OF TEENAGE IGNORANCE

Adolescents who are ignorant or casual about sex run a high risk of contracting a venereal disease (VD), sometimes called a sexually transmitted disease (STD). Of all infectious diseases, only the common cold is more prevalent than VD. More than 1 million cases of gonorrhea and 80,000 cases of syphilis are reported every year in the United States. Experts estimate that at least twice as many cases of gonorrhea go unreported. Approximately one-fourth of all VD cases occur among 15- to 19-years-olds.

When ignorant about sex, adolescents and young adults are also vulnerable to unwanted pregnancy. Over one-third of adolescent girls become pregnant at least once before reaching 20. More than 1 million teenage girls aged 15 to 19—plus 30,000 girls younger than 15—become pregnant every year in the United States. Three out of 10 teenage pregnancies end in abortion; one out of 10 ends in miscarriage. The remaining six out of 10 pregnant teenagers face health risks during pregnancy and delivery that are much higher than those for adult women; in addition, their babies are at increased risk of *prematurity,* low birth weight, and death.

For teenagers who keep their babies and want to be self-supporting, social and economic consequences are usually serious. These young parents usually become isolated from school friends, with whom they no longer have much in common.

Unless they finish high school or receive some type of marketable vocational training, they are unlikely to be able to earn sufficient income, particularly if they must pay for daycare. Many single teenage mothers must resort to collecting government assistance.

OBTAINING HELP

A pregnant teenager has three options: to have a baby and keep it, to carry the pregnancy to term and give the baby up for adoption, or to have an abortion. Any pregnant young woman should discuss these choices carefully with her parents, her partner (if possible), and her physician.

If the teenager, or any woman, finds it difficult or impossible to seek help and confide in anyone who is close to her, she can seek reliable, anonymous advice of a qualified health professional (female or male) at a hospital, neighborhood health clinic, or the nearest office of a pregnancy counseling center, such as Planned Parenthood. All of these health resource agencies ensure confidentiality, an essential protection for the individual which continues to be guaranteed by law. They provide explanations of the full range of choices and the consequences of each, especially the possible risks and benefits involved. In almost all cases, fees are based on a sliding scale that takes into account a client's financial status.

Counselors at these centers will support and assist a pregnant young woman in whatever choice she makes. Any decision regarding the outcome of a pregnancy needs to be made after careful, informed consideration. If an abortion is chosen, the medical procedure used during the first trimester (first 13 weeks) of pregnancy is simpler and faster than those which may be used later on.

If a woman of any age has missed a menstrual period, she should consult a doctor or nurse. A woman should never rely upon a home pregnancy test kit (prepared by various pharmaceutical companies) to determine whether she is pregnant. Pregnancy testing offered at any of the health resource agencies mentioned above is inexpensive, and a client's privacy is protected by law. Although a home pregnancy test kit may seem at first to be a less expensive and faster alternative than having a health professional perform the test, a mistaken conclusion and its consequences can prove much more costly in both human and financial terms.

VENEREAL DISEASES

It is essential that young men and women know how to avoid acquiring or spreading venereal diseases (VD). Misinformation and misconceptions about these diseases are more prevalent than accurate information and can have tragic consequences. Accurate information and, if needed, proper medical attention are the most effective public health measures available in the effort to control VD.

Venereal diseases are those infections spread predominantly by sexual activity. VD can be spread by someone who is infected or by a carrier, a person who harbors the disease organism without displaying any signs of the disease itself. Common venereal diseases include *syphilis, gonorrhea,* nongonococcal urethritis, and *genital herpes.* An increasingly common, fatal disease, acquired immune deficiency syndrome (AIDS), is transmitted through direct genital contact and the exchange of infected body fluids such as blood or semen. Research to find a cure for AIDS continues; at present, medical treatment can provide only partial relief from some effects of the disease.

The most common signs of VD are sores, warts, lumps, or bumps anywhere in the genital region; discharge from the vagina, penis, or anus; burning during urination; sore throat; itching in the genital or anal region; rashes, especially on the soles of the feet or palms of the hands; and lower abdominal pain or pain in the groin.

Anyone of any age who may have VD should seek medical help from a private physician, local board of health, birth control clinic, women's health clinic, hospital emergency room, chapter of Planned Parenthood, local VD hotline, or the national VD hotline: 1-800-227-8922 (Monday–Friday, 11 A.M.–11 P.M., Eastern Time.). Individuals who suspect that they may have contracted any of these diseases should seek qualified medical help immediately. The U.S. Public Health Service hotline for AIDS is 1-800-342-AIDS. Diagnosis and treatment by anyone other than a health professional with considerable experience is dangerous and could have long-term consequences. Self-diagnosis and treatment is both dangerous and irresponsible. Parents and adolescents are urged to read the articles on each of the diseases: *AIDS; genital herpes; gonorrhea; syphilis.*

BIRTH CONTROL

Since about two thirds of the adolescent men and one half of the adolescent women in the United States are sexually active (engage in intercourse), accurate information about birth control (contraception) is essential.

The condom is a simple, time-tested form of male birth control. Condoms (also called rubbers, prophylactics, safes, or protections) are sheaths made of extremely thin rubber or animal membranes. They look like the finger of a surgical glove and are designed to encase the erect penis. After orgasm and ejaculation, the condom traps and holds the sperm and seminal fluid released. Condoms prove about 95 percent effective against pregnancy.

Condoms are sold in drugstores and variety stores, are available at birth control clinics, and can be found in coin machines at various other places (such as rest-rooms). Males or females of any age can usually purchase condoms without a prescription. Condoms come in one size because their elastic material adjusts to the size and shape of the penis.

Condoms, when used properly, serve as effective protection against infectious microorganisms that cause venereal diseases (see discussion earlier in this chapter).

Contraceptive foam is a light, airy cream resembling shaving cream. The foam contains spermicide, a sperm-killing chemical, which coats the lining of the vagina, including the mouth of the cervix. The foam is applied before intercourse with a small plastic stem called an inserter. Used by itself, foam is somewhat effective against pregnancy. When used in conjunction with a condom, foam proves to be about 98 percent effective.

Anyone can buy contraceptive foam without a prescription in drug and variety stores, in supermarkets, and in birth control clinics. It is usually packaged in aerosol cans that hold about 20 applications or in disposable packages containing six individual applications.

Contraceptive foam offers minimal protection against VD, but offers excellent protection when used together with a condom.

A diaphragm is a flexible, soft rubber cup two to three inches in diameter which, when inserted into the vagina, covers the cervix, the entrance to the uterus. The diaphragm serves as a partial barrier against sperm reaching the cervix. When covered with special cream or jelly containing spermicide, the diaphragm also serves as a chemical shield against conception.

Every diaphragm must be fitted by a physician or nurse; the procedure is brief and painless and the cost at a birth control clinic or women's health clinic is quite small. A physician's fee to fit a diaphragm is usually the same as for a routine office visit. The prescription from the physician must then be filled at a drugstore for a diaphragm of the proper size.

When used with scrupulous care, a diaphragm with spermicidal cream or jelly is about 97 percent effective against pregnancy. (When inserted without a spermicide simply as a barrier to the cervix, a diaphragm is ineffective, since sperm can enter the cervix around the diaphragm's edges.) A diaphragm used properly with spermicidal cream or jelly rarely produces side effects for females or males. A diaphragm used with a spermicide is somewhat effective against VD but not as effective as a condom and foam.

A cervical cap is another type of rubber cup contraceptive device that is designed to fit snugly around the cervix. It should be used with special spermicidal jelly or cream, and must be individually fitted by a physician or other health professional. Although the cap itself is slightly more costly than a diaphragm, the price remains modest. The cap is available at women's health clinics and at drugstores with a physician's prescription indicating the proper size. The cervical cap is not generally advised for use by teenagers unless a physician specifically recommends it. A cervical cap used in conjunction with special spermicidal jelly or cream is minimally effective against VD.

A vaginal contraceptive sponge is a soft, polyurethane disk resembling a dimpled powder puff. The sponge contains the same spermicide used in most contraceptive jellies and creams. When inserted into the vagina, the sponge kills sperm, absorbs sperm and seminal fluid, and may serve as a barrier to the cervix. The sponge is inexpensive and available to anyone at drugstores without a prescription. It is said to be slightly less effective than the diaphragm at preventing conception, presumably because it is not fitted to each woman's vagina: one size fits all. The contraceptive sponge has limited effectiveness as protection against VD.

The birth control pill, sometimes called simply "the pill," is a small tablet composed of synthetic (laboratory-produced) hormones. The pill is used by women to stop ovulation by supplying the synthetic female hormones, estrogen and progesterone, almost continuously throughout a woman's menstrual cycle. The pill comes in several different types according to the amount and types of synthetic hormones used. Most types are combinations of hormones.

Combination pills are 99 percent effective against pregnancy. The minipills are 97 to 98 percent effective and may be somewhat safer for certain women because they do not entail using estrogen. Birth control pills of various types have been associated with some severe side effects—one reason they must be prescribed by a physician after a health history has been recorded and a complete physical examination performed.

No form of the birth control pill provides any protection against VD.

The intrauterine device (IUD) is a small plastic invention, available in several shapes, that a physician inserts into a woman's uterus to prevent pregnancy. The IUD works for reasons that are still not entirely agreed upon by members of the medical community, but it does prevent pregnancy about 97 to 98 percent of the time. The IUD is a device that must be precisely chosen and properly fitted by a skilled physician following a complete health history and physical examination. The cost of an IUD is the cost of a regular visit to a physician's office. Once it has been properly fitted and implanted by the physician and the woman has become accustomed to how it feels, the IUD is perhaps the least complicated form of birth control.

The IUD, however, can cause a number of unpleasant side effects, especially excessive bleeding during the menstrual cycle. And it increases the risk of infection by gonorrhea and other infectious microorganisms. The IUD also increases the chances of a woman's contracting pelvic inflammatory disease (PID), a frequent cause of recurrent infection and even of sterility. Therefore, the IUD is not recommended for use by teenagers, unless specifically advised by a physician. No type of IUD offers any protection against any form of VD.

For information on all facets of children's physical and emotional health, write for the annual catalog of publications from the American Academy of Pediatrics, Department of Publications, P.O. Box 927, Elk Grove Village, IL 60007. Reliable information on child care is also available from the Association for the Care of Children's Health, 3615 Wisconsin Avenue, Washington, DC 20016; and the National Association of Education for Young Children, 1834 Connecticut Avenue NW, Washington, DC 20009.

A wealth of child health information is available in *Imprints* magazine, published quarterly by the Birth and Life Bookstore, 7001 Alonzo Avenue NW, P.O. Box 70625, Seattle, WA 98107.

Promoting Mental Health

WHAT IS MENTAL HEALTH?

Mental health is a general term that refers to emotional, behavioral, and social well-being. Each of these components is connected with the others. Feeling sad, for example, is likely to affect the way people behave and, in turn, the quality of their social activities. Conversely, the quality of people's social relationships usually bears on the way they behave and how they feel. Thus, any mental-health problem is likely to have emotional, behavioral, and social implications.

CATEGORIES OF MENTAL HEALTH

Although an emotional, behavioral, or social problem rarely becomes apparent in isolation, it can be useful to make distinctions among the categories.

Emotional Problems

Emotions, or "feelings," include such states as happiness, sadness, anger, joy, guilt, love, hopelessness, and jealousy. They can be felt only by the person who experiences them. Other people receive clues to the way a person is feeling only from the way he or she behaves. Examples of behavior that reveal feelings include smiling, laughing, crying, and screaming. In addition, feelings are often conveyed by gestures or tone of voice.

When a person is mentally healthy, he or she has some control over how emotions are experienced and managed. A person can often temper unpleasant emotions—anger, for example—by consciously trying to feel better. Rational thought, sometimes called cognition, also helps control emotions. A mentally healthy, stable person can cope with situations that engender "bad feelings," in part by thinking through what happened.

A problem exists when a child cannot express feelings or manage the frequency, intensity, or duration of an emotional state. For example:

- Persistent problems coping with difficult situations. A child becomes unreasonably fearful in new situations and cannot be comforted or encouraged.
- Persistent disquieting or distressing emotions. A child is convinced that personal harm or harm to others will come and remains anxious even when comforted.

- Expressions and behavior that do not adequately reflect what one could logically assume a person should be feeling. A child acts as if he does not care about the death of his father when the actual feeling is one of devastation. Such an event usually elicits sadness, fear, anxiety, and anger in children.
- Feelings that are inappropriate to the situation. A child frequently breaks down crying for no apparent reason during school. A child's anger is out of proportion to the situation, or expressed violently.
- Too narrow a range of emotions, or "blunted" feelings. A child who is recovering from surgery seems apathetic, never smiles or cries.

Behavior Problems

Behavior is directly influenced by emotions; in fact, as mentioned earlier, emotions can be discerned only by observing behavior. In addition, behavior always needs to be considered in context. What is desirable or "healthy" behavior varies over the course of development. A child who is just learning to eat will necessarily have messy times with food and poor table manners—behavior that would not be acceptable for a school-aged child. Also, behaviors acceptable in one culture might be viewed as insulting or offensive in another.

A behavior problem exists when a person refuses or is unable to control his or her own behavior. The standards can be the person's own, or those of society. For example:

- A child wants to quit wetting the bed but is unable to stop.
- A child regularly ransacks any room he or she is in and appears unaware of the disruption caused.

Social-Relationship Problems

Many different kinds of social relationships exist. Examples include the relationship between husband and wife, between brother and sister, between student and teacher, and between salesclerk and customer. Each kind of relationship plays a different role in a person's life. Relationships both influence and are influenced by a person's self-esteem. For children, relationships with their parents, friends, and role models (such as teachers) are extremely important for healthy mental development. When a social relationship is disordered, the result may be a loss of self-esteem, followed by emotional and behavioral problems.

Examples of problems in social relationships:

- The number or, more significantly, the quality of friendships is so unsatisfactory that the child's daily life is impaired. An adolescent who has difficulty making friends in school joins a gang of vandals.
- A child has difficulty relating to others in an emotionally satisfying way. A school child becomes withdrawn and does not respond to any overtures from parents, friends, or teachers.
- A child is constantly fighting with people.

EFFECTS OF MENTAL HEALTH

Like the body, a child's mind and emotions grow rapidly during childhood. And just as certain levels of physical growth and development are associated with certain minor health problems (acne during adolescence, for example), so certain childhood stages have come to be associated with minor mental-health problems and challenges. Irrational fears involving animals and monsters, for example, are almost universal among preschoolers. Most people have minor emotional problems such as recurring sadness—"feeling blue"—at some point in their lives, just as most people have minor physical-health problems, such as colds and bruises. As with physical-health problems, the severity of mental-health problems depends on their frequency and intensity, and on how long they continue.

Success in treating a mental-health problem is greatly enhanced if the problem is detected and treated early. Unfortunately, early intervention is uncommon. This may be because the idea of "mental health" is often misunderstood, and mental-health problems tend to be equated with bizarre or incurable illnesses. People often fear others who are known to be "mentally ill," and they avoid thinking of the possibility that someone they love has a mental-health problem. As a result, many minor mental-health problems are neglected. What begins as attention-getting behavior, for example, may turn into a more serious behavioral or emotional disorder if attention is not given to the original problem.

Although a child's mind can be just as resilient as the body in recovering from disease, an unacknowledged, untreated mental-health problem during childhood can mar normal childhood experiences. Moreover, if a child is allowed to pass into adulthood without ever receiving help for a problem such as dealing with anger, for example, then the likelihood is great that the problem will affect the person's behavior and social relationships as an adult.

A child's state of mental health can affect physical health. Children sometimes reveal emotional problems through physical signs and symptoms. Sometimes, for example, a child who is distressed about parental marriage problems develops stomachaches. The stomachaches are not faked, nor is the child "trying" to feel sick. Rather, a feeling of powerlessness in this situation and the difficulty of putting these concerns into words can cause the child to express them through physical symptoms (see *psychosomatic disease and symptoms*).

WHAT PARENTS CAN DO

Just as parents can promote good nutrition, sufficient sleep, and adequate hygiene, so too can they promote good mental health.

PROMOTING A POSITIVE SELF-IMAGE

A positive image of oneself is very important to good mental health. If a person —especially a child—thinks that he or she is not a capable, likable, valuable person, then he or she is likely to exhibit behavior indicative of low self-esteem. Examples:

- difficulty managing such emotions as anger
- shy, unassertive behavior or, alternatively, arrogant, overbearing, or overaggressive behavior
- difficulty establishing or maintaining mutually supportive relationships with others

Self-esteem is not the same as conceit or egotism; these qualities, in fact, are often products of low self-esteem. A boy who does not feel self-confident, for example, may behave defensively and act arrogantly as a way of protecting himself from what he perceives to be the rejection and superiority of others. A boy who has a solid sense of self-esteem, on the other hand, feels accepted by others and is tolerant of his own and other peoples' weaknesses.

Building a positive self-image during childhood can be difficult because life's demands change constantly as a child grows and develops. Conquering one challenge, such as learning to read, does not necessarily ensure self-esteem, because physical and social challenges may seem overwhelming. A child who has been a secure toddler may need special support if he or she encounters difficulty learning in school. Most children continue to need support and encouragement from other people, especially parents, as they struggle to find themselves. Helping a child achieve a stable, positive self-image can be the most important—and gratifying—task of parenthood.

Parents can help their children feel good about themselves in many ways. One effective method is to help discover a child's strengths and then to encourage them. All children, no matter how disabled, have valuable potential. Sometimes talents are obvious; for example, a child may have a lovely voice and a sure sense of rhythm. Often, however, talents are more subtle. Some children, for instance, are remarkably sensitive to the needs of other people. Other children have extraordinary imaginations that help them find novel solutions to many problems. Still others simply have sweet dispositions. Regardless of what their strengths or weaknesses are, all children need to know that their parents love them and are proud of them. To the degree that children feel lovable, they are able to perform at their best.

Situations often arise that threaten a child's sense of self-worth. Society expects much of children—that they obey authority figures, sit still in the classroom, learn to read, work with numbers, use money, and so on. Children struggle either to meet or resist these externally imposed standards. For some children, especially those with *learning problems,* routine developmental and academic challenges represent major obstacles to achieving a sense of self-esteem. It may be necessary for parents to help a child compensate for disappointments and a sense of failure by making a special effort to draw out the child's strengths. For practical advice, see *hyperactivity* and attention problems; *language disorders; learning problems; speech problems.*

PROMOTING EMOTIONAL WELL-BEING

A person in good emotional health successfully copes with the various problems life presents every day. Coping involves recognizing, controlling, and expressing emotions in appropriate ways.

Helping a Child Recognize Emotions

Before children can control their emotions, they need to begin to label and talk about them. This task is particularly difficult for children because their ability to communicate verbally is more limited than that of most adults. Thus, after doing poorly on a test, losing a toy, watching another child become the teacher's pet, or waiting in a long line, a child may not know how to express a sense of failure, rejection, and frustration, and may resort, for example, to angry behavior.

Parents can help a child by confirming what they think the child is feeling and, depending on the age of the child, by suggesting ways to deal with the feelings or the opportunity to talk about them. If, for example, an older child lashes out when asked to wash the dishes, a parent might say, "You must have had a rough day, since you're usually so willing to help with the dishes. It's hard to cooperate when you're feeling angry. Did I do something to upset you?" Such an approach can ease a child into discussing his or her feelings and perhaps discovering what triggered them.

Parents should listen carefully to the details the child provides about any emotion-provoking situation. They may want to follow up on the first discussion by showing continuing interest in the situation as time passes. Such concern may help a child feel more comfortable about bringing problems to parents in the future.

Helping a young child talk about his or her feelings may make it easier for the child to deal with a variety of problems later on. Such early learning can lead not only to better control over the expression of feelings but can also improve personal relationships in the long run.

Helping a Child Control Emotions

Having recognized and talked about feelings, a child is then likely to be better able to decide how to deal with them. Children are not naturally inclined to control powerful feelings, even when they recognize them. It is important for parents to help their children learn ways to gain some control over emotions.

Suppose, for example, that a child is having difficulty dealing with an irrational fear of monsters. Parents can reassure children that no monsters are allowed in the house, and suggest that they remember this or say it aloud when they feel afraid. Or if an adolescent has a powerful crush on a teacher, parents can tactfully suggest that the child find a more attainable object of affection. They can also help find diverting activities that take his or her mind off the lovesick feeling. It is important to remember, however, that controlling a feeling does not mean denying or even softening it. Rather, control means not allowing a feeling to dominate one's thinking or behavior. If a child understands that feelings are legitimate but that they also can be transient—and can be controlled with thought and behavior—then he or she has gained valuable insight and power.

Helping a Child Express Emotions

Children are bound to express emotions to parents, other family members, or friends. The issue is not whether to express feelings, but how to do so. Children have options. A child who is angry with a friend, for example, may scream and shout at parents. An alternative would be to act morose for the next several days. More constructive options could include approaching the friend and explaining how he or she feels, or releasing tension through some sort of constructive physical activity, such as running or bicycling. To be aware of and to use these options, children need the advice, empathy, and encouragement of parents.

Every person has different coping styles, and it may be difficult for parents to influence the way a child expresses emotions. Parents should resist the temptation to remake their child in their own image and should not expect that a child's coping style necessarily will—or should—coincide with their own. Exploring various options with the child can allow the child to save face and feel more in control. Requiring a child to "be a man" or "act like a lady" may be inappropriate to his or her developmental stage or temperament and may add shame to the problem at hand.

Suppose, for example, that a child takes out frustrations on parents every time he or she does poorly on a test. A parent might say, "I think I understand how you're feeling. It's very difficult to prepare for a test and then find you did not do well on it. But we feel bad, too, when you yell at us afterward. We understand that you *almost* can't help it, but that doesn't make it fair. Can you think of any other way to get rid of that angry feeling?" Parents may find that children, in a calm moment, are surprisingly open to self-evaluation and, perhaps, to the idea of modifying their style of expressing emotions.

PROMOTING HEALTHY BEHAVIOR

How can parents help children toward healthy behavior—to find a workable balance between their own needs and desires and the rights of others? One obvious and popular approach is to point out that other people have rights and to teach the child how to act in a way that respects these rights, as far as his or her age and development permit.

A somewhat different approach is to watch what a child does and to listen quite carefully to what he or she says, in order to find out what the underlying feelings are. It may then be possible to talk with a child in such a way as to acknowledge the child's feelings and at the same time to affect or modify behavior. When children believe that parents truly hear and understand their point of view and feelings, even the most painful or stubborn problems are likely to be open to some change. Parents need to be patient and allow children to express their feelings and concerns. Once these are communicated, the parent, often with the child, can choose what seems most appropriate—helping the child to choose a different tack independently or suggesting alternative behavior that can then be positively reinforced.

Modifying behavior in relation to the desires, needs, or rights of others is not a manipulative attempt to ingratiate oneself into another's favor. Rather, much can be gained by avoiding offending others, including more meaningful social relationships. Respecting the rights of others does not mean conforming to someone else's whims. In fact, respecting the rights of others sometimes is the most effective way to encourage others to look critically at themselves.

In helping a child learn how to behave appropriately, parents should try to distinguish issues of development from true behavior problems. All children go through developmental stages that predispose them to behave badly. For example, toddlers tend to throw tantrums as a way of expressing strong feelings, school-aged children may tell small lies in an attempt to demonstrate their growing independence, and adolescents sometimes boldly defy rules as a way of testing their own values and independence. In many cases, the best way to deal with these types of behavior is to respond honestly but briefly and not emotionally. Children usually will abandon attention-getting behavior that is unsuccessful.

This is not to say that an adolescent who steals cars does not need parental attention or guidance. Rather, parents need to judge the source and degree of the child's behavior problem so that they may decide when firmness or outside help is needed.

Explaining the Rules

If an adolescent experiments with smoking cigarettes (as most do when they are in their early teens, see *drug and alcohol abuse*), he or she is not necessarily engaging in defiant behavior. Smoking cigarettes can be a way of testing independence and trying to gain peer acceptance. If parents realize this, they will avoid remarks that will embarrass or "put down" the child, such as, "We are not worried about your smoking because it is just a phase that you're going through to test your independence." To the child, the desire to smoke cigarettes often is real. Such a parental reaction is likely to provoke anger, for a child may assume that parents are being condescending or sarcastic.

Instead, parents can try pointing out why certain types of behavior are not in the child's best interests. In the case of cigarettes, a parent might try saying, "I know how tempting it is to smoke. I tried cigarettes when I was young because all my friends were smoking. But after a while I quit because smoking got to be pretty expensive, and I was always reading about how smoking caused all kinds of terrible diseases, like cancer and emphysema. I care about you so much, and I don't want you to be hurt." In addition, parents may want to provide their children with pamphlets and other information about the problems associated with smoking.

Defiance of and experimentation with rules are not the only motives that prompt children to behave "badly." Sometimes children do not understand the rules, and sometimes the rules are unreasonable. To prevent the first problem, parents should explain the rules in a straightforward, sympathetic way. If a child, especially an adolescent, believes that rules are unreasonable—either when they are introduced or later as the child grows out of them—then parents should take complaints seriously and at least consider adjusting their standards. If the existing rules still seem reasonable to parents, they should explain to a child that they intend to enforce them. Parents should outline clearly their expectations and punishments, which should be appropriate, reasonable, and above all, consistent. Parents also should explain the reasons underlying their rules.

The time to think about a child's behavior, however, is not just when rules are broken. Perhaps the surest way to influence a child's behavior is to offer immediate praise and reassurance when rules or guidelines are followed. Not only does this raise a child's self-esteem, it also demonstrates the benefits of respecting the rights of others.

Controlling Habits

One of the familiar ways that children—and adults—often cope with tension, stress, anxiety, and other difficult or painful feelings is by engaging in some sort of rhythmic or repetitive behavior. Rhythm and repetition are soothing. For example, a mother will rock a crying baby in her arms, or children will rock themselves in a chair if they are upset. Virtually all adults use some sort of rhythmic or repetitive activity to calm themselves; a few examples are pacing back and forth, rapidly tapping a foot, and nail-biting.

In general, such movements last only a short while and appear just occasionally. Paying no attention to them—or occasionally diverting the child—is the best response. In some cases, however, a movement is repeated so often that it becomes routine, and its frequency or intensity may be increased during times when soothing is needed. When this happens, a habit has been formed. Common childhood habits include *hair-pulling, nail-biting,* and *thumb-sucking.* These habits tend to be relatively harmless, and should concern parents only if they become physically harmful to the child, interfere with social relationships, or diminish a child's sense of control.

It is easy to overreact to a child's repetitive movements and assume that a harmful habit is about to develop. The key is to try to determine if the habit is, in fact, harmful. Should parents be uncertain, they can discuss their concern with their child's physician.

To help a child break a habit, parents can try to ignore it—at least outwardly. When the child begins engaging in the habit, parents can try subtly to divert his or her attention to other things. If such an approach fails, parents may wish to try a modest form of behavior modification, which involves praise for not engaging in the habit and praise for trying not to do so even when the child fails to exercise self-restraint. Some parents find it helpful, for example, to put a star on a calendar each day that the child does not engage in the habit. Others promise equivalent small rewards. The positive effects of behavior modification are largely lost, however, if parents are inconsistent and sometimes punish the child for engaging in the habit.

PROMOTING SOCIAL WELL-BEING

The best way to help a child establish meaningful relationships with others is to promote actively his or her emotional and physical behavior. Children need to become familiar, as well, with social conventions, including how to be polite and share with others. Here are some simple ways parents can help:

- A child should feel free to invite other children over to play; when the child is very young, parents can invite children of different ages and sexes to play with their child at their home. While inviting several children over every day can be overwhelming to a child, regularly inviting one or two of a group of playmates of the child's choosing can encourage early development of social skills.

- Engaging a child in a group activity, such as kickball or tag, can teach valuable lessons about getting along with others and meeting new people. Games and sports can also improve a child's sense of physical confidence and coordination and simultaneously alleviate or resolve feelings of awkwardness.
- Parents can make a point of talking with a child's teacher—and, perhaps, guidance counselor—about how a child behaves and interacts with other children in school. Parents might also want to check to see if teachers are reinforcing a child's positive, outgoing behavior.
- Parents, while encouraging a child's friendships, can help their child understand the important difference between being popular and having friends. Parents can take an interest in their child's friends, yet not worry about them unless they obviously seem to be causing harm.
- Parents should try to set realistic expectations for a child's success in school or any other activity. When improvement is called for, parents should be pleased with a child's modest rate of change and substantial—but not enormous—gains in a reasonable amount of time.
- Children often need help in developing sensitivity and learning to be thoughtful of others. They should be encouraged not to tease their playmates, and, in turn, taught how to handle teasing. Ignoring good-natured teasing and developing a sense of humor can be two helpful responses. However, if a child is continually being teased for a disability such as a hearing impairment, parents might consider placing the child in a school where the staff is more sensitive to the child's needs and limitations.
- Parents should feel free and relaxed about hugging their children and giving them other clear physical signs of affection as long as children seem comfortable in receiving these gestures. At certain stages of development (during some periods of adolescence, for example), children may resist almost all physical signs of affection from parents and relatives. Some children, however, at any age appear to have difficulty with overt physical gestures of affection. They may need to have their parents' love and esteem communicated in verbal and other reassuring tangible forms.
- Children need to feel confident that parents are available and ready to talk; however, children should not feel pressured or obliged to do so. Children universally profit from their parents' attention when they talk, especially when children are very young. Parents can make a helpful habit of communicating to children their strong belief that children's opinions are significant and worthwhile.
- It is unwise to encourage children to trust everyone they meet in every situation. Children need help in learning to evaluate the behavior of others in a variety of contexts. In general, however, a child can be encouraged to have a positive, optimistic attitude about new people and unfamiliar situations.
- Parents can encourage a child to be independent and responsible. Household tasks, such as helping with meal preparation, often help convey these "lessons" to a child. Children need to sense, as well, that part of becoming independent is learning how to be alone and feel self-confident.
- Parents are in a position to explain that not everyone who criticizes the child is justified or right. Children over 5 or 6 years old are often able to evaluate the source of an opinion before putting too much or too little stock in it.
- Many children need help in learning to take appropriate risks, one small step at a time. A parent's guidance can be instrumental in preparing a child for both successes and failures and in demonstrating how to accept and learn from both.
- A child needs encouragement and assistance in breaking habits such as

thumb-sucking or nose-picking if they are causing embarrassment (see above). Certain habits, of course, make children vulnerable to being teased or ignored, and parents can give gentle, consistent reminders when children engage in habits that could make them targets of ridicule or ostracism.

- It is painful for a child to be forced to wear clothes that are extremely out of fashion or to wear their hair in a style that marks them as "different." Seemingly trivial details such as the type of cartoon on a lunchbox can be absolutely crucial to the child; when possible, parents should be flexible about such details.
- Parents are responsible, usually by their natural daily example, for teaching a child basic social skills, such as answering the telephone politely, meeting guests without fear, and accepting compliments naturally and graciously.

FINDING RELIABLE, LOVING CHILDCARE

Increasingly, American parents are sharing the care of their children with others. During all or part of the workday, for example, more than 11 million preschool children in the United States (about 40 percent of the total) are in the care of someone other than their parents. The child's emotional and social well-being, of course, will be affected by the quality of that care, as will his or her physical health. Yet, alternative care available to most working families is limited, and not just because of financial considerations. The most sought-after kind of care—that found in daycare centers—is very scarce. Only about 2 million children find places in public daycare centers. All the other children are placed with caregivers who possess greatly varying skills. Such caregivers include other mothers with children at home, independent proprietors of small, unlicensed neighborhood daycare facilities, and untrained teenaged baby-sitters. Additional uncounted thousands of children, unfortunately, do not receive consistent supervision or care of any kind. One of the most important steps a parent can take in promoting a child's well-being is to evaluate and monitor all care given by others.

VARIETIES OF CARE

Full-time care can be given in the child's own home, in the home of a professional or amateur caregiver, or in a daycare center. Part-time care may be available at home, in some of the full-time facilities, in a nursery school, or in a small playgroup organized to accommodate a parent who needs part-time childcare.

Care in a child's own home by a relative, friend, or experienced child caretaker can be the most reassuring and least threatening. Home care may also have the advantage of keeping a number of preschool siblings together.

Care in a daycare center is the best publicized and most generally approved form. Daycare centers in the United States range in size from 15 to 300 children; the average size is about 50, usually divided according to age. Good daycare centers will have public accountability through local or state licensing, quality and stability in their staffs, diversity of their children, and safety in their environments.

Part-time daycare includes innumerable formal and informal arrangements. The traditional forms in the United States are nursery schools and playgroups. Nursery schools are organized, mostly morning sessions for 3- and 4-year-olds. Playgroups, usually designed to provide spontaneous social experiences for both children and parents, are informal gatherings of mostly 2- and 3-year-olds.

GETTING INFORMATION

Selecting care for a child is difficult because the choices usually are extremely limited. Some communities have an information referral system or a coordinating service for childcare—or children's services generally. Even if a home or center can boast a license, such certification is a guarantee only of minimal environmental standards, not of skilled personnel nor quality care.

Some municipal social service departments and public health departments are prepared to refer parents to daycare providers. Bulletin boards in town government offices, stores, or religious institutions, newspapers, or telephone directories may contain information about available services. Even so, most parents are likely—or forced—to rely on suggestions offered by informal sources such as friends, relatives, or neighbors.

Daycare and Nursery Schools

Getting reliable, accurate information about the actual daily life of a daycare facility takes time and effort. Most community social service departments still are not permitted to provide recommendations, evaluations, or opinions about the performance of any daycare provider or the quality of any daycare facility. Even with carefully prepared questions, a parent can usually acquire only limited amounts of useful information from a telephone conversation with a daycare provider.

One reliable source of "inside information" is the parent of a child who currently attends a particular daycare facility. A list of questions prepared in advance may elicit important details of how daycare is provided, though it cannot give a comprehensive picture. Visits and interviews provide the most direct information. Some suggestions for making wise choices about daycare centers and nursery schools:

1. Visit twice for more than an hour each time, if possible, and (a) observe how staff members deal with a child's emotional needs, especially how much holding, comforting, and talking occur and how anger and conflict are handled; (b) take into account how many creative, flexible play materials (not commercial games and standard toys) and what kinds of equipment are available and how they are used; (c) see how much freedom children are given to set their own pace, follow their own rhythms, and make their own decisions about what they prefer to do; (d) listen to how much reading aloud and storytelling staff members do with children.

2. Talk after daycare hours to the director or a staff member to hear in detail about the staff's outlook on children's needs at various stages of development.

3. Talk later in detail with two or more parents whose children currently attend that facility.

4. Consider or ask the following questions (some suggested by the Children's Bureau of the United States Department of Health and Human Services):

- Is the staff professionally trained? (Credentials may include a college degree or a CDA—Child Development Associate—certificate offered by the National Association for the Education of Young Children.)
- Is the center licensed or approved by a child health or welfare department?
- What is the adult-to-child ratio? (Some experts suggest one adult for every four or five children, with 24 as the absolute maximum number of children; and one for every three or four babies, with 12 as the absolute maximum number of babies.)
- Does the facility appear to be safe and clean?
- Is there adequate space to play? to nap? to eat?
- Is there a safe outdoor play area, with supervision?
- Is the food nutritious? tasty? varied?
- How does the staff handle discipline? rewards? minor injuries?
- Are teaching and play appropriate to the childrens' ages and levels of development?

- What efforts does the staff make to encourage cooperation? sharing? independence? manners?
- What kind of written records are kept for each child?
- How does the center deal with accidents, serious injuries, illness, or contagious disease?
- What are the hours of operation? Are the hours flexible enough to accommodate a parent who occasionally must be late in picking up the child from the center? Is the center closed on holidays?
- What are the arrangements for parent conferences?

Above all, parents should trust their own impressions of and emotional responses to the personal qualities of daycare staff members. Children's transactions with staff members are crucial to the quality of the time they spend in daycare.

Home Care

Parents must also be selective and diligent when choosing childcare that will be provided in the child's or someone else's home. Again, visits and interviews will provide parents with much information about the type of setting the child will be in. Some suggestions for making these interviews and visits as illuminating as possible:

1. Interview the caregiver or sitter at length, both with and without the child present. A parent should feel quite comfortable with the person who is going to spend so much time with the child. It is of paramount importance to establish rapport and to feel that he or she is someone worthy of the highest trust.

2. Find out in detail about the caregiver's particular experiences with children both at home and outside his or her immediate family.

3. Ask about any education and training in childcare and childhood education.

4. Ask why he or she wants to do this work, aside from financial considerations.

5. Try to estimate how imaginative and flexible he or she may be, and be alert for playfulness and a ready sense of humor.

6. Most important, observe how the individual relates to the child throughout the entire interview, especially whether he or she talks to the child or directs all remarks to the parent. People who respond spontaneously and unselfconsciously to children of all ages can be their most satisfying, nurturing, and reliable companions.

7. Ask for at least four references, two personal (excluding relatives) and two vocational.

Discussions and interviews, whether for a daycare center, nursery school, or home care, can give parents a clearer image and firmer feel of what their child's experiences might be like. Initially, parents may not feel that they have sufficient time for such careful screening. If they consider, however, what crucially formative hours in a child's life will be spent in the care of others, they will want to make a special effort to inform themselves fully before making decisions. The enhanced quality of their children's lives—and their own—will more than repay the time and energy parents spend in making that "extra effort."

TELEVISION AND MENTAL HEALTH

In the United States television is sometimes used as a free electronic "baby-sitter" for children of all ages. Television occasionally becomes a substitute for commercial childcare—or even a part of it. The cumulative negative effects of this kind of passive entertainment can be substantial, as television is one of the most powerful influences on children's imaginations and emotions. It filters and shapes their view of reality. In addition to entertainment, television provides powerful images of how people get along with each other—or more often, fail to get along.

The terms "fixation" and "addiction" seem appropriate for the hold that television can exert on children. Anyone who has watched television with children can testify to how deeply absorbed they become; young children seem helpless to resist the magnetic attraction of televised sights and sounds.

By their nature, children are energetic, curious, mobile, and eager for variety, but often they are stripped of those qualities by televised "entertainment." Children under 5 are extremely vulnerable to whatever images and messages are conveyed to them. Overexposure to the programming and advertising on commercial television can seriously impair their ability to separate truth from deception, real harm from staged violence.

Commercial television regularly serves up large doses of violence and adult forms of sexuality that may mobilize powerful fantasies for young children. Fear and anxiety can be triggered by these images. Few children have any way of expressing the fantasies that are evoked or dealing appropriately with the accompanying feelings. So they try to suppress these feelings or to act them out afterward, usually with unhappy results. Rarely do children have an opportunity to explore fully how they feel about what they see.

What can parents do to protect the emotional health and ethical sensibilities of their children? First, they can inform themselves about programming for children. Action for Children's Television (ACT, 20 University Road, Cambridge, MA 02138) is an independent organization that monitors children's programming and provides reliable information for families and governmental groups. *Parents' Choice,* a review of children's media, can provide various kinds of information about television, videos, and other forms of popular entertainment, especially books (Box 185, Newton, MA 02168). Well-informed parents can exchange information and help each other decide which programs their children may watch during any given week.

For many parents it is unrealistic to try to keep track of all of their children's television watching. Whenever possible, however, parents should consider watching television with their children; when it is impossible to do so, they should emphasize that they are available to discuss anything that their children see. No matter what messages, images, and feelings arise during a television program, the child should always be able to rely upon a parent for discussion afterward.

Sexually explicit "entertainment" that is labeled "adult" almost never is what children, no matter how mature, should see. Even small doses of such programming can be disturbing and stimulating to children, especially adolescents, who have little experience coping with the feelings so aroused. With adolescents, discussing why a particular show may be unsuitable is more effective than a ban imposed without explanation or justification.

For children less than 6 years old, an hour or so of television each day is probably enough. For older children, an additional hour daily may be acceptable as long as the program's content is appropriate to the child's age and development.

Parents should resist using television as a baby-sitter. That practice deprives children of supervision and the opportunity for discussion of what they see. Such a misuse of television ultimately is destructive of children's imaginations and abilities to entertain themselves creatively.

GETTING HELP

Whenever parents become seriously concerned about a child's emotional, social, educational, and behavioral development, it is time to seek help. Often the most difficult decisions parents face are when and where to get counseling if their efforts to help their own child don't appear to be working.

One of the most reliable sources of information for parents is their child's physician, who usually can provide a referral, if necessary, to a reputable mental-health clinic. All facets of a problem can be discussed with an appropriate specialist, and if necessary, further diagnostic work be performed. Psychiatrists, psychologists, and social workers can usually be helpful. The appropriate consultation can help clarify a normal developmental stage and can result in some suggestions for parent and child. If the problem proves serious, help should be found as quickly as possible. For a child with particularly complex emotional (and physical) problems, an interdisciplinary clinic affiliated with a regional medical center or medical school may be able to provide diagnosis, a treatment plan, and a local referral. For parents who do not have a private physician, a call to the school guidance counselor, the local department of public health, or the state medical society may be a practical first step in getting useful information and a referral.

Many common problems may stress children and their families. Parents should not feel guilty, hesitant, or shy about sharing their concerns with a psychologist, psychiatrist, or social worker. Such specialists deal successfully and confidentially with children's problems daily. Some of the most common—and distressing—problems that these mental-health specialists regularly discuss with parents and children (either separately or together) include death, divorce, illness, hospitalization, school problems, weight problems, suicidal thoughts, frequent accidents, and bed-wetting.

See also *autism; bed-wetting; bruxism; eating disorders; failure to thrive; hairpulling; head-banging; hyperactivity and attention problems; movement disorders; nail-biting; neurotic disorders; phobias; psychosis; sleep disorders; stress; suicide; thumb-sucking; tics and Tourette's syndrome.*

4 Accident Prevention

In the United States each year, accidents (including automobile accidents) are the leading reason for children's visits to hospital emergency rooms, and they account for more children's deaths than the next five most frequent causes of childhood death combined. Most childhood accidents, however, can be avoided with preventive planning and action by alert parents and children themselves.

Although children are capable of assimilating some basic safety concepts after they become toddlers, most young children comprehend and retain limited amounts of information. Accordingly, it is essential that parents and children work together regularly to learn and apply safety rules. As an example, a toddler can learn not to touch a hot stove, but often does not fully understand why. While preparing meals, a parent can remind the child of how hot the stove is and how easy it is to get burned when near one. As the child grows older, more complex lessons can be mastered, and the child can then assume more responsibility for mastering information and preventing accidents.

Supervision and guidance are important, but the best ways to teach safety consciousness are by example and instruction. For young children especially, parents serve as role models—good, bad, and mixed. Older children, in addition to following examples set by parents, can take safety courses that teach valuable, pain-saving, even lifesaving lessons.

Although parents need to take precautions to prevent accidents, they can also try to be realistic and not excessively protective. Children need to explore; inevitably, they get bumps and bruises.

In addition to the preventive measures discussed in this chapter, parents should become familiar with the information in Part Three (Emergencies).

CHILDPROOFING

When infants and toddlers begin to move around the home on their own, their natural curiosity leads them to "get into everything"—cabinets, closets, bookcases, and virtually every other household niche. Usually nothing more serious occurs than the scattering of cans, books, and other objects. In some instances, however, access to household areas and objects can result in severe accidents. To prevent such accidents, parents should "childproof" their homes by the time a child is 6 months old, well before children start crawling or moving in walkers.

Childproofing a house means making it safe for young children by removing possible hazards. To childproof a home effectively and thoroughly, parents should examine each room individually for potential hazards that are within the child's reach. It may be necessary to make inaccessible any areas that contain high safety risks to children. A list of possible hazards follows, but parents should be alert for others, because each house is different.

- Electrical wires and outlets. All wires should be covered with strong vinyl insulation and fastened, if possible, to baseboards with approved electrical tape or electrical safety staples. Unused electrical outlets should be covered with plastic safety caps (available at any hardware store).
- Cabinets. Cabinets should be secured with plastic locking fasteners that hook around cabinet handles from the outside. Fastening or locking cabinets is essential if they contain hazardous items such as cleaning supplies or tools. It is preferable to move dangerous or hazardous objects to overhead cabinets and shelves.
- Doors. Safety latches (hooks and eyes) should be used on both interior and exterior doors to prevent them from being opened. Doorchecks can keep children from opening doors at the top of stairs. Clear glass doors should be marked with large colored stickers or tape to alert children visually.
- Radiators and fireplaces. Radiators should be protected with wooden or metal covers. Locking metal grates or screens should be placed in front of fireplaces. Tempered glass fireplace doors should be protected with screening. Fireplace tools and long fireplace matches should be set well out of a child's reach.
- Curtain cords and sashes. All curtain and window blind accessories should be tied up or placed out of a child's reach.
- Movable objects. All household tools—including brooms, vacuum cleaners, and small appliances—should be stored out of a child's reach. Decorative objects—including vases, pictures, and lamps—should be kept out of a child's reach.
- Furniture. Chairs, couches, and footstools should not be placed near un-screened, open windows.
- Windows. Windows should be opened, if possible, from the top only. Screens or storm windows should be used, particularly if windows open from the bottom.

In addition to identifying these general safety hazards, parents should conduct a room-by-room search for specific dangers, as follows:

- Kitchen. All cleaning supplies, including furniture polishes and waxes, should be kept entirely out of the reach of children under 8. A locked cabinet reserved for such materials is a good investment. Small electrical appliances should be stored well out of reach and, when in use, be set away from the edges of counters. Electrical cords should never hang over counters. Matches should be stored out of a child's reach. When pots and pans are on the stove, their handles should be turned toward the rear; pots containing hot liquids should always be placed on the back burners. Dishwashing machine doors should not be left open. Tablecloths should not be left on tables after use. If no one is available to supervise a small child during meal preparation, he or she should be occupied in play or placed in a child carrier on the parent's back to avoid accidents.
- Bathroom. Medicines, pills of any kind, cosmetics, shaving creams, and other toiletries should be stored in medicine cabinets that lock or are securely

latched. Parents should check bathroom doors to make sure they do not stick and cannot be locked accidentally from the inside. The hot water temperature should be set no higher than 120° F (49° C) to avoid accidental scaldings. Nonskid stripping or mats should be used on tub and shower floors.

- Bedroom. Perfumes, jewelry, and other swallowable items should be stored out of a child's reach. Clocks, radios, and television sets should be anchored or moved so that they cannot be toppled by a child pulling on their electrical cords.
- Laundry area and utility room. Washing machine and dryer doors should not be left open. All detergents and household cleaners should be kept on overhead shelves, well out of a child's reach. Tools should be stored out of reach or in locked cabinets. Young children should not have open access to laundry areas or utility rooms.
- Staircase and hallway. Gates with safety latches at top and bottom of stairs should be used so that young children cannot gain access to halls or stairways. In apartment buildings, young children should be kept away from stairs and should not be allowed to play in hallways.
- Yard. Grills and accessories, lawn mowers, rakes, and other outdoor tools should be stored out of a child's reach. Permanent fences with securely latching gates and safety locks should be erected around swimming pools. Swings and other play equipment should be checked periodically.
- Garage. Young children should not be allowed to play in garages.

POISON PREVENTION

One of the most devastating childhood accidents is poisoning from ingestion of toxic substances (materials that can cause illness or death if swallowed, touched, or inhaled). Parents should place all toxic substances out of the reach of children. It is important to keep the number of the local or regional poison information center near the telephone. Ipecac syrup, which causes vomiting, can be purchased inexpensively at all pharmacies; every home with a child should be equipped with a small container to be given if—and only if—the poison center recommends vomiting. (See discussion of poisoning in Chapter 10, "Basic First Aid," p. 142.) Parents should insist on childproof containers for all medications, both prescription and over-the-counter. Child-resistant caps on medicines and household products serve to remind parents which are the most toxic substances. Parents should pay particular attention where they store these products and not use them when children are around.

Potentially poisonous substances that can be consumed include detergents, fuels, polishes, shampoos, automobile fluids, insect or animal poisons, weedkillers, ammonia, solvents, liquids containing lye, and many acids. Such substances should be stored in original containers that clearly label their contents. Toxic substances should never be transferred to other containers, especially beverage bottles, even if descriptive labels are placed on bottles—since children often don't or can't read them.

Lead can easily be eaten by young children. *Lead poisoning* usually occurs when small amounts of lead are ingested over time. This most often occurs among young children who live in homes built before 1960, where the walls and woodwork are often painted with lead-based paints. When children chew on window sills painted with leaded paint or swallow chips of leaded paint, or put fingers in their mouths after playing in lead-contaminated dust or dirt, lead enters the body. If lead ingestion continues, poisoning eventually occurs (see *lead poisoning*).

In addition to the poisons discussed here, medications, taken in sufficient quantities, can poison young children. Medications that taste good, such as flavored aspirin, vitamins, and cough syrups, are particularly appealing—and hazardous—to young children.

Plants are another potential source of ingested poisons. Potentially dangerous indoor plants include philodendron, pothos, diffenbachia, mistletoe, and poinsettia. Potentially dangerous outdoor shrubs include rhododendron, hemlock, yew, holly, boxwood, and mountain laurel; poisonous flowers include bleeding heart, crocus, narcissus, jonquil, and sweet pea.

Some species of mushrooms are also quite toxic (see *food poisoning*). If a child gets as much as a bite of certain wild mushrooms, he or she may have to be given ipecac syrup, *but only when prescribed by a health professional.* Parents should call the nearest poison information center for assistance if a child has consumed any plant material.

Children can also be poisoned by inhaling toxic fumes. Because most young children have no experience in recognizing hazardous odors, they should be taught how to identify such odors and what to do if they are present. It is very important, for example, that children recognize the odor of natural gas, understand the dangers of a gas leak, and respond to the need to evacuate an area as quickly as possible. Many state and local health departments distribute educational materials about toxic fumes. Chemically impregnated paper strips, often called "scratch and sniff," can be effective educational materials for older children when explained by a qualified instructor. The odors of pesticides, natural gas, propane gas, kerosene, and gasoline are among the most common hazardous odors.

When substances that give off toxic fumes are in use in and around the home, children should be kept as far away from the odor as possible. Common substances used at home that give off toxic fumes include turpentine and other paint thinners, varnishes, glues, gasoline, and pesticides. Any area in which toxic fumes are present should always be well ventilated. Carbon monoxide is odorless (and invisible). It can escape from improperly vented kerosene heaters and is persistent in exhaust fumes from all gasoline engines. Automobiles should never be warmed up or allowed to idle in a garage when the door is not fully open. If the garage is an integral part of a house, a car should never be warmed up in the garage, as exhaust fumes may drift or circulate into the living areas.

FIRE SAFETY

FIRE SAFETY RULES

Children need to know the basic rules of fire safety as soon as they are old enough to understand them. Even when fires cannot be prevented, related injuries can often be avoided if precautions are taken.

Matches and candles

- Caution children not to play with matches or lighted candles. Matches should never be used near open flames or red-hot surfaces.
- Submerge used matches in water before discarding them.

Stoves and Ovens

- Watch out for all clothing near the flames of a gas stove.
- When using an oven broiler, be alert for grease catching fire. Small grease fires can often be smothered with a handful of baking soda or a lid from a pot.

- Do not leave the door of a hot oven open, and never use a stove to heat the kitchen.

Trash

- Remove trash from the house regularly so that flammable materials do not accumulate.

Flammable Liquids

- Keep flammable liquids in capped metal cans. If flammable liquids are used indoors, make sure the area is well ventilated. Do not use extremely flammable substances indoors.
- Never use or store combustible liquids near sources of high heat, including lighted matches, because fumes from such liquids can ignite easily. Such liquids include pressurized hair spray, lighter fluid, and cleaning fluids, especially gasoline and turpentine.
- When oiling wood or refinishing furniture, work in a well-ventilated space and never leave oily rags or cloths lying around. Spontaneous combustion can start a vigorous fire in a surprisingly short time—sometimes in as little as half an hour in hot weather.

Gas Leaks

- Check gas pipes periodically for leakage. If a mild gas odor is noticed, call the local gas company. If the odor is strong, evacuate the home immediately and call for assistance from a neighbor's home.

Building Materials

- Cover any exposed, flammable construction materials, such as urethane insulation, with flame-retardant gypsum wallboard, or call the local building code inspector for help.

Parties and Holidays

- Keep paper hats, long hair, and loose clothing away from candle flames at parties or celebrations. Candle lighting should always be supervised by an adult.
- If the family uses a cut evergreen at Christmas, make sure that the tree is fresh. The needles on fresh trees should bend rather than break. Water evergreens frequently to prevent dryness.
- Check indoor light fixtures, including Christmas tree bulbs, for exposed wires (stripped of insulation) or broken or cracked sockets. Never use electric lights on a metal or plastic Christmas tree. Never use candles on or near a live Christmas tree or evergreen boughs. All Christmas lights should be unplugged from wall sockets when no one is at home, at bedtime, or when everyone is sleeping.

Heating and Air-Conditioning Equipment

- Maintain heating equipment properly. Keep the furnace clean and regulated. Motors, blowers, and pumps should be lubricated regularly. Keep oil-burning or kerosene appliances clean and adjusted. Rooms where space heaters are in use must be adequately ventilated. Keep boxes of trash and other combustibles at least five feet from any heating device.

- Position portable heaters so that they cannot fall over and are far from any flammable materials such as curtains and bedding. Make sure there is a suitable permanent shield over the heating coils. Turn heaters off or set them on low at night.
- Make certain that chimneys are clean and free of excessive soot and creosote deposits. Chimneys should be cleaned every one to two years. Only reputable and qualified professionals should inspect and clean a chimney. Be sure that the flue is open before a fire is started in the fireplace, and do not close the flue until the fire is completely out. Embers should be raked, spread, and doused repeatedly with water to ensure that the fire is completely out.
- Protect the area around the fireplace from sparks with a sturdy, nontipping metal screen. Never hang flammable materials from the mantel.
- Never start or try to rekindle a fire in a fireplace with combustible liquids such as gasoline or lighter fluid.
- Never use a hibachi or other portable outdoor grill indoors.

Electricity

- Do not overload electrical circuits. If a fuse blows more than once in 24 hours, the circuit is probably overloaded. Never replace a fuse with one of a higher amperage. Use heavy-duty fuses only for high-voltage equipment, as indicated on the fuse box instruction plate. Circuit breakers may be needed to replace defective fuse boxes. Call an electrician if any repair work needs to be done.
- Keep appliance cords and extension cords in flawless condition; replace cords that are cracked or frayed. Do not overload a wall outlet with multiple cords or plugs. Do not staple extension cords to walls, and never lay them under rugs or carpets. Keep lamp cords close to the baseboards. Do not use an ordinary extension cord for high-voltage appliances. (Appliances usually are plainly labeled as requiring high voltage. Use only extension cords that are designed to handle high voltages.)

  Never use an appliance that is not working properly. If an appliance starts smoking, feels unusually hot, or produces an odor, immediately pull the plug or shut off the electricity. Do not use the appliance until it has been checked and repaired.
- Always provide a ground connection for any outside television antenna. Television sets should be unplugged when they will not be in use for a few days or longer.

Warning Devices

- Smoke detectors should be installed in every home regardless of its size. Since they are the most valuable device for alerting occupants to fires, smoke detectors should be placed on every floor of a dwelling and in corridors and staircases, especially outside bedrooms.

  Another device, a heat detector, can be used to sense rapid increases in air temperature. Alone, heat detectors are less effective than smoke detectors because most fires are characterized first by smoke.

TEACHING CHILDREN ABOUT FIRE SAFETY

When teaching children how to respond to fire, it is wise to introduce the signs of fire, including the crackling sound of fire and the odor of smoke, hot walls, and doors. Children can be taught that as soon as they suspect fire they should shout to wake up the rest of the household. Then they must try to escape the fire and smoke. It is essential, however, that parents instruct children not to run from their rooms in fear. Opening a bedroom door and entering a smoke-and-fume-filled hallway can be fatal; as many as four out of five fire-related deaths are caused by smoke inhalation rather than burns. On the other hand, children should be told never to try to hide from fire.

Family fire drills are invaluable in teaching children how to react to fire. Since most home fires that cause fatalities occur between midnight and 6 A.M., parents may want to hold a drill after dark. A flashlight should be available in each room.

Parents and children together should map out two or three escape routes from individual bedrooms and from other rooms of the house. Older children should be instructed to help younger children follow these routes. During a drill, parents should trigger a smoke alarm or heat detector so that children can recognize the sound.

Escape plans should minimize exposure to smoke and fumes. Parents should emphasize the importance of staying low in smoke-filled areas (since smoke and fumes tend to rise), and of moving as quickly as possible—without stopping to look for or pick up personal possessions. Children should be told not to spend time looking for pets. Seconds are precious in escaping safely.

Children should learn what to do if all escape routes through the house are blocked. If fire is in the hall, and the child is in the bedroom, the bedroom door should be shut securely. The child should open a window and, if possible, use a fire-department-approved folding metal ladder to escape. (Each bedroom should contain a collapsible ladder or a heavy piece of wood with sheets or rope attached.) If the child is unable to escape through the window, he or she should lean out, if possible, and breathe fresh air while waiting and calling out for help.

Children should learn what to do if their clothing catches fire. They must act fast. They need to "drop and roll" immediately: lie down, cross their arms over the chest, and quickly roll over and over on the floor (or ground) until the fire is out. Children should be shown how to roll themselves up in a rug or blanket, or how an older child can roll up a younger child. If hair catches fire, the child should be shown how to beat out or smother the fire with a towel or piece of clothing. Children should be told never to try to pull burning clothing over their heads.

As children get older, they can acquire additional information. For example, they can be taught how to put out small fires on their own. Because putting out a fire can be dangerous if not done properly, supervision must be expert and instructions clear.

FIRE EXTINGUISHERS

There are several types of fire extinguishers, each designed to fight a specific class of fire. Some can be used to fight two or three classes of fire. Fire extinguishers contain one of the following active ingredients: pressurized water, dry chemicals, carbon dioxide, potassium bicarbonate, or special chemical compounds called halogenated hydrocarbons. Before purchasing an extinguisher, find out what type of extinguisher best suits the needs of the household. It is important to read the owner's manual before the extinguisher is installed. An older child can be taught how to use an fire extinguisher properly.

If adults or children are unfamiliar with the use of a fire extinguisher, it is much safer to improvise and use what is at hand. Water is often available to drown a small fire (except one involving grease), or a blanket or small rug can be used to smother a well-contained fire. If a grease fire starts on a stove or in the broiler, it is best to try to smother the flames. If the fire is in a pan, cover the pan with a lid and turn off the gas or electricity. If the fire is in the oven, keep the oven door closed and turn off the oven. If baking soda is in the kitchen, it can be sprinkled on a grease fire to smother it. <u>Water should never be used on a grease fire, no matter now small</u>. If fire-fighting measures do not seem to be effective within <u>one minute</u>, evacuate the home and call for help without delay.

CAR SAFETY

Motor vehicle accidents are the leading cause of death and serious injury among American children. Many of these accidents could be prevented by simple safety precautions. Research shows that if parents buckle up their children in car seats and safety belts, they can reduce the chance of death by more than 60 percent and the chance of injury by more than 50 percent.

When a moving car hits something and stops suddenly, its unsecured contents—including human occupants—continue to move forward at the same speed until something stops them. This object is usually the steering wheel, dashboard, windshield, or some other hard part of the car's interior. This second, or human, collision, is what injures and kills; it can be prevented by the use of seat belts for adults and older children and special crash-tested safety seats for infants and toddlers.

During an accident a safety belt will hold an adult firmly against the seat, allowing the strong, mature pelvis and rib cage to absorb most of the impact. Children under the age of 4, however, have softer bones, which may not be able to withstand such intense pressures. Young children need to have the force of the crash distributed more evenly over their bodies. Infant and toddler car seats are designed specifically for this purpose.

Unfortunately, too many parents think that the safest place for an infant is in their arms—even in an automobile. They believe that they can restrain a child during an accident. But when riding in a motor vehicle, children in the arms of adults may be in more danger than children who are not restrained at all. The impact of an accident could cause the adult's body to crush the child against the dashboard or windshield. Even if the adult were wearing a lap and shoulder belt, the child could easily be torn from the adult's grasp and fly forward like a missile.

One safety belt should never be placed around both the adult and the child. In an accident, the weight of the adult coupled with the force of the crash could press the belt into the child's body, causing serious—sometimes fatal—injuries.

Restraining children in car safety seats may help prevent those accidents that occur when a child distracts the driver. Having a child secured properly in a safety seat allows the driver to concentrate on the road. Safety seats also help prevent the bumps and bruises that can occur when an unrestrained child falls during a sudden stop or swerve.

It is also true that children tend to behave better when they are buckled up in their car safety seats. These special seats, which are made to fit small shapes and sizes, are more comfortable and satisfying for children because they lift them high enough to see out of the window. Studies show that children are less likely to feel carsick and more likely to fall asleep when properly restrained in a safety seat.

A child accustomed to riding in a car seat all his life will expect to be placed in one when in an automobile. A child who is not used to riding in a car seat may initially resist and struggle against the idea of being restrained. Children should be allowed to test the seat before their first ride, and parents should explain to their children how the seat works and why it is important. It is advisable, at first, to take the children on some short rides—perhaps around the block—to help them become comfortable with the seat. Children should be praised for sitting quietly. Allowing children to bring some toys that are associated with quiet play may help make the first few rides easier. <u>A child should never be allowed to get out of the seat during the ride</u>. If this happens, the driver should pull over, and the child should be placed back in the seat.

CHILD RESTRAINT SYSTEMS

Choosing the right restraint system is essential to ensure adequate protection. Some seats are built for use by infants only, while others are designed expressly for toddlers, preschoolers, or children old enough to sit up by themselves. Other safety seats, called convertibles, are designed for both infants and toddlers. Parents should be aware that some seats have special features, such as top anchors, which may require drilling into the body of the car for installation. Other seats may be difficult to fit in the back seat of compact cars. Cars with low ceilings may present problems if armrests or shields must be lifted over the seat.

There is no "best" car seat. The best seat turns out to be the one that fits the needs of parents and child, one that will be used for every ride.

Infant

The baby's first ride should be a safe ride. That means parents should have a car seat ready to take their newborn home from the hospital. Infant seats, which are usually tublike devices, and convertible seats, which are larger than infant seats and shaped more like a small chair, are the only types of car safety seats recommended for use with babies less than 17 pounds. (See Fig. 4.)

FIG. 4. INFANT CAR SEAT

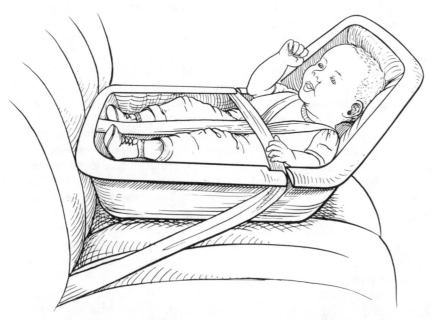

Infant tub-style seats are designed so that the baby rides in semireclining position facing backwards. In the event of an accident, the back absorbs the force of the crash.

The safest place for the infant to ride is in the center of the back seat. Infants ride in a semireclining position facing backwards. In the event of an accident, the baby's back absorbs the force of the crash.

Infant seats are usually lined with soft padding. Folded blankets may be placed around the baby to help keep the head steady. A safety harness holds the baby firmly in the chair, and the chair is anchored to the car with the vehicle's regular safety belt.

Infant seats should be used until the baby's legs become cramped or until the child exceeds the weight limitations set by the seat's manufacturer. When the child outgrows the infant seat, parents should have a toddler seat installed in the car and ready to use.

Convertible seats are usually economical, because the same seat can be used for infants and toddlers. Infants ride in the semireclining, backward-facing position in the convertible seat. When the child approaches 20 pounds, the seat is turned toward the front of the car, the harness system is revised according to manufacturing specifications, and the frame of the seat is converted to an upright position.

Parents should keep in mind that convertible seats are heavier and bulkier than the infant tub-style seats and are therefore more difficult to carry into restaurants or grocery stores. Flimsy, lightweight, plastic feeding seats or car beds, which may be more convenient for carrying infants into buildings, should be restricted to household use. Infants should be transported only in federally approved car seats, which have been crash-tested under strict government guidelines.

Toddler

Several types of restraint systems are available for children who weigh more than 17 pounds and can sit up by themselves. All types of toddler seats face forward and are anchored by the vehicle's lap belt, which is either fastened around the front of the seat or threaded through the back of the car seat frame. (See Fig. 5.)

The first type of restraint is known as the five-point harness system. The harness consists of two shoulder straps, two lap straps, and a crotch strap. All the straps converge at a buckle, and all can be adjusted to the size and shape of the child and the thickness of the child's clothing. The crotch strap should be as short as possible to hold the lap straps in their proper positions, low and flat across the child's thighs.

In an accident, the five-point harness spreads the force of the crash over the child's shoulders and hips. The crotch strap keeps the lap belt from riding up into the child's delicate abdomen. This type of restraint system is usually quite comfortable for the child because it allows free movement of hands and arms.

Some of the harness safety seats have a top anchor strap, or tether, which fastens the top of the restraint to the structure of the car. The tether must be used to ensure adequate crash protection. This usually involves drilling a hole in the rear-window shelf or in the floor of a hatchback, station wagon, or van. Proper installation is essential to prevent the seat from tipping forward or collapsing in an accident.

A second type of toddler safety seat is known as the protective shield. This restraint fits over the front of the child's lap and chest and is designed to cushion the child and prevent forward movement in a crash. The seat is a padded C-shaped shell structure. It is anchored to the car by the lap belt, which fastens around the front of the shield. In an accident, the shield spreads the crash forces evenly over the child's upper body.

An advantage of the shield restraint is that parents do not have any harnesses or buckles to fasten. Children, however, can climb in behind some shield models while the seat is secured in place. However, children may also be able to climb out of the

FIG. 5. TODDLER CAR SEAT

Toddler car seats, which face forward, usually have some sort of harness system. In the event of an accident, the child's upper body and possibly the hips absorb the force.

shield while the car is moving, so this type of restraint often works best with older toddlers. A disadvantage of the shield is that it comes up high on the child's chest, restricting some hand and arm movements.

The third type of toddler car seat is part harness and part shield. This seat offers a compromise by eliminating some of the adjustment difficulties associated with harness systems as well as the restricted movement associated with the shield. The partial shield, which replaces only the lap portion of the harness, is a reinforced pad that is attached to the shoulder straps. Shoulder belts must be used with this type of seat.

Older Children

Booster seats are specially designed to fill the gap between the time a child outgrows the car safety seat and when he or she can use the adult belt and comfortably see out the window. Pillows or cushions should <u>never</u> be used to lift a child higher in a car. These can slide out easily, allowing the child to slip under the lap belt or causing the child's head to move far enough forward to strike something.

Booster seats should be used with some sort of upper torso support, preferably in the back seat with a harness. The body harness is secured to the car in the same manner as the standard tether used with toddler seats. The car's lap belt and shoulder belt can also be used to hold the child in the booster seat, but parents should make sure that the shoulder belt does not cut across the child's neck.

Accident Prevention **69**

Adult safety belts can be used for children who have outgrown booster seats. Safety belts can also be used for small children who can sit up by themselves, but they should only be used as a last resort when no car seat is available. The safety belt should ride in a snug, low position on the child's hips. If the shoulder belt crosses the child's face or neck, it should be placed behind the child's back after the buckle has been fastened. If a shoulder strap cannot be used, parents should check to make sure the child's head will not hit the dashboard in a crash or a sudden stop. If this could happen, the child should be placed in the back seat.

Family Safety

Parents should buckle up <u>every time</u> they get into the car, to set a good example for their children, for their own safety, and for the safety of other passengers. Because unrestrained occupants can crash into other occupants who are belted in, for maximum safety of all persons in a car, everyone should be restrained.

Other car safety tips:

- Two children should never be strapped into one belt. Doing this makes a proper fit impossible.
- Lawn mowers, bicycles, luggage, or any hard, heavy objects should be carried in the trunk or on a roof rack. Unsecured objects inside a car pose a hazard. Nothing should be placed on the shelf under the back window. If the car stops suddenly, flying objects could be lethal.
- Children should be reminded to keep all parts of their bodies inside the car.
- All doors should be kept locked while the vehicle is moving.
- Small children should not be left in the car alone.

Detailed information on child restraint systems and car safety is available from either of the following:

The United States Department of Transportation
National Highway Traffic Safety Administration
400 Seventh Street SW
Washington, DC 20590
Phone: 800-424-9393

The National Child Passenger Safety Association
P.O. Box 841
Ardmore, PA 19003
Phone: 215-525-4610

CAR SAFETY FOR ADOLESCENTS

Before teenagers can obtain drivers' licenses in many states, they must pass a driver education course. Taking such a course is a good way to learn driver safety rules and the rules of the road. Even after teenagers pass a driving test, however, they must gain substantial on-the-road experience before they can become competent drivers.

Because of the increasing number of inexperienced teenagers who drive drunk or drugged, teenage drivers and their passengers run a high risk of accidents. An estimated 15,000 Americans between the ages of 15 and 24 are killed in car accidents each year. Substantially fewer deaths might occur if more teenagers followed safety rules and avoided driving recklessly or while drunk or drugged.

Although schools, police departments, and community organizations continue their efforts to reduce teenage traffic fatalities, solving the problem remains largely in the hands of teenagers and their parents. Parents must rely on their own judgment about how best to work with their children to ensure automobile safety. Parents and teenagers should discuss this problem candidly, exploring the options for safe driving. Parents must set good examples when driving and encourage their teenagers to follow them.

Teenage drinking, however, is not a subject that many adolescents are comfortable discussing with their parents. As a result, teenagers feel ambivalent about calling to ask for rides when they and their friends have been drinking. Too many teenagers take their chances on riding in a car driven by a friend who drinks but drives anyway.

Parents may have to bring up the subject of drinking and driving. Such conversations must be conducted frankly but diplomatically so that teenagers do not feel that their independence is being diminished or that the parents are trying arbitrarily to curtail social activities. Parents need to be sympathetic and patient with their teenagers when discussing this issue. If handled successfully, arrangements can be agreed upon so that teenagers feel comfortable calling for rides and parents are less worried about the safety of their children. It is, of course, vital that parents practice what they preach about never driving while drinking.

TRICYCLE SAFETY

In general, children who can climb stairs one foot at a time can ride Big Wheel pedal vehicles and similar toys. If ridden in safe areas, tricycles rarely bring about serious accidents, usually only cuts or bruises.

Children should ride their tricycles only on their own (or a neighbor's) driveway, or with supervision on the neighborhood sidewalk, or in a park. Tricycles should not be ridden in the street. Riding "double" on a tricycle can be dangerous for both children involved.

BICYCLE SAFETY

Bicycle-related injuries are most frequent among children between the ages of 6 and 12. Most minor bicycle-related injuries result from falling off a bike because of a lack of balance, stopping short, skidding, or catching clothing in the bicycle chain. Such injuries usually involve no more than scratches, cuts, or bruises.

Serious bicycle injuries—those caused by a fast-moving cyclist falling off the bicycle or colliding with another object—occur most often when a cyclist turns too sharply or emerges suddenly from an alley, driveway, or parking lot, or when a careless motorist ignores the presence of a cyclist. Serious accidents also occur in heavy traffic when maneuvering room for cars and bicycles is limited. Injuries from such accidents usually require emergency room treatment and may include severe lacerations and broken bones. If internal injuries occur, hospitalization may be necessary. (See Chapter 10, "Basic First Aid," for treatment techniques for all injuries.)

SELECTING A BICYCLE

In general, children are not ready to start riding bicycles until at least 5 years of age. A bicycle should be chosen so that a child can ride comfortably, since one that is too large or too small can lead to injuries. A knowledgeable bicycle shop owner can recommend a safe, suitably sized bike for any child.

RIDING A BICYCLE

Children under 8 should never ride in the street. Children from 8 to 12 or so can ride in the street but should be accompanied by a responsible teenager or adult if

FIG. 6. BICYCLE SAFETY HELMET

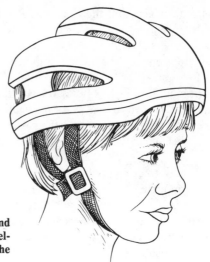

When riding bicycles, children and teenagers should wear protective helmets, especially when riding in the street.

there is moderate or heavy traffic or when visibility is marginal (at dusk and during evening hours, for example). Safe places for young children to bicycle include parks, bike paths or lanes, and sidewalks.

Children of all ages should dress sensibly when bicycling. Rubber-soled shoes that grip pedals are best. Clips or rubber bands should be worn around the bottoms of trouser legs to prevent them from getting caught in bicycle chains. Loose clothing and long coats should be avoided. Children and teenagers should always wear bicycle helmets when riding in the street. (See Fig. 6.) When riding at night, cyclists should always wear light-colored clothes or, preferably, reflective armbands, legbands, or vests. Cyclists who ride in the street must learn and obey all traffic rules, signals, and signs.

MOTOR BIKE SAFETY

A variety of motorized bicycles, 2-, 3-, and 4-wheeled, are available for children and adolescents. Minicycles, minibikes, and trail bikes are advertised for children as young as 4 or 5 years old. These vehicles are relatively unstable and have poor visibility. The American Academy of Pediatrics recommends that the use of any unlicensed two-wheeled motorized cycle, especially by children less than 14 years old, be discouraged. If a child rides one, an adult should supervise the activity at all times.

An all-terrain vehicle (ATV) is a motorized recreational cycle with 3 or 4 very large soft tires. ATVs are intended for off-the-road use on many hilly terrains. Because of their demonstrated instability and high center of gravity, ATVs are inherently dangerous. The Committee on Accident and Poison Prevention of the American Academy of Pediatrics "recognizes ATVs as a major hazard to the health of children." The Committee has called for a suspension of sales of new ATVs for recreational use until engineering improvements can assure greater safety.

The American Academy of Pediatrics states that "the safe use of ATVs requires skill, judgment, and experience. Their use by children less than 14 years old should be prohibited." Adolescents who choose to ride ATVs should always wear helmets and protective clothing and be required to hold a valid operating license.

STREET SAFETY

FOR YOUNG CHILDREN

Motor vehicle accidents are the single greatest cause of death to children between 5 and 10. A child of this age is likely to die from multiple injuries sustained when hit by a car while walking or riding a bicycle. Young children do not comprehend the dangers associated with playing in the street. Even when old enough to understand these dangers conceptually, children usually take a long time to develop enough caution for street safety. To keep accidents to a minimum, parents should supervise children who are crossing the street until they fully grasp vehicular dangers, usually between the ages of 8 and 10.

The first step for parents to take when teaching street safety is to set a good example. Being conscientious about crossing with the green light or Walk sign and carefully looking both ways before starting across a street are good practices to pass on to a child.

FOR UNACCOMPANIED CHILDREN

When a child is old enough to walk or bike along a street without supervision, parents should clearly designate safe routes to certain destinations. In determining safe routes, families may want to consider hazards such as construction sites or abandoned buildings, as well as positive safety factors such as crossing guards. During these sessions, parents should give clear instructions about not talking to strangers and explain why. It is important that parents impress upon their children that they should never go anywhere with a stranger.

A child's first walk without a parent should be taken in the company of siblings or other children. In general, these first trips should be to places where parents can learn quickly if a child has reached a destination within a reasonable amount of time. For many children, the walk to school or to the school bus stop is the first trip. The child's teacher or school bus driver should be aware when unsupervised trips are beginning so that if a child does not arrive on schedule parents can be notified quickly.

As a child gets older, he or she needs to learn extra street safety precautions. For example, older children should try to wear light-colored clothes or fluorescent vests when outside at night. Children should be warned against hitchhiking, and teenagers who drive should be warned strongly against picking up hitchhikers.

TOY SAFETY

Toys that are not carefully selected can pose serious safety hazards. Parents should examine toys carefully to determine their safety, especially if toys are handed down or purchased secondhand; most new toys made in the United States must now conform to safety standards set by the United States Consumer Product Safety Commission.

Toys for very young children should be unbreakable and made of nontoxic materials. They should be too large to swallow and should be free of sharp edges or points. Toys that may be hazardous include stuffed animals with plastic or glass eyes that can be pulled or chewed off; arrows or darts with sharp points; wooden toys that may splinter; and toys with long cords that might get wrapped around a child's neck. For children less than 18 months old, toys such as miniature telephones with cords longer than 18 inches are unsafe.

Certain hobby supplies used by older children—woodworking tools and chemistry sets, for example—as well as electrical equipment such as record players, may prove dangerous for both younger and older children. Parents should teach children the proper uses of such equipment.

FURNITURE SAFETY

In general, furniture designed specifically for an infant or young child requires more attention than do furnishings for the rest of the house. If used furniture is bought, it should be inspected thoroughly to make sure it is safe for children.

Some guidelines for furniture safety:

- <u>Cribs</u>. Side slats should be less than 2½ inches apart so that a child's head cannot get stuck between them. The mattress should fit snugly in the crib, leaving no extra space between its edges and the crib sides. Crib sides, head, and foot should come up at least to the chest of a child who is standing in the crib.
- <u>Playpens</u>. The only playpens that are safe for children are those with very narrow spaces between the vertical slats or with very small-gauge fabric mesh. Playpens with expandable wooden latticework sides or with mesh large enough to catch buttons on clothing are significant strangulation hazards. Parents should always keep sides of playpens up, as an infant can smother if caught between the floor and a lowered side of a playpen.
- <u>High chairs</u>. High chairs should have legs spaced for maximum stability and trays that latch securely.
- <u>Portable chairs</u>. Portable chairs should be stable and equipped with harnesses.
- <u>Toy chests</u>. Toy chests should not have hinged tops that can close unexpectedly. The Consumer Products Safety Commission has a list of distributors of safety props that can be placed on toy chests to reduce the risk of accidental closings.

WATER SAFETY

Playing in water can be hazardous to anyone if safety precautions are not followed. Each year an estimated 7,000 children drown; approximately one third are less than one year old. Childhood drownings most often occur because unsupervised children cannot swim adequately, overestimate their physical strength, or do not know water-survival techniques.

Young children must always be supervised when in or near water. This is true even when children are playing in very shallow water—the ocean, a pool or a bathtub—because drowning can occur in less than three minutes in as little as three or four inches of water. Most children are capable of learning water-safety rules by the ages of 4 to 6. As they begin to participate in water-related sports, children should be taught appropriate water-safety rules. In addition, they should be taught water-survival techniques, the most valuable water-safety lessons children can learn. The Red Cross and other organizations offer courses in water-safety rules and water-survival techniques, especially drownproofing, which most children enjoy practicing.

SWIMMING

No matter what their age, children should never be allowed to swim alone or unsupervised. Children and teenagers should swim with an individual trained in lifesaving techniques or should limit their swimming to areas patrolled by lifeguards.

Although all places to swim pose hazards, some are so dangerous that they should be avoided. Dangerous locations include beaches subject to strong or shifting currents or heavy surf; pools with defective ladders or diving boards; quarries and other swimming places with steep banks or submerged rocks; any area with heavy boat traffic; and swift-flowing streams and rivers. Swimming is never safe during an electrical storm.

All private swimming pools, above ground and underground, should have a fence around them. Many drownings and near drownings occur when an unsupervised child notices an unprotected pool and, moved by curiosity, topples in.

BOATING

Most boating accidents are caused by miscalculation or ignorance. Following safety rules can substantially reduce boating accidents. Copies of the basic boating safety rules are available through the United States Coast Guard and private boating organizations.

Boating with children requires extra precautions because children often do not understand the logic of safety rules. All children should wear life jackets that fit properly. If an older child or adolescent is allowed to go out without a life jacket, it is essential that other flotation devices such as floating seat cushions be aboard the boat. (Boat owners are required by law to carry such devices; those who do not are liable to fine and loss of their operating license.) Children should be taught not to stand up in canoes or small boats nor to stand close to the edge in large ones.

Before an older child or adolescent is permitted to operate a boat alone, he or she first needs training. A child must be able to recognize the first signs of hazardous weather conditions, to read a compass and a simple map so that the boat stays on course, and to interpret different navigational markers, as well as understand the dangers of operating a boat near swimmers, in unknown waters, or at excessive speeds.

ICE-SKATING AND SLEDDING

Skating can be an enjoyable and healthy winter activity if basic precautions are observed. Children should be warned of the dangers of thin ice. If a child plans to go skating on a pond, lake, or river, parents should check to determine that the ice is at least three inches thick. The skating area should always be checked for sections of thin ice, which are common near the entrance and exit points of the pond's water supply. Children should always skate under the supervision of an adult or adolescent. (See discussion of *drowning* in Chapter 10, "Basic First Aid," for instructions on how to treat a child who has fallen through ice.)

Parents should advise children to be careful when they are either on a sled or pulling one so that they avoid hitting other children or being hit themselves. On a sled, small children should sit snugly, in front of an older, responsible child or an adult. Children should be taught how to steer a sled before they are allowed to use one by themselves. Children should never sled too near a pond, whether it is frozen or not. When children ride on snowmobiles, they should be supervised <u>at all times</u>.

Children should dress warmly to avoid internal chilling (see discussion of frostbite in Chapter 10, "Basic First Aid"). Clothing should include a hat or earmuffs, a scarf, and gloves or, preferably, mittens. For maximum retention of body heat, clothing should be applied in layers: a thin cotton layer against the skin (T-shirts, tights, or long underwear) followed by a thick cotton (flannel) or thin wool layer. A heavy wool layer with windbreaker or a warm outer garment should be worn to protect the child from the cold. One pair of cotton socks (to absorb moisture) and one or two pair of wool socks (for skaters, depending on how much space remains inside the skate) should be worn on the feet.

FIREWORKS

Years ago, fireworks were readily available. As a result, serious injuries occurred frequently, especially on the Fourth of July. The most common wounds included eye injuries, sometimes leading to loss of sight; severe burns; and the loss of fingers or a hand.

Since the sale of fireworks to the public is now prohibited in many states, the incidence of fireworks-related injuries has decreased substantially. Injuries still occur, however, because some children are able to obtain potentially dangerous fireworks. It is easy to use firecrackers in unsafe ways—such as exploding them inside cans or bottles and thereby scattering sharp fragments of metal or glass. Injuries frequently stem from "safe" fireworks, such as sparklers, especially when children are neither careful nor supervised carefully.

All fireworks should be kept out of the reach of children. If parents wish to set up a fireworks display, children should watch from a safe distance. If children are permitted to use sparklers, parents must instruct them not to get close to the flame, which can burn skin or eyes. To ensure safety, children and parents should leave fireworks displays to professionals.

GUNS

An estimated 500 children die each year in shooting accidents. Studies show that most accidental shootings occur at or near the home rather than on hunting trips or at firing ranges. Tragic shooting accidents occur when a parent mistakes a family member for a burglar.

Accidents involving firearms happen when guns are stored within a child's reach (or persistent search, in some cases). A child who finds a loaded gun in the home, for example, usually does not realize that it can hurt someone. Pointing a loaded gun at a playmate and squeezing the trigger can occur in seconds.

Unless having one at hand is essential, a gun should not be kept in the home. If a parent must keep a gun, it should be stored and locked out of the reach of children. Ammunition should always be stored and locked separately.

If parents wish to teach their children how to use guns, instruction should not start until the child is old enough to manage the weapon responsibly, usually during the teenage years. The child should use the gun only after careful instruction and under close supervision. Children who want to use air rifles and BB guns should receive similar instruction and supervision.

PET SAFETY

Pet safety involves caring daily for animals kept at home so that the risk of health problems for family members is minimized. Children derive many important benefits from learning to care responsibly for a pet. We are dealing here only with concerns for children's safety. Rarely does a well-cared-for pet strike out or bite without provocation.

CHOOSING A PET

A pet should suit the owner's needs and living conditions, particularly the size of the home and grounds. Prospective owners must be sure that they can give the pet sufficient care and attention. The entire family should become knowledgeable about the desired pet before it becomes one of the family.

A reliable way to find out what a young animal will be like when full-grown is to talk in detail with someone who has owned that kind of pet. Checking an animal's breeding often leads to fairly accurate predictions of adult height, weight, coloring, hair length, temperament, and related matters. In many cases, mixed breeds ("mongrels") are less excitable and adapt more easily to children. Pets should be examined thoroughly by a veterinarian before being brought into the home.

PET CARE

Before a pet is brought home, parents should discuss with children in detail pet care responsibilities. Books on pet care may supply helpful advice and suggestions. If the pet is to belong to only one member of the family, it should be made clear how much time is required for performing pet-related duties and whether other family members may help out as necessary. Many children are initially eager to have a pet, but most need encouragement when they discover that responsibilities are continual. Parents, however, should be supportive of a child's determination to care for a pet if he or she is old enough to take responsibility. A 10-year-old child is usually ready to take seriously the demands of owning and caring for a dog. Parents should expect, however, to watch out for the animal's well-being, whenever necessary.

AVOIDING PET-RELATED INJURIES

Children should be taught not to provoke animals, for reasons of kindness, as well as the risk of being bitten or scratched. Children should not tease their pets, take away food, or disturb a sleeping animal. Because a bird may peck at anything stuck through the bars of a birdcage, children should be taught not to poke at the bird. Recent studies show that the great majority of children less than 4 years old who are bitten by dogs are attacked at home while parents are present. These incidents usually involve dogs that have never bitten people before. Pit bulls, German shepherds, Doberman pinschers, Scottish Terriers, dachshunds, miniature French poodles and schnauzers tend to be temperamental animals and, unless parents are experienced and careful, should not be kept in a home where there are children.

Children should not stroke or approach pets that they never have seen before unless the owner can supervise. They should be encouraged to get to know the pets in the neighborhood only when the owners are present. If a cat hisses or pounces, the child should try to back away slowly. When approached by unknown dogs, children should drop any food they might be eating, slowly tuck parcels under their arms instead of dangling or swinging them, and avoid sudden movements. If the strange dog then growls or snaps, children should stand perfectly still, hands at their sides, and avoid looking into the dog's eyes. In most such encounters, the dog loses interest and goes away.

Experts recommend that if a dog attacks, children should fold their arms, grabbing each elbow with the opposite hand, and thrust their arms in front of their faces. If the dog knocks the child down, the child should lie perfectly still, arms protecting his or her head and neck. Screaming or flailing about further antagonizes an attacking animal.

Pet safety also involves prevention of pet-related diseases (see *pets, diseases caused by*). If the skin is broken because of an animal bite, immediate medical attention is needed, as animal saliva can carry infectious organisms (see *rabies*). Washing hands with soap and water is essential in preventing transfer of infectious organisms contained in pet droppings. Children should be taught always to wash their hands after changing cat litter, cleaning a bird or rodent cage, or washing a fish tank.

SAFETY RULES TO PREVENT KIDNAPPING

The agony of missing children affects as many as 1.5 million families each year in the United States. Various estimates indicate that about 1 million children are runaways, 25,000 to 50,000 may be taken by a parent, and 3,000 to 20,000 are kidnapped by strangers. A runaway child may stay away from home as briefly as an hour or two or for weeks, months, or years. Parental kidnapping usually occurs in the course of a custody dispute when a separated or divorced spouse abducts a child out of anger or frustration. Many children kidnapped by strangers are released within minutes or hours; some manage to make their own escapes.

As is true with childproofing a home, prevention is parents' most effective tool in ensuring a child's safety from kidnapping. The following list of safety tips can be followed and taught to children to help them avoid potential dangers.

- Children should be told they have a right to say no, even to an adult. They do not have to obey strangers.
- Children should know their full name, complete address, and phone number, including area code.
- Make sure children know how to reach the operator and how to call long distance.
- Teach children that a stranger is someone you and they don't know. They should be told never to go anywhere with a stranger, not even for a "minute," and never to accept presents of any kind, including candy and gum.
- Teach your children to tell you about strangers they meet and about anyone who asks them to keep a "secret."
- Children should know that adults rarely ask children for directions and that they should ignore anyone who does ask. They should never go near a car with a stranger in it, even if they are called by name.
- If children believe that they are being followed by someone in a car or on foot, they should be taught to run to the nearest <u>public</u> place and yell "Help!" Rehearsing this advice with small children may be helpful.
- If children become separated from adults while shopping, they should be taught to go immediately to the nearest clerk and ask for assistance. They should not wander about searching and should never go to the street or a parking lot alone.
- Never leave children alone or in an unattended car, not even for a "minute."
- Be sure that the school or daycare center policy is never to release children to anyone but parents or someone designated by parents. Set up a code word with children if an unfamiliar adult must be sent to pick them up.
- Tell children that no one has the right to touch them or make them feel uncomfortable.
- Teach children never to admit to anyone over the phone that they are home alone, never to answer the door when home alone, and to call the police or a neighbor if someone tries to get into the house.
- Know your children's friends.
- Listen when children say they do not want to be with someone: there may be a reason that they initially are reluctant to reveal. Take time to talk with them about their concerns, anxieties, or fears.
- Take photos of children at least yearly and keep a copy of their fingerprints and dental records.

These recommendations come from ACTION, a national volunteer agency, and from

The National Center for Missing and Exploited Children
(in association with the U.S. Department of Justice)
1835 K Street NW
Washington, DC 20006
Hotline (toll-free): 800-843-5678

The shared goal of these organizations is to promote child safety through the Missing Children Project.

Part II
Finding Health Care for Children

5 Choosing Health Care

All parents want to maintain sound health for their families. However healthy children may be, parents will want the help of a pediatrician, family physician, or other professional for checkups, advice about health care, and treating illness. A family living almost anywhere in America has choices, but must become aware of what to look for among the various types of providers, care, costs, and professional services. The type of health insurance is another important choice.

TYPES OF CARE

There are three general categories of health care. Primary health care involves treating and preventing common health problems. A primary health care team performs routine examinations, provides information about nutrition and accident prevention, immunizes against infectious disease, assesses growth and development, provides teaching and counseling, helps handle common childhood problems, and if necessary coordinates medical care with physician specialists. Secondary care is provided by a specialist to whom a child is usually referred by a member of the primary care team, often the physician. Tertiary care focuses on complicated or unusual problems that require extensive investigation and elaborate treatment by several specialists, who often work as a team at a hospital or regional health center.

For primary care, depending upon geography, income, and health insurance, parents can choose among three broad types of health care systems:

Private Medical Practices. The most familiar American system for pediatric health care is the private medical practice. Typically, a physician has an office where he or she sees patients and performs routine diagnostic laboratory tests. Some physicians locate their offices in residential neighborhoods to be close to their patients' homes. Others choose locations close to or in the hospital with which they are affiliated and to which they send patients for various specialized tests and treatment. The physician in private practice often has a nurse or nurse practitioner (see below) assisting with certain kinds of medical services and information.

Neighborhood Clinics. In some places, especially large cities, primary health care for children is available through independent or hospital-based clinics or neighborhood health centers. Such facilities, sometimes called well-child clinics, are staffed by primary-care teams which include physicians, nurses, and other health professionals. At many clinics, members of the same team see a child during each visit. To find the nearest clinic, parents can call their local health departments.

Health Maintenance Organizations. Health maintenance organizations (HMOs) are prepaid medical insurance plans which provide a variety of primary health care services as well as selected specialty and emergency services. HMO services may include general medicine, surgery, pediatrics, gynecology, obstetrics, nursing, nutrition, and mental health. Some HMOs offer dental and eye care as well.

HMOs differ in the size and scope of services offered. One popular type of HMO enables members to receive most of their primary health care at one location and the health professionals work exclusively for the HMO. Another type of HMO offers the services of private-practice physicians with various specialties who participate in the plan. Members can choose among these participating physicians and in this way have continuity of care. Hospital care is provided in affiliated institutions.

HOW TO CHOOSE

Over the years, a solid working relationship based on mutual confidence is essential. Parents should try to find physicians, nurse practitioners, or nurses who are available and informative, and have reassuring personal styles. For example, some parents may find it difficult to communicate successfully with a busy pediatrician who can give little time to interpreting a child's problem. On the other hand, a general practitioner who is more available may have to rely upon a medical center to perform and interpret some kinds of diagnostic tests. Often it is useful to ask friends and relatives who have children for detailed recommendations.

A physician's training, credentials, and hospital affiliation are also important. A physician is a medical doctor (M.D.) who is registered by the state board of medicine. A pediatrician is a physician who specializes in child care and is certified by the American Board of Pediatrics or is eligible for certification (having completed training but not yet taken or passed the certifying examination). Information on training and credentials can be found in the *American Medical Directory* (published by the American Medical Association) or the *Directory of Medical Specialists,* both available in public libraries. The local or state medical society can also provide this information. A physician should have admitting privileges at a children's hospital or a general hospital with a respected pediatric service. If the hospital is affiliated with a medical school, a physician may be more likely to know highly qualified specialists and have access to the latest diagnostic techniques, treatments, and research findings.

Establishing rapport with the rest of the health care team is valuable for the family. Parents should be sure that their child is reasonably comfortable with the nurse or other professionals in the office or clinic. The child's and parents' questions should be answered patiently and satisfactorily by everyone involved.

In addition to dealing with problems, the physician, nurse practitioner, and others should anticipate questions and give advice about promoting a child's overall physical and emotional health (see Chapter 2, "Promoting Physical Health," and Chapter 3, "Promoting Mental Health").

Here are further questions to consider when making a choice about primary care:

Is the office or clinic easily accessible? Consider distance, access to public transportation, traffic, and parking.

Are office hours convenient?

Is obtaining an appointment difficult? How long is the average waiting-room time?

Does the physician or other members of the health care team ever make house calls?

What are the fees? Are they affordable?

HEALTH PROFESSIONALS CARING FOR CHILDREN

Pediatricians. The medical specialty concerned with the care of children is called pediatrics. In addition to having a thorough knowledge of general medicine, a pediatrician is trained to understand and treat children's physical, emotional, and developmental problems.

Family Physicians. While not trained exclusively in pediatrics, a family practice physician, or general practitioner, is fully qualified to provide health care for children. Some parents may prefer to have the same physician care for the whole family. Others obtain pediatric services from general practitioners and nurses because no pediatricians are available in their areas. In rural locations, one physician may care for the entire community: he or she delivers babies, gives screenings and immunizations to school children, and treats virtually all child and adult health problems.

Nurses. Nurses are trained in certified schools of nursing, which are usually affiliated with universities, hospitals, or both. They receive certification as registered nurses (R.N.'s) after completing two to four years of study and supervised training and then passing a state-administered examination.

In almost every health care setting—hospitals, clinics, HMOs, and physicians' offices—R.N.'s perform physical examinations, give injections and provide other forms of medication (including immunizations), help parents carry out a physician's recommendations, provide health education by informing and guiding parents and children of all ages, and frequently answer questions and give advice over the telephone.

Some R.N.'s, especially public health nurses, also make house calls—for example, to help new parents with their babies. A nurse can evaluate a baby's problems and assist parents in developing skills such as breastfeeding and bathing the baby. A nurse can also answer questions and, generally, help parents feel more comfortable and become more skillful health care providers themselves. Visiting nurses, or public health nurses, are available in many cities and towns. For more information, parents can call a visiting nurse association, the local health department or clinic, or their municipal government office.

Nurse Practitioners. Nurse practitioners (N.P.'s) are nurses who, frequently after having worked for several years, return to graduate school for additional education and supervision. Or nurses may enroll in a special nurse practitioner program that grants certification. This additional education and experience coupled with national certification allows nurses to practice as N.P.'s.

An N.P. with a specialty in pediatrics usually focuses on health promotion and illness prevention, which includes taking health histories, giving physical exams, handling common childhood illnesses and developmental problems, and providing health education. Although qualified to practice independently, N.P.'s usually choose to practice collaboratively with pediatricians. N.P.'s usually provide continuing care to children and their families and consult with physicians as necessary. In some practices, however, the M.D. and N.P. alternate health care visits to assure double supervision and to keep in continuous touch with their patients.

Physician Assistants. Physician assistants (P.A.'s) are trained to work under the supervision of a physician. P.A.'s are prepared in a special one-year course of study to take patient histories, perform physical exams, and treat minor health problems at the supervising physician's direction. P.A.'s sometimes deal with pediatric patients in private physicians' offices or HMOs.

Specialists. A physician may recommend that a child be seen by a specialist because of the severity or complexity of a particular health problem. To become a fully qualified doctor of medicine, most students study and train for at least seven years beyond college: four years of medical school (leading to a medical degree) and three or more years of clinical training (experience serving in a hospital as an intern and resident). In some states a physician may begin practice immediately after graduating from medical school and passing a state medical society examination. Most states, however, require that a general practitioner (any physician without a specialty) have one, two, or three years of supervised clinical training in a hospital before beginning the independent practice of medicine. A medical specialist must go on for several years of additional clinical training beyond the first three.

In those areas where health care services are abundant and comprehensive, families often receive their health care from several specialists. Adults may seek care for hay fever from an allergist, while teenagers may see a dermatologist for treatment of acne. Health care can become too specialized; patients may have several specialists for specific problems but no primary physician to integrate their health care.

Here is a list of some of the major specialists and their specialties.

cardiologist	heart
dermatologist	skin
endocrinologist	glands, hormones, and internal secretions of the body
gastroenterologist	digestive system
gynecologist	female reproductive system
hematologist	blood and blood-forming tissues
immunologist	resistance to disease
neonatologist	newborn babies, especially those born early or of low birthweight
nephrologist	kidneys
neurologist	nervous system, including the brain and spinal cord
obstetrician	pregnancy and childbirth
oncologist	cancer
ophthalmologist	eyes
orthopedist	bones, other connective tissue, and joints
otolaryngologist	ears, nose, and throat
pathologist	origin, course, and effects of disease
pharmacologist	drugs and medications and their use
plastic surgeon	restoration, construction, reconstruction, or improvement of the shape and appearance of body structures that are malformed, damaged, or missing
psychiatrist	emotional and behavioral problems and mental diseases and disorders (M.D. with a specialty in psychiatry)
psychologist	same focus as psychiatry, but without authority to perform physical examinations or prescribe medications (Ph.D., M.S., or M.S.W. with a specialty in psychology)
radiologist	the use of X-ray and other imaging techniques to diagnose and treat health problems
surgeon	treatment of diseases, injuries, or malformations by operation
toxicologist	treatment of the effects of poisons

Dentists. A dentist is not a medical doctor but may be a doctor of dental medicine (D.M.D.) or a doctor of dental surgery (D.D.S.). (No substantive difference exists between these degrees; the designation depends on the dental school attended.)

Most dentists maintain private practices; others participate in dental clinics at hospitals, neighborhood health centers, or HMOs. In smaller communities one dentist usually cares for the whole family. In larger areas pedodontists (dentists who specialize in the care of children's teeth) are often available. Pedodontists have special training to deal with children and their special needs and problems. They focus on making the visit to the dentist less difficult emotionally and more educational. Many dental practices and clinics include a dental hygienist who cleans the teeth and instructs the family about proper dental care. In addition to private dentists, hospital-based dental clinics and clinics staffed by dental faculty members who supervise dental students are available in some communities.

From time to time a child may need the care of one of several dental specialists. Children whose permanent teeth are crooked, protruding, crowded too tightly, spaced too far apart, or otherwise misaligned may be referred by their dentist to an orthodontist, a dentist who specializes in the correction of such problems. A specialist who identifies and treats gum problems is called a periodontist. Oral surgeons, as their name implies, specialize in correcting tooth and gum problems through surgery. An endodontist treats the problems of the roots of the teeth and the jawbone. (See *bruxism; gum problems; teeth, developmental problems of; teething;* and *tooth problems.*)

HEALTH INSURANCE

Parents need to educate themselves about the range of available health insurance options. Once they have selected an insurance plan, parents should remain alert to future changes in health care coverage and be ready to consult their insuror and consumers' groups about newly available options that might prove valuable for their family.

Prospective parents who have health insurance should review their policy before their baby is born to see what types of child health services are covered. How long must a policy be in effect before obstetric coverage is provided? Is hospitalization covered before, during, and after delivery? What kind of coverage is provided for the baby? Is preventive care, including well-child medical exams, covered?

Health insurance can be "individual"—the individual subscriber or family pays the premiums—or "group"—the individual belongs to a group of insurees (typically, company employees, union members, and other organization members) which is granted reduced premiums for each member because of the size of the subscribing group. Although group insurance is less expensive than individual insurance, a prospective group subscriber may be permitted to join only during an annual designated enrollment period or there may be a waiting period before a policy takes effect.

Many policies stipulate that policyholders annually pay the first $100 to $1,000 (called a "deductible") of certain health-care costs. Emergency care is usually covered in full as soon as coverage begins, but the deductible amount applies to other costs. Once the deductible is paid, insurance usually reimburses for 75 to 80 percent of medical costs; the policyholder (or his or her group) pays the rest.

Basic hospitalization insurance covers most hospital charges (certain types of rooms and meals, medications, laboratory tests, X rays, operating-room fees). Insurance covers a certain number of days (often 120) in the hospital, annually. In general, the greater the number of days covered, the more expensive the policy. Basic hospitalization covers some of the tests and laboratory procedures included in both inpatient and outpatient care but does not always pay for all physicians' fees charged to a family member when an outpatient or during a hospital stay.

Basic medical-surgical insurance includes basic hospitalization plus the fees of physicians who care for the hospitalized patient. Some policies cover certain services offered by private practitioners, including, for example, oral surgery.

Major medical insurance provides additional coverage beyond basic hospitalization and medical-surgical insurance. Major medical often covers any expense incurred as a result of an accident or major illness, such as a broken leg or an appendectomy. Policies vary widely in coverage and cost. A typical policy covers hospitalization, surgery, diagnostic tests, physicians' fees, private nursing services, home medical care, prescribed medications, and certain kinds of therapy and rehabilitation services. Visits to a physician's office are not usually covered.

Medicaid is the largest single government medical program providing care for children. If a family's income is below a designated minimum, the state's Medicaid program may pay for some or all child health care expenses. The Medicaid program is funded by both the federal and state governments. Services covered vary from state to state, and benefits are subject to periodic revision when governmental fiscal policies change.

Medicare, the other major government-sponsored medical program, pays for health care for people ages 65 and over and for certain services for disabled people of all ages. Major specialized child care services covered by Medicare include kidney dialysis and kidney transplantation.

COST OF ROUTINE CHILD CARE

Office visits to a private pediatrician or family physician are not usually covered by health insurance. Some comprehensive health insurance plans cover routine dental checkups and treatments. Most community well-child clinics base their fees on a sliding scale that takes into account a family's ability to pay. In extreme financial circumstances, it may be possible to make special arrangements for deferred payments.

Unlike other insurance plans, HMOs cover routine checkups, primary health care, and hospitalizations. Members of most HMOs pay a fixed amount every month and then receive most medical services for a nominal fee (or without additional charge) for each visit.

Going to the Doctor

For many children going to see the doctor is part of growing up. Whether the doctor is a general practitioner in a small town, a family practice specialist in a suburban health maintenance organization, or a pediatrician in an urban health clinic, a child can often look forward to a special relationship with "my doctor."

REGULAR CHECKUPS

NEWBORN CHECKUP

The first 4 weeks of life—the newborn period—is the most crucial period for monitoring health and disease. Physicians want to keep a close check on the newborn's health and usually examine a child twice during the first 28 days. If a child is premature, has problems present at birth (congenital), or becomes ill during those first 4 weeks, a physician, of course, will see the child as often as necessary.

A child's first detailed examination occurs within the first 6 to 8 hours of life. At birth, the physician (often an obstetrician) or other birth attendant surveys the child for any life-threatening conditions. A few hours later a more thorough examination is performed by the pediatrician if one has been selected and consulted before a child's birth. If a pediatrician has not been selected and the baby is in a hospital, a member of the residential medical staff usually performs the examination. If the baby is at home, a family practice physician or pediatrician must be called to perform the examination.

A physician's examination is both general and specific. A physician wants to get a general impression of the newborn's health. It also is important to take accurate measurements of a variety of physical characteristics. By observing a baby's physical actions (neuromuscular behavior), the physician also can observe a baby's relative "maturity." The entire checkup resembles those that will continue throughout childhood.

The first procedure is weighing and measuring the baby. At birth, the head is the largest part of a baby's body, larger in circumference than the chest. When measured from the top of the skull to the bottom of the chin, a newborn's head is about 25 percent of body length.

After the baby is weighed and measured, a complete physical examination, head to toe, begins. Most physicians examine a baby in three ways: with their eyes, with their hands, and with instruments. The physician begins by observing how the baby looks: general appearance, level of activity, and alertness. The physician notes whether the skin looks normal and is free of rashes, and if the baby's physical actions are equally vigorous on both sides of the body.

In handling the baby the physician usually begins with procedures that are least likely to disturb the baby, and works up to those that may prove temporarily upsetting.

When examining a newborn's head, for example, the physician checks for the size and number of soft spots (fontanels). The baby is lifted up by the arms from a lying-down position to check for head control. Muscle tone is checked by holding the baby by the arms in a standing-up position. With the baby faceup, the physician draws up the hips and stretches them into a froglike position to see whether any tendency exists for the hipbone to slip out of its socket, and stretches out the legs to see if they are the same length. The pulses located on either side of the groin are felt to make certain that the blood is flowing normally from the heart.

To examine the heart, the physician first feels the chest manually, then moves the stethoscope to various positions to hear the heart sounds. To examine the lungs, the physician watches the chest and abdomen as the baby breathes and listens to the baby's breathing through the stethoscope placed first on the chest and then on the back.

The entire newborn examination may require less than 10 minutes of what appears to be almost casual looking, touching, and turning. The skilled pediatrician moves thoughtfully and deliberately through the examination, checking carefully all the while.

Preventive medicine is a key part of pediatrics. Most of what a child experiences in the physician's care is intended to augment and protect a growing child's health. From the first visit with parents and child, a physician gives whatever advice and encouragement is appropriate for the child's age and physical and emotional condition. A substantial portion of each office visit is devoted to the physician's addressing the concerns of the parents and raising issues that are likely to become significant to the child in the weeks and months ahead. Most first-time parents need some reassurance that their baby's movements, noises, and facial expressions are normal. Parents of newborns should ask questions and ask for medical help if they are uncertain of a child's health and well-being. They should learn to trust their instincts or intuition but be ready to ask for guidance: they know their child better than anyone else. Most pediatricians maintain regular call-in hours during which they are available to answer questions and interpret babies' behavior.

As a general rule, parents of newborns should seek medical assistance if any of these medical conditions occur: difficulty in feeding, vomiting, diarrhea, noisy or labored breathing, fever higher than 100° F (37.8° C).

Responsible physicians and nurses will remind new parents that the baby must ride in an approved car seat or safety restraint, beginning with the very first ride. In the United States, the law requires car seats for children.

ONE-MONTH VISIT

The 1-month checkup duplicates many of the physical measurements of the newborn exam. Height, weight, and head circumference are measured. Reflexes and body movement are checked, including an evaluation of head movement.

During this checkup, a physician wants to see if the infant has "outgrown" any jaundice experienced during the first 4 or 5 days of life. He or she checks to make certain that no congenital, metabolic, or genetic abnormalities have become evident. A check of the heart is particularly significant in order to rule out abnormal sounds that could indicate congenital structural defects. At all visits, personal and social (interactive) skills and fine motor and gross motor development of the child are checked.

TWO-MONTH VISIT

The 2-month checkup consolidates the information and impressions gained during earlier examinations. Physical measurements are repeated, reflexes checked, and all the problems or questions involving feeding and sleeping are discussed. As an infant grows, increasing neurological control of the body is evident, moving down the body from the head to the legs.

At the end of the examination, the physician gives the baby the first dose of two immunizations—polio vaccine and DPT (diphtheria, pertussis, tetanus). Polio vaccine is a small capful of flavored liquid for the infant to swallow. DPT is an injection into the fleshy part of the thigh or hip. Polio vaccine causes no reaction. DPT can produce two common reactions: the first, a sore, sometimes warm leg, which may hurt to move for a day or two (cold compresses can be soothing); and the other, generalized irritability, which can be accompanied by a self-limited fever of 100°–102° F (37.8°–38.8° C). (Fever-reducing and pain relieving medications may be helpful. Consult the physician for specific recommendations and read discussion of nonprescription medications in Chapter 7.) Only rarely does an infant experience severe reactions from DPT vaccine. (See *poliomyelitis; tetanus; whooping cough.*)

FOUR-MONTH VISIT

At the 4-month visit the physician repeats the standard physical measurements. Reflexes and general neurologic control are monitored. Another ear, nose, and throat survey may be performed. The physician reviews feeding and bowel habits and checks on how much breastmilk or formula an infant is getting. At the end of the visit the second dose of DPT and oral polio vaccine is given.

SIX-MONTH VISIT

By the time a child is 6 months old, physical development begins to progress dramatically as does complex interaction between child and parents. Physical measurements are made and the physician checks for further development of neurological control of muscles. Diet and sleep patterns are evaluated with the parents, making certain that the solid foods are not causing problems. Parents' questions are answered.

At the end of the visit the third DPT immunization injection is given. Slight reactions may occur as before.

NINE-MONTH VISIT

The usual physical measurements are made and reflexes checked. Somewhere between the ninth and fourteenth or fifteenth month, the first teeth will be erupting. The child's hearing will be checked again by the physician's whistling or clicking and watching for a response.

The physician usually gives more guidance now on subjects such as childproofing the home. He or she makes certain that the parents are monitoring the child's diet, rest, and exercise.

A blood sample (hemoglobin or hematocrit) may be checked for the possibility of anemia. A tuberculin (tine) test and a blood test of lead level in the blood sometimes are performed for urban children who may be vulnerable to *tuberculosis* or *lead poisoning.*

ONE-YEAR VISIT

The usual physical measurements and observations are performed by the physician. The ears, nose, and throat are checked visually. The chest is checked by stethoscope sound. The heartbeat and breathing are monitored at the same time. Both fine and gross motor skills are evaluated.

The physician checks teething and also whether a child is beginning to say a few words. He or she inquires about activities such as feeding and drinking and how much initiative the child is taking. Parents' questions are answered.

VISITS FROM ONE TO THREE YEARS

During the second year the physician usually wants to see a child three times—at 15, 18, and 21 months of age. The general procedure remains much the same. The standard physical measurements and observations are made and the child is evaluated for normal growth and development. Parents' questions and concerns are discussed. If a parent has questions at any other time, the physician or another member of the health care team—often a nurse practitioner—can be called for information and assistance.

After the second birthday the physician usually schedules checkups every six months for the next year or two.

The toddler usually is an energetic child who is exploring and mastering the skills involved in walking and talking. The physician will ask about and observe these activities. Apart from the standard physical examination, and checking for growth in weight, height, and head circumference, blood pressure may be checked for the first time around the age of $2\frac{1}{2}$ or 3. Ears, nose, and throat are checked and a standard neurological survey is completed.

The physician checks cognitive development by listening to the child's speech and evaluating his or her responsiveness to the speech and gestures of others. A routine screening test may be given to test for normal language development. The screening test for levels of lead in the blood is often given annually (perhaps twice) to children who live in the inner cities of metropolitan areas. Screening tests for vision and hearing normally are not given until around age 4 unless a significant problem becomes obvious earlier.

Because toddlers are so active and curious, the physician usually wants to know how thoroughly parents have childproofed their home and whether the child has had any major or minor accidents. Falls and the swallowing of foreign objects or substances are major health concerns for young children (see Chapter 4, "Accident Prevention"). The physician customarily inquires about a child's progress in, or mastery of, toilet training, which can be a source of tension between child and parents (see Chapter 2, "Promoting Physical Health").

Again, because of toddlers' high activity level, the physician often asks their parents about their personal levels of frustration stemming from their child's energetic explorations and experimentations. Many parents, but especially single ones or those with other small children, may have great difficulty in managing a toddler without becoming frustrated, angry, exhausted, or all three. Parent support groups and counseling may provide important stabilizing influences for weary parents and contribute indirectly to the well-being of children.

A *German measles* (rubella), *measles,* and *mumps* vaccine, the fourth dose of DPT, and the third dose of oral polio are given at the end of the 15-month visit. For complete schedule of immunizations, see p. 96.

VISITS FROM FOUR TO TWELVE YEARS

Annual visits to the physician and health care team for preschool and school children are important, in order to keep track of physical, mental, and emotional development.

The physician continues to update the record of growth based upon a complete history and physical examination. Immunizations and screening tests are given as needed (see p. 96).

The "real work" of the physician through the school years is to monitor sensitively how well the child is doing at his or her "job"—that is, establishing a secure role in the family, performing well in school, making and keeping friends, and generally gaining a sense of self-confidence, self-mastery, and self-definition. Because children's bodies are changing so rapidly, the physician observes how a child is dealing with his or her body and its ongoing changes.

Children need private time with the physician in which to review how things are going in their lives. Stresses of many kinds tend to multiply, and preadolescents slowly learn how to deal with them. For instance, deviations from the norm weigh heavily on the school-age child. How does it feel to be the tallest, shortest, thinnest, chubbiest, fastest, slowest, smartest, "coolest," most confident, or least secure girl or boy in the whole class? These are concerns for the physician's private time with a child. During these years of increasing independence, self-motivation, and self-sufficiency, a physician's interest adds to the emotional support all children need from family members, friends, teachers, and coaches.

Children of grade school age, for example, sometimes shy away from physicians because they associate "going to the doctor" with being sick, taking medicine, or getting injections. The physician who can listen to the child's own concerns in a warm, nonjudgmental way will often overcome this reluctance.

Parents should trust the physician and other members of the health care team. Parents need to come to the physician with a clear impression of how their child is doing with the major personal—intellectual and social—challenges of the preceding year. Questions, concerns, and satisfactions relating to their child can be shared either at the beginning or conclusion of the visit.

Any serious physical or mental health problems need to be considered seriously and investigated, perhaps in consultation with a specialist. The preschool and school years are times of testing and blossoming. A good relationship with the entire health care team can nurture both child and parents during these demanding years.

VISITS FOR ADOLESCENTS AND YOUNG ADULTS

Continuity of care for the broad developmental and personal concerns of the adolescent and young adult years is crucial. Young women and men need to be seen regularly—at least once a year—by their physicians and health care teams.

Parents must allow their daughters or sons to spend most of the visit alone with the physician with the understanding that what is appropriate for parents' knowledge will be communicated at the right time. Trust is the essential ingredient in the patient-physician relationship at this stage of growing maturity for the adolescent. The young woman or man must feel that all topics of health, in the broadest sense of the term, are safe to explore. Then, emotional growth and development, so important at this age, can be evaluated by the physician.

Adolescents begin to take increasing responsibility for managing their own bodies and health needs. If medications, diet, or both are required for an illness or chronic condition, such as *arthritis* or *diabetes,* the physician gives over increasing responsibility to the young woman or man.

Adolescents and young adults need to become thoughtful, responsible health consumers. If a young woman or man finds that a physician is unprepared or uncomfortable with a more comprehensive role as adviser, confidant, and medical guide, the parent and daughter or son may want to consider seriously how to find more helpful health care. In some cases a young adult attending college will choose to be cared for by the physician and health care staff in attendance there.

Adolescent patients often feel some discomfort or embarrassment with a physician of the opposite sex. It is important that a physician be made aware of this situation either by the parent or by the parent and child. A parent can give the adolescent a careful explanation of why complete physical examinations, including those of the genital organs, are essential and how they can be performed with complete dignity and empathy by the physician. An adolescent can then have full opportunity to respond. If after visiting the physician once or twice more, an adolescent still feels strongly that he or she needs to see a physician of the same sex, the parents should ask the current physician for a referral. This situation occurs often enough so that a physician, especially a pediatrician, understands this sensitive problem and will usually make a referral.

The physician and health care team continue to provide standard physical checkups and developmental monitoring and to give immunization boosters, if needed. Preventive medicine takes on added significance. Since sound nutrition and adequate exercise are lifelong necessities, the physician can be expected to review these needs in detail. Conversations about contraception and personal sexual practices often become a regular part of the medical interview. Teenagers usually need to explore realistically with someone other than their own parents sensitive topics such as the control of alcohol and other drug use and how to handle a variety of impulses effectively. The physician may feel comfortable in initiating such conversations or be open to having the young adult raise the issues.

The relationship between the physician and the adolescent and his or her family can be a most valuable, instructive, and mutually satisfying experience. However, some teenagers do not want to be subject to one more adult's authority, no matter how well-intentioned. Adolescents may also rebel against going to see the same physician, especially a pediatrician, whom he or she has been seeing since early childhood. He or she may feel embarrassed at having to sit in a waiting room with a group of noisy little children, some babes in arms.

Some pediatricians attempt to meet this problem by setting aside a separate waiting area for teenagers so that they do not have to mingle with "little kids." Pediatricians often anticipate this kind of friction and raise the question of a patient's emotional discomfort around the age of 11 or 12. By stating candidly that he or she understands how a maturing young man or woman must feel in a pediatrician's office, the physician is sometimes able to give the patient an opening to share these feelings.

Somewhere in late adolescence or young adulthood a young person will begin to want "a doctor of my own." A pediatrician can then give a referral to an internist or other primary care physician.

PREVENTIVE MEDICINE

SCHOOL SCREENINGS

To ensure that potentially serious medical conditions are identified and treated, most school systems in the United States sponsor screening programs designed to detect a range of common problems. Such screenings can reveal conditions that may produce no symptoms but could become serious if left untreated. They do not, of course, replace regular checkups with a physician or clinic. Screening programs include:

- Vision and hearing tests. These are often the most important screening procedures for young children. They can begin as early as 3 or 4 years of age.

- *Tuberculosis* screening. Most public health departments recommend routine screening every two or three years for possible exposure to tuberculosis.
- *Anemia* screening. Iron-deficiency anemia. (see *anemia, nutritional*) may develop if a child does not receive sufficient dietary iron or iron supplements. A simple blood test can determine whether iron-deficiency anemia is present.
- Urine screening. A routine screening of urine can detect problems such as a bacterial infection of the urinary tract (see *urinary tract infections*).
- Lead screening. Particularly among infants and toddlers in older urban areas, screening for *lead poisoning* is extremely important, as pointed out above. Screening is the most effective method of determining lead levels in the blood and preventing severe lead poisoning.

School screening programs are not meant to be comprehensive assessments of a child's health. If a school test shows that a child has difficulties with hearing or vision, for example, parents are urged to arrange for a more complete set of tests before deciding how to deal with the problem. The child's pediatrician and various professionals specializing in sight or hearing problems can help parents arrange for additional testing.

IMMUNIZATIONS

Vaccines are available today to prevent the most severe communicable diseases of childhood. The most common vaccines are those for diphtheria, *German measles, measles, mumps, polio, tetanus,* and *whooping cough* (pertussis). Even though it may seem that vaccines have virtually eliminated these diseases, they continue to occur in the United States. It is very important, therefore, that parents see that their children receive all needed immunizations.

Public health authorities estimate that one in three preschoolers has not had all the recommended immunizations and that as many as half of all children under 11 years old are not completely protected. Because of the possibility of epidemics, health officials periodically initiate local campaigns to reach all unimmunized children. Currently, health departments in all 50 states require parents to present proof of certain immunizations before their children begin school and, in some cases, at the beginning of each school year.

Immunization is based on a remarkably simple principle. Many infectious diseases can be contracted only once during a lifetime because in the process of recovery the body produces a permanent defense response against the organism causing the particular illness. Immunization artificially triggers this defense response so that a person can become immune without actually contracting the disease.

All vaccines are delivered by injection except the one against polio, which is usually given orally. Vaccinations are often delayed if a child is running a fever. Reactions to vaccines generally are mild and may include headache, mild fever, redness, and mild to moderate muscle soreness at the site of injection for a day or two. A mild rash, 5 to 10 days in duration, may develop after a child receives the measles vaccine. If a child has ever experienced a convulsion (see *seizures*), parents should so advise the physician before the DPT vaccine (see below) is given. The physician may decide to omit the pertussis vaccine because of the possibility of a severe reaction for a child who has had a convulsion, previous vaccine reactions, or who suffers from suppressed immunity. (For details, see discussion in prevention section of *whooping cough*.)

Vaccines are best administered at specified times in early childhood, when "peak immunity" can be obtained. During the first few months of life, vaccines create only transient immunity, so dosages must be scheduled at designated intervals throughout childhood to ensure maximum protection.

Although every health team administers vaccines and maintains records of a child's immunizations, parents should keep their own up-to-date record at home. Parents should also think about preparing their children psychologically for immunizations. For children, the diseases against which they are being protected are unknown and abstract, but the brief pain of a needle is immediate and vivid.

Immunization Schedule

Recommended age	Immunization
2 months	DPT—diphtheria, pertussis, tetanus (first dose) OPV—oral polio vaccine (first dose)
4 months	DPT (second dose) OPV (second dose)
6 months	DPT (third dose) OPV (optional dose given in areas where the risk of polio might be high)
15 months	MMR—measles, mumps, rubella (single injection) DPT (fourth dose) OPV (third dose)
2 years	H. influenza (type b)—for bacterial infections including meningitis, epiglottitis, and pneumonia
4–5 years	DPT (fifth dose) OPV (fourth dose)
14–16 years and every 10 years thereafter	Td—tetanus and diphtheria (adult variety)

A child may miss an immunization inoculation or a whole series of regular infant and toddler examinations have not been performed. If an initial DTP shot or OPV dose has been given, the usual schedule can be resumed where it left off (the whole series need not be started over). If an entire series is missed, a physician usually will begin a catch-up schedule, designed for the child's age and need for immediate protection.

For children not immunized as infants, the American Academy of Pediatrics' Committee on Infectious Diseases recommends the following:

Catch-Up Schedule

First Visit	DTP, OPV; tuberculin test
One month later	MMR (at least 15 months old)
Two months later	DTP; OPV
Four months later	DTP; optional OPV
Ten to sixteen months	DTP; OPV
Preschool	DTP; OPV
Age 14–16	Td (every 10 years)

SECOND OPINIONS

If parents have questions about how a physician is handling the treatment of a particular illness or problem, they should make an appointment to discuss the matter in person. If a physician's explanation does not fully satisfy the parents or if they subsequently feel that the child is not responding to the treatment, they should ask for a second opinion. Such a request is standard medical practice; an experienced physician usually agrees immediately to make a referral and is not offended by such a request.

CONSULTATIONS

The child's physician is often best qualified to select an appropriate person to act as a consultant. In some cases parents will know of other physicians through their own doctor, or by reputation. The consultant performs an independent examination and evaluation of the child's condition, then reports the findings to the referring physician and to the parents. If the second opinion confirms the physician's judgment, the parents' confidence in their child's care by the physician is renewed and enhanced. If the second opinion is different from their physician's treatment of the child, the parents can decide how best to proceed: they may want either to ask their physician if the differing opinion will modify the way their child's care will be handled in the future, or to select another physician for their child by asking the local medical society or a respected senior physician in the community.

Parents may also want to obtain a second opinion if a child's physician makes a diagnosis or recommends a future course of treatment about which the parents have reasonable concerns or questions. Such a second opinion is very common when elective surgery is recommended. (Elective surgery is an operation designed to improve the quality of a patient's life but is not considered essential for survival.) Surgeons regularly provide second opinions regarding their colleagues' recommendations, since consultation is part of sound medical practice.

A physician may also refer a child to a specialist for consultation. Such a request can be made for any of several reasons. The physician may want to get a confirming opinion for a diagnosis, treatment, or both. The physician may feel that a patient might be better served by a specialist and wants to find out whether the problem is one that the consultant is well equipped to manage. Or the physician may simply need expert advice. Whatever the reason for a recommended consultation, parents should respect their physician's attempt to identify and obtain the best possible care.

CHANGING PHYSICIANS

Parents and child need to feel comfortable with their physician. Parents should have confidence that the physician is competent, caring, and committed to the total well-being of the child. When talking with the physician, parents should feel relaxed and able to discuss any topic or raise any questions relating to their child's health. The child, too, should feel comfortable and trusting.

If at any time parents are not fully satisfied with their child's care, they should share their concerns privately with the physician. If a conference fails to answer all their questions or to relieve their uneasiness, they may decide to find another physician. Sometimes, changing physicians comes about because a family prefers to have someone who is associated with a particular hospital, clinic, or HMO. Also, as mentioned, a young person may want his or her own physician when grown up.

A local, county, or state medical society can almost always provide the names of physicians who are qualified and who might give more confidence-inspiring care. The experience of other responsible parents can also be helpful.

CARE FOR CHRONIC ILLNESS

A chronic disease or condition is one that recurs periodically and which can be lifelong.

Children with chronic diseases and their families require extra time, attention, and care on the part of all caregivers. Not only do many chronic diseases require more frequent visits to the physician, but affected families must have a variety of health services. Parents and child often need considerable amounts of the physician's energy and resourcefulness because the course of most chronic diseases requires periodic adjustments in treatment and hospitalization.

The emotional burden of coping with a child who has a chronic illness almost always affects the entire family. A specialist can help parents anticipate the physical and emotional demands of a chronic disease. The physician may recommend counseling with a psychiatrist, psychologist, or psychiatric social worker. Working with a qualified, experienced counselor often provides a chronically ill child with a feeling of having a completely reliable ally, one who may be depended upon no matter what the illness brings. Parents may also find counseling helpful if the stress of the child's illness feels overwhelming.

Parents may find it helpful to consult with parents of children with similar chronic conditions. General emotional support and specific practical steps for coping with the demands of the illness usually are welcome. The child's primary-care physician or the specialist is often the best source of referrals to families with children similarly affected.

7 Caring for the Sick Child at Home

Children, especially those less than 6 years old, can become ill many times. Illness often occurs among the very young because of their organ systems, which are not fully developed, and the immune system, which is still immature. Infants and young children usually develop 6 to 9 viral infections each year, with first-graders averaging about 6 colds a year.

Many illnesses of childhood are self-limiting and tend to run their course with rest, proper nutrition, and perhaps mild medication. Even when mildly ill, it may be possible for a child to continue normal activities, including school. Sometimes, however, sick children require home care, including bed rest. This is common with illnesses such as *chicken pox, colds,* middle-ear infections (see *earache and ear infections*), *influenza,* and *strep throat.*

HOW TO TELL IF A CHILD IS SICK

Infants and young children may not be able to tell you when they are sick. Parents should be alert for any change in the child's usual appearance or behavior. A normally contented child may become irritable; a baby who enjoys eating may turn away from food; a child who is usually energetic may appear listless. In most cases, such changes occur suddenly and are accompanied by other indications of illness.

Some common signs and symptoms of illness:

- fussiness (especially during the first three years of life) and restlessness
- irritability or crankiness
- unusual fatigue or listlessness
- unexplained crying (especially during infancy)
- flushed or pale face
- headache or earache
- warm or very cool forehead
- rash
- sweating
- shivering or "goose bumps"
- loss of appetite

- abdominal pain
- change in the frequency and consistency of bowel movements
- increase or decrease in urine output
- sleeplessness

A child with any of these problems should be encouraged to rest while parents keep an eye on him or her. Parents should also take the child's temperature to check for fever. The only reliable way to take a temperature is with a thermometer. Feeling a child's forehead may provide some hint of a fever, but it is never an accurate method. (See *fever.*)

WHEN TO CALL A PHYSICIAN

In many cases parents can trust their judgment about a child's illness because they know the child's health, moods, and habits. However, parents should call a physician if a child looks or acts much different from normal, especially if fever is present. During the first few months of life it is important to seek a physician's advice, because a baby can become ill quickly without having a fever or other specific signs and symptoms of illness. A physician should also be consulted if an ill child has not improved with home treatment or if parents do not know enough about a child's condition to feel confident that they can handle the situation.

In addition to these situations, a physician should be called immediately if a child has a severe accident or has any of the following signs or symptoms:

> *acute abdominal pain*
> *blood in the stools or in the vomit*
> eye inflammation (see *conjunctivitis*)
> extensive *rash*
> projectile *vomiting*

If the child is turning blue, has breathing difficulty, experiences *seizures,* becomes unconscious, or has active bleeding which doesn't stop when direct pressure is applied (see Chapter 10, "Basic First Aid"), summon an emergency squad, police, or fire department as quickly as possible.

Many physicians and health centers have regular call-in times for nonemergency situations. Call-in times are offered so that parents can phone in and ask questions or express concern about a child's health and physical and mental development. Parents should ask their physician or health center about telephone hours.

When called, a member of the primary care team (often a nurse or nurse practitioner, if not the physician) may recommend home treatment or ask that the child be brought to the office or a hospital for examination. The physician or nurse can also give concerned parents advice and guidance about their child's health.

BASIC HOME CARE

Rest

Rest is essential for recovery from illness. A child's body needs sufficient time and energy to combat infectious organisms or other causes of illness. Sick children should be allowed to rest and sleep until they feel better. Of course, children should not be confined unnecessarily; depending on the illness, they may not have to stay in bed. A child should not be pressured, however, to get out of bed before feeling well enough to do so. Children are generally good at assessing their own need for rest and are always eager to resume normal activities when feeling better.

Reducing the Discomforts of Fever

Children should not be given fever-reducing medication unless recommended by a physician. Some excess body heat usually can be released by removing some of the child's clothing, by cooling a child's head and neck with lukewarm washcloths, and by giving sponge baths. (Sponge bathing is described at the end of this chapter.) For additional information on fever reduction, see discussion of nonprescription medications below (see also *fever*).

Reducing Aches and Pains

A sick child often feels achy. To ease discomfort and soothe tender areas, heating pads and hot-water bottles may be used. A hot-water bottle or a heating pad must be used carefully to avoid burns. Neither a hot-water bottle nor a heating pad should be placed directly on the skin. Always wrap the rubber water bottle in a towel or baby blanket and be sure to check the child's skin for telltale signs of redness every 10 to 15 minutes. Fever-reducing medications can sometimes be helpful for aches too. See discussion below.

Activities

Children need both attention and company when they are sick, especially if they are frightened, lonely, or sad. If children want to rest, however, parents should encourage rest and provide a quiet environment conducive to rest. It is wise not to try to entertain them or force them to play. Sick children are often comforted by having their favorite stuffed animals, blankets, or toys with them. Young friends can be enjoyable and comforting for a sick child, but parents must take care to monitor the level of activity and also be sure that the illness is not contagious.

Parents can participate in many activities with a sick child, such as reading books, coloring, working on crafts, doing puzzles, playing with favorite toys, or watching television. For a child who is recuperating and whose disease is no longer contagious, activities can include baking cookies or helping with meal preparation. Children should not participate in strenuous play until they have recovered fully. Remember that children are quite good at limiting their own activities until they feel able.

Comfortable Clothing

A sick child should be kept warm. Even a child with a fever should avoid becoming chilled. While in bed, children can be dressed appropriately: in the summer (or when running a fever) a child can wear summer pajamas, shorts, or a cotton T-shirt and underpants or a diaper. In cooler weather a child can wear warm pajamas, sweat pants and a sweatshirt, or long underwear and socks. To avoid overheating, however, a sick child should not be overdressed.

A sick child who is out of bed can also dress according to the room temperature: light clothes in a warm room or, if the room is chilly, socks or slippers and a bathrobe or sweater.

TYPES OF MEDICINES

Parents should give medicines to children as prescribed. Nonprescription, or over-the-counter (OTC), medicines should be administered according to instructions on the package label or as a health professional has recommended. In addition, parents should consult a health professional for advice about starting another medicine if a child already is taking either a prescription or OTC medicine for any medical problem.

Parents should remember that most nonprescription medicines, including pain relievers, fever reducers, decongestants, and cough preparations, can only relieve symptoms; they do not cure the illness or eliminate the underlying cause. In many cases of mild to moderate physical discomfort, an old-fashioned "treatment" consisting of rest and plenty of fluids without medication, can be quite effective.

All medicines, especially those that are flavored to taste good to children, should be kept out of reach (see discussion of childproofing in Chapter 4, "Accident Prevention"). The bright colors and pleasant flavors of some liquid medications can be attractive to young children.

All medicines labeled "Keep Refrigerated" should be kept in the refrigerator, preferably in a location well out of the reach of all small children in the house, not just the child who is ill.

NONPRESCRIPTION MEDICINES

Aspirin

Aspirin has served as one of the most common medicines for childhood illnesses. Although aspirin cannot cure an illness or disease, it can relieve symptoms and make a child more comfortable. Aspirin reduces three important discomforts: fever, pain, and inflammation. In the past, aspirin was often given to children for headaches, aching muscles, the fevers associated with many childhood illnesses, and the inflammation associated with *arthritis.*

In recent years, research has identified a link between aspirin therapy used for *chicken pox* and *influenza* and the development of *Reye's syndrome,* a potentially fatal illness of the liver and brain. Parents should be alert to the possibility that an illness with fever which their child develops may prove to be either *chicken pox* or *influenza.* Aspirin, therefore, should be avoided when a child has a fever until a physician diagnoses the illness.

In general, "children's" aspirin is preferable because the dosage per tablet is smaller than that in regular aspirin tablets, and the amount given can be adjusted more easily to the child's need. Specific dosages may be recommended by a health professional. Parents should also read carefully the dosage instructions on the label or in the package insert. If children's aspirin is not available, regular adult-strength aspirin tablets (325 mg) may be used. Extra-strength (500 mg) tablets and capsules are available for aspirin and acetaminophen; therefore, parents should read labels carefully. Tablets can be broken into halves or quarters to obtain the proper dosage.

Parents should also be aware of the dangers of routinely giving their children aspirin. *Aspirin poisoning* can occur with frequent ingestion of excessive amounts of aspirin over a period of time.

Acetaminophen

Acetaminophen is a pain reliever and fever reducer that is as effective as aspirin. Acetaminophen to reduce a fever should be given according to directions on the label unless otherwise recommended by a health professional. Acetaminophen can be particularly useful for a child if aspirin causes allergies or stomach irritation. It can be helpful and safe when a possibility exists that an illness with fever may prove to be influenza or chicken pox (see discussion of Reye's syndrome above).

Acetaminophen is available in a number of tablet, capsule, or liquid forms. Because acetaminophen comes in a variety of product forms, it is possible to confuse one form or strength with another. For example, some brands come in "baby" and "junior" strengths. Parents should follow a health professional's recommendations or carefully follow the dosage directions on the container of medicine before using.

Decongestants

Decongestants can shrink swollen mucous membranes in the ear, nose, and throat, thereby relieving stuffy noses and clogged ears. Many decongestants are sold over the counter as tablets, liquids, nose drops, or nose sprays.

In many cases, childhood colds or other illnesses causing congestion do not require the use of decongestants. If needed, however, decongestants should be administered carefully according to a health professional's recommendation. A "rebound effect" may occur. (Rebound develops when the effect of decongestants wears off and, in reaction, the nose and ears become severely clogged.) Before discontinuing or changing a decongestant, it may be helpful to consult a health professional. Children should not be given decongestants for more than a few days, or permanent damage to mucous membranes is possible.

Some children may experience side effects after taking certain decongestants. For example, lethargy, sleepiness, irritability, restlessness, and inability to concentrate or sit still occasionally occurs.

Cough Syrups

Because a *cough* is the body's way of clearing mucus secretions from the throat and bronchial tubes, a child should be encouraged to cough deeply rather than suppress a cough. Sufficiently large amounts of liquids help keep the mucus loose, and a teaspoon of honey in warm water or tea may soothe a dry, scratchy throat. (Honey should not be given to children less than 1 year old.) Many parents believe that mucus that is spit up should be spit out and not swallowed. As a result, some children often avoid coughing because they do not feel comfortable trying to spit out mucus. Parents should tell children that swallowing mucus does no harm and is better than not coughing and allowing mucus to remain in the respiratory tract.

If mucus cannot be loosened by coughing, a health professional should be called for advice. An "expectorant" cough syrup may be prescribed to liquefy mucus so that it can be coughed up. If a cough is deep and painful or keeps a child awake at night, a health professional may recommend a cough suppressant, a stronger medicine that reduces the urge to cough. Unless recommended, cough suppressants should not be given to children (see *cough*).

PRESCRIPTION MEDICINES

Precautions

A physician's instructions should always be followed when giving prescription medicines to children. If after taking a medicine a child experiences an adverse reaction, no matter how mild, a physician should be consulted immediately. If a parent is concerned about the effectiveness of a medicine, the physician also should be consulted.

If a physician happens to prescribe a medicine which the parents believe they have on hand, the available medicine should not be used without first checking with the physician or pharmacist to be sure it is exactly the same as the one currently prescribed, and that the strength and dosage are correct. No child should be given a prescription medicine ordered for someone else—not even for a brother or sister—unless the physician specifically approves such action. Medicine strength and dosage must be exactly suited for each child's individual needs.

It is always important to check the prescription label for the expiration dates of medicines. All outdated (or no longer used) medicines should be discarded, preferably by flushing them down the toilet. This practice eliminates the possibility of a child's finding bottles of pills or capsules in the wastebasket or garbage.

Antibiotics

The most commonly prescribed medicines for children are antibiotics. Antibiotics kill or significantly reduce infection-producing bacteria in the body. Antibiotics, however, *cannot kill viruses,* and thus are ineffective against ailments such as colds or the flu.

Physicians are cautious about prescribing antibiotics because excessive use can lead to the development of antibiotic-resistant strains of bacteria which then become difficult to treat.

Antibiotics are usually prescribed for a 10-day course. To ensure that bacteria causing an infection have been killed, the prescription should be taken exactly as the physician ordered, even if a child begins to feel well within two or three days. Antibiotics given at home are in liquid or tablet form although a physician may want to give an initial dose by injection. Occasionally, antibiotics cause side effects such as upset stomach or *diarrhea*. Parents should inquire about possible side effects if an antibiotic is prescribed for their child. Certain antibiotics (tetracyclines) cause staining of developing teeth, and therefore they are almost never prescribed for children.

Many types of antibiotics are available, each specific for a certain type of bacteria; no one type of antibiotic works against all types of bacteria.

HOW TO GIVE MEDICINE TO A CHILD

BY MOUTH

Medicine should be measured accurately with a measuring spoon or dropper. Pharmacies stock measuring spoons designed especially to administer medicine accurately: plastic tube-shaped spoons that are particularly handy because, once measured, the medicine is less likely to spill and a child can hold it before swallowing the liquid.

Acetaminophen or aspirin tablets can be ground up and mixed with food or dissolved in a little water and given by spoon. Acetaminophen in liquid form is often preferable, because it is flavored.

Infants and young children can be given medicine mixed with foods such as cereal, jam, applesauce, or pudding. If parents add medicine to a baby's bottle, they must make certain that the baby gets all of the medicine; an effective strategy is to mix the medicine with an ounce or two of the formula or other liquid, and when the child is finished with that small portion the bottle can be filled with the rest.

Capsules should not be opened or pills crushed unless parents are directed to do so by a health professional.

The entire course of any prescribed medication should be administered according to a physician's instructions. If a child misses one dose of a prescription medicine, the usual treatment dosage should be continued; the next dose should not be doubled.

SUPPOSITORIES

If a child who is vomiting cannot be given oral medication, a physician may prescribe a suppository, a medicine that is inserted into the rectum. Most suppositories are cylinder-shaped with a tapered end. Suppositories should be stored in the refrigerator, as they usually contain medicine mixed with a glycerin base that melts when warm. Suppositories should be at room temperature when inserted: 15 minutes (less time in the summer) outside the refrigerator usually warms them sufficiently.

A suppository should be gently inserted into the child's rectum and the buttocks should then be held together for five to ten minutes. If a child cannot keep the suppository in the rectum for one half hour, the physician should be consulted before any medication is repeated.

DIET FOR A SICK CHILD

In addition to rest and medication, sick children may require a special diet. Because children often lose their appetites when ill, they may not want to eat much. A child should not be forced to eat unless a physician orders a special diet. Instead, a child should be encouraged to eat whatever is appealing. In most cases, children should be encouraged to drink more fluids than usual.

FEVER WITHOUT VOMITING

When a child has a fever above 101° F (38.3° C), the appetite usually decreases, especially for solid foods. During the first day or two of fever, a child may not want any food; the child should not be forced to eat except on physician's orders. Instead, the child should drink plenty of liquids such as fruit juices, water, or in some cases, skim milk. Babies are likely to want milk; older children may not.

A hungry child can be served bland foods such as toast, crackers, cereal, soup, custard, gelatin, applesauce, or scrambled or soft-boiled eggs. Foods that are not well-digested during fever include fresh fruits and vegetables, meats, sweets, and foods with high fat or salt content.

NAUSEA AND VOMITING

A child's stomach should be allowed to rest completely for an hour or two after vomiting. The child should then be given fluids sparingly, especially if vomiting is severe.

After an infant vomits, a parent should consult with the physician about the child's diet, especially liquids. Very young children who have vomiting illnesses can run the risk of dehydration. (See *dehydration; vomiting.*)

After vomiting, children should first be given sips of water or other clear liquids such as apple juice, ginger ale, gelatin or gelatin water, or herbal tea. (Canned soups, consommé, or bouillion should be avoided because of the high salt content.) If small amounts of liquids do not upset the stomach, more can be given. Gradually, fluid intake can be increased to a full glass. A child can also be given small amounts of a less acidic fruit juice, such as apple juice. If the child is hungry, he or she can be offered dry, bland foods like toast, crackers, or arrowroot cookies. As the child's appetite returns, easily digested foods—such as those recommended for a child ill with fever—can be added.

If the child vomits again, the procedure should be repeated more slowly, allowing the stomach plenty of time to recover and rest.

HOW TO TAKE A CHILD'S TEMPERATURE

There are two types of thermometer: rectal and oral. A rectal thermometer has a round, smooth bulb, designed to slide easily into the rectum (see Fig. 7A); an oral thermometer a long, thin bulb (see Fig. 7B). Usually an arrow or red mark points to the "normal" human body temperature, 98.6° F (37.0° C). A slender band of silver or red mercury appears parallel to the line of temperature markings.

A thermometer should always be held at the top, the end opposite from the bulb.

FIG. 7. RECTAL AND ORAL THERMOMETERS

7A. A rectal thermometer has a short, round mercury bulb to ensure safe and easy insertion. The rectal thermometer shown uses the Celsius (centigrade) scale. Normal temperature is 37° C.

7B. An oral thermometer has a long, slender mercury bulb that provides greater surface area to register heat. The oral thermometer shown uses the Fahrenheit scale. Normal temperature is 98.6° F.

Finding the band of mercury is sometimes tricky. By holding a thermometer near a good light and rotating it slowly with the fingertips, it should be possible to locate the band of mercury that indicates the child's temperature.

Before taking a child's temperature, the thermometer must be "shaken down" until the mercury is at or below 96° F (35.6° C). This should be done by holding the upper end of the thermometer (nonbulb end) and shaking it with a vigorous snapping of the wrist. It is best to take a child's temperature early in the morning and late in the afternoon. If the temperature seems to be rising rapidly, however, more frequent readings are needed.

There are three ways to take a child's temperature: rectally, under the armpit, or orally. Rectal temperatures run about 0.5° F (0.3° C) higher than mouth temperatures; armpit temperatures fall in between the other two temperatures.

Rectally. The rectal method is best for infants and young children because they are not patient enough to hold a thermometer under their tongues. A very young child should be placed face down across an adult's knees so that he or she cannot easily squirm out of position. An older child should lie on one side with knees bent slightly to relax the buttocks. The bulb end of the rectal thermometer should be dipped in petroleum jelly and then gently inserted about 1 inch into the rectum. The thermometer should be released once it is in the rectum so that a sudden motion does not cause it to twist or jab against the rectal wall. The thermometer can then be steadied between the index and middle fingers while the baby's buttocks are held still with the other fingers and the palm of the hand. The thermometer should be kept in place for three minutes, two at the very least.

Under the Arm. The underarm method is often used for toddlers who do not like rectal thermometers but cannot yet hold an oral thermometer under the tongue. It is also used when older children cannot breathe through their noses because of nasal congestion. Either an oral or rectal thermometer should be shaken down and placed in an armpit that has been wiped dry. To keep the thermometer in place, the child's elbow should be held flush against the side while the child's hand is placed on the opposite shoulder. The child's arm should be kept in this position with the thermometer tucked in the armpit for about four minutes.

Orally. In general, oral temperature readings can be taken with children 5 years of age and older who can hold a thermometer firmly between the lips without biting it.

To avoid incorrect readings, a child should not drink anything for about 15 minutes before oral temperature-taking. The oral thermometer should be shaken down and the bulb end placed under the tongue and just to one side. The child's mouth should be closed around the thermometer but it should not be kept in place with the teeth. A child should never be left alone with an oral thermometer in place. An accurate reading takes about three minutes.

Following temperature-taking, the thermometer should be washed with cold water and soap. (Hot water will crack it.) The thermometer should be rinsed with cold water, then dried and wiped with isopropyl rubbing alcohol. After being shaken down again, the thermometer should be replaced in its case. A cracked thermometer should be thrown out, no matter how small the crack.

If the thermometer indicates that a child has a fever, parents should consider calling the child's pediatrician. A physician should be called if an infant under 2 months of age has a fever of 100° F (37.8° C) or higher; if a child from 3 months to 2 years has a fever of 102° F (38.8° C) or higher; if a child of any age has a fever above 103° F (39.4° C); or if a child of any age has a fever that is accompanied by drowsiness, labored breathing, or a sick or markedly unusual appearance. (See also *fever.*)

Sponge bath

Physicians often recommend a sponge bath if a child has a high fever. A child should never be put in an icy bath or rubbed with isopropyl alcohol; such treatment is usually too severe. In fact, such treatment often produces shivering, which can cause the body temperature to climb even higher. Instead, a child should be given a cool-water sponge bath.

To give a child a sponge bath, a bathtub or basin should be filled with lukewarm water. If it feels comfortably warm when tested by an adult elbow, it will feel cool to a feverish child. The child should sit navel-deep in water. Using a brisk stroke, a parent or the child can move a wet sponge or washcloth rapidly across the child's skin with enough friction so that blood is drawn to the surface. Some of the heat given off by the blood is absorbed by the bathwater, thereby cooling the child's skin. Cold water should trickle into the tub during the bath to keep the temperature cool. If the child starts shivering, if his or her teeth begin chattering, or if the lips turn blue, the water can be warmed. A sponge bath should last as long as 20 minutes for effective temperature reduction.

After the bath, the child should be patted, not rubbed, dry and dressed in light clothing. A temperature reading should be taken 30 minutes after the bath. Because of the bath, fever usually drops one or two degrees; if it does not, a sponge bath should be repeated within an hour or two. Rarely does a feverish child require more than two consecutive nights (or days) of sponge baths.

# Going to the Hospital

Almost every patient, young or old, is anxious about going to the hospital. For a child, the experience is often especially difficult. Parents and hospital staff who are sensitive to the child's needs, expectations, and fears can help prepare the patient for the experience, but even then a hospitalization can be a very unsettling time.

PREPARING FOR THE HOSPITAL EXPERIENCE

THE PARENTS' ROLE

It is helpful if the parents (and if possible, the child) meet with hospital staff before the child's admission. This provides an opportunity to discuss the hospitalization process, the people involved, the child's condition, the tests and treatment, and the possible results of any procedures. Parents who know what to expect are better able to prepare their child.

When discussing hospitalization, parents should be as detailed as is appropriate for a child's development. Parents can describe the hospital and its staff, and explain the daily routine in detail appropriate for a child's age. They can also be sure the child knows when the hospitalization is scheduled to begin and approximately how long the child will be in the hospital. Hospital staff can advise parents about the content and timing of such a discussion.

Children often need to be encouraged to ask questions and express their fears. Some children believe they are going to the hospital as a punishment, that they are to blame for being sick, that they may not wake up after surgery, or that they may never return home. Parents who deal realistically with their children's concerns can help reduce fears. Many children are too young or just unable to put these fears into words. Parents who realize the common misconceptions can help their child by verbalizing the child's fears and reassuring the child that they are unfounded.

Parents should emphasize that hospitals and their staff exist to make people of all ages well. Parents and children can read books together that are designed specifically to prepare children for hospitalization. Some books present a realistic description in words and pictures of a typical child's experience in a hospital and of the different kinds of facilities and services offered. For younger readers there are storybook accounts of what goes on inside a hospital. Many of these books are available in libraries and bookstores. One of the very best is *The Hospital Book,* by James Howe (New York, 1981), available in hard- and soft-cover editions. Some hospitals publish special booklets of their own to prepare children for admission.

Parents should be supportive and honest during these reading and discussion sessions. If they don't know the answers to their child's questions, they should say so and try to acquire the necessary information from their physician or from hospital staff members. Above all, parents should emphasize that they care deeply for their child and will be as available and close as possible.

PREADMISSION PROGRAMS AND TOURS

Many hospitals offer preadmission programs that give children and their families opportunities to learn firsthand about a hospital stay. Generally, orientation sessions are presented for small groups of soon-to-be patients. A nurse or other staff member may discuss a typical hospital stay and answer parents' and children's questions. Individual problems, fears, or confusions are often successfully resolved at sessions like these. Presentations such as puppet shows, films, or slides help to explain a child's hospital stay.

A tour is often included to help familiarize a future patient with at least some of the hospital. Young children may be encouraged to dress up and play the roles of doctors and nurses, using stethoscopes, paper surgical masks and caps, tongue depressors, and plastic syringes fitted with plastic points. During preadmission sessions, older children—preteens and teenagers—may want to talk with their physician or another member of the medical staff to get detailed, specific answers to their questions and to begin establishing a personal link with the people who will soon be caring for them.

If preadmission programs or tours are not available, parents should at least arrange a visit for the child to the physician and walk around part of the hospital.

PREPARING FOR OUTPATIENT VISITS

Preparation is equally useful and reassuring for a child's visit to the hospital as an outpatient. Even though such visits are usually less frightening, because the child does not stay overnight at the hospital, children still worry about examinations, diagnostic tests, evaluations, referrals, or treatment as well as about who will be taking care of them.

For ambulatory, or outpatient, surgery, the procedure usually takes only a few hours and the child goes home the same day. Before going to the hospital, however, it is important for parents to talk about surgery with the child, to answer any questions, and to be reassuring and informative about the parent's constant presence and availability during the time in the hospital. Occasionally a child undergoing surgery as an outpatient may be required to stay overnight for observation, and that possibility needs to be explained in advance. Many children's hospitals also have special preparation programs for ambulatory surgery patients.

ADMISSION PROCEDURES

INPATIENTS

For an inpatient, the first stop is usually the admitting office. The admitting process can be lengthy. It often takes place in several different areas of the hospital, and involves a variety of people, including resident physicians, nurses, technicians, and clerks. First a child is registered and insurance data is obtained; then a room or ward assignment is made. In addition, it is determined whether the patient is properly immunized or may have been recently exposed to a contagious disease. The child receives a plastic identification bracelet.

Blood Test

The admitting process usually includes taking a blood sample, and parents should prepare their child for the brief pain of this procedure.

For very fearful children, role-playing at home can help prepare for a blood test, with a parents playing the role of the child. In this way, parents can let their children know that it is acceptable to cry or yell but that it is important to try to stay still—and that they will be with them for support. Children are reassured when they know that just a small amount of blood will be taken, that adults understand their fears, and that there will be a Band-Aid ready when the blood test is finished.

Admission Forms

Parents are required to fill out multiple hospital forms. During this time parents may want to involve the child in the admitting process by reading certain parts aloud, or by asking some of the questions aloud. Some teenagers may want to fill out these forms themselves.

In some hospitals or in certain cases (for example, when a child is transferred from another hospital or when the admission is an emergency), the details of the admitting process may be taken care of at the bedside.

Orientation

After the child has been admitted, a nurse or other staff member will explain the features of the child's room and hospital recreation areas if available. Getting to know staff members and other patients often helps children feel more comfortable and secure, especially at those times when their parents cannot be there. Children may become puzzled or frightened by the sight of bandages, intravenous tubing, drainage apparatus, and other medical equipment, or by crying or obviously ill patients, and parents should be as reassuring and honest as possible in their explanations.

EMERGENCY ADMISSION

Emergencies are frequently hectic and confusing for parents and children alike, allowing little or no time for preparation. Whenever possible, parents should try to have someone call ahead to the hospital emergency room before setting out for the hospital (see Chapter 9, "Preparing for Emergencies").

A hospital staff member in the emergency room supervises all admissions work and can answer questions and help with problems. In an effort to reassure their child, parents should stay with the child whenever possible and accompany him or her everywhere—to the laboratory, X-ray area, and if permitted, as far as the operating-room door if surgery is required.

INTENSIVE CARE UNIT

A child who is severely injured or ill may be admitted directly to an intensive care unit (ICU). Patients in an ICU are monitored constantly and receive the most technically advanced, highly specialized care available from a team of physicians and nurses. Some common occasions of ICU admissions for children are near-drownings, life-threatening breathing problems, poisonings, and motor vehicle accidents. Transfer of children to the ICU for recovery is a common practice after lengthy or complicated surgical procedures. Children should be told in advance of surgery if an ICU stay may be a possibility. If it can possibly be avoided, a child should not wake up in the ICU without some prior explanation.

If a community hospital is not equipped to treat a young child's particular needs, he or she may be transferred to the nearest hospital where an ICU or specialized equipment and care are available. Babies born prematurely or who are seriously ill may be admitted to a special neonatal intensive care unit (NICU) if one is available.

PARENT PARTICIPATION

Fears can be eased considerably if a parent can stay with the child, preferably in the child's room. Because the presence and support of the family are essential to a child's well-being and sense of security, visiting hours for parents, brothers and sisters, and grandparents, especially in children's hospitals, are usually liberal and flexible. A child's emotional well-being is considered as important as his or her physical condition in most enlightened hospitals today.

Facilities for "rooming-in" (staying overnight)—including bedside chairs that convert into beds, or cots that are set up in or near the child's room—are often available for parents. Parents can usually call ahead to learn about rooming-in policies. Sometimes space at the bedside is limited, especially in older hospitals. If rooming-in facilities are not provided, special rooms for parents may be available elsewhere on the hospital premises.

If parents find that hospital rules make continual close contact between them and their child difficult, they should stress to the hospital staff the importance of maintaining their usual closeness. For example, if there was not time to make arrangements for staying overnight before the child was admitted to the hospital, parents can often negotiate with the nursing managers or the child's physician to ensure that their child is not separated from them.

Parents are encouraged to participate in their child's care. Arrangements can be made with the nursing staff regarding how and to what extent this may be done. For example, parents should make every effort to cooperate with daily routines and hospital policies. In some hospitals parents may visit in ICUs and can often participate in care as soon as they become familiar with the environment and hospital routines.

For most hospitalized children and adolescents, visits from friends and family are important and reaffirm that the family cares about them and misses them. Photographs, letters, cards, or cassette tapes also bring the family closer to a hospitalized child.

The Association for the Care of Children's Health publishes excellent informational brochures for parents about hospitalization (3615 Wisconsin Avenue, Washington, DC 20016). Around the country parents' groups exist that can help inform and support families dealing with a child's illness and hospitalization. For names and addresses of some of these groups, parents can write to (or phone) what is perhaps the most resourceful and knowledgeable of these organizations:

Children in Hospitals, Inc.
31 Wilshire Park
Needham, MA 02192
(617-482-2915)

SUPPORT STAFF

Many hospitals have staff members who work with patients to discuss feelings of anxiety, fear, or depression. Hospital <u>social workers</u> work with families and patients to deal with the emotional problems arising from a child's illness or injury. They can also help with living or housing arrangements or with financial concerns.

In most hospitals activity therapists involve patients in organized activities appropriate to their age. Such activities provide lively outlets for feelings and energy. At many hospitals volunteers provide toys, games, or craft materials and entertain children, especially at night and on weekends.

School districts and hospitals frequently arrange to have tutors help hospitalized children with their studies. State laws commonly require that children who miss more than two weeks of school receive tutoring.

Work and family commitments sometimes make it impossible for parents to spend every day with their hospitalized child. Occasionally a child may be hospitalized far from home to receive specialized care. The separation of parents from children during a hospital stay can be painful and problematic for all family members. Parents should discuss in detail the circumstances that make separation unavoidable with their child's physician or nurses. Many children's hospitals have patient care specialists who can be especially helpful in easing and minimizing the pains of separation. Parents who find themselves in this situation should inquire about the availability of such help.

In their operating policies and professional staff, hospitals—and especially children's hospitals—make every effort to be responsive to the material and emotional needs of patients and their families, regardless of how complicated. The social service department usually has staff members who can act as personal advisers and advocates. They often can be helpful if financial assistance is necessary. Parents should feel no hesitation in seeking out many kinds of professional assistance at the hospital.

PLANNING AHEAD FOR SURGERY

When facing surgery, regardless of its scope or complexity, children's concerns vary according to their developmental level. Children under 5 or 6 are most concerned about being separated from their families and being left in the midst of strangers. Children from about age 10 through adolescence worry about having to bear "unsightly scars," losing control of their bodies, being completely dependent upon strangers, and even of waking up during the operation because the anesthesia "has worn off too soon." The concerns of children older than 12 generally resemble those of adults: they are often anxious about the appearance and integrity of their bodies. They almost always want to know what their bodies will look like after surgery and how long it will take to recover.

Hospital personnel, especially those connected with the admissions office and preadmission program, if one exists, can provide factual information and emotional reassurance.

Parents who feel sufficiently well informed may wish to try to explain surgery and anesthesia in terms appropriate for a child's age and maturity. This can help alleviate some of the child's anxiety. Often, however, it is highly desirable and reassuring for a member of the surgical team to provide that kind of preoperative explanation, especially to an older child who wants to know details and is able to understand the information.

An anesthesiologist can explain to an older child what to expect, what the anesthesia is intended to do, and how long it takes for the effects to wear off. The appropriate anesthesia is chosen by the anesthesiologist in consultation with the child's surgeon. The precise drug or, more often, combination of drugs is chosen specifically for each patient.

The goal of anesthesia is to furnish the safest possible freedom from pain during surgery while using the smallest effective amount(s) of drug(s). During the operation and afterward the child's condition is continuously monitored by the anesthesiologist, using the equipment that is constantly checked for reliability and safety. In the recovery room following surgery, the child is checked constantly by a nurse or physician until consciousness returns. The anesthesiologist or an assistant makes certain that the process of awakening proceeds smoothly.

Once conscious, the child is regularly reassured by recovery room staff regarding his or her well-being and the outcome of the operation. Parents may be able to visit the recovery room briefly to see the child and confirm what staff members have been saying.

It can be particularly reassuring to a child to have someone the same age who has successfully undergone the same operation describe what the experience is like. Surgeons and anesthesiologists may be able to provide the names of patients willing to share their experiences.

PATIENT AND PARENT RIGHTS

It is important for parents to be able to trust members of their child's health care team. The best way to establish this trust is to stay well-informed about the child's condition and progress. In conversations with physicians and nurses, parents should ask questions and express concerns about any part of their child's care. Often the "simplest" questions are the most important. Parents, of course, have a right to informative explanations. If anything remains unclear, parents should ask again until they receive information and interpretations that satisfy them.

The parents are asked to give their "informed consent" before a child undergoes surgery, certain diagnostic tests, or potentially hazardous treatments. Often, beginning at about the age of 12, patients are asked to sign consent forms as well. Of course, in an emergency, hospital staff may begin treatment without first obtaining consent. In most circumstances a physician and nurse explain in detail to the parents—or parents and child, where appropriate—all relevant details and implications of the course of treatment proposed by the health care team. When giving such consent in writing, parents and patients acknowledge that they have received an explanation of the proposed procedure, understand the risks and benefits, and agree to the proposed care.

The primary purpose of informed consent is to make certain that all treatment is fully explained and that any foreseeable risks are described in detail and to protect an individual from unknowingly serving as a subject for medical research. To ensure that parents and patients understand the consent form, physicians are required to offer an oral explanation or paraphrase to supplement the written form. If this is not offered, parents should ask the child's physician or specialist for a complete explanation.

At a minimum, these issues should be discussed:

- the specific diagnosis
- the nature of the illness
- the proposed test, treatment, or operation
- the risks and benefits of the procedure
- the potential complications
- any possible alternative treatments and the benefits and risks of those treatments
- the possible results for the child, both short-term and long-term, with and without the treatment

Hospital patients have many other rights in addition to informed consent. While these may vary from state to state, standard patient rights include the following:

- the right to confidentiality of medical records
- the right to have all reasonable requests fulfilled promptly if within the capacity of the hospital
- the right to obtain a copy of any hospital rules or regulations that apply to the patient's conduct
- the right to receive, upon request, information about financial assistance and free care
- the right to inspect the patient's own medical records
- the right to refuse to be examined, observed, or treated by a medical student or a particular hospital staff member without jeopardizing access to medical care
- the right to as much privacy as the hospital can provide during treatment
- the right to receive, upon request, a copy of the hospital bill submitted to any third party (such as an insurance company)

REHABILITATION

For some children the end of a hospital stay means the beginning of a long-term period of rehabilitation and recovery. Such periods of rehabilitation are necessary if a child requires recuperation under medical supervision or if a child has a long-term condition that cannot be managed at home. Whenever possible an attempt is made to return the child home and bring appropriate health services there. When extended periods of care are required, children may be transferred from a community or acute-care hospital to a long-term or rehabilitation hospital. In such long-term cases, visits by parents and other family members become even more important.

LONG-TERM HOSPITALS

Long-term and rehabilitation hospitals offer services in addition to medical and specialized nursing care, including dental care, counseling, school programs, and comprehensive evaluations for special needs.

The child's parents and physician should decide together whether the child can be cared for at home or which type of hospital is appropriate. If choosing a hospital, parents should consider the distance from home, the estimated length of stay, the severity of their child's condition, the services provided, and the cost. Many long-term facilities have several levels of care to accommodate patients with different types of needs.

Because of the high cost of long-term care, parents should investigate all available means of coverage and then choose the most appropriate level of care. For example, skilled nursing care for a severely handicapped child may be entirely covered by Medicaid, while intermediate nursing care may be only partially covered. In addition, visiting or public health nurse services may be available. For families that choose to provide most nursing care themselves, respite care personnel may be ideal to give valuable weekend help occasionally. For information about visiting and public health nursing and respite care, parents should inquire at local health departments.

NURSING HOMES

In addition to long-term and rehabilitation hospitals, pediatric nursing homes are available in some areas to provide long-term health care. Such homes are classified according to the level of care provided.

- Extended care facilities. Round-the-clock nursing care and medical supervision are provided. Extended care facilities closely resemble hospitals.

- Skilled nursing facilities. Round-the-clock nursing services are provided, as well as preventive, therapeutic, social, and emotional care.
- Intermediate care facilities. Very little medical service is provided. Intermediate care consists primarily of nursing care for patients who need help with treatments.
- Residences or rest homes. Medical and nursing services are not available, but a residence provides supervision and a protective environment. If a child needs help with dressing, bathing, eating, or other daily activities which cannot be provided at home, but does not need medical care, a residence may be appropriate.

Moving a child to a long-term hospital or nursing home is a very difficult decision, but at certain times such a move can be in the best interest of both the child and family. The community in a quality pediatric nursing home strives to provide companionship and stimulation; health care is always available; the environment is secure, protective, and designed to accommodate special needs; special education may be available.

The decision to place a child in a nursing facility may be difficult and painful for parents. Parents may fear that their child will not receive proper care or may worry that they are evading their parental responsibilities. If they decide that a nursing home is best after much discussion and consideration, parents and physicians need to choose carefully an appropriate institution for the child. It is important for parents to investigate the credentials of the staff and standards of the facility, to inspect the premises, and to talk at length on several occasions with the health care personnel. They may then be able to make a sound judgment about the capabilities of the nursing facility to care for their child.

Part III
Emergencies

Preparing for Emergencies

BASIC PREPARATION

Being prepared for an emergency can prevent complications from injury or illness, and can save lives. Being prepared includes instituting and following safety precautions, knowing where to get help, having emergency supplies on hand, and knowing first aid (see Chapter 10, "Basic First Aid"). Too often families establish safety precautions after an accident has occurred; for example, smoke detectors are installed after a fire.

Many health care organizations offer first aid courses for parents and children. A basic program can provide useful information, such as how to estimate the extent of injury and how to react to a life-threatening situation. Training is often provided in life-saving techniques, such as artificial respiration, cardiopulmonary resuscitation (CPR), the Heimlich maneuver, and how to stop external bleeding. Training for CPR can be particularly important since using this technique incorrectly can cause injury. (See next chapter for descriptions of these techniques.)

In addition to becoming trained in first aid techniques, families should find out exactly what emergency assistance is available in their community.

- Does the fire department or police department provide emergency services and transportation?
- Are trained paramedics part of the rescue squad and is the service fully certified?

- How close in time and distance is the nearest hospital emergency room?
- Are there alternate routes to the hospital if one route is inaccessible or blocked?

Information such as alternate routes should be posted near each telephone with a list of emergency phone numbers:

- Fire department
- Police department (and state police)
- Physicians (names and specialties)
- Emergency assistance (nearest emergency room)
- Local rescue squad or ambulance service
- Poison information center

Instructions should also be posted for an emergency in which it is possible only to give vital facts over the telephone:

Dial "O" or 911, where applicable, and give the operator the following information:
 (1) name and nature of the emergency
 (2) street and number
 (3) city or town
 (4) telephone number

Children should carry personal identification at all times, listing their names and addresses. Children who have long-term medical conditions, such as diabetes or epilepsy, or who suffer severe allergic reactions to medications or insect bites or stings, should carry such information along with personal identification. (One convenient method is wearing a MedicAlert bracelet or necklace; write to MedicAlert, Turlock, CA 94355.)

EMERGENCY SUPPLIES

To deal with emergency situations, the home should be equipped with a first aid kit, fire extinguishers, and other fire safety equipment. (See Chapter 4, "Accident Prevention," for discussion of fire safety and firefighting equipment.) A first aid kit is usually kept in the bathroom medicine cabinet or closet. Wherever these supplies are stored, they should be kept out of the reach of small children. (See childproofing information in Chapter 4, "Accident Prevention," for tips on storing such supplies.)

First Aid Kit

Commercial first aid kits are available for use at home or while traveling. A basic kit usually contains rolls of two-and three-inch-wide gauze bandages, a dozen two- and four-inch-square gauge pads, adhesive tape, and assorted sizes of adhesive-strip bandages. To make a complete home set of emergency supplies, the following additional items should be added:

- a three- or four-inch-wide elastic (Ace) bandage
- two slings—pieces of cotton material about 36 inches square
- scissors with rounded tips
- tweezers
- large and small safety pins
- syrup of ipecac (to induce vomiting)
- acetaminophen or aspirin
- antihistamine
- petroleum jelly
- rubbing (isopropyl) alcohol (used to relieve itching and to clean skin)
- calamine lotion (used to relieve itching)
- two thermometers (one oral, one rectal)
- cotton swabs
- cotton balls
- ice bag
- hot-water bottle or heating pad
- an approved first aid manual, preferably published by the American Red Cross.

Prescription insect bite kits should be kept on hand if a child is known to have severe allergic reactions to bee or wasp stings.

First Aid Kit for Traveling

When traveling by car or planning to be outdoors camping or hiking, the following additions should be made to the basic first aid kit:

- prescription medications, if needed
- moleskin (for blisters)
- insect repellent
- a snake bite kit
- sunscreen (containing PABA)
- lip balm
- a flashlight with extra batteries
- safety flares
- a whistle
- a pocketknife
- a reliable first-aid manual, preferably published by the American Red Cross.

An excellent first aid kit especially designed for automobile travel can be purchased from local chapters of the American Red Cross.

INSTRUCTIONS FOR BABY-SITTERS

A baby-sitter should be prepared for an emergency. Even if a home is well equipped, emergencies can be disastrous if a baby-sitter is uninformed about emergency supplies and procedures.

Parents should arrange to have the baby-sitter visit the house prior to the first baby-sitting engagement. At this time parents can discuss with a sitter both regular duties and emergencies. The sitter should be given a thorough tour of the house and shown where to find emergency resources, including the first aid kit, phones and emergency phone lists, fire escapes or portable ladders, fire extinguishers, flashlights, and first aid instruction manuals.

Parents should also explain the operation of emergency home warning systems, such as smoke detectors or burglar alarms. Sitters should understand exactly what each family member is to do in the event of emergency. For example, it should be emphasized that children must leave the home immediately at the first sign of smoke or fire, and the sitter should know the fastest exit routes.

This visit is also an opportunity for the sitter and child (or children) to become acquainted. An introductory visit is a good time to discuss medications, nighttime emotional needs (such as a favorite blanket or stuffed animal), and other special needs.

If an introductory meeting with a baby-sitter is not possible, parents should allow an unhurried 15 to 30 minutes with the sitter before they leave. At this time parents should be certain to leave a phone number where they can be reached in case of emergency or an alternate phone contact in case they are not going to be near a phone. Sitters always should be warned not to let anyone into the house unless the visitor is well known to the sitter or expected by the parents.

In case of emergency or injury, a sitter should be prepared to make a quick assessment of the seriousness of a problem, based on the child's physical appearance, behavior, and other circumstances. If the injury or illness appears minor, such as a small cut or upset stomach, the sitter should call the parents or the alternate telephone contact. If the injury or illness is major, the sitter should call immediately for emergency help (according to the emergency phone list) and then contact the parents. If properly trained, the sitter should apply appropriate first aid techniques. Older children and teenagers should be encouraged to learn the techniques of artificial respiration, CPR, and the Heimlich maneuver (see next chapter).

10 Basic First Aid

RECOGNIZING AND EVALUATING EMERGENCIES

Parents—and anyone else who is often with children—should be able to do the following:

- **recognize** an emergency situation so that they can be alert to respond.
- **distinguish** between medical problems that can be treated at home and others that require professional medical attention.
- **deal with** certain life-threatening problems. Sometimes it is better to begin immediate treatment of the child's condition than to wait for medical assistance or to transport a seriously ill or injured child to the emergency room. (See previous chapter for information on first aid courses.)

When an emergency arises, it is necessary to choose among three options:

- begin treatment immediately
- call for emergency assistance
- transport a sick child to a hospital emergency room

Follow common sense. This chapter suggests the course to follow in each type of emergency. Parents would do well to become familiar with its contents. The ideal solution may be to have someone call a hospital emergency room, rescue squad, or police or fire department while another person begins first aid. If only one person is present, emergency help should be sought only if leaving a child will not result, as far as can be determined, in a worsening of the child's condition.

Before transporting the child, call the hospital to alert medical personnel about whom and what to expect. (If a child has serious injuries, especially those of the head or neck, checking for movement may be risky.)

While waiting for emergency help, administering first aid, or transporting a child to a hospital, parents should try to remain calm themselves and keep the child calm. Anyone attending an injured or ill child should explain to the child what is happening, step by step, in simple words spoken in a quiet voice.

Life-threatening problems deserve attention first, and parents need to act deliberately—not frantically. Even if the child's condition seems to grow worse before emergency medical help arrives, parents are urged to continue providing the kind of care indicated in this chapter. A few more seconds or minutes of needed first aid can prove lifesaving.

REPORTING AN EMERGENCY

When calling about emergency medical attention, it is important to be as specific as possible about the child's injuries and condition:

- What happened?
- What is the child's general condition? In other words, what is wrong
    (1) that a parent can see by looking at and quickly checking a child (referred to as "physical signs")?
    (2) that the child describes, if able, about how he or she feels (known as "symptoms")?
- What about a child's vital functions and systems?

    Airway. Is the child coughing or choking or making noises when breathing in?

    Respiration. Is the child breathing quickly or slowly; is the pulse rapid or slow?

    Pulse rate. Rapid or slow?

    Circulation. Is the child pale or flushed; what is the color of the lips and skin; is the child faint or nauseated; is there any bleeding?

    Consciousness. Is the child awake, arousable, irritated, consolable?

LIFE-THREATENING CONDITIONS

In any crisis situation involving

- unconsciousness,
- an absence of pulse (heartbeat), or
- breathing failure,

FIRST TAKE TIME TO EVALUATE WHAT NEEDS TO BE DONE. Making such an evaluation may take a minute or two, but in the long run a calm, overall appraisal of the priorities for emergency aid can be timesaving and lifesaving.

Basic Steps

- Call for emergency assistance immediately or send someone to make a call if a child's condition seems serious.
- Try to deal with the child's most serious problem first. See list of priorities below.
- Try to find out what happened, by asking either the child or others at the scene.
- Look for emergency medical information a child may carry on a necklace, bracelet, or card.
- Begin to treat the child wherever he or she is, according to priority list below. Do not move the child unless failing to do so would be likely to cause more

harm. DO NOT PICK UP THE CHILD AND TRY TO RUN FOR HELP.

- Move and speak deliberately as a way of keeping yourself calm and as a way of reassuring the child when he or she regains consciousness.

Priorities

1. Check breathing by bending over the child's nose and mouth. Listen for breathing sounds, try to feel the child's breath against your cheek or ear, or hold a mirror near the nose and mouth to check for mist produced by breathing. If child is not breathing, see p. 124.

2. Take the pulse at the body location appropriate for the child's age and size (see p. 000). If there is no pulse, see CPR, p. 127.

3. Check to see if the child is fully conscious. If not, see p. 123.

4. Check the rest of the head, neck, and body for bleeding (p. 132) and signs of possible broken bones (p. 133).

5. Be alert for any signs of poisoning, that is, stains or burns on the child's mouth or the presence of chemicals or medicines. (See p. 142.)

6. Be prepared to treat the child for shock (p. 144).

7. In hot or cold weather, be alert to the possibility of either hypothermia (p. 140) or heat exhaustion (p. 141).

Unconsciousness

Call for emergency assistance immediately if a child fails to respond when he or she is (1) called by name in a loud voice, (2) tapped on the chest, or (3) shaken gently as you would do if trying to rouse someone asleep.

Always seek medical attention for a child who loses consciousness for any reason—injury, disease, exposure to temperature extremes, allergic reaction, or shock. An unconscious child is unresponsive and unaware of his or her surroundings. The face, gums, or inner eyelids may be flushed, white, or blue, depending on the cause of unconsciousness.

Do not move the child unless he or she is in a hazardous location. Do not attempt to rouse the child again. Loosen the child's clothing, especially around the neck and waist. Raise the child's legs.

Turn the head to one side to encourage drainage of saliva and prevent choking. DO

NOT DO THIS IF A SERIOUS HEAD OR SPINAL INJURY IS SUSPECTED. Check for injuries, and if necessary, give first aid. Even if the child regains consciousness, keep him or her lying down until medical attention is available.

Carefully monitor the child's pulse. If it stops, begin cardiopulmonary resuscitation (p. 127). If breathing stops, give artificial respiration (see below).

Artificial Respiration

A child may stop breathing for any of several reasons, some involving an obstructed airway, usually the windpipe. (The windpipe is the breathing tube [trachea] which begins in the throat and leads to the lungs.) Food or toys lodged in the windpipe can cause breathing to stop, as can severe swelling as a result of illness such as *croup* or *epiglottitis.* Smoke inhalation, near drowning, and near suffocation can also cause interruption of breathing.

When a child is deprived of oxygen (hypoxia), the lips turn blue. If the child's chest is rising and falling, even with difficulty, and the rescuer can feel the child's breath on his or her face, air exchange is going on despite partial blockage of the airway. In this case, it is best to try to transport the child as quickly as possible to an emergency room. If the lips are blue and the child is unresponsive to gentle shaking and calling, immediately try to open the airway.

Opening an Airway

It is possible that establishing an open airway is all that is needed to restore breathing. With the child lying on his or her back on a firm surface, tilt the head back into a neutral position for an infant, or slightly farther back for an older child. Place your fingers against the bony part of the lower jaw and gently lift the chin while gently pushing back on the forehead with your other hand. This extension of the head usually will be enough to move the tongue so that it does not block the airway.

If a neck injury is suspected, move the child as little as possible and be sure to keep the neck and back straight. Do not tilt the head back, but open the airway by gently lifting the jaw upward.

If the child does not begin to cough or struggle for air within a few seconds after opening the airway, the rescuer must begin to provide breath for the child.

Artificial respiration, sometimes called rescue breathing, is a first aid technique used when a person is not breathing. It allows a rescuer to provide some breath for the child until emergency help arrives. (If a child is not breathing because he or she is *choking,* see p. 137). If a child is not breathing and has no pulse, start cardiopulmonary resuscitation (see p. 127).

Taking a Child's Pulse

An infant's pulse is felt most easily from the brachial artery, which is located in the middle of the inner arm, just above the elbow. Press your index and middle fingers into the infant's arm and feel for the pulse. (See Fig. 10A.)

An older child's pulse is felt most easily from the carotid artery, a major blood vessel in the neck. To check the carotid pulse, place two or three fingers on the child's Adam's apple (the lump in the middle of the front of the neck). Then slide these fingers sideways into the groove formed by the Adam's apple and the neck muscles to feel for the pulse. (See Fig. 10B.)

If a pulse can be detected but the child is *not* breathing, begin artificial respiration immediately.

- Try to have someone else call for emergency help, or call for help by dialing an emergency number.
- *Do not leave the child alone for more than 30 seconds to call for help* except in unusual circumstances. Begin artificial respiration immediately. It is essential to continue breathing for the child while emergency help is sought.

As long as the child is not breathing, continue artificial respiration until emergency help arrives. Continue to check for a pulse. If the child begins coughing or breathing independently before help arrives, try to keep the child calm by speaking in a slow, reassuring manner. If the child does not begin to breathe independently, the pulse may stop and cardiac compressions should be started. CPR should be continued while transporting the child.

Artificial Respiration Technique
For an infant (younger than 1 year old)

Leave the infant lying where he or she is; a firm surface usually is best. To avoid further damage if an injury to the head or spine is suspected, keep the infant's body from bending or twisting. Immobilize the head by using heavy objects such as bags of flour, sugar, sand, or rolled towels. Clear the mouth of any readily visible foreign material that can be reached easily.

1. Open the infant's breathing passages by making sure the head is in a normal neutral resting position. Lift the jaw open gently while supporting the head with one hand. (See Fig. 8A.)

2. Take a breath and place your mouth over the infant's mouth and nose, forming an airtight seal. (See Fig. 8B.)

3. Give two slow breaths (1 to 1½ seconds per breath), with a pause between, allowing you to take a breath. An infant's lungs will fill easily with very little force. Give the infant just enough air to make the chest rise and fall gently. BREATHING FOR AN INFANT SHOULD BE AT A STEADY, MODERATE PACE.

4. Check to see if the infant's chest is rising and falling (see Fig. 8C). If not, it may be because the airway is still obstructed. Adjust the position of the head, usually by tilting it back very slightly, unless a head or spinal injury is suspected.

FIG. 8. ARTIFICIAL RESPIRATION—INFANT

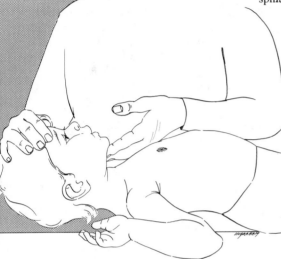

8A. Open airway by lifting up on the bony part of jaw and gently pushing back on forehead to put infant's head in a neutral position.

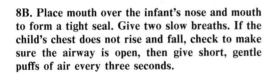

8B. Place mouth over the infant's nose and mouth to form a tight seal. Give two slow breaths. If the child's chest does not rise and fall, check to make sure the airway is open, then give short, gentle puffs of air every three seconds.

8C. Look to see whether the infant's chest is rising and falling. Listen for breathing sounds, and try to feel for breath.

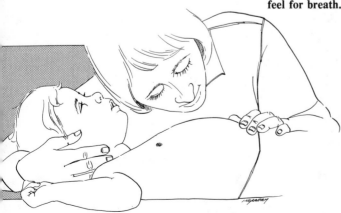

5. Repeat the artificial respiration procedure, and if the chest still does not rise and fall, assume that the infant has a foreign object obstructing the airway (unless a head or neck injury is likely). Treat for *choking*. (See p. 137.)

6. If the airway is open but the infant is still not breathing, continue giving a short, gentle puff of air *every three seconds, or 20 times per minute*. Between puffs, count seconds aloud: "One-one thousand, two-one thousand, three-one thousand."

7. Continue artificial respiration until the infant begins to cough or breathe alone or until medical help arrives. <u>DO NOT STOP EVEN IF YOU GET TIRED, DISCOURAGED, OR FRIGHTENED!</u>

For a child

Leave the child lying where he or she is; a firm surface usually is best. To avoid further damage if an injury to the head or spine is suspected, keep the child's body from bending or twisting. Clear the child's mouth of any readily visible foreign material that can be reached easily.

1. Open the child's breathing passages by gently tilting the head back and pulling the jaw open while gently supporting the head with one hand (see Fig. 9A). Do not tilt the head if a serious neck or spinal injury is suspected. Instead, pull the jaw open gently.

2. Take a breath. Pinch the child's nose, and place your mouth over the child's mouth, forming a tight seal. (See Fig. 9B.)

3. Give the child two slow breaths (1 to 1½ seconds per breath), with a pause between to let you get more air and to check

FIG. 9. ARTIFICIAL RESPIRATION—CHILD

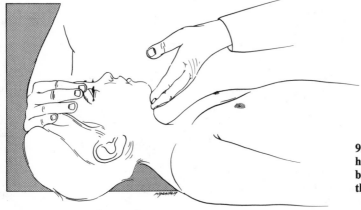

9A. Open child's airway by tilting head back slightly, lifting up on the bony part of jaw, and pushing back on the forehead.

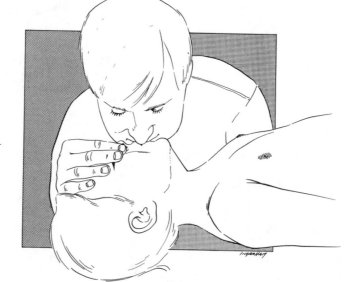

9B. Pinch the child's nose and place mouth over child's mouth, forming a tight seal. Give two slow breaths. If child does not begin to breathe alone, check to make sure the airway is open, then give short, gentle puffs of air every three to four seconds.

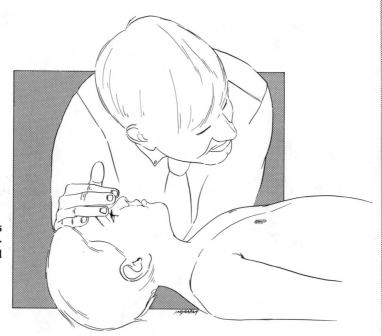

9C. Look to see if the child's chest is rising and falling. Listen for breathing sounds, and try to feel the child's breath.

for signs of breathing. Give just enough air to make the chest rise and fall gently.

4. Look for the child's chest to rise and fall and listen for the sound of air leaving the child's lungs (see Fig. 9C). If air is not getting into the child's lungs, tilt the head again to open the breathing passages, unless a head or spinal injury is suspected.

5. If the child still is not breathing, continue blowing air into the lungs once every four seconds, or 15 breaths a minute. Count seconds aloud: "One-one thousand, two-one thousand, three-one thousand, four-one thousand."

6. Be persistent: Do not stop artificial respiration until the child begins to cough or breathe unaided and the child's breath can be felt on your cheek, or until medical help arrives. Try to remain calm, even if the seconds seem like hours.

Cardiopulmonary Resuscitation (CPR)
Remember: Never perform CPR on a person who has a pulse.

Cardiopulmonary resuscitation (CPR) is a first aid technique used to save a person who has stopped breathing and whose heart has stopped beating. CPR can sustain circulation and maintain breathing until professional help takes over. The technique serves to get air into the lungs as well as squeeze blood out of the heart and into the arteries.

Except in the most extreme of emergencies, it should be performed only by those with CPR training. However, if a child is not breathing, the heart appears to have stopped, and no one trained in CPR is available, proceed as follows:

If the child is severely injured or unconscious, check for signs of breathing or coughing. If two rescuers are present, one should do this while the other goes or calls for help. If there is no breathing or coughing, check the pulse (see p. 127).

At the same time, check for bleeding. If bleeding seems severe, try to stop or reduce it by applying strong, sustained pressure with a compress, a clean cloth, or a bare hand (see p. 132).

For an infant
An infant's pulse is most readily felt from the brachial artery, which is located on the inner arm, just above the elbow. Press down with the tips of the index and middle fingers until the pulse is felt. (See Fig. 10A.)

If there is no sign of a pulse, nor cry or coughing, check the child's mouth, and carefully clear away any visible obstructions that can be reached easily.

Start artificial respiration (see p. 124). If this procedure fails to produce breathing or coughing and a pulse, start cardiac compressions.

1. To find the correct place for chest com-

FIG. 10. CPR—INFANT

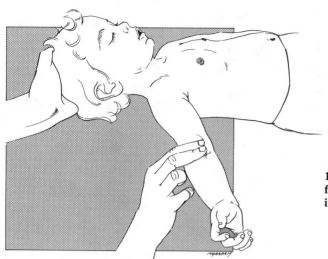

10A. Check infant's pulse by feeling for the brachial artery on the inside inner arm, just above the elbow.

10B. Using two or three fingers, push down 1/2 to 1 inch on the infant's breastbone, just below the internipple line. Do this about 100 times a minute. Continue giving short, gentle puffs of air after every fifth compression (every 3 seconds).

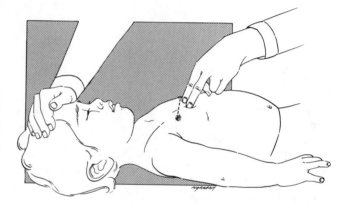

pressions, draw an imaginary line between the infant's nipples. Place the index finger of one hand just under the nipple line over the breastbone. The chest compression site is one finger's width below this place, or at the location of the middle finger. (See Fig. 10B.)

2. Using two or three fingers, push down on the infant's breastbone so that the chest goes in about 1/2 to 1 inch. Repeat chest compressions at a rate of at least 100 compressions per minute, but do not be overly concerned with the exact rate. After each compression release the pressure, allowing the breastbone to come to its normal position, but keep fingers in place on the chest. The compressions should be as rhythmic and smooth as possible.

3. *External chest compression always must be accompanied by artificial respiration. To be effective, the two must be coordinated.* Make sure the infant's head is in a neutral position to open the airway. Take a breath and place your mouth over the infant's mouth and nose, forming a tight seal.

4. At the end of every fifth chest compression (every three seconds), pause very briefly to give a breath to the infant, checking to see that the chest rises and falls. Each breath should last about 1 to 1 1/2 seconds.

5. Check the infant after one minute to see if vital functions have been restored. If not, continue CPR and check the infant every few minutes until medical help arrives.

6. If an ambulance or other help has not been called, and after 15 minutes of CPR there is still no pulse or breathing, take the infant along with you while calling for help, continuing the CPR if possible.

7. If breathing and pulse start, and as long as the infant continues to breathe, check for any problems, such as *shock* (see p. 144) or bleeding (see p. 132), which require treatment. If there is a pulse but no breathing, continue artificial respiration. (See p. 124.)

For a child

The child should be placed in a face-up position on a firm surface. Kneel beside the child. A child's pulse is most easily felt from the carotid artery, a major blood vessel in the neck. To check the carotid pulse, place two fingers on the Adam's apple (the lump in the center of the neck) (see Fig. 11A) and then slide these fingers to the side into the crease formed by the Adam's apple and the neck muscles (see Fig. 11B). If the child has a fleshy neck, the carotid pulse may be difficult to detect. Try to feel for a pulse for about 10 seconds.

If there is no sign of a pulse, nor cry or coughing, check the child's mouth and carefully clear away any visible obstructions that can be reached easily. Start artificial respiration (see p. 124). If this procedure does not produce signs of breathing, coughing, and a pulse, start cardiac compressions.

1. To find the correct place for chest compressions follow along the lower edge of the child's rib cage with your middle finger. Move finger up toward the middle of the chest until you reach the notch where the rib cage meets the breastbone. Keep the middle finger on the notch, and place the index finger next to the middle finger. Place the heel of your hand next to the index finger with the fleshy pads of the palm on the breastbone. <u>DO NOT WASTE VALUABLE TIME CHECKING AND RECHECKING THE EXACT LOCATION FOR COMPRESSIONS.</u>

2. For children younger than approximately 8 years of age, use the heel of one hand for compressions. If the child is older,

FIG. 11. CPR—CHILD

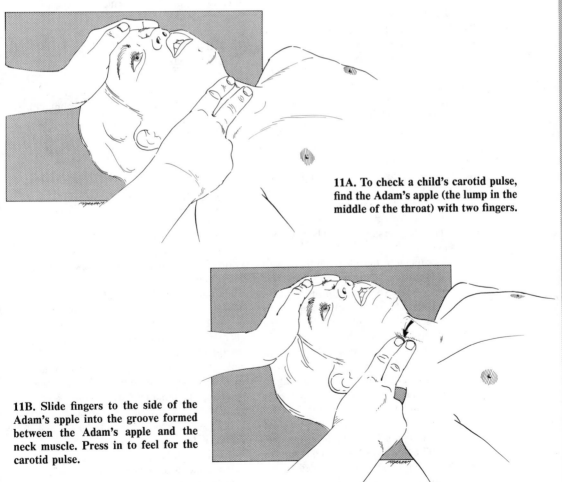

11A. To check a child's carotid pulse, find the Adam's apple (the lump in the middle of the throat) with two fingers.

11B. Slide fingers to the side of the Adam's apple into the groove formed between the Adam's apple and the neck muscle. Press in to feel for the carotid pulse.

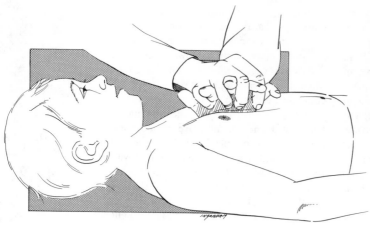

11C. Place the heel of the hand on the breastbone. Place the other hand on top of the first, interlacing the fingers. Compress the chest 1 to 1½ inches for a young child and 1½ to 2 inches for an older child. Do this about 80 times a minute. Continue giving short, gentle puffs of air after every fifth compression (every 3 to 4 seconds).

rest your free hand on top of the first, interlacing the fingers so that only the heel of the bottom hand touches the breastbone. (See Fig. 11C.)

3. Hold your arms straight and keep your shoulders squarely in position over the child's chest, then press down. The chest should be compressed about 1 to 1½ inches for a younger child, and 1½ to 2 inches for an older child.

5. Repeat chest compressions at the rate of 80 times per minute. Do not be overly concerned about the exact rate. Count aloud the compression rate—"One and two and three and four and five," compressing on the number and releasing on the "and." After each compression, release the pressure, allowing the breastbone to come to its normal position, but keep the heel of the hand in place. The compressions should be rhythmic and smooth.

6. Coordinate artificial respiration with chest compressions. Open the child's airway by tilting the head back and lifting the chin gently. Take a breath, tightly pinch the child's nose, and place your mouth over the child's mouth, forming an airtight seal.

7. At the end of every fifth compression (every three to four seconds), pause briefly and give a breath to the child, checking to see that the chest rises and falls. Each breath should last about 1 to 1½ seconds.

8. If an ambulance or other help has not been called, and after 15 minutes of CPR there is still no pulse or breathing, then take the child along with you while calling for help, continuing CPR if possible.

9. If pulse and breathing start, and as long as the child continues to breathe alone,

check for any problems, such as *shock* (see p. 144) or bleeding (see p. 132), which require treatment. If there is pulse but no breathing, continue artificial respiration. (See p. 124.)

LEARNING FIRST AID TECHNIQUES

Do not wait until the first emergency occurs before learning lifesaving techniques. Read Chapter 9, "Preparing for Emergencies." Anticipate the emergency situation so that you—and everyone in your household —know what steps to take.

BITES AND STINGS

Allergic Reactions

Allergic reactions from bites or stings develop rapidly and can affect a child's entire body. Signs of a severe allergic reaction include severe swelling, breathing difficulty, *hives,* severe itching, *dizziness,* and *shock* (see p. 144). If a child seems to be having an allergic reaction to a sting or bite, call for emergency help or immediately take the child to the nearest hospital emergency room. An allergic reaction may be alleviated by giving the child an antihistamine, if it is available and a physician so directs.

Insect Bites

Bee, Hornet, Wasp

If a child who is allergic to stinging insects has been given an emergency self-treatment kit by a physician, immediately administer the antidote (epinephrine). If the antidote is not at hand, seek immediate medical help.

If a child is stung by a honeybee but does not have an allergic reaction, try to remove the stinger without squeezing it. (Squeezing can speed the spread of insect's venom.) Instead, gently scrape it out of the skin with the edge of a fingernail or the blunt edge of an ordinary, clean table knife. If the stinger is buried too deep to remove easily, seek medical attention.

To reduce swelling and itching once the stinger is removed (or if a stinger is not present, as in the case of a wasp or hornet sting), promptly apply cool, wet cloths (compresses) or a paste made of baking soda and water.

Mosquito, Red Ant, Black Fly

Reduce swelling and itching with cool compresses. Itching can also be reduced by applying calamine lotion or a paste of baking soda and water. If further care seems necessary, call for medical advice.

Tick and Leech

Never remove a tick or leech with your fingers. Cover the pest with a heavy petroleum jelly or oil or touch with a hot (not burning) match head. Wait 30 minutes. Remove the pest with tweezers.

Spiders and Other Arachnids

If a child is bitten by a black widow spider, brown recluse spider, scorpion, or tarantula, call a poison information center or immediately bring the child to the nearest hospital emergency room. Bites from arachnids (the class to which spiders, scorpions, and tarantulas all belong) can be dangerous and even life-threatening. They may cause severe, general reactions which can involve the central nervous system.

On the way to the hospital, reassure the child and try to prevent movement. Do not give the child food, liquids, or medications. Place the child in a position that aids breathing. If necessary, restore breathing (see artificial respiration, p. 124).

If possible, keep the affected area lower than the heart to slow the flow of blood and the spread of venom. Apply cool compresses to the wound. Follow any instructions given by the poison center or hospital emergency room.

Snake Bites

Call a poison information center for emergency help or immediately take the child to the nearest hospital emergency room. If it is apparent that the child has been bitten by a poisonous snake, inform the hospital by phone or at the time of arrival. Health professionals can have antivenin (antivenom serum) ready upon your arrival at the hospital or can start a regional search for it. If possible, describe the snake's appearance. The telltale sign of a poisonous snake bite is the presence of one or two fang marks at the site of the bite. (Nonpoisonous snakes lack fangs.)

While waiting for help or en route to the hospital, apply cold compresses (cloths) to the wound, but do not use ice. Keep the child warm and try to restrict movement. If possible, keep the bitten area lower than the heart to slow the flow of blood and the spread of venom through the body. Do not give the child food, liquids, or medication. Place the child in a position that aids breathing. Restore breathing if necessary (see artificial respiration, p. 124). Follow any additional instructions given by the poison center or the emergency room. Watch carefully for signs of *shock* and start treatment, if necessary (see p. 144).

Animal Bites

Wash the wound with soap under warm running water for at least five minutes. Control bleeding, if necessary (see p. 132).

If the bite is deep, place the wounded area lower than the rest of the body to slow the flow of blood. Do not use any medication, ointment, or antiseptic. Put a sterile bandage or clean cloth over the wound. Seek immediate medical attention.

An effort should be made immediately to capture the animal involved so that it can be examined for *rabies*. If the animal cannot be captured safely, provide police and health department officials with as accurate a description as possible. Try to remember coloring, markings, and other distinguishing characteristics.

If it seems likely that the animal is rabid, the child must begin immediate medical treatment for rabies.

Human Bites

Wash the wound with soap under warm running water. If the skin is broken, the wound should be examined by a physician or nurse. Control bleeding if necessary (see p. 132). Do not use any medication, ointment, or antiseptic. Put a sterile bandage or clean cloth over the wound. A tetanus shot may be needed (see *tetanus*).

Marine Life Bites and Stings

Seek immediate medical attention if a child is stung or bitten by any form of marine life.

Portuguese Man-of-war or Other Jellyfish. Wearing gloves, if possible, gently remove any tentacles from the child's skin. Clean the area with rubbing (isopropyl) alcohol. If stung by a Portuguese man-of-war, a child may suffer *shock* (p. 144) and require artificial respiration (p. 124) if breathing stops. Seek immediate medical attention.

Sea Anemone, Hydroid, Stinging Coral, Cone Shell, Sea Urchin, or Stingray. If possible, remove any stinger. Wash the area with soap and warm water for at least five minutes. Soak in warm water or apply warm compresses. Seek immediate medical attention.

BLEEDING

Internal bleeding

A sharp or crushing blow to the abdomen or chest can cause internal bleeding. Look for vomit containing bright or dark red blood or dark brown specks, stools that are streaked with bright red blood or are black and tarry; coughed-up blood, or symptoms of *shock* (p. 144).

Call for emergency help. If none is available, take child immediately to an emergency room. In the meantime, do not give the child food, liquids, or medications. Keep the child lying down and covered with a blanket or jacket for warmth. Make sure the child can breathe easily. Restore breathing if necessary (see artificial respiration, p. 124). Comfort the child and keep him or her as quiet as possible.

If necessary, treat the child for *shock* (p. 144).

External Bleeding

If bleeding is severe, call for emergency help or take the child to the nearest hospital emergency room.

Pressure

While waiting for help or en route, have the child lie down, if possible. Try to control the bleeding by applying direct pressure to the wound. (See Fig. 12A) Place a thick, clean compress (gauze, towel, or clothing) directly over the wound and press down firmly with the palm of the hand. (Fig. 12B) If no clean compress is available, use your

FIG. 12. BLEEDING

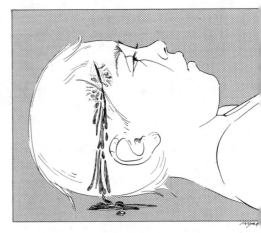

12A. A severe wound to the head will bleed profusely.

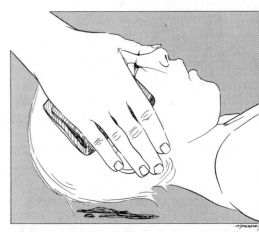

12B. Control severe bleeding by applying direct pressure to the wound. Place a thick, clean compress, such as a towel or washcloth, directly over the wound and press down firmly.

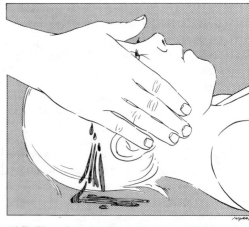

12C. If a clean compress is not available, apply steady pressure with bare fingers or the heel of the hand.

bare fingers or hand. (Fig. 12C) Steady pressure may cause the child some pain, but the pressure is absolutely necessary.

Without relaxing pressure, always raise the wounded area *above* the level of the child's heart. Do not do this if it is painful or the child shows signs of internal bleeding and injuries or broken bones. If the wound is on the head or neck, raise the child's head and shoulders—unless a fractured skull or spine is suspected or obvious. If skull or spine is fractured, the child SHOULD NOT BE MOVED AT ALL. In case of a possibly severe head injury, immobilize the child's neck by placing supports—such as bags of sugar, flour, or rice or rolled up towels—on both sides.

If blood soaks through the compress, replace it with a clean one and reapply pressure. Avoid disturbing blood clots that may form around the compress. If a clot has started to form and the compress is sticking to the wound, add another compress to the original rather than replace it. Apply more pressure when adding compresses. Remember that too many compresses could diminish the pressure.

After bleeding is controlled—in perhaps 2 or 3 minutes—wrap and tie the compress firmly, but not too tightly, using a bandage made of strips of gauze or cloth. In some cases it may be necessary to continue applying pressure until professional medical help arrives.

To ensure that the compress is not tied so tightly that it hinders adequate circulation, try to find a pulse below the wound. If no pulse is felt, loosen the bandage until the pulse returns. If finding a pulse is not possible, feeling the child's fingers or toes for numbness, cold, or pain is another way to check for adequate circulation. If necessary, treat the child for *shock* (p. 144).

Tourniquet

If direct pressure fails to stop bleeding in an arm or a leg, a tourniquet can be applied. USE A TOURNIQUET ONLY AS A LAST RESORT, when emergency help or a hospital emergency room is not accessible, and when it appears that a child may bleed to death unless blood supply to the injured limb is stopped completely. A tourniquet blocks the flow of blood and can be extremely dangerous if used incorrectly. A properly applied tourniquet can so deprive a limb of blood that the affected arm or leg

may have to be amputated if the tourniquet is allowed to remain in place too long.

A tourniquet must be at least two inches wide. Use a belt (but cover the buckle with a handkerchief), sock, tie or scarf—anything long and flat enough to wrap around the limb two times and tie.

Place the center of the tourniquet just above the wound (between the wound and the heart). If a joint is in the way, place the tourniquet above the joint.

Wrap the tourniquet around the limb two times and firmly tie a half-knot (intertwining the two ends of the strip as in the first step of tying a bow). Place a short, strong stick or something similar—a ruler or kitchen utensil will do—on top of the half-knot. Tie a second half-knot over the stick and then complete the knot with another half-knot. Twist the stick until all bleeding stops. Tie the loose ends of the tourniquet around the limb and over the stick to anchor it in place.

The exact time the tourniquet was applied must be recorded and highly visible. Attach a note to the child's clothing or print the information on the child's forehead or any other uninjured area using lipstick or a marking pen.

Do not cover the tourniquet. Call for or seek medical care immediately.

BREATHING FAILURE

See p. 124.

BROKEN BONES

A child may have a broken bone if

- intense pain, severe swelling, and limited motion are present following an accident (see Fig. 13);
- a snap is heard or felt at the time of injury; or
- bones feel as if they are grating together.

Call for or seek medical help as soon as possible. Do not try to straighten or push bones back into place. If possible, apply ice packs. (Do not apply ice directly to the skin; make an ice pack by wrapping a plastic bag of ice in a towel.) Try to avoid moving the broken bones. Do not give the child food, liquids, or medication.

If the skin is punctured, do not wash the

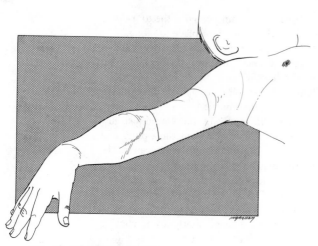

FIG. 13. BROKEN BONE

A broken bone is often accompanied by intense pain, severe swelling, and limited motion.

wound. If sterile gauze or dressing is available, cover the wound. If a sterile dressing is not available, leave the wound uncovered.

If the child is having difficulty breathing, a broken rib may have punctured a lung. Immediate medical treatment is essential to prevent lung collapse (see *lung rupture).* Never attempt to tape or otherwise immobilize fractured ribs, as this step may interfere with breathing.

If a serious head or spinal injury (see *head and spinal injury*) is suspected, <u>DO NOT MOVE THE CHILD AT ALL.</u> Immobilize the child's neck by placing weights on either side of it. Five-pound bags of sugar, flour, or rice may be used. Call for emergency medical assistance. If required, maintain an open airway (see p. 124).

If necessary, treat the child for *shock* (p. 144).

If any fragments of bone have broken off, put them into a clean container and take them with the child to the nearest hospital emergency room. If trained professional help is not available and a child must be transported to a physician or hospital emergency room, immobilize broken bones for the trip as follows:

Arm, Elbow, Wrist, and Hand Fractures

Make a splint with flat objects, such as magazines, pillows, boards, or pieces of cardboard. Pad the splint with pieces of cloth, towels, or blankets. (See Fig. 14.)

Put a flat object on each side of the broken arm, or wrap a padded magazine or pillow around the break as follows:

If the break seems to involve the <u>UPPER ARM,</u> the splint should reach from the shoulder and armpit to the elbow.

If the break seems to involve the <u>LOWER ARM</u> or <u>WRIST,</u> the splint should reach from the elbow well past the wrist.

If the <u>FINGERS</u> seem to be broken, do not move them. If only one finger is involved, immobilize it against an adjacent finger using tape or cloth. If more fingers or <u>HAND BONES</u> seem involved, cushion the hand with a pillow.

If the <u>ELBOW</u> seems broken, do not try to change the arm's position. If the arm is straight, the splint should reach from the child's armpit and shoulder to the hand. If the arm is bent, do not try to splint it.

FIG. 14. SPLINT

A flat object such as a padded magazine can be used as a splint to immobilize a broken arm. The splint should reach from the elbow well past the wrist.

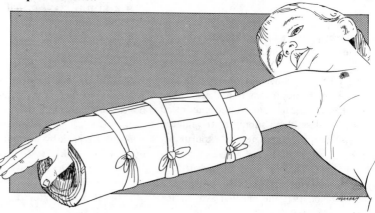

Carefully bind the splint together by wrapping the arm with strips of cloth, neckties, belts, or similar pieces of material. Tie above and below the break. Make sure the bindings are snug but do not interfere with circulation.

Except in cases where the elbow seems broken, gently place the affected arm or wrist in a sling after splinting. Adjust the sling so that the lower part of the arm is held across the child's chest and the hand is raised 4 to 5 inches above the elbow. If the upper arm seems to be involved, gently bind the arm to the body with a bandage or strip of cloth. Tie the bandage snugly around the child's shoulders and over the sling.

Seek medical attention as soon as possible.

Leg, Knee, Ankle, and Foot Fractures

If possible, gently remove the shoe and sock from the injured leg. Immobilize a broken leg, knee, or ankle by splinting it with long, flat objects, such as boards, or flat objects such as magazines, pillows, or pieces of cardboard. Pad the splint with cloth, towels, or blankets. Put a long, flat object on each side of the broken area or overlap several short objects on each side as follows:

If the break seems to involve the UPPER LEG, the outer part of the splint should reach from the hip to the heel and the inner part from the groin to the heel.

If the break seems to involve the LOWER LEG, the splint should reach from above the knee to the heel.

If the break seems to involve the ANKLE or FOOT, make the splint out of a pillow, folded blanket, or folded towel. The splint should reach from the child's calf well past the foot.

If the KNEE is painful to move, do not try to change the position of the leg. If the leg is straight, place a splint under the leg, extending from the child's buttocks to the heel. If the knee is bent, the leg is not splinted.

Broken TOES are not splinted.

Carefully bind the splint together with neckties, belts, strips of cloth, or similar pieces of material. Tie the splint above and below the break; if a splint goes the length of the leg, also tie it near the ankle and on the upper thigh. Make sure the ties are snug but not so tight as to interfere with circulation.

If a sturdy splint cannot be made for a broken leg, knee, or ankle, place a thick padding of blankets, towels, or sheets between the child's legs and bind the legs together above and below the break. Keep the limb elevated by placing it on a pillow or a stack of books or magazines. Apply ice in an ice bag or plastic bag to the leg, knee, or ankle. Do not apply the ice directly to the skin.

Seek medical attention as soon as possible.

Facial Fractures

Immobilize a broken jaw by gently wrapping a piece of cloth, elastic bandage, or similar piece of material around the head and under the chin. Do not try to immobilize or straighten a broken nose. Seek medical attention as soon as possible.

Collarbone and Shoulder Fractures

For children who have collarbone or shoulder injuries, it is often not necessary to immobilize the shoulder area. It is possible to immobilize a broken collarbone or shoulder by wrapping an elastic bandage or strips of cloth around the shoulders, back, and chest in a figure eight. Bind the involved arm securely but not tightly to the body by tying a bandage or piece of cloth snugly around the child's shoulders. Seek medical attention.

Pelvis and Hip Fractures

If possible, place a thick padding of blankets, towels, or sheets between the child's legs without moving them.

It is usually difficult to determine whether the spine is involved. If in doubt, do not move the child at all and seek emergency assistance.

If emergency assistance is unavailable and a child must be moved to receive medical attention, immobilize an injured pelvis or hip by strapping the child to a stretcher, board, door, or any other long, flat, sturdy object that reaches from the child's shoulders to the heels. Using ties, belts, or strips of cloth, bind the child securely to the board in several places above and below the injured area. While transporting the child, keep the splint as nearly horizontal as possible.

After emergency medical help is secured, see *ankle injuries; arm injuries; facial fractures; fractures; head and spinal injury; knee injuries.*

BURNS

Never cover any burn with ointment, sprays, or butter. Try not to break burn-related blisters. Cut away any loose clothing, but do not remove anything sticking to the child's skin. Do not give a child medications or alcohol. See *burns*.

Third-Degree Burns

Third-degree burns (those that extend deep into the tissue below the skin) can be life-threatening. They usually are caused by scalding or contact with flames or high-voltage electricity. Third-degree burns are characterized by little or no pain (although other, less severe burns may cause considerable pain) and by tough, leathery, charred or white skin. A third-degree burn can be deceiving in severity if it covers a very small area.

If a child is severely burned, call for emergency help or go to the nearest hospital emergency room immediately. Do not wait to start home treatment. Even relatively small areas of burn may require hospitalization for an infant or toddler. If necessary, treat the child for *shock* (p. 144) on the way to the hospital. Have the child lie down unless the face is severely burned or this position is extremely uncomfortable. Start cardiopulmonary resuscitation (p. 124) if a child's heart and lungs stop functioning.

If help is unavailable for an hour or more and the child is conscious, try to prevent dehydration by having him or her sip water. Give a child about one-quarter cup (2 ounces) of water, an infant about half that amount. If vomiting occurs, do not give any more water.

Second-Degree Burns

Second-degree burns (which affect only the first layer of skin and a small amount of the second layer), are usually caused by contact with hot liquids that stick to the skin, such as grease, or extended overexposure to the sun. Second-degree burns are characterized by redness, pain, swelling, and blisters.

Stop the burning action by submerging the affected area in cold water or covering it with layers of clean dressing soaked in cold water. Submerge or cover the area for at least 5 minutes or until pain subsides. Do not use ice or ice water, because the sudden cold may cause the child to go into *shock* (p. 144).

Gently pat the wound dry with a clean cloth, trying not to break blisters. If blisters do break, cut off loose skin with clean first aid scissors. Cover the burn loosely with a clean cloth or sterile bandages. Prevent contact between burned areas such as the fingers by wrapping each individually with loose, dry, sterile bandages or clean cloth. Seek medical attention.

First-Degree Burns

First-degree burns (those that affect only the outer portion of the skin) are usually caused by brief contact with hot objects, hot water, hot steam, or by overexposure to the sun. First-degree burns are characterized by redness, mild swelling, and pain.

Stop the burning action using the same method as for a second-degree burn. Gently pat the area dry with a clean cloth.

If desired, cover the burn loosely with a clean cloth or sterile bandage. A physician or nurse should examine any first-degree burn larger than about one square inch.

Chemical Burns

Chemical burns are severe third- or second-degree burns caused by contact with corrosive substances such as cleaning solvents, battery acids, or industrial chemicals.

Immediately flush a child's skin for several minutes with cool running water from a shower, faucet, or hose, or pour large amounts of water over the burn.

As soon as possible, remove and dispose of any clothing containing the chemical.

If an eye is involved, turn the head so that the injured side is down and the chemicals will not flow into the unaffected eye during washing. Hold the eyelids open. Immediately flush the affected eye with running water for 10 to 15 minutes.

Cover the affected eye with a clean cloth. Seek medical attention immediately.

Respiratory Burns

Respiratory burns are caused most often by inhalation of smoke and hot gases during a fire or after an explosion. Such burns are especially dangerous to infants and very young children who may appear unharmed but cannot communicate their pain and difficulty in breathing.

The symptoms of respiratory burns often grow progressively worse during the first hour or two following the accident: coughing, wheezing, shortness of breath, and sneezing. Any child who has been exposed to fire and smoke, even briefly, should be examined promptly by a health professional so that appropriate treatment, if necessary, can be given. If a health professional or hospital emergency room is not immediately accessible, keep the child quiet—lying down, perhaps—and warm. If the child is thirsty, give water or other nonacidic liquids. Seek medical assistance as soon as it is available.

After emergency medical help is secured, see *burns*.

CHOKING

If a child gasps, clutches at his or her throat, cannot speak, and begins to turn blue, he or she is probably choking. If the child can breathe, is coughing, or can make any noise, do not interfere by attempting to clear a foreign object from the breathing passages. Unless the object in the mouth or throat is visible and easily attainable, do not attempt to remove it with your fingers or any device. Such attempts could push the object farther down the child's throat. Do not pull the child's neck backward.

Calmly try to tell the child to relax and cough. If, after a few seconds, the child continues having difficulty breathing, call for emergency help or, preferably, have someone else call. In addition, immediately do the following:

Back Blows and Chest Thrusts

For an infant or small child, whether conscious or unconscious, give a series of four back blows followed by four chest thrusts.

Begin with four back blows: Keep the infant straddled over your arm so that the head is lower than the body. Support the head by firmly holding the baby's jaw. Rest the forearm that is holding the infant on the thigh for support. With the palm of the other hand slap the child firmly but not too forcefully between the shoulder blades four times in succession, counting "one thousand one, one thousand two," and so on, slapping on the number at the end of each phrase. (See Fig. 15A.)

Follow with four chest thrusts: If the back blows do not expel the object, place your free hand on the infant's back, sandwiching the baby between your two hands. Turn the infant face up while continuing to support the head and neck and keeping the infant's head lower than the body. Keep the arm on

FIG. 15. CHOKING INFANT—CONSCIOUS OR UNCONSCIOUS

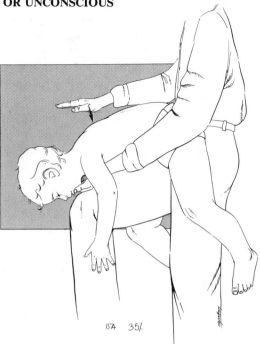

15A. Keep the infant straddled over your forearm with the head lower than the body. Firmly slap the infant four times between the shoulder blades. If difficulty persists, follow with four chest thrusts (Fig. 15B).

15B. Turn the infant face up, keeping head lower than body. Place two or three fingers for a new-born or the heel of hand for an older infant below the internipple line, on the breastbone. Push in and up four times.

Emergencies/Choking   **137**

which the infant is resting on your lap for support. (See Fig. 15B.)

Place two or three fingertips for a newborn or the heel of the hand for an older infant just below the internipple line on the breastbone. Push in and up four times in rapid succession. Be careful not to push so forcefully as to injure the child.

Continue alternating four back blows followed by four chest thrusts until the object is freed and the child begins to breathe or until medical help arrives. Seek medical attention as soon as the child seems to be breathing without difficulty.

Heimlich Maneuver

For an older child who is <u>conscious,</u> see Fig. 16 and perform the Heimlich maneuver as follows:

Stand behind the child, who may be either standing or sitting. Wrap your arms around the child's waist, make a fist, and place the thumb side against the child's stomach between the navel and the rib cage. The fist should not be touching the child's breastbone.

Place your free hand over the fist and repeatedly thrust inward and upward four times, or until the object is dislodged. Each thrust should be a separate, distinct motion. Seek medical attention as soon as the child seems to be breathing without difficulty.

Remember: Artificial respiration is useless until the object is dislodged. Once an object is dislodged, however, the child may require artificial respiration if breathing is inadequate or if he or she is unconscious. See artificial respiration instructions on p. 124.

As soon as the child begins to cough or breathe alone, seek medical help. The child should be examined by a physician for treatment of any damage that might have been caused by choking (or by the Heimlich maneuver).

For a child who is <u>unconscious,</u> see Fig. 17. Place the child face up on the floor. Turn the child's head to one side. Kneel beside a small child, or straddle the body of an older child. Place the heel of one hand on the child's abdomen in the midline, slightly above the navel and below the bottom of the rib cage. Place your free hand on top of the first.

Thrust the heel of the bottom hand into the child's stomach with quick upward thrusts. Do this in a series of four thrusts, making sure each motion is separate and distinct.

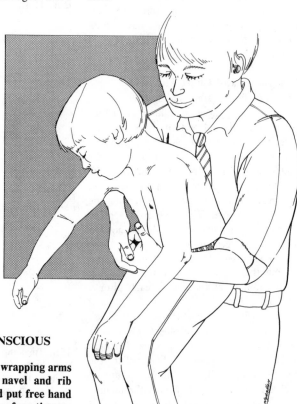

FIG. 16. CHOKING CHILD—CONSCIOUS

Perform the Heimlich maneuver by wrapping arms around the child's waist between navel and rib cage. Make a fist with one hand and put free hand over the fist. Thrust hands in and up four times.

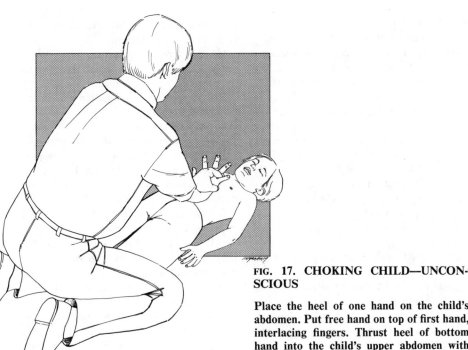

FIG. 17. CHOKING CHILD—UNCON-SCIOUS

Place the heel of one hand on the child's abdomen. Put free hand on top of first hand, interlacing fingers. Thrust heel of bottom hand into the child's upper abdomen with four quick upward thrusts.

Remember: Artificial respiration is useless until the object is dislodged. Once the object is dislodged, however, the child may require artificial respiration if breathing is inadequate. See artificial respiration instructions on p. 124.

As soon as the child begins to cough or breathe alone, seek medical help. The child should be examined by a physician for treatment of any damage that might have been caused by choking or rescue attempts.

After emergency medical help is secured, see *choking*.

CONVULSIONS

A convulsion can be caused by high *fever,* head injury (see *head and spinal injury*), poisoning, *shock,* epilepsy (see *seizures*), or brain inflammation (such as *encephalitis*), or it can be part of an allergic reaction (see *allergies*). A child having a convulsion typically exhibits a stiffening of the body followed by jerky, flailing movements, drooling, and unconsciousness.

Stay with the child. Try to ease him or her toward an open space on the floor or ground. Try to clear the area of any objects (tables, lamps, and chairs).

Do not interfere with the child's movements in any way. Do not try to hold the child or force anything, including liquids, into the child's mouth.

Wait for the convulsion to end. If it lasts for more than 10 minutes (a rare occurrence), call for emergency assistance. If it ends sooner (as is typical), allow the child to rest or sleep. Call a physician, describe the incident, and arrange for a consultation.

DROWNING

Do not swim to a child in distress in deep water unless swimming is the only possible way to reach the child.

Do not walk near open ice if a child has fallen through. Instead, try to reach the child from land, from firm ice, or by wading in and extending a hand, leg, pole, or piece of clothing, such as a belt.

If using a floating object to reach the child, throw it past the child, then pull it slowly within the child's grasp.

If a swimming rescue is necessary, keep watching the child or the spot where you last saw the child until you reach it. Try to bring a towel, rope, or something sturdy enough for the child to hold onto while being towed to land.

Avoid pulling a child, especially one who is heavy, while swimming to land.

Not Breathing

If the child is not breathing, call for emergency help immediately or have someone else do so. Do not try to drain the child's lungs. Instead, immediately begin artificial respiration (p. 124).

If the child has fallen through ice into icy water, it may take several hours of continuous artificial respiration to restore the child's natural breathing pattern. DO NOT STOP ARTIFICIAL RESPIRATION UNTIL THE CHILD BEGINS TO COUGH OR BREATHE ALONE OR UNTIL MEDICAL HELP ARRIVES.

If necessary, have someone else treat the child for *shock* (p. 144).

If the child has no pulse, begin CPR (p. 127).

Once the child begins breathing, remove his or her wet clothing. Watch for hypothermia (see below). Wrap the child in blankets, a sleeping bag, or any other warm covering as soon as possible.

Coughing or Breathing

Stay with the child until breathing returns to normal.

If necessary, treat the child for *shock* (p. 144). Watch for hypothermia (see below).

Remove the wet clothing and wrap the child in blankets, a sleeping bag, or any other warm covering.

Call for medical advice promptly as a precaution. If the child is or has been in *shock,* seek immediate medical attention.

EXPOSURE TO TEMPERATURE EXTREMES

Hypothermia

Internal chilling, which is known as hypothermia, can be life-threatening and must be treated at once. It can affect children quickly in cold weather: because their body surface area in relation to body mass is quite high, children lose heat much more quickly than adults do.

Hypothermia most often strikes children who are not adequately protected from the cold, such as those who play outside during the winter without enough layers of clothing. Hypothermia is characterized by shivering followed by numbness and muscle weakness. Children who are outdoors in cold weather and become uncharacteristically quiet and lethargic may be suffering the effects of hypothermia. If drowsiness and in-

coherence develop, life-threatening hypothermia may be present.

If hypothermia is suspected, call for emergency help or immediately take the child to the nearest hospital emergency room.

If it is necessary to wait for emergency help while away from home, try to carry the child indoors or wrap in a jacket or blanket, shelter the child from wind, and start a fire.

If symptoms of *shock* (p. 144) are apparent, start emergency treatment. If the child is unconscious and has stopped breathing, start artificial respiration (p. 124).

Remove any wet clothing. Wrap the child in warm blankets, clothing, or a sleeping bag. If possible, have an adult crawl into the sleeping bag or blankets with the child to share body heat. Body heat will be transferred to the child and trapped within the sleeping bag or layers of blankets.

Even if hypothermia seems mild (the child is simply shivering, for example) or the child seems fully recovered, don't forget to seek medical assistance. During transportation, be sure the child is well insulated (with blankets, for example) and cover the head with a cap, scarf, or other warm piece of clothing.

Frostbite

A child's toes, fingers, nose, ears, or cheeks are the most likely parts of the body to develop frostbite (freezing of external skin) during winter. If frostbite is mild, skin temporarily feels cold, loses color, and then becomes sticky. Severely frostbitten skin is painful and develops a burning sensation. The affected area becomes hard and numb and turns white, yellowish-white, or mottled blue-white. Blisters may form. In rare, extreme cases, bone freezes. A child may become incoherent, unconscious, or go into *shock* (p. 144).

Seek medical assistance as quickly as possible if a child has severe frostbite.

Do not rub frostbitten parts or break blisters. If the child is outdoors, cover affected areas with clothing or scarves. If possible, bring the child indoors immediately.

Once indoors, remove all clothing from around the affected area. Immerse mildly frostbitten toes, fingers, feet, hands, or limbs in lukewarm water—never hot. Pat the child dry thoroughly to avoid chilling. Gently wrap frostbitten ears or cheeks with scarves and blankets.

Do not place the child close to a stove or radiator. Do not use direct heat, hot water bottles, heat lamps, or heating pads on the frostbitten area. If possible, keep frostbitten fingers and toes separated with strips of gauze or clean cloth.

Seek medical assistance immediately if color and feeling do not return to frostbitten areas within 20 minutes.

Heat Stroke

Heat stroke occurs in cases of extreme overexertion and subsequent dehydration during hot weather. It is a life-threatening condition, which results when a child's internal temperature-regulating mechanism shuts down completely.

Heat stroke is characterized by a body temperature of 105° F (40.6° C) or higher, flushed skin, complete absence of sweating, weakness, dizziness, nausea, and abdominal cramps. The child may seem confused, lose consciousness, or go into a coma. It is essential to lower body temperature immediately, as follows:

Remove the child's clothes and place the child in a cold—not icy—shower or tub of water. If a shower or tub is not available, use water from a garden hose or generously sponge the child with cold water or rub him or her with ice wrapped in towels. The child can also be cooled by wrapping cold, wet towels or sheets around the body and placing the child in front of a fan or air conditioner. Massage the arms and legs to restore circulation. Do not give any medication. If necessary, treat for *shock* (p. 144).

Check the child's temperature every 10 or 15 minutes. Continue cooling until the temperature drops to 102° F (38.8° C) or lower but avoid chilling the child.

As soon as body temperature drops sufficiently, wrap the child in a blanket and seek medical attention.

Heat Exhaustion

Heat exhaustion develops when a child becomes severely overexerted and dehydrated during hot weather. It is characterized by low or normal body temperature, cold, clammy skin, shallow breathing, and a loss of appetite. The child may be weak or dizzy, have a headache, or complain of nausea. Vomiting or fainting may occur.

Move the child indoors or to a shaded area. Loosen or remove the child's clothing.

If the child is not vomiting, he or she must be given liquids (water, lemonade, or juice is best) to restore the body's supply of fluids. Give the child sips of the liquid every 15 minutes for an hour, but stop if vomiting occurs.

If the child's condition seems to grow worse or symptoms last longer than an hour, seek immediate medical attention.

Heat Fatigue

Heat fatigue develops when a child becomes mildly overexerted and dehydrated. It is characterized by headache, excessive sweating, shallow breathing, poor appetite, and overall weakness.

Treat as for heat exhaustion.

Heat Cramps

Muscular in origin, heat cramps are caused by loss of large amounts of fluids and body salts through excessive sweating. Most often occurring in the legs, arms, and abdomen, heat cramps are characterized by painful muscle spasms, sweating, and cold, clammy skin.

Heat cramps should be treated the same way as heat exhaustion. A child older than 3 years (or anyone who has perspired very heavily) should drink one or two glasses of liquids—water or juice—over the next hour. (Give a younger child one glass of liquid per hour.) Place warm, moist compresses then firm but gentle pressure on the involved muscles. Do not try to massage out cramps.

HEAD INJURY

Severe Head Injury

The following combination of symptoms may signal a severe head injury: unconsciousness lasting longer than a few seconds; drowsiness; vomiting; convulsions (p. 139); clear or bloody fluid flowing from the nose or ears; extensive bleeding from head wounds; slow pulse; or a severe change in mental alertness such as incoherence or delirium.

If a child displays symptoms of a severe head injury, call for emergency help as quickly as possible.

Treat a child who has a potentially serious head injury with the utmost care: <u>DO NOT MOVE THE CHILD WHILE WAITING FOR HELP TO ARRIVE</u>.

For a sports-related injury, do not remove mouth guards, helmets, or other equipment unless removal is the only way to provide an airway for a child who cannot breathe. If necessary, give artificial respiration (p. 124) or cardiopulmonary resuscitation (p. 127) and treat for *shock* (p. 144). Do not give food, liquids, or medication.

Do not attempt to clean a severe, open head wound. If bleeding is profuse, press a clean cloth or gauze on the wound (p. 132). Use several layers of dressings if necessary. Do not apply heavy pressure. After the bleeding is controlled, wrap the dressing firmly but not too tightly with strips of bandages or cloth. Tie the dressing to secure it, being careful to move the head as little as possible.

Minor Head Injury

These symptoms may accompany a minor head injury: loss of consciousness for a few seconds; headache; momentary confusion or double vision; a lump or slight cut on the head; and drowsiness for an hour or two. The child should have no trouble moving uninjured body parts and answering simple questions, such as "What is your name?" and "Where are you?"

Keep the child lying down and quiet. Gently clean any minor scalp cuts with soap and water. Apply gentle direct pressure to control any bleeding (p. 132). Cover the wound with a sterile bandage, if available, or clean cloth. Seek medical attention promptly.

If the child has a lump on the head but no bleeding, apply cold compresses or an ice pack to reduce the swelling. A mild pain-relieving medicine may be helpful. Consult the physician for specific recommendations and read discussion of nonprescription medicines in Chapter 7, "Caring for the Sick Child at Home." If the lump is very swollen or increases dramatically in size over the next few hours, a slight skull fracture may exist. Seek immediate medical attention promptly.

If symptoms are very mild and immediate medical attention does not seem necessary, watch the child carefully for a day or two. WAKE THE CHILD FULLY 3 TIMES DURING THE NIGHT AFTER INJURY. If the child shows any change in mental alertness, seek medical attention promptly.

LOSS OF LIMB OR FINGER OR TOE

Call for emergency help or immediately take the child to the nearest hospital emergency room. If possible notify the hospital of the emergency ahead of time.

If possible, wrap the severed limb or digit (finger or toe) in a dry, clean cloth or plastic wrap. Place it in a plastic bag and pack the bag in cold water or keep it in a cool place. Do not freeze or pack the limb or digit directly in ice. Bring the limb or digit with the child to the nearest hospital emergency room.

The most important thing to do while waiting for help or on the way to the hospital is to control bleeding (p. 132). In addition, if necessary, treat the child for *shock* (p. 144).

POISONING

Many ordinary substances in and around the home are poisonous: common cleaning products, perfumes and colognes, household plants, and medicines. (See Chapter 4, "Accident Prevention.") Suspect poisoning if a child suddenly becomes ill or shows a sudden change in appearance or behavior. The first *2 hours* after ingestion of a poisonous substance are critical for treatment and recovery. However, most poisoning emergencies can be fully handled at home with accurate instructions.

Step I. Act Promptly

- MOUTH Remove any suspected poisonous material from the child's mouth. Use a wet cloth to wipe the mouth clean. Examine the mouth for cuts, burns, or unusual coloring.
- EYES If poison has entered the child's eyes, bathe the eyes with cool, clean water for at least 10 minutes. If just one eye is affected, lean the head over to that side so that water does not wash poison into the other eye.
- SKIN If poison has affected the skin, rinse the skin thoroughly with water and then wash thoroughly with soap and water.
- DIGESTIVE TRACT If the child has swallowed a caustic, such as Drano, Liquid Plumber, Lysol, or Clinitest tablets (used to test urine for sugar content), give two glasses of water immediately. Caustics can severely burn the esophagus and other parts of the digestive tract unless treated promptly.
- RESPIRATORY TRACT If poisoning results from breathing fumes or gases, move the child immediately into fresh air. (Before entering the area, take a

deep breath of clean air and hold it. Cover your mouth and nose with a cloth or a mask. If the air is hot, crawl along the floor to reach the child.)

After the child is removed from the area, loosen his or her clothing and, if necessary, treat for *shock* (p. 144). Watch the child's breathing closely. If breathing stops, start artificial respiration (p. 124). If necessary, treat for chemical burns (p. 136). Call for medical assistance.

Step II. Get Expert Help

Phone the local poison information center or a regional center (call the toll-free number in your state). Identify yourself and your relationship to the child. Describe the child by name, age, and sex. If possible, have the poisonous substance or its package in hand, and explain what and how much was taken and when. Describe any symptoms, such as drowsiness, or signs, such as cuts or burns in the mouth, which the child may show.

The health care provider at the poison information center will give instructions in a matter of minutes according to the class of poisons involved:

Poisonings from noncaustic, nonpetroleum household products, drugs, and plants. The instructions will be either to

(1) do nothing;

(2) induce vomiting by giving the child syrup of ipecac, keep the child moving, and monitor the recovery at home; or

(3) induce vomiting with syrup of ipecac and take the child immediately to an emergency room or physician. (Ipecac is available at all pharmacies and should be on hand in all home medicine cabinets.)

Poisonings from caustic agents. The instructions will be to give two glasses of water immediately (if you have not already done so), and to take the child to an emergency room or physician. Do not try to make the child vomit!

Poisonings from petroleum products, such as gasoline, lighter fluid, or cleaning fluid. The instructions will be to

(1) do nothing, or

(2) take the child to an emergency room or physician. Do not try to make the child vomit!

If the health professional at the poison center recommends medical attention, take the child, along with the suspected poison, the package it came in, and a sample of any vomit, to the emergency room or physician's office.

UNCONSCIOUS, see p. 123.

PUNCTURE WOUNDS, SPLINTERS, AND FISHHOOKS

Seek immediate medical attention for a deep wound if any doubt exists about a child's immunity to *tetanus* or if the wound seems severe. Treat a mild puncture wound —one caused by a splinter, for example—at home only if no doubt exists that it is superficial and that the child has been immunized against tetanus. (If in doubt, check the child's immunization record at home or call the physician's office.)

Puncture Wounds

Do not wash a large, deep puncture wound. Do not try to remove any deeply inbedded object. Simply cover the wound with a sterile bandage or clean cloth and seek immediate medical attention. Do not give the child food, liquids, or medication.

Splinters

Wash your hands. Use metal tweezers to remove the splinter. Before using the tweezers, sterilize them by holding them in a flame until they are red hot or by immersing them in boiling water for five minutes. (Make sure tweezers cool before using them.) After removing the splinter, press gently at the edge of the wound; however, do not force the wound to bleed.

Wash the wound with warm, soapy water and cover it with a sterile bandage or clean cloth.

If you cannot remove a splinter, cover it with a sterile bandage or clean cloth and seek medical attention.

Fishhooks

Never remove a fishhook if it is embedded in a child's eye, face, head, or neck. Seek immediate medical attention.

If the barbed end of the hook is embedded somewhere else in the skin, try to push the other end of the hook gently through the skin until the barb comes out. Cut the hook below the barb with pliers or clippers. Carefully withdraw the remainder of the hook from the skin. Never attempt to pull or twist an embedded fishhook.

Clean the wound thoroughly with warm, soapy water.

Call a physician to determine whether the child needs a tetanus shot. Check the child's immunization record at home.

See *puncture wounds and splinters.*

SHOCK

Shock is a life-threatening condition that can occur in cases of serious injury or illness. It results from sudden decreases in blood pressure, circulation rate, and blood oxygen levels. Shock is characterized by cool, clammy, pale skin; weak, rapid pulse; thirst; dizziness or faintness; and increased breathing rate. When shock is suspected, call for emergency help or take the child to the nearest hospital emergency room.

Until medical help is available, carefully monitor the child's breathing. If necessary, restore breathing through artificial respiration (p. 124).

Keep the child in the most comfortable position possible, preferably lying down. If outdoors, cover the child lightly with a jacket, sheet, or blanket. <u>DO NOT MOVE THE CHILD IF A SERIOUS HEAD OR SPINAL INJURY IS SUSPECTED</u>. Otherwise, if the child has chest pain or difficulty breathing, raise the head and shoulders without raising the feet. For all other injuries, raise the feet only.

Treat any injuries as necessary.

After securing emergency medical help, see *shock.*

UNCONSCIOUSNESS

See p. 123.

Part IV
Diseases and Symptoms

ABDOMINAL MASSES

DESCRIPTION

An abdominal mass is a lump or an area of swelling anywhere in the abdominal region. Among young children, an abdominal mass is often associated with the kidneys, but it can also appear in the intestinal tract, adrenal glands, genital organs, liver, or spleen.

Abdominal masses are unusual occurrences. They can appear at any age. Often a parent is the first to notice the mass, while a child is at play or taking a bath. Or a newborn may have a mass which is obvious to a physician during the first physical examinations. More often, a mass becomes apparent only if pain occurs or a vital bodily function is affected. Occasionally an abdominal mass may go unnoticed even during routine physical examinations if the lump is not large enough to be obvious on sight or to be felt when a hand is run over the surface of the child's body.

An abdominal mass may appear as a slight swelling above the surface of the body or as a substantial bulge, sometimes the size of a golf ball or even a tennis ball. Conversely, it may be obvious only when the skin of the abdomen is pressed with the fingers. Sometimes the location of a mass is so deep as to be unapparent to either sight or touch, but there is pain.

When visible, an abdominal mass is usually not inflamed (red-looking), bruised, or otherwise discolored. If it can be felt, an abdominal mass is usually firm to the touch and painful. Most abdominal masses cause pain sooner or later, and pain is usually accompanied by some change in the function of whatever structures are affected.

An abdominal mass requires medical attention, as only specialized diagnostic tests can determine the severity of the condition. Since treatment is almost always needed following diagnosis, the more promptly a physician is consulted the better. The outlook for a child who is diagnosed as having an abdominal mass varies according to the nature and location of the problem.

CAUSE

Abdominal masses are either abnormal growths, unusual extensions of a body structure, or the result of an injury. Masses can be abnormal growths on a kidney, the genital organs, the stomach, the small and large intestines, the adrenal glands, the liver, the spleen, or a bile duct. Each kind of mass must be treated differently, according to its size, its location, the type of tissue involved, and the general health of the child.

Abdominal masses in newborns are commonly the result of conditions or abnormalities present at birth (congenital), requiring immediate treatment. Occasionally, especially among newborns, abdominal masses can be the cause or result of an obstruction which must have emergency corrective treatment. Rapidly growing abdominal masses often need immediate attention because their rate of increasing size may indicate a malignant, or cancerous, condition.

Newborns (birth to one month old)

More than half of all abdominal masses affecting newborns are associated with the kidneys. Almost half of these masses are caused by hydronephrosis (see *nephrosis*), a condition in which urine cannot escape from the kidney. Other common kidney-associated masses stem from kidney malfunction caused by the development of cysts (encapsulated collections of fluid or semisolid matter) inside or on the surface of a kidney. The rarest kidney-related mass affecting newborns is a cancerous growth (a mass of abnormal, rapidly dividing cells), such as *Wilms' tumor.*

Genital masses account for about 15 percent of newborn abdominal masses, and they develop only among females. One form of mass is a fluid-filled, enlarged vagina, uterus, or both. An ovarian cyst (see *ovarian tumors and cysts*) can also grow into an abdominal mass.

Gastrointestinal (GI) masses account for another 15 percent of all newborn abdominal masses. The most common kinds of GI masses are those arising from duplication or volvulus (see *abdominal pain*). Duplication, a congenital (present at birth) abnormality, is an abnormal, nonfunctioning offshoot of a segment of the intestine. It usually involves the lower right side of the small intestines. Volvulus is a twisting of a segment of the GI tract because of a congenital structural or functional problem. The most common tumors in the abdomen during infancy, however, do not involve the GI tract (esophagus, stomach, and intestines).

Other masses that affect newborns arise from or near the adrenal glands (one located at the top of each kidney). These masses can be caused by bleeding from one of the adrenal glands (see *adrenal problems*) or from a rare adrenal gland tumor (see *neuroblastoma*).

The remaining 5 percent of newborn abdominal masses are problems associated with the liver, spleen, or bile ducts, including the gall bladder.

Older Children (One Month Through Adolescence)

More than half of all abdominal masses among infants and older children are associated with the kidneys. The risk that masses associated with the kidneys are cancerous increases with age. In fact, among children from 1 to 3 years old, almost half of all kidney masses are Wilms' tumors. A smaller number of children of this age develop masses associated with hydronephrosis, a noncancerous condition.

Among older children, the number of masses associated with the adrenal gland doubles; many of these are the result of neuroblastoma.

The number of masses associated with the GI tract remains about the same for older children, but of these almost half are the result of localized infections resulting from acute *appendicitis*.

Older girls experience far fewer genital masses than do newborns; 75 percent of these masses are caused by ovarian cysts.

A newborn or an older child can develop an abdominal mass as the result of an injury suffered in a fall, automobile collision, or some other kind of accident. Blood or other fluids can collect in the abdomen, producing a mass or swollen area.

DIAGNOSIS

An abdominal mass is difficult to diagnose until it is large enough to be felt. However, if a newborn or an infant cries and cannot be comforted, even in the absence of any abdominal mass or swelling, a physician

should be notified. If an older child complains of pain in the abdomen and reacts with distress when any part of the abdomen is touched, a physician should examine the child.

Initially, a physician performs a thorough examination. A child's medical history may help identify any prior instances of abdominal distress or illness. Blood and urine tests may be performed.

The process of identifying and defining abdominal masses relies heavily on tests performed in X-ray departments, usually in hospitals. All these tests are performed under the supervision of a radiologist (a physician who specializes in diagnosing disease by means of X-ray films and related studies.)

Among the X-ray studies most frequently used are X rays of the abdomen, intravenous pyelography (IVP), voiding cystourethrography (VCUG), upper gastrointestinal series (upper GI), and barium enema (lower GI). The IVP involves the injection into a blood vessel of a solution that is concentrated by the kidneys, allowing them to be seen on X-ray film. The VCUG involves injection of a similar solution into the bladder through a catheter, a flexible plastic tube inserted into the urethra. These tests may be done even if the physician does not think the mass originates in the kidneys. The upper GI and the barium enema illuminate the upper and lower portions of the intestines, respectively. Occasionally a physician may want to outline the blood vessels in the abdomen by using dye-contrast X-ray films.

Ultrasound is a pain-free procedure that outlines abdominal structures on a television screen by using sound waves. A child is not exposed to any X-ray radiation. A CT (computed tomography) scan can provide highly detailed X-ray pictures on both film and a television monitor. Ultrasound and CT scan are particularly helpful in distinguishing fluid-filled masses from solid ones.

Newer diagnostic tests involving nuclear medicine use small amounts of radioactive material to define the location, size, and function of various abdominal organs. Tiny radioactive particles, injected through a blood vessel, are concentrated in specific areas of the body, causing patterns to form on a television screen or X-ray film. These patterns can sometimes be enhanced by a computer to aid the radiologist's interpretation.

TREATMENT

Specific treatment depends upon the underlying cause, the organ involved, and the location of an abdominal mass. If an abdominal mass causes partial or total obstruction of the affected organ or system, surgery may be necessary, possibly on an emergency basis. Regardless of the kind of treatment necessary, abdominal masses often require hospitalization.

For more information on methods of treatment, see individual sections for details about the various causes of abdominal masses.

PREVENTION

An abdominal mass can be prevented only if its underlying cause is preventable.

ABDOMINAL PAIN
(ACUTE)

EMERGENCY ACTION

A child who suffers severe pain anywhere in the abdominal region should be checked by a medical professional. Regardless of the time of day, consult a physician and, if so directed, take the child to the physician's office, a hospital emergency room, or clinic for evaluation. Any abdominal pain that continues for more than an hour should not be dismissed as "just another stomachache." Rely upon a child's complaint of pain until a physician's examination can clarify the cause of distress.

DESCRIPTION

Acute abdominal pain can strike a child at any age with or without warning. ("Acute" means a brief and severe episode of any symptom or disease.) If an infant, child, or adolescent has been ill, particularly with a fever and cramps, abdominal pain may come on as a worsening of earlier abdominal discomfort. An internal injury following an accident can also produce abdominal pain.

Acute abdominal pain is associated with a variety of gastrointestinal (GI) tract problems and other internal organ conditions, some of which may need medical attention, while others require surgery. For example, acute *appendicitis* can cause great pain and almost always requires surgery.

Abdominal pain is intense, occasional or continual (regular with few interruptions),

often localized, but can travel. Such pain almost always slows a child's movement or halts it entirely. Although it may develop as an ache that gradually grows worse, abdominal pain sometimes begins at peak intensity. Intense pain can awaken a sleeping child. In such circumstances, the child may describe the sensation as "grabbing," "sharp as a knife," or "hot as fire."

Pain usually is confined to one area in the upper or lower abdomen, on the right or left side, or in the middle, although sometimes the pain travels (radiates) back and forth across the abdomen or all the way through to the back. Such pain can be so severe that it renders a child speechless; more often, it provokes moans, cries, or screams. Pain can cause a child to double over or faint. Nausea and vomiting may occur; fever may be present. A child may feel a repeated need to urinate or defecate.

Abdominal pain can sometimes be evaluated and diagnosed in a matter of hours and treatment begun to alleviate the pain and deal with its underlying cause. If treatment of a surgical emergency is handled as soon as diagnosis is confirmed, the outlook for most children is good.

The outlook, however, for a child with abdominal pain may be described as uncertain if treatment is delayed or is inappropriate, or external or internal injury, bleeding, shock, or loss of healthy intestine interferes with the body's recuperative capabilities.

CAUSE

Acute abdominal pain may be the result of a variety of illnesses, accidents, or abnormalities. In infancy some of the most common causes are *hernia;* twisted testicle; *intussusception* (intestine that has telescoped in upon itself); infectious intestinal illness (viral or bacterial *diarrhea,* for example); a twisted digestive organ; and stomach ulcer.

In childhood, in addition to those already listed, among the most common causes are adhesions (fibrous bands of tissue) resulting from previous surgery around which loops of small intestine become twisted, causing partial or total obstruction and great pain; *pneumonia; food poisoning;* severe irritation or inflammation of the stomach (gastritis); gallbladder disease (often gallstones); inflammatory bowel disease (such as *ulcerative colitis* or *Crohn's disease);* inflammation of the liver *(hepatitis);* chronic constipation; pain caused by emotional problems such as severe *phobias* or anxiety; kidney infection *(see urinary tract infections); sickle cell anemia* (with acute inflammation of the abdominal organs caused by clumps of sickled blood cells); and inflammation of the pancreas (pancreatitis).

Among the most common additional causes in female adolescents are *menstrual pain,* ovarian cysts, and pelvic inflammatory disease (PID). (See *gonorrhea* for discussion of one type of infectious PID.)

Injured internal organs which are bruised or bleeding following an accident (such as an automobile collision) can cause abdominal pain.

DIAGNOSIS

Diagnosis varies according to the age and sex of the patient, location and kind of pain, and when the pain began and how long it has lasted. A patient's physical and emotional condition are also important as is information about fever, nausea, vomiting, or changes in defecation or urination. An examining physician takes a detailed history, noting prior conditions—an accident, chronic disease, and previous operations.

Physical examination focuses upon the painful area and the overall effects of pain upon the child. The abdomen is checked carefully and an internal rectal exam is performed. Blood and urine samples are analyzed. Further tests, including X-ray films, may be postponed until initial tests can be evaluated along with the medical history and results of the physical examination.

COMPLICATIONS

Complications depend upon the cause of pain, the organ or system involved, and the speed with which diagnosis can be made and treatment begun. If a child is in the care of experienced medical personnel, especially in a hospital emergency room, the threat of serious complications and long-term aftereffects is reduced significantly. Life-threatening complications may develop if diagnosis is delayed or inappropriate treatment is begun.

TREATMENT

Treatment depends upon diagnosis of the cause of acute pain. Surgery may be necessary. In certain situations, such as acute *appendicitis,* surgery is almost always chosen. In the case of appendicitis, an infected appendix could burst, causing, perhaps, a serious infection in the abdominal cavity (peri-

tonitis). In others, where a choice exists between surgery and medical management, the physician discusses with the parent (and child, if appropriate) alternative methods of treatment and any risks that may be involved. Then medical or surgical treatment begins.

It is never wise to delay an examination by blaming abdominal pain on "bad food" or "just a bug that's going around." In addition, using home remedies for persistent abdominal pain—such as baking soda, medications (including over-the-counter antacids or laxatives), and heating pads or hot-water bottles—should be avoided until a physician has evaluated the child's condition.

PREVENTION

Most causes of acute abdominal pain cannot be prevented.

ACETAMINOPHEN POISONING

EMERGENCY ACTION

If a child has swallowed large amounts of acetaminophen, call a poison information center or physician immediately. If recommended, try to induce vomiting with syrup of ipecac (a nonprescription preparation). A child should drink a glass of water immediately after swallowing syrup of ipecac; vomiting should occur within 20 minutes. Consult a poison information center or physician again for further instructions immediately after vomiting occurs.

If a child does not vomit within 20 minutes, repeat treatment. If vomiting still does not occur, seek medical attention immediately. At this point a child's stomach may need to be washed out by a physician to prevent further absorption of acetaminophen.

If a child is seen shortly after swallowing pills, a physician will take a blood sample to determine the level of acetaminophen in the blood (see below). If the level is high, an antidote is necessary to counteract the effects of acetaminophen overdose. This medication has an unpleasant taste and is usually diluted in a soft drink to make it easier to swallow. It may cause a child to become nauseated and vomit.

DESCRIPTION

Acetaminophen is a common, over-the-counter medication often used as an aspirin substitute to reduce pain and fever. When excessive amounts of acetaminophen are swallowed, poisoning occurs. Young children are the most frequent victims of accidental poisoning, but the incidence of poisoning from intentional overdoses is increasing among teenagers.

The most serious effect of acetaminophen poisoning is liver damage. Damage is not caused by acetaminophen itself, but rather results from chemical compounds called metabolites that are produced as acetaminophen is broken down. Ordinarily, these are neutralized by the liver. However, when an excess of metabolites is present, the protective processes of the liver are overwhelmed and liver damage occurs. If damage is severe, liver functioning is severely impaired.

With prompt treatment, a child usually recovers fully from acetaminophen overdose. Death is very rare and usually occurs only if treatment is delayed for more than 24 hours.

CAUSE

Poisoning results from swallowing excessive amounts of acetaminophen (either in pure tablet form or as a component of other medications). The minimum toxic dose of acetaminophen is estimated to be approximately 150 milligrams per kilogram (2.2 pounds) of weight. The average children's tablet contains 70 mg of acetaminophen, and a regular-strength adult tablet contains 325 mg. For example, if a child weighs 100 pounds, he or she will become poisoned after swallowing approximately 95 children's acetaminophen tablets or 20 adult acetaminophen tablets.

SIGNS AND SYMPTOMS

Within 2 to 4 hours of ingestion, a child becomes pale and nauseated, and may vomit and perspire heavily. These symptoms may last up to 24 hours. More advanced symptoms of acetaminophen poisoning occur 36 to 48 hours after ingestion and include tenderness over the liver, mental confusion (see *delirium*). If liver damage is severe, *jaundice* (yellow staining of the skin by bilirubin, a waste product of the breakdown of red blood cells), and abdominal swelling may be present.

DIAGNOSIS

Acetaminophen poisoning may be sus-

pected initially if a child suffers characteristic signs and symptoms of acetaminophen poisoning. However, acetaminophen-related damage is often not apparent until 24 to 48 hours after ingestion. Unless a child is discovered while swallowing tablets or the empty container is found, a parent cannot be certain that a child has swallowed large amounts of acetaminophen. A poison information center or physician should be consulted immediately if poisoning is suspected.

A physician must rule out other possible causes of liver damage (such as damage caused by other medications and *Reye's syndrome*) before making a positive diagnosis of acetaminophen poisoning. Among adolescents, such causes as drug abuse (particularly alcohol and narcotics) must also be ruled out.

Laboratory tests are necessary to determine the level of acetaminophen in a child's bloodstream. High levels of acetaminophen four hours or more beyond ingestion confirm a diagnosis of acetaminophen poisoning.

COMPLICATIONS

In addition to liver damage there may sometimes be kidney damage, heart damage, and *hypoglycemia* (abnormally low levels of sugar in the blood), although these occurrences are rare.

TREATMENT

Treatment of acetaminophen poisoning focuses on immediate removal of acetaminophen from a child's stomach by stomach washing or by induced vomiting. Hospital treatment includes neutralization of the ingested acetaminophen with an oral antidote to prevent subsequent liver damage (see Emergency Action, above).

In addition to removing acetaminophen from the stomach, a physician usually gives a child activated charcoal to bind the drug in the gastrointestinal tract. The charcoal bound to the drug is then excreted in the stool. If a child is to receive the antidote, however, charcoal should not be given, as it binds with and inactivates the antidote.

Fluid losses caused by vomiting and dehydration are corrected by intravenous administration of fluids. These fluids usually contain glucose (a sugar) and potassium to correct sugar and mineral depletion.

PREVENTION

Parents should be aware of a child's curiosity and tendency to explore. Keeping medications out of a child's sight and reach helps prevent accidental acetaminophen poisoning. Limiting the number of tablets per package and equipping bottles with childproof caps help decrease the number of accidental acetaminophen poisonings.

ACNE

DESCRIPTION

Acne is a common skin eruption characterized by whiteheads, blackheads, and pimples. Five types of acne are frequently found: infantile acne; acne vulgaris, almost universally occurring when a child's or an adolescent's hormones become highly active; steroid acne, resulting from cortisone treatments; halogen acne, resulting from the surface application of halogenated hydrocarbons; and drug-induced acne (caused by lithium, iodides, bromides, antiseizure medicines, or antituberculous medicines).

Infantile acne usually erupts on male infants 3 to 6 months old. A temporary condition, this form of acne occurs on the forehead, cheeks, and chin, and less frequently on the scalp and genital area. It usually appears as white pimples; scarring is rare. Infantile acne may recur, but will usually clear up within the first few years of life. The disturbance may be due to poorly understood hormonal factors.

Acne vulgaris may appear initially at age 6 or 7 among girls, age 7 or 8 in boys, and is most common among teenagers (girls 12 to 17, boys 16 to 19). Somewhat more common among boys than girls, this condition occurs on the face, chest, and back. The whiteheads, blackheads, and pimples that characterize acne may all be present. Skin, scalp, and hair may appear very oily. Acne vulgaris tends to disappear, slowly but spontaneously, by early adulthood, but it may persist until the third and fourth decades.

Steroid acne can occur when a child is receiving cortisone medication for an illness or disease. Eruptions usually appear two or more weeks after treatment begins, arising on the face, neck, chest, shoulders, arms, upper back, and rarely, the scalp. Eruptions are usually composed of many small red lumps. Severe eruptions and scarring are rare.

Halogen acne appears when large amounts of halogenated hydrocarbons (cutting oils) are applied to skin or when drugs containing iodides or bromides (which are sometimes found in medicines, health foods, and vitamin supplements) are consumed. Halogen acne appears as bright red lumps. Acne due to lithium, antiseizure medicine, and antituberculosis drugs may appear as red lumps or cysts. Pitch and tar may cause blackheads.

CAUSE

Mild cases of acne are usually due to collection of dead skin and hardened oils in the oil gland canals.

More severe acne eruptions (including halogen acne) are caused by rupture of clogged oil glands and bacteria in the passageways (ducts) into the skin. Oil, bacteria, and dead skin in the ducts are forced into surrounding skin and inflammation occurs.

Overproduction by oil glands is most often stimulated by hormonal changes which may occur temporarily during infancy, puberty, and adolescence. Why these hormonal changes occur is unknown.

Severe acne is usually aggravated by bacteria in the oil ducts. Swelling occurs when bacteria produce a natural acid irritating to the skin, or stimulate inflammation when bacteria from the oil ducts rupture into the skin.

SIGNS AND SYMPTOMS AND DIAGNOSIS

Acne may occur in one or more forms: whiteheads, blackheads, pimples, and cysts. The severity of eruption is related to the amount of oil secreted by the body, the tendency of oil ducts and glands to rupture into the skin, and the degree of irritation caused by bacteria in the oil ducts. Mild eruptions are composed of whiteheads and blackheads. Whiteheads are small, raised, pus-filled bumps. These occur when a duct is closed at the skin surface and oil in the duct pushes toward the surface. If the ducts are widely dilated at the skin surface, the dead skin and hardened oils give a dark appearance (blackhead).

More severe acne eruptions occur as pimples and cysts. The clogged oil ducts provide an environment for bacteria to multiply. As the bacteria break down the oils, an irritating substance is produced that causes redness and swelling when the material ruptures into the skin. A pimple results from the combined effects of irritation and hypersensitivity to bacteria. Pimples may be slightly itchy, but may be painful, particularly when pressed.

COMPLICATIONS

Squeezing or picking acne eruptions can lead to increased irritation and redness.

If a duct becomes severely inflamed, a large, painful cyst can develop. This occurs below the skin surface. A physician should be seen for treatment of cystic acne and red pimples or pustules.

TREATMENT

Infantile acne can be observed at home without consulting a physician unless it progresses or persists beyond 12 months.

Acne vulgaris of the blackhead and whitehead type usually can be treated satisfactorily at home. Effective treatment is directed toward unclogging oil ducts and removing the dead skin and oil deposits.

The most effective medicated preparations available without prescription for the treatment of acne contain benzoyl peroxide, which prevents the growth of acne-causing bacteria and helps unclog the oil ducts. Vitamin A acid applied to the skin is also effective in the control of acne because it helps unclog oil ducts. Vitamin A acid however, can also increase the skin's sensitivity to the sun. Avoidance of sunbathing and use of a sunscreen are advisable if topical vitamin A acid is being used. All medicated surface treatments require a minimum of 6 to 12 weeks to be completely effective. Surface treatment should be applied to dry skin, and excessive washing and scrubbing of the skin should be avoided. Otherwise, the skin will be irritated by the surface treatments using benzoyl peroxide and vitamin A acid.

Although exposure to ultraviolet light (either from the sun or a sunlamp) may help clear acne vulgaris, it is not recommended because long-term exposure to ultraviolet light may cause skin cancer.

Creams or oil-containing preparations applied to the face or scalp may aggravate acne. Contrary to popular belief, diet usually plays no significant role in the duration or severity of acne eruptions.

A physician may prescribe an oral antibiotic to combat severe acne vulgaris. An oral antibiotic remains in the skin and reduces bacterial growth, and reduces redness caused by the skin's reaction to the bacteria. Surface treatment must be continued while antibiotics are being taken. Surface antibiotics may also be prescribed. Improvement resulting from oral antibiotics should become apparent within 6 to 8 weeks. For young women, estrogen (the female sex hormone) may sometimes be prescribed to treat very severe cases of acne. Estrogen suppresses hormonal activity that stimulates excess oil secretion. Steroid injections are sometimes used to reduce inflammation of cysts.

Steroid acne can persist as long as a child is taking steroid medication. Surface medications containing vitamin A acid may be effective in treating steroid acne. Halogen acne will not clear as long as halogenated hydrocarbons are being applied to the skin. Acne induced by iodides, bromides, lithium, and antiseizure or antituberculosis medicines will persist as long as the drug is continued, but may be improved with oral and topical medication.

PREVENTION

Infantile acne and acne vulgaris cannot be prevented. Drug-induced acne and halogenated hydrocarbon acne will disappear when use of the medication in question is discontinued.

ADRENAL PROBLEMS

EMERGENCY ACTION

Any child with loss of appetite, *abdominal pain, vomiting,* and *diarrhea* must receive medical attention within 24 hours of the beginning of symptoms to prevent possible life-threatening complications from *dehydration,* the severe loss of body fluids and salts. (Signs and symptoms include cold, clammy, pale skin, sunken eyes, dry tongue, listlessness, and rapid pulse.)

DESCRIPTION, CAUSE, SIGNS, AND SYMPTOMS

The endocrine system is a network of glands and tissues in the body that controls growth, certain body processes, and sexual development. (See Fig. 18.) Each endocrine gland secretes hormones (chemical messengers) into the bloodstream. Endocrine glands function in response to changes in activity, sleep, and feeding in order to keep essential nutrients such as blood glucose available in adequate amounts. The body's response to daily changes is controlled by a complex interrelationship among blood

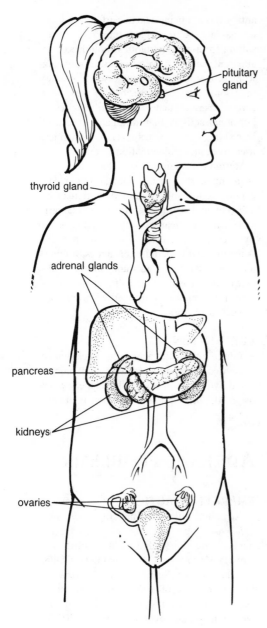

FIG. 18. ENDOCRINE SYSTEM

Labels (top to bottom): pituitary gland, thyroid gland, adrenal glands, pancreas, kidneys, ovaries

levels of nutrients and hormones and the brain (hypothalamus) and pituitary gland.

There are six major parts of the endocrine system: the hypothalamus-pituitary system (see *pituitary problems*), the thyroid gland (see *thyroid problems*), the parathyroid glands, the pancreas, the adrenal glands, and the gonads (ovaries and testes). Hormones of the adrenal glands are involved in metabolism (the sum of all the complex chemical and physical processes of matter and energy

that occur within living cells), in maintaining body fluids by controlling salt retention, in producing pubic, underarm, and facial hair (called sexual hair), and in the functioning of the involuntary (autonomic) nervous system.

The adrenal glands are located at the upper ends of the kidneys. Each is composed of two sections, the cortex and the medulla. Each section secretes specific hormones and is regulated by the hypothalamus and hormones of the pituitary gland. Factors such as salt intake, fasting, and stress from injury or illness also can influence function of the adrenal glands.

Hormones of the cortex include cortisol, aldosterone, corticosterone, and androgens. Cortisol controls inflammation; stimulates enzyme activity in the muscles, blood cells, and fatty tissues; and helps store sugar in the liver. Aldosterone, required for survival, is responsible for salt retention and is needed to maintain blood volume. Corticosterone has both a cortisol and aldosterone effect. Androgens are responsible for the appearance of sexual hair at puberty and may play a role in initiating hypothalamic-pituitary-gonadal functions.

Hormones of the medulla include epinephrine (adrenaline) and norepinephrine, both of which are involved in regulation of blood pressure and certain metabolic functions required to maintain blood sugar and fatty acid levels. Excesses of either hormone can increase blood pressure.

If functioning of the adrenal glands is impaired, a severe, life-threatening situation may develop. With prompt treatment, however, children with acute adrenal problems usually recover fully.

Adrenal cortex problems are divided into two major categories: hypoadrenocorticism, which occurs when the adrenal output of hormones is abnormally low, and hyperadrenocorticism, which occurs when excess hormones are produced. The most common forms of hypoadrenocorticism of childhood are Addison's disease and congenital adrenal hyperplasia. The most common form of hyperadrenocorticism is Cushing syndrome. The most common problem of the adrenal medulla is pheochromocytoma.

Adrenal Insufficiency (Addison's Disease)

Adrenal insufficiency, or Addison's disease, is a disorder that arises when the adrenal cortices are underdeveloped or structurally damaged by disease (such as severe hemorrhaging, *tuberculosis,* or autoimmune disease—when the body's defense system attacks its own cells) and produce only a limited supply of hormones. Because some hormones are produced, symptoms may not appear until a greater demand for hormone production is placed on the adrenal glands. Such a demand arises, for example, when a child has a concurrent illness, suffers a severe injury, or experiences the stress of surgery.

Adrenal insufficiency is often the result of an autoimmunological disorder and is associated with a similar destruction of special cells of the stomach leading to *anemia,* and of cells of the thyroid gland, the parathyroid glands, and the pancreas. Symptoms of adrenal insufficiency include loss of appetite, weight loss, loss of fluids, *hypoglycemia,* and *seizures.* Diarrhea, vomiting, and abdominal pain usually occur. A child's skin may be overly pigmented (tan to bronze), particularly in skin creases on the face, neck, back of the hands, and knuckles. Skin of the genitals, anal area, and elbows may also become overly pigmented, and scattered black spots or freckles may appear. A child may develop irregular brown, gray, or bluish patches on the lips, gums, tongue, or lining of the cheeks.

With treatment, most signs and symptoms of adrenal insufficiency disappear, and a child grows and develops normally.

Congenital Adrenal Hyperplasia

Congenital adrenal hyperplasia (overgrowth) is caused by a deficiency in the enzymes necessary for the production of certain hormones, especially cortisol. Since this disorder is carried by a recessive gene, the affected child must inherit it from both parents (see *genetic disorders).*

When enzymes required for hormone synthesis are missing, cortisol is not produced in adequate amounts and the pituitary gland increases output of a hormone called ACTH in an attempt to compensate for the deficit. This causes an excess of ACTH, enlargement of the adrenal glands, and overproduction of androgens. Androgen synthesis is usually not affected by the missing enzymes, however. Excess production of androgens causes abnormal growth and genital development. For about half of the affected children, aldosterone synthesis is impaired, and children suffer from decreased aldosterone production and salt loss, leading to dehydra-

tion, collapse of blood vessels, and possibly death.

The effects of androgen overproduction are most noticeable at birth among female infants because the hormone causes masculinization of the external genitals. Masculinization involves enlargement of the clitoris (resembling a tiny penis) and fusion of the labia (external lips of female genitals), but the internal female sex organs—the ovaries, fallopian tubes, and uterus—are not affected. The excess androgen production among male infants may increase the size of the penis and development of the scrotum, but the testes do not enlarge. Penile erections occur frequently, but sperm are not produced. Male children develop sexual hair much earlier than normal, and voice deepening occurs if they are untreated.

Because of the increase in ACTH, the genitals of both sexes may show increased pigmentation. Rarely, the enzyme deficit may block the synthesis of androgens. In this case, the genitals of affected female infants are normal, but the penis of affected male infants may be small, and hypospadias (in which a defect in the wall of the urethra causes the canal to be open on the underside of the penis) may occur.

Children with congenital adrenal hyperplasia usually begin to show masculinization caused by excess adrenal androgens by 1 to 3 years of age. Pubic hair appears first, followed by underarm hair, *acne,* and *seborrheic dermatitis.* Rapid growth, including increase in muscle development and bone length, occurs. Children are usually above normal height for their age, but do not reach their expected adult height because bone growth stops prematurely.

Without treatment, children with congenital adrenal hyperplasia retain abnormal sexual characteristics and never fully develop sexually. Female children become progressively more masculine, developing thick, stocky bodies, heavy facial and body hair, and deep voices. Eventually they may become bald. Neither breast development nor menstruation occurs. With treatment, however, affected children can grow and develop normally. The abnormal sexual development present at birth can be corrected surgically.

Cushing Syndrome

Cushing syndrome is rare in infancy and childhood except when induced by the use of glucocorticoids (including cortisol, prednisone, and dexamethasone) for the treatment of other diseases (such as *nephrosis* and long-term *asthma*). When not caused by the use of glucocorticoids, Cushing syndrome usually results from an adrenal or pituitary tumor (see *neuroblastoma* and *pituitary problems*). These tumors usually develop after a child's first birthday and seldom spread to other areas of the body.

Signs and symptoms of Cushing syndrome are caused by excess cortisol (or other synthetic glucocorticoids) and include excess weight gain with a decreased growth rate, decreased muscle mass, muscle weakness, thinning of the skin, bruising, and glucose intolerance *(diabetes)*. Fat deposits develop in the abdominal area, chest, and shoulders. A child's face becomes fat and round (called a "moon face"), and reddish or purple stretch marks may develop on the abdomen, waist, thighs, and chest. Blood pressure and blood volume may increase if there is increased sodium and water retention from the excess cortisol production.

Isolated increased production of aldosterone or androgens is usually linked to noncancerous adrenal tumors. Increased production of aldosterone causes *hypertension* (high blood pressure). When androgen production increases, signs and symptoms resembling those of untreated congenital adrenal hyperplasia develop, but labial fusion does not occur because these tumors usually form after birth. Rarely, cancerous adrenal tumors develop, producing excess cortisol, aldosterone, and androgens. While prompt surgical, medical, or radiation treatment of pituitary and benign adrenal tumors is usually successful, the outlook for children with cancerous adrenal tumors is poor because cancer cells tend to spread early.

Pheochromocytoma

The major adrenal problem involving the medulla is the formation of an adrenal medullary tumor (pheochromocytoma). This tumor is associated with marked periodic or continuous hypertension and oversecretion of epinephrine and norepinephrine. Excess epinephrine causes an increase in cardiac output, a rise in heart rate, a rise in body temperature, and hyperglycemia (increased blood sugar levels). A child may become apprehensive, nervous, and overexcited, and heartbeat may be irregular. Excess norepinephrine does not produce these effects, but instead may even slow an individual's heart rate. A child may develop severe hypertensive retinopathy, a disorder that damages the retina of the eye, interfering with normal vision.

A pheochromocytoma is often found among several family members and can be associated with other tumors. Treatment involves surgical removal of the tumor.

DIAGNOSIS

Parents should suspect an inherited adrenal problem if an infant is born with abnormal genitals, becomes dehydrated or goes into shock during the second week of life, or subsequently shows abnormal growth and sexual development. Acquired adrenal problems may develop at any age, indicated by signs and symptoms of adrenal hormone deficiencies or excesses.

Many parents do not recognize abnormalities or seek appropriate medical attention after a child becomes seriously ill. This is particularly true in cases of Addison's disease, because the onset of symptoms tends to occur slowly and subtly.

If parents seek medical attention in time, however, a physician can usually diagnose an adrenal problem based on signs and symptoms and the results of blood and urine tests.

Adrenal problems and related complications may be identified using the child's medical history, evaluation of past growth and development, and the findings of a complete physical examination. A CT (computed tomography) scan can detect an adrenal or pituitary tumor if none is found using routine X-ray films of the abdomen or skull. Further blood and hormonal analyses are required to detect metabolic abnormalities caused by adrenal problems.

COMPLICATIONS

A major complication of adrenal problems is the adrenal crisis, inability of the adrenal cortex to function adequately to meet specific hormonal needs of the body during stress of illness, injury, or elective surgery. Crises can be life-threatening if severe and untreated. (An adrenal crisis may also occur if a child develops bacterial *meningitis*.)

A child with congenital adrenal hyperplasia suffers an adrenal crisis if he or she loses excessive amounts of salts and fluids. This often happens 7 to 11 days after birth, when dietary salt intake is normally low and the disorder has not been recognized. An affected child becomes dehydrated, and the cardiovascular system collapses because of electrolyte (essential body salts) losses in the urine. Without immediate treatment, infants are at high risk for cardiac arrest. Similar crises can occur at any age if, during even a mild illness or a period of stress, a child significantly decreases his or her intake of food, fluids, or medications for several days.

TREATMENT

Any child having an adrenal crisis must receive immediate medical care in a hospital. (See Emergency Action, above.) Treatment involves administration of fluids and salts to combat shock and large doses of cortisol to replace the missing hormone.

A physician often refers a child with an adrenal problem to an endocrinologist, a specialist in treating complex endocrine system problems.

Adrenal Insufficiency

Children with adrenal insufficiency caused by hypopituitarism often require treatment, with cortisol only, when suffering other illnesses or during periods of stress (injuries or operations).

Treatment of children with adrenal insufficiency usually includes giving cortisol (or synthetic substitutes such as cortisone, prednisone, and dexamethasone). The response to treatment must be monitored by a physician to ensure that therapy is effective and does not alter a child's growth and development.

If a child with adrenal insufficiency is losing salt, a salt-retaining hormone is required; additional salt may be taken by older children and adolescents. If an illness, injury, or surgical stress is present, cortisol is required in larger, more frequent doses given orally, intravenously, or intramuscularly. As soon as the period of stress is past, dosage is reduced to the previous maintenance level.

Congenital Adrenal Hyperplasia

To achieve the best results, a child with congenital adrenal hyperplasia should be treated from birth. Initial treatment of adrenal hyperplasia involves giving somewhat larger doses of cortisol to suppress secretion of ACTH and androgens. Once secretion is suppressed, cortisol dosage is reduced to a maintenance level that suppresses excess androgen production. As a result of suppressed secretion, further development of male characteristics among female children is halted.

Surgery is required to correct abnormally developed external female genitals caused by congenital adrenal hyperplasia. If clitoral enlargement is slight, correction may not be required. Initial surgery to correct the abnormal sexual development should occur during the first year of life.

If treatment is begun early, children with adrenal hyperplasia grow and develop normally. Once they reach puberty, these individuals are capable of reproduction. If treatment is delayed until later childhood, administration of cortisol stops abnormal growth and development. The resulting advanced bone maturation and early onset of gonadal development, however, invariably leads to early cessation of bone growth and short stature (see *height problems*).

Hyperadrenocorticism

Treatment of hyperadrenocorticism most often involves treatment of tumors. Successful surgical removal of noncancerous adrenal or pituitary tumors restores normal secretion of cortisol and ACTH. Following surgery, children may require cortisol therapy as they recover.

Cancerous tumors are also removed surgically. If the cancerous cells have spread, chemotherapy and radiation therapy may help eliminated them, although as yet such therapy has not been very successful. (For further discussion of cancerous tumors, see *cancer*.) Following surgery, a child should be seen periodically by a physician to check for recurrence of a tumor and to monitor adrenal gland functioning.

Pheochromocytoma

Children with pheochromocytoma require medication both before and during surgical removal of the tumor to prevent rapid changes in blood pressure.

PREVENTION

While adrenal problems cannot be prevented, early treatment of infants with congenital adrenal hyperplasia can prevent subsequent abnormal growth and development. In addition, adrenal crises can be prevented by recognition of the extra needs of children with adrenal insufficiency during periods of illness, injury, or surgery. Children should wear identification tags specifying their hormonal requirements so that appropriate action can be taken in crisis situations if people familiar with the child's condition are not available.

Parents with a child who has adrenal problems or prospective parents with a family history of adrenal problems should consider genetic counseling (see *genetic disorders*).

AIDS
(ACQUIRED IMMUNE DEFICIENCY SYNDROME)

DESCRIPTION AND COMPLICATIONS

AIDS (acquired immune deficiency syndrome) is a recently recognized disease that affects many of the body's systems. Most of the symptoms of AIDS are the result of a breakdown in the body's natural ability to defend itself against infection. The impaired immune system becomes unable to remove or destroy disease-causing microorganisms. As a result, people with AIDS experience many infections, some of which would not ordinarily be a threat to healthy people.

These infections, called opportunistic infections, are caused by certain unusual bacteria, fungi, parasites, and viruses. People with AIDS may also develop rare forms of cancer. In addition, AIDS affects the central nervous system, causing gradually progressive paralysis and mental deterioration. As the symptoms worsen, for example, swallowing may become difficult. This, in turn, can result in bacteria being inhaled into the lungs, which can cause *pneumonia*.

The syndrome, identified in the spring of 1981, was first noticed with significant frequency among homosexually active men. Soon after the first cases were diagnosed, AIDS also appeared among intravenous drug users and hemophiliacs. More recently, the disease has been identified among sexual partners of those at risk (members of groups that account for more than 90 percent of AIDS cases), people who received blood products donated by AIDS-infected individuals, and infants and children of parents in at-risk groups.

Males make up more than 90 percent of those diagnosed with AIDS, and homosexual males account for nearly 75 percent of the cases. The majority of individuals with AIDS are in the 25-to-45-year-old age range. More than half the people diagnosed with AIDS have been Caucasians, but all races have been affected. AIDS has occurred in every one of the United States and in most countries of the world. More than 90 percent of the cases involve people who live in or near major cities.

More than 36,000 cases of AIDS were reported in the United States by the middle of 1987. Of these, about 1 percent involved children less than 13 years old. Since 1981 the number of AIDS cases has doubled every 13 months. While this rate of increase continues at an alarming pace, it appears to be gradually slowing down.

No person diagnosed with full-blown AIDS is known to have regained immune-system function. Some people who have a milder but similar condition known as AIDS-related complex (ARC) have failed to develop AIDS, but in other cases, AIDS-related complex has progressed into full-blown AIDS. It is estimated that about half of the adults and children with AIDS die within one year of diagnosis.

CAUSE

AIDS is considered to be caused by a virus called human immunodeficiency virus (HIV). HIV has been isolated from the blood, semen, saliva, and tears of individuals with AIDS. The origin of the virus is unknown, although there are suspicions that it is related to similar viruses in certain African monkeys.

The most common source of AIDS transmission is sexual contact, either homosexual or heterosexual. Other means of transmission include injections with contaminated needles, transfusions of blood containing HIV, and for hemophiliacs, injections of contaminated blood-clotting factor concentrates.

Among infants, AIDS is transmitted from an infected mother to the fetus, probably through the placenta, while the baby is still in the uterus. Like adults, children may also contract the AIDS virus from contaminated blood products or clotting factors.

While full-blown AIDS has been identified in only 36,000 people as of 1987, many times this number are infected with the HIV. All of these individuals are probably capable of transmitting the virus to others, and a proportion of these, currently estimated to be 40 to 50 percent, will eventually develop AIDS.

AIDS transmission occurs only through well-defined routes: sexual intercourse, sharing of intravenous needles, blood or blood-product administration, and birth from an infected mother. The virus clearly is not transmitted through common infectious exposures such as talking, sneezing, coughing, touching, sharing food, or even sleeping in the same bed, using the same bathroom, or living together for many years.

SIGNS AND SYMPTOMS

When HIV is acquired from the mother before or during birth, the signs are somewhat different from those characteristics of adults with AIDS. The first symptom is likely to be an unusual frequency and severity of infections. These can be *pneumonia, ear infection* (see *earache and ear infection*), *meningitis* (inflammation of the lining of the brain), *diarrhea,* or other infections. These infections can be caused by common bacteria or viruses. As in adults, lymph-node swelling is common, as is enlargement of the liver, spleen, and salivary glands. Infants may have particularly severe thrush and may fail to gain weight. Later signs are loss of ability to walk and talk, and lack of coordination.

AIDS in teenagers is quite similar to AIDS in adults. The first signs of disease usually are swollen lymph nodes (most often in the neck, armpits, and groin—see *swollen glands*), fever, and weight loss. After several weeks, lymph nodes grow larger and more tender, weight loss accelerates, and fever may increase. As time passes, people with AIDS may feel extremely weak and fatigued. They may experience severe *diarrhea,* dry *cough, breathing difficulty,* joint swelling, abnormal bleeding, weakness, lack of coordination, and muscle pain.

DIAGNOSIS

Physicians may suspect the presence of AIDS after evaluating an individual's medical history and learning of intimate contact with or receipt of blood products from a person who is at risk for AIDS. Gradual worsening of symptoms is another warning sign. Laboratory tests may show decreasing numbers of white blood cells and abnormal ratios of various types of immune-system cells. Both of these conditions are common with AIDS. AIDS is usually confirmed when a severe opportunistic infection or rare cancer develops.

A test is available to determine if HIV antibodies are present in a person's blood, and this screening is now used routinely by blood banks to identify potentially infectious do-

nors. Physicians can use negative test results to help rule out AIDS in cases where a severe immune-system disorder is suspected.

A positive test for HIV antibodies does not mean people will necessarily develop AIDS. Nevertheless, if the test does return positive, it is an indication that HIV infection has occurred and that the virus is probably still present. Such a person, even if entirely well, must not give blood and should consult a physician.

TREATMENT

Currently, no treatment is available that can destroy or control the HIV virus or restore function to the weakened immune system. Several special antiviral medications, however, are being used for adults with AIDS with varying degrees of success.

People with AIDS are usually hospitalized for extended periods of time. Treatment involves attempting to control infections and, in advanced stages of the disease, using life-support systems.

Infants and children with AIDS can be protected from many infections by the intermittent administration of large doses of gammaglobulin, a preparation made with antibodies from normal adults. Some antibiotics may also be given on a regular basis to prevent infections.

PREVENTION

Prevention of AIDS is a major public health concern, and as a result, blood banks screen for HIV antibodies to identify people at risk for spreading the virus. People in one of the AIDS at-risk groups and sexual partners of people at risk must not donate blood and blood products.

People who know that their blood carries HIV antibodies should inform doctors, dentists, and other health-care providers so precautions can be taken to curb spreading of the virus. Also, razors, toothbrushes, and other items that may be contaminated with the blood, semen, or saliva from people at risk should not be shared.

Women who have been in sexual contact with a member of an at-risk group, women who use intravenous drugs, and women who test positive for HIV antibodies should postpone becoming pregnant until they have consulted a physician.

People can reduce their risk of contracting AIDS by avoiding sexual contact with anyone who has AIDS and anyone in an at-risk group who displays AIDS symptoms. Members of at-risk groups should limit the number of sexual partners, use condoms, and avoid anal intercourse to reduce their chance of acquiring AIDS.

No incidents of AIDS transmission to children through normal family, school, or neighborhood contacts had been reported as of mid-1987. Children who have AIDS should be allowed to attend school if they are well enough, if they have no open sores, and if they exhibit no unusual behavior such as biting. Children in homes where AIDS is present can attend school and take part in normal activities. Local health professional and family groups can often provide valuable emotional support.

People who suspect they have AIDS or parents in at-risk groups whose children display AIDS-like symptoms may fail to seek medical help because they fear the stigma associated with the disease. Medical personnel, however, assure confidentiality when dealing with AIDS.

Early medical intervention is vital to combat infections and preserve immune-system function for as long as possible. Medical professionals need to test and monitor anyone with AIDS or AIDS-like symptoms so that research efforts on this new disease can be as comprehensive as possible.

Information about AIDS is available on the United States Public Health Service hotline 800-342-AIDS, or from a local chapter of the American Red Cross or the AIDS Education Office of the American Red Cross, 1730 D Street, N.W., Washington, D.C. 20006 (phone: 202-737-8300).

ALBINISM

DESCRIPTION

Albinism is an inherited disorder characterized by a lack of normal coloration of skin, hair, and eyes. Present at birth, the disorder is due to absent or insufficient pigment (coloring matter). Albinism is rare, occurring once every 10,000 births worldwide and once every 20,000 births in the United States. The disorder affects all races in all parts of the world.

Albinism occurs in six types. The most common type is complete albinism, characterized by milk white or light, fine, silky hair; white eyelashes and eyebrows; white or pinkish skin; and pink to red eyes (which may look pale gray or blue in certain lighting). The other, less common types of albinism tend to involve a greater degree of coloration.

CAUSE

Albinism can appear only if each parent carries and passes along one recessive defective gene to the baby. If two persons with the same type of albinism have children together, all of their children will have that type of albinism (see *genetic disorders*).

Albinism has been linked to intermarrying and inbreeding, and studies show a high incidence of shared ancestry among parents of affected children. If two persons with albinism have different types of albinism, however, they may have normal children.

Any child inheriting two defective genes will lack or have defective tyrosinase, the enzyme necessary for full coloring of skin, hair, and eyes.

SIGNS AND SYMPTOMS

In addition to having characteristic coloring of skin, hair, and eyes, some people with albinism are short.

In complete albinism, the eyes are abnormally intolerant of light and, if confronted by light, may move rapidly. A vision problem called astigmatism (because of which a child has difficulty focusing on vertical and horizontal objects at the same time) is also common (see *focusing problems*).

DIAGNOSIS

Albinism is diagnosed by observation of a baby's skin, hair, and eye coloring. The diagnosis may be confirmed with a lab test to detect the absence of tyrosinase. Albinism cannot be detected prenatally through amniocentesis.

COMPLICATIONS

Albinism often leads to impaired vision, because of extreme sensitivity to light. If the skin is damaged by either excessive or normal sunlight, a severe burn may occur and skin cancer may develop. Victims of albinism may suffer decreased fertility and life expectancy.

TREATMENT

No cure exists for albinism. Affected people, however, may adapt by taking certain precautions. It is extremely important that children with albinism be protected from exposure to any sunlight. They must wear total sunscreening ointments or lotions when outdoors even briefly in cloudy weather. Sunscreens must be reapplied if the skin becomes wet or sweaty.

Before children with albinism start school, they should be seen by an ophthalmologist in order to obtain protective (dark) glasses or, if their vision is impaired, corrective glasses or contact lenses.

PREVENTION

Parents who have a family history of albinism should receive genetic counseling so that they know in advance their chances of having affected children.

Any couple aware of a shared or close family lineage should consider genetic counseling to try to determine the presence or probability of inherited diseases in their family histories. (See genetic counseling section of *genetic disorders.*)

ALLERGIES

An allergy is an extreme sensitivity to a specific substance (allergen). Children of all ages can have allergies, and some are allergic to more than one substance at a time. Many children outgrow their allergies by adolescence, while others are affected throughout their lives. Allergies tend to run in families.

The most common childhood allergies or allergic reactions include *food allergy* (which may be caused by almost any food), *asthma* (breathing difficulty and wheezing), *hay fever* (also called allergic rhinitis), *poison ivy, oak, and sumac,* and *eczema* (a skin reaction to swallowed or touched allergens). Asthma and hay fever can be caused by many allergens, particularly those that are inhaled, such as pollen, dust, and animal dander. Children may also be allergic to the venom of stinging insects (see *stinging insect reactions*).

Symptoms of an allergic reaction to food may include swelling of the lips and mouth, *rash, hives, asthma, wheezing,* stuffy nose, *vomiting, abdominal pain, diarrhea,* and if the reaction is severe, *shock.* Hay fever symptoms include runny nose, sneezing, *tearing, eye itching and irritation,* mouth breathing, *headache,* and fatigue. The major symtoms of poison ivy are red, itchy pimples and tiny blisters.

Symptoms of a reaction to stinging insect venom include swelling and itching at the site of the sting and surrounding skin areas. If the reaction is severe, hives, wheezing, *dizziness,* nausea, weakness, diarrhea, and stomach cramps may be present.

With proper treatment, symptoms of most allergic reactions can be reduced or eliminated. Specific medications, a desensitization program, and avoidance of reaction-causing substances are the most effective forms of treatment.

See individual sections mentioned above for complete discussion.

ANEMIA

Read *Blood Disorders.*

If too few red blood cells are in the circulating blood, or if the concentration of hemoglobin in red cells is decreased, a condition called anemia exists. As a result of anemia, insufficient oxygen is in the blood (hypoxemia) and not enough oxygen reaches body tissues and organs. Signs and symptoms of anemia include weakness, an excessively rapid heart rate, rapid breathing, and pale skin.

Except in cases of abnormal blood loss, anemia is the result of an imbalance between red blood cell production and destruction. This balance is normally maintained by proper functioning of the bone marrow (the spongelike tissue that fills the cavities of most bones). Constant production and destruction of red blood cells is necessary because the cells naturally wear out after about four months. Old red blood cells must be destroyed, and young red blood cells must take their place.

In a number of different ways, this process can be disrupted, producing anemia. For each cause of anemia, treatment (and, sometimes, signs and symptoms) is different. The two major categories of causes are excessively rapid destruction of red blood cells or hemoglobin (see *anemia, hemolytic),* and impairment of red blood cell or hemoglobin production.

Specific causes of impairment include the following:

1. Bone marrow failure. If the bone marrow does not produce enough red blood cells, anemia results. This is the case in *aplastic anemia* (See *anemia, aplastic*).

2. Nutritional problems. If the body is deficient in a certain nutrient—specifically iron, folic acid, or vitamin B-12—red blood cells cannot form or mature properly, and nutritional anemia results (see *anemia, nutritional*).

Lead poisoning can also lead to anemia because it causes a decrease in the production of heme (the iron compound in blood responsible for color and carrying oxygen).

See also *hereditary spherocytosis; jaundice; Rh and ABO incompatibility; sickle cell anemia; thalassemia.*

ANEMIA, APLASTIC

DESCRIPTION

Aplastic anemia is a blood disorder resulting in the failure of the bone marrow to produce 3 blood cell lines. (See *blood disorders* for a description of the types of blood cells and how they are produced.) The first form is leukopenia, in which there is an insufficient number of white blood cells. The second is thrombocytopenia, in which there are too few platelets. The lack of white cells and platelets leaves aplastic anemia victims at high risk of infection and bleeding, which are the chief causes of death of children with aplastic anemia. The third form is *anemia,* caused by a deficiency of red blood cells. Of the three disorders, anemia generally develops last. ("Aplasia" means physically undeveloped or lacking.) Children who have aplastic anemia have progressively lost function of the bone marrow. Other causes of bone marrow failure in children include *leukemia* and tumors.

Aplastic anemia is generally categorized as severe or mild. In the mild form of aplastic anemia, sometimes called hypoplastic anemia, the blood cells are less drastically reduced in number. ("Hypoplasia" means physically underdeveloped or incomplete.) Sometimes, a deficiency of one type of blood cell precedes the full-blown development of aplastic anemia.

An individual case of aplastic anemia may initially be moderate and then become severe, or vice versa. Often, mild aplastic anemia develops into a severe form of the disease. Mild aplastic anemia and, less frequently, severe aplastic anemia may resolve (blood cell levels return to normal). In moderate cases a child may suffer frequent

nosebleeds, occasional or mild infections, and mild anemia. In severe cases, a child may suffer from heavy or prolonged bleeding, frequent or severe infections, and severe anemia.

Aplastic anemia may be acquired or inherited. Acquired aplastic anemia occurs three times as often as the inherited variety. A child can acquire aplastic anemia at any age; inherited aplastic anemia may be apparent at birth or become apparent later during childhood. It occurs most frequently before the age of 12.

Fanconi's anemia, a severe disorder, is the most common form of inherited aplastic anemia. Problems with the blood typically develop when a child with Fanconi's anemia is between 5 and 10 years old. Children with Fanconi's anemia often have bone or kidney abnormalities. Abnormalities of the thumbs or wrists are the most common type of bone abnormality. Kidney abnormalities can include having only one kidney, having extra kidneys, or having an abnormally placed kidney.

The outlook for recovery of children with Fanconi's anemia is poor. Available treatment provides only temporary control of the disorder. About 10 percent of affected children eventually develop *leukemia* and another 10 percent develop other malignancies.

As many as 80 percent of children with mild, acquired aplastic anemia (and about 15 percent of children with severe, acquired aplastic anemia) recover without treatment within two to three weeks.

For a child with severe aplastic anemia, the outlook for recovery is poor if the disease develops suddenly, numbers of all three types of blood cells are very low, and the child is bleeding or infected when brought for medical attention. In addition, when diagnosis or treatment is delayed, the outlook for recovery is worse than when children are treated immediately after the onset of the disease. Of severely affected young children who receive the recommended form of treatment (bone marrow transplantation), however, four out of five survive and are considered cured.

Without transplantation, children with aplastic anemia are not considered to be completely cured, despite lengthy remissions, unless blood cell counts return to normal. Even during remission, blood cell counts are not usually normal; however, they may remain for decades in ranges that are not life-threatening. The rate of leukemia for aplastic anemia patients is higher than that for the non-aplastic population.

CAUSE

Half the cases of acquired aplastic anemia have no identifiable cause and are called "idiopathic." The remainder of cases of acquired aplastic anemia result from exposure to factors that suppress the blood-forming activity of the bone marrow. Suppression may be caused by certain medications (including antibiotics such as chloramphenicol), radiation therapy, or medication used for chemotherapy. Aplastic anemia can be caused by exposure to both home-use and industrial-use toxins (poisons) and chemicals; for instance, the toxin benzene is a common component of insecticides, petroleum products, and model-airplane glue. Not all people with the same exposure will develop aplastic anemia. For unknown reasons, some children are more susceptible than others.

Bacterial infections (such as a form of *tuberculosis* that spreads through the body via the bloodstream) or viral infections (such as infectious *mononucleosis* or viral *hepatitis*) occasionally result in aplastic anemia.

Fanconi's anemia can be inherited only if both parents carry a defective gene for the disorder. Each of their children has a 1-in-4 chance of inheriting a defective gene from each parent and subsequently developing the disorder.

SIGNS AND SYMPTOMS

In addition to the manifestations of aplastic anemia that have already been described, Fanconi's anemia almost always is marked by at least one of the following conditions (before blood problems become apparent): low birthweight; an abnormally small head; abnormal or absent thumb and outer-forearm bone; an abnormal increase in skin pigmentation indicated by flat café-au-lait spots; squinting; deafness; *mental retardation;* short stature; decreased functioning of the ovaries or testes; slowed sexual development; and structural abnormalities of the kidneys. Siblings may have these disorders without having aplastic anemia.

Adolescent females with severe aplastic anemia may have persistent menstrual bleeding as a result of thrombocytopenia. (Bleeding can be controlled with the administration of hormones.)

DIAGNOSIS

If a child has a severe infection or repeated infections and an abnormally low number of white blood cells, a blood problem may exist. Accurate and prompt diagnosis of the problem and appropriate treatment are essential.

When a child has aplastic anemia, blood tests reveal a depletion of the three types of blood cells. Since a deficiency of all cell elements of the blood can also result from leukemia or a tumor, examination of a sample of bone marrow as well as blood is important.

Both the outlook and treatment differ for acquired and inherited cases, so it is essential that the form of aplastic anemia be diagnosed. A family medical history should be taken, as families with a history of Fanconi's anemia tend to have a high incidence of the abnormalities noted above. All children with aplastic anemia should be examined for indications of Fanconi's anemia whether or not any characteristic abnormalities appear. X rays may reveal abnormalities (such as abnormal kidney structure) that are characteristic of Fanconi's anemia. If no characteristic abnormalities are found, a child's chromosomes should be studied for evidence of Fanconi's anemia.

TREATMENT

The first and most important step in treatment is to remove the child from any causative agent. The second step involves the wise and careful use of blood products. The child's ultimate recovery can be endangered by ill-advised transfusions. Infections are treated with antibiotics. Transfusions and analysis of blood require treatment by experienced hematologists (specialists in diagnosing and treating blood and bleeding disorders) with access to a sophisticated blood bank.

The preferred treatment for severe aplastic anemia is bone marrow transplantation, performed at special marrow transplantation centers as soon as possible after the disease is diagnosed. Without bone marrow transplantation, aplastic anemia may rapidly and progressively become worse, resulting in death within a few months. Children who seem to recover from severe aplastic anemia may suffer relapses years later.

The success of bone marrow transplantation depends upon three factors. The first factor is the affected child's age; the younger he or she is, the better. The second factor is the compatibility of the donor's and the recipient's (the affected child's) bone marrow. The bone marrow of one in four siblings will completely match the patient. Rarely, a parent will be a compatible donor.

The third factor is the avoidance of previous blood transfusions. If a transfusion contains white blood cells with what are called transplantation antigens, the child's immune system might become sensitized to them and later reject the donated marrow. If red blood cell transfusions are absolutely necessary before bone marrow transplantation can take place, related donors are avoided and specially preserved and treated red blood cells are used to prevent sensitization. Platelets are avoided, if possible, because the chances of sensitization are very high.

After bone marrow transplantation, a condition called graft-versus-host disease can be a major problem, particularly if the donated marrow is not perfectly compatible. This disease occurs if the white blood cells of the donated bone marrow reject the recipient and attack major organs such as the skin, liver, and intestines. This disorder may be acute (occurring soon after transplantation) or chronic (occurring later and persisting), severe or mild. Graft-versus-host disease seldom occurs, however, one or more years after the transplant. Because of the possibility of graft-versus-host disease, bone marrow transplantation currently is limited to children with completely matched donors. Research currently is under way to overcome this limitation.

Graft-versus-host disease is not the only risk of bone marrow transplantation. Host-versus-graft disease (or graft rejection), an opposite problem, also can occur. To keep the donor's bone marrow from being rejected by the recipient's remaining white blood cells, the recipient's immune system must first be suppressed with chemotherapy and, in some cases, radiation. Although the suppression of a child's immune system allows the donated bone marrow to be accepted, it also makes the child even more vulnerable to infection for a period of months following the transplant. As a result, the child also must receive protection from infection. For instance, a child may stay in a sterile environment, eat sterile food, and be given special oral antibiotics. Unfortunately, such protective treatment usually exists only at major medical centers and is sometimes

unavailable even there because of great demand. In addition, this form of treatment is extremely expensive.

If compatible bone marrow cannot be found for transplantation, supportive care may be given. Transfusions of specially preserved red blood cells can be given. If severe bleeding occurs as a result of thrombocytopenia, platelet transfusions can be administered. If necessary, platelets can be given to prevent bleeding within the central nervous system. White blood cells, which normally fight infections, are not routinely transfused for a number of reasons. First, even if white blood cells of the donor and affected child are perfectly matched, a very high risk exists that the child's immune system will attack the antigens of the donated white blood cells. Second, transfused white blood cells do not prevent infections in cases of aplastic anemia, and may not be useful in treating infections either, particularly if available antibiotics are effective in combatting a particular infection. The main difficulty is that current technology does not allow the collection of adequate numbers of white blood cells.

In addition to red-blood-cell and platelet transfusions, which only temporarily treat symptoms, other forms of treatment have been tried to control or cure aplastic anemia itself in cases where bone marrow transplantation is not an option. Unfortunately, these alternative forms of treatment have been largely ineffective in cases of severe aplastic anemia. New therapies are being studied continually at major blood research centers.

No measures are taken initially in cases of mild or moderate acquired aplastic anemia except to remove any suspected cause of the disease and to avoid the use of drugs or blood transfusions. Children with mild or moderate aplastic anemia that does not disappear spontaneously may respond at least in part to therapy with androgen (a hormone). For those children with moderate disease who have no prospective bone marrow donor and who need red blood cell transfusions, androgen therapy reduces the number of transfusions required.

For children with Fanconi's anemia, androgen therapy seems to be effective at least initially in controlling the disease. (Androgens may need to be given for an indefinite period of time.) However, side effects such as slowed growth may occur. Bone marrow transplantation has not been used extensively for Fanconi's anemia patients because of increased sensitivity to the preparatory therapy. Other than androgen therapy, treatment for Fanconi's anemia basically consists of relieving symptoms: transfusions of platelets for hemorrhaging and of red cells for anemia. In addition, antibiotics are given for infection.

PREVENTION

Inherited aplastic anemia cannot be prevented. However, parents with an affected child or with family histories of Fanconi's anemia may want to seek genetic counseling to determine the likelihood that subsequent children may have the disease. (See genetic counseling section of *genetic disorders.*)

Some cases of acquired aplastic anemia can be prevented by avoiding exposure to harmful drugs, chemicals, poisons, and radiation.

ANEMIA, HEMOLYTIC

DESCRIPTION

See *Blood Disorders* for a description of the types of blood cells and a definition of anemia.

Anemias caused by excessive destruction of red blood cells are called hemolytic anemias. ("Hemolysis" is the destruction of red blood cells at an abnormal rate.) Destruction of red blood cells may be short-term, long-term, or intermittent. The severity of any hemolytic anemia depends upon the difference between rates of red blood cell destruction and production. The outlook for a person with a hemolytic anemia depends upon the specific disorder involved.

CAUSE

Hemolytic anemia can be congenital (caused by abnormalities present at birth) or acquired.

Each type of congenital hemolytic anemia results from one of three types of defects:

- A defect in the structure of red blood cells. Examples of anemias caused by this type 'of defect are *hereditary spherocytosis,* in which red blood cells are shaped like spheres instead of disks, and elliptocytosis, in which red blood cells are shaped like ellipses (ovals).

- A defect in the production of hemoglobin. Examples of anemias caused by this type of defect are *sickle cell anemia,* in which hemoglobin is abnormal and has a tendency to congeal (sickle), and *thalassemia,* in which the production of hemoglobin is reduced or never occurs.

- A defect in an enzyme of red blood cells (an enzyme is a chemical messenger that can induce changes in other substances and is essential for certain metabolic processes). The most common disorder caused by this type of defect is inherited G-6-PD deficiency, in which the activity of the enzyme G-6-PD within the red cells is greatly reduced. In the most common form of this deficiency, certain drugs or infections can induce episodes of hemolysis and subsequent anemia in affected people.

Each type of acquired hemolytic anemia results from one of two types of disorders: immunologic or nonimmunologic.

- Immunologic disorders are caused by antibodies, either passively acquired, as in the case of Rh incompatibility (see *jaundice*), or actively formed, as in some types of *lupus erythematosus* or *lymphoma* (tumor of the lymphoid tissue). These antibodies attack, reject, or crowd out red blood cells. (For more information about antibodies, see *immune disorders.*)

- Nonimmunologic disorders can be caused by poisons (toxins), such as certain drugs or chemicals, or infections, such as malaria. Exposure to these toxins or infections can cause excessive destruction of red blood cells.

SIGNS AND SYMPTOMS

Signs and symptoms of hemolytic anemia resemble those of other anemias and include weakness, an excessively rapid heart rate, rapid breathing, and pale skin and mucous membranes. Unlike other forms of anemia, there can be a yellowish tinge to the skin of a child with hemolytic anemia because of the color of products (bilirubin) resulting from red cell destruction. This condition is called *jaundice.*

DIAGNOSIS

Hemolytic anemia is diagnosed by a physician, who determines the cause as well as the presence of anemia. The physician takes individual and family medical histories and performs a physical examination. If jaundice and an enlarged spleen are detected, a hemolytic anemia is suspected. Blood tests are taken for several purposes: to analyze the structure of red blood cells; to determine the number of new, young red blood cells being produced, and to measure the level of bilirubin in the blood (a high level of bilirubin occurs in response to excessive destruction of hemoglobin, which is then converted to bilirubin). Urine may be tested for the presence of free hemoglobin and a form of iron in the urine.

COMPLICATIONS

For children with long-term and persistent hemolytic anemia, the anemia may be aggravated by an aplastic crisis, a temporary failure of red blood cell production caused by infection. In addition, the formation of gallstones and occurrence of gallbladder disease can occur at a younger age.

TREATMENT

Treatment varies for each type of hemolytic anemia and for each individual. For instance, some types of hemolytic anemia require replacement of lost iron, others require removal of the spleen.

PREVENTION

Inherited types of hemolytic anemia are not preventable. Anemia caused by nonimmunologic disorders can be prevented if the toxins or infections causing the disorders can be avoided. Anemia caused by immunologic disorders, with the exception of Rh incompatibility, cannot be prevented.

(See also *anemia; hereditary spherocytosis; jaundice; lupus erythematosus; Rh and ABO incompatibility; sickle cell anemia; thalassemia.*)

ANEMIA, NUTRITIONAL

DESCRIPTION

See *anemia* and *blood disorders* for general description.

There are three types of nutritional ane-

mias, which are distinguished by the size, shape, and color of the red blood cells: microcytic, macrocytic, and normocytic. (The suffix *-cytic* means "pertaining to cells.")

MICROCYTIC ANEMIAS

DESCRIPTION

The red blood cells of a person with microcytic anemia are abnormally small and contain insufficient hemoglobin as a result of disorders that interfere with the production of heme (the iron-carrying component of hemoglobin) or of globin.

One example of a microcytic anemia is iron-deficiency anemia. Iron deficiency interferes with the production of heme and therefore of hemoglobin. Anemia occurs only after all the body's stored iron has been depleted and normal physical development begins to be affected.

Iron deficiency is the major cause of anemia during childhood. It is most common among preschool children and, in this age group, usually results from insufficient iron in the diet. Although iron deficiency caused by an inadequate diet is preventable, the high incidence of subsequent anemia among preschool children remains a cause for concern to parents, physicians, and public health officials.

The body's requirement for iron changes with age. Iron deficiency is most likely to occur at times when the need for iron is greater than normal: during pregnancy, during the first two years of life, and during adolescence. (See Chapter 2, "Promoting Physical Health.")

During adolescence, females lose iron when they menstruate and have a greater need for iron for the production of extra hemoglobin.

Microcytic anemia may also appear if iron is not transported from storage in the liver to be used for hemoglobin production or reused for red blood cell production. (Iron cannot be reused properly if red blood cell production is decreased because of infection or inflammation.)

Lead poisoning can also cause anemia by inhibiting production of heme by the bone marrow.

CAUSE

Iron deficiency in newborns can result from acquiring an insufficient amount of iron from the mother before birth. Conditions that can cause this problem include prematurity, severe iron deficiency in the mother, or blood loss from a tear in the placenta (the vascular organ in the uterus that connects the mother and fetus) or from "fetal-maternal bleeding" (meaning that the fetus bleeds into the mother's circulation). After the age of 6 months (2 months for premature infants), iron deficiency results from lack of iron in the diet. Throughout the preschool years, all children grow rapidly and their blood volume increases; they are vulnerable to iron deficiency as a result of an increased need for dietary iron.

After about age 5 and until adolescence, children seldom develop an iron deficiency because of inadequate dietary iron. Instead, iron deficiency is caused by the decreased absorption of iron or, most often, by iron lost through bleeding, whether rapid or persistent and slow. Conditions that can cause blood loss include intestinal parasites and inflammatory bowel disease.

DIAGNOSIS

A physician may diagnose iron-deficiency anemia after a blood test detects small red blood cells with low concentrations of hemoglobin. The presence of signs of pica (in which a child eats nonfood substances) may indicate iron deficiency (see *eating disorders*).

If iron deficiency is probable, a physician prescribes iron supplements to see whether a child's anemia lessens.

To distinguish between iron deficiency and lead poisoning, a test is performed to detect lead in the serum (blood medium minus blood cells). The trait (carrier state) for *thalassemia* can also produce symptoms similar to those of iron deficiency; a blood test rules out one condition or the other. To diagnose anemia caused by blood loss, stool is analyzed to detect evidence of gastrointestinal bleeding. Tests may also be performed on the blood of the child's parents to identify any signs of hereditary blood disorders.

TREATMENT

If congestive heart failure has occurred or is about to occur as a result of iron-deficiency anemia, a transfusion of red blood cells may be necessary.

Less severe cases of iron-deficiency anemia are treated by taking iron supplements at least an hour before meals so that the iron can pass into the intestines for absorption before food in the stomach interferes. (Iron supplements should not be taken with milk.) Even after anemia is eliminated, iron continues to be given so that iron supplies can be replenished. In addition, because iron-deficiency anemia may occur with either lead poisoning or folate deficiency, every contributing cause requires treatment before anemia can be eliminated.

Treatment for anemia resulting from lead poisoning can be a slow process. An affected child should be examined by a physician every one to two months until most lead in the body is gone. If there is also an underlying nutritional anemia, treatment is begun with the help of a nutritionist.

PREVENTION

To help prevent iron-deficiency anemia, a physician may prescribe supplemental iron (usually in the form of iron-fortified formula or iron-fortified cereal) when an infant is 6 months old (or 2 months for premature babies). If an infant is being breast fed exclusively, iron supplementation is unnecessary until any other type of milk or food is introduced. Premature infants and babies who have not yet begun eating solid foods should drink milk or formula that has been fortified with iron.

If taken in excess, iron is dangerous. Parents should never give infants more than the prescribed dosage or begin supplements too early.

At each meal, infants who are not breast-fed and who have begun eating solid foods should receive one food that is high or moderate in iron content. Foods high in iron content include fortified hot cereals, dry breakfast cereals, liver, raisins, fortified bread, and fortified milk. Foods moderate in iron content are meats, beans and peas, egg yolk, spinach, and other dark green leafy vegetables. It is best for children to receive added iron through foods rather than through supplements because the supplements are not always taken consistently.

MACROCYTIC ANEMIAS

DESCRIPTION

Macrocytic anemia is uncommon during childhood. People with macrocytic anemia produce too few red blood cells; those red cells that are produced are abnormally large, but have normal concentrations of hemoglobin. The most common macrocytic anemias are caused by folate deficiency and vitamin B-12 deficiency. Both deficiencies cause anemia by stopping or slowing the development of red blood cells.

Folic acid is required for the production of new red blood cells and for normal physical growth. The body can store only enough folate to last two or three months, so deficiency occurs rapidly if insufficient folate is taken in through the diet. Folic acid is available in fresh green leafy vegetables. Within one month of the onset of inadequate folate intake, folate deficiency may become noticeable; anemia usually becomes apparent within three or four months.

It is common for dietary intake of folate to be barely adequate. Some groups of people have an increased demand for folate and develop anemia unless their diets include extra folate. Groups at highest risk of folate deficiency are newborns (especially premature infants), pregnant or breast-feeding women, and people with long-term hemolytic anemia. (See *anemia, hemolytic*.) If a child has a slight folate deficiency, long-term illness or *malnutrition* can aggravate the condition.

Vitamin B-12 is needed to stimulate the production of red blood cells. For the small intestine to absorb B-12, not only must adequate B-12 be ingested, but also a special protein called an "intrinsic factor" must be secreted by the stomach lining. After B-12 is absorbed, it is stored in the liver, then released when it is needed for the production of hemoglobin.

Without sufficient B-12, too few red blood cells are produced and those that are formed are abnormal. Vitamin B-12 deficiency typically develops over a period of years because the body can store large amounts of B-12. In severe cases of B-12 deficiency, nervous system damage may occur.

CAUSE

Folate deficiency can be caused by an inadequate diet, congenital or acquired intestinal malabsorption, or any condition—such as pregnancy, leukemia, or chronic hemolytic anemia—that stimulates increased production of red blood cells (and, consequently, an increased need for folate). Persistent liver disease makes a child vulnerable to folate deficiency, as does long-term kidney dialysis (mechanical cleansing of impurities from the blood). Folate deficiency may also appear as a side effect of long-term treatment with drugs such as anticonvulsant medications (see *seizures*) or oral contraceptives.

Vitamin B-12 deficiency can be caused by an inadequate diet or insufficient intrinsic factor, both of which contribute to decreased absorption of the vitamin by the intestines. Deficiency of intrinsic factor can be present at birth (a rare condition) or acquired; this condition is called pernicious anemia. Acquired deficiency of intrinsic factor is the most common cause of vitamin B-12 deficiency. A rare cause of vitamin B-12 deficiency is an inadequate diet. Very strict vegetarian diets (without milk products or eggs) cause some cases of B-12 deficiency. In other cases, women with B-12 deficiency breast-feed their babies, who in turn develop the deficiency. Malabsorption diseases, stomach surgery, tapeworms, and certain drugs can also lead to B-12 deficiency.

DIAGNOSIS

Folate deficiency is indicated by signs and symptoms of anemia, test results indicating abnormally large red blood cells, and, early in the course of the disorder, a change in the normal shape of a specialized white blood cell called a multilobed neutrophil. A low level of folate found in serum also indicates folate deficiency.

With vitamin B-12 deficiency, anemia usually develops slowly and is not readily apparent. Blood tests, however, may indicate the presence of abnormally large red cells in the blood. Other indications of deficiency and anemia can be a low level of B-12 in serum and a decrease in the number of young red blood cells. A special test (the Schilling test) determines whether the intrinsic factor is present in sufficient amounts.

TREATMENT

Folate deficiency is treated by the daily administration of oral folate and nutritional consultation.

If vitamin B-12 deficiency is caused by inadequate dietary intake or any other cause where intestinal absorption is normal, B-12 supplements are given orally three times daily. If intestinal absorption is the problem (as in pernicious anemia), injections of vitamin B-12 are given, because taking pills would not help.

Unless the cause of the deficiency can be

corrected (for example, by improving the diet, ending the use of offending drugs, or taking medication to kill tapeworms), vitamin B-12 must be taken for a lifetime.

PREVENTION

Folate deficiency can be prevented through supplementation or diet. Vitamin B-12 deficiency can be prevented if children eat meat, eggs, milk, cheese, and liver, or receive supplements.

NORMOCYTIC ANEMIAS

DESCRIPTION AND CAUSE

The red blood cells of people with normocytic anemia are normal in size, shape, and concentrations of hemoglobin, but insufficient in number. Although most normocytic anemias are caused by blood loss, in rare cases vitamin E deficiency can bring on normocytic anemia. Premature infants are most vulnerable to this type of anemia because they usually have a persistent, mild vitamin E deficiency. The amount of vitamin E that a child needs depends in part on how much the child's body has in storage and in part on the amount of polyunsaturated fat in the child's diet. The more polyunsaturated fat in the diet, the more vitamin E the child needs. Breast milk contains very little polyunsaturated fat, so breast-fed babies are less likely to have deficiency problems than are bottle-fed babies.

DIAGNOSIS

Vitamin E deficiency is indicated by signs and symptoms of anemia along with the presence of normally sized red blood cells, normal concentrations of hemoglobin, and a mild increase in the number of young red blood cells. The level of vitamin E in the blood also may be measured.

TREATMENT AND PREVENTION

Vitamin E deficiency is treated by the administration of vitamin E supplements once a day. If this approach fails, vitamin E is given through injections. Premature infants who are fed cow's-milk formulas can avoid vitamin E deficiency if they receive daily supplements to offset excess polyunsaturated fat found in such formulas.

ANIMAL BITES

EMERGENCY ACTION

Immediately wash out a bite with soap and water. Flush with running water for at least five minutes to remove any saliva. Apply a sterile gauze dressing to reduce chances of infection. Begin first aid if bleeding is heavy. (See section on bleeding in Chapter 10, "Basic First Aid.") Seek immediate medical attention.

DESCRIPTION

Most animal and human bites are categorized as either cuts (see *cuts and lacerations*) or *puncture wounds*. See also *snake bites* for further discussion of bites. In the United States an estimated 2 to 3 million people are bitten by dogs each year; more than half the victims are children. Most bites occur on exposed areas such as the hands, arms, ankles, legs, and face.

With proper treatment, most wounds from animal or human bites heal without complications.

CAUSE

Abrupt behavior toward an animal, such as grabbing or teasing, can provoke a pet to bite. Many animal bites, however, are inflicted by nervous or unprovoked animals that are trained to attack, such as guard dogs. Wild animals are most likely to bite when cornered or frightened.

SIGNS AND SYMPTOMS

The most obvious sign of a bite is the presence of one or more puncture wounds. Symptoms include bleeding, swelling, and pain. A bite that does not break the skin usually results in a bruise (see *bruises).

DIAGNOSIS

A bite is obvious. A history of a child's recent whereabouts and activities and the type of animal involved helps determine whether there is danger of severe complications.

COMPLICATIONS

Bacterial and viral infections are the most common complications or animal or human bites. Infections are easily transmitted through saliva when a victim is bitten or even licked. One of the most common infections is *tetanus.*

Perhaps the most dangerous infection is *rabies,* caused by the rabies virus. The most frequent carriers of the rabies virus are wild animals such as skunks, foxes, and raccoons. Less common carriers are cattle, dogs (domestic or wild), and cats. Squirrels, chipmunks, rats, and mice are rarely infected. There is no risk of infection from housebound pets such as gerbils, guinea pigs, hamsters, and white mice. Symptoms of rabies usually do not appear until 10 days after a child is bitten. They can include drooling, head pain, swelling, confusion, increased activity, paralysis, and ultimately, *coma.* Once symptoms develop, rabies almost always results in death.

Another bite complication, though quite rare, is *osteomyelitis,* an infection of the bone.

TREATMENT

Prompt treatment of bites is important to prevent infections and scarring. The wound should be washed thoroughly with soap and water and then flushed with running water for five minutes to remove any remaining saliva. A sterile gauze dressing should then be applied to protect the wound from infection. If a bite is deep, the wounded area should be placed lower than the rest of the body to slow blood flow. The affected area should be moved as little as possible. The child should be taken to the nearest medical facility immediately.

Unless a child has received a *tetanus* shot within the preceding year, a physician usually administers one to prevent tetanus infection. A physician may also prescribe an oral antibiotic to reduce the chances of other bacterial infection.

A physician must be consulted immediately if a bite is inflicted by an animal. All efforts should be made to locate the animal so that it can be retained and observed for signs of rabies. If the animal shows unusual, vicious behavior, foams at the mouth, is extremely active, or is partially paralyzed, rabies is likely and the animal must be killed to confirm the diagnosis and prevent further injury. If diagnosis is confirmed, a bite victim must receive treatment for rabies immediately.

If the animal has been identified and shows signs of rabies but cannot be caught safely, it should be killed immediately. The head is then examined for the presence of the rabies virus. Again, if the virus is found, a bite victim must receive treatment for rabies immediately. Because many people have a reaction to the antirabies serum, a physician tries to be sure that vaccination is necessary. A child bitten by an immunized and well-cared-for animal does not usually require vaccination. Vaccination is also not required if the animal's history is not known but no symptoms of rabies are present. Incidence of rabies in the area also helps determine the chances of rabies infection (see *rabies).*

If a wound from a bite is large or deep, surgery may be required to ensure proper healing.

PREVENTION

To prevent animal bites, children should be cautioned about dogs and other animals. They should not try to pet or hold animals unless owners give permission. When outdoors, dogs should be kept on a leash or behind a fence. Children should learn to be gentle with animals. They should be taught to avoid teasing family pets or pets in the neighborhood, and never to try to trap a wild animal.

Development of *rabies* can be prevented if a child bitten by a rabid animal receives immediate treatment. To prevent rabies in pets, owners should have them immunized each year.

ANKLE INJURIES

EMERGENCY ACTION

If a fracture is suspected, the ankle should be immobilized immediately with a splint (anything sturdy to prevent movement). Ice packs (ice wrapped in a towel or ice bag) should be applied to reduce swelling, and medical attention should be sought immediately. (See Chapter 10, "Basic First Aid.")

DESCRIPTION

The ankle is the point where the bottom of the shinbone (tibia) meets the rear footbone (talus). These bones are held in place by ligaments (strong ropes of tissue), and moved by tendons and muscles. Injury of any of these parts is regarded as an ankle injury.

Ankle injuries occur in children of all ages, particularly those active in sports. The most common ankle injuries during childhood are *sprains,* torn ligaments, strains, and *fractures.* A sprain occurs when a ligament is stretched or partially torn; complete tearing results in a torn ligament. A strain occurs when a tendon or muscle is stretched or partially torn; a "pulled muscle" is actually a muscle strain.

These childhood ankle injuries are similar to those that occur among adults. However, the possibility of a growth plate (zone of growth near either end of a bone) injury having occurred rather than a sprain must always be suspected when actively growing children are involved. Damage to the growth plate of a bone many cause permanent problems if not treated properly. Injuries range in severity from quite mild, requiring only rest, to severe, possibly requiring surgery for full recovery. Mild injuries of ligaments, tendons, or muscles do not involve tearing; tissues are injured but retain their elasticity and ability to function. More severe injuries, involving partial or complete tearing of tissue, require several weeks rest to regain normal functioning. Fractures usually require a physician's care to ensure proper healing.

With prompt treatment, most injured ankles regain their normal strength and functioning without complications.

CAUSE

Sprains, torn ligaments, and strains usually occur when a child forcefully twists or overstretches an ankle. These injuries may occur while a child jumps and lands in games such as soccer and basketball. Fractures may also occur in this manner, but are more likely when a child falls from a considerable height or is involved in an accident.

SIGNS AND SYMPTOMS

Signs and symptoms of an ankle injury include swelling (due to bleeding around the bony bump of the ankle and throughout the area), tenderness of the surrounding area, often severe pain, and decreased joint movement. Swelling reaches its peak 24 to 48 hours after injury and the skin turns blue-black as a bruise forms. The foot may become discolored. An ankle almost always looks unusual and functions abnormally if it is severely fractured or if connecting ligaments are severely torn.

DIAGNOSIS

An ankle injury is identified by the presence of characteristic signs and symptoms.

At certain stages of a child's development, particularly during periods of rapid growth, the ligaments may actually be stronger than the growth plates; growth plate damage should always be suspected when a child complains of a "sprained ankle." If an injured ankle can bear weight and is only mildly painful, a minor sprain or strain has probably occurred. Any ankle that is quite painful and cannot bear weight is usually severely injured. Abnormal appearance and impaired movement accompanied by severe pain also indicate a fracture or torn ligaments.

Positive identification of severe ankle injuries should be made by a physician. X-ray films may be taken to reveal the exact nature of the injury.

COMPLICATIONS

Even with treatment, a severe ankle fracture may result in pain, limited motion, disruption of normal bone growth due to injury of a growth plate, bone deformities, and failure of a bone to heal. Deformities can also occur if a fractured bone is not positioned properly during casting.

TREATMENT

If a fracture is suspected, the ankle should be immobilized immediately with a splint (anything sturdy to prevent movement). Ice packs should be applied to reduce swelling and medical attention should be sought immediately.

The first step in home treatment of other ankle injuries is to reduce swelling. An injured ankle should be raised to slow the flow of blood through damaged blood vessels. The ankle should be moved as little as possible and an ice pack (ice wrapped in a towel or ice bag) should be applied for 10 minutes. Thereafter, ice packs or cold compresses should be applied at 30-minute intervals, 10 minutes each time, over the next few hours to reduce swelling. A pain-relieving medication may be helpful. Consult the physician for specific recommendations and read discussion of nonprescription medications beginning on p. 102.

In addition, an elastic bandage can be wrapped around the ankle to provide support and ease pain. An ideal combination is an elastic bandage soaked in ice water. The bandage should not be stretched too tightly or it may interfere with blood circulation. When applying a bandage, consult a person trained in first aid about correct wrapping techniques. Ankle pain lessens as swelling decreases. When pain is less severe, a child should begin to move the ankle, gently rotating it in all directions several times an hour to increase mobility. Stiffness or ache is expected during these exercises. If a particular movement is painful, however, a child should not exercise the ankle.

A child should use crutches to walk with an injured ankle. The top of the crutch should reach just below a child's armpit when he or she stands upright. This position ensures that a child's weight rests on the hands, not on the nerves and blood vessels of the armpit, which are easily damaged. A child should continue to use crutches until able to put weight comfortably on an injured ankle. The ankle should remain wrapped in an elastic bandage for support, although bandaging does not prevent reinjury.

With home treatment, pain usually subsides significantly 24 to 48 hours after injury. If pain does not subside and home treatment is not sufficient to restore original elasticity to ligaments, muscles, or tendons, a physician should be consulted.

Severe ankle injuries must be treated promptly to prevent permanent weakness. An orthopedist (a bone and muscle specialist) may recommend casting a special "air splint" to immobilize severe sprains. Surgery is rarely required. Fractures require a physician's treatment to ensure proper healing. Since a fractured bone begins to mend shortly after injury, prompt action is needed to prevent incorrect healing. A physician moves the ends of a fractured bone into place and aligns, or "sets," them. The bones are then immobilized with a cast made either of plaster or a lightweight casting material. A child should use crutches to move about. When the cast is removed, a child should strengthen the ankle through exercises recommended by an orthopedist or physical therapist.

With proper treatment, an injured ankle usually regains its original strength and functioning. A child can slowly begin to use a sprained or strained ankle when pain is almost gone. The ankle is fully healed when swelling and pain have disappeared. A child should not resume vigorous activity for at least a week, however, even if pain has disappeared. Complete healing of a mild sprain or strain requires approximately 7 to 10 days. Severe sprains, torn ligaments, and fractures may take 2 to 6 weeks to heal fully.

PREVENTION

Ankle injuries are almost impossible to prevent. Twisting, straining, or tearing of ligaments, tendons, and muscles is less likely, however, if a child stretches the ankle area thoroughly before vigorous activity. Supporting a previously injured ankle with an elastic bandage may reduce chances of reinjury.

APNEA

EMERGENCY ACTION

Babies or children who are unconscious or turn blue from lack of oxygen require immediate artificial respiration (see Chapter 10, "Basic First Aid").

DESCRIPTION AND CAUSE

For adults, breathing generally follows patterns. Infants, however, often demonstrate irregularity in their breathing; it may be uneven, shallow, fast, or slow. When breathing is both uneven and slow, apnea may occur.

What physicians refer to as an apneic spell or apneic episode is a prolonged pause in breathing, accompanied in more severe cases by a falling heart rate and, frequently, *cyanosis* (bluish skin, lips, and nails, caused by inadequate oxygen in the blood). During an apneic episode, the instinct to breathe is suppressed. In mild cases, a breathing pause is temporary (10 to 15 seconds) and a baby automatically starts breathing again. In more severe cases—if breathing ceases for longer than 20 seconds (or even fewer in small premature infants)—a baby retains carbon dioxide while inhaling no oxygen and may need help to start breathing again. Otherwise, the baby will lapse into unconsciousness. Apnea usually occurs during sleep. In fact, short apneic pauses are a normal characteristic of a certain state of sleep (REM, or active, sleep) in newborns, both premature and full-term (see *prematurity*). Most episodes of normal-sleep apnea, however, are fleeting, and breathing automatically starts again.

Apnea is distinct from periodic breathing, which follows a different pattern. Periodic breathing is characterized by deep breathing for 10 to 15 seconds, a pause for 5 to 10 seconds, another period of deep breathing, then another pause. Pauses in periodic breathing last for a shorter length of time than do those in apnea. Periodic breathing more commonly occurs when a baby is awake; sucking movements and rapid eye movements may be apparent. A baby's heart rate does not slow. Periodic breathing is much more common than apnea and much less serious.

Two groups of infants tend to have apnea. The first group comprises premature infants born before 34 weeks of pregnancy (or gestation). During the first few weeks of life the majority of premature babies tend to demonstrate irregular breathing. The younger an infant's gestational age and the less developed the central nervous system, the more likely the occurrence of apnea. Very small premature babies (born before 30 weeks of gestation) are very susceptible to occasional apneic episodes. Any procedure or condition causing an infant's airway to be blocked may be associated with apnea.

Small babies have limited oxygen reserves. As a result, an apneic episode of, for instance, 30 seconds, may have a greater effect on a smaller baby than a larger baby.

Apnea is sometimes associated with lung disease such as hyaline membrane disease (see *respiratory distress syndrome*). Most often, apnea first occurs on the first or second day of a premature infant's life, and recurs until the infant's original due date is near. Normal premature infants usually outgrow mild cases of apnea when they reach the time they were supposed to be born.

Occasionally, babies born from 34 to 42 weeks of gestation have persistent apnea beginning at the age of 6 weeks or older. This so-called "late apnea" may sometimes be associated with serious underlying disorders such as infection, *seizures, congenital heart disease, anemia, meningitis,* or gastroesophageal reflux (see *hiatus hernia and gastroesophageal reflux*). With treatment of these disorders, or at least with treatment of the apnea itself, spells of late apnea may disappear during the first year as the baby begins to outgrow apnea.

Repeated episodes of apnea for a prolonged period of time may lead to developmental delays or may even be life-threatening. Late apnea that persists may result in either near-miss, or resuscitated, *sudden infant death syndrome* (SIDS) or actual SIDS.

DIAGNOSIS

Premature infants nearly always need to spend time in a hospital intensive care unit.

While they grow and develop in incubators, their vital functions, including heart rate and breathing, are monitored. A heart monitor sounds a warning if an infant's heart rate falls. This warning, possibly combined with bluish color of the skin and low body temperature, indicates apnea.

Late apnea occurs at home rather than in the hospital. Unfortunately, parents often have no warning that apnea may occur. They are not likely to notice temporary pauses in the baby's breathing during sleep. Parents do not usually seek immediate medical attention unless they happen to check on their baby during a severe apneic episode and notice the baby's pale or bluish skin, decreased muscle tone, and unresponsiveness to stimulation by touch.

COMPLICATIONS

Complications of apnea differ, depending on the age of an affected infant, the duration of an episode, the frequency of recurrence, the persistence of the apnea, and the underlying cause.

Reduced oxygen entering the lungs can lead to accumulation of acid in the blood and body tissues (acidosis) and to constriction of small arterial branches in the lungs, producing persistently high arterial blood pressure in the lungs (pulmonary hypertension). Prolonged and excessive administration of oxygen during treatment of a premature infant's apnea may result in retrolental fibroplasia (an eye problem that in its most severe form may lead to partial or complete detachment of the retina and subsequent blindness). The risk of this disorder may be reduced by monitoring the oxygen level in the baby's blood. Severe or persistent apnea can lead to brain damage and subsequent *cerebral palsy*. If a baby suffers a severe apneic episode at home during sleep, and the episode goes unnoticed or artificial respiration is ineffective, the baby could die.

TREATMENT

Treatment of apnea differs, depending on the age of an affected infant, the duration and frequency of apnea, and the underlying cause, if it is known.

An infant under 34 weeks of gestation should be observed in a hospital intensive care unit. If a heart monitor detects a fall in the heart rate to fewer than 100 beats per minute, it sounds an alarm. Gentle physical stimulation—such as stroking the baby with a finger—is often all that is needed for an infant to begin breathing normally again. ("Water bed" incubators, or incubators that rock, may provide continuous gentle stimulation of breathing.) Sometimes, more vigorous stimulation, such as repeatedly snapping the soles of a baby's feet with fingers, is necessary. During a severe apneic episode, particularly after 30 to 45 seconds, an infant may not respond to stimulation by touch. In these cases a special resuscitating bag and mask may be necessary to end an apneic episode.

If an apneic episode occurs more than two or three times per hour, or if episodes are frequently severe enough to require bag and mask ventilation, further treatment is necessary. Lowering incubator temperatures, increasing oxygen, blood transfusions, or medication can all reduce the number of spells. On rare occasions all of these treatment methods fail, and an infant requires mechanical ventilation.

For cases of late apnea, home monitors may be recommended until an infant outgrows apnea or an underlying cause is corrected. Home monitors check both respiration and heart rate.

PREVENTION

Good prenatal care, which lessens the likelihood of prematurity, can reduce the incidence of apnea. Specialized care in a high-risk hospital nursery can help prevent the consequences of apnea.

APPENDICITIS

EMERGENCY ACTION

If a child complains of pain, tenderness, or cramps in the stomach, around the navel, or in the lower right side of the abdomen, and if such discomfort continues without relief for three hours or more, consult a physician or take the child to an emergency room for examination. Acute appendicitis can result in perforation (puncture) of the intestine. It is important to respond promptly to a child's complaint of continual *abdominal pain.*

DESCRIPTION

Appendicitis is usually a sudden, severe inflammation of the appendix, a small branch extending fingerlike from the beginning of the large intestine, or colon. (See Fig. 30, p. 437.) Appendicitis is not unusual between ages 2 and 30; teenagers and young adults are affected most often. (It is estimated that in the United States 4 out of every 1,000 children less than 14 years old undergo appendectomies each year.) Males suffer from appendicitis more often than females, and most cases occur in spring or autumn. Acute appendicitis almost always occurs just once, and surgery is required.

CAUSE

Appendicitis is usually caused by a blockage of the channel inside the appendix. Hardened feces become trapped inside the appendix, which is, in effect, a short, dead-end alley. Inflammation sets in, accompanied by infection, usually fast-developing.

SIGNS AND SYMPTOMS

Pain around the navel is usually the first sign of appendicitis (see *abdominal pain*). After an hour or so, the child may become nauseated, then vomit; *vomiting,* however, does not always occur in appendicitis. The pain often increases in intensity and moves over and down to the lower right portion of the abdomen. That entire area becomes extremely tender to the slightest touch, sometimes even to the slightest movement of any part of the body. *Diarrhea,* loss of appetite, flushing or whiteness of the cheeks, mild *fever,* rapid heartbeat, and increased frequency and urgency of urination may also accompany the later stages of the illness.

Appendicitis in children, however, is unpredictable. Some experience a gradual beginning of illness, with pain starting, subsiding, then becoming more severe over several days. So a parent cannot rely upon severe pain as a foolproof guide to whether a child may be suffering an attack of acute appendicitis. Infrequently, a child may experience repeated mild appendicitis attacks, which subside with or without medication.

DIAGNOSIS

The primary symptom in diagnosing appendicitis is a child's complaint of steady abdominal pain. A physician carefully examines the child, evaluating the painful abdomen and performing a rectal exam as well. Blood tests identify the presence of infection. X-ray films may be needed to try to confirm blockage or inflammation of the appendix.

COMPLICATIONS

If untreated, acute appendicitis may result in perforation (puncture) of the appendix, spilling feces and bacterial infection into the entire abdominal cavity. Peritonitis, a potentially life-threatening inflammation and infection of the lining of the abdominal wall, can follow.

Sterility may sometimes occur for a female who suffers a severe pelvic infection following a perforated appendix.

TREATMENT

An emergency appendectomy, or surgical removal of the inflamed, usually infected, appendix is the standard treatment. Whenever possible, in order to prevent perforation, surgery takes place on the same day that a diagnosis is made. The more quickly a child is seen by a physician, the sooner a diagnosis can be confirmed and, if necessary, surgery begun.

If surgery goes well, as is almost always the case in a modern hospital, recovery is rapid. Children can often leave the hospital within three to five days following surgery. Antibiotics may be given after surgery to prevent or combat infection. In case of perforation, antibiotics are required to prevent or combat peritonitis. Recovery for a child whose appendix has perforated may be somewhat longer, 10 to 14 days in the hospital.

The outlook for children who have undergone an appendectomy is excellent, even if perforation has occurred. Complete recovery from surgery without complications or any lasting aftereffect is customary.

PREVENTION

Appendicitis cannot be prevented.

ARM INJURIES
(INCLUDING WRIST, ELBOW, AND SHOULDER)

EMERGENCY ACTION

If a fracture or dislocation is suspected, the joint should be immobilized immediately. Immobilize a fractured collarbone by wrapping an elastic bandage or other narrow cloth around the shoulders, back, and chest in a figure eight. Bind the involved arm to the chest by wrapping the band around the child's shoulders, back, and chest. For more information on bandaging, see section on broken bones in Chapter 10, "Basic First Aid."

DESCRIPTION

A joint is made of bones held together by ligaments and moved by tendons and muscles. Injury to any part of these joints can occur among children of all ages.

Among children, the wrist is the most frequently injured joint of the arm. The most common wrist injuries are *sprains*, strains, and *fractures*. Most commonly, wrist fractures affect the ends of the long bones of the forearm.

The most common elbow injury is a partial dislocation, called nursemaid's elbow, which most often occurs among young children. This injury may appear to be a wrist injury, because it hinders rotation of a child's arm and causes the hand to appear abnormally positioned.

Shoulder injuries most often include dislocation (which occurs when the end of the upper arm bone is pulled out of the shoulder socket), sprains (which occur when the ligament that attaches the collarbone to one of the shoulder bones is partially torn), and collarbone fractures (which may result in loss of shoulder and arm movement). A shoulder sprain is the most common shoulder injury. Shoulder dislocations are rare except among young athletes.

See *dislocation of joints* for further discussion.

CAUSE

Injuries to the wrist most often occur when a child falls on an outstretched arm. Nursemaid's elbow usually develops when a child is picked up or swung around by the forearms, wrists, or hands. Shoulder and collarbone injuries usually result from forceful blows, such as those received during contact sports or an automobile accident.

SIGNS AND SYMPTOMS

Signs and symptoms of a sprain, strain, or fracture include tenderness in the surrounding area, severe pain, decreased joint movement, and swelling. Swelling reaches its peak 24 to 48 hours after injury and the skin turns blue-black as a bruise forms. Signs and symptoms of dislocation include severe pain and decreased joint movement. A joint almost always looks unusual and does not function if it is severely fractured or dislocated.

A child cradles an arm with a dislocated elbow. The collarbone may be slightly deformed when it is fractured. A dislocated shoulder gives the shoulders an extremely uneven appearance.

If an injured joint can bear weight and is only mildly painful, a minor sprain or strain has probably occurred. Any joint that is quite painful and cannot bear weight is severely injured. If a severe injury is suspected, a physician should be consulted to determine the type and extent of damage. X-ray films are taken if necessary.

COMPLICATIONS

Rarely, severe joint injuries result in long-term pain and limited motion, disruption of normal bone growth due to injury of a growth plate (area of actively growing bone), bone deformities, failure of a bone to heal, and bone infection (see *osteomyelitis*). Dislocated shoulders often redislocate because of stretched, ineffective ligaments and require preventive surgery.

TREATMENT

A child with a suspected dislocation or fracture should see a physician as soon as possible, unless the problem is a recurrent nursemaid's elbow and parents have been trained to treat it. Sprains and strains usually heal with home treatment. Rest is essential for proper healing of all injuries: the more an injured joint is used, the more slowly it heals.

The first step in home treatment of sprains and strains is to reduce swelling. The injured joint should be moved as little as possible. Ice packs (ice placed in an ice bag or in a plastic bag wrapped in a towel) should be applied for 30 minutes. If swelling does not decrease, ice packs may be applied at 30-minute intervals, 15 minutes apart, until swelling begins to subside. A pain-relieving medication may be helpful. Consult the physician for specific recommendations and read discussion of nonprescription medications on p. 102.

When swelling subsides, a sprained or strained wrist can be wrapped in an elastic bandage or splinted to provide support and ease pain. Before applying a bandage it is wise to consult a medical professional, or person trained in first aid, about correct wrapping techniques. The bandage should not be stretched too tightly or it may interfere with blood circulation. An injured wrist can be cradled in a sling to minimize movement. A sprained shoulder should not be wrapped in an elastic bandage, although the affected arm should be immobilized against the body with a sling.

With home treatment, pain from mild sprains and strains should subside significantly within 24 to 48 hours. When pain is less severe, a child can try rotating the joint slowly several times a day to increase mobility. Soaking the affected area in warm water may help relax injured ligaments and muscles and ease movement. If movement remains painful, however, a child should not move the joint, and a physician should be consulted again.

If a parent does not know how to correct a nursemaid's elbow, a physician should pop the joint back into place. Emergency action is usually needed to correct a dislocated shoulder. (See *dislocation of joints* for complete discussion of treatment.)

Fractures require medical treatment to ensure proper healing (see *fractures* for complete discussion of treatment). Surgery may be required to restore severely stretched or torn ligaments or severely strained muscles or tendons to their original elasticity and strength.

With proper treatment an injured joint slowly regains its original strength and functioning. A child can slowly begin to use the joint when pain is almost gone, but should avoid vigorous activity for 4 to 6 weeks after injury.

PREVENTION

Wrist, elbow, and shoulder injuries are difficult to prevent. Nursemaid's elbow can be prevented, however, if young children are lifted under the armpits or upper arms instead of by the forearms, wrists, or hands. Toddlers should never be swung, even briefly, by the lower parts of the arms.

ARRHYTHMIAS

DESCRIPTION

An arrhythmia is any variation from normal heartbeat rhythm. Arrhythmias frequently occur in children and most require no treatment. Occasionally, however, an irregular heartbeat may be a symptom of a serious heart disorder.

To comprehend arrhythmias, it is important to understand generally how the normal heart beats. Contraction and relaxation of the heart muscle, the components of the heartbeat, pump blood through the heart's chambers to the arteries, which carry blood throughout the body. The steady rhythm of the contraction and relaxation is maintained by a group of "pacemakers," or specialized muscle fibers within the heart. The heart's principal pacemaker, a group of muscle fibers in the right atrium (upper chamber) at the sinoatrial (SA) node, generates tiny electrical impulses that stimulate contraction and relaxation of the heart.

The normal heart rate of adults ranges from 60 to 100 beats per minute. The resting heart rate of young children and infants, however, is faster. A normal newborn's heart beats between 110 and 150 times per minute; a toddler's heart rate is between 85 and 125; the heart rate of a preschool child is between 75 to 115 beats per minute. After age 6, a child's heart rate will level off between 60 and 100 beats per minute.

Sinus arrhythmia is the most common irregularity of rhythm among young children and is normal. It is characterized by an increase in the heart rate when breathing in and a decrease when breathing out. The most common abnormal rhythms, however, are those that are either (1) too slow (bradycardia) or (2) too fast (tachycardia) for the child's age, or are (3) irregular because the beats come too early. Under certain conditions, however, a child may be expected to have a heart rate that is markedly slower or faster than the normal range.

The child with a slow heartbeat may in fact have a more efficient heart. Children who are highly athletic are likely to have a slower resting heart rate than normal. Their bradycardias are due to physical training, which allows the heart to beat more slowly, pumping out a greater volume of blood with each beat. The child who is not athletic and has an abnormally slow heartbeat, however, may have a problem with the proper conduction of the electric impulses through the heart muscle.

It is common for a child's heart rate to accelerate in response to fever, exercise, and emotions such as anxiety, excitement, and fear, but an abnormally fast heart rate may indicate a more serious cardiac disorder.

Newborns sometimes experience arrhythmias, especially tachycardias, which often correct themselves during the first year of life. Male infants who show no other sign of heart disease often develop an abnormally fast heart rate. Children between the ages of 8 and 12 may develop arrhythmias that correct themselves with time.

Children born with heart defects are more likely to have an arrhythmia than children with structurally normal hearts. Most children with arrhythmias have structurally normal hearts. Most arrhythmias are not serious. Under certain conditions, however, severe disturbances in the heart's rhythm can be fatal.

Children who experience either extreme tachycardia, with a sustained heart rate of 300 or more beats per minute, or extreme bradycardia, with a sustained heart rate of less than 40 beats per minute, may suffer heart failure, an inability of the heart to pump enough blood to meet the body's demands. If the principal pacemaker, the SA node, stops firing electrical impulses to stimulate the heartbeat and another group of pacemaker cells does not immediately begin sending impulses, the child may experience cardiac arrest and die unless successful emergency treatment is provided.

Another rare and potentially fatal rhythm disturbance is ventricular fibrillation, which occurs when the lower chambers of the heart begin sending out their own chaotic, very rapid beats.

CAUSE

Arrhythmias may be caused by conditions within the heart itself or by external factors affecting the heart rate. Rheumatic heart disease (see *rheumatic fever*) and heart defects present at birth (see *heart disease, congenital*), may cause arrhythmias. Rare causes of disturbances in the heart rate include excessive production of thyroid hormones (hyperthyroidism—see *thyroid problems*) and blood clotting. In excess amounts, digitalis, a drug prescribed to stimulate the heart, may cause irregular rhythms, as may drugs given for other purposes. Corrective surgery performed on the heart or any surgical operation may also produce arrhythmias.

SIGNS AND SYMPTOMS

Often the child with a mild arrhythmia show no symptoms.

The major sign of tachycardia is an extremely rapid heart rate. The child may have a heart rate as consistently high as 300 beats per minute. Severe episodes of tachycardia in an infant may cause a pulse rate too fast to count. The infant may turn extremely pale and vomit. Older children, experiencing a spell of tachycardia, may complain of chest pain or of feeling that the heart is racing. Spells of tachycardia may occur repeatedly over several months and then subside spontaneously. Attacks may occur in infancy and then cease, only to recur in teenage years or later life.

The fainting, dizziness, and light-headedness that accompany a sudden decrease in blood flow to the brain are the major symptoms of bradycardia, caused either by a malfunction of the pacemakers or by a heart block. Convulsions may also occur (see *seizures).

DIAGNOSIS

Since children with arrhythmias often show few symptoms, the irregular heartbeat may not be detected until the time of a physical examination when a physician listens to sounds of the child's heart. The diagnosis can be confirmed by using an electrocardiogram (EKG), a record of the electrical activity of the heart. By using the EKG, simple and complex arrhythmias can be analyzed. Continual recorded tape monitoring of the child's heartbeat during rest and activity has also proved helpful in diagnosing arrhythmias.

TREATMENT

Children with premature or extra beats usually do not require treatment. In general, arrhythmias will not require treatment unless severe. Treatment is usually reserved for children with extremely fast or slow heart rates, shock or heart failure, or those with fainting spells and convulsions.

The primary purpose of treatment for extreme tachycardia is to slow a galloping heart rate. A number of available drugs are quite effective, but because they may produce severe or even toxic side effects, they are administered with great caution.

Other techniques include electrical shock therapy and a number of maneuvers that exert pressure on nerve endings near the heart that inhibit the action of the heart's pacemakers. Children who suffer episodes of tachycardia sometimes learn to manage the attack themselves by gagging, coughing, applying ice packs (ice wrapped in towels or in ice bags) or cold compresses to the forehead, or the Valsalva maneuver (closing the mouth and nose and then forcing air up from the lungs).

When the child with an extremely slow heartbeat is experiencing cardiac failure, drugs that stimulate the heartbeat may be prescribed. Drug therapy for bradycardia is usually only temporary, however, since these drugs themselves may over time cause irregular heartbeat. Children who experience the ill effects of severe, long-term bradycardias usually require an artificial pacemaker.

PREVENTION

Arrhythmias in children cannot be prevented.

ARTHRITIS, ACUTE

DESCRIPTION

Arthritis is inflammation in one or more joints and in their tendons and ligaments (connective tissues). Signs of inflammation include swelling of the joint, limitation of motion, heat, pain, and redness. Arthritis can occur in over 100 different conditions, including infections and blood disorders.

When a case of arthritis lasts less than six weeks, it is called acute arthritis. Infectious arthritis most often affects children less than 5 years of age. In most cases, only one joint is affected, although as many as four joints can be involved. Most cases of bacterial arthritis are treated successfully with no resulting complications. For chronic arthritis, see *juvenile rheumatoid arthritis.*

CAUSE

Most cases of acute arthritis are bacterial in origin, but they may also be associated with *blood disorders,* such as *hemophilia.* Most cases of bacterial arthritis are caused by staphylococcal or streptococcal bacteria, although pneumococcal and gram-negative bacteria may also be responsible. Among children 6 months to 2 years old, the most common cause of bacterial arthritis is *Hemophilus influenzae* (not related to the virus that causes influenza).

SIGNS AND SYMPTOMS

The sequence of pain, stiffness, warmth, redness, swelling, and, finally, some loss of function in one or more joints is typical of arthritis. Limited motion of an affected joint may be caused by muscle spasms and accumulation of fluid around the particular joint.

Fever is usually present, either low-grade and persistent or high and spiking, reaching peaks once or twice daily above 102° F (38.8° C). Loss of appetite and weight can sometimes occur.

DIAGNOSIS

Acute arthritis is diagnosed on the basis of a careful history and physical examination by a physician who notes the signs and symptoms. Blood tests, blood cultures, and analysis of joint fluid are performed if bacterial arthritis is suspected. A physician may order X-ray films of the affected joints. Sometimes a definite diagnosis is postponed until other known causes of signs and symptoms are eliminated as possibilities (see *juvenile rheumatoid arthritis)*.

COMPLICATIONS

Complications in cases of acute arthritis may develop even if treatment is ultimately successful in controlling the inflammation. For example, permanent stiffness may result. Rarely, bacterial arthritis may be preceded by or lead to *osteomyelitis,* which may result in loss of function. In rare cases, children may die from overwhelming infection.

TREATMENT

Bacterial arthritis is treated with specific antibiotics to eliminate the bacteria involved, as well as by removing any pus present in the joint. Physicians choose antibiotics according to which bacteria are present. For example, penicillin or a semisynthetic antibiotic with similar properties is used to treat staphyloccocal or streptoccocal arthritis. Cases caused by other bacteria or disease organisms require different medications. If no organism can be identified, a combination of several antibiotics may be used.

If rapid improvement in the acute joint inflammation does not occur, draining the pus from the affected joint is performed. If a child's hip is involved, surgical opening and drainage, under general anesthesia, must be performed as primary treatment because of the sensitivity of that hip to excess fluid in the joint. If other affected joints need to be drained, a physician can often do this with a needle aspiration (withdrawing the fluid through a needle) instead of by surgery.

PREVENTION

Prevention of acute arthritis during childhood is not yet possible.

ASPHYXIA

EMERGENCY ACTION

If a baby is unconscious, with absent or random heartbeat and breathing, and with bluish, bright red, or discolored (black and blue) skin, cardiopulmonary resuscitation (CPR) should be started immediately. (See Chapter 10, "Basic First Aid.") The infant should be taken immediately to a hospital emergency room, even if consciousness returns.

DESCRIPTION

Asphyxia is a life-threatening condition in which the oxygen level in the blood is dangerously low, the carbon dioxide level is far too high, and the acid level is too high. Sometimes the terms *hypoxia* and *anoxia* are used interchangeably with *asphyxia,* but *hypoxia* indicates only a reduced supply of oxygen and *anoxia* an absence of oxygen.

Asphyxia can result from any severe breathing problem. Severe asphyxia may be associated with unconsciousness. Asphyxia may coexist with *shock,* in which blood flow to tissues far from the heart is diminished. Shock is characterized by cool, clammy, pale skin; weak, rapid pulse; dizziness or faintness; and increased breathing rate. Asphyxia almost always occurs as a severe complication for a sick or injured infant.

Premature and dysmature infants are especially susceptible to asphyxia as newborns (see *prematurity).* Asphyxia can recur, especially among premature babies, due to immaturity of their lungs or to prolonged pauses in breathing *(apnea).*

Asphyxia is the leading primary cause of permanent brain damage or death during the four weeks before and four weeks after birth. The outlook for a child of any age is poor if asphyxia is severe, prolonged, and untreated.

CAUSE

A fetus may suffer from asphyxia resulting from any of a number of causes, particularly anything that interferes with blood flow from the mother or the fetus through the placenta. Placental blood flow may be affected by inadequate attachment or early separation of the placenta; an inadequate placenta due to postmaturity (pregnancy lasting longer than 42 weeks); very low maternal blood pressure; toxemia (a condition in which the mother experiences high blood pressure, fluid retention, and protein in her urine); or decreased blood circulation through the umbilical cord as a result of compressing or knotting of the cord. Other causes of fetal asphyxia include heart failure or respiratory failure of the mother and, in some cases, inappropriate use of anesthetics during labor and delivery.

Asphyxia for the newborn may be caused by any problem in initiating breathing after placental blood flow is cut off at birth. Newborns may fail to breathe adequately if they have suffered from a brain defect or injury, or from narcosis (a deep stupor caused by a narcotic, an anesthetic, or carbon monoxide). Any lung disease (such as *pneumonia)* or structural defect can also lead to asphyxia. Poor circulation of blood may lead to asphyxia in the newborn.

Among infants beyond the newborn period the clearest case of asphyxia occurs in *sudden infant death syndrome* (SIDS). Affected infants are unable to regulate their breathing properly. When they pause in their breathing for too long a time, asphyxia may occur and spontaneous breathing does not resume.

SIGNS AND SYMPTOMS

Signs of fetal asphyxia may occur at any time from a few minutes to a few days before delivery. Excessive acid may accumulate in the blood, lungs, and cells of the body.

After birth, signs of asphyxia are unconsciousness, pale or bluish skin, shallow breathing, *apnea* (prolonged pauses in breathing), slow heart rate, unresponsiveness to stimulation of the senses, and limp muscle tone. However, victims of carbon monoxide poisoning have red or discolored (black and blue) skin.

DIAGNOSIS

Asphyxia is diagnosed by observation of the signs named above and the presence of a recognized cause that could have been responsible for insufficient oxygen intake. A low Apgar score (which rates the condition of a newborn) may also indicate that asphyxia has occurred. Definitive diagnosis of asphyxia is made by measurement of blood gases and blood acidity. Ultrasound, fetal monitoring, and tests of fetal blood (obtained from the scalp through the birth canal) are all used to check for fetal asphyxia.

COMPLICATIONS

In fetal asphyxia, the excessively high acid level of the blood may be associated with a reduction of calcium in the blood, which can lead to decreased bone and cartilage formation. Asphyxia during birth can cause depletion of stored sugar in the liver, leading to low blood sugar *(hypoglycemia).* Asphyxia may also lead to *seizures.* Asphyxia can cause an increase in blood pressure within the blood vessels of the lungs, leading to massive hemorrhaging. Severe asphyxia may cause brain damage leading to *cerebral palsy* or *mental retardation.*

TREATMENT

Emergency treatment of asphyxia in the newborn consists of prompt administration of CPR or of artificial respiration combined, in severe cases, with mechanical administration of oxygen, external heart massage, circulatory support, and correction of acid accumulation. Acid accumulation can be resolved with an intravenous solution of sodium bicarbonate. An intravenous sugar solution, if given promptly, can correct low blood sugar caused by asphyxia at birth.

Cases of fetal distress require that the baby be delivered as quickly as possible while the mother is given high concentrations of oxygen. Immediately after birth, resuscitation may be necessary.

Other treatment is directed at correcting conditions that may cause asphyxia.

PREVENTION

Most causes of prenatal and neonatal asphyxia cannot be prevented. The risks of fetal asphyxia can be reduced through adequate prenatal care, with special attention to those pregnancies at higher than normal risk (involving, for example, a mother who has previously had a stillbirth or a premature baby). Babies should be delivered at a location where asphyxia beginning during labor can be promptly detected and treated. Often, skilled health professionals who have resuscitation equipment available must deliver the baby quickly.

ASPIRIN POISONING

EMERGENCY ACTION

If a child has swallowed excess amounts of aspirin, call a poison information center or physician immediately. If the center recommends that you induce vomiting, use syrup of ipecac (a nonprescription preparation). A child should drink a glass of water immediately after swallowing syrup of ipecac; vomiting should occur within 20 minutes. Immediately after vomiting occurs, consult the center again—or call a physician—for further instructions.

If a child does not vomit within 15 to 20 minutes, repeat the treatment. If vomiting still does not occur, or if the child is suffering symptoms of aspirin poisoning (rapid deep breathing, confusion, unresponsiveness), seek medical attention immediately. A child's stomach must then be washed out by a physician to prevent further absorption of aspirin.

DESCRIPTION

Aspirin poisoning results from swallowing large amounts of aspirin, usually in tablet form. Poisoning most often occurs among children under 6 years of age. Generally, aspirin poisoning is accidental, but cases of deliberate overdose occur among adolescents.

Large amounts of aspirin increase a child's breathing rate, leading to respiratory alkalosis (a loss of carbon dioxide caused by rapid breathing). In addition, the kidneys excrete excess amounts of potassium and sodium, resulting in depletion of the body's supply of these minerals.

Excessive amounts of aspirin also increase the body's rate of metabolism (sum of all complex and physical processes of matter and energy that occur within a living cell). As a result, a child's heart and breathing rates increase and stores of oxygen and sugar are depleted. *Hypoglycemia* (very low levels of blood sugar) may develop. Energy (heat) production increases, and a child may develop a fever. In addition, aspirin hinders breakdown of carbohydrates and fats and increases the acidity of the bloodstream. Liver damage may occur. Aspirin poisoning may interfere with normal blood clotting.

Even though aspirin poisoning temporarily affects many body functions, a child usually recovers fully when given prompt treatment.

CAUSE

Aspirin is removed from the body by the liver and kidneys. If the mechanisms involved become saturated by excessive amounts of aspirin, further removal cannot take place, excess aspirin accumulates in the bloodstream, and aspirin poisoning occurs.

Saturation occurs when a child swallows more than 150 milligrams of aspirin per kilogram (2.2 pounds) of weight. The average children's tablet contains 70 mg of aspirin, and a regular-strength adult tablet contains 325 mg. For example, if a child weighs 100 pounds, he or she will develop signs and symptoms of aspirin poisoning after swallowing more than 95 children's aspirin tablets or 20 adult aspirin tablets. A 50-pound child becomes poisoned after ingesting more than 10 adult aspirin tablets.

Poisoning most often occurs when a small child swallows a large number of aspirin tablets or preparations containing high concentrations of aspirin such as oil of wintergreen (used for treatment of muscle pain). Children's aspirin is often swallowed because it has a relatively pleasant flavor and color. Poisoning sometimes occurs because an adolescent has intentionally swallowed large amounts of aspirin.

SIGNS AND SYMPTOMS

Symptoms of mild aspirin poisoning include rapid breathing, vomiting, fever, lethargy, and confusion (see *delirium*). Symptoms of severe poisoning include *seizures* and *coma.*

DIAGNOSIS

Unless a child is discovered while swallowing tablets or the empty container is found, a parent cannot be certain that a child has swallowed large amounts of aspirin. If aspirin poisoning is suspected, a poison information center or physician should be consulted immediately.

Before aspirin poisoning can be diagnosed, other conditions that cause confusion and rapid breathing (such as *encephalitis, meningitis,* and *Reye's syndrome)* or an increase in body acidity and rapid breathing (such as *diabetes, kidney failure* and *pneumonia)* must be ruled out.

A physician can positively diagnose aspirin poisoning through blood and urine tests. These tests detect elevated levels of aspirin in the blood. Blood tests also help determine the severity of aspirin poisoning.

COMPLICATIONS

See *dehydration* for dangers of fluid loss due to vomiting. Other complications may include temporary *bleeding disorders;* fluid accumulation within the brain or lungs (called pulmonary edema); and, rarely, heart or kidney failure.

TREATMENT

Excess aspirin must be removed from the body as quickly as possible to prevent further absorption (see Emergency Action, above).

Once aspirin is removed from a child's stomach (by vomiting, stomach washing, or binding with activated charcoal given by mouth), hospital treatment of severe aspirin poisoning focuses on restoring normal body functions. A child is given sodium bicarbonate to treat excess acidity and to increase excretion of aspirin in urine. Fluid losses caused by vomiting and dehydration are corrected with intravenous fluids. These usually contain glucose (a sugar) and potassium to correct sugar and mineral depletion.

If poisoning is severe, more involved procedures are used to remove aspirin from the child's body, such as dialysis (a process in which a special machine removes excessive amounts of certain substances from the bloodstream). If a child suffers seizures, anticonvulsants (medication that prevents seizures) are given. Complications such as heart failure and fluid within the lungs require more involved treatment.

PREVENTION

Parents should be aware of a child's curiosity and tendency to explore. Keeping medications out of a child's sight and reach helps prevent accidental aspirin poisoning. Limiting the number of tablets per package and equipping bottles with childproof caps help decrease the incidence of accidental aspirin poisoning.

ASTHMA

DESCRIPTION

Asthma is a condition characterized by *cough, wheezing,* and *breathing difficulty* that occurs when the air tubes leading to

FIG. 19. LOWER RESPIRATORY TRACT

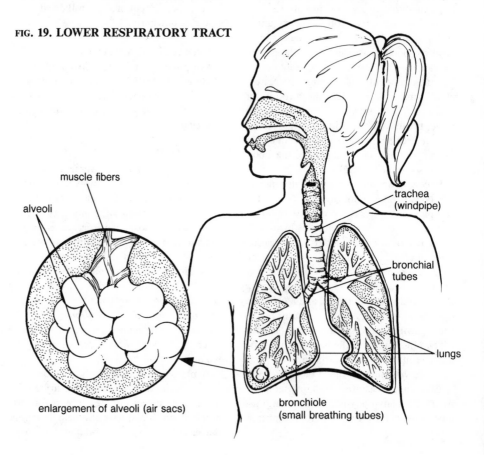

muscle fibers

alveoli

enlargement of alveoli (air sacs)

trachea (windpipe)

bronchial tubes

lungs

bronchiole (small breathing tubes)

and inside the lungs become blocked. More children are hospitalized for asthma than for any other childhood disease or illness. Asthma most often develops around age 4 or 5, but may occur at any age. Most children have only occasional mild or moderate attacks; others have severe asthma all year long, which interferes with school attendance and daily activity. Many children outgrow asthma; others continue to have asthma of varying severity as adults.

An asthma attack occurs when a child's airways become blocked (or narrowed) and breathing, particularly exhaling, is difficult. A child cannot empty the lungs of air, available effective lung space is reduced, and the child can take only short, shallow breaths. During an asthma attack a child constantly feels that not enough air can get into the lungs.

Airway blockage or narrowing can occur in several ways. If thick mucus accumulates in the airway, breathing is impaired. Spasms in smooth muscles lining the airways cause airway narrowing. If the membrane that lines the airway swells, the airway also narrows.

Asthma varies in severity. A child with mild asthma usually leads an active, healthy life with little disruption of daily routine. Between attacks, a child breathes normally and does not always require continuous medication.

Children with moderate asthma often cough between attacks and may not sleep well at night. These children often miss school and cannot participate in vigorous activities. Medication is usually required between and during asthma attacks.

Severe asthma is characterized by continual wheezing and frequent attacks. Affected children often sleep poorly and sometimes cannot participate in even mild physical activity such as climbing stairs. Severely affected children require continual medication and often need to be hospitalized for treatment. Even for such children, however, symptoms of asthma can most often be controlled with proper treatment.

CAUSE

The most common cause of asthma is a viral infection of the lungs and airways, such as *colds* or *influenza*. Asthma also can be caused by sensitivity to specific substances (allergens), such as animal dander, pollen, dust, feathers, mold (see *hay fever*), and certain foods and medications (see *food allergy*).

Asthma can be triggered by vigorous exercise or inhalation of irritants such as smoke (especially tobacco smoke) or fumes. Sudden exposure to very cold air or an extreme change in temperature can also bring on an asthma attack. During later childhood and adolescence, when children are going through both physical and psychological changes, asthma may be triggered by emotional *stress.*

Sometimes it is impossible to identify a specific cause of asthma.

SIGNS AND SYMPTOMS

Wheezing may begin slowly and remain mild or be abrupt and severe. Other symptoms may include restlessness, shortness of breath, labored breathing, *coughing, vomiting,* and *abdominal pain.* Low- or high-pitched sounds may also accompany a child's breathing.

The chest of a child suffering from long-term severe asthma may become barrel-shaped to accommodate overexpanded and enlarged lungs. During a severe, acute episode, a child's skin may take on a bluish color *(cyanosis)* or turn very pale. Heartbeat may rise, and a child may sweat heavily.

DIAGNOSIS

Before asthma can be diagnosed, other possible causes of wheezing must be ruled out. Children under 2 years of age may actually have *bronchiolitis,* congestive heart failure (see *heart failure, congestive),* or *cystic fibrosis.* Foreign objects trapped in the air passage can also cause asthmalike wheezing (see section on choking in Chapter 10, "Basic First Aid"). If no underlying illness is detected, wheezing during childhood usually indicates asthma.

A child's medical history, particularly multiple episodes of wheezing, helps a physician diagnose asthma, as does the physical examination, X-ray films of a child's lungs and airways, and if the child is old enough, breathing tests. A physician may also perform a series of skin-sensitivity tests to check for allergies.

COMPLICATIONS

During an acute asthmatic attack, two complications may occur. A swollen airspace may rupture, permitting air to flow into the pleural cavity (the space between the chest wall and the lungs). An air pocket forms between the rib cage and the lungs, causing sharp chest pain, lung collapse, and respiratory problems. In addition, sufficient pressure may develop from accumulated air to interfere with heart function and cause heart failure.

The second major complication of an acute asthmatic attack is respiratory failure. This usually occurs after a prolonged, severe attack when the child has become very tired from breathing with great difficulty. When this occurs, the child may need mechanical ventilation to maintain an adequate amount of oxygen in the blood, and to exhale sufficient carbon dioxide.

TREATMENT

Treatment of mild or moderate asthma initially focuses on treating underlying conditions such as a cold, influenza, or allergy. To relieve a child's runny nose, cough, and fever, decongestants, cough medicines (available over the counter or by prescription), and a fever-relieving medication are usually helpful. Consult the physician for specific recommendations and read discussion of nonprescription medications beginning on p. 102.

Treatment of an asthma attack begins by opening blocked airways. If mucus is clogging a child's airways, it must be thinned and loosened to ease breathing. Large amounts of fluids tend to thin mucus, and a child should be encouraged to drink plenty of fluids, preferably at room temperature, since cold drinks tend to cause coughing. Breathing moist air may also be helpful; moisture can be added to dry air by using a humidifier or by placing pans of water on warm radiators.

Mild asthma attacks are often effectively treated with a prescription medication that relaxes smooth muscle in the breathing tubes. Some asthma medication can cause side effects, however, such as nausea, abdominal pain, vomiting, heart palpitations, and excitability. To ensure complete recovery, a child who does not experience side effects usually takes medication for 2 to 7 days after wheezing has stopped.

A physician may treat a child with moderate asthma with smooth muscle relaxants. In addition, corticosteroids (artificial hormonelike medications), which reduce swelling and inflammation of the airways, may occasionally be required to control asthma attacks. Administration must be supervised by a physician aware of potential side effects such as heart palpitations, trembling, anxiety, nausea, and vomiting.

To prevent asthma attacks triggered by vigorous physical activity, a child can be given an inhaled membrane stabilizer (such as cromolyn). With its use, children may require medications less frequently. Cromolyn is especially effective for children who are allergic to inhaled allergens or who develop asthma after exercise.

When stress acts as the trigger for asthma attacks, parents should consult their child's physician for possible referral to a pediatric mental health professional. The most effective treatment a child can receive for stress-induced asthma, in addition to relieving immediate symptoms of asthma, is to learn to cope with some of the stresses of childhood and adolescence.

A child who has severe asthma usually requires hospitalization during an attack. Intensive care includes monitoring of vital signs, replacing essential body fluids and salts (lost during vomiting), giving oxygen, and removing mucus from clogged airways by suction. Smooth muscle relaxers and corticosteroids may be prescribed as part of treatment.

PREVENTION

If possible, a child should avoid asthma-inducing substances or situations. Controlling dust, animal hair, and animal dander at home (particularly in a child's room) and frequently changing heating and air-conditioner filters help prevent contact with allergens. Children who suffer severe reactions to pollution or pollen should remain indoors during pollution alerts (usually on hot, still summer days in industrial areas) or windy days during pollen seasons.

Children prone to exercise-induced asthma attacks should not be discouraged from participating in sports. A physician can help select appropriate sports and provide advice and precautions. Children susceptible to asthma caused by viral infections should try to avoid contact with people who have respiratory infections that may be contagious. A child who is particularly susceptible to asthma caused by viral infections may need a flu vaccination every year (see *influenza*).

AUTISM

DESCRIPTION AND COMPLICATIONS

Autism is a developmental disorder characterized by a lack of responsiveness to other people and by deficits in development and use of language. These deficits are associated with severe difficulties in processing and responding appropriately to every day stimuli (such as sounds) and adapting to and initiating changes in environment and routine. Autism is evident before an affected child is 2½ years old and, although some symptoms may become less severe, persists throughout life. Two children of every 10,000 born each year in the United States are affected.

Autism is a behavioral syndrome—a group of specific problems that appear together. Although the way these problems influence a child's behavior varies, the syndrome of autism always includes some degree of difficulty in the following areas:

Difficulty Relating to Other People

Autistic children have serious difficulty forming emotional attachments to parents and other people. This disability is sometimes apparent as early as infancy; a baby may, for example, be indifferent or even averse to being held. In addition to having a continued lack of desire for affectionate physical contact, an autistic toddler characteristically does not make meaningful eye contact with other people, does not respond socially to others by smiling or using other facial expressions, and seems, in general, not to recognize people as individuals—or sometimes even as people. Typically, an autistic child seems to live in a world of his or her own.

As autistic children grow, they tend to become more aware of parents and other familiar adults and to develop some emotional attachments to them. Development of peer friendships, however, continues to be lacking, as is the ability to play cooperatively with others. In addition, autistic children seem to lack a sense of empathy; they are unable to "put themselves in the other person's shoes." While such disabilities may lessen in severity over time, most autistic children continue to have social problems in adulthood.

Difficulty Understanding and Communicating With Language

Language disorders are universal among autistic children. Although hearing difficulties are not a component of autism, young autistic children are often first thought to be deaf. Experts believe that autistic children have great difficulty processing the meaning of speech, even though they hear clearly. Autistic children suffer from long delays in language development or, in severe cases, from a lifelong inability to speak.

If an autistic child does begin using language, it is usually not for communicative purposes, at least at the outset. Autistic children seem to enjoy language for its sound alone. A characteristic feature of an autistic child's early use of language is echolalia, the tendency to repeat the sounds and words of others. While echoing may occur immediately after another person speaks, some autistic children have an unusual capacity for remembering whole passages from conversation or television programs for a surprisingly long period of time.

If an autistic child develops meaningful speech, it is often peppered with grammatical errors and other peculiarities. One common characteristic is a tendency to mix up pronouns; a child requesting an apple, for example, may say "you want apple." It is also common for autistic children to have difficulty remembering the names of objects, talking about abstract ideas, and using metaphors.

The speech of an autistic child tends to be flat, lacking tone, emotion, and other subtleties. When tone does change, it is often inappropriate. Appropriate nonverbal expressions of emotion, such as gestures and facial expressions, often do not accompany speech. All of these problems tend to persist through adulthood.

Difficulty Processing and Reacting to Sensory Stimuli

Autistic children tend to have unusual and erratic reactions to routine sensory stimuli—things that they can hear, see, feel, taste, or smell. A child may, for example, ignore a very bright light but become distressed by the sound of a distant neighbor's lawn mower. Stimuli that other people do not even perceive may prompt an autistic child to become frenetically active or passive and unmoving for long stretches of time. It is possible for an autistic child not to express pain after receiving an injury and not to show fear of dangerous situations. In general, autistic children seem better able to use touch, taste, and smell than vision and hearing to explore their environment—and other people.

Difficulty Adjusting To or Initiating Changes in Environment or Routine

Autistic children seem to have a great desire to maintain sameness in their lives. An autistic child may become extremely distressed over even minor changes, such as the relocation of a piece of household furniture. In addition, many autistic children develop strong attachments to meaningless objects— pieces of string or rubber bands, for example —and become quite upset if such objects are taken away. They also tend to engage in rituals, such as continually touching certain objects in an ordered sequence.

A desire for sameness may also explain why some autistic children have bizarre *movement disorders,* such as frequent, purposeless hand-flapping, *hair-pulling, head-banging,* rocking, whirling, lunging and darting, or statuelike posturing. In addition, autistic children tend to be fascinated by repetitive movement and to be utterly absorbed by spinning objects, such as fans and toy tops, though they are often unable to use toys in an imaginative, "pretend" play.

Older autistic children and adults tend to show a special interest in rote activities, such as memorizing bus schedules or historic dates.

Difficulty Maintaining an Even Rate of Development

The rate of an autistic child's development tends to vary as much as its character does. A child may, for example, sit up at an unusually early age but not begin walking for years. Often, a child's developmental rate in one area is far behind that in another. A 7-year-old autistic child may, for example, be able to dress and undress but be unable to use a toilet.

For a child to be diagnosed as autistic, all of these problems must exist. Other difficulties may be associated with autism. It is estimated, for example, that about three quarters of all autistic children suffer from mild to serious *mental retardation,* which can complicate the syndrome. In addition, about 25 percent of autistic children eventually develop *seizures.*

About two thirds of all autistic children remain severely handicapped throughout adulthood. Usually, the remaining third are able to function more independently because they have higher intelligence and better language development. However, even these children usually manifest difficulties in social functioning and concrete thinking. This is often referred to as residual autism. While some children improve spontaneously, the best outlook seems to be obtained by participation in specialized, intensive educational programs.

CAUSE

Despite considerable research, the cause of autism remains unknown. Experts do not know how the body malfunctions to produce the syndrome. Since autism severely restricts perception and communication, some experts have proposed that it is caused by problems with the brain centers that regulate sensory input and processing, especially of language.

Another question yet to be answered is why autism sometimes appears in conjunction with certain conditions present at birth (congenital). Such conditions include *encephalitis, meningitis, mental retardation, PKU,* retrolental fibroplasia (see *prematurity*), congenital rubella (see *German measles*), congenital *syphilis,* and tuberous sclerosis (see *seizures*). Experts speculate that the same factors that can cause these conditions may also lead to autism.

Medical researchers are investigating the possibility that autism may result in part from genetic factors. It is significant that the incidence of autism is 50 times greater among siblings of autistic children than in the general population. The incidence of other disorders, such as in language, also is higher than usual among families with autistic children.

One fact about the cause of autism has now become clear: the syndrome is not caused by improper parenting. It is certain that a child who is autistic is born with the disorder, that all different types of parents— regardless of their child-rearing practices— have autistic children, and that child-rearing practices have no bearing on the cause of the disorder. The way parents respond to their child's autism can, however, have some bearing on how far the child can go within the confines of his or her disabilities.

DIAGNOSIS

Any child suspected by parents of having a developmental problem should be seen by a pediatrician, preferably one specializing in developmental disorders. Although the signs and symptoms of autism are thought by experts to be evident in most cases from birth, parents may not notice them until the child is a toddler or even older. The majority of children are diagnosed at age 2 or 3, when their language deficits and social difficulties become obvious, especially compared with their peers' development.

Obtaining an accurate, detailed diagnosis for a child who seems to be autistic is absolutely essential. Because the behavioral problems associated with autism are so varied, the syndrome is easily mistaken for other disorders, especially when some problems are quite mild and others quite severe. Parents should be especially wary of physicians who casually contend that their child is "slow" or is "mentally retarded with autistic tendencies (or features)." Although the degree of severity may vary, autism is diagnosed only when all its symptomatic behaviors are present.

The best place to obtain a thorough, precise diagnosis is a university-affiliated developmental evaluation clinic. These clinics are more likely than other facilities to have an interdisciplinary approach; they usually employ a team of specialists who are trained to rule out the wide variety of conditions that can easily be confused with autism. Such conditions include *depression, hearing loss,* developmental *language disorders, mental retardation,* other developmental disorders, schizophrenia (see *psychosis*), and abnormally slow development caused by environmental deprivation. (For information on how to find a university-affiliated diagnostic program, see Chapter 5, "Choosing Health Care.")

Diagnosis of autism can be a lengthy process; a child may be seen several times over a period of weeks or even months by professionals such as a physician who specializes in developmental disorders, a psychiatrist, a neurologist (nervous-system specialist), an otolaryngologist (ear, nose, and throat specialist), and a speech pathologist (a speech and language expert). Diagnostic procedures are likely to include thorough physical and psychological examinations, lengthy observation of the child's behavior, intelligence testing, and hearing and language tests. A child may be hospitalized for various central nervous system tests.

If parents have any doubts about a diagnosis—whether it is thorough or accurate, for example—they should seek a second opinion. In addition, children diagnosed as autistic should be reevaluated at least once a year so that their treatment program can be adapted to their current needs.

TREATMENT

Autistic children may be helped through a combination of specialized education and training. The goal is to teach them how to make maximum use of the skills they do possess so that they can compensate for their disabilities. Autistic children require constant care.

It is extremely important for parents to learn about autism and their child's form of the syndrome. Parents should press diagnosticians and other professionals to explain everything. They should also join the National Society for Autistic Children (NSAC, 1234 Massachusetts Avenue NW, Washington, DC 20005; phone: 202-783-0125), through which they can obtain information on autism, news about research and new treatment programs, and general support.

No universally effective program currently exists for autism. While institutionalization of autistic children is almost never necessary, most experts agree that affected children should attend yearlong day programs starting as soon as the child is diagnosed. In selecting such a program, parents should avoid those that use only one type of therapy or that claim overwhelming success. Parents should be suspicious, for example, of claims that medication can cure autism. No conclusive evidence exists that any medication is helpful in curing the disorder. Some medications, however, may be helpful in modifying certain symptoms that interfere with learning.

As in choosing a diagnostic facility, parents should look for an interdisciplinary program that tailors treatment methods to the needs of individual children. Parents should ensure that any potential treatment program is realistic—that it does not ask more of each child than he or she is capable of achieving. The program should also be able to teach family members how to provide home therapy. To this end, it is essential that parents and professionals trust and respect each other and that they have frequent opportunities to discuss a child's progress.

In general, a good treatment program should be structured and should promote the development of language and social skills. Many treatment programs use intensive behavior modification techniques, which praise and reward children for following instructions and, sometimes, provide appropri-ate punishment for disobeying them.

The newest, most promising approach to the education of young autistic children is home-based. Specialists from a developmen-tal disabilities center spend considerable time with the child's family, teaching family members appropriate educational, stimula-tion, and behavior management techniques at home. This education should be started as soon as diagnosis is made, and supplemented later by enrollment in a day school.

In the United States, federal law mandates that the public school system provide educa-tion for all handicapped children. Too few communities, however, have adequate pro-grams for autistic children. Parents of autis-tic children should join together to discuss options and seek help from authorities. In addition, parents can contact NSAC for ad-vice on promoting an adequate public-edu-cation program in their area. NSAC can also provide information on weekend- and sum-mer-care programs, special residential treat-ment centers for adolescents, and programs that offer care for autistic children while family members take much-needed vaca-tions.

Accepting that a child is autistic can be extremely difficult. It can also be challenging to maintain reasonable expectations of an autistic child and to persevere in administer-ing a demanding home-treatment program. Many families of autistic children find coun-seling an invaluable source of support and advice.

PREVENTION
As yet, autism cannot be prevented.

BACK PAIN

DESCRIPTION
The lower back is the most common loca-tion of back pain. It occurs infrequently among younger children, but becomes more prevalent among teenagers, especially ath-letes. Lower-back pain can appear immedi-ately after overexertion or several hours later. It may be constant or may come and go. The pain can vary from mild to so severe that the child cannot move without extreme discomfort.

CAUSE
The most common causes of lower back pain are muscle strains due to strenuous physical exertion (see *muscle pain);* sprained backs due to sudden twisting movements, es-pecially in sports (see *sprains);* and muscle spasms caused by an injury, especially from sports or car accidents.

Minor backaches can be caused by mat-tresses that are too soft or by poor posture. Children who lift heavy objects are likely to suffer muscle strains and backaches, as are obese children, who carry significantly more weight than other youngsters (see *weight problems). Stress* can cause sharp pain and tenderness in muscles near the shoulders and neck.

Bladder or kidney infections may result in lower back pain. Although uncommon in children, kidney stones (see *urinary tract de-fects and obstruction*) also cause lower back pain. Children who have the flu may com-plain of low backache (see *influenza*), and adolescent girls may experience backaches when or just before they menstruate (see *menstrual pain*), but neither of these prob-lems is serious.

Most other causes of back pain can be traced to problems of the skeletal or muscu-lar systems. Stress fractures of bones are fairly common among athletic teenagers. Dislocations due to sports injuries or other injuries (such as from accidents) occur. Stress fractures and dislocations require im-mediate medical attention. Painful injuries can result when a child falls on his or her tailbone, but these injuries are rarely serious.

Rare causes of back pain among children include cysts at the base of the spine, *arthri-tis,* ruptured or slipped disks, nerve distur-bances, developmental hip or spine abnor-malities, leg length discrepancies, diseases of the spine, and *leukemia.* Tumors of the spine are rare but are frequently identified as a painful *scoliosis,* often with muscle weak-ness.

SIGNS AND SYMPTOMS
Young children who have back pain usu-ally have some other problem. It is easier to identify that problem if other symptoms ap-pear along with the backache. If a child uri-nates frequently, experiences painful urina-tion, or has bloody or discolored urine, with fever, a urinary tract infection may be to blame; the child should see a physician. Sig-nals of a possibly serious problem include

weakness of the legs, back pain extending into one or both legs, upper back pain, or a condition that causes a limp. In these cases, a physician should examine the child.

DIAGNOSIS

A careful medical examination, including X rays, is generally recommended for any prolonged and unexplained back pain.

TREATMENT

Back pain caused by muscle strains or sprains will disappear only as muscles heal. However, back pain can be eased by home treatment, including a pain-relieving medication, rest, and heat. Consult the physician for specific recommendations and read the discussion of nonprescription medications in Chapter 7. This combination is as effective as muscle relaxants, which should not be used unless prescribed by a physician. Heat treatment can consist of a lukewarm bath, hot-water bottle, or heating pad. Bed rest is recommended for children with sprained backs and muscle strains; a pillow beneath the thighs to flex the hips and knees can lessen discomfort. Sometimes back problems are alleviated by sleeping on a firm surface with no pillow.

Medical treatment sometimes includes a brace (fitted by a physician), prescribed for stress fractures or for hip or spine disorders. A physician may recommend crutches for certain back problems to relieve the stress caused by walking. Activity should be increased gradually.

A physician might use low-back strappings or might recommend heat therapy or orthopedic exercises for severe back pain. If intense pain persists, the patient may need to be immobilized by being put in traction in bed. Infrequently, surgery is recommended (e.g., to remove, repair, or fuse a ruptured or slipped disk).

Muscle spasms can bring intense back pain and stiffness. Severe muscle spasms usually last 48 to 72 hours. If no improvement of severe muscle spasms is felt after 48 hours, the child should be examined by a physician.

For kidney or urinary tract infections, antibiotics are prescribed.

PREVENTION

Children should exercise regularly to increase the strength and flexibility of their backs, so they are less susceptible to strains and sprains. Children should also avoid lifting very heavy objects. Many backaches could be prevented through proper posture and adequate support for the back—firm mattresses or well-structured chairs, for example. Low-heeled shoes are helpful in avoiding back sprains.

Simple precautions to avoid back pain from injury include taking steps to reduce the risk of accidents—seat belts, car seats, safety gates, for example. To prevent reinjury through strenuous activity, an exercise program to build up back strength is often recommended.

BAD BREATH

DESCRIPTION

Bad breath is unpleasant mouth odor. It is rare among young children, though common among adults. At one time or another, however, every child has had bad breath. Bad breath caused by poor oral hygiene usually clears up immediately with good dental care; however, if it is a symptom of a more serious disorder, it usually persists until that problem is solved.

CAUSE

The most common cause of bad breath is poor dental hygiene. Mouth bacteria cause tooth decay by breaking down tooth enamel. Severe decay can result in an infection of the tooth (an abscess), and infection gives off an unpleasant odor. Bad breath may also occur when particles of food become stuck between teeth. Food is broken down by bacteria, and this process gives the mouth an unpleasant smell. Breathing through the mouth, a result of congested nasal passages, and coated tongues (associated with illnesses such as *colds* and *mononucleosis)* also cause bad breath.

Bad breath can also be a symptom of a more serious or generalized problem. Local infections of the mouth (for example *thrush,* a yeast infection) and throat (see *tonsillitis and adenoiditis)* can cause mouth odors. Bad breath can also be caused by problems of the stomach and intestines or, more uncommonly, by heavy ascaris (worm) infestations. When a child has problems such as *sinusitis* or *pneumonia,* bad breath also may develop.

DIAGNOSIS

Bad breath is obvious. A parent can examine a child for obvious signs of tooth decay or poor dental care. If bad breath persists and no cause can be found, or a serious problem is suspected, a child should be examined by a physician or dentist or both.

TREATMENT

Most bad breath can be eliminated by regular use of a toothbrush and toothpaste, and careful brushing of teeth, gums, and tongue. Dental floss and mouthwash can also be effective. If mouth odors are not caused by poor dental hygiene, however, mouthwash is useless, since it eliminates odors temporarily but not the cause.

If bad breath is not due to poor dental hygiene, a physician should examine a child for an underlying problem. For positive diagnosis of an infection, a physician takes a throat or mouth culture. Antibiotics may be prescribed for the infection. If more serious problems are found, a physician prescribes treatment accordingly.

PREVENTION

In most cases, good oral hygiene prevents bad breath. To prevent or reduce mouth infections, objects such as spoons or toothbrushes, which children may put in their mouths, should be boiled. Toothbrushes should be replaced by new ones two or three times a year.

BED-WETTING

DESCRIPTION

Bed-wetting (enuresis) results from a bladder-control variation that is not considered unusual or abnormal unless an underlying condition is present. The ability to sense a full bladder and to control urination depends on the development of nerve and muscle systems, which varies from child to child just as height and weight do. Slow development of nighttime bladder control should not be considered a problem unless it is accompanied by signs and symptoms of an underlying condition or affects a child's activities, family relationships, or self-image.

Urination during sleep is virtually universal among very young children not yet toilet-trained. By the age of 5, most children develop sufficient bladder control and toilet habits to avoid accidents during both day and night. For some children, however, acquiring bladder control—especially at night—takes a few more months or even years.

Between 10 and 15 percent of 5-year-olds (slightly more boys than girls) wet their beds more than once a month. Some accidentally urinate every night at exactly the same time; others have occasional nighttime accidents. Some also have bladder-control problems during the day or bowel-control problems (see *encopresis*).

Of a given group of 5-year-old bed-wetters, 15 percent naturally develop nighttime bladder control by age 6, another 15 percent by age 7, and likewise for the next few years. Only 2 percent of all 12-year-olds wet their beds. More than 99 percent of children who wet their beds eventually develop nighttime bladder control naturally. The remaining 1 percent almost always have a developmental problem or physical disorder.

If bed-wetting creates a problem for a child who does not have an underlying disorder, various forms of treatment are available that encourage faster development of nighttime bladder control than might occur naturally.

CAUSE

Bed-wetting tends to run in families. About 70 percent of children who wet their beds have siblings who are bed-wetters, and about 40 percent have parents with a history of bed-wetting. It is believed that patterns of nerve and muscle (neuromuscular) development may be passed down from generation to generation, just as external-growth patterns are.

Some children have neuromuscular problems and poor nighttime bladder control associated with developmental disabilities such as *mental retardation* or *autism*. Bed-wetting is also common among children who suffer from small-capacity bladders, *diabetes, seizures, sickle cell anemia, kidney failure,* and lower-spine disorders, such as *spina bifida.* (See also *urinary tract infections; urinary tract defects and obstruction.*) Some physicians believe bed-wetting results when the bladder is irritated by certain foods, such as dairy products and chocolate. Evidence also exists that babies of low birthweight, including premature babies (see *prematurity*), are more likely than others to wet their beds when they are older. Less than 10 percent of all 5-year-olds who wet their beds, however, are affected by any of these physical factors.

Extremely few children lack nighttime bladder control because of long-term emotional or psychological disorders. Such problems may result, however, if a child's negative feelings about bed-wetting are not alleviated. In rare cases, a single upsetting event, such as the death of a parent, may cause temporary bed-wetting. In very rare cases, children purposely wet their beds to rebel against premature toilet-training attempts; this practice usually ends when a child's desire to stay dry outweighs the desire for revenge. Bed-wetting has nothing to do with a child's sleep patterns, although it seems to be associated with other *sleep disorders.*

DIAGNOSIS

If bed-wetting is causing a child to feel unhappy or if an undiagnosed underlying disorder is suspected, a physician should be consulted. (Difficulty with daytime as well as nighttime bladder control is often an indication of an underlying problem if a child is toilet-trained and more than 5 years old.)

The goal of diagnosis is to detect or rule out any underlying disorder causing bed-wetting. A physician bases the diagnosis on a child's medical history, a physical examination (with particular attention to the lower abdomen and genital area), and an analysis of the child's urine (to detect infection or diabetes). It is helpful for parents to tell the physician details such as when the child was toilet-trained, how often accidents occur, and whether they tend to occur at the same time each night. In addition, symptoms such as lack of daytime bladder control or complaints about painful urination should be mentioned. The physician may also want to know how many times a day a child urinates as well as details about such things as the force of the urinary stream. Such information may indicate that a child has a physical disorder, such as a small bladder, blocked urinary tract, or urinary tract infection. If a child has had many urinary tract infections or if the force of the urinary stream is abnormal, a physician may recommend X-ray films, hoping to detect a cause.

COMPLICATIONS

No complications are associated with bed-wetting per se. However, negative family attitudes can lead to problems. If, for example, bed-wetting is viewed by a family as a bad habit that is the child's fault, the child is likely to experience anxiety and embarrassment (see Chapter 3, "Promoting Mental Health"). If family members are openly angry with or taunt a child, more serious psychological and family problems can result.

TREATMENT AND PREVENTION

In clear and simple language, parents should explain to a child that bed-wetting, though not his or her fault, is a nuisance because it causes discomfort. Parents should not complain about washing sheets or any other inconvenience not directly related to the child.

In an effort to prevent wet nights, parents should encourage urination at bedtime and should discourage the child from drinking large amounts of fluid during the evening. It is a good idea, however, for a child who will be home most of the day to drink large amounts of fluid in the morning and early afternoon and then to practice controlling urination. If a child has a small bladder, drinking large amounts of liquid is also helpful because it stretches the bladder and increases its capacity.

Children who have small bladders should be encouraged to wake up and go to the toilet in the middle of the night. Lifting a sleeping child out of bed and bringing him or her to the toilet usually does nothing but prevent the bed from becoming wet that night. Parents are usually able to wake a child who is more than 6 years old, so that the child is fully conscious of walking to and using the toilet. If, just before bedtime, parents and child discuss the child's intention to wake up and use the bathroom, he or she may wake up automatically in the middle of the night. A light should be left on in the bathroom for encouragement and safety.

After dry nights, a child should be rewarded with praise and physical expressions of affection from everyone in the family. Putting a star or some other symbol on a calendar is a good reward as well as an incentive for more dry nights. Almost all bedwetters feel ashamed after wet nights. Everyone in the family should sympathize with the child after these nights, praising him or her for trying and offering reassurance that bed-wetting will eventually be overcome. Telling a child about any other family bedwetters who eventually developed bladder control is often a source of great relief and encouragement.

A toilet-trained child who wets the bed regularly should not be forced to wear diapers, plastic pants, or any other clothing that seems "babyish." Wearing two pairs of underpants helps prevent wetness from spreading on the bed. Mattresses can be protected with a plastic cover or a vinyl mattress pad.

Having a child participate in the clean-up procedure sometimes increases a child's sense of control over bed-wetting. A towel and an extra set of underpants and pajamas can be kept by the bed so that if the child wakes up in the middle of the night, he or she can change clothes and lay the towel over the wet spot without disturbing anyone else.

If these approaches are unsuccessful for a child who feels unhappy about bed-wetting, consultation with a physician may be helpful. A physician can choose an appropriate form of treatment on the basis of diagnostic procedures, information about the child's bed-wetting and urination habits, and the child's age. When a physical disorder underlies bed-wetting, a physician may refer a child to a urologist (a urinary system specialist). If an emotional disorder is suspected, referral may be made to a psychologist, psychiatrist, or other mental health professional. Urinary problems can often be corrected with medication or surgery; the outlook for other underlying disorders varies.

If a physician determines that bed-wetting has something to do with the small size of a child's bladder, exercises to stretch the bladder may be advised. A physician and child may also discuss bladder control and how to become more sensitive to the need to urinate. Some children can be taught to hypnotize themselves before bedtime so that they can wake upon sensing a full bladder. If a physician believes that certain bladder irritants are causing bed-wetting, a special diet may be recommended.

In certain cases, moisture-sensing devices are attached to a child's underpants, and at the first signs of wetness an alarm attached on or near the neck of a child's pajamas sound. Many children begin to wake up and control further urination after using an alarm for just a couple of months. Following through consistently for the necessary length of time may prove difficult if a family's sleep patterns are disrupted by the alarm.

It is common for an initial treatment program to be successful only temporarily, especially for older children. Any recurrence of bed-wetting should not be discouraging, however; the second round of treatment is often permanently successful. Carefully designed behavior management programs produce success for about 85 percent of children who work with a health professional.

If bed-wetting does not respond to treatment, individual or family counseling may be a helpful measure of support. There is every reason for families to stay optimistic that bed-wetting will eventually disappear. Time is the most reliable cure.

BILIARY ATRESIA

DESCRIPTION

Biliary atresia is a severe, often fatal defect in the network of small tubes (ducts) that carry bile through and away from the liver, where it is produced. This defect occurs once in every 25,000 live births; twice as many girls as boys are affected.

Normally, tiny ducts in the liver carry bile, a thin yellow fluid, from liver cells, where it is produced, to larger ducts. These ducts empty into the common bile duct, which connects the liver to the duodenum, the beginning of the small intestine.

When bile ducts are absent, underdeveloped, or malfunctioning, bile backs up in the liver with two harmful results. First, waste substances in the bile, normally excreted from the liver, cannot pass through the common bile duct into the intestines for elimination from the body. Second, fatty foods cannot be digested completely. A newborn, therefore, cannot obtain full benefit from food as it moves through the intestinal tract.

If bile outflow from the liver is blocked completely, substances normally excreted in the bile gradually back up and accumulate in the blood as it circulates through the liver. One of these substances is bilirubin, a major waste product from the breakdown of red blood cells. When enough bilirubin accumulates in the infant's blood, the result is *jaundice,* a yellowing of the skin, mucous membranes, and whites of the eyes. Bilirubin and other waste products increasingly clog the tiny ducts inside the liver, obstructing bile flow. If unrelieved for an extended time,

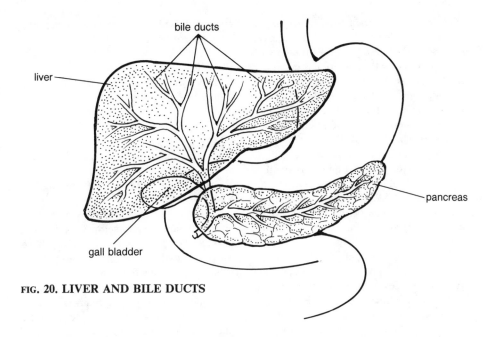

bile ducts

liver

pancreas

gall bladder

FIG. 20. LIVER AND BILE DUCTS

this obstruction results in enlargement of the liver and such extensive liver cell destruction (cirrhosis) that a child dies.

One surgical procedure can provide temporary relief, but unless liver transplantation can be performed, few children who suffer from biliary atresia live beyond childhood.

CAUSE

For many years biliary atresia was thought to be caused by a congenital malformation. Research has proved this view incorrect, but a definite cause has not yet been identified. It is currently believed that the disease may be the result of a viral blood infection (perhaps contracted in the uterus), a metabolic defect, or a biological poison (toxin) present in bile duct cells.

SIGNS AND SYMPTOMS

Jaundice occurs 3 to 6 weeks after birth. The liver becomes enlarged and feels firm to a physician's touch. Bilirubin levels, measured by a blood test, climb steadily after the first 2 months of life. The abdomen becomes swollen and is occasionally tender to the touch. The great majority of infants with biliary atresia have stools that are sticky, resembling putty. Such stools are white, light gray, or tan, indicating an absence or deficiency of bile pigments. Conversely, urine is caramel-colored, like tea or root beer, indicating an excessive amount of bile pigments (bilirubin).

In the first 6 months, some infants may look well otherwise, but their skin, mucous membranes, and eyes remain deep yellow, even light bronze. General itchiness may occur because of accumulation of bile salts in the skin.

In the second 6 months of life, nutritional deficiencies and problems with blood chemistry become severe. Growth may no longer be possible. Because of a lack of adequate protein absorption, swelling around the lungs, heart, and gastrointestinal tract may occur. By their first birthday, children with biliary atresia are generally in declining health and appear weak and irritable.

DIAGNOSIS

Biliary atresia is diagnosed by a physician's examination and evaluation of a child's history and signs and symptoms. Prolonged jaundice (quite different from the temporary jaundice often found in newborns), low weight, and retarded growth are common indications of biliary atresia. Blood tests detect excessive levels of bilirubin in the blood and often reveal moderate anemia (low levels of red blood cells). In many cases exploratory surgery is the only way to make a definite diagnosis of biliary atresia.

TREATMENT AND COMPLICATIONS

Surgery is the only means of correcting

Biliary Atresia **193**

biliary atresia. The sooner the surgery is performed, the better the chances of success. If successful, the surgery relieves the obstruction, but whether the condition is cured cannot be predicted. Unfortunately, because of complications that develop later, only a small number of those children who do have corrective surgery live beyond childhood.

Infants who have a clear portion of the common bile duct between the liver and the duodenum (the first portion of the small intestine) may undergo surgery. During this operation, a child's duodenum is connected directly to the base of the liver, where the network of internal bile ducts delivers the bile.

After successful surgery, bile flow may begin, jaundice and itching subside, and growth and development resume. But for about half of these children progressive inflammation of the bile ducts occurs later regardless of precautions and care. Even for the other 50 percent—children whose surgery is successful and whose external bile ducts remain free of inflammation—internal bile duct inflammation often occurs later, leading eventually to cirrhosis.

Another surgical alternative is liver transplantation, a procedure available at several pediatric medical centers in the United States. Transplantation replaces the diseased liver with a healthy one donated by a child of approximately the same age and weight. Before any child with biliary atresia is selected to receive a liver transplant, highly specialized examinations and tests are required. These are designed to evaluate general health, blood chemistry, and immune characteristics. Physicians can then weigh the chances of a successful operation should a donated liver become available for transplantation.

An infant whose biliary atresia recurs and for whom liver transplantation is not a possibility can be made more comfortable and given increased mobility with the help of various supplements and medications. Vitamin K promotes clotting of the blood and may delay the onset of internal bleeding. Vitamin D prevents *rickets* and bending or permanent distortion of the bones. Antihistamines and starch baths may relieve itching. By reducing salt in their diet and taking medications that increase urine production (diuretics), children with biliary atresia may be relieved of fluid accumulation in their abdominal cavities (ascites) that can make walking difficult. Medication, however, provides short-term relief only.

PREVENTION
Biliary atresia, as yet, cannot be prevented.

BIRTHMARKS

DESCRIPTION AND SIGNS AND SYMPTOMS
By definition, birthmarks are present at birth, although they sometimes are not fully obvious until childhood or adolescence. They are divided into two categories: pigmentary (including those that have no color) and vascular. Most birthmarks are harmless. Occasionally, their presence may be troublesome cosmetically, may indicate a serious underlying disease, or may be precursors of a cancer called melanoma. Some birthmarks fade over time, while others persist for life. Pigmented birthmarks may be caused by excess numbers of melanocytes, the cells that produce the skin's pigment (melanin), or by excess production of melanin by a normal number of melanocytes.

Pigmented Birthmarks
Nevocellular Nevi Nevocellular nevi (NCN) may be acquired or congenital. In general, acquired NCN are harmless pigmented growths caused by an increased number of special melanocytes, called nevomelanocytes. The majority of older children and adolescents have at least one nevus which developed after the first few years of life.

Approximately 1 percent of infants have a nevocellular nevus at birth (congenital). Congenital nevi are usually small, although in rare cases (approximately 1 out of every 20,000 to 1 out of every 500,000 newborns), they may be quite large (called "gigantic" or "garment" NCN). Small congenital nevi are round or oval, slightly raised, and light to dark brown in color. Gigantic congenital nevi often have a hairy, irregular or lobulated surface; they also may itch.

When a child has a congenital gigantic NCN, the risk of developing melanoma is high, perhaps 1 out of every 10 cases over a lifetime. A significant risk of melanoma also exists for small congenital nevi—as high as 5 percent by age 60. In cases of small congenital nevi, melanoma does not usually develop until a child reaches puberty. However, congenital nevi that are very darkly or irregularly pigmented may have an increased risk for problems before puberty. Very large congenital nevi have a markedly increased risk of developing melanoma even in the first several years of life.

Mongolian Spots Mongolian spots are present at birth in about 90 percent of black and Oriental infants. They result from overproduction of melanin by active melanocytes deep in the skin. These harmless spots are flat, smooth, and blue-gray, and usually appear on the buttocks, lower back, or shoulders. More than one Mongolian spot may be present, and they may be fairly small in size or cover large areas. Mongolian spots usually disappear within the first five years of life but may persist into adulthood.

Café-au-lait Spots Café-au-lait spots are small, flat, well-defined, tan spots that are present at birth or appear during early infancy and childhood. They are more common among black children than among white children and are caused by increased melanin in the skin. Café-au-lait spots usually appear individually and may appear anywhere on the body.

The presence of one or two café-au-lait spots is common and does not indicate an underlying problem. The presence of three or more café-au-lait spots may indicate an underlying medical problem, such as *neurofibromatosis* (a condition in which nerve cell tumors grow anywhere in the body or on the skin surface). Additional diagnostic factors are required to make a diagnosis of neurofibromatosis. Café-au-lait spots have no malignant potential.

Other Pigmented Birthmarks Epithelial nevi occur because of structural defects of the skin. They are usually harmless, hairless, linear marks that can appear anywhere on the body. These birthmarks are raised, tan or brown in color, and may be large or small.

Becker's nevi are brown spots covered by coarse hair, often mistaken for giant congenital nevi. They most often occur on the chest or back and usually appear after the first 10 years of life. After a child reaches puberty, these brown areas become increasingly hairy. Unlike gigantic congenital nevi, however, these pigmented spots are not precursors of melanoma.

Like congenital nevi, acquired dysplastic melanocytic nevi may be precursors of mela-noma. These pigmented nevi usually develop around the time of puberty. They are raised and irregularly shaped with poorly defined borders; they are usually large in size and darkly or irregularly pigmented. Dysplastic melanocytic nevi are composed of many structurally unusual melanocytes. Dysplastic melanocytic nevi often occur in families, especially in families with one or more members with melanoma.

White Birthmarks White birthmarks are the result of malfunctioning melanocytes that do not produce melanin. They are frequently associated with serious medical conditions. For example, flat white patches occur on almost 90 percent of infants with tuberous sclerosis. (Tuberous sclerosis is a rare genetic disease characterized by *seizures* and *mental retardation.*) These patches may be small or large and are usually shaped like a thumbprint, an oval leaf, or a confetti spot. A white spot present at birth may also indicate a "skin-only" condition not associated with an underlying medical problem.

Vascular Birthmarks

There are two types of vascular birthmarks: hemangiomas and vascular malformations. Hemangiomas are common, abnormal growths of infancy that characteristically increase in size rapidly and then begin to shrink after several years; they are usually harmless and usually disappear completely. Vascular malformations are structural errors of vascular development and formation; in severe cases, they may be associated with abnormalities of growth, infection, and dysfunction.

Hemangiomas Hemangiomas, also called strawberry birthmarks, usually appear during the second to fourth week of life, but may be present at birth. By 1 year of age, approximately 12 percent of all infants have a hemangioma. They can occur in several areas of the body at the same time, a rare condition called hemangiomatosis, which may affect the gastrointestinal tract (the esophagus, stomach, and intestines), the liver, the central nervous system (the brain, spinal cord, and their protective covering, the meninges), and the lungs, as well as the skin.

A hemangioma first appears as a pale spot or reddened swelling surrounded by a ring of pale skin. It then grows rapidly to form a raised, bright red mass. If a hemangioma develops below the skin surface, its presence is indicated by swelling with normal or slightly bluish overlying skin. Rapidly growing surface hemangiomas may develop ulceration, but bleeding rarely occurs.

Hemangiomas usually begin to shrink before the first 8 to 10 months of life. Shrinking begins at the center of the hemangioma and is indicated by a change in color from the original bright red to a deeper cherry red. The surface of the hemangioma turns gray, and white flecks can be seen on close inspection. As the interior of the hemangioma shrinks, the surface loses its smoothness and becomes wrinkled. Approximately 50 percent of all hemangiomas disappear by age 5; another 40 percent are usually gone by age 7.

When shrinking of a small hemangioma is complete, the skin involved may look completely normal or it may be slightly wrinkled. The skin may not regain its original elasticity, and a layer of fatty tissue may be visible under the skin surface.

Vascular Malformations Vascular malformations are always congenital, although they may not become obvious until several months after birth. They are structural problems, errors of vessel formation which occur during early pregnancy. Capillaries (tiny blood vessels), arteries (vessels that take blood away from the heart), veins (vessels that take blood to the heart), and lymphatics (vessels that circulate lymph, a clear liquid involved in immunity) may be abnormal in a vascular malformation. These malformations grow with the child; they also may enlarge with changes in hormone levels, such as during puberty or pregnancy, or blood flow. Vascular malformations can also enlarge after injury to the involved area. Some vascular malformations are associated with bone overgrowth.

Port-wine stains are vascular malformations that usually appear on the face, trunk, arms, or legs. These birthmarks are initially pink but gradually deepen to a dark red as an infant grows; occasionally they lighten in color instead. When an infant cries, has a fever, or is exposed to high environmental temperatures, port-wine stains further deepen in color. Extensive port-wine stains usually do not fade; during adulthood, they become purple and the stained skin may become raised, bumpy, and loose. These birthmarks are usually harmless but may indicate the presence of a deeper vascular disorder.

Another common vascular birthmark, called a stork bite or a salmon patch, is a harmless, flat, irregularly outlined pink area on the neck, forehead, or eyelids. Stork bites on the forehead or eyelid usually fade by an infant's first birthday. Stork bites on the back of the neck may persist indefinitely for half of affected children. At birth, stork bites may also occur over the bridge of the nose or upper lip.

DIAGNOSIS

Birthmarks are identified by their appearance and duration, and a child's age. Some white or tan birthmarks may not be clearly visible at birth but can be identified by examination under black light.

At birth, newborns are usually examined for the presence, number, and location of café-au-lait spots, pigmented nevi, and vascular lesions.

COMPLICATIONS

If a child breaks the skin of a birthmark by scratching or other trauma, it may become infected.

Occasionally, extensive pigmented birthmarks may be associated with problems of the skeletal system, eyes, teeth, or central nervous system.

Pigmented birthmarks may be troublesome cosmetically.

If hemangiomas interfere with vision, breathing, functioning of any internal organs, or are troublesome cosmetically, a physician should see the infant.

TREATMENT

In general, hemangiomas do not require treatment; they disappear by themselves, leaving only a faint skin change. Hemangiomas that develop sores during their rapid growth phase usually require medical attention. If these birthmarks interfere with the functioning of body structures, cortisone may be prescribed to hasten shrinking. When shrinking is completed, plastic surgery may be desired to correct wrinkled skin. Sometimes hemagiomas are removed surgically before a child goes to school.

Not all vascular malformations require treatment. If prescribed, treatment is highly individualized and based on the extent of the malformation, the degree to which blood flow is impaired, and the nature of problems resulting from the malformation.

Café-au-lait spots and Mongolian spots are harmless and require no treatment. Many physicians recommend evaluation for removal of all congenital nevi to avoid the possibility of melanoma (see *cancer).* Since small congenital nevi do not lead to melanoma until puberty, a physician may decide to observe the birthmark until it can safely be removed during late childhood. If a congenital nevus has very dark pigmentation or an uneven surface, however, a physician may decide to remove it during infancy. Very large congenital nevi are frequently removed in the first year or two of life. Appropriate time for removal depends on the congenital mole's appearance, size, and location, and the health of the child.

PREVENTION
Birthmarks cannot be prevented.

BLEEDING DISORDERS

EMERGENCY ACTION
If a child experiences prolonged, excessive, or unexpected bleeding, seek immediate medical attention. For emergency measures, see Chapter 10, "Basic First Aid."

DESCRIPTION
Children with bleeding disorders experience more prolonged, excessive, or unexpected bleeding than normal children. For instance, the socket of an extracted tooth may begin to bleed 4 to 6 hours after the tooth is removed. A joint may swell with blood following a minor fall. Bruises may form too easily following minor bumps. A cut may begin bleeding again a few hours after being stitched, or may bleed excessively at the time of injury.

Bleeding disorders usually result from one of three major causes. One cause involves an abnormality in the quantity or quality (or both) of one of the blood proteins—also called blood factors—responsible for the formation of blood clots (semisolid clumps of blood that help stop bleeding). The most common of these factor abnormalities is known as *hemophilia*. A second cause involves an abnormality in the quantity of the platelets, the specialized blood cells that initiate the formation of a blood clot and stop bleeding from damaged blood vessels. Platelet abnormalities are called thrombocytopenias. The third bleeding disorder, known as Von Willebrand's disease, is relatively common and involves both an abnormality in the quality of the platelets and a clotting factor abnormality. However, Von Willebrand's disease usually takes a mild form. In rare cases, blood platelets are extremely sensitive to aspirin, and the child is particularly susceptible to blood-clotting problems when aspirin is given. (This condition is not the same as *aspirin poisoning*.)

Another condition that can cause blood-clotting problems among certain susceptible children is vitamin-K deficiency. Vitamin K helps stimulate the production of substances necessary for blood clotting. Normally, vitamin K is released from foods by the action of bacteria and is absorbed by the intestines and stored in body fat. As a result, the normal person would have insufficient vitamin K only if his or her diet were sorely lacking in the vitamin. Vitamin K is found in green, leafy vegetables as well as in cabbage, cauliflower, peas, potatoes, liver, and cereals.

Supplementary vitamin K is needed by children who have been taking antibiotics, especially sulfa drugs, for a prolonged time period, as long-term use of antibiotics can destroy the intestinal bacteria that normally release vitamin K from food. In addition, newborn babies and children with impaired fat absorption (see *malabsorption), cancer,* kidney disease, liver disease, *jaundice,* bowel diseases, or chronic *diarrhea* need extra vitamin K because their bodies either cannot absorb vitamin K or cannot use it efficiently.

The severity of each bleeding disorder varies. Depending on the effectiveness of treatment, severity can range from no practical consequences to crippling. Even for one child, the severity of symptoms can fluctuate over time.

See also *blood disorders.*

CAUSE
Children with thrombocytopenia may have reduced numbers of platelets as a result of reaction to drugs or infection. More often the cause is unknown and the deficiency of platelets is called idiopathic thrombocytopenic purpura (ITP). (Idiopathic means "of unknown origin.") ITP does not appear to be inherited and often improves without treatment.

Von Willebrand's disease is an inherited disorder. A baby can inherit Von Willebrand's disease if one parent has it and passes along the defective gene. Each child of an affected parent has a 50-percent chance of inheriting the disorder. However, the severity of the disease may differ from parent to child (see *genetic disorders).*

Aspirin irreversibly affects an enzyme in

blood platelets so that platelets cannot perform their usual function of stopping bleeding and initiating clotting. (An enzyme is a chemical messenger that can induce changes in other substances and is essential for certain metabolic processes.) However, new platelets that the body routinely produces are unaffected unless they, in turn, are exposed to aspirin.

Vitamin-K deficiency is an acquired blood-clotting disorder, resulting from insufficient dietary vitamin K to meet the extra needs of a child with illnesses such as kidney disease or jaundice.

See also *hemophilia.*

SIGNS AND SYMPTOMS

Platelet abnormalities associated with thrombocytopenia are characterized by easy bruising and prolonged, excessive bleeding following injury. Bleeding can usually be observed in the skin, in the mouth, and from the rectum. Among adolescent girls, heavy menstrual periods may be the first sign of a platelet problem.

Bleeding in Von Willebrand's disease is usually expressed as immediate problems of bleeding after injury or surgery. A prolonged bleeding time is characteristic of the disease. The skin and mucous membranes are most frequently involved; nosebleeds and easy bruising are common problems. In mild cases a child may have no symptoms at all or may experience only increased bruising. In severe cases blood escapes from blood vessels and collects in joints. Other serious bleeding problems, such as gastrointestinal bleeding and prolonged menstrual periods (see *menstrual irregularities)* may occur.

The effects of one aspirin can last up to 10 days. After taking aspirin, a child with sensitive platelets bleeds spontaneously and is subject to *blood in the stools,* bruising (see *bruises),* and *nosebleeds.* A menstruating female who takes aspirin for dysmenorrhea (pain just before or during menstrual periods) will have a heavy menstrual period. If a child is cut or otherwise injured within 10 days of taking aspirin, it is difficult to stop the bleeding. In addition, bleeding problems can arise during surgery if a child has taken aspirin within the previous 10 days.

A newborn infant with vitamin-K deficiency may hemorrhage (i.e., large quantities of blood escape from blood vessels). Hemorrhaging is most likely to occur 3 to 5 days after birth and consists of bleeding into

the navel, gastrointestinal tract (esophagus, stomach, and intestines), and less often, the brain. Hemorrhaging may also occur following circumcision.

See also *hemophilia.*

DIAGNOSIS

If a child bleeds excessively, unexpectedly, or for prolonged periods of time after minor injuries, tooth extraction, or the use of any medications, a physician should be consulted (see *hemophilia).*

If a child bruises easily, a physician should be consulted. Thrombocytopenia is diagnosed by a physician when a blood test reveals low platelet counts.

Diagnosis of Von Willebrand's disease involves detection of factor abnormalities and clotting activity in the blood, along with noting platelet response to ristocetin, an antibiotic. When exposed to ristocetin in the test tube, the platelets of children with severe Von Willebrand's disease do not clump together as normal platelets would.

Review of the use of medications is part of the evaluation of the child with a bleeding problem. For instance, if use of aspirin is linked to the bleeding problem, a physician must determine if the child has an underlying bleeding disorder that is being aggravated by aspirin use. If a child has a history of prolonged bleeding times associated solely with the use of aspirin, special tests of platelet function can confirm the diagnosis.

The possibility of vitamin-K deficiency is explored if a child with illnesses such as liver or bowel disease has blood that clots slowly.

COMPLICATIONS

Among children with any of the three main types of bleeding disorders, certain common drugs—such as aspirin, tranquilizers, and some antihistamines and expectorants that are widely used in cough medicines—have the potential to aggravate bleeding. These drugs apparently interfere with platelet function among normal people as well as people with bleeding disorders. Their inhibiting effect on clotting, however, is much more pronounced in the person with a clotting disorder. In fact, sometimes a bleeding disorder first becomes evident after the use of such drugs.

For a child with a bleeding disorder, surgery may pose risks of blood loss from excessive or prolonged bleeding. Prior to surgery, a child needs to be evaluated for such risks.

During and after surgery, patients with hemophilia and Von Willebrand's disease must receive large concentrated doses of the blood factors that they are missing. Children with thrombocytopenia receive platelet transfusions.

See also *hemophilia*.

TREATMENT

Most bleeding disorders cannot be cured. Much is known, however, about how to manage and treat bleeding problems. Eliminating the use of aspirin usually prevents recurrence of blood-clotting problems among children with Von Willebrand's disease. In the cases of hemophilia and Von Willebrand's disease, the defective or reduced blood-clotting factor can be replaced by injections of concentrates of the factor to restore the blood to an acceptable clotting level. It is possible for many children with hemophilia to keep a supply of the factor concentrate at home and give it to themselves (or have their parents give it) as needed. Minor injuries, including bruises and nosebleeds, can be treated with pressure dressings (bandages that are applied snugly to reduce bleeding).

When a platelet deficiency causes severe symptoms, platelets obtained from donors (by removal from whole blood) can be transfused to restore the platelet level in the patient's blood to normal or near normal. ITP is commonly treated for a short time with hydrocortisonelike hormones. (ITP does not respond well to platelet transfusions.)

A child with aspirin sensitivity and aspirin-induced uncontrolled bleeding may need a transfusion of normal platelets to perform the clotting functions that his or her malfunctioning platelets cannot perform.

Children who are susceptible to vitamin-K deficiency require supplements of the vitamin. However, children with severe liver disease are unlikely to be helped by supplements. If hemorrhaging occurs, a child may need to receive blood or plasma.

See also *hemophilia*.

PREVENTION

Hemophilia, Von Willebrand's disease, and most cases of thrombocytopenia cannot be prevented. A woman who has a family history of hemophilia should receive genetic counseling so that she can discuss in advance her chances of having affected sons or of passing the trait along to her daughters.

Anyone who has Von Willebrand's disease should also receive genetic counseling. (See discussion of genetic counseling in *genetic disorders*.)

Negative effects upon blood clotting can be eliminated by avoiding aspirin and aspirin-containing products (such as many cold preparations and pain pills) and using acetaminophen instead.

Vitamin-K deficiency can be prevented in most cases (except those involving malabsorption) if susceptible children receive supplements of the vitamin. Parents should not give their children extra vitamin K unless it is prescribed by a physician, and they should make sure that their children take only the prescribed doses. Excessive vitamin K can be poisonous.

BLINDNESS

DESCRIPTION

Blindness is the absence of vision. It may occur as a single disability or in conjunction with some other disease or disabling condition. Four out of every thousand children are blind.

Federal and state laws define blindness to include anyone whose vision in both eyes is severely impaired. A person who is legally blind has a visual acuity of 20/200 or worse in the better eye, even when wearing corrective eyeglasses or lenses. Normal clear sight is referred to as 20/20 vision. A person with 20/20 vision sees at 20 feet what people with normal vision see at 20 feet. A person with 20/200 vision sees at 20 feet what people with normal vision see at 200 feet.

The examining ophthalmologist (eye specialist) is required by law to report newly diagnosed blind individuals to the appropriate state agency. A child need not be legally blind to qualify for federal or state aid for children with developmental disabilities, for teaching materials from the American Printing House for the Blind, and for state programs and other services. The state department of special education should be informed of all children so affected to ensure provision of special educational opportunities.

Of those children older than 5 who are considered legally blind, 50 percent have vision that is near 20/200 with corrective glasses or lenses. Those children can read large-type books and be independent. Approximately another 25 percent of the legally blind have some light perception, and can distinguish shapes a foot or so away. These children can probably move around a room unassisted but may not be able to read. The remaining 25 percent are totally blind or can barely distinguish light from dark. They must rely on braille, talking books, and tutors, and may need some assistance in walking.

Despite their disability, many vision-impaired individuals lead exceptionally productive lives. Totally blind or partially sighted persons can attain all levels of education and work at most professions. Blindness does not rule out participation in sports; some totally blind and partially sighted athletes run marathons, ski, swim, scuba dive, and enjoy most athletic and recreational activities.

CAUSE

Currently, congenital defects (present at birth), such as congenital cataracts (opaque lens), congenital *glaucoma,* and disorders of the retina (the rear portion of the eye that receives light rays) and the optic nerve (a part of the brain involved in vision) are the most common causes of blindness among newborns. Loss of sight may also be caused by an acquired eye disease, by disorders of the brain, by diseases affecting the whole body, or by accidents. Cancer of the retina *(retinoblastoma)* may also cause blindness.

Some former major causes of blindness during childhood have become much less common, including retrolental fibroplasia (RLF) (see *prematurity*), maternal rubella *(German measles)*, and *gonorrhea* during pregnancy. RLF, once one of the most frequent causes of blindness among premature newborns, is also one of the most preventable. High concentrations of oxygen given to premature newborns with breathing difficulties damaged the children's eyes. Approximately 10,000 adolescents and young adults in the United States are blind from RLF. Now, with more careful control of oxygen treatment of premature newborns, blindness from RLF has become rare.

Childhood blindness caused by maternal rubella (German measles) during the first three months of pregnancy often occurs with congenital heart disease (see *heart disease, congenital*), *hearing loss,* or *mental retardation.* Maternal rubella, however, has become uncommon because of childhood immuniza-tion against the disease. Blindness from maternal gonorrhea, which once accounted for nearly 30 percent of all congenital blindness, is now prevented by the application of silver nitrate or antibiotic ointment to a newborn's eyes.

SIGNS AND SYMPTOMS

Several signs indicate lack of vision among infants and young children. A child whose vision is severely impaired does not blink or cry at a sudden or threatening movement. Eye movements may be random, jerky, and uncoordinated. Eyes neither fix on an object nor follow it. Pupils (the circular opening that allows light to enter the eye) do not constrict if a light is shined in the eyes. A child's eyes may drift out of alignment and the child may appear unusually timid and clumsy for his or her age.

The onset of blindness among older children may be marked by poor performance in school and a lack of interest in normal childhood activities. Young school-age children may not understand what is happening to them and may try to hide their disability and embarrassment.

DIAGNOSIS

Observation of a child's visual behavior combined with a thorough examination of the eye, including the cornea, the lens, the pupil, the retina, and the optic nerve, confirms the diagnosis of blindness. A special electrical study of the retina of the eye, the optic nerve, and the visual pathways of the brain may help determine the source of the blindness.

COMPLICATIONS

A child who is blind from birth or early childhood at first experiences some developmental delays regardless of the level of intelligence. Motor skills requiring large and fine muscle coordination are delayed, since early development depends on visual perception. The child may not sit until 8 months of age and may not crawl at all. Walking may be delayed until the child is 2 years of age or older. Language is delayed. The blind child learns to speak by ear alone, a slow process without the visual cues of lip and mouth movement.

It is not unusual for blind children to engage in self-stimulation, such as poking the eye, *head-banging*, and rocking. Such behavior usually disappears by the time a child is about 4 years old and starts school.

Other complications may arise as a child without sight learns to function in a world of sighted people. A blind child requires special education, and to some extent depends on special equipment to minimize disability. Emotional problems can arise as the family adapts to a child's disability.

TREATMENT

If any evidence exists of vision loss, a child should be examined thoroughly by an opthalmologist. In some cases, such as the presence of cataracts, eye damage may be reversible and surgery may restore vision. If vision loss is not complete, corrective glasses and lenses may help a child use what vision he or she has.

Most of the treatment for a child who is blind, however, is educational and takes place at home and in school, involving the child's family and teachers. A child without sight uses touch and sound to explore the world, and parents should take fullest advantage of those senses when communicating with the child.

A blind child, especially as an infant, needs to be loved and cuddled more than the child who can see. It is important for parents to talk to the child continually, even when he or she is a tiny infant. Textured objects should be placed within and just outside the child's reach, and the child should be encouraged to explore without fear.

Both a blind child and his or her family need the support of a pediatrician and education specialists. A child should be encouraged to become as independent as possible. Family efforts can foster an attitude of self-sufficiency and self-confidence, but this is not an easy task. While a family's inclination may be to protect a blind child from possible harm, pampering or sheltering because of disability deprives a child of deserved and helpful experiences.

The education of a blind child is much the same as for a child with sight, but special educational services are needed. As the child reaches school age, the extent of the visual loss should be known, and an appropriate special education plan can be implemented.

A child whose vision is near 20/200 can use large-type books, while children with less vision more often need talking books, tutors, and braille. Braille is a written language formed as a series of raised dots on a page and read left to right. A skilled reader of braille can read about one quarter as fast as the average reader with sight. Many blind college-age children have studied in regular classrooms and gone on to graduate using some or all of these methods.

Severely blind children and adults need the assistance of an orientation and mobility specialist to learn to move about. Approximately 5,000 blind individuals in the United States rely on seeing-eye dogs. Canes and sonar-guided obstacle-detecting devices are also commonly used. No single method is necessarily better than another and a blind child should be allowed to use whichever method works best.

PREVENTION

Blindness among newborns caused by maternal rubella during pregnancy can be prevented if the mother is vaccinated against the infection at least three months before she plans to become pregnant. RLF-related blindness can be prevented through strict control of oxygen therapy for premature infants. Gonoccocal eye infections can be prevented through treatment at birth of the eyes of all newborns with silver nitrate or antibiotic ointment. Accidental blindness can be prevented if a child wears protective goggles or lenses when participating in hockey, racquet sports, and other activities in which eye injuries are a common hazard.

BLISTERS

DESCRIPTION

When skin is damaged by rubbing, injury (trauma), or suction, it may respond by developing a raised red bump, filled with a clear or almost clear fluid (serum), forming at the site of injury. This eruption, or blister, is a response to injury and will not disappear until the underlying skin has healed. Blisters range in size from very small to several inches in diameter and may be tender to touch.

Blisters can form anywhere on the body. If left undamaged, a blister heals by itself in a short time. With proper treatment, broken blisters also usually heal quickly.

CAUSE AND DIAGNOSIS

Blisters have many causes. Rubbing from ill-fitting shoes frequently results in blisters. Allergic reactions to plants (see poison ivy, oak, and sumac) and insects (see lice; scabies), may produce small red blisters. Burns of any kind result in eruptions of blisters on the damaged skin. Bacterial or viral diseases such as *chicken pox,* staphylococcus, *impetigo,* herpes simplex, and athlete's foot (see *ringworm*) may cause blisters. Knowledge of a child's recent activities or exposure to infectious diseases helps identify the cause of a blister.

COMPLICATIONS

Infection may occur if a blister breaks and is not treated. Red streaks spreading from a blister or cloudy fluid in a blister and redness at the blister base indicate the presence of infection.

TREATMENT

Treatment of blisters should begin by first eliminating the disease or skin irritation that caused the eruption. While the underlying cause is being treated, it is important to prevent infection of the blisters. The area should be well protected with a gauze wrap or bandage.

If a blister is accidentally broken or opened, the exposed skin should be washed gently with soap and water. A mild antibiotic (available without a prescription) should be applied, and the area covered with a clean bandage.

If a blister becomes infected, a physician should be consulted. An infected blister is usually opened and drained. Antibiotics or medicated soaking compounds are often prescribed.

A physician should also be consulted if the cause of a blister eruption is unknown. Blister fluids can be analyzed to determine the underlying cause.

PREVENTION

Long pants, long-sleeved shirts, shoes, and gloves should be worn to prevent contact with poison ivy. To prevent blistering from rubbing, a child's shoes should be checked to ensure a proper fit. Physical contact with children infected with diseases such as chicken pox and impetigo should be avoided.

BLOOD DISORDERS

Blood carries oxygen and nutrients throughout the body and transports waste products to the kidneys and liver. Blood consists of a liquid portion, called plasma, and three types of cells: red blood cells (which make up about 99 percent of all blood cells and which are alternatively called erythrocytes), white blood cells (called leukocytes), and platelets.

Red blood cells are composed almost entirely of hemoglobin, a red pigment that transports oxygen from the lungs to body organs and tissues. White blood cells are part of the body's immune system, involved in fighting infections caused by foreign organisms. Platelets serve to clot blood and prevent leakage of blood between cell walls. All three types of blood cells originate in the bone marrow (the spongelike tissue that fills the cavities of most bones).

Depending on what type of blood cell becomes deficient, different blood disorders may develop. If too few red blood cells are present in the circulating blood, or if the concentration of hemoglobin in red cells decreases, a condition called *anemia* exists. As a result of anemia, an insufficient amount of oxygen is carried in the blood (hypoxemia) and thus not enough oxygen reaches body organs and tissues. Signs and symptoms of anemia include weakness, an excessively rapid heart rate, rapid breathing, and pale skin and mucous membranes.

Many conditions impair production of red blood cells or hemoglobin and lead to anemia. Inadequate nutrition, for example, leads to nutritional anemias (see *anemia, nutritional),* in which a specific nutrient such as iron, folic acid, or vitamin B-12 is deficient. *Lead poisoning* causes a decrease in the production of heme, the iron component of hemoglobin.

Another type of anemia is hemolytic anemia (see *anemia, hemolytic),* in which red blood cells are destroyed at an excessively rapid rate. Examples of hemolytic anemia are *hereditary spherocytosis,* hereditary elliptocytosis, *sickle cell anemia,* G-6-PD deficiency, erythroblastosis fetalis (the disease caused by *Rh incompatibility*), and *thalassemia.*

An insufficient number of white blood cells is called leukopenia. Leukopenia is caused either by excessive destruction or reduced production of white blood cells. Children who have too few white blood cells cannot fight disease properly.

A deficiency in platelets, called thrombocytopenia, can cause a bleeding disorder in which small blood vessels leak, leading to frequent nosebleeds and small bleeding spots under the skin.

A severe bone marrow disease called aplastic anemia (see *anemia, aplastic*) impairs production of all three types of blood cells. A child with aplastic anemia develops anemia, leukopenia, and thrombocytopenia simultaneously.

The production of red blood cells and platelets is also inhibited by *leukemia,* a malignant (cancerous) bone marrow disease caused by overproduction of abnormal white blood cells.

See also *bleeding disorders.*

BLOOD IN THE STOOLS, VOMITING OF BLOOD

EMERGENCY ACTION

A child who vomits blood or bleeds rectally requires immediate medical attention. Consult the child's physician or take the child to a hospital emergency room. Significant blood loss can lead to *shock,* a condition characterized by cool, clammy, pale skin; weak, rapid pulse; thirst; dizziness or faintness; and increased breathing rate.

DESCRIPTION

Bleeding from the gastrointestinal (GI) tract—esophagus, stomach, and intestines—can happen to a child at any age. Blood may appear when a child vomits or has a bowel movement. Vomiting blood usually indicates that bleeding originates in the esophagus or stomach. Blood in the stools is usually a sign that bleeding originates in the small or large intestines.

Upper GI Bleeding

Vomiting of blood may be accompanied by pain or cramps, or it may occur without symptoms. A child may become pale quickly, the skin grow cold and clammy, dizziness or light-headedness begin, and pulse rate increase—the first signs of *shock.* A child can suffer several episodes of vomiting in just a few hours. Blood in vomit may be bright red or it may resemble brown coffee grounds, indicating that it stayed in the stomach long enough to be partially digested.

Estimating blood loss can be difficult, because blood stains the entire contents of the vomit. In addition, if a child vomits into a toilet, the toilet water dilutes and spreads blood, giving the sometimes misleading appearance that a large volume of blood has been lost.

Lower GI Bleeding

Bloody bowel movements or rectal bleeding may be accompanied by pain, cramping, gas, and abdominal bloating. If bleeding is massive, a child may quickly become pale as signs of shock appear. A child may suffer several bloody bowel movements in a few hours. Again, estimating blood loss can be difficult since toilet water dilutes blood, producing the appearance of a large blood loss. If unchecked, bleeding from any part of the GI tract can lead to shock, loss of consciousness, and eventually, death.

Blood in bowel movements varies in color from bright red to dark brown or black. Blood from the rectum or bloody stools can vary: bright red blood mixed with clots; blood-streaked or blood-permeated stools; brown or black stools with a tarlike consistency; stools with the consistency and color of currant jelly (appearing to be dark red and gelatinous). The appearance of such stools can provide clues to the seriousness of the condition and possible origin of bleeding.

CAUSE

Upper GI Bleeding

Bleeding can result from a variety of causes. Among children less than 1 year old, vomiting usually occurs because of a clotting defect in the blood rather than as a result of an abnormality in the GI tract. Any break in a blood vessel, regardless of how small, may result in substantial internal bleeding. An ordinary coughing spell may become a potential bleeding hazard for an infant with a clotting defect.

If a newborn vomits blood, the most obvious cause is mother's blood swallowed by the child while being born. An ulcer in the stomach is another fairly common cause of an infant's vomiting blood. In addition, vomiting blood may be an early indication that a systemic infection is present.

The most common causes of vomiting blood among children over 1 year old, in order of frequency, are severe inflammation of the stomach (gastritis); networks of enlarged blood vessels in the esophagus that may bleed (as a result of high blood pressure); stomach *ulcers;* and an injury to or a growth in the nose or throat.

Lower GI Bleeding

Among children less than 1 year old, rectal bleeding or bloody stools may be caused by a crack (fissure) in the mucous membrane of the anus. Fissures result most often because of *constipation,* which produces large, hard stools capable of tearing the soft tissue of the anus. Other causes of rectal bleeding in infants are intestinal blood vessels that rupture because of defects of development. A severe intestinal infection or reaction to a food, such as cow's milk protein, may cause severe *diarrhea* or colitis, which then leads to ulceration or bleeding in the small or large intestine. Other leading causes of rectal bleeding or bloody stools among children less than 1 year old include *intussusception* (telescoping of a loop of small intestine, often into the adjoining large intestine) and enterocolitis (severe massive inflammation of the small and large intestines). Infants may also bleed rectally from unknown causes and from locations difficult or impossible to pinpoint.

In children older than 1 year, rectal bleeding most often may be caused by an anal fissure; multiple *polyps* (small growths) in the large intestine; inflammatory bowel disease such as *ulcerative colitis* and *Crohn's disease;* birth abnormalities, such as duplication or twisting of a part of the GI tract; or severe infection in the small or large intestine.

It is possible for bleeding from the upper GI tract to appear first as dark brown or black stools with a tarlike consistency. Blood acts as a laxative in the GI tract and can pass through the small and large intestines in a few hours.

DIAGNOSIS

For any kind of vomiting of blood or rectal bleeding, diagnosis is made by a physician, often a specialist in GI disease (gastroenterologist), sometimes in consultation with a surgeon. A careful history is taken, followed by a physical examination. The history is of particular importance in confirming whether signs and symptoms such as cramps, pain, nausea, vomiting, diarrhea, or fainting have occurred in the recent past. In order to identify potentially irritating or harmful substances, a physician asks about diet in detail and any medications taken by a child. The examining physician needs to know about any accidents, chronic illnesses, surgery, and infections in a child's medical history.

Blood and urine samples are analyzed. X-ray films of various kinds may be performed as necessary depending upon when

the bleeding subsides or is brought under control by medical means. Since a child who has experienced GI bleeding can rapidly lose essential body fluids and salts, possibly leading to dehydration and shock, intravenous fluids may be started while the examination is going on. If active bleeding is going on, blood transfusions may be necessary to replace blood already lost and to help prevent shock.

COMPLICATIONS

Complications depend upon the cause and source of bleeding, the physical condition of a child before bleeding begins, and occasionally, upon how quickly a diagnosis can be confirmed. Both shock and dehydration can be dangerous when large amounts of blood are lost.

TREATMENT

Massive bleeding is a medical emergency that requires immediate attention, in a hospital emergency room if possible. Intravenous fluids and salts may be given to combat dehydration and shock. In order to replace blood loss, blood transfusions may be started even as the examination is being performed and a medical history is being taken.

Treatment depends upon the cause and source of bleeding and the physical condition of a child before bleeding begins. Whenever possible, before surgery is chosen, medical procedures are employed to stop or slow bleeding. New and more effective medical procedures are reducing the need for surgery for children who suffer certain kinds of bleeding from the upper and lower GI tract.

Some causes of GI bleeding can be managed best by surgery, but it is always better for an operation to be performed after a patient's condition has been stabilized. The relative impact of surgery upon a child's body can be reduced if all vital signs are satisfactory and active bleeding has stopped.

When GI bleeding occurs, children usually suffer from fear and anxiety, both of which can complicate or even accelerate blood loss. Parents should try to comfort and reassure a child from the first sign of bleeding through the sometimes worrisome processes of examination and diagnosis.

PREVENTION

Prevention of unexpected bloody stools, rectal bleeding, or vomiting of blood is not possible.

BLOOD IN THE URINE

EMERGENCY ACTION

In the great majority of cases the cause of blood in the urine is not serious. Still, blood in the urine can be indicative of one of several rare but potentially serious conditions. Therefore, seek an immediate medical evaluation whenever a child's urine appears red, pink, rust-colored, or smoky.

DESCRIPTION

Blood in the urine may be a symptom of a variety of health problems, most of which are not common. Many affected children have microscopic amounts of blood in their urine, amounts that can be detected only through urinalysis (laboratory analysis of urine). For every thousand visits to an emergency room, only one involves a complaint of obviously bloody urine.

The medical term for blood in the urine is hematuria ("hema" means blood and "uria" means urine). When urine is obviously bloody—when it looks red, pink, rust-colored, or smoky—a child is said to have gross hematuria. When blood in the urine can only be discerned through urinalysis, a child is said to have microhematuria. Whenever a child has a medical problem that may involve the urinary tract, a physician orders a urinalysis, and one of the conditions that laboratory technicians look for is microhematuria. The urinary tract consists of the kidneys, ureters (tubes which carry urine to the bladder), bladder, and urethra (the tube from the bladder to the outside of the body).

Children of any age can develop a health problem that involves hematuria, although children 3 to 4 years old have bloody urine more often than children in any other age group, according to most studies. The amount of hematuria does not, however, depend on an affected child's age—or, for that matter, whether it is gross or microscopic. The important issue is the severity of the condition that is causing hematuria.

About 7 percent of children who seek medical attention for discolored urine do not actually have hematuria. Certain food dyes —natural and artificial—can discolor urine, as can certain medications. Substances that can discolor urine include certain pain-relieving and fever-reducing medications, certain dyes often added to sweets, the natural dyes in beets and certain berries, and certain laxatives. Diapers left in a pail sometimes turn red because a particular strain of reddish bacteria tend to breed on wet diapers. Finally, a small number of people have an inborn chemical defect that causes their urine to appear discolored.

CAUSE

Hematuria during childhood (usually microhematuria) is most commonly caused by *urinary tract infections* (UTI). More rare urinary tract problems that can cause hematuria include *urinary tract defects;* blood-vessel malformation in the tract (see the discussion of hemangiomas in *birthmarks);* and injury to the tract from, for example, insertion of a foreign object.

Urinary-tract problems that specifically involve the kidneys are rare, but they frequently involve hematuria. Such problems include kidney cysts (capsules of fluid or semisolid matter within the kidney), any type of *nephritis,* and kidney stones.

In some cases of hematuria the cause can be traced to use of a medication that irritates the urinary tract and causes it to bleed. Such medications include certain agents that prevent blood from clotting, certain antibiotics (used to fight bacterial infections), and some medications used to combat cancer. Sometimes the benefits of using such medications outweigh the risk that hematuria may develop.

Irritation of the urinary tract and hematuria can also result from a variety of conditions that affect the entire body or that primarily affect a part of the body that is not a urinary-tract structure. Such conditions include blood-clotting problems, such as *hemophilia* or thrombocytopenia; *blood disorders* that interfere with the oxygen-carrying capacity of blood, such as *sickle cell anemia;* inflammation of blood vessels; malformation of blood vessels; very high fever; high blood pressure *(hypertension)*; hemolytic uremic syndrome; *lupus erythematosus; bloodstream infection;* subacute bacterial endocarditis (see *heart disease, congenital*); anaphylactoid purpura; *appendicitis;* inflammation or irritation of the lining of the abdominal cavity and the abdominal organs (peritonitis); and epididymitis (see *scrotal and testicular problems*).

In some cases blood in the urine indicates injury to the kidneys, which can occur accidentally or because of child abuse or, specifically, sexual abuse (see *child abuse*).

Some of the most rare cases of blood in the urine include benign or cancerous tumors in the urinary tract. (See, for example, *Wilms' tumor* and the discussion of rhabdomyosarcoma of the bladder in *genitourinary tumors*.)

In a small minority of cases, the cause of hematuria never becomes clear. Sometimes, inexplicable hematuria runs in the family, and a physician labels the condition "familial hematuria." In other cases, there is no family history, and hematuria is labeled "benign recurrent hematuria."

DIAGNOSIS

Whenever a child appears to have blood in the urine, an immediate medical evaluation should be sought. Microhematuria can only be discovered through urinalysis, a common diagnostic procedure. In about three quarters of all cases involving blood in the urine, a pediatrician or family doctor can diagnose the cause of the problem without consulting a kidney specialist (nephrologist) or urinary-tract surgeon (urologist). In general, the cause of a case of gross hematuria is easier to identify than that of a case of microhematuria.

A physician diagnosing the cause of hematuria considers a child's personal and family medical histories, performs a physical examination, and asks the child to provide a urine sample for analysis.

After the sample is collected, it may be examined in a laboratory immediately to discern if the discoloring factor is blood or if an unusually large number of bacteria are evident. Other tests can be performed on a urine sample using chemically treated paper or other laboratory materials. These tests can identify additional problems, such as excess protein in the urine (which can be associated with nephritis) and excess sugar in the urine (which can be an indication of *diabetes*).

If urinalysis and other preliminary procedures fail to reveal the cause of blood in the urine, further tests are necessary. Blood samples may be taken and analyzed to test for such problems as sickle cell anemia, kidney impairment, or clotting problems. A physician may order an ultrasound of the urinary tract, a procedure that produces an image of the structures using sound waves. In addition, two types of X-ray films may be taken. The first, called an intravenous pyelo-

gram (IVP), is a film of the kidneys and ureters. A vein is injected with a special fluid, which is first excreted by the kidneys, but the residual fluid illuminates the urinary tract on X-ray film. The second, a cystourethrogram, is a film of the bladder and urethra. It involves placing a tube in the urethra to instill a special fluid in the bladder.

In rare cases, when the cause of blood in the urine remains unclear, tests using various direct viewing techniques are performed. These can include cystoscopy (examination of the urinary tract through a small, lighted tube), X-ray films of arteries, or a biopsy (removal of a small tissue sample) from the kidneys.

If, after all diagnostic procedures have been performed, the cause of blood in the urine remains unclear, the child is reevaluated after a short period of time. Even if the cause is identified, diagnostic procedures are often repeated at a later date to monitor the severity of the condition. In some cases urinalysis is repeated periodically for months even after normal results first appear.

COMPLICATIONS, TREATMENT, AND PREVENTION

The complications, treatment, and prevention of hematuria depend on its underlying cause.

BLOODSTREAM INFECTION

EMERGENCY ACTION

Call a physician promptly if

- an infant under the age of 3 months has a temperature of 100° F (37.8° C) or higher;
- a child from 3 months to 2 years old has a temperature of 102° F (38.8° C) or higher;
- any child has a temperature of 104° F (40° C) or higher;
- a child with *sickle cell anemia, thalassemia,* aplastic anemia (see *anemia, aplastic*), *hereditary spherocytosis,* or *leukemia* has a temperature of 100° F (37.8° C) or higher; or
- a child with a skin injury (such as a burn) has a temperature of 100° F (37.8° C) or higher.

A child who fits into any of these categories could have a bloodstream infection, which can become very serious very rapidly.

Seek medical attention immediately if a feverish child shows signs of *shock* (a potentially life-threatening condition characterized by cool, clammy, pale skin; weak, rapid pulse; thirst; dizziness or faintness; and increased breathing rate). While waiting for medical attention, keep the child warm.

DESCRIPTION AND CAUSE

During everyday life, as well as during illness, bacteria can get into the bloodstream. When this happens, a type of bloodstream infection called bacteremia exists. Bacteremia can cause few or no signs and symptoms of illness and is detectable only through a laboratory test called a blood culture. Normally the body's immune system immediately eradicates these bacteria, so bacteremia is brief.

Unlike older children or adults, however, young children do not yet have immunity to many types of bacteria. As a result, the bacteria that get into their bloodstreams may persist and cause signs and symptoms of severe and overwhelming illness to appear. When this happens, a type of bloodstream infection called septicemia, sepsis, or blood poisoning exists.

A bloodstream infection can be classified as primary (with no apparent source of infection) or secondary (with an apparent source of infection). Secondary bloodstream infections can be caused by a bacterial infection anywhere else in the body. Diseases or conditions that are common sources of bloodstream infection include *pneumonia, urinary tract infections* (including pyelonephritis), gastroenteritis, *boils* and other skin infections, and a perforated appendix (see *appendicitis*). In addition, intravenous therapy, surgery, burns, and other skin injuries (or the abscesses—pockets of pus—that can develop if they become infected), and intravenous drug abuse (see *drug and alcohol abuse*) can be sources of bloodstream infection. Primary bloodstream infections occur most often among newborns, infants under 6 months, and infants of low birthweight congenital illness. The outlook for infants with a bloodstream infection depends upon the age at which the infection began; the older the infant, the better the outlook.

Other children susceptible to primary bloodstream infection are those from the ages of 6 months to 3 years and children of any age who have a severe underlying disease such as *sickle cell anemia, thalassemia,* aplastic anemia (see *anemia, aplastic*), *hereditary spherocytosis, leukemia,* or any other disease that impairs the function of the spleen (an organ located in the upper left abdomen that filters blood and stores red blood cells).

The chief concern when a child has a bloodstream infection is to keep the bacteria from spreading in the blood to other parts of the body such as the skin, bones, and brain. Prompt and adequate treatment can usually eradicate the bacteria before they cause complications. Some bloodstream infections are self-limited; the bacteria do not spread even without treatment. However, since it is not always possible to tell which cases will be self-limited and which will not, treatment is usually advisable.

After treatment for a bloodstream infection, the child usually starts to feel better and bacteria do not spread. In a few cases, however, the child's condition does not improve and the infection requires long-term intravenous antibiotics.

SIGNS AND SYMPTOMS

Symptoms of bloodstream infection vary and can be subtle. Bacteremia usually, but not always, causes children to be intensely sick with shivering, high (or spiking) fever, and marked decrease in level of activity. Severe headache, nausea, vomiting, diarrhea, exhaustion, and loss of appetite may also occur.

In addition to having the above signs and symptoms, a newborn with a primary bloodstream infection may be limp and have *jaundice.* Signs that the infection is rapidly becoming very serious include convulsions (see *seizures)* and shock.

DIAGNOSIS

To make a tentative diagnosis of bloodstream infection, a physician notes any signs and symptoms of illness and takes a medical history. The physician also performs a physical examination, which may reveal a rapid pulse rate and low blood pressure, and looks for an apparent source of infection. The diagnosis of bloodstream infection can usually be inferred from analyses of samples of blood, cerebrospinal fluid, and in some cases, urine. In addition to culturing blood to see if bacteria are present in excess numbers, laboratory technicians will determine the number of white blood cells. A high or very low white blood cell count indicates infection.

Diagnosis of a bloodstream infection can be difficult. If signs and symptoms indicate septicemia, a source of infection is apparent, or a blood culture has revealed the presence of bacteria, treatment can be started immediately in efforts to prevent complications. If a child has only a high fever, however, parents might not suspect a serious illness and might not seek medical attention. A physician may suggest evaluation of a child less than 24 months of age who has a high fever. If no reason for a fever is found during a physical examination, and the level of white blood cells is found to be high, then a blood culture may be ordered. It can take from one to three days for results of blood cultures to be ready. Delay of treatment could be dangerous. As a result, if bacteremia is suspected, physicians may begin treatment with antibiotics without waiting for test results.

If a child has a positive blood culture (meaning that bacterial infection is present), other tests might be conducted to determine sources of infection and whether complications have arisen; these tests include chest X rays and spinal taps.

COMPLICATIONS

If bacteria in the blood are not eradicated with treatment, they can spread in the bloodstream to other parts of the body and cause disease there. If the bacteria spread to the brain, they can cause *meningitis.* If they spread to the bones, *osteomyelitis* can result. If they spread to the joints, septic *arthritis* can occur. If they spread to the skin, they may lead to cellulitis, a purplish red swelling, often of the face or neck.

In cases where bacteremia is untreated, is treated too late or ineffectively, or is unresponsive to treatment, affected children may suffer permanent brain or bone damage or may die. Complications occur more frequently among children who have spleens that do not function normally.

TREATMENT

A child with a bloodstream infection is given antibiotics, either on an impatient or outpatient basis. Any affected child is carefully watched or is followed up to make sure that the fever is going down and that the child is feeling better. If the child's condition

does not change, the child is often hospitalized and given antibiotics intravenously.

Aside from administration of intravenous antibiotics to eradicate the disease-causing bacteria, supportive care is crucial in the treatment of bloodstream infections. It includes reduction of body temperatures to normal levels, maintenance of normal circulation and fluid levels, maintenance of a balance between levels of acids and bases in the blood, and attainment of adequate levels of oxygen in the blood.

PREVENTION

Some cases of bloodstream infection cannot be prevented.

An effective vaccine against infections stemming from influenza bacteria is available. All children should be immunized against H. influenza (type b) disease at 2 years of age (see immunization schedules in Chapter 6, "Going to the Doctor"). A child 2 years old or older who has a damaged spleen may receive a pneumococcal and meningococcal vaccine as well. For a younger child who has a poorly functioning spleen (as in cases of *sickle cell anemia* or *thalassemia*) or who has had the spleen removed (as in some cases of *hereditary spherocytosis*), preventive administration of penicillin is often recommended to help prevent bloodstream infections.

BOILS

DESCRIPTION

Boils (sometimes called furuncles) are skin infections caused by common bacteria. Resembling oversized pimples, they form in the lower layers of the skin and appear as red lumps, pea-sized or larger, that eventually fill with pus, come to a head at the surface of the skin, break, and drain. (Pus is the liquid produced in certain infections, consisting of bacteria, white blood cells, and other matter.)

Although they may erupt anywhere on the body, boils most commonly appear on the face, neck, buttocks, and upper back. The formation of a boil begins when bacteria (usually staphylococci, which are often harmlessly present among healthy people) invade an opening in the skin, such as a hair follicle or scratch, and cause an infection.

Any child can get a boil, which is among the most common of skin conditions. In most cases only one boil at a time forms on a child's skin; with proper care it usually disappears within a week. In rare instances, a cluster of boils called a carbuncle may form. This condition can be extremely painful and may be accompanied by other symptoms of infection, such as fever or *swollen glands* (enlarged lymph nodes).

Sometimes a severely infected lymph node resembles a swollen red boil. If infection destroys a lymph node, it may follow the same course as a boil, breaking down into pus, coming to a head, opening, and draining.

Some physicians refer to boils as abscesses. Not all abscesses are boils; the term "abscess" also includes collections of pus that can be caused by bacteria other than staphylococci and appear in the brain, muscles, bones, and internal organs.

CAUSE

A boil can develop if bacteria invade a break in the skin. Conditions that cause breaks in the skin and can therefore increase a child's risk of getting a boil include hair follicle inflammation, insect bites (see *stinging insect reactions*), *cuts and lacerations,* and *eczema.* Pus can drain directly from one boil into a break in the skin, or bacteria from another person's drained boil can reach skin openings from unsterilized towels or linens. In general, therefore, poor hygiene increases susceptibility to the formation and spread of boils.

Certain long-term systemic conditions, including *diabetes* and *malnutrition,* can increase a child's chances of getting a boil. Sometimes multiple, persistent, recurrent boils are signs of an immune disease which produces low resistance to infection. In addition, young children seem to be somewhat more susceptible to boils than older children, perhaps because their resistance to infection is still developing (see *infections, frequent*).

Finally, studies show that ointments like petroleum jelly may block natural openings in the surface of a child's skin, trapping bacteria below and causing a boil to form.

SIGNS AND SYMPTOMS

Until they break and drain, boils are usually painful, especially when they form where skin is tight, such as on the nose or outer ear. A single boil does not usually affect other parts of the body or overall health, but infection may cause a nearby lymph node to become swollen and tender. Swollen lymph nodes and fever are fairly common when a child develops a carbuncle or multiple boils.

DIAGNOSIS

A boil can almost always be identified on sight by its characteristic appearance.

COMPLICATIONS

Complications involving boils usually result from improper treatment. Squeezing a boil may cause scarring and may force pus into uninfected areas or into the bloodstream, spreading infection. (One common complication caused when pus gets into the bloodstream is a bone infection called *osteomyelitis.*) Puncturing a boil near the nasal area may spread the infection to a child's sinuses or to the veins on the surface of the brain.

Ignoring a boil completely may increase the chances of further infection. This is especially true in the case of a carbuncle because of the large, open sore remaining after drainage.

TREATMENT

A physician should be consulted as soon as possible under the following circumstances:

- a boil is present for 5 days without coming to a head;
- a boil is in an awkward or sensitive location such as a child's face, armpit, or buttocks (especially a child in diapers);
- red streaks are seen on the skin near the boil or a general sign of infection (swollen glands, *fever*) is present;
- a child has a carbuncle or multiple boils;
- a drained boil does not seem to be healing after 2 or 3 days.

If none of these signs or symptoms is present, home treatment may be sufficient and should ease a child's discomfort and speed recovery. The skin around a boil should be kept clean and dry. A boil can be brought to a head quickly by soaking it frequently or even constantly in a saltwater solution. This solution can be made by dissolving 1 teaspoon of salt in 1 quart of boiling water and allowing the mixture to cool to body temperature—about 100° F (37.8° C). A piece of sterile gauze or cotton should be used to apply the solution to the boil.

If doubt exists about whether or when to prick a boil, it may be helpful to have a physician perform the procedure. A physician may also want to analyze pus from a boil to determine the exact cause of infection and to prescribe surface antibiotic creams or oral antibiotics, especially for a carbuncle of multiple boils. If a child develops boils repeatedly, a physician may take cultures of bacteria in the nose and throat.

PREVENTION

The best way to prevent boils is good hygiene. In addition, all skin irritations should be treated correctly and promptly. Regular use of antibacterial soap may help in keeping bacteria-sensitive skin as clean as possible. Also, monitoring conditions such as *diabetes* may decrease a child's chances of getting a boil.

BONE CANCER

DESCRIPTION

Cancer is a general term describing over 100 diseases marked by abnormal and uncontrolled growth of cells (see *cancer).* These abnormal, rapidly multiplying cells form a mass or tumor. A benign tumor is a mass that stays in one area and does not expand out of control by invading healthy tissues. A malignant tumor expands uncontrollably and invades healthy tissue. Abnormal cells originating in a tumor can spread (metastasize) throughout the body in the blood or lymph (the clear fluid that bathes and protects many cells in the body), and "seed" additional or secondary cancers in other parts of the body.

Bone cancers are malignant tumors that may develop anywhere in the skeletal system. Although bone cancers represent the second most common form of solid tumor that occurs among children and young adults between 10 and 20 years old, they are rare diseases: just slightly more than five cases per million children occur each year in the United States.

Any tumor that originates in the bone and connective tissues of the skeleton is called a primary bone cancer. The two most common primary bone cancers occurring among children and adolescents are osteogenic sarcoma, which originates in bones, and Ewing's sarcoma, which usually begins in the marrow of bones. Less common bone cancers include chondrosarcoma and non-Hodgkin's lymphoma of the bone.

Osteogenic Sarcoma

Sarcoma is the term for a malignant tumor that develops in the supportive and connective tissues—the hard or tough, sinewy tissues. Osteogenic sarcoma, the most common bone cancer, accounts for about 60 percent of all cases. It most frequently affects people between 10 and 25 years of age, with most cases occurring between 13 and 18, the adolescent period of rapid skeletal growth. Osteogenic sarcoma affects slightly more males than females.

The disease usually occurs in a growth zone at either end of a leg bone. Half of these tumors develop around the knee: many have their origin in the lower end of the femur (the thighbone), just above the knee. Other frequent sites of origin include, in order of occurrence, the shinbone, the upper arm (near the shoulder), the upper end of the thighbone, and the pelvis.

Osteogenic sarcoma of the bone can spread through the veins into the bloodstream, most often to the lungs. Such spreading occurs if a tumor penetrates into the bone marrow, and tumor cells then spread. Osteogenic sarcoma is a painful, life-threatening disease; it requires prompt, multidisciplinary treatment in a cancer hospital or center. Physicians can often eliminate all signs and symptoms of disease for extended periods. These periods, called "remission," now occur regularly.

Ewing's Sarcoma

Ewing's sarcoma is responsible for 25 percent of all bone cancers. About half of those with the disease are between 10 and 20 years old. About 1½ times as many males as females develop the disease. Tumors occur in the middle of long bones (especially the upper leg, the marrow of the leg bones, pelvis, upper arm, ribs, vertebrae, lower leg, shoulder blade, and lower back.

Statistics show that about 1 in 4 individuals with Ewing's sarcoma exhibits spreading of the cancer in the form of a detectable tumor. At the time of diagnosis, however, more than 90 percent of people with Ewing's sarcoma exhibit spreading of tumor cells (called micrometastatic disease) that is undetectable with current diagnostic techniques. The outlook frequently depends upon the stage of the disease: if the disease is micrometastatic (not in the form of a gross tumor) at the time of diagnosis, the chances for successful treatment are better.

CAUSE

The causes of all types of bone cancer are unknown.

Although an injury in the vicinity of the affected bone often precedes the detection of a bone cancer, there is no evidence that any injury (trauma) causes a tumor. Bone cancer can arise in bone that has previously received heavy radiation therapy for other tumors.

SIGNS AND SYMPTOMS

Pain, the most common symptom of bone cancer, may be periodic and severe, or a continuous, dull ache, and is usually confined to the bone itself and adjoining tissues. Swelling often follows, accompanied by warmth in the area and, rarely, by *fever*. Discomfort may grow worse at night and interfere with a child's sleep, but unless the tumor has begun to spread at the time of diagnosis, few children show signs and symptoms of general illness. If the tumor is in a leg bone, a child may stumble or trip. If an arm is affected, some other kind of difficulty with movement may be apparent.

DIAGNOSIS

A child who complains of persistent bone or joint pain should see a physician. Children's complaints of bone pain are sometimes not taken seriously because parents believe that *growing pains* or *sprains* are more likely to be causing bone pain. If a bone tumor exists, a close examination of the affected area usually reveals a specific tender area or mass that may be warm to the touch. If a tumor has reached an advanced stage, blood vessels may be visible or apparent to a physician's examining touch.

If a bone tumor is suspected, the child may be referred to a cancer center for diagnosis by a team of medical specialists, including a pediatric oncologist (a physician specializing in diagnosis and treatment of childhood cancers). For further details, see *cancer*.

To detect newly forming bone cancers, a bone scan may be performed. This test involves injecting tiny, harmless amounts of radioactive materials into a vein to locate bone tumors.

A CT (computed tomography) scan may be required to locate cancer in other sites, such as the lungs. A CT scan provides highly detailed X rays of small cross sections of the body that can be seen on a TV screen and X-ray film.

If X rays, bone scans, and other tests indicate the possibility of bone cancer, a biopsy (small sample of tumor tissue) is surgically removed from the tumor or withdrawn through a needle and then analyzed.

TREATMENT AND COMPLICATIONS

The type, location, and extent of disease determine how a child's bone cancer should be treated. Bone cancers can be treated with surgery, chemotherapy, and radiation therapy.

Treatment for Osteogenic Sarcoma

Physicians may begin by surgically removing the entire tumor. Or the condition may be treated first with chemotherapy, followed by surgery. In the case of a tumor in an arm or a leg, tumor removal may involve either amputation, or simply resection, if the growth is small and well located for this type of surgery. The goal of surgery is to remove all cancerous cells before disease spreads.

Resection involves removing a portion of bone in which a tumor has grown. Sometimes, if a tumor is not extensive and can be removed entirely without interfering with the major nerves and blood vessels, the diseased segment of bone (sometimes including a joint) is replaced by a metallic rod (or artificial joint), or by a substitute bone transplant from a bone bank. Bone transplants do not have the same problems with tissue rejection that accompany other organ transplants. Some bones (ribs, for example) can be removed with little loss of function, and replacement is usually not required.

Following surgery, chemotherapy is usually given in an attempt to destroy any remaining cancer cells over a period of months or years. Anticancer medications are very powerful and can kill normal cells as well as tumor cells. An oncologist must monitor a child's chemotherapy to try to prevent damaging large numbers of healthy cells.

If osteogenic sarcoma spreads to the lungs, surgery to try to remove the secondary tumor is usually followed by chemotherapy. Radiation therapy may also be given following lung surgery.

The outlook for children who receive combined treatment for osteogenic sarcoma is good. After primary tumor removal and chemotherapy, about 50 to 75 percent of patients whose cancer has not spread at the time of diagnosis may expect to live disease-free for at least five years. If a child survives disease-free for five years, the chances of cure may be quite good. Those children who receive further treatment because their disease has spread face a more difficult future, but more and more of them are surviving for longer periods of time. All children who have completed treatment need to be checked periodically by a physician and have X rays or bone scans performed to make certain the disease has not recurred.

Treatment for Ewing's Sarcoma

Physicians more often find metastatic tumor from Ewing's sarcoma at the time of diagnosis than from osteogenic sarcoma. For children who have Ewing's sarcoma, radiation is the usual treatment of their primary tumor. The disease often spreads to lungs and other bones, and further treatment with radiation and chemotherapy is necessary.

The goal of radiation therapy is to focus a high-energy X-ray beam on a tumor at levels sufficiently high to destroy cancer cells while damaging as little healthy tissue as possible. Even though X rays may not show any spread of cancer cells, migration of cells through the bloodstream often occurs.

The success rate for Ewing's sarcoma is increasing. If metastatic disease is not evident at diagnosis and the child is treated by a combination of chemotherapy and radiation, about 50 percent of children with the disease live at least five years. If the tumor is located in an arm or leg, rather than in the lower spine or pelvis, chances of successful treatment and five-year survival increase to about 80 percent. If the disease has spread in the form of a gross tumor, only about 20 to 30 percent of patients can expect to live as long as five years.

Long-term treatment can be stressful for both child and family. Chemotherapy, for example, may go on for 2 years. Families often find that the beginning and end of chemotherapy are especially trying because of the uncertainties of how a child may respond to treatment and, later, to life without it. Networks of relatives and friends as well as health professionals and self-help organizations can provide emotional support during these periods of adjustment.

See also *Cancer.*

PREVENTION

No form of bone cancer can be prevented, as yet.

BOWED LEGS

DESCRIPTION

A child whose ankles touch but whose knees do not has bowed legs, a condition involving the shin and thigh (tibia and femur) bones. During childhood, bowed legs are a part of normal growth and development and are obvious by 2½ months of age. Most infants are bowlegged until they have been walking for a few years, at which time they may become *knock-kneed.* If a child remains bowlegged, however, bone malformation or an underlying bone disease, such as Blount's disease, may be present.

Blount's disease occurs more frequently during infancy (1 to 3 years of age), but also may appear during late childhood and adolescence (9 years and older). Female children, obese or short children, or children who walk at an early age are most often affected by this disorder.

The upper part of the shinbone, where bone growth occurs, is affected by Blount's disease. As a result, the shinbone sharply bows or curves out just below the knee. Since the shinbone is no longer securely connected to the thighbone, a child with Blount's disease is forced to walk with the affected knee flexed, which increases bowing of the leg.

Bowed legs caused by natural growth and development usually correct themselves by the time a child is 4 or 5 years old, but may persist until 8. Bowed legs caused by other conditions may appear at any age and persist into adolescence and beyond.

CAUSE

Bowed legs most often develop as a part of natural growth. Certain diseases may cause a child's legs to bow. *Rickets* is a disease caused by vitamin D deficiency which affects and often weakens a child's bones. Bone malformations present at birth also may cause bowed legs.

COMPLICATIONS

Severe knee joint problems may develop if a child's bowed legs are due to Blount's disease. Abnormal stress from excess weight placed on a slightly bowed leg may increase bowing.

DIAGNOSIS

Bowed legs are obvious when a child stands with legs straight and toes pointed forward. A physician can determine the severity of bowed legs by observing the position of a child's legs, knees, and ankles, and by measuring the distance between the knees. A physician may recommend X-ray films of the knees to look for underlying bone deformities.

TREATMENT

A physician should be consulted if a child has bowed legs. Even if bowing is severe, a physician may advise delaying treatment to give leg bones a chance to straighten naturally.

If bowing of the legs does not correct itself, or increases after a child has been walking for some time, a physician may recommend corrective appliances. Night braces help to pull the legs slowly into a straighter position.

Bowed legs caused by an underlying disease cannot be corrected completely until the disease itself is treated. A child usually wears a corrective brace during part or all of treatment of the disease.

If leg bowing is severe and cannot be corrected through the use of appliances, a physician may recommend surgery. Treatment of Blount's disease often involves surgery upon the upper part of the shinbone.

PREVENTION

Bowed legs caused by *rickets* can be prevented if a child is given at least 400 units of vitamin D daily. Bone diseases and malformations that cause bowed legs cannot be prevented.

BRAIN TUMOR

DESCRIPTION

A brain tumor is any abnormal growth developing within the brain or inside the skull. Such a growth may be a solid tissue mass or a fluid-filled cyst. A brain tumor is considered malignant if it is very rapidly growing. It is considered benign if it is very slow growing. This can be determined only by examining some of the tissue microscopically. Brain tumors rarely spread to other parts of the body and therefore do not behave like *cancer*. They may spread within the head and spine, however.

Statistics show that brain tumors are rare: just one American in 20,000 develops a brain tumor. Approximately 1,400 new cases of brain tumor occur each year among American children.

Among children, however, brain tumor is the second most common malignancy and the most common solid tumor of childhood; only *leukemia* occurs more often and claims more lives each year in the United States. Of the tumors occurring among children less than 15 years old, brain tumors account for about 20 percent of the total. Most children who develop brain tumors are less than 10 years old; boys are affected slightly more often than girls. Brain tumors may occur more often among children who have inherited diseases such as *neurofibromatosis* and tuberous sclerosis (see *seizures*).

The central nervous system (CNS) includes the brain, spinal cord, and their covering, the meninges. The brain and spinal cord consist of highly specialized tissues that direct and coordinate voluntary and involuntary activities. They receive information from and send messages to the vast network of nerves throughout the body.

Both the brain and the spinal cord are protected from shock by the cerebrospinal fluid (CSF) and the meninges. CSF is a clear, thin liquid that bathes and insulates the brain and spinal cord. The meninges consist of three layers of protective membranes that enclose the entire brain and spinal cord, forming an envelope within which the CNS rests in CSF.

The brain is divided into three main parts: the hindbrain, the midbrain, and the forebrain. The hindbrain, located in the back of the skull, contains the medulla oblongata (including centers that control breathing, heart rate, and blood pressure) and the cerebellum, which provides balance and coordinates voluntary movement. The midbrain, located just above the hindbrain in the center of the skull, contains the reflex centers for control or influence of alertness, waking, sleeping, and various reflexes. The forebrain, located in the front and top of the skull, consists of the cerebrum, which divides into two large cerebral hemispheres containing centers for controlling and integrating activities of the entire nervous system. (See Figs. 33–35, p. 634.) The left hemisphere serves the right side of the body; the right hemisphere, the left side. A right-handed person writes and speaks with the left hemisphere.

A tumor can affect any or all of the brain's complex functions in subtle or obvious ways. Both malignant and benign brain tumors can exert damaging pressure on delicate nerve tissue in the CNS, interfering with virtually any physical and mental function of the body that is controlled or dependent upon the brain.

Because the entire brain is especially sensitive to increased pressure and because brain tissue requires an uninterrupted supply of freshly oxygenated blood, a brain tumor threatens the function of the affected part of the brain and that part of the body with which it is associated.

Tumors can occur anywhere in the brain. A tumor arising from the insulating cells between the nerve cells is called a glioma, of which there are several types; the most common is called an astrocytoma. A particular type of astrocytoma, which occurs in the cerebellum, is the most common childhood brain tumor. It often causes disturbances of movement and equilibrium. Astrocytomas of other parts of the brain are less common in childhood and can range from slow-growing tumors curable by surgery to very malignant tumors (such as glioblastomas), which do respond somewhat to radiation and chemotherapy.

The second most common brain tumor in childhood is medulloblastoma, which begins in structures of the hindbrain. It is a malignant tumor that can spread quickly. An example of a benign tumor is the craniopharyngioma which originates in the region of the pituitary gland (see *pituitary problems*).

The outlook for a child with a brain tumor depends on the tumor's location and its exact type (especially whether malignant or benign). These factors determine whether it can be removed. If surgical removal is possible, full recovery may follow. Radiation and chemotherapy sometimes prove effective if surgery cannot be performed.

Through the development of better surgical techniques, better radiation therapy, and the application of newer drugs or combinations of drugs, the control of brain tumors is improving gradually.

CAUSE

The cause of brain tumors is unknown.

SIGNS AND SYMPTOMS

Because some brain tumors develop slowly, signs and symptoms can go unnoticed for a long time. If, on the other hand, a tumor grows quickly, symptoms can develop with alarming speed.

Signs and symptoms of brain tumors vary according to the size of the tumor and the part of the brain affected. Even a small tumor may obstruct the spinal fluid circulation, which will accumulate and cause signs and symptoms of increased pressure in a child's head, including vomiting upon arising in the morning and headache. Morning vomiting, sometimes without nausea, occurs frequently among children with cerebellar tumors that obstruct CSF. In some cases a child may have a stiff neck or tilt the head to one side because of a tumor pushing normal structures down beside the spinal cord.

Children with brain tumors in the cerebral hemisphere may experience *seizures*. Irritation of brain cells which control the limbs may produce uncontrolled twitching of parts of the body and, as this spontaneous electrical activity spreads, may lead to loss of consciousness. Other signs and symptoms of a brain tumor may include increasing listlessness, unusual sleepiness, growing irritability, and changes in emotional and intellectual behavior. Deciding when changes in behavior warrant medical investigation is difficult; parents should consult a physician if they are uncertain as to the cause of unusual behavior.

Trouble with vision or speech or loss of coordination can indicate a tumor. Unduly rapid enlargement of a baby's head or persistent bulging of the soft spot on top of the head (fontanel) may indicate an increase in pressure, in some cases due to a tumor.

Although any of these signs and symptoms may indicate the presence of a brain tumor, other less worrisome problems may turn out to be the cause.

DIAGNOSIS

If a physician suspects an abnormality of the central nervous system, a specialist such as a neurosurgeon or neurologist may be consulted. First, the physician performs simple tests, almost like a game, to check the function of various parts of the brain. Next, the physician inspects the interior of the eyes with a lighted instrument called an ophthalmoscope. At the point where the optic nerve enters the back of the eye, there may be swelling in the presence of increased pressure in the head.

Special tests may be ordered to search for the presence of abnormalities in the brain, for example:

- An X-ray of the child's skull. X-ray films reveal changes in the skull caused by a tumor. In addition, if tiny deposits of calcium (calcifications) are detected in the brain, they may indicate a tumor.
- A CT (computed tomography) scan. This test provides a series of highly detailed images on a television screen and on X-ray film which show not only the skull but also the brain itself and any tumor that may be present.
- An MRI examination (magnetic resonance imaging). This examination by a complex electronic machine equipped with a powerful magnet enables a physician to gather extraordinarily detailed images of internal organs—in this case, the brain. This test does not invade the body in any way, and is accomplished magnetically without radiation.
- An EEG (electroencephalogram). This test records on graph paper the minute yet measurable electrical activity (voltage) of the brain. Tiny electrical contacts (electrodes) are pasted to the scalp and connected to a machine that automatically traces electrical activity in 25 locations in the brain. A patient feels nothing during the course of the test.
- A cerebral angiogram (arteriogram). This test reveals changes in the arteries and veins that carry blood to and from the brain. A special dye, injected into a blood vessel, illuminates the cerebral arteries on X-ray film. Sedation (medication to dull sensation) given before this examination relaxes a child. (Now that CT is more widely available, arteriograms are performed less frequently.)

After locating a tumor by use of such tests, a brain biopsy may be requested to make a definitive diagnosis. If so, a small sample of tissue is removed, under general anesthesia, by a neurosurgeon. A pathologist examines this sample under a microscope to determine the nature of the tumor and whether it is benign or malignant. In cases where tests indicate that a tumor can be removed surgically, a biopsy may be performed at the beginning of the operation, thereby avoiding an extra surgical procedure.

COMPLICATIONS

Because of the extremely delicate nature of nerve tissue, any kind of brain disease or injury (trauma), as well as the surgery performed to save a patient's life, can have severe, long-term consequences. Pressure on important areas may lead to the malfunctioning of part of the body served by that area. Irritation caused by pressure may cause *seizures.* Prompt diagnosis and treatment of these problems can be lifesaving.

TREATMENT

A multitreatment approach may be required for cases of brain tumor. Surgery, radiation therapy, and chemotherapy are useful in dealing with different kinds of brain tumors. The appropriate treatment approach depends upon the type, size, and location of a tumor and a child's age and general physical condition.

Surgery, when it is possible, is the most effective treatment for brain tumors and can provide a cure. A neurosurgeon may be able to remove all or part of a tumor. For example, the most common type of astrocytoma, which occurs in the cerebellum, can usually be cured surgically. Sometimes, however, it proves impossible for a surgeon to reach a tumor for successful surgery because removal of certain tumors can cause irreparable damage to adjacent nerve tissues. Nerve cells do not regenerate. For the same reason, it is sometimes impossible to perform even a biopsy. In such cases, treatment is chosen after evaluating results of the other tests.

Radiation therapy may be able to destroy benign or malignant tumor cells that cannot be reached by surgery. Therapy involves exposure to high-energy radiation, usually X-ray waves. The process is designed to eliminate tumor cells while damaging adjacent healthy tissue as little as possible. A radiation therapist (a physician who specializes in treatment involving high energy rays) supervises therapy and determines how much of the brain is to be exposed to radiation. Some tumors can be treated with localized radiation; others, because of their location or tendency to spread elsewhere (by shedding cells into the CSF), must be treated by irradiating the entire brain and spinal cord. Radiation dosage varies according to a child's age and the type and size of a tumor. Radiation treatment may continue for as long as 6 or 7 weeks.

Chemotherapy has been used much less often for brain tumors than for other kinds of malignant tumors. Anticancer medications may be given orally or intravenously (by injection into a vein). The choice of method depends upon the medication involved, the kind of tumor, and its location.

Other medications given to control the effects of tumors include anticonvulsants to prevent *seizures* and corticosteroids (synthetic hormonelike medications) to reduce pressure within the skull and swelling of the brain.

A child may take medication over a period of months or years at intervals specifically designed for the child and tumor involved. The duration of any medication and how often treatment takes place depend upon the tumor involved, the medication being given, and the severity of any side effects experienced.

The outlook for any child with a brain tumor depends upon the type of tumor being treated, its size, and its location. The type of tumor and its behavior are the most important predictors. If treatment of a malignant tumor is possible, the critical question is whether the entire tumor can be eliminated by one or more methods. If it cannot be, the tumor recurs and destruction of additional healthy brain tissue is certain.

Life expectancy for children with brain tumors, malignant and benign, varies from individual to individual, although in many cases treatment of benign tumors is more promising. It is worth recalling that the most common childhood brain tumors can usually be cured by surgical removal.

PREVENTION

As yet, brain tumors cannot be prevented.

BREAST DEVELOPMENT AND DISORDERS

DESCRIPTION

Breasts contain fat and fibrous (connective) tissue, milk-producing glands, and milk-transporting ducts. These ducts carry milk to the nipple, which is surrounded by the pigmented, circular-shaped areola. The anatomical function of female breasts is to secrete milk. The size of a female's breasts is determined by the amount of glandular tissue and fat within the breasts; any size breasts can secrete milk.

Breast budding is one of the signs of puberty. The first indication of breast budding is the protrusion of the nipple from the chest, followed by the growth of glandular tissue within the breast. A breast bud feels like a tender, grainy lump. One breast may bud before the other does. (Sometimes a breast bud that develops before the other bud is mistaken for a breast mass or lump.) Growth and development of breasts are initiated and regulated by the body's production of female reproductive hormones.

In most cases development problems of the breasts are not disorders at all, but simply involve delayed, rapid, or uneven development. Most girls begin to develop breasts when they are 9 to 14 years old; the average age is 10 or 11. Each girl develops at her own rate. A girl's breasts may not be fully developed until she is 17 or older. Breast size varies greatly but has nothing to do with function.

It is very common, especially early in adolescence when breasts are budding, for breasts to be uneven in size. The unevenness usually lessens or disappears by the time a young woman's breasts are fully developed. Fully developed breasts are often slightly different in size. Generally the difference is noticeable only to the girl herself.

In contrast to normal breast irregularities, true disorders of the breasts occur only occasionally:

- Development of breasts before age 8 may be a sign of precocious, or abnormally early, puberty. Complete lack of development of one or both breasts by age 14 may be a sign of congenital abnormality (one that is present at birth). Some females develop excessively large breasts. Such disorders of the growth rate or size of breasts require medical attention.

- Sometimes a girl is born with nipples that turn inward, a harmless condition called inverted nipples; the condition usually is not particularly noticeable. Breast development sometimes causes inverted nipples to turn outward by themselves. Nipples that are normal at birth and later become inverted, however, require a physician's attention.
- Breast masses or lumps are fairly common among teenage girls. Most "masses" are normal breast tissue. Harmless cysts (typically, liquid-filled sacs) can appear just before a menstrual period and disappear after the period. They may recur, following the same pattern, for two or three months, then usually go away for good. Cysts may be single or multiple, tiny or egg-sized, and concentrated in one area or spread throughout a breast. Breast cysts are usually tender or painful just before menstrual periods.
- Aside from cysts and normal breast tissue, breast masses among females under the age of 25 are almost all fibroadenomas, which are persistent but harmless solid tumors. Fibroadenomas may be small or large, single or multiple; they are round, smooth, painless, and firm or rubbery. In contrast, the texture of normal glandular tissue is irregular and grainy. They may stay the same size or grow larger with each menstrual period. Breast masses are almost never cancerous during childhood and adolescence, but all lumps should be examined by a physician. Fibroadenomas are surgically removed.
- Bruising of a breast can produce a tender breast mass that is poorly defined in shape and size. The mass generally disappears after a few weeks, but occasionally, in the case of a severe blow, a mass takes several months to heal.
- Breast infections are uncommon in females other than newborn infants and nursing mothers. Teenagers occasionally have breast infections near the areola. (A minor infection may be signaled by a discharge from the areola or nipple.) In rare instances an adolescent suffers from mastitis (inflammation of the breast). (A warm, tender mass that appears suddenly underneath the areola plus redness of the overlying skin may indicate breast inflammation.)
- Hair growth around the areola occurs fairly frequently among healthy teenagers. Such hair growth is normal.
- Galactorrhea (flow of milk from the nipples) occurs occasionally and may be associated with amenorrhea (see menstrual irregularities).
- Rarely, nipples secrete other discharges. A barely noticeable amount of fluid is commonly secreted to keep the nipple ducts from closing. Occasionally, a small gland at the edge of the areola becomes blocked or discharges a small amount of brownish fluid for several weeks. If a discharge contains pus, is bloody, pinkish, brownish, or milky, or is persistent, a physician should be consulted.
- About 1 out of every 100 adolescent girls has an extra (accessory) nipple and areola and, rarely, associated breast tissue as well. An accessory nipple looks like a large mole and is not noticeable to most girls. Accessory breasts are rare.

Frequently, an adolescent boy's breasts temporarily develop. (For more information, see gynecomastia.)

CAUSE

The onset and rate of development and the ultimate size of a girl's breasts (and her nipple and areola) are determined by heredity, the level of female hormones and their effects, and nutrition; weight problems can also play a part.

Lack of breast development may result from congenital absence of breast glandular tissue, defective development of the ovaries, or decreased functioning of the ovaries caused by low levels of pituitary hormones. The latter may occur because of functional problems (such as stress, depression, athletic competition, weight loss, or delayed development) or rarely because of an organic problem (pituitary tumors, cysts, or hormone deficiency). Certain conditions can cause an excess of an androgen (male hormone), which may inhibit normal breast development in some girls. These conditions include congenital adrenal hyperplasia (a rare condition in which there is a lack of an

Breast Development and Disorders   **217**

enzyme in the adrenal glands) and adrenal or *ovarian tumors and cysts.*

Lack of breast development may also result from an underlying condition affecting the entire body's growth, such as *malnutrition* or *Crohn's disease.*

The cause of excessive breast development is unknown. Pregnancy, the use of oral contraceptives, and weight gain may cause breasts to enlarge in adolescents.

Congenitally inverted nipples are generally caused by abnormal development of the milk ducts, which causes connective tissue within the breast to pull the nipple down. Nipples that become inverted later in life can be caused by a breast tumor.

The exact cause of most breast masses is unknown. Bruising resulting in breast masses is generally due to blows to the breast.

Minor breast infections often have no apparent cause; occasionally, a hair shaved from the areola causes infection. Infections may also occur during nursing.

Galactorrhea can be caused by hypothyroidism (low level of thyroid gland activity) or factors that cause an increase in the secretion of the hormone prolactin (see also *thyroid problems*).

Prolactic secretion is normal during pregnancy and immediately after childbirth or an abortion. Women who are not pregnant sometimes secrete excess prolactin if their bodies are undergoing major stress (such as surgery or running a marathon), if their breasts are stimulated, or if they are taking oral contraceptives or certain other drugs. Chronic kidney failure (see *kidney failure, chronic*) and kidney and lung tumors can cause galactorrhea, as can conditions and procedures that affect the chest area, such as surgery, *burns,* injury, shingles, and atopic dermatitis (see *eczema*). Some cases of galactorrhea have unknown causes. The most important cause of galactorrhea, especially if associated with amenorrhea, is a tumor of the pituitary gland (see *pituitary problems*).

A discharge containing pus may indicate a breast infection, and a brownish discharge may indicate a cyst and infection. In rare cases, a teenager has a blood-tinged discharge, which can be caused by a wartlike growth in a major breast duct.

The cause of accessory nipples or breasts is unknown.

DIAGNOSIS

If breast development occurs before a girl is 8 years old or none has occurred by the time she is 14, a physician should be consulted. If one breast is significantly different from the other in size, a physician should also be consulted.

If a girl is concerned about her breast development, her breasts and areola are measured at each exam. However, if a girl with small breasts has normal pubic and underarm hair, widening hips, normal genitals, and regular menstrual periods, it is unlikely that she has a developmental disorder of the breasts.

As a matter of course the physician examines the breasts, looking for abnormal masses. If one or more are found, the physician may ask the girl to return at a different point during her menstrual cycle to see if the mass has disappeared. If the mass is still present or has grown larger, aspiration often is performed. Aspiration involves using a small syringe and needle to determine if fluid is present within the lump. If the breast mass then collapses, it is assumed to be a liquid-filled cyst. After 3 months the physician reexamines the area to be sure that the mass is gone. If there is no fluid within the lump or the lump is persistent, the lump is removed by a surgeon. Incisions can often be made in such a way that scars are barely noticeable.

Infections are diagnosed by the presence of a discharge or an inflamed area on the breast.

Galactorrhea is diagnosed by a physician, who may take lab tests to check levels of prolactin in the blood and the function of the thyroid gland. If the prolactin level is high, a CT (computer tomography) scan is done to look for a pituitary tumor. A girl may be referred to an endocrinologist (a physician specializing in disorders of hormone-secreting glands) if her physician suspects the possibility of a pituitary tumor.

A key part of medical consultation involves teaching an adolescent how to examine her own breasts. Pamphlets describing breast self-examination can be found in most physicians' offices.

COMPLICATIONS

Excessively large breasts can result in back pain and the appearance of being round-shouldered.

Inverted nipples may trap normal discharges, possibly leading to infection. If the nipples become infected, they may drain pus.

TREATMENT

Lack of development occurring because of delayed puberty will be reversed with the onset of puberty. For example, the girl involved in competitive ballet or running may be encouraged to alter her training schedule and improve nutrition. Lack of development secondary to inadequate function of the ovaries is treated with hormone tablets.

Lack of development resulting from congenital adrenal hyperplasia can be treated with a drug that suppresses certain hormones. Once these hormones are suppressed, breasts should begin to develop normally.

Research efforts are being made to find better treatment of excessively large breasts that are still growing.

Minor asymmetry requires no treatment, although a bra pad for one breast can be used for cosmetic purposes.

If a young woman is very unhappy about the size or asymmetry of her breasts after they have stopped growing, she may wish to undergo cosmetic surgery either to enlarge or reduce one or both breasts. Surgery presents risks, however, and is best undertaken when breasts have failed to grow at all, are excessively large, or are quite asymmetric.

Inverted nipples that are present at birth are harmless and require no treatment.

If breast masses persist, enlarge, or cause symptoms, surgical removal using local or general anesthesia, usually on an outpatient basis, may be performed. Because a patient who has a fibroadenoma can develop additional fibroadenomas, follow-up examinations are essential.

Breast inflammation is treated with antibiotics and, if a mass is present, incision and drainage of the mass.

Treatment of hair around the areola is unnecessary; however, if a girl feels self-conscious about the hair, she may wish to pluck or clip it. She should not shave the area.

Treatment of galactorrhea caused by hypothyroidism involves treating the thyroid problem.

If a pituitary tumor is causing galactorrhea, the form of treatment depends on the size of the tumor. Therapies include hormonal medications, surgery, and radiation therapy.

Abnormal nipple discharge requires treatment of the underlying condition.

No treatment is necessary for accessory nipples or breasts unless it is desired for cosmetic reasons or problems arise because of engorgement of an accessory breast during nursing.

PREVENTION

Breast disorders cannot be prevented, but regular examinations—both self-exams and medical exams—during adolescence can prepare the teenager for this aspect of important health care for adult women (discussion of self-examination in Chapter 2, "Promoting Physical Health").

BREATHING DIFFICULTY

DESCRIPTION

Children of any age may experience difficult or labored breathing (dyspnea) from various causes. They may have difficulty inhaling or exhaling, through either the mouth or nose. A child's breathing may be uneven, shallow, fast or slow. A child may wheeze, which is most obvious when breathing out. Breathing may be noisy or sound abnormal. In severe cases a child may gasp for air. Breathing difficulty may often be associated with shortness of breath.

CAUSE

Breathing difficulty is commonly caused by *asthma, allergies* (including allergic reactions to insect bites or stings; see *stinging insect reactions*), and *colds* and other viral respiratory infections. Other disorders causing breathing difficulty include *croup, epiglottitis, pneumonia,* bronchitis, lung disorders, and grand mal seizures (see *seizures*). Less common disorders causing breathing difficulty include *heart disease,* kidney disease, and *cystic fibrosis.* Premature infants commonly suffer *apnea* or *respiratory distress syndrome,* both of which involve breathing difficulty.

When anxious, some children, especially adolescents, begin to hyperventilate (breathe so rapidly or deeply that they exhale too much carbon dioxide). They feel as if they cannot breathe. Competitive swimmers may also hyperventilate. Hyperventilation can lead to a fainting spell.

See cross-referenced entries for discussion of diagnosis and treatment.

BRONCHIOLITIS

DESCRIPTION

Bronchiolitis is a common infectious disease of the lower respiratory tract (trachea, or windpipe, bronchi, and lungs). (See Fig. 19, p. 182.) It causes partial blockage of the small airways in the lungs, which in turn produces overinflated lungs. Bronchiolitis usually affects infants less than 2 years old; most often, infants less than 6 months come down with it. Bronchiolitis usually strikes in winter and early spring, either in single cases or in epidemics. Among older children, it sometimes may be mistaken for other lung illnesses, most notably *asthma.*

Bronchiolitis usually occurs just once, although it may recur because it can be caused by several viruses and immunity is often not complete, even in otherwise normal infants. Although it makes infants and young children extremely uncomfortable, bronchiolitis rarely becomes life-threatening. Most children recover completely from bronchiolitis within a week; children with only mild illness may recover within as little as three days.

CAUSE

Bronchiolitis is almost always caused by a virus. In the winter, the most common viral cause is respiratory syncytial (RS) virus. A contagious disease, bronchiolitis is usually transmitted by person-to-person contact, especially from hands and personal materials contaminated by the virus. An older child or adult usually develops only a cold from this virus, which if spread to an infant may produce bronchiolitis.

SIGNS AND SYMPTOMS

Bronchiolitis typically begins with a runny nose and sneezing. A fever of 101° to 103°F (38.3° to 39.4°C) may follow. A wheezing cough and labored breathing almost always cause a child to become irritable. These signs and symptoms usually develop quickly, sometimes in a matter of hours, and last for days.

The most critical period occurs two or three days after the cough and breathing difficulties begin, when air becomes trapped in the small airways of the lungs, making breathing difficult and painful. Children begin to suffer from what is called "air hunger," a physical inability to get enough air in and especially out. This problem is made worse by growing anxiety and fear resulting from the increasing number of breaths which a child must take each minute.

Flaring nostrils, rattling sounds (rales) in the throat or chest, pallor, and a blue color *(cyanosis)* in the area around the mouth and under the finger nails are additional signs that bronchiolitis has become severe. Infants encounter difficulty feeding because there is just not enough time to breathe and either eat or drink. Rest increasingly becomes a problem because sleep is possible only in short naps.

DIAGNOSIS

A physician examines a child, giving close attention to the nose, throat, chest, and lungs. X-ray films of the lungs can help to indicate the degree of blockage of the airways and the amount of air trapped in the lungs. Cultures of mucus can be used to identify the specific virus causing the infection.

COMPLICATIONS

Without treatment, it is possible for a young child with bronchiolitis to suffer respiratory failure—inability to breathe. Infection in the respiratory tract prevents the sick child from getting enough oxygen from inhaled air and from breathing out adequate amounts of carbon dioxide.

Because of fever and breathing difficulties, *dehydration* (a condition characterized by cool, dry, pale skin; a dry tongue; thirst; listlessness; rapid pulse; sunken eyes; and for an infant, sunken fontanel—soft spot on top of the head) may become a problem. If drinking is difficult or impossible, intravenous fluids may be necessary to replace essential body fluids and salts.

TREATMENT

In most cases infants with breathing difficulty, fever, and inability to eat or sleep properly require hospitalization for diagnosis and treatment. Older children may be able to recover at home with attentive care. In the hospital much of the treatment consists of parents and medical staff giving attention and encouragement to a frightened child. Parents need to stay close to an infant and provide comfort and support to help young children through a crisis.

Antibiotics are ineffective against bronchiolitis because it is caused by a virus. Young children, however, may be treated at first with antibiotics since it can sometimes be difficult to distinguish between bronchiolitis and bacterial *pneumonia.* Some children may be helped by the use of a medication to widen the airways (bronchodilator). Cold, humidified oxygen is often given to ease labored breathing. A fever-reducing medication may be helpful. Consult the physician for specific recommendations and read discussion of nonprescription medications beginning on p. 000. Because any form of sedation may be dangerous for a child with breathing difficulties, sedative medications are not prescribed.

Although most children hospitalized with bronchiolitis recover completely within a week, longer recuperation periods may be required for children who have especially severe cases or for children who have chronic diseases. For several months or even years after recovering from bronchiolitis, some children may have recurring episodes of wheezing, particularly when they have a cold.

PREVENTION

Infants less than 6 months old should be kept away from adults or older children with *colds,* if possible. Soap and water handwashing is particularly useful in limiting the spread of infection. Such precautions are particularly important during the winter and with infants who have some other problem such as *prematurity* or congenital heart disease (see *heart disease, congenital*).

Breast-feeding, through transfer of immunity, may reduce the severity of respiratory viral infections among infants and young children.

BRUISES

EMERGENCY ACTION

Most bruises are "well-earned" and appear on the shins, arms, and foreheads of active children who have multiple small injuries during the course of their busy day at play. Most bruises need no special attention unless the injury that caused them is severe. In contrast, multiple bruises that appear spontaneously—without injury and in unusual spots, such as the trunk or back—may indicate that the child has a bleeding disorder. Spontaneous bruising, especially when associated with other bleeding tendencies—such as *nosebleeds,* gum bleeding, or excessive bleeding from minor cuts—requires immediate medical attention. These problems may be the first symptoms of hereditary *bleeding disorders* or of an acquired disorder such as *leukemia.*

DESCRIPTION

A bruise is a collection of blood that has escaped from broken blood vessels because of injury or disease. The blood has settled in a space between muscle and skin and is visible through the surface of the skin. A bruise can be virtually any size. It usually appears reddish at first (or purple if very close to the surface of the skin) and changes to black and blue and finally to yellow-green as the blood cells composing the bruise die and are reabsorbed by the circulatory system. The bruises of fair-skinned children are usually more visible than those of dark-skinned children. Bruises of the whites of the eye are always blood-red.

A bruise can almost always be identified by its characteristic appearance. It can be distinguished from a rash or other skin discoloration when pressure is applied to the area: if it does not appear lighter, the mark is a bruise. All other red-purple marks on the skin blanch under pressure.

Virtually every normally active child gets an injury-related bruise at one time or another. Such a bruise is likely to be accompanied by swelling and pain. A physician may refer to the bruise as a hematoma or a contusion. In general, a hematoma is any collection of blood that has escaped from blood vessels because of injury. A contusion is any surface injury that does not involve a break in the skin. It is common for tiny blood vessels (capillaries) to break and a bruise to appear when the following injuries occur: *cuts and lacerations, fractures, dislocation of joints,* and muscle injuries (see *muscle pain).*

In general, the farther a broken blood vessel is from the skin, the longer it takes for blood to reach the surface of the skin as a bruise. A bruise related to a torn ligament or fracture may not appear until several days after an injury occurs. In some cases, escaped blood does not travel to the skin directly above an injury but settles with gravity, which is why, for example, a blow to the forehead may result in a black eye.

Unfortunately, one cause of injury-related bruises is *child abuse.* Bruises caused by child abuse are frequently not limited to the arms and legs. Children who are the victims of child abuse often appear to have bruises constantly. Many such children have no symptoms except their painful bruises.

Causes of spontaneous bruises include *leukemia,* aplastic anemia (see *anemia, aplastic*), hemophilia and other clotting disorders, and thrombocytopenia (see *blood disorders*). In addition, certain infections and allergic reactions can injure the capillary walls and cause bleeding. Disease-related bruises almost always appear spontaneously, and they usually develop in areas and in numbers that make unnoticed injury a highly improbable cause. They are not usually serious in and of themselves, but the condition that causes them almost always needs medical attention. Sometimes the presence of patches of bruises, a condition known as <u>purpura,</u> is the only visible sign that an underlying disease exists.

In some cases diseases produce pinpoint-to-pinhead sized bruises called <u>petechiae.</u> Often present by the hundreds, petechiae may also appear on the neck as a result of forceful vomiting or coughing or on another part of the body because of harsh contact.

Most bruises disappear naturally, without treatment, in a few days or weeks.

DIAGNOSIS

A child with a very painful bruise, or one of unknown origin, should be seen by a physician as soon as possible. A physician who suspects an underlying disease may recommend a complete physical examination, including blood tests and other diagnostic examinations. If a serious injury is suspected, appropriate diagnostic procedures are carried out (see entries on specific injuries).

TREATMENT

Bruises themselves need no treatment unless a child complains of pain. To ease pain or swelling, cold compresses or an ice pack should be applied to the bruise for about 30 minutes immediately following the injury. In general, ice should never be applied directly to the skin. An ice pack can be made by wrapping a plastic bag of ice cubes in a towel.

Having a child raise a bruised arm or leg above heart level eases swelling by reducing the flow of blood to the injured area. To speed reabsorption of dead blood cells into the blood stream, warm compresses can be applied to a bruise 24 hours or more after the injury occurs.

PREVENTION

While avoiding all minor bruises is impossible, parents can take steps to protect against injury. When possible, children should wear protective gear during sports activities. At home, parents should make sure children are not exposed to furniture with sharp corners. Finally, all children should use car-safety equipment, including car seats or seatbelts. (See also Chapter 4, "Accident Prevention.")

Anyone with a tendency to punish children harshly should seek help and advice from a mental health professional.

BRUXISM

DESCRIPTION

Bruxism is the habit of grinding or clenching the teeth together, usually during sleep.

Many children experience malocclusion (an imperfect fit between closed upper and lower teeth) while they lose their primary ("baby") teeth; an imperfect fit exists between remaining primary and new permanent teeth. Bruxism is most commonly found among children going through this in-between stage, most of whom probably grind their teeth mildy during sleep at one time or another. Bruxism is more uncommon among children who have all their permanent teeth; malocclusion among these children is most likely to result if permanent teeth come in crooked (see *teeth, developmental problems of*).

Children who habitually grind their teeth do not, as a group, have more serious emotional or psychological problems than other children. Bruxism may seem to indicate a severe problem, however, because of the loud grating noises it can produce. These sounds, often loud enough to wake other family members, are misleading; a better measure of the severity of bruxism is the appearance and condition of the teeth, as well as the absence or presence of pain in the mouth.

Even when bruxism is severe enough to cause abrasion of tooth enamel, it can be caught in time to prevent permanent dental problems. When the malocclusion is corrected, bruxism usually decreases.

CAUSE

Certain children develop physical tension in their jaw muscles in response to everyday stress; bruxism helps release this tension. Some children develop simple emotional *stress* in response to physical discomfort caused by malocclusion; bruxism acts as a release for this stress. Most experts agree that bruxism occurs during sleep because the bite reflexes that normally prevent teeth-grinding are suppressed.

SIGNS AND SYMPTOMS

The most obvious indication of bruxism is the loud screeching noise it typically produces.

When bruxism is severe, a child may develop a muscle spasm (tensing of a muscle in an uncomfortably tight position) in the jaw, which can produce extreme local discomfort or even overall *headache*. In addition, a child with severe bruxism may develop tooth problems such as fractured fillings or excessively loose or worn teeth (see *teeth, developmental problems of*).

DIAGNOSIS

A dentist diagnoses and treats bruxism that is unrelated to the gradual eruption of permanent teeth.

COMPLICATIONS

Unchecked severe bruxism involving permanent teeth is a major cause of injury to the structures supporting the teeth, including gum tissue (see *gum problems*), ligaments, and bone. It is also a main cause of excessively loose, prematurely worn, or cracked teeth.

TREATMENT

The type of malocclusion that occurs while permanent teeth are erupting disappears naturally. Some parents, however, may wish to consult a dentist because the noise caused by a child's teeth-grinding is continually waking other family members.

If treatment for malocclusion is necessary, a dentist usually realigns or reshapes teeth. If bruxism is affecting permanent teeth, orthodontic devices such as braces may be used.

If a child has worn down a permanent tooth, a dentist may round sharp edges with a file or bond an enamellike substance to the tooth. These procedures are usually painless. Other treatment methods include medications to relax jaw muscles and soft plastic mouthpieces that fit over teeth during sleep.

PREVENTION

While nothing can be done to prevent the type of malocclusion that occurs as permanent teeth are coming in, routine dental examinations can identify treatable malocclusions that can lead to severe bruxism and its complications.

BURNS

EMERGENCY ACTION

Immediate action is needed when a child is burned, no matter how minor the injury. Never apply butter or ointment on any type of burn because salves can interfere with the healing process and frequently lead to severe infection of the wound. Never break burn blisters, and do not give a child alcohol of any kind. Do not induce vomiting. Be sure that a child can breathe. Start immediate resuscitation if a child's heart and lungs stop functioning. (See Chapter 10, "Basic First Aid.")

Take any child with severe burns or burns covering a large portion of the body to a hospital emergency room immediately. Chances of wound infection are high and immediate medical attention is required. Watch for signs of *dehydration* (characterized by cool, dry, pale skin; dry tongue; thirst; listlessness; rapid pulse; sunken eyes; and for an infant, sunken fontanel, the soft spot on top of a baby's head) and *shock* (characterized by cool, clammy, pale skin; weak, rapid pulse; thirst; dizziness or faintness; and increased breathing rate).

If burns are caused by chemicals, immediately wash a child's skin for several minutes under cool, running water from a shower, faucet, or hose. Remove any contaminated clothing. If the eyes are involved, immediately flush with running water for 10 to 15 minutes to remove chemicals. Turn the head so that the injured side is down and the chemicals will not flow into the unaffected eye. Hold the eyelids open. Cover the affected eye with a clean cloth and seek immediate medical attention.

If emergency medical care for burns is not available immediately, cut away any loose clothing, but do not try to remove any clothing that sticks to the skin. If possible, submerge the burned area in cold water or cover it with several layers of clean dressings soaked in cold water to stop the burning action. Do not use ice water—it may cause the child to go into shock. Cover the burned area loosely with dry, clean bandages. Prevent contact between burned areas such as the fingers by wrapping each individually with loose, dry, clean bandages. The child should lie down unless he or she has severe facial burns or this position is extremely uncomfortable.

If help is unavailable for an hour or more and the child is conscious, give the child fluids. A weak solution of one-half teaspoon baking soda in one quart of water is sufficient. Give a child approximately two ounces (one-quarter cup) of this solution; give an infant one ounce. If vomiting occurs, do not give any more solution.

DESCRIPTION

Burns are among the most common severe injuries of childhood. Severe burns are second only to automobile accidents as the leading cause of accidental death among 1- to 4-year-olds. Among 5- to 14-year-olds, severe burns are the third most common cause of death. All children are susceptible to burns; children under 2 years of age are at higher risk of getting severe burns than others because of their thin, delicate skin. Almost all burns are preventable.

Burns are classified in two ways: by degree or by depth. Both are measures of the depth of the burn. Partial-thickness burns damage the outer part of the skin and can heal with time; full-thickness burns damage all layers of skin and require skin grafting. Severe partial-thickness burns may be difficult to distinguish from full-thickness burns.

A first-degree burn is the least severe type of burn. It affects only the outermost portion of the skin and is characterized by reddening of the skin, pain, and occasionally, slight swelling.

Second-degree burns may be mild, involving only the first layer of skin (the epidermis) and a small amount of the second layer (the dermis), or may be deep, damaging a great deal of the second layer of skin. Affected skin is red, tender, swollen, and blistered. Skin with a deep second-degree burn is usually tough and may be numb for a day or two after injury because of nerve damage.

Third-degree burns extend deep into the tissues below the skin. Swelling may be extensive. Skin surface is tough, leathery, and numb; blisters do not form. The burned tissue is charred and is usually brown, tan, or black in color (although it may be white or even red if the child has a fair to medium skin color). If an electrical burn has occurred, the point of entry is a sunken gray or yellow area.

CAUSE

Burns are caused by contact with extreme heat, flames, corrosive chemicals, electricity, or extended exposure to radiation. First-degree burns most often result from contact with very hot water, with very hot objects such as irons or stoves, or from overexposure of unprotected skin to the sun (see *sunburn*).

Second-degree burns are caused by extended exposure of unprotected skin to the sun; contact with very hot liquids that cling to the skin, such as grease; or contact with small amounts of corrosive substances such as strong cleaning solvents.

Third-degree burns are most often caused by contact with scalding water. This occurs when a child is immersed in extremely hot bathwater or when a scalding liquid is spilled on the child's skin. Spilling often occurs when a curious toddler overturns a container of hot liquid, such as a coffeepot or a cup of hot coffee or tea. Immersion burns are usually more extensive and more severe than spill burns because more skin area is affected. Young children may receive third-degree burns if they chew on plugged-in electrical cords or put small metal objects into unprotected electrical sockets. Third-degree burns are also caused by contact with high-voltage electricity (such as from lightning or a high-tension power line), flames, or extended contact with corrosive substances such as cleaning solvents.

DIAGNOSIS

Burns are obvious because of red skin color, blisters, and in severe cases, charring of skin. However, unless a child has received a first-degree burn, a physician must determine the extent of injury, the type of burn inflicted, and the threat of complications. It is extremely important that a physician have full knowledge of a child's activities at the time of injury so that the type of burn and all possible complications can be determined. To help assess the severity of a deep second-degree or third-degree burn, a physician may use a sterile needle to scratch the skin to see if it bleeds. The most severe burns do not bleed. This test is also helpful in evaluating the severity of burns to darker skin colors, where burns might be masked by the natural complexion.

The size of a burn is described as the percentage of total body surface area affected. Determining the size of a burn also helps define the severity of an injury, the type of treatment required, and a child's chances of successful recovery. However, severe burns are not always associated with extensive skin damage. For example, a high-voltage burn may leave only a small mark on the skin but can cause extensive damage to internal tissues as the current passes through the body.

Partial-thickness burns may be differentiated from full-thickness burns so that proper emergency treatment can be provided. A physician differentiates between these two types of burns by applying gentle pressure with a fingertip to the injured area. If the skin turns white under pressure but resumes its original red color when pressure is relieved, a partial-thickness burn is present. Full-thickness burns do not whiten under pressure. A scratch test with a sterile needle, as described above, may be used for assessing burns to darker-colored skin, where the pressure test would obviously not be helpful.

If a third-degree burn has occurred, a thorough internal examination is performed to detect any damage to the upper and lower airways, the lungs, the gastrointestinal tract (the esophagus, stomach, and intestines), and other parts of the body. Muscle and bone destruction caused by electrical injury must be determined. Lung function must be evaluated frequently to determine whether respiratory failure may occur.

COMPLICATIONS

A child suffering second- and third-degree burns usually loses a great deal of water, bodily fluids, and salts and easily becomes dehydrated. *Dehydration* can lead to other problems, such as extremely low blood pressure, increased heart rate, decreased heart function leading to low blood-pumping output, and constriction of blood vessels. Sudden kidney failure can occur (see *kidney failure, acute*).

Bacterial infections occurring with burns are always a serious threat to a child's health. Such infections may include bacterial *pneumonia* and *urinary tract infections.* If a deep second-degree burn becomes infected, it may deteriorate into a third-degree burn.

Treatment methods have improved vastly in the past few years, however, and the incidence of infection has greatly decreased. Infants are at highest risk for developing infections, as they have not had time to build up sufficient immunity to infectious organisms. Older children with underlying medical problems such as *diabetes* or congenital heart disease (see *heart disease, congenital*) are also at high risk of infection.

Extensive swelling occurring with full-thickness burns may restrict blood flow in surrounding areas or may block the airway and interfere with breathing. Surgery to restore air or blood flow is required to prevent a life-threatening situation.

High-voltage electrical currents cause extensive damage to internal organs and tissue, and may even melt bone. Electrical burns near the head may cause development of cataracts (opaque lens) in the eyes 4 to 6 months after injury. Bleeding may occur deep in internal tissues; hemmorhaging (severe, difficult-to-control bleeding) may occur. If damage is extensive, a child may never recover fully from severe burn complications.

Severe burns can also cause peptic *ulcers.* This occurs because the decreased rate of blood flow caused by severe burns increases the susceptibility of the stomach and beginning of the small intestine to developing open sores (ulcers). This complication is rare among burn victims, however, because antacids which help prevent ulcers from forming are routinely administered upon admission to a burn unit or center.

Today the most common cause of death related to severe burns is respiratory failure. This complication most often results from bacterial pneumonia but may also result from inhalation injury (including heat injury to the airways, carbon monoxide poisoning, or inhalation of toxic gases), fluid collection in the lungs, constriction of the chest wall because of a severe burn injury, or inhalation of foreign matter into the air passages. A child wheezes and gasps for air as the lungs begin to malfunction. Artificial respiration and medication to widen breathing tubes are necessary to prevent respiratory failure.

TREATMENT

Most first- and second-degree burns can be treated at home. However, severe second-degree burns and third-degree burns always require a physician's treatment. A child with severe burns should be taken to a hospital emergency room immediately.

Mild Burns

At home, treatment of mild burns should begin with immediate immersion of the injured area in cold (not icy) water or covering of the area with cold, moist dressings. These precautions prevent further damage to the skin and ease pain. The area should remain submerged or covered for at least 5 minutes or until the pain lessens. Care must be taken, however, to ensure that the injured area does not become numb, since frostbite (see *exposure to temperature extremes*) can occur. If pain flares up again, the area can be reimmersed in cold water.

After pain has lessened, first-degree burns should be dried gently; a sterile-gauze dressing may be applied. Very mild soap can be used to clean an uncomplicated second-degree burn, but a washcloth or other washing implement should not be used because it could irritate the wound. After being washed, second-degree burns should be covered with a loose, sterile bandage. A pain-relieving medication can be helpful. Consult a physician for specific recommendations and read discussion of nonprescription medications beginning on p. 102. Surface-numbing preparations are not recommended, as they can be absorbed into the skin and then the bloodstream.

Blisters forming because of a mild second-degree burn should not be broken unless they cover a joint or the hand, because they act as natural protection for underlying damaged skin. If a blister does break, the loose skin should be removed, unless this is too painful to accomplish. If left in place, the loose skin may increase the risk of infection. After the wound is wrapped in clean bandages, a child with a second-degree burn should be seen by a physician.

A physician rewashes a second-degree burn gently and removes any loose skin. The wound is wrapped in fresh, sterile bandages. The physician will instruct the parents to change the bandages twice a day and to keep the wound clean. The pain caused by changing bandages may be lessened if the bandages are soaked with warm water just before removal.

If a child has not received a tetanus immunization during the previous year, a physician administers a shot to prevent tetanus. If the wound has become infected, a physician prescribes oral antibiotics. In most cases a physician does not prescribe a surface antibiotic because most preparations produce side effects or allergic reactions. The physician asks to see the child again within a few days if the burn is severe.

With effective treatment, first-degree burns usually heal 48 to 72 hours after injury; 5 to 10 days later, the damaged skin peels off and no scar remains. Mild second-degree burns heal with minimal scarring within 10 to 14 days, although burns caused by hot grease or flames usually require a longer healing time. Deep second-degree burns heal slowly, usually within 25 to 35 days, and scarring is common. If a second-degree burn becomes infected, healing is prolonged and hospitalization is required to treat infection.

Severe Burns

A severely burned child always requires immediate hospitalization in a hospital burn unit or burn center. The treatment of severe burns is complicated. A child with severe burns over 30 percent or more of the body can suffer as many as 4 to 6 major complications during recovery, any one of which may be life-threatening.

All burned children under the age of 2 and any older child suffering burns on the face, hands, or perineum (the area between the legs) must be hospitalized. Children with first- or second-degree burns over 30 percent or more of their bodies or with third-degree burns over 10 percent or more of their bodies also must be hospitalized. Any child burned by chemicals or high-voltage electricity or suffering inhalation injury caused by inhaled flames or toxic fumes must be hospitalized. A child with a medical condition that may be aggravated by burns should also be admitted to a burn center or hospital.

If a burned child's parents cannot provide adequate care at home, for whatever reason, a physician may decide to hospitalize the child. If a physician suspects that a burn was intentionally inflicted, the child must be hospitalized for his or her own safety (see *child abuse*).

Before burns are treated, life-threatening complications must be alleviated. This includes treatment of shock; administration of oxygen and respiratory support; conservation of body heat, fluids, and salts, including control of environmental temperature and intravenous fluid replacement; and administration of antibiotics, including, if necessary, tetanus immunization. Burn victims require diets high in protein and calories so that the body has adequate nutrients and energy for tissue regeneration.

Once a child's life is no longer in danger, treatment focuses on care of burns. Treatment includes careful cleaning of the wound, removal of dead tissue, administration of antibiotics, and dressing of the burns with sterile bandages, which are changed daily. The burned area should be skin-grafted as soon as possible, using the child's own skin from an unburned area. If the burn is very extensive, a temporary skin graft made of pigskin or artificial skin may be applied; this graft acts as a temporary living bandage. It is effective at preventing fluid loss and infection and at lessening pain caused by the burn. Temporary pigskin grafts survive for 5 to 7 days; artificial skin grafts last up to 40 days. Temporary grafts can be used on any burn but are particularly effective in areas that are difficult to bandage. In most cases children who are burned over less than 50 percent of their body surface recover fully with skin grafts within 3 to 6 weeks after injury.

Permanent skin grafts can replace destroyed skin at the site of the full-thickness burn. Burns of the face and neck and around the joints are usually treated first. Burns are covered with healthy skin taken from unaffected areas of the body; the graft acts as a permanent covering for the damaged area. Grafting of a burn may be a lengthy project, as only small patches of healthy skin can be removed at any one time. Healthy skin must regrow in donor areas before more skin tissue can be removed for grafting.

Skin grafting is the most effective treatment of third-degree burns. Newer techniques are being developed that will allow severely burned individuals to survive. Researchers are developing an artificial skin that may be used in the same way as grafts from the child's own skin and thus hasten the healing process and make possible the survival of children burned over much of their bodies. However, the use of this artificial skin continues to be limited to a relatively small number of individuals.

Once a burn begins to heal, it is extremely important that functional motion of the affected area is not impaired. A physician and a physical therapist recommend special exercises to prevent stiffening or contracting of muscles and loss of movement in the joints. If damage to muscles is extensive, traction (which gently stretches muscles) or pressure treatments designed to prevent muscle stiffening and contractions are needed.

Severe burns and skin grafts require special care as they heal. Exposure of the skin to sunlight should be avoided; sunscreens containing PABA should be used for maximum protection. Moisturizing creams or lotions that do not contain alcohol can be used to help prevent drying, cracking, and itching of skin as it heals. A physician may prescribe special creams to help reduce scarring, but these preparations are very strong and should be used in small areas only.

If a full-thickness burn causes skin or muscle constriction or major scarring when it heals, further skin grafting may be needed. Although some improvement can be achieved, some scarring will always remain.

Children burned by high voltage electricity require extensive care of internal injuries as well as treatment of burns. Intensive, often prolonged care is usually required.

In addition to care of burns and internal injuries, severely burned children need emotional guidance and understanding. They frequently relive the experience of being burned in their minds, and must deal not only with the fear and emotional pain involved but also with the constant physical pain of healing. Children may go into self-hypnotic states in an effort to escape the experience. Frequent hospitalization may separate burned children from their parents and friends and can be a frightening and lonely experience. In addition, severely burned children are constantly faced with unanswered questions about their future, their health, their chances of recovery, and "why this awful thing happened to me." Consequently, an important member of the burn treatment team is an experienced, compassionate psychiatric nurse, psychiatrist, psychologist, or social worker. This professional can also help other members of the family work through their personal reactions to the child's condition.

PREVENTION

In most cases burns can be prevented. Children should wear sunscreens containing PABA to prevent sunburn. Fireplace screens or guards should be placed around fireplaces, heaters, furnaces, and radiators to prevent a child from coming in contact with flames or extremely hot surfaces. Hot-steam vaporizers and portable heaters should be placed well out of the reach of children. Vaporizer thermostats should be set at a warm rather than a hot temperature. The temperature of bathwater should be carefully checked before a child is placed in a bathtub. Running the cold water first for a bath is a sound safety precaution. Children should always be supervised while bathing.

Infants or small children should be placed in playpens or highchairs while a stove or an electrical appliance is in use. Pot handles should be turned toward the back of the stove so that a child cannot reach them. The oven door never should be left open when a child is nearby. Matches should be kept on a shelf or in a drawer well out of a child's reach.

Electrical outlets that are not in use should be covered with plastic safety caps, available at all hardware stores. Active electrical cords should be placed out of a child's reach. Children should be warned not to play near electrical power lines or electrified railroad tracks. Fencing should be erected around areas of high electricity.

Flammable liquids, such as gasoline, kerosene, and other fuel oils, should be stored in locked cabinets or storage rooms. All such liquids should be clearly marked and left in their original containers. Gasoline or kerosene stored in soft-drink bottles or fruit juice jars may present small children with an attractive danger. For full discussion of childproofing, see Chapter 4, "Accident Prevention."

CANCER

DESCRIPTION

Cancer is a general name for more than 100 different diseases characterized by uncontrollable growth of cells. This growth most often involves very young cells that keep dividing and cannot be stopped.

Cancer causes the destruction of normal cells, often interfering with normal growth and development. As a result, childhood cancers are among the most harmful of all children's diseases. It is important to remember, at the same time, that remarkable progress has been made over the past 25 years in understanding how to combat and control cancers.

Cancers are often referred to as tumors—masses of abnormal cells. A cancerous tumor is referred to as malignant, because the growth of abnormal cells is uncontrolled and spreads to adjacent healthy tissue. A noncancerous tumor is referred to as benign, because growth is confined to a specific location and does not invade and destroy healthy tissue. Because size and location of tumors are crucial factors in treatment, however, a benign tumor sometimes can be as injurious to health as a malignant one. For example, a benign brain tumor located in a crucial but inaccessible site may be permanently disabling and prove much more of a problem than a malignant tumor of the arm, which is easily accessible for surgical removal.

A cancer that originates in one kind of cell or tissue is called a primary cancer (primary tumor). Cells from a malignant tumor can spread through the blood or the lymph (a clear fluid that bathes cells and circulates through the vessels of the infection-fighting lymphatic system) and "seed" additional tumors—called secondary tumors—in distant parts of the body such as the lungs, liver, bones, brain, and spinal cord. Sometimes secondary tumors are more obvious than primary ones, because they are the first to produce noticeable signs and symptoms of disease. When a cancer spreads, it is said to metastasize, and the secondary tumors are sometimes referred to as metastases.

Tumors appear in three different forms. Carcinomas are cancers that develop in the tissues lining body organs. Sarcomas are cancers that develop in the connective and supportive tissues, such as tendons and bones. A lymphoma is a cancer that develops in the specialized, infection-fighting lymphoid tissue of which the lymph nodes and the spleen are examples. Leukemia is a cancer of both the bone marrow and the circulating blood. Many types of lymphomas exist, each with its own treatment (although many courses of treatment have substantial similarities), and its own probabilities of control or cure.

Cancer among children remains a rare disease. There are about 6,000 new cases of childhood cancer annually in the United States. At least half of all children with cancer in the United States survive the disease.

Leukemia is the most common type of cancer among children, comprising about one-third of all malignant childhood diseases. Cancers of the central nervous system (including *brain tumor* and spinal cord tumors) rank second (20 percent) among childhood cancers. The next most prevalent, in order of frequency, are *lymphoma* (11 percent), *neuroblastoma* (8 percent), soft-tissue sarcoma (7 percent), *Wilms' tumor* (6 percent), *bone cancer* (5 percent), *retinoblastoma* (3 percent), liver cancer (2 percent), ovarian cancer (1 percent; see *ovarian tumors and cysts*), and testicular cancer (1 percent; see *genitourinary tumors*). All other cancers of childhood account for the remaining 7 percent.

Cancer specialists, called oncologists, have come to regard cancer as a chronic disease in the sense that it requires lifelong observation. Although treatment may be successful and a child judged to be disease-free, for many types of childhood cancer it is difficult to predict how long a "cure" may last. Today children treated successfully for some types of childhood leukemia remain healthy into their 20s and 30s. While the term "cure" is used cautiously, there is good reason to be hopeful. Because at least half of all childhood cancers are now being cured or are curable, in the future a majority of children with cancer should receive even more effective treatment and be considered permanently free of the disease.

The outlook for a child with cancer varies according to the type of cancer, its location and size, the child's general health and strength, and the success of the therapies used.

CAUSE

The cause of cancer remains unknown. Although research efforts have made remarkable progress in the past 20 years, not a single definite cause for any type of cancer has yet been identified. One question about the cause of cancer can be answered: cancer is not contagious—it cannot be transmitted from person to person.

Cancer-triggering agents, such as carcinogens or viruses, are presumed to work by damaging (changing or mutating) genetic material—genes. Accordingly, they are called mutagens. In human cells the target of carcinogens is DNA (deoxyribonucleic acid)—a complex molecule, present in each cell of every living organism. Segments of DNA, or genes, serve as the bearers of information for all biological functions. By mutating the structure of DNA, mutagens can create new patterns of genes that encourage or promote the growth of tumor cells.

Carcinogens often enter the human body through the lungs or the intestinal tract. By chance they encounter the DNA in cells of some tissues, and abnormal gene patterns are created. Human cells that have been exposed to carcinogens may slowly accumulate damaged genes and duplicate them. Sequences of mutated genes that control growth in cancer cells are called "oncogenes"—cancer genes. Instead of permitting growth only when appropriate, oncogenes compel a cell into endless growth. A cell with mutated genes can reproduce billions of copies of its abnormal self that eventually constitute a tumor.

Even after an oncogene is created by a spontaneous rearrangment of genes or possibly by invasion of a particular virus, other changes must occur before it can become a full-fledged cancer cell. It is theorized that perhaps one or more altered genes must cooperate with the oncogene at several points of development in order to accomplish the task of stimulating and producing cancer.

Some evidence suggests that a predisposition to certain cancers runs in some families, although exactly how this mechanism operates is only partially understood. For example, an identical twin of a child with *leukemia* runs a somewhat higher risk of acquiring leukemia than does a child in the general population.

Certain risk factors also increase the chances of acquiring cancer. Studies of survivors of nuclear bombing, workers exposed to radiation, and cancer patients who have received radiation therapy or diagnostic X rays for various medical conditions have shown that excessive doses of ionizing radiation can induce human cancers. Drugs and medications—including, ironically, some used in cancer treatment—can increase the risk of acquiring cancer. In addition, some hormones, including diethylstilbesterol (see *DES exposure)* can also increase the risk of developing cancer.

Certain chemicals in air, water, soil, and food can lead to cancers, especially those of the lung, bladder, skin, and blood. Cigarette smoking causes one of every four cases of adult cancer; smoking among children and adolescents guarantees many future cancers of the lung.

Dietary factors (such as food additives, pesticides, and exposure to water that is contaminated) are associated with development of cancers of the breast, colon, stomach, and other organs. No causal relationship, however, has been proved. Infectious agents, especially several viruses (see *AIDS*), are thought to be associated with specific human cancers, but a direct relationship has yet to be demonstrated.

Children who have certain *genetic disorders* display unusual susceptibility to various kinds of cancer. In most of these genetic disorders, a child is identified as having that disorder before a cancer appears. Children with genetic disorders who develop cancer usually share several common features, including being very young at the time of diagnosis or having several primary cancers. Chromosomal abnormalities can be either inborn, as in *Down syndrome,* or acquired through exposure to environmental factors, such as radiation or certain hydrocarbons (chemical compounds found, for example, in petroleum products).

SIGNS AND SYMPTOMS

Leukemia, brain tumor, lymphoma, neuroblastoma, Wilms' tumor, bone cancer, and *retinoblastoma* are cancers of childhood whose signs and symptoms are discussed in detail in individual entries.

Many cancers produce general signs and symptoms of illness; others produce quite specific ones. Some have common signs and symptoms, such as fatigue, loss of appetite and weight, and recurrent infections, and may not, at first, seem like cancer at all. Cases in which the signs and symptoms are unusual and persistent, however, such as swelling or the appearance of a lump, are noticeable from the start and usually receive attention more promptly. However, by their very nature, some types of cancer are "silent tumors": they give few, if any, indications of their presence until fairly well developed.

DIAGNOSIS

The most caring parent has no way of knowing the possible long-term significance of the general signs or symptoms of illness (e.g., aches and pains, irritability, loss of appetite) which precede or accompany some types of childhood cancer. A child who experiences swelling, persistent pain, or convulsions, on the other hand, is usually brought at once to a physician. If any general signs or symptoms of any illness persist for a week, it is probably wise to call a physician and describe what is going on. He or she may advise an additional period of watchfulness or may ask to see the child promptly. Parents should keep the physician

fully informed of the child's physical and emotional condition as long as illness persists.

A physician who suspects cancer but is not certain may refer a child and parents to a cancer hospital or cancer center, where a team of medical specialists, many of them oncologists, cooperatively investigates whether an individual may, indeed, have cancer of some type.

After recording in detail the history and signs and symptoms of illness, an oncologist performs a careful physical examination, seeking to locate specific indicators of abnormality or disease. A series of laboratory examinations is performed, beginning with blood tests and X rays. Descriptions of various tests are included in the diagnosis section of individual sections about cancer.

When leukemia is suspected, a sample of bone marrow is removed and analyzed for abnormal cells. This procedure is a type of biopsy. A lumbar puncture (sometimes called a spinal tap) may be performed to withdraw and analyze a sample of spinal fluid for the presence of abnormal cells or infectious agents. When solid tumors are suspected or located, tissue biopsies are performed. A variety of X-ray techniques, often highly sophisticated forms of technology, are used to locate and identify tumors. A radiologist (a physician who specializes in diagnosing disease by using these techniques) assumes responsibility for this phase of the investigation. Specialized X rays may include intravenous injection of specific dyes to illuminate affected organs or systems. Scans of various organs using intravenous injection of tiny amounts of harmless radioactive materials may be helpful. Ultrasound, the use of high-frequency sound waves, is used to provide images of certain tissues and organs on a TV screen and on film.

The entire diagnostic process may take only one day or it may require as long as a week or more for systematic investigation and study. The diagnostic process may take place in a hospital, or tests may be performed on an outpatient basis. The choice depends in large part upon the preference of the medical team and the physical condition of the child. While undergoing these tests, an ill child may feel more comfortable and secure in a hospital with his or her parents on hand for explanations and support.

Parents of children who are found to have cancer sometimes blame themselves for not having sought medical attention or the help of oncologists at the very first sign of illness or abnormalities. Feelings of guilt and anger over having "delayed" in seeking medical attention are understandable but usually unjustified. It is essential, however, that accurate treatment be started as soon as diagnosis is confirmed.

Parents who are troubled by or uncertain of a diagnosis of cancer may want to get a second opinion, especially if the diagnosis is not made by a cancer specialist. Some physicians suggest that parents seek another opinion. If a physician does not recommend a particular oncologist or cancer center, parents may call the local or state medical society to get names of physicians, hospitals, or centers specializing in cancer diagnosis and treatment. Parents should NEVER seek second opinions from nonlicensed practitioners who profess to be expert in "nontraditional diagnosis" or "guaranteed cure" of cancer.

TREATMENT AND COMPLICATIONS

If a diagnosis of cancer is confirmed, parents and physicians can decide on the best location for treatment. Because most forms of childhood cancer are complicated, a regional cancer center or a teaching hospital is usually preferable to a local hospital. The National Cancer Institute, a branch of the United States Public Health Service, recommends that treatment be given at a cancer center that has an experienced staff and the resources to apply the most effective form(s) of treatment from the beginning. Treatment for cancers of all types changes constantly as experience and research provide new, better methods and therapies.

Before any treatment begins, a physician should discuss the program with the parents, explaining possible benefits and risks. It is necessary for the physician to obtain parental consent before therapy begins. Depending upon the institution's policy on the age at which a patient's consent is necessary to begin treatment, a child may be encouraged to approve the treatment as well. The child's local physician can continue to play an active role in patient care, even if treatment occurs some distance from home. The local physician can coordinate and perform routine medical care, can serve as a source of ongoing advice and reassurance, and may also be asked by cancer center physicians to perform follow-up blood tests and to give and monitor chemotherapy as prescribed by them.

The kind of treatment given any child varies according to the type of cancer diagnosed. Most cancer patients receive surgery, radiation therapy, or chemotherapy, or a combination of these therapies. The goal of therapy is to create a remission—the decline or disappearance of cancer cells as well as associated signs and symptoms. Treatment goes through two major phases—remission induction and remission maintenance.

If remission induction is successful, maintenance therapy aims to eliminate any cancer cells that cannot be detected by any test. Such a course is followed because experience in treating cancer indicates that cells often travel far from the site of the original tumor.

The summary of the three therapies that follows is intended as an introduction; it is neither detailed nor comprehensive.

Surgery

The best form of therapy for many solid tumors is often surgery. In the case of extensive or large tumors, radiation or chemotherapy may be used to reduce the size of the tumor before surgery is attempted.

Surgery involves general anesthesia, some postoperative pain, and intravenous fluids for several days during recuperation. In cases of sarcoma, if other therapies do not succeed, surgery may involve amputation of a limb.

A child should be prepared for all of these new experiences before the operation itself. The child should learn as much as he or she is interested in or capable of learning about the nature of the operation. A surgeon or nurse might show the child the uniforms and masks worn by operating-room personnel, or a member of the surgical team might drop by in advance, wearing the surgical outfit, to describe the operating procedure. A nurse or physician can explain anesthesia, how it is administered, and how it feels while it is wearing off. A nurse or physician can discuss the purpose of pain medication and intravenous fluids before and after surgery.

A parent should be present during such conversations so that he or she is prepared to answer any questions that the child may ask later. Honesty about the experience of surgery and its aftermath is essential. What a parent does not know or is unsure of should be discussed with a member of the hospital staff.

Chemotherapy

Treatment with a combination of powerful anticancer medications is known as chemotherapy. These medications may be given by mouth (pills or liquids) or by injection into a muscle, into a vein, or just below the skin. They can also be injected directly into the spinal fluid (which cushions and protects the brain and spinal cord). Such an "intrathecal" injection takes place either into the spinal canal between two vertebrae in the lower back or directly into the brain through a small tube which is surgically implanted in advance for that purpose.

Anticancer medications interfere with a cancer cell's ability to duplicate and grow, either killing the cell or preventing its division by blocking DNA production.

Unfortunately, anticancer medications affect not only cancer cells but other rapidly dividing cells such as those in the hair follicles, bone marrow, and gastrointestinal tract. As a result, certain side effects of chemotherapy are unavoidable. Among the most threatening to physical health is reduction or suppression of the capacity of bone marrow to produce normal amounts of blood cells. The consequences include greater risk of *anemia* (from reduced levels of red blood cells), bleeding (from reduced levels of platelets), and infection (from reduced levels of white blood cells; see *infections, frequent)*. Nothing has yet been discovered to reverse or avoid the suppressive effects of anticancer medications on bone marrow during chemotherapy.

A child may suffer hair loss as a side effect of chemotherapy. Hair may fall out gradually or all at once and regrow slowly over several months following the completion of chemotherapy. A child may feel more comfortable wearing a cap, a scarf, or a wig during the course of chemotherapy. Such a child may find it comforting and reassuring to talk with someone who has coped with the same experience and regained both hair and a sense of well-being afterward.

Other side effects vary in kind and severity from person to person and medication to medication. Nausea and vomiting are common immediate side effects that may occur soon after a child takes a dose of medication. Mouth soreness and ulcers are common delayed side effects; they may develop days or weeks after medication has begun. Constipation can result from taking one of several medications. Some side effects can be controlled; a child's physician can suggest ways of dealing with many of them.

Radiation

High-energy X rays or other sources of ionizing radiation such as radioactive cobalt or radium are used to treat many types of cancer. The radiation rays strike cell tissue, damaging the DNA within. Cancer cells are more sensitive to radiation than normal cells because radiation tends to kill cells that divide rapidly. Most surrounding healthy tissue is not affected. The size of a tumor is reduced proportionally to the number of cells that are destroyed.

Radiation is painless during the treatment itself. The therapy resembles having a diagnostic X-ray film taken except that it takes longer; the child receiving the treatment must not move for several minutes at a time, depending upon the kind of tumor, its size, and the dosage of the treatment. Radiation therapy may occur daily or every other day, for as long as 4 or 5 weeks.

A radiation therapist explains to the child and parents the duration of therapy, the number of treatments, the dosages, and the possible side effects. The area of the body to be irradiated is often marked with a dye pen to provide guidelines for radiation during each individual treatment. A radiation therapist or technician can explain what happens in the course of treatment and can show the child the radiation therapy room and what radiation machinery looks like.

During radiation therapy, for a child's protection against possible long-term side effects, parts of the child's body other than those being irradiated are shielded with lead. Radiation side effects can vary according to the part of the body being irradiated. Skin around the site of radiation may become somewhat sensitive, reddened, and sore, but blistering is unusual. Creams, ointments, or powders may be prescribed by the physician to relieve any pain, itching, or burning. Any skin receiving radiation loses its hair, but hair loss is temporary and new hair begins to grow about three months after completion of radiation treatments. Nausea, vomiting, and headaches may bother a child who receives radiation therapy of the abdomen or head. Diarrhea can occur after radiation therapy of the abdomen or pelvic area.

Some children who receive radiation therapy to the brain or central nervous system may become drowsy afterwards and begin to require longer sleep periods. This change in sleep habits can occur immediately or as long as 5 to 7 weeks after the completion of therapy. Fever, headache, nausea and vomiting, general irritability, and loss of appetite may precede this temporary need for additional sleep. The most serious long-term aftereffect of radiation therapy can be development of a second tumor in the same area several years later because of the previous radiation therapy. The chances of such recurrence are not great; they vary according to the amount of radiation given and the body part irradiated.

Frightened parents sometimes seek out untested or controversial treatments. "Cures" induced by unproved therapies, such as "miracle diets," controversial, unlicensed "wonder drugs," or a series of treatments using unusual "medical equipment" or physical manipulations raise false hopes and benefit only the promoter. Because legitimate cancer treatment is usually complicated and time-consuming, profit-seeking individuals prey upon cancer patients and their families. Occasionally, well-meaning relatives and friends may offer suggestions regarding "alternative" treatment methods. If this happens, it is usually best to describe briefly the child's treatment program and to say quite firmly that such a course seems safest and most promising in the long run.

Cancer affects everyone in a family. The overall psychological impact of a child's cancer treatment is profound. At the time of diagnosis, many families feel overwhelmed by the knowledge that a child has a potentially life-destroying disease. Fear for a child's welfare and future often becomes tinged with anger as family members begin to ask the question that plagues every victim of a life-threatening disease: "Why me?" or "Why us?" Even when it becomes evident to a young person that there is no answer to such a question, painful emotions often continue to cast shadows over the daily life of the family.

When treatment stops, the family wonders whether the remission of signs and symptoms will continue without therapy; how the child will feel without the support of therapy and the accompanying medical team; and what will happen when the child resumes a normal routine.

Relapses, recurrence of illness following termination of treatment, can signal a period of apprehension and even depression for the entire family. If resumption of therapy brings about a remission of signs and symptoms, inevitable anxiety-producing questions loom even larger: "How long will the remission last?" and "What happens next if cancer recurs?" If treatment is not successful, the time comes when the parents must decide with the medical team whether to abandon all treatment and prepare for the inevitable or, instead, to attempt an experimental course of therapy based on research efforts to find more effective ways of treating cancer in the future. This time is often marked by feelings of desperation mixed with hope that a new discovery, at last, will save the child.

Cancer centers and other hospitals usually have psychologists, psychiatrists, and social workers on their staffs who are trained to deal with the range of problems that cancer can pose for patient and family. Dealing with the emotional complications of the disease can contribute significantly to the overall success of treatment.

Cancer patients who are as old as 3 or 4 years want to know when they will get better. In response to specific questions, children should be told as much as they can comprehend intellectually and process emotionally. "Humanely tempered truth" is the way one physician describes the sensitive choice of facts and interpretation that a thoughtful adult is capable of conveying.

Cancer means different things to children of different ages. The preschool child, for example, wants to know why so much time is spent in a hospital. The school-aged child wants to know when the treatments will end and life become normal again—returning home and to school. The adolescent wants the side effects to disappear quickly and yearns to be independent even while depending upon the medical team and parents for help. Regardless of age, children with cancer know with varying intensities that their illness is serious and their treatment unusual. Many struggle inwardly and outwardly with feelings about death and dying. Each child with cancer should be treated as an individual whose needs for information and protection vary with health and age.

Even now when so much more is understood about cancer, some people hesitate to come into contact with an individual who has cancer, perhaps for fear of "catching" it. Such unfounded fear can have an isolating effect upon children who are often eager for company and support as they undergo treatment and fight their disease. A parent can say candidly to relatives, friends, and a child's classmates and teachers that cancer is impossible to catch: even though the cause of cancer remains unknown, we do know that cancer is not transmitted from person to person.

Cancer is too often considered a taboo subject. Some people avoid anyone with cancer, perhaps because they cannot bear to be reminded of their own frailty or mortality. Others may feel embarrassed or uncomfortable because they are uncertain of what to say to a child with cancer or to the parents. Reassurance often overcomes avoidance: parents who realize this can help others reach out.

Sources of institutional support are available. Parents of a child with cancer can call upon a number of excellent resources for information and assistance:

The American Cancer Society (ACS) is a public service organization specializing in providing public information and education about the disease and in fundraising to promote research efforts. For the nearest ACS office, consult local telephone directories or write to the national headquarters: 90 Park Avenue, New York, NY 10016 (212-599-8200).

The National Cancer Institute (NCI) sponsors programs of cancer research in Washington and in laboratories across the country. In addition, the NCI publishes many types of printed and taped information about cancer for the public (adults and children) and health professionals. These excellent materials are available from the NCI (Office of Cancer Communications, NCI, Bldg. 31, Room 10A24, Bethesda, MD 20892) and through medical offices and hospitals. One especially helpful book is *Young People with Cancer: A Handbook for Parents.*

NCI sponsors the Cancer Information Service, a telephone network that provides excellent information about cancer to anyone who calls (toll-free): 1-800-4-CANCER.

Parents can find information on services for children with cancer and a national network of families through an organization called Candlelighters Childhood Cancer Foundation, Suite 1011, 2025 Eye Street NW, Washington, DC 20006 (202-659-5136).

PREVENTION

Parents should try to be alert to the probable existence of any environmental hazard to health (see Cause, above). Children should not be exposed to any agent known to cause cancer among humans, especially tobacco in any form—smoking, chewing, or inhaling. The American Academy of Pediatrics warns that children who simply breathe tobacco smoke in their environments (i.e., who are subject to "passive exposure") run higher risks of contracting other health problems as well, especially respiratory infections.

CANKER SORES

DESCRIPTION

Canker sores are painful, recurrent mouth sores that appear on the inner lips, gums, inner cheeks, tongue, palate, and throat. They appear as small, shallow hollows in the lining of the child's mouth, with sharp borders covered by a gray membrane and surrounded by a bright red circle. The sores usually occur singly but may appear in clusters. Canker sores are very common, occurring in approximately 20 to 50 percent of the population; they appear more frequently in females. The sores are not associated with general symptoms such as fever, and tend to recur in cycles. Most sores heal by themselves without scarring within one to two weeks.

Canker sores should not be confused with fever blisters or cold sores, which are caused by the herpes simplex type 1 virus and commonly are found on the outer lips or nearby skin (see *oral herpes).* Children often think they have a toothache when they actually have a canker sore.

Rarely, a more severe form of canker sore occurs, with larger sores that do cause scars.

CAUSE

The cause of canker sores is not known, although *stress* plays an important role. Alternative causes that have been considered include viruses and bacteria, extreme sensitivity to certain foods, allergic reactions, toxic drug reactions, hormonal factors, or trauma.

SIGNS AND SYMPTOMS

A tingling or burning sensation sometimes precedes canker sores by 24 hours.

DIAGNOSIS

A parent can diagnose canker sores by examining the child's mouth where the child feels pain and noting the sore.

COMPLICATIONS

During the first 2 to 3 days, canker sores are extremely painful and can interfere with eating or speaking.

TREATMENT

No cure exists for canker sores. Only the pain caused by the sores can be treated. If the pain is mild, the child should avoid acidic foods, such as oranges or tomato dishes, which cause the sores to sting. If the pain is more severe, a variety of numbing ointments and solutions are available that may help relieve pain temporarily. Some of these require a prescription. These medications should not be used on a large area of the mouth.

Good oral hygiene can help to speed the healing process. If sores persist for longer than 2 weeks, the child should see a physician.

PREVENTION

Canker sores cannot be prevented.

CARDIOMYOPATHY

DESCRIPTION

Cardiomyopathy is any disease of the heart muscle. A child may develop cardiomyopathy as a single, isolated illness or, more often, as a result of systemic disease, infection, or a metabolic problem. Cardiomyopathy and the problems that can lead to it are often congenital (present at birth) and can be hereditary. Cardiomyopathy may be associated with other diseases or conditions. For example, chronic cardiomyopathy is characteristic of a number of congenital abnormalities that affect the nervous system, circulation, muscles, and growth and development. Cardiomyopathy can follow an injury or can occur as a severe reaction to certain medications. One of the most common forms of cardiomyopathy is called myocarditis, an inflammation of the middle (and thickest) layer of heart muscle.

Cardiomyopathy is often limited to a small area of the heart muscle. If a sufficiently large portion of heart muscle becomes involved, however, a weakened heart muscle may not be able to pump enough blood to meet the body's needs, despite increased heart rate. This condition is called congestive heart failure (see *heart disease, congenital*).

Prospects for a child with cardiomyopathy depend on the cause and severity of the condition. Sudden, severe cardiomyopathy may be fatal for a newborn, but for an older child the disease may be so mild that few troublesome signs or symptoms occur. Children with chronic cardiomyopathy usually develop enlarged hearts and some permanent damage to the heart valves, often leading to periodic congestive heart failure.

If a child is born with heart defects, the condition of the heart muscle must be evaluated and monitored throughout childhood and adolescence. A child may grow and be active if the heart muscle can provide sufficient circulation of blood in spite of abnormal structure. The long-term prospects can be uncertain, however, for a child whose congenital heart defects are complicated by chronic cardiomyopathy.

CAUSE

Cardiomyopathy has multiple causes. When it occurs as an isolated disease, cardiomyopathy is usually of unknown origin.

When cardiomyopathy occurs as a result of preceding physical conditions, its causes vary. Generalized viral infections may have a secondary effect on the heart even though the signs and symptoms are those of the systemic illness, such as *mumps*. Certain viruses (Coxsackie, for example) tend to cause infections which primarily affect the heart. The bacteria that cause diphtheria and *typhoid fever* may cause bacterial myocarditis. Toxic myocarditis can occur when toxins (chemical poisons) reach the heart muscle through the bloodstream (see *bloodstream infections*). Included among common blood-borne toxins are those produced by certain infections or by exposure to unsuitable medications or inappropriate dosages of suitable medications.

Infections caused by parasites, insects, and fungi may inflame the heart muscle, causing myocarditis.

Chronic cardiomyopathy can be associated with severe forms of *muscular dystrophy*, such as Freidrich's ataxia, a progressive disease that causes muscle wasting. More than half of those children with muscular dystrophy experience damage to the heart muscle; many of them have episodes of congestive heart failure (see *heart disease, congenital*).

Several blood diseases, including *anemia* and *leukemia*, may cause cardiomyopathy. Inflammatory diseases of the joints, such as *arthritis, rheumatic fever,* and *lupus erythematosus,* may damage the heart muscle. Malnutrition or vitamin deficiency diseases occasionally cause cardiomyopathy. Other suspected causes include disorders of the endocrine system, such as *diabetes,* and certain metabolic disorders, such as a child's inability to store complex sugars in the liver.

SIGNS AND SYMPTOMS

The signs and symptoms of cardiomyopathy can differ according to the cause. Often, as is true in the case of a disease as severe as *muscular dystrophy,* symptoms of cardiomyopathy may be overshadowed by the predominant characteristics of the disease itself.

Generally, signs and symptoms of cardiomyopathy include an irregular heartbeat *(arrhythmia)*, chest pain, and in severe cases, congestive heart failure. A galloping heartbeat, lung congestion, breathlessness, weakness, and paleness can be indications of congestive heart failure.

DIAGNOSIS

A physician performs a careful physical examination and records the history of illness. Examination of a child with cardiomyopathy may reveal low blood pressure, poor circulation, or heart murmur. Various X-ray studies can usually determine the general condition of a child's heart, including its size. An electrocardiogram (EKG) examination can be helpful in recording a child's heart rhythm. An EKG machine painlessly traces the pattern and intensity of a child's heartbeat on graph paper.

All children whose signs and symptoms indicate possible heart problems are examined with an ultrasound examination called echocardiography. Echocardiography is a painless, noninvasive evaluation of how well the heart is functioning. Sound waves are bounced off the heart and monitored by an electronic device that converts the echoes into an image of the heart on a television screen. Additional diagnostic tests may be ordered if needed.

COMPLICATIONS

Complications of cardiomyopathy include collection of excess fluid in the lungs (edema) and breathlessness. Over many years, chronic cardiomyopathy may prove to be incapacitating, even life-threatening.

TREATMENT

When cardiomyopathy occurs as a single, isolated disease whose origin is unknown, a child can usually be treated only to relieve the signs and symptoms of the illness. When it occurs as a result of another physical condition, its underlying cause is treated. When that treatment is successful, the signs and symptoms of cardiomyopathy may subside. For instance, a child with cardiomyopathy caused by a bacterial infection is usually treated with antibiotics, while one whose cardiomyopathy is the result of *anemia* receives treatment effective for anemia.

It is not usually possible to predict how completely a child may recover from cardiomyopathy. Most children who make even a partial recovery from signs and symptoms of disease can resume normal activities, although strenuous, competitive sports may be restricted. Children whose cardiomyopathies are congenital or hereditary may improve gradually as they grow and mature.

PREVENTION

Cardiomyopathy is preventable only insofar as some of its underlying causes, such as certain infectious diseases, are preventable.

CELIAC DISEASE

EMERGENCY ACTION

A child suffering a celiac crisis (see Description, below) should be taken to an emergency room immediately so that fluids and salts lost through *diarrhea* can be replaced intravenously.

DESCRIPTION

A child suffering from celiac disease (also called gluten-sensitive enteropathy) cannot break down (digest) gluten, a protein found in wheat and rye. Gluten is found in many common foods, including those containing flours or cereals made of wheat or rye, such as baby foods, cakes, breads, and pastries. Many prepared meats and packaged foods contain wheat or rye gluten. Undigested gluten remaining in the intestine irritates the intestinal lining and interferes with normal digestion.

Symptoms of celiac disease usually appear once an affected child has been eating gluten for at least six months, usually within the first 2 years of life. Onset of symptoms is called a celiac crisis, the simultaneous onset of abdominal distension (bloating) and cramps, *diarrhea,* and *dehydration.* Crises result from the combined effects of irritation of the small intestine, insufficient nutrition and fluids (caused by digestion problems, diarrhea, and rarely, *vomiting),* and occasionally, sugar intolerance (a form of *malabsorption*). Celiac crises recur as long as a child continues to eat gluten.

Celiac disease is a lifelong problem. If a strict gluten-free diet is followed, however, celiac disease does not interfere with a child's health or activities.

CAUSE

The exact cause of celiac disease is unknown. Celiac disease may run in families, although the method of inheritance has not yet been determined.

SIGNS AND SYMPTOMS

A child suffering from celiac disease has little appetite; is irritable; has bulky, greasy, foul-smelling diarrhea; and develops abdominal distension. Because the body is not absorbing nutrients, a child's growth and weight gain are slowed. In some cases the onset of puberty is delayed.

Less common symptoms include *abdominal pain, vomiting,* and occasionally, *constipation.* In severe cases, a child develops a smooth tongue, long eyelashes, and clubbed fingers; tooth development may be delayed.

DIAGNOSIS

A physician first suspects celiac disease if a child has characteristic *diarrhea,* is irritable, and has little appetite.

Before a physician confirms a diagnosis of celiac disease, however, other possible causes of diarrhea must be ruled out. Intestinal infections (such as giardiasis—see *malabsorption*) and lactose intolerance (inability to break down the sugars found in cow's milk) produce symptoms that resemble those of celiac disease. Diarrhea may also be a symptom of immunoglobulin deficiency (an immune-system problem, see *infections, frequent*).

If celiac disease is suspected, a physician performs a small-intestine biopsy (examination of a small sample of tissue from the intestinal lining). If the biopsy demonstrates features of an abnormal flattening of the intestinal lining, celiac disease is usually present and a child is placed on a gluten-free diet for 12 months.

After this period, and providing stool has become normal and the child is growing appropriately, a second intestinal biopsy is performed to confirm intestinal healing (flattening should disappear). Gluten is then reintroduced into the child's diet (a procedure called a gluten challenge). This should reproduce the flattening observed in the first intestinal biopsy (detected through a third intestinal biopsy), thereby confirming the diagnosis.

COMPLICATIONS

Gluten irritates the lining of a child's intestine so that it cannot absorb needed nutrients, and a condition called *malabsorption* develops.

Malnutrition can occur in children suffering long-term, untreated celiac disease because the intestines cannot absorb necessary nutrients. If malnutrition is severe, a child's muscles may deteriorate as the body begins to break down its own tissue in an effort to obtain protein and nutrients. Permanent short stature (see *height problems*) may develop if malnutrition persists. Dehydration may occur from fluid loss caused by *diarrhea.*

TREATMENT

The most effective treatment of celiac disease is to remove all foods containing gluten from a child's diet. Package labels containing words such as gluten, wheat or rye flour, bran, farina, wheat germ, semolina, or cereal additives indicate the presence of gluten. Corn, rice, or potato flour can be substituted safely for wheat or rye flour. To ensure that a child's diet is nutritionally balanced, meats, eggs, milk, cheeses, fish, fruits, and vegetables should be included.

If a child also has sugar intolerance resulting from gluten intolerance, sugars should be avoided until gluten *malabsorption* is corrected, usually 4 to 6 weeks after removing gluten from the diet. Some children may also need supplements of vitamins (particularly B and D), minerals (particularly iron), and folic acid (for proper digestion).

If an affected child's intestinal digestion is severely impaired, intravenous feeding in a hospital may be required. Severely impaired digestion most often occurs if a child is severely malnourished at the onset of a crisis.

When gluten is removed from the diet, the child's appetite usually returns, stool consistency becomes normal, and characteristic bloating disappears. If significant improvement does not occur within a month, celiac disease may not be the problem. Within 6 to 12 months a child with celiac disease who is receiving treatment usually reaches normal weight. A child usually reaches normal height after 2 years of a gluten-free diet.

PREVENTION

Celiac disease cannot be prevented. Celiac crises and complications of long-term, untreated celiac disease can be avoided, however, if a child follows a gluten-free diet.

CEREBRAL PALSY

DESCRIPTION AND SIGNS AND SYMPTOMS

Cerebral palsy is a disorder of muscle, movement, and posture resulting from damage to a child's developing brain. The term "cerebral" refers to the brain. "Palsy" means impairment or abnormality of muscle functioning.

Cerebral palsy is not a single disease but a group of conditions caused by malfunction, usually early in development, in the brain's motor pathways (those areas of the brain responsible for movement). For a condition to be classified as cerebral palsy, the damage must be nonprogressive and must have occurred prenatally, during birth, or in childhood. The brain reaches 90 percent of its adult weight by the time a child is 5 years of age.

Cerebral palsy includes a range of movement disorders of varying symptoms and severity. A child with mild cerebral palsy may be merely awkward. A child with severe cerebral palsy may be seriously physically disabled, with or without *mental retardation,* or subject to convulsions (see *seizures*) or other brain abnormalities.

Infants at high risk for cerebral palsy include those who are premature or dysmature (see *prematurity*), who experienced complicated births, and whose blood type is incompatible with their mothers'. Cerebral palsy may, however, develop in babies born at full term and full weight. The United Cerebral Palsy Association estimates that between 1 and 3 of every 1,000 live-born infants develop cerebral palsy, translating to about 9,000 new cases every year in the United States.

Cerebral palsy is often not evident at birth, as all newborns have little control over their bodies. Their movements and actions are dominated by their primitive reflexes, automatic responses built into the nervous system. Primitive reflexes cause changes in both muscle tone and in movements of the limbs. As the brain matures and an infant's development progresses, a normal baby gradually loses the primitive reflexes and gains increasingly fine voluntary control over the movement of the body's separate parts.

When a child has cerebral palsy, however, primitive reflexes persist beyond the usual 6 months of age, interfering with normal movement and significantly delaying motor development. The child has difficulty mastering such familiar landmarks of growth as sitting, rolling over, crawling, walking, smiling, or making speech sounds. The persistence of the primitive reflexes, even into adulthood, is a principal sign of cerebral palsy.

Cerebral palsy interferes not only with the brain's function of controlling and coordinating movement but with the further development of a child's gross and fine motor skills, normally achieved by a precise and delicate balance between voluntary and involuntary controls. An example of a gross motor skill is walking; an example of a fine motor skill is drawing. Although motor development is delayed, cognitive skills (perceiving, thinking, and remembering) and language skills may be unaffected and progress at a normal rate.

Cerebral palsy is usually described according to the limbs it affects and the kind of movement disorder that occurs.

When one arm or one leg has been affected by cerebral palsy, the condition is called monoplegia. ("Plegia" means muscle disorder.) Hemiplegia involves the arm and leg on the same side. Paraplegia involves only the legs; diplegia refers to major involvement in the legs, and minor involvement in the arms. Triplegia means that one arm and both legs are affected; quadriplegia refers to major involvement of all the arms and legs.

Types of Disorders The most common types of muscle and movement disorders associated with cerebral palsy are spasticity, athetosis, and mixed muscle reactions. Spasticity is the muscle disorder most frequently associated with cerebral palsy, and is the characteristic form seen in premature and low-birthweight babies.

A child with spastic cerebral palsy finds it difficult to initiate movement. In contrast, a child with athetoid cerebral palsy finds it difficult to control movement and maintain posture. Damage is done to the nerves that regulate movement rather than those that initiate it, as in spastic cerebral palsy. When several motor centers in the brain have been injured, the cerebral palsy may be mixed, causing both spasticity and athetosis. Since, in these cases, brain damage is often extensive, children with mixed muscle reactions have a higher incidence of mental retardation and other associated brain disabilities.

The muscles in the affected arms and legs of a child with spastic cerebral palsy are extremely taut, or hypertonic, and strongly resist sudden movement or stretching. A child whose muscles are spastic has what is referred to as a "clasped knife" muscle response to movement. The muscle will at first be very tight, and resistant to efforts to move it, then will snap open. Once a spastic muscle begins to move, it may contract repeatedly and interfere with coordinated movement, a condition called "clonus."

A child with spastic cerebral palsy who can walk is likely to have a gait disturbance called "scissoring." Sometimes, however, leg muscles may be so contracted that a child's heels cannot touch the floor, resulting in a gait disturbance called "toe walking." A child with cerebral palsy may walk in a crouched position, because of increased flexing of the muscles.

In athetoid cerebral palsy, muscle tone may be normal, but affected body parts move constantly in involuntary, purposeless writhing motions. This condition, called athetosis, is characterized by turning and twisting of the hands, facial grimacing, and involuntary movements of the tongue and mouth. Associated with athetosis may be involuntary flailing or jerking motions of the body, referred to as "chorea" (from the Greek word for dance).

A person examining a child with choreathetoid cerebral palsy can "shake out" muscle tone by rapidly flexing and extending the arm or leg. Increased tone will disappear briefly and the muscle will be flaccid and limp. Muscle spasms are less likely to occur in choreoathetoid cerebral palsy than in spastic cerebral palsy. Facial muscles, however, of a child with choreathetoid cerebral palsy are more affected and the child has more trouble swallowing, sucking, and speaking than does a spastic child.

Cerebral palsy has a major effect on muscle tone, causing a condition of either hypertonicity or hypotonicity. Hypertonic muscles are in a condition of contraction, and are hard and resistant to stretching and movement. They are associated with spastic cerebral palsy. Hypotonic muscles are loose, flaccid muscles with little muscle tone, and are sometimes associated with athetoid cerebral palsy.

Many differences exist in the effects of various forms of cerebral palsy. Symptoms vary according to the movement disorder involved and the location and extent of brain damage. In general, infants with cerebral palsy sleep excessively, have a weak cry, a poor suck, and show little interest in their surroundings.

Associated Disabilities Children with cerebral palsy often suffer from associated disabilities, some having a greater impact than their physical handicap. Approximately two thirds of the children with spastic quadriplegic cerebral palsy have some degree of *mental retardation,* although those with other types of cerebral palsy have a lesser degree of mental retardation. The severity of the mental retardation depends upon the location and degree of injury to the brain. Many children with cerebral palsy develop *seizures* at some time in their lives.

More than 40 percent of all children with cerebral palsy have associated eye problems; about half have *speech problems* and *language disorders.* Speech difficulties may be associated with physical disabilities in the muscles of the mouth and throat that interfere with the forming of words. These children have problems speaking, chewing, and swallowing, and may drool involuntarily. The injury or disease that caused the cerebral palsy may also have affected speech centers in the brain, causing a language problem, such as an inability to select and organize speech.

About one fifth of all children with cerebral palsy experience *hearing loss.* Other associated disorders include a loss of sensation in affected limbs of hemiplegics, and perceptual disorders, the inability to perceive spatial relationships.

Children with cerebral palsy often have behavior problems, such as *hyperactivity*, that may develop as they attempt to adjust to a lifelong disability. These problems tend to intensify during adolescence, especially among children of normal or above-average intelligence.

Most children with cerebral palsy live to be adults, but in severe cases their life expectancy is less than that of the population in general. The outlook for people with cerebral palsy depends on the severity of the condition and of associated disabilities.

One third of all people with cerebral palsy have normal or above-average intelligence. In spite of many difficulties, a few have been able to achieve independence and success in work and personal life. For example, many monoplegics and paraplegics, and some hemiplegics and diplegics, are able to live on their own. About half of those affected with cerebral palsy work in sheltered workshops. Many have enough self-help skills to be partially independent while remaining at home with their families.

CAUSE

Causes of cerebral palsy have been identified in only 60 percent of all cases; no cause is known for the remainder. About 85 percent of all cerebral palsy is congenital (present at birth); the remaining 15 percent is acquired from injuries to the brain, such as those received in accidents.

Prematurity and its many complications still rank as major causes of cerebral palsy that occurs shortly before or after birth. A baby born before 37 weeks of pregnancy or gestation is considered premature. Most premature infants weigh less than 5½ pounds.

Other prenatal causes include lack of oxygen to the fetal brain caused by irregularities of the placenta, pinching or kinking of the umbilical cord, and *shock* because of the mother's blood loss. Poor prenatal care and factors such as a mother's smoking or heavy drinking of alcohol during pregnancy are suspected as causes of prenatal brain damage leading to cerebral palsy. Maternal infections such as *German measles* (especially in the first 3 months of pregnancy), toxoplasmosis, *genital herpes,* and cytomegaloviral infection may cause cerebral palsy in a newborn. Severe *jaundice* in a newborn because of RH incompatability (see *RH and ABO incompatibility*), now preventable by injecting the mother with a drug called RhoGAM or by giving the fetus or newborn blood transfusions, was a major cause of cerebral palsy in the past. ABO incompatibility, however, is still an occasional cause of cerebral palsy. Metabolic diseases, such as *diabetes* of the mother (if she suffers complications from the disease), may cause cerebral palsy.

Damage to the brain at birth is a major cause of cerebral palsy. Motor centers may be affected; lack of oxygen to the brain because of lung collapse, *respiratory distress syndrome* (also known as hyaline membrane disease), *pneumonia,* or oversedation with obstetric drugs used to relieve labor pains may also cause cerebral palsy at birth.

During infancy and early childhood, head injuries (see *head and spinal injury*), including skull fractures and brain lacerations, can cause cerebral palsy. Cerebral palsy during early childhood may also be caused by brain infections, such as *meningitis* and *encephalitis,* and by *lead poisoning.* Sudden, spontaneous brain hemorrhages may cause cerebral palsy in young children, as can lack of oxygen to the brain, caused by *asphyxia* from carbon monoxide poisoning, suffocating, choking, drowning, and congestive heart failure (see *heart failure, congestive*). Cerebral palsy may be one complication of a *brain tumor.*

DIAGNOSIS

Cerebral palsy is almost always diagnosed on the basis of a child's medical history (prenatal, birth, and developmental) and a physician's examination. The most important component of diagnosis is examination of the child's nervous system.

Certain exploratory tests may be used to confirm a diagnosis of cerebral palsy, to determine the extent and location of brain damage, and to exclude the possibility of progressive brain disease. These tests include a CT scan (computerized tomography, a complex form of multiple X-ray films that provide a cross-sectional image of the brain), electroencephalography (which measures electrical activity of the brain), and electromyography (which measures the electrical activity of muscle during movement). Blood and urine analyses are used to look for chemical abnormalities that may cause cerebral palsy.

A multidisciplinary team including a physical therapist, orthopedic (bone) surgeon, speech therapist, psychologist, and neurologist (nervous-system specialist) may be consulted to determine the degree of disability.

COMPLICATIONS

A child with cerebral palsy and his or her family have difficult problems to resolve in accepting the disability. These difficulties are likely to be compounded by attitudes often encountered in others toward a child with cerebral palsy, especially if the child has unusual posture or bone structure, makes involuntary facial grimaces, or has speech difficulties.

Children with mild cerebral palsy may have problems because they are just different enough not to be accepted by their peers. Children with normal or above-average intelligence may find their disability extremely frustrating and may suffer related emotional conflicts.

Discrimination against the disabled still exists despite laws and regulations that require equal educational opportunities for the disabled and that prohibit discrimination on the basis of disability. For instance, most buildings and transportation systems even in major cities are still inaccessible to individuals confined to wheelchairs. Until recently, individuals with noticeable cerebral palsy and speech difficulties were often placed in institutions for the mentally retarded no matter what their intellectual abilities.

TREATMENT

There is no cure for cerebral palsy; treatment focuses on dealing with the effects of the irreversible damage to the motor centers of the brain. Treatment goals are to encourage a child with cerebral palsy to become as independent as possible by developing skills to minimize the level of disability and to compensate for limitations. Whether a child will walk depends upon the type and severity of cerebral palsy.

Treatment is interdisciplinary and involves physical therapy, special education, speech therapy, vocational training, social services, medical treatment, and perhaps orthopedic surgery and supportive psychological services. *Seizures* may require drug therapy or the services of a neurologist.

Infants and young children with cerebral palsy, especially those who cannot walk, need opportunities to learn about their environment. It is important for their treatment to include learning experiences in the home that are normally part of an infant's education. Children's "work" is to play and explore the world around them. Part of their growth and development includes feeling and touching things and putting things in their mouths. Therefore, early intervention is important not only to arrest physical problems but to stimulate normal development. Children who are confined to their cribs by disability lack opportunities to bang pots together, splash in water, and creep around at home exploring, all important aspects of growing up.

Orthopedic Treatment Orthopedic treatment may improve some of the disabling effects of cerebral palsy. Orthotic support (using orthopedic appliances such as braces, splints, and casts) may maintain arms and legs in positions necessary to prevent contractions and other deformities in bone and muscle structure.

Orthopedic surgery may increase range of motion in bones and joints. Surgical techniques used in treating spastic cerebral palsy include cutting contracted muscles and tendons to provide greater stretching and flexibility, and fusing bones together to stabilize joints. These techniques may help a child with cerebral palsy walk or maintain balance. For instance, a child's dislocated hip may be replaced in the socket, or the socket, if malformed, can be rebuilt. Such operations may prevent inward curvature of the spine *(scoliosis)* and allow a child more movement.

Physical, Occupational, and Other Therapies Physical therapy is crucial in developing a child's abilities and reducing the level of disability. Methods include exercise, relaxation, and the practice of walking activities by using parallel bars or by transferring from wheelchair to bed or chairs.

Physical therapists can offer parents advice on incorporating therapeutic techniques into daily routines. Parents can learn ways to pick up, hold, and carry their child to help stimulate good movement patterns.

Occupational therapy is important in helping a child with cerebral palsy develop daily living skills. Seemingly routine tasks, such as feeding and dressing, can be frustrating, impossible experiences for a child who cannot control head, trunk, or hand movements. Occupational therapy can help a child with cerebral palsy learn to perform these tasks, often compensating for disability by adapting utensils or developing techniques to aid the child. Later efforts of occupational therapy are directed toward the development of vocational skills. For example, rather than trying to write with pen and paper, a child with cerebral palsy may use an electric typewriter.

Muscle weakness may affect lips, tongue, and jaw, and interfere in sucking and swallowing movements or heighten gag and bite reflexes, causing feeding difficulties. Children with cerebral palsy may need nutritional therapy to correct deficiencies. They may also have increased caloric needs because of increased movements and constant muscle rigidity. In contrast, if they are immobile and have decreased muscle tone, they may require fewer calories.

A child may need traditional speech and language therapy or, if speech is not possible, alternate communication systems, such as a spelling board or electronic alphabet board.

Special Education For proper educational placement, early evaluation of a child's capabilities and neurological function is essential. Federal and some state laws now require cities and towns to provide equal educational opportunities to children who have special needs; such special education is required to be provided in the "least restrictive environment." These laws have made available many therapeutic services to families who in the past could not have afforded such therapy. Many children with cerebral palsy now attend regular public schools, while more severely disabled children attend developmental day care programs.

Recent advances in rehabilitation engineering, a new field linking science and technology to the service of the physically handicapped, may help children with cerebral palsy. For example, microprocessors operating an environmental control system allow totally disabled persons to operate electric lights, television or radio, and the telephone from a bed or wheelchair, providing an independence not previously possible.

Parents who want to encourage a child with cerebral palsy to achieve optimal independence while minimizing disability need to understand their child's condition and be committed to involvement in therapy. Parents need to know what the motor problem is, how to interpret their child's development, and how to detect skeletal changes such as *dislocation of joints*.

A child with cerebral palsy and his or her family may need social and psychological services to adjust to the lifelong disability. Parents may need help finding financial aid for wheelchairs, braces, and other equipment and may need guidance in finding community resources, such as special nursery schools, infant stimulation programs, visiting nurses, and recreational programs. Parents may want to join other parents of children with cerebral palsy in support or advocacy groups.

As adults, people with cerebral palsy may need continued support to maintain their independence. Adults with slight or moderate cerebral palsy can live independently in the community. An increasing number of disabled adults will probably live in group homes or apartment clusters, with some supervision or nursing care, depending on their level of intellectual functioning and physical disability.

PREVENTION

Prevention of cerebral palsy depends upon the cause.

The incidence of cerebral palsy has decreased because of immunizations against maternal infections such as *German measles,* preventive measures against *jaundice* associated with *RH incompatibility,* and the development and availability of neonatal intensive care units. However, the incidence of cerebral palsy resulting from head injuries sustained in automobile accidents has risen. The incidence of cerebral palsy in premature infants of very low birthweight and those with congenital heart defects has also increased because of the advancing survival rate of these babies.

Information about support services is available from local chapters of the United Cerebral Palsy Association or from its headquarters, 66 East 34th Street, New York, NY 10016 (phone: 212-481-6300).

CHEST DEFORMITIES

DESCRIPTION

Two types of structural deformities of the chest are fairly common among children. The first type is a depression or hollow caused when the breastbone, the bone in the middle of the ribcage, is pushed abnormally inward. This condition is known as <u>funnel chest</u>. The second type of chest deformity is caused when the breastbone is pushed outward, like the keel of a boat; this condition is called pigeon breast.

Funnel Chest

Approximately 1 of every 300 children has funnel chest, which is either congenital (present at birth) or develops within months of birth. Mild cases on occasion correct themselves, usually by the age of 3 years. In moderate and severe cases, however, funnel chest may grow progressively worse and require surgery.

Other children with what appear to be funnel chests do not require treatment. For example, it is common for infants with breathing difficulties to have intermittent drawing in (retractions) of their chests. In addition, some infants and young children have mild to moderate hollows in the center of their chests during inhalation and appear normal during exhalation; true funnel chest exists when the chest remains sunken even when a baby exhales or is resting. When a baby with funnel chest is examined either sitting or lying on the back, face up, the hollow in the chest is unchanged or rigid.

For those children who undergo surgery, normal breathing returns. In fact, the outlook is excellent for 90 to 95 percent of those who are treated for this problem; for about 1 in 30 children, a second operation may be required.

Pigeon Breast

Pigeon breast is about one third as common as funnel chest. Three out of four cases of pigeon breast involve boys. Girls usually develop pigeon breast at a somewhat younger age than boys, who do not develop the condition until adolescence, usually from 11 to 14 years of age.

As with funnel chest, pigeon breast may interfere with a child's physical health. The deformity often leads to *emphysema* early in life and increases in severity each year until a child reaches full growth. *Scoliosis* is common and becomes more controllable after treatment. Surgery can correct pigeon breast, and the outlook for children who have the operation is excellent.

CAUSE

The cause of both chest deformities is unclear. Both conditions tend to recur in families, however, about 65 percent of the time. Excessive growth and structural abnormalities of the cartilage (tough, elastic tissue) of the ribs and breastbone are present in both conditions. If pigeon chest is present during infancy, it may be associated with premature fusion of the segments of the breastbone, a short wide breastbone, and congenital heart disease (see *heart disease, congenital*).

SIGNS AND SYMPTOMS

Symptoms of funnel chest usually appear after infancy. The condition interferes with a child's breathing ability. If symptoms do appear during infancy, they include frequent, lingering colds which often develop into *pneumonia*. The severity of funnel chest varies greatly. The depression may be broad and shallow, deep and narrow, or asymmetric. For example, it is not unusual for one side—typically the right side—to be more sunken than the other.

Older children may be inactive, become fatigued easily, experience *breathing difficulty* upon exertion and exercise, have chest pain, and contract a greater number of respiratory infections than children of the same age who do not have funnel chest. About 20 percent of affected children may have lateral curvature of the spine, absence of the curve of the upper back (a condition called "straight back"), hooked shoulders, and a broad, thin chest.

Pigeon breast rarely causes symptoms other than difficulties in playing and exercising, tenderness and intermittent pain in the area of the overgrown cartilage, and concern for self-image.

DIAGNOSIS

A physician diagnoses chest deformities. A child's chest is observed when a child is well and while he or she inhales, exhales, and rests. The physician also calculates the depth of the chest from front to back using X-ray films of the chest to determine whether the diameter is shorter than average (funnel chest) or longer than average (pigeon breast). The heart is usually widened and displaced to the left. Lung capacity can be measured by exercise tests and lung scans, which often reveal mismatched lungs. An electrocardiogram (EKG) reveals heartbeat and rhythm. An echocardiogram, a graphic recording of the position and motion of the heart, can detect *heart murmurs*. Murmurs can often be relieved by surgery for children under 14, but older children show little improvement.

COMPLICATIONS

Emphysema can become a long-term problem in a severe pigeon breast since it is rigid and locked in the position of full inhalation. In a severe funnel chest, the heart's capacity to pump blood is impaired, the function of the left lung is reduced, and *scoliosis* may occur at any age.

TREATMENT

Children with moderate to severe cases of funnel chest require surgery, ideally between 3 and 5 years of age. When surgery is performed in adolescence, lung function may not improve unless additional growth is expected. Corrective surgery for funnel chest should never be performed before 2 years of age. The sooner surgery is performed after age 3, the better, however, because results are superior then, and spontaneous improvement of a severe problem is unlikely. If severe cases are not corrected, deformity of the bones, scoliosis, and asymmetry develop, making surgery more difficult. By adolescence, surgery cannot produce a normal, balanced chest.

Surgery is necessary for most children with pigeon breast, which always grows worse until late adolescence. Surgery involves removal of the involved rib cartilages and repositioning of the breastbone, essentially the mirror image of that performed for funnel chest. Surgery always restores normal chest contour.

PREVENTION

Neither funnel chest nor pigeon breast can be prevented.

CHEST PAIN

EMERGENCY ACTION

Seek immediate medical attention if a child has severe chest pain, fever, and *breathing difficulty.* Injury to the lung may be present and should be treated immediately to prevent possible *lung rupture.* Do not immobilize fractured ribs, as doing so may interfere with breathing.

DESCRIPTION

Chest pain is very common during childhood. It can be caused by many problems, most of which are no cause for alarm. Causes of chest pain during childhood rarely indicate the presence of a serious disease.

The most common causes of childhood chest pain are severe coughing, physical overexertion, or injury to chest structures.

When a severe cough makes the lungs work very hard, the chest muscles under the breastbone (sternum) become sore. This is particularly true in cases of severe coughs caused by *colds.* The diaphragm (the large muscle of the chest wall) may also become sore from a child's coughing, and a child may experience tenderness in the area of the lower edge of the ribcage.

A child may feel chest pain when participating in physical activities after a lengthy period of inactivity. This pain, commonly called a "stitch in the side," occurs as a stabbing pain in the lower front chest, usually on the left side. If a child rests for a minute or two, the pain goes away. Such pain may be caused by a spasm of the diaphragm.

Injuries to the chest or abdominal area usually result in chest pain. For example, muscle bruises or fractures of the breastbone or ribs cause chest pain, which is aggravated by breathing or movement of the chest. Overexertion of chest or abdominal muscles (from doing too many sit-ups, for example) may lead to mild muscle strains and chest pain. Pain recurs when a child moves, and the affected area is tender to the touch.

Less often, chest pain is caused by infections of the lungs. Pleurisy, or inflammation of the membrane surrounding the lungs, may occur with *pneumonia* and cause chest pain, *fever, cough,* and shortness of breath.

Pneumothorax, the condition in which a lung ruptures and air escapes into the chest cavity, also causes chest pain. The escaped air compresses the lung and gradually leads to its collapse. Children with severe *asthma* are susceptible to pneumothorax, but this condition may arise without an apparent cause. Pneumothorax develops quickly, often with a sharp pain, and causes shortness of breath. Emergency medical care is required.

Occasionally, children suffering severe anxiety develop chest pain. Blood pressure and heart rate increase. The muscles of the upper left chest wall may become tender from the rapid pounding of the heart. A child may also hyperventilate (breathe very rapidly and take in excess oxygen), become dizzy, and develop a tingling sensation in the fingers. In other cases chest pain associated with anxiety may have no direct pattern or location, or may resemble angina pectoris, a severe, constricting chest pain that travels from the upper diaphragm up to the left shoulder and down the left arm. Anxious children with harmless chest pain may be overly concerned about it if a close friend or family member has died of heart failure recently. Parental reassurance and understanding are needed to ease these fears.

In rare cases, a child with a heart problem experiences chest pain. Chest pain caused by heart problems is rare among individuals under 30. *Arrhythmias* (irregular heartbeats) may cause some chest discomfort or pain. A child may experience a fluttering or turning sensation in the heart area, and may become pale and anxious and perspire heavily. Pericarditis (inflammation of the pericardium, the membrane surrounding the heart) may also cause chest pain, as well as fever. Other causes of chest pain include structural defects in the pericardium; narrowing of the main artery of the heart, the aorta; and high blood pressure in the blood vessels of the lungs. (See *cardiomyopathy; heart disease, congenital; heart failure, congestive.*)

DIAGNOSIS

In most cases a parent can determine the cause of chest pain based on a child's recent activities and physical health. If no cause can be found, however, or if pain is persistent or severe anywhere in the chest or abdomen, a physician should be consulted.

Diagnosis of the cause of chest pain is based on the location of the pain, a child's present health and medical history, signs and symptoms, and the results of a complete physical examination. In many cases it is not possible to determine the exact location of chest pain, and a physician takes X-ray films of the chest, lungs, heart, and abdomen to detect possible injury or illness. If necessary, electrocardiography, an examination that electronically records the heart's actions, or echocardiography, an examination that uses sound waves to form a picture of internal structures, may be needed to detect heart or lung problems.

TREATMENT

Treatment of chest pain depends on the underlying cause. Most childhood causes of chest pain can be treated at home. A warm heating pad, warm hot-water bottle, or warm compresses may help relax sore muscles and ease pain. Cough suppressants may be given to reduce cough and rest sore muscles. A pain-relieving medication may be helpful. Consult the physician for specific recommendations and read discussion of

nonprescription medications beginning on p. 102.

A physician should be consulted if chest pain is caused by injury. Broken ribs are not taped (unless there is danger of puncturing the lungs), because holding the chest in place sometimes interferes with breathing.

For detailed discussion of treatment of underlying disorders mentioned, see the individual entries.

PREVENTION

Chest pain can be prevented only if its underlying cause can be avoided or corrected.

CHICKEN POX

DESCRIPTION

Chicken pox (varicella) is a common, highly contagious, but usually mild childhood disease, characterized by *fever* and a *rash* that starts as red spots and eventually becomes itchy blisters. Nearly every American child is infected with chicken pox, usually between 3 and 9 years of age. The second case in a family is often more severe (more blisters, higher fever) than the first.

One attack usually gives lifelong immunity. The virus that causes chicken pox, however, becomes latent (present but invisible) and can appear again later in life in the form of a disease called shingles.

CAUSE

Chicken pox is caused by the varicella zoster virus. The virus is transmitted through direct contact with an infected person and may be spread by contact with the skin lesions or secretions from the mouth or nose. The disease is contagious from a day or two before the rash appears until the blisters have formed scabs. An adult or older child with shingles can transmit the varicella zoster virus to a younger child, who will develop chicken pox if he or she is not immune.

The incubation period for chicken pox ranges from 10 to 20 days, usually 14 to 16 days.

SIGNS AND SYMPTOMS

The first sign of chicken pox may be a low fever, perhaps accompanied by headache, tiredness, and lack of appetite.

Simultaneously (among children) or

within a day or two (among adolescents), a rash of flat, red, splotchy dots will appear, which may erupt in tiny, raised pimples. Next, the pimples quickly become small, soft, clear blisters. All stages of the rash may be present at the same time. The dots, pimples, and blisters usually appear in clusters on the upper body, although the rash may show up on any part of the body, including the inside of the mouth. If blisters appear in the eyes, a physician should be notified. Rarely, the rash covers the entire body. However, some children infected by the chicken pox virus do not have a recognizable rash.

The rash itself lasts from 3 to 7 days and the child begins to feel better 3 or 4 days after the rash first appears. The blisters form scabs 6 or 7 days after the start of the rash. Scabs fall off after 5 to 10—occasionally 20—days. Usually no permanent scarring occurs.

The fever is highest when the rash is at its peak and subsides when scabs form over the broken blisters. The blister stage of the rash itches intensely until scabs have formed, although children under age 2 or 3 seem not to be bothered.

DIAGNOSIS

Chicken pox is diagnosed by a physician, usually by phone due to risk of infecting other patients. The appearance of fever and the characteristic rash are the key signs. If the scabs become infected with bacteria, the physician may then want to see the child.

COMPLICATIONS

The most common complication of chicken pox is bacterial infection caused by scratching. If not treated, permanent scars can form. If the scabs come off too early, scarring may also occur.

Rarely, the varicella zoster virus spreads to the brain, causing *encephalitis,* a potentially severe illness.

Patients with low resistance, infants, and adults can become extremely ill if they contract chicken pox. Adults who contract chicken pox are susceptible to *pneumonia* and *hepatitis.*

Babies born to women who contract chicken pox during pregnancy are almost always normal. A few cases of fetal infection have occurred, but this is most unusual.

One fifth to one fourth of babies born to women who contracted chicken pox or shingles during the last three weeks of pregnancy acquire chicken pox. If the rash is present at birth or erupts within a few days, the disease can be severe or fatal.

Children recovering from chicken pox sometimes develop *Reye's syndrome,* a severe illness characterized by brain disease and deterioration of liver function. A link may exist between aspirin and the development of Reye's syndrome. Children with chicken pox should not be given aspirin.

TREATMENT

Home treatment for a child with chicken pox includes

- rest (not necessarily in bed),
- lukewarm sponge baths several times a day (to reduce the chance of blisters becoming infected; the child's skin should be patted, not rubbed, dry), and
- calamine or Caladryl lotion (without phenol) or antihistamine lotion to dry the blisters.

Gargling with salt water may provide relief if blisters form in the mouth. Acetaminophen may be helpful in reducing fever and muscle aches and pains. Aspirin should never be given to any child with chicken pox because of a possible connection between its use and the development of *Reye's syndrome* in the aftermath of chicken pox. (See discussion of medications and home care in Chapter 7, "Caring for the Sick Child at Home.") Children with chronic or immune-deficiency diseases often recuperate much more slowly.

Until all the blisters have scabbed, the infected child should be kept away from children who have not had chicken pox. To keep the young child from scratching the blisters or scabs, it may help to cover the child's hands with clean cotton gloves or socks or at least to keep the child's nails cut short and to wash the child's hands often with antibacterial soap. If nothing will keep the child from scratching, a physician may prescribe an oral or topical antihistamine to reduce itching. If the rash becomes infected, antibiotics may be prescribed.

PREVENTION

At this time chicken pox cannot be routinely prevented. However, a vaccine has been developed that soon may be available to high-risk patients (such as those with *leukemia).*

Until chicken pox is universally preventable, it is best for children to get the disease over with during childhood. However, whenever possible, parents should try to keep infants away from children with chicken pox.

CHILD ABUSE

Child abuse is one of the most disturbing problems in America today. Although most parents recognize the distinction between loving care and overt abuse, the line between discipline and abuse is often blurred.

Q: *What is child abuse?*
A: Child abuse is any kind of mistreatment or deprivation that threatens the welfare of an infant, child, or adolescent. Most often it occurs at home.

Mistreatment can be physical, emotional, or sexual. Physical abuse consists of physical violence of any kind. Emotional abuse may include rejection, blaming, threats of violence or terror, or constant criticism. Sexual abuse may involve molestation, rape, or incest.

Deprivation includes physical neglect (abandonment or the withholding of proper food, clothing, protection, schooling, or medical care) and emotional neglect (lack of affection or stimulation).

Q: *How common is child abuse?*
A: Every year, about 2 to 6 percent of all children in the United States suffer severe injuries from assault or neglect; many more children suffer other health problems that are caused by neglect. More children die from abuse or neglect than from car accidents, leukemia, or all diseases combined. Approximately 600,000 cases are reported each year in the United States, but some experts estimate that annually from 1 million to 4 million American children are abused by their parents or other caretakers.

Q: *Who abuses children?*
A: In 9 out of 10 cases an abusing person is a close relative, usually a parent, although occasionally a brother or sister. The parent who spends the greatest amount of time with a child is most likely to act on impulse.

Parents who abuse or neglect their chil-dren come from every ethnic group, socio-economic class, and geographical area. Contrary to popular opinion, only about 10 percent of parents who abuse their children are mentally ill. The other 90 percent are people who are frequently under a great deal of stress and whose home life is often confused or chaotic. Abuse is usually not intentional but is a result of uncontrollable anger or frustration. Most abusing parents say they feel guilty afterward about hurting their children.

Q: *Why do parents abuse their children?*
A: Child abuse is usually an extreme response to *stress*. It often stems from a complex combination of stress-related factors, including difficult living conditions, short-term and long-term economic problems, and a lack of appropriate childrearing information and skills. The vast majority of abusing parents want to be good parents. Especially during crises, however, they tend to return to behavior learned from their own parents: the majority of child abusers were abused themselves as children.

To many parents who physically abuse their children, being a parent means keeping children under control. They respond to their children's "bad" behavior with the only type of discipline they know—physical violence. Similarly, emotional abuse of children may be caused by the parents' emotional deprivation in their own childhoods. Sexual abuse that takes the form of molestation or rape can also be prompted by nearly all of these factors. Incest, however, often seems to occur in families in which marital problems exist and both parents are emotionally needy.

Q: *What are signs and symptoms of child abuse?*
A: The most evident signs and symptoms of physical abuse are bruises, welts, bumps, burns (including small, round cigarette burns), black eyes, cuts, lacerations, human bite marks, scars, and broken bones. A school-aged child may suddenly lose or gain a noticeable amount of weight.

Emotional symptoms include nightmares and night terrors, inability to sleep (see *sleep disorders*), irrational fears (see *phobias*), and illnesses with a substantial emotional element (see *psychosomatic disease and symptoms*). An abused child may seem overly eager to please, unusually submissive and cooperative, or guarded. An abused child may also act passive, withdrawn, listless, anxious, or depressed. Abused children tend to avoid eye contact and may cling to their parents. A child may appear to be mentally retarded but score within the normal range on standard tests. An older child may suddenly fail or skip school, or run away.

About 25 percent of abused children have very different emotional reactions. They are extremely aggressive, impulsive, disruptive, negative, and hyperactive (see *hyperactivity and attention problems*). They show violent tendencies and may take out their hostility and rage on toys, animals, or other children.

Abused children sometimes become excessively demanding of loyalty and affection, and as a result, they scare away potential friends. They may find it difficult to trust anyone because their own parents' behavior is so unpredictable.

Sexual abuse or incest is suspected if a child too young to give "informed consent" has a venereal disease or is pregnant. Injuries in a child's genital area may also be signs of sexual abuse. In some cases *blood in the urine* may indicate sexual abuse. Psychological symptoms such as *phobias* or sexualized play also may be present.

Preteen or teenage runaways, especially but not solely girls, may have been victims of incest. Other signs of possible incest include sudden changes in behavior, rebellion, delinquency, isolation, low self-esteem, *depression,* attempted *suicide,* drug abuse (see *drug and alcohol abuse*), and prostitution. In one type of family in which incest takes place, a teenage girl who is involved in an incestuous relationship with her father or stepfather often seems to have been delegated the mother's traditional role within the family; she may serve not only as the father's sexual outlet but as a homemaker—cooking, cleaning, and taking care of younger siblings.

The chief sign of physical neglect during infancy and early childhood is *failure to thrive.* An affected infant or young child looks small and underweight, may not have been kept clean, may suffer frequent infections, and is often delayed in physical and intellectual development. A neglected child has usually not received routine medical care.

An emotionally deprived child may engage in compulsive masturbation or try to cling to his or her mother. In contrast, an emotionally deprived child may act aggressively.

Q: *Are there any warning signs of potential severe abuse or neglect?*
A: Parents themselves may indicate their potential for severe abuse or neglect of their children. Parents who spank infants, seldom change an infant's diaper, or do not respond to an infant's crying may be experiencing difficulties that could lead to more severe abuse or neglect.

Q: *How is child abuse diagnosed?*
A: Child abuse is often difficult to diagnose. Physical abuse is frequently inflicted in ways that are not obvious, and injuries are often not visible. For instance, a whiplash injury from a severe shaking can cause brain damage with no outward sign of abuse. Physical abuse is nearly always suspected by physicians when a small child is injured in an unexplained way, particularly if parents delay seeking medical treatment or if their explanation does not fit the extent of their child's injuries. Very few children are "accident prone."

Physically abused children may have more than one injury, old wounds that have never been treated, bruises in odd locations, and repeated injuries to the same part of the body. A physician may suspect that a head or abdomen injury is not accidental if skull fractures, brain damage, bruised or fractured ribs, a ruptured spleen, or kidney damage occurs. Internal injuries are common. X rays often reveal previously broken bones.

A physician diagnoses sexual abuse by carefully interviewing the child alone, by interviewing family members, by performing a physical examination of the child, and perhaps by performing laboratory tests.

When physical neglect is suspected, a physician performs a thorough physical examination and may refer the child to child development specialists for testing. In cases of emotional neglect in which a child appears to be physically healthy, the child may also be referred to a child development specialist. In addition, the family is likely to be referred to a psychologist.

Q: *What happens if child abuse is suspected?*
A: By law, a physician or any other person working with a child in a professional capacity must report suspected child abuse to the proper authorities. When a child is being

treated in an emergency room for serious or life-threatening injuries that seem to be caused by abuse, medical staff are likely to notify both the hospital's social service staff and the police. Without making any accusations, a social worker calmly and tactfully interviews parents and child (if the child is old enough to talk).

Usually, parents do not readily admit to abuse, especially in a stressful situation like an emergency room. To admit to injuring or neglecting their child may mean punishment for the parents. The child may cover for the parents, in fear of retaliation or in an effort to keep the family together—a heavy responsibility for a young child.

A teacher, school nurse, youth worker, or other professional who discovers possible evidence of child abuse can notify either school officials or a state or community agency responsible for child welfare. Neighbors and acquaintances can always report abuse anonymously to child welfare agencies.

Q: *What happens to the family after abuse has been reported?*
A: With more enlightened methods of treatment, efforts are often focused on keeping a functioning family together, if possible. Removal of children from the home is not the main goal unless such drastic measures are necessary for safety reasons. Intervention is intended to be positive and constructive and to prevent abuse from recurring.

Q: *What happens to an abused child after abuse has been reported?*
A: The first objective is to treat the child's injuries and to protect the child from further abuse. This often involves hospitalization until the home situation can be evaluated as safe or until temporary foster care is found. Children tend to be fearful in a strange environment and miss their families. The Foster Grandparent Program and other volunteer groups assist the social service staff at a hospital in comforting fearful children and helping them express feelings of anger, rage, frustration, and guilt.

Q: *How are the parents and child helped?*
A: Treatment involves separate therapy, preferably long-term, for both parents and child. Therapy for the parent is often even more crucial than for the child. Abusing parents may be so emotionally needy that

they resent their child's receiving special attention. Therapy for both the parents and child should help them express feelings in nonviolent ways.

The goal of treatment is to teach parents how to find support in times of stress or crisis, face their problems, and help rather than harm their children.

Q: *What must happen before a child can return home?*
A: Most abusing parents do not want to lose their children. Usually, health professionals or social workers who intervene allow a child to return home if parents have learned to deal with their children without using violence and if they show genuine affection for their child. Other important indications of positive change are the development of a friendship with a supportive, mature, reliable adult; the use of available social service resources; and improvement during therapy as time passes. If a family benefits from treatment, the child is usually able to return home after 6 to 9 months.

Q: *What happens when a child returns home?*
A: When a child returns home, a family should be encouraged to use available social services. Ideally, these include homemaker's services (regular visits from a homemaker, who may offer ideas about housework and child care); parents' aides or advocates, who become friends with isolated parents and aid them in seeking any needed help; crisis nurseries (24-hour-a-day nurseries where distraught parents can bring children of any age for a few hours until a crisis abates); and daycare centers, where parents can watch skilled workers play with and discipline children appropriately.

Q: *What kinds of support services are available for abusing parents and abused children?*
A: If both mother and children are in danger of physical abuse, they can go to a shelter for abused women and children, if one is available. Job counseling and training, employment services, and transportation are other services often available to a distressed family.

Another source of support for abusing parents is a national organization called Parents Anonymous (1-800-882-1250), which has local chapters composed of abusing parents in the process of recovery, who offer each other support and counseling. Some parents, as well, may desire family planning services. Prevent Child Abuse (Box 2866, Chicago IL 60690) offers advice on how and where to find help.

Statistically, only half of treatable parents have been able to stop emotionally abusing their children, although they can stop physically abusing them. Those who find it hard to stop especially need the support of Parents Anonymous, crisis centers, and daycare centers.

Q: *How can further child abuse be prevented?*
A: In cases where children cannot be returned to their families because the parents are untreatable and the children are at high risk for reinjury, parental rights can be terminated legally in order to free children for speedy adoption. Simply removing a child from a dangerous home situation and placing him or her in a series of foster homes is emotionally damaging to that child. Such a child may feel confused, unwanted, and distrustful later in life. Early, appropriate adoption can give a child a sense of belonging and security.

Q: *What can parents do who fear they may abuse their children?*
A: The key to preventing child abuse is early, effective intervention. Regular, effective prenatal care can reduce the risks of prematurity, birth defects, and illness, thereby reducing the chances that a child will suffer developmental disabilities that may trigger abuse from a parent with a potential for abuse. Warning signs of potential child abuse may surface even before a baby is born.

Fathers can be helped to form an attachment to their babies if they are involved in planning, delivery, and child care. If newborn babies are given to parents right after birth, parents and baby become attached more quickly to each other. Ideally, the baby should be allowed to "room in" with the mother (stay in the mother's hospital room when she so desires).

When babies are premature or born with other difficulties that require a stay in an intensive care nursery or incubator, parents especially need contact with their babies so that they can begin to feel emotionally close to them. Parents who show no desire to cuddle or talk to their babies are cause for concern. Medical caretakers may refer the family to a community or private agency where they can receive supportive services.

If paternity leaves (paid or unpaid time off for new fathers) are not offered by an employer, it may be a good idea for the father to schedule his vacation around the time of the baby's birth. That way, the father can begin immediately to establish a close relationship with his child.

A network of friends, relatives, and a supportive spouse are crucial to helping a parent avoid feeling completely alone. Grandparents and other members of the extended family may be available to offer both practical help and emotional support. Baby-sitters can help parents get away from the children and spend time alone or together.

Parents of children whose disabilities require constant attention especially need periodic vacations. In addition, parents of children with disabilities may need someone to relieve them in providing everyday care for their child. Many communities offer respite services for both short and long periods. If a parent of a disabled child ever feels sudden anger and loss of control, he or she should call Parents Anonymous or a community child abuse hotline.

Education can reduce child abuse. Family living courses can provide teens with invaluable information about the 18-year, 24-hour-per-day responsibility of having and raising children. Students can learn that parents need to be consistent and reliable role models for their children and that children are not the "property" of their parents. A sensitive teacher can describe the stages of a child's physical and intellectual development and explain alternatives to physical violence for discipline.

Q: *How should child abuse be reported?*
A: It is essential that all adults consider themselves the protectors of children. Child abuse should be reported to a health professional, a child welfare agency, the police, or a community child abuse hotline. For parents who want confidential help and guidance with their childrearing problems, Parents Anonymous is always available: 1-800-882-1250.

CHLAMYDIAL INFECTION

DESCRIPTION AND CAUSE

Chlamydia is a special type of bacterium capable of causing several health problems, some of which affect newborns and adolescents. In adolescence, chlamydial infections cause a common group of venereal diseases. In infancy, chlamydia can produce *conjunctivitis* (an eye infection) or *pneumonia.*

Among adolescent males, chlamydial infections account for approximately 40 percent of the nongonorrheal cases of urethritis (inflammation and possible infection of the urethra—the tube that carries urine from the bladder out of the body). In addition, approximately 45 percent of the sexual partners of persons with chlamydial infections will contract the same infection. If treated properly, such an infection lasts only a short time, has no complications, and leaves no aftereffects.

Infection of adolescent females is very common (5 to 10 percent of sexually active girls may carry chlamydia in their genital tracts), but they often have no symptoms.

Approximately one third of all babies born to women who have chlamydia in their cervix (the portion of the womb that protrudes into the vagina) develop conjunctivitis, and about 10 percent of babies born to chlamydia-infected women become ill with pneumonia.

With chlamydial conjunctivitis, a baby's eyes become red, swollen, and watery and may contain pus 3 to 20 days after birth. Chlamydial pneumonia, which is marked by a dry cough, may occur from 3 to 20 weeks after birth. If untreated, both conditions persist for several weeks or months.

SIGNS AND SYMPTOMS

Among young males, genital chlamydial infections usually produce a white or gray odorless discharge from the penis, accompanied by a burning sensation with urination. Females with genital chlamydial infections often have no symptoms, but they may experience increased vaginal discharge or pain during urination (see *urinary tract infections*).

Chlamydial *conjunctivitis* usually begins in one or both eyes with a watery discharge that may contain pus after several days. The child's eyelids often become red and swollen.

This infection is rarely accompanied by fever.

The onset of chlamydial *pneumonia* is gradual. The first signs of a problem may be difficulty in feeding, closely followed by a repeated, dry cough. Breathing may become rapid, shallow, and labored, and the infant may vomit. Fever is not present.

DIAGNOSIS

A physician may suspect a genitourinary chlamydial infection if an adolescent has had sexual contact with a person known to have the disease. A chlamydial infection may also be suspected if tests for *gonorrhea* prove negative. Gonorrhea and chlamydia may occur together, and in such cases chlamydia is suspected when problems persist after completion of penicillin treatment. Presence of the infection is confirmed when the microorganisms are isolated through laboratory studies.

Chlamydial *conjunctivitis* and *pneumonia* may be diagnosed among infants whose mothers are identified as having genitourinary tract chlamydial infections. Because there are several types of bacteria and viruses that cause conjunctivitis and pneumonia, laboratory tests—blood tests, stains, and cultures—may be performed to rule out other possible causes and to identify chlamydia.

COMPLICATIONS

Untreated genitourinary chlamydial infections may result in swelling in part of the testes among males (epididymitis). Among females, chlamydia may lead to an inflammation and infection of the fallopian tubes. In rare severe cases, sterility may occur.

TREATMENT

A physician usually prescribes 2 to 3 weeks of antibiotic treatment (usually erythromycin for infants and tetracycline for adolescents). Antibiotic eye drops were at one time given for conjunctivitis, but now oral antibiotics are preferred for this disease as well as for *pneumonia* and venereal chlamydia.

PREVENTION

Genitourinary tract chlamydial infections can be prevented if adolescents refrain from sexual contact with persons who have or suspect they have the disease. Sexual partners of persons with chlamydial infections should be treated to prevent recurrence and spread of the organism.

Among newborns, chlamydial conjunctivitis can be prevented by placing erythromycin drops in the eyes immediately after birth. Most American hospitals now routinely use these drops instead of silver nitrate. If conjunctivitis occurs, oral antibiotics may be given to help prevent the onset of chlamydial *pneumonia.*

CHOKING

EMERGENCY ACTION

If a child begins to choke or cough repeatedly after swallowing a foreign object or a large chunk of food, seek medical assistance. Do not attempt to dislodge an object that interferes with breathing, because complete obstruction may follow.

If an *infant* is gasping, cannot breathe, and begins to turn blue, give a series of four back blows followed by four chest thrusts as follows:

(1) Keep the infant straddled over your forearm with the head lower than the body.

(2) Firmly slap the infant four times between the shoulder blades (Fig. 15A, p. 137).

(3) Turn infant face up, keeping the head lower than the body. Place hand just below the internipple line on the breastbone. Push in and up four times. The object should pop out of the infant's throat. If it does not, continue alternating four back blows with four chest thrusts. (See Fig. 15B, p. 137.)

If a *child* is gasping, cannot breathe, and begins to turn blue, but is still *conscious,* apply the Heimlich maneuver as follows:

(1) Stand behind the child and reach around with both arms to encircle the waist.

(2) Make a fist with either hand, placing the thumb side against the child's abdomen midway between the navel and rib cage.

(3) Grasp the fist with the other hand and pull quickly inward and upward into the child's abdomen. The object should pop out of the child's throat. If it does not, repeat the maneuver several times.

(4) While applying the maneuver, you should hold your elbows away from the child's body to avoid squeezing the child's sides and perhaps injuring the ribs. (See Fig. 16, p. 138.)

If a *child* is *unconscious* because of choking, apply the Heimlich maneuver with the child lying down as follows:

(1) Position the child face up on his or her back.

(2) Kneel beside a small child or straddle the body of an older child.

(3) Place the heel of one hand in the middle of the child's abdomen between the navel and rib cage. Place free hand on top of the first.

(4) Push the heel of the bottom hand into the stomach with four quick upward thrusts. The object should pop out. If it does not, repeat the maneuver several times. (See Fig. 17, p. 138.)

If a child swallows a sharp object such as a pin, tack, nail, staple, paper clip, bottle cap, pull-tab from a can, fish bone, or shell, consult a physician immediately. If a child swallows a poisonous object such as a mothball or miniature ("button") battery, consult a poison information center or a physician immediately. (See section on poisoning in Chapter 10, "Basic First Aid," p. 142, and *foreign objects, swallowed.)*

DESCRIPTION AND CAUSE

Choking involves either partial or total blockage of the throat or windpipe by an object. Choking on foreign objects is a common childhood accident and children of all ages are vulnerable.

Children under the age of 4 years are most likely to choke on food or foreign objects. A wide variety of small, common household objects are potentially dangerous, including buttons, pins, staples, thumb tacks, nails, bobby pins, paper clips, small knobs, miniature ("button") batteries, marbles, coins, rings, bottle caps, pull-tabs from cans, toy rattles, eyes from stuffed animals, and seeds.

Foods that can be dangerous for a small child to eat include hard candies, nuts, hotdogs, popcorn kernels, raw carrots and celery, shellfish, and fish with bones. In addition, sharp objects or foods may damage the throat, windpipe, or possibly the stomach and intestines. In addition, objects such as button batteries are poisonous and occasionally cause serious gastrointestinal problems if they do not pass promptly out of the intestinal tract. Older children are most likely to choke on food such as meat or large nuts.

If a child's oxygen supply is blocked for more than four minutes, permanent brain damage or death can occur. If an object is dislodged before four minutes have passed, however, the chances of complete recovery are excellent.

SIGNS AND SYMPTOMS AND DIAGNOSIS

A child who is choking usually clutches at his or her throat. The child is unable to speak and looks panic-stricken. The child may make gurgling or choking noises or, if the airway is partially blocked, may gasp or breathe noisily. If the airway is completely blocked for more than three minutes, the child's skin, tongue, lips, and nails begin to turn pale or blue from lack of oxygen. After about 4 minutes the child becomes unconscious.

COMPLICATIONS

Cracked or broken ribs can occur if rescue maneuvers are performed incorrectly or too energetically. The risk of prolonged choking and its consequences, however, obviously outweighs the risk of broken ribs.

TREATMENT

See choking section of Chapter 10, "Basic First Aid," p. 137, as well as instructions for artificial respiration, p. 124, and cardiopulmonary resuscitation (CPR), p. 127.

PREVENTION

The best way to prevent young children from choking on foreign objects is to try to put all potentially dangerous objects out of their reach. Since infants discover many such objects while crawling on the floor, it is wise for parents to childproof the floor by getting down on their hands and knees and looking for pins, buttons, nails, and the like, before allowing a child to crawl around. (See childproofing section of Chapter 4, "Accident Prevention," p. 59.)

Children under 3 years old should not be given dried beans or beanbags, peas, or other hard, small objects. Parents should also not let small children play with any toy that is smaller than the child's fist or that has small removable parts, such as the eyes or nose of some stuffed animals. Parents should pull on such parts to make sure that a child cannot tug, suck, or chew them off.

Young children should not be given hard candies, nuts, food containing seeds or pits, or hard, small pieces of raw vegetables or fruits like carrots or apples. As a rule, all food given to young children should be cut into small pieces and should be easily chewable. Small children should be taught to chew each bite of food thoroughly before swallowing. Parents should remove bones and shells from any meat or seafood. Hotdogs should be cut into very small pieces for young children. If the hotdog skin or casing is tough or thick, it should be removed.

Older children should not play or run while eating. They may need to be reminded to thoroughly chew their foods, especially meat, before attempting to swallow it. Children should also be told to spit out food into a napkin if they are about to cough or sneeze. Children should be cautioned about chewing gum while lying down, in case they fall asleep with gum in their mouths.

Parents and children should learn how to properly perform the Heimlich maneuver on themselves and others. Self-help can involve the standard method or sudden pressure of the diaphragm against a solid object such as a chair or countertop. (See Chapter 10, "Basic First Aid," p. 138.)

CHOLESTEROL AND TRIGLYCERIDE PROBLEMS

DESCRIPTION, CAUSE, AND SIGNS AND SYMPTOMS

Triglycerides are the body's most important reserve of energy. They make up most of the natural fats and oils of the body, which are either saturated, monounsaturated, or polyunsaturated. In addition to the triglyceride fats, the body produces other fats such as cholesterol. Cholesterol is vital to bodily function and has specific roles in such processes as cell membrane formation and hormone secretion.

Most triglycerides and cholesterol are produced by the liver, but they also enter the body in foods containing fats. In the bloodstream, cholesterol and triglycerides bind to proteins, forming lipoproteins, to be transported through the body for use or storage.

Problems may develop when levels of cholesterol or triglycerides (or both) in the blood are too high. High levels may cause deposition of cholesterol in the blood vessels, including the aorta, the main artery of the heart. The vessels eventually become clogged, and blood flow and heart function are reduced. This process is called atherosclerosis, or hardening of the arteries. It is estimated that 40 to 45 percent of deaths in the United States are caused directly or indirectly by atherosclerosis and related heart disease.

Diet-Induced High Lipid Levels

A diet high in saturated fats (containing triglycerides) and cholesterol may play an important role in the development of high blood fat levels and atherosclerosis. Saturated fats and cholesterol are found in many foods, including eggs, red meats, butter, some margarines, some oils, nuts, and whole milk products. In the United States most diets contain more saturated fats and cholesterol than necessary. The average daily intake of cholesterol by Americans is about 750 milligrams, about 450 to 550 mg higher than is healthy.

Inherited High Lipid Levels: Hyperlipidemias

Hyperlipidemias, or inherited high levels of lipids, are caused by defective genes inherited by children from their parents; the disease usually affects more than one family member. These genes interfere with lipid metabolism (the breakdown and use of fats by the body). Hyperlipidemias are the most common of all inherited diseases; approximately 0.5 to 1 percent of all people have an inherited form of hyperlipidemia, including familial hypercholesterolemia, familial combined hyperlipidemia, and familial hypertriglyceridemia.

The defective gene responsible for familial hypercholesterolemia causes an absence of a specific agent that allows lipoproteins to enter cells and be broken down. The resulting decreased cellular supply of fats triggers increased liver production of cholesterol. As a result, levels of lipids in the bloodstream and the blood vessels increase. The defective genes responsible for familial combined hyperlipidemia and hypertriglyceridemia are not well understood (see *genetic disorders*).

Levels of cholesterol become elevated during childhood in cases of familial hypercholesterolemia. In cases of combined hyperlipidemia and hypertriglyceridemia, however, this usually does not happen before age 25. Familial hypercholesterolemia may be accompanied by xanthomas, yellow-orange nodules of accumulated cholesterol, but this does not usually occur until 30 to 40 years of age. These nodules are found most often on the tendons of the fingers or on the Achilles tendon at the heel of the foot. Affected tendons can become inflamed and sore. If atherosclerosis has developed, chest pain may be present. A dense, grayish ring may develop around the rim of the cornea (the transparent membrane covering the eye) because of fatty deposits.

DIAGNOSIS

A physician may have difficulty diagnosing an inherited lipid problem, particularly when signs and symptoms do not appear until adulthood. A child's dietary intake of saturated fats, as well as the presence of a weight problem such as obesity (see *weight problems*), can make diagnosis difficult by affecting lipid levels in the blood.

A physician's diagnosis of a lipid problem is based on a child's medical history, the family's medical history, and the results of a thorough physical examination. Blood samples from the child and other family members are usually analyzed to measure levels of cholesterol and triglycerides. If a family history of lipid problems exists, a child should be examined as early in life as possible, even if no signs of a problem are present.

COMPLICATIONS

Individuals with hyperlipidemia have a greater chance of developing early heart disease, usually between ages 40 and 60, than unaffected individuals.

TREATMENT

Lowering levels of blood cholesterol and triglycerides can be attempted with a diet that is low in saturated fats, low in cholesterol (under 200 mg per day), and high in polyunsaturated fats. Caution must be taken, however, because excessive amounts of polyunsaturated and monounsaturated fats may produce gallstones. Prolonged use of lowfat or skim milk may deprive growing infants and children of needed calories or essential fatty acids (see Chapter 2, "Promoting Physical Health").

No diet modification is recommended before 2 years of age. Once a child reaches his or her second birthday, however, the diet should be modified so that saturated fats are replaced by polyunsaturated fats. Such diet modifications include consuming only three eggs per week, including those used in cooking; consuming less meat and more fish and poultry; substituting skim or lowfat milk and lowfat dairy products for whole milk and whole-milk products; substituting polyunsaturated margarines for saturated margarines or butter; and substituting corn, olive, or other unsaturated oils for saturated oils, such as palm or coconut oil. If a child with high levels of cholesterol in the blood follows a diet with these modifications, cholesterol levels usually decrease markedly, about 15 to 20 percent.

Treatment of inherited hypercholesterolemia also focuses on such dietary modifications. However, treatment of hypertriglyceridemia initially focuses on reduction of caloric intake because many patients are overweight. Reduction of saturated fats usually occurs as well, but is not the major focus of diet modification. Once ideal body weight is achieved and maintained, the focus of a child's diet is on restriction of saturated fats.

Many children with inherited lipid problems respond well to diet therapy. However, if diet therapy does not correct hyperlipidemia by 10 to 12 years of age, a physician may recommend the use of medications. Before prescribing treatment, a physician determines whether the potential benefits of medication therapy outweigh the risk of potential side effects.

PREVENTION

Inherited problems cannot be prevented. Atherosclerosis may be prevented if cholesterol buildup is prevented during childhood. All children older than 2 years should follow lowfat diets; children with inherited problems must also take any medications prescribed by their physicians.

CLEFT LIP AND CLEFT PALATE

DESCRIPTION

A cleft lip is a congenitally split upper lip; a cleft palate is a congenitally split palate (roof of the mouth). In either case, the cleft represents an incomplete fusion of skin, muscle, or bone during fetal development. The condition is almost always apparent at birth; rarely, a partial cleft of the soft palate (the fleshy area toward the back of the roof of the mouth) is discovered in later childhood.

The conditions may occur separately or together. Cleft lip (alone or with cleft palate) is more prevalent in males; the incidence is about 1 in 1,000 births. Cleft palate alone is more prevalent in females; the incidence is about 1 in 2,500 births. Clefts are sometimes associated with other birth defects. Children with clefts, especially cleft palate, may also have teeth problems. The teeth may be out of position, misshapen, or rotated; there may be more or fewer teeth than normal.

Both cleft lip and cleft palate interfere with the natural functioning of the mouth, which must be closed and hollow to perform normal speaking, drinking, and chewing functions. Lip and palate clefts can be closed by surgery. Cleft-lip surgery leaves a minor scar on the upper lip; speech is not affected. Children who have cleft-palate surgery are more likely to have speech problems, although over 80 percent of the children who have a repaired palate attain normal speech.

CAUSE

Causes of clefts are not known. Some children born with clefts have a family history of similar conditions, and some have not (see *genetic disorders*).

Cleft lip is a birth defect. Normally, the lip is formed in the fourth to sixth week of fetal development; two tissue tabs that grow in from the sides of the face join with a central tab that grows down from the tip of the nose. If this union is not complete, a baby is born with cleft lip.

Cleft palate is also a birth defect. Normally, the palate is formed during the first 8 to 12 weeks of fetal development. Bone and tissue grow in from the sides of the upper jaw to join in the middle. This forms the roof of the mouth (palate), which is also the floor of the nose. It is composed of a bony part (hard palate) and a muscular part (soft palate). When the sides do not grow together properly, a cleft (or opening) between the mouth and the nose results.

SIGNS AND SYMPTOMS

Cleft lip can be as minor as a small notch in the upper lip or slight nasal asymmetry (unevenness). It can also involve a complete separation of the upper lip, extending up into the floor of the nose. Clefts can appear on one or both sides of the lip. The nostrils are usually displaced or malformed.

Cleft palate appears as a hole in the roof of the mouth. The defect varies greatly in width and length, depending on when and where the growth process stopped. A cleft may involve only the soft palate, or the soft palate and part or all of the hard palate. A cleft may also appear in one or both sides of the upper gum.

DIAGNOSIS

The conditions are nearly always readily apparent at birth. Even a partial cleft will almost always be noticed by a physician during routine checkups.

COMPLICATIONS

Recurrent inflammation of the middle ear (see *earache and ear infections*) and subsequent temporary hearing loss are frequently associated with uncorrected cleft palate. Children who have cleft palates are more susceptible to *colds, sore throat,* and earaches, and tonsils and adenoids may become persistently infected and enlarged (see *tonsil and adenoid problems*).

Teeth of children with palate defects may not be naturally cleaned by the lips, cheeks, tongue, and saliva; as a result, cavities may develop more readily.

Speech problems are also associated with cleft palate. An open palate gives nasal speech. The problem is compounded by the inadequate formation of the muscles of the palate and throat. Without the proper working of these muscles, it is difficult to build up enough pressure in the mouth to make explosive sounds like *p, b, d, t, h, g, sh,* and *ch.*

TREATMENT

An immediate concern for those with clefts is adequate nutrition. Infants with clefts cannot feed in the usual way—by sucking. A special syringe (called a cleft-lip feeder) can be used to feed a child with cleft lip or cleft palate. Infants should be held in an upright position while feeding.

Surgery is the treatment of choice for clefts. The goals of surgery are symmetrical appearance of lip and nose, normal speech, normal hearing, and functional and attractive teeth. Surgical closure of cleft lip is usually performed at 1 to 3 months of age, if an infant weighs enough and is otherwise healthy. The age at which cleft palate is repaired depends on the size, shape, and degree of the defect; it normally takes place between 8 and 12 months of age.

Following surgery, precautions must be taken to keep the stitches clean and to avoid straining them (this is to prevent infection and to achieve the best cosmetic results). Patients are often fed by medicine dropper or cleft-lip feeder, and sometimes wear arm restraints to restrict movement and to keep them from touching the stitches.

Because years of treatment may be required for children with clefts, especially cleft palate, many specialists are involved in a child's care, including a pediatrician; a plastic surgeon; an ear, nose, and throat specialist (otolaryngologist); several specialized dentists (orthodontist to straighten teeth, prosthodontist to fit the child with special appliances, and pedodontist to treat general dentistry problems in children); a speech therapist; a social worker; a psychologist; and a psychiatrist.

Clear speech is accomplished through careful cooperation between the family and various members of the medical-surgical team. A small percentage of children with repaired cleft palate continue to have speech problems. These children may benefit from a secondary operation on the palate; once this is done, they can expect to have near-normal speech.

PREVENTION

Cleft lip and cleft palate cannot be prevented. Parents whose child has a cleft may want to discuss with a genetic counselor the risk of having another child similarly affected (see genetic counseling section of *genetic disorders*).

CLUBFOOT

DESCRIPTION AND SIGNS AND SYMPTOMS

One of the more common foot malformations present at birth is clubfoot. Occurring in approximately 1 out of every 1,000 births, clubfoot appears almost twice as often among boys as among girls. In half the cases of clubfoot, both feet are affected.

When clubfoot is present, foot bones and anklebones are malformed. Characteristically, the heel turns in under the ankle, the inner edge of the foot turns upward, and the front of one foot turns in toward the other. The entire sole of the foot and the toes flex downward.

With proper treatment, clubfoot can be corrected. However, the calf of the affected leg remains thin because the muscles of the foot and leg are poorly developed. Clubfoot tends to recur, and a child needs frequent medical monitoring until maturity.

CAUSE

Clubfoot is an inherited malformation; if a family history of clubfoot is present, a child has about a 1 in 20 chance of developing it (see *genetic disorders*).

DIAGNOSIS

A physician diagnoses clubfoot at birth according to the appearance of a child's foot and ankle. X-ray films are taken during the first year of life to identify the precise bone malformations.

TREATMENT

To ensure successful results, treatment of clubfoot should start within a few days of birth. An infant's joints and bones are most flexible then and can be repositioned most easily. Treatment usually involves moving the feet into a straight position and holding them with casts. This procedure must be gentle, however, to avoid damaging an infant's skin and crushing the soft bones. For infants less than 3 months old, new casts are usually applied every week to accommodate rapid growth. If progressive repositioning of the foot by casting fails to correct a clubfoot completely, surgery is necessary. Surgery often but not always corrects a clubfoot completely, although malformations such as a short broad foot or abnormally small leg muscles may persist. After surgery, corrective casts are needed for at least 3 months and corrective shoes are worn for at least 3 months more.

COMPLICATIONS

If a child's clubfoot is not treated at an early age, permanent walking difficulty may result. In addition, foot and leg ligaments may become more resistant to correction, and foot cartilage may grow progressively deformed. Complications may also arise if treatment of clubfoot is interrupted before the foot bones are fully straightened. If treatment is resumed at a later age, the process is longer and more difficult. Problems may also develop if improper casting procedures are used to treat clubfoot. Careful surgery is more conservative than forceful casting if gradual correction is not taking place.

PREVENTION

Clubfoot cannot be prevented.

COLDS

DESCRIPTION

A cold is a viral infection of the upper respiratory tract characterized by stuffiness and sneezing. It is one of the most common illnesses among people of all ages. Children are particularly susceptible to colds because they have not had a chance to build up immunity to many of the viruses in the environment. Each time a child suffers a cold, however, he or she becomes (at least temporarily) immune to the virus involved and the risk of subsequent infections decreases.

Colds most often affect the nose and throat, but may also involve other areas of the respiratory tract. The eyes, ears, sinuses (cavities in the face bones that drain into the nasal passage), and lymph nodes (disease-filtering tissues that are part of the body's infection-fighting mechanism) of the neck may also be affected.

No cure has yet been discovered for the common cold, and symptoms usually last for 5 to 7 days. If complications develop, symptoms may persist.

CAUSE

Colds can be caused by approximately 200 different types of viruses. Contrary to popular belief, cold, wet weather does not by itself cause or increase the chances of developing a cold. However, people stay indoors more often during cold weather, which increases the risk of coming in contact with a cold virus.

Healthy children acquire a cold virus by breathing air laden with contaminated mucus droplets produced by a cold sufferer's sneeze or cough. A child can also acquire a cold virus through contact with an infected child who has not washed his or her hands after coughing or nose blowing, or by touching recently contaminated objects, often a toy or a table top.

SIGNS AND SYMPTOMS

The most common signs and symptoms of a cold are sneezing, stuffy nose, headache, and a nasal discharge. The nose may feel heavy and full because sinuses are clogged and cannot drain. A child's throat may be dry and scratchy, and a cough may develop. Red, watery eyes, ear pain, and mild swelling and tenderness of the neck lymph nodes also may be present. *Fever* as high as 103° F

(39.4° C) may develop, particularly among young children.

DIAGNOSIS

To most parents, cold symptoms are obvious. It is difficult, however, to identify the specific virus responsible for a cold.

If parents suspect a more serious respiratory infection, such as *pneumonia, influenza, bronchiolitis,* or *allergies,* a physician should be consulted to identify the condition. Diagnosis is based on signs and symptoms, results of a physical examination, and occasionally laboratory test results.

COMPLICATIONS

Obstruction of the openings that normally allow the sinuses to drain into the nose occurs when the nasal mucous membranes become swollen. This obstruction allows bacteria to multiply, and *sinusitis* may develop. By the same mechanism, the space behind the ear drum (the middle ear), which normally is open to the nasal passage, can be cut off and become infected. This can lead to otitis media, a bacterial infection of the middle ear. (See *earache and ear infections.*)

Occasionally, a child suffering a cold can develop a more severe infection, including *laryngitis, bronchiolitis, pneumonia,* and rarely, *encephalitis* (inflammation of the brain).

TREATMENT

Since no cure exists, treatment of a cold focuses on easing symptoms. A child should get plenty of rest, although complete bed rest is not necessary. Drinking plenty of fluids (particularly warm ones) is recommended to help thin mucus and unclog nasal passages. Gargling with salt water or medicated mouthwashes temporarily eases a sore throat.

Decongestants, available without prescription as tablets, nose drops, or nose sprays, can be used to open a child's clogged nose and sinuses temporarily. Nose drops or sprays should not be used for an extended period of time, however, because they can cause nasal mucous membranes to thicken and further block the nasal passages. Membranes do not return to normal size until use of the decongestant is stopped.

Adding moisture to dry, scratchy throat membranes can help reduce throat irritation and prevent coughing. This can be done by having a child breathe air moistened with steam from a cool-mist vaporizer or a shower. Nonprescription cough drops and syrups are available to temporarily ease a child's cough.

A fever-reducing medication may be helpful. Consult the physician for specific recommendations and read discussion of nonprescription medications beginning on p. 000. In some instances, vitamin C may lessen the severity of some symptoms.

PREVENTION

A child should be taught to cover the nose and mouth when sneezing or coughing to avoid spreading a cold virus. An infected child should wash his or her hands frequently, especially after nose blowing.

Contrary to popular belief, large doses of vitamin C cannot prevent the common cold.

COLIC

DESCRIPTION

Colic is characterized by prolonged periods of intense crying. Some studies estimate that almost 80 percent of infants in the United States are affected during their first 3 months of life.

Colic usually begins suddenly with loud, sustained crying. The infant's face may be flushed, the abdomen is usually tense and distended, the legs are drawn up to the abdomen, the feet are cold, and the hands are clenched. An episode of colic generally ends when the infant is completely exhausted. Occasionally the passing of feces will calm the child.

Although daily crying would seem to indicate a sickly child, it is usually the case that an infant with colic appears quite healthy, gaining weight at acceptable rates.

Of the two patterns of colic that exist, the more common is infantile or "3-month" colic. The infant makes up for peaceful daytime hours by crying long and hard, beginning at nightfall and continuing until well after parents and child have passed their level of tolerance. No amount of cajoling, burping, or amusement will divert the infant from its pained crying.

The less common variety includes infants who wake every few hours and cry fitfully. These babies may drink small amounts of milk, then fall into a restless sleep.

An infant may suck eagerly on a pacifier, a hand, or a finger during a colic episode. When offered milk, the child may drink greedily at first, then abruptly push away a bottle or a mother's breast and begin to cry.

In most cases, symptoms of colic diminish rapidly after a child is 3 months old.

CAUSE

The traditional explanation of colic, that it is a reaction to abdominal pain, has recently been tempered with the suggestion that it results from large amounts of swallowed air trapped in the intestines. It has also been suggested that colic is an infant's frustrated reaction to his or her inability to interact with the environment. Colic probably results from a combination of these conditions.

Since colic usually appears in the late afternoon and early evening, fatigue may contribute to the severity of an episode. Household activity and tension often increases later in the day, when more family members are present. Family difficulties that occur at this time may contribute to a colic episode.

DIAGNOSIS

Diagnosis of colic consists largely of eliminating other possible causes of prolonged crying. Intestinal allergy, *intestinal obstruction, constipation,* or a gastrointestinal infection must be ruled out before colic can be diagnosed.

TREATMENT

Since the cause of colic is not known, it is difficult to provide effective treatment. Colic eventually disappears, however, and the best management is to comfort and reassure a colicky infant. Cuddling, rocking, holding, backrubbing, and other reassuring actions will help an infant feel more secure. Placing an infant on his or her stomach on a warm heating pad or a warm hot-water bottle may help ease muscle cramps.

If an attack of colic lasts more than 4 hours, a physician should be consulted. A physician may perform a thorough physical examination, paying particular attention to the ears, throat, chest, and abdomen for signs of infection or illness that may cause crying. Laboratory urine tests may be performed to check for *urinary tract infections.* A physician may recommend changing an infant's formula and diet to eliminate the possibility of *food allergy.* A physician again should be consulted if colic episodes have not stopped by the time an infant is 4 months old.

PREVENTION

Since an exact cause is unknown, it is almost impossible to prevent colic. A stable emotional home environment will help reduce *stress* and tension. Proper feeding and burping techniques and identification of possible allergies may also be helpful.

COLOR BLINDNESS

DESCRIPTION

Color blindness is the inability to distinguish certain colors. Usually color blindness is not total; an affected individual retains some color vision but is unable to discern shades of a particular color, usually red and green.

Color blindness occurs much more frequently among males, especially of European and Asian descent, than among females.

Color blindness is not serious, although it can be annoying when color discrimination is necessary. The exception is a rare condition called monochromatic vision, or total color blindness. A child with this condition sees only one color and may have difficulty seeing well in daylight.

CAUSE

Color blindness is inherited; the responsible gene is passed on by mothers to their children, most often their sons. Approximately 8 percent of all white males inherit this disorder, while only 4 percent of black males do so. Fewer than 1 percent of all females develop color blindness. (See *genetic disorders.*)

SIGNS AND SYMPTOMS

A child with red or green color blindness is likely to confuse red, brown, and green. A child with blue color blindness confuses shades of blue.

DIAGNOSIS

An opthalmologist (eye specialist) diagnoses color blindness by using color plates (in which a child is asked to identify various numbers or shapes by color) and colored disks (which are placed in characteristic order by children with color blindness).

TREATMENT

No cure exists for color blindness. As children develop, they learn to recognize colors by association. For instance, the affected child learns that the top light of a traffic signal is red and means stop, while the bottom light is green and means go.

Tests for color blindness are often included in routine physical examinations (see Chapter 6, "Going to the Doctor"). Screening for color vision defects can be performed with a child about 4 years old or older.

PREVENTION

Color blindness cannot be prevented.

COMA

EMERGENCY ACTION

Any child who is unconscious because of injury, disease, or poison needs medical attention immediately. If necessary, call the police for assistance. In any event, do not transport the child to the hospital unaccompanied by at least one other person unless no alternative exists; it is vitally important that an unconscious child be watched at all times in case breathing or circulation become impaired.

If a person trained in cardiopulmonary resuscitation (CPR) or first aid is available, that person should monitor the condition of an unconscious child until medical help is available.

The first step in emergency treatment is to ensure that the child can breathe. If the child is unconscious because of head or spinal injury (see *head and spinal injury*), do not move his or her head, neck, or back, unless providing an airway is otherwise impossible. If it is certain that injury is not a factor, lay the child on his or her side with the chin extended away from the chest. This position prevents an unconscious child from *choking* by encouraging saliva (and, if present, vomit) to drain out of the mouth. If necessary and possible, administer cardiopulmonary or artificial resuscitation (see Chapter 10, "Basic First Aid," pp. 124 to 127).

An unconscious child should be kept warm but not hot. Even if consciousness returns, do not give the child food, drink, or medication. The stomach should be as empty as possible for certain diagnostic and surgical procedures; if an unconscious child vomits, a danger exists that he or she will inhale the vomitus and choke. If external injuries such as cuts are present and first aid can be used, administer treatment.

These steps are imperative no matter what the cause of unconsciousness. If it is known that the cause is *diabetes,* see that entry for information on emergency treatment.

DESCRIPTION

Coma (a Latin word meaning "deep sleep") is a state of unconsciousness from which a person cannot be roused. It is caused by a malfunction of the complex brain system that controls being awake, aware, and alert. This system can malfunction as a result of injury, disease, or poison.

How often coma occurs is difficult to estimate, partly because almost all comatose patients progress through various stages of unconsciousness and decreased responsiveness, not all of which are considered coma. The condition develops most often following head injuries, poisonings, and other problems affecting the brain.

The majority of comatose patients—even those who have sustained severe head injuries or are very ill—remain in actual coma for only a few days, although full recovery may be impossible or may take weeks, months, or even years. The long-term outlook is virtually impossible to predict at the outset of coma. It depends on the cause, severity, duration, and treatment of coma. In general, the longer it takes to rouse a comatose patient, the worse the prognosis.

Death, however, rarely results because of unconsciousness, even when coma lasts for years. Advances in other areas of medicine have prolonged the lives of many comatose patients. These advances have inspired a variety of new treatment methods designed to rehabilitate comatose patients with mild to moderate brain damage. In addition, medical advances have raised ethical questions about the best way to treat comatose patients who have suffered severe, irreversible brain damage.

CAUSE

Coma can be caused by any substance, disease, or injury that disrupts the brain system controlling alertness and awareness.

Coma can result from inhalation or swallowing of toxic substances, such as carbon monoxide or lead (see *lead poisoning*). Certain combinations of substances (alcohol and sedatives, for example) can produce coma. Children who are highly allergic to chemicals found in certain foods or medications can lapse into coma after swallowing them.

The most common disease-related causes of coma are *meningitis* (infection of the membranes encasing the brain and spinal cord); *encephalitis* (brain inflammation); metabolic disorders such as *diabetes* and *hypoglycemia;* and *seizures.* Also among the most common causes of coma during childhood are diseases that affect the supply of oxygen to the brain. These diseases include congenital heart disease (see *heart disease, congenital*), severe *anemia,* and *sickle cell anemia.* Other disease-related causes of coma include liver disorders (sometimes caused by diseases such as *Reye's syndrome),* *hydrocephalus* (a condition marked by a buildup of fluid in the brain), *stroke,* severe hypothyroidism (see *thyroid problems),* and *brain tumor.*

Head and spinal injury is a frequent cause of coma, most often because of motor vehicle and sports accidents. Accidents that can affect the supply of oxygen to the brain and cause coma include *choking,* drowning, strangulation, and suffocation (see *asphyxia).*

SIGNS AND SYMPTOMS

Signs and symptoms can be grouped into levels of decreased responsiveness:

- Drowsiness. Lethargy, sleepiness, lack of interest; child lapses into sleep easily but also is roused easily, gives appropriate verbal responses, and does not need constant stimulation to stay awake.
- Stupor. Dullness, disorientation, *delirium;* child lapses into sleep without constant stimulation but can be roused to make simple—but sometimes inappropriate—verbal responses.
- Deep stupor (child is considered semicomatose). Strong, painful stimulus is needed to rouse child, who may moan during rousal attempts and make attempts to brush away the stimulus.
- Coma. Eyes are closed at all times; child cannot be roused even with painful stimuli and makes inappropriate attempts to get rid of stimuli, such as placing limbs in odd positions (arms flexed on chest with hands fisted and legs extended, for example) or curling up into a fetal position.
- Deep Coma. Child does not respond to any stimuli, has no reflexes, and is relaxed and flabby without any muscle tone.
- Brain Death. Total absence of brain activity, as indicated by monitoring of brain waves; it may be possible to maintain breathing and circulation with the use of machines.

In any of these stages, pulse may be slower than normal and blood pressure may be higher. The child's breathing may be rapid and shallow (a condition called hyperventilation—see *breathing difficulty).* Many comatose patients have unusually large pupils and may stare straight ahead even while a physician rolls the head from side to side. In cases of deep coma, lack of breathing *(apnea)* may be a problem.

DIAGNOSIS

When a child is unconscious, a physician administers lifesaving treatment, such as cardiopulmonary resuscitation, even before determining the cause of the condition.

Once an unconscious child's condition is stable, a physician diagnoses the level of decreased responsiveness and its cause. In addition to performing physical tests (such as taking a patient's pulse), a physician usually orders sophisticated laboratory tests that show how the patient's brain is functioning. These tests may include a CT (computed tomography) scan and an electroencephalogram (EEG). Other body functions are tested in an attempt to determine whether an undiagnosed disease exists or whether a child has been poisoned. These tests may involve, for example, examination of the blood, cerebrospinal fluid, liver, or lungs.

COMPLICATIONS

Many causes of coma, especially severe head injury, can cause a buildup of fluid in the brain, which increases pressure within the skull. Such pressure can interfere with circulation and, consequently, with the supply of oxygen to the brain. Permanent brain damage, then death, can result if this pressure is not relieved very quickly.

Because physical activity ceases while a

child is in a coma, muscle problems such as extreme flaccidity (a condition marked by poor tone and relaxation of muscles) can result. Absence of movement can also increase a child's chances of developing skin irritations and infections and metabolism problems. All these problems can be prevented with proper treatment.

TREATMENT

Treatment of coma involves the following steps: stabilization of respiration and circulation, treatment of any increased intracranial pressure and of the cause of coma, and monitoring of body functions with special machines. Treatment can involve medication or surgery (used, for instance, if other forms of treatment cannot prevent or lower increased intracranial pressure). The ultimate goal is to prevent brain death, which is considered medically and legally the stage at which life has ended.

The goal of treatment is also to prevent complications while bringing the patient to progressively higher levels of responsiveness. This process can take months or even years. Acute-care hospitals do not usually have the facilities or resources to provide long-term, intense therapy programs. Many nursing homes, however, are equipped to treat coma patients, and a few facilities exist exclusively for them. (See Chapter 5, "Choosing Health Care.")

As long as coma lasts, circulation, respiration, and other body functions must be monitored constantly. Ideally, a rehabilitation program should provide near-constant stimuli for revivable patients. One popular method of therapy aims to revive one sense at a time; when focusing on reviving the sense of hearing, for example, a therapist may place a radio at the patient's bedside for hours at a time. This type of therapy has been successful at rousing patients slowly into higher levels of responsiveness.

Even with intensive therapy, some coma patients improve very slowly—or not at all. The uncertainty can be extremely stressful to a family, and individual or group counseling may provide relief, as can support groups. Families should be aware that personality and behavioral changes, as well as emotional problems, are common among coma patients undergoing rehabilitation. Readjustment to a daily routine can be difficult even if the child regains full consciousness in a short period of time. A counselor can help

a child meet this challenge. Family support is essential.

PREVENTION

Many head injuries leading to coma could be prevented by simple measures of safety, such as using seat belts and car seats and wearing quality protective headgear while engaging in sports or riding bicycles and motorcycles. Diabetics should be aware of the factors that bring on diabetic and hypoglycemia coma and should avoid them. Prevention of coma caused by other diseases varies with each disease. Parents should keep all known poisons out of the reach of children. Older children should be warned of the danger of combining alcohol with prescribed medication or illegal drugs.

CONJUNCTIVITIS

DESCRIPTION

Conjunctivitis is an inflammation of the conjunctiva, the mucous membrane lining the inner eyelid and the whites of the eyes (see Fig. 23, p. 362). Conjunctivitis, the most common eye problem of young children, can have many causes. When affecting children, it is most often called pink eye. If promptly treated, conjunctivitis is not serious.

CAUSE

Pink eye may be caused by a variety of bacteria, including staphylococcus, streptococcus, and pneumococcus. The mucous membrane of the eye becomes infected by bacteria rubbed in the eye (usually by the hand), by infections of the nose traveling up the tear duct, and by contact with the eye secretions of someone who has pink eye. Bacterial conjunctivitis is mildly contagious and can be carried on anything—books, toys, papers, or towels—touched by the discharge from the infected eye. Children who have conjunctivitis in one eye often quickly spread the infection to the other with their hands.

A much more serious form of bacterial conjunctivitis occurs in newborns whose mothers have *gonorrhea*. The newborn child's eyes become infected with the gonococcus bacteria during passage through the birth canal. Until the discovery of antibiotics, gonorrheal conjunctivitis was a major cause of blindness.

Conjunctivitis is also commonly caused by viruses. Some viruses cause only conjunctivitis. Conjunctivitis can also be a symptom of a systemic viral disease, such as *measles*. Children often contract a mild form of viral conjunctivitis from swimming pools contaminated by urine, particularly if the eyes have been irritated by chlorine. Viral conjunctivitis is highly contagious.

Chemicals in the child's environment can irritate the membrane of the eye, causing conjunctivitis. Household cleaning substances, smog, smoke, and industrial pollutants are all potential causes of chemical conjunctivitis (see *eye injuries*). Silver nitrate, administered as eye drops to newborns as a preventive measure against gonorrheal conjunctivitis, may itself cause a mild conjunctivitis, which lasts 2 or 3 days. Conjunctivitis may also occur in allergic children who encounter substances to which they are sensitive, such as ragweed pollen.

SIGNS AND SYMPTOMS

Pink eye is easy to identify because of the bright pink color of the conjunctiva and the typical yellowish discharge from the eye. Upon waking, the child may find the eyelids stuck together and caked with crusts. The child may feel as if sand is in the eye and will be uncomfortable.

The discharge from an eye infected by a virus will be more watery than the yellowish pus of bacterial conjunctivitis. Conjunctivitis caused by a generalized viral infection is characterized by fever, sore throat, and diarrhea. When a child has viral conjunctivitis, the eyes may be sensitive to light, an unusual occurrence with bacterial conjunctivitis.

DIAGNOSIS

A diagnosis of conjunctivitis is usually made by a physician's visual examination of the child's eye and differentiation from other possible disorders such as periorbital cellulitis (inflammation of the tissue lining the eye socket). Mucous discharge, the feeling of sand in the eye, and redness of the conjunctiva indicate conjunctivitis. The child's vision and pupil (the circular opening that allows light to enter the eye) will be normal, and the cornea (the transparent membrane covering the eye) will be clear.

COMPLICATIONS

Among newborns, conjunctivitis caused by contact with gonococcus bacteria in the mother's genital tract can cause corneal opacification and blindness. If chemical conjunctivitis is not treated promptly and effectively, long-term damage can result. Chemical solutions that linger in the eye tissues can inflict extensive damage, including the permanent loss of sight.

TREATMENT

Except in cases of mild conjunctivitis—such as that which occurs with the common cold, the swelling of the newborn's eyelids after an application of silver nitrate drops, and the mild irritation that results from swimming in chlorine pools—parents should generally seek medical attention when their child has a red and swollen eye. Conjunctivitis itself is easily treatable but may be the symptom of another disease or eye problem.

The physician will probably treat bacterial conjunctivitis with antibiotics, either in drop or ointment form. If discharge is excessive, the physician is likely to suggest drops, although the ointment produces less discomfort and is easier to administer. The eyelids must also be washed to keep the lids from sticking together. The eyes should not be rubbed or touched.

Allergic conjunctivitis is often treated for 3 to 5 days with hydrocortisone drops (an anti-inflammatory medication). Antihistamine drops may help relieve itching and discharge, and cool compresses may make the child more comfortable.

In the case of chemical conjunctivitis, parents should thoroughly flush the chemical from the eye with water immediately to prevent permanent damage. The eye should be rinsed often until no chemical remains on sensitive eye tissues (see *eye injuries*).

PREVENTION

Conjunctivitis cannot be prevented. To limit the spread of the infection, however, the parent should use disposable towels, discourage rubbing of the eyes, and insist upon frequent hand washing during treatment of an infectious case of conjunctivitis.

CONSTIPATION

DESCRIPTION

Constipation is the tendency toward abnormally infrequent bowel movements. The frequency of bowel movements varies widely: some children have bowel movements 2 or 3 times a day and others as infrequently as once every 5 to 7 days.

When a child is constipated, his or her stool is unusually hard and dry, and the child experiences pain or difficulty with bowel movements. The child usually expresses a desire to defecate but is unable to do so.

In most cases constipation is not a serious condition, medically speaking, but it can become a persistent problem and cause the child physical and emotional discomfort.

CAUSE

The causes of constipation are many, and may be nutritional, behavioral, or physical. Dietary causes include a lack of bulk and an excess of fats and protein. A sudden change in diet, or the introduction of a new food, like chocolate, can also cause difficulty.

Constipation can occur because a child first resists having a bowel movement, then later cannot. Babies who experience discomfort during bowel movements because of *diaper rash,* dermatitis, or other irritations near the rectum may resist defecating and thus become constipated.

Toddlers rebelling against toilet training may experience constipation. Others become constipated as a reaction to premature or overenergetic training. Children who experience family *stress* during toilet training, such as that caused by the birth of a sibling or the death of a loved one, may hold back bowel movements and become constipated. Children who are generally anxious, depressed, or agitated may experience constipation. In school-age children, the fear of using the school bathroom may provoke constipation.

Another cause may be traced to anal fissures (small tears in the rectal area). Anal fissures may cause the child to hold back the bowel movement in the first place, or they may be caused by the abnormally hard stool. (See *rectal itching; rectal prolapse.*)

Developmentally disabled children often suffer from persistent constipation, as do children with *celiac disease, lead poisoning,* or hypothyroidism (see *thyroid problems*), and those who take certain medications.

In rare instances constipation is caused by an obstruction of the intestines, a condition called *Hirschsprung's disease,* which is usually recognized in infancy.

DIAGNOSIS

Constipation is diagnosed when a child's bowel movements become excessively infrequent, his or her stool is unusually hard and dry, and pain or difficulty with bowel movements occurs.

COMPLICATIONS

Constipation can sometimes lead to a loss of control over bowel movements, a condition called *encopresis.* This usually develops when school-aged children withhold stools and then develop a loss of muscle tone in the bowel. As a result, unexplained accidents occur at various times of the day. A physician should be consulted for proper treatment of encopresis.

TREATMENT

A physician should be called if the child feels severe pain while attempting to have a bowel movement, if there is *blood in the stools,* or if the examination of the child's rectum reveals cracks or tears. Persistent constipation should also be brought to the physician's attention.

Enemas and commercial laxatives should never be used except on the advice of a physician.

PREVENTION

Constipation can sometimes be prevented by a balanced diet rich in fruits, vegetables, whole-grain products, and bran. A child should also be encouraged to go to the toilet as soon as he or she feels the urge and to remain there as long as necessary, but overenergetic toilet training practices should be avoided—for physical and emotional reasons.

COUGH

EMERGENCY ACTION

If a child coughs up blood-tinged mucus or bloody fluid, consult a physician immediately. Coughing up blood can occur suddenly following severe injury to the chest, respiratory system, or esophagus and stomach.

Intense coughing may cause *vomiting.* If a sick child who is exhausted or dizzy accidentally inhales vomit, *choking* or even asphyxiation can occur. Stay with a child who is vomiting to guard against choking. In rare instances artificial respiration may be required (see Chapter 10, "Basic First Aid").

If a child's breathing is rapid, noisy, and

high-pitched, and if an accompanying cough sounds like a bark, especially while the child is inhaling, *croup* may be the problem. Seek medical attention; severe croup can be life-threatening.

DESCRIPTION

Coughing is one of most helpful defense mechanisms in the body. The cough reflex can be triggered by a mechanical or chemical irritation in any part of the respiratory system—throat (pharynx); voice box (larynx); windpipe (trachea); breathing tubes (bronchi), which both lead to and are inside the lungs; or the lungs themselves.

Coughing may be a passing occurrence or one sign of an underlying problem. Sometimes coughing begins suddenly when a child inhales a small piece of food (such as a peanut, part of a hotdog, or a piece of popcorn) or a foreign object (such as a coin, marble, or small part of a toy). Over a period of several days, coughing can develop as a cold grows worse (see *colds*). When bacterial *pneumonia* occurs, coughing can develop as a fever rises. *Allergies* can trigger coughing; so can *asthma*.

Coughing may be loud and gasping, as in *whooping cough,* or harsh and high-pitched, as in *bronchiolitis.* It may sound like a bark, as when *croup* is present. Wheezing or whistling can occur when a child is breathing out, as happens during an asthma attack. Coughing may be associated with noisy or labored breathing (see *breathing difficulty*).

Coughing may bring up fluids (sputum) from anywhere in the respiratory tract. Sputum can include mucus, pus, blood, or any liquid inhaled into the lungs, such as water after a near-drowning. Coughing also protects the lungs from mucus that drips down from the throat and the back of the nose (postnasal drip). During sleep, when swallowing (the normal way of clearing nasal drippings) is interrupted, coughing can be especially helpful. Swallowing nasal dripping does no harm and is preferable to allowing mucus to remain in the respiratory tract.

If severe and continual, coughing can be tiring, even exhausting, and can interfere with rest or eating. Coughing may lead to aching chest muscles and sore ribs, sometimes even to muscle tears and broken ribs.

Almost all coughs begin to subside as soon as treatment of the underlying problem is effective. Any child with a recurring or long-term cough should be checked by a physician, who may suggest that a specialist be consulted.

CAUSE

Many coughs that affect children occur because of underlying infections; any member of seven large categories of disease can cause coughing. Following are examples of each:

- Infectious diseases: viral *(cold, measles, influenza)*
  bacterial (bacterial *pneumonia, sinusitis, tuberculosis, whooping cough, epiglottitis*)
  spirochetal *(syphilis)*
  parasitic *(parasitic infections)*
- Irritative diseases: chemical (poisons, noxious fumes, smoke, gases)
  mechanical (foreign bodies, voice strain, accumulated secretions, postnasal drip)
  thermal (exposure to extremes of temperature)
- Allergic diseases: *asthma*
  food allergy
- Tumors: malignant or benign, inside or outside the lungs (see *cancer*)
- Diseases of the heart and blood vessels: inflammation of blood vessels in the heart
- Psychological diseases: tension (see *stress; psychosomatic disorders; tics*)
- Diseases whose cause is unknown: *lupus erythematosus,* scleroderma, *cystic fibrosis*

DIAGNOSIS

Coughing is obvious. Diagnosis by a physician is aimed at discovering an underlying cause. A physician records the history of illness and performs a careful physical examination, concentrating upon the respiratory tract. A culture of nose, throat, or lung secretions may be helpful in identifying a bacterial infection. Additional diagnostic tests vary according to other signs and symptoms. Any young child whose cough persists may require a sweat chloride test to check for the possibility of *cystic fibrosis.*

COMPLICATIONS

If untreated, some cough-producing bacterial infections can develop into *pneumonia.* Irritative coughs over a long period of time may damage or destroy lung tissue (see *emphysema*).

TREATMENT

Treatment for cough depends upon the specific underlying cause. When the cause subsides or is relieved, coughing usually decreases. Two to four weeks may pass before a persistent cough disappears entirely.

A child should be encouraged to drink water as often as possible to help eliminate a cough, especially one that persists for more than a week. Rest and a light diet that includes warm, clear liquids (broth, bouillon, and tea) are often helpful for a child suffering from illness with cough. Inhaling steam from a pan of boiling water or kettle or hot shower or cool mist from a vaporizer may help to liquefy thick mucus and keep moist the mucous membrane lining a child's respiratory system. A physician may prescribe medication for relief of both underlying disease and accompanying cough.

Over-the-counter cough medicines are probably overrated as reliable sources of relief. Temporary coughs resulting from mild irritation do not generally require treatment. Some cough medicines may prove effective for a few hours in reducing discomfort and in resting an overburdened respiratory system, but it is impossible to guarantee that such medications will always work.

Cough medicines available include cough suppressants, cough looseners (or "expectorants"), antiallergy preparations, and throat soothers. Some cough suppressants are narcotic. In most states medicines containing a narcotic, no matter how small the amount, require a prescription. They work by reducing the nerve impulse that triggers the cough reflex. Cough looseners typically include an ingredient called an expectorant that loosens mucus, helping a child bring it up and spit it out. They may also contain a decongestant, which helps relieve the feeling of heaviness in a child's chest by reducing secretions, thereby clearing fluid from breathing tubes.

Antiallergy drugs usually rely upon an antihistamine to combat a strong reaction in the body (the release of a powerful chemical called histamine) provoked by an allergy-causing substance, such as dust or pollen. As an antihistamine takes effect, coughing and other allergic signs slowly subside.

Throat soothers, such as the old-fashioned remedy of lemon and honey, serve to coat an irritated throat and relieve pain temporarily.

Cough medicines should be chosen with the advice of a health professional, such as a physician or pharmacist. Since so many cough medicines with so many different ingredients and strengths are available, it is important to know what to ask for. The most widely advertised or the sweetest-tasting cough medicine may not be helpful for the cough or well suited to a child's age, weight, and physical condition and to the particular signs and symptoms of illness. Parents should not use price—either high or low—as any indication of a cough medicine's value or effectiveness.

In choosing an over-the-counter cough medicine it is worthwhile to read carefully the list of ingredients printed on the package. Some cough medicines contain relatively large amounts of alcohol and should not be given to children. Others may contain ingredients unsuitable for a child with a simple irritative cough.

Cough drops and lozenges should be chosen with the same care one would take in selecting a cough medicine. The purpose of most cough drops or throat lozenges is to soothe sore or "tickling" throat, not to combat coughing. Giving a child a lollipop may produce the same general effect.

Cough medicines should not be given to children who have *croup* or who may have inhaled a foreign object, nor should they be given to children who have difficulty breathing. If a child has *asthma,* however, medication prescribed by a physician should be given at the first indication of breathing difficulty. (See Chapter 7, "Caring for the Sick Child at Home" and the choking section of Chapter 10, "Basic First Aid.")

PREVENTION

Most coughs cannot be prevented. The risk of a cough brought on by an inhaled foreign object or piece of food can be reduced, to some degree, by keeping very small toys away from infants and young children and by not giving nuts, hard candies, or popcorn to them. Children should not be exposed regularly to tobacco smoke, exhaust fumes, or smog, which can irritate the respiratory system severely. Children of all ages should be urged not to smoke.

CRADLE CAP

DESCRIPTION

Cradle cap is a skin disorder in infants

caused by excessive oil (sebum) and scale deposits on the scalp. It looks like patches of dirty, crinkled skin. Most often it occurs on the top of a baby's head.

Though unattractive, cradle cap itself is not harmful. It may, however, weaken the scalp skin and lead to greater susceptibility to bacterial or yeast infections. Temporary hair loss is common. With treatment, cradle cap clears up, but often recurs. In most cases, infants outgrow cradle cap by the end of the first year of life.

CAUSE

A child's hormones are very active at several stages of development and cause oil glands to secrete large amounts of oil. In addition, scaling is excessive. Oil builds up in the glands, and scales accumulate, eventually causing cradle cap in young infants. The exact mechanism of disease is unknown.

SIGNS AND SYMPTOMS

Cradle cap appears as yellow or brown crusty patches, composed mostly of oil and dead skin cells.

DIAGNOSIS

A physician can distinguish cradle cap from other skin disorders such as *seborrheic dermatitis, eczema,* fungal infections (*ringworm*), and contact dermatitis (see *poison ivy, oak, and sumac*) by the condition of the underlying skin and the location of the rash. The characteristic greasy scale and scalp film of cradle cap is not found in other skin conditions. Occasionally scrapings from the patches are examined under a microscope to exclude fungal infection.

TREATMENT

Mild to moderate cases of cradle cap can be treated easily at home. Mineral or baby oil is usually very effective in loosening scales; it is rubbed into the scalp and left on overnight. This treatment can also be used around the eyebrows and forehead. The next morning the scalp and hair should be washed thoroughly with a gentle shampoo. Daily hairbrushing helps minimize cradle cap by preventing the collection of dead skin cells.

Cradle cap often returns and treatment must be repeated. If home treatment is not successful and cradle cap does not improve or worsens, the child should be examined by a physician.

PREVENTION

Cradle cap contracted during early infancy cannot be prevented. Frequent applications of oil and hairwashings with mild shampoo will help prevent recurrence.

CROHN'S DISEASE

DESCRIPTION

Crohn's disease is a chronic inflammatory disease of the gastrointestinal (GI) tract.

The disease is characterized by abdominal pain and *diarrhea,* sometimes accompanied by mucus and bleeding. Inflammation results in pain and swelling of the mucous membrane lining the GI tract (esophagus, stomach, and intestines). If untreated, the inflammatory process can progress to ulceration of portions of the mucous membrane and, eventually, to scarring and narrowing of the walls of the GI tract. A severe attack may involve hemorrhaging from an affected area of the GI tract and occasionally may be life-threatening.

Crohn's disease usually begins after 6 years of age; the teen years are a common time of first appearance. Approximately 4 of every 5 individuals with Crohn's disease experience their first symptoms before reaching 40 years of age. As many as 10 out of 100,000 in the population 10 to 30 years old experience the disease each year.

Crohn's disease is unpredictable. It tends to flare up and then, after weeks or months of treatment, subside (go into remission), and recur months or years later. If a "typical pattern" exists, it involves initial symptoms during the teen years, followed by recurrent episodes of intestinal inflammation, sometimes accompanied by at least one other non-GI tract symptom, requiring different kinds of treatment. It can cause impairment of normal GI tract function, especially that having to do with absorption of nutrients during digestion. In some cases the disease can produce various signs and symptoms resembling those typical of *juvenile rheumatoid arthritis, anorexia nervosa* (see *eating disorders*), *rheumatic fever,* or *lupus erythematosus.*

Most people with Crohn's disease require lifelong medical supervision. Few are permanently free of all signs and symptoms of disease, even though the disease can be in remission for extended periods of time. In a hospital a single episode can usually be managed successfully. Adults with Crohn's disease run a somewhat higher than average risk of developing intestinal cancer later in life.

CAUSE

The cause of Crohn's disease is unknown, despite some claims to the contrary. Because diarrhea is a major symptom, as it is in *food poisoning,* bacterial infection is sometimes suspected as a cause. The disease may begin after a child has returned from foreign travel or after recovery from an intestinal illness. Specific foods or eating habits do not cause the disease, nor is there scientific evidence of psychological or emotional causes. As is true of many chronic illnesses, *stress* from whatever source—work, emotions, food—does affect how a person with Crohn's disease feels.

Although no genetic basis for its origin has been identified, Crohn's disease sometimes strikes several members of a family; it occurs frequently among Jews and infrequently among blacks. In some families, one form or another of chronic inflammatory bowel disease appears in more than one generation.

SIGNS AND SYMPTOMS

The principal symptom of Crohn's disease is *diarrhea,* ranging from sporadic loose bowel movements to multiple watery ones. Mucus, pus, and blood in any combination may be in the stools.

Other intestinal symptoms may include abdominal cramping and pain, gas and bloating, and loud bowel sounds. Nausea and *vomiting* occur uncommonly. Loss of appetite, weight loss, and failure to grow are common. *Anemia* and protein loss are two of several blood irregularities, and listlessness is frequently the result of anemia and *malnutrition.* The inflamed mucous membrane lining of the small intestine often becomes ulcerated and bleeds. Blood in the stools ranges from invisible amounts, detectable only by chemical test, to substantial amounts of bright or dark red blood, which masks stool in a bowel movement (see *blood in the stools, vomiting of blood*).

Long-term inflammation of the GI tract often leads to fever (around 100° F, or 37.8° C). In severe flare-ups, a spiking fever reaching 104° F (40° C) can continue until the episode subsides.

Inflammation of weight-bearing joints (ankles, knees, and hips) can often produce pain, stiffness, and swelling almost identical to the signs of *juvenile rheumatoid arthritis.* Walking may become difficult if the inflammation is not treated promptly.

DIAGNOSIS

Crohn's disease is diagnosed by a physician, often a pediatric gastroenterologist (specialist in diseases of the digestive system), who evaluates all signs and symptoms. After a physical examination, X-ray films are usually taken of the small and large intestines to locate the extent and severity of disease. An internal examination is made of the lining of the lowest end of the large intestine (rectum and sigmoid colon) using a slender, illuminated, plastic or metal instrument (sigmoidoscope). A similar, longer, flexible instrument called a colonoscope is often used to view the interior of the entire colon. Stool specimens are analyzed to determine the presence of blood or infection.

Special tests of intestinal ability to absorb nutrients may be required. In some cases a physician may want to analyze a small sample of intestinal tissue (biopsy) to decide what specific disease may be present.

COMPLICATIONS

Failure to grow is the most frequent serious complication of Crohn's disease among children. Intestinal surgery may be required for the management of bleeding, intestinal obstruction, perforation, or persistent growth failure. Joint inflammation may interfere with walking and vigorous physical activities, but subsides when GI tract signs and symptoms subside. Other nonintestinal problems may include rash, changes in or blurring of vision, and changes in liver function.

Dehydration can become a major complication in severe cases of Crohn's disease.

TREATMENT

A mild attack of Crohn's disease (cramps, diarrhea, fever, and loss of appetite) can often be treated adequately at home with rest, proper medication, and nutrition. The most frequently prescribed medications for intestinal inflammation, mild to severe, include sulfa drugs, corticosteroids (synthetic hormonelike drugs), and several nonsteroid, anti-inflammatory medications.

A moderate attack of Crohn's disease (moderate diarrhea marked by mucus, pus, and blood in stools, a high fever, and perhaps swollen joints) may require hospitalization to ensure adequate rest, suitably high-calorie nutrition, and medication. Blood transfusions, medications, vitamins, and perhaps intravenous feeding may also be needed.

A severe attack of Crohn's disease (moderate to severe diarrhea with serious rectal bleeding, dehydration, and fever) requires hospitalization. Stomach suction (to relieve gas and nausea), medications, intravenous feeding, and blood transfusions are common in treating severe cases. Significant numbers of children with these complications—at least one half of all patients—respond well to vigorous medical treatment.

If bleeding cannot be brought under control or if a child's overall condition worsens steadily, surgery may be necessary. Surgery may also be needed if a child fails to grow over a substantial period of time and permanent stunting of growth becomes likely.

Surgery may result in (1) removal of the large intestine (colon), called a colectomy, or (2) removal of a section of the small intestine, called a small-bowel resection. In some cases an opening of the intestine onto the surface of the abdomen, called a colostomy or ileostomy, must be created by the surgeon. Fecal matter thereafter is collected in a small, inconspicuous plastic or rubber pouch, which is attached to the artificial opening. These procedures usually result in effective bowel function.

Just as no two children with Crohn's disease have exactly the same pattern of illness, so no two patterns of treatment will be identical. One key is finding an experienced, patient, knowledgeable physician who takes enough time to explain the nature and variability of the disease. In some instances it is helpful for the family to see a skilled counselor who can help the child and the family discuss the complexities that living with a long-term illness creates. Above all, perhaps, both family and child need to be willing to experiment with diet, activities, and medication.

A close, working relationship with a registered dietitian or other qualified nutritionist is often helpful. A high-calorie, high-protein, low-fiber, nutritious diet that avoids raw fruits and vegetables, nuts, and spices is sometimes recommended. Many children with Crohn's disease do not tolerate milk or milk products well. Even a small amount of alcohol can be an irritant and a depressant. Megavitamin plans are rarely helpful, although appropriate amounts of vitamins, iron, folic acid, zinc, and special supplements may be recommended by a physician. Occasionally tube feeding is necessary.

Information is available from local chapters of the National Foundation for Ileitis and Colitis (headquarters: 444 Park Avenue South, New York, NY 10016; phone: 212 685-3440).

PREVENTION

Crohn's disease cannot be prevented.

CROSS-EYES AND WALLEYES

DESCRIPTION

A child with strabismus (cross-eyes or walleyes) cannot focus both eyes on the same object at the same time. An affected child's eyes are not aligned or parallel. While one eye is focused on an object, the other turns either inward (cross-eyed, estropia), outward (walleyed, extropia), upward, or downward.

In some cases of strabismus, only one eye is ever deviated; in other cases each eye is deviated in turn (the latter condition is called alternating strabismus).

A child with strabismus may begin to favor one eye without ever realizing it, usually suppressing the vision in the deviating eye. This allows the child relatively comfortable, normal vision in only the normal eye. A condition called "lazy eye" (amblyopia) develops in the eye not being used as it loses at least some of its ability to see. Lazy eye does not develop in cases of alternating strabismus, because each eye is used intermittently.

Approximately 4 percent of all children have some form of strabismus. The incidence is much higher among children with developmental disorders. For instance, about one half of children with *cerebral palsy* have some form of strabismus.

Strabismus most often appears during the preschool years, and is present from birth in 20 to 30 percent of cases.

It is important to note that, for infants under the age of 6 months, brief misalignment of the eyes is normal. A baby learns to focus and control the eye muscles between the ages of 3 and 6 months. During this time, the infant's eyes sometimes "unlock" and wander. However, if constant strabismus occurs at any age, or if occasional strabismus occurs after the age of 6 months, a child's eyes should be examined by a physician.

Sometimes an infant may appear to have strabismus even though both eyes are actually focused on the same object. This condition, called pseudo-strabismus, occurs when an infant looks slightly to the left or right and one eye seems to cross. The impression of strabismus is heightened if the child has a broad, flat nose or has narrowly set or almond-shaped eyes. The appearance of pseudostrabismus diminishes as a child grows older, and it requires no treatment. However, an affected child's eyes should be examined by a physician to ensure that the child does not have true strabismus.

The outlook for a child with strabismus is excellent if the condition is detected early and corrective treatment is prompt. It is important to realize that if strabismus is left untreated, the child may lose some of the vision in the unused eye. Once a child with strabismus is 6 to 8 years old, full vision in the unused eye cannot usually be regained even with treatment.

In the past, some believed that children would outgrow strabismus. Unfortunately, many adults have poor vision in one eye because of that mistaken belief. Even today, strabismus is a major cause of reduced vision in one eye.

CAUSE

Strabismus is most often caused by imbalance or incoordination of the eye muscles, which control eye movements. The cause of the incoordination itself is usually unknown. Far less commonly, strabismus is caused by paralysis of an eye muscle. Such paralysis results from nerve damage, caused by a disease or injury.

Although strabismus may cause disuse of an eye, the reverse is true in some cases. For instance, in cases of severe *focusing problems* (such as nearsightedness or farsightedness), if one of a child's eyes focuses differently from the other eye, the eye with the greatest focusing problem may become an unused eye, causing strabismus. Disuse of an eye—and resulting strabismus—may also be caused by impaired vision resulting from disease or injury. A blind eye may turn inward or outward.

SIGNS AND SYMPTOMS

The major sign of strabismus is misalignment of an eye—crossing or drifting. Strabismus may be most obvious when an affected child is tired or daydreaming. Any form of strabismus may be intermittent or constant. When a child has cross-eyes, the degree of deviation may be most pronounced when the child is looking at near objects; when a child has walleyes, the opposite may be true.

If strabismus is caused by eye muscle paralysis, the affected eye is limited in motion and the child experiences double vision, about which children complain when old enough to talk. However, if eye muscle paralysis is present at birth (a rare occurrence), double vision does not occur, as vision in the defective eye is suppressed.

DIAGNOSIS

Strabismus may first be recognized by parents when their child is tired or daydreaming. As soon as they suspect a problem, parents should consult their child's physician.

To diagnose strabismus, an ophthalmologist (a physician who specializes in eye and vision problems) first performs a complete eye examination, including observing the relationship of a child's eyes to each other as the child focuses on nearby and distant objects, looks to the left and right, and looks up and down. The physician may observe an infant's eye reflexes when the eyes focus on a light being held by the physician. A method of diagnosing strabismus among older children involves covering first one eye and then the other while the child looks steadily at an object. The eye that has not been covered moves if the child has strabismus.

The physician also tests the child's vision. Impaired vision can be detected soon after birth. In addition, the physician may perform neurological tests (to check the nervous system).

TREATMENT

Treatment for strabismus begins as soon as deviation of a child's eye is diagnosed. The primary purpose of treatment is the development of the best possible vision in both eyes. To achieve that goal, a child's lazy eye needs to be used and then realigned.

In cases of strabismus caused by muscle imbalance and incoordination, the most effective way to force the child to use the lazy eye is to cover or patch the normally functioning eye. If the child has suppressed the vision in the lazy eye for a long time, it may take months for normal vision in that eye to return.

Treatment may also consist of wearing glasses or contact lenses, administration of eye drops that cause the pupil to contract, or if those methods are not successful, surgery to correct eye muscle balance. More than one operation may be needed to bring the eyes close to correct alignment.

Strabismus caused by a difference between the eyes' focusing abilities may be corrected with glasses.

Follow-up examinations of the eyes are essential until a child is 10 years old.

PREVENTION

Strabismus cannot be prevented, but if detected and treated early, progressive impairment of vision can be prevented. Regular vision screening is the best way to detect the problem, since a slight degree of strabismus is likely to be unrecognized by parents, but amblyopia can be detected through vision testing.

CROUP

EMERGENCY ACTION

In certain rare circumstances, croup can be a life-threatening problem. A child with several of the following symptoms should be taken to the nearest hospital emergency room immediately: *breathing difficulty;* very noisy breathing; breathing more than 40 times per minute; chest sinking in deeply during intake of breath; a frequent, harsh, barking cough; paleness or turning blue (especially around the lips or base of the nails); uncontrollable restlessness and fear.

Keep calm and try to keep the child as calm as possible. A calm parent can do much to soothe the child's anxiety. Allow the child to assume any comfortable position, such as sitting or lying down. Do not force the child into a position he or she does not like. In the car, open the windows and keep the child near the cold air; do not use the heater. Tell the child: "Breathe slowly and evenly."

Croup can resemble *epiglottitis,* which can be fatal if immediate emergency action is not taken. If a child has some of the above symptoms, has high fever, is drooling, and has become ill very suddenly, with no prior cold, the child may have epiglottitis. (See epiglottitis entry to be sure that the child does not have that illness.)

DESCRIPTION

Croup is a swelling of the area just below the vocal cords. This common illness occurs most often in infants and children from 3 months to 5 years old and is more prevalent in males than in females. Croup occurs most often in late fall and winter, during an upper respiratory tract infection, usually coming either suddenly or gradually during the evening or night, though severe cases can occur at any time.

Croup often is a severe form of childhood *laryngitis.* Croup can resemble *choking;* however, unlike a child choking on a foreign object, a child with croup is usually able to talk. Croup is a self-limited disease and can occur with or without a fever.

A child may develop croup more than once. Until age 6, some children develop croup or laryngitis each time they get a head cold. Symptoms of croup may last for a period as short as an hour; it may become better and worse over a period of days before clearing up entirely.

The younger the child, the more likely that the disease will be serious. The outlook for the illness depends on the severity of tracheal swelling, but in general the outlook is excellent.

CAUSE

Croup develops from a mild cold in conjunction with *cough* and *sore throat.* It is usually caused by a common cold virus that infects the area just below the vocal cords, causing it to swell. The virus also causes mucus to accumulate in and block the airway. Rarely, croup is caused by a bacterium. The virus causing croup is contagious and is spread by coughing, sneezing, direct contact with an infected child, or possibly through indirect contact with objects such as the child's drinking glass or handkerchief. In approximately 15 percent of cases, a strong family tendency exists. Occasionally, croup is caused by an allergy (see *allergies*). Anxiety and extremely dry air can make croup symptoms worse. Spasmodic croup occurs rapidly and intermittently but can also rapidly clear. Its cause remains uncertain.

SIGNS AND SYMPTOMS

A frequent, harsh, barking cough is the most striking characteristic of croup. Since an infant's or young child's airway is narrow, the swelling of the airway affects the child's ability to breathe. Thus, along with violent fits of coughing, the child will have difficulty breathing in (in contrast to difficulty breathing out, as in *asthma*) and those breaths will sound like squeaking gasps. The child's nose may flare when he or she is trying to breathe, and the breathing may be rapid. The child may have trouble drinking, may be restless and cry, and may want to sit or be held upright.

DIAGNOSIS

Croup is diagnosed by hearing the child cough and breathe and by observing the child's signs. The physician may want to listen to the child's breathing over the phone. If a physical examination is advised, it may include an X ray to detect the narrowing of the airway. The physician will also ask about the child's previous illnesses (especially a history of croup) and any *allergies*.

COMPLICATIONS

Complications are based on the severity of the tracheal swelling. In a minority of cases, the infection spreads to the middle ear or lungs.

TREATMENT

Most cases of croup can be handled at home as long as the parent can keep calm and keep the child calm. An anxious child usually has even greater difficulty breathing. As soon as the parent notices prolonged coughing, a cool-mist vaporizer (hot-mist vaporizers are not safe in the home) should be turned on in the child's bedroom or the child should be taken into the bathroom to breathe in steam from a warm (not hot) shower. The child should not be left alone. Taking a rocking chair into the steamy bathroom and gently rocking the child can help to relieve anxiety as well as breathing. The parent should not try to force the child to change head position. Sometimes cool night air can help. Cool mist and warm steam help thin the mucus in the windpipe and open the airway. If cool mist or air does not cause the child's condition to improve after 10 or 15 minutes, parents should call a physician promptly.

If breathing improves, the child should be kept warm and given clear, room-temperature liquids such as water, tea, or ginger ale (not milk or orange juice) to drink. Fluids are important both to keep the child from becoming dehydrated (due to fever or exertion from difficult breathing) and to help thin the mucus in the child's breathing passages. No solid food should be eaten. If the child's temperature rises above 101° F (38.3° C), acetaminophen suppositories should be given and the child should be taken to an emergency room.

A parent should sleep within hearing range of the child for the first few nights when the child has croup, periodically checking on the child during the night. A cold-mist vaporizer should be used in the child's bedroom for a few nights.

In an emergency room the child is given oxygen and humidity. If this fails, the child is admitted to the hospital so that medication can be administered to shrink the mucous membranes of the throat. Often fluids are given intravenously if the child is not able to drink. Some medications may be added to the intravenous fluids, while others may be given by face mask. Such treatment is usually successful; on the rare occasions when it is not, the physician may insert a throat tube while the child is under anesthesia in order to relieve the obstruction and ease breathing problems.

PREVENTION

Nothing can prevent a child from getting a virus, except for avoiding others known to have it. Prompt treatment of prolonged coughing—using a cold-mist vaporizer and giving the child extra fluids—may make an episode of croup less severe. A child with a tendency to get croup should sleep with a cold-mist vaporizer in the bedroom when he or she has an upper respiratory tract infection.

CUTS AND LACERATIONS

EMERGENCY ACTION

For information about dealing with all types of bleeding from cuts or lacerations, and for information about dealing with shock (from blood loss), see Chapter 10, "Basic First Aid."

DESCRIPTION

A cut is any wound in the skin that bleeds. Lacerations are torn, ragged, or mangled wounds, which may bleed severely. Lacerations are more serious than cuts because they frequently involve greater tissue damage. Injuries to blood vessels, nerves, muscles, tendons, or ligaments may also occur. In addition, infection may develop in cuts and lacerations contaminated by bacteria or fungi.

CAUSE

Cuts and lacerations are typically caused by accidents. Knives, broken glass, sharp or rusty toys, bicycles, and sports equipment, among other things, can cause lacerations of varying severity. Falls, especially involving young children, can produce lacerations. Automobile accidents may inflict extensive lacerations, especially if a child is hurled against a dashboard or windshield in a collision. When lacerations involve damage to blood vessels, bleeding can be considerable, sometimes even life-threatening.

SIGNS AND SYMPTOMS

Lacerations generally slice through the skin and underlying fatty tissues, damaging blood vessels, nerves, tendons, ligaments, and even bone in the process. Bleeding, moderate to severe, often results, depending upon the location and depth of the wound and how it was inflicted. Severe lacerations can injure multiple blood vessels.

If arteries (vessels that carry oxygen-rich blood from the heart and lungs to organs and tissues all over the body) are damaged or severed, bright red bleeding comes rapidly in spurts. If veins (vessels that carry oxygen-poor blood back from the body to the heart) are damaged or severed, bleeding is dark red and comes more slowly and steadily. Of the two kinds, bleeding from an artery is more serious and difficult to stop because it occurs with greater force and speed. Sometimes, as the result of a serious injury, bleeding from both arteries and veins occurs. Pain may be severe, although sometimes numbness and tingling develop in a laceration because of nerve damage.

DIAGNOSIS

The diagnosis of cuts and lacerations is obvious in nearly every case.

COMPLICATIONS

If a cut or laceration begins to throb or swell, becomes red, or oozes pus, or if the child begins to run a *fever,* a physician should be consulted. Infection or allergy to stitches occurs occasionally. The physician should be consulted if redness or swelling persists longer than 24 hours.

TREATMENT

Medical assistance should be obtained if any of these conditions exist:

- The wound is extensive or deep.
- Bleeding continues even after applying pressure.
- A dirty or rusty object, no matter how small, caused the laceration.
- The wound is marked by any of the following: throbbing; red or purple color along its edges; puffiness or swelling; pus; red lines or streaks leading away from the wound.
- Pain or tenderness in the wound increases rather than decreases after the first 24 hours.
- Foreign material, no matter how small, is embedded in the wound. Such material should be removed only by a physician.
- There are cuts or lacerations on the palm of the hand or on the neck. These are a special concern. Professional attention is advisable if a possibility exists of injury to underlying nerves and tendons.
- A child's tetanus immunity cannot be confirmed promptly following an injury. A tetanus booster injection may be necessary (see *tetanus).*

At Home

When bleeding from a cut or laceration slows, the wound should be covered with a sterile pad, which is taped in place, preferably with strips of nonbinding paper or cloth tape. A sterile "butterfly bandage" may hold together the irregular edges of many lacerations.

In Physician's Office or Emergency Room

The wound is examined, cleaned of foreign matter, and usually cleansed with an antiseptic solution. Medical professionals do not routinely stitch (suture) cuts and lacerations. In fact, a physician usually stitches a cut or laceration only if one of these conditions exists:

- The edges of the wound cannot be held together in any other way long enough to permit healing to begin.
- The wound is located somewhere on the face or neck where an obvious scar might be disfiguring.
- A wound is located where motion (of a knee or elbow, for example) or frequent contact (against a shin or palm of the hand, for example) makes complete, uninterrupted healing a problem.
- Fat tissue (soft and pinkish white) protrudes from an open wound.

It may be necessary to stitch a cut or laceration if a child suffers from an immune-deficiency disease or is taking corticosteroid medication, which tends to delay healing. In those circumstances a child often benefits from stitching and the accelerated healing it usually provides. Stitching a laceration may be necessary, as well, for very young children who may not tolerate a simple bandage over a wound long enough to permit healing.

A physician or physician's assistant who performs the stitching specifies when and under whose supervision stitches can be removed. Stitch removal is generally an uncomplicated procedure at the hospital, in a physician's office, or at home. If a physician permits removal of simple stitches at home, a parent should be sure to get step-by-step instructions.

PREVENTION

Knives, obviously sharp objects, and toys that can shatter if dropped or thrown should be kept out of children's reach. A child-proofed home is a safety necessity for all children under 4 years old (see Chapter 4, "Accident Prevention"). A well-supplied first aid kit should be available in the kitchen or bathroom at all times; it should include compresses, bandages, gauze strips, and tape (see Chapter 9, "Preparing for Emergencies").

When riding in any motor vehicle, children should use approved safety seats or restraints to reduce the risk of injury (see Chapter 4, "Accident Prevention").

CYANOSIS

EMERGENCY ACTION

If a child's skin, lips, or nail beds suddenly take on a dusky blue or purple tint for any reason other than nausea or prolonged exposure to cold, seek immediate medical attention. A bluish tint may be a sign that insufficient oxygen, necessary for all body functions, is circulating in the bloodstream. This condition is called cyanosis. In many cases, cyanosis is mild and does not pose an immediate threat. However, when cyanosis occurs unexpectedly, an explanation for oxygen insufficiency should be sought. Cyanosis caused by prolonged exposure to cold usually disappears after a short exposure to a sufficiently warm environment. (See *exposure to temperature extremes* for information on emergency treatment of other symptoms.)

Emergency treatment methods depend on the cause of cyanosis. If a child is *choking*, follow the directions in Chapter 10, "Basic First Aid," and then call a physician. If a child cannot breathe because of a near-drowning, a blow to the head, or a similar injury, perform artificial respiration (also in "Basic First Aid,") and seek medical attention.

If a baby with congenital heart disease (see *heart disease, congenital*) turns blue, cries uncontrollably and suffers from *breathing difficulty,* hold him or her in a burping position against the shoulder and try to comfort the child. Such symptoms may be signs of a heart-related cyanotic attack. Although holding the baby in a burping position eases discomfort temporarily, medical assistance is necessary because recurrences are possible.

DESCRIPTION

Normally, before circulating through the rest of the body, blood is pumped by the heart to the lungs to receive oxygen. This process also gives blood its characteristic bright red color; oxygen-poor blood is blue. If blood circulates to the body from the heart without a sufficient supply of oxygen, a condition exists called <u>hypoxia</u> (which means, literally, a less-than-normal amount of oxygen).

The duration of cyanosis depends largely on its cause. A child with a severe lung infection, for example, may be slightly cyanotic until the infection has cleared. A child with a congenital heart defect, on the other hand, may have cyanosis all the time.

If hypoxia is severe, body tissues do not receive enough oxygen to maintain themselves, and permanent damage or death can result. If the cause of hypoxia is correctable, however, the outcome is rarely tragic. The blue skin tint characteristic of cyanosis is one of the body's most obvious signs of malfunction, and medical attention is usually sought in time to administer successful emergency treatment. The long-term outlook varies with the underlying condition. Structural abnormalities of the heart and lungs can often be corrected or improved with surgery, and the outlook for an affected child is constantly improving with advances in medical technology.

The extreme form of hypoxia is called *asphyxia,* a life-threatening condition in which oxygen levels in the blood are dangerously low and carbon dioxide levels far too high. Permanent disability or death can result unless effective medical action is taken immediately.

CAUSE

All babies are slightly cyanotic for the first 5 to 10 minutes of life, until they have inhaled enough oxygen to turn characteristically pink. The circulatory system of an infant is delicate, and certain environmental stresses may cause cyanosis to recur during the first few weeks of life. In a cold environment, for example, the circulation automatically adjusts to conserve heat and energy. The resulting blueness is usually observable only in the hands (and sometimes feet), which may also be cold.

Persistent, overall cyanosis in an infant, however, is usually a sign of a more serious problem. When a newborn's cyanosis is severe, it usually signals a heart defect. Less severe cyanosis in newborns can be caused by *respiratory distress syndrome* or bronchopulmonary dysplasia, two conditions that interfere with breathing and are most common among premature babies (see *prematurity).* Congenital breathing problems can also be caused by brain injury during birth, fetal alcohol syndrome, or a reaction to an anesthetic used during delivery. Other respiratory problems that can be present at birth and cause cyanosis include lung-related infections, such as *bronchiolitis, croup,* or *pneumonia,* and breathing-mechanism abnormalities such as *tracheoesophageal fistula.* (Also see *breathing difficulty.)*

Cyanosis can also result from congenital *blood disorders.* Abnormally thick blood, for example, can interfere with the rate of circulation. Another blood disorder, <u>methemoglobinemia,</u> can cause a child's skin tone to appear brown-blue because it involves an abnormal form of the oxygen-carrying components of the blood. Other congenital problems often appearing with cyanosis are *hypoglycemia* and <u>thrombocytopenia</u> (see *bleeding disorders);* the connection between cyanosis and these conditions is not clear.

Episodes of cyanosis can also be caused by acquired conditions, such as *asthma,* congestive heart failure, (see *heart failure, congestive),* and *emphysema.* Other problems that can cause severe breathing difficulty include *apnea, choking,* breath-holding spells, *lung rupture,* and near-drownings. In addition, although older children are more resilient in cold temperatures than infants, extreme cold can produce cyanosis at any age (see also *exposure to temperature extremes).*

SIGNS AND SYMPTOMS

The cyanosis associated with exposure to cold occurs in parts of the body furthest from the heart (such as fingers and toes), and results from a reduction in circulation to conserve heat.

When the cause of cyanosis is a heart or lung problem, however, all areas of the body can appear bluish. The most visibly affected are those that contain many blood vessels: the lips, mucous membranes, and nail beds. Typically, these areas appear deep blue or violet, and other areas of the skin appear dusky blue. Some rare heart defects, however, produce odd cases of cyanosis; one half of the body, for example, may appear blue while the other appears normal.

Episodes of cyanosis are common among children with severe heart defects. The episodes may become apparent gradually or, if a respiratory infection is also present, may develop suddenly. An affected child is likely to become irritable, cry uncontrollably, suffer from *breathing difficulty,* and take on the characteristic blue tint.

Other signs and symptoms characteristically accompany cyanotic congenital heart disease (see *heart disease, congenital*).

DIAGNOSIS

A child who becomes cyanotic for any reason other than prolonged exposure to a cold environment requires immediate medical attention. After administering emergency treatment, a physician attempts to identify the cause of cyanosis if it is not already apparent from a child's medical history or in light of a triggering event or underlying disease.

Shortly after birth, all American children are routinely examined for skin color. This process is one way physicians identify possible victims of congenital heart disease.

COMPLICATIONS

Children with cyanotic congenital heart disease develop thickened tips of the fingers and toes. Their growth is frequently below normal and their ability to exercise is limited by fatigue and shortness of breath. A child who experiences cyanotic attacks is likely to be frightened, even inconsolable, and afflicted with recurrent deep cyanosis and rapid breathing. Without treatment, such a child may suffer permanent brain injury.

TREATMENT

Emergency treatment of cyanosis caused by anything other than extreme cold always involves medical administration of oxygen or facilitation of oxygen intake. An oxygen mask or tent can be used, or in instances of upper-airway obstruction, a surgical procedure called a tracheostomy may be performed. This procedure involves cutting a small hole through the throat and inserting an oxygen-carrying tube from the outside into the airway. How oxygen is given varies according to the cause and severity of cyanosis.

If the cause of cyanosis is a long-term problem, emergency treatment cannot usually eliminate recurrent or persistent hypoxia. The type of follow-up treatment required depends on the long-term problem. (See entries individual diseases and conditions mentioned in Cause, above.) Many children with congenital heart defects, for example, eventually require surgery.

Cyanosis caused by extreme cold usually disappears after brief exposure to warmth. If any signs of medical abnormality persist, however, a physician should be consulted. (See also *exposure to temperature extremes*.)

PREVENTION

See individual entries mentioned.

CYSTIC FIBROSIS

DESCRIPTION

Cystic fibrosis (CF) is a serious, incurable hereditary disease that impairs a child's breathing and digestion. The disease is characterized by fits of coughing, severe *breathing difficulty,* extreme thinness, and frequent infections. Although the effects of CF vary considerably from child to child, the disease commonly causes abnormal regulation of certain bodily fluids (such as mucus and sweat). Various types of secretions in the lungs and pancreas (and occasionally other organs such as the liver) are thicker than normal. These thick secretions block the small bronchial (breathing) tubes of the lungs, the pancreatic ducts, and when the liver is affected, the bile ducts, causing these organs to malfunction.

CF is the most common of the childhood lung diseases. It is also the most common genetic disease among white Americans. Approximately 1 out of every 2,000 white Americans has CF, and about 1 out of every 20 is a healthy carrier of the gene for CF. CF occurs considerably less often among black Americans than among other parts of the population.

Children with CF have trouble clearing substances from their lungs. When a weakened infant or small child has CF, large amounts of sticky mucus fill the lungs and can flood the windpipe, causing *asphyxia* (loss of consciousness due to insufficient oxygen and excess carbon dioxide in the blood) and possibly death. When a stronger and usually older child has the disease, mucus-clogged lungs increase susceptibility to respiratory infections (such as *pneumonia* and bronchitis). During an infection, disease-fighting white blood cells attack bacteria or viruses. As a result, the lungs also become clogged with pus (a combination of white blood cells and dead bacteria or viruses) and the bronchial tubes become stretched.

Untreated or severe lung infections can cause abscesses (collection of pus) to form.

When the abscesses dry up either spontaneously or, more often, with treatment, they leave scar tissue in the lungs. Each time the lungs of a child with CF are infected, healthy tissue is destroyed.

One of the functions of the pancreas is to secrete enzymes that aid digestion. CF, however, damages the pancreas and causes it to malfunction. As a result, digestion is disturbed because sufficient amounts of digestive enzymes (such as trypsin) are not produced and the amounts that are produced cannot be secreted through the blocked pancreatic ducts. Without these enzymes the intestines cannot absorb fats and certain vitamins required to meet the body's energy and growth needs. Even if a child eats adequately, the body cannot be adequately nourished.

A child with CF also has excessively salty sweat because the body's regulation of the amount of salt in sweat is abnormal.

Normally the liver secretes bile; when secretion is impaired by blocked bile ducts, the liver's ability to filter and excrete waste products from the blood is decreased. Some researchers theorize that substances that cannot be excreted cause damage to tissue. About 5 percent of children with CF have significant liver disease.

The severity of CF and outlook for any child vary widely. If serious lung infections recur frequently, the outlook is bleak. Eventually breathing is completely impaired and death results. The effects of a malfunctioning pancreas are less crucial, though still important, since a child needs nourishment to survive.

The average life expectancy for a child with CF is 19 years. Some CF patients have lived as long as 40 or 50 years. However, life expectancy is expected to continue to increase as treatment methods improve and research progresses. The prognosis is best if the disease is detected and treatment is begun before permanent lung damage occurs. With or without treatment the disease grows progressively worse, but treatment usually slows the rate of decline.

CAUSE

The basic defect of CF is unknown.

A baby can inherit CF only by acquiring a gene for the disease from each parent. If one parent has CF, each child will be a carrier. If both parents have CF, each child will inherit the disease. This situation is highly unlikely, since nearly all men with CF are sterile and most women are less fertile than normal (see *genetic disorders*).

The disease does not affect sexual maturation or activity.

SIGNS AND SYMPTOMS

The timing and severity of onset of CF vary. A child may be an adolescent before symptoms appear, although they usually appear when the child is much younger.

Most newborns with CF fail to gain weight (see *failure to thrive*). Occasionally a newborn's intestines are blocked with meconium (waste products of the fetus, which are normally excreted as the first bowel movement of a newborn); the meconium must be removed. As time passes, the infant remains undersized and undernourished, even with a good appetite. The baby's abdomen is bloated (resembling a potbelly) and stools are foul-smelling, fatty, and bulky. A persistent, hacking cough may be present and may be followed by breathing difficulty and fatigue. Sweat is salty and fingers and toes may be unusually broad.

A child with CF may continue to have a protruding abdomen, diarrhea (or, occasionally, constipation), and foul-smelling stools. Failure to gain weight is still a problem; the child may even lose weight, despite an increasing appetite. The child may have a nasal voice and suffer postnasal drip (the leaking of mucus from the sinuses down the throat). The child's skin may appear pale and bluish with tiny bruises. The child may cough up blood or blood-stained mucus. It may be difficult for the child to see well in the dark due to a deficiency of vitamin A.

DIAGNOSIS

CF is suspected in newborns when there is a plug of meconium in the intestines. A physician performs other tests to confirm the suspicion. If CF is not suspected when a baby is born, parents usually notice, when kissing their baby, that the baby's skin tastes salty even right after the baby has been bathed. Parents also will notice that the baby does not gain weight normally. In these cases a physician should be consulted.

A physician performs a physical examination of the infant. In addition, a chest X ray reveals whether breathing tubes are clogged. If the liver is diseased, low-grade inflammation and clogged bile ducts will be detectable through routine diagnostic tests.

The physician may also take a family medical history. If after all these procedures CF is suspected, a test can be performed to measure the level of salt in the child's sweat. A child with CF has an abnormally high level of salt in sweat. A sweat test can be performed within the first week of life. However, a sweat test, though simple and definitive, should <u>NOT</u> be used as a routine, universal screening test for every child who has minor breathing problems.

The physician may also analyze intestinal juices for amounts of pancreatic digestive enzymes and the baby's stools for excess fats and nitrogen. Mucus secretions from the lungs may be tested for thickness and stickiness. An older child with CF may have a history of chronic lung infections, such as recurrent pneumonia; a physician needs that information as well.

Even if they have few or no symptoms, siblings of any child diagnosed as having CF should have a sweat test, since mild cases of CF are often undiagnosed for years. A sibling of a child with CF has a 1 in 4 chance of having CF.

CF cannot be detected prenatally, nor can carriers be detected. Research continues on methods of detection of carriers and detection of disease in a fetus affected by CF.

COMPLICATIONS

Children with CF are vulnerable to *dehydration,* heat exhaustion (see *exposure to temperature extremes*), and *shock* due to excessive amounts of salt and fluids lost through profuse sweating during hot weather. They are also more susceptible to *rectal prolapse* and to inguinal hernia (see *hernia, inguinal and umbilical*).

Diabetes can be a complication of CF. The type of diabetes that occurs is not juvenile-onset diabetes; it is more similar to adult-onset diabetes.

Blockage of the lungs in some cases leads to *breathing difficulty,* chronic bronchitis (which does not appear until adulthood) and bronchopneumonia (see *pneumonia*), and lung collapse. Heart function can be impaired, and the spleen and liver can become enlarged. Scarring of the liver (cirrhosis) can occur. In severe cases of CF, puberty may be delayed and height stunted.

Certain complications are more common among CF patients who are older than 15. These complications include the development of nasal polyps (protruding growths of mucous membrane of the nose, leading to nasal obstruction), *sinusitis,* and air in the pleural cavity (see *lung rupture*). Women with CF may have difficult pregnancies because of the increased demands of pregnancy on lungs, heart, and liver.

TREATMENT

Since no cure exists for CF, treatment is aimed at control of the disease. Efforts to alleviate symptoms and to fight or prevent complications of CF continue throughout an affected child's life.

It is important that a child with CF be given the chance to lead as normal a life as possible. Activities should be restricted only if they adversely affect the child's condition.

For evaluation of severity of a child's case and for education in home management of the disease, hospitalization may be required. Families meet with a physical therapist and possibly a social worker (specializing in medical cases) and a psychologist. Following the initial hospital stay, children with CF must have physical examinations anywhere from every 2 weeks to as far apart as a year, depending upon many factors, including the severity of the case. (If complications develop, hospitalization is usually required.) Home treatment of CF, including prescription of antibiotics and physical therapy, is usually a key part of every affected child's daily routine.

Home treatment of the lungs is most crucial. As much mucus (and pus) as possible must be removed from the lungs regularly by physical-therapy methods. One type of physical therapy, called postural drainage therapy, involves shaking loose the accumulated plugs of mucus and pus blocking the bronchial tubes. The child is positioned so that gravity drains the clogged areas of the lungs. The child's chest is thumped to aid in drainage.

In addition, antibiotics are prescribed by a physician to fight bacterial respiratory infections. In many cases antibiotic therapy continues for months or even years in an attempt to control the progression of CF. Other drugs are available that may help clear the airways of children with CF; some studies have shown that these drugs increase the amount of sputum that can be coughed up.

Children with CF follow a diet that is high in calories and protein and low in fat, and they take supplements of vitamins A, D, and E to compensate for their inability to get these vitamins from food. A physician prescribes extracts of pancreatic enzymes to replace those not naturally secreted, which are given orally with each meal to improve digestion.

Extra salts and fluids are necessary to replace those lost through sweating and to avoid *dehydration,* heat prostration, and *shock.*

All children with CF who are not immune to *measles* should receive a measles vaccine, unless they are too ill to be immunized. Complications of measles may be serious or even fatal for a child with CF. An *influenza* vaccine should be given yearly, particularly to a child who is beginning to have frequent lung infections. Flu can lead to serious lung infections or can aggravate a child's condition.

A child with CF should be hospitalized if breathing is severely impaired. Oxygen can be administered in conjunction with antibiotics and physical therapy. A child who cannot receive adequate nutrition from a special diet, vitamins, and pancreatic enzymes may require hospitalization to receive nutrients intravenously. Complications of liver disease can require hospitalization and sometimes surgical treatment. A child might need surgery to remove nasal polyps or meconium plugs or to repair damage within the chest or abdomen.

PREVENTION

CF cannot be prevented. Couples who have a family history of CF should receive genetic counseling, so that they can estimate their risk of having affected children (see *genetic diseases*).

Research into the cause of CF is sponsored by the Cystic Fibrosis Foundation, which also provides information and support services for families with a child with CF. (National headquarters: 6000 Executive Blvd., #510, Rockville, MD 20852; phone: 800-344-4823.)

DEHYDRATION

EMERGENCY ACTION

Dehydration can develop quickly among newborns and infants who have *diarrhea* or are *vomiting.* Consult a physician or take the child to an emergency room without delay.

Seek medical attention if a child of any age who is experiencing diarrhea, vomiting, *fever,* or excessive sweating develops one or more of these signs:

- decreased intake of all fluids
- decrease in frequency or quantity of urination
- dry mouth and dry tongue
- sleepiness, lethargy, listlessness, or irritability
- rapid pulse rate
- loss of weight, especially for children less than 2 years old
- pale, dry skin (lacking in elasticity)
- sunken eyes and, for an infant, a sunken fontanel—the soft spot on top of the head
- blood in the vomit or diarrhea

Shock (impaired blood circulation and low blood pressure) sometimes follows severe dehydration. Shock can be life-threatening if not treated promptly.

If medical help is not available immediately, try to get the child to drink small sips of water or other clear liquids to help compensate for fluid losses.

DESCRIPTION

Dehydration is the excessive loss of body fluids. It occurs when the total volume of water in the body is less than that needed to provide for normal metabolism—the complex energy conversion processes of the cells.

The rate of metabolism for infants and young children is much higher than that for older children and adults. As a result, children less than 3 years old require large amounts of fluids. When excessive amounts of fluid are lost through *diarrhea, vomiting,* or the sweating that often accompanies *fever,* for example, children's metabolism can be impaired. Body salts, such as sodium, potassium, calcium, and magnesium, are almost always washed out along with the fluids. Depletion of necessary salts further reduces the activity involved in the normal exchange of solids and gases that provides the body with energy for life activities. If prolonged, dehydration can be life-threatening (see Emergency Action, above).

Children who have mild to moderate dehydration can usually be treated successfully without aftereffects. Children with severe dehydration require hospitalization for replacement of fluids and body salts, checking of vital signs and body systems, and treatment of the underlying cause.

It is particularly difficult to keep up with a sick infant's fluid losses, since a very young child can lose fluids quickly and replacement through drinking may not be possible because of rapid fluid loss from the stomach or intestines. Immediate medical attention is usually necessary.

CAUSE

A variety of diseases and illnesses can lead to dehydration. Any disease that produces extensive fluid loss from *diarrhea, vomiting,* urination, sweating, or the failure to drink enough fluids may cause dehydration. For example, any of the following could suffer some degree of dehydration: an infant who is vomiting from *pyloric stenosis,* a child who has diarrhea from *influenza,* or an adolescent who has *diabetes* and urinates excessively after strenuous exercise. Dehydration may even develop from extreme *malnutrition.* Diarrhea continues to be the major cause of dehydration among children worldwide.

DIAGNOSIS

A physician diagnoses dehydration on the basis of a child's recent medical history, the signs and symptoms of illness, and the results of a physical examination. If a child is admitted to a hospital for treatment of dehydration, blood and urine tests can determine the amounts of body fluids and salts and nutrients that have been lost.

COMPLICATIONS

Severe dehydration can seriously affect body systems, making normal physical and mental functioning difficult or impossible. Depending on the severity of the problem, the following systems could be impaired or damaged by dehydration: the central nervous system (brain, spinal cord, and their protective covering, the meninges); the heart and circulatory system; the kidneys and urinary system; and the respiratory system.

Long-term complications are unusual, although an infant could suffer brain damage if deprived too long of the proper combination of fluids and salts. In the United States death from dehydration is rare, but dehydration (usually as a complication of diarrhea and malnutrition) remains a prime worldwide cause of death for infants and young children.

TREATMENT

It is essential to replace depleted body fluids and body salts during illness. A child who is losing large volumes of fluids should be encouraged to drink clear liquids—water, juices, flat carbonated beverages (especially ginger ale), tea, and broth. Commercial bouillon and broth should not be given, because they are much too salty. Getting a child to take regular sips of fluids can be helpful. If a child feels unable to drink because of nausea and vomiting, helpful alternatives include sucking on crushed ice, frozen juice pops, or segments of an orange. (Read treatment sections of *diarrhea* and *vomiting* for suggestions about home treatment, and see also Chapter 7, "Caring for the Sick Child at Home.")

A physician may recommend that the child be given a special oral replacement (rehydration) solution called Pedialyte RS or Infalyte. These preparations are clear, odorless, bland fluids that contain exactly the right combination of body salts and calories for a child suffering the effects of dehydration. These solutions can be remarkably effective in combatting dehydration and making a child feel much better in a matter of hours. Pedialyte RS and Infalyte are available over the counter in most drug stores. Directions are included in the package. If the bland taste of the solution is not appealing to the child, parents may add a bit of lemon or orange juice for flavor. Nothing else should be added.

If the physician decides that hospitalization is necessary, the child is usually given intravenous fluids, salts, and nutrients. After initial intravenous treatment, depending upon a child's overall physical condition, it may be possible to give the balance of rehydration fluid by mouth over a period of hours or days. The physician orders the proper combination and concentration of liquids. The nursing staff encourages and helps the child to drink the proper amounts at regular intervals.

The length of time required to recover varies according to the child's overall health and the severity of dehydration.

PREVENTION

Dehydration can be prevented if its causes, especially diarrhea and vomiting, are successfully treated and controlled. Once children are ill, dehydration can sometimes be prevented if children are able to drink adequate liquids. Regular intake of sips and small amounts of clear liquids can be helpful. Because of the nature of the illness and a child's age or physical condition, it may prove impossible to keep up with fluid losses except with intravenous replacement available in a hospital. In addition, precise monitoring of a very young child's progress in recovery may require hospital care.

DELIRIUM

EMERGENCY ACTION

If a child, especially one with a *fever,* undergoes a sudden change in mental alertness, seek immediate medical attention. Such a change may be a sign of delirium, a condition which can be caused by any one of a number of underlying problems, all of which should be detected and controlled immediately. A child who is delirious may have any of the following problems:

- disorientation—child appears "out of it," confused
- severe anxiety—child is unusually and excessively afraid or fretful for no apparent reason
- misinterpretations—child repeatedly mistakes obvious sounds or objects for other things (a door slamming is interpreted as a gunshot, for example)
- illusions—child becomes convinced that certain objects have properties that they actually do not have (the folds of bedsheets indicate to the child that the sheets are alive, for example)
- hallucinations—child is convinced of the presence of something completely fictitious (imaginary people or animals may appear to the child to be hovering over his or her bed)
- *hyperactivity*—child engages in an unusually high level of physical activity
- *movement disorders*—child suddenly engages in purposeless, repetitious motions
- insomnia—child suddenly cannot sleep at night (when sleep does come it is often accompanied by nightmares or other *sleep disorders,* and insomnia may be replaced during the day by intense drowsiness)
- *depression*—child is unusually unhappy, perhaps morose

Until medical help is available, carefully observe a child who suddenly develops one or more of these symptoms. Children who are extremely anxious may be indifferent to hazards and may hurt themselves in attempts to run away from illusions or hallucinations. Do not give food, drink, or medication to a child whose state of mental alertness changes suddenly: he or she may be unable to swallow without *choking.*

DESCRIPTION

Delirium is an altered state of consciousness marked by a tendency to misperceive and misinterpret reality (see Emergency Action, above). It results from a brain malfunction which can be caused by a wide variety of diseases, poisonings, or injuries.

The severity of delirium usually varies dramatically during a single episode. At times a delirious child may merely seem confused or sleepy, and his or her behavior and speech may simply seem inappropriately fast or slow. Hours later the same child may show signs and symptoms of severe delirium, including total disorganization of thought, hallucinations, restlessness, and hyperactive behavior. Still later the same child may appear to be fine, only to show signs and symptoms of delirium as time passes. In general, delirium is most severe at night, when darkness aggravates confusion and heightens related symptoms.

Children are more susceptible to delirium than adults are, presumably because their brains are not completely developed. Children with a history of brain damage or delirium episodes seem more likely than other children to have future episodes.

CAUSE

Diseases producing fever are most often the cause of delirium among children; the incidence of delirium during peak periods of childhood fever is high. The second most common cause of childhood delirium is severe head injury (see *head and spinal injury).*

Poisonings are another common cause during childhood. Routine anesthesia given before surgery can cause a child to become delirious for a short period of time upon awakening. In addition, some children become delirious because they have sensitivities to certain medications, such as antihistamines (often found in cold medicines) or antinausea preparations. Another common source of toxins causing delirium is the family of jimsonweed plants (characterized by a strong, foul smell; prickly fruit; and trumpet-shaped flowers).

Among adolescents and adults, delirium is often caused by ingesting excessive amounts of alcohol or some other drug (see *drug and alcohol abuse*). After abrupt withdrawal from prolonged periods of heavy drinking or drug taking, a variation called delirium tremens can set in, characterized by severe agitation and fever.

Other conditions that sometimes produce childhood delirium include petit mal *seizures, psychosis,* and disorders affecting metabolism (the sum of all the complex chemical and physical processes of matter and energy that occur within living cells), such as *hypoglycemia.*

SIGNS AND SYMPTOMS

If the cause of delirium is head injury or poison, signs and symptoms of mental confusion usually appear suddenly. The same is often true when disease is the cause of delirium, although warning signs sometimes precede the actual onset of delirium. Such signs can include restlessness, difficulty in thinking clearly, oversensitivity to everyday stimuli, insomnia at night, drowsiness during the day, vivid dreams, and nightmares.

All these warning signs may be present during the more mild periods of a delirium episode. During such periods a child is usually able to answer simple questions but cannot maintain normal conversation because of problems with thinking, memory, perception, and attention. Speech is often disjointed; a child may stop in midsentence and abruptly change his or her train of thought, for example. Delirious children have acute, overwhelming problems maintaining attention, as evidenced by their distractibility and purposeless behavior. During severe periods of a delirium episode, a child is likely to have hallucinations. Signs and symptoms of mild delirium are typically present in a more severe form.

The behavior of a delirious child often swings between extremes during a single episode. At times a child may appear quiet, uninterested, and withdrawn. At other times the child may be sweaty, shaky, and agitated. Speech may be halting and sparse or just the opposite—pressured and incoherent. At times a child may appear to be stuporous or semicomatose; at other times insomnia and hyperactivity may be overwhelming.

The behavior of a delirious child tends to vary with emotional changes. During delirium the following emotions are common: anxiety, fear, depression, irritability, anger, euphoria (intense happiness), and apathy (total uninterest). In addition, it is common throughout an episode of delirium for a child to appear at least slightly confused and disoriented and to have a diminished intellectual ability and memory.

Medical signs of delirium include rapid heartbeat and breathing, elevated blood pressure, sweating, flushed face, and abnormally large pupils.

DIAGNOSIS

Delirium should always be diagnosed by a physician, who begins the diagnostic procedure by looking for evidence of an altered state of consciousness. A physician usually speaks with a child (or provides another type of stimulus) in an attempt to determine whether problems with attention, orientation, and perception exist.

A physician also reviews a child's recent behavior, focusing on whether the child has perceptual problems, incoherent speech, sleep disorders, or an unusually low or high level of activity. If at least two of these problems are present (especially if they developed suddenly and tend to fluctuate in type and severity), delirium is likely to exist.

Physical and laboratory examinations are conducted to establish the cause. An electroencephalogram (EEG), which measures brain waves, is often helpful. Throughout the diagnostic procedure a physician is interested not only in confirming the presence of delirium but also in determining its cause. Appropriate tests are given to confirm a physician's suspicion.

COMPLICATIONS

If the condition underlying delirium is untreated or becomes increasingly severe, brain function can deteriorate and lead to *coma,* permanent brain damage, or death.

If a child is not monitored closely during a severe period of delirium, he or she may be injured in an attempt to flee from hallucinations. In extreme cases delirious children suffering from terrible hallucinations may attempt *suicide.*

TREATMENT

Treatment of delirium focuses on eliminating its underlying cause. To control severe signs and symptoms of delirium, a child should be monitored in a hospital. Hospital personnel can try to minimize confusing stimuli—such as the blaring of a television. Another way hospitals attempt to lower confusion is by keeping a child's room well lighted when the child is awake. In some cases medication is given to lower a child's anxiety level and help him or her rest. Parents can greatly aid the efforts of hospital staff members by reassuring and comforting their child.

PREVENTION

Delirium can be prevented only if its underlying cause can be prevented. Examples of preventive measures include wearing car and sports safety equipment to prevent head injury, avoiding medications to which a child is sensitive, and taking steps to educate the child about the dangers of drugs and alcohol (see *drug and alcohol abuse).*

DEPRESSION

EMERGENCY ACTION

Suicides among young people are often but not always preceded by signs and symptoms of depression. Treat remarks about *suicide* very seriously. If an adolescent begins talking about suicide-related ideas, consult a mental health professional immediately. (If necessary, call a physician, suicide hotline, local hospital, or member of the clergy for names of qualified mental health professionals.)

DESCRIPTION

Depression is a term used to describe an episode of mental illness characterized by feelings of unhappiness and by loss of interest in usual activities. Feelings of unhappiness may include sadness, melancholy, misery, discouragement, hopelessness, or despair. Associated behavior may reflect a loss of interest in previously satisfying activities, such as going to school, working in school, being with friends, engaging in sports, and participating in activities outside of school. When such feelings and behavior significantly interfere with a child's home, social, or school life, depression is frequently the cause.

In the past, experts believed that depression was related to the interaction of psychological forces that were not fully developed until adulthood. Childhood depression, therefore, was considered impossible. Any signs and symptoms of depression among children seeking professional help were attributed to other mental health problems. Recently, however, this belief has changed. Depression exists during childhood, although its signs and symptoms can differ from those of adult depression. The way a child experiences depression is thought to depend on the child's stage of development; in general, depression among adolescents is more like that of adults, while depression among children is different. It is now thought that a significant number of children who previously might have been diagnosed as having some other problem are actually suffering from depression.

The percentage of children who suffer from depression is difficult to ascertain, however, because age-appropriate diagnostic criteria are still being developed. A relatively large number of children may have age-related symptoms of depression. Some studies show that of all children who receive treatment for mental health problems, one out of four may have depression and about half have some symptoms of the condition. Symptoms of depression are sometimes associated with other mental health problems such as obsessive-compulsive disorders and *psychosis.* Symptoms of depression among children with serious or long-term physical diseases are very common.

Depression is thought to be uncommon among prepubertal children and to increase among older children. Depression seems to be virtually nonexistent among children younger than 5 years, although exposure to stressful situations may produce symptoms of sadness among some preschoolers. Some experts believe that very young children suffer depressionlike symptoms when separated from their parents for a significant length of time. Children from 5 to 9 years old seem to be capable of experiencing longer and deeper periods of sadness, which also seem to be prompted by stressful situations.

As children approach puberty, they begin to form judgments about self-worth and the worth of others, and they become capable of interpreting problems in terms of self-worth. A child may, for example, feel guilty about the marital problems of parents. A child who experiences recurrent guilt can lose self-esteem and become depressed. Low self-esteem is often a key component of adult depression.

Childhood depression occurs most often

among adolescents, who are struggling to establish identity and meet the challenges of becoming adults. Some adolescents become obsessed with the future and overreact to setbacks. Some adolescents tend to envision themselves as failing at challenges such as leaving the home, causing severe depression. Suicides among adolescents may be preceded by severe depression.

Tragic outcomes, however, can often be prevented. Although an episode of depression can last weeks or months, it can almost always be alleviated or resolved with treatment if a more severe, underlying disorder does not exist.

CAUSE

The exact cause of depression is unclear. It appears to be caused by a combination of internal and external factors that varies from child to child.

Statistically, children of parents who have suffered from bouts of depression are more likely than other children to suffer from depression themselves. A family history of psychiatric problems also seems to be more common among children who are depressed than among other children. Environmental and genetic factors may contribute to depression, but this remains to be determined.

Evidence exists that some forms of depression have a biochemical basis. One such form is manic-depressive disorder, which is characterized by extreme mood swings and is rare among children.

Other factors that can contribute to depression include a persistently poor self-image or major *stress* in the family, such as divorce or the death of a parent or sibling.

Finally, depression may be a complication of severe short-term or long-term medical problems. When a short-term problem is involved, depression usually disappears when the illness ends. Depression caused by illness affects younger children more often than older ones; depression among children 5 to 9 years old is most likely to be prompted by illness or a similar environmental stress.

SIGNS AND SYMPTOMS AND COMPLICATIONS

Although unhappiness may not be the most prominent symptom of depression, it is one of the most persistent. Unhappiness is characteristically accompanied by a loss of interest in customary activities.

The behavioral signs and symptoms accompanying depression vary with a child's age, personality, and environmental influences. A child may withdraw from usual activities and perform below par at others, such as schoolwork. A child is likely to spend time brooding or doing nothing and to show less energy and enthusiasm than usual. Some children, however, respond to depression by filling their days with frenetic overactivity to cover their sadness. Likewise, it is common for a depressed child to lose interest in eating (see *eating disorders)* and to lose weight.

Many aspects of a child's life can be interrupted because of depression. *Sleep disorders* —especially insomnia (sleeplessness) or hypersomnia (excessive sleeping)—are common. A child may have difficulty concentrating on even simple tasks and may show unusual signs of irritability and aggressiveness. Physical health may be disturbed by psychosomatic symptoms (see *psychosomatic disease and symptoms),* such as persistent *headache* or stomachache (see *stomachache, stomach pain).*

A depressed child's feelings of sadness may be accompanied by anxiety, a sense of apprehension and worry about something specific or about things in general. Some children also suffer from periodic panic attacks. Guilt, anger, and feelings of low self-esteem often accompany these emotions. The combination of these feelings may cause a child to dwell on morbid subjects, such as disasters or death.

These symptoms are rare among children younger than 5, partly because they have difficulty expressing themselves verbally. One sign of depressionlike symptoms in a very young child may be a sad or vacant expression.

Children from 5 to 12 years old are likely to have symptoms resembling those of younger children. A child in this age group may complain of a general feeling of sadness without being able to verbalize what is causing it. In addition, depression may be associated with friendship problems.

Depression among teenagers tends to be marked by a sense of hopelessness and linked with the pressures of adolescence.

DIAGNOSIS

A pediatrician, child psychiatrist, child psychologist, social worker, or other mental health professional should be consulted if a child has signs and symptoms of depression that persist for more than two weeks. (See Chapter 3, "Promoting Mental Health," for information on mental health care specialists.) A professional should be consulted sooner if the child refuses to go to school or seems paralyzed by sadness, and immediately if a child talks about *suicide.*

The professional assesses a child's symptoms and overall functioning. Diagnosis is based on a thorough consideration of a child's developmental, mental, medical, and family histories, in addition to physical and psychological examinations. The professional talks with both parents and child about the child's recent activities and feelings. Parental participation is essential, because parents often observe things about a child's behavior that a child does not perceive.

In diagnosing depression, a professional must rule out underlying psychiatric conditions such as psychoses. In addition, the professional attempts to determine what factors may be contributing to depression. The consultant also attempts to discern the role of the family in a child's life in an effort to determine how the family can help the child recover. If a mental health professional who is not a medical doctor (such as a social worker or psychologist) suspects that a child has an underlying medical problem, referral is made to a medical consultant.

TREATMENT

Parents should talk compassionately with a child who is depressed and should not tell the child to "snap out of it." Parents should recognize that mild depression can become severe if it is unacknowledged or downplayed. Professional treatment should be sought without guilt if family talks are unsuccessful at resolving depression.

The most widely used treatment method for depression is psychotherapy, which involves one or more discussion sessions between an affected child and a mental health professional. During psychotherapy sessions, a child and consultant discuss a child's life and feelings in an attempt to strengthen the child's ability to cope. With treatment, mild depression usually improves after one or two months. More severe cases —or recurring episodes of depression—may require therapy for weeks, months, or years.

When a preadolescent child is undergoing psychotherapy, a therapist usually keeps parents informed of the general content of discussions as well as the child's progress. Parents usually participate in some of the discussions or have their own sessions with the consultant. Sometimes parents, child, and therapist are able to come up with new activities that can interest a child and help resolve depression.

When teenagers are involved, however, a therapist is likely to withhold specifics about discussion sessions from parents to gain the adolescent's trust. Finding an identity as an individual is one of the most difficult challenges of adolescence, and a teenager may perceive parental participation in therapy as intrusive. In general, psychotherapy for adolescents lasts longer than treatment for younger children because an adolescent's emotions are more developed. In addition, many adolescents resist psychotherapy because they regard it as an acknowledgment of failure.

If depression is severe and long-lasting, a therapist may recommend medication, prescribed by a physician. Psychotherapy always continues in conjunction with medication.

In very severe cases of depression—those that involve suicide threats or attempts, for example—a child may be hospitalized temporarily in a mental health care facility. Parents should always check the reputation of a mental health care facility before agreeing to have their child placed in it.

If depression is a complication of an underlying medical or psychological problem, treatment usually focuses on the underlying problem. In many cases depression disappears naturally as the underlying condition clears up.

Helping a child who is depressed can be stressful for parents. They should not hesitate to consult a counselor—either their child's or, perhaps, one whom that counselor recommends—for advice, support, and encouragement.

PREVENTION

Parents should strive to create a home environment of warmth and understanding. A child needs to feel comfortable talking to other family members about anything on his or her mind, and parents should regularly set aside time for this purpose.

Since the cause of a child's depression is likely to be complex, however, absolute prevention is impossible. If a child does become depressed, the best way parents can try to prevent the condition from becoming worse is to acknowledge and address the problem, and, if necessary, seek professional treatment promptly.

DES EXPOSURE

DESCRIPTION

Between 1946 and 1971 a synthetic form of estrogen (a female reproductive hormone) called diethylstilbestrol (DES) was commonly prescribed for certain pregnant women in the belief that it would prevent repeated miscarriages, premature births, and stillbirths. It was thought by some physicians that DES might help sustain pregnancy by stimulating the production of progesterone, a female reproductive hormone vital to the success of a pregnancy. To women who had suffered repeated miscarriages, DES then seemed to be their best hope for carrying babies to term. If a woman experienced vaginal bleeding during pregnancy or if she was a diabetic, DES or a similar form of synthetic estrogen was likely to have been prescribed.

The effectiveness of DES in preventing miscarriages was first questioned in 1953, but the drug continued to be used for 18 years, until its safety was challenged in 1971. Researchers found a link between women's use of DES during pregnancy and the development in their daughters of a rare type of cancerous tumor (called clear-cell carcinoma) of the vagina (the canal leading from the external genital organs to the uterus), the cervix (the narrow, lower end of the uterus), or both. As a result, the United States Food and Drug Administration immediately issued a warning about using DES during pregnancy. Since then further studies have shown a statistically significant incidence, though still a relatively low one (about 1.4 cases in 10,000 DES daughters, or about 500 total reported cases), of this type of cancer in daughters exposed to DES before birth. Not every person exposed to DES before birth develops reproductive-system abnormalities. Only .01 percent of DES-exposed offspring develop a malignancy; from 40 to 90 percent develop benign changes. DES was used most often from 1951 to 1968, so daughters born during those years are at highest risk.

Although cancerous tumors as a result of DES exposure before birth are relatively rare, DES daughters commonly develop noncancerous tissue changes of the vagina or cervix. Other abnormalities of the reproductive tract, such as structural changes in the vagina, cervix, uterus, or fallopian tubes (two slender tubes that carry eggs from the ovaries to the uterus) may also occur.

It is unknown exactly how many women and their offspring were exposed to DES or similar forms of synthetic estrogen, as medical records may be unavailable or unreliable. Researchers estimate, however, that DES daughters alone probably number at least 1 million.

Sons exposed to DES before birth can also suffer side effects, although it does not appear that there is an increased risk of malignancy (cancer). Some have been found to have urinary or genital abnormalities such as narrowing of the urethra (the canal through which urine and semen are discharged), hypospadias (in which the urethra opens on the underside of the penis), an abnormally small penis, cysts within the testicles, underdeveloped or *undescended testicles,* and varicoceles (a varicose vein condition within the scrotum; see *urinary tract defects and obstruction*). Other genital abnormalities include absence of sperm, fewer sperm than normal, abnormally shaped sperm that are less active than normal, and decreased volume of semen. It is not known yet what effect, if any, some of these genital abnormalities may have on fertility.

Women who took DES during pregnancy do not appear to experience an increased risk of cancer of the cervix, uterine lining, or ovary.

Despite its negative effects during pregnancy, DES is still used to prevent pregnancy in rare situations (in the form of the "morning-after pill"), infrequently to dry up unwanted breast milk, and to treat some advanced cancers of the breast and prostate.

Very few women develop cancer as a result of exposure to DES, but regular follow-up physical examinations are essential if tumors that do appear are to be detected while they are still small (in the earliest stage of development) and chances of controlling or curing them are still high. Noncancerous tissue changes may eventually disappear without treatment.

Since DES and similar drugs were first

used during the 1940s, their long-term effects on mothers and offspring cannot yet be determined. Research into DES exposure and its implications continues.

CAUSE

Whether or not any abnormality does appear depends in part upon the timing and duration of DES exposure and the doses given. The earlier in pregnancy that DES treatment began (especially if it began before the eighteenth week), the greater the chances of subsequent abnormalities in offspring. It is now apparent that treatment begun after the fourth or fifth month of pregnancy carries a very small risk of either malignancy or benign structural changes.

SIGNS AND SYMPTOMS

Most DES daughters have no symptoms of reproductive-system abnormalities, regardless of whether any such abnormalities exist. In the earliest stage small tumors can cause no symptoms. Occasionally an abnormal vaginal discharge or bleeding is reported.

DIAGNOSIS

All persons with known or suspected exposure to DES, including women exposed during pregnancy, should be examined by a physician. If a DES daughter of any age experiences unusual vaginal bleeding, spotting, or discharge, she should receive immediate medical attention. (Any female should consult a physician if such symptoms occur.)

A daughter who knows or suspects that she was exposed to DES or similar drugs before birth should try to obtain a medical record of her mother's use of any drugs during pregnancy. A physician will consider this, her mother's subsequent health, and the daughter's medical history when DES exposure is suspected. When a DES daughter is age 14 or has begun to menstruate, whichever comes first, a gynecologist should be consulted for a pelvic exam. Such an exam includes palpation (examination by touching) and observation of the vagina and cervix (using a speculum to separate the walls of the vagina gently to aid examination). A Pap smear (in which cell specimens are obtained for analysis) is taken. In addition, the vagina and cervix are usually examined through a procedure called coloscopy, in which, as the vaginal walls are stretched, a binocular, low-power microscope is used to aid observation. Coloscopy is useful for diagnosis of noncancerous tissue changes, and detects those changes in 80 to 90 percent of DES daughters. If an area of the vagina or cervix appears abnormal, tiny specimens of tissue may be removed (in a procedure called a biopsy) and analyzed.

DES daughters should have pelvic exams performed annually; more frequent exams may be necessary if any problems are detected. Any benign (noncancerous) tissue changes that are found may require follow-up examinations every six months. Typically, cancerous tumors have not been diagnosed until a female patient is 17 to 21 years old (but they have been found in patients from ages 7 to 29).

To help evaluate cases in which DES daughters have had trouble with miscarriage or stillbirth, an opaque dye (colorless and harmless) is injected into the uterus and X-rays are taken of the uterus and fallopian tubes.

Immediately after puberty a DES son should be examined by a pediatrician. A son who knows or suspects that he was exposed to DES or similar drugs before birth should try to obtain copies of medical records of his mother's use of any drugs during pregnancy.

COMPLICATIONS

DES daughters may have more difficulty becoming pregnant than other women do, and they also seem to run a higher risk of miscarriage, tubal pregnancy, stillbirth, and premature delivery (see *prematurity*). These complications are especially likely if the uterus is malformed or the muscles of the cervix are weak, a condition which also appears among women not exposed to DES. If a DES daughter becomes pregnant, she is considered to be a high-risk case and should be examined frequently. Most DES daughters, however, have normal pregnancies, since noncancerous tissue changes generally have no effect on fertility or reproduction.

TREATMENT

Treatment for DES-exposed individuals is generally necessary only if a cancerous tumor is found. If a cancerous tumor is diagnosed early, surgical removal is necessary to cure the cancer. Basic information, along with new research findings, about DES exposure and its implications is provided by the medical community on a continuing basis, not only for the sake of individuals known to be affected but for general public awareness. Counseling may be helpful in alleviating any family tension resulting from the consequences of a mother's use of DES.

PREVENTION

DES mothers and daughters should use estrogen and estrogen-containing medications with caution and only after thorough medical evaluation to rule out the presence of a cancer or a precancerous condition. During pregnancy, every woman should avoid taking any drugs unless the gynecologist prescribes one for her or her baby's health.

DEVIATED NASAL SEPTUM

DESCRIPTION AND SIGNS AND SYMPTOMS

A septum is a partition that divides a body cavity. The nasal septum is a pliable structure that divides the nasal cavity into two chambers (see Fig. 000, p. 000). These chambers are not identical in size and shape for about 80 percent of all people, because their nasal septums are irregularly shaped or "deviated."

Many septal irregularities are not noticeable. Sometimes, however, the nose appears crooked, slightly off center, or rounded or bulbous on one side or at the bridge. Some people with deviated septums have difficulty breathing through their noses. A septum can form an S-shaped curve that changes the shape of both nasal cavities. It can curve completely toward one nasal cavity, making one cavity very large and the other very small. Or a septum can lean toward one nasal cavity (so that the septum is not vertical), making the cavities uneven in size.

The majority of septal irregularities are acquired (through injury) while some are congenital (present at birth). Even quite minor contact with an object such as a ball, an elbow, or a swinging screen door can injure or dislocate the septum.

Congenital septal irregularities occur less often. Studies have shown, however, that as many as 13 percent of infants delivered vaginally show some nasal or septal deformities.

During childhood many septal irregularities are insignificant and unnoticed. Unless

having a septal irregularity interferes with breathing or significantly detracts, in a child's view, from his or her appearance, it should not be cause for concern.

COMPLICATIONS

During adolescence the septum grows more rapidly and an irregularity can become prominent. This change may be only cosmetic, however, and causes no functional problems.

In cases of extreme septal irregularity, airway obstruction can result either at birth or right after injury, causing breathing difficulty.

TREATMENT

A physician can easily correct most cases of noticeable congenital septal irregularity by gentle realignment. Some cases of severe displacement require surgery to correct airway obstruction and to improve appearance.

PREVENTION

Wearing proper headgear while engaging in sports, using car seat restraints and seat belts, and other accident prevention measures may protect a child's nose from injuries that lead to acquired septal irregularities. Congenital septal irregularities cannot be prevented.

DIABETES

EMERGENCY ACTION

Any child with diabetes, even one whose condition is relatively stable, may develop diabetic *coma,* become dehydrated, or have an insulin reaction. All are emergencies.

Diabetic ketoacidosis (sometimes called diabetic coma or severe hyperglycemia) is an extreme medical emergency that usually comes on gradually over a period of several days. It is preceded by frequent urination and increased thirst. Key signs and symptoms: flushed face; dry skin; dry mouth and great thirst; excessive urination; headache; nausea; vomiting and abdominal pain; drowsiness and lethargy; blurry vision; fruity-smelling breath; rapid heartbeat; and deep, labored breathing. Without immediate treatment a child who exhibits these signs and symptoms can eventually lose consciousness and die. Seek medical assistance immediately, preferably from the child's own physician or in a hospital emergency room. An injection of insulin must be given only by someone who knows exactly what the correct strength and dosage are. The child who has reached this condition usually also requires intravenous fluids and salts to replace those lost by the body.

Dehydration (loss of essential body fluids and salts) can develop quickly—within several hours—in a diabetic child whose treatment is inadequate. Dehydration is a major part of diabetic ketoacidosis. Key signs and symptoms: thirst; dry tongue and lips; cool, dry, mottled skin; rapid pulse; listlessness; sunken eyes; and, for an infant, sunken fontanel (the soft spot on top of the head). Children with uncontrolled diabetes who are developing ketoacidosis often complain of abdominal pain. In mild cases or early in the course of diabetes, give the child sugar-free drinks, water, and salty fluids. If that proves inadequate or if vomiting makes such treatment impossible, intravenous infusion of fluids and salts given in a hospital may be necessary. Notify a physician.

Insulin reaction (sometimes called insulin shock or, if severe, hypoglycemic coma) comes on rapidly, within minutes or a few hours. Key signs and symptoms: a general feeling of weakness; hunger; headache; dizziness; confusion, trembling, and inattention; inappropriate responses or strange behavior; nausea; cool, pale, sweaty skin; and rapid heartbeat, sometimes with heart palpitations. Urination is not more frequent nor is thirst increased. An insulin reaction usually develops after (1) an excessive amount of insulin, (2) a missed or partially eaten meal, or (3) strenuous exercise carried on without enough food in the system. The usual remedy is rapidly absorbed sugar, such as that contained in a glass (6 or 8 ounces) of orange or apple juice; candy, such as 6 or 7 small hard candies; or 2 to 3 teaspoons of plain table sugar. Diabetic children should have glucagon available at home, and family members should be familiar with its use and how to inject it. Glucagon, available by prescription in drugstores, rapidly mobilizes sugar stored in the liver. If an insulin reaction is severe, intravenous glucose may be necessary. Notify the physician and take the child to the hospital.

DESCRIPTION

Diabetes is a serious, lifelong disease affecting children and adults. The lack of insulin is often more severe for children than for adults, making children's illness more difficult to treat and live with. Diabetes occurs as either type I (juvenile or insulin-dependent) diabetes or as type II (adult onset or non-insulin-dependent) diabetes. The adult variety is usually more easily controlled.

Diabetes affects approximately 12 million Americans of all ages. There are about 1.5 million juvenile diabetics, and 13,000 new cases are diagnosed annually. About as many boys as girls are affected. The disease may begin at any age, but the rate of occurrence peaks among children 5 to 6 years old and again at puberty, between 11 and 13 years old.

What Diabetes Does to the Body

Diabetes mellitus (the medical term means "honey siphon") seriously disrupts metabolism, the chemical processes in the cells that convert food into energy. The disease interferes with the normal amount of sugar in the blood and its delivery to meet the energy needs of cells in the body. When the cells are deprived of glucose for energy, fat tissue begins to break down into fatty acids that the body uses for energy instead of glucose. This abnormal fat consumption leads to weight loss and to increased appetite. Because the blood is burdened with ketones (the by-products of fatty-acid breakdown), it becomes increasingly acidic, a condition called acidosis.

The kidneys begin to pass excess ketones into the urine along with sugar. Without treatment this disease process intensifies and the child begins to lose weight, suffers dehydration, and grows progressively weaker.

What Insulin Does for Metabolism

Dietary carbohydrates are consumed in the form of sugars and starches. They are all converted into simple sugars in the intestinal tract and finally enter the blood as glucose. At the end of the digestive process glucose is delivered by the blood directly to cells throughout the body to provide energy necessary to sustain life activities. Additional glucose is carried in the blood to the liver and muscles for storage as glycogen until needed. Beyond that, any excess glucose is converted to and stored as adipose (fat) tissue.

A vital hormone called insulin regulates how much glucose is present in the blood at any time. (A hormone is a chemical secreted into the bloodstream by an organ or gland that affects the activity of another organ.)

Insulin also permits just the right amount of glucose to move out of the bloodstream for either immediate use or storage. For a diabetic person, digestion proceeds as usual, but the glucose level in the bloodstream rises excessively because not enough insulin is available to permit passage of glucose out of the blood and into body tissues.

The kidneys, which continuously filter and purify the blood, at a certain point can no longer handle such a high level of glucose in the bloodstream. When that point is reached, glucose spills into urine along with other usual wastes from the kidney filtration process. This condition is called passing sugar. As it spills into the urine, glucose carries with it large quantities of water and salts from the bloodstream and leads to excessive thirst. Since the bladder rapidly fills up, frequent urination follows.

With careful treatment, diabetic children can lead successful, active lives, participating in virtually all vocations and activities. Statistics indicate, however, that the life expectancy of a person with juvenile-onset diabetes is somewhat shorter than for individuals without the disease.

CAUSE

Diabetes is caused by a lack of insulin, a hormone produced in specialized cells (called beta cells) in the pancreas, a 6-inch-long, comma-shaped gland located in the abdomen just behind the stomach. Why the beta cells fail to function normally in diabetics is not completely understood.

SIGNS AND SYMPTOMS

The signs and symptoms of diabetes usually begin rapidly and become dramatically evident in a matter of one to several weeks. Increased urination, in both frequency and quantity, is the most common complaint. This is most noticeable at night, when a child awakens with an urgent need to urinate or when *bed-wetting* begins for a child who has never had the problem before.

Parents may take the child to a physician, assuming that a urinary tract infection is the problem. Other symptoms are usually present as well, most notably excessive thirst and a noticeable, steady loss of weight; occasionally there may be an increase in appetite. The child may look pale and have dark circles under the eyes. Dry, itchy skin is sometimes a problem. Irritability, listlessness, and fatigue are characteristic of a child's behav-ior when diabetes is developing. The signs or symptoms of diabetes in children rarely go unnoticed.

DIAGNOSIS

A physician carefully examines the child and takes a detailed history of previous illnesses, especially infections. It is important to know whether diabetes has occurred before in the family, as heredity may play a role in the transmission of the disease (see *genetic disorders*). Urinalysis detects sugar and ketones in the urine. A blood test measures the amount of sugar in the bloodstream.

In unusual or very mild cases a physician may also want to perform a glucose tolerance test. For this a child drinks a measured volume of sugar water, often carbonated, and over the next several hours blood samples are drawn and urine samples collected in order to measure the level of glucose in the blood.

Urinalysis and blood chemistry tests can be performed in a physician's office or in a hospital if a child is ill.

COMPLICATIONS

The major complications of diabetes are the result of damage to the large and small blood vessels. Diabetics develop atherosclerosis (narrowing and hardening of the arteries) at an accelerated rate. This accounts for the higher incidence of heart attacks and strokes in adult life. Of more immediate concern for children is disease of tiny blood vessels in both the kidneys and retinas of the eyes, which can lead, respectively, to kidney failure and visual impairment. Cataracts may develop as a result of the effects of high blood glucose on the metabolism of the lens of the eye. Diabetes also frequently causes disturbance in the function of nerves in the legs, arms, and involuntary nervous system. There is currently good evidence that these complications can be prevented or significantly delayed by maintaining excellent control of the diabetes throughout the individual's life.

TREATMENT

Since children with newly diagnosed diabetes usually feel quite sick, hospitalization may be required. *Dehydration* (loss of essential body fluids and salts) and ketosis (excessive concentration in the body of acidic byproducts of fat breakdown) must be treated promptly.

Consistent, carefully monitored treatment is a necessity if a diabetic of any age is to lead as normal a life as possible. The management of juvenile diabetes consists of four essential elements: insulin, diet, exercise, and education of the diabetic child and his or her family.

Insulin

In order to return the blood sugar level to near normal, insulin is given by injection under the skin. In the hospital and afterward, the dose of insulin is adjusted until the appropriate dose is achieved—one that causes signs and symptoms to disappear and reduces or stops the spilling of sugar into the urine. Initially, stabilization of insulin dosage takes about a week. A child's requirement, however, usually decreases during the first three months and has to be adjusted during this time in consultation with a physician. It usually takes several weeks or months, depending upon the particular child and family involved, before everyone feels comfortable with the entire insulin-taking routine.

Just as there are subjective symptoms reflecting insulin deficiency, so also does the body react to hypoglycemia (excessive lowering of blood sugar). Hypoglycemia can be caused by an inadequate or missed meal, too much exercise, or an unduly large dose of insulin. Hunger, headache, irritability, drowsiness and inattentiveness, sweating, and coolness of the skin commonly mark hypoglycemia. If not treated, severe hypoglycemia can lead to loss of consciousness and *coma.* Convulsions may also occur (see *seizures).*

The immediate treatment for early symptoms of hypoglycemia is simply to restore blood sugar as described in Emergency Action, above.

Since insulin is needed daily and the child who has insulin-dependent diabetes cannot live for long without it, the responsibility for insulin injections must be assumed by the parents until a child is at least 12 years old. At any time during childhood a child can be encouraged without coercion to learn to carry out some of the injections under parental supervision. Disposable plastic syringes are used, tipped with very sharp, slender needles designed to minimize pain. Injection sites must be alternated in order to reduce chances of local injury or infection: the back and side of the upper arms, the front of the thighs, the buttocks, and the lower abdomen.

Insulin dosages for children and adolescents are an individual matter. A single injection before breakfast may be all that is required early in the course of the disease. Most children, however, require a second injection before supper or at bedtime in order to regulate blood sugar adequately. Insulin requirements increase with the growth of the child. At puberty rapid growth and increased food consumption invariably necessitate an increased amount of insulin to achieve satisfactory diabetes control. All diabetic children and their parents should remember that a child's daily insulin requirement is not an indication of the severity of disease. Insulin requirements stabilize when growth is complete.

Delivering a steady, more controllable supply of insulin to diabetics is one goal of specialists in insulin therapy. In recent years a device known as an insulin pump has been developed for adults and children. It permits a constant infusion of insulin by means of a small, battery-powered pump, which is carried in a pocket or on a belt. The insulin is delivered through a small plastic tube to a needle that is inserted under the skin, usually somewhere on the abdomen. The needle must be repositioned about once every 3 days. The pump is programmed to deliver a constant dose of regular insulin and extra doses at mealtimes. To take advantage of the added convenience of the insulin pump requires expert medical and parental supervision as well as advanced knowledge of intensive insulin therapy.

Delivering insulin by nasal spray is an even newer method of insulin delivery. At present, this convenient, flexible, and theoretically easy-to-control way of providing insulin remains the subject of careful medical experimentation in only a few research centers. If proved reliable and safe, insulin delivery in a nasal spray may one day become widely accepted and generally available.

Diabetic children routinely check the concentration of sugar in their urine by using one of several acceptable methods of testing. In one test, drops of urine and water are mixed, a chemical tablet is added, and when the reaction is complete, the color of the solution is matched against a color chart in order to determine the level of sugar. In another, a paper strip impregnated with chemicals can be used to estimate the amount of sugar in the urine. These checks are done quickly before breakfast (before insulin injection), lunch, supper, and at bedtime, before the final snack of the day.

Blood sugar levels can be monitored at home using a chemically treated strip of paper. A drop of blood is obtained by quickly pricking a finger or earlobe with a disposable, sterile lancet. The blood is placed on the paper, then wiped off after a specified length of time. The color change on the strip is compared to a chart that gives the actual blood glucose level. Many diabetic children, their families, and their physicians prefer this method, as it is more accurate and reliable than urine testing. Frequent monitoring of blood glucose levels is a valuable aid in attempting to control a child's diabetes and identify patterns of blood glucose fluctuation, which are not readily apparent with urine testing.

Diet

A diet designed specifically for the child by a physician and a dietitian is the second essential part of treatment. Suggested proportions of the three major food groups are 50 to 55 percent carbohydrate, 30 percent fat, and 15 to 20 percent protein. Of the carbohydrate share, the bulk should come from complex carbohydrates—starches—and the rest should be lactose (sugar from milk) or fructose (sugar from fruits). Concentrated carbohydrates (refined sugars) should be restricted. Foods high in fiber are recommended, because fiber slows the rate of carbohydrate absorption into the blood. Vegetable fats, such as safflower, corn, and sunflower oil, are preferable to animal fats, which should be limited in order to reduce cholesterol and retard the development of atherosclerosis (hardening of the arteries).

For a growing diabetic child, diet must be appealing, satisfy growth requirements, and provide for the energy necessary for physical activity. Three meals and three snacks are suggested. Snacks usually come at midmorning, at midafternoon, and before bedtime. The goal of six feedings is to prevent swings between high and low blood sugar concentration.

It is important that a child eat meals and snacks at nearly the same times each day to provide food at the times that the injected insulin is most active. Becoming accustomed to this routine may take some time for young children, but it should eventually become a way of life. Adolescents, neverthe-

less, may find dietary restrictions annoying and confining, particularly when junk foods and fast foods seem irresistible and peer pressure not to conform to parents' expectations is strongest. Patience, resourcefulness, and a willingness to talk regularly with their adolescent are indispensable for parents who want to help their child with dietary control.

Physical Fitness

Physical fitness that grows out of regular planned exercise increases the body's sensitivity to insulin and assists in maintaining an ideal body weight. Athletes who have diabetes participate in nearly all sports at every level of skill and endurance. Diabetic people who maintain excellent physical condition often need less insulin.

Both individual and group sports can promote fitness and overall sound health for diabetic children. Parents should take the lead in encouraging regular, age-appropriate physical activity for their diabetic child. As is true for all dimensions of a diabetic child's life, it is best to increase gradually both physical conditioning and demanding athletic exercise.

Education

With a physician's guidance, the entire family needs education about diabetes and how a child with this serious, periodically unpredictable, lifelong disease can learn to live a full and active life. As he or she grows, a child should understand just how many activities and challenges remain unaffected by having diabetes as well as the limitations imposed by the disease.

Support and encouragement for a diabetic child are essential throughout childhood and adolescence. It is often helpful for a child to meet diabetic people, especially children, who are managing their disease well. Going to a summer camp for children and adolescents with diabetes can be a valuable experience for many children. Brothers and sisters who understand the disease can play an important role in providing support and encouragement for a diabetic sibling who must adhere to a daily routine of injections, dietary restrictions, and blood and/or urine testing.

Friends, classmates, and teachers should know enough about diabetes to assist a diabetic child if signs of either insulin reaction or uncontrolled diabetes should appear. The child's friends should receive reliable, age-appropriate information so they are not fearful of what the disease may do to their diabetic friend or to themselves. Parents should inform themselves by asking their child's physician for educational materials and by learning about support organizations (see *Prevention,* below).

PREVENTION

Diabetes, as yet, cannot be prevented or cured.

Information about diabetes and services for the families of diabetic children is available from the headquarters and local chapters of the following organizations:

- The Juvenile Diabetes Foundation, 60 Madison Avenue, New York, NY 10010 (phone: 800-223-1138).
- The American Diabetes Association, 2 Park Avenue, New York, NY 10016 (phone: 212-683-7444).
- The Joslin Diabetes Center, One Joslin Place, Boston, MA 02215 (phone: 617-732-2400)—a pioneer in diabetes treatment, research, and education.

DIAPER RASH

DESCRIPTION

Irritation of an infant's sensitive skin by wet diapers usually results in diaper rash. Appearing on an infant's buttocks, upper thighs, and genitals, diaper rash is an eruption of rough, red patches.

With treatment, diaper rash usually clears up in 3 to 4 days. As an infant grows, skin becomes less sensitive and diaper rash usually disappears permanently.

Rashes other than diaper rash may also appear in the diaper area. These may be an allergic reaction to some external substance *(eczema),* an eruption of *seborrheic dermatitis* (which is usually also present on the scalp and behind the ears in the form of *cradle cap), thrush* (a yeast infection), or the first signs of a contagious disease such as *chicken pox.*

CAUSE

Diaper rash is caused by frequent contact with diapers. It is not contagious. The rash may be severe if urine produces ammonia, a harsh substance that usually inflames an infant's sensitive skin. Use of some disposable plastic-coated diapers or of close-fitting plastic pants aggravates diaper rash because moisture is retained and air cannot reach an infant's skin.

DIAGNOSIS

A parent can usually recognize diaper rash by its appearance and location. Because urine cannot get into skinfolds at the top of a child's legs, redness in these areas often results from a skin problem other than diaper rash. If a parent is not certain that the red patches are diaper rash, a physician can identify the skin problem.

COMPLICATIONS

Bacterial or yeast infections may develop when skin is severely irritated. Rarely, *impetigo,* contagious bacterial infection, appears as very small pus-filled blisters.

TREATMENT

Treatment of diaper rash focuses on keeping an infant's skin dry and as open to the air as possible. The most effective treatment is to allow an infant to go without diapers. The absence of moisture and a plentiful supply of air quicky clears up the rash.

If a child cannot go without diapers, other steps should be taken to reduce skin irritation and diaper rash. Diapers should be changed frequently to avoid extended contact with urine. If plastic pants must be used, make sure they are large enough to "breathe."

With each diaper change, the buttocks area should be thoroughly washed with water (if only urine is in the diaper) or mild soap (if stool is also in the diaper) and dried well. Mild unscented powders help dry the diaper area. Protective skin coatings such as zinc oxide ointment can be used to help protect the diaper area, but should be avoided if the skin is severely inflamed and cracked.

Diaper rash should improve in 48 to 72 hours with treatment, though it may not clear up completely for several days. If diaper rash does not clear up, or if the rash is very severe or accompanied by a fever, irritability, or loss of appetite, a physician should be consulted.

PREVENTION

Diaper rash is difficult to prevent completely. Almost every infant has it at least once. To reduce recurrence of diaper rash, protective skin coatings (zinc oxide ointment, vitamin A and D ointment, or petroleum jelly) and mild drying agents (unscented powders) should be used to help keep moisture away from an infant's skin. Use of disposable plastic-coated diapers or close-fitting plastic pants should be avoided if diaper rash is present.

A mild soap is recommended when washing an infant's diapers at home because detergent may irritate already tender skin. Extra rinse cycles may be needed to ensure that all soap is removed.

DIARRHEA

EMERGENCY ACTION

If severe pain anywhere in the abdomen makes a child uncomfortable and persists for half an hour or longer, see a physician or go to an emergency room immediately. Do not give the child any fluids, foods, or medicine.

Seek medical assistance for any child, especially an infant, who cannot retain fluids because of diarrhea or vomiting. *Dehydration,* severe loss of essential body fluids and salts, can occur rapidly and be life-threatening, especially for infants under 6 months old. This condition is characterized by cool, dry, pale skin; dry tongue; thirst; listlessness; rapid pulse; sunken eyes; and for an infant, sunken fontanel—the soft spot on top of the head.

If a child's stool is red, rust-colored, or streaked or flecked with blood, notify a physician promptly.

DESCRIPTION

Diarrhea is an increase in the frequency, liquidity, and volume of stools, or bowel movements. A common symptom of many disorders which affect the digestive, absorptive, and secretory functions of the gastrointestinal (GI) tract, diarrhea is one of the most common illnesses among children. During the first 3 or 4 years of life, many children in the United States have an episode or two of diarrhea severe enough to interrupt normal activities and require treatment at home or, occasionally, in a hospital. Only illnesses resulting from infections of the upper respiratory tract (such as *colds)* occur more frequently during childhood than diarrhea. Often a child develops diarrhea at the same time as or immediately following the start of an infection of the upper respiratory tract.

Diarrhea can be either acute (short-term) or chronic (long-term). Most childhood diarrheas are short-term; they are usually self-limited (i.e., they run their course and improve without medication) and infectious. Long-term diarrhea may stem from any of a variety of chronic conditions or diseases which are either present at birth or acquired as a child grows. Long-term diarrhea requires medical diagnosis and treatment of the diarrhea and its underlying cause, if one can be identified.

Infectious diarrhea results in a condition called gastroenteritis, an inflamation of the stomach and small and large intestines. When the stomach is affected, *vomiting* usually occurs. Although infectious diarrhea is not usually severe, even mild inflammations, such as those resulting from common childhood GI infections, can impair the functions of the intestinal tract.

Diarrhea can be especially dangerous to infants and very young children because of the speed with which *dehydration* (excessive loss of essential body fluids and salts) sometimes develops. Food and fluids tend to move through the intestinal tract with abnormal speed because the intestines become abnormally active. As a result, far less water and many fewer salts and nutrients are absorbed into the bloodstream for use in metabolism by cells throughout the body.

Long-term diarrhea can be either a continual or a recurrent illness. If untreated, it can weaken a child, cause loss of appetite and weight, and lead to long-term growth failure.

Diarrhea affects children in many different ways. A 2-year-old child, for example, may have as many as 8 or more completely liquid stools a day, while an 8-year-old may have just 3 or 4 soft-to-runny stools daily. On the other hand, a well, breast-fed infant may have as many as 8 to 12 runny stools daily. Stool frequency alone does not indicate diarrhea.

Variations also exist among children with diarrhea in terms of the color, consistency, and volume of their stools. Diarrheal stools may vary in color from light brown to yellow to green; a tendency toward green is typical of diarrhea. Partially digested food may appear in the stool. With some kinds of diarrhea, children may have mucus in their stools; other types of diarrhea may be colored by blood. The volume of fluid and the amount of fecal material in diarrheal stools vary substantially, depending upon the underlying problem and a child's health. In watery stools, almost no fecal matter may appear, and substantial fluid may pass in a single stool.

Home treatment of children with short-term infectious diarrhea is usually successful in a few days; severe cases may require a week or more until all signs and symptoms disappear. Long-term diarrhea may require that a child be hospitalized for diagnosis and treatment. The goal in treating some types of chronic diarrhea may be to control, rather than cure, the condition.

CAUSE
Infections

Infections produce more childhood diarrhea than any other cause. The principal causes of infectious diarrhea are viruses, bacteria, microscopic animal organisms, fungi, and parasites. These agents of infection can attack the small intestine, the large intestine, or both. They either invade the mucous membrane lining of the intestine directly or manufacture toxins (biological poisons) which interfere with intestinal function. Infectious diarrhea results in a condition called gastroenteritis. It is not always possible—or necessary—to identify which particular organism causes gastroenteritis. In as many as half of all cases of childhood infectious diarrhea, no organism is ever identified. Many mild cases of acute diarrhea are simply assumed to be viral in origin. Viral and bacterial agents of infection may be present simultaneously.

Just two common viruses may be responsible for as much as 50 to 80 percent of all acute diarrheal illness among American children. After an incubation period lasting from 1 to 3 days, these viruses can produce abdominal pain, diarrhea, nausea, vomiting, and fever. In many cases, when an upper respiratory tract infection, such as a cold, precedes or coincides with other symptoms, the *fever* and *vomiting* often disappear within two days but the diarrhea may last as long as a week.

Bacteria account for approximately 10 to 15 percent of all infectious diarrhea. After a variable incubation period, diarrhea, vomiting, and fever occur. Stools are often watery an sometimes marked by mucus or pus. If blood appears in the stool, more severe illness is usually present. Diarrhea subsides gradually during a period lasting from a few days to 2 weeks or more, depending upon the specific bacterium involved. One bacterium is responsible for a particularly severe type of diarrhea called dysentery. If a child contracts this form of illness, the colon is severely affected and bloody diarrhea, often with pus, occurs. Recovery time following bacterial diarrhea can vary from 2 or 3 days for a mild case to 2 weeks or more for dysentery. Two forms of bacteria, salmonella and staphylococcus, are usually responsible for *food poisoning.*

Microscopic animal organisms sometimes infect the human intestine. *Giardia* (a species of protozoa) is a common cause of a highly contagious diarrhea often transmitted from child to child in daycare centers. An amoeba causes amebic dysentery, a form of diarrhea frequently found in tropical and subtropical climates and one which Americans sometimes acquire while traveling abroad.

Candida (a species of fungus) can cause diarrhea, particularly among children who have been weakened by other illnesses or who have immune-deficiency diseases, which make them susceptible to fungal infestation.

Each of several species of parasitic worms (including *hookworms* and whipworms) can sometimes cause acute or chronic diarrhea among children (see *parasitic infections).* Two species of roundworm can cause diarrhea and are usually transmitted to children by pets (see *pets, diseases caused by).*

Infections not associated directly with the GI tract occasionally cause diarrhea (see *urinary tract infections; earache and ear infections).*

Many viral and bacterial diarrheas are contagious. They can be transmitted by person-to-person contact, by secretions from the nose and mouth, by contaminated water or food, and by fecal-oral contamination which frequently occurs because of failure to wash hands following defecation.

Congenital Defects of the Intestinal Tract and Mechanical Problems

A variety of congenital defects (those present at birth) can cause diarrhea. Among the more are *Hirschsprung's disease* (in which a portion of the lower colon is abnormal and nonfunctional) and malrotation (in which a portion of the GI tract becomes twisted or knotted). One rare congenital abnormality is called short-bowel syndrome (in which the small intestine is too short to provide adequate absorption of liquids and nutrients during the digestive process). Among mechanical problems often causing diarrhea are partial obstructions of the small intestine (including *appendicitis)* and fistulas (abnormal passages leading to or from the intestinal tract).

Pancreas and Liver Disorders

A variety of abnormalities of the pancreas and liver can cause diarrhea. Liver problems include *hepatitis,* an inflammation of the liver, and *biliary atresia,* chronic abnormality and blockage of the bile ducts present at birth. Pancreatic problems include *cystic fibrosis,* a severe disease of digestion and breathing, and pancreatitis, often a recurrent inflammation.

Metabolic or Biochemical Causes

Several problems associated with the metabolism of carbohydrates, sugars, and proteins can cause chronic diarrhea. Among the most prominent are lactose intolerance, an inability to digest milk sugar; *celiac disease,* an inability to digest gluten, a complex protein found in grains; and *malabsorption* syndrome, an inability to metabolize sugars. Malabsorption may in turn be caused by *malnutrition,* which may then be perpetuated by the diarrhea.

Dietary Problems

Among the most common of the dietary problems that can cause acute diarrhea are overfeeding and introduction of new foods into an infant's diet. Diet can also be a cause of chronic diarrhea.

Allergies

Diarrhea is a fairly common allergic reaction to certain foods (see *food allergy).* Offending elements of "problem foods" are cow's milk protein (also found in standard infant formulas) and, less often, soy protein. For some children, whole milk itself may cause an allergic form of colitis with diarrhea. In addition, certain antibiotics used to fight infections may cause a strong reaction that involves diarrhea.

Emotional Stress

A chronic diarrhea can be provoked by several factors including diet and emotional stress. Chronic nonspecific diarrhea syndrome, or irritable bowel syndrome, is one such problem that affects many children.

Poisoning

Diarrhea can be the result of the accidental eating, drinking, or breathing of poisonous chemicals, such as arsenic and iron. It may also develop following the accidental or excessive use of laxatives by children. (See Poison section in Chapter 10, "Basic First Aid.")

For other, rarer, causes of diarrhea see *adrenal problems; Crohn's disease; lymphoma; neuroblastoma; thyroid problems; ulcerative colitis.*

DIAGNOSIS

Diarrhea is usually obvious, except in cases where an infant's normally loose stools are difficult to distinguish from diarrheal stools.

If a child becomes ill with diarrhea, a mild *fever,* and *vomiting,* a physician who is consulted may assume from the description of signs and symptoms that a viral infection is causing the problem. In those cases where additional signs and symptoms point to a cause more complicated than a common virus or bacterium, a physician examines a child carefully and records the history of illness. Blood tests may be helpful. Stool specimens may be studied for the presence of microorganisms, such as bacteria, and for hidden blood.

If the cause of diarrhea is not readily apparent, further diagnostic tests, including appropriate X-ray studies, may be necessary.

COMPLICATIONS

Dehydration is the most common complication of diarrhea. It can be a serious condition and often requires medical attention (see *dehydration). Malnutrition* and *failure to thrive,* a complex problem which includes growth failure and its psychological complications, are possibilities in certain cases of long-term diarrhea.

TREATMENT

Treatment varies according to the underlying cause of diarrhea. If the underlying cause can be eliminated or alleviated, diarrhea almost always disappears or is reduced. In addition, for certain types of illness specific treatment of the diarrhea itself may be necessary; such treatment usually involves medication and careful adjustment of diet.

No specific medication is effective for acute infectious diarrhea caused by any virus. Viral diarrhea is usually a self-limited illness. Antibiotics may be helpful for certain bacterially caused varieties of infectious diarrhea, identified in a stool culture. In other cases, bacterial diarrhea can be expected to run its own course. Specific antibiotics often prove effective against microscopic animal organisms, parasitic worms, and fungal infestations. If hospitalization is required, intravenous fluids may be given to combat *dehydration* and to correct fluid and salt imbalances.

For treatment of diarrhea with causes other than infections, see *Cause,* above. If the physician recommends home treatment, see the advice below.

Chronic nonspecific diarrhea syndrome, or irritable bowel syndrome, may improve with certain medications and dietary adjustments and, sometimes, with improved skills in coping with *stress.* A child may outgrow the problem, or it may recur throughout life.

Home Treatment for Infectious Diarrhea

In most cases, if the debilitating effects of infectious diarrhea can be reduced and a child's strength restored, the body's natural recuperative capabilities bring about complete recovery.

Preventing *dehydration* is a major goal of treatment. The younger the child, the greater is the threat of dehydration. Because infants and young children have a greater turnover of body fluids each day than do older children or adults, they must drink more liquids per pound of body weight to meet their needs. Children also have a smaller "reserve" of fluid from which to draw when they are ill and lose fluids or are deprived of them. Although most infants and young children do not experience a major problem during episodes of diarrhea and *vomiting* (a common associated symptom), a few children become severely dehydrated and require hospitalization.

If a child has diarrhea, it is helpful for the physician to know the number of bowel movements, when they occur, and their appearance. A parent can keep a written record of this information by the phone for reporting to the physician. In addition, if a child has a *fever,* temperature readings should be recorded. It may be useful to weigh a child when diarrhea begins, because a physician may ask for weighings later in any prolonged illness. Noting weight change can be crucial in determining possible dehydration.

Diet

Diet is essential in proper treatment of diarrhea. The goal is to restore water, salts, and nutrients lost in frequent stools and through urination. Fluids are most important, even if no solid food at all is eaten during the several days of an episode of diarrhea. As the frequency of stools increases, so does the need for fluids to keep up with losses.

When a child is having frequent stools, a liquids-only diet is recommended. Most children do not want solid food anyway while having many bowel movements each day. When diarrhea begins to diminish, soft solid foods may be introduced. When diarrhea stops completely, the child can return to a normal diet.

Whole milk should be avoided.

Simple, clear liquids are most helpful. For infants, diluted versions of whatever formula they are taking are also usually satisfactory and well tolerated. Water or premixed fluid replacement solutions, such as Rehydralyte (available at pharmacies), are alternatives for infants and young children. Tea with sugar, dissolved and diluted fruit-flavored gelatin, and flat soda, such as ginger ale, are other soothing drinks for the weakened child who lacks appetite.

It is best to give frequent, small amounts of liquids rather than large, occasional drinks. Children with diarrhea are likely to vomit everything if encouraged to drink liquids beyond their quite limited capacities.

Guidelines for Drinking

- For infants: 2 ounces every hour (12 ounces—a cup and a half—every 6 hours).
- For preschool children: 4 ounces every hour (24 ounces—3 cups—every 6 hours).
- For school-age children: 5 ounces every hour (30 ounces—almost 4 cups—every 6 hours).

These suggestions are upper limits. A child should be offered a drink once an hour while awake, but a parent should note the 6-hour cumulative totals rather than try to force a child to drink an hourly "quota." If a child finds it unpleasant to drink regularly, taking sips may be easier. Sucking on ice cubes or ice chips from time to time may also be a welcome variation.

Guidelines for Continuing Care

Here are "rule of thumb" suggestions for children with diarrhea who have no additional symptoms or whose accompanying symptoms are limited to fever under 102° F (38.8° C) and moderate listlessness or lack of energy. After diarrhea begins, it is usually safe to wait for 2 to 4 hours to observe a child's overall condition before informing a physician. If diarrheal bowel movements begin to occur rapidly during this observation period, the physician should be informed promptly.

- If diarrheal bowel movements occur no more than twice in 24 hours, a child may continue on a regular diet, including milk, if desired. A physician should be informed if stools are still loose after 36 hours.
- If diarrheal bowel movements occur as often as once every 4 hours, clear liquids and a soft diet are indicated. This is often called the BRAT diet—binding fruits and bland carbohydrates: mashed bananas, rice cereal, applesauce or pulp, refined grain toast, bread, or crackers, sherbet, and gelatin. If no change in the diarrhea occurs within 24 hours, a physician should be consulted.
- If diarrhea occurs once every 2 to 3 hours, the regular diet should be stopped and soft solids and clear liquids, as described, substituted. No milk should be given. A physician should be notified if diarrhea continues at this frequency for 8 hours or more or if the stools begin to be especially large and watery in volume.
- If diarrhea occurs once or more an hour, all solid food should be stopped and only clear liquids given in recommended amounts. If bowel movements continue at this frequency for 3 or 4 hours, a physician should be notified.
- If any change occurs in the frequency of bowel movements, the diet should be adjusted accordingly as can any decision about whether and when to notify the physician.

For many mild cases of diarrhea effective, commonsense treatment at home is usually sufficient to comfort the child. Bed rest conserves and increases strength. Unless a physician prescribes one, a bulking agent, such as Kaopectate or Kaolin, is not usually helpful. Prescription antispasmodic drugs, to quiet the intestinal tract, are not usually given unless diarrhea stems from chronic inflammatory bowel disease (see *Crohn's disease; ulcerative colitis*).

PREVENTION

Many of the diseases that cause diarrhea cannot be prevented. Soap and water handwashing after using the toilet continues to be the single most effective precaution against infectious diarrhea. Transmission of contagious bacterial, viral, protozoan, and amoebic causes of diarrhea can be reduced by modern public and private sanitation methods. Sanitary food preparation practices are always important (see *food poisoning*).

DISLOCATION OF JOINTS, CONGENITAL AND DUE TO INJURY

(See also *Dislocation of the Hip, Congenital.*)

EMERGENCY ACTION

If any of an injured child's joints or bones seem awkward or out of line, seek immediate medical help. A dislocated joint must be repositioned by a physician as soon as possible. To prevent the injury from worsening and to avoid damaging nearby blood vessels and nerves, exercise extreme care while transporting a child to a physician or hospital emergency room. Never attempt, for example, to move an out-of-line joint or to bend an injured limb. If possible, try to splint the affected limb (see Chapter 10, "Basic First Aid").

If an injury is severe or a child unconscious, stay with the child, keep him or her warm, and if possible, have someone else call for emergency help. If a child also has an open wound, put a clean, preferably sterile cloth over the injury and, if necessary, use first aid procedures to stop bleeding (see Chapter 10, "Basic First Aid").

Do not give an injured child food, drink, or medication, as it may be necessary to administer anesthesia for medical or surgical treatment.

DESCRIPTION

A joint is the meeting of two or more bones to form a movable part. Whenever any bone in a joint slips from its normal position, the joint is said to be dislocated. Congenital dislocation of a joint is the absence of a correct or sufficiently snug and sturdy fit between the bones of a joint. A baby is diagnosed as having a congenital dislocation whenever the structure of a joint allows for easy dislocation of a bone, regardless of whether the bone is actually dislocated at birth.

All joints are held together by tough, fibrous, connective bands called ligaments. If ligaments are torn when a joint is forced to move beyond its normal range, a *sprain* may result (see *sprain*). When the tearing is serious enough, the bone slips out of place and the joint dislocates.

Because ligaments are strong, dislocations are not common injuries. The only common type of dislocation due to injury occurs when the forearm bones slip out of position at the elbow. This condition is commonly known as nursemaid's elbow. It occurs frequently among children 1 to 3 years old who grab for an adult's hand while stumbling or whose arms and hands are yanked. After a nursemaid's elbow dislocates once, it is likely to do so again, but relocating the joint is relatively easy and can be done at home with a physician's recommendation and instructions. Nursemaid's elbow is rare after 4 years of age because a child's skeletal system is stronger and because the number of situations in which the arms are yanked usually decreases.

Injury-related dislocations of the shoulder, fingers, toes, and other joints are most commonly the result of sports activities. They are usually quite painful and may be accompanied by *fractures* and other injuries. (See *also nose, injuries to and foreign objects in.*)

If any of an uninjured child's joints—especially the hip or kneecap (patella)—appear to be out of line, the child may have been born with a congenital dislocation, which usually becomes more obvious as a child grows.

Dislocation of the hip is a common congenital problem (see *dislocation of the hip, congenital*). The following congenital dislocations are far less common than those of the hip:

- The kneecap (the patella—a round, flat bone) is dislocatable from the rest of the knee and "floats" in and out of the correct position as the leg is bent and straightened. This problem is rarely evident before a child reaches 4 or 5 years of age, and often does not become obvious until a child reaches adolescence.
- The shinbone is dislocated from the knee joint.

These dislocations are usually more obvious among newborns than congenital hip dislocation is. Severity and prognosis differ from case to case.

Like fractures, dislocations usually heal completely after being relocated and held immobile for several days or weeks.

CAUSE

Nursemaid's elbow is caused by a sudden pull on a child's hand or arm. It can result when a parent grabs a child's arm to prevent a fall, lifts a child by the hands, wrists, or forearms, or swings a child by the lower part of the arms. It also is common for a child learning to walk to get nursemaid's elbow while grabbing someone's hand.

The elbow is composed of two joints, the most obvious of which is the large one that allows the arm to bend. The other joint involves the connection at the elbow between the two bones of the forearm and allows the forearm to rotate. This less obvious joint is the one that dislocates when a child's arm is yanked. The forearm bones are not actually pulled entirely apart; the condition is known as a subluxation (partial dislocation).

Any joint forced severely beyond its normal range of motion may dislocate. In rare cases children are born with joints—usually kneecaps—that are likely to dislocate as a result of minor strain or even normal movement. Orthopedists presume that many causes also exist for congenital dislocation of joints other than the hip.

SIGNS AND SYMPTOMS

A child with nursemaid's elbow immediately experiences pain anywhere from the wrist to the injured joint. The child is likely to refuse to use the injured arm and to clutch it to the side of the body with the good arm. The hand on an injured arm faces palm down (instead of, as is usual, palm up) in relation to the upper arm. Several hours after the injury, the hand and wrist may begin to swell.

A child with an injury-related dislocation other than nursemaid's elbow usually has an obvious deformity in the injured area. Pain is likely to be severe (see *joint pain*) and is usually accompanied by swelling, tenderness, decreased joint movement, and internal bleeding (see *bruises*). A dislocated kneecap may actually "float" in and out of place, and a child may refuse to bend or extend the affected leg.

People with dislocating patellas usually experience pain when bending the knee during certain activities. Congenital dislocation of the elbow usually limits bending and rotational motion; an affected elbow also looks abnormal. When a knee is congenitally dislocated because of a slipped shinbone, the shinbone appears abnormally long and the knee is usually bent in a backward direction.

DIAGNOSIS

An injury-related dislocation is usually obvious because of the awkward position of the affected joint. Home diagnosis alone, however, is usually insufficient: a badly swollen sprain may also cause a joint to appear out of line; dislocations may entail other, less obvious injuries requiring medical care; or nursemaid's elbow may appear to be a wrist injury because of the way a child holds the injured arm.

A physician diagnoses nursemaid's elbow by the presence of a cause for the dislocation and by the characteristic palms-down position of the forearm.

X-ray films are always ordered when dislocation or a fracture is a possibility, although they are usually of little help in diagnosing nursemaid's elbow. X rays are used to confirm preliminary diagnosis of other types of injury-related dislocations and to indicate the extent of damage.

If a dislocatable kneecap is suspected, a physician may extend the affected leg fully and attempt to push the kneecap to the side. If the kneecap is dislocatable, the thigh muscles in the affected leg flinch involuntarily during this procedure.

A physician can identify a congenitally dislocated elbow or knee (shinbone) by its characteristically abnormal appearance. Diagnosis is confirmed by X-ray films. Congenital dislocation of the kneecap is identified by its characteristic signs and symptoms, but X-ray films are usually of little help in confirming the diagnosis since the kneecap often floats in and out of position.

COMPLICATIONS

Attempting to move a dislocated joint before it is treated by a physician is likely to cause further injury or to damage surrounding tissues. The exception is recurring nursemaid's elbow, which parents can relocate if a physician has shown them how.

On the other hand, it is important to get the joint relocated immediately after the dislocation. If a bone remains out of joint too long, a child may experience pain and inflammation of the joint later in life. This is especially true of the hip joint. If a hip remains dislocated too long (more than 12 to 14 hours), blood supply to the area may be diminished or cut off, and bone cells may die (a condition called necrosis). As a result, a child may have difficulty moving the hip properly. Movement problems and pain

sometimes do not appear until weeks or even months after the injury occurs.

Other complications tend to vary according to the joint affected. When a shoulder dislocates, the nerves around the joint may be damaged and the shoulder may be permanently weakened. If the skin around a dislocated finger is broken, a risk exists that bacteria will get into the joint and cause an episode of *arthritis*. A dislocated finger may never regain its full flexibility. Finally, when a kneecap dislocates, a risk develops that it may become malaligned again in the future. In addition, dislocation of a kneecap sometimes predisposes a child to the development of long-term problems with knee infections.

TREATMENT

Medical attention should be sought as soon as possible for a child with a suspected dislocation unless the problem is recurrent nursemaid's elbow and parents know how to treat the condition themselves.

Nursemaid's elbow is relocated by bending the arm to a 90-degree angle, holding the forearm near the elbow, and sharply twisting the wrist so that the palm faces upward. If this procedure is performed within a few hours of injury, a sharp click is sometimes heard but usually felt near the elbow. Pain disappears and normal movement returns within minutes. Sometimes nursemaid's elbow automatically clicks back into place while it is being positioned for X rays. If nursemaid's elbow is not treated until several hours after injury, relocation may be more difficult, soreness may persist, and a physician may advise keeping the arm in a sling for a day or two after the procedure. Once nursemaid's elbow occurs, the probability that a child will dislocate the joint again is high for the next 3 to 4 weeks.

After being taught how to diagnose and relocate nursemaid's elbow, parents can perform the procedure themselves as long as no doubt exists that diagnosis is correct. If a child gets nursemaid's elbow frequently, however, a physician may advise immobilizing the arm in a cast in a fully extended, palms-up position for a week or two to reinforce proper position of the joint.

Treatment for an injury-related dislocation other than nursemaid's elbow depends on the type of dislocation and the extent of a child's injuries. In most cases treatment involves relocating the joint as soon as possible and holding it immobile in a cast until tissues heal—but no longer: a joint that is held immobile for too long may feel stiff and painful even after the dislocated bone has been repositioned and the joint has healed.

Another common component of treatment for a dislocated joint is isometric exercise, which involves tensing certain muscles to build strength and control. In some cases, traction (stretching muscle and connective tissue near the joint) or surgery may be necessary before or during relocation. If a particular joint dislocates several times, surgery may be necessary to strengthen tissues in the affected area. Sometimes a physician recommends surgery after only one dislocation if a joint seems likely to dislocate again; most such cases involve the shoulder. Surgery may also be necessary to treat necrosis of the hip.

More than 75 procedures have been developed to help correct congenital dislocation of the patella. Isometric exercises are often part of treatment.

A congenitally dislocated elbow is usually treated by immobilizing the joint in a plaster cast. A new cast is applied periodically to allow for gradual repositioning of the joint and normal tissue growth. In rare cases an elbow is relocated surgically. Prognosis is good for complete recovery.

Congenital dislocation of the knee (shinbone) is treated much the same as that of the elbow, with traction often being used first to stretch muscles in the lower leg.

The use of artificial joints to replace congenitally dislocated ones is almost never considered for children; artificial joints are virtually certain to loosen or break within a very few years.

PREVENTION

Injury-related dislocation of joints other than nursemaid's elbow usually occur accidentally and are almost impossible to prevent. Subsequent dislocations of an injured joint may be prevented by following a physician's precautions or, in rare cases, by preventive surgery.

Nursemaid's elbow may be prevented if young children are lifted by the armpits or upper arms and not by the forearms, wrists, or hands. Likewise, toddlers should never be swung by the lower parts of the arms. (These precautions are especially important during the month or so after nursemaid's elbow occurs.) If a child continually gets nursemaid's elbow, parents should look for any consis-

tent and preventable cause and, if necessary, should seek a physician's help.

It is important to diagnose and treat congenital dislocations as early as possible.

DISLOCATION OF THE HIP, CONGENITAL

DESCRIPTION

The movable part formed where two or more bones come together is called a joint. Whenever any bone in a joint slips from its normal position, the joint is said to be dislocated. Congenital dislocation of a joint is the absence at birth of a correct or sufficiently snug and sturdy fit between the bones of a joint. A baby is diagnosed as having this condition whenever the structure of a joint allows for easy dislocation of a bone, regardless of whether the bone is actually dislocated at birth.

Most congenital dislocations are of the hip and involve an instability between the thighbone and hipbone socket in either or both legs. The rounded end (head) of the thighbone may be totally or partially out of the socket or may simply have the potential to slip. It is common for the ligament connecting the hipbone socket to the head of the thighbone to be somewhat loose at birth.

In most cases congenital dislocation of the hip can be easily and entirely corrected within the first few months of life. Correction is possible because a newborn's bones are pliable at their ends. If poorly fitting bones are repositioned early enough during the development of the musculoskeletal system, tissues are likely to set in the correct position.

If the condition is not corrected early enough or at all, or if it is complicated by other congenital problems, congenital hip dislocation may lead to poor posture, walking difficulties, and persistent discomfort. Later in life a poorly treated case of congenital hip dislocation greatly increases a person's chances of developing *arthritis*.

About 1 out of every 100 newborns has some form of congenital hip problem, but the majority of these infants simply have unstable connections between the thighbone and socket that usually strengthen on their own during the first few days after birth. About 4 out of every 1,000 newborns have some form of congenital hip dislocation requiring treatment.

Congenital hip dislocation is rarely obvious. It is painless to the infant and an affected joint may appear normal, since the musculoskeletal and nervous systems of all newborns are underdeveloped. To detect the condition as early as possible, physicians routinely examine newborns for hip dislocation. This procedure has dramatically reduced the need for surgery and the incidence of severe complications due to late diagnosis.

Approximately 70 percent of infants affected by congenital dislocation of the hip are girls. The left hip is affected about 60 percent of the time, the right about 20 percent, and both about 20 percent. Approximately 20 percent of all congenital hip dislocations affect babies whose position in the uterus is abnormal and who are delivered in the breech position (legs first). A female delivered in the breech position has 1 chance in 35 of having congenital hip dislocation. The incidence of newborns with congenital hip dislocation also seems to be higher for those born with other bone or muscle problems, such as *clubfoot*. Congenital hip dislocation runs in families to some extent.

In about 90 percent of newborns with congenital hip dislocation, the hipbones become poorly positioned around the time of birth, and dislocation can almost always be corrected completely with no complications if detected in infancy.

Some newborns with congenital hip dislocation also have a disease affecting nerves and muscles in the hip area, such as *poliomyelitis* or *cerebral palsy*. In these newborns a dislocated hip can usually be relocated but often continues to slip after treatment because of disease-associated problems such as weak pelvic muscles.

CAUSE

The exact combination of factors that leads to congenital hip dislocation is not clear, but statistics indicate that more than one cause is present.

Since the incidence of congenital hip dislocation is higher for newborns with affected siblings and since girls have it far more often than boys, heredity is considered a causal factor (see *genetic disorders*).

Heredity is clearly not the only cause, however, since incidence is also higher among babies who were incorrectly positioned either in a mother's uterus or at birth. Congenital dislocations of the hip are associated with a mother's first pregnancy more often than later ones. This may indicate that tight uterine muscles play a role in causing congenital hip dislocation.

SIGNS AND SYMPTOMS

Before better methods of detection were developed, an infant was thought to have congenital dislocation of the hip if skin folds were not in identical places on both legs or if it was impossible to spread the legs of an infant lying on his or her back with the knees bent so that each thigh touched the surface the baby was lying on. This is essentially the diapering position.

This method of detection is now considered inaccurate. Many normal babies exhibit these signs during the first few weeks of infancy because of normal musculoskeletal underdevelopment. As a baby with normal hips grows, however, these signs almost always disappear. If they persist in a baby 1 month of age or older, they should be taken as possible signs of congenital hip dislocation.

As a child grows older, the signs of dislocation become more obvious. In just a few months the hip joint may look out of line and a baby may begin to hold the affected leg awkwardly. Muscles may set in an incorrect position, sometimes making the thigh appear shorter and making the spreading of legs for diapering difficult.

As a child begins to walk, more signs of congenital hip dislocation become evident. If only one hip is affected, a child limps. If both legs are affected, a child walks with a distinctly abnormal waddle. In both cases the pelvis is tilted, the abdomen and buttocks protrude abnormally outward, and the lower back curves abnormally inward.

The presence at birth of a neuromuscular disease such as *cerebral palsy* is a sign that a newborn may have congenital hip dislocation as well.

Pain is not a reliable sign of congenital hip dislocation. A painful hip is more likely to be a sign of injury, infection (see *osteomyelitis*), arthritis (or some other inflammation problem), or *leukemia* (see also *joint pain*).

DIAGNOSIS

Every infant should be tested by a physician for congenital hip dislocation soon after birth and should be reexamined at routine checkups over the next year. To check for congenital hip dislocation, a physician feels an infant's hip joint for a "clunk" as the baby's legs are moved.

X-ray films are unreliable in diagnosing an infant's congenital hip dislocation, as the tissue in the hip area of every newborn is not developed enough to show up on X rays. As a newborn grows, however, the "clunk" disappears and diagnosis by examination can be more difficult. Fortunately, X rays become helpful in diagnosis as early as 3 months after birth.

COMPLICATIONS

If a child under walking age (about 18 months) is treated correctly for congenital hip dislocation, chances are good for complete adjustment.

The longer congenital hip dislocation goes untreated, the more likely that complications such as painful *arthritis* of the hip or *scoliosis* (spine curvature) will affect the child later in life. If a congenitally dislocated hip has remained out of place more than 6 years, arthritis is likely to develop later, even if relocation is at first successful. Children older than 8 years of age tend to develop relatively early complications even if the thighbone is successfully relocated. Therefore, up to about 6 years of age, previously untreated hip dislocations should be repaired. Over 6 years, only unilateral dislocations should be treated.

The greatest risk in treating a child with congenital hip dislocation is that pressure may be put on the sensitive blood vessels to the femoral head, stopping the flow of blood to this area. Without blood, cells die and permanent damage is done to tissue. The result may be disturbed growth and shape of the bones in the hip area.

TREATMENT

Treatment of congenital hip dislocation varies with the age of the child at the time of diagnosis and with the nature of each case.

As soon as congenital hip dislocation is suspected or diagnosed, a child should see an orthopedist for treatment. An orthopedist classifies a hip as "dislocated" if the thighbone is totally out of the hip socket; as "dislocatable" if the thighbone tends to slip in and out of the socket; or as "subluxated" if the thighbone is partly but incorrectly attached to the socket. If treating a condition poses a great risk of stiffening joints or persistent pain, treatment may be withheld permanently.

In most cases a congenitally dislocated or subluxated hip discovered before a child is 3 months old can be corrected by having an orthopedist gently stretch the leg and ease the thighbone into place in the hip socket. The hip joint is then held in position using a special harness, brace, splint, or pillow. If a child's hip joint is extremely loose, a plaster cast called a spica, which encompasses the child's lower trunk and upper legs, is used to prevent the hip from slipping as it sets.

If congenital dislocation is diagnosed before an infant is 1 month old, immobilization of the hip joint with some type of brace or cast usually corrects the problem entirely within 2 to 4 weeks. The repositioning of the hip in a child younger than 3 months may take place gradually in a harness.

If hip dislocation is not diagnosed until after an infant is 3 months old or if treatment before this age is unsuccessful, it may be necessary for an orthopedist to loosen any abnormally tight tendons, ligaments, and muscles in a child's rapidly developing leg before using an immobilizing device. Loosening such tissue tightness also guards against damaging blood vessels to the hip during subsequent relocation. The most common stretching method is skin traction, in which the leg on an affected side is wrapped and gently stretched by an overhead mechanism for up to three weeks. If further stretching is necessary, pins may be inserted temporarily in a child's legs as part of the traction procedure, or tight tendons may be loosened surgically. Relocation consists of a gentle setting of the hip while a baby is under general anesthesia.

After stretching and relocation, hips are usually enclosed in a spica cast, which is changed about every 6 weeks to allow for natural growth. Immobilization continues for a time equal to or double the child's age at the time of diagnosis, but no longer than 6 months. A splint may be necessary for several months after this procedure to ensure continued proper development of a child's hipbone socket.

If stretching and immobilizing procedures are not entirely successful, surgical relocation of the thighbone is necessary, although orthopedists rarely resort to surgery before a child reaches walking age. To prevent stiffening after surgery, the hip joint is rarely held immobile in a cast longer than 8 weeks.

Once an untreated child reaches walking age, prognosis for a full recovery is not good. A toddler's musculoskeletal system is so well set at walking age that surgical reshaping of bones may be necessary before attempting relocation. The need for surgery becomes greater as an untreated child grows. After initial treatment, the individual should be examined by an orthopedist until maturity.

PREVENTION

The importance of early diagnosis and treatment in preventing disability from congenital dislocations cannot be overemphasized.

DIZZINESS

DESCRIPTION

Dizziness is the sensation that one's body or the environment is whirling around. Children often use the word "dizzy" to describe feelings of faintness and lightheadedness, but true dizziness, also called vertigo, always involves a spinning sensation.

Dizziness always results from a disturbance of the body's balancing mechanism, which is located in the inner ear. If a sense of balance is not restored within a few minutes of disruption, nausea and *vomiting* are likely to develop. Malfunction of the balancing mechanism usually lasts just a few minutes, although underlying causes such as inner-ear disease can produce dizziness for days or longer.

Most people have experienced dizziness; the balancing mechanism can be disrupted momentarily by spinning quickly in the same spot until the room seems to reel. This kind of physical activity is by far the most common cause of dizziness among children. Much less often, a child's dizziness is caused by disease, injury, or substance use.

A very small number of children experience frequent, inexplicable dizzy spells for a few months or years during early childhood (ages 1 to 4). This condition is known as *benign* paroxysmal vertigo. ("Benign" indicates that the condition is mild and does not involve complications; "paroxysmal" indicates that dizziness attacks come on suddenly.)

Children with benign paroxysmal vertigo have dizzy spells at varying intervals, and each attack typically lasts just a few minutes. During an attack the severity of dizziness tends to vary according to the position of the child's head. As soon as an attack passes, the child feels completely well and resumes normal activities.

The outlook for a child with benign paroxysmal vertigo is excellent; medication is available to prevent attacks, and the condition is likely to disappear altogether as mysteriously as it appeared. Dizziness caused by a temporary medical problem also tends to disappear when the underlying condition clears up. Children are likely to experience recurrent dizziness only when an underlying cause, such as head injury, affects the balancing mechanism over a long period of time.

CAUSE

Many routine activities can cause dizziness or lightheadedness. Bending over backwards even for a few seconds, for example, can temporarily affect blood flow to the head and produce lightheadedness. Similarly, a child affected by *motion sickness* can become lightheaded or dizzy simply by riding in a car.

The diseases, injuries, and substances that, in rare cases, produce vertigo during childhood include middle-ear and inner-ear infections (see *earache and ear infections*), certain brain tumors, (see *brain tumor*), *meningitis, encephalitis,* head injury (see *head and spinal injury*), cigarettes (nicotine), and alcohol.

The exact cause of benign paroxysmal vertigo is unknown. The condition appears not to be associated with any past or ongoing disease. The number of children with benign paroxysmal vertigo who eventually develop migraine headaches (see *headache*) is greater than that for the general population, but the significance of this fact is not clear.

SIGNS AND SYMPTOMS

During a dizzy spell caused by anything other than physical activity (such as spinning around), a young child may appear pale and frightened. The child is usually unsteady on his or her feet and may clutch another person or a piece of furniture in an attempt to maintain balance. Mental alertness, however, is unaffected. The likelihood that a child will become nauseated and vomit increases as dizziness persists.

These signs and symptoms are also common when a child suffers from benign paroxysmal vertigo. In addition, the eyeballs of a child with this condition may move rapidly and rhythmically back and forth during a dizzy spell.

DIAGNOSIS

Parents usually discover that a child feels lightheaded or dizzy because the child cries, complains of the feeling, or has signs and symptoms of dizziness. Before attempting to determine the underlying cause of the problem, parents should ask their child for a detailed description of the dizzy feeling to ensure that the problem is not nausea, faintness (see *fainting*), or *focusing problems.*

If dizziness is not obviously related to physical activity and if it lasts for more than a few minutes, a child should also be asked to describe any other symptoms. The diseases that can cause dizziness also commonly produce symptoms such as earache (see *earache and ear infections), fever,* and *headache.* If any of these symptoms accompanies dizziness, a physician should be consulted about how to proceed. A physician should also be consulted if a child is delirious (see *delirium),* lacks coordination, complains of buzzing in one or both ears, wants desperately to lie down, is dizzy for more than a few hours, or suffers from repeated dizzy spells for no apparent reason.

A physician consulted about dizziness usually asks a child to describe signs and symptoms and asks parents about the child's medical history and recent activities. The physician is also likely to perform a comprehensive physical examination in an attempt to determine the cause of dizziness. A physician may flush a child's ears with water to see whether rapid, rhythmical eye movement begins spontaneously. If it does not, a child may have an ear infection or benign paroxysmal vertigo. A physician who suspects an ear problem may refer a child to an otolaryngologist (ear, nose, and throat specialist) for further tests and final diagnosis.

A physician may refer a child to a neurologist (nervous-system specialist) if the cause of dizziness is still unclear. The signs and symptoms of dizzy spells can resemble those of *seizures,* which must be ruled out. (During a seizure, however, a child's mental alertness is usually affected.) A child may be hospitalized for a day to undergo neurological tests, such as skull X rays, CT (computed tomography) scans, which produce highly detailed X-ray films of the brain, and electroencephalogram (EEG) monitoring of brain activity.

TREATMENT

A child who becomes dizzy after spinning or some other form of physical activity should feel fine after a few minutes of rest.

When disease, injury, or the use of some substance produces dizziness, treatment depends on the underlying cause. Lying down or holding the head in a comfortable position may alleviate dizziness momentarily.

An attack of benign paroxysmal dizziness can be treated with an over-the-counter preparation containing an antihistamine, the same type of medication used to prevent *motion sickness.* Before giving a child medication, however, parents should always consult a physician.

PREVENTION

Benign paroxysmal dizziness cannot be prevented. Some causes of dizziness, such as head injury, can sometimes be prevented by following simple health and safety guidelines (see Chapter 4, "Accident Prevention"). Prevention of dizzy spells is one of many reasons parents should discourage cigarette smoking and alcohol overconsumption.

DOWN SYNDROME

DESCRIPTION

Down syndrome is the name given to a variation in human form and development. People with this condition typically have short stature (see *height problems*), diminished muscle tone, a skin fold at the inside corner of the eyelids, small nose, short fingers, and *mental retardation.*

The degree of mental retardation varies widely among children with Down syndrome. In general, however, a child with Down syndrome will be delayed in all aspects of development, including cognition (the processes of perception, thought, and memory), gross motor skills (such as walking), fine motor skills (such as writing), learning skills, and language skills. Impaired cognition has an influence on a child's social adaptability as well, although the chief influences for this are the guidance and support that a child with Down syndrome receives. Like children of normal intelligence, those with Down syndrome develop faster in some areas than in others.

For educational purposes a child with Down syndrome is classified as having a developmental disability. Affected children need special supportive and educational services to function to the best of their ability.

Between 30 and 40 percent of all children with Down syndrome also have congenital heart disease (see *heart disease, congenital*). Possible heart defects include a hole between the chambers of the heart and abnormalities of the valves. A heart defect may be so severe that it is apparent at birth, or it may be detected in the first few months of life. Most of these defects can be corrected surgically. Approximately 10 to 20 percent of all children with Down syndrome have a heart defect so severe that they could not survive beyond the first 2 to 4 years of life without heart surgery.

The educational progress of a child with Down syndrome depends in large part upon the degree of mental retardation. It is also influenced by the severity of the medical complications and by the use of support services such as early intervention programs.

CAUSE

Down syndrome is the most common example of a disorder caused by a chromosomal abnormality. In approximately 95 percent of cases, a child with Down syndrome has 47 rather than 46 chromosomes in the cells of the body. (Chromosomes carry a person's genes.) The extra chromosome is present at (or very soon after) conception; the occurrence of the extra chromosome is spontaneous, not hereditary. The extra chromosome is located with the number 21 pair of chromosomes; Down syndrome is sometimes called trisomy 21, meaning that there are three number 21 chromosomes. It is not known just how this extra chromosome interferes with the development of a child, either before or after birth.

The extra chromosome may come from the egg or sperm. Research indicates that the extra chromosome comes from the father in one fourth to one third of cases. Typically, at conception, the cell with 47 chromosomes starts to divide, making an exact copy of itself so that each new cell has an identical set of 47 chromosomes.

The extra chromosome may also result from an error during the first cell division after fertilization. Why cells divide incorrectly remains unknown.

It is known that the risk of a baby's being born with Down syndrome increases with the age of the mother. The incidence of children with Down syndrome is considerably less than 1 per 1,000 babies born to women who are 25 years old, about 1 per 100 for women 35 years old, and about 2 to 3 per 100 for women 45 years old.

In about 5 percent of cases, Down syndrome is caused by a hereditary translocation (rearrangement) of the number 21 chromosome.

A child with Down syndrome is never the result of anything the mother did or did not do during pregnancy (see *genetic disorders*).

SIGNS AND SYMPTOMS AND COMPLICATIONS

Children with Down syndrome have many physical features in common. They also, however, resemble members of their family, since they have many traits inherited from their parents that are not masked or dominated by Down syndrome features.

The head of a child with Down syndrome is somewhat smaller than the head of a normal newborn. The back of the head is slightly flattened, giving the head a round appearance. The fontanel (the soft spot on top of an infant's head) is larger than normal and may take longer to close. The hair of children with Down syndrome is often sparse, silky, and straight.

A skin fold at the inside corner of the eyelids is characteristic of babies with Down syndrome. The eyes appear wide-set, and the iris (the colored part of the eye) often has white speckles due to thinning of the iris tissue. *Focusing problems,* such as nearsightedness and farsightedness, are present more often among children with Down syndrome than among other children. Ears are usually small and low-set, and the ear canals are narrow. Fluid accumulation associated with infection of the middle ear (see *earache and ear infections*) is common, which often leads to a mild hearing defect (see *hearing loss*). The mouth and jaw are usually small, and as a result, the tongue may protrude. Eruption of teeth is often delayed. The face of a child with Down syndrome appears somewhat flat due to the underdeveloped nasal bone, and the nose itself is small.

Infants with Down syndrome have poor muscle tone, limited muscle coordination, and reduced strength. Hands and feet tend to be small. There may be a single crease across the palm. Because of the laxity of muscles and tendons, many children with Down syndrome have flat feet and are loose-jointed.

Down syndrome can be associated with other birth defects—such as obstructions in the gastrointestinal tract (the esophagus, stomach, and intestines)—which, if untreated, can cause death (see Complications section in *mental retardation*).

DIAGNOSIS

Down syndrome can be diagnosed prenatally (before birth), but its severity cannot be determined before birth.

Prenatal diagnosis of Down syndrome involves amniocentesis (removal of amniotic fluid by a needle inserted into the uterus through the abdominal wall) and the analysis of chromosomes in fetal cells. The best time to have the procedure performed is some time during the 16th to 18th week after the first day of the mother's last menstrual period.

After birth, Down syndrome may first be diagnosed by a pediatrician who examines the newborn baby. Within days of birth, any medical complications are usually identified. During infancy some clues about a baby's development become apparent. Developmental testing is of limited usefulness, however, until the preschool years (ages 3 and 4), and is most helpful during the early school years. As childhood proceeds, the degree of a child's disability can be evaluated by a team of medical and psychological specialists. A full evaluation is a complex process and involves assessment of a child's development of gross and fine motor skills, language and cognitive skills, and social adaptation.

TREATMENT

No cure exists for Down syndrome. However, the achievements of a child with Down syndrome can be significantly enhanced through special education. Early intervention programs are becoming increasingly available, starting shortly after birth. Later in the school years, and following them, vocational training becomes highly useful.

At least initially, a child with Down syndrome may require medical or surgical treatment of heart defects. A child who has problems with muscle coordination will benefit from physical therapy. In addition, many children with Down syndrome need treatment for vision and hearing problems. It may be advisable to check for thyroid deficiency and for abnormalities in the alignment of the bones of the spine in the neck.

It is crucial that parents of a child with Down syndrome make long-term plans regarding their child's education and support. For instance, children with Down syndrome need to receive training in self-help skills so that they may become as self-sufficient and independent as they are able to become.

In cases where family difficulties are pressing, arrangements can be made for intervals of respite care or, on infrequent occasions, placement in specialized foster care. Rarely, a child with Down syndrome is put up for adoption. Waiting lists exist of people who want to adopt children with Down syndrome.

Parents of a child with Down syndrome need to learn how to provide a supportive environment for a child with special needs. At the same time they must be careful not to neglect their own needs or those of any other children. Many families find that counseling helps them resolve issues of conflicting needs. Counseling may also help parents deal with their anxiety about their emotional capacity to care for their child; they may find internal and external resources. Parent groups can be invaluable in providing support.

Parents of a baby with Down syndrome may also be concerned about their practical ability to care for their child. However, they will find that support services and programs such as special preschool and school programs, homemaker services, daycare, and summer camps are more available than in the past because of the presence of various helping organizations and the passage of state and federal laws that guarantee the education of children with developmental disabilities. Virtually all families who resolve to raise a child with Down syndrome succeed in doing so.

As parents become older, they must consider the available options regarding their dependent child's future. As an adult, their child may be able to work at unskilled or semiskilled jobs or in sheltered workshops. Adults with Down syndrome and moderate mental retardation often live in community group homes or apartment clusters. In the current atmosphere of improved attitudes toward the developmentally disabled, people with Down syndrome are encouraged and aided in living full and productive lives.

PREVENTION

Down syndrome cannot be prevented, although the birth of a baby with Down syndrome can be prevented through prenatal diagnosis and interruption of pregnancy.

Women who are 35 years old or older may want to receive genetic counseling during pregnancy (see Prevention section in *genetic disorders*). Women with a family history of Down syndrome caused by translocation (which is hereditary) should receive genetic counseling.

Information about Down syndrome and local support services is available from the National Down Syndrome Congress, 1640 West Roosevelt Road, Chicago IL 60608 (phone: 312-226-0416).

DRUG AND ALCOHOL ABUSE

EMERGENCY ACTION

A child who shows any inexplicable, significant change in mental alertness or functioning requires immediate medical attention. Such a change may be a sign of a toxic reaction to prescription medication, illicit drugs, household chemicals, or alcohol. Signs of decreased mental alertness and function include lethargy (extreme drowsiness and sluggishness), insomnia (severe sleeping difficulty), confusion, *dizziness, seizures, delirium* (marked in some cases by misinterpretations, illusions, and hallucinations), and unconsciousness or *coma.*

Other possible signs that can indicate a mild to severe reaction to drugs or alcohol include dilated or constricted pupils, nausea, *vomiting,* coordination problems, profuse sweating, chills, tremors, and *headache.* These signs are frequently accompanied by a sudden change in behavior that appears for no apparent reason and reflects panic, anger, fear, a pervasive feeling of well-being and confidence, *depression,* or other emotions.

Before seeking emergency medical help, try to determine the cause of a change in mental alertness by asking an affected child whether any drugs, alcohol, or other chemicals were recently taken. Be sympathetic. The goal of questioning must be to deter-

mine the best course of emergency action based on the probable cause of the child's signs and symptoms. Questions of moral and legal significance must wait. If the child is fearful or panicky, it is especially important to provide reassurance without reservation or condemnation.

If the cause of a child's change in mental alertness cannot be determined, take the child to a hospital emergency room immediately.

If the specific cause of a child's change in mental alertness can be determined, decide how to proceed by considering the nature of the substance and the apparent severity of signs and symptoms. These topics are discussed below. When doubt exists, seek assistance promptly from a physician, hospital emergency room, or poison information center.

DESCRIPTION, SIGNS AND SYMPTOMS, AND COMPLICATIONS

Although drugs and alcohol are the most commonly abused substances, this section concerns anything taken into the body to alter consciousness, perceptions, thought processes, personality, behavior, energy level, or mood. Many health professionals now refer to such behavior as "substance abuse" to emphasize that a wide variety of foods, chemicals, and medications can be used for this purpose. Abuse occurs when using a substance interferes in the short or long term with a person's physical or mental health—or with activities, relationships, daily functioning, capacity to achieve, and happiness.

Tobacco

Tobacco smoked in cigarettes, cigars, and pipes, sniffed in the form of snuff, or chewed is one of the most physically harmful substances used by human beings. Tobacco smoke is the main cause of lung cancer, and tobacco in all forms plays a role in causing other cancers, heart disease, and *emphysema.* Using tobacco during pregnancy can increase the risk of having a miscarriage; a stillborn, premature, or dysmature baby (see *prematurity*); birth complications; and birth defects. Using chewing tobacco or snuff often leads to persistent sores in the throat, mouth, and nasal passages and sometimes causes cancer in these areas. It is estimated that the incidence of all cancers would be reduced by almost one third if no one used tobacco.

Smoking cigarettes poses the highest risk of developing major physical problems from tobacco. Smoke inhalation is the major contributing factor to lung problems because it produces carcinogenic (cancer-causing) "tar." A person who smokes a pack of cigarettes a day takes, on the average, 75,000 puffs a year.

Tobacco contains nicotine, which is as addicting as "hard drugs" like heroin. Smoking draws more nicotine into the body than any other method of tobacco use. The tobacco withdrawal syndrome usually includes depression, irritability, and weight gain, as well as an intense craving for more tobacco. Many ex-smokers also report the following symptoms during withdrawal: nervousness, a feeling of social awkwardness, drowsiness during the day, difficulty sleeping at night, lightheadedness and dizziness, headache, sluggishness, constipation or diarrhea, sweating, muscle cramps, tremors, heart palpitations, and loss of energy.

Alcohol

Alcohol is available in "hard" liquors, such as whiskey, and in beverages with less alcohol content per portion, such as beer and wine.

Drinking alcohol to the point of intoxication ("drunkenness") tends at first to produce self-confidence, a brightness in personality, and a fluency of speech (which, nonetheless, may be slurred). These effects are achieved at the enormous cost of disrupting a person's abilities to think in a complex way, remember, concentrate, and use sound judgment.

The amount of alcohol required to produce intoxication varies according to a person's weight, metabolism, experience with alcohol, rate of drinking, and food intake. One drink is enough to make some people intoxicated; two is enough for many people, and enough to make driving risky for most.

For people who take alcohol occasionally and in moderate amounts, few negative side effects are likely to occur. But for those who get extremely drunk on occasion or habitually—and for the sober people in their presence at the time—alcohol can have devastating consequences. Not only can it cause direct damage to physical and mental health, it can also alter judgment and emotional and physical control so dramatically that the drunk person and others are often indirectly harmed. Among adolescents, for example, the number one cause of death is accidents, and most of these accidents involve a drunk person.

Possible damaging results on the body of long-term, heavy use of alcohol include high blood pressure, nerve degeneration, gastrointestinal problems, partial loss of sight, brain disease or degeneration, confusion, severe memory problems, liver problems (including cirrhosis, a progressive disease that permanently damages the liver), damage to cardiac and skeletal muscles, *sleep disorders, psychotic disorders* (see *psychosis*), impotence and *gynecomastia* (abnormal breast development) in males, sterility, and a shorter life expectancy.

Pregnant females who drink—even in moderation—run the risk of bearing children with fetal alcohol syndrome (FAS). No exact measurement yet exists to determine how much and how often a pregnant female can drink before she begins to endanger her unborn baby, but medical experts agree that when a woman drinks heavily on a regular basis during pregnancy she exposes her baby to the greatest risk of developing FAS. Heavy drinking is defined as at least two ounces of absolute alcohol per day; for example, 2 or more hard drinks, beers, or 3-ounce glasses of wine. The effects of moderate drinking are not known. However, the greater the amount and frequency of alcohol consumption during pregnancy, the greater the likelihood of causing FAS in the unborn baby.

A baby born with FAS is likely to be microcephalic (i.e., to have a small head). The infant may have a low nasal bridge and skin folded over the inner corner of the eye (a normal trait in people of Asian ancestry). One or both eyes may be abnormally small. The nose may be short and upturned, and the upper lip thin and underdeveloped. An affected infant may also suffer from joint, limb, or organ abnormalities, such as a malformed hip or a congenital heart defect (see *heart disease, congenital*). The most serious problem associated with FAS is *mental retardation.*

People who subject themselves to the hazards of being drunk or of being around drunk people run a significantly higher risk than others of being involved in accidents (especially automobile accidents), suicides, child abuse, rape, and crimes involving weapons. Alcohol is involved, for example, in at least half of all car accidents, half of all murders, and one quarter of all suicides. Intoxicated people also suffer far more accidents such as *fractures* and head injuries (see *head and spinal injury*) than other people. They are also more susceptible to *exposure to temperature extremes* because of impaired ability to feel pain and discomfort. Intoxication can also affect the immune system and increase the risk of developing infections. Death by respiratory failure or inhalation of vomit can result from a single episode of intoxication.

Tolerance of alcohol varies. A hangover is a common withdrawal syndrome, however, that produces *headache,* nausea, *vomiting,* tremors, anxiety, lethargy, and a general feeling of malaise. The withdrawal symptoms for heavy drinkers are severe, including *seizures* and *delirium.*

For a teenager, signs of a severe drinking problem include drinking before school, drinking to "steady nerves" for an exam or a similar situation, or drinking alone regularly.

Caffeine

Caffeine is a chemical that stimulates the central nervous system (the brain and spinal cord and their protective covering, the meninges) and the heart.

Caffeine is found in everyday beverages—such as coffee, tea, cola, and cocoa (and in some other forms of chocolate). On average, coffee contains more caffeine than any other food source. For example, 1 cup of coffee contains about twice as much caffeine as 1 cup of tea and about 3 times as much as an equivalent serving of cola. The amount of caffeine in chocolate products varies. Over-the-counter caffeine preparations contain about the same amount of caffeine per tablet as a cup of coffee.

The amount of caffeine in 1 cup of coffee —about 100 to 150 milligrams—can enhance the speed and clarity of train of thought; reduce tiredness; increase the capability to concentrate on something for a sustained period of time; provide a keener perception of sights, sounds, and other stimuli; decrease the amount of time it normally takes to react to such stimuli; and encourage greater body movement.

Drinking more than 1 cup of coffee can increase the drinker's heart rate, can affect pulse rhythm, blood vessel width, circulation, blood pressure, and frequency of urination, and can produce restlessness, nervousness, excitement, and sleeping difficulty.

One gram of caffeine, the amount contained in about 7 to 10 cups of coffee, can produce muscle tension and twitching, inability to relax, physical agitation, rambling train of thought and speech, rapid breathing,

and rapid, irregular heartbeat. In slightly higher doses, caffeine can produce symptoms of mild *delirium,* such as ringing in the ears, flashes of light in the visual field, and similar sensory effects.

For years parents warned their children not to drink coffee because it would "stunt your growth." In and of itself, neither coffee nor caffeine has any effect on growth, but drinking coffee can suppress a child's appetite, and subsequent poor nutrition can cause growth problems. Frequent ingestion of caffeine has also been linked to gastrointestinal problems and heart disease.

In addition, habitual users of caffeine—even those who start out drinking only a cup of coffee a day—tend to need more and more to achieve desired effects. Habitual use of caffeine also produces addiction (physical or mental dependence), which means that adverse effects—withdrawal symptoms—occur if the usual dosage of caffeine is decreased or terminated.

Sedatives

The barbiturates constitute a class of drugs used mostly for treating anxiety and insomnia. Two large classes exist: long-acting barbiturates, which are used to treat certain seizure disorders and high blood pressure, in addition to anxiety; and short-acting barbiturates, which are used to help induce sleep and calm nerves. A common long-acting barbiturate is phenobarbital. Common short-acting barbiturates include pentobarbital (manufactured under the brand name Nembutal and nicknamed "yellow jackets") and secobarbital (Seconal, "red devils").

Tranquilizers, hypnotics, and other sedatives have uses and effects that are similar to those of the short-acting barbiturates; they are the most common types of "sleeping pills," for example. Common tranquilizers include chlordiazepoxide (Librium), diazepam (Valium), and oxazepam (Serax). Common hypnotics include ethclorvynol (Placidyl), flurazepam (Dalmane), glutethimide (Doriden), methyprylon (Noludar), chloral hydrate (manufactured under a variety of brand names), paraldehyde (no specific brand name), and methaqualone (Quaalude, "ludes"). Another common sedative is meprobamate (Equanil, Miltown). All of these are available as pills, capsules, or both. All of them are prescription medications and can be used legally only under the supervision of a physician.

Most people who take long-acting barbiturates for medical purposes do not become addicted, but short-acting barbiturates pose a great risk of addiction. The other medications mentioned usually do not lead to addiction when used according to prescription but have a significantly higher likelihood of leading to addiction when used for nonmedical purposes.

One danger of sedatives is overdose—accidental or intentional—which usually causes *coma,* severe respiratory problems, or other serious symptoms. Death can occur. The combination of alcohol and sedatives is dangerous because of synergy: the effect of the two substances combined may be greater than the user expects or can tolerate.

Amphetamines

Amphetamines are synthetic drugs capable of powerful stimulation of the central nervous system. Types of amphetamines include amphetamine (Benzedrine), dextroamphetamine (Dexedrine), methamphetamine (Methedrine, Desoxyn). Other drugs that stimulate the central nervous system and are much like the amphetamines include phenmetrazine (Preludin), diethylpropion (Tenuate, Tepanil), and methylphenidate (Ritalin). Each is available through a physician's prescription in either tablets or capsules. Amphetamines are often called uppers, ups, or dexies (for Dexedrine). Crystalline methoamphetamine can be manufactured illegally and is often called crystal. Crystalline methamphetamine (or any other dissolved amphetamine) injected into a vein is often called speed. Crystal amphetamine can also be ground into a fine powder and sniffed ("snorted").

Effects are variable, but people who take moderate doses of amphetamines by mouth generally experience euphoria (an intense sense of happiness) and alertness, a decreased appetite, and less of a sense of boredom about fatiguing activities. Side effects of a moderate dose sometimes include anxiety, irritability, insomnia, and talkativeness.

When amphetamine is injected, the effects are typically far more intense than when it is taken orally or sniffed. In addition to feeling euphoria, a user feels physically and mentally stronger and may lose all desire for sleep and food. Immediately following injection ("shooting up"), a user feels a "flash" or "rush" of pleasure. Many users report increased pleasure during sexual activity.

The danger of becoming addicted to amphetamines is comparable to that for sedatives, except that dependence tends to be more psychological than physical. The chances of addiction are highly increased when the route of administration is injection.

At a threshold that is different for every habitual user, odd behavior appears. A user may show signs of hyperactivity (see *hyperactivity and attention problems)* and signs of anxiety such as tooth-grinding (see *bruxism).* Many users, for example, eventually perceive imaginary insects or worms crawling on or under their skin. Even though they understand that such perceptions originate because of drug use, most scratch and pick at their bodies. Many speed addicts are intensely suspicious of other people or even paranoid (see *psychotic disorders).* Eventually signs and symptoms of full-blown psychosis—such as hallucinations—may appear.

To counteract these unpleasant effects, many speed addicts turn to other drugs, which can aggravate the psychotic symptoms of amphetamine influence. They are often taken to avoid the unpleasant effects of withdrawal, which include great depression, fatigue, sleep problems, and a craving for more amphetamines.

The life-style of a speed addict is often altered dramatically by drug addiction—perhaps more so than by any other type of drug dependence. Most addicts inject speed every few hours for several days, remaining awake continuously and eating nothing or very little. This period is called a run, and it typically ends only when the drug supply is depleted or the user becomes too paranoid or disorganized to continue shooting it. A few hours after stopping, the user "crashes"— falls into a deep sleep that lasts for 12 hours, a day, or even longer. Sleeping is usually followed by intense feelings of hunger and sluggishness, signs of withdrawal. A new run eradicates these unpleasant symptoms. Amphetamine addicts commonly suffer from malnutrition and insomnia. Some former addicts continue to suffer from mild memory-loss problems.

Opioid Prescription Pain Relievers

The opioids (formerly and incorrectly known as narcotics) are a group of drugs used in medical practice largely to relieve pain and thereby induce sleep. They can produce physical dependence quickly.

The following medications, which are legal when prescribed by a physician for medical uses, contain opioids: codeine (found most commonly in cough syrups, even over-the-counter ones), oxycodone (Percodan, Percocet), dihydrocodeine (Synaglos-DC and other brand names), hydromorphone (Dilaudid), meperidine (Demerol, Pethadol, and other brand names), anileridine (Leritine), and oxymorphone (Numorphan). Two other substances sometimes used to achieve opioidlike effects are propoxyphene (Darvon, Dolene, and other brand names) and pentazocine (Talwin).

Taken according to directions, these preparations do not, in general, pose a risk of addiction. Taken in excess or for an excessive period of time, they can cause physical dependence.

The Strongest Opioids

The opioids, which produce stupor and relieve pain, are either natural derivatives from the opium plant or synthetic imitations. Opium is the dried juice of the unripe seed pod of the opium poppy. The chemical morphine is the chief ingredient in opium; each portion of opium is about 10 percent morphine. Heroin is a derivative of morphine made by heating it with acetic acid, a main ingredient in vinegar.

The opioids mainly affect the central nervous system, but they also affect many other body systems. They can be taken orally, inhaled, or injected under the skin or into a vein. Most nonmedical users take opioids intravenously, a practice popularly called mainlining. Almost immediately after injection, sometimes called a fix, the user feels a warm flush on the skin and an intense, pleasurable sensation in the lower abdomen. This feeling is called a rush, kick, or thrill, and achieving it is the goal of many opium users. During a high from opiod injection, a user is likely to feel elated. Sometimes, however, opioids produce a feeling of sadness; and often they produce effects—mostly negative ones—other than mood changes. The first time a person uses opioids for nonmedical purposes, for example, he or she is likely to feel nauseated and may vomit. In addition, use of opioids often produces apathy and slows mind and body functioning. Other common effects include drowsiness and constricted pupils; slurred speech; attention, memory, and judgment problems; constipation; and a reduced ability to feel physical pain. Other unwanted side effects include anxiety and shortness of breath. An opioid overdose can lead to *coma, shock,* pinpoint-

sized pupils, breathing difficulty, and sometimes death, although an antidote is available to counteract the overdose before permanent damage results.

Far more likely than overdose is the possibility that an opioid user—especially a mainliner—will become addicted; opioids are among the most addicting substances known. A person who uses small amounts of codeine in cough syrup for medical purposes has a slim chance of developing an addiction. A person who mainlines heroin, on the other hand, is at high risk of becoming a lifelong addict. For an addict physical dependence on opioids is almost always intense, with tolerance high and the withdrawal syndrome severe.

Tolerance typically becomes so great, in fact, that the addict eventually needs to take daily doses of an opioid just to feel normal. The goal of an addict eventually changes from achieving a rush to avoiding withdrawal symptoms. The physical symptoms of withdrawal tend to resemble those of severe influenza. They can include eye secretions, nose secretions, dilation of pupils, sweating, *diarrhea,* yawning, mild elevation of blood pressure, rapid heartbeat, tremors, *fever,* muscle and joint pain, weakness, nausea, *vomiting,* and insomnia. Behavioral and psychological symptoms can include restlessness, irritability, depression, and an overwhelming craving for more opioids. Withdrawal also causes an addict to develop skin roughness that makes him or her resemble a plucked turkey, a characteristic that spawned the expression "cold turkey." In addition, an addict undergoing withdrawal may make bizarre kicking motions, an unusual symptom from which the expression "kicking the habit" may have originated. For some addicts, withdrawal symptoms are so extreme that death results.

If withdrawal from opioids is successfully withstood, an addict is likely to suffer from anxiety, depression, and a strong craving for opioids. These feelings can persist for months or even years, often becoming most strong during periods of *stress.* Statistics show that most ex-opioid addicts eventually become dependent on alcohol or some other substance. The overwhelming number of addicts, however, never become ex-addicts; it is estimated that about half a million heroin addicts live in the United States.

Long-term opioid addiction seems to do no unusually severe physical damage, although some addicts complain of lessened sexual interest, restriction of night vision, *constipation,* profuse sweating, *headache,* joint pain, hiccups, nervousness, runny nose, difficulty urinating, and persistent melancholy. Women addicts sometimes suffer from menstrual problems and childbirth complications. Babies of women addicts are often physically dependent on opioids themselves and suffer withdrawal symptoms immediately after birth.

Addicts who have access to needed doses of opioids are virtually indistinguishable from nonaddicts. Many addicts, however, commit criminal acts to support their expensive habit. It is these acts, more than their behavior during intoxication, that have given opioid addicts their bad reputation.

The Inhalants

A number of substances can be inhaled to produce a feeling of drunkenness similar to that achieved by drinking intoxicating amounts of alcohol.

In some communities nitrous oxide (laughing gas) is as easily obtainable as many other illicit drugs. Much more accessible to children are common household solvents. The most talked-about household inhalant is probably hobby glue (also called airplane glue). Other household substances that produce similar effects when inhaled include gasoline, paint thinner, lacquer, enamel, varnish, varnish remover, cigarette lighter fluid, charcoal lighter fluid, nail polish, nail polish remover, and spot remover and other dry-cleaning substances.

Inhalants are particularly attractive to children because they are often more accessible than other substances.

They are also more likely to be taken in overdose than are most other substances. Breathing in nothing but inhalant fumes for a sufficient period of time (sometimes just seconds) can produce *asphyxia,* a condition in which the supply of oxygen to the brain is seriously threatened. Death can result. Permanent damage to body systems is also possible. For example, gasoline and some other solvents contain a chemical called benzene, which, when inhaled habitually, can produce aplastic anemia (see *anemia, aplastic)* and *leukemia,* two life-threatening blood disorders. Heart problems, such as *arrythmias,* are particularly common complications of substance inhalation. Smoking while inhaling a flammable substance often leads to severe *burns* and, sometimes, death.

Less drastic effects of an overdose of inhalants can include lack of coordination, restlessness, excitement, confusion, disorientation, *headache,* blurred vision, *dizziness,* ringing or buzzing in the ears, nausea, loss of appetite, weakness, and even *delirium* and *coma.*

A person who regularly uses inhalants may experience persistent muscle weakness, fatigue, lack of interest in usual activities, nausea, *vomiting, abdominal pain,* weight loss, confusion, lack of coordination, muscle tremors, itching, and problems with nerves (such as paralysis of certain nerves). Some of the short-term and long-term effects of inhaling substances are reversible; others, such as brain damage, are not.

Marijuana

Marijuana is made by drying the leaves and flowering shoots of the cannabis plant. The active ingredient in marijuana is called THC. Hashish is produced by drying the resin of cannabis flowers. It has the same properties as marijuana but is somewhat more potent. Marijuana has many nicknames, including pot, dope, weed, reefer, grass, Mary Jane, and tea. Most commonly it is crumbled into small pieces and rolled in cigarette paper; the resulting "joint," or "jay," is smoked. It can also be smoked through a bowl (a type of pipe) or inhaled through a bong (a type of water pipe). Sometimes marijuana is mixed with food, such as brownies, and ingested.

Marijuana stimulates the cardiovascular (heart and circulatory) system to produce much the same effects as *stress.* It also has a variety of effects on the central nervous system. The specific effects tend to vary widely depending on the potency and size of the dose, the situation and the manner in which the user takes it, and the user's experience and expectations. (Smoking marijuana is about 3 times as potent as swallowing it because the substance reaches the bloodstream much faster and in higher concentrations from the lungs than from the stomach.)

In general, smoking 1 marijuana cigarette (approximately 20 milligrams of THC) produces a feeling of well-being and relaxation. If the user is alone, 1 marijuana cigarette may also encourage sleep. If the user is with others, a feeling of tiredness is less likely to develop; instead, the user may get "the giggles" and laugh frequently and spontaneously. Balance and muscle strength are often somewhat decreased. The ability to perform simple physical tasks is usually unaffected, but the ability to perform complex tasks involving perception and the processing of information is likely to be impaired. One such task is driving a car. The ability of the eyes to adjust to glare also is reduced.

Other common results of smoking 1 marijuana cigarette are hunger, dry mouth and throat, and intensified perception of stimuli (such as sounds and sights). The usual sense of time is altered; minutes, for example, tend to feel like hours. Speech may be delayed or pressured; it can also be slurred. Heart rate and blood pressure are increased, and eyes become bloodshot.

If a user takes more marijuana, he or she usually has problems with short-term memory and has difficulty carrying out tasks requiring more than one step. There is sometimes difficulty distinguishing between the immediate past and future and the present. Depersonalization, a feeling of unreality and of separation from self (see *neuroses)* is common.

At doses higher than those needed to produce these effects, a marijuana user may feel markedly confused and disorganized with even greater feelings of altered time and depersonalization. Some users develop severe anxiety or panic, largely due to a feeling that the marijuana high will never end. Another common result is paranoia—feelings that, for example, others are plotting against him or her or that others detect and are critical of the effects of marijuana. Hallucinations and delusions may develop.

Long-term use of marijuana is linked with *asthma,* persistent *bronchitis, laryngitis, cough, hoarseness,* and other breathing-system problems. (The same is true of cigarette smoking.) Smoking marijuana produces more carcinogens (cancer-causing agents) than smoking tobacco does. Using marijuana in any form puts a strain on the heart and can cause complications for people with heart problems. Scientific studies show that some long-term marijuana users become apathetic and dull, have difficulty with judgment, concentration, and memory, and lose interest in self-care. Research remains in progress on how smoking marijuana affects the mind and body years after using it and also on how the chemicals sprayed on large cannabis crops affect human health.

Whether or not marijuana produces tolerance or dependence is a subject for debate. In general it appears that taking low doses of marijuana—even daily—does not produce significant tolerance or dependence. Taking higher doses still does not produce dependence but may produce tolerance to some but not all of the drug's effects. It is clear that abrupt withdrawal from long-term use of high doses of marijuana can produce irritability, restlessness, nervousness, decreased appetite, weight loss, sleeping difficulty, tremors, increased body temperature, and chills.

Cocaine

Cocaine, a stimulant of the central nervous system, is found in the leaves of the South American coca plant. Once used as an anesthetic, especially on mucous membranes, it has largely been replaced by comparable synthetics. Cocaine cannot be obtained legally in any nonmedical product. Illegally, cocaine is sold as a white, crystalline powder resembling saccharin. It is usually diluted by the seller with about 50 percent talcum powder or dried milk. Most commonly, the crystals are arranged into narrow "lines," sometimes with a razor blade, and are sniffed up the nose with the aid of a straw, a rolled-up piece of paper or currency, an empty pen barrel, a special glass or plastic tube, or a tiny spoon. Habitual users sometimes dissolve the crystals in ether or a similar substance, heat the mixture in a special pipe, and inhale the vapors. This technique, which runs the risk of an explosion, is called freebasing. Some habitual users inject cocaine into veins, alone or with heroin (a combination called a speedball). Nicknames for cocaine include coke, snow, gold dust, nose candy, lady, and toot. Snorting cocaine is often called "doing lines" or "tooting."

In comparable doses the effects of cocaine are virtually identical to those of amphetamines. Use of cocaine produces a strong feeling of well-being and confidence and a heightened perception of sensory stimuli. It may also produce physical agitation, talkativeness, and pressured speech. Physical effects can include rapid heartbeat, dilation of pupils, elevated blood pressure, sweating or chills, nausea, *vomiting,* loss of appetite, and insomnia.

A person severely intoxicated with cocaine may experience confusion, incoherence of speech, anxiety, *headache,* and heart palpitations. Freebasing or injecting large amounts of cocaine can produce paranoia, a feeling that one's thoughts are more profound than they are, an increased interest in sexual activity, ringing in the ears, a sensation of hearing one's name called, and a feeling that insects or other creatures are crawling on or in the skin. Curiosity may be increased, and a user may demonstrate strange behavior, such as sorting things into piles. Repetitious, involuntary movements of the mouth and tongue sometimes occur. After using very large doses, a user may experience *fainting, chest pain, seizures, arrythmias,* or respiratory failure.

An hour or so after the effects of cocaine lessen, a user may experience anxiety, trembling, irritability, fatigue, or *depression.* These effects, which usually subside after 24 hours, constitute a "crashing" syndrome akin to that experienced following withdrawal from amphetamines. While cocaine does not seem to produce physical dependence, it does seem to produce tolerance and a significant psychological dependence; habitual use of cocaine almost invariably leads to an extremely strong craving for the substance and depression in its absence, particularly among intravenous users and freebasers. Most professionals, therefore, consider cocaine to be an addicting drug.

Crack

Crack is highly purified cocaine, which is usually smoked directly from a pipe or by first sprinkling it in a marijuana cigarette. Crack produces a temporary feeling of well-being or happiness and is said to heighten sexual enjoyment. Since crack is relatively inexpensive, it tends to be widely distributed and easily purchased. As a result, many young people begin using it without having any knowledge or warning of its potency and great dangers. Of particular importance is the fact that when crack is smoked, it reaches the brain almost immediately in highly concentrated, often damaging levels.

Because crack, which is addictive, takes effect so swiftly, users often try to maintain their high by taking repeated "hits" of the drug. This tendency to overuse the drug can have harmful physical and psychological effects for a user of any age. Among the more common problems resulting from using crack are *arrhythmias* of the heart (irregular, often accelerated beats), *seizures,* and other central nervous system problems, and even sudden death as a result of a heart attack or cardiac arrest.

PCP

PCP (phencyclidine) is a synthetic drug developed in the 1950s for use as an anesthetic for animals. Its common nicknames include angel dust, peace pill, crystal, hog, and horse tranquilizer. Drug peddlers frequently misrepresent PCP as a psychedelic such as LSD (see below) or as THC, which is actually the active ingredient in marijuana. Illegally, PCP powder is smoked, snorted, swallowed, or taken intravenously. PCP smokers often sprinkle the substance on tobacco, marijuana, or parsley.

PCP can depress or stimulate the central nervous system, and it sometimes has hallucinogenic effects. A small dose of PCP produces a feeling of intoxication, a feeling of happiness (or sometimes, mood swings from happiness to anxiety), balance and coordination problems, speech articulation problems, jerking movements of the eyes, a feeling of weightlessness, a sense of slowed time, and numbness of the hands and feet. It can also produce sweating, muscular rigidity, a blank stare, disorganized thinking, drowsiness, apathy, bizarre or violent behavior, paranoia, and distortions in physical self-perception. A larger dose of PCP intensifies all these effects and can lead to stupor, *coma,* convulsions, or death.

The number of deaths associated with the use of PCP is higher than comparable figures for most other substances. Some of the deaths are caused directly by PCP; most, however, are caused by accidents or *suicide* associated with the behavioral effects of the drug. Although tolerance seems to develop to the drug, dependence and withdrawal do not seem to exist. Long-term users of large doses of PCP often report persistent problems with short-term memory, speech, and thinking, which sometimes last up to a year after cessation of use of the drug. Personality problems, such as persistent nervousness or social withdrawal, also seem to be common after long-term, heavy use of PCP. Users report both short-term and long-term psychotic symptoms.

LSD, Mescaline, and Other Psychedelics

The psychedelics differ from other substances in their ability to produce altered mental states that are rarely experienced otherwise, except sometimes during dreams or intense religious experiences. The most commonly known psychedelic is LSD (lysergic acid diethylamide), a synthetic, commonly referred to as acid; taking LSD is commonly called dropping acid. Lesser known synthetic psychedelics include peyote, natural mescaline, certain types of mushrooms, large amounts of the spice nutmeg, and seeds from the morning glory plant.

Psychedelics are usually taken orally. Peyote, for example, comes in "buttons," which are cut from the top of certain cactus plants, dried, and eaten. Most psychedelics, including LSD, are available in their illegal form in sugar cubes or some similar food or on tiny paper tabs popularly called blotter acid; each tab is called a hit. Illegal manufacturers of blotter acid sometimes mark their paper with identifying cartoons, and the hits are nicknamed accordingly. A user might say, for example, that he or she "does monkeys" or "does Mickey Mouses."

With most psychedelics, a miniscule amount can produce a bizarre under-the-influence experience called a trip. A psychedelic-induced trip usually lasts longer than trips caused by other substances. Normal functioning is significantly impaired during a trip because psychedelics are capable of inducing dramatic psychological changes. It is common for a user to believe that a psychedelic has given him or her profound insight into basic truths about existence.

Sensory stimuli may seem more intense. Hallucinations, illusions, and distortions in perception (such as visual distortions in how other people look) are also common. Unlike people with psychotic disorders or those under the influence of certain other substances, the psychedelic user realizes that these phenomena are drug-induced. All these perceptions and feelings are accompanied by a strong sense of being fully awake and alert, often with abnormally acute hearing and attention to detail. Physical symptoms of psychedelic intoxication can include dilated pupils, rapid heartbeat, heart palpitations, sweating, blurred vision, tremors, and lack of coordination.

Psychological effects can be elating and thrilling, producing a "good trip." In certain situations, however, they can be terrifying. Instead of enjoying the experience, a psychedelic user may become fearful that it will never end, that he or she will never regain normality, and that sanity is permanently lost. Anxiety or depression may set in. A user may become paranoid and may begin to behave irrationally. Virtually all the deaths associated with use of psychedelics are related to irrational behavior during a "bad trip."

Once a trip is over, feelings of being under the influence of a psychedelic may persist for a day or two. Also, depression may begin. It is relatively common for users to feel anxious or guilty after a trip and to wonder whether they have caused themselves irreparable harm from using a psychedelic. Some users complain that they experience periodic "flashbacks," brief reexperiences of some aspect of a trip, months or even years later. The existence of such experiences is controversial; evidence does exist, however, that psychedelics can draw out psychotic disorders in people who are prone to developing them.

Tolerance to psychedelics builds up quickly, but no evidence exists that they are physically or psychologically addicting or that they can induce withdrawal symptoms. In fact, statistics show that most people eventually abandon the use of psychedelics because of one or more bad trips; because the thrill of good trips has worn off; because predicting when a bad trip will occur is difficult; or because the range of social and occupational functioning possible under the influence of a psychedelic is so small.

CAUSE

Today most children experiment with at least one substance before entering high school, and many substances are readily available to elementary-school-aged children who want to try them. Explanations emphasizing the emptiness of modern-day life, the pressures on today's children to achieve, and similar theories may be significant but tend to be vague. Some of the more specific reasons follow.

Availability of Alcohol, Medications, and Other Substances

With the exception of marijuana, the majority of substances commonly used by children are available at home or obtainable in stores. When one child gets hold of a substance, he or she is likely to share it with friends. Thus, a child whose parents do not keep any alcohol in the home nonetheless may be exposed to the substance by a peer who obtains liquor from his or her own parents' supply.

Misinformation About Substances

The average child is given similar information and warnings about all substances, namely, "Do not smoke; do not drink; do not smoke pot; do not take drugs. These things will harm your health." A child who consumes a modest amount of alcohol, who feels happy, and who suffers no hangover is likely to believe that trying other substances can produce similarly nonthreatening results. In addition, other substance users often provide potential experimenters with misinformation.

Mixed Signals About Certain Substances

Ironically, the child who is told not to take any substances often observes adults using caffeine, alcohol, or tobacco. The message is that these substances are "okay" and that taking them before adulthood is not a good idea only because it is considered too early by authority figures.

Misinformation About Addiction

Many children are still taught that if addiction to a substance does develop, the habit can be kicked. Unfortunately, this message stems largely from well-intended campaigns to induce cigarette smokers to quit. For motivational purposes, such campaigns sometimes give the false impression that quitting is merely a matter of will and that most people who try to stop are successful. In fact, most of the people who want to break a physical addiction cannot. For these people, substance addiction is not a thrill-seeking phase but a lifelong struggle. Children also tend to believe mistakenly that certain substances are not addicting because they do not induce physical dependence. A common misconception, for example, is that marijuana and cocaine are not addicting. While this statement is, in limited contexts, true, a significant number of users of both substances find themselves psychologically hooked after frequent use.

A Desire to Be Grown Up

When adults socialize by, for example, drinking alcohol, it is reasonable for a child to feel that drinking alcohol is an adult thing to do.

The Influence of Peers

Peer influence is an obvious reason that some children use substances. What is less obvious is why children choose friends who are inclined to use substances, how the influence of peers counteracts the influence of parents and other adult role models, and fundamentally, who influenced the peers in the first place. The answers to these questions probably vary greatly from child to child.

Parental Preferences

Many parents send out the message to their children, spoken or unspoken, that if they have to use an intoxicating substance, it should be alcohol.

Fearlessness

On the whole, children have a stronger sense of immortality than adults do. They may feel, for example, that they will not be hurt while driving under the influence of alcohol simply because "I'm too young to die" or "It can't happen to me."

Lack of More Satisfying Alternatives

Often children turn to alcohol or drugs because they cannot think of alternative activities that will make them happy. They temporarily "escape from reality" with drugs rather than find pleasure through activities such as sports, music, and hobbies.

DIAGNOSIS, TREATMENT, AND PREVENTION

All parents should assume the task of developing their own understanding of drug and alcohol abuse and making it known to their child before they are forced to consider the issue. Following are a few suggestions about what parents should do.

Educate themselves about the various drugs and other substances described above.

Evaluate their own use. Parents should take account of the substances they use, how old they were when they began using them, why they chose to use them, why they continue using them, and related issues. This process can help parents understand the processes their child will inevitably undergo.

Evaluate their child's environment. This process includes consideration of the availability of substances in the home, in peers' homes, in schools, and in the community at large. Children themselves can provide some information, and school and community officials may be able to provide other details. Such an evaluation can help show parents what type of temptations face their child.

Educate children about the consequences of using drugs, alcohol, and other substances. Such efforts should be made in the home, in schools, with the physician, and in the community at large.

Keep potentially dangerous substances in the home unavailable to children. When necessary, substances should be stored under lock and key.

Encourage a child's social, intellectual, and special strengths in an attempt to lessen the temptation of substance use.

Develop guidelines for the child. Parents may, for example, decide that all substances should be off limits to a child until he or she reaches a certain age. In adopting such a standard, however, parents should realize that their guidelines may be difficult for a child to follow and may simply induce a child to experiment secretly. On the other hand, few parents decide to allow their children to experiment with any substance as long as experimentation is done at home. In general, it is wise to choose guidelines that fall somewhere between these extremes.

Discuss guidelines with a child. The goal of such a discussion should be to clearly lay out the rules and the consequences that will ensue if they are not followed. The punishments to be given if rules are broken should be reasonable and appropriate; they should not, for example, be so stringent that they anger a child enough to make him or her break the rules again. A child should be given an opportunity to voice his or her own opinion, which may or may not result in guideline modification. Parents should emphasize—and believe—that the topic is always open to discussion and that the rules are always subject to modification.

If parents suspect their child of using some substance, the best way to confirm or nullify the suspicion is to ask their child. In talking with a child, parents should use an approach consistent with their ultimate goal: if their primary goal is to punish their child as long as any positive evidence exists, they may choose to be confrontational; if their primary goal is to obtain as much information as possible, they should speak with their child without threats or immediate condemnation.

Be prepared to seek help. A child who seems to be in imminent danger of developing severe physical or mental problems needs immediate medical help, regardless of the cause. If any doubt exists about whether to consult a physician, it is best to err on the side of safety. A telephone call to a physician, hospital emergency room, or poison information center may reveal the proper course of action. In addition, most areas have a 24-hour telephone hotline staffed by people trained to recognize the signs and symptoms of substance problems. Parents should keep the phone number with other emergency listings and should never hesitate to call either for an emergency or for general information. The United States Department of Health and Human Services drug hotline, 800-662-HELP, is available for anyone requiring information or guidance.

Many approaches exist for dealing with a single episode of severe intoxication. Some of these approaches follow.

Taking a child to a hospital to obtain treatment for an overdose. In addition to administering antidotes, which are available for opiates, psychedelics, sedatives, and certain other substances, emergency techniques used by hospital personnel to deal with overdose include emptying out the user's stomach, administering needed fluids and salts or blood transfusions, and providing oxygen. Other techniques vary and depend largely on signs and symptoms.

Reassuring a child who is on a bad trip. The best way to keep a bad trip from becoming worse is to reassure the user that he or she is not losing sanity, is merely intoxicated, and is among people who will take care of him or her until the trip ends.

Letting a child "sleep it off" or waiting to deal with the episode until it is over. This approach may be the best way to handle alcohol, barbiturate, and marijuana intoxication when parents are sure that their child is not in imminent physical or mental danger. Attempting to confront a child about his or her use of substances while the child is still intoxicated is futile.

Never allowing any intoxicated child or any child who is likely to become intoxicated in the near future to drive a car or operate any other complex piece of machinery. Parents should also stress to their child that he or she should never ride in a vehicle driven by an intoxicated person, even if finding another source of transportation is extremely inconvenient or expensive.

Approaches for dealing with substance dependence:

Placing a child in a residential treatment center. In recent years the popularity of treating children in such centers has declined somewhat because many experts now believe substance abuse among children can be treated as effectively on an outpatient basis.

Seeking outpatient treatment. Many programs exist to help substance addicts. Because the mechanism of addiction is not precisely understood, each of these programs tends to stress a particular theory. Some programs try to enhance a person's will and motivation to quit using a substance; others address the biochemical basis of addiction and use other substances to wean an addict from the primary one. Programs designed to help cigarette smokers quit, for example, often emphasize psychological factors. Some programs for heroin addicts assume that opioid addiction is lifelong; the policy of such programs is to prescribe daily doses of methadone to supply the addict legally. Treatment methods are constantly changing; for the most up-to-date information, parents should contact a physician, medical society, or local drug abuse program.

EAR, FOREIGN OBJECTS IN

EMERGENCY ACTION

If an object—visible or not—is tightly lodged in a child's ear canal, do not try to remove it. Seek medical attention immediately.

DESCRIPTION

Young children are usually curious and explore their environments in many ways. They tend to put things in their mouths, ears, and other body openings. Most often these objects are small and round, such as seeds, beans, nuts, dried corn, raisins, beads, marbles, or small wads of paper. Most of the time these objects are too large to be pushed very far into the ear. Occasionally, however, they become lodged and cause irritation and discomfort. If an object is deeply lodged in the canal, temporary hearing loss or eardrum damage may result. With prompt removal, however, foreign objects rarely cause permanent damage to a child's ears or hearing.

SIGNS AND SYMPTOMS

A child may experience pain and itching when a foreign object is lodged in the ear canal, and may scratch or rub the affected ear. Irritation of the external ear canal may cause a draining ear.

DIAGNOSIS

If a parent cannot see the object or the object is tightly lodged into the ear, a physician should be consulted for identification and removal of the object.

COMPLICATIONS

A foreign object can block the ear canal and temporarily impair a child's hearing. A foreign object can also interfere with a child's hearing by packing down ear wax, which prevents vibration of the eardrum.

A bacterial infection may develop if the walls of the ear canal are injured by a foreign object. A foul-smelling discharge usually indicates the presence of an infection.

If an object is pushed far enough into the canal, it can puncture the eardrum. A punctured eardrum usually heals spontaneously in two to three months or can be corrected surgically. If a punctured eardrum does not heal spontaneously or with treatment, permanent hearing loss can result.

TREATMENT

If a foreign object is visible and not lodged in the ear canal, it can often be removed at home. Care must be used, however, so that the object is not pushed farther into the ear during a removal attempt. Never attempt to remove a foreign object by sticking something into the child's ear.

Grasping the top of the outer ear and pulling up and out straightens the ear canal. To remove a foreign object, a child should point the affected ear toward the floor while the canal is straightened. When the child shakes his or her head in this position, the object usually falls out.

If an object does not fall out of the ear canal after headshaking, it may come out when the ear is flushed with a gentle stream of water from a spigot. This also may remove packed ear wax. However, if the object is identified as paper or a piece of dried food, the ear should not be flushed, because the object will swell and make removal more difficult. If an object cannot be removed at home, or if signs of an infection are present, a physician should be consulted. Special instruments and small suction apparatus may be used to remove the object and avoid forcing it through the eardrum or dislocating one of the small bones in the ear. If an infection is present, an antibiotic ear drop is prescribed.

When more specialized procedures are needed to remove an object from the ear canal, or if the canal is injured, a physician usually refers a child to an otologist (ear specialist) or an otolaryngologist (ear, nose, and throat specialist). An otologist may administer a general anesthetic during object removal. Since a general anesthetic relaxes the whole body, a child will not move during the removal procedure, which lessens the chances of further ear damage. Medication is prescribed to reduce swelling. If an infection is present, antibiotic ear drops are prescribed. Surgery is rarely required to remove a foreign object.

Hearing lost by canal blockage usually returns almost immediately once the foreign object is removed. Eardrum damage requires 2 to 3 months for complete healing.

PREVENTION

Small objects should be kept out of a child's reach. Toddlers should be taught not to put anything in their ears. (See Chapter 4, "Accident Prevention," for childproofing information.)

EAR ABNORMALITIES, CONGENITAL

DESCRIPTION

A congenital ear abnormality exists when an infant is born with an ear that deviates in any way from the structure or position of a normal ear (see Fig. 21, below). The external, middle, or inner ear—or more than one part—can be affected in one or both ears.

By the time a fetus has been developing for 4½ months, the inner ear has reached its adult size and shape. The middle and external ears, in contrast, keep growing at least until puberty. As a result, any structural abnormalities of the inner ear develop during the first half of prenatal development. Ear abnormalities can be associated with disorders of the skull or face.

Inner ear abnormalities are rare, but generally serious. External and middle ear abnormalities are relatively common, but are usually minor.

Congenital ear abnormalities can be cosmetic—ears may stick out, for example—or impair function—the inner ear may be malformed, for example, leading to *hearing loss*—or both. Severity of both appearance and functional problems varies greatly.

Functional problems resulting from congenital ear abnormalities range from slight hearing loss to total hearing loss. There are two types of hearing loss, depending on which part of the ear is affected. Conductive hearing loss occurs when the external or middle ear is malformed. Sensorineural hearing loss—usually more severe—occurs when the inner ear is malformed, rarely associated with a malfunction of part of the central nervous system. In a few cases, mixed hearing loss—a combination of conductive and sensorineural—occurs. Sensorineural hearing loss is rarer than conductive hearing loss.

Abnormalities of the external or middle ear can be corrected surgically; those of the inner ear cannot.

CAUSE

Congenital abnormalities of the ear arise during the first 4½ months—usually the

FIG. 21. EXTERNAL, MIDDLE, AND INNER EAR

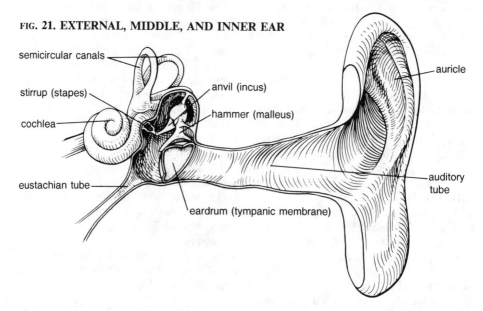

semicircular canals
stirrup (stapes)
cochlea
eustachian tube
anvil (incus)
hammer (malleus)
auricle
auditory tube
eardrum (tympanic membrane)

first 3 months—of development of the fetus. Some abnormalities are genetic, and some of those are inherited. About half of all cases of sensorineural hearing loss are caused by inherited structural defects (see *genetic disorders*).

Less commonly, cases of sensorineural hearing loss result from injury—such as a lack of oxygen during the birth process—or disease. If the mother contracts a viral infection during the first 3 to 4½ months of pregnancy, her baby may suffer from a congenital ear abnormality. Viral infections that have been linked to congenital deafness include toxoplasmosis (see *parasitic infection*), *syphilis, German measles,* cytomegaloviral infection (see *heart disease, congenital*), *measles, mumps, chicken pox,* and *genital herpes.*

Some congenital ear abnormalities are believed to result from exposure to radiation or drugs during pregnancy. For instance, use of an anticancer drug called methotrexate during the first 3 months of pregnancy can lead to ear malformations. Some congenital ear abnormalities occur spontaneously, for no apparent reason.

SIGNS AND SYMPTOMS

The most visible congenital ear abnormalities are those of the external ear. A common minor deformity is excess flaps of skin (called skin tags or pedicles). Another is protruding ears (called lop ear). Some children have excessively small external ears, which are set closer to the face and lower than normal. Some children have no external ear at all.

Although signs and symptoms of middle and inner ear abnormalities are not readily observable, parents are likely to notice functional problems. An infant who is born with a moderate to profound hearing loss shows subtle signs of the loss during the first few months of life. The baby may show little awareness of sounds and may not be responsive to vocal comforting or alerting. Unlike other babies, those with hearing problems do not search for the source of a sound with their eyes.

DIAGNOSIS

An infant who has an obvious structural deformity of the ear is referred by a pediatrician to an otolaryngologist (ear, nose, and throat specialist) for examination. Otolaryngologists are skilled in pinpointing structural and functional ear abnormalities.

Because many ear abnormalities are not visible, parents should not dismiss any suspicions they may have about their child's hearing, but should consult a physician.

Diagnosis and treatment of hearing problems is often accomplished by a team, consisting of an otolaryngologist, an audiologist (who conducts hearing tests and makes evaluations), and a speech and language therapist.

In addition to taking medical histories of both the pregnancy and the family, the team may perform a combination of tests in making a diagnosis. Tests include audiometry (assessment of hearing) and tympanometry (measurement of flexibility of the eardrum).

COMPLICATIONS

Congenital ear abnormalities that result in hearing loss can cause *language disorders, speech problems, learning problems,* and delays in achieving any developmental milestones—such as toilet training—in which language plays a part.

Deformities that affect physical appearance can contribute to emotional distress if the deformity is severe enough to make a child feel different from peers. Individual and family counseling can be very helpful.

TREATMENT

Methods of treatment depend on the nature of a structural or functional problem. Children with cosmetic problems and conductive hearing loss can often benefit from surgery; those with either type of hearing loss may be helped by hearing aids. In general, sensorineural hearing loss is more severe and no treatment is available apart from amplifiers.

Early intervention is of great importance in alleviating emotional and learning problems.

PREVENTION

Congenital ear abnormalities that are genetic cannot be prevented. Parents of a child with such a condition may seek genetic counseling to learn their risk of having other children similarly affected (see discussion of genetic counseling in *genetic disorders*). Deformities caused by exposure to drugs, radiation, or certain infectious agents during the first several months of pregnancy can be prevented by avoiding such exposure.

Any woman whose blood test shows that she is not immune to *German measles, mea-*

sles, or *mumps* should be vaccinated at least three months before she plans to become pregnant.

EARACHE AND EAR INFECTIONS

DESCRIPTION AND CAUSE

An ear infection can affect the external, middle, or inner ear (see Fig. 21, p. 320). The external ear consists of the auricle (the visible part of the ear) and the ear canal, which is lined by skin and which ends at the eardrum. The middle ear is a small chamber between the eardrum and inner ear. During upper respiratory infections, such as *colds,* fluid and mucus may accumulate in the middle ear, especially if the eustachian tube is not functioning. Normally, the eustachian tube (a short, narrow passage) drains fluid and mucus from the middle ear into the nasal passages. The eustachian tube also regulates the balance between the pressure of the atmosphere and that of the middle ear. The inner ear is made up of a system of connected cavities called a labyrinth.

The inner ear reaches its adult size and shape by the end of the first half of prenatal development. As a result, any structural abnormalities of the inner ear develop before birth. The external ear, by contrast, keeps growing at least until a child reaches puberty.

Eustachian tubes are small during early childhood. As a result, young children are susceptible to infections of the middle ear. Next to colds, middle ear infections are the most common early childhood disease: they affect half of all children by their first birthday and 90 percent by age 6.

Ear infections vary in severity. All ear infections—even mild ones—require prompt treatment by a physician to prevent complications.

Because infections of the external, middle, and inner ear are quite different, each type is described separately.

External Ear Infections

Of the two parts of the external ear, the auricle (the visible, outer ear) is least commonly infected. One infection that can develop is cellulitis, a bacterial infection in which the skin of the auricle becomes red and hardened. *Eczema* (an allergic skin eruption) may also develop on the auricle.

The external ear canal is more susceptible to infection. Normally, the canal is protected by ear wax. If this coating of wax gets too wet, moisture makes it soft, swollen, and eventually cracked. If the coating becomes too dry, the skin of the ear canal becomes flaky, like dandruff. Either of these conditions can make the ear canal more vulnerable to infection.

The mildest type of ear infection—and the most common infection of the external ear—is external otitis (also known as swimmer's ear, because inflammation of the ear canal often develops after a large amount of water gets in the ear). It can also result from cleaning of the ear canal or from hair spray (or other irritants) in the ear canal. Children with certain *allergies* are susceptible to swimmer's ear. The infection takes the form of a rash on the skin of the ear canal. It is usually caused by bacteria or a fungus.

The skin of the outer third of the ear canal can become scratched or injured by insertion of a foreign object (such as a cotton swab), and *boils* (bacterial skin infections resembling oversized pimples) can develop.

Middle Ear Infections

Inflammation of the middle ear is called otitis media. It occurs most often among infants 6 to 24 months old and children 4 to 6 years old. It occurs less frequently after 8 years of age. Middle ear infections, which can be caused by viruses or bacteria, are the most common cause of earache. The severity and intensity of an earache is often affected by chewing, swallowing, or nose blowing, which affect pressure inside the middle ear.

Middle ear infections, like *colds,* occur most frequently during the fall and winter when people congregate indoors with windows closed, and bacteria and viruses can be circulated by hot-air heating.

Otitis media usually develops when the eustachian tube becomes swollen and subsequently blocked, usually as a result of upper respiratory infections (such as colds), some *allergies,* or enlarged or infected adenoids (see *tonsillitis and adenoiditis*). The eustachian tubes can also sometimes become irritated and blocked if babies are given milk to drink while lying flat on their backs. Obstruction of the eustachian tube results in a buildup of pressure and fluid in the middle ear.

Otitis media has many variations: it can be acute (occurring once or infrequently) or chronic (persistent or recurring frequently). Many children experience a minor, temporary *hearing loss* during and just after an earache. When the cause of an earache is properly treated, permanent damage rarely occurs. Other causes of earache are ear wax plugs; a foreign object in the external ear canal; irritation of the external canal (caused primarily by scratching or use of bobby pins or paper clips to clear the ears); and sometimes a *sore throat* or disease in the mouth. In addition, earache can be caused by high altitudes.

Otitis media can be resolved simply—it sometimes clears up spontaneously—or it can cause complications. It is an unpredictable problem: it can last for 10 days or 10 weeks.

The eardrum can become inflamed. Viral or bacterial infections can cause a number of related problems: buildup of pressure and fluid in the middle ear, eardrum inflammation, and sometimes eardrum perforation. Fluid then leaks out of the middle ear, alleviating the pressure and pain. Perforation of the eardrum is usually self-healing in cases of acute otitis media. In cases of chronic otitis media, the eardrum is permanently perforated, resulting in hearing loss. The eardrum can usually be repaired with surgery.

A bone located behind the ear, called the mastoid, can also become infected and inflamed. Such an inflammation is called mastoiditis; it can develop if a middle ear inflammation is not treated properly.

Inner Ear Infections

Infections of the inner ear are less common than those of the external or middle ear but are usually more serious.

The most common inner ear infection is viral labyrinthitis. A virus causes inflammation of the membranous labyrinth of the inner ear. If a virus—such as the rubella virus—is contracted by a woman during the first third or half of pregnancy, it may invade and cause inflammation in a fetus's developing inner ear (see *German measles*). This prenatal inflammation usually causes permanent hearing loss for the baby.

If a virus—such as from *measles, mumps, influenza, chicken pox,* or infectious mononucleosis (see *mononucleosis, infections*)—invades the inner ear during childhood, subsequent inflammation causes sudden, profound, but usually temporary hearing loss (10 to 14 days), often in one ear.

In contrast to viral labyrinthitis, bacterial labyrinthitis develops during early childhood when either an acute middle ear infection or mastoiditis spreads to the inner ear. Bacterial labyrinthitis usually results in complete hearing loss. Bacterial labyrinthitis also can be caused by *meningitis* (inflammation of the meninges, the protective covering of the brain and spinal cord).

SIGNS AND SYMPTOMS
External Ear

The initial symptom of external otitis, known as swimmer's ear, is itching, followed by earache, tenderness, redness in the ear canal, swelling, and smelly discharge of pus. Even after treatment is begun, pain, itching, and discomfort can persist for four or five days.

Middle Ear

Some children with otitis media seem healthy. Signs and symptoms that can occur include pulling at the ears, severe earache, fussiness or irritability, and prolonged crying. A child may also experience *diarrhea,* nausea, *vomiting,* loss of appetite, and weakness or lethargy. A feeling of pressure or fullness within the ear is common, as is a noise, such as ringing or buzzing, in the ears (called tinnitus). If the eardrum ruptures, a discharge containing blood, then pus, drains from the middle ear. A slight, temporary hearing loss results.

If a child with otitis media develops *fever,* chills, *headache, dizziness,* (a sensation of revolving movement, called vertigo), and sudden, profound *hearing loss,* complications are likely to arise. Inflammation of the eardrum is often signaled by sudden persistent pain and *fever.*

Inner Ear

Viral labyrinthitis that develops during childhood is marked by tinnitus and vertigo. These problems are rare. Bacterial labyrinthitis is signaled by *fever,* severe vertigo, by an involuntary rapid movement of the eyeball, and by a discharge of pus from the ear. Pain, tenderness, swelling, and redness of the mastoid—or an abscess behind the ear—also indicate that bacterial labyrinthitis has developed.

DIAGNOSIS

Parents who suspect ear infection or earache should seek medical advice within 24 hours of beginning of pain. All ear infections are diagnosed by a physician, who examines the ears, usually with the aid of an otoscope (a lighted instrument for examining the interior of the ears). The physician also inspects a child's nose, throat, and mastoid bones. If a child has otitis media, physical examination may reveal a bulging eardrum, a sign of increased air pressure or the presence of fluid in the middle ear. The eardrum may also be red and immobile.

In addition the physician checks the child's medical history for a record of frequent ear infections and asks if the child has recently experienced or is currently experiencing nasal discharge or obstruction, *sore throat,* upper respiratory infection, *allergies, headache,* or *fever.*

COMPLICATIONS
External Ear
Swelling caused by swimmer's ear can lead to temporary hearing loss.
Middle Ear
When otitis media causes fluid buildup in the middle ear, a minor hearing problem can result. Should fluid remain in the middle ear (if, for example, otitis media is untreated or if a eustachian tube remains blocked), it can become a breeding ground for bacteria and lead to a secondary infection. A serious hearing problem then can result because accumulated, pus-filled fluid blocks the conduction of sound. In most cases, however, *hearing loss* is temporary and reversible.

The major complications of otitis media—particularly if it is untreated—are hearing loss, labyrinthitis, mastoiditis, and perforation of an eardrum. If the infection is allowed to spread, more serious diseases could develop, such as *meningitis, encephalitis* (brain inflammation), or brain abscess.
Inner Ear
Bacterial labyrinthitis may be associated with serious complications involving the brain and central nervous system, including meningitis, and can be fatal.

TREATMENT
Treatment of ear infections depends upon the location and cause of the infection.
External Ear
Treatment of an external ear infection can sometimes be supplemented at home with fever-reducing and pain-relieving medications. The physician should be consulted for specific recommendations. (See the discussion of nonprescription medications in Chapter 7, "Caring for the Sick Child at Home.") The physician first cleans pus and debris from the ear canal, then prescribes ear drops containing antibiotics and cortisone. The ear drops clear up the infection and reduce swelling. A physician may also place a fabric wick in the ear canal; this device carries medicated drops to all affected areas. If the child's symptoms do not clear up promptly, it is important that antibiotics be given for the prescribed period (usually 10 days) to ensure elimination of the bacteria.

The most important part of treatment of external ear infections is keeping the ear canal dry. No water, shampoo, hair spray, or bubble bath should get into the affected ear until the infection is completely eliminated. When a child with swimmer's ear is bathing or showering, cotton should be placed in the affected ear and covered with petroleum jelly to make a watertight seal.

If cellulitis is spreading, a child is treated with antibiotics. Mastoiditis is also treated with antibiotics, which can prevent the spread of a mastoid infection to the inner ear.
Middle Ear
Home treatment of otitis media may be supplemented by fever-reducing and pain-relieving medications. The physician should be consulted for specific recommendations. (See the discussion of nonprescription medications in Chapter 7, "Caring for the Sick Child at Home.")

Treatment of otitis media by a physician focuses on opening the blocked eustachian tube and allowing air to reach the middle ear. Medicated nose drops can help unblock the eustachian tubes by reducing swelling. Antibiotics may be prescribed to relieve symptoms (especially inflammation of the eardrum), combat infection, and lessen chances of serious complications. After the first few days of antibiotic treatment, a physician may prescribe breathing exercises that a child can do at home to help replace air in the middle ear.

For severe or recurrent cases of otitis media, a physician may recommend making a small incision in the eardrum (myringotomy), then placing a tube through it. This procedure allows fluid to drain from the middle ear and prevents reaccumulation of fluid and reinfection of the middle ear. A permanently perforated eardrum caused by chronic otitis media can often be repaired surgically through a procedure called tympanoplasty.
Inner Ear
Treatment of bacterial labyrinthitis involves antibiotic therapy and drainage of accumulated fluid from the inner ear. Surgery is sometimes necessary to remove infected tissue. If mastoiditis has caused bacterial

labyrinthitis, a mastoidectomy (removal of the mastoid bone) may be performed.

PREVENTION

If a child has suffered an ear infection and resulting hearing impairment in one ear, special care must be taken by parents and child alike to ensure continued good health in the unaffected ear.

Children susceptible to swimmer's ear can have their ears cleaned by a physician before the start of the swimming season, and parents can administer medicated ear drops at the end of the day to keep the ear canals clean and dry.

Most cases of otitis media cannot be prevented. However, infants should not be allowed to drink milk while lying flat on their backs. Nor should a child or his or her parents insert anything into the child's ear for any purpose. Parents should ask their child's pediatrician about how ear wax should be softened and removed.

In addition, children who have a history of middle ear infections developing after colds may receive antibiotics to prevent bacterial middle ear infections.

German measles infection of the inner ear during the first several months of prenatal development can be prevented. Any woman whose blood test shows that she is not immune to German measles (rubella) should be vaccinated at least 3 months before she plans to become pregnant.

To prevent ear pain due to high altitudes, older children can relieve pressure by chewing gum or swallowing repeatedly. Infants can accomplish the same thing by nursing or drinking fluids. For children with congestion due to colds, pediatricians can prescribe decongestants prior to a trip by air.

EATING DISORDERS

DESCRIPTION

Most disturbances in eating behavior among infants, children, and adolescents fall into five categories: anorexia nervosa, bulimia, pica, rumination, and overeating.

Anorexia nervosa

Anorexia nervosa is a serious eating disorder involving persistent denial of any appetite for food; it is not a loss or decrease of appetite. The majority of affected individuals are adolescent females, many of whom have just reached puberty. From 4 to 10 percent of individuals with anorexia nervosa are male.

Typically, as anorexia nervosa develops, affected individuals begin to use enormous will power to refrain from eating even when they are very hungry, in a kind of self-imposed starvation. Weight loss follows.

As the disorder is developing, concerned parents who notice their child's progressive weight loss may try to persuade him or her to eat. To pacify parents, the child may pretend to eat or may actually eat, then induce *vomiting*. If the disorder becomes chronic (persistent or recurring regularly), adolescents with anorexia nervosa occasionally may give in to hunger pangs and binge on food. Then they will often force themselves to vomit secretly or they will use a diuretic, laxative, or enema, so that they retain few calories.

Eventually the mere thought of eating food becomes repulsive and can trigger nausea. An affected individual's body changes so much from starvation and severe weight loss that eating ultimately becomes physically, not just psychologically, repellent. The stomach becomes smaller, and emptying of it is delayed; hunger pangs cease.

The number of cases of reported anorexia nervosa has increased in the last 2 decades. Currently, as many as 1 million individuals in the United States are affected by anorexia nervosa or associated eating disorders.

The duration and severity of anorexia nervosa vary. For many, anorexia nervosa is a serious long-term disorder. The outlook for adolescents with anorexia nervosa is better when the disorder occurs in early rather than late teen years, is diagnosed and treated early, and is of short duration. The outlook is worse for individuals who vomit regularly or use laxatives. A few individuals with severe anorexia nervosa "diet" to the point of death.

Bulimia

Bulimia is a serious long-term eating disorder involving secretive cycles of rapid overeating (binging) and self-induced *vomiting* (or some other form of purging, such as using laxatives, diuretics, or enemas). Some bulimics fast after gorging. A binge usually ends only when abdominal pain becomes severe, when sleep overpowers the urge to eat, or when the binge is interrupted. After binging and purging, a person with bulimia typically feels extreme self-hatred and self-disgust. With severe depression, a person with bulimia may have suicidal thoughts (see *suicide*).

Because the habit is hidden, incidence is unknown. More than 95 percent of bulimics are female, and the typical bulimic is single, white, and from a middle- or upper-class family. Bulimics can be as young as 10 or as old as 50, although most are from 13 to 31 years old.

Repeated vomiting eventually causes the body to become less accurate at detecting when hunger is satisfied; as a result, bulimics always feel as if they are hungry.

Bulimic people realize that their eating behavior is abnormal; nonetheless, usually at least once a day, they feel compelled to eat uncontrollably. (Some bulimics consume over a week's worth of food in one binge.) In addition, bulimics tend not to have good control over their impulses in areas other than eating. Alcoholism and drug addiction (see *drug and alcohol abuse*) can be associated with bulimia.

Bulimics tend to be achievement-oriented perfectionists, who seek approval from others and are eager to please. They also tend to fear intimacy and avoid making adult decisions about their own sexuality by isolating themselves with their habit and telling themselves that no one would want to develop a close relationship with an overeater.

Bulimics are usually of normal weight or slightly overweight. A person with bulimia tends to try various crash diets, and frequent weight fluctuations of 5 or 10 pounds are common. Over the long term, the binge-and-purge cycle usually causes neither weight gain nor loss. Unlike anorexia nervosa, bulimia often goes unnoticed for years.

Bulimics commonly resist treatment, denying that anything is wrong, either physically or psychologically. The outlook for control, if not cure, of bulimia is better if the disorder is diagnosed and treated early, before a habit becomes an obsession. Chronic, severe bulimia can result in death.

Anorexia nervosa and bulimia are not always separate problems. An affected person may alternate between a binge-purge pattern and refusal of food. This combination can be even more difficult to treat than either bulimia or anorexia nervosa.

Pica

Pica involves the persistent searching for and eating of nonfood items. The disorder is somewhat rare but occurs most often among children under the age of 3. Children may be more likely to practice pica if affected by *mental retardation* or *psychosis*. Infants who have the disorder tend to eat hair, wool cloth, paper, string, paint chips, putty, or plaster, while toddlers tend to eat animal feces, charcoal, ashes, sand, pebbles, leaves, or bugs. Affected children are indiscriminate in the nonnutritious substances that they eat.

It is normal for young children to taste objects and put things into their mouths, but if a child actually eats nonnutritious objects, a physician should be consulted without delay, because almost all nonfood items, if eaten, can cause medical problems. Pica is usually outgrown during the ages of 3 to 5 but can persist into late childhood or, in rare cases, into adulthood.

Rumination

Rumination is a persistent and self-induced regurgitation of partially-digested food. The disorder is rare but, when present, occurs among infants from the ages of 3 to 12 months. Before or during regurgitation the infant usually makes sucking or chewing movements, and may put fingers in the mouth, perhaps to stimulate regurgitation. Characteristically, an infant sits with the back arched, the abdominal muscles stiff, and the head held back. After regurgitation some of the brought-up food is spit or dribbled out of the mouth, and some is chewed and swallowed again. An infant who ruminates does not retch and is not nauseated or physically ill.

Some cases of rumination are resolved spontaneously; others require treatment. Rumination can lead to serious nutrition problems and can be fatal if not controlled.

Overeating

A child who habitually eats an excessive amount of food for emotional rather than physical reasons suffers from an eating disorder. No clear line exists between normal eating and overeating nor between normal weight and overweight; eating patterns and body proportions that are regarded as normal vary from culture to culture and family to family. However, if a child becomes obese (according to medical standards) as a result of his or her eating habits, the child is considered an overeater.

Feeding Problems of Infants and Toddlers

Feeding problems of infants and toddlers occur when a child's eating habits change and the parents begin to worry about the quantity and type of foods that a child will eat. No harm is generally caused by the child's eating habits, but parents should consult their child's pediatrician for advice on nutrition (see Chapter 2, "Promoting Physical Health," for advice on nutrition).

CAUSE
Anorexia Nervosa

The causes of anorexia nervosa are unknown. Why some dieting teenagers carry reduction of food (or caloric) intake to the point of anorexia nervosa while others stop at a reasonable weight has not yet been determined. It is known, however, that anorexia nervosa often begins as an ordinary voluntary diet. Dieting may be provoked by an inappropriate desire to be as thin as fashion models, or even by someone's harmless comment about "chubby cheeks." Adolescents who have anorexia nervosa—or who have the potential to develop the disorder— equate slimness with attractiveness (and eventually equate near-emaciation with attractiveness). They have an intense fear of becoming obese. In actuality, when beginning their diets, only some adolescents who eventually develop anorexia nervosa are above normal weight. These teenagers voluntarily and methodically begin to deny themselves food in an effort to become thinner and, eventually, to maintain a very low weight. Thinness becomes an obsession, and self-starvation a way of gaining control over their bodies and their parents. This passive defiance eventually gains parents' attention, and concern over the illness begins to dominate family life.

Most adolescents with anorexia nervosa come from middle- or upper-class, white, close-knit families. (Anorexia nervosa has been called a "disorder of affluence.") Teenagers with anorexia nervosa usually have loving but overprotective, overinvolved, inflexible, and controlling parents. The families of affected teenagers appear to be harmonious because negative feelings are rarely expressed; thus conflicts are suppressed rather than resolved. The appearance of happiness is essential to these families, even at the unwitting cost of honest personal relationships within the family.

Most clinicians believe that many individuals with anorexia nervosa either have failed to develop a sense of self or are afraid to grow up. Typically, they are still "good" children, causing few problems for their parents. They are eager to please, seek approval from others, and tend to become perfectionists. Yet in interviews they reveal that they feel inadequate and helpless, having little control over their lives, except for their power over their own food intake and how that affects their bodies.

Some individuals with anorexia nervosa have a fear of becoming a sexual person. Affected teenagers who were overprotected by parents may not feel able to cope with more independent, complicated social situations, including pressure to experiment with sexual activity.

Bulimia

The cause of bulimia is unknown; medical experts theorize that environmental, genetic, family, and sociocultural factors contribute to the disorder. Bulimia is associated with conflicting obsessions with food and thinness. What causes an obsession with food is not certain, although such an obsession may be a response to *stress.* Food, like alcohol, can reduce tension; it is often soothing to someone feeling inadequate, empty, or lonely.

An obsession with thinness usually stems from an attempt to become model-thin and, therefore, "attractive" and—above all—accepted. Bulimics insist that they feel fat and need to lose weight, even when they are of normal weight. Apparently bulimics never feel thin enough. This obsession with thinness leads to an obsession with dieting (which is in conflict with an obsession with food).

Pica

By definition, pica is a behavioral problem; however, the exact cause is unknown. Some medical experts believe that children with pica suffer from a habit disorder or from *stress,* particularly family-related stress, such as that resulting from instability or disruption of the family and neglect or inadequate supervision of the child. Another theory is that pica is a simple extension of the tendency of many infants to put things into their mouths. A few medical experts believe that some affected children crave certain nonfood substances because they lack minerals (such as iron or zinc) and other vital nutrients in their diets.

Rumination

Problems with an infant's interactions with parents during feeding can contribute to rumination. Mealtimes can become a battle of wills. Sometimes problems that cause rumination are quite simple. Parents may feed babies too frequently or may try to give too much food at one sitting, resulting in *vomiting*. To compound the problem, parents may be unsure or confused about how to take care of babies, including when, how, what, and how much to feed them at each stage of development.

Another contributing factor may be insufficient stimulation of an infant (for example, inadequate talking to and playing with the baby) resulting from the lack of a close bond between parents and baby. For instance, an infant who was ill at birth and who required a prolonged hospital stay may not have been able to develop close attachments to his or her parents.

Some cases of rumination are believed to be related to family stress. Numerous losses and persistent stresses in a parent's life can affect his or her ability to deal with children.

Overeating

Many emotional factors can cause a child to overeat. The habit of overeating usually starts early in life when parents consistently try to comfort their fretful baby by feeding him or her even though the baby may be seeking another kind of nourishment, such as cuddling. The baby comes to expect and want to be fed whenever feelings of frustration arise. Parents reinforce this habit when they offer a child cookies when the child scrapes a knee, for example. These children may eventually equate food with love.

Throughout childhood and usually into adulthood, food can continue to be a form of emotional comfort. Friendship problems, family problems, *stress, depression,* low self-esteem, and poor self-image may influence a child's eating patterns. Food may be used to overcome internal distress.

In addition, children may become overeaters as a way of pleasing parents who encourage them to eat large meals because of the mistaken belief that children need to eat heartily to be healthy.

SIGNS AND SYMPTOMS

Anorexia nervosa

The first noticeable indication of anorexia nervosa may be bizarre eating habits, such as cutting food into extremely small pieces, crumbling food, or refusing to eat with the family. An affected adolescent may also hoard food or make odd food choices (such as eating only one or two foods). Even though individuals with anorexia nervosa

will not eat, they are obsessed with food; this obsession may be expressed by a desire to prepare food for others.

The next sign of anorexia nervosa is marked weight loss. Teenagers with anorexia nervosa may become adept at hiding their bodies by avoiding undressing in front of others and by wearing bulky or baggy clothing. They may also hide weights on their bodies or may drink large quantities of water if they know that they are going to be weighed. They may deny looking too thin (for, in their eyes, they are never thin enough) and try to avoid the issue of eating. They are likely to refuse to admit that they are ill, and resist suggestions that they gain weight, maintain a normal weight, or receive treatment. In contrast, they may insist that they do not intend to lose weight, that they have no idea why it is happening, and that they actually wish to gain weight. When alone, they may exercise excessively, appearing to use nervous energy. As a teenage girl's body fat decreases, her menstrual periods are likely to stop, although she may hide the fact (see *menstrual irregularities*).

In general, teenagers with anorexia nervosa may seem immature and have unrealistic or distorted perceptions of themselves and their bodies, criticizing themselves as being less smart, capable, likable, and attractive than they really are. They may demonstrate compulsive behavior, such as frequent handwashing. Eventually they may become depressed.

As body weight dwindles and individuals with anorexia nervosa become more and more malnourished, they will suffer from increasing weakness, fatigue, lightheadedness, *constipation,* low blood pressure, and a slowed heart beat. A susceptibility to hypothermia (abnormally low body temperature) may develop, and extremities may feel numb. Swelling may appear as a result of fluid retention. Scalp hair will start to thin; fine hair will grow on other parts of the body; skin will dry out and may appear yellowish; muscle tone will diminish. A girl's breasts, hips, and pubic hair will cease to develop or grow; sexual desire will be lacking.

Bulimia

Bulimics usually look and act normal except that they may seem depressed at times. Secretly they have low self-esteem, are terrified of weight gain, and are afraid of losing control over themselves or their environment. Persistent *vomiting* can cause dental erosion or salivary-gland swelling. Parents may notice behavioral changes or food refusals. Family members, friends, or dentists may notice dental erosion or salivary-gland swelling, caused by repeated vomiting.

Pica
A child with pica may feel nauseated or may vomit after eating nonfood objects.

Rumination
An infant who ruminates appears emaciated and may be irritable from hunger between episodes of regurgitation.

Overeating
The most obvious symptom of overeating is obesity.

DIAGNOSIS

Anorexia nervosa
Unfortunately, anorexia often progresses to a point of serious emaciation before parents seek medical intervention. A physician diagnoses anorexia nervosa by evaluating physical appearance, weight in proportion to height and bone structure, proportion of body fat, physical development, and the individual's distorted sense of body or appetite. The physician will record the individual's history of illnesses and of growth, noting especially the weight at earlier points in life and when the individual stopped growing taller. The physician may also make a note of any family or individual history of psychiatric disorders. In addition, a physician may order laboratory tests (to measure electrolytes, serum protein, thyroid function), and a full physical and psychological evaluation.

Bulimia
Parents may suspect that their child is bulimic if a dentist notices abnormal and severe tooth decay. If no one makes such an observation, bulimia may go unnoticed until the bulimic's muscle function begins to be impaired, partially as a result of a loss of potassium from excessive vomiting.

Any individual who seems obsessed with dieting and losing weight should be seen by a physician. Bulimics are likely to refuse to admit that a problem exists, however, and may resist seeking help because they are ashamed to admit that they binge and purge regularly.

A physician who suspects bulimia usually checks the patient's teeth, throat, stomach, and muscles (including the heart), and looks for signs of dehydration (a condition characterized by cool, dry, pale skin, dry tongue, thirst, listlessness, rapid pulse, and sunken eyes). A physician also checks the patient's blood electrolytes to determine if the level of potassium is low.

Pica
Unless a child is observed eating nonfood items, pica is difficult to detect. A physician must eliminate other causes of any nausea or *vomiting* before determining that a child has pica.

Rumination
In diagnosing rumination, a physician notes an infant's habit of regurgitating and the loss of weight or failure to gain weight. However, the physician must differentiate among rumination and other disorders that can cause regurgitation, such as *pyloric stenosis, hiatus hernia, and gastroesophageal reflux, chronic kidney disease* (see *kidney failure, chronic*) and *ulcers.*

Overeating
In diagnosing overeating, a physician compares a child's weight to standard measurements and asks about his or her eating habits.

COMPLICATIONS

Anorexia nervosa
Menstrual periods of an affected girl may not resume until adequate weight is regained; even then they may appear on an irregular basis. Some girls never menstruate again.

Congestive heart failure (see *heart failure, congestive*) may also result when a person with anorexia nervosa suddenly drinks large amounts of fluid. The most serious complication is hypokalemia (abnormally low potassium concentration in the blood), which occurs in teenagers who vomit repeatedly and which can result in cardiac arrhythmia and death.

Bulimia
A bulimic's health is threatened by continual binging and purging. Common complications of bulimia include abnormal and severe erosion of tooth enamel and irritation of the throat and esophagus because of excessive stomach acid brought up by frequent *vomiting.* Pain in the chest and swelling of salivary glands may also result from repeated vomiting.

Bulimics may become dehydrated and suffer vitamin and mineral deficiencies. The menstrual cycles of bulimic women may become irregular or may cease (see *menstrual irregularities*).

Chronic overuse of laxatives can lead to rectal bleeding and other colon malfunction, and loss of potassium. Vital organs—such as the liver, kidneys, pancreas, or gallbladder—may also suffer damage.

If bulimia is serious, prolonged, and undetected, the loss of potassium could cause the bulimic's heart to stop, leading to death. In rare cases a bulimic's stomach stretches too far and ruptures, a condition which can also lead to death.

Bulimia interferes with a person's life, leaving time only to work or study, sleep, binge, and purge—not to socialize. In severe cases, work or studies may also be impaired. A bulimic is likely to encounter financial difficulty as a result of spending a great deal of money on food.

Pica

Many nonfood substances that are eaten can spread infection, damage the stomach and intestines, or be potentially poisonous. For instance, if a child with pica swallows lead paint chips, *lead poisoning* can result. In very rare cases, if hair is eaten, hairballs may form in the stomach and block the intestines.

Rumination

Severe, long-term rumination that is untreated or does not respond to treatment results in *dehydration* and *malnutrition,* followed by a loss of weight or failure to gain the weight expected for the infant's age (see *failure to thrive*). A child who ruminates is also likely to suffer developmental delays resulting from malnutrition. In some rumination cases the disorder is not controlled and eventually results in the child's death.

Overeating

Overeaters tend to eat snack and dessert foods rather than more nourishing foods and, as a result, are likely to suffer from nutritional deficiencies. Children who become obese from overeating suffer the additional burden of feeling guilty every time they eat too much. In addition, their peers may not accept them socially because of their appearance. For some children, unhappiness leads to overeating, which leads to obesity, which leads to further unhappiness, and the cycle begins again.

TREATMENT AND PREVENTION
Anorexia Nervosa

Most cases of anorexia nervosa require hospitalization, not only to ensure gradual weight gain but to remove affected teens from the cycle of the parents' pleading and the child's denial or refusal. An individual with anorexia nervosa requires both physical and psychological treatment, as the disorder will recur if all underlying causes are not confronted.

For the emaciated patient, treatment begins with nutritional rehabilitation. Many programs use positive reinforcement and behavior modification, including the withholding of privileges (use of a phone, books and magazines, writing materials, TV, use of activities room, having visitors, and visits home), which are earned as the patient gains weight. Only as a final lifesaving measure is a patient ever fed through nose or stomach tubes.

At first therapists usually talk with the teen and his or her parents separately to hear 2 or 3 perspectives about family life and the teen's illness. Eventually, however, most therapists insist upon family therapy. Family members often need to work at learning how to better communicate with each other and how to confront and resolve problems. In some cases parents need to work at reaching decisions with each other about their child.

People with anorexia nervosa are unlikely to make a lasting recovery until they decide on their own that they want to get well and stay well. Placing trust in a physician can be a crucial step in recovery.

In addition to being helped by behavior modification, teenagers with anorexia nervosa benefit from eating with companions, participating in group activities and group therapy with other patients, and talking with other patients and with the medical staff.

When a target weight has been attained and the family situation seems to have improved sufficiently, the patient may go home. Some patients require a change in living place—to live with a relative or at a boarding school—before their weight stabilizes. Weekly follow-up visits to the hospital are scheduled until both physician and therapist agree that the patient is ready for independence. Community support groups, made up of recovered and recovering teens along with a group leader, can keep the teenager from feeling isolated or ashamed. Individual or family therapy may continue on a long-term basis.

Parents can help their children become comfortable with and accepting of their bodies: their appearance, growth, and development. Food should not be equated with love or approval, but instead regarded as a pleasurable means of satisfying hunger and, more important, gaining energy, just as sleep averts exhaustion and restores energy.

Any adolescent who seems obsessed with dieting or losing weight should see a physician.

Bulimia

The first order of treatment of bulimia is to replace the potassium lost from excessive *vomiting*. If a bulimic is cooperative and the case is mild, home treatment may be sufficient to meet physical needs. Such treatment consists of eating bananas or drinking tomato or orange juice. If the affected person is not cooperative or if the case is moderate to severe, hospitalization may be required.

After a bulimic's physical health seems stable, the goals of treatment are for the patient to learn to deal with anxiety and to eat normally. Until a bulimic admits that the problem exists, however, successful treatment is virtually impossible. To control bulimia and to keep it from recurring, a bulimic needs long-term treatment to deal with the underlying causes of the disorder. Psychotherapy may be useful; it involves communication between a trained person and the bulimic and is designed to produce a response. It includes counseling, support, and education (about the dangers of bulimia and about when and how much to eat). Therapy involves reducing anxieties about thinness and food, particularly the latter.

Behavior modification is often used to treat bulimics. Other forms of treatment include exercising, learning how to relax, keeping a diary, and making contracts with oneself.

In cases where depression is severe, it may be necessary for a bulimic to receive antidepressants. Some physicians try hypnosis. Group therapy, community support groups, and self-help groups (with other bulimics and possibly parents) can keep bulimics from feeling ashamed and isolated and from falling back into their compulsive behavior.

Medical professionals widely agree that the pressure, especially upon females, to be thin contributes greatly to the growing incidence of bulimia. Parents should accept their children's appearance, growth, and development and should help their children become comfortable with themselves. Parents should also avoid equating food with love or approval; food should be regarded as a pleasurable means of satisfying hunger and gaining energy.

Pica

Elimination of underlying causes is necessary for pica to be completely cured. Cases of pica can sometimes be prevented through proper supervision of young children. If necessary, a social worker may be able to arrange for parents to have access to child care. (A pediatrician can refer parents to a social worker.)

If pica is triggered by family *stress,* it cannot be controlled if family problems persist. Medical social workers, psychologists, or psychiatrists may help ease family-related problems by offering counseling and other support services.

Pica can sometimes be controlled through behavior modification. Parents can learn to encourage their child's acceptable behavior, mostly through positive reinforcement, and to discourage unacceptable behavior by providing the child with distractions.

Rumination

Rumination can be extremely hard to control.

A child who ruminates may need to be hospitalized for treatment of *malnutrition.* For instance, an affected child must receive extra calories, particularly of protein, to initiate and sustain growth. *Dehydration* must also be treated.

An infant needs stimulation to develop physically and intellectually, as well as to learn how to interact with parents. To accomplish these goals, a physician may recommend that an infant who ruminates be involved in special infant stimulation programs and receive treatment from physical and occupational therapists. Parent-infant therapy, designed to help strengthen relationships, can be beneficial and improve the outlook for children who ruminate. In this therapy, a therapist observes a parent and baby interacting at mealtimes, identifies problems as they occur, and offers suggestions. The most successful method of treatment involves holding an infant during and after feeding and distracting him or her from regurgitating by providing close attention. Eye contact and verbal contact are important in this treatment method. The importance of creating an affectionate bond between parent and child at feeding times is emphasized.

A complete, lasting recovery from rumination is more difficult to achieve if contributing family problems persist. If necessary, a social worker may be able to arrange for parents to have access to child care, family counseling, and other social support services.

A child with rumination is likely to need long-term care. For instance, a child may benefit from speech therapy as well as from remedial instruction to improve comprehension or language skills. Early intervention may help prevent or lessen learning problems. Pediatric follow-up is important to monitor the progress of treatment.

Overeating

Medical treatment of children who overeat combines attempts to pinpoint the psychological causes of overeating and efforts to change the child's eating habits. The whole family should participate in both facets of treatment.

Dealing with the psychological influences that lead to overeating and subsequent weight problems is an important step in correcting negative eating habits. In addition, a child must learn to modify eating behavior. A physician can recommend an appropriate behavior modification program, which includes adopting new eating patterns, becoming aware of the types and quantities of food eaten, learning to eat more slowly so that the body has time to feel full, and increased activity to burn calories. If possible, parents should avoid having highly caloric foods in the house and should discourage children from frequent snacking. A reward system may give a child incentive to change eating patterns; it can involve toys, weekly allowances, special television time, or going to special events.

Motivation, patience, and determination are constant requirements for successful treatment of overeating. It is important that an affected child receive support and encouragement from family members and friends when trying to change eating patterns.

Parents can help prevent overeating by encouraging their child's good eating and exercise habits. A child's diet should be suitable to age and development, high in fiber, and well balanced.

Reliable information about eating disorders is available from either a local chapter of the National Association of Anorexia Nervosa and Associated Disorders, or its headquarters, 550 Frontage Road, Suite 2020, Northfield, IL 60093 (phone: 312-831-3438).

ECZEMA

DESCRIPTION

Eczema is a skin eruption that is characterized by redness, oozing, scaling, and thickening of the skin. It results from an allergic reaction to substances that are either swallowed (such as certain foods and medications) or come in contact with the skin (such as urine in wet diapers or poison ivy). Itching is usually present.

The predominant symptoms of eczema during infancy are redness and oozing. Thickening of the skin does not usually occur unless eczema is long-term. Scaling occurs among older children if eczema is long-lasting and the skin is dry. In addition, children tend to scratch itchy skin, causing eczema to become worse.

There are two major varieties of eczema. Each is identified by its symptoms, pattern of distribution over the body, and if known, the underlying causes. These categories are atopic dermatitis (also called infantile or atopic eczema) and contact dermatitis, divided into primary irritant and allergic contact dermatitis. Contact dermatitis, caused by external factors, usually clears up in 1 to 2 weeks with treatment. Atopic dermatitis is often more difficult to treat and may persist into adulthood.

Atopic dermatitis usually affects infants 2 to 3 months old, but sometimes it does not occur until a child is 2 or 3 years old. It is the most common type of long-term childhood eczema and affects 2 to 4 percent of children under 7 years of age. This eczema variety is often associated with other allergic conditions such as *hay fever* and *asthma*.

Atopic dermatitis first appears on an infant's cheeks as red patches. The patches eventually spread to the rest of the face, the neck, the wrists, and the hands. If atopic dermatitis persists, the rash tends to involve the skin behind the knees and in front of the elbows, the eyelids, and the backs of the hands and feet. Atopic dermatitis, like all eczema, is quite itchy, and an infant will try constantly to scratch the eruption. Rubbing his or her face against blankets or crib sides causes eczema patches to ooze and develop crusts and scales.

Most eczema found among children other than infants is contact dermatitis. Primary irritant dermatitis most often occurs in the diaper area as the skin's reaction to contact with and irritation by damp or soiled diapers.

Allergic contact dermatitis (the second type of contact dermatitis) usually develops when a child's skin comes in contact with a substance that causes an allergic reaction. Children may be particularly sensitive to certain skin preparations, shoes, clothing, and plants. This type of eczema develops at the point of contact.

With proper treatment most cases of eczema clear up in 1 or 2 weeks. However, eczema, particularly atopic dermatitis, can recur throughout childhood until it is outgrown.

CAUSE

Eczema, a noncontagious skin eruption, occurs as an allergic reaction to certain external or internal substances. The tendency to develop eczema may be inherited.

Atopic dermatitis is an inherited form of long-term eczema. It may become worse when new foods are introduced into an infant's diet, or when an infant comes in contact with inhaled allergens, such as animal dander.

Allergic contact dermatitis often appears after contact with an external substance, such as metal alloys found in inexpensive earrings. Substances found in shoe rubber, tanned leather, shoe and clothing dyes, fabric finishers, and cleaning solutions may also cause allergic contact dermatitis, as do certain skin medications and preparations such as antihistimines, anesthetics, and preservatives. All types of cosmetics can affect facial skin if a child is extremely sensitive. Sensitivity to nail polish fumes is usually indicated by eczema on the eyelids.

Primary irritant dermatitis usually occurs on skin that is constantly in contact with irritating substances. For example, detergent bubble baths, skin antiseptics, and harsh soaps when combined with scrubbing and rubbing irritate the skin and lead to an eczematous skin reaction. Inadequate cleaning, such as infrequent changing of urine-soaked or soiled diapers, can also lead to contact dermatitis. Frequent contact with saliva, either from drooling or constant licking of the lips, is the most common cause of eczema on the face.

DIAGNOSIS

Eczema can be identified by the characteristic appearance of eczema eruptions, such as redness, scaling, and thickened skin, and the presence of intense itching. A careful examination by a physician is often needed for specific diagnosis, since eczema varieties often resemble each other. An eczematous skin response may also occur in association with other skin conditions, such as scabies, or skin eruptions associated with phenylketonuria *(PKU)*. Laboratory tests and a careful medical history may be needed for positive identification.

COMPLICATIONS

Children with eczema may develop secondary bacterial or viral infections because of constant scratching. Hay fever and asthma can develop later during childhood if a child has long-term atopic dermatitis.

TREATMENT

It is almost impossible to control eczema if a child continues to scratch. Before eczema is treated, measures should be taken to reduce itching and scratching. Cool, moist compresses can help soothe itchy skin. A physician may prescribe antihistamines. A child's fingernails should be kept as short as possible.

Once itching decreases, attention can be given to the causes of eczema. Substances that cause an allergic reaction must be avoided. Hot, dry conditions and sweating (salt in sweat is irritating) should be avoided. Exposure to strong sunlight, especially during the summer months, for brief periods of time is helpful because the ultraviolet light reduces underlying inflammation of the skin.

Since eczema becomes worse if skin is dry, one of the most important treatment measures is to add moisture to affected areas and to prevent existing moisture from being removed. Harsh soaps and detergents should be avoided, and oils or moisturizers should be applied to the skin. Cool, wet dressings can be applied several times a day.

Soaking in warm water is another way to add moisture to a child's skin. After the child soaks for about 20 minutes, oil should be applied to the skin. Oil acts to "seal" moisture in the skin, and will also soften coarse skin and scales.

After moisturizing, surface corticosteroid preparations (available by prescription) can be applied to eczema patches to help reduce inflammation. Infant eczema is treated with a mild hydrocortisone ointment. Long-lasting eczema often requires more potent surface steroids (available by prescription). Bacterial infections should be treated with antibiotics prescribed by a physician.

Atopic dermatitis is best treated by eliminating substances that may cause eczema. All suspect foods and beverages should be removed from a child's diet. During infancy these foods can include cow's milk, milk products, wheat flour products, eggs, tomatoes, citrus and tropical fruits, chocolate, nuts, fish, and shellfish. Any medications started within a month of an eczema eruption should be stopped. Once eczema has cleared up, foods can be reintroduced into the diet, one at a time, at weekly intervals. If eczema reappears, the offending food then can be identified. A restricted diet should be planned by a dietician and a physician to ensure that the child receives adequate nutrition.

Primary irritant dermatitis usually clears up when the irritating substance is removed. To avoid further irritation, a child with eczema should wear smooth-textured cotton clothing. Infants should not be allowed to crawl on wool carpets. Thorough but gentle cleaning will help control primary irritant dermatitis in the diaper area. Frequent diaper changings, gentle washing of the buttocks and genital areas, and the replacing of tight-fitting plastic pants with loose-fitting pants are helpful. Application of a protective surface preparation (petroleum jelly, mild, nontalc powders, and zinc oxide ointment) after thorough cleaning often helps to prevent further eczema eruptions.

If primary irritant dermatitis is severe, a physician may prescribe a mild hydrocortisone ointment. Applied after each diaper change, hydrocortisone ointment effectively reduces inflammation.

Wearing inexpensive jewelry or the use of surface medications should be discontinued if allergic contact dermatitis appears. A child should not wear items of clothing that seem to cause eczema eruptions, particularly wool or acrylic clothing. If eczema does not disappear after these materials have been removed and appropriate treatment is given, a child should see a physician.

PREVENTION

Prevention of an initial outbreak of eczema is almost impossible unless a child's allergies are identified. Recurrent eruptions can usually be prevented once sensitivities are identified. Labels in clothes, shoes, and fabrics should be checked for processing chemicals. Allergy-causing foods should be removed from a child's diet.

EMPHYSEMA

EMERGENCY ACTION

If a child inhales or swallows a foreign object of any size, then cannot cough it up, and experiences breathing difficulty of any kind—coughing, wheezing, or inability to breathe deeply—consult a physician immediately. Emphysema can begin almost unnoticed with the smallest inhaled object, even a bit of food. The sooner foreign objects are removed, the smaller the chances of lung irritation or danger of permanent lung damage. Depending upon how difficult it is for the child to breathe without distress, do one of the following immediately: try to perform the Heimlich Maneuver yourself (see page 138); summon the local rescue squad or emergency team; or take the child to the nearest hospital emergency room for treatment.

DESCRIPTION

The term "emphysema" refers to several similar diseases of the lung, all characterized by overinflation or overexpansion of the lungs. Depending upon which disease is involved, emphysema may affect both lungs, one lung, or part of one lung (see Fig. 19, p. 182).

Two emphysema diseases particularly affect children: localized obstructive emphysema and congenital obstructive lobar emphysema. ("Lobar" refers to any one of the three lobes or segments of each lung.) In both diseases, one of the two large bronchial (breathing) tubes leading from the windpipe to the lungs is partially or completely blocked. Inhaled air becomes partially or completely trapped in the lung, causing the lung to become gradually and uncomfortably overinflated.

If not treated promptly and correctly, both forms of emphysema in children grow worse, making a child's breathing increasingly difficult and painful. Localized obstructive emphysema can occur at any age; the congenital variety is a disease of early infancy, making its appearance at any time from birth to around six months of age.

CAUSE

Localized obstructive emphysema is caused by aspirating (breathing in) a foreign object of any kind—a peanut, a button, a part of a toy or game, for example. The object often lodges in one of the smaller bronchial tubes inside the lung.

Congenital obstructive lobar emphysema is caused by a malformation of one bronchial tube, which makes it impossible for all the air already inhaled to come back out again. The particular lobe of the lung supplied by that bronchial tube slowly overexpands, causing the child discomfort and pain.

SIGNS AND SYMPTOMS

In localized obstructive emphysema, the foreign object stuck in a bronchial tube causes coughing, wheezing, or occasionally shortness of breath. A child may not recall breathing something into the throat or chest; the inhaled object may not cause any specific pain that would enable a parent to guess its location. Congenital obstructive lobar emphysema causes newborns and young infants extreme difficulty and pain in breathing. Skin that begins to turn blue from lack of oxygen is the most obvious sign.

DIAGNOSIS

Breathing difficulty and distress, wheezing, and shortness of breath provide the physician with the clearest signs of lung disease. X-ray films are used most often to determine the presence and extent of emphysema. If X rays fail to locate a malformation or a foreign object in a bronchial tube, a bronchoscope may be used. (A bronchoscope, a flexible, lighted tube, is passed down the windpipe so that the bronchial tubes may be examined and, in many cases, foreign objects removed.)

COMPLICATIONS

If left untreated, localized obstructive emphysema almost always leads, to permanent damage to part of a lung, to *pneumonia,* or to chronic emphysema. Congenital obstructive lobar emphysema can be fatal if not treated when first observed.

TREATMENT

In cases of localized obstructive emphysema, an inhaled object can be removed by bronchoscope or by surgery. In cases of congenital obstructive lobar emphysema, surgery is always required to remove the affected lobe in order to prevent further damage to the entire lung. Bronchoscopic or surgical treatment, if done promptly, is almost always successful, leaving little or no permanent impairment of breathing capability.

PREVENTION

Parents need to be watchful about the size of all materials children use as playthings. Since small edible nuts are so often accidentally inhaled, children under 5 should not be given whole nuts of any size to eat.

ENCEPHALITIS

EMERGENCY ACTION

If a child who is *vomiting* or has *diarrhea* or a *sore throat* suddenly develops a high *fever* (101° to 106° F; 38.3° to 41.1° C), extreme sleepiness or lethargy, and a stiff neck, seek medical assistance immediately.

DESCRIPTION

Encephalitis is an inflammation, usually an infection, of the brain, characterized by *headache, fever,* and sometimes lethargy and confusion.

Encephalitis can occur at any age. Although the severity of illness depends partly upon the particular cause, encephalitis usually affects infants and young children more severely than adults. Severe illness can leave long-lasting aftereffects.

Encephalitis can occur in isolated cases, localized outbreaks, or in epidemics, depending upon the particular cause and circumstances. The illness can occur at any time, but insect-carried illness often begins in summer and fall.

Encephalitis can affect the brain in sudden, damaging ways. Without warning, high *fever,* nausea, *vomiting,* stiff neck, and *seizures,* in any combination, may occur and be followed, occasionally, by paralysis, *coma,* and even death. Or encephalitis may produce only mild illness with or without fever, and it may pass so quickly that it is never known to be encephalitis. A mild case may last a few days, but severe illness with complications can go on for several weeks or more. Fewer children die of encephalitis now than in the past, but the mortality rate remains high for children who contract some particularly destructive varieties of the disease.

CAUSE

Encephalitis is usually caused by one of a wide variety of viruses, which may be divided into those causing primary encephalitis and those causing postinfectious (or postvaccinal—occurring after certain vaccinations) encephalitis.

In the case of primary encephalitis, infection of the central nervous system (brain, spinal cord, and their protective covering, the meninges) develops directly from exposure to a virus. Primary encephalitis viruses include *mumps,* herpes simplex, lymphocytic choriomeningitis, and *rabies* as well as three large groups called enteroviruses, arboviruses, and adenoviruses.

Encephalitis caused by arboviruses can be carried by rodents and birds and transmitted by biting insects, especially mosquitoes and ticks. When an insect's salivary glands are infected by the virus, the infection can be transmitted to a human being through the insect's bite. (Arbovirus-caused encephalitis cannot be transmitted from human to human.) A bite from an arbovirus-infected mosquito that produces only a mild disease may be sufficient to provide immunity against later bites with similar infection. For a child or adult who does not possess antibodies against that particular encephalitis virus, such a bite might lead to a serious case of encephalitis.

In the case of postinfectious encephalitis, inflammation of the brain or spinal cord develops as a complication of an infection that begins elsewhere in the body. Postinfectious encephalitis may occur, for example, following *measles, German measles* (rubella), *chicken pox,* or *influenza.*

Very rarely, live-virus vaccines, such as those for measles or smallpox, can cause postinfectious encephalitis.

SIGNS AND SYMPTOMS

Encephalitis is marked by a sudden moderate to high fever (101° to 106° F; 38.3° to 41.1° C), *headache,* nausea, *vomiting,* stiff neck and upper back, and *seizures.* Drowsiness, listlessness, lack of coordination, mental confusion, paralysis, lapses of consciousness, and *coma* may develop as the disease progresses.

DIAGNOSIS

Since diseases of the central nervous system frequently produce similar signs and symptoms, exact diagnosis of cause is difficult. For example, *meningitis,* an inflammation of the meninges, may be mistaken at first for encephalitis. In addition, one disease affecting the central nervous system can grow worse and lead to another; meningitis, for instance, can progress into encephalitis.

Diagnosis of encephalitis is made by a physician's examination and by testing a sample of cerebrospinal fluid, which is obtained by making a lumbar puncture (sometimes called a spinal tap). Because many viruses are extremely difficult to isolate from spinal fluid, a blood sample is taken early in the illness and then compared to one taken later. If antibody levels increase sufficiently, identification of a virus can usually be confirmed.

X-ray films of chest, spine, skull, and sinuses may aid in diagnosis. Changes in the skull, brain, and vertebral column can be detected by taking a CT (computed tomography) scan.

COMPLICATIONS

Recurrent *seizures* may affect children who have had encephalitis. *Mental retardation,* hearing and speech difficulties, paralysis, or spastic muscle movements can affect children who have recovered from severe illness. For many of these children, skilled care and treatment can produce significant improvement, even when paralysis or retardation has occurred.

TREATMENT

If a child loses consciousness or suffers a seizure, hospitalization is necessary. Since viruses are not affected by antibiotic medications, treatment is generally directed toward making a child as comfortable as possible. Specialized antiviral medications may be helpful in some cases; viral encephalitis caused by the herpes simplex virus is the only variety that now responds even partially to such treatment. Antibiotics can be effective in cases of complicated bacterial encephalitis.

Specialized hospital care may be necessary for a child who has *seizures,* experiences difficulty breathing, or cannot eat or drink. If the aftereffects of encephalitis are severe, a child may require lengthy rehabilitation when well enough to leave the hospital. Various kinds of assistance may be necessary from specialists in physical therapy, speech, nutrition, education, and counseling.

PREVENTION

Vaccines have nearly eliminated encephalitis that arises as a complication of *poliomyelitis* and *measles* and have reduced the number of cases related to *German measles* and *mumps*.

Tick-borne infection can be avoided if adults and children wear protective clothing while walking through wooded and brush-filled areas when ticks are in season—usually the spring and summer months. Mosquito repellent may be helpful. It is also a good idea to bathe children and change their clothes after exposure to tick-infested areas or animals.

ENCOPRESIS

DESCRIPTION, CAUSE, AND COMPLICATIONS

Encopresis is the passage of stool at inappropriate times and places. By definition, encopresis does not occur until sufficient attempts have been made to toilet train a child, although bowel control problems can occur before or after training has been accomplished. In general a child can be said to have encopresis when bowel control problems persist or recur regularly; one or two isolated accidents may not constitute encopresis. It is estimated that 1 percent of 5-year-old children have persistent bowel control problems. For reasons that remain unclear, most of these children are boys. About one quarter of all children with encopresis also have bladder control problems (see *bed-wetting*).

Encopresis commonly results from *constipation,* a condition in which stools are not passed out of the body at regular intervals. Normally, stool is formed in the intestines, which absorb excess liquids from waste matter. When constipation occurs, the intestines at first continue to absorb liquids, causing stool to become hard and dry. If severe constipation occurs, build-up of stool can become so great that the last portion of the intestine, the colon, is stretched well beyond its normal size. This condition can provoke the intestines to secrete instead of absorb liquids. The secreted liquids can mix with loose stool, slip past the area of severe constipation, and pass out of the body. This process is beyond the affected child's control.

Constipation sometimes results from physical factors, such as an inadequate diet. Voluntary withholding of stools can also cause constipation and subsequent encopresis. The most common cause of voluntary constipation is overzealous toilet training, which can provoke anxiety and *stress* (see *mental health*) in a child and cause him or her to resist moving bowels at an appropriate time and place. (For more information on toilet training, see Chapter 2, "Promoting Physical Health.") Other situations that can lead to emotional strain and encopresis include attending school for the first time and experiencing the birth of a sibling.

In rare cases the cause of encopresis is malformation, disease, or injury of the intestines or anus. *Hirschsprung's disease,* for example, involves a congenital (present at birth) absence of nerve cells in the lower portion of the colon, a condition that leads to persistent constipation and encopresis. In addition, certain severe intestinal diseases can lead to loss of bowel control. Finally, an injury such as a tear in the mucous membrane lining of the anus can lead to great pain during bowel movements with resulting encopresis.

The most rare form of encopresis is the deliberate emptying of bowels by a child who has a severe mental health problem, such as *psychosis.* This problem is often accompanied by bizarre behavior, such as smearing stools with the hands after elimination. Such behavior should not be confused with that of a child who has an involuntary bowel movement and then desperately tries to cover up the accident out of shame and embarrassment.

Emotional conflicts are common among children with encopresis. Friendship problems and a desire to avoid social situations may ensue, especially if a child's self-esteem is not boosted and constructive help is not available (see Chapter 3, "Promoting Mental Health"). With understanding and prompt, proper care, however, the chances are excellent that complications will not develop and that encopresis will be overcome.

DIAGNOSIS AND TREATMENT

Regardless of the underlying cause, loss of bowel control never is a child's "fault." Parents should always extend sympathy and support. Whenever a child has more than one unexplained episode, parents should seek a physician's help promptly to prevent possible emotional complications.

The diagnostic procedure always includes

a thorough physical examination, with emphasis on the gastrointestinal tract. If a physical cause of encopresis cannot be found, a physician is likely to ask for a detailed history of the child's physical and emotional health and toilet-training experience. The goal of a physician is not to place blame but to provide appropriate treatment.

Virtually all physical causes of encopresis can be successfully treated. Similarly, the consequences of inadequate toilet training can often be overcome after one or more discussion sessions involving a physician, the affected child, and the parents. Working through other trying situations can take more time, but again, the outlook is excellent. The older the child, the greater the motivation: the urge to retain the feces is eventually overwhelmed by a strong desire to control bowel movements.

PREVENTION

Some causes of *constipation* can be prevented. Proper toilet training can also help prevent encopresis (see Chapter 2, "Promoting Physical Health").

EPIGLOTTITIS

EMERGENCY ACTION

Epiglottitis can be fatal if immediate action is not taken. Call a physician, or if it would be faster, call a rescue squad and take a child to the nearest hospital emergency room immediately if the child wakes up day or night, is drooling, and exhibits any of the following symptoms: a desire to sit or be held up, with the head tilted forward, the jaw pointed out, the mouth open, and the tongue protruding; gasping for air; severe difficulty breathing; difficulty swallowing; a fever from 103° to 105° F (39.4° to 40.6° C); and a severe sore throat. These symptoms can appear very suddenly and can come after the child has had a normal and active day.

Keep calm and try to keep the child as calm as possible. A calm parent can do much to soothe the child's anxiety. DO NOT USE A TONGUE DEPRESSOR OR IN ANY WAY TRY TO LOOK DOWN THE CHILD'S THROAT OR FORCE THE CHILD TO CHANGE HEAD POSITION. These actions could instantly block the child's airway. In the car, open the windows and keep the child near the cold air; do not use the heater. Tell the child, "Breathe slowly and evenly."

DESCRIPTION

Epiglottitis, a moderately common childhood illness, is caused by the swelling of the epiglottis (the tissue covering the opening of the windpipe during swallowing). Epiglottitis occurs most often from November to March, and in children from age 2 to 12, though it may happen at any time and at any age. Typically the child seems to be well at bedtime but awakens later feeling very ill.

The swollen epiglottis blocks air flow, causing extreme breathing difficulty. Mucus lodges in the child's throat, compounding the breathing problem. The illness can be confused with *croup* or *laryngitis,* but unlike a child with either or these illnesses, a child with epiglottitis drools. Also, the child with croup or laryngitis usually has just had a cold and either has a barking cough or a hoarse voice. Epiglottitis can also be confused with *choking,* but a child choking on a foreign object cannot talk; a child with epiglottitis continues to talk, although painfully. The child with epiglottitis looks feverish and is quite anxious.

Without treatment, the illness grows worse rapidly; immediate medical attention is needed. The outlook is excellent if proper care is given swiftly.

CAUSE

Epiglottitis is caused by a bacterial infection. In three fourths of cases there is no related illness or advance warning. In the remaining cases the child has an infection of the upper breathing passages. Anxiety may add to breathing difficulties.

SIGNS AND SYMPTOMS

A previously well and active child awakens at night, drooling, and prefers to sit or be held up, with the head tilted forward, the jaw pointed out, the mouth open, and the tongue protruding. The child experiences difficulty in swallowing and breathing, gasps for air, has a high (103° to 105° F; 39.4° to 40.6° C) *fever* and severe *sore throat,* and often becomes irritable and restless. Some children eventually become pale or turn blue, and even suffer brief blackouts.

DIAGNOSIS

A physician who observes a drooling

child, sitting with head forward, mouth open, and tongue protruding, will suspect that the child has epiglottitis. It can be difficult for a physician to examine the child's throat and accurately determine if the epiglottis is swollen, since this examination itself can cause blocking of the child's airway. Often the recommended diagnostic procedure calls for an X-ray film of the child's throat to determine the location of the swelling.

COMPLICATIONS

If untreated, epiglottitis can lead to closing of the airway and, because of a lack of oxygen, bring on *coma,* convulsions, and death within hours. In fewer than 10 percent of cases, epiglottitis leads to *pneumonia,* swollen lymph nodes in the neck, pericarditis (inflammation of the membrane surrounding the heart), or pleural effusion (an escape of fluid into the chest cavity).

TREATMENT

Epiglottitis is <u>always</u> regarded as an emergency, one that cannot be treated successfully at home with any simple remedies.

Emergency room treatment usually requires that a tube be placed in the child's airway under anesthesia to allow him or her to breathe freely. An X-ray film of the child's throat is usually taken for signs that a swollen epiglottis is blocking the airway. The child receives intravenous antibiotics to fight the bacterial infection and intravenous fluids to maintain the body's fluids and to provide nutrients. A cool-mist tent can provide humidification and keep the airway tube moist. The child's heartbeat and breathing rate are monitored.

The child usually stays in the hospital for 5 to 7 days and requires antibiotics for 7 to 10 days.

PREVENTION

To prevent the child's family from developing the same bacterial infection and subsequent epiglottitis, antibiotics are recommended for family members and are prescribed by a physician.

EXPOSURE TO TEMPERATURE EXTREMES

EMERGENCY ACTION
Heat Stroke

Immediately begin treatment if a child shows signs of heat stroke, including weakness, *dizziness,* nausea, abdominal cramps, complete lack of sweating, high fever (often over 104° F; 40° C), pounding pulse, flushed skin, *delirium,* and possible unconsciousness or *coma.* Remove clothing and plunge the child into cold, but not icy, water. If no body of water is available, generously sponge the child with cold water or rub with ice wrapped in towels. Massage the arms and legs to restore circulation. Do not give any medications. Immediately begin treatment for *shock* if signs and symptoms appear, including cool, clammy, pale skin; weak, rapid pulse; thirst; dizziness or faintness; and increased breathing rate. Once temperature is lowered to 102° F (38.8° C) or below, wrap the child warmly to prevent chilling and seek medical attention immediately.

Frostbite and Hypothermia

Seek medical attention immediately if a child exposed to very cold weather shows signs of severe frostbite (freezing of external tissue) or hypothermia (internal chilling), including violent shivering, muscle weakness, numbness, incoherence, or eventual unconsciousness. Immediately begin treatment for *shock* if signs and symptoms appear. If the child is not breathing, start artificial respiration. (See p. 124.) Remove any wet clothing and, to trap as much body heat as possible, wrap the child in warm blankets with one or two other people. If the child is conscious, give warm, nonalcoholic liquids and quick-energy foods such as chocolate or raisins. Get the child to the nearest warm environment immediately.

Frostbitten areas must be rewarmed rapidly to prevent permanent tissue damage. Placing frostbitten fingers in the armpits or between the thighs will help warm them. However, if there is a chance that a frostbitten area may become frozen again, do not warm it. It is better to wrap the area well and seek immediate medical help, because refreezing can cause severe damage.

Place a child with mild frostbite (indicated by coldness and loss of color) or mild hypothermia (indicated by moderate shivering) in warm water; make sure the water remains warm. Never treat severe cases of hypothermia in this manner. To avoid chilling, be sure to dry the child thoroughly afterward. Do not use hot-water bottles or heat lamps and do not place the frozen areas near a source of high heat, such as a stove, because burning can occur easily. Once a child with mild hypothermia is warm, wrap him or her in blankets to maintain body temperature. Seek medical attention.

If possible, separate frostbitten fingers and toes with sterile gauze or any available clean cloth. Do not massage frostbitten areas; rubbing can damage the skin further. Encourage the child to bend and move frostbitten areas gently. Do not break any blisters. A mild pain-relieving medication may be helpful if severe pain is present. Seek medical attention if color and feeling do not return to frostbitten areas within 20 minutes of beginning treatment.

DESCRIPTION AND CAUSE
Heat-Related Problems

When the body is hot, the hypothalamus (a tiny part of the brain that controls internal heating and cooling mechanisms) stimulates increased blood flow and movement of water to the skin surface in an effort to release heat. If the temperature is so high that the body cannot sufficiently cool itself, a child may become ill.

Problems caused by high heat and humidity include heat fatigue, heat cramps, heat exhaustion, and heat stroke. If proper precautions are not taken, these conditions can occur even in weather that is not excessively hot or humid. Children with long-term illnesses, especially those with heart or lung difficulties, are particularly susceptible to heat-related problems.

Heat fatigue is the least severe of all heat-related problems; it develops when a child mildly overexerts and becomes dehydrated in hot and humid conditions. Symptoms include *headache,* excessive sweating, shallow breathing, poor appetite, and general weakness (see *dehydration*).

Heat cramps are muscle cramps that are caused by loss of large amounts of fluids and salts through heavy perspiration. Cramps most often occur in the legs, arms, and stomach, and frequently affect physically active children, such as runners or bicyclists, who overexert themselves during hot and humid weather. Heat cramps are indicated by painful spasms of certain voluntary muscles, heavy sweating, and cold, clammy skin.

Heat exhaustion, a more severe heat-related problem, may develop if a child severely overexerts and becomes dehydrated in very hot, very humid weather, particularly when participating in strenuous physical activities. In addition to the mild symptoms characteristic of heat fatigue, symptoms of heat exhaustion include cold, clammy skin, weak pulse, low blood pressure, temperature normal or below normal, *dizziness,* and possible *vomiting* and *fainting.*

The most severe heat-related problem is heat stroke. It occurs only in cases of extreme overexertion and dehydration in which a child's internal temperature-regulating mechanism completely shuts down. Children most susceptible to heat stroke are those who are ill, who are taking medications, or who have circulatory problems from such disorders as *diabetes* or vascular problems. Heat stroke produces the most severe heat-related signs and symptoms. These can include weakness, dizziness, nausea, muscle cramps, complete lack of sweating, high fever (often over 106° F; 41.1° C), high blood pressure, pounding pulse, flushed skin that turns ashen or purple, and possible *delirium,* unconsciousness, or *coma.*

With prompt treatment, most children recover completely from heat-related problems. If treatment for severe heat-related problems is delayed, however, children may suffer permanent brain damage.

Cold-Related Problems

When the body is cold, the hypothalamus triggers shivering in which muscles move involuntarily to generate heat. If the environmental temperature is so low that the body cannot sufficiently warm itself, a child may become ill.

Frostbite and hypothermia are caused by lengthy exposure to cold temperatures. The children most susceptible to these problems are those exposed to cold temperatures who are not dressed properly for cold weather. In addition, children who are inactive or overly tired, who have inadequate diets or little body fat, or who have medical problems that cause poor blood circulation are at risk for frostbite or hypothermia.

Frostbite occurs when the fluid between skin cells freezes and when the water inside the cells themselves moves out of the cells.

This condition most often occurs when unprotected or poorly protected skin is exposed to extreme cold. If bare skin touches very cold metal or very cold caustic substances such as gasoline, severe frostbite may occur immediately. Fingers, toes, ears, and the nose are most often affected.

Mild frostbite affects only the top layer of skin; the skin temporarily feels cold, loses color, and becomes sticky. If frostbite is severe, all three layers of skin are affected and resulting damage may destroy the cells permanently. The affected area is painful; a burning sensation usually develops. The frostbitten area eventually becomes numb and hard and turns white, yellowish-white, or mottled blue-white. In extreme cases bone may freeze and a child may become incoherent or unconscious or go into *shock*.

Whereas frostbite affects the surface of the body, hypothermia affects the body internally. It develops when the body becomes chilled internally and cannot generate enough heat to become and remain warm. This condition most often occurs in very cold weather and is aggravated by windy, wet conditions. The body temperature of a child with hypothermia drops drastically, often as much as 20° F (11.1° C); the body temperature remains below 95° F (35.0° C). Immediate action is crucial because the drastic drop in body temperature can lead to severe infection, shock, or a heart attack.

Hypothermia most often affects children who are not adequately protected from the cold, such as those who play outside for extended periods of time without enough layers of warm clothing or hikers who are caught unprepared by a severe change in the weather. Children are also susceptible to hypothermia if they play outside for more than an hour in clothes dampened by perspiration or snow and ice. Fatigue, poor nutrition, and alcohol consumption can predispose a child to developing hypothermia in cold weather.

The first sign of hypothermia is intense shivering, the involuntary action of muscles as the body attempts to generate heat. If severe hypothermia develops, numbness and muscular weakness follow shivering. Drowsiness and incoherence indicate life-threatening hypothermia.

With proper and prompt treatment, children almost always recover from cold-related problems. In severe cases, however, delayed or inadequate treatment may result in permanent complications or even death.

DIAGNOSIS
Heat-Related Danger Signals
A health professional diagnoses exposure problems according to weather conditions, the child's signs and symptoms and recent activities, the child's medical history, and the results of a physical examination.

Indications that a child is suffering from heat exposure include *headache,* excessive sweating, shallow breathing, poor appetite, and general weakness. Cramps in legs, arms and stomach may result from overexertion in hot and humid weather. If exposure is severe, weakness, *dizziness,* nausea, lack of sweating, high fever, high blood pressure, pounding pulse, ashen or purple skin, possible *delirium,* unconsciousness, or *coma* may result.

Cold-Related Danger Signals
A health professional diagnoses exposure problems according to weather conditions, a child's signs and symptoms and recent activities, the child's medical history, and the results of a physical examination. If the top layer of skin loses color and becomes sticky, it is an indication that a child is suffering from mild frostbite. If frostbite is severe, all three skin layers are affected. A burning sensation is followed by numbness; the skin hardens, turns white, yellowish-white, or mottled blue-white. A child may become incoherent or unconscious or go into shock.

If a child is suffering from hypothermia, intensive shivering is followed by numbness and muscular weakness, drowsiness, and incoherence.

COMPLICATIONS
Frostbitten skin remains permanently sensitive to cold temperatures even after it heals. In rare cases extensive frostbite may destroy all the tissue of a finger or toe and amputation may be required. A child may suffer brain damage because of severe heat stroke. Long-term effects of brain damage may include developmental delays and *mental retardation.*

TREATMENT
In cases of heat fatigue, heat cramps, and heat exhaustion, children should move out of the sun and into cooler surroundings immediately. Use of fans or air conditioners is helpful. A cool-water sponge bath or cool shower or bath can cool a child's skin and lower body temperature. Fluids and salts must be given to replace those lost through

heavy sweating. When heat-related problems are mild, children should drink water, lemonade, or juice. Children older than 3 who suffer heat cramps or perspire very heavily should drink 1 or 2 glasses of water or juice in 1 hour's time. If a child vomits, however, no more salted fluids should be given. Rest is extremely important. Children should not resume vigorous physical activities for 1 to 2 days, even if feeling completely well.

In addition to replacing fluids and salts, parents should treat heat cramps by placing warm, moist compresses and firm but gentle pressure on the involved muscles. Cramps should not be kneaded out, because this action may make them worse.

Heat stroke and most problems caused by cold temperatures require emergency medical care (see Emergency Action, above).

PREVENTION

With proper precautions children can avoid problems caused by exposure to temperature extremes. During hot days children should drink plenty of fluids. They should avoid long-term exposure to the sun or high temperatures and should not participate in strenuous physical activities during very hot, humid weather. Frequent cool baths or showers can help keep the body comfortable. Loose-fitting cotton clothes allow air to reach a child's skin. If even mild symptoms of a heat-related problem appear, such as *headache* or mild weakness, children should get out of the sun, drink plenty of fluids, and reduce activity for at least a few hours.

Cold-related problems can also be avoided. Layering is the most effective way to dress for protection against the cold. A child should wear an absorbent cotton layer next to the skin, followed by a heavier cotton layer. Wool or down outer layers are best; if the weather is wet, a waterproof jacket or coat can keep a child dry. Two pairs of socks, one cotton and one wool, and an insulated pair of boots can keep feet warm and dry. Mittens, a scarf, and a hat are essential for conserving body heat. For activities such as skiing a child should protect the face with a scarf or face mask.

In addition, on particularly cold days children should eat well and perhaps add extra carbohydrates and fats to ensure an adequate calorie supply. Overexertion should be avoided in extreme cold because it makes the heart work very hard and because excessive breathing of cold air can prevent internal warming. At the first sign of chilling or shivering, a child should go indoors to warm up.

EYE INJURIES

EMERGENCY ACTION

A child should be taken immediately to an emergency room if severe eye pain is present or an eye injury (such as a cut or a puncture) has occurred. Severe injuries of the eye and eyelid often require some type of surgery.

If chemical substances come in contact with the eye, immediate emergency action is necessary to prevent severe burning and possible blindness. Immediately flush the eye thoroughly with running water for at least 15 minutes to remove as much of the harmful substance as possible, protecting the other eye from the substance being washed out. Call a physician immediately or take the child to an emergency room.

If a child's eye is hurt by an explosive substance, such as a firecracker, a penetrating injury may occur. Seek medical help immediately. Do not attempt to wash out the eye.

DESCRIPTION

Eye injuries can be serious; about one third of all children's blindness is caused by eye injury. Injuries may involve several parts of the eye and are usually quite painful (see Fig. 23, p. 362).

The most common cause of pain in a child's eye is the presence of foreign matter such as sand or dust. When a child blinks, foreign matter is pressed against the eyeball, causing pain and tearing. If the conjunctiva (mucous membrane) covering the sclera (white of the eye) and the eyelid are scratched, blood may accumulate on the surface of the eye. Foreign matter can also become imbedded in the eyeball. Holes or notches may appear in the iris (colored part of the eye) if the eyeball is penetrated.

The cornea (the surface of the transparent membrane covering the eyeball) can also be damaged by foreign matter, or can be burned by ultraviolet light. When the cornea is damaged, a child's eye is usually painful and very sensitive to light. As a result, the child squints or closes the eye in bright light.

Severe cuts or punctures of the eyeball are

always serious, and even small wounds can be dangerous. Injuries may involve the cornea, the sclera, the retina (rear portion of the eye, which receives light rays), or other membranes of the eye. Occasionally the retina may become detached, and serious eye problems such as hemorrhaging, infection, and *blindness* may result.

A child's eyes can also be seriously injured through contact with chemical or explosive substances. Severe pain, swelling, and blurred vision usually result.

Eye injuries can also damage a child's eyelid. Cuts on the eyelid may involve the eyelid margin, the openings to the tear ducts, or the tear canals themselves. If nerves of an eyelid are damaged, its upper fold may disappear and the eyelid may droop. The eyelid usually swells and turns black, though this does not always indicate a serious eye injury.

When a child's eye is struck with force or by a heavy object, the bones of the eye socket can be fractured or chipped. The injured eyelid turns black and swells, and a child may not be able to raise or lower it. Sensitivity of the eye may decrease, and vision may be affected. Blunt blows to the eye may also cause bleeding inside the eye or tearing of tissues (for example, the iris or retina) in the eye.

With immediate medical treatment, many eye injuries heal successfully, without permanent loss of vision.

CAUSE

Eye injuries occur in many ways. A piece of foreign matter in the eye or under the eyelid can scratch the eye or become embedded. Sharp objects such as sticks, tools, darts, arrows, and fishhooks can puncture the eye or eyelid. The eye and the eye socket bones can be damaged by forceful blows. Burns occur when the eye comes in contact with explosive or chemical substances such as battery acid, cleaning agents, or the explosives in firecrackers. The eye can also be burned if overexposed to ultraviolet light from the sun or a sunlamp.

SIGNS AND SYMPTOMS

Obvious signs of eye injury are blood in the eyeball and changes in the shape of the iris or the pupil. Eye pain is usually present, and vision may be blurred. A serious eye injury may exist, however, even if no symptoms are present.

DIAGNOSIS

Some eye injuries are not detected because no symptoms are present. When an eye injury is suspected, a physician should be consulted.

A physician can usually locate foreign matter in the eye by examination with a magnifying glass under good light. If no foreign matter is found, a child's eyes and the surrounding area are examined to determine the presence and possible seriousness of an injury. During examination anesthetic eye drops may be administered to lessen eye pain.

To help locate scratches and other small injuries, the eye is stained with an orange dye called fluorescein. This dye appears bright yellow under a blue examining light; with it, highlighted scratches and scrapes on the eye can be detected.

COMPLICATIONS

Damage to the eye socket can cause blood to collect behind the eye, sometimes pushing the eye forward. If the rear wall of the eye socket, which separates the eyeball from the brain, is punctured, the brain may be damaged.

When a child's eye is injured, bacterial or fungal infections may develop, sometimes weeks after the injury occurs. Embedded metallic objects that are not removed may result in retina problems, cataracts (opaque lens) or *glaucoma*.

TREATMENT

Foreign matter in the eye usually requires only simple treatment. Blinking often forces sand or dust out of the eye, but a moistened cotton swab can also be used for removal. If the foreign matter is embedded in the eye, treatment should not be attempted at home; a child should be taken immediately to an emergency room. A physician may apply surface antibiotics once the object is removed.

A scratched cornea usually heals without complications. Pain relievers and surface antibiotics may be prescribed by a physician. If one cornea or both have been burned by ultraviolet light, both eyes should be kept closed until healing occurs, usually 24 to 48 hours later.

Treatment of cuts varies according to the extent of injury. A small cut in the conjuctiva does not usually need stitches. If the cut is large, an ophthalmologist (eye specialist) should be consulted. A severe cut on the eyeball requires immediate treatment and usually requires surgery. If the tear ducts are affected, more extensive surgery may be necessary. A child should not be active until an eye specialist determines the condition of the eye.

Emergency action is required when a child's eye has come in contact with chemicals (see Emergency Action, above). Immediately following water flushing of the affected eye, a child should be taken to an emergency room. To ease the pain, a physician may apply a surface anesthetic. If eye damage is severe, surgery may be necessary.

When the eye socket is damaged, cold compresses may help reduce swelling. Eye socket injuries, however, usually require immediate medical attention. If the bones of the eye socket have been damaged, surgery may be necessary.

Internal bleeding in the eye may require close observation by a physician and treatment in the hospital. Occasionally surgery is necessary. A torn retina and retinal detachment also usually require surgery.

PREVENTION

Many eye injuries can be prevented if a child takes safety measures when at work and at play. Protective helmets and face masks should be worn when playing games such as baseball, football, and ice hockey; sports glasses should be worn when playing racquetball, squash, lacrosse, field hockey, basketball, and soccer. When working with tools or harsh substances of any kind, including home chemistry sets, a child should wear protective eye goggles. (See Chapter 4, "Accident Prevention," for details.)

EYE ITCHING, IRRITATION, AND TEARING

DESCRIPTION AND CAUSE

In general, eye itching is a symptom of allergic inflammation (see *allergies*). Eye irritation is usually a symptom of foreign matter in the eye (see *eye injuries*) or of diseases such as *conjunctivitis* (an inflammation of the membrane lining the white part of the eye and the insides of the eyelids) or

blepharitis (an inflammation of the eyelids). Depending on the underlying problem, itching or irritation may affect the eyelids, eyelashes, or the structures of the eye itself.

Allergic reactions can affect the transparent covering of the whites of the eyes, the insides of upper and lower lids, the outer skin of the lids, and the area around the eyes. Many allergies that affect the eyes are caused by airborne materials; these may be seasonal, such as pollen, grasses, and ragweed in spring and summer, or present all the time, such as animal fur, feathers, and dust. Allergic reactions may also result from exposure to household products and chemicals, cosmetics (including nail polish and hair spray), and playthings (including materials found in stuffed animals and finger paints).

Itching may be a byproduct of a healing eye wound, because the body chemicals involved in reducing pain during the healing process are related to the itching sensation.

Foreign matter that can irritate the eye includes everything from tiny particles of dust or sand, which cause minor irritation, to chemical substances, such as cleaning agents, which may cause serious eye injuries if untreated. Although most children rub their eyes when they are tired or when the eyes are strained from overuse, itching and

FIG. 22. THE EYE (front view, showing tear duc

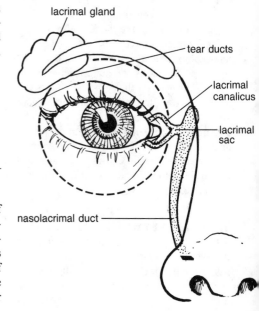

lacrimal gland

tear ducts

lacrimal canalicus

lacrimal sac

nasolacrimal duct

irritation both cause a child to rub the eyes excessively.

Tears are produced continually by the tear glands (located under the upper eyelid) to keep the eyes clean, lubricated, and free of foreign matter. Normally tears produced by the glands wash over the surface of the eye and are drained away into the nasal passages through the tear ducts, located where the upper and lower eyelids meet, near the nose.

When the output of tears exceeds the capacity of the tear ducts to drain the tears, watering or tearing of the eyes results. The most obvious example of this process is crying, a normal part of infancy and childhood. Aside from crying (and tearing resulting from administration of silver nitrate at birth), tearing of one or both eyes usually indicates a treatable medical condition. For instance, any source of irritation or itching can cause tearing. Other causes of tearing include eye injury, *colds,* or an underlying eye disease.

Among infants, tearing commonly results indirectly from a congenital (present at birth) obstruction of the tear duct. The obstruction is usually a thin membrane at the nasal (lower) end of the duct. There may be mucous or pus along with the tearing. About 85 percent of the time this obstruction clears up spontaneously.

Tearing is also a symptom of serious eye diseases, all of which require prompt medical attention.

- *Glaucoma* occurs when pressure inside the eyeball increases to a dangerous point.
- Dendritic keratitis is an eye infection caused by a virus.
- Corneal ulcers are caused by infected eye injuries. (The cornea is the transparent tissue that covers the iris and pupil.) Corneal ulcers account for 10 percent of blindness in the United States.
- Uveitis is inflammation of a layer of blood vessels in the pigmented portion of the eye. It can be caused by disease, injury, or chemical substances.

Many infants do not cry tears until several months after birth, and some people never do. Absence of reflex tearing with crying is not necessarily abnormal, but parents should mention it to their baby's pediatrician.

DIAGNOSIS

Itching and irritation may be accompanied by redness and tearing of the eye. A child with itching eyes may blink more than normal and his or her eyes may be sensitive to light. A child with irritated eyes may describe a grainy feeling in the eyes. Itching should be distinguished from pain. If a child complains of eye pain, a physician should be consulted.

Eye tearing is obvious. A physician should be consulted when tearing could be caused by underlying eye disease.

COMPLICATIONS

When tears cannot drain because of tear duct obstruction, they may collect in the tear sac and cause the tear sac to become swollen, sore, and red. This complication, called dacryocystitis, is unusual and requires medical treatment.

TREATMENT

Treatment should focus on the cause of itching, irritation, or tearing rather than on the symptom itself.

For itching caused by allergy, a physician may prescribe medicated eye drops to ease discomfort. Cold compresses applied over the eyes may also bring temporary relief from itching.

In many cases eye irritation has a simple solution. If blinking or tearing does not rid the eye of foreign matter, washing the eye with water may flush out small floating pieces such as dust, sand, eyelashes, or hairs. A clean, moist cotton swab is often effective in removing some of these particles. If the foreign matter is embedded in the eye, home treatment should not be attempted; medical attention is needed. Generally treatment of *conjunctivitis* should be supervised by a physician.

Home treatment may help infants with blocked tear ducts. Massaging the tear duct in a downward direction with warm, moist compresses may relieve the obstruction. Discharge can be wiped away from the lids, and an antibiotic ointment can be applied. Occasionally the blocked tear duct may have to be surgically opened by inserting a very small probe into the tear duct opening. This treatment is successful for about 90 percent of children; occasionally surgery may have to be repeated.

Treatment of dacryocystitis involves giving the child antibiotics. Rarely, an infected tear sac requires drainage.

PREVENTION

Avoiding exposure to harmful chemicals or known causes of allergies can prevent eye itching.

Eye irritation can be prevented by avoiding direct contact with people who have bacterial or viral conjunctivitis. Both eye irritation and injury can be avoided by wearing goggles when involved in activities such as swimming or woodworking.

Eye tearing cannot usually be prevented unless underlying causes are prevented.

FACIAL DEFORMITIES, CONGENITAL

DESCRIPTION AND CAUSE

Facial abnormalities can involve skin, bone, fat, muscles, nerves, and cartilage. About 80 percent of all facial abnormalities are congenital, meaning that they are present at birth, having occurred during prenatal development. The remaining 20 percent are acquired—caused later in life by tumors or injury.

The face and the hands form, more or less simultaneously, during the first 4 to 6 weeks of embryonic development. The anatomical areas most affected by congenital facial deformities are the forehead, eye sockets, nose, cheeks, upper lip, upper and lower jaws (including the teeth), mouth, and chin (see Figs. 36A and B, p. 679).

The most commonly found congenital facial deformities are *cleft lip and cleft palate.* There are numerous other examples of congenital deformities: retruding (opposite of protruding) or small upper or lower jaw, small ears, and varieties of birthmarks on the skin. The relatively rare, major congenital craniofacial deformities are described as follows:

Craniofacial Dysostosis

Dysostosis occurs when certain bones are prematurely and incorrectly joined together during fetal development. This causes overexpansion or underdevelopment of adjacent parts of the skull and face, as in Crouzon syndrome and Apert syndrome.

In Crouzon syndrome, dysostosis results in the underdevelopment of the bones in the middle third of the face and a malformed skull. Crouzon syndrome is characterized by a high and prominent forehead, downward slant to the eyelids, widely spaced eye sockets and resulting protruding eyeballs, a form of *cross-eyes* in which one eye turns outward while the other is focusing on an object (see *cross-eyes and walleyes),* a beaklike nose, retrusion of the upper jaw, protrusion of the lower jaw, poorly aligned teeth, a high and narrow palate (roof of the mouth), and a prominent lower lip. Protruding eyeballs can lead to complications such as damage to the cornea and progressive loss of vision.

Crouzon syndrome occurs in about 1 in 10,000 births. Approximately 65 to 75 percent of all cases of Crouzon syndrome are inherited from one of the parents. If one parent has Crouzon syndrome and passes along the gene for the syndrome to a baby, the baby is affected. Each child of an affected parent has a 50-percent chance of inheriting the gene. However, although nearly all people with that defective gene show some signs of the disorder, the severity of Crouzon syndrome varies within families (see *genetic disorders).*

The remaining 25 to 35 percent of the children with Crouzon syndrome also have one gene for the disorder, which became mutated (altered spontaneously, for no known reason, in either the sperm or egg cell prior to conception or after conception). In those cases neither parent has the disorder.

A child with Apert syndrome has facial deformities that are similar to those of Crouzon syndrome. In addition, however, Apert syndrome is characterized by an associated hand or foot deformity: an affected child has webbed fingers or toes or both. This deformity is more severe and difficult to correct than the more common forms of webbed fingers. Children with Apert syndrome have an abnormally shaped skull (usually pointed or conical), a horizontal forehead skin furrow, rather widely spaced eye sockets, severe malpositioning of the eyelids, uneven protrusion of the eyeballs, and anterior open bite (the inability of the teeth on upper and lower jaws to make contact). Approximately 30 percent of affected individuals have cleft palate.

The incidence and type of Apert syndrome is about the same as that of Crouzon syndrome, but many people with the gene for Apert syndrome show few or no signs of the disorder.

Orbital Hypertelorism and Hypotelorism

Orbital hypertelorism is the condition of having greater than normal distance between the eye sockets (orbits). The average distance between a normal adult's eye sockets is 25 millimeters in females and 28 mm in males. If an individual has orbital hypertelorism, the distance ranges from 30 mm to 40 mm or greater. In extreme cases the shape and positioning of the eye sockets are markedly abnormal. The distance between the optic nerves is not increased; only the location of the eye itself varies. Children with severe orbital hypertelorism often have a form of cross-eyes (see *cross-eyes and wall-eyes*).

Orbital hypertelorism is thought to be caused by a prenatal disruption of the normal narrowing process of the distance between the eye sockets.

Orbital hypotelorism is the opposite of hypertelorism: the distance between the eye sockets is less than normal. Extremely rare, it occurs only when there is underdevelopment of the central forehead and face.

Mandibulofacial Dysostosis

The characteristics of mandibulofacial dysostois (known as Treacher Collins syndrome) appear on both sides of the face in a symmetrical pattern. The condition is marked by any combination of the following features: downward-slanting eyelids, notching of the lower eyelids, lack of middle-lower eyelashes, flat cheekbones, unusual hair growth extending onto the cheeks, a large and beaklike nose, low-set and malformed external ears, underdeveloped chewing muscles, a large mouth, underdeveloped teeth, bite problems, and a receding chin. About 30 percent of individuals with Treacher Collins syndrome have an excessively high or cleft palate. Conductive *hearing loss* is common because of abnormalities of the external and middle ear. In turn, developmental delays or *learning problems* can be caused by hearing loss.

Treacher Collins syndrome occurs in approximately 1 of every 10,000 births. In about half of the cases it is inherited, but the severity varies. In the remaining cases children have no conclusive family history for the problem (see *genetic disorders*).

Hemifacial Microsomia

Hemifacial microsomia (also called first and second branchial arch syndrome) occurs when the structures on one side of the face do not develop normally. The condition is characterized by unilateral (one-sided) underdevelopment of any or all of the following: cheekbone, upper or lower jaw, chewing muscles, and the external ear (these areas are called first branchial arch structures); temples, external ear, part of the middle ear, facial nerve, and facial muscles (these areas are derived from the second branchial arch). The mouth opening on the affected side is often wider than normal. In most cases the lower jaw is deformed; in mild cases the size of the jaw is abnormally small; in more severe cases, the shape and size of the jaw are affected.

Normally the line between the pupils of the eyes is parallel to the line of contact of the upper and lower teeth (called the occlusal plane). In hemifacial microsomia, if the lower jaw is too short, growth of the upper jaw may be impaired. As a result, the occlusal plane often tilts upward on the affected side of the face.

In hemifacial microsomia the lower jaw needs to be lengthened to avoid impairing growth of the upper jaw and to achieve a horizontal occlusal plane. If treatment is delayed, the upper jaw must also be corrected —either by lowering or lengthening it, depending on the case—to allow it to mesh with the lower jaw.

Hemifacial microsomia is the second most common congenital facial deformity (after *cleft lip and cleft palate*), occurring in 1 in 5,642 births. It is rarely inherited; most often the alteration occurs spontaneously and randomly.

Encephalocele

Encephalocele is a rare congenital hernia (protrusion) of the brain through an opening in the skull. The hernia is contained in an external pouch or sac, filled with brain tissue. Because an encephalocele affects brain tissue, there is a slight possibility of impaired intellectual or motor function.

In less than 25 percent of cases the encephalocele protrudes through the facial skeleton, usually of the forehead or the area between the eyes (both are referred to as frontal encephaloceles). When the encephalocele is in the forehead, it may extend into the eye sockets, forcing them out of position, and resulting in the appearance of widely spaced eyeballs. When the malformation is in between the eyes, it sometimes causes the bridge of the nose to widen, but usually it is observable only by internal examination—by looking in the nasal passages. Frequently it can seem to be a nasal polyp (see *polyps)* and, as a result, is not accurately diagnosed.

Encephalocele frequently occurs alone; however, it can occur as part of many other syndromes, such as hemifacial microsomia. A frontal encephalocele between the eyes may be accompanied by cleft palate or nasal obstruction. An encephalocele in the back of the head (called occipital encephalocele) can occur with *hydrocephalus.*

Encephalocele appears to be caused by a number of factors in combination (multifactorial cause), unless it occurs as part of a syndrome (a set of symptoms that occur together).

All of these deformities except encephalocele are associated with normal intelligence.

DIAGNOSIS

Because these facial deformities are present at birth, they are most often recognized through routine examination of the newborn baby by a pediatrician. The pediatrician refers the infant to craniofacial specialists, who make a complete diagnostic assessment.

Extensive diagnostic studies are performed before specialists develop a comprehensive treatment plan. These diagnostic studies may include a series of close-up photographs, several kinds of radiographic examinations, plaster models, hearing and vision evaluations, and psychological evaluations.

COMPLICATIONS

Specific complications exist for each particular deformity. Some deformities are accompanied by functional complications, such as problems with swallowing, hearing, speaking, breathing, and seeing. Some are associated with developmental delays or learning problems.

A child's self-image and relationships with family and other people are emotional issues that are always related to facial malformations. Resolving these issues is as important a part of treatment as is correction of the physical deformity.

TREATMENT

New techniques have been developed in the last decade that allow surgery to be performed on virtually every part of the facial skeleton. Today, in almost all cases, congenital facial deformities can be corrected or improved significantly. The ultimate goal of treatment is to help the child feel normal— to aid in development of a good self-image. In addition to correcting the appearance of a child's face, treatment is aimed at correcting functional deficits. Early diagnosis and treatment are keys to success in correcting facial deformities. If the defects can be corrected when a child is at a proper age, the facial bones can begin to grow normally.

Because the treatment of congenital facial deformities is complex, the professional team involved in a child's care includes many specialists. Depending on the specific condition, team members may include any of the following:

- a plastic surgeon, who usually coordinates the treatment and performs the operation, often with the help of an oral surgeon or neurosurgeon;
- an oral surgeon, who coordinates dental and orthodontic preparations for the operation
- a neurosurgeon, who is involved in operations that require exposure and correction of the upper skull
- an anesthesiologist
- a pediatrician
- a nurse
- an orthodontist, who aligns and straightens teeth
- a pedodontist, a dentist who specializes in treating children
- an ophthalmologist, who is concerned with eye problems that may be associated with certain of the conditions
- an otolaryngologist, who cares for ear, nose, and throat problems that may be present
- a speech and language therapist
- an audiologist, who evaluates hearing
- a psychologist
- a social worker
- a prosthodontist, who makes special appliances that may be needed
- a geneticist, who answers questions about inherited conditions
- a radiologist, who is responsible for X-ray studies that help in developing the treatment plan

In most cases an operation is required to correct or improve congenital facial deformities. If more than one area of the facial skeleton needs repairing, surgeons can often correct 2 or more deformities in one operation using several procedures. Frequently, however, more than 1 operation is necessary to achieve the best results.

This type of surgery often involves obtaining bone grafts, taken from the patient's rib, hip, or skull. Composite grafts can consist of layers of skin, muscle, fat, nerve, and bone.

If the jaws are moved, they must be immobilized by wiring, or binding with elastic bands, the upper jaw to the lower jaw. The wire or elastic bands are connected to arch bars—metal bars with hooks that are wired to upper and lower teeth. Metal orthodontic bands with brackets ("braces") are also glued onto the teeth. This process allows the cut facial bone to heal.

During the time that the jaws are wired shut, only liquids and pureed foods can be consumed. This stage of recuperation usually lasts about 6 weeks (1 to 2 weeks in the hospital, the rest at home).

Recuperation and follow-up include regular checkups, supportive therapy, and family counseling.

PREVENTION

Congenital facial deformities are not preventable. Parents of a child who has a congenital facial deformity may want to seek genetic counseling to learn their risk of having another child similarly affected (see *genetic disorders*).

FACIAL FRACTURES

EMERGENCY ACTION

Seek medical attention immediately, if a facial fracture is suspected. Breathing may be impaired after a facial fracture. The airway can be blocked by bone fragments, swollen tissue, blood clots, dislodged teeth, or pieces of debris. In cases of multiple fractures, a tracheotomy (surgery to create an exterior opening to the airway through the throat) may be necessary to create an adequate breathing passage. Control of bleeding is also essential (see Chapter 10, "Basic First Aid").

Try to keep the child quiet and calm until help arrives.

DESCRIPTION

Facial fractures are broken bones of the face. Fractures may involve the bones of the upper jaw, lower jaw, cheeks, nose, or eye sockets. (See Fig. 36A and B, p. 679.) A closed fracture is one in which the skin is not broken; an open or compound fracture involves laceration of the skin.

Only about 10 percent of all facial fractures involve children. Because children's bones are not completely hardened, their fractures are usually of the "greenstick" variety—an incomplete fracture in which the bone is partially bent and partially broken. Most children's facial fractures heal rapidly, with very few complications.

Two thirds of all facial fractures involve the lower jaw. Although the strongest of the facial bones, the lower jaw is also the most vulnerable because of its position. Upper jaw fractures occur about one forth as often as those of the lower jaw. The nose and the cheekbones, because of their prominence, are also damaged frequently.

Facial fractures may be associated with other problems, including head and neck injuries, infection (from open fractures), vision problems, and breathing problems.

CAUSE

A majority of facial fractures during childhood are caused by falls, being struck with a blunt object, and motor vehicle accidents. A smaller percentage are caused by disease.

Fractures of the lower jaw are most often caused by car, bicycle, and motorcycle accidents; fistfights; falls; and sports or industrial accidents. They may also result from diseases such as *osteomyelitis* (an infection of the bone), metabolic disorders, or tumors. Upper jaw fractures result most commonly from car accidents (called smash injuries, because a child hits the dashboard or the back of the front seat during impact). Less often, upper jaw fractures result from a blow from a fist.

Fractures of the nasal bones and cheekbones can result from any severe impact to the area. Common causes include blunt objects, falls, fistfights, and athletic encounters.

Fractures of the floor of the eye bone socket (the orbit) are called blowout fractures of the orbit. They most often result from a sudden increase in pressure around the eye area due to an external force such as a fist or a baseball. All the connecting bones in the eye area are compressed, and the system of bone structures gives out (blows out) at its weakest point—the floor of the eye bone socket.

SIGNS AND SYMPTOMS

Symptoms of lower jaw fracture include pain, excessive salivation, and difficulty in swallowing. Signs apparent to a physician include swelling, malocclusion (improper meshing of the upper and lower jaw and teeth), skin discoloration, a crackling noise when ends of the broken bone are rubbed together, visible jaw deformity, and bad breath.

Symptoms of upper jaw fracture include those already mentioned, plus nosebleed. Signs apparent to a physician, in addition to those mentioned above, are swelling in and around the eyes, visible dislocation (especially around the eye socket), and an apparent elongation of the face.

Symptoms of nasal fracture include pain, nosebleed, and trouble in breathing. Signs apparent to a physician include swelling, cuts or lacerations either inside or outside the nose, visible displacement of the nose, and the crackling noise already mentioned.

Symptoms of cheekbone fracture include pain; numbness of the cheek, eye, and upper teeth on the affected side; swelling of the eyelids; and an inability to close the mouth properly. Signs apparent to a physician include swelling around the eyes, a flatness of the cheek, irregularity of the eye bone region, or a sunken cheekbone or eye bone on the affected side.

Symptoms of blowout fracture of the orbit include pain, especially when looking up or down, and double vision. A physician may notice limited motion of the eyeball and a sunken eyeball.

DIAGNOSIS

Diagnosis of facial fracture involves careful observation of the facial structures, followed by studies of X-ray films. A physician feels the facial bones—orbital rims, nose, upper and lower jaw, and cheekbones—to discover bone fragments or irregularities of shape. A physician may also look inside the nose and ears for blood clots or discharge of cerebrospinal fluid (such a discharge from the ears could mean a basal skull fracture). X-ray films are needed to diagnose a facial fracture and to rule out other problems such as dislocation or fracture of the neck.

COMPLICATIONS

Generally children's broken bones heal rapidly and with few complications. Fractures that involve the upper or lower jaw, however, may affect tooth development. For example, teeth about to grow in may come through abnormally or may be deformed.

TREATMENT

The usual treatment for facial fractures—and indeed for most fractures—involves two steps: reduction and fixation. Reduction, or "setting" the bone, involves restoring broken pieces to their proper position. In many cases of facial fracture, reduction can be accomplished several days after the injury, once the swelling has subsided.

The second step is fixation, the process of holding the broken pieces together until they have rejoined and the fracture has healed. Most often, this means immobilizing the broken parts.

Many jaw fractures during childhood require only a soft diet. Sometimes jaw fractures require intermaxillary fixation, (IMF): temporary locking of the upper and lower jaws together by wire or rubber bands. The wire or rubber bands are connected to arch bars (metal bars with hooks that are wired to upper and lower teeth). Metal orthodontic bands with brackets ("braces") are also glued onto the teeth. While the jaws are wired shut, only liquid nourishment is possible. The length of time the IMF is in place varies with the extent and severity of the fracture; the usual length of time is 3 to 6 weeks.

In nasal fractures fixation is usually accomplished by external splinting and occasionally by packing the inside of the nose with soft material.

A blowout fracture may require careful exploration and restoration of the orbital floor.

PREVENTION

The great majority of facial fractures result from accidents, many of which could be prevented (see Chapter 4, "Accident Prevention").

A child should always wear protective headgear or teeth guards (as well as protective clothing or other safety equipment in good repair) when playing contact sports or when involved in any other potentially hazardous activities.

FAILURE TO THRIVE

DESCRIPTION

Failure to thrive (FTT) is a nutritional disorder of infants and young children in which an affected child loses weight or fails to gain weight. The disorder develops over time. "Poor growth" or "growth failure" are terms sometimes used to describe the disorder. If a child's weight for age and height are persistently and abnormally less than those of 97 percent of normal children of the same age and a similar ethnic background, that child may be suffering from failure to thrive. Of course, a child may be small naturally—for instance, because his or her parents are small—but perfectly normal and healthy.

Children who fail to thrive lack sufficient nutrition to sustain growth. The problem can stem from the inadequate intake of calories, excessive loss of nutrients, an abnormally high need for calories, or from a combination of these factors. Whatever the cause, poor nutrition can lead to medical problems (see *malnutrition*). The degree of FTT varies widely; in severe cases the disorder can be life-threatening.

The incidence of FTT in the general population of children is unknown, although one recent study indicated that as many as 5 percent of all poor children (who are less likely to have access to adequate nutrition) suffer from FTT.

FTT is classified by physicians as organic, nonorganic, or mixed. By definition organic FTT is caused by illness or other physical factors that interfere with the retention or use of nutrients or that create an unusually high metabolic demand for nutrients. Nonorganic FTT is said to result from eating problems (see *eating disorders*) that are complications of emotional difficulties. These difficulties, in turn, usually result from economic, psychological, or family problems. Most cases are mixed FTT, caused by a combination of organic and nonorganic factors.

For 4 out of 5 children, failure to thrive becomes evident before the age of 18 months. Overall, the majority of children who develop nonorganic FTT do so under the age of 1 year, many under 6 months.

Factors that tend to place a child at risk for FTT include multiple minor birth defects (such as those caused by fetal alcohol syndrome—see *drug and alcohol abuse*) and prenatal malnutrition. Malnutrition before birth can result from severe infection, a mother's inadequate diet, or problems with the placenta that interfere with transfer of nutrients from the mother to the fetus. Premature babies who suffer medical complications, as well as children who were small for gestational age at birth, are also at risk for FTT (see *prematurity*).

The outlook for children with FTT depends upon the duration and severity of the disorder and upon the age at which the disorder develops and is identified. The earlier the problem is diagnosed and growth is reestablished, the better the outlook for complete recovery with no developmental delays.

Nonorganic FTT appears to be associated with multiple problems during childhood. For instance, from 25 to 50 percent of affected children continue to be underweight, and more than half have *learning problems* (especially with speech and language), difficulty in adjusting to school, and behavioral problems (see also *speech problems* and *language disorders*). Affected children may also have *sleep disorders* and elimination problems (such as *bed-wetting*). Because of these persistent problems, long-term care and regular follow-up examinations are essential.

CAUSE

Organic FTT

Chronic (persistent or long-term) illness of a child can be a risk factor for organic FTT. Illnesses that are most likely to lead to organic FTT are often congenital (present at birth) and usually involve the gastrointestinal tract (esophagus, stomach, and intestines) or less frequently, the central nervous system, genitourinary tract, endocrine system, heart, or immune system. Diseases that commonly lead to organic FTT include *malabsorption, cystic fibrosis, sickle cell anemia,* heart disorders (see *heart disease, congenital*) and *celiac disease.* Some diseases (such as congenital heart disease) increase a child's need for calories, others (such as *diabetes* or hypothyroidism—see *thyroid problems*) keep a child's body from using calories in his or her diet.

Physical problems such as nasal obstruction or a cleft palate can discourage a child's eating (see *cleft lip and cleft palate*). *Pyloric stenosis* can cause a child to vomit food.

The risk of either organic or nonorganic

FTT may be increased if an infant has poor feeding capabilities. For instance, an infant may be unable to suck properly or may suffer from tongue-thrusting, which interferes with feeding.

Nonorganic FTT

Nonorganic FTT occurs when a child has not taken, retained, or been offered adequate nutrition.

A number of different family or individual problems can contribute to FTT. When a parent is unhappy, depressed, or under *stress* because of a job, health, loss of a family member, etc., the risk increases, as it does when a parent is unprepared for or uneducated about the responsibilities of childcare. When a mother cannot establish a fulfilling relationship with her child, because she sees it as "bad," or because she feels isolated and overwhelmed, lacking support from a father or relatives, FTT becomes more likely. A withdrawn or hypersensitive or colicky baby, or a "mismatch" in the temperaments of baby and parents can strain the parent-child relationship and increase the risk of FTT. Anything that impairs the parents' response to the emotional needs of the baby adds to this risk.

Mixed-Cause FTT

Often children have an organic predisposition to *not* grow well but are not clearly medically ill. For example, some children may have an uncoordinated swallowing mechanism and are thus difficult to feed. Other children might have an underlying hyperactivity or irritable state that makes them difficult to feed and makes it difficult to be good parents to them. Often the combination of such minor organic problems with a parent who is depressed or unable to cope may result in FTT even though the child is not suffering from severe health problems.

Cases of mixed-cause failure to thrive can also involve a chronically ill child who suffers from a physical nutritional disorder. Parents can become overwhelmed with the care of such a child, complicating the FTT picture. For instance, in trying to ensure that their chronically ill child receives enough nutrition, parents may be anxious and unable to help the child develop normal eating habits. Or parents may become frightened at the prospect of caring for a disabled child, and without consciously intending to do so, they may withdraw emotionally from the child.

Children who have *Down syndrome, Turner's syndrome,* another chromosomal abnormality, or a rare skeletal disorder are also at risk for FTT, as are children who had prenatal *German measles.*

Occasionally, no cause (either organic or nonorganic) can be identified for FTT.

SIGNS AND SYMPTOMS

A child who fails to thrive is noticeably underweight and may be of less-than-normal height. An excessively limp or rigid posture and a pasty or pale, rough, or dry skin tone are seen in some cases of FTT (especially in severe cases). Organic FTT may be accompanied by *vomiting, diarrhea,* bulky or foul-smelling stools, excessive urination, and excessive thirst. Although nonorganic FTT does not have physical origins, affected children frequently have physical symptoms such as diarrhea or vomiting. They may also be irritable and may prefer to play with toys instead of people. A child who is emotionally deprived may display rocking behavior or *head-banging.* A child with nonorganic or mixed-cause FTT may display rumination (see *eating disorders).*

DIAGNOSIS

If parents are concerned about their child's size or general well-being, they should consult their child's physician.

The diagnosis of failure to thrive is made by a physician, who looks for a pattern of growth failure by comparing a child's weight, height, head circumference, hand size, and skeletal age with medical standards. A physician also evaluates a child's emotional and physical development during a physical examination. Children with FTT are often developmentally delayed or have emotional problems.

To help identify the cause of failure to thrive, a physician performs a complete examination (which may include checking a child's hearing and vision and looking for birth defects and signs of neglect or abuse) and orders necessary lab tests. In addition, a physician or nurse takes the child's medical history, seeking information about the child's birth (such as birth weight, prematurity, complications before or after birth, and exposure to any harmful substances), hospitalizations, and persistent or recurrent symptoms. A chart is begun to document the rate of change between visits. The physician pays close attention to any family history of short stature (see *height problems*), slow development, disease, FTT, or neglect or abuse that the parents experienced when they were children.

Most children with FTT are diagnosed and treated by a pediatrician, who may—if diagnosis is difficult and complicated—consult specialists from the fields of nutrition and child development, as well as a social worker or psychiatrist.

Typically, medical tests include blood tests, urine tests, stool tests (for such conditions as *parasitic infections* and *diarrhea),* a tuberculin test (for *tuberculosis),* and a sweat test (for *cystic fibrosis).* If a child has diarrhea or is *vomiting,* further tests may be ordered.

Evaluating how well a hospitalized child is eating is another approach; if a child begins to gain significant weight soon after hospitalization, then his or her physician may suspect nonorganic FTT. If a child does not eat or gain weight while in the hospital, nonorganic FTT is not necessarily ruled out, since the child may feel anxious in the hospital, especially if a parent does not stay with the child. In addition, infants who have been seriously deprived may not respond quickly, even in a safe place.

If a child eats well but does not gain weight, organic FTT is more likely, and further tests may be necessary.

COMPLICATIONS

Children with severe FTT are likely to suffer delays in their intellectual and behavioral development and in their physical coordination, even when FTT is treated.

TREATMENT

Both short-term and long-term care are necessary in almost all cases. Follow-up care can be crucial until a child is well into school years.

Nutritional rehabilitation. Treatment of FTT first involves meeting the nutritional needs of affected children. A child with FTT must get extra calories, particularly of protein, to begin and sustain growth. A child may resist feeding, so various forms of food are offered in a quiet setting with few distractions. A parent participates whenever possible, and a physician or nutrition specialist can offer advice to parents about solving feeding problems. The importance of creating warmth between mother and child at feeding times is emphasized. Practical ad-

vice is also given on preparation of food, feeding methods and times, and nutritional needs so that the child is neither overfed nor underfed.

Stabilization and clarification of medical problems. Illnesses such as *dehydration, anemia,* and infections must be treated and any physical causes corrected. An important part of this stage of treatment is determining how much any associated illness contributes to FTT.

Developmental stimulation. An infant needs stimulation to develop physically and intellectually, as well as to learn how to interact with parents. To accomplish these goals, a physician may recommend that an infant be involved in special infant stimulation programs and receive treatment from physical and occupational therapists, or that parents receive supplementary training and support. A child may benefit from speech therapy as well as from remedial instruction to improve comprehension or language skills. Early intervention may help prevent or lessen learning problems.

Social intervention. A complete, lasting recovery from nonorganic FTT is difficult to achieve if contributing family problems persist. If necessary, a social worker may be able to arrange for parents of FTT children to have access to child care, social-service homemakers, housing assistance, and financial counsel. Crisis-intervention centers or hot lines may also help parents cope with ordinary problems or crises in childrearing. Parent groups may provide support and understanding to isolated parents or to parents who simply need to air their feelings. For instance, parents of a child with organic FTT, who have to cope with a taxing physical illness, often need support to deal with the psychological and social problems that such an illness causes.

Parent-infant therapy. This form of therapy is designed to help parents and infants strengthen their relationships. Typically, a therapist observes a mother and baby interacting, particularly at mealtimes, identifies problems as they occur, and offers suggestions to the mother. Parent-infant therapy has the advantage of directly dealing with the mother's frustrations and the baby's nutritional needs. In addition, the therapist can offer guidance regarding child development and appropriate expectations for each stage in the child's development.

Close pediatric follow-up. Pediatric follow-up is important to monitor the progress of treatment.

PREVENTION

In cases of organic FTT, growth delays or failure occur because of the child's underlying physical condition. Improved care may minimize the problem of growth failure. Organic FTT can often be prevented, or at least improved, by providing psychological, educational, and social help to parents of children with chronic illnesses. Both treating the "whole child" and aiding the family are crucial.

FAINTING

EMERGENCY ACTION

If a child has fainted, check for breathing and a pulse. If breathing is absent, start artificial respiration; if there is no pulse, start cardiopulmonary resuscitation (CPR) (see Chapter 10, "Basic First Aid"). Call an ambulance or a physician.

If a child has a pulse and is breathing normally, but is still unconscious, keep him or her lying down, with feet elevated. (If the child is conscious, have him or her sit with body bent forward, head between the knees.) Loosen clothing around the child's neck and waist. Turn the child's head to one side; keep his or her mouth clear. Check for injuries caused by falling. Keep the child warm.

Give nothing to swallow. Do not splash the child's face with water or shake the child.

If the child remains unconscious, call a physician. Check frequently for weak pulse or failing breathing. Check for a medical identification tag.

DESCRIPTION

Fainting is a sudden, temporary loss of consciousness fairly common among children and adolescents. Fainting spells most often are brief.

Before fainting, pulse rate may slow or, more rarely, become excessively rapid, and the blood pressure drops abnormally. In a simple fainting spell the child feels dizzy or lightheaded. Other symptoms include blurred vision or decreased hearing, chills or hot flashes, clamminess, and nausea. The child may look extremely pale, have glazed eyes, and may appear limp. The child then collapses.

Fainting is often confused with seizures (see *seizures*). A child who has had a seizure is disoriented, difficult to arouse, and may have been unable to control urination and defecation while having the seizure. A child who has regained consciousness after fainting is coherent, alert, and aware of the surroundings even if he or she cannot recall what happened. After a child regains consciousness, fatigue and *headache* may appear.

Fainting may be the first sign of a serious illness if there is not an obvious cause such as change of position, the sight of blood, or fright. Regular fainting episodes may also signal a more serious underlying condition.

CAUSE

The cause of fainting is a sudden drop in blood pressure which prevents adequate blood and its oxygen from reaching the brain.

Fainting is often triggered by a combination of factors, which can include standing still too long (especially with knees locked); a hot, stuffy room; too much clothing; bright lights or hot sun; an empty or upset stomach; fatigue; or *fever*. Emotional stress, fright, the sight of blood, and sudden sharp pain (such as from shots or having splinters removed) may cause some children to faint. Children who have been in bed for several days with a cold or flu virus often faint when they try to stand up. Very rarely, children faint because of an allergic reaction to an insect bite (see *stinging insect reactions*).

Fainting may be a sign of a physical health condition such as *arrhythmias* (unusual heart beats), *anemia,* and rarely, *hypoglycemia* (low blood sugar). Children with low blood pressure are especially susceptible to fainting spells. Children taking medication for *hypertension* (high blood pressure) may faint as a side effect. Ear infections (see *earache and ear infections)* or other illnesses caused by viruses can cause *dizziness* and sometimes fainting. Occasionally a child with *asthma* will faint after a prolonged coughing attack.

Adolescent girls may faint during their menstrual periods because of heavy blood flow or severe cramps. Teenaged girls who are pregnant or miscarrying may faint. Adolescents of both sexes may faint from taking drugs, prescription or over-the-counter.

The susceptibility of some children to fainting might be explained by a defect in the involuntary nervous system that controls circulation.

DIAGNOSIS

A fainting spell may be diagnosed if a child who has lost consciousness makes a complete recovery within 15 minutes, particularly when a frequently recognized triggering factor is present.

If the cause of a fainting spell cannot be determined, a physician should be consulted. A complete physical exam may be indicated. Occasionally a physician will order blood or urine tests, chest X rays, a heart rhythm evaluation (electrocardiogram), or a brain evaluation (electroencephalogram).

COMPLICATIONS

Although fainting is not generally serious, children are occasionally injured as they fall.

TREATMENT

Emergency medical treatment is necessary if a child faints because of an allergic reaction to an insect bite or is injured from falling (see Emergency Action, above).

In addition to treatment described in Emergency Action, parents should not allow a child who has fainted to stand or walk until recovery is complete (after 5 to 15 minutes of full consciousness). Smelling salts, basically ammonia, are not necessary.

A child should see a physician if recovery is slow or incomplete, fainting episodes recur, signs of seizure exist, or the child's skin turns blue. Treatment depends on the underlying cause.

PREVENTION

Children with low blood pressure should not try to sit or stand up suddenly. They should sit or lie down immediately if they feel dizzy. Children susceptible to fainting can lie down when receiving shots and blood tests.

Fainting from most other causes is preventable only by avoiding or removing the underlying cause.

FEVER

EMERGENCY ACTION

Call a physician promptly if

- a child under 6 months old has a fever of 100° F (37.8° C) or higher;
- a child from 6 months to 3 years old has a fever of 102° F (38.8° C) or higher;
- any child has fever of 103° F (39.4° C) or higher that doesn't begin to subside after 4 to 6 hours of fever-reduction treatment;
- a child of any age who has fever accompanied by unusual drowsiness and loss of mental alertness, labored breathing, or an appearance that disturbs or worries a parent.

Fever above 105° F (40.6° C) can cause *delirium* and may damage the brain and spinal cord. Always consult a physician promptly, since serious infection may be present.

Fever can be life-threatening for an infant, especially because *dehydration* can develop quickly. (Signs of dehydration include cool, dry, pale skin; dry tongue; thirst; listlessness; rapid pulse; sunken eyes; and for an infant, sunken fontanel—the soft spot on top of an infant's head.)

If a child experiences a convulsion (see *seizures),* clear the airway (nose and throat) during the convulsion but do not force anything into the mouth in an attempt to prevent breathing difficulty. Ease the child to the floor or ground and turn the head to one side to allow saliva to drain out of the mouth. Nothing should be given to eat or drink until the child is fully alert. When the convulsions stop, the child may either awaken slowly or lapse into a deep sleep. A physician should be notified. Give artificial respiration if breathing stops, which is a rare occurrence (see Chapter 10, "Basic First Aid"). Consult a physician as soon as possible following the convulsion.

The high fever that accompanies heat stroke requires immediate medical attention. To promote radiational cooling, undress a child who may be suffering from heat stroke and go immediately to a hospital emergency room.

If a health professional is not available for consultation, fever reduction can be started immediately with a lukewarm sponge bath (see Treatment section below).

DESCRIPTION

Fever is an elevation of body temperature at least 1° above 98.6° F (0.6° above 37.0° C) or whatever temperature is normal for the particular child. Normal body temperatures can range from 97° to 100.5° F (35.0° to

37.8° C), and a physician can determine what is normal for a particular child if there is any question. The figure 98.6° F (37.0° C) represents the midpoint of the normal range of temperature readings among healthy people.

During the course of a day, body temperature usually varies a degree or two—lower from about 3 A.M. to 6 A.M. and higher from about 5 P.M. to 7 P.M. These fluctuations are due in part to changes in levels of physical activity. Very strenuous exercise may push temperature up. Additional body heat is produced as the body burns more food to produce energy needed for increasing activity.

Children can also develop higher body temperatures because of their special sensitivity to the temperature of the environment. When it gets cold outside, their bodies begin to shiver. The motion of shivering stimulates production of body heat, and contraction of blood vessels closest to the skin reduces heat loss. Extra and heavier clothes further insulate their bodies against heat loss. When it gets hot, the body begins to sweat and surface blood vessels expand so that heat radiates out of the blood and away from the skin.

Fever prevents infection from spreading by stimulating production of white blood cells and by speeding up the body's inflammatory response, the essential defense mechanism for fighting disease and promoting healing.

Fever raises the metabolic rate, meaning that a child's body uses energy more quickly as breathing rate, heartbeat, kidney function, and conversion of food to sugars and fats speed up. Weight loss and *dehydration* can result.

Partly because their temperature centers in their brains are not yet completely developed, infants and young children develop fevers more often than do older children. In addition, infants and young children may develop fever more quickly because the body's natural cooling system—sweating—does not function effectively in the very young. Simply overdressing or overcovering an infant or toddler, for example, can sometimes cause fever. Similarly, adding blankets to the bed of an infant who is already running a fever or putting heavier pajamas on a feverish toddler prevents normal cooling.

Children's fevers vary widely. A mild or low-grade fever runs in the range of 100° to 101° F (37.8° to 38.3° C) and a moderate fever in the range of 101° to 103° F (38.3° to 39.4° C). Any fever above 103° is considered high. In situations of illness, even a mild fever can make a child feel quite uncomfortable.

Fever is a sign of disease, not a disease or illness itself. In addition to bacterial and viral infections, many noninfectious childhood diseases and conditions can cause fever. Poisons and drugs of many kinds are also fever producers.

Children generally handle fever well. Fever may begin slowly or develop quickly in a matter of hours. The speed with which a fever comes on and the height it reaches are not necessarily indications of the severity of its underlying cause. A fever may rise as a child's overall condition grows worse and then subside as the condition improves. Some fevers may spike to a high point at about the same time each day and then subside, or they may run high throughout the course of illness. Fever usually runs its course without treatment.

The outlook for children who suffer fever resulting from common infectious diseases is excellent. Fever usually subsides without aftereffects if the underlying cause is treated. Recurrent fever, however, associated with long-term disease (such as arthritis (see *arthritis, acute*), ulcerative colitis, a tumor, or *leukemia*) can affect both physical and emotional health.

Occasionally fever is persistent. A fever of unknown origin (FUO) is a prolonged elevation of temperature the cause of which is very difficult to diagnose. It is a sign of disease, not a disease itself, and may affect a child at any age.

A fever designated FUO usually has three general characteristics:

- An elevation of more than 100.5° F (38.1° C) as measured several times over several days. To confirm the existence of a prolonged fever, it is necessary to obtain repeated temperature readings that clearly lie above the normal range. For a young child, rectal temperature readings are preferred.
- A duration of one week or more.
- A cause that remains unidentified even after investigation in a hospital for at least 1 week. If examination and testing of a child with a prolonged fever over a week or more at home fails to identify

a cause, a physician may recommend hospitalization for further evaluation. Extended observation in a hospital of a child with a fever allows a variety of experts to study the child in a controlled environment, evaluate various test findings, and consult about possible causes. If a cause cannot be identified after an entire week of such procedures and observation, then the puzzling fever is designated FUO and investigation continues, usually until a cause is found or the fever subsides spontaneously.

FUO may be accompanied by signs and symptoms typical of those appearing with any fever. Fever may remain nearly constant or may fluctuate by several degrees during the day or night.

In some children FUO resists diagnosis. Estimates vary, but perhaps 10 percent of all FUOs go undiagnosed. Fever reduction methods may be successful in some cases, while other children may recover spontaneously before diagnosis can be made.

CAUSE

Fevers have many causes. They may generally be divided into two kinds: acute (of short duration with a clearly defined end) and chronic or recurrent (occurring repeatedly over time). Here are some examples of those best known.

Acute

- bacterial infections, such as earaches, *urinary tract infections,* and *pneumonia*
- viral infections, such as *colds, influenza,* and *chicken pox*
- allergic or toxic reactions to certain drugs or poisons, of which sulfa and atropine are examples
- heat stroke, in which high, life-threatening fever occurs
- *dehydration,* often occurring in children as a result of *diarrhea* and *vomiting*

Chronic or Recurrent

- chronic inflammatory diseases (characterized by fever, swelling, redness, pain, and some loss of function) of connective tissue, such as *arthritis* and *lupus erythematosus*

- chronic inflammatory disease of the GI tract, such as *Crohn's disease* and *ulcerative colitis*
- infections commonly associated with *cystic fibrosis,* a chronic lung disease
- tumors and cancers, such as *leukemia* and *lymphoma*
- disorders of the central nervous system, such as brain tumors and cerebral hemorrhage, and congenital abnormalities of the central nervous system
- endocrine gland disorders, such as hyperthyroidism (excessive secretion of thyroid hormone, see *thyroid problems)*

The causes of FUO usually fall into four broad categories: viral and bacterial infections, inflammations of connective tissue (ligaments and tendons), malignancies (see *cancer),* and miscellaneous illnesses. Other signs and symptoms of these diseases can be subtle or nonexistent in early stages of development, and fever can be the predominant or only indication of illness.

Causes of FUO tend to vary, depending on whether a child is older or younger than 6 years. Younger children more often have viral and bacterial infections underlying prolonged fever. For older children an inflammation of connective tissue more often underlies a prolonged fever.

DIAGNOSIS

A parent can sometimes tell that something is wrong by an overall impression that a child "just doesn't look right," but the most effective way to detect fever is to take a child's temperature with a fever thermometer.

When consulting a physician about a fever, it is helpful to report the length of time the fever has been present, exactly how high it is, whether it has a particular pattern day by day, and if the child has any other signs and symptoms. A written record of temperature readings comes in handy.

A physician who examines a child with fever attempts to determine underlying causes or conditions. A history is taken of a child's recent health, activities, diet, and if applicable, travel. A physical examination may be supplemented by urine and blood analyses. Any medication being given to reduce the fever is usually discontinued during medical evaluation.

If fever persists and its cause remains unidentified, blood and urine analyses are usually ordered. In addition, mucus and saliva from the nose and throat may be cultured for possible growth of bacteria. Cultures are also ordered on any body materials that may be suspect, such as fluid from a skin rash or pus from a swollen eye. X-ray films can provide additional valuable information. A physician may perform these studies either at an office or in the hospital, depending upon how sick and uncomfortable a child appears to be.

If the first tests do not produce a diagnosis and FUO may be a possibility, the physician may want to repeat some of them or perform others. Some of the more complicated ones —CT (computed tomography) scans, ultrasound, and nuclear tracing, for example— must be done in a hospital, but typically they are ordered only after all other means of identifying the cause have been exhausted.

How To Take a Temperature

Temperatures can be taken orally, rectally, or using the armpit. Rectal temperatures run higher than the other two because they record from a well-insulated location within the body. Mouth temperatures run lower than the others since air breathed through the nose cools the mouth and the oral thermometer. Especially when ill with *colds* or coughs, children have a difficult time keeping their mouths closed and the thermometers under their tongues. Armpit temperature usually falls in between rectal and mouth temperatures. The difference between a rectal reading and a mouth reading is usually about one-half to 1 full degree F (0.2 to 0.5 degrees C).

Rectal or armpit temperatures should be taken for babies and children up to about 6 years old (about the age when cooperation in keeping the mouth closed for an oral temperature may be assured and the chances of a child's biting the glass thermometer are reduced.) Armpit temperatures should be taken when children have *diarrhea*. This technique often works better than the rectal one with active infants and young children whose sudden movements could bump the rectal thermometer and cause injury to the rectum.

An oral or rectal thermometer can be used for taking armpit temperatures. The mercury bulb of an oral thermometer is long and slender as opposed to the short, fat mercury bulb at the end of a rectal thermometer. An oral thermometer provides greater surface area upon which the mouth or armpit can register heat, while the rectal thermometer ensures easier, safer insertion. (See Fig. 7, p. 106).

A thermometer should always be held at the top, the end opposite from the bulb. A slender ribbon of mercury, silver or red in color, appears parallel to the line of temperature gradations etched into the glass of the thermometer. These gradation lines mark the degrees between 94° and 106° F (34.4° to 41.1° C). Often a red line or arrow points to the "normal temperature," 98.6° F (37.0° C). Sometimes the gradation lines below the arrow are marked in blue and those above are marked in red.

Finding the ribbon of mercury in the narrow channel can sometimes be tricky, especially in the middle of the night. By holding a thermometer near a good light and rotating it very slowly with the fingertips, it should be possible to locate the ribbon of mercury and to read the number or line closest to its upper end, which indicates the child's temperature. (See Fig. 7, p. 106.)

Small battery-powered electronic temperature-taking devices are also available. Many hospitals use them because they register body temperature quickly. It is important to make certain by inquiring before purchase that such a device is accurate and durable. Temperature-sensitive plastic strips of various designs are also available for measuring temperatures but may not be accurate. Using such a device is not a reliable substitute for a thermometer reading.

It is best to take a child's temperature early in the morning and again in the late afternoon. Following are directions for using the two types of thermometers.

Rectal Temperature The rectal thermometer should be shaken down and the bulbed end lubricated with a little petroleum jelly. A baby or small child should lie down across the lap of a seated adult. The child's legs hang down and rarely kick in this position; wriggling free is possible only with great effort. An older child should lie on one side with knees bent slightly to relax the buttocks. The thermometer should be inserted gently into the rectum, pushed lightly, allowing it to take its own path. Holding it tightly may hurt the child.

Once the thermometer is in about an inch, the end of the thermometer should be released so that a sudden motion doesn't cause it to twist or jab against the wall of the rectum. Then the thermometer can be held between the index and middle fingers with the palm down so that the buttocks can be held together with the thumb, ring, and little fingers. If a child is especially active, the child's hips can be held down tightly with the other hand. The thermometer should stay in place for 3 minutes if possible, 2 at the very least.

After the thermometer is removed, the petroleum jelly can be wiped off. If there is any uncertainty, the readings should be double-checked.

Armpit Temperature The thermometer should be shaken down and the bulb end placed in a dry armpit. To keep the thermometer in place, the child's elbow should be flush against his or her side and the hand placed on the opposite shoulder. It is essential that the thermometer be placed between two skin surfaces and that clothing not interfere with temperature taking. The child's arm should be kept in this position with the thermometer tucked in the armpit for about 10 minutes for an accurate reading.

Oral Temperature Oral temperature taking requires a child's cooperation. To avoid false readings, a child should not drink anything for 15 minutes before taking an oral temperature. The oral thermometer should be shaken down and the mercury bulb end should be placed under a child's tongue and just to one side. The child should keep lips closed but should not hold the thermometer with the teeth. (Holding the thermometer lightly in place with the fingers is permissible.) A child should never be left alone with an oral thermometer in place. An accurate reading takes about 3 to 5 minutes. If a child breathes through the mouth the reading may be inaccurate; if this cannot be avoided, temperature should be taken by armpit or rectum.

Thermometer Cleaning Thermometers should always be washed with cold water and soap. (Hot water will break the thermometer or crack the glass.) A cracked or chipped thermometer should be thrown out, or the user may be cut. The thermometer should be rinsed with cold water, then dried. Ideally, it should be wiped lightly with a tissue soaked in rubbing (isopropyl) alcohol. After being shaken down, a thermometer should always be replaced in its case to guard against breakage.

COMPLICATIONS

High fever, up to 105° F (40.6° C) can cause a child, most often between 6 months and 4 years old, to have a febrile seizure (sometimes called a convulsion) in which the face, trunk, or arms and legs undergo violent spasms or a series of uncontrollable jerking movements (see *seizures*). The tendency to have a febrile seizure is inherited, and often other members of the family, including parents, have had this difficulty. Common illnesses (such as viral *pneumonia* and *roseola*) that cause a sustained high fever are often associated with such a seizure. In rare cases a febrile seizure may be the result of *meningitis*. The central nervous system (brain, spinal cord, and their protective coverings, the meninges) overheats, altering the normal pattern of nerve impulses. Dehydration can be a threat, especially to infants and young children.

TREATMENT

Whether and when to call a medical professional for assistance for a child with fever depends upon several factors, including a child's age, overall health before beginning of fever, associated symptoms of illness, a parent's experience in caring for ill children, and the individual physician's own policy about reporting fever.

In certain cases children with fever require prompt medical attention (see Emergency Action, above).

If a child 3 years of age or older has a fever of less than 102° F (38.8° C) unaccompanied by any other signs or symptoms (except indications of mild illness, such as a decrease in appetite and activity), a parent can wait a day or two before consulting a physician. Such a wait-and-see attitude applies especially with older children who can reliably report symptoms. If any fever persists beyond several days, a physician should be informed regardless of the child's overall condition. If a parent has any doubt about what to do for a feverish child, a physician should be consulted.

As soon as a child begins to run a fever, one impulse is to treat and so eliminate it. Yielding to such an impulse immediately, however, may not be wise.

Fever reduction usually provides some immediate comfort, whatever the underlying cause of fever may be. If the fever is below 102° F (38.8° C), parents may want to reduce a fever to alleviate a child's discomfort. If any question exists about the advisability of trying to reduce a child's fever, regardless of degree, parents should consult the physician.

Three methods of fever reduction are available: radiational cooling to allow excess heat to leave a child's body; sponge baths to increase circulation to the skin and to allow heat to be absorbed by the lukewarm water touching a child's body; and medication to reduce or eliminate fever.

Cooling by Radiation If a child's body temperature is 103° F (39.4° C) or less, some clothing can be removed to allow excess body heat to escape and radiate into the cooler surrounding air. Cotton clothing is preferable to synthetic, as sweat is absorbed better by natural fabric. Summer pajamas or underpants or diapers and a short-sleeved shirt should make a feverish child more comfortable.

Sponge Bath If a child's fever remains above 103° F (39.4° C) for longer than an hour, a lukewarm-water sponge bath can be helpful.

A child with a high fever feels consumed by heat. Any relief is welcome and needed, but the shock of being put in a cold bath or being rubbed with isopropyl alcohol is usually too severe. In fact, such treatment often produces crying and shivering, which can cause temperature to climb even higher.

A bathtub or basin should be filled with lukewarm water. If it feels comfortably warm when tested by an adult's elbow, it will feel cool to a feverish child. The child should sit navel-deep in water. Cold water should be permitted to trickle into the tub so that the overall temperature will continue to drop while the bath progresses. It is helpful to use two washcloths or sponges during the bath so that one is cooling in the water while the child is being washed from head to toes with the other.

The person giving the bath can move the dripping sponge or washcloth rapidly across the child's skin so that the water washes over the skin continuously. Body heat slowly radiates into the bath water and warmed water and perspiration evaporate into the air, lowering the child's temperature in time. As the cloth or sponge is warmed slowly, it can be exchanged for the cooler one in the bath water. The water must be warmed if the child starts shivering, his or her lips turn blue, or the teeth begin chattering. If a sponge bath can be extended to as long as 20 minutes, a child should feel much more comfortable and relaxed. Of course, if a child will not sit still for 20 minutes, even a 5- to 10-minute sponge bath can be helpful. The tub bath is usually a welcome relief from the miseries of high fever. Music, especially singing, and bathtub games and toys may help divert a younger child so that the bath can be prolonged.

After a sponge bath, the child should be patted, not rubbed, dry. Moisture left on the skin usually evaporates and cools the body even further. After the child is dressed in light clothing, the temperature can be taken again 30 minutes after the bath. Usually fever drops 1 or 2 degrees F (0.6 to 1.1 degrees C); if it does not, the sponge bath should be repeated within an hour. If a high fever develops at night, as it often does, a child may need 2 or 3 baths. After a fever has dropped by morning only to rise again during the late afternoon or early evening—as fevers often do—sponge bathing may be needed again, even if fever-reducing medication is prescribed and given. If fever persists, the physician should be consulted again.

Medication It is wise to wait and see how a child's body deals naturally with fever. Giving a child medication always entails some risk, however small, which should be considered before proceeding. A physician should be consulted if a parent has questions about the advisability of giving fever-reducing medication.

Read the full discussion of choosing and giving nonprescription medications in Chapter 7, "Caring for the Sick Child at Home."

Fevers usually disappear as soon as an underlying condition or cause is identified and treated successfully. In the case of recurrent disease, fever may return with each new flare-up.

Once diagnosis of an FUO is made, appropriate treatment for the underlying cause can be started. Fevers caused by infections usually begin to subside within a day or two of the beginning of treatment. Fevers due to other causes may respond more slowly.

PREVENTION

Fever cannot be prevented; however, some specific diseases that cause fever can be prevented by means of vaccination, medication, nutrition, or improved methods of sanitation.

FLAT FEET

DESCRIPTION

When a child's foot does not have an arch, the foot is flat. An infant always has flat feet because of a thick pad of fat present on the soles. Once a child begins to walk, fat pads begin to disappear. Normal activity strengthens and shapes the ligaments, tendons, and bones of the feet into an arch. After several years of walking, the arch of the foot is fully formed, usually by the time a child is 3 or 4 years old.

Flat feet may result from bone or ligament problems present at birth that can persist into adulthood.

Children usually outgrow mild flat feet. With effective treatment, severe flat feet can usually be corrected.

CAUSE

Flat feet not part of natural development may be caused by loose ligaments in the foot. Loose ligaments cannot hold bones in position, and as a result, the rear of the heel and the front of the foot abnormally turn outward. This repositioning flattens the arch of the foot.

SIGNS AND SYMPTOMS

When a flat-footed child stands, the entire sole of the foot touches the ground. Flat-footed children usually walk on the inside of the foot and break down the inner side, heel, and sole of their shoes.

DIAGNOSIS

Flat feet are obvious when a child stands. A physician can make a diagnosis of flat feet by observing the presence of characteristic signs. A physician also examines the feet for possible complications. The mobility of the foot joints and the strength of the tendons may be tested, and X-ray films of the feet may be taken.

COMPLICATIONS

Flat feet that cause painful muscle spasms in the leg and interfere with a child's daily activities are known as symptomatic flat feet. Symptomatic flat feet may develop when a child is between the ages of 3 and 5.

TREATMENT

Depending on the severity of the condition, a child's flat feet may or may not require treatment. Treatment is usually not needed if the foot is twisted only slightly at the heel but is otherwise normal, particularly if a child has reached adolescence.

Treatment of severe flat feet in a child involves repositioning the foot bones so that they develop into a normal arch. A physician or physical therapist can prescribe walking exercises to be repeated at home that help straighten the foot bones and strengthen and tighten the ligaments. Children ages 4 to 6 years old with flat feet should walk barefoot on tiptoe for 5 to 10 minutes each day. An older flat-footed child should walk barefoot on the outer edge of the affected foot or feet with toes clenched for about 10 minutes each day.

If exercises are not sufficient to correct flat feet, a physician may recommend special shoes or appliances that help reposition bones and ligaments into an arch. All children's shoes should fit well in the heel and have room at the toe.

Orthopedic appliances such as plastic inserts that hold the foot straight, heel wedges, heel "seats" or cups, or sole wedges can be placed in a regular shoe. These appliances work by gradually straightening the bones at the rear of the foot, eventually resulting in the formation of an arch. Arch supports may be recommended in cases of very severe flat feet.

If flat feet cannot be corrected through exercise or orthopedic appliances, and are troublesome and painful, a physician may recommend surgery.

PREVENTION

Flat feet cannot be prevented. Effective treatment may prevent feet from becoming permanently flat.

FOCUSING PROBLEMS

DESCRIPTION

The most common focusing problems during childhood are nearsightedness (myopia), farsightedness (hyperopia), and astigmatism. These are all "errors of refraction" involving defects in the child's focusing mechanism.

In normal vision, the lens (an inner part of the eye involved in focusing), which is behind the pupil (the circular opening that allows light to enter the eye), projects the image onto the retina (the rear portion of the eye that receives light rays) in the back of the eye. The image is focused first by the cornea (the transparent membrane covering the eye), which bends the light rays before they strike the lens. The lens performs the final focusing in this process, which is called refraction. (See Fig. 23, p. 362.)

A child who is nearsighted, or myopic, cannot see objects in the distance clearly be-

FIG. 23. THE EYE (side view)

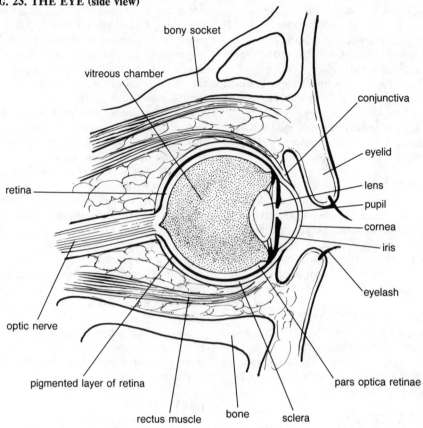

cause the image is focused in front of the retina. Myopia can develop quite gradually between age 6 and adolescence. It is also possible that the school-age child who once was able to read the blackboard easily may a year later see only a blur, even though he or she may have no trouble reading a book.

When a child is farsighted, or hyperopic, the eyes must focus more to see objects at close range because the light rays are focused behind the retina. Farsightedness occurs more frequently than nearsightedness during early childhood, but children are usually able to adjust and keep their eyes in focus.

A child with astigmatism has difficulty focusing on vertical and horizontal objects at the same time. Light entering the eye is refracted irregularly, making vision hazy. Astigmatism may occur alone or with nearsightedness or farsightedness. A mild degree of astigmatism is common among children and may produce no problems. The more irregular the bending of light rays, however, the greater the blurring of vision.

CAUSE

The shape of the cornea, the shape or position of the lens, the dimensions of the eyeball, especially the distance from the lens to the retina, or any combination of these factors may contribute to focusing problems. These traits may be inherited, causing certain focusing problems to affect more than one family member. *Eye injuries* or foreign objects in the eye can also cause vision problems.

SIGNS AND SYMPTOMS

A child with focusing problems may hold a book very near to the eyes, may sit very close to the television, and may squint to improve focus. Older children may notice an inability to see the blackboard, street signs, or other distant objects clearly.

DIAGNOSIS

A physician or ophthalmologist (eye specialist) may test a very young child's vision by watching the way the child follows brightly colored, moving objects. When a child has a sufficient vocabulary, he or she can identify and name small pictures held at increasing distances. For children between the ages of 3 and 6, the ophthalmologist may use the E chart, which contains only the letter E in different sizes and positions. The Snellen eye chart, which is composed of letters and numbers in different sizes and positions, is usually used to test vision among children who can read. Most pediatricians use such tests in their general examinations of children.

COMPLICATIONS

Focusing problems that are not treated can lead to eyestrain and fatigue. Untreated focusing problems may be a handicap in reading but usually do not cause learning difficulties.

TREATMENT

Eyeglasses usually correct a child's vision to normal levels. Children with focusing problems may begin wearing eyeglasses as young as 1 year old. Shatter-resistant lenses are recommended for all children who need glasses. During adolescence, contact lenses may be an alternative to glasses. Corrective contact lenses are not usually recommended, however, until a child is old enough to be responsible for the meticulous cleaning and care regimen they require.

PREVENTION

There are no generally accepted ways of influencing the development of refractive errors. Early detection allows the prescription of glasses, when appropriate, so that the child can see more clearly. Prompt treatment can spare the child the disabling effects of faulty vision and can reduce other problems, such as poor school performance, that may result from poor vision.

There are misconceptions about the prevention of focusing problems. Holding books close when reading, prolonged reading, or reading in dim light do not damage vision. Sustained visual activity may lead to eye fatigue, a condition easily corrected by adequate rest.

FOOD ALLERGY

EMERGENCY ACTION

If a child has signs of *shock* (weak, rapid pulse, increased breathing rate, thirst, dizziness or fainting, and cool, clammy, pale skin) or airway obstruction, start emergency first aid (see Chapter 10, "Basic First Aid") and seek immediate medical attention. Epinephrine is usually administered to control such severe allergic reactions. (For a discussion of severe allergic reactions see *allergies.)*

DESCRIPTION

If a child has an allergic reaction after eating certain foods, a food allergy (extreme sensitivity to specific foods) exists. Any child can have a food allergy.

Most children with food allergies are able to eat limited amounts of offending foods without reaction. Other children, however, are so sensitive that eating even the smallest amount of certain foods produces violent reactions. Severe allergic reactions (leading to *shock)* are rare in children, however.

All children with food allergies can prevent allergic reactions by avoiding offending foods. In addition, many children outgrow food allergies, although nut and fish allergies are usually permanent.

CAUSE

An allergic reaction affects a child with extreme sensitivities to certain substances (allergens). When a child eats a particular food, the immune system produces an antibody, a protein compound specific for the offending allergen. Production of this antibody is the first step in a chain of events which together create a severe allergic response. Since children possess widely varying sensitivities, every food has the potential to cause an allergic reaction. The most common allergens are cow's milk, eggs, nuts, fish, and shellfish. Less common allergens are wheat, corn, berries, citrus fruits, peas, beans, and certain spices.

SIGNS AND SYMPTOMS

Characteristic signs and symptoms of a food allergy usually appear within a few minutes to an hour of eating an offending food. These include swelling of the lips and mouth, *hives, rash, asthma, wheezing, vomiting,* stuffy nose, *abdominal pain, diarrhea,* and, if the reaction is severe, *shock.*

DIAGNOSIS

If a child has a reaction for the first time after eating a particular food, a physician should be consulted to confirm the diagnosis.

A physician must rule out other possible

causes of a reaction to certain foods when diagnosing a food allergy. Children may be sensitive to contaminants (such as bacteria), food additives (such as dye or preservatives), or natural toxins (such as penicillin in milk) found in certain foods. Lack of an enzyme (such as lactase) often produces symptoms that resemble an allergic reaction.

Once other possible causes are ruled out, diagnosis of food allergy is based on a history of reactions occurring after eating the suspected food. Skin and blood tests are also performed.

An elimination diet is often used to determine which foods produce an allergic reaction. Suspect foods are removed from a child's diet for 7 to 10 days to see if symptoms disappear. If symptoms reappear when suspect foods are returned to a child's diet, a specific allergen can usually be identified.

A more accurate method of establishing a diagnosis, however, is a double-blind challenge in which food or a placebo (a neutral compound, identical in appearance with the food being tested) is given to the child without the parents or the physician knowing which is which. If a child reacts to the placebo, the reaction is not caused by a food allergy.

Allergylike symptoms may affect children who have emotional reactions to certain foods (such as association with an unpleasant occasion). These children experience allergylike symptoms when specific foods are returned to their diets. To avoid this reaction and to determine accurately whether or not an allergy exists, foods should be disguised (mixed in with other foods, for example) when used in an elimination diet.

If characteristic symptoms do not disappear and reappear with an elimination diet, the reaction is probably not caused by an allergy.

TREATMENT

The first step in treatment of a food allergy is to remove offending foods from a child's diet. Symptoms should disappear within a short time.

Until symptoms disappear, steps can be taken to make a child more comfortable. Children should drink plenty of clear liquids to replace fluids lost through *vomiting* or *diarrhea*. Itching from *hives* can be lessened with antihistamines, cool compresses, or calamine lotion, and decongestants can be used to clear up a child's stuffy nose. If *asthma* is present, a physician can prescribe medication to ease breathing difficulty. A physician may also prescribe an epinephrine kit for emergency home use if a child experiences a severe reaction following eating.

Since children often outgrow food allergies by age 2 or 3, they should be tested (through an elimination diet) every 3 to 6 months to see if the allergy still exists.

PREVENTION

The best way to prevent an allergic reaction to food is to avoid eating the offending foods. This is not always easy, however, because offending foods (particularly flour, corn starch, eggs, milk, legumes, and spices) may be hidden in processed foods or foods prepared in restaurants.

FOOD POISONING

EMERGENCY ACTION

Consult a physician, the nearest hospital emergency room, or a poison information center for information and assistance for any child who may have consumed spoiled, infected, or contaminated food.

Any child who has severe *diarrhea* or is *vomiting* repeatedly should be taken to an emergency room immediately. *Dehydration* (severe loss of essential body fluids and salts) can occur rapidly and be life-threatening to children, especially infants and young children. Dehydration is characterized by cool, dry, pale skin; dry tongue; thirst; listlessness; rapid pulse; sunken eyes; and for an infant, sunken fontanel—the soft spot on the top of the head.

DESCRIPTION

Sometimes when children become ill with *vomiting* or *diarrhea* after eating or drinking what parents suspect may have been spoiled, infected, or contaminated food, the problem is referred to as food poisoning. Often, however, a child's vomiting or diarrhea is caused by bacteria, viruses, or parasites that have no connection with food or drink.

Two common bacteria, types of *Staphylococcus* and *Salmonella,* produce illness under certain conditions. In addition, food-related illness can be caused by botulism, poisonous mushrooms, and contaminated shellfish. Each of these types of food poisoning is described in detail below.

Food poisoning causes signs and symptoms of illness in the gastrointestinal (GI) tract—esophagus, stomach, and intestines—and affects other organs in the body. Characteristic problems include nausea, vomiting, diarrhea, and low-grade fever. Breathing, nerve, and muscle functions may also be affected.

Bacteria may attack the body directly or indirectly. Most bacteria operate indirectly by first secreting a toxin (an irritating biological poison) which then invades specific organs or entire systems of the body. In spoiled food, for example, a variety of staphylococci secretes a toxin that invades the stomach, causing nausea and vomiting. Other toxins may attack nerves, as sometimes happens with botulism, mushroom poisoning, and paralytic shellfish poisoning. A direct attack may not involve the action of a toxin. Salmonella, for example, works on the lining of the intestine, producing an infection and causing diarrhea.

Pasteurization, refrigeration, and improved preparation and preservation of foods have greatly reduced illness and deaths during infancy caused by food poisoning. Illness caused by contaminated food, however, continues to strike thousands of children and adults every year, and food poisoning is sometimes serious enough to require hospitalization.

STAPHYLOCOCCAL FOOD POISONING

SIGNS AND SYMPTOMS
Within 1 to 6 hours of eating food contaminated with staphylococcal toxin, a child typically develops one, often all, of the following symptoms: nausea, retching, *vomiting,* and severe cramps. These symptoms often affect many, though not necessarily all, members of a family or a group of children exposed to the contaminated food. Less common symptoms include *fever, headache,* chills, *dizziness, diarrhea,* and muscular weakness. The most severe phase usually lasts about 12 hours but can persist from 24 to 48 hours.

CAUSE
Each year more than half of all identified cases of food poisoning in the United States are caused by staphylococcal ("staph") bacteria toxin that affects the stomach and intestinal tract. Staph food contamination usually occurs when dairy products, prepared foods, and meats are inadequately refrigerated, allowing the bacteria to multiply rapidly.

Any meat not kept uniformly cold in refrigerators and salad dressings (especially mayonnaise-based dressings such as those used for potato and tuna salads and cole slaw) that spoil quickly in summer heat are two of the most common carriers of staph food poisoning.

Staphylococcus bacteria, commonly present in animal carcasses at the time of slaughter, sometimes multiply before carcasses are refrigerated. Once inside the human stomach, staph bacteria begin to produce a toxin that primarily affects the stomach.

Staph bacteria may also be introduced into foods during preparation and handling by a person with an open staph sore—any break in the skin infected by staph bacteria.

DIAGNOSIS
A physician makes a diagnosis of food poisoning based upon a history of a child's *vomiting* and cramps as well as identification of anyone else who has become ill after eating similar food (typically: meat, fowl, or fish; homemade-mayonnaise based salad dressings; or custard- or cream-filled pastries). A physician often wants to examine a child who has become particularly ill with what may be food poisoning. Laboratory tests to identify a specific toxin are complicated and not usually necessary.

COMPLICATIONS
Children who have lost excessive amounts of fluids through *vomiting* may become dehydrated (see *dehydration*). Hospitalization may be required for intravenous replacement of essential body fluids and salts.

TREATMENT
During the period of severe nausea and *vomiting,* a child requires bed rest, small amounts of fluids, and reassurance. If repeated vomiting persists longer than 4 hours and the child is unable to retain fluids, a physician should be consulted. Parents should be alert for any signs of *dehydration* (see Emergency Action, above), especially if babies or young children are involved.

When symptoms begin to subside, the child should be encouraged to drink more fluids (such as clear soups and tea, gelatin water, and flat soft drinks, such as ginger ale). Milk and milk products should be avoided. Over the next few days, as the appetite returns, soft, easily digested foods may be tried. These might include rice cereal, pureed chicken, milk-free mashed potatoes, or sweet potatoes. Feedings should be small, and the child should be encouraged, but not forced, to drink liquids. Fruit juices should be given only in very small amounts. Apple juice should be avoided. If the child continues to improve, a normal, well-balanced diet can be resumed gradually over the next 1 to 3 days. No medication is usually required.

PREVENTION

Uninterrupted refrigeration below 40° F (4.4° C) of meats, fowl, dairy products, and sauces, salads, and dressings, especially during warm weather, is essential to help reduce the risk of staph food poisoning. Staph bacteria toxin contaminates food in a few hours in warm temperatures. It is usually impossible to detect deterioration of food by either telltale odors or discoloration.

Staph toxin, once having entered food, is heat-resistant. No amount of heating or cooking can destroy the toxin and its potential danger to those who consume it. When any doubt exists about the safety of food in which staph may be present, it is wise to dispose of that food immediately. Even a small dose of staph toxin can sicken a child.

Picnic foods should never be taken outdoors without sufficient insulated cooling material to ensure freshness. If food cannot be adequately refrigerated or cooled during hot weather, it should not be eaten. If children's lunch boxes are left in a warm room, they become ideal containers for breeding staph bacteria. When eating out, particularly in summer months, it is important to be reasonably sure of proper food preparation, especially of meats, sauces, gravies, and dressings.

SALMONELLA INFECTIONS

SIGNS AND SYMPTOMS

Within 12 to 48 hours after eating food contaminated by *Salmonella,* a child usually develops one or more of the following symptoms: abdominal cramps, *diarrhea,* chills and fever up to 104° F (40.0° C) and *headache.* Occasionally nausea and *vomiting* occur.

Stools are watery and may occasionally contain mucus, pus, or blood. For about half the affected individuals, symptoms subside within 24 hours. Young infants or children who have difficulty fighting infections or who have consumed a large dose of a powerful type of bacteria may be more severely ill for a week or longer.

CAUSE

Salmonella bacteria affect the stomach and intestinal tract. They can flourish in raw or incompletely cooked meat, particularly pork or fowl, eggs and egg products, including cracked eggs contaminated by stool from chickens; dairy products; shellfish; and pet foods. These bacteria can also be present on household pets, such as turtles and hamsters. Illness may occur when food or drink is consumed that has been contaminated by the droppings of animals, such as cattle, rodents, and household pets.

Some salmonella bacteria are spread by carrier individuals who unknowingly or carelessly contaminate food in a public institution, such as a restaurant, hospital, or school; or during a large meeting or at a picnic. Salmonella bacteria typically are transmitted by persons who use the toilet and afterwards do not wash hands carefully with soap and water.

DIAGNOSIS

A physician notes the signs and symptoms of illness and may want to examine a severely ill child. Specific diagnosis of salmonella food poisoning requires analysis of a stool or blood sample and sometimes analysis of the suspected food, if it is still available.

COMPLICATIONS

A severely dehydrated child may require hospitalization in order to replace body fluids and salts. Infants and very young children can quickly become dehydrated. If an infant is not treated promptly, salmonella can invade an infant's bloodstream and cause a life-threatening infection.

TREATMENT

Bed rest is recommended. When diarrhea begins to subside, juices in small amounts (with the exception of apple juice, which aggravates the problem) and warm, clear fluids, such as tea, are helpful to replace lost fluids and salts. Milk and milk products should be avoided. Over the next few days, as the child's appetite returns, soft, easily digested foods may be tried. These might include rice cereal, pureed chicken, milk-free mashed potatoes, or sweet potatoes. Feedings should be small, and the child should be encouraged, but not forced, to drink liquids. If the child continues to improve, a normal, well-balanced diet can be resumed gradually over the next 1 to 3 days. No medication is usually required.

Infants and very young children are given antibiotics to reduce their risk of developing a *bloodstream infection.*

PREVENTION

The most effective means of preventing salmonella infections is to make certain that all foods are cooked completely, particularly poultry, meats, fish, shellfish, eggs, and unpeeled vegetables.

Salmonellae can sometimes multiply rapidly when food is cooled and later reheated. Leftovers should be refrigerated immediately at a temperature lower than 40° F (4.4° C), then reheated fully for the next serving. Soups and gravies should be reheated to the boiling point. Slow cooling and slow, incomplete reheating provide *Salmonella* bacteria with time to multiply. For example, a common problem is contamination of stuffing not cooked immediately after preparation or left inside fowl after the first roasting. Slow cooling and slow reheating of the carcass permit the bacteria to grow quickly to dangerously high numbers. Dressings or stuffings should always be removed from fowl immediately after the first serving.

Cleanliness can also help prevent salmonella poisoning. Unclean hands, particularly when contaminated by human waste, spread *Salmonella* bacteria. Thorough soap-and-water handwashing after using the toilet helps to prevent salmonella infection. Children should also be urged to wash their hands after handling household pets or other animals.

BOTULISM

Botulism, a rare but powerful food poisoning, involves an extremely dangerous toxin produced by one type of bacterium.

CAUSE

Botulism occurs most frequently in improperly prepared home-canned food, particularly vegetables, meat, and poultry. On rare occasions botulism has been traced to commercially prepared foods, such as canned tuna and salmon that are improperly processed—without sufficient sustained heat to destroy all botulism bacteria. The bacteria can then produce a highly potent toxin inside cans, jars, or vacuum-sealed packages.

Children under 1 year of age are susceptible to microscopic botulism cells called spores, which may be present in commercially or home-packed honey. After a child has eaten contaminated honey, bacteria may grow from the spores in the intestinal tract and secrete toxin which then is absorbed by the intestines.

SIGNS AND SYMPTOMS

Within 16 hours to 5 days of eating food contaminated by toxin from the botulism bacteria, a range of progressively worsening symptoms can occur, beginning with *headache* and *dizziness* and progressing to double vision, muscle paralysis, *vomiting,* and breathing and swallowing difficulties. In severe cases death may occur because of paralysis that interferes with breathing.

Botulism affecting newborns ("infant botulism") can cause *constipation,* which leads to weak sucking when breastfeeding. The infant becomes hungry and often thirsty. A condition sometimes called "floppy baby" can develop, characterized by listlessness and extremely poor muscle tone.

DIAGNOSIS

If botulism is suspected, immediate consultation with a physician or poison information center is necessary. Neither food nor fluids should be given. A physician records the details of a child's signs and symptoms and inquires about food the child has consumed during the preceding week. A careful physical examination follows. A sample of the suspected food or the patient's blood and stool can be analyzed for the presence of botulism toxin.

TREATMENT

Hospitalization is usually required so that a child may be given antitoxin and other necessary treatment. Children with botulism poisoning whose signs and symptoms are recognized early in their illness usually recover fully. The length of time in the hospital varies according to the severity of a child's illness. Advances in pediatric intensive care in hospitals, including use of antitoxin, also enhance the chances of complete recovery. Only in cases of untreated severe botulism poisoning are children in danger of dying.

PREVENTION

Extreme care should be exercised in home canning and preserving of vegetables, meat, and poultry. Parents should be alert to any public announcement of commercial manufacturers' recalls of improperly canned foods such as fish, soups, or liver paste. Because botulism bacteria spores can also contaminate honey, it is recommended that honey not be given to children less than 1 year old.

MUSHROOM POISONING

DESCRIPTION

Although just 100 or so of the 5,000 species of wild mushrooms in the United States are poisonous, one taste of any of several poisonous mushrooms can cause a child to become sick enough to require medical attention or hospitalization. Death from mushroom poisoning, however, is rare.

Differentiating harmless mushrooms from poisonous mushrooms and toadstools is difficult even for experts: many mushrooms change shape, color, and texture in the course of a few days. Even with the aid of a full-color guide to mushrooms, an amateur can make mistakes—and in certain rare cases a single mistake can be fatal. No method of identification is foolproof.

Common mushrooms of the Amanita family are those most responsible for poisonings: fly agaric, death cap, and destroying angel. Lesser known mushrooms, such as those containing muscarine, can produce reactions ranging from uncomfortable to life-threatening.

SIGNS AND SYMPTOMS

Almost immediately after eating poisonous wild mushrooms, several symptoms may begin to develop: *abdominal pain, vomiting,* excessive salivation, severe *diarrhea,* sweating, double vision, twitching, lack of muscle coordination, *seizures,* and slowed heartbeat. If Amanita is involved, vomiting is delayed.

CAUSE

A number of different toxins cause illness among humans. The severity, duration, and complications of poisoning depend upon the particular toxin involved and the amount consumed.

DIAGNOSIS

A physician notes a child's signs and symptoms and performs a careful physical examination. A specific diagnosis can be made by identifying the species of mushroom through analysis of the cap, stalk, and root ball of the mushroom itself, and if possible, through analysis of the spores (cells) contained in the child's vomit. If mushroom poisoning is suspected, a fresh sample of the mushroom should be taken along when seeking help.

TREATMENT

If mushroom poisoning is suspected, the nearest poison information center or nearest available physician should be consulted immediately. A poison center staff member or a physician may recommend that *vomiting* be induced as quickly as possible. Ipecac syrup, available in all pharmacies, is the most reliable preparation for inducing vomiting. Never give ipecac syrup to a child without specific instructions to do so.

Hospitalization may be necessary depending upon the type of mushroom poisoning and the severity of symptoms.

PREVENTION

Parents should warn children of the hazards of picking and sampling even a small part of any wild mushroom or fungus, no matter how harmless or inviting it may appear.

PARALYTIC SHELLFISH POISONING

SIGNS AND SYMPTOMS

Within a half hour of eating certain contaminated shellfish—clams, oysters, mussels, and scallops—children may begin to complain of a burning sensation inside the nose; tingling and numbness in the lips, mouth, and face; breathing difficulties; and then an overall muscular weakness, sometimes resulting in partial paralysis of one or more of the arms and legs.

CAUSE

Tiny poisonous organisms are responsible for the "red tide" which occurs from time to time along any of the coasts of the United States. When humans eat shellfish that have fed upon these toxic organisms, various symptoms of "paralytic shellfish poisoning" can occur. Temporary paralysis is the most severe result of consuming this poison.

DIAGNOSIS

Parents should call the nearest poison information center or a physician if any possibility exists that a child has consumed infected shellfish. A physician notes the child's physical signs and symptoms and performs a careful physical examination. The physician needs to know if the child has recently eaten clams, scallops, mussels, or oysters from beds or tidewaters known or suspected to be contaminated by red tide. Blood tests may not be necessary to make a specific diagnosis.

TREATMENT

Home treatment usually consists of rest, adequate fluids, and a normal diet. If muscular weakness or paralysis occurs, a child is hospitalized. A physician should be asked to monitor even mild symptoms that require only home treatment.

PREVENTION

No one should go clamming or shellfish harvesting on beaches or tidal flats that have been closed because of a red tide warning. If a red tide alert occurs, parents should buy shellfish only from reputable, well-known dealers.

FOOT ABNORMALITIES

DESCRIPTION

Some abnormal foot problems result from bone and muscle malformations in the foot and ankle that develop before birth. *Flat feet, pigeon toes, clubfoot,* metatarsus adductus, and calcaneovalgus are the most common abnormal foot malformations. Vertical talus is rare form of abnormal foot.

Metatarsus adductus, one of the most common foot malformations present at birth, is a condition in which the front of the foot turns inward (unlike pigeon toes, in which the entire foot turns in toward the opposite foot). This condition affects approximately 70 percent of newborns; the majority of problems correct themselves without treatment within the first few days of life. The condition may persist, however, if an infant sleeps on his or her stomach with the feet turned inward. If metatarsus adductus is not corrected, it may be difficult to find shoes that fit the child properly.

Another foot malformation, calcaneovalgus, affects approximately 30 percent of infants. In this case the entire foot bends upward toward the knee, occasionally bending far enough so that the toes touch the front of the shin. The heel of the foot turns outward. An infant cannot flex the foot downward because the muscles in the front of the foot are short and tight and restrict movement.

Vertical talus is an uncommon foot malformation which, if uncorrected, interferes with an infant's ability to walk. The rear of an infant's foot is held off the ground and the front of the foot flexes upward toward the leg. The center of the sole remains on the ground, resulting in a "rocker bottom," or upward bowing of the foot. An orthopedist (bone specialist) should be consulted as soon as vertical talus is identified.

With early treatment most foot abnormalities can be corrected. Approximately 1 percent of cases of metatarsus adductus, however, persist into childhood regardless of treatment.

CAUSE

Abnormal feet are caused by bone malformations and muscle problems that develop in the feet before birth.

DIAGNOSIS

An orthopedist can identify each type of abnormal foot by the appearance of an infant's foot and by taking X-ray films of underlying bones and muscles.

COMPLICATIONS

An infant with a calcaneovalgus foot may also have a flat foot. Walking difficulties persist for life if an abnormal foot is not properly corrected.

TREATMENT

Treatment of metatarsus adductus is usually successful if begun before an infant is 8 months old. If the front of an infant's foot can easily be moved outward, treatment may involve only vigorous stretching exercises prescribed by an orthopedist or physical therapist.

If the front of an infant's foot cannot be moved easily, the use of special open-toed shoes that gently straighten an infant's foot may be recommended. An infant should wear these shoes 24 hours a day except when bathing or swimming. If an infant's leg also turns in, an open-toed shoe may be attached to each end of a bar. This procedure prevents the leg from turning in while an infant sleeps on his or her stomach.

Use of open-toed shoes should continue until a child no longer sleeps on the stomach, although metatarsus adductus may already be corrected. If treatment does not begin until age 6 months, a child may need to continue wearing open-toed shoes past the age of 2.

If treatment with open-toed shoes is not successful, an orthopedist may recommend the use of casts to move the front of an infant's foot gradually into a straight position. Casts are changed at weekly intervals to accommodate a child's growth and to straighten the foot further; 2 or 3 changes are usually needed. Once metatarsus adductus is corrected, an open-toed shoe should be worn to ensure that the front of the foot does not turn in when a child lies on the stomach.

Unlike metatarsus adductus, calcaneovalgus is usually corrected with plaster splinting. An orthopedist places a splint along the top (bridge) of the foot and holds it in place with an elastic bandage. This procedure gradually pushes the foot down into a normal position. At home the splint is removed several times a day so that the foot can be exercised to lengthen and loosen muscles further. Splints are adjusted at weekly intervals by an orthopedist; complete straightening usually takes 2 to 4 weeks. Stretching exercises should be continued after a foot is straightened to ensure that muscles are no longer tight.

Vertical talus should always be treated by an orthopedist. In some cases a child's foot may be treated successfully through casting. Surgery, however, is usually required for complete correction.

See also *clubfoot; flat feet; pigeon toes.*

PREVENTION

Abnormal feet cannot be prevented.

FOREIGN OBJECTS, SWALLOWED

EMERGENCY ACTION

If a child begins to choke or cough repeatedly after swallowing a foreign object of any kind, seek medical assistance. Do not attempt to dislodge an object that interferes with breathing because complete obstruction may follow.

If an *infant* is gasping, cannot breathe, · and begins to turn blue, give series of four back blows followed by four chest thrusts as follows:

(1) Keep the infant straddled over your forearm with the head lower than the body.

(2) Firmly slap the infant four times between the shoulder blades.

(3) Turn infant face up, keeping the head lower than the body. Place hand just below the internipple line on the breastbone. Push in and up four times. The object should pop out of the infant's throat. If it does not, continue alternating four back blows with four chest thrusts. (See Figs. 15A and B, p. 137.)

If a *child* is gasping, cannot breathe, and begins to turn blue, but is still *conscious,* apply the Heimlich maneuver as follows:

(1) Stand behind the child and reach around with both arms to encircle the waist.

(2) Make a fist with either hand, placing the thumb side against the child's abdomen midway between the naval and rib cage.

(3) Grasp the fist with the other hand and pull quickly inward and upward into the child's abdomen. The object should pop out of the child's throat. If it does not, repeat the maneuver several times.

(4) While applying the maneuver, you should hold your elbows away from the child's body to avoid squeezing the child's sides and perhaps injuring the ribs. (See Fig. 16, p. 138.)

If a *child* is *unconscious* because of choking, apply the Heimlich maneuver as follows:

(1) Position the child face up on his or her back.

(2) Kneel beside a small child or straddle the body of an older child.

(3) Place the heel of one hand in the middle of the child's abdomen between the navel and rib cage. Place free hand on top of the first.

(4) Push the heel of bottom hand into the stomach with four quick upward thrusts. The object should pop out. If it does not, repeat the maneuver several times. (See Fig. 17, p. 139.)

If a child experiences steady or intermitten pain or vomits after swallowing a foreign object, intestinal bleeding may occur. Seek medical assistance promptly if it is known—or even suspected—that a pointed or sharp object has been swallowed.

DESCRIPTION

As part of learning and exploring, small children frequently put things in their mouths. Some are edible and digestible, others are not. Children 2 to 4 years old seem more likely than others to put nondigestible objects in their mouths and swallow them accidentally or deliberately. The size of a foreign object relative to the size of a child is often the critical consideration.

The foreign objects most commonly swallowed are slippery and smooth or nearly so: parts or pieces of toys, coins, marbles, buttons, stones, eyes from dolls, fruit pits, and button-size alkaline or mercury batteries, including those that power watches, hearing aids, and other miniaturized electronic equipment. Such batteries are popularly referred to as button batteries.

Pointed or even rough foreign objects similarly, if less frequently, find their way into children's mouths and down their throats: pins of all kinds (including hairpins and safety pins); puzzle pieces; pieces of glass, tile, and bone; nails; and doll house equipment, especially toy spoons, knives, and forks.

Whether smooth or pointed, most foreign objects pass through the digestive system harmlessly. (The digestive system consists of the esophagus, stomach, and small and large intestines.) Sometimes even razor blades pass through without doing harm.

A large or irregularly shaped object may lodge in the esophagus, the tube that connects the throat to the stomach, and cause considerable discomfort. If the object is not removed promptly, it can severely irritate or ulcerate (cause a small wound that does not heal) the lining of the esophagus or even perforate (puncture) it. Once foreign objects pass the midpoint of the esophagus, they usually enter the stomach directly without further difficulty. And once objects reach the stomach, 90 percent or more of them work their way through the small and large intestines without additional difficulties.

The outlook for children who swallow objects is almost always excellent and without complications. For the small number of children who must have the objects removed by a physician, both treatment and recovery are usually swift and uncomplicated.

SIGNS AND SYMPTOMS

An object stuck in a child's esophagus can produce a tight, constricted feeling, coughing, gurgling sounds in the throat, or difficulty swallowing. Sometimes it is possible to swallow liquids, but any attempt to swallow solid or semisolid foods may cause a child to choke, vomit, or both. If the esophagus is scratched or scraped, inflammation or ulceration can follow. If either occurs, a child usually experiences soreness or pain in the area of the breastbone when swallowing.

In most cases a child experiences no signs or symptoms once an object is swallowed and has entered the stomach. This is true even if the object is pointed or has sharp edges or angles. It is possible, of course, for a large object to become stuck as it progresses slowly through the intestines or for a sharp one to scrape the intestinal wall. The probability of this happening, however, is slight.

Occasionally when foreign objects are swallowed, choking and coughing occur. Throat pain may occur if the object is large or irregularly shaped. The throat may be scraped, and slight bleeding may result. If an object lodges in the pharynx (throat) or trachea (windpipe), coughing, gagging, *choking,* and breathing difficulty may occur.

A foreign object usually moves through the intestinal tract in anywhere from 2 to 12 days, but as long as 3 weeks may be required for a large object to pass through. Progress of a fairly large object through the digestive system is occasionally slowed at one of three junctions: where the stomach empties into the small intestine; where the upper and middle parts of the small intestine join; and where the small intestine empties into the large intestine. If the object is smooth, it usually clears the anus without difficulty. Sharp- or rough-edged objects, however, can cause considerable pain as they pass through the lower rectum and anus. Rectal bleeding rarely occurs, as most objects become embedded in feces by the time they reach the anus.

DIAGNOSIS

If an object is stuck in the esophagus, it can be located with an instrument called an esophagoscope, a slender, flexible, lighted tube that allows a physician to see the interior of the esophagus.

Finding the exact location of a foreign object once it has entered the intestines can be difficult; occasionally it proves impossible. X-ray films are the single reliable means of identifying a metallic swallowed object; nonmetallic objects may not show up on an X-ray film. X-ray films are also helpful in cases where doubt exists whether something has actually been swallowed. Sometimes what a parent suspects has gone down an infant's throat is found later on the floor, in the crib or bed, or between the pillows of a chair or sofa.

Once an object has been located, its progress through the intestines is usually checked weekly by X-ray film. A physician may consider surgery if X-ray films show an object has not moved at all during a 7-to-10-day period.

COMPLICATIONS

If a foreign object causes ulceration of the esophagus, bleeding occurs. Infection may develop in the esophagus and spread to the airways. *Pneumonia* can further complicate a child's recovery.

If an irregularly shaped or sharp-edged object becomes stuck as it progresses through the intestines, a child may have bloody bowel movements or rectal bleeding. If perforation of the intestine occurs, abdominal pain, rigidity, bloating, nausea and *vomiting,* and *fever* can occur. These conditions require immediate medical attention.

A button battery can be especially hazardous if it leaks, although this problem is quite rare. Its corrosive contents can cause extreme irritation, ulceration, or perforation of the esophagus, stomach, or intestine.

TREATMENT

If a foreign object is swallowed, do not attempt to feed anything to the child.

After an object stuck in the esophagus has been located by an esophagoscope, a child is given local anesthesia (medication that reduces or deadens sensation) and a physician can remove the object with a pair of surgical tongs called forceps. If the object is far down in the esophagus, a surgeon may decide to push it down into the stomach and allow it to pass out of the body through the intestinal tract.

For those swallowed objects that reach the stomach, no treatment except patience and the passage of time is necessary. Because of their size, sharp edges, or material, however, certain objects are sufficiently hazardous to require intervention.

If a child has *abdominal pain,* bloating, nausea, *vomiting,* a bloody bowel movement, or rectal bleeding, a physician should be informed.

Diet should not be changed. Emetics (preparations that cause vomiting) and laxatives never should be given. Often a smooth object passes unnoticed in a bowel movement. If an object is rough or sharp, however, some physicians may ask parents to check all stools to see if it passes. This can be done by placing stools in a sieve and dissolving them with running water.

Surgical removal of a swallowed object is performed only when a child experiences one of these problems: failure of an object to progress through the intestinal tract; abdominal pain; bloody bowel movements or other signs and symptoms of possible perforation. In rare cases a button battery may require surgical removal if it is lodged in the esophagus. If a button battery passes into the stomach or the intestinal tract, it is almost always eliminated naturally. Surgical removal involves resection: cutting the intestine at the point of blockage, removing the object, and repairing the intestine.

No object made of or containing lead should remain in the intestinal tract longer than about two weeks. It is possible for a child to suffer *lead poisoning* from such a swallowed object if it rests in the digestive tract too long. Surgical removal may be necessary if a lead object remains stationary in the intestinal tract.

PREVENTION

Even when supervised, infants and young children should not play with very small objects. Children older than 4 years may comprehend some of the hazards involved, but it is unrealistic to assume that explanations or warnings will be entirely effective. Childproofing play areas can be protective (see Chapter 4, "Accident Prevention").

Through the teen years some children chew or gnaw on something habitually—even it is nothing more palatable than a pencil eraser or the cap of a ballpoint pen. An occasional, good-natured reminder about this type of habit may serve to alert an older child to the risks involved if a small object is swallowed accidentally.

FRACTURES

EMERGENCY ACTION

If a child suffers a fracture of any bone, seek immediate medical attention, especially if the child seems to be in *shock* (characterized by cool, clammy, pale skin; weak, rapid pulse; thirst; dizziness or faintness; and increased breathing rate). Do not give the child food or drink. Do not try to push a protruding bone back into the skin. If possible, immediately apply ice packs (ice wrapped in a towel or ice bag) to reduce swelling. Do not allow the child to use the involved area until the injury is examined by a medical professional.

If a child experiences extreme *breathing difficulty,* injury to the lung may be present and should be treated immediately (see *lung rupture).* Do not attempt to tape or otherwise immobilize fractured ribs, as this may interfere with breathing.

If a serious head or spinal injury (see *head and spinal injury)* is suspected, do not move the child at all. Maintain an open airway (see p. 124).

If a fracture involves bones other than the spine, skull, or ribs, immobilize the involved area if possible. (Nose and toe fractures do not require immobilization.) Do not straighten a deformed bone, unless the foot or hand is white and cold, indicating a circulatory problem. Use a sling for shoulder, elbow, and arm fractures. If the collarbone is fractured, immobilize it by wrapping an elastic bandage or other cloth around the shoulders, back, and chest in a figure eight. Immobilize a fractured pelvis by strapping the child to a stretcher or board, and use a splint (anything sturdy, such as a firm pillow, board, or even cardboard) to immobilize leg, ankle, or foot fractures. (Remove the shoe before splinting an ankle fracture.) Immobilize the jaw by wrapping a bandage around the head and chin. For detailed guidance on slings, splints, etc, see pp. 133–135.

If the skin is punctured by a broken bone, cover it with a sterile gauze dressing to prevent infection. If a sterile dressing is not available, do not cover the wound.

DESCRIPTION

A fracture is a break, crack, or buckling of a bone. Most children break a bone at least once during their lives; athletic children often break bones during their most active years. Bones most commonly fractured during childhood include those of the nose, the arm, the hand, the fingers, the thigh (femur), the shin (either the large bone, tibia, or the small bone, fibula), the ankle, the foot, and the toes. Less frequently, a collarbone or the pelvis is fractured. Fractures of the thigh and pelvis occur only with extremely forceful blows or impact (see Fig. 24, p. 374). A fracture may damage surrounding nerves and blood vessels.

The two major categories of fractures are open and closed. A closed fracture is usually a single, complete or incomplete break that does not puncture the skin. The most common simple fractures affecting children are greenstick, torus (or buckle), and compression fractures. Greenstick fractures are common only among children, because their bones are not fully developed and tend to bend and break incompletely. Torus fractures occur horizontally along the side of a long bone (such as the shinbone or an arm bone) and cause the bone to buckle rather than break. A compression fracture occurs when force "compresses" a bone and causes it to shatter.

A comminuted fracture results in several breaks in the same bone, and the bone may shatter into splinters. Open fractures usually cause only one break, but the broken ends of the bone can puncture the skin, exposing the bone to possible bacterial infection.

Open and closed fractures can be divided into more detailed categories. If a bone breaks but the broken ends do not move apart, the break is called a nondisplaced fracture. A displaced fracture occurs when the broken bone ends become separated and angulated or twisted. An angulated fracture can also occur when a bone bends and cracks but does not break.

Another fracture common during childhood is a stress fracture, a crack that results from repeated pressure on or injury to a bone, often because of frequent participation in a new activity. During childhood, stress fractures most often occur in the foot and the fibula and are common among young dancers, runners, or athletes who jump frequently (such as basketball players).

A child's bones heal quickly, and normal

FIG. 24. SKELETON

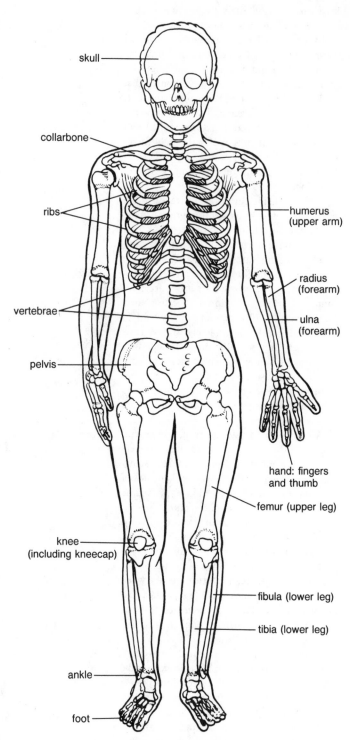

- skull
- collarbone
- ribs
- vertebrae
- pelvis
- humerus (upper arm)
- radius (forearm)
- ulna (forearm)
- hand: fingers and thumb
- femur (upper leg)
- knee (including kneecap)
- fibula (lower leg)
- tibia (lower leg)
- ankle
- foot

shape and function can usually be restored if a fracture is treated promptly. Severe fractures, however, often require involved treatment and rehabilitation, and full recovery is not always possible, particularly if joint surfaces or growth plates are damaged.

CAUSE

Most childhood fractures result from falls, forceful blows inflicted during sports (such as by physical contact with another person or by being hit with a ball), or repeated impact from activities (such as jumping or kicking). Severe fractures, particularly those involving the spine and skull, are most often the result of motor vehicle accidents or falls from a height.

SIGNS AND SYMPTOMS

Swelling, pain, and tenderness in the involved area are generally present with all fractures. The affected area cannot bear any pressure. In addition, bone deformity (such as a bend in a normally straight bone), lumps (caused by overlapping bones), and bruises (caused by blood leaking from broken blood vessels) may be present. If a fracture is open, broken ends of the bone may poke through the skin, and bleeding may occur.

In addition to characteristic fracture symptoms, shallow breathing may be present with rib fractures. Nose fractures are usually accompanied by breathing difficulty. Skull fractures may be accompanied by *headache* or unconsciousness. Rarely, a skull fracture at the base of the brain is accompanied by drainage of clear fluid from the nose. Symptoms of a spinal fracture may include numbness in the back, neck, arms, or legs.

The most common symptom of a stress fracture is a dull bone ache. A stress fracture often is often overlooked because the ache initially tends to go away when the affected area is at rest. After a week or so of repeated stress, however, aching becomes persistent.

DIAGNOSIS

A fracture should be suspected if a child complains of intense pain and limited motion in a limb following an accident. In some cases a child hears and feels a snap, which is followed by intense pain. Bone deformities, such as a bend in the middle of the shinbone, are more obvious indications of a fracture.

A physician determines the presence and

type of fracture based on a child's complaint of pain, obvious signs of deformity, and X-ray films. (Torus, compression, and stress fractures, however, can be difficult to detect even with X-rays.) History of a child's recent activities, including any accidents, also helps in diagnosis of a fracture. A physician also checks for injury to blood vessels (usually indicated by bruises) and nerves (often indicated by numbness).

COMPLICATIONS

Even with treatment, some fractures do not heal properly. As a result, a child may experience limited motion and persistent pain in the affected area. Bone deformities may occur if the broken bone does not set properly. Fractures involving the growth plate (located near the ends of long bones) may result in shortening or progressive deformity of a limb.

One or both lungs can be punctured by a broken rib, making breathing extremely difficult. If the spinal cord is injured when the spine is fractured, partial or complete paralysis may occur.

If an open fracture is not treated immediately, the bone may become infected. In severe cases, *osteomyelitis* (a severe bone infection) may develop.

TREATMENT

Emergency medical treatment of fractured bones is required to prevent complications (see Emergency Action, above). A broken bone must be properly aligned and immobilized to ensure correct healing. If a fracture involves bones of the arm, lower leg, hands, or feet, realignment is accomplished by manipulation, usually performed by an orthopedist (bone specialist). The ends of the bone are aligned as accurately as possible. Then the affected bone is placed in a cast to immobilize and protect it as healing occurs. Most casts are made of plaster or one of the newer, lightweight casting materials. To ensure complete immobilization, casts are applied so that the joints at both ends of the fractured bone are immobilized.

If a fracture occurs in a large bone (such as the thigh or pelvis), traction (which continuously pulls the muscles around the broken bone in opposite directions) is required to counteract strong muscle contractions, which can cause a bone to buckle and shorten. Traction may be needed for several weeks and is continued until broken bones line up properly and some healing occurs. A cast is then applied to immobilize the affected area and ensure proper healing.

Treatment of a fractured nose or toe involves taping to immobilize the area, since casting these bones is virtually impossible. Broken ribs are not taped (unless there is danger of puncturing the lungs) because holding the chest in place may interfere with breathing. If a lung is punctured, surgery is required.

If a child has fractured bones of the leg, ankle, or foot, crutches can be used. The top of the crutch should reach just below the armpit when the child stands erect. This position ensures that a child's weight rests on the hands, not on the nerves and blood vessels of the armpit, which are easily damaged. A child can use crutches until healing is complete. If a hand, arm, shoulder, or collarbone is broken, moving around is easier when the arm is held still with a sling.

If a bone cannot be set and immobilized easily, surgery may be required. However, this is necessary only when the risk of complications or permanent damage is high. Surgery is most often required for hip, elbow, and ankle fractures. When a cast is removed, a child should follow an exercise plan recommended by an orthopedist or physical therapist. Exercises focus on restoring a normal, painless range of motion and strength. Once healing is complete, a child gradually can return to normal activity.

Fractures of the spine or the skull require hospitalization and surgery. If nerves are damaged because of a spinal fracture, surgery, long-term therapy, and rehabilitation are needed.

PREVENTION

Some fractures can be avoided if children wear protective athletic gear such as helmets and pads when participating in contact sports. Seat belts and approved car seats should be used at all times when a child is riding in a motor vehicle. Children should wear approved helmets when riding bicycles, skateboards, or minibikes, or when riding as passengers on motorcycles. (See Chapter 4, "Accident Prevention.")

GENETIC DISORDERS

DESCRIPTION

Genetics is the science of heredity. It studies how characteristics are transmitted from parents to children through special inborn materials called genes and chromosomes. Genetics is also concerned with how individuals change, over time, as the result of highly complex interactions between their genetic materials and the environments in which they live.

A genetic disorder may be defined as any physical or mental abnormality that can be inherited from parents or transmitted to offspring.

Disorders present at birth are called congenital. Some genetic abnormalities are not apparent at birth, but a problem develops as the affected individual grows, and signs and symptoms become apparent. An abnormality may not make itself known until the individual reaches puberty or even adulthood.

To understand genetic disorders it is helpful to learn some of the basic terms of the science of genetics and rules of inheritance.

- Birth defects is the popular term for those disorders and abnormalities associated with a physical deformity, most of which are genetic. However, the term "birth defects" sometimes refers to malformations that are not caused by genetic defects, or its use is mistakenly restricted to physical abnormalities.
- Genetic refers to genes, the basic units of heredity. In a discussion of congenital physical or mental abnormalities, the term "genetic" refers to any problem that originates or stems from the presence of one or more abnormal genes or chromosomes.
- Hereditary refers to any characteristic of an individual that can be passed on to his or her offspring. Some genetic disorders, such as *hemophilia* (a defect of blood-clotting mechanisms), are inherited; others, such as *Turner's syndrome* (an abnormality of female sexual development), are not. In other words, to say that a disorder is genetic does not necessarily mean that it is inherited or that it will be present in one or all of a couple's offspring. In addition, some congenital problems, such

as *birthmarks,* are believed to be inherited, but in fact, many are not.

Genetic disorders are a universal problem. They affect all races and ages and both sexes. Certain genetic disorders, however, occur much more frequently among certain racial groups. For example, *sickle cell anemia,* a rare defect of red blood cells, occurs most frequently (once in about every 600 births) among black children. *Tay-Sachs disease,* a rare, fatal degeneration of the nervous system, appears almost exclusively among Jews of Eastern European descent.

Each year in the United States about 1 in 20 live births shows some type of genetic abnormality. Many are not significant, but others represent the principal cause of complex difficulties; for example, it is estimated that the problems of perhaps 4 out of 5 mentally retarded people in the United States can be attributed to various genetic abnormalities. In addition, studies now confirm that many diseases not thought to be genetic bear a genetic component: abnormalities in genetic material are being identified as the sole or partial cause of a growing number of human illnesses.

Every person carries, on average, approximately 1 gene for serious genetic abnormalities that could be passed on to descendants. Geneticists estimate that every childbearing couple runs an approximately 3 percent risk of having a child with a birth defect or genetic abnormality that is readily apparent at birth.

Certain defective genes, however, cause only a predisposition for abnormality, which will not be expressed except in the presence of some "environmental factor." One such factor is diet. Children with phenylketonuria (PKU), for example, cannot tolerate normal amounts of dietary protein because their bodies lack a certain enzyme necessary to metabolize one component of proteins completely. If fed a normal diet, such children will become severely retarded. But if their protein intake is strictly limited and their diet otherwise modified, these children can lead normal lives.

Strictly speaking, most genetic abnormalities and disorders are presently incurable, at least as far as the underlying cause is concerned. However, medical science is now able to diagnose and treat successfully more and more genetic disorders. In the last 3 decades genetic research into the problems of human heredity has made remarkable discoveries about the origins of human disease. Over 100 serious genetic problems can be identified before birth by various tests. In addition, it is possible in some cases to use "carrier tests" to identify carriers of a trait that might be expressed in a child under certain conditions.

A relatively new health care speciality, clinical genetics, applies the principles of genetics to the health care of adults and children. Physicians trained in both genetics and medicine provide diagnostic and referral services for many genetic disorders. One of the most useful and far-reaching activities of clinical genetics is genetic counseling (see Prevention, below).

CAUSE

Almost every living cell in the human body contains highly complex information that guides the activities and production of the cell throughout its life. This "operating code" is transmitted to every one of the cell's descendants. The operating code is contained in microscopically small, rod-shaped structures called chromosomes located in the nucleus of every cell. Normally, each cell contains 22 pairs of chromosomes known as autosomes, plus a 23rd pair known as sex chromosomes, which determines the sex of the individual.

Each chromosome contains long, threadlike strands composed of many hundreds or thousands of genes—each submicroscopic gene positioned precisely in special order along the length of the tiny chromosome. Genes, the basic unit of heredity, are composed of a variety of nucleic acid called DNA. Every gene is responsible for a specific characteristic of the organism. In human beings, for example, a specific gene or combination of genes exists for hair color, eye color, ear shape, and hundreds of other physical characteristics.

The 23 chromosome pairs in each cell are identical to those contained in almost every other cell in the body. At conception, the very first cell, which is to become a human fetus, normally receives half of the total contained in each parent's standard chromosome pattern: 23 chromosomes, one of each pair, from the mother's egg and 23 from the father's sperm. That first cell containing the unique combination of 23 pairs of chromosomes then divides millions of times as the fetus grows; each new cell is identical in its

number and pattern of chromosomes. As the body grows, cells differentiate to perform specialized functions. A normal human body consists of hundreds of different cell types, all containing exactly the same chromosomes. Occasionally a problem develops: a chromosome or gene is defective because it was inherited as defective from a parent or because of a spontaneous change in a chromosome or gene which occurs occasionally during formation of eggs and sperm.

Genetic disorders can be divided into three general types: single-gene defects, chromosomal abnormalities, and complex "multifactorial" disorders.

1) Single-gene defects occur in slightly more than one percent of all live births. These conditions may be divided into three general categories: autosomal dominant, autosomal recessive, and X-linked (sometimes called sex-linked).

1a) An autosomal dominant, single-gene abnormality can be transmitted (passed on) by one parent who is affected by it. About 1,000 disorders caused by such abnormalities have been identified. If one parent possesses the defective gene, there is a 50 percent risk of transmitting the gene. In the unlikely circumstance that both parents possess that defective gene, a 75 percent risk exists of transmitting the gene.

Parents should remember that the risk for a particular type of single-gene defect remains the same for every child of the same parents. For example, those parents who already have a child affected by a disorder caused by dominant inheritance may believe mistakenly that a 50 percent (or 1 in 2) risk means that their next child will not be endangered by the same genetic problem. In fact, the risk factor is a constant for each of their children.

Examples of autosomal dominant, single-gene abnormalities include certain forms of polydactyly (extra fingers or toes), neurofibromatosis (a complex nerve, skin, and muscle disease), achondroplasia and some other forms of dwarfism accompanied by other physical defects, and some adult-onset disorders such as Huntington's disease (an irreversible degeneration of the brain). See Fig. 25.

1b) An autosomal recessive single-gene abnormality can be transmitted by a parent who has either the trait or the disorder itself. However, the disorder appears in the child only if the child inherited that particular recessive, single-gene abnormality from each parent. A person is said to be a "carrier" if he or she carries a single recessive gene for that trait but does not exhibit the disorder. If both parents carry the trait, each of their children runs a 25 percent chance of having the condition and each child has a 50 percent chance of being a carrier (as were both parents). Approximately 1,000 recessive, single-gene disorders have been identified.

Among the best-known recessive, single-gene disorders are *sickle cell anemia, Tay-Sachs disease, PKU,* certain forms of albinism, and *cystic fibrosis.* Unusual recessive, single-gene disorders include dysautonomia (a lifelong, complex impairment of the involuntary nervous system) and Wilson's disease, a disorder marked by abnormal deposits of microscopic copper in the liver, brain, kidneys, and eyes. (See Fig. 26.)

1c) X-linked single-gene defects are so designated because the abnormality is carried on the X chromosome, one of the sex chromosomes. Most X-linked single-gene defects are recessive. Most inherited traits stem from individual genes or combinations of genes. One exception is sex: a person's sex is determined by genes, as yet undefined, most probably located on the special sex chromosomes. Each female carries two X chromosomes, but each male carries X chromosome and one Y chromosome. During chromosome division, each of the male parent's sperm cells receives either an X or Y chromosome; during division, each of the female parent's egg cells gets an X chromosome. Offspring receiving a Y chromosome from the father normally become male (XY) and those receiving the father's X chromosome normally become female (XX).

If a male has a defective gene on his X chromosome, he has the genetic makeup to exhibit the disease because he does not possess another normal X chromosome to counterbalance it. This defective gene on his X chromosome either occurred spontaneously or was inherited from his mother. Each male birth to a carrier mother would run a 50 percent risk of expressing the recessive, sex-linked, single-gene defect. More than 150 sex-linked single-gene disorders are known. Some examples of X-linked disorders include *color blindness, hemophilia,* and Duchenne *muscular dystrophy* (progressive wasting of muscles). (See Fig. 27.)

2) The second and most diverse category of genetic disorders, called complex or "multifactorial," is apparently caused by the combined interactions of a gene (or genes) and environmental influences. The number of multifactorial diseases has not been determined, but the total may be in excess of 2,000; perhaps as many as 3 percent of all live births are affected by one of these disorders.

As yet no accurate test exists for determining or predicting the potential risk of contracting a multifactorial disorder. It is estimated roughly that a family with 1 child who has a multifactorial disorder runs a risk of almost 5 percent of having another similarly affected child. However, a second child with the abnormality increases even more the risk that a third child also will be affected.

Exactly how multifactorial disorders are transmitted remains a highly technical subject, one that is only partially understood by geneticists. Examples of multifactorial disorders include *clubfoot, cleft lip and cleft palate, diabetes,* congenital *dislocation of the hip,* and *spina bifida.*

Research continues to explore how multifactorial abnormalities are transmitted. It is likely that some children inherit a greater susceptibility than others to existing environmental factors. When triggered by an environmental factor (or "agent"), such a susceptibility subsequently can lead to a disease or abnormality. It is believed that this mechanism operates, for example, when certain children acquire some forms of heart disease (see *heart disease, congenital), cancer,* some forms of mental illness (including *schizophrenia), allergies,* and perhaps certain types of *hypertension.*

3) Chromosomal abnormalities occur because of an error in the number or defect in the structure of an individual's chromosomes (or both). Most chromosomal abnormalities occur spontaneously as genetic "accidents," producing chromosomal patterns that did not exist in the parents. Some may be transmissible to future generations. Chromosomal errors occur most often during the formation of reproductive cells (eggs and sperm). If such a reproductive cell fertilizes or is fertilized and implants, the developing fetus would have either a numerical or a structural chromosome abnormality.

Chromosomal abnormalities are usually associated with major and minor physical abnormalities and with varying degrees of *mental retardation* or with abnormalities of sexual development. *Down syndrome,* usually caused by an extra chromosome number 21, is the best known chromosome abnormality; it constitutes about one fifth of all chromosomal disorders. A couple who has one child with a chromosomal abnormality may run an increased risk of having another child with a chromosomal abnormality. The actual risk depends upon the type of abnormality.

Significant chromosomal abnormalities occur in about 1 of every 150 live births. Of these most are obviously harmful or interfere substantially with the usual activities of life.

SIGNS AND SYMPTOMS

The signs and symptoms of genetic disorders vary according to the specific problem.

DIAGNOSIS

A growing number of genetic disorders can be diagnosed by various prenatal examinations. Others can be detected almost immediately after birth—before a child displays a recognizable sign or symptom. *PKU,* for example, can be identified by a routine screening—a blood test performed immediately after birth. Still other disorders become apparent gradually over a period of weeks, months, years, or even decades. Genetic disorders such as *cystic fibrosis* and many metabolic abnormalities may go undetected and untreated for months or even years either because they produce few symptoms or their symptoms are so nonspecific.

The term "prenatal diagnosis" refers to various examinations which can be performed prior to birth to determine the genetic characteristics and general health of a fetus.

Chromosome study is usually performed from a blood sample, specially prepared so that a geneticist can observe chromosomes in the nuclei of the cells just before they divide. Special staining techniques "fix" the chromosomes for detailed study and interpretation. The process of arranging magnified photographs of a person's chromosomes for genetic interpretation is called preparing a karyotype.

If the karyotype indicates the probability of a chromosome problem for the fetus of a pregnant woman, for example, the genetic counselor may recommend ultrasound examination and amniocentesis to gather more information. Should the results of ultrasound examination and amniocentesis be ambiguous, direct examination of the fetus may be recommended by means of a highly sensitive diagnostic probe called a fetoscope. A fetoscope is a flexible plastic, lighted examining instrument through which a physician can observe the fetus inside the uterus. If necessary, samples of fetal blood or skin can be withdrawn from the uterus through the fetoscope to determine whether certain genetic disorders exist.

Amniocentesis (literally, puncture of the amniotic sac), through which a sample of amniotic fluid and cells shed by the fetus in the amniotic fluid is withdrawn for chromosomal and biochemical analysis, is an established and often-used procedure. Careful analysis of the enzyme levels in those cells can detect as many as 100 different metabolic problems in the growing fetus. (An enzyme is a protein that acts upon another substance to cause a chemical change without undergoing any change itself.) Some of the common genetic disorders detectable by amniocentesis include chromosomal abnormalities, such as *Down syndrome,* and biochemical abnormalities, such as *Tay-Sachs disease.*

Because amniocentesis is a procedure that carries some risk to the fetus (see below), amniocentesis is usually recommended only for certain situations or individuals:

- Any pregnant woman who is 35 or older. The incidence of Down syndrome or other similar "extra chromosome" problems is markedly higher among newborns whose mothers have reached the age of 35 and the risk increases each year thereafter. Pregnant women with an unusually low maternal serum alpha-fetoprotein measurement also appear to be at slightly increased risk for having a child with Down syndrome due to trisomy 21 and probably other autosomal trisomies as well.
- Any couple who already has had a child with certain chromosomal abnormalities (especially those characterized by problems associated with carrying an extra chromosome).
- Couples in which one or both partners possess a chromosomal abnormality. Even if that trait has proved harmless for the parents, a child of theirs might experience a severe disorder because of

having received extra chromosome material from one or both parents.

- Any couple who has a child born with a neural tube (spinal cord) abnormality or a couple at increased risk for the birth of such a child because of the results of a mother's elevated alpha-fetoprotein measurement (see below).
- Couples who have certain biochemical disorders or who are carriers for such disorders.
- Pregnant women whose family history includes X-linked recessive disorders.

Amniocentesis is a relatively simple procedure that can be performed in 15 minutes or less either in a physician's office or in the hospital. After cleaning the skin and, sometimes, applying local anesthetic to dull sensation, the physician inserts a long, thin needle through the abdominal wall and into the uterus and amniotic sac. A few tablespoons (15 to 25 cubic centimeters) of amniotic fluid are withdrawn into a laboratory syringe. Within a few hours the body replaces the amniotic fluid.

Amniocentesis is performed about 16 weeks after a pregnant woman's last menstrual period, so that enough amniotic fluid is present while enough time still remains in the second trimester of pregnancy to conduct the laboratory tests. (Chromosome analysis requires about 3 to 4 weeks and biochemical analysis of fluids about 4 to 6 weeks.) Medical records show that in about 98 percent of amniocentesis testing the fetus is found to be free of abnormalities.

Just prior to or, optimally, during the amniocentesis examination itself, an ultrasound examination is performed. Ultrasound, a painless, rapid procedure, involves passing sound waves through the woman's abdomen; the examiner uses a small electronic transmitter, which is passed lightly over the skin. An image of the fetus in the uterus appears on a television monitor, allowing the physician to determine the least hazardous location for the insertion of the needle for amniocentesis. Ultrasound examination may also reveal other information, such as the sex of the fetus or the presence of twins.

Certain known risks are associated with the amniocentesis procedure. The true risk of miscarriage following amniocentesis is unknown; currently it is estimated to be in the range of one half of one percent. In addition, it is possible for the fetus or placenta to be touched when the needle is inserted. This risk is quite small when the procedure is performed by an experienced physician who is assisted by a colleague providing an ultrasound visualization. In a very small percentage of cases infections occur which, if not treated promptly, could lead to a spontaneous abortion.

Chromosome analysis is accurate more than 99 percent of the time, but in the case of a fetus possessing both chromosomally normal and abnormal cells a chance remains that the less prevalent cell type could go undetected. For each laboratory study a specific set of uncertainties exists; the physician should describe all possible uncertainties and explain how results can be cross-checked to reduce or eliminate the possibility of error.

Amniocentesis can also detect birth defects which do not show up in a chromosome analysis. Many—but not all—forms of *spina bifida* or a severe brain defect (anencephaly) can be detected by analysis of alpha-fetoprotein, a special protein present in the amniotic fluid. A test for alpha-fetoprotein level can be performed on the same sample of amniotic fluid withdrawn for chromosomal analysis.

Other specialized tests. For those pregnant women who do not undergo amniocentesis, alpha-fetoprotein levels can be checked by a special blood test that can be performed as early as the fifteenth week of pregnancy. This alpha-fetoprotein measurement alone, however, will not detect 10 to 15 percent of open neural tube defects. Most elevations of this substance in the mother's blood are due to other causes, which means the tests must be carefully interpreted. Low levels of this substance have recently been found to indicate an increased risk for a fetus with an autosomal trisomy. This alpha-fetoprotein screening test of the blood serum is inexpensive and noninvasive. Urinary screening, indicating the probability of a genetic abnormality, is sometimes helpful if mentally retarded children are already part of a family.

Chorionic villi sampling (CVS) is a newer examination that can detect the presence of genetic problems in the fetus. CVS has two major advantages over amniocentesis: it can be performed as early as the eighth week of pregnancy, and results of some of the examinations can be available as early as a day or two after testing.

The chorion is a layer of tissue that surrounds the fetus during its first 2 months and later develops into the placenta. Chorionic villi are microscopic strands of tissue that serve to transfer oxygen, nutrients, and waste between mother and fetus. The examining physician uses a thin, flexible tube which is inserted into the uterus through the vagina. The tube is guided into place between the lining of the uterus and the chorion. A second physician or technician visualizes the procedure on an ultrasound monitor and helps the examining physician maneuver the tube into exactly the right spot. Samples of the villi are quickly and painlessly suctioned into the tube and then analyzed in a laboratory.

Because the chorionic villi cells are identical (with few and occasionally important exceptions) to those in the fetus, any genetic abnormalities present in the fetus should be revealed in lab studies of the villi cells. The major risks involved in CVS are bleeding and/or infection that could lead, for some women, to a spontaneous abortion. If the risks of infection and spontaneous abortion are not resolved or reduced as the CVS technique is further improved, the examination may be used primarily or only for high-risk pregnancies where the chance of abnormalities is known to run high. A major advantage of CVS is that if a woman decides to terminate a pregnancy because of the severity of genetic abnormalities revealed by CVS, an abortion can be performed as early as the ninth week rather than as late as the twentieth, which often occurs when amniocentesis is performed for diagnosis.

Testing for rare biochemical diseases, some having to do with specific metabolic abnormalities, can be done before birth. A specific, complex diagnostic test for a rare biochemical disease is not performed unless a woman is known to run a high risk of having a fetus affected by one of these conditions. For example, a highly technical analysis of a pregnant woman's amino acids can be performed by using a chromatogram, which could reveal abnormalities in the structure of basic proteins. If there is a history in any generation of a genetic disorder or abnormality in the families of either the prospective father or mother, the physician caring for the woman needs to be informed as early in the pregnancy as possible so that appropriate diagnostic tests can be performed.

Some genetic disorders and abnormalities cannot be detected by any test devised. Many of these defects are multifactorial; among the best known examples are *cleft lip and cleft palate,* congenital heart defects (see *heart disease, congenital),* and *clubfoot.* Certain forms of congenital heart defects and cleft lip, however, can be detected with ultrasound.

TREATMENT

Although most genetic disorders are incurable, a variety of treatment methods before and after birth can deal with certain kinds of disorders and abnormalities.

Increasingly, various kinds of prenatal treatment are being employed. Some techniques are well established and highly effective. Transfusions, for instance, can deal with severe cases of Rh blood disease. Medicines can occasionally prevent fetal heart failure. Fetal surgery is still experimental. In certain cases surgery is performed to correct prenatal abnormalities of anatomy diagnosed by ultrasound or the use of a fetoscope; such procedures include reducing hydrocephalus (abnormal accumulation of fluid in the brain). Such surgery is a risk to both fetus and mother, and in the foreseeable future its use will be limited to a few pediatric medical centers.

Some genetic diseases and abnormalities can be diagnosed and treated immediately after birth. For example, *PKU* is treated at once following diagnosis. A specific diet with protein substitute is begun and recovery is almost always rapid and complete. Prenatal testing for PKU is also being developed. For *diabetes,* a genetic disease (or more precisely, a group of diseases many of which, if not all, have a genetic basis), insulin, a special diet, and exercise can be lifesaving.

Surgery can correct structural abnormalities of the heart, *cleft lip and cleft palate, clubfoot,* and certain obstructions of the gastrointestinal tract, among others, early in life. Results are remarkably successful. Transplantation surgery can provide corneas, kidneys, and livers for some children whose sight, kidney function, or liver function is impaired or has failed. Mechanical devices (called prostheses), such as hearing aids and artificial limbs, can compensate for certain physical disabilities.

Mental, sensory, and physical disabilities that are the result of a variety of genetic abnormalities can be improved with sustained, expert rehabilitative education and training. The outlook for children with such disabilities depends upon the accuracy of diagnosis, the severity of the condition, and the kind and duration of treatment given.

Some genetic diseases, such as *Tay-Sachs disease,* are not treatable today. With other now incurable genetic diseases, such as *cystic fibrosis,* methods of treatment are becoming increasingly more successful, thereby lengthening life and improving its quality remarkably.

PREVENTION

Prevention is the most effective and least costly way of dealing with genetic disorders and abnormalities. Thoughtful planning and investigation in advance of a pregnancy can help to protect against the occurrence of genetic disorders. Individuals and couples are turning increasingly to genetic counseling for accurate information and emotional support.

Genetic Counseling

Genetic counseling is an invaluable health service for individuals and couples who have questions about the possibility of transmitting a genetic disorder to a child or who are having difficulty becoming pregnant. Genetic counseling involves specialized, individualized communication about fertility and the range of human problems associated with the occurrence or risk of occurrence of a genetic disorder in a family. The process helps an individual or couple to

- grasp the medical facts, including the diagnosis, the ways that genetic disorders can affect children, and the kinds of treatment available;
- appreciate how heredity contributes to the disorder, and comprehend the risk of having a disorder appear;
- understand what options exist for dealing with this risk;
- choose and act upon a course of action that seems appropriate to them in view of their risk, their family goals, and their ethical and religious principles;
- make the best possible adjustment to the disorder as it currently affects a member of their family or to the risk of having that disorder recur in their family should they try to have another child.

Clinical genetics, an interdisciplinary medical specialty, combines the knowledge and insights of genetics, medicine, molecular biology, ethics, psychology, and sociology (among others) as they bear upon questions of the nature and quality of human life. Physicians who are also trained in genetics work in this relatively new field of medicine.

Genetic counseling is an allied specialty. Genetic counselors may be physicians or genetics associates. (Genetics associates earn a two-year master's degree in genetic counseling by completing an accredited graduate school program.) The field, however, is not limited to health professionals. Significant numbers of medical ethicists, members of the clergy, psychologists, and social workers, among others, have been trained to provide highly informed, sensitive genetic counseling. (An increasing number of qualified genetic counselors are achieving board certification by the American Board of Medical Genetics; certification involves a highly selective process of testing.)

Who Should Seek Genetic Counseling? Any individual, couple, or family whose risk of transmitting a genetic disease or disorder may be high or who is worried about that risk should seek genetic counseling. Here are some examples:

- a pregnant 36-year-old woman who is concerned about her risk of having a child with Down syndrome;
- a couple with one child suffering from a disease of the central nervous system (brain, spinal cord, and their covering, the meninges), and concerned about their risk of having another child with the same or a related problem;
- Jewish couples of Eastern European heritage worried about their risk of having a child affected by *Tay-Sachs disease.*

What Do Genetic Counselors Do? A genetic counselor's role is to inform and educate individuals or couples about their unique genetic profiles and the choices available to them in planning a family. After informing their patients as completely as possible, genetic counselors attempt to be nondirective and allow patients to make their own decisions. Once individuals make a decision—for example, to try to become pregnant, to carry through a pregnancy, to have amniocentesis, to choose to terminate a pregnancy—genetic counselors are usually as supportive and encouraging of their choice as possible.

During the course of an initial interview, a genetic counselor tries to elicit as much information from the patients as possible about medical history including all severe illnesses, familial and chronic diseases or illnesses, former marriages, birth defects, miscarriages, abortions, and causes of death in the immediate family. Other information often includes ethnic background, education, work, hobbies, athletic activities, and diet. Questions are asked about exposure to harmful viral or bacterial infections and to environmental hazards such as toxic (poisonous) chemicals, drugs, and X rays. The genetic counselor will diagram a family tree which identifies and provides vital statistics for at least three generations, if possible, to create the broadest perspective on the health history of the family. Diseases that can be inherited are often identified simply from the history-taking process.

A complete physical examination may be ordered and appropriate medical specialists consulted if the personal history so warrants. If preliminary information seems to suggest to the counselor a higher-than-normal risk of any kind of genetic disorder or abnormality, any of the specialized tests described in the Diagnosis section (above) may be ordered.

What Genetic Counseling Can and Cannot Do Once all the data and test results are available, the counselor may be able to say whether a genetic problem exists or if a problem triggered by an environmental problem is possible. The evidence and tests results are reviewed with the patient(s). The mode of inheritance (i.e., whose genes or chromosomes could transmit the abnormality) is explored, and the risks of recurrence are described. Finally, available options are reviewed and explained.

Individuals or couples who are going to have genetic counseling can prepare for the experience. They can think ahead of time about their own and their family's health histories. (Two excellent resources are an informative booklet, "Genetic Counseling," and a family medical worksheet, both available from the March of Dimes Birth Defects Foundation, 1275 Mamaroneck Avenue, White Plains, NY 10605.)

During the first visit with the counselor, individuals should not hesitate to ask questions, even ones that may seem simple, obvious, or even repetitive. One research survey of the patients of genetic counselors revealed that almost half of them did not understand what they had been told well enough to be

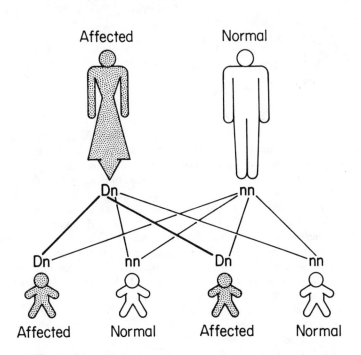

Affected / Normal

Dn / nn

Dn / nn / Dn / nn

Affected / Normal / Affected / Normal

How Dominant Inheritance Works
One affected parent has a single faulty gene (<u>D</u>) which *dominates* its normal counterpart (<u>n</u>).
Each child's chances of inheriting either the <u>D</u> or the <u>n</u> from the affected parent are 50%.

Affected Mother	<u>Dn</u>
Normal Father	<u>nn</u>
Affected	<u>Dn</u>
Normal	<u>nn</u>

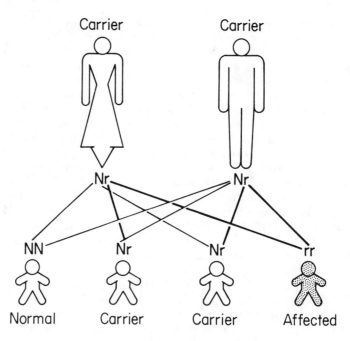

How Recessive Inheritance Works
Both parents, usually unaffected, carry a normal gene (N) which takes precedence over its faulty recessive counterpart (r). The odds for each child are

- a 25% risk of inheriting a "double dose" of r genes, which may cause a serious birth defect
- a 25% chance of inheriting two Ns, thus being unaffected

- a 50% chance of being a carrier, as both parents are

Carrier Father	Nr
Carrier Mother	Nr
Normal	NN
Carrier	Nr
Carrier	Nr
Affected	rr

able to make well-informed decisions. Genetic counselors are patient: they do not expect—or want—instantaneous decisions from clients.

Genetic counseling, like all disciplines, has its limits. Occasionally tests results are erroneous (show a false positive or false negative, that is, indicate a problem when none exists, or vice versa). Regardless of a counselor's competence and reliability, patients should ask about the possibility of error and whether other tests exist that can cross-check the accuracy of an initial test finding. Geneticists and genetic counselors can often estimate quite precisely the chances of a child's being born with a particular defect or combination of defects. On the other hand, they cannot foresee the extent or severity of the particular defect (or combination of defects), or whether a particular child will be able to cope with the problem successfully.

More significantly, the quality of life for a child affected with a particular genetic disease or disorder cannot be predicted with precision nor can parents forecast with certainty whether they will have emotional, social, and financial resources to raise such a child competently and lovingly.

Referrals to organizations specializing in genetic counseling services are available from the National Health Information Center, P.O. Box 1133, Washington, DC 20013 (phone: 800-336-4797).

GENITAL HERPES

DESCRIPTION

Genital herpes is a venereal disease characterized by a pattern of infection, latency

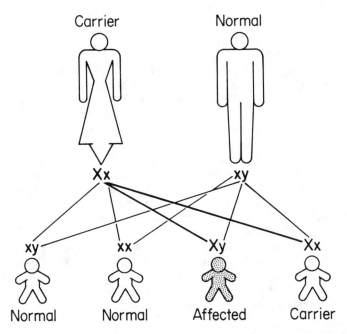

Carrier

Normal

Xx

xy

xy
Normal

xx
Normal

Xy
Affected

Xx
Carrier

How X-Linked Inheritance Works

In the most common form, the female sex chromosomes of an unaffected mother carry one faulty gene (X) and one normal one (x). The father has normal male x and y chromosome complement.

The odds for each *male* child:

- 50% risk of inheriting the faulty X and the disorder
- 50% chance of inheriting normal x and y chromosomes

The odds for each *female* child:

- 50% risk of inheriting one faulty X, to be a carrier like the mother
- 50% chance of inheriting no faulty gene

Carrier Mother	Xx
Normal Father	xy
Normal Male	xy
Normal Female	xx
Affected Male	Xy
Carrier Female	Xx

(present but invisible and inactive), and reactivation. The disease has reached epidemic proportions the world over and is now the most common sexually transmitted disease in the United States. Approximately half a million Americans become infected with a genital herpes virus each year, and more than 20 million suffer reactivations.

When a person becomes infected with a genital herpes virus, no signs or symptoms may appear. More frequently, however, small blisters are present and remain for about 2 weeks. The reactivation form of the disease also appears as blisters in the genital or anal area.

Most people infected with the genital herpes virus suffer reactivations, though the frequency of such reactivations may lessen as a person grows older. Reactivations are more common in men than in women; however, they are often more severe in women. Reactivations can occur at any time, without further contact with an infected person. Blisters usually reappear in groups in the same place(s), and remain for 5 to 10 days.

Genital herpes is a serious public health problem because the virus causing the disease is stubborn and resistant. A person can build up antibodies to the virus, but they do not prevent recurrences. The disease, though painful and extremely frustrating in its frequency of reactivation, is not life-threatening to adolescents or adults but is highly dangerous to newborn babies.

CAUSE

About 80 percent of cases of genital herpes are caused by the herpes simplex virus type 2; herpes simplex virus type 1 (which causes *oral herpes)* is the culprit in 20 percent of cases of genital herpes. The virus is transmitted through direct contact with genital herpes blisters or sometimes with oral herpes blisters, usually during sexual contact, including oral-genital sex. Fingers can also carry the virus from the lips to the genitals. Inanimate objects rarely carry the virus and spread the infection. The virus can enter the body through any opening. The blisters are highly contagious and can spread the virus for about 10 days, from a few days before they break out on the surface of the skin until after their appearance. People who carry the herpes simplex virus type 2 and who have no symptoms can rarely spread the virus.

Reactivations can be triggered by *fever,* general ill health, diseases that suppress immune responses, fatigue, emotional *stress,* pregnancy, friction, and sunlight. Genital reactivations of the type 2 virus are more frequent and severe than those of type 1.

SIGNS AND SYMPTOMS

One third of those people who become infected with a genital herpes virus for the first time have *fever, headache,* swollen lymph nodes, muscle pain, difficult or painful urination, and a vague feeling of physical discomfort. In women, small blisters usually appear on the labia or cervix, in the vagina, or all three. The area around the blisters will feel irritated as the blisters break and form ulcers. After 2 to 3 weeks symptoms disappear.

Symptoms of reactivations are usually less noticeable. The first indication is mild irritation and burning or itching in the genital area. Then painful blisters appear on the surface of genital organs, including the penis or the vulva and labia, and on the buttocks or thighs. The scrotum usually has no blisters. Fewer blisters appear with reactivations. Many women can be unaware of their blisters, which may not be visible. The blisters break, scab, and heal within 7 to 11 days.

DIAGNOSIS

Genital herpes is diagnosed through observation of the sores and through laboratory studies of the blisters. A Pap smear will detect only about half of active genital herpes cases in females.

COMPLICATIONS

A baby delivered vaginally to a woman with an active case of genital herpes has a small but significant chance of becoming infected during the passage through the birth canal and subsequently developing neonatal herpes, which, if untreated, is fatal or severely and permanently damaging in 8 out of 10 cases. Sometimes even women with latent genital herpes pass the disease to their newborn babies. A woman who delivers a baby at a time when she has just become infected (i.e., who has a primary infection) is at a higher risk of transmitting the virus to her baby than is a woman suffering a reactivation. The risk of danger to the baby is also increased.

Typically, the baby appears well until the fifth to ninth day of life (sometimes for as long as 3 weeks), then refuses to eat and develops such symptoms as *fever* or hypothermia (body temperature below normal), *vomiting,* lethargy, irritability, *jaundice,* difficult or labored breathing, convulsions (see *seizures), cyanosis* (bluish skin, caused by lack of oxygen in the blood), *apnea* (failure to breathe regularly), or, often, myocarditis (inflammation of heart muscles). An enlarged spleen and liver failure are common; the kidneys may also be affected. Blisters similar to those of genital herpes may appear on the skin or mucous membranes, or in the mouth or eye. *Blindness* can result. If the central nervous system is affected, the prognosis is very poor. Eventually, if the heart and lungs stop functioning, the baby will die. Half of surviving infants suffer brain damage.

Occasionally an infant suffers a milder case of neonatal herpes, with only a skin, mouth, or eye infection and low fever.

Meningitis can be a complication of genital herpes, both in infants and adults. Affected infants suffer severe meningitis combined with *encephalitis;* complications are severe. Affected adults, on the other hand, suffer transient viral meningitis; this complicaton does not appear after reactivations.

TREATMENT

Although no cure now exists for genital herpes, a person with genital blisters should see a physician immediately. Antiviral medications—in surface, intravenous, or oral forms—can reduce the duration of blisters and sometimes lessen pain and reduce fever, but only if applied right after symptoms appear. It is much less effective against reactivations and has no value in destroying the virus during the latent stage. A person with blisters should rest, take sitz baths (in plain, warm water), avoid tightly fitting, nonabsorbent clothes, and abstain from sexual contact until the blisters have disappeared. Burow's solution applied 3 or 4 times daily may ease symptoms. Infected persons should make sure that any people with whom they have had sexual contact have been notified.

Neonatal herpes is often treated with antiviral medications. These can greatly increase an infected infant's survival chances, but they do not always prevent severe damage. Infected infants must be isolated in incubators.

PREVENTION

Issues of sexuality are especially difficult to sort out during adolescence. It is important for teenagers to remember that decisions about when to have sex and with whom should not be made lightly. Open conversation and trust in his or her sexual partner is perhaps the best way for any adolescent to prevent herpes.

A number of additional actions can be taken to reduce the risk of infection. Condoms may help prevent the virus from being transmitted during sexual contact. Avoidance of oral-genital sex while one or both partners have active oral herpes is another precautionary measure. (Each partner also should avoid touching the oral herpes blisters with his or her fingers.)

Most cases of neonatal herpes can be prevented if women with active genital herpes have their babies delivered by cesarean section. Delivery must take place prior to or within 4 hours of the breaking of the amniotic sac to keep the virus from spreading. Infants must be isolated in incubators while laboratory tests are performed to determine the presence of the herpes virus.

GENITOURINARY TUMORS

DESCRIPTION

The word "genitourinary" refers to all the body structures involved in reproduction and in the formation and excretion of urine. (Obviously these two functions are not strictly related, but since they are physically close, medical classification groups them together; see Fig. 38, p. 698.)

Although a benign or malignant tumor can develop in any genitourinary structure, the structures most commonly affected are the kidneys, bladder, testicles, and ovaries. Among children, tumors in other parts of the genitourinary system are exceedingly rare. The most common form of genitourinary tumor is called *Wilms' tumor,* a cancerous growth that originates in the kidneys.

The second most common form of genitourinary tumor is a cancer of the bladder called rhabdomyosarcoma, which originates in the muscular wall of the bladder. Although rhabdomyosarcoma of the bladder affects fewer than 5 out of every million children, it represents 13 percent of all solid tumors among children. For reasons that remain unclear, this tumor is most common among children 2 to 6 years of age, affecting slightly more males than females. Its abnormal cells tend to multiply with extraordinary rapidity and to spread quickly throughout the bladder and to surrounding tissues.

Even rarer than rhabdomyosarcoma of the bladder are testicular tumors, which represent only 1 percent of all tumors—malignant and benign—among children. Testicular tumors (which usually develop in only 1 testicle) tend to affect boys younger than 4 years old and those in late puberty. Less than half of all testicular tumors are benign and can be removed without complications.

Even malignant testicular tumors are often successfully controlled. Sterility (inability to father a child) is a fairly common complication of treatment.

The most rare form of genitourinary tumor affects the ovaries (see *ovarian tumors and cysts*).

CAUSE

The cause of tumors that originate in the genitourinary tract is unknown. In addition to arising as "primary" growths, malignant genitourinary tumors can develop as the result of the spread of other cancerous tumors (see *cancer*).

SIGNS AND SYMPTOMS

The most common signs of bladder tumors are those associated with obstruction of the urinary tract by tumor growth, a condition in which the flow of urine through the tract is partially or totally blocked. As a result, an affected child may have difficulty urinating. In addition, retained urine encourages bacterial growth and can lead to *urinary tract infections.* In severe cases urine clogs not only the bladder but also the ureters and the kidneys, and acute kidney failure (see *kidney failure, acute*) a possibly life-threatening condition, can result.

The most prominent sign of a testicular tumor is enlargement of the affected testicle. In many cases the testicle swells up to twice its normal size. While enlargement of the testicle is likely to be the only sign of a testicular tumor for an affected teenaged boy, a small boy with the condition may also feel some pain and have a slight fever. (See *ovarian tumors and cysts; Wilms' tumor.)*

DIAGNOSIS

A physician checking for a genitourinary tumor considers a child's medical history and performs a physical examination with special emphasis on the lower abdominal area. Diagnostic tests include specialized X-ray films and, if necessary, surgical exploration of the affected area.

COMPLICATIONS

Testicular tumors can interfere with the production of male sex hormones and cause sexual-development or sexual-function problems such as *gynecomastia,* enlargement of the breasts.

Rhabdomyosarcoma tends to spread rapidly and can interfere with the function of the urinary system and with other nearby structures.

TREATMENT

Benign genitourinary tumors are usually removed surgically. The risks associated with surgery depend on the size of a tumor as well as its location.

Like all cancerous tumors, malignancies of the genitourinary system are currently treated with a combination of surgery, chemotherapy, and radiation (see *cancer).*

PREVENTION

Genitourinary tumors cannot be prevented.

GERMAN MEASLES (*RUBELLA*)

EMERGENCY ACTION

German measles, known to physicians as rubella, can cause birth defects if a woman contracts the disease during the first 4 months of pregnancy. Any pregnant woman who suspects that she has been exposed should see a physician immediately.

DESCRIPTION

Rubella is the medical term for German measles (also sometimes called three-day measles). Throughout this essay, for the sake of brevity, we shall refer to German measles as rubella.

Acquired Rubella

Acquired rubella is a mild, preventable disease, which before a vaccination was developed, was common during childhood. Today adults and adolescents (who are 15 years old or older) who have not been immunized are most susceptible to contracting the disease. It strikes most often during the spring.

Rubella is a viral disease and is usually accompanied by a characteristic rash. However, the disease is often confused with other viral diseases that cause rashes and often goes undiagnosed. In addition, in about 1 out of 4 cases rubella is so mild that it causes no symptoms and is thus unrecognized. A significant number of adults are not immune to the disease, indicating that they never contracted rubella or that they failed to receive vaccine, since one dose of vaccine or one attack of the disease generally brings permanant immunity.

Until 1969, when a rubella vaccine became available, a major epidemic occurred every 6 to 9 years. The last epidemic in the United States was in 1964.

Congenital Rubella

Rubella that is contracted during the first 4 months of pregnancy can cause chronic (persistent) disease in the fetus. It can result in miscarriage, stillbirth, birth defects, or death (usually within the first 6 months after birth). After the fourth month of pregnancy chronic rubella and resulting birth defects do not generally occur.

CAUSE
Acquired Rubella
Rubella is caused by a virus. The virus is contagious and is transmitted by coughing or sneezing. The virus can be spread from 7 days before the characteristic rash erupts until 5 days afterwards.

Congenital Rubella
If a pregnant woman contracts rubella and the virus spreads into her bloodstream (see *bloodstream infection),* the virus may be transmitted to the fetus through the placenta.

Babies who suffered from chronic rubella before birth may spread the virus for many months after birth. However, infants with congenital rubella spread the virus through physical contact rather than through coughing or sneezing.

SIGNS AND SYMPTOMS
Acquired Rubella
No signs or symptoms of acquired rubella appear until 14 to 21 days after a child has been exposed to the rubella virus. The disease may occur with only very mild symptoms and the child may not be very sick. The first indication of the disease among children is usually a rash of tiny, flat or slightly raised, pink-red spots that may appear behind the ears, on the forehead, around the mouth, or elsewhere on the face. Within a day the rash spreads to the trunk, then to the arms and possibly legs. By the time the rash appears on the arms and legs, it may have started to fade on the face and may linger on the trunk only in the form of flushed-looking patches. Within three to four days the rash is gone. In some rubella cases no rash appears at all.

An early, common finding among adolescents is swollen lymph nodes (see *swollen glands*) in the neck, behind the ears, and on the lower back of the head. From 1 to 7 days after the lymph nodes become swollen, the characteristic rash appears. Other than swollen lymph nodes, possible early (pre-rash) symptoms among adolescents include fever under 102° F (38.8° C), *headache,* inflamed eyes, runny nose, slight *sore throat, cough,* mild loss of appetite, and a vague feeling of physical discomfort.

Congenital Rubella
Congenital rubella varies widely in sever-ity. If severe, it can cause slowed growth of a fetus, causing it to be dysmature (abnormally small in weight and length at birth) and to suffer from a variety of severe defects (see *prematurity*).

In serious cases there is a significant chance that fetal development will be severely affected and damage may be caused to the fetal heart (see *heart disease, congenital*), eyes (causing *cataracts, glaucoma,* or *blindness*), brain (causing an abnormally small head, *mental retardation,* or both), or ears (causing deafness; see *hearing loss*).

Pneumonitis, *thyroid problems,* precocious puberty (abnormally early puberty), or *diabetes* may also result from congenital rubella. Temporary problems of the liver, spleen, bone, or skin may occur. Hemolytic anemia (see *anemia, hemolytic*) may also be a short-term condition.

DIAGNOSIS
Acquired Rubella
If the characteristic rash does not appear and parents are unaware that a child has been exposed to rubella, the disease can be difficult for a physician to diagnose through observation. The physician can confirm a diagnosis of rubella either by performing blood tests or examining throat cultures.

Congenital Rubella
Congenital rubella may be suspected if the mother has been exposed to the virus during the first 4 months of pregnancy, if the baby is of low birthweight, and if one or more of the conditions or problems listed above is present. The diagnosis may be confirmed through laboratory testing of throat secretions, urine, or blood.

COMPLICATIONS
Acquired Rubella
Complications are uncommon in acquired rubella although adolescents and adults may experience temporary muscle or *joint pain* and, rarely, joint swelling.

TREATMENT
Acquired Rubella
After a physician has diagnosed childhood rubella, home treatment is fairly simple. A fever-reducing medication may be helpful. Consult the physician for specific recommendations and read discussion of nonprescription medications beginning on p. 102. Calamine lotion may relieve itching. Generally the child can eat a usual diet. The

child does not have to be kept in bed but should be kept at home and away from pregnant women.

Antibiotics are not effective against viruses.

Congenital Rubella

If a woman who is pregnant—especially in her first 4 months—suspects that she has been exposed to rubella, she should see a physician immediately for a blood test to find out whether or not she is immune.

PREVENTION

Rubella can be prevented with a vaccine. All children, both boys and girls, should be vaccinated so that they will not be able to spread the virus to a pregnant woman. Children should be vaccinated when they are 15 months old. If for some reason children are not vaccinated at that age, they certainly should be vaccinated before puberty. (See vaccination schedules in Chapter 6, "Going to the Doctor.")

All adult women should have blood tests to find out if they are immune to rubella. People should not assume that they are immune simply because their medical histories indicate that they have had rubella. All adult women who are not immune should be vaccinated.

Premarital blood tests for rubella immunity should be required in all states. Women should be vaccinated at least 3 months before they plan on becoming pregnant. No woman should be vaccinated during pregnancy.

The rubella vaccine is generally given in the form of an injection in combination with *mumps* and *measles* vaccines. Like the disease, the vaccination occasionally causes temporary joint pain in adolescents or adults.

Pregnant women should avoid physical contact with infants who have congenital rubella. In addition, anyone with rubella—or who has been exposed to rubella—should stay away from pregnant women.

If a pregnant woman is shown to have contracted rubella, she may want to consider a therapeutic abortion because of the risk of serious birth defects in the baby.

GLAUCOMA

EMERGENCY ACTION

If a child suddenly becomes extremely sensitive to light, sees halos around lights, has severe headaches, eye pain, profuse tearing, or clouding of the cornea (the transparent membrane covering the eye), seek immediate medical attention.

DESCRIPTION

Glaucoma is a group of visual disorders characterized by an increase in pressure within the eye. This pressure can damage the optic nerve and blood vessels in the eye, resulting in blindness as early as 2 to 5 days after the beginning of the elevated pressure. (See Fig. 23, p. 362.)

An estimated 2 million Americans suffer from glaucoma, 90 percent of them victims of long-term (chronic) glaucoma. Chronic glaucoma affects adults; it develops gradually as the flow of the aqueous humor through the eye becomes obstructed, usually for unknown reasons. The aqueous humor is the watery fluid that fills the chambers between the iris and the lens, and between the cornea and the iris. This fluid nourishes the cornea and the lens and regulates pressure within the eye. When flow of the aqueous humor is obstructed, pressure within the eye increases and the eye receives insufficient blood, leading to glaucoma.

Children most often suffer from infantile glaucoma, which may be present at birth (congenital) or may develop during infancy or early childhood. Infantile glaucoma occurs when, for unknown reasons, the drainage area between the cornea and the iris (the colored part of the eye) is obstructed, and the aqueous humor cannot circulate through the eye.

If glaucoma is diagnosed and treated immediately, the outlook is excellent and the child may retain normal vision. Untreated glaucoma remains a major cause of *blindness;* the importance of prompt treatment cannot be overemphasized.

CAUSE

Congenital glaucoma and glaucoma that occurs during infancy and early childhood are usually caused by abnormal development of the eye.

Although the disease is usually an isolated abnormality, congenital and infantile glaucoma are occasionally associated with other disorders affecting a child's development. For example, glaucoma may occur either with other eye disorders, such as *retinoblastoma,* or with diseases such as *neurofibromatosis* and Sturge-Weber syndrome. It may occur with inflammatory conditions such as *juvenile rheumatoid arthritis* or with infections, such as congenital rubella (see *German measles).*

Severe *eye injuries* or eye tumors may also cause glaucoma among children.

SIGNS AND SYMPTOMS

The most common sign of both congenital and infantile glaucoma is enlargement and clouding of the cornea. Other signs include profuse tearing and extreme sensitivity to light.

DIAGNOSIS

Glaucoma is usually suspected because of the characteristic symptoms. Positive diagnosis is made by an ophthalmologist (eye specialist) with an instrument called a tonometer, which, when placed on the eyeball, measures pressure within the eye. Any information concerning a family history of glaucoma can help the ophthalmologist make a positive diagnosis.

TREATMENT

Surgery is required for childhood glaucoma. If surgery is performed very early, the outlook is excellent and the child may retain full vision.

PREVENTION

Glaucoma cannot be prevented, but proper treatment prevents further, possibly permanent, damage.

GONORRHEA

DESCRIPTION AND CAUSE

Gonococcus bacteria are responsible for a number of diseases (gonococcal infections) among humans, the most well known of which is gonorrhea, usually transmitted by sexual contact with an infected person. Gonorrhea is the most common venereal (sexually transmissible) disease, and is also the most commonly reported infectious disease in the United States. In 1983 there were 897,833 reported cases of gonorrhea in the United States. Its epidemic proportions have made it a major public health problem.

Gonococcus bacteria are highly contagious. The bacteria can enter the body through any opening lined with mucous membrane (such as the urethra, vagina, mouth, and anus) and cause an infection at that site.

When a male of any age has a gonococcal infection, it most often involves the urethra (the canal conveying urine from the bladder to the exterior of the body (see Figs. 37 and 38, p. 698). This particular infection is called gonococcal urethritis. When an adolescent or adult female has a gonococcal infection, it most often involves the cervix (the narrow, lower end of the uterus) and possibly the urethra (see Figs. 3A and B, p. 39). The former infection is called gonococcal cervicitis. When a prepubertal female (one who has not yet reached puberty) has a gonococcal infection, it most often involves the vulva (region of the external genitals) and vagina (the birth canal, which leads from the vulva to the uterus). This infection is called gonococcal vulvovaginitis.

Because men are much more likely to have early noticeable symptoms of gonorrhea than women are, they are much more likely to seek diagnosis, receive treatment, and stop spreading the bacteria to other people, as well as avoid complications. Moreover, even if untreated, gonococcal urethritis among males usually disappears spontaneously without causing complications (although a man could still transmit bacteria to sexual contacts). In contrast, untreated gonococcal cervicitis often leads to complications.

If the bacteria spread beyond the urethra or cervix, complications arise elsewhere within the genitourinary tract. Or if the bacteria spread into the bloodstream (see *bloodstream infection*), complications can arise in other parts of the body such as the joints or skin.

Gonococcal infections affect people of all ages; one fourth of those infected are between the ages of 10 and 19. Gonococcal infection among adults and adolescents is sexually transmissible. The risk of contracting gonorrhea increases with the number of sexual partners. Adolescent and young adult males are most often infected with gonococcus bacteria because they tend to have a greater number of sex partners than females do.

Any form of sexual contact, not just sexual intercourse, can transmit gonococcus bacteria from an infected person to another person. The bacteria infect the male urethra and the female cervix during sexual intercourse. Bacteria can spread to the female urethra from the vagina during or after sexual intercourse.

Gonococcus bacteria can also be transmitted during oral or anal sex. During oral sex, the bacteria infect the pharynx (throat), and gonococcal pharyngitis develops. Gonococcal pharyngitis is found most often among females and homosexual males who practice fellatio; it is found less often among heterosexual males who practice cunnilingus.

During anal sex, gonococcus bacteria infect the anus and rectum, and gonococcal proctitis develops. In a few cases, the bacteria can spread along the perineum (the small area between the vulva and the anus) to the female anus from the vagina during or after sexual intercourse.

Young children who have a gonococcal infection usually contracted the bacteria from infected adults, most often through sexual abuse, including incest. A child may be subjected to oral or anal sex and develop, respectively, gonococcal pharyngitis or proctitis. Prior to puberty, females have gonococcal infections more often than males do because young female children are more frequently victims of sexual abuse. The person inflicting the abuse is usually familiar to the girl and is often an older male family member.

Less frequently, a prepubertal child contracts gonococcus bacteria during sexual play with siblings or playmates who have been infected by adults or other children.

Among all age groups the bacteria may be transmitted via the hands from one person to another or from one part of the body to another, although this means of transmission is uncommon.

Among all age groups the conjunctiva (the mucous membrane lining the inner surface of the eyelids and covering the front part of the eyeball) of the eyes can be infected by touching of the eyes with hands contaminated with gonococcus bacteria. This infection is called gonococcal *conjunctivitis.*

A gonococcal infection continues to be contagious until treatment has lasted a day or two. If the infection is never treated, a person continues to be a carrier of the bacteria for a year or possibly more, even though symptoms usually disappear. Reinfections with gonococcus bacteria are common.

The outlook for a person with a gonococcal infection is excellent if the disease is treated promptly.

SIGNS AND SYMPTOMS

From 60 to 80 percent of females show no early symptoms of gonococcal cervicitis or urethritis. Even if symptoms such as abnormal discharge or a swollen vulva do appear, they may go unnoticed or be ignored. Only a few women experience fever, pain on urination, frequent urination, or pain during sexual intercourse.

From 10 to 40 percent of males also have no early symptoms of gonococcal urethritis, although most males notice pain on urination, frequency of urination, and a discharge of pus from the urethra.

Gonococcal vulvovaginitis may cause no symptoms or may be marked by a discharge of mucus or pus. Other symptoms that may occur include painful urination, itching of the vagina, or pain of the vulva.

During adolescence or adulthood, gonococcal pharyngitis may or may not cause symptoms. The symptoms may resemble those of *strep throat.* Sometimes red patches appear in the throat. Less often, the uvula (the small outgrowth hanging above the back of the tongue) is red and swollen and blisterlike, pus-filled sores appear on the top of the back of the mouth and near the tonsils. Prepubertal children who have gonococcal pharyngitis usually have a sore throat, with or without fever.

Gonococcal proctitis often causes no symptoms. Discomfort of the rectum or anus occurs occasionally. Other symptoms that sometimes occur include ineffectual and painful straining when trying to defecate, pain upon defecation, or discharge of blood, pus, and mucus from the anus.

Gonococcal conjunctivitis is indicated by a discharge of pus.

DIAGNOSIS

Screening for gonorrhea during gynocological exams is becoming common practice. As a result, infections that have caused few or no symptoms are discovered.

A gonococcal infection is diagnosed by a physician, who performs a physical examination. The physician also carefully questions the patient about the history of any signs or symptoms. One or more laboratory tests (such as a smear of the obviously or possibly infected areas or, as confirmation, cultures of any discharges) will be ordered to check for the presence of gonococcus bacteria. Cultures may also be taken of the cervix or urethra to look for a symptomatic gonorrhea even when no discharge is apparent. A blood test is likely to be given to check for the presence of the bacteria that cause syphilis.

If a gonococcal infection is suspected or diagnosed, the physician is likely to check for concurrent gonococcal infections. For instance, if gonococcal cervicitis or vulvovaginitis is found, the physician will probably check for the presence of gonococcal pharyngitis and proctitis. If a male has gonococcal proctitis, he is likely to have gonococcal pharyngitis as well. (Gonococcal pharyngitis will usually be missed on a standard throat culture that tests for strep throat.)

If a girl has gonococcal vulvovaginitis, she is interviewed by a social worker, psychologist, pediatrician, or another appropriate health worker, who gently and carefully tries to determine how she received the infection. By law, suspected sexual abuse must be reported.

In addition, all of her family members and caretakers are tested in efforts to find the source of her infection. If sexual abuse is suspected, it is important that the person who infected her is identified, not only in order to spare the girl further sexual abuse and reinfection, but to determine whether her mother and sisters have also been infected by the same person. Also, the person who is the source of the girl's infection must receive treatment.

COMPLICATIONS

If treatment of a gonococcal infection is delayed or never administered, gonococcus bacteria may spread to other parts of the body and serious complications may arise. These complications can develop years after the infection.

Bacteria can spread through the reproductive tract and cause a number of complications.

- Acute or chronic pelvic inflammatory disease (PID). If the bacteria spread to and infect the fallopian tubes (through which eggs must pass on their way to the uterus), PID has developed. PID is the chief complication of gonococcal cervicitis; about 20 percent of women with gonococcal cervicitis develop noticeable PID; many of the other 80 percent may have hidden PID. The fallopian tubes may become partially or totally blocked, leading to sterility or

ectopic (tubal) pregnancies. (An undetected ectopic pregnancy can be life-threatening.) During the first trimester (approximately 3 months) of pregnancy, PID can cause a miscarriage. PID can also be followed by pelvic peritonitis (inflammation of the peritoneum, the membrane lining the abdominal and pelvic walls). The most noticeable symptoms of PID are lower abdominal pain and tenderness. Fever, vaginal discharge of pus, and pain during menstruation may also occur.

- Perihepatitis. Among females, gonococcus bacteria can spread through the fallopian tubes into the peritoneum (the membrane lining the abdominal cavity and covering certain organs, including the liver). If the peritoneal membrane covering the liver and the tissues around the liver becomes inflamed, perihepatitis occurs. Occasionally perihepatitis occurs in males.

- Endometritis. Gonococcus bacteria spread upward from the cervix onto the endometrium (lining of the uterus). The infection can cause abnormal menstrual bleeding.

- Bartholinitis. Gonococcus bacteria can spread along the perineum from the vagina and infect one of the two Bartholin's ducts, sometimes causing an abscess. A woman's labia (the folds of skin of the vulva) may be swollen and painful on the side of the infected duct.

- Periurethral abscess. Rarely, gonococcus bacteria cause an abscess (pocket of pus) near the urethra in males.

- Epididymitis. Men who have untreated gonococcal urethritis are susceptible to epididymitis, inflammation of the epididymus (consisting mainly of ducts in the testicles that excrete sperm). The testicles become enlarged and painful.

Gonococcus bacteria can spread through the bloodstream to any part of the body and, unless eradicated, can cause rare but serious complications. These complications more often affect females than males.

- Septic *arthritis*. The primary source of this complication is typically gonococcal cervicitis that caused no symptoms. The septic arthritis is characterized by pain in many joints (most commonly, the wrist, fingers, knees, and ankles); inflammation of tendons; fever; chills; and a rash consisting of a small number of red, pimplelike sores that may become blisterlike or pus-filled sores, usually on the arms and legs. Later symptoms can include fluid, sometimes pus-filled, on the knee or other joint.

- Endocarditis. Bacteria may infect part of the heart, leading to inflammation and alteration of the endocardium (the lining of the cavities of the heart). This is a rare complication.
- *Meningitis.* Bacteria may infect the brain and spinal cord leading to inflammation of the meninges (the protective covering of the brain and spinal cord). This is a rare complication.

Newborn infants who develop a gono-coccal infection typically acquired the bacteria during passage through an infected birth canal. Most often, the conjunctiva of both eyes are affected and gonococcal *conjunctivitis* develops. If untreated, gonococcal conjunctivitis can cause scarring of the eye or blindness.

Infrequently, an unborn baby is infected with gonococcus bacteria when the amniotic membranes rupture prematurely. Gono-coccal conjunctivitis, pharyngitis, or procti-tis can develop.

TREATMENT

No effective home treatment for a gono-coccal infection exists. Usually, however, if the disease is identified and treated early, it is readily curable with prescription antibiot-ics. Typically, a physician treats gonococcal infection with penicillin. (People who are al-lergic to penicillin are given another antibi-otic. Tetracycline should not be taken during pregnancy.) Contacts of infected people should be treated.

Careful follow-up is essential in all cases of gonococcal infections in order to be sure that the bacteria have really been eradicated. Some strains of gonorrhea are resistant to penicillin, so they must be treated, or re-treated, with other antibiotics. Gonococcal pharyngitis is more difficult to cure than other forms of gonorrhea, and treatment must be adjusted accordingly. Other consid-erations in selecting treatment include the possibility that the individual may also be incubating *syphilis* or an accompanying

nongonococcal sexually transmitted disease, such as chlamydia (see *chlamydial infec-tion*).

Gonococcal *conjunctivitis* in newborns is treated with irrigation of the conjunctiva and intravenous penicillin.

PREVENTION

No vaccine exists to prevent gonococcal infection.

One of the most important ways of preventing both infection and reinfection is education about how gonococcus bacteria are transmitted. Such education is especially important for teenagers, many of whom wrongly believe that gonorrhea is a disease of the past. Parents should instruct their children ages 10 or older about venereal dis-eases, including how they can be transmit-ted, identified, prevented, and treated.

The spread of gonococcus bacteria can be reduced. The regular use of condoms by sex-ually active people is recommended. Some research indicates that diaphragms and spermicides may reduce the risk of gono-coccal cervicitis or urethritis. The pill and IUD, however, offer no protection against gonorrhea.

Public health measures to curb the spread of gonococcus bacteria include the notifica-tion, examination, and treatment of infected persons' sexual contacts.

It is becoming common practice to screen pregnant women for gonococcal infection at their first prenatal care visit. (If the woman is at high risk of developing a gonococcal infection, she is also screened late during the third trimester of pregnancy.) If the preg-nant woman's gonococcal infection is identi-fied and treated early, infection of her baby may be avoided.

Most states now require the routine appli-cation of silver nitrate drops to newborns' eyes to prevent gonococcal *conjunctivitis* caused by passage through an infected birth canal. Erythromycin is sometimes adminis-tered instead. As a result, infants today sel-dom suffer from *blindness* due to conjuncti-vitis caused by their mothers' gonococcal infection.

The above measures are ineffective if the baby's eyes have already become infected be-fore birth. Obstetricians try to deliver at-risk babies as soon as possible after the amniotic sac ruptures, because risk of infection in-creases with time. If infection does occur, antibiotic treatment must be given.

GROWING PAINS

DESCRIPTION, SIGNS AND SYMPTOMS, AND CAUSE

Growing pains are normal, temporary, harmless aches and pains in a growing child's limbs and joints. They are not, however, caused by growth but result from vigorous use of incompletely developed muscles and bones. Almost all children, particularly those ages 6 to 12, experience growing pains, although they may be so mild as to go unnoticed. In general, growing pains worsen as a growing child's physical activity becomes more strenuous.

Most often, growing pains occur in a child's thighs, calves, and feet, but may also develop in other parts of the body that are used vigorously, such as the arms. They characteristically occur only when a child is at rest; an affected child experiences stiffness and limited joint motion. No signs of illness are present, and growing pains generally do not interfere with a child's daily routine.

Muscle cramps, which are painful contractions of muscle fibers, are severe growing pains that can last from a few seconds to a few hours. Cramps vary from mild to so severe (such as a charley horse) that they wake a child during the night.

DIAGNOSIS

Growing pains are different from other muscle and bone pains because they occur only when a child is at rest. If pain is severe or persistent, a physician should be consulted to ensure that the cause is not an underlying condition, such as a *sprain,* a *fracture,* or muscle inflammation caused by childhood illnesses such as *influenza, arthritis,* and *osteomyelitis* (a bacterial bone infection). A physical examination will be performed and X rays will be taken.

TREATMENT

Growing pains require little treatment. A pain-relieving medication may be helpful. Consult the physician for specific recommendations and read discussion of nonprescription medications beginning on p. 102. Gentle massage, application of a heating pad, or a warm-water soak may help relax sore muscles.

The best treatment for cramps is to gently stretch and massage the affected muscle. For example, cramped calf muscles should be massaged while the front of the foot is pushed upward. This procedure should be continued until the muscle relaxes.

PREVENTION

Growing pains cannot be prevented.

GUM PROBLEMS

DESCRIPTION

The gums (also called the gingiva) are the slightly soft, pink (although color may vary according to a child's skin color and the texture of the gums) mouth tissues that support the teeth and cover the dental arches (the upper or lower curved row of teeth and bone surrounding the roots of the teeth). When the structure of gum tissue changes or gum tissue becomes infected, a gum problem exists.

Gum problems vary in severity and duration, and most children experience at least one during childhood. With proper treatment most problems can be corrected.

Gingivitis

Gingivitis is a reversible gum disease, caused by build-up of plaque, deposits of dead cells, bacteria, and components of saliva that form when particles of food remain on or between teeth. It is characterized by gum swelling, redness, and tenderness without involvement of bone surrounding the tooth's root. It is the most common type of childhood gum disease, and mild cases occur in approximately 85 percent of children under age 15. Gingivitis may be associated with tooth eruption (both primary or permanent) and the onset of puberty.

If plaque is not removed from the teeth for a prolonged period of time, gum tissue can be severely damaged. Severe gingivitis is rare in healthy children but may develop if a child's ability to fight infection is low because of such problems as *malnutrition* or *parasitic infections.* It develops more often in young adults, ages 15 to 30. In rare cases severe gingivitis is quite painful and does not improve with treatment. Signs and symptoms of severe gingivitis appear suddenly and include red, swollen, tender gums (which may bleed), bad breath, and fever up to 104° F (40.0° C). The child usually feels ill and experiences loss of appetite. In severe cases associated with bacterial infection of the gum, areas of dead tissue may develop between the teeth.

Periodontitis

If gingivitis is not treated, it can progress to a more destructive form of gum disease called periodontitis. Periodontitis is much more common in adults than in children, and is characterized by swollen, tender, grooved gums. Teeth become loose because bone surrounding the tooth's root is lost. If the condition is untreated, underlying bone may be damaged extensively and teeth may be lost.

Juvenile Periodontitis

Juvenile periodontitis (also called periodontosis) is rare in young children but occurs in about 1 percent of healthy American adolescents. This condition is similar to adult periodontitis, but damage of supporting bone and gums is much more rapid. (Loss of bone may be so rapid that it is not noticed until affected teeth are very loose.) As a result, teeth may be lost.

Thrush

Thrush is a fungal infection characterized by white filmy spots on the gums and the lining of the mouth.

Viral Gum Infection

Children under 5 years of age often develop a viral infection of the mouth that affects the gums as well as the tongue, the inside of the lips, and the roof and sides of the mouth. This infection may be the initial stage of *oral herpes,* the most common oral viral infection. An affected child is usually irritable and feels ill. Signs and symptoms of infection develop suddenly and include swelling, redness, and soreness of the gums; headache; and mild fever. Blisters develop on the gums and rupture in a few days to form painful sores covered with a whitish-gray membrane. Symptoms usually disappear 10 to 14 days after onset.

After the initial childhood infection the virus remains inactive in the child's body, possibly for years. In some cases it may reactivate and produce symptoms of recurrent *oral herpes,* commonly known as cold sores.

CAUSE

Gingivitis and periodontitis are caused by a bacterial infection, occurring when large amounts of plaque build up and remain on the teeth. Plaque buildup usually results from poor or difficult teeth cleaning (which can occur because of orthodontic appliances such as braces), faulty fillings or caps, and crowded or eroded teeth (see *teeth, develop-*

mental problems of). Gum disease is more likely to be severe if a child cannot fight infection sufficiently because of nutritional deficiency or underlying illness.

The herpes virus can be picked up by sharing spoons, forks, or other objects that have come in contact with saliva carrying the virus.

SIGNS AND SYMPTOMS

Gum swelling, bleeding, and tenderness often occur with gum disease. Gum swelling can also be associated with more serious diseases, such as *leukemia,* or with allergic reactions to medications. Gums return to normal when the offending substance is eliminated or disease is controlled. Other symptoms can include redness or ulceration of the gums, loose teeth, and *bad breath.*

DIAGNOSIS

Gum disease is identified by a dentist according to characteristic signs and symptoms detectable upon oral examination and with X-ray films. A child's dental and medical histories are also helpful in making a diagnosis. Viral and fungal infections are identified by the presence of signs and symptoms and can be confirmed by a blood test if necessary.

COMPLICATIONS

An abscess (a collection of pus caused by a severe infection) may develop if gingivitis is severe. Primary or permanent teeth may be lost prematurely if juvenile periodontitis is severe, resulting in dental malocclusion (see *teeth, developmental problems of*).

TREATMENT

If gum problems result from an underlying disorder, successful treatment must involve treatment of the disorder.

Two of the most important steps in treatment of gum disease are the practice of good oral hygiene (including toothbrushing and flossing) at home and having a dentist or dental hygienist remove plaque deposits periodically.

Mild gingivitis can usually be controlled with good oral hygiene and professional care. Antibiotics may be prescribed if an abscess has developed. Pain and swelling of gum tissue should be lessened after one to three days of treatment.

If gingivitis is severe, a child will require more involved treatment and may be referred to a periodontist (a dentist specializing in treatment of gums). Deep cleaning may be required to remove dead tissue and plaque. If tissue damage is extensive, gums can be surgically reshaped. Severely affected primary teeth may be removed to prevent potential infection and involvement of permanent teeth.

Conditions that reduce a child's ability to fight infection (such as malnutrition) must be treated to achieve effective control of gum disease. A child's physician can recommend a nutritionally balanced diet and prescribe medication, if needed, to fight other infections.

If gum disease is diagnosed and treated early, a child usually recovers fully. Treatment of juvenile periodontitis may be difficult, however, because the cause is not known and the disease progresses so quickly.

Since no cure is available for herpes infection, treatment focuses on easing symptoms. Treatment involves good oral hygiene and nutrition and numbing preparations to lessen pain during infection. A fever-reducing medication may be helpful. Consult the physician for specific recommendations and read discussion of nonprescription medications beginning on p. 102.

PREVENTION

Good oral hygiene, regular visits to the dentist, correction of poorly spaced or poorly structured teeth (see *teeth, developmental problems of)*, and a nutritious diet (including firm, fresh fruits and vegetables, which help clean teeth) can help reduce plaque and the incidence of gum disease. Viral infections cannot generally be prevented.

GYNECOMASTIA

DESCRIPTION

Gynecomastia is development of breast tissue in males. Like females, all males have mammary glands. These glands are capable of swelling if stimulated by estrogen, a female hormone. Normally, all males have a certain level of estrogen in addition to male hormones (androgens) in their bodies. If the balance between estrogen and androgens in a boy's body is disrupted, gynecomastia can result. Gynecomastia should be distinguished from tissue growth caused by fat deposits (obesity) or chest muscle development.

Gynecomastia can involve any degree of breast development, from a barely noticeable "button" of swelling under the areola (the circular, brownish area that surrounds the nipple) to a full breast, resembling that of a woman. In most cases gynecomastia involves both breasts, although often there are minor variations in breast size.

Readily noticeable swelling of breasts is rare among boys. About half of all boys, however, develop slight gynecomastia during adolescence, when the balance of hormones in a boy's body is naturally changing. In most cases gynecomastia develops during the onset of puberty, when hormonal changes are most pronounced. Most boys enter puberty between the ages of 10 and 16. It appears that some boys develop gynecomastia because their bodies are more sensitive than others' to the normal hormonal changes that occur during this time.

As this hormonal activity subsides, gynecomastia usually disappears—often within 12 to 18 months of its onset. In rare cases, however, when breast development is quite pronounced or occurs late in adolescence, gynecomastia may not disappear for years and breasts may never reduce completely in size. Fortunately, relatively simple surgery can be performed to remove excess breast tissue and reduce breasts to normal size.

Even mild, temporary gynecomastia commonly causes an affected boy to feel embarrassment. With strong sympathy and support, emotional complications can usually be kept to a minimum, and a boy need not make any adjustments in his activities.

CAUSE

The exact way in which hormones can produce gynecomastia is unclear. Experts speculate that several different situations can lead to the condition. The only common cause of gynecomastia seems to be a sensitivity to normal hormonal changes in early puberty.

A far less common cause is an abnormal disruption in the body's hormonal balance. Such an imbalance can result from ingestion of estrogen-containing substances, such as birth control pills (which some young boys have mistaken for candy), or use of estrogenic skin creams. When ingestion of the substance stops, breast development recedes completely. An even rarer cause of a hormonal imbalance is an internal problem that interferes with normal hormone production, such as a testicular tumor (see *genitourinary tumors*) or an adrenal tumor (see *adrenal problems*). Among adults, alcohol abuse can seriously damage liver tissue, thereby prompting a hormonal imbalance which leads to gynecomastia.

Another rare cause of a hormonal imbalance is a genetically inherited problem with hormone production. In some cases the nature of such a problem is not altogether clear; a physician may suspect it exists because of a family history of pronounced gynecomastia. Boys with pronounced gynecomastia—and their male relatives—also tend to mature markedly faster than other boys. It is not clear what role, if any, rapid maturation plays in causing gynecomastia.

A very rare cause of gynecomastia is a *brain tumor*, which stimulates the pituitary gland to secrete prolactin, a hormone that promotes production of breast milk. Accumulation of fluid in the male breast can produce gynecomastia.

SIGNS AND SYMPTOMS

In most cases of gynecomastia the only sign is a slight swelling of the areola. Often this swelling is palpable (capable of being discerned by touch) but not particularly visible. The degree of swelling tends to be temperature-dependent; in warm weather, swelling increases.

In rare cases gynecomastia is associated with minor pain, which tends to appear during vigorous physical exertion, such as participating in sports activities. Such pain almost never necessitates curtailment of activities.

If the cause of gynecomastia is a *brain tumor*, fluid may flow spontaneously—or it may be possible to squeeze fluid—from one or both breasts.

DIAGNOSIS

If gynecomastia is not obvious, diagnosis and treatment are unnecessary. If gynecomastia is obvious to an affected boy or his parents, a physician should be consulted to explore the possibility that the boy has a problem causing an abnormal hormone imbalance, especially if gynecomastia appears before puberty or late in adolescence. A physician's counsel can also be useful in helping a boy cope with temporary enlargement of breasts.

In an attempt to discern a possible cause

for gynecomastia, a physician performs a physical examination and takes a family history as well as a history of recent activities. Such preliminary procedures may reveal a possible cause (ingestion of birth control pills, for example), and no further tests may be necessary. The results of these procedures can also raise a physician's suspicions about, for example, the possibility of hereditary gynecomastia or a *brain tumor*, in which case the physician orders further tests.

In very rare cases mammary-gland swelling is not gynecomastia but the result of a mammary-gland tumor or *neurofibromatosis*. Should a physician suspect such a problem, appropriate diagnostic tests (such as chest X rays) are performed.

COMPLICATIONS

Gynecomastia causes no significant physical complications. In some cases the skin of a nipple may erode slightly from rubbing against clothing. This problem can be eliminated by wearing looser shirts. Emotional and behavioral complications are more common. Boys with gynecomastia may shun peers or curtail athletic or other activities out of embarrassment. In some cases boys suffer from anxiety because they do not understand what is causing gynecomastia and fear a chest tumor or that they are not fully "male." Such worries can be particularly acute because of the social, academic, and other pressures of adolescence. Without sympathy and support, they can persist even after gynecomastia disappears.

TREATMENT

In most cases the only treatment needed is emotional support from the family and a physician. A boy should be helped to understand gynecomastia and should be reassured that it will eventually disappear. A physician can offer suggestions for situations such as changing clothing during gym classes. Although medical treatment is rarely necessary, in some cases medication is used to correct a hormone imbalance or decrease sensitivity to normal hormonal changes. If a boy is suffering emotionally from pronounced breast enlargement, plastic surgery is a viable option. Surgery involves making a small incision on the underside of the areola and removing mammary-gland tissue. A tiny, hairline scar may remain; gynecomastia, however, does not recur.

If the cause of gyncomastia is a *brain tu-*

mor, treatment focuses on eliminating the tumor.

PREVENTION

Substances known to contain estrogens should be kept out of the reach of children. It is not now known whether other causes of gynecomastia are preventable.

HAIR LOSS

DESCRIPTION

Hair loss can occur at any stage of childhood. Newborns' first hair usually falls out, but new hair regrows during childhood. If hair loss occurs during childhood, any of a variety of factors may be responsible, such as infections; severe illnesses accompanied by high fever; continual rubbing trauma of the head with a surface such as the mattress of a crib; pulling or twisting of the hair; emotional upsets; *burns;* hormonal problems such as hypothyroidism (see *thyroid problems);* iron deficiency; and spot baldness.

Many children lose some hair at one time or another, usually in random patches, but it grows back within a short time. Rarely, severe balding may result in a permanent loss of hair. Approximately 40 percent of all children affected by spot balding (alopecia areata) lose their hair again 4 to 5 years after the first hair loss.

Hair loss during childhood may appear as small, smooth, hairless patches. A stubble of broken hair shafts may be a sign of *ringworm.* Impetigo and ringworm may cause yellow crusts to form on the scalp in the balding area.

CAUSE

During infancy, hair loss occurs most often because of constant rubbing against crib and playpen mats. Young children may pull their hair, causing patchy hair loss. Playing with hair or pulling it tightly into ponytails, braids, and pigtails also leads to hair loss because of the strain on the roots and the hair shaft itself. *Ringworm* causes hair to become brittle and break off. *Impetigo,* a skin infection caused by staphylococcus or streptococcal bacteria, may cause the hair to fall out at the roots.

Spot baldness results in sudden hair loss. Its cause is unknown, although it frequently is triggered by emotional upset. Balding may last for weeks, months, or years.

Severe illness, drastic weight loss, or other marked metabolic changes also cause hair loss. The changes cause many of the growing hairs to enter a resting (nongrowing or "sleeping") phase. Approximately 6 to 12 weeks after entering the resting phase, hair loss occurs. This type of hair loss is not permanent.

Iron deficiency, calcium deficiency caused by parathyroid problems, or thyroid excess or deficiency, can also lead to a resting phase and subsequent hair loss. *Burns* caused by intense heat, X rays, acids, or chemicals may damage the growth center of the hair, resulting in scarring and permanent balding.

Inherited family traits may result in premature baldness. In the male pattern of hair loss, balding usually occurs at the temples and on top of the head and may spread over the entire scalp. A rare, inherited disorder called <u>anhidrotic ectodermal dysplasia</u> is associated with brittle, sparse hair, abnormal teeth, and the absence of sweat glands. There are other inherited hair disorders as well (see *genetic disorders).*

DIAGNOSIS

Parents can often diagnose hair loss caused by a child's habits such as hair pulling and hair twisting. Other causes of hair loss require a physician's diagnosis.

Diagnosis of a fungus infection and *impetigo* can be made by a physician. Since there are no visible signs other than hair coming out at the roots when hair loss is caused by calcium or iron deficiency, diagnosis is made by the presence of other characteristic signs and symptoms and a blood test.

COMPLICATIONS

Fungal and bacterial infection may lead to permanent baldness if not treated early.

TREATMENT

Because treatment methods often produce side effects and hair loss often corrects itself, therapy for spot baldness may not always be recommended. Hair loss caused by continual rubbing against crib mattress or playpen mats corrects itself when the rubbing is halted.

Treatment of *impetigo* and fungal infections usually requires oral medication prescribed by a physician. Encrusted sores can be soaked with warm water compresses several times a day to speed healing and reduce crusting.

Treatment of underlying illnesses is recommended according to the condition present.

PREVENTION

Hair pulling should be discouraged. Ponytails, braids, or pigtails should be kept loose to reduce stress on the hair. *Burns* can usually be prevented or reduced by keeping household chemicals, acids, or hot substances out of the reach of children (see Chapter 4, "Accident Prevention").

To prevent fungal and bacterial skin and scalp infections, a child should not borrow combs, brushes, or hats. The spread of *impetigo* can be prevented by keeping an infected child at home until the sores have stopped oozing. Frequent shampooing is a good preventive measure against bacterial and fungal infection.

Spot baldness, baldness caused by marked metabolic changes, and baldness caused by inherited traits cannot be prevented.

HAIR-PULLING

DESCRIPTION

Playing with hair in a harmless way is one of the most common habits of childhood. Many young children finger, stroke, and twirl their hair. Practiced in moderation, such actions are not unusual or abnormal. They most likely fulfill a universal need for self-comforting, in much the same way that a habit like *thumb-sucking* does. In fact, many children who suck their thumbs play with their hair simultaneously, especially at times such as bedtime when the need for self-comforting can be greatest. Before or during the first few years of school, many children learn to give up habits of early childhood and seek comforting through other means.

A small number of children, however, play with their hair for reasons that go beyond self-comforting. These children are often deeply troubled by a long-term problem or a sudden crisis, and the manner in which they play with their hair can be self-destructive. Instead of caressing their hair, they may pull out single strands or even tufts. After pulling out hair, a child may discard, caress, or even eat it. Caressing or eating hair may actually function as self-comforting. Other signs and symptoms of psychological *stress,* such as crying, may accompany hair-pulling. A hairball on rare occasions may cause intestinal obstruction.

Hair lost through hair-pulling grows back, but unlike cosmetic problems, a child's distress is unlikely to disappear spontaneously. The help of a physician or counselor may be required.

CAUSE

Psychological stress leading to hair-pulling can arise in a variety of situations, including the birth or death of a sibling or the illness of a parent, a persistent family problem, or sudden drastic changes in surroundings, such as moving. Why some children cope with these situations by pulling out their hair is unknown.

Children with developmental disabilities such as *mental retardation* may pull at their hair or may continue to play harmlessly with their hair longer than other children. These children may use habits to compensate for difficulties in perceiving and responding to stimuli.

Rarely, a child may yank at his or her hair because of scalp irritation caused by *psoriasis, ringworm,* and *seborrheic dermatitis.* Scratching the scalp, however, is more common.

DIAGNOSIS

If parents know that a child is pulling out hair, a physician's diagnosis is necessary.

Usually it is obvious if a child habitually plays with or pulls his or her hair. Parents who are unsure whether a child's hair-playing is harmless or destructive should look for evidence of hair-pulling such as small bald patches on the child's head and strands or tufts of hair on the floor. Children who habitually eat their hair may complain of stomach pain and may vomit (see *vomiting*).

If a child is merely playing with his or her hair now and then, professional diagnosis—as well as parental worry—is unnecessary. One exception exists: a child who plays with his or her hair using the same rapid, rhythmic, uncontrollable movement may have a tic (see *tics and Tourette's syndrome*) and should be examined by a physician.

If a tic is suspected, the physician may refer the child to a psychiatrist or neurologist for further testing. If, as is most common, hair-pulling seems to be related to psychological *stress,* a physician may refer the family to a counselor.

COMPLICATIONS

Hair-pulling can be extremely painful. In severe cases it can cause the scalp to bleed. A child who has obvious bald spots because of hair-pulling may be ridiculed by peers. A hairball on rare occasions may cause intestinal obstruction.

TREATMENT AND PREVENTION

Unless signs and symptoms of hair-pulling or of a psychological or physical problem are present, parents should not scold a child for hair-twisting and other harmless habits. Reprimands intensify a child's need for self-comforting.

If a child continually twists his or her hair into knots that cannot be worked out, parents may suggest to the child that hair be twirled more gently. It is also helpful for parents to try to interest a child in a more constructive activity whenever hair-twisting begins.

If the underlying cause of hair-pulling is physical—*psoriasis,* for example—a physician may be able to provide medical treatment for the problem. Parents of a child who engages in hair-pulling can work with a physician or other health professional to find out what is bothering the child and how best to help him or her deal with stress.

It may be possible to curtail a child's hair-pulling. A child can usually be encouraged by a counselor to modify his or her behavior and avoid hair-pulling through a system of daily rewards (such as stars on a calendar) or other incentives.

If necessary, ointments can be prescribed or recommended to alleviate certain scalp problems.

HAND DEFORMITIES, CONGENITAL

DESCRIPTION

A congenital hand deformity exists when an infant is born with a hand that deviates in any way from normal. The severity of the deformity may vary greatly, from a small defect in a nail or bone to total absence of the hand. Sometimes all normal structures may be present but are abnormally positioned.

Problems associated with congenital hand deformities also vary greatly and may be directly related to the severity of the hand or limb defect. Developmental milestones such as crawling, sitting, standing, and walking may be severely affected by hand and other upper-limb malformations. Many children with hand deformities have associated conditions such as cardiac (heart), gastrointestinal (stomach, esophageal, and intestinal), and craniofacial problems (see *facial deformities, congenital*).

Flexed Thumb

Flexed thumb is the most common hand deformity found among children, although it may be difficult to recognize at birth because the newborn normally holds the thumb flexed in the palm for the first 3 to 4 months after birth. This deformity exists when the thumb cannot be completely extended. It usually affects both thumbs at birth and corrects itself without active treatment.

Flexed thumb is caused by a thickened flexor (flexing) tendon at the base of the thumb. This tendon normally passes through a series of pulleys, much like those on a fishing pole, that keep it from bowstringing. When the tendon thickens, it cannot glide freely beneath the pulleys, and the thumb is held in a flexed position. If the problem persists, a simple surgical procedure can correct it and permit full function.

Webbed Fingers

The second most common deformity involves fingers that are joined together and have not completely separated. In its simplest form, webbing between fingers contains skin and abnormal ligaments. In the more complex forms, bones, joints, nails, tendons, nerves, and arteries may be shared by two or more fingers.

Extra Fingers

Extra bones or complete fingers can be found anywhere in the hand. Often, extra bones are contained within the central portion of the hand covered by webbing between fingers. Rarely, an entire hand may be duplicated and have 9 or 10 fingers. The size and configuration of extra or duplicated parts may vary, but most are small and incompletely developed. It is unusual for the extra part to be normally sized or to have the normal number of tendons, nerves, bones, and joints.

Bent Fingers

Bent fingers are usually caused by tight

flexor tendons, which bend the first joint of the finger beyond the palm. This deformity may involve all fingers but most commonly appears as a flexed fifth finger on both hands. If recognized early in life, especially at or soon after birth, bent fingers can be successfully corrected by passive stretching and splinting. If treatment is delayed, bent fingers can be corrected to some extent through surgery.

Deviated Fingers

Instead of being bent or flexed, deviated fingers and thumbs are curved to one side or another. Any part of the hand may be involved, but most commonly the fifth finger is deviated toward the thumb. This deformity occurs because of abnormal development of the middle bone of the fifth finger, the last bone of the hand to develop. Often the thumb deviates away from the rest of the hand so that it looks like a hockey stick. When the thumb is affected, neurologic and facial deformities are usually present.

Incurving of the fifth finger alone may be associated with other congenital hand deformities but most commonly occurs as an isolated inherited deformity.

Missing Fingers

One or more fingers may be missing from the hand. One of the most common occurrences is a small hand with a thumb and fifth finger but a very small or missing index, long, and ring finger. These three fingers are often represented by small, undeveloped fingers called nubbins. The causes of these deficiencies are unknown; no genetic pattern has been identified. Isolated absence of either the thumb or fifth finger can occur as part of other deformities such as clubhand. Missing fingers are often classified as amputations.

Clubhand

A clubhand occurs when one of the two forearm bones—the radius on the thumb side of the arm or the ulna on the little-finger side of the arm—is either missing or smaller than normal. As a result, the hand and wrist deviate to one side and look like the head of a golf club. If the radius is small or absent, the unsupported hand and wrist deviate inward toward the body. The thumb is often absent or small, and it may appear as a "floating thumb," attached to the rest of the hand by a small skin bridge. Almost half of the cases of radius clubhand that involve both arms are accompanied by malformations of the genitourinary tract, gastrointestinal tract, skeletal system, and cardiovascular (heart and blood vessel) system. In addition, various types of *anemia* may develop during childhood.

Cases of ulnar clubhand are much less common than radial clubhand. In such cases the entire ring and small fingers are usually missing.

Constriction Ring (or Annular Band) Syndrome

Over the past 10 to 20 years a deformity known as the constriction ring (or annular band) syndrome has occurred with increasing frequency. Any part of the hand, forearm, or upper arm may appear with a depressed, circular or semicircular band or ring around it. This ring appears to be caused by an invisible thread.

In most cases constriction rings occur because of irritation of the uterus during early pregnancy. As a result of this irritation and resulting uterine spasms, parts of the lining of the amniotic sac separate and float within the fluid-filled cavity. Eventually these parts wrap around parts of the developing embryo, such as the arms, hands, fingers, and toes. In severe cases tight rings may act as a tourniquet and prevent the rest of the finger or hand from developing. This results in an "intrauterine amputation."

There is no genetic basis for constriction rings. Approximately 10 percent of children with constriction rings involving their hands also have facial or skull deformities such as cleft lips and palates.

Amputations

Part of a finger, an entire finger, or an entire hand may fail to develop. The most common congenital amputation involves an absent top half or third of a finger, although amputations at the wrist, forearm, and upper arm level also occur. As already stated, amputations may be caused by constriction bands. However, not all amputations are associated with this syndrome. There appears to be no genetic basis for amputations. Occasionally, the upper arm or forearm (or both) may be absent, with an intact but abnormal hand attached to the shoulder, as occurs among children whose mothers took thalidomide during pregnancy.

Short Fingers

Short fingers and/or thumbs commonly occur as isolated deformities or as part of many congenital syndromes, such as short stature (see *height problems*). Joints of these fingers often fuse and do not move. Despite their limited motion, these fingers usually function quite well, and corrective surgery is not usually recommended.

Large Fingers

Abnormally bulky and long fingers occur quite commonly and are often overlooked. The most common cause of this deformity is a blood vessel malformation or abnormal collection of blood vessels that greatly increase the size of a finger or hand when filled with blood. Approximately one half of these blood vessel masses disappear spontaneously by the third year of life. The other half of large fingers grow proportionately with the child, but later may increase rapidly during growth spurts and pregnancy.

Children with *neurofibromatosis* may have enlarged fingers with or without webbing. Two fingers are usually affected and may reach huge proportions if surgery is not performed. Enlargement of fingers and hands may also be caused by bone or soft-tissue tumors. Although this is much less common than vascular malformations, the possibility must always be considered during diagnosis. Treatment of very enlarged fingers, thumbs, or hands is difficult.

Associated Deformities

Most congenital upper-limb deformities occur alone; others occur in combination with other deformities or as part of complex syndromes. The three most common deformities—webbed fingers, extra fingers, and congenital flexed thumb—occur alone with a few exceptions.

Webbing of fingers can be part of a complex syndrome in which other parts of the body are also abnormal. Simple webbing is common among children with *Down syndrome.* Cranial or skull defects, congenital facial deformities such as *cleft lip and cleft palate,* cardiac abnormalities, and kidney malformations may be present along with webbing of fingers.

Complex webbed fingers involving bone fusions are frequently associated with congenital facial abnormalities. Webbed fingers with associated short fingers is frequently one of many musculoskeletal abnormalities involving the entire side of the body.

Approximately 20 percent of all children with craniofacial abnormalities have associated upper-limb abnormalities. Because upper-limb and hand defects are so often associated with other problems, these malformations are considered initially as a symptom or indicator of an underlying problem.

CAUSE

Exactly why congenital hand deformities occur is not well understood. From 10 to 15 percent of congenital upper limb deformities are caused by environmental factors, and another 10 to 15 percent result from genetic factors (see *genetic disorders*). The causes of the remaining defects are unknown.

The constriction ring syndrome is an example of an environmentally caused deformity: radiation delivered to the developing fetus results in abnormal development and lack of growth. Other causes include abnormal positioning of a fetal finger or hand within a crowded space and poor fetal growth because of the mother's illness or malnutrition.

Medications can have significant effects; an example would be the deformities caused by thalidomide. Mothers who have metabolic problems related to heroin addiction or alcoholism frequently give birth to children with hand defects such as extra fingers, small hands, and bent joints. (See discussion of fetal alcohol syndrome in *drug and alcohol abuse.*) Defects may also result from diseases acquired during pregnancy, such as *chicken pox* or *German measles.*

Genetic defects account for a number of well-known hand malformations. Abnormal shortness of fingers and missing joints within fingers are commonly carried as a dominant trait and will appear in most members of the same family. Deviation or incurving of the fifth finger is so common in some families that it is often thought to be normal. Hundreds of genetic syndromes exist in which a hand problem is present, but most of these are infrequent.

DIAGNOSIS

Hand and upper-limb defects are usually present at birth and are obvious on routine medical examinations of the newborn. By the time an infant is 6 months of age, most abnormalities become obvious because of the functional problems they present. If any abnormalities are noted, a complete physical examination is performed, and careful pregnancy and medication histories of the mother are taken. In addition, family medical histories are obtained.

A child with a hand or upper-limb deformity is usually referred during infancy by a pediatrician to a plastic or orthopedic surgeon for assessment and treatment. Diagnostic studies may include X-ray films; photographs; measurements of strength, coordination, and motion; and plaster models. The correct diagnosis and treatment plan are then discussed with parents.

TREATMENT

The hand surgeon who is treating the child may consult a clinical geneticist to determine whether the deformity is part of an identified syndrome. Other professionals such as radiologists, occupational hand therapists, physical therapists, and psychologists may be consulted to develop a comprehensive, long-range treatment plan for the child. Severe deformities with significant limitation of function require a team approach.

During the first 6 to 12 months of life, treatment consists primarily of hand therapy in which deformed joints are stretched, moved, and splinted. Early treatment during this period may avoid the necessity of surgery later.

If surgery is necessary, it is usually performed after a baby is 1 year old. Surgeons aim to complete most hand reconstructions by school age. Surgery cannot eradicate the deformity but can usually improve it significantly. Improvement of function is given highest priority.

Many ingenious methods of improving the function and appearance of the hand have been devised by plastic surgeons. A living bone graft (a transplant of bone that grows with an intact blood supply) can be used to reconstruct an incomplete or missing finger. Artificial joints can be inserted where one is missing. Short bones can be stretched and lengthened using external devices that look like erector sets. The tissue and fused bones of webbed fingers can be divided. With microsurgery, toes may even be transferred to the hand to make a thumb or fingers. Simple releases of abnormal tendons can straighten a bent finger. In cases of amputation or reduction, a prosthesis (artificial limb) may be made. Use of prostheses early in life is essential to ensure the best possible limb function. Parts of a hand can be rearranged to improve function, such as moving the index finger into the thumb position when the thumb is missing.

While a child is recuperating from surgery, occupational and physical therapy may be beneficial to help the child learn how to maneuver and use a reconstructed thumb, finger, or hand, or a newly attached prosthesis. Frequent follow-up appointments are necessary.

Helping a child and parents resolve psychological problems stemming from the deformity is as important as correcting the deformity itself. Any deformity, regardless of severity, has an emotional impact upon the child and may greatly affect self-image development. Individual and family counseling can be helpful.

PREVENTION

During pregnancy, women should avoid radiation and drugs (including alcohol and medications) unless a physician considers them to be absolutely necessary. It is also very important for women to receive regular prenatal care from the beginning of pregnancy. Pregnant women should take reasonable precautions—such as wearing car seat belts—to avoid injury.

At least three months before becoming pregnant, a woman should be tested to see if she is immune to *German measles* (rubella). If she is not, she should be vaccinated.

Parents who have a child with severe multiple deformities may wish to receive genetic counseling (see *genetic disorders*) so that they will know the chances of having another affected child.

HAND, FOOT, AND MOUTH DISEASE

DESCRIPTION

Hand, foot, and mouth disease is a viral infection characterized by *fever;* mouth sores and blisters; a body rash, especially on the buttocks; and small, flat, red spots or raised blisters on the hands and feet. The disease affects infants and older children alike, occurring most often in the summer and fall months. Mouth sores and blisters affect a child's appetite, make chewing painful, and diminish the sense of taste.

Signs and symptoms of the disease appear 2 to 5 days after a child has been exposed to the virus, and usually last less than 2 weeks. Hand, foot, and mouth disease is not a serious illness, and most infants and children recover without any aftereffects.

CAUSE

Hand, foot, and mouth disease is caused by one of several types of virus collectively known as Coxsackie. These viruses are found in human feces, in sewage, and in contaminated drinking water. Children are exposed to the virus through contact with contaminated food or water or through unsanitary disposal of feces. The virus is also transmitted in mucus droplets produced by a cough or a sneeze.

SIGNS AND SYMPTOMS

Hand, foot, and mouth disease usually begins with moderate fever (100° to 103° F; 37.8° to 39.4° C), and eruption of small, round blisters inside the mouth. Blisters appear most often on the inside of the cheeks and on the tongue, but also may affect the lips, gums, and roof of the mouth. These blisters begin to break within a day or two, leaving shallow sores. Small, round, well-defined, fluid-filled blisters may also develop on the palms of the hands, the soles of the feet, and between the fingers and toes. About 25 percent of children develop a rash, especially over the buttocks.

DIAGNOSIS

Hand, foot, and mouth disease is diagnosed by a physician by observing typical symptoms, especially fever and mouth blisters and sores.

COMPLICATIONS

Hand, foot, and mouth disease is occasionally accompanied by viral *meningitis,* an inflammation of the central nervous system that is usually self-limited.

TREATMENT

Because hand, foot, and mouth disease is caused by a virus, antibiotics are not effective. The disease runs its course in a week or two, however, and care is aimed at making a child as comfortable as possible. Fever-reducing and pain-relieving medications may be helpful (see discussion of nonprescription medicines beginning on p. 102).

It is important that the child receive plenty of fluids, even if eating is too painful. Cold liquids are preferable in almost all cases. Sucking on frozen juice pops or ice cubes can temporarily numb sores on lips, cheeks, gums, and tongue.

PREVENTION

Hand, foot, and mouth disease cannot be prevented, except by avoiding contact with contaminated water or infected individuals. No vaccine yet exists.

HAY FEVER

DESCRIPTION

Hay fever (allergic rhinitis) is a reaction of nasal membranes and sinuses to certain inhaled substances (allergens). Two types of hay fever affect people of all ages. Seasonal hay fever, occurring during spring and summer, affects people who are sensitive to various pollens and molds. Approximately 5 to 9 percent of all children have seasonal hay fever. Perennial hay fever exists all year round and affects people who are sensitive to substances such as dust, pet hair or fur, and feathers.

The nose, sinuses, roof of the mouth, eyes, and ears are affected by hay fever. Allergies that cause hay fever can persist throughout life, though some may be outgrown. Severity and duration depend on the number and types of allergens to which a child is sensitized.

Hay fever often accompanies or follows an eruption of *eczema,* and may be associated with *sinusitis* and *conjunctivitis.*

CAUSE

Seasonal hay fever is usually caused by a sensitivity to the pollens of trees, grasses, or weeds. Ragweed pollen is one of the most common causes of hay fever. Flower pollens rarely cause hay fever, as they are usually too heavy to be airborne.

Perennial hay fever is caused by substances present year round. Animal dander, feathers, dust, and mold are common allergy-causing substances. Small children are often sensitive to dust or animal dander; older children are often allergic to several substances.

Hay fever seems to run in families, although specific sensitivities are not inherited.

SIGNS AND SYMPTOMS

Nasal membranes become swollen, inflamed, and itchy. Sneezing is the body's response to constant irritation of the nose. Large amounts of mucus are produced, causing nasal congestion and clogged sinuses. A child may develop characteristic actions such as a "rabbit nose" (wrinkling of the nose) or an "allergic salute" (frequent rubbing of the nose) in attempts to scratch the itchy nasal passages. Breathing through the nose is difficult, and mouth breathing and nighttime snoring are common.

Nasal problems may be accompanied by red, itchy, tearing eyes and bluish circles below the eyes. The roof of the mouth may itch. Headaches often develop, due to congested sinuses, and ears may ache and feel clogged. Hearing may be reduced or blocked. Tiredness, known as an allergic fatigue syndrome, is common.

DIAGNOSIS

A physician will examine a child and take a detailed medical history. Normal nasal membranes are pink, but a child with allergic rhinitis will have pale, bluish membranes. Identification of hay fever can occasionally be made through laboratory tests of nasal secretions. To identify specific allergens, a child can be given a series of skin tests. These expose a child to small amounts of potential allergy-causing substances. A local skin reaction identifies the allergen.

If an infant has hay fever, elimination of various foods from the diet may determine possible cause. Foods are uncommon causes of hay fever in an older child.

COMPLICATIONS

Secondary bacterial infections are common. Symptoms include *fever,* earache (see *earache and ear infections),* swollen neck glands, and opaque nasal discharge.

TREATMENT

The first step in treatment is avoiding contact with known allergy-causing substances. Windows can be kept closed to minimize infiltration of pollen; air can be filtered indoors by air conditioners or air-filtering devices. All rooms of the house, particularly a child's bedroom, should be cleaned frequently to prevent dust collection. Children with mold allergies should avoid damp areas. Basements can be dried out through the use of cross ventilation, dehumidifiers, or air conditioners. Children allergic to feathers can use rubber or synthetic pillows.

To reduce the symptoms of hay fever a child can be given an oral antihistamine (to reduce sneezing, runny nose, and itching) and decongestants (to unclog the nasal passages). Antihistamines should be administered carefully, since they may make a child drowsy. If nasal passage inflammation is severe, a physician may prescribe a short treatment of corticosteroids in nasal spray form.

Once an allergen has been identified and if a child cannot avoid contact with it, the most effective treatment of hay fever is immunotherapy (desensitization). This treatment can effectively control a child's allergies by producing an immunity to the allergy-causing substances. Administered by a physician, immunotherapy consists of a series of injections of the identified allergen. These injections are usually administered once each week in slowly increasing doses.

Once immunized, usually 3 months after therapy begins, a child is transferred to a maintenance immunotherapy program of injections at monthly intervals. The dosage of each maintenance injection remains constant; injections continue as long as the program controls allergy symptoms. To be most effective, year-round immunotherapy is recommended for both seasonal and perennial hay fever. Treatment is usually discontinued in 3 or 4 years. Short-term or long-term side effects are rare with treatment.

PREVENTION

Symptoms of hay fever can be controlled by avoiding known allergens and by the use of antihistamines and decongestants. They can be prevented by immunotherapy, when indicated.

HEADACHE

EMERGENCY ACTION

Most headaches are nothing but short-term annoyances. Occasionally, however, head pain is a warning sign that an underlying problem needs medical attention. Treat a headache as an emergency under any of the following circumstances:

- Head pain is so severe that a child cries, clutches his or her head, or wants desperately to lie down.
- Head pain interferes significantly with routine activities for more than an hour.
- Head pain is accompanied by unexplained *fever,* violent *vomiting,* or a stiff neck (see *wry neck, neck pain).*
- A child seems confused, disoriented, delirious (see *delirium),* or excessively drowsy.

A headache should be taken even more seriously if any of these conditions is present when a child awakes from a night's sleep; minor headaches almost always disappear after extended rest.

DESCRIPTION

Just as its name suggests, headache is internal head pain. It is always a symptom of another problem, which could be anything from minor, everyday tension to a life-threatening disease. Almost without exception, headaches resulting from serious underlying problems are accompanied by other signs and symptoms.

Very generally speaking, headache results from irritation of nervous-system structures called pain fibers, which are located throughout the head in tissues such as muscle and blood vessels. A headache can originate in virtually any part of the skull, including blood vessels, nerves, and the membrane covering the brain. Tension headache, for example, occurs when stress causes neck and temple muscles to contract, which in turn irritates pain fibers.

Headaches are almost as common among children as adults, and a child may develop a headache at any age. About 40 percent of children get at least one headache by age 7; about 75 percent have had at least one by age 15. Headache duration and severity vary greatly. Most headaches—about 95 percent —result from mild, uncomplicated conditions. Headaches affecting toddlers, however, are usually a sign of something more serious. Regardless of the prognosis for any underlying condition, headache itself can usually be relieved, if not prevented.

For diagnostic and treatment purposes, headaches may be classified into three broad categories according to cause: migraine, disease- or injury-related, and tension or psychological.

Migraine Headaches

Migraine, a lifelong condition, is one of the most common causes of headache among children, and about 5 percent of all children are affected. In childhood the condition is characterized by repeated attacks, lasting for an hour or more each, of throbbing headache, loss of appetite, and nausea. The length of time between attacks varies from several times per week to several times per year, and the severity and duration of each attack may be different. Some attacks are accompanied by more severe signs and symptoms, such as visual problems and *vomiting,* which can persist for a day or two.

The typical migraine headache lasts an hour or so, affects the front portion (temple areas) of the head, is accompanied by loss of appetite and nausea, and is relieved by sleep. During an attack a child may be irritable, lethargic, withdrawn, confused, or dizzy. Paleness is a telltale sign of a migraine headache.

More rarely, other signs and symptoms are part of a migraine attack. Immediately before a migraine headache, a child may experience an "aura" in one or both eyes characterized by blind spots, brilliant flashes, or blurriness. During an aura, a child may also have a communication problem such as difficulty speaking. Within minutes or, at most, a few hours, one or both sides of the head throb with pain and one or both sides of the child's body may be slightly numb. Nausea may be accompanied by abdominal pain and *vomiting.* Children with migraine are often prone to *motion sickness.*

For some children who suffer from migraine, headache is not the most prominent symptom. These children may have recurrent spells of nausea and vomiting or abdominal pain lasting minutes, hours, or even days. If headache is a factor, it usually develops between attacks instead of during them. Many children who have migraine-related episodes of vomiting, nausea, and abdominal pain eventually develop more common signs and symptoms of migraine.

In most cases migraine attacks first appear in late childhood and early adolescense, but the condition has been diagnosed in children as young as 2 years of age. Almost all children who suffer from migraine attacks have a family history of the condition. Although it seems clear that heredity plays a role in causing migraine, the exact cause is not well understood. Studies show that certain emotional and physical factors may have some bearing on the onset of individual attacks. These factors include *stress* (from any source, including *learning problems*), missed meals, head injury (see *head and spinal injury*), certain foods (chocolate and cheese, for example), oral contraceptives, and menstrual periods.

Disease- or Injury-Related Headaches

Headache commonly accompanies many diseases, injuries to the head or central nervous system, and other signs and symptoms.

Common infectious diseases that often cause headache include *influenza, colds,* ear infections (see *earache and ear infections*), *strep throat, sore throat,* and *eye infections.* Headache also commonly appears with *fever,* which causes blood vessels within the skull to enlarge.

In rare cases the cause of headache is a physical disturbance within the head. Such problems include head injury (see *head and spinal injury*), *encephalitis* (brain disease), *meningitis* (a serious infection of the membranes covering the brain and spinal cord), and malformation of blood vessels in the head.

In very rare cases the cause of headache is a *brain tumor.* Only about 1 of every 40,000 children develops a tumor of the brain or any other part of the central nervous system. Headaches caused by brain tumors may develop following changes in the position of the head. They tend to awaken a child at night or be present when a child wakes up from a night's sleep. These headaches are frequently accompanied by vomiting and slight nausea and may be followed by a feeling of well-being. An affected child usually has other obvious symptoms of a brain tumor.

Tension or Psychological Headaches

Although tension is a common cause of headache among adults and although it may play a role in bringing on migraine attacks, tension-caused headaches are not common among children. It is more common for children to express stress and anxiety in other ways—by, for example, behaving in an unusual way or developing stomach pain (see *stomachache, stomach pain).* When tension or a psychological or emotional problem is the underlying cause, headache is usually dull and steady. It is likely to increase in intensity as the day wears on and to be relieved by sleep—only to begin again the following day. A child may complain of extreme head pain virtually constantly; and other symptoms, such as poor appetite, *constipation,* and insomnia (see *sleep disorders)* are likely to be present.

DIAGNOSIS

An older child may indicate a headache by complaining of head pain. A younger child with a headache may be irritable and may cry in pain and distress.

Awareness of the presence of a headache, however, is not sufficient to determine treatment. Attempts always should be made to identify the underlying cause, and a physician's help may be necessary. Diagnosis is based on the nature of the headache and any other signs and symptoms; a child's medical history; physical examination; and, sometimes, laboratory or psychological tests.

It is good practice to be alert for other symptoms if a child has a headache of unknown origin. Such information may help a physician diagnose an underlying disease. In addition to signs and symptoms such as fever or nausea, more subtle irregularities—refusal to play, eat, or socialize, for instance—should be noted. A parent should also try to tell a physician where a child's head pain is located, how long it lasts, what time of day it appears, any circumstances that may be provoking it, and response to any medication a child has been given.

When a physician suspects that a child's headaches may be caused by migraine, a thorough knowledge of the family's history of headaches is particularly helpful. If any of a child's close relatives has had similar attacks, it is likely that migraine is the cause of the child's headaches.

If no family history of migraines is present, a physician or a consulting neurologist (nervous-system specialist) may order sophisticated diagnostic tests, such as three-dimensional X-ray films (called CT scans). These tests are used to determine whether blood vessel malformation, *brain tumor,* or some other physical disturbance within the head is the cause of the headache.

It is important, however, to rule out more common and less serious causes of headache before considering complicated diagnostic procedures requiring hospitalization. Headaches caused by migraine are often misdiagnosed, and unnecessary tests may aggravate an undetected psychiatric condition by heightening a child's anxiety. If a physician orders complicated tests, the child should be reassured and comforted.

COMPLICATIONS

An underlying condition could persist and become worse if the cause of a headache is misdiagnosed or improper medication is prescribed. In addition, a persistent headache could interfere seriously with a child's routine activities, such as going to school.

TREATMENT

Tension headaches are usually relieved by comforting and rest. A pain-relieving medication may be helpful. Consult the physician for specific recommendations and read the discussion of nonprescription medications beginning on p. 102. This treatment is also applicable to headache caused by common infectious diseases such as *influenza*. In some cases cool compresses applied to the forehead or a gentle neck massage may relieve tension and pain. Some parents have found it helpful to try one or both of the following:

- Encourage the child to rest quietly in a dimly lit room and, if possible, to nap.
- Feed the child a light meal, but do not insist that he or she finish it.

If headache persists after home treatment or recurs frequently, a physician should be consulted.

In general, the best method of treatment for any headache is one that focuses on the cause of head pain as well as the pain itself. More than half of all children who suffer from migraine can prevent attacks by taking prescription medication that controls the expansion and contraction of blood vessels in the skull. A physician usually prescribes such medication for 4 to 6 months and recommends more only if frequent attacks recur. A physician may also advise changes in the child's diet and life-style.

If headaches recur despite attempts to prevent attacks, pain may be eased by a mild pain-relieving medication. Consult the physician for specific recommendations and read discussion of nonprescription medications beginning on p. 102. A physician can also prescribe stronger medicine which, taken at the first signs of headache, may provide relief and shorten its duration.

One highly successful form of treatment for migraine and other recurring headaches involves teaching a child how to recognize the onset of an attack (often through a technique called biofeedback) and control it using an appropriate relaxation method.

Sometimes headache caused by tension or psychological problems can be alleviated if the child talks with a counselor. A psychiatrist's help may be necessary, and in extreme cases antidepressant medication (see *depression*) may be prescribed.

PREVENTION

Providing a warm, supportive environment for a child may help prevent frequent tension headaches. Prevention of other types is possible only when the causes are preventable.

HEAD AND SPINAL INJURY

EMERGENCY ACTION

Seek medical assistance immediately if any of the following signs and symptoms appears after a child receives a blow to the head, neck, or back:

- unconsciousness for more than a few seconds (see also *coma*)
- signs of diminished mental alertness, such as loss of memory, confusion, disorientation, *dizziness,* or *delirium* for more than 5 minutes
- increasing drowsiness
- *apnea* (absence of breathing) or abnormal breathing
- cold, wet, pale skin or any other sign of *shock*
- slow pulse (less than 50 to 60 beats per minute)
- convulsions (see *seizures*)
- stiff neck, awkwardly held head, or other signs of neck injury or fracture
- bent or oddly shaped spine
- extensive or profusely bleeding cuts (see *cuts and lacerations*)
- flow of clear or bloody, unclotting fluid from an ear or nostril
- a depression or unusually large lump on the skull or other signs of skull fracture
- walking problems (such as limping) or severe weakness or paralysis of the head, neck, arms, or legs
- inability to speak or slurred speech
- eye pupils of different sizes or vision problems such as seeing double for more than 5 minutes
- persistent, severe *headache* that is unrelieved by pain-reducing medication
- recurrent *vomiting* (more than two episodes)

All of these signs and symptoms indicate the possibility of severe head or spinal injury. Some, such as decreased mental alertness, may not appear until days or even weeks after an injury. To prevent complications and irreversible damage, medical attention must be sought as soon as any sign or symptom appears.

If no one trained in first aid procedures is available, treat a child who has a potentially serious head or spinal injury with the utmost of care until help arrives (see Chapter 10, "Basic First Aid). Do not move the child unless there is no other way to get the child out of a life-threatening situation. Even if it appears that only a head injury has been sustained, do not move the child's neck or back. If the child is wearing a sports helmet, do not remove the helmet unless the child cannot breathe and removal is the only way to provide an airway. No food, drink, or medication should be given; a child's stomach should be empty in case general anesthesia or certain diagnostic tests are needed.

DESCRIPTION

In the majority of cases, injury involving the head or spine is mild: a bump on the forehead after running into a low beam or a sore tailbone after falling on the floor, for example.

Although nearly all children sustain such minor injuries, they can become a source of alarm for parents because of the possibility of damage to the brain or spinal cord. Parents may perceive a young child's sobs as an indication of serious injury. Likewise, the "goose egg" that forms when an infant hits his or her head can inspire fear. In general, however, brain and spinal cord injuries are rare. The skull and backbone are good buffers against injury to the central nervous system, and children are remarkably able to tolerate blows to the head and spine (see Fig. 24, p. 374).

Head Injuries

Mild head injuries include cuts (see *cuts and lacerations*), *bruises,* and bumps. Because blood supply to the head is abundant, bleeding is often heavy, and mild injuries may appear more serious than they actually are. These injuries rarely require medical attention, however, except when cuts are deep or extensive or facial structures are involved. (For discussion of specific facial injuries see *eye injuries; facial fractures; nose, injury to and foreign objects in.*)

A severe head injury can result in temporary or permanent paralysis of a portion of the body, but it is far more common for intellectual functions, such as memory, to be affected.

Severe head injuries involving open wounds include skull-depression fractures and penetration of the skull by a foreign object, such as a bullet. These injuries almost invariably involve brain tissue.

An open wound does not have to be present, however, for injury to the brain to occur. One of the most common severe head injuries occurs when the brain shakes against the skull as the result of a blow. This type of injury is called a concussion, and it always results in at least a few seconds of unconsciousness. In general, the longer unconsciousness lasts, the more serious the head injury is. A person who cannot be roused from unconsciousness is said to be in a *coma.*

One of the most serious types of head injury occurs when a blood vessel within the brain breaks. Blood can hemorrhage (seep or rush) into brain tissue and form a partially clotted mass called a hematoma. If bleeding cannot be controlled or the hematoma cannot be removed, serious complications—including brain damage and death—can result.

Head trauma is one of the major causes of serious disability and death among children. Most serious head injuries occur during motor vehicle accidents; the next leading cause is sports accidents. At any given time about 1 million people in the United States are living with complications from head injuries that require long-term professional attention.

Spinal Injuries

The severity of spinal injuries depends on the location of the injury and the structures involved. Each year about 10,000 people suffer permanent paralysis because of spinal-cord injury. (The extent and duration of any paralysis depend on the location and severity of the injury.) Most commonly, however, spinal trauma involves structures other than the spinal cord: vertebrae (the bony rings that form the backbone), the spongy disks between vertebrae, or the ligaments connecting these structures. A vertebra can crack or slip, a ligament can be pulled, or a disk can slip. Even though these injuries are more common than spinal-cord damage, they are quite rare among children; they occur most often among athletes who engage in contact or acrobatic sports. (See also *back pain.*)

The most common—though still rare—type of severe spinal injury is the "broken neck," which results when upper-spine vertebrae are fractured. The spinal cord is easily injured by a blow to the neck, and temporary or permanent paralysis can result. (For further discussion of neck problems, see *wry neck, neck pain.*)

In very rare cases children who have had several spinal injuries develop more serious spinal problems because reinjury occurs. A disk or bone that has been injured several times, for example, can slip into the spinal cord. This new injury can put pressure on or cut into the spinal cord and cause temporary or permanent paralysis.

SIGNS AND SYMPTOMS
Head Injuries

A mild head injury is likely to be followed by *headache* in the area of impact, a lump or cut, paleness, crying, and perhaps drowsiness for an hour or two. Young children with mild head injuries may also vomit once or twice (see *vomiting*). If a bump on a child's head is very swollen or increases dramatically in size within a few hours, a skull fracture may be present.

The most common signs and symptoms appearing immediately after brain injury are unconsciousness, diminished mental alertness, weakness, altered vision, and prolonged vomiting. When a mild concussion (just a few seconds of unconsciousness) is sustained, signs and symptoms may include headache, confusion, physical and mental fatigue, memory problems, and concentration difficulty. These symptoms may not become evident until an injured child attempts to resume routine activities.

When a blow causes bleeding within the brain, a child may be unconscious for a few minutes, wake up, and appear to have no other signs or symptoms. Over the next few hours or even days, however, the child may begin to develop progressively more severe signs and symptoms, including an excruciating headache and diminished mental alertness. These delayed signs and symptoms develop as pressure from escaped blood within the brain increases.

A severe head injury can involve damage to the meninges, the tough membranes that envelop and protect the brain and spinal cord. The space between these membranes and the central nervous system structures is filled with a shock-absorbing liquid called cerebrospinal fluid (CSF). If a head injury tears the meninges and breaks the lining of the skull, CSF may escape and leak out of the child's ears or nose. It can also escape into brain tissue, causing pressure to build and producing signs and symptoms of severe head injury, such as unconsciousness, severe headache, and disorientation.

Spinal Injuries

Injury to the spinal cord, no matter how mild or severe, is usually followed by a drop in blood pressure, collapse, and problems with body functions, such as bladder control. This condition, known as spinal shock, is temporary. More telling signs and symptoms, such as pain around the area of injury, often do not appear for at least several hours.

In rare cases children who have had several injuries in the same area of the spine experience long-term, recurring pain and weakness. These symptoms may mean a vertebral crack. Signs and symptoms of a ruptured disk include severe back pain (worsened by certain movements); muscle spasms in the affected area; and pain, numbness, or weakness of one or both legs resulting from pressure on the spinal cord.

DIAGNOSIS

If a child has any signs or symptoms of severe head or spinal injury, immediate medical attention should be sought.

If doubt exists about the state of a child's mental alertness, the rescuer should ask the child questions, such as, "What is your name?" and "Where are you?" The rescuer should check to see if the child has difficulty moving uninjured body parts. If the child answers all questions correctly and appears to show no other signs or symptoms of severe injury, the injury is probably mild.

A child who has sustained a seemingly mild blow to the head should be watched carefully for the next day or two to ensure that no new signs and symptoms are developing. During the first night it is a good idea for parents to wake the child fully once or twice. Since pressure from any escaped fluid within the skull can build slowly and since symptoms indicating severe head injury may not appear until a child resumes a routine requiring nonphysical skills (such as school), parents should be alert to any changes in the child's health or mental state for a few weeks. If head or spinal injury is serious, signs and symptoms always appear eventually.

A physician consulted for diagnosis of head or spinal injury usually treats any symptoms needing immediate medical attention (such as profuse bleeding) before determining the seriousness of the injury.

Several types of X rays can be used by a physician or consulting neurologist (nervous system specialist) to detect internal damage. A physician may want to take three-dimensional X-ray pictures of the brain (called CT scans). These pictures are particularly helpful in locating the site of brain injury. Spinal X rays called myelograms may also be ordered. These X rays are preceded by injection of dye into the CSF, a procedure that produces a better picture of the spinal cord than is possible with standard X-ray films.

A physician may want to hospitalize a child with a severe head or spinal injury while performing these tests. Other diagnostic tests often requiring hospitalization are the electroencephalogram (EEG), which involves monitoring brain waves with a machine, and the lumbar puncture ("spinal tap"), which involves extracting CSF from the spinal canal and analyzing it.

COMPLICATIONS

Unchecked buildup of intracranial pressure can lead to permanent brain damage or death. If the meninges are torn, infectious agents (bacteria, for example) may enter the cerebrospinal fluid through the tear, and a severe infection such as meningitis can develop.

By definition, victims of severe head injury suffer complications for weeks, months, or even years. Possible complications may include any of the following:

- physical: difficulty communicating or an inability to communicate (by speaking, writing, or signs); visual impairment; hearing and auditory-perception problems; problems controlling arm and leg motions; spasticity; slight paralysis of one side of the body; paralysis from the waist down; *headache;* sensitivity in the area of direct injury; *seizures;* bowel and bladder control problems; *urinary tract infections; pneumonia*
- intellectual: short-term or long-term memory deficits; perceptual problems, inability to concentrate; short attention span; lack of foresight; inability to plan ahead or understand the concept of time; judgment problems (see also *learning problems*)
- behavioral and emotional: personality changes; obstinacy; tendency to become bored or tired easily; impulsiveness; euphoria (exaggerated feeling of well-being); denial that problems exist; anxiety; restlessness; lack of motivation; self-centeredness; poor self-image; emotional instability or blunting of emotions; lack of behavioral control; inability to cope; depression; agitation

Very severely injured children suffer most of these problems over a long period of time. With therapy, some or all complications may disappear. The long-term outlook is often impossible to predict immediately after a head injury occurs and becomes clearer only as time passes. In general, other problems tend to linger after physical problems disappear.

TREATMENT

Most minor bumps are best treated by comfort, attention, and a few minutes or hours of rest. If a child has a *headache,* acetaminophen may be given to help relieve pain. No stronger medication should be given. An ice pack applied to the sore spot for about a half hour should help swelling go down. (Ice should never be applied directly to the skin; if an ice bag is not available, an ice pack can be made by wrapping an ice-filled plastic bag in a towel.) If a minor cut is present, firm pressure applied to the area using a clean (preferably sterile) cloth for about 10 minutes should stop the bleeding by reducing the flow of blood to the area.

When medical attention is necessary, the type of treatment used depends on the nature of the injury. If intracranial bleeding is present, surgery is necessary to remove any hematoma (blood-filled swelling) and stop further bleeding. Surgery is also necessary to stop any CSF leakage and to relieve pressure on the spinal cord. Surgery involving any part of the central nervous system is usually performed by a neurosurgeon.

Fractured vertebrae require rest and immobilization, usually in a cast encircling the trunk. (Skull fractures are difficult to immobilize; typically, the crack is bandaged and the child is encouraged to be careful of reinjury.) If a brain or spinal cord membrane is torn and bacterial meningitis is a possibility, a physician may prescribe an antibiotic to fight infection.

If a child is in a *coma* for more than a few days, a physician may suggest that parents begin looking for a facility that specializes in monitoring and rousing comatose patients.

If physical problems persist, a physician may recommend that a child undergo long-term physical therapy. The use of devices such as crutches, braces, and wheelchairs may be suggested.

Persistent nonphysical problems resulting from head injury are best treated by long-term therapy administered by head injury professionals and recommended by the child's physician. The method of treatment varies from patient to patient and can involve anything from discussion sessions to playacting to computer games.

Statistical studies indicate that head injury victims who enter a long-term rehabilitation program within a month after injury make progress twice as quickly as those who postpone long-term treatment. The most rapid recovery is usually seen in the first 6 months after injury, although therapy may be needed for years.

Counseling for family members can be extremely helpful—and, in fact, is usually essential—in helping a child with complications from a head or spinal injury adjust to his or her disabilities. Active participation by the family in the rehabilitation of a head-injured child is crucial if the best possible results are to be achieved.

PREVENTION

Many accidents resulting in injury to the head or spine are preventable. Parents and children should practice simple accident prevention measures, such as using safety belts and approved car seats. In the event that head or spinal trauma does occur, both parents and children should be familiar with first aid procedures (see Chapter 10, "Basic First Aid"). If a child participates in sports, parents should be aware of potential hazards and teach their child the importance of wearing appropriate protective equipment. Information is available from the National Head Injury Foundation, Box 567, Framingham, MA 01701; phone: 617-879-7473.

HEAD-BANGING

DESCRIPTION

Head-banging is a common, usually harmless habit that is said to exist when a child frequently hits his or her head against a solid object (such as a crib mattress or headboard) in a rhythmical way. In the absence of other symptoms, head-banging almost always disappears in early childhood with no aftereffects. In general, it is not linked to physical, neurological, psychological, or social problems, and babies rarely bang their heads hard enough to cause even temporary damage.

Most commonly, head-banging first appears when a child is between 6 months and a year old and disappears before a child's third birthday. It is usually practiced at bedtime. Between 5 and 10 percent of children engage in head-banging. For reasons unknown, the habit is three times as common among boys as among girls. Occasionally a family history of head-banging is present, but head-banging is characteristic of 2 siblings or more in only about 20 percent of cases.

Head-banging is closely associated with rocking, also considered a harmless habit. Babies are said to rock when they sway back and forth on their hands and knees in a rhythmical way. Rocking is most common during the day, and about half the children who rock during the day will rock at bedtime as well. Rocking or head-rolling is equally common among boys and girls. About 20 percent of all children have rhythmical-motion habits and engage in rocking frequently; half of the children who engage in head-banging also engage in rocking before, during, or after the onset of head-banging.

CAUSE

In the absence of other symptoms, the cause of head-banging is unclear. The prevailing theory among experts is that babies engage in rhythmical motion because it is soothing and pleasurable.

Some medical experts believe that infants passing through early growth and development stages—such as *teething*—comfort themselves and release tension through rocking or head-banging. Babies may engage in these motions at bedtime because the need for self-comforting is felt more acutely when a child is alone. If a major disruption occurs in the relationship between a parent and child (which could happen, for example, because of parental depression), head-banging may occur or increase in frequency. If the parent-child problem persists, the baby may continue to engage in head-banging during early childhood.

Head-banging may also be a source of

physical release for babies who are inactive because of temporary physical illness. When a baby is capable of resuming normal physical activity, head-banging usually stops.

Head-banging also occurs among children with developmental problems such as *autism, mental retardation, blindness,* and *hearing loss.* Head-banging is fairly common among children with such problems, who apparently engage in rhythmical motion to compensate for their inability to take in, comprehend, or respond to stimuli.

DIAGNOSIS

The central concern of parents and physician is usually whether the rhythmical behavior is within "normal" limits. Furthermore, does it represent a sign of a child's heightened need for self-stimulating or self-consoling? Parents should share their questions and concerns with the child's physician. Of course, if suspicion exists that head-banging is related to an undetected developmental disability, a physician should be consulted for diagnosis. Usually other obvious symptoms—failure to respond to sound and severe physical uncoordination, for example—are present if a developmental disability does exist.

If a rhythmical behavior starts when a child is 18 months or older, or if such behavior goes on for a long time (an hour or more), there may be cause for concern. If a child with no other obvious symptoms continues to engage in head-banging after the age of 3, a physician should be consulted for physical, neurological, and psychological examinations.

TREATMENT

The best thing parents can do for a child who engages in head-banging is to avoid expressing concern about the habit to the child. Transferring parental worry to a child only increases the chances that habits like head-banging will persist.

To prevent injury—and to reduce parental worry about injury—parents may have to place the child's crib-size or full-size mattress on the floor. Padding a child's crib with pillows and anchoring it so that it does not roll almost never prove to be successful preventive measures.

An otherwise normal child who engages in head-banging almost never needs a helmet. However, a few children—who usually have severe associated developmental problems—bang their heads so hard that they are in danger of injuring themselves. In such cases a physician may advise that the child wear a helmet to prevent head injury.

If head-banging remains a source of worry for parents, a physician can be consulted for guidance. When an underlying disorder or family tension seems to be associated with head-banging, a physician may refer the child and parents for consultation with a specialist, such as a hearing-problems expert or a child psychiatrist.

PREVENTION

In the absence of any associated problem, most physicians consulted about head-banging conclude that it is a harmless habit and concentrate on reassuring parents to that effect. Some believe, though, that a child can be taught to replace head-banging with hand-clapping games; elementary, rhythmical, music-making exercises; or other purposeful rhythmic activities.

HEARING LOSS

DESCRIPTION

Hearing loss is an inability to hear the range of sounds that the human ear is normally capable of detecting. Many different degrees of hearing loss are possible; it can be slight or total, temporary or permanent, congenital (present at birth) or acquired at any age. One or both ears can be affected. The degree of hearing loss depends largely on which structure in the hearing mechanism is adversely affected and on the cause of the problem (see Fig. 21, p. 320).

The Hearing Mechanism

Sounds travel in ripples, much like the ripples created by dropping a stone in a body of water. These ripples have a pitch and an intensity. The human ear is sensitive to a certain range of pitches and intensities—that is, a certain range of high-to-low sounds and a certain range of soft-to-loud sounds. A person with a hearing loss has deficits in hearing the range of possible pitches or the range of possible intensities or both.

Normally, when a ripple capable of being heard by human beings reaches the ear, it is captured by the external ear in much the same way that a satellite antenna dish captures radio waves. The ripple then passes down the ear canal, another portion of the external ear. It reaches the eardrum, a thin membrane separating the external ear from the middle ear, and causes it to vibrate. These vibrations in turn cause three tiny bones in the middle ear to vibrate. The inner ear membrane, which separates the middle ear from the inner ear, picks up these vibrations and passes them to the inner ear. In the inner ear, highly specialized structures convert the vibrations into electrical impulses, which are sent via a special nerve to the brain. The brain completes the process by interpreting the impulses as sound. This entire process takes a tiny fraction of a second.

Hearing Loss Due to Structural Malfunctions

When a part of the external or middle ear is malfunctioning, conductive hearing loss results. "Conductive" denotes that something is interfering with the travel of a sound ripple from structure to structure. When a part of the internal ear, nervous system, or brain is malfunctioning, sensorineural hearing loss results. "Sensorineural" indicates that something is wrong with the structures that convert and interpret sound waves. Both conductive and sensorineural hearing losses can be partial or total. In general, sensorineural hearing loss is more severe and more difficult to treat or reverse because the inner-ear and nervous-system structures are more delicate and less accessible than the middle- and external-ear structures.

Sensorineural hearing loss is rarer than conductive hearing loss. By far the most common cause of temporary conductive hearing loss is fluid buildup in the middle ear due to inflammation. In fact, about one-third of all children have at least three bouts of inflammation resulting in temporary hearing loss before their second birthdays. Fluid buildup can hamper or prevent vibrations of the eardrum and middle-ear structures, thereby affecting the reception and transmission of sound. It commonly occurs when a child has an ear infection (see *earache and ear infections*) or an upper-respiratory infection, such as a cold (see *colds*).

Inflammation and hearing problems typically last a few days or, less often, weeks, but some children seem prone to develop frequent infections that result in hearing problems for months at a time. Short-term inflammation tends to be the most painful and obvious; sometimes the most prominent symptom of long-term inflammation is hearing loss.

Degrees of Hearing Loss

Hearing loss can be mild, moderate, severe, or profound. With mild hearing loss, an affected child mostly has trouble hearing distant noises. If the child has already learned to speak, speech is usually normal and conversation is unhindered. If the child is in the process of learning to speak, however, the acquisition of speech and language may be affected. In some cases such delays have ramifications that persist into the first few years of school.

Moderate hearing loss significantly affects a child's ability to participate in conversation. If moderate hearing loss persists, articulation of words is impaired, regardless of whether the child has learned to speak.

With severe hearing loss a child is unable to participate in oral conversations. Typically, however, the child can catch a word here and there and can hear certain loud noises. If severe hearing loss persists, retaining the ability to speak coherently is difficult. If a child develops severe hearing loss while in the process of learning to speak, further acquisition of spoken language is likely to be greatly impeded.

A child who has a profound hearing loss cannot hear most sounds, including normal speech. The child may be able to hear very loud sounds and is likely to be sensitive to the vibrations produced when sound ripples hit walls, floors, and other structures. Retaining or acquiring spoken language is extremely difficult for a child with a profound hearing loss.

Incidence

Approximately one half of 1 percent of the population has some degree of permanent hearing impairment. (The term "hearing impairment" implies that hearing problems are permanent; "hearing loss" and "deafness" are general terms used to describe either a temporary or a permanent hearing problem.) Four of every five hearing-impaired people have problems in both ears. For about 40 percent of these people impairment is mild; about 20 percent have moderate problems, another 20 percent have severe problems, and the remaining 20 percent have profound problems. In the United States approximately 35,000 children are in special education programs because of permanent severe or profound hearing loss.

No matter what the degree of impairment, all children with permanent hearing problems are subject to handicapping receptive and expressive *language disorders* and to *speech problems*. Children with temporary hearing loss usually have difficulty with speech and language only if loss is prolonged and occurs during the crucial phase of language development that takes place from birth until about the age of 8.

Outlook

The long-term outlook for a child with hearing loss varies. Typically conductive hearing loss can be reversed with no complications, or treatment methods are successful at enhancing hearing and providing an affected child with speech and language skills. Children with mild to moderate sensorineural hearing loss can also develop adequate speech and language skills, although this type of hearing loss is rarely reversible.

Most children with severe to profound sensorineural hearing loss never learn to speak clearly; if they lost their hearing after speech was acquired, they lose the ability to some extent. In addition, studies show that, for reasons that are unclear, the thought processes of children with profound hearing impairment from birth tend to be different from those of children with no hearing problems; many affected children who are taught in conventional education programs have reading difficulties (see *learning problems*). The incidence of *mental retardation,* however, is no higher among children with profound hearing loss than among other children.

The long-term outlook for a child with permanent, profound hearing impairment depends largely on the approach used by parents, school officials, and other professionals. To be successful, an approach must equip a child with adequate communication skills and address a child's emotional needs.

CAUSE

In about half of all cases of hearing loss, the cause is unknown. For the other half the cause of hearing loss is traceable to a specific malformation, disease, injury, or other factor.

Malformations that can cause conductive hearing loss include congenital ear abnormalities (see *ear abnormalities, congenital*) and *cleft lip and cleft palate*. A child with a cleft lip or palate often has malformations that hinder equalization of pressure in the middle ear by the eustachian tube. Consequently, such children are highly susceptible to long-term, recurring middle-ear inflammation.

Most diseases associated with conductive hearing loss involve middle-ear inflammation, which is the cause of about 90 percent of all types of hearing loss (see *earache and ear infection; strep throat*). Other causes of conductive hearing loss include the accumulation of wax in the ear canal and obstruction of the canal by a foreign object in the ear (see *ear, foreign objects in*).

About 50 percent of all cases of sensorineural hearing loss are caused by inherited structural defects. About 70 different types of such defects exist. Less commonly, sensorineural hearing loss is present at birth because of disease or injury. Such problems include complications of *drug and alcohol abuse* by the mother during pregnancy (including fetal alcohol syndrome), and lack of oxygen during the birth process. A child may also be born with hearing impairment if during pregnancy the mother had a viral disease such as *German measles, measles,* cytomegaloviral infection, *genital herpes, chicken pox, syphilis,* or *mumps* or a parasitic infection such as toxoplasmosis (see *parasitic infections*).

Two other conditions associated with congenital hearing problems are a family history of hereditary kidney disease (such as *nephritis*) and severe *jaundice* during the newborn period because of a problem such as Rh incompatibility (see *Rh and ABO incompatability*).

Acquiring any serious viral infection during infancy can cause sensorineural hearing loss in a child. Damage to the inner ear can also cause sensorineural hearing loss. In rare cases a foreign object in the ear damages the inner-ear membrane or inner-ear structures. More commonly, exposure to loud sounds—either once or over a prolonged period of time—can lead to temporary or permanent sensorineural hearing problems.

SIGNS AND SYMPTOMS AND COMPLICATIONS

A child who is born with a moderate to profound hearing loss or develops one during infancy shows subtle signs of the loss during the first few months of life, regardless of the severity of the problem. The child may show little awareness of sounds and may not be responsive to vocal comforting or alerting. A baby with a hearing loss may be surprised to see someone in front of the crib because of not having heard the person approaching. Unlike other babies, those with hearing problems do not search for the source of a sound with their eyes. They do not babble along with music, although they are likely to babble and coo like other children. At 9 to 12 months of age, when most other children begin to form words, children with hearing loss do not; they may even stop making noises altogether.

A toddler with a moderate to profound hearing loss shows no recognition of oral commands without visual signs. The child does not know when others call his or her name unless the caller is visible. Little or no recognition is given of common household sounds, such as the radio, television, stereo, doorbell, and telephone; the child may seem confused, for example, about why others seem to know when to answer the door. While other children of the same age are beginning to form simple sentences, the child with a hearing loss has obvious speech deficits and relies on gestures to communicate. Toilet training may be difficult.

By the time a child is 3 or 4 years old, moderate to profound hearing loss is usually obvious. A mild hearing loss at this age, however, is generally more difficult to identify. Common signs include not having as large a vocabulary as other children and not pronouncing words as easily or clearly. A child may also have difficulty understanding new words and structuring sentences correctly. Abstract concepts, such as time, may be particularly difficult for an affected child to grasp. He or she may not understand the difference between comparable terms such as "who" and "what."

After age 10 or so, most children report any hearing problems to parents. When mild or moderate hearing loss develops between ages 5 and 10 because of temporary middle-ear inflammation, however, changes in behavior may be the most prominent signs. A child may ignore parents' comments and seem to be stubborn or disobedient. He or she may talk unusually loudly or may seem to withdraw into a dream world. Turning the television volume up too high and sitting too close to the TV are also common. The child may have trouble hearing the phone ring.

In school the child may pay poor attention to the teacher unless addressed loudly or more than once. He or she may watch other children in an attempt to understand what the teacher is saying. If hearing loss is prolonged, the child's academic performance may slip, especially in areas requiring reading. The child may not recognize the or-igin of a sound, may complain of pain or ringing in the ears, may have *dizziness* or balance problems, or may become excessively annoyed upon hearing loud sounds.

DIAGNOSIS

Hearing loss is difficult to diagnose and is often confused with specific development disorders such as primary *language disorders, speech problems,* and developmental disabilities that affect language acquisition, such as *mental retardation* or *Down syndrome.*

In general, if parents have suspicions about a child's hearing or general development, they should always consult a physician. Specifically, if a child is 12 to 18 months old and speaks no words, shows little or no understanding of words, and responds inconsistently to sounds, a medical examination is in order. It is essential to diagnose a hearing problem early to avoid long-term or permanent speech and language problems and their ramifications. Mild hearing loss is usually the most difficult to detect; about 80 percent of children with moderate to profound impairment are diagnosed before the age of 18 months.

When a physician suspects that a child has a hearing loss, he or she usually refers a child to an otolaryngologist (ear, nose, and throat specialist) for a complete—and painless—examination of the ears and upper respiratory tract. If the cause of hearing loss is a temporary medical problem, the otolaryngologist provides appropriate treatment.

If the otolaryngologist determines that hearing impairment is permanent, the child may be referred to a certified audiologist, who determines the extent of hearing difficulty. If less than 3 years old, the child is tested in a soundproof room while sitting on a parent's lap. Sounds are issued from loudspeakers to the right and left of the child, and the child's reactions are noted. If a child is older than 3, this test is performed with earphones. Before going to an audiologist, parents should, if possible, explain to a child that such a test is completely painless and that it can be fun, like "playing spaceman."

An otolaryngologist may also refer a child to a certified speech and language pathologist, an expert in diagnosing speech and language problems. Sometimes an otolaryngologist consults an otologist, an ear specialist, for help in determining the cause of a child's hearing loss.

To detect hearing problems among children between the ages of 5 and 10, most schools conduct standard hearing tests each year. Parents should take the results of such tests seriously and should consult a physician for further diagnosis when necessary.

TREATMENT

Temporary hearing loss is treated by resolving the underlying cause. Support treatment by an audiologist or speech and language pathologist is not usually necessary. During the time that hearing remains difficult, parents can aid their child by talking to him or her more, speaking exceptionally clearly, and placing their mouths in the child's line of vision as they speak. If only one ear is impaired, it is a good idea to address the "good ear" when reading to the child. These approaches may minimize any speech and language delays or difficulties that might otherwise develop.

Almost all children with permanent hearing impairment, even those with profound hearing problems, can benefit from hearing aids. Many different types of aids are available. Some children benefit from using one during all waking hours; others find that the aids amplify annoying background noises and interfere with hearing more than they help. Many children fall somewhere between these extremes.

Communication aid is essential for all children with permanent hearing problems. For children who have mild to moderate problems, the help of a speech and language pathologist should be engaged (see *speech problems* and *language disorders*). Controversy exists, however, over whether attempts should be made to teach children with severe to profound problems to understand and use oral speech. Some experts maintain that not making such attempts prevents a child from understanding the majority of other people. Others believe that mastering oral communication sufficiently can be agonizing for many children with profound hearing problems and can ultimately prove fruitless. These experts sometimes emphasize the use of manual sign language.

Most experts believe that affected children benefit most from a combination of treatment approaches. Typically, treatment involves teaching a child to compensate for hearing deficits with many tools, including a hearing aid, gestures, body language, pantomime, sign language, fingerspelling, lipreading, and sometimes oral speech.

Less conventional alternatives have also proved successful for some children. One is a communication board with pictures, letters, numbers, and words; a child points to the appropriate symbols to communicate. Electronic devices are also available to aid communication with the hearing world. One such device is programmed with certain commonly used words. To call up a word a child presses a code number, and the word is heard by listeners through a speaker. A more recent variation of this machine is a calculator-sized typewriter. A child types in the desired word to have it "spoken" by the machine.

To aid long-distance communication for people with permanent hearing loss, special telephones called teletype or "TTY" machines, which operate using written communication, are available, and their use is widespread. In addition, television executives have become increasingly sensitive to the needs of people with hearing impairment; some television programs are "close-captioned"—accompanied by written dialogue that can be seen when a special device is attached to the set. More and more communication devices ae continually being developed for people with severe and profound hearing loss.

In addition to communication aid, most children with severe or profound hearing loss require special education to compensate for their disabilities. By federal law the public school system is required to provide such education. It is a good idea, however, to seek dayschool education for a preschool-aged affected child immediately after diagnosis. To find an appropriate facility, parents should call local groups for the hearing-impaired. Information is also available from the National Association of the Deaf, 814 Thayer Avenue, Silver Spring, MD 20910 (phone: 301-587-1788).

A disability such as hearing loss can engender special emotional needs. Parents should be sensitive to such needs and should seek advice and treatment when necessary. Local groups for the hearing-impaired can be especially helpful.

PREVENTION

Some types of hearing loss can be prevented. Parents can

■ ensure that before becoming pregnant the mother has vaccinations against

German measles and, when possible, against other severe viruses.

- caution children against putting anything in their ears; even cotton swabs can cause a buildup of wax or damage middle-ear structures.
- warn children about the hazards of using portable stereos with headphones and sitting too close to speakers at rock concerts. Federal law mandates that any employer requiring personnel to be exposed to excessively loud noise—such as the roar of airplane engines—provide workers with earplugs or other protective devices. Parents should advise a child of this provision in the event that he or she takes such a job.
- help protect children from head injury by insisting on the use of proper car restraints and sports-safety equipment.
- be alert to signs of middle-ear inflammation among children who already are hearing impaired, because inflammation can aggravate existing problems.

HEART DISEASE, CONGENITAL

DESCRIPTION

"Congenital heart disease" is a general term for several heart defects caused by abnormal prenatal development (see Fig. 28). A defect may be obvious at birth or may go unnoticed for years. Heart defects may occur as single structural problems or in complex combinations. More than 35 known congenital heart defects occur among newborns, but fewer than 10 are common.

The annual incidence of congenital heart disease in the United States is 8 out of every 1,000 live births; 2 or 3 of those 8 suffer from potentially fatal heart defects.

Of the approximately 25,000 infants born in the United States each year with congenital heart disease, 25 percent also suffer from other disabilities, including a number of chromosomal disorders (see *genetic disorders*). For instance, 30 to 40 percent of all children with *Down syndrome* also have congenital heart disease.

The outlook for a child with congenital heart disease varies with the severity of the defects and the timing and success of treatment. For some children whose severe heart disease is not treated, death can occur shortly after birth. In most cases, however, the defect is minor, or can be surgically repaired, so that the child can live a long healthy life with few or no restrictions.

Septal Defects

The most common heart problems affecting newborns are septal defects, abnormal openings in the septum (the wall that divides the right and left chambers of the heart). Nearly 20 percent of all children born with congenital heart disease have ventricular septal defects, holes in the wall between the lower chambers. Less than 5 percent of infants are born with an atrial septal defect, an abnormal opening in the wall between the upper chambers.

Many septal defects are small and may close spontaneously during the first year of life. These small defects usually pose no problem to the child's development. For larger defects, however, corrective surgery is likely to be required.

FIG. 28. HEART WITH BLOOD CIRCULATION IN GREAT ARTERIES
(viewed from front of body)

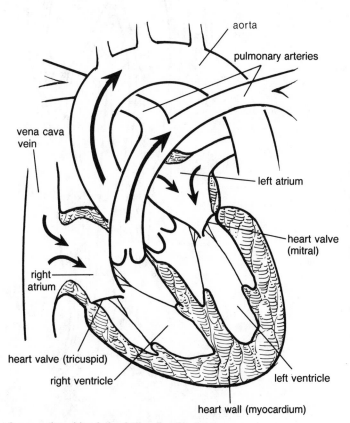

(arrows show blood circulation directions)

FIG. 29. CIRCULATORY SYSTEM

(showing heart, great vessels leading to and away from heart, and supplying head, lungs, kidneys, arms, and legs)

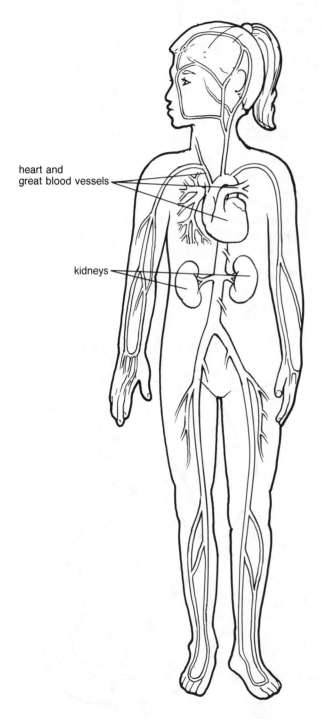

heart and
great blood vessels

kidneys

Patent Ductus Arteriosus

Before birth, the fetal circulatory system bypasses the unused lungs of the fetus by rerouting the blood through a special channel (ductus arteriosus) between the pulmonary artery carrying blood to the lungs and the aorta, the artery that carries blood through the body. Normally this channel closes within a few days or weeks after birth. When it fails to close, the condition is called patent (open) ductus arteriosus. Because the duct does not close, blood already oxygenated by the lungs is pumped needlessly back through the lungs, placing extra strain on the heart.

Less than 10 percent of all children born annually in the United States with heart defects have patent ductus arteriosus; it is particularly common among low birthweight and premature infants. Surgery to close the patent ductus arteriosus is now performed routinely with few resulting complications. Patent ductuses of premature babies may be closed by administration of an intravenous medicine.

Tetralogy of Fallot

A less common but more serious defect is a condition called tetralogy of Fallot, a combination of four different structural problems in the heart. The child born with this defect suffers from (1) a hole between the lower right and left chambers of the heart (known as a ventricular septal defect), (2) misplacement of the aorta, the artery that sends blood throughout the body, (3) decreased blood flow to the lungs (known as pulmonary stenosis), and (4) an enlargement of the right ventricle (the lower right chamber). Because this defect interferes with blood flow to the lungs, some of the blue blood returning from the body is sent back through the body without picking up oxygen, and the baby's skin takes on a blue tint (see *cyanosis*). Tetralogy of Fallot is a major cause of "blue babies."

Without surgery early in life, babies who suffer from tetralogy of Fallot rarely live past childhood. The development of modern surgical techniques, however, allows repair of this defect in almost all cases.

Transposition of the Great Arteries

In some babies the pulmonary artery arises from the left ventricle and the aorta from the right ventricle, instead of the reverse, which is normal. This transposition of the two largest arteries in the body is the most common cause of severe cyanosis in newborns. If not treated, these infants almost invariably die within the first days or weeks of life. Prompt surgery is necessary. The outlook for such children is excellent.

Coarctation of the Aorta

Another common heart defect affecting newborns is coarctation of the aorta, a narrowing of the main artery, which carries blood from the heart to the rest of the body. This defect, which occurs twice as often among males as among females, affects the flow of blood throughout the child's body, causing high blood pressure *(hypertension)*. Before corrective surgical techniques were developed, most infants with this condition failed to survive. Today coarctation of the aorta can be repaired surgically.

Aortic and Pulmonary Stenosis

Other common heart defects include abnormally narrow valves between the lower chambers of the heart and the two great arteries leading out of the heart. If the narrowed valve occurs between the left ventricle and the aorta, the disease is called aortic stenosis. If it occurs between the right ventricle and the pulmonary artery, leading to the lungs, it is known as pulmonary stenosis. Often the narrowing is minor and no specific treatment is needed and no restrictions need be placed on the child. Surgery, with low risk, is available for those with more severe stenosis.

CAUSE

If during the prenatal period the fetal heart or a major blood vessel near the heart fails to develop properly, congenital heart defects will result. Physicians do not know the causes of 90 percent of all congenital heart defects. Causes that have been identified include maternal infections during pregnancy, genetic mutations, heredity, and excessive radiation, such as X rays. Congenital heart disease may also be inherited (see *genetic disorders*).

Maternal *German measles* (rubella) during the first three months of pregnancy, cytomegaloviral infections, and herpes virus infections have been linked to abnormal development of the fetal heart. Children born with fetal alcohol syndrome, resulting from their mother's excessive consumption of alcohol during pregnancy, often suffer from congenital heart defects. If a mother takes diet pills or anticonvulsant medication during pregnancy, the course of prenatal heart development may be changed.

SIGNS AND SYMPTOMS

Symptoms of congenital heart defects vary. Many children with minor defects have no symptoms; others show only mild symptoms. Infants with severe defects may die within the first days or weeks of life unless surgery is performed. Heart failure manifested by rapid breathing and *cyanosis* are the major symptoms.

Children—even those with serious defects—rarely suffer heart attacks. The most common evidence of heart disease in young people is fatigue, shortness of breath, and blueness. They also may fail to gain weight.

DIAGNOSIS

Congenital heart disease may be diagnosed by a physician, who observes a child's symptoms, growth, and development, and listens to the child's heart with a stethoscope. If a congenital heart problem is suspected, the infant is usually referred to a medical center that specializes in cardiac care. The existence of a heart defect can be confirmed by X rays, electrocardiograms, ultrasound, and other diagnostic tests that examine the structure of a child's heart and measure its work capacity.

One important tool developed within the past 40 years to diagnose heart disease is cardiac catheterization. Thin plastic tubes with tiny electronic sensing devices at their tips are inserted through the veins and arteries of the arms and legs and passed into the chambers of the heart and the aorta. The sensing devices take readings from within the heart itself. Blood samples are drawn through the tubes, and special material is injected into the heart so that X rays can be taken of blood flow through the heart's chambers and valves. This information provides the cardiologist (heart specialist) with a clearer view of the heart's interior, including any structural defects, their size, location, and degree of severity.

COMPLICATIONS

Children with congenital heart disease must be protected from developing infective endocarditis, an infection and inflammation of the inner layer of the heart tissue. This infection may be triggered among children with congenital heart disease by most dental procedures, including the cleaning of teeth, filling of cavities, and root canal work. Throat and mouth surgery and examinations or procedures involving the gastrointestinal tract (the esophagus, stomach, and intestines) or urinary tract (kidneys, ureters, bladder, and urethra) also may cause infective endocarditis. Infective endocarditis may occur following open heart surgery. Once in the bloodstream, bacteria or fungi usually migrate to the heart where they infect abnormal heart tissue, subject to turbulent blood flow, especially the valves. Although many microorganisms can cause infective endocarditis, staphylococcus and streptococcus bacteria are most often responsible for the infection.

Many adolescents with cardiac defects experience curvature of the spine *(scoliosis)*. Scoliosis can complicate respiratory problems for children who already have difficulty breathing.

TREATMENT

Treatment varies according to the particular defect and its severity, the age of the child, and the child's general health. Children with minor heart defects may require no treatment. Children whose defects are severe may require surgery during early infancy and medical care during later childhood. Nearly 25 percent of all children born with heart defects require surgery at a very early age. These children usually need cardiac catherterization during the first weeks of life to determine location and severity of the defects.

Remarkable recent achievements in pediatric medicine allow pediatric heart surgery even among newborns. In the past, infants with complicated but correctable heart defects requiring open heart surgery usually underwent 2 operations. Now in many centers a child may undergo a single open-heart operation within the first year of life, thereby reducing the risk posed by 2 operations and ensuring a more normal pattern of growth, activity, and development.

Major heart surgery can be performed on tiny infants by using intense cold, called deep hypothermia. This process drastically lowers body temperature, slows body processes, and reduces the body's oxygen requirement, allowing the circulatory system to rest. This provides a still, bloodless heart, which gives the surgeon a clear field of vision. Heart tissue relaxes, allowing complex repairs on the delicate organ which, among newborns, may be the size of a walnut.

A child with infective endocarditis is hospitalized to receive antibiotic treatment. If the child is seriously ill or has recently had heart surgery, antibiotics may be administered before blood tests have identified the particular organism causing the infection. Antibiotic therapy is usually given for at least 4 weeks.

A great majority of children with cardiac defects have no restrictions on their physical activities. A physician should determine how much activity is appropriate at school. Children should be encouraged to function near the peak of their physical capacity, taking part in school physical education classes even though they may need to skip some of the more strenuous activities. A balance must be maintained so that these children are challenged but not embarrassed by being asked to exceed their physical capacities.

Children with cardiac defects usually determine for themselves how much exercise is comfortable. At these children's exertion points, their bodies force them to rest when they have reached their physical limits.

Body image may be a problem for children who have experienced heart surgery; they should be helped to develop positive self-images and provided with situations where they can physically succeed.

Children with heart defects may be absent from school frequently. They need encouragement to keep up with their school work. Since some children with severe heart defects cannot perform manual labor as adults, they need appropriate educational and vocational guidance.

PREVENTION

At present, most congenital heart defects cannot be prevented.

Heart defects caused by a mother's having *German measles* during pregnancy can be prevented if a mother is vaccinated against the disease at least 3 months before becoming pregnant. A mother who refrains from using medication or alcohol during pregnancy and avoids high concentrations of radiation reduces the risk to her unborn child from these potential causes of congenital heart defects.

For children with structural heart disease, prevention of infective endocarditis is essential. Before dental or surgical procedures, a physician or dentist should be informed of a child's heart condition. An affected child should be given an antibiotic before and after dental work or a surgical procedure that may cause any bleeding. Children with structural heart disease should not participate in school dental screening programs without antibiotic treatment to prevent endocarditis. Prevention also includes good dental hygiene and protective dental care.

Genetic counseling may be helpful in weighing the chances of a couple's having a child with a congenital heart defect. This is especially applicable for individuals considering parenthood who have congenital heart defects themselves or whose family histories include *Down syndrome* or *muscular dystrophy* (see *genetic disorders*).

HEART FAILURE, CONGESTIVE

DESCRIPTION AND SIGNS AND SYMPTOMS

Congestive heart failure is a condition in which the heart is unable to pump enough blood to supply body tissues with oxygen and other nutrients. This problem may occur if the heart muscle is weakened and cannot supply ordinary bodily needs. It also may occur if there are excessive demands on a poorly functioning heart muscle, as may develop during respiratory disease or in strenuous play. Congestive heart failure is often a symptom of serious heart disease during childhood.

Among children, the entire heart is usually affected by congestive heart failure. Because the heart's ability to pump blood effectively is impaired, blood may collect in the heart, lungs, liver, and blood vessels throughout the body.

Congestive heart failure differs from a heart attack, a severe symptom of heart disease among adults. A heart attack occurs when oxygen flow to the heart is blocked by severely diseased blood vessels or heart muscle. Heart attack strikes suddenly and often results in the destruction of heart tissue, causing permanent disability or death. Congestive heart failure is usually a long-term condition and may occur in episodes. A child who suffers intermittent attacks of congestive heart failure is likely to be chronically ill.

A child with congestive heart failure is frequently fatigued, and finds physical effort difficult. The child may have a poor appetite and experience occasional abdominal pain. Because of the accumulation of blood in the lungs and blood vessels, a child may breathe rapidly, be short of breath, have a persistent cough, and be susceptible to recurrent respiratory infections. Older children may have swollen ankles or legs, much like adults suffering congestive heart failure. Sweating may be excessive and heart rate increased. Infants may have feeding difficulties and be irritable, with a weak cry.

Children rarely suffer heart attacks, since their heart and blood vessels are still young and strong, despite a structural defect or diseased tissue. Children may, however, suffer from congestive heart failure at any age. Infants born with heart defects sometimes experience congestive heart failure at birth.

CAUSE

Congestive heart failure during childhood is almost always associated with heart defects present at birth (see *heart disease, congenital*). Infections of the heart muscle, such as myocarditis (see *cardiomyopathy*), or of the heart valves and muscle, such as *rheumatic fever* and infective endocarditis, also cause congestive heart failure during childhood.

DIAGNOSIS

A diagnosis of congestive heart failure is based on observation of a child's symptoms and identification of a cause such as congenital heart disease. By means of a physical examination, an electrocardiogram (EKG), and an echocardiogram, a physician diagnoses heart failure and its cause. These diagnostic tests are painless and brief. In the EKG, electrical impulses from the heart muscle are recorded on graph paper. In the echocardiogram, sound waves are used to visualize the structures of the heart and blood vessels. X-ray films of the chest and abdomen may be taken to detect heart and liver enlargement because of blood accumulation.

TREATMENT

The primary goal of treatment is to correct the underlying cause of the heart's inability to pump blood effectively throughout the body. Surgery may be required to correct heart defects, and medication may be used to rid the heart of an infection.

Children with congestive heart failure must often limit their physical activity. Congestive heart failure can usually be controlled so that children can tolerate near-normal levels of activity.

Digitalis or other medications are prescribed for a child with severe congestive heart failure. Drug dosage is adjusted according to a child's weight and continued until symptoms have been eliminated. Diuretic medications, which reduce fluid in the body, and a low-sodium (low-salt) diet may also be needed.

PREVENTION

Medications that increase the ability of the heart to meet the body's needs may prevent congestive heart failure among children with congenital heart defects or diseased heart tissue. Ultimate prevention, however, depends on correction or elimination of the underlying cause.

HEART MURMURS

DESCRIPTION

A heart murmur is an extra heart sound. Most heart murmurs are harmless, or "innocent." They are simply extra sounds produced by the heart as blood is pumped through its chambers to the arteries and veins.

Heart murmurs are common among children. More than half of all newborns have a heart murmur for the first 48 hours. Approximately 65 percent of all children have a heart murmur sometime during childhood.

A child with an innocent, or functional, murmur has a structurally normal heart. Such a heart murmur is of no significance, and a child's activity should not be limited in any way. In a very small percentage of children with heart murmurs, however, extra heart sounds may signal serious disease.

CAUSE

Research has not yet identified all the causes of innocent heart murmurs.

Heart murmurs may be associated with heart defects present at birth (see *heart disease, congenital*). Such defects may include narrowing of the blood vessels, defective or diseased heart valves, and abnormal openings in the heart wall or in a blood vessel near the heart. If a child has an infection that affects the heart, such as *rheumatic fever* or myocarditis, heart murmurs often develop. Children with *anemia* have been known to develop extra heart sounds.

SIGNS AND SYMPTOMS

A child's heart murmur is likely to be detected first by a physician during a routine examination. Heart murmurs have distinctive sounds. The murmur may sound like the vibration of a tuning fork, or may rise to a crescendo. Various murmurs have been described as cooing, rumbling, musical, or high-pitched. Innocent murmurs vary in loudness. The murmur is probably loudest when the child's heart rate increases, such as after exercise or when the child has a fever or is excited. An innocent murmur may become louder or disappear when a child changes physical position.

DIAGNOSIS

A physician or cardiologist (heart specialist) uses a stethoscope to diagnose the existence of a heart murmur. He or she listens to the quality of the heart sounds, their location, and duration. The normal heart sound is often described as a "lub-dup" sound. Any sounds other than that are diagnosed as a heart murmur. It is possible to distinguish innocent murmurs in normal hearts from heart sounds that are signs of serious disease. Methods such as cardiac catheterization, in which a thin plastic sensor tube is guided through the veins to the heart, allow a precise diagnosis.

TREATMENT

No treatment is necessary for innocent or functional heart murmurs. In fact, it is important not to limit a child who has an innocent heart murmur but a normal heart.

PREVENTION

Heart murmurs cannot be prevented.

HEIGHT PROBLEMS

DESCRIPTION AND CAUSE

A child's height potential is determined by his or her genetic makeup as inherited from the parents. Children who are short often have a short parent, and children who are tall often have a tall parent. A child's pattern of growth from birth also seems to be determined genetically, although it can be affected by enviromental factors, organ malfunctionings, and hormonal disorders.

Attaining genetic height potential depends

upon many factors, including a child's rate and duration of growth, intake of nutrition and calories, and body metabolism (the sum of all complex and physical processes of matter and energy that occur within living cells). A child's growth is also influenced by hormones, such as those secreted by the pituitary gland (see *pituitary problems*), the thyroid gland (see *thyroid problems*), the adrenal glands (see *adrenal problems*), and the gonads (ovaries and testes). (A hormone is a chemical messenger, formed in one organ and carried in the blood to another organ, where it acts.)

If a child fails to reach his or her height potential, or exceeds it, a height problem exists. Short stature (resulting from a decreased growth rate), or being well below one's height potential, is more common among children than tall stature (resulting from an increased growth rate), or being well above one's height potential. Height problems caused by skeletal abnormalities (usually accompanied by other structural malformations) cannot usually be corrected; those caused by disorders that disturb normal bone growth are reversible if the disorder is recognized and treated in time.

Short Stature

An infant may be born with temporary short stature if fetal growth is delayed. Delayed fetal growth can be caused by several factors, including maternal ingestion of alcohol or nicotine (see *drug and alcohol abuse*), exposure to radiation, or incompletely treated long-term maternal illnesses such as *diabetes* or kidney failure (see *kidney failure, chronic*). Growth-delayed infants may have low birthweights for gestational age. Subsequently, they may show catch-up growth and reach their genetic height potentials.

Short stature caused by a decreased growth rate during childhood may be associated with long-term illnesses, nutritional and emotional deprivation, and hormonal problems. The severity and duration of the underlying problem determine the degree of short stature. For example, a severe nutritional deficiency (see *malnutrition*) occurring with heart failure (see *heart failure, congestive*), liver or gastrointestinal disorders, long-term *anemia* (such as *sickle cell anemia* or *thalassemia*), or kidney failure (see *kidney failure, chronic*) may cause slowing of skeletal growth and lead to short stature. Children so affected by these disorders also tend to be underweight for height.

Short stature may also be caused by chromosomal or *genetic disorders*. Chromosomes and genes are the components that determine a child's physical characteristics. Affected children often have normal growth rates for their height but remain well below the range of heights for most children. When they become adults, these individuals are called "little people." In the past the term for little people was "dwarfs." Some chromosomal disorders are accompanied by mental retardation and slowed sexual development. Such disorders include *Down syndrome,* a well-known disorder that causes mental retardation and retention of infantile characteristics and stature, and Prader-Willi syndrome, a rare genetic disorder characterized by marked obesity, mental retardation, sexual immaturity, and short stature. *Turner's syndrome,* a chromosomal disorder affecting females, is associated with short stature and problems such as abnormal development of the ovaries. Affected females require hormonal treatment to develop sexually at puberty.

Endocrine disorders may cause short stature. These disorders include hypothyroidism (insufficient secretion of thyroid hormones—see *thyroid problems*) and hypopituitarism (insufficient secretion of pituitary hormones—see *pituitary problems*). Adult short stature can result from the early onset of puberty (precocious puberty), causing the production of sexual hormones at an inappropriate age and premature cessation of skeletal growth. As a result, affected individuals are tall as children but short as adults.

Delayed adolescence, which occurs more frequently among boys than among girls, can result in a significant slowing of bone growth and even short stature. Long-term use of certain medications (such as cortisol; see *adrenal problems*) can also slow a child's rate of growth. When a child stops taking such medications, rate of growth increases rapidly, although a child may never completely catch up and reach a normal adult height.

Tall Stature

Most cases of tall stature are not the result of disease but reflect a child's genetic height potential. Such cases are called familial tall stature; more than one family member is usually affected. This form of tall stature does not require treatment, but parents and children may request hormonal therapy to bring about an earlier puberty and thus reduce mature height.

Tall stature resulting from an increased childhood growth rate may be caused by increased secretion of hormones of the pituitary, thyroid, and adrenal glands and of the gonads. A child's adult height, however, will surpass his or her genetic height potential only when a pituitary tumor is present that causes excess production of growth hormone (a condition called <u>gigantism;</u> see *pituitary problems*). Other disorders causing accelerated childhood growth also cause accelerated sexual maturation and usually result in adult height below the genetic height potential. If children with growth-hormone-producing pituitary tumors are treated unsuccessfully or not treated at all, sexual development may be delayed. These children may continue to grow into their thirties, because the actively growing portions of their bones do not close. Excessive adult height is usually accompanied by enlargement of the facial bones, the hands, and the feet (features of a condition called <u>acromegaly</u>).

Disorders such as *obesity* (see *weight problems*) and Marfan syndrome may also be associated with tall stature during childhood. Bone growth of an obese child is frequently 1 to 2 years ahead of his or her chronological age. Children with Marfan syndrome, an inherited disease of the connective tissue, are tall and thin; their limbs, hands, and fingers are usually longer than normal. Muscle problems, *scoliosis* (any curvature of the spine to the right or left side of the body), and joint problems often develop.

DIAGNOSIS

A parent should be concerned about a height problem if a child fails to grow or grows excessively during childhood. The earlier such a problem is detected and diagnosed, the better the chances of recovery with appropriate treatment. It often is not difficult to determine the cause of a height problem, since characteristic signs and symptoms of underlying illnesses or conditions are present. A physician can usually determine the cause and prescribe appropriate treatment for a height problem based on a child's growth pattern and medical history, parental heights, a careful physical examination, and appropriate laboratory tests, including measurement of bone age. If an endocrine disorder is suspected, specific tests

to evaluate hormone production and regulation can be performed.

TREATMENT

A child should receive treatment of height problems as soon as a diagnosis is made to prevent permanent short or tall stature. Treatment focuses on correction of underlying causes of height problems. (See entries on individual diseases mentioned under Description, above, for complete discussions of treatment.)

Short Stature

Growth-delayed infants may reach their genetic height potential if they naturally catch up in their growth and height rates following infancy.

If a child's height problem is caused by a long-term illness, nutritional or emotional deprivation, or a hormonal problem, growth may resume and genetic height potential be attained if the underlying disorder is treated successfully and in time. If treatment either of a nutritional deficiency or an underlying disease is unsuccessful or absent, pubertal development is delayed and the growth rate is further decreased.

Short stature caused by a genetic disorder cannot usually be increased in adulthood by any form of treatment. However, height problems caused by some endocrine disorders may be corrected if the underlying endocrine problem is recognized and appropriate treatment begun immediately (see *adrenal problems; pituitary problems; thyroid problems*).

A height problem caused by delayed adolescence is self-correcting if onset of adolescence is not extremely late.

Tall Stature

Treating female children with familial tall stature involves high doses of estrogen to accelerate puberty and complete skeletal growth. Before therapy begins, the risk of possible estrogen-induced side effects must be thoroughly discussed. To have a significant effect on a girl's adult height, treatment should begin before the adolescent growth spurt or the onset of the menstrual cycle, usually between 10 and 12 years of age. Estrogen therapy is usually given daily. At monthly intervals a progesteronelike hormone is used to induce menstruation. Therapy is continued until a child's growth stops, usually by age 14 or 15.

See also *adrenal problems; pituitary problems; thyroid problems.*

PREVENTION

Height problems caused by genetic conditions cannot be prevented. Those that are symptoms of underlying conditions can be prevented only if the condition is diagnosed early and treated successfully. If treatment is delayed, height problems may become permanent.

HEMOPHILIA

DESCRIPTION

Hemophilia is a serious genetic disorder in which the blood does not clot properly, due to an insufficient amount of a protein, called a "factor." Thus, episodes of persistent and excessive bleeding may occur from minor injuries or even just the stress and strain of body motion. Although hemophilia can be controlled with proper management, it is a lifelong condition that, beginning at birth, imposes some physical limitations on an affected child. Although the hereditary trait for the disorder is carried by females, hemophilia affects males almost exclusively. The incidence of hemophilia is 1 in 10,000 births.

Three types of hemophilia exist. Hemophilia A (also called classical hemophilia or factor VIII deficiency) is the most common, accounting for 80 percent of hemophilia cases. Hemophilia B (Christmas Disease or factor IX deficiency) occurs in 15 percent of hemophilia cases. Hemophilias A and B affect the body in much the same way. Severity of these two types of hemophilia varies according to the amount of the blood-clotting factor an affected child lacks; the less clotting factor present, the more severe the hemophilia. The third and mildest type is hemophilia C (PTA deficiency), which appears in only 5 percent of hemophilia cases. This type is more correctly termed factor XI deficiency; it is quite different from hemophilias A and B.

The seriousness of hemophilia is due more to uncontrolled internal bleeding than to a loss of blood from prolonged external bleeding. Blood from internal bleeding can collect anywhere in the body. By far the most common site of bleeding is into the joints, but other parts of the body, such as muscles, skin, kidneys, gastrointestinal tract, abdominal cavity, the brain and spinal cord, and mucous membranes, can also be affected. If

bleeding episodes are not treated promptly and properly, or if repeated hemorrhaging is not prevented, hemophilia can lead to permanent joint damage or death from interference with functioning of vital organs such as the brain. Both permanent joint damage and death are increasingly uncommon today, and most children with hemophilia can look forward to a normal life expectancy and a basically normal life-style.

CAUSE

Hemophilia is a genetic disorder. Hemophilias A and B are nearly always inherited. The trait is sex-linked, transmitted only by females on an X chromosome (see *genetic disorders*).

If a man with hemophilia has sons with a normal, noncarrier woman, those sons will be normal. Their daughters, however, will all be carriers.

In the very rare instance of a man with hemophilia having children with a woman who carries the trait, a 50 percent chance exists that each daughter will have hemophilia, and a 50 percent chance that she will be a carrier. Each son has a 50 percent chance of having hemophilia and a 50 percent chance of being normal.

In one fourth to one third of severe cases, there is no family history for hemophilia. Spontaneous mutation is probably responsible for most of these cases, since neither the mother nor the maternal grandmother can be shown to be carriers.

Factor XI deficiency is inherited but is not carried on a sex chromosome; both sexes can be affected.

Carriers of hemophilia genes are unaffected by the disease; that is, they do not bleed excessively.

SIGNS AND SYMPTOMS

Children affected by hemophilia do not start bleeding more easily than normal children, but they do bleed longer. The severity of the bleeding depends on whether the factor deficiency is mild, moderate, or severe. Children who have mild hemophilia bleed excessively only at times of major injury or surgery. With severe hemophilia, there can be prolonged bleeding from minor injuries. The bleeding is usually internal, under the skin, into muscles or inside joints. Small bumps on the shins, for example, may lead to large bruises in the child with hemophilia. One of the most common effects of severe hemophilia is blood collecting in the joints spontaneously or after slight injury. When this happens, the child suffers pain, tenderness, swelling, heat, and limitation of movement. A frequent observation is the appearance of small amounts of blood in the urine, which does not indicate serious problems. When undergoing surgery or when a tooth is pulled, children with hemophilia bleed persistently. Often the bleeding seems to stop but late oozing of blood appears several days later. This happens because the initially formed clot is disturbed, and bleeding recurs. People with hemophilia do not bleed excessively from small cuts or scrapes. Their tendency toward internal bleeding, however, can lead to hemorrhage into joints, resulting in crippling unless appropriate treatment is given.

Head or spine injuries may be signaled by bumps or bruises, unusual headaches that do not respond to medication, unexplained *vomiting,* confusion, disorientation, unexplained sleepiness, or inability to move an arm or leg. Abdominal injuries may be marked by *abdominal pain,* paleness, weakness, or sudden sweating.

Children with factor XI deficiency rarely suffer excessive bleeding or the collection of blood in the joints. However, they may bleed excessively after surgery.

DIAGNOSIS

If a newborn baby boy is circumcised, his hemophilia may be discovered by the attending physician. If that does not occur, parents may suspect hemophilia when their son is learning to walk and shows unusually large, dark bruises from falling down. A dentist may detect hemophilia after pulling a child's tooth. Severe cases of hemophilia are almost always detected by the time a child is 3 or 4 years old. A blood test in which the amount of clotting factor is measured confirms the diagnosis. In severe hemophilia a person has less than 1 percent of the normal amount of clotting factor, while in mild hemophilia the factor level is 5 to 40 percent of normal.

A physician takes a family history. Carriers of the trait for hemophilia often have an affected brother, uncle, or grandfather (in the mother's family); women who have a family history of the disorder should be tested to see if they are carriers. Carriers now can be detected by a special blood test with 95 percent accuracy. This testing is performed in most hemophilia centers.

COMPLICATIONS

Since injury can lead to prolonged bleeding and resulting joint damage, the activities of children with hemophilia need to be somewhat restricted. They cannot play contact sports, although exercise like swimming is beneficial because it improves strength but does not place stress on the joints. They may be unable to run long distances because of the risk of bleeding in the joints.

Rarely, there may be a spontaneous brain hemorrhage, an emergency situation.

Patients with hemophilia receive blood products from thousands of blood donors. Therefore, they are at risk for allergic transfusion reactions and for *hepatitis* and other blood-transmitted infections. However, serious hepatitis is rarely a problem for people with hemophilia.

TREATMENT

Hemophilia cannot be cured. Treatment and management methods, however, have improved tremendously in recent years. Early, effective treatment can reduce disability dramatically.

Currently, most treatment can be provided at home, supported only by routine outpatient care. Minor injuries, including bruises and nosebleeds, can be treated with pressure and ice dressings. If bleeding does not stop, a concentrate of the missing clotting factor can be injected by a parent or by a child who is old enough. This treatment is quick and effective.

Until recent years children and adolescents with hemophilia spent long periods in the hospital, being treated for and recovering from bleeding episodes. Ice applications, bandages, and bed rest were standard procedures. Blood plasma was given by transfusion, but plasma infusions can correct the defect only partially. Limbs had to be immobilized to prevent further damage. Patients were often in casts or braces or on crutches for weeks. Current treatment is aimed at early treatment of bleeding before significant joint damage occurs.

During and after any surgery, large doses of the concentrated blood factor must be administered. Children with hemophilia used to require hospitalization after dental care, but now simple outpatient therapy is usual. Good dental hygiene and regular preventive care are recommended.

Approximately 10 percent of patients with hemophilia A have inhibitors or antibodies to the clotting factor that their bodies lack. When the clotting factor is infused, it becomes inactivated. A number of forms of treatment can be used for inhibitor patients, but they are of limited effectiveness. These patients usually suffer from chronic joint damage and joint disease as a result of bleeding.

PREVENTION

A woman who has a family history of hemophilia should be tested to see if she carries the trait for the disorder; if she does, she should have genetic counseling so that she will know in advance her chances of bearing affected sons and carrier daughters (see Prevention section of *genetic disorders*).

In a prenatal test using a fetoscope, fetal blood samples can be drawn for analysis and determination of hemophilia.

To prevent the worsening of bleeding episodes, males with hemophilia should avoid aspirin and other medicines that interfere with clotting. Patients with hemophilia should consult a physician about medications to reduce fever, pain, or inflammation. See also discussion of nonprescription medications beginning on p. 102.

Modern comprehensive hemophilia care aims at early treatment of bleeding and prevention of the complications of the disease.

HEPATITIS

EMERGENCY ACTION

If a child with *jaundice* (indicated by yellowness of body fluids, the whites of the eyes, and occasionally, the skin) suddenly becomes confused, restless, dehydrated (characterized by cool, dry, pale skin; dry tongue; sunken eyes; listlessness; rapid pulse; and thirst), is unable to retain fluids, or goes into a *coma,* seek immediate medical attention. Severe, life-threatening hepatitis may be present.

DESCRIPTION

Hepatitis is any inflammation of the liver (see Fig. 20, p. 193). It is most often caused by a viral infection, but it may also result from ingestion of excess chemicals or toxic substances. Liver inflammation may be mild, causing only slight swelling, tenderness, and discomfort. More severe inflammation may lead to permanent liver damage and mal-

functioning. The severity of viral hepatitis varies according to an affected individual's age, health, and the type of virus involved. Severity of toxic hepatitis is determined by the amount of chemicals or toxic substances ingested.

Viral Hepatitis

There are three types of viral hepatitis; hepatitis A, previously called infectious hepatitis; hepatitis B, previously called serum hepatitis; and non-A, non-B hepatitis.

Hepatitis A Hepatitis A affects approximately 1 out of every 250 Americans at least once. People of all ages can develop hepatitis A, although it is most common among children and adolescents. Hepatitis A is usually a very mild childhood infection.

In most cases no cure exists for hepatitis A. About 98 percent of children recover fully when the infection runs its course in a few months. Those children who do not recover fully may suffer liver damage.

Hepatitis B Approximately one out of every 500 people gets hepatitis B at least once. It is usually more severe than hepatitis A, particularly among infants. Children with long-term or severe illnesses, such as immune deficiencies or kidney failure, (see *kidney failure, chronic*) those receiving immunosuppressive therapy (given to prevent adverse immune responses), or those with *Down syndrome* are also susceptible to hepatitis B.

As with hepatitis A, a cure does not exist for most cases of hepatitis B. In most cases not at high risk, however, affected children recover fully. A vaccine has been developed against hepatitis B virus, that is used for those at high risk for contracting the infection. Such cases include children who are receiving dialysis treatment for malfunctioning kidneys and infants who are born to women who have hepatitis B.

Non-A, Non-B Hepatitis Little is known about non-A, non-B hepatitis. It represents about 90 percent of all hepatitis cases resulting from blood transfusions and can develop in people of all ages. It also has been found among individuals receiving kidney dialysis.

No cure exits for non-A, non-B hepatitis, but most children recover fully.

Chronic Hepatitis

If hepatitis persists for more than 6 months, chronic hepatitis exists. One percent of all children and adolescents with viral hepatitis develop this condition; it also may develop with toxic hepatitis. Exactly why chronic hepatitis develops is unknown, but it most often affects young children with hepatitis B and those with immune deficiencies. A child with chronic hepatitis may carry the hepatitis virus for years. If extensive liver damage does not occur, chronic hepatitis may eventually resolve without treatment.

As liver function deteriorates because of chronic hepatitis, normal body processes and development may be hindered. Problems involving hormones frequently develop, because liver damage prevents hormonal regulation. These include an increase in body hair, obesity, development of abnormal facial features, acne, and breast development in men (see *gyneconastia*). In addition, a child may have high blood pressure *(hypertension), arthritis,* hemolytic anemia (see *anemia, hemolytic), ulcerative colitis,* thyroiditis (inflammation of the thyroid gland; (see *thyroid problems*), inflammation of the membrane surrounding the lungs, or inflammation of the kidneys.

About 10 percent of cases of hepatitis B and non-A, non-B hepatitis progress to chronic hepatitis.

CAUSE

Viral hepatitis is caused by hepatitis A virus, hepatitis B virus, or hepatitis non-A, non-B virus. (The exact viruses of non-A, non-B hepatitis, however, have not been identified.) These viruses are believed to be extremely contagious. Hepatitis A virus is usually acquired through contact with soil and water contaminated by stool carrying the virus. In addition, hepatitis A virus can be passed on through close physical contact with an infected individual; he or she is most contagious about 2 weeks before his or her own signs and symptoms appear. The virus also can enter an individual's body in shellfish contaminated by polluted water. Use of unsterilized needles or surgical tools or transfusions with infected blood or blood products may also transmit hepatitis A virus.

Hepatitis B virus is most often transferred in contaminated blood, although incidence with blood transfusions has greatly decreased because of donor screening. It can also be transferred on contaminated needles, syringes, or surgical or dental instruments that are not properly sterilized. Less often, hepatitis B virus can be transmitted sexually or orally; the virus has been found in semen and saliva. If a pregnant woman develops hepatitis B during the last three months of pregnancy, she may transfer hepatitis B virus to the fetus; severe birth defects may result.

Viral hepatitis may also occur as a secondary infection with other viral infections. This most often occurs with *German measles* (rubella) and *syphilis.* Rarely, viral hepatitis occurs with neonatal herpes (see *genital herpes*).

Toxic hepatitis develops when a child ingests certain substances that damage liver tissue or when the liver is not developed enough to handle certain food products. Some substances, such as phosphorus, are essential to body functioning; excessive levels in the body, however, can injure the liver. Some drugs, both prescription and over-the-counter, can cause toxic hepatitis. Excessive doses of acetaminophen, for example, can produce toxic hepatitis. Ingestion of chemical substances, such as carbon tetrachloride (a spot remover and carpet cleaner) and arsenic (frequently found in food, water, and air contaminated by industrial pollution) also cause toxic hepatitis.

SIGNS AND SYMPTOMS

Childhood symptoms of viral hepatitis are usually milder than those produced during adulthood. Symptoms of hepatitis A do not always develop; if they do, they usually appear suddenly between 10 and 50 days after hepatitis A virus enters the body. Symptoms of hepatitis B and non-A, non-B hepatitis usually develop slowly and appear 50 to 180 days after infection.

Initial signs and symptoms of viral hepatitis include fever, headache, muscle achiness, loss of appetite, and itchy rash. Within a few days symptoms become worse and include nausea, *vomiting, abdominal pain,* joint pain, foul breath, and a bitter taste in the mouth. The liver, spleen, and lymph nodes may become swollen and painful when pressed. *Jaundice* may develop, although it is rare during childhood. When jaundice does appear, it is preceded by the appearance of dark urine. Symptoms often lessen when jaundice develops during childhood cases of hepatitis, but they usually become more severe when older children and adults are affected.

Signs and symptoms of toxic hepatitis resemble those of viral hepatitis, although headache, organ enlargement, and jaundice are rare.

DIAGNOSIS

A physician should be consulted if a child has signs and symptoms of hepatitis or if an ill child has been exposed to an individual known to have viral hepatitis. If *jaundice* is not present, a physician must be sure that signs and symptoms are not caused by another disorder, such as mononucleosis (see *mononucleosis, infectious*), *appendicitis, influenza,* or *food poisoning.* If jaundice is present, disorders such as cirrhosis of the liver, a tumor in the liver, or syphilis must be ruled out.

A physician diagnoses hepatitis on the basis of signs and symptoms, history of a child's recent activities, a child's medical history, and results of tests analyzing blood, urine, stool, and liver function. Liver function tests usually reveal abnormal liver functioning. A liver biopsy (removal and analysis of a sample of liver tissue) may be performed if liver inflammation and malfunctioning persist after the appearance of signs and symptoms.

When a viral infection develops, the virus produces antigens, substances that provoke the body's immune system to produce antibodies to fight infection. When a child has hepatitis B, a special antigen called Australian antigen (hepatitis-associated antigen—HAA) develops that is found in all body fluids and secretions, including blood, saliva, semen, and breast milk. Presence of Australian antigen is detected by special blood tests and indicates hepatitis B. Australian antigen can be detected in blood 6 to 30 days after the virus is transmitted in blood and 6 to 160 days after it is passed sexually or orally.

Non-A, non-B hepatitis is diagnosed by excluding the possibility of hepatitis A virus or hepatitis B virus.

COMPLICATIONS

If tissue damage in the liver is extensive, liver failure occurs. Other organs may be affeted, including the stomach, intestines, spleen, and kidneys. The child may go into a *coma.* Encephalopathy (brain disease resulting in bizarre behavior and coma) may occur suddenly. Even with treatment, 70 percent of children in hepatic coma die from severe, irreversible liver damage and resulting complications. If severe liver damage has not occurred, toxic hepatitis disappears a few days after removal of offending substances.

TREATMENT

Because there is no cure for viral hepatitis, treatment focuses on relieving symptoms until the infection runs its course. In most cases home treatment is sufficient; bed rest is essential.

Diet is best regulated according to a child's appetite. Liquids such as broths and juices should be given if a child has little or no appetite; when a child's appetite returns, a nutritious, well-balanced diet should be resumed. A physician usually recommends vitamin supplements, particularly vitamin B, to replenish depleted supplies.

Medications are not recommended for treatment of hepatitis. Affected individuals should avoid alcohol, because filtering it taxes the liver. A child can resume normal activities gradually; children, however, usually recover more quickly than adults.

Severe hepatitis requires immediate hospitalization. Treatment focuses on reducing nitrogen levels—which rise because the damaged liver cannot process the nutrients—to prevent toxic effects to the brain. Nitrogen levels are lowered by reducing a child's dietary protein intake and removing protein from the gastrointestinal tract with laxatives and washings. In addition, the normal bacterial population in the intestines is suppressed with medications to prevent breakdown and retention of protein and its components. If a child is vomiting, intravenous feedings may be administered. Potassium supplements may be needed to maintain electrolyte and fluid balances in the body.

If a child with hepatitis is highly contagious, isolation in a hospital may be required. A child with hepatitis should not have contact with others for at least 3 weeks after the onset of symptoms.

PREVENTION

Good hygiene helps prevent transmission of hepatitis viruses. Children should wash their hands carefully after playing outside, after going to the bathroom, and before eating. In a home where anyone with hepatitis lives, all utensils used in food preparation should be washed thoroughly with hot water and detergent, preferably in a dishwashing machine.

Any individual exposed to hepatitis A virus can be given gamma globulin, a protein of the immune system that combats infections, to reduce or prevent symptoms of hepatitis. Gamma globulin cannot relieve hepatitis symptoms, however, if the infection is already established. If an individual plans to travel to areas of the world where hepatitis virus is present constantly, a physician usually recommends administration of gamma globulin before the trip begins.

Prevention of hepatitis B depends mainly on the identification and avoidance of contaminated blood and blood products. Blood tests to detect Australian antigen are extremely helpful when screening potential blood donors. Anyone who has had hepatitis B at any time in life is not considered a suitable blood donor. Regular gamma globulin is ineffective against hepatitis B, but a special, more potent globulin has been effective in preventing or reducing symptoms of hepatitis B in about 70 percent of cases. In special cases, infants and children can be given the anti-hepatitis B vaccine. Ordinarily this expensive vaccine is given only to those children who cannot avoid exposure to a known carrier of hepatitis B. Any baby born to a mother who is a carrier of hepatitis B should receive the anti-hepatitis B vaccine.

The chances of toxic hepatitis can be lessened by keeping toxic drug and household substances out of a child's reach.

HEREDITARY SPHEROCYTOSIS

EMERGENCY ACTION

If a child who suffers from hereditary spherocytosis (HS) has a cold, flu, or some other viral infection and seems abnormally pale or lethargic, parents should seek immediate medical attention. If a child who has had his or her spleen removed develops a high fever, a physician should be notified immediately.

DESCRIPTION

Hereditary spherocytosis is a blood disorder characterized by *anemia, jaundice,* and sometimes an enlarged spleen (the organ located in the upper left abdomen that filters blood). Red blood cells of children with HS are destroyed at an excessively rapid rate. (Because of this increased rate of destruction, HS is classified as a type of hemolytic anemia. See *anemia, hemolytic*).

HS is congenital (present at birth). From 200 to 400 cases of HS exist in every million children in the United States. The disease occurs most frequently among people of Northern European ethnic backgrounds.

Normal red blood cells are disk-shaped and flexible; the red blood cells of people with HS have an inherent defect that makes them become shaped like spheres. The cells then are less flexible and more fragile than usual. This inflexibility causes problems only in the spleen, through which the blood must pass during circulation. The spleen destroys old or defective red blood cells and also produces antibodies, which provide continuous immunity against certain types of infection.

Because portions of the spleen's filtering channels are very narrow, red blood cells need to be very flexible to pass through quickly and continue circulating throughout the body. Rigid spherocytic (sphere-shaped) red blood cells, however, pass through the channels with difficulty. During each slow journey through the spleen, many spherocytic cells are engulfed and destroyed by cells called phagocytes, which routinely destroy bacteria and other foreign particles.

When red blood cells are destroyed more rapidly than they can be made in the bone marrow, anemia develops. As a consequence, the heart rate must increase to maintain adequate oxygen delivery and exercise tolerance is reduced. When large numbers of spherocytic cells are destroyed, the spleen becomes enlarged and jaundice develops.

From 20 to 30 percent of HS cases are mild; a balance exists between red cell destruction and production. Usually no symptoms are present and often no anemia is found.

From 60 to 75 percent of HS cases are "typical." In such cases the children have mild to moderate anemia, periodic slight jaundice, and a moderately enlarged spleen. The remaining 5 to 10 percent of HS cases are severe. Here the rate of destruction of red blood cells is far greater than the rate of production. An affected child has severe anemia and sometimes requires transfusions of red blood cells.

CAUSE

The genetic defect for HS is inherited. The cause appears to be a deficiency in the red-cell membrane protein called spectrin.

In three fourths of the cases, one of the parents has detectable HS, and each child has a 50 percent chance of inheriting the defective gene that causes the blood disorder. In the remaining one fourth of cases, HS appears in children with seemingly normal parents (see *genetic disorders*).

SIGNS AND SYMPTOMS

About half of newborns with HS are jaundiced. Older children with signs and symptoms of HS typically have mild to moderate *anemia,* enlargement of the spleen, and intermittent mild *jaundice.* Children with moderate to severe anemia may have a rapid heart rate or a heart murmur, or they may breathe rapidly. In severe cases a child may be extremely pale or jaundiced.

DIAGNOSIS

If a child appears pale or jaundiced, a physician should be consulted. A physician looks for indications of HS in a child's family history. Often a family history reveals *anemia, jaundice,* surgical removal of the spleen, or gallstone formation. If a parent has HS, each newborn infant should be tested for the disease. Diagnostic blood tests will identify HS. A physician also feels the child's spleen to check for enlargement.

COMPLICATIONS

The most common complication of untreated HS is gallbladder disease. A certain type of gallstones forms as a result of persistent, excessive destruction of red blood cells and the increased amount of bile formed by the liver from bilirubin.

A hemolytic crisis may occur, usually as the result of a viral infection, which causes the spleen to enlarge. Such a crisis is characterized by a brief, usually mild increase in *anemia, jaundice,* and spleen enlargement. Mild hemolytic crises leave no lasting effects.

An aplastic crisis is often more serious, and lasts 10 to 14 days. Aplastic crises are usually brought on by certain types of viral infections, which suppress production of red blood cells, causing severe anemia. Transfusions are often required. Typical symptoms are *fever, vomiting, abdominal pain, headache,* weakness, excessively rapid heart rate, rapid breathing, and pale skin and mucous membranes.

Another type of aplastic crisis can develop if a child does not consume enough folic acid. Folic acid, necessary for the production of red blood cells, is found in meats such as liver and kidneys, dark green leafy vegetables, wheat germ, and dried beans and peas. For patients with HS or other hemolytic anemias, physicians often recommend daily folic acid supplements.

Another complication of HS may occur in severely affected children as a result of insufficient oxygen reaching body tissues. They may experience slowed growth, delayed sexual development, and increased prominence of the forehead and cheekbones.

TREATMENT

Splenectomy (surgical removal of the spleen) is the usual treatment for children with HS. With no spleen, spherocytic cells no longer have difficulty circulating or surviving; in fact, after a splenectomy, spherocytic cells last as long as normal red blood cells. Thus, splenectomy effectively cures HS, although the spherocytic cells remain. To allow for development of some natural immunity against infection before the organ is removed, splenectomy is usually performed when a child is between 5 and 10 years old.

Before the spleen can be removed, treatment of symptoms is sometimes necessary. For instance, newborns at risk of developing complications from jaundice may require exchange transfusions or phototherapy (in which fluorescent light rays break down bilirubin. See *jaundice* for explanation of this treatment). Older children with severe anemia may require transfusions of red blood cells, especially during aplastic crises.

Splenectomy is nearly always successful in eliminating an affected child's anemia, jaundice, crises, excessive destruction of red blood cells, and abnormally high risk of gallstone formation.

After the spleen is removed, however, a child loses some immunity and is at increased risk of *bloodstream infection.* Removal of the spleen does not increase the risk of infections other than bloodstream infections. This complication is very rare, even in the absence of the spleen, but because it may be very serious, precautions are taken to prevent it. For example, to guard against bloodstream infections by the most common germ causing this complication, an inoculation called a pneumococcal vaccination is given to children with HS. In addition, many physicians recommend that a child have a preventive daily low dose of penicillin at home. Despite these precautions, a child whose spleen has been removed still runs a slight risk of serious bloodstream infection. Parents should immediately notify their physician whenever their child develops a temperature greater than 101° F (38.3° C) or seems unusually ill.

PREVENTION

Hereditary spherocytosis cannot be prevented. Individuals with HS, however, may seek genetic counseling to discuss the chances of passing on the defective gene causing the disease to their children (see genetic counseling section of *genetic disorders*).

HERNIA, DIAPHRAGMATIC

DESCRIPTION

The diaphragm is the large, musclelike membrane that serves as a major respiratory muscle and as a partition between the chest and abdominal cavities. Diaphragmatic hernia is present when one of the organs normally found in the abdomen (stomach, small or large intestines, or spleen, or, rarely, the liver, or kidneys) protrudes up into the chest cavity through a hole or tear in the diaphragm.

Appearing most often on the left side, this protrusion crowds the heart and lungs, severely interfering with breathing. Consequently, the life of a newborn with this condition is threatened. Diaphragmatic hernia occurs about once in every 3,000 to 4,000 live births.

Diaphragmatic hernia may be congenital (present at birth) or caused by an injury. The more common congenital variety must be repaired surgically. This condition is often associated with inadequate development of the lungs. Children with diaphragmatic hernia and lung problems usually have *breathing difficulties* and may experience oxygen deprivation (see *prematurity*). If the respiratory system of a newborn is sufficiently developed, the chances of full recovery and a normal life thereafter are good.

CAUSE

Diaphragmatic hernia may be present at birth due to an abnormality of prenatal development. It occurs when segments of the diaphragm of the fetus fail to fuse completely. Diaphragmatic hernia may also occur as the result of an injury involving a se-vere blow to the chest and abdomen, as in an automobile collision or a sports accident.

SIGNS AND SYMPTOMS AND COMPLICATIONS

Signs and symptoms of diaphragmatic hernia are usually present at birth. Signs include dyspnea (severe breathing difficulty) and *cyanosis* (turning blue from inadequate oxygen). An infant may reach several weeks or even several months of age before signs of difficulty are evident.

If a loop of small or large intestine becomes caught or twisted in a gap in the diaphragmatic membrane, *vomiting, colic,* cramps and pain after feedings, and *constipation* may result because of intestinal obstruction.

DIAGNOSIS

A physician diagnoses diaphragmatic hernia on the basis of signs and symptoms. X-ray films can confirm the diagnosis.

TREATMENT

Surgical repair is the only treatment for newborns with diaphragmatic hernia. Usually an operation must be performed within the first few hours of life because of insufficient lung function resulting in severe oxygen shortage. This occurs because the lung is markedly compressed and cannot expand with air. Because of inadequate development of the lungs, the chances of survival for a newborn with this condition may be less than 50 percent despite surgical correction. In some cases the infant may be placed on a respirator for several days to allow the lungs to attain more mature and self-sustaining development. Those infants who survive in relatively good condition for 24 to 48 hours are less likely to have serious problems.

PREVENTION

Congenital diaphragmatic hernia cannot presently be prevented. The traumatic type can be prevented by avoidance of high-impact accidents.

HERNIA, INGUINAL AND UMBILICAL

EMERGENCY ACTION

If a child complains of continuous pain or a lump in either groin (where the upper thigh meets the pubic area of the lower abdomen) and then has abdominal cramps, *vomiting,* and bloating of the lower abdomen, a strangulated hernia may be the cause. Seek medical attention without delay, especially if a child has a history of hernia.

DESCRIPTION

A hernia occurs when a loop or segment of an organ or tissue protrudes through an abnormal opening in the membrane or muscle that surrounds it. Such an opening is commonly due to an opening present at birth, often enlarged by straining or to a tear caused by an injury.

Inguinal hernia, the most common hernia in infancy and childhood, is sometimes mistakenly called a "rupture." About 1 child in 20 has an inguinal hernia; boys are affected 9 times as often as girls. The condition occurs more often on the right side than on the left, but frequently it affects both sides.

Another relatively common childhood hernia is the umbilical hernia, which occurs at the navel. Umbilical hernia is less common than inguinal and occurs more often among black children.

Inguinal and umbilical hernia often occur because the peritoneum, the membrane which lines the abdominal cavity, does not develop properly while the baby is still in the womb. Around the third month of prenatal development, a small saclike projection of the peritoneum extends down through a tunnel between the abdomen and thigh (inguinal canal) into the scrotum of a boy or the labia majora (outer skin folds of the vulva, the external genital organs) of a girl. Just before birth the peritoneal pouch normally seals itself off and dissolves, and eventually the canal between abdominal cavity and testis or labia ceases to exist. If this process is incomplete, an intestinal loop could protrude into the pouch, causing an inguinal hernia.

In approximately 5 to 10 percent of normal male infants, the pouch never seals off. Among these individuals a hernia may appear at some time in childhood or during adult life. In hernias that occur during infancy, nothing tears; rather, the muscles of the inguinal canal are stretched after straining. Inguinal hernia may be associated with hydrocele, a fluid accumulation in a pinched-off section of the pouch.

While emergency surgical relief of a trapped inguinal hernia is often necessary, a trapped umbilical hernia is rare.

Umbilical hernia is an incomplete closure or weakness of the abdominal wall at the navel. It appears as a skin-covered swelling that may protrude much more noticeably during coughing, crying, or straining. The swelling can be reduced temporarily by gently pushing it back through the abdominal wall. Umbilical hernias that occur before a child is 6 months of age usually disappear without treatment by the first birthday.

Surgical repair is the standard treatment for inguinal hernia. Most umbilical hernias subside without treatment. Surgery for umbilical hernia is indicated only if a loop of intestine is trapped or if the size of the protrusion continues to increase, or if the defect persists beyond 2 years of age.

CAUSE

Inguinal hernia is caused by a failure of the normal sac leading to the scrotum to disappear. This condition may be aggravated by the excessive straining of bowel movements, coughing, sneezing, or extremely stressful physical activity.

Umbilical hernia is caused by weakness of the abdominal wall at the navel, an area called the umbilical ring. Sometimes this hernia occurs when the muscle layers of the abdominal wall separate abnormally. Loops of intestine within the fibrous lining of the abdominal wall bulge through the umbilical ring and are restrained only by the skin.

SIGNS AND SYMPTOMS

In the case of inguinal hernia, a telltale bulge occurs in the groin. Such a bulge, which often resembles a lump just under the skin, may move downward into the scrotum in a boy or toward the labia majora in a girl. The lump may be visible continually or it may appear only when abdominal muscles are under pressure, such as when a baby strains during a bowel movement or cries intensely. For an older child the lump usually develops gradually during the course of a day's activities or it may "pop out" after an especially strenuous twist, stretch, or lunge while the child is participating in sports or play.

Inguinal hernias usually do not cause sharp pain, but a gradually increasing dull ache can accompany bulging. Trapped intestine in an inguinal hernia can cause cramping, *vomiting,* and bloating of the abdomen, even if strangulation has not occurred.

DIAGNOSIS

Diagnosis can usually be made by observation. Pressing the abdomen when a baby is crying usually produces a characteristic inguinal hernia bulge. When an older child stands and strains down while the abdomen is pressed firmly inward, the appearance of a bulge usually indicates inguinal hernia. Umbilical hernia is obvious without applying external pressure.

COMPLICATIONS

If an inguinal hernia becomes irreversibly trapped, the loop of intestine cannot be manipulated free by a physician. That loop may be pinched shut, cutting off circulation. Without a supply of nutrients and oxygen from the blood, tissue becomes gangrenous (decays) and will die. Redness and extreme tenderness follow swelling of the lower abdomen; cramping and *vomiting* may occur as well. This condition is known as strangulation. Infants may reveal their discomfort only by becoming increasingly fretful and irritable.

Strangulation of an umbilical hernia occurs rarely.

TREATMENT

A strangulated inguinal hernia is an extreme surgical emergency. A surgeon may need to remove the strangulated section and rejoin the two healthy ends of intestine.

For an infant in good physical condition whose inguinal hernia does not require emergency treatment, surgical repair is performed promptly in order to prevent an unexpected trapping of intestine. For an older child with an obvious inguinal hernia, surgery is usually recommended when convenient. A hernia operation is relatively simple, and although it requires general anesthesia, a child is usually treated as an outpatient and can return home later the same day. Following surgery, the child is normal and may engage in any physical activity. Inguinal hernia repair removes the sac and strengthens the inguinal canal by stitching the weakened muscles together.

Trusses and support belts do not cure or permanently reduce inguinal hernias. They may lead to serious complications and are not recommended.

Many mild umbilical hernias in infants and young children are not treated surgically. If the hernia grows larger after the second birthday, or if at any age it repeatedly causes symptoms or gives indications

that it may become trapped, surgery may become necessary. The surgical procedure for umbilical hernia is much the same as in inguinal hernia: the umbilical ring is reduced by stitching. Although parents sometimes try to strap in an umbilical hernia with a belt or elastic band to try to reduce or eliminate it, this treatment is both ineffective and dangerous.

PREVENTION

Neither inguinal nor umbilical hernia can be prevented.

HIATUS HERNIA AND GASTROESOPHAGEAL REFLUX

DESCRIPTION

A hernia is the protrusion of an organ beyond its normal confines. This problem can be congenital (present at birth), or it may develop at any age. Most hernias develop during adulthood, and childhood hernias tend to be congenital.

Congenital hiatal hernia is rare. It occurs when the stomach protrudes beyond the abdominal cavity into the chest cavity through the hiatus, or opening, of the diaphragm, the muscular wall that separates the two cavities (see Fig. 30, p. 437). Normally the diaphragmatic hiatus allows the esophagus, or foodpipe, to extend into the abdominal cavity, where it connects to the stomach. When the stomach protrudes up through this opening constantly or intermittently, a hiatus hernia exists. However, for reasons that are not altogether clear, hiatus hernia may be associated with a condition called gastroesophageal reflux. (The word "reflux" means "backward flow," "gastro-" denotes the stomach, and "esophageal" refers to the esophagus.)

Gastroesophageal reflux is the backward flow of the contents of the stomach into the esophagus, which is the tube connecting the throat to the stomach. This problem affects many people; its most prevalent symptom is commonly called heartburn, and its causes among older children and adults are complex.

Among infants, however, gastroesophageal reflux involves a problem with the sphincter mechanism between the esophagus and the stomach. There is a muscle and a flaplike valve which together prevent stomach contents from returning into the esophagus. For some infants this system functions poorly. As a result, a child can experience a number of symptoms, including frequent *vomiting*. Potentially serious consequences, such as *failure to thrive,* recurrent *pneumonia,* or bleeding are rare.

Fortunately the sphincter muscle and valvelike mechanism usually mature well within the first year of life, and gastroesophageal reflux often disappears without permanent complications. Almost all infants who have persistent vomiting beyond 15 months of age or who experience complications of gastroesphageal reflux, such as growth failure, recurrent pneumonia, or bleeding, need further evaluation to determine the exact cause of the problem. For those children who deviate from the normal pattern, treatment is available to ease symptoms and, if necessary, correct structural problems.

CAUSE

The cause of hiatal hernia is unclear. Genetic factors may be involved, since the frequency of certain other congenital malformations is somewhat higher among children with hiatus hernia than among those who do not have the condition (see *genetic disorders*).

SIGNS AND SYMPTOMS

Typically symptoms of gastroesophageal reflux are relatively mild and first appear in early infancy. Occasionally symptoms do not develop until late childhood or even into adulthood.

The most common, uncomplicated symptom of gastroesophageal reflux during infancy is *vomiting*. About 90 percent of all children born with gastroesophageal reflux experience this symptom during the first week of life, especially after meals. Vomiting may be forceful, is usually effortless, but is never tinged with bile (yellow or green). All other symptoms are related to complications of the condition.

COMPLICATIONS

The vast majority of children with gastroesophageal reflux never develop any complications and do not require further testing.

Children who experience severe gastroesophageal reflux may fail to gain weight or grow according to schedule. This problem results directly from *vomiting* and the consequent failure to derive adequate nutrients.

FIG. 30. GASTROINTESTINAL TRACT

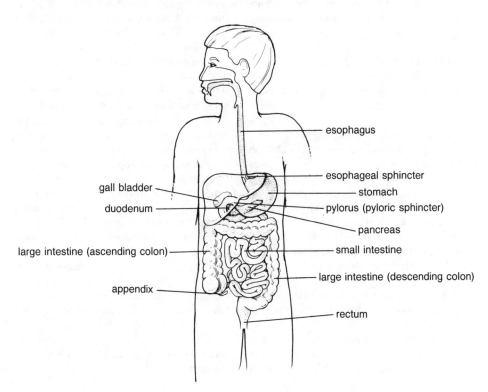

esophagus

esophageal sphincter

gall bladder

stomach

duodenum

pylorus (pyloric sphincter)

pancreas

large intestine (ascending colon)

small intestine

large intestine (descending colon)

appendix

rectum

Hiatus Hernia and Gastroesophageal Reflux **437**

Another common problem is inflammation (swelling and redness) of the lining of the esophagus, a condition called esophagitis, which results from irritation of the lining by acidic stomach secretions. If esophagitis is severe, the walls of the esophagus may bleed, and blood may appear in vomit or may travel through the rest of the gastrointestinal (GI) tract (esophagus, stomach, and intestines) and turn stools black. Esophageal bleeding can also lead to iron-deficiency anemia (see *anemia, nutritional*). In some cases of esophagitis, the esophagus swells so much that the pathway to the stomach becomes partially or completely blocked. Even before this problem develops, having a swollen esophagus can hinder swallowing of food.

Some children with persistent gastroesophageal reflux may experience respiratory complications. Such problems include frequent bouts of *coughing,* wheezing (see *breathing difficulty*), or *apnea* (temporary cessation of breathing). In addition, pneumonia can develop from inhaling vomit into the lungs. Such problems, some of which are potentially life-threatening, may occur because gastroesophageal reflux can trigger a spasm in the windpipe that interferes with normal breathing.

Over 90 percent of children with gastroesophageal reflux get better with medical evaluation. A physician should be consulted if the vomiting is excessive or if any complications develop.

DIAGNOSIS

If a baby appears to have signs and symptoms of gastroesophageal reflux, a physician should be consulted. The diagnostic procedure begins with a history of the child's general health and vomiting patterns and a thorough physical examination. For children who have experienced one of the complications of reflux, the most reliable way to tell whether a baby has episodes of gastroesophageal reflux indicative of an underlying problem is to insert a probe that detects the presence of acid in a child's esophagus. This simple and relatively painless procedure provides objective data about the severity of the gastroesophageal reflux. Infants who vomit and have not experienced any of the complications of gastroesophageal reflux usually do not require such testing.

If a physician suspects that the cause of gastroesophageal reflux is related to an anatomic abnormality, such as hiatus hernia, an X-ray study of the upper abdomen may be performed. A child drinks a sweet-tasting liquid containing barium sulfate, which illuminates the upper GI tract on X-ray film and eventually passes easily out of the body in a bowel movement. In some cases, usually when inflammation is suspected, a physician wants to get a direct look at the upper gastrointestinal tract. For this purpose the physician inserts into the esophagus a special, flexible, lighted tube (endoscope) through which the esophageal lining can be viewed. Obtaining tiny scrapings of the lining of the esophagus for microscopic evaluation is the most sensitive test for determining the severity of damage to the esophageal lining.

TREATMENT

Treatment for hiatus hernia alone is not necessary unless symptoms of gastroesophageal reflux are present. In that case the goal of treatment is to minimize the symptoms until reflux disappears naturally or, if it persists, to correct the condition surgically.

Traditionally physicians have used a special "infant seat" to treat gastroesophageal reflux. This device is composed of a board with a padded peg. The board can be tilted at various angles, and a child can be placed on it face down with his or her legs toward the ground and straddling the peg. The idea is to use gravity to enhance emptying of the stomach. A baby can be placed on the infant seat for an hour or so after each meal or for much longer periods.

Recent evidence has shown, however, that this treatment method is less successful than simply ensuring that the baby rests on his or her stomach with the head slightly elevated. While neither strategy can "cure" gastroesophageal reflux, both are designed to prevent complications as the condition resolves naturally. It is also important to burp a child thoroughly after meals (see Chapter 2, "Promoting Physical Health"). In addition, some physicans recommend giving the child a thicker formula than usual.

If a child's gastroesophageal reflux persists or if potentially serious complications develop, a physician may recommend medication to improve the function of the gastroesophageal sphincter or to treat inflammation. Fewer than 10 percent of all children with gastroesophageal reflux require surgery, which is completely successful for about 90 percent of the children who have the operation.

PREVENTION

Congenital hiatal hernia and gastroesophageal reflux cannot be prevented.

HIRSCHSPRUNG'S DISEASE

DESCRIPTION

Hirschsprung's disease (named after the Danish physician who first described the condition) is a birth defect involving a deficiency of nerve cells in the colon (see Fig. 30, p. 437). As a result, the colon becomes partially blocked, regular bowel movements become difficult or impossible, and *constipation* results. At first, newborns afflicted with Hirschsprung's disease are unable to pass the thick green fetal contents (meconium) of the intestines. Curiously, many babies experience *diarrhea* as the first sign of this disease. A rectal examination by a physician may stimulate the passage of meconium and gas, but the symptoms of blockage or diarrhea soon appear again.

The colon above the area of partial blockage or obstruction becomes enlarged to 2 or 3 times normal size, a condition called megacolon ("large colon"), and this can progress to *enterocolitis* (severe inflammation of the intestines). As the internal pressure increases, the colon wall begins to secrete the fluids of digestion instead of absorbing them, and this can result in diarrhea with *dehydration*. The condition does not improve without treatment.

Sometimes symptoms of Hirschsprung's disease are not apparent until a child is 6 to 12 months old. If this is the case, recurring constipation, gas, and bloating of the abdomen signal the presence of Hirschsprung's disease. Feces are usually small in volume and may be watery. The condition may vary: general health can appear almost normal, or severe intestinal blockage can result in growth failure. Severely affected children can also develop *anemia* and are subject to periodic attacks of intestinal blockage, pain, and fever.

Hirschsprung's disease is the second most frequent cause of intestinal blockage among newborns (after *pyloric stenosis*). Its incidence is estimated at 1 out of 10,000 births. It may occur even more frequently, however, since infants may die of undiagnosed enterocolitis stemming from untreated megacolon. Hirschsprung's disease affects siblings or successive generations of the same family about 10 percent of the time. Males develop this disease 4 times as often as females. Unless surgery is performed, Hirschsprung's disease may be fatal.

CAUSE

Hirschsprung's disease is a congenital defect caused by the partial or total absence of nerve cells in the lower end of the colon, leading to its partial or complete blockage. Without adequate nerve cells, muscles in the colon wall cannot relax properly to allow normal bowel movements to occur. Normally the muscles of the colon wall remain contracted; when a bowel movement is necessary, the nerves in the colon wall permit relaxation of these muscles. Rarely, the entire colon can be involved, and even more rarely, the absence of nerve cells may extend further upward to include part of the small intestine as well.

SIGNS AND SYMPTOMS

All newborns are unable to pass meconium until after a physician has performed a rectal examination which stimulates the muscles at the lowest end of the large intestine. If Hirschsprung's disease is present, an infant subsequently has *constipation* or *diarrhea* instead of normal bowel movements.

In addition to constipation or diarrhea, symptoms of Hirschsprung's disease include loud gurgling noises from the abdomen, gas, and bloating that becomes increasingly more pronounced. Stools are usually small in volume. Older children with megacolon can have *abdominal pain,* gas, and bloating along with loud bowel noises and constipation. Poor appetite and weight loss may result. In such a situation *failure to thrive* may be unavoidable. Bowel movements, when they do occur, are likely to be painful and explosive because of accumulated gas.

DIAGNOSIS

A physician's examination often reveals a bloated abdomen. A rectal examination usually discloses an empty rectum. In other forms of constipation, the rectum is full of stool. A physician orders X-ray films of the colon, followed by a test to measure the internal pressure of the rectum. Finally, a biopsy (tissue sample) of the colon may be analyzed to detect the presence of nerve cells.

The absence of nerve cells confirms a diagnosis of Hirschsprung's disease.

COMPLICATIONS

The major complication of Hirschsprung's disease is enterocolitis, a condition which occurs without warning and can cause death in 24 hours. Unless treated immediately with intravenous fluids, blood transfusions, antibiotics, and surgery to relieve extreme pressure building in the colon, death occurs because of *bloodstream infection. Failure to thrive* among older children can be a serious, common complication.

TREATMENT

Hospitalization is necessary for all children with Hirschsprung's disease. The defective section of colon causing blockage must be removed and the healthy ends of colon sewn together.

If a newborn has Hirschsprung's disease, or if an older child has suffered enterocolitis and needs emergency treatment, a temporary colostomy is often the safest first treatment to relieve the bloated bowel. A colostomy is an artificial opening of the colon created by the surgeon on the outside of the abdomen. Fecal matter is collected in a small bag attached to the abdomen. Several months later the defective colon is removed and the small intestine is reconnected to the rectum and anus.

Complications from either operation are rare. Most children who undergo this operation (or, in some cases, two operations) come to have almost normal bowel movements and anal control, so that soiling is not a problem. During adolescence and adulthood those individuals who have had successful surgical treatment can lead normal lives.

PREVENTION

Hirschsprung's disease cannot be prevented.

HIVES

EMERGENCY ACTION

If hives develop on a child's tongue or throat and interfere with breathing or swallowing, seek medical treatment immediately. A physician can give the child epinephrine (also called Adrenalin) to reduce swelling.

DESCRIPTION

Hives (urticaria) is a skin reaction that affects children who are allergic (extremely sensitive) to certain substances (allergens) or have certain medical conditions. Hives are itchy, red lumps or welts that can develop anywhere on a child's body. Anyone can develop hives; more than 20 percent of children have hives at least once.

There are several categories of hives, classified either by duration (acute, long-term, and recurrent) or cause (allergic; physical, including cold and solar; stress-related; infectious; or related to systemic disease).

Acute hives are extremely itchy and usually develop on a child's chest and face, sometimes causing the eyelids and lips to swell. These hives usually appear suddenly and disappear without treatment within a few days. Acute hives are most often caused by an allergic reaction to swallowed or injected allergens (foods or medications) or allergens that have touched the skin. For example, hives erupt immediately after an allergic child receives a bee sting or a penicillin injection.

Long-term hives are often caused by an underlying medical illness, although the cause frequently cannot be determined. They resemble acute hives in appearance but develop more slowly and last until the underlying cause is resolved, occasionally persisting for months or even years. Long-term hives usually disappear spontaneously.

Papular hives affect children between the ages of one and five who are sensitive to bites from insects such as fleas, bedbugs, chiggers, and mosquitoes. These hives develop suddenly around the bite, but also appear on unbitten areas of the body (except the chest and buttocks). Papular hives itch intensely.

Cholinergic (stress-related) hives most often affect adolescents and young adults. They are bright red and itchy and develop on the neck and chest immediately following vigorous exercise, hot showers or baths, or emotional stress. Cholinergic hives usually disappear in a few minutes or hours. If the physical or emotional strain accompanying cholinergic hives is severe, excessive salivation, sweating, *abdominal pain,* and *diarrhea* may also be present.

Cold hives result from exposure to cold air, cold drinks, or cold water. They usually appear suddenly on exposed body areas such as the face and hands and are extremely itchy or painful. When a child's skin comes in contact with cold substances (such as a cold glass or cold foods) hives develop.

Solar hives appear within minutes of exposure to sunlight. These hives are most often associated with diseases that increase a child's sensitivity to the sun, such as *lupus erythematosus*.

CAUSE

Ingested substances that most often cause hives include medications (particularly aspirin and penicillin) and foods (particularly shellfish, nuts, eggs, chocolate, strawberries, and food additives). Hives can also be caused by surface allergens such as animal saliva, ointments, plants, or less frequently, inhaled allergens.

Hives may be caused by viral infections, such as *hepatitis* and infectious mononucleosis (see *mononucleosis, infectious)*, and bacterial infections, such as *sinusitis* and tooth abscess. *Parasitic infections,* such as ascaris and underlying diseases such as arthritis (see *arthritis, acute),* and *rheumatic fever* may also cause hives.

DIAGNOSIS

Hives are obvious. The underlying cause, however, is not always easy to determine, even by allergy skin testing and eliminating suspect foods or medications.

A child's medical history may help a physician identify possible causes. History of a child's activities, diet, and medications immediately preceding the appearance of hives is also helpful.

TREATMENT

Unless the underlying cause is known, treatment of hives focuses on relieving the itching and swelling. Soaking affected areas in cool water and applying cool compresses or calamine lotion may lessen itching. An oral antihistamine (often available without prescription) is the most effective treatment. If antihistamines do not relieve itching or if swelling is severe, a physician should be consulted.

If hives are widespread or affect a child's eyes, lips, and upper respiratory tract, an injection of epinephrine may be required to reduce swelling. If a child has frequent bouts of hives, a physician should be consulted to determine the underlying cause.

Aspirin may increase itching and is not recommended for treatment of hives.

PREVENTION

The best way to prevent hives is to avoid contact with or exposure to hive-inducing substances or situations. Foods and medications known to cause hives should be avoided. A child's sheets and clothes should be changed regularly if hives result from certain insect bites. Children susceptible to cold or solar hives should avoid exposure to strong sunlight or sudden changes in temperature. A sunscreen lotion or insect repellent can be used when a child is outdoors.

Hives caused by a disease cannot be prevented until the underlying condition is treated. Children who are prone to recurrent hives should keep diaries of events and situations that often precede an eruption in order to uncover possible causes.

HOARSENESS

EMERGENCY ACTION

Difficulty speaking can be a symptom of *epiglottitis,* a life-threatening condition that requires emergency action. If a child awakens at night and is drooling, feverish, or anxious, has difficulty breathing, refuses to drink, and suddenly appears very ill, he or she could be suffering from epiglottitis.

Hoarseness more often is a symptom of *croup,* which is rarely a life-threatening condition that requires emergency action. If a child experiences several of the following symptoms, he or she could be suffering from croup: difficulty breathing; very noisy breathing; breathing more than 40 times per minute; chest sinking in deeply while breathing; a frequent, harsh, barking cough; paleness or turning blue (especially around the lips or base of the nails); and uncontrollable restlessness and fear.

In either emergency situation, take the child immediately to the nearest hospital emergency room. Keep calm and try to keep the child as calm as possible. If epiglottitis is suspected, DO NOT USE A TONGUE DEPRESSOR OR IN ANY WAY TRY TO LOOK DOWN THE CHILD'S THROAT OR FORCE THE CHILD TO CHANGE HEAD POSITION; these actions could completely block the child's airway. In the car, open the window and keep the child near the cold air sitting upright; do not use the heater. Tell the child: "Breathe slowly and evenly."

DESCRIPTION

Hoarseness is a harsh and grating or rough and husky quality of the voice. It can develop among children of all ages, and may alter the voice in pitch, intensity, or both. Hoarseness is a common sign of any condition (such as upper respiratory tract infections) that causes the vocal cords to become inflamed, thereby interfering with normal vibration patterns.

Severe hoarseness tends to linger. Hoarseness caused by a cold, for example, may remain after other symptoms have disappeared. At times severe hoarseness leads to total but temporary loss of voice, such as in severe cases of *laryngitis.*

CAUSE

Hoarseness is usually caused by an infection of, or excessive strain on, the vocal cords. The most common cause in childhood is simple irritation from yelling or screaming. Very young children may become hoarse after prolonged or excessive crying. Among children under 5 years old, viral infections—such as *colds, laryngitis,* or *croup* —are the most common cause of hoarseness. School-age children also contract colds frequently and become hoarse as a result. Adolescents sometimes become hoarse from prolonged singing, especially if it is loud, too high-pitched, or too low-pitched. Around the time of puberty, boys whose voices are changing may sound hoarse.

Children of all ages may become hoarse from exposure to cigarette smoke, excessive dust, or irritant fumes. *Allergies* also cause hoarseness.

More rarely, hoarseness is caused by inhaled foreign objects or injuries of the larynx (voice box). Infants less than 3 months old may become hoarse because of birth defects of the larynx or serious adrenal or thyroid disorders, such as hypothyroidism (deficient thyroid hormone; see *thyroid problems). Polyps* in the throat can also cause hoarseness.

DIAGNOSIS

Hoarseness itself is quite evident. The underlying condition may be diagnosed by a physician or an otolaryngologist (ear, nose, and throat specialist). The physician performs a physical examination, and may look at a child's vocal cords using a small mirror if the child is old enough to cooperate or else may have to examine the vocal cords under anesthesia.

COMPLICATIONS

Frequent vocal abuse may lead to the formation of small, wartlike growths called screamer's nodes or singer's nodes on the vocal cords. These may result in long-term hoarseness.

TREATMENT

Resting the vocal cords is the best treatment for hoarseness. It may help for the child to drink warm liquids and sleep in a room with a cool-mist vaporizer. A warm washcloth or hot-water bottle applied to the neck may also speed recovery. If hoarseness persists for a week, grows worse by the day, or appears with a fever and sniffles, a child should see a physician.

PREVENTION

To prevent hoarseness, children should avoid excessive screaming or yelling. Children should not be exposed to tobacco smoke, excessive dust, or fumes. A cool mist vaporizer moistens air indoors, especially during the winter.

HYDROCEPHALUS

DESCRIPTION

Hydrocephalus is a condition characterized by abnormal accumulation of cerebrospinal fluid (CSF) within the cavities (ventricles) of an infant's brain, leading to enlargement of the head (see Figs. 33 and 34, p. 634).

The circulation of cerebrospinal fluid (a clear watery liquid that bathes and protects the brain and spinal cord) can be compared to the circulation of blood. A constant flow of CSF through the brain and around the spinal cord protects them from sudden pressure changes and helps nourish them. The amount of spinal fluid remains fairly constant but can accumulate in the brain when normal circulatory pathways are blocked.

Hydrocephalus may develop before birth, at birth, during infancy, or anytime during childhood. If it occurs before birth, at birth, or during early infancy, abnormal enlargement of the head occurs. The fetal or infant brain expands by pushing open the pliable bones of the skull and drastically increasing head size, thereby avoiding sudden increases in pressure within the skull. Among older children, however, when the bones of the skull have fused and the brain has no room to expand, hydrocephalus can lead to a dramatic increase in pressure within the skull, causing a child to vomit, become lethargic, and possibly go into a *coma*. Damage to the brain and spinal cord may also occur.

Surgical procedures have improved the outlook for children with hydrocephalus, and most children now survive past infancy. Many have normal intellectual abilities and are not disabled in any way. When brain or spinal cord damage has occurred, however, hydrocephalic children can be disabled in various ways. Some experience difficulties in understanding language while others suffer from problems including *mental retardation* and *cerebral palsy*. The outlook for these children depends upon the severity of these problems and the extent of damage to the brain or spinal cord.

CAUSE

Serious injury to an infant's head during delivery—most likely to happen to premature and firstborn infants—can lead to hemorrhaging, the primary cause of hydrocephalus among newborns. Hemorrhaging may block the cerebrospinal fluid pathway.

Hydrocephalus may also be caused by tumors in the brain (see *brain tumor)* that block the circulation or absorption of cerebrospinal fluid, or by any of a number of birth defects (such as *spina bifida)* or diseases (such as *meningitis).*

Spina bifida, an abnormal opening in the spine (which encases the spinal cord), is a major cause of hydrocephalus among infants. Abnormal formation of the spine often causes the lower brain to slide back into the spinal canal, blocking circulatory pathways of the cerebrospinal fluid.

Before or after birth, meningitis (an inflammation of the membranes covering the brain and spinal cord) can lead to a progressive thickening of the walls of cerebrospinal fluid pathways at the base of the brain, causing eventual blockage of fluid circulation. Meningitis is a frequent complication of spina bifida.

Rarely, hydrocephalus is a genetic disorder, transmitted to male children by their mothers (see *genetic disorders).*

SIGNS AND SYMPTOMS

Signs and symptoms of hydrocephalus de-pend on the age at onset and the severity of the imbalance between production and absorption of cerebrospinal fluid.

Hydrocephalus that occurs during prenatal development or infancy is always marked by abnormal enlargement of the head. In the most severe cases of prenatal hydrocephalus, massive enlargement of the head during the fetal period interferes with normal delivery of an affected infant. In milder cases an infant's head is normal size at birth but then grows at an excessive rate. The skull expands in all directions, especially in the forehead and front of the head. Scalp veins may be swollen and obvious and the scalp skin may be shiny and thin. An infant's cry may become high-pitched as pressure within the skull increases. In severe hydrocephalus, an infant's eyes focus downward (as the result of pressure) and a child's development may be delayed.

A delay in the closing of the fontanel (the soft spot on top of an infant's head) may indicate hydrocephalus. A fontanel that seems to be enlarging from month to month may be a sign of increased pressure within the skull.

If hydrocephalus first occurs late in childhood, no obvious enlargement of the head will exist. Instead, pressure within the skull will increase suddenly and dramatically. A child may periodically lose control of the sphincter muscle (which controls the bladder) or leg muscles. Mental activity may decline and judgment and reasoning be affected. Speech may become nonsensical.

DIAGNOSIS

A physician diagnoses hydrocephalus through CT (computed tomography) scans, which provide a cross-sectional image of the skull. This diagnostic test can detect an enlarged brain cavity and thinning and separation of the skull bones.

TREATMENT

Treatment of hydrocephalus usually involves surgical implantation of a shunt, a plastic tube that is used to bypass the obstruction. A shunt enables the fluid to drain from the brain into some other part of the body, such as the chest or the abdominal cavity. In this way pressure within the skull is decreased and further enlargement of the head is prevented.

Children who have had shunt implantations early in childhood may need one or more shunt revisions to accommodate growth spurts.

COMPLICATIONS

Many of the complications of hydrocephalus are related to shunt implantation. For example, the shunt may become infected. In addition to antibiotic treatment of the infection, shunt removal may be necessary.

Shunt tubing can become pinched, plugged, or separated, requiring replacement. A child's rapid physical growth may also necessitate replacement of a shunt. In addition, shunts may malfunction, causing dramatic increases in pressure within the skull, accompanied by *headache, vomiting,* and stupor, which, if untreated, could lead to *coma.* Long-term shunt failure may result in school failure, lethargy, and unsteady walking patterns.

PREVENTION

Hydrocephalus present at birth cannot yet be prevented. Maintaining normal circulation of cerebrospinal fluid and pressure within the skull with the use of surgically placed shunts may prevent further hydrocephalus.

HYPERACTIVITY AND ATTENTION PROBLEMS

DESCRIPTION

Virtually all children appear hyperactive at one time or another in the eyes of their parents. A small child who seems impatient during an adult social occasion may, for example, be considered hyperactive. The term "hyperactive" is most appropriately used, however, when a child's level of activity interferes significantly with home, school, and social life. A hyperactive child typically seems to be in constant motion, "getting into everything," and always full of energy.

Hyperactivity is often accompanied by attention problems, such as an inability to concentrate and by impulsiveness (a tendency to begin an activity without thinking about its merits or drawbacks). Other attention problems that tend to affect such children include excitability, restlessness (being "squirmy" or always "up and on the go"), a tendency to deny mistakes or blame others,

failure to finish things, "childishness" or "immaturity" (clinging to others, needing constant reassurance, and wanting help when it is not needed), distractibility, quick and drastic mood changes, and a tendency to become frustrated easily. An affected child may also have behavioral problems, such as frequent temper tantrums (see Chapter 3, "Promoting Mental Health").

Because those parts of the brain that control attention and filter out unwanted stimuli seem to be impaired, physicians call this syndrome attention-deficit disorder (ADD). About 5 percent of all children have ADD, and it is one of the behavioral problems most frequently brought to the attention of pediatricians. Boys are affected at least 4 times as often as girls. Although hyperactivity frequently accompanies ADD, it is not necessarily a part of the syndrome. Some children with ADD are not hyperactive, and those who are hyperactive often become less so as they get older.

Even when ADD is accompanied by hyperactivity, it is often difficult to identify the syndrome in a preschool child. Typically, however, signs of ADD are present in infancy. Babies with ADD are often slow to develop daily feeding and sleeping rhythms. They sometimes squirm away from parental attempts to hold and cuddle them.

Toddlers with ADD are more likely than other children to get into mischief and danger. Trips to stimulating places like supermarkets, for example, can turn into fiascoes. At home, toddlers with ADD tend to explore everything with insatiable curiosity, to demand constant attention, and to intrude physically and verbally into other peoples' interactions. They may have difficulty sitting still for meals, stories, or television programs. Their curiosity about everything overwhelms any fears of danger, and they are prone to damage household objects and injure themselves. Unless this behavior is severe, however, preschool children with ADD may be difficult to distinguish from other active children.

The distinction between children with ADD and other children typically becomes much more evident when an affected child enters school or is placed in groups or in situations that provide many distractions. Classroom situations require a level of self-control and self-discipline that children with ADD find extremely difficult to maintain. These children may find sitting still at a desk and finishing work—or even organizing it—

virtually impossible. Most children with ADD tend to be disruptive; they may call out in class, disobey instructions, and defy discipline. They may also be quick to anger, may pick fights, and may refuse to share or wait their turn.

Because an affected child's capacity to learn is interrupted, ADD is considered a learning problem (see *learning problems*). Children with ADD often perform at academic levels well below their ability. In addition, attention problems often precipitate behavioral problems, which contribute to learning difficulties as well as social problems. Children with ADD tend to be moody and given to temper tantrums. Because of their impulsive behavior, children with ADD frequently alienate themselves from their peers and fail to make friends. Peers may taunt children with ADD for their apparent clumsiness. Unsympathetic teachers may reprimand these children and aggravate their other social problems.

Children with ADD may complain to parents about problems with people at school, but they seldom associate social difficulties with their own behavior. Affected children may, however, develop an awareness of basic differences between their behavior and the conduct of people who do not have the syndrome. They may also experience *stress,* anxiety, *depression,* and other emotional problems because of other people's negative reactions to their behavior.

Some school-aged children with ADD also exhibit what medical experts refer to as "soft" neurological signs. These include difficulty standing on one foot without falling, distinguishing right from left, and moving fingers on one hand without imitating the motion with the other.

By adolescence most children with ADD become less overtly hyperactive, and other symptoms of ADD may become less obvious or disappear. In some cases, however, ADD is a lifelong condition; an affected person continues to experience difficulty with concentration and organization and to exhibit impulsivity.

While the behavior of school-aged children with ADD is remarkably similar from case to case, the severity of lingering symptoms in adulthood varies greatly and depends to some extent on treatment.

CAUSE

Hyperactivity can be associated with a long-term neurological problem such as *cerebral palsy* or *seizures.* Certain psychiatric disorders, such as anxiety, *depression,* or *psychosis,* can also be accompanied by hyperactivity. *Lead poisoning* and prenatal alcohol exposure (see *drug and alcohol abuse*) contribute to some cases of hyperactivity. In addition, certain drugs can temporarily produce hyperactive behavior. There has been much research on whether hyperactivity is sometimes caused by certain foods, by food additives such as artificial flavors and colors, and by aspirin and similar medications. It appears that a small percentage of children may experience hyperactivity because of food additives, but the results remain inconclusive.

The exact cause of attention-deficit disorder is unclear because little is yet known definitely about how the brain controls attention. Medical experts believe they have identified a brain mechanism, called the reticular activating system, that enables a person to screen out certain noises and sights at will. When a person decides to concentrate on something, chemicals may be released by the brain in the reticular activating system. For instance, this mechanism may help a person to speak and listen to someone in a crowd while blocking out other conversations. One theory is that people with ADD do not release enough of these chemicals. Another contributing factor to the problem among growing children may simply be the immaturity of frontal brain systems.

Heredity may play a role in some cases of ADD. Specialists believe that some parents pass along to their children a tendency toward slow maturation of certain parts of the brain—including the part that controls attention. Other major causes of ADD are thought to include improper fetal development, injury or deprivation of oxygen at birth, and other birth complications.

DIAGNOSIS

Although signs and symptoms are evident as early as infancy, most children with hyperactivity are not diagnosed until they begin school. Many teachers are trained or otherwise experienced in recognizing hyperactive behavior. A teacher may recommend that a child suspected of having the problem see a professional, in which case a physician —preferably one familiar with a child's medical history—should be consulted.

Physicians base a diagnosis of hyperactivity on a child's symptoms and medical history. No specific test exists to detect hyperactivity, although evidence of neurological immaturity, obtained from sophisticated neurological tests, may suggest ADD. Nonetheless, it is crucial for physicians to test for possible causes of hyperactivity. A physician can be expected to perform vision and hearing tests as well as psychological and physical examinations. The physician initially consulted may refer a child to a psychiatrist or neurologist for further tests or treatment.

Because a physician's office usually contains fewer distractions than a classroom, a hyperactive child may be fairly calm during the examination procedure. For this reason, parents should be prepared to report in detail their own and teachers' observations of a child's behavior. With parental consent, a physician may request intelligence test scores and other academic measurements from a child's teacher. It may also be helpful for a physician to speak directly with a teacher about a child's classroom behavior.

Historically, the label of hyperactivity has been incorrectly applied to any child who seemed "abnormally" active. Mistaken labels of hyperactivity have been applied to children who simply were too active for rigid or fussy teachers or parents. This mistake has caused problems for many children whose true maladies are *stress,* anxiety, other emotional disorders, or auditory-perception problems (see *language disorders).*

COMPLICATIONS

The most common complications affecting hyperactive children are psychological problems stemming from other peoples' reactions to their behavior. A child may develop anything from a poor self-image to periodic depression to severe friendship problems. In the absence of proper diagnosis and treatment, such complications are likely to develop.

TREATMENT

The goal of treatment is to minimize the ill effects of a child's hyperactivity and related problems by providing a small, structured, supportive environment that is conducive to improved attention. Ultimately, any approach should seek to motivate a hyperactive child to understand his or her behavior and thereby to undertake increasing responsibility for achieving greater success in social and learning situations. Any treatment plan should be administered with much love and understanding. Success should be measured

by how comfortable a child becomes and not by any arbitrary standards.

Treatment for hyperactivity or ADD may involve medication, behavior modification, family counseling, special education, psychotherapy, or special diets. The exact treatment approach used varies from child to child, but almost all children benefit from a tailor-made combination of several methods. Even if some symptoms disappear, treatment may be necessary throughout childhood.

Many children with ADD benefit from medication. Although it may seem to parents that an affected child needs tranquilizers, such drugs tend to aggravate a child's hyperactivity without improving behavior. The most effective drugs used by physicians in treating ADD are stimulants, notably amphetamines. Some people use stimulants illegally just to stay awake or lose weight; taken frequently for such reasons, these drugs may become addictive (see *drug and alcohol abuse).* Addiction among children with ADD, however, does not occur, nor do children taking stimulants for ADD experience a sense of euphoria or any other "high." The incidence of drug abuse in children with ADD has been documented as being no higher than the incidence for the general population.

About 80 percent of children with ADD respond to stimulant drug therapy. However, some children with ADD do not improve while taking stimulants, and certain emotional disorders may become worse with use of such drugs. For these reasons, stimulant drugs should always be prescribed and monitored by a physician. And although often enormously effective, medication should never be the sole method of treatment for children with ADD. The best way to encourage the progress initiated by drug therapy is to provide simultaneously a program that teaches a child how to deal with social and educational situations.

Certain children who improve only slightly with medication can receive additional help from a behavior modification program designed by medical and educational experts. Such a program begins by providing a child with a structured and supportive environment. Routine activities, such as eating, sleeping, bathing, and going to school, take place at the same time each day. Initially, a child is protected from overstimulating situations such as trips to crowded places and supermarkets. The goal of behavior modification eventually becomes teaching the child appropriate conduct for real-life situations.

Parental involvement throughout behavior modification is essential. The child always needs to be rewarded for even the simplest positive behavior, such as arriving on time for a meal. The best reward is an expression of happiness and love, although more tangible rewards are at times appropriate. A child's failure to follow rules should always be pointed out. Extremely negative behavior, such as temper tantrums, should be ignored; paying attention to such behavior or giving in to a child's unreasonable demands usually indicates to the child that desirable results can be produced by negative behavior. The best way to deal with such behavior is to construct a "time-out" period for calming down by removing the child from his or her immediate locale for a few minutes.

At the outset of any behavior modification program, expectations, rules, rewards, and reasonable punishments should be clearly explained to a child. Response to a child's behavior in any situation should always be consistent, immediate, and unmistakable. At the same time, the child should be well aware that he or she is not being punished for hyperactivity or attention problems per se and that the condition is *not* his or her fault.

Although behavior modification almost always results in improvement, it can be extremely taxing for a child's family. Family counseling may be necessary to provide understanding, support, and advice for other family members. In general, the better a family understands ADD, the faster the family and the child learn to adjust to the condition.

A special learning environment, part-time or full-time, is often helpful, at least at the outset, especially when a child's behavior is disruptive in standard classroom situations. Parents should be sure that the special education classroom is actually helpful and challenging, and not just a place to get rid of a difficult but intelligent child. Many special-education teachers are well trained in teaching children with hyperactivity and ADD. They look for improvements and setbacks in these children, and their assistance and reports can be invaluable to a physician monitoring drug and other therapy.

Sometimes treatment for hyperactivity and attention problems is accompanied by psychotherapy, which can be of great help in promoting a child's self-image and confidence. Ultimately, psychotherapy often aids a child in exercising better self-control.

PREVENTION

Some cases of hyperactivity and ADD may not be preventable. However, reduction of environmental lead, control of alcohol intake by mothers during pregnancy, and improvements in prenatal care and birth (delivery) procedures may well prevent many cases.

HYPERTENSION

DESCRIPTION

Blood pressure is expressed as a term of two numbers: the systolic pressure followed by the diastolic pressure, as in 120/80 (read "120 over 80"). Systolic pressure is the pressure existing in the large arteries of the body when the heart contracts and pumps blood forcefully into the arteries. Diastolic pressure is the pressure existing in the large arteries when the heart is at rest and, momentarily, blood is not being pumped into the arteries. Of the two, diastolic pressure may be considered the more significant because a high resting pressure means that the heart muscle and arterial walls are constantly under excessive stress.

Normal blood pressure varies with age, height, and weight and is affected by a variety of physical, chemical, emotional, environmental, and unknown factors. Blood pressure usually rises with age; the amount of increase is the critical factor.

"Hypertension" is the medical term for high blood pressure. If arterial blood pressure (the force exerted against blood vessel walls by the circulating blood) is above normal for age, then hypertension exists. Hypertension may be said to occur in two general circumstances: when the heart must pump too large a volume of blood through normal blood vessels, or when the heart pumps a normal volume of blood through vessels which, for a variety of reasons, have grown inelastic or are too narrow, even partially blocked.

Hypertension may exist as a disease in itself (called either primary or essential hypertension) or may be caused by a variety of underlying diseases (secondary hypertension). Secondary hypertension is more common than primary hypertension among young children. As children near their tenth birthday, primary hypertension becomes more common. Although hypertension can occur at any age, it is not a common disease among children. Exactly how many children are affected by it is difficult to estimate, since some cases probably go undiagnosed.

When caused by an underlying disease or abnormality, secondary hypertension may go away when the underlying problem resolves or is successfully treated. Primary hypertension, however, is a disease in itself or, perhaps, as some physicians believe, a number of closely related diseases. It must be treated as a chronic (lifelong) problem. Secondary hypertension becomes chronic only in those cases where the underlying cause has no known cure.

Primary hypertension is a progressive (increasingly damaging) condition in which noticeable signs and symptoms may be almost totally absent. For children with secondary hypertension, however, the underlying problem may produce obvious signs and symptoms, even if the hypertension itself is not particularly noticeable. Should signs and symptoms of hypertension become evident, damage to specific organs or systems may be quite far advanced.

If primary or secondary hypertension is diagnosed promptly and treated systematically and successfully, most children can look forward to near-normal lives. Even primary hypertension, a lifelong problem, can usually be controlled effectively and relatively simply.

CAUSE

By definition, the origin of primary hypertension is unknown.

In childhood, about 80 percent of secondary hypertension is related to some kind of kidney problem, either an anatomic or functional irregularity. Many of these irregularities are congenital (present at birth). Other common causes include the narrowing of blood vessels leading to one or both kidneys and narrowing of the aorta, largest artery in the body—a condition called coarctation of the aorta. Problems of the endocrine system (see *thyroid problems* and *adrenal problems*) also lead to secondary hypertension among young children, as do systemic diseases such as *lupus erythematosus*. Malignancies, such

as *Wilms' tumor* and *neuroblastoma*, can cause secondary hypertension by producing hormones which elevate blood pressure by compressing blood vessels leading to the kidneys. Usually brief problems, such as overdose with poisons or medications, also can cause hypertension.

Among the most common miscellaneous causes are *burns* and severe injuries (traumas) to bones and muscles. Some children who are overweight may experience hypertension.

DIAGNOSIS

Hypertension is usually discovered by a physician during a routine examination or, less often, during an investigation of another illness. If the child is being checked routinely for the first time, the physician is likely to ask about any family history of hypertension. If another illness is being investigated, the physician asks for details of the signs and symptoms. In either situation, the obtaining of preliminary information is followed by a careful physical examination.

Weight and height are measured, as are the vital signs. Weight measurements are important because a certain number of overweight children are predisposed to hypertension as they grow older, and a young child who is overweight may be on the threshold of difficulty. The proportional relationship of weight to height is crucial in deciding whether a child or adolescent is overweight: appropriate weight for a child's height is checked. Whenever hypertension is found to exist, a physician may need to evaluate the relative importance of excessive weight (see *weight problems*).

The standard method of detecting hypertension is by taking a careful blood pressure reading. A child's physical examination from the age of 6 on almost always includes such a reading (unless there is reason for it, a physician seldom checks it earlier). Secondary hypertension among younger children is sometimes signaled by a particular illness or medical problem known to cause or be associated with hypertension.

If hypertension is suspected, a child's blood pressure is measured on each arm and one leg, and then while the child is standing, sitting, and lying down. Such care is exercised to determine if variations exist from limb to limb and to try to reduce any possible temporary increase in blood pressure caused by a child's anxiety during blood pressure readings.

Blood pressure is usually measured with a blood pressure cuff, a rectangular cloth which encloses an inflatable rubber bladder. The cuff encircles an arm or leg, and a stethoscope or other device that detects sounds is placed on top of a large artery at the surface of the skin. When the bladder is inflated with air, the cuff stops blood flow in the artery and no sound can be heard. As air is released from the bladder, pressure in the cuff begins to fall. When pressure falls below that of the systolic phase of the individual's blood pressure, blood resumes flowing in the artery and the sound is picked up by the stethoscope. At that moment the examiner notes the systolic pressure on the pressure gauge; seconds later, when all sound of blood flow ceases, the diastolic pressure is noted.

Hypertension is determined by checking the measured pressure against a chart of normal pressures for age and sex. Because children's blood pressures within the normal range vary, "normal blood pressures" for growing children are not included here.

A series of increasingly specific tests is usually performed in an effort to diagnose an underlying cause of hypertension. Evaluation for hypertension is usually phased—that is, not all tests are needed immediately for an individual. Diagnostic tests are designed to rule out kidney problems, blood vessel abnormalities, and endocrine system (glandular) problems as possible underlying causes. When those more common possibilities have been eliminated, tests for rare causes of secondary hypertension are considered and tested for.

A blood test, urinalysis, and urine culture are usually performed first. A chest X ray and an electrocardiogram (EKG), a painless electronic examination of heart muscle function, often follow. The timing and ordering of subsequent tests depends upon what information is obtained from the preliminary ones.

An intravenous pyelogram (IVP) may help to determine the structure and function of the urinary tract (kidneys, urine-carrying tubes called ureters, bladder, and urethra). A harmless contrast dye is injected intravenously, and X rays are taken as the dye passes through the structures of the urinary tract.

Other diagnostic studies include nuclear medicine scans of the kidneys and ultrasound examinations of the abdomen to visualize kidneys and areas where adrenal glands are located. Nuclear medicine scans, more sensitive and specific than an IVP, are performed by injecting a small amount of harmless radioactive material into a vein and then monitoring the amount of radioactivity absorbed by an organ or system. Ultrasound bounces sound waves off of internal body structures and a monitor then reveals images of the internal organs.

If any of these tests gives evidence of a disease or abnormality known to produce hypertension, additional tests may be necessary to identify the exact cause. Specialized X-ray examinations are often helpful. In a hospital, arteriograms of kidneys may be ordered so that blood supply to the kidneys can be checked. After injecting contrast dye, a radiologist can visualize the condition of the arteries leading to and within the kidneys; X rays can also be taken. (A radiologist is a physician who specializes in the diagnosis of disease using X rays and other imaging techniques.) Blood samples from the veins leading from the kidneys may be obtained at the same time as the arteriogram. These may be useful in determining the presence of excessive quantities of certain enzymes in the blood. Such excesses can trigger chemical reactions which produce hypertension.

A CT (computed tomography) scan can provide highly detailed X rays of extremely small segments of the kidneys or adrenal glands. Such studies can reveal the presence of abdominal masses and other abnormalities.

COMPLICATIONS

Any child who is diagnosed as being hypertensive (having hypertension) needs to be checked regularly by a physician, who monitors possible development of any serious related disorders, such as heart, nervous system, eye, or kidney problems. It is now believed that even mild, or "borderline," hypertension during childhood may have serious consequences for health later on. Regular blood pressure checks afford a simple, reliable indicator for anyone with hypertension.

TREATMENT

For secondary hypertension, treatment varies according to the underlying cause. Medical management, surgery, or both may be necessary, depending upon the cause and severity of hypertension and a child's general health.

Treatment for primary hypertension depends upon the severity of the condition. Some children with mild primary hypertension can control the problem with diet (including reduction of salt intake), weight reduction (if necessary), regular exercise, and biofeedback and relaxation techniques.

If diet, weight reduction, exercise, and behavior modification do not bring blood pressure within the normal range, a child may have to take one or a combination of special antihypertensive medications.

Most children with primary or secondary hypertension respond well to appropriate treatment. For some children, depending upon its cause, secondary hypertension may be a short-term problem. Primary hypertension must be understood and managed as a lifetime condition whose characteristics and requirements for treatment change as a child grows and matures.

PREVENTION

Primary hypertension cannot usually be prevented. Many physicians believe, however, that excluding large amounts of salt from children's diets may reduce the severity of primary hypertension, or even prevent it from developing.

In certain cases, if underlying causes of secondary hypertension are correctable, hypertension can be averted or cured.

HYPOGLYCEMIA

DESCRIPTION

Hypoglycemia is a condition in which the blood contains an abnormally low concentration of sugar (glucose). A child with hypoglycemia reacts by becoming hungry, irritable, sweaty, confused, and—if an episode is unchecked—unconscious. In extreme cases a child may have a *seizure*.

Anyone can develop hypoglycemia under certain conditions. Hypoglycemic reactions characteristically occur among children, however, when their food intake has decreased or their diet is inadequate (e.g., lacking sufficient carbohydrates), often in association with excitement or tension, minor illnesses like *colds*, excessive activity, or an indifferent appetite.

Any prolonged period without food (called a fast) can trigger a hypoglycemic re-

action; spells most often occur, however, before a child eats breakfast, thus ending the longest daily period without food. Most episodes of symptomatic hypoglycemia among children occur in this fasting state; as a result, this type of hypoglycemia is called fasting hypoglycemia.

Infections may contribute to hypoglycemia because they lead to *vomiting* and/or loss of appetite. Repeated vomiting or, in extreme cases, starvation or voluntary fasting may also trigger hypoglycemia.

Many misconceptions exist regarding hypoglycemia, and a diagnosis is sometimes made without proper confirmation. Diverse nonspecific complaints may be attributed incorrectly to a "low blood sugar level."

To understand hypoglycemia it is necessary to understand the role of sugar in the body and how it is regulated. The brain is the major user of blood sugar; it requires a constant and sufficient supply to function properly. As a result, the brain is the first organ to be affected by diminished blood sugar. In addition to acting as nourishment for the brain, blood sugar acts as fuel, providing heat as well as energy required for the body's movement, cell functions, and cell growth.

Normally a constant supply of sugar enters the circulating blood. Sugar is provided to the body initially by the food we eat. If, several hours after a good meal, a normal person has eaten nothing more or has eaten foods that have little nutritional value (such as diet drinks and foods), the body has to depend solely on the release of sugar that has been stored (as glycogen) in the liver in order to maintain a constant supply of blood sugar to body tissues. With an even longer fast, glucose must be made in the liver from other body sources, such as muscle and fat. If the body's need for sugar is greater than the amount of sugar that can be made by conversion of other tissues, fasting hypoglycemia develops.

Blood sugar levels are regulated in two ways. First, the insulin is secreted by the pancreas at increased levels when glucose from food enters the bloodstream. Insulin enhances metabolism of blood sugar by the body. (Metabolism is the chemical and physical breakdown of sugars and fats, mainly within the liver.) Insulin thus decreases the amount of sugar in the blood and increases the storage of sugar in the liver. If too much insulin is produced by the body, or is injected into the body (for instance, when a child has diabetes), the blood-sugar level falls and the typical symptoms of hypoglycemia result. The counterregulatory hormones (glucagon, epinephrine, cortisol, and growth hormone) increase the release of glucose from the liver and mobilize other substances (amino acids, glycerol) from muscle and fat for conversion in the liver to glucose and thus keep blood sugar from decreasing to levels that produce hypoglycemic symptoms.

A low blood sugar level is caused by a prolonged fast more often among children than among adults because their rates of glucose use are greater. Normally, during childhood, sugar stored in the liver becomes depleted after a few hours without food and children become dependent on conversion from body muscle and fat. When this supply cannot keep up with their need—which for some young children occurs in as little as 8 to 12 hours—hypoglycemia develops. In adults, blood sugar can be made from other sources rapidly enough to permit very long periods of fasting without the development of hypoglycemia.

Fasting Hypoglycemia

Typically, fasting hypoglycemia occurs among small, thin children who are indifferent eaters but quite active and between the ages of 18 months and 6 years. Boys are affected 2½ times as often as girls. This form of fasting hypoglycemia is sometimes called intermittent hypoglycemia. Children with a tendency to develop intermittent hypoglycemia typically do so only when they do not eat at regular intervals (e.g., when they skip breakfast, thus prolonging the nighttime fast). The problem is aggravated sometimes by the fact that special diets prescribed to promote weight gain cause these children to become more indifferent to food and thus to reduce their intake and become more susceptible to hypoglycemia. Intermittent hypoglycemia can usually be anticipated and prevented, and when it occurs, it is correctable. Fortunately, by the time children with intermittent hypoglycemia are 6 to 8 years of age, they can make sufficient glucose with fasting to meet their needs so they no longer develop fasting hypoglycemia. Usually there are no long-term complications.

Reactive Hypoglycemia

A second type of hypoglycemic reaction is reactive hypoglycemia, which is not common in childhood. It occurs when the body's blood sugar regulating system overreacts. After a person eats a meal high in carbohydrates, a large amount of sugar flows through the digestive tract and is absorbed into the bloodstream. Subsequently a large dose of insulin is released, followed (approximately 2 to 4 hours after the meal) by a drop in blood sugar to a level below normal. The severity of reactive hypoglycemia depends upon the rate of fall in blood sugar.

Fasting hypoglycemia develops more slowly than reactive hypoglycemia. In addition, fasting hypoglycemia continues until food containing sugar is eaten or until an underlying disease is controlled or cured. An episode of reactive hypoglycemia is much less likely to be prolonged, although episodes may occur regularly.

CAUSE

Reactive hypoglycemia, not common in childhood, is caused by the body's overreaction to large amounts of carbohydrates.

The most common form of hypoglycemia during childhood is transient symptomatic hypoglycemia, which affects newborns who are small for their gestational age. Newborn infants in certain other high-risk categories are also susceptible to hypoglycemia. Included are infants of diabetic mothers (who tend to produce excessive amounts of insulin), premature and dysmature infants, and the smaller of some sets of twins (see *prematurity*). All of these infants have limited stores of sugar in the liver.

Many conditions that occur among newborn infants are associated with hypoglycemia, including *asphyxia* during birth, *respiratory distress syndrome,* cyanotic *congenital heart disease* (see *heart disease, congenital*), and the disease caused by Rh incompatibility (see *Rh and ABO incompatibility*). Others include blood poisoning (see *bloodstream infection*), brain hemorrhaging, drug withdrawal (see *drug and alcohol abuse*), and low body temperature (hypothermia). Infants of toxemic mothers and those infants who suffer placental abnormalities are also susceptible, as are those infants who were malnourished before birth. Malnutrition of a fetus reduces stores of sugar in the liver, and hypoglycemia follows if these babies are not fed promptly after birth.

From 10 to 15 percent of newborns with hypoglycemia experience recurrent hypoglycemia later in infancy whenever they go too long without being fed (see *diabetes*).

Fasting hypoglycemia occurs more readily among infants and children who have underlying diseases that interfere with the release of stored sugars or that disturb the production of hormones that regulate blood sugar levels. These diseases include acquired or inherited enzyme deficiencies (liver disease), serious hormonal deficiencies (e.g., cortisol or growth hormone), *malabsorption* syndromes, tumors or other disorders of the pancreas, and *PKU* or other inherited metabolic problems. Previous stomach surgery may also be a factor in the development of hypoglycemia.

Children with *diabetes* are more likely than other children to develop hypoglycemia because they receive daily (often twice daily) injections of insulin.

A small child may develop hypoglycemia from accidentally drinking alcohol, since alcohol interferes with the ability of the liver to provide a constant supply of sugar. Such accidental drinking of alcohol is a problem more prevalent among small children than commonly realized. Alcoholism among teenagers may also cause fasting hypoglycemia.

SIGNS AND SYMPTOMS

Symptoms of hypoglycemia may include paleness, sweating, rapid heartbeat (palpitations), shakiness, dizziness or *fainting,* weakness, tiredness, extreme hunger, anxiety, or nervousness. Because the brain is the first organ to be affected by diminished blood sugar, people who develop fasting hypoglycemia begin to show signs of effects upon the brain, such as trembling, *headache, vomiting* (occasionally), weakness, irritability, "lightheadedness," drowsiness, and speech and visual disturbances. These symptoms may be followed by confusion, unusual behavior, and ultimately, *seizures* and hypoglycemic coma (see *diabetes).*

Between episodes of hypoglycemia, affected children are healthy.

Newborns with hypoglycemia may have no symptoms or may exhibit any of the following: jitteriness, *seizures, apnea,* rapid breathing, weak or high-pitched cry, limpness, unresponsiveness, excessive drowsiness, irritability, feeding difficulty, eye rolling, sweating, paleness, or low body temperature. Low birthweight infants usually have symptoms; apnea is especially common.

DIAGNOSIS

Early diagnosis of hypoglycemia is important so that treatment may begin promptly to restore a normal level of glucose in the blood. Until a normal blood sugar level is restored, a risk exists of damage to the brain.

Hypoglycemia is diagnosed by finding a low blood sugar level. A physician asks about a child's eating habits, particularly those of the days when hypoglycemic reactions have occurred. Family and individual medical histories are taken and a physical examination is performed.

When hypoglycemic reactions occur, a physician looks for a cause requiring specific treatment (such as alteration in diet). The cause of hypoglycemia is defined by appropriate laboratory tests that evaluate liver and hormonal functions. These tests are best done in medical centers where there are physicians specializing in defining the cause of hypoglycemia.

COMPLICATIONS

If hypoglycemia is severe, prolonged, or frequent and uncorrected, it can be associated with significant brain damage. Seizures or hypoglycemic *coma*—the most serious complications of fasting hypoglycemia—can then occur. Both can be followed by serious, permanent brain damage. (Results of brain damage include *mental retardation, learning disabilities,* behavioral problems, failure of muscular coordination, or *seizures.)*

TREATMENT

Treatment of hypoglycemia depends on its cause. Fasting hypoglycemia can usually be controlled by avoiding periods of fasting that are not tolerated and by treating the cause if it is due to a specific disease.

If a hypoglycemic reaction is serious (for instance, if the child becomes unconscious), an intravenous infusion or injection of glucose is often necessary. For some medical emergencies, parents can inject glucagon, available by prescription, to raise the blood sugar level.

All high-risk newborns should have their blood sugar levels monitored repeatedly before feeding until it is clear that, on their feeding schedule, blood sugar levels are normal. These infants should be fed frequently. Hypoglycemia in infants can be corrected with an intravenous sugar solution if the condition is identified early.

An infant whose pancreas produces excess insulin may require surgery of the pancreas.

PREVENTION

To prevent episodes of fasting hypoglycemia, parents should pay careful attention to their children's eating habits and not allow prolonged periods without eating to occur. Teenagers should be discouraged from attempting to lose weight through fad diets, which can prove dangerous. Very thin children, children with indifferent appetites, and very active children should be permitted to eat frequently. When a susceptible child is ill and *vomiting* occurs, medical attention should be sought if the child is unable to retain clear liquids with sugar in them.

Children should not have access to alcohol, including rubbing alcohol and leftover party drinks.

See also *diabetes.*

IMMUNE DISORDERS

DESCRIPTION, CAUSE, AND SIGNS AND SYMPTOMS

The immune system is the body's defense against invading infectious organisms, including bacteria, viruses, fungi, and parasites. It is made up of four components: cell-mediated immunity, antibody-mediated immunity, the phagocytic system, and the complement system.

Cell-mediated immunity is created by special infection-fighting white blood cells called T-lymphocytes. These cells work in the blood and body tissues to prevent autoimmune disease, a condition in which the body's immune system attacks its own tissue. They also activate antibody-mediated immunity.

Antibody-mediated immunity is created by another type of infection-fighting white blood cell called B-lymphocytes. These cells produce antibodies (proteins called immunoglobulins) that fight infectious agents; they work in plasma (the clear fluid portion of blood), body secretions, and the fluids between cells.

The phagocytic system consists of special cells called macrophages and polys (special white blood cells) that live in tissue and blood and ingest and kill infectious microorganisms.

The fourth component, the complement system, is made up of special proteins that work with the other immune components to maintain the body's resistance to infection.

Each time an infectious agent enters the body, the immune system responds by creating organism-specific antibodies. Even after the infectious agent is destroyed, these antibodies remain in the body and prevent future infection by the same organism. Each time a new infectious organism enters the body, the immune system creates new antibodies; as a result, immunity increases. By adulthood, individuals have built up a large supply of antibodies and a high level of immunity.

Most of the time childhood infections are no cause for alarm; the combination of medication, rest, fluids, and the body's immune system usually eliminates infectious agents successfully. Occasionally, however, a young child has a disorder of the immune system, and the frequency and severity of infection increases greatly. One or more areas of the immune system may be involved; the child's susceptibility to infection is determined by the severity of the immune disorder. Most immune-system disorders are inherited, and symptoms appear very early in an infant's life. Life-threatening complications frequently develop.

Disorders of the immune system are usually inherited (see *genetic disorders)* and include *Wiskott-Aldrich syndrome,* in which cell-mediated immunity and certain antibodies are missing; SCID *(severe combined immunodeficiency disease),* in which both antibody- and cell-mediated immunity are missing; *agammaglobulinemia,* in which gamma globulin, the protein needed to make antibodies in the blood, is completely absent; absent or abnormal thymus, an organ of the immune system located at the base of the neck; incomplete synthesis of antibodies; and *transient* or *permanent hypogammaglobulinemia,* in which levels of gamma globulin are low. Certain other diseases, such as *lupus erythematosus,* in which antibodies attack the body's connective tissues, apparently stem from abnormal functioning of the immune system. See AIDS, p. 158, for details on that immune disorder.

Transient hypogammaglobulinemia, which contributes to frequent infections, is a delay in an infant's ability to produce immunoglobulin (IgG), a protein substance that helps the body fight common infections. The problem can become evident when the baby is about 6 months old and persist until the child is 3 or 4 years old.

In addition to immune-system disorders, children may suffer diseases that impair immune-system functioning. These diseases include tumors, such as *leukemia,* granuloma, and *lymphoma;* disorders of red and white blood cells, including aplastic anemia and neutropenia (see *anemia* and *anemia, aplastic),* and severe *malnutrition.* In addition, immunosuppressive medications (given to prevent adverse immune responses) or frequent exposure to radiation may impair the immune system's ability to function properly.

Depending on the severity of an immune deficiency, affected children are susceptible to bacterial, viral, fungal, and parasitic infections. Severe viral infections include *oral herpes, genital herpes, chicken pox, colds, hepatitis, measles, mumps, mononucleosis,* and viral *encephalitis.* Bacterial infections include bacterial pneumonia and bacterial *meningitis.* Fungal infections include *thrush* and *ringworm;* common parasitic infections include toxoplasmosis and pneumocystis (see *pets, diseases caused by),* trichinosis and worm infestations (see *parasitic infections).* In addition to decreasing a child's defenses against infection, a problem of the immune system may allow infectious agents that are normally confined to one area to spread extensively throughout a child's body. For example, the fungus causing ringworm usually stays on the scalp of children with healthy immune systems, but may spread to other areas of the skin when affecting a child with an immune deficiency.

A child with an immune deficiency may respond adversely to "live" vaccines—those that work by exposing the child to tiny numbers of infectious agents. Live vaccines include those against polio, measles, mumps, rubella, and smallpox. Instead of prompting the body to build up protective immunity against a particular disease, a live vaccine causes the child with an immune deficiency to develop the disease—usually in a severe form. The vaccines for *diphtheria, tetanus,* and *whooping cough* are not live and do not cause infections among children with immune deficiencies.

Children with immune disorders usually are constantly ill, pale, and irritable. Affected children usually have many common problems simultaneously. Such problems include *eczema, vitiligo, rash, conjunctivitis,* persistent draining of fluid from the ears, and *diarrhea.* Less common problems include growth failure (see *pituitary problems),* and *osteomyelitis.* Spleen, lymph node, and liver enlargement, common signs of infection, usually occur. Occasionally, partial *albinism* and increased heart rate are present. If infection spreads, nervous system complications may develop.

In addition to the above problems a child with an immune deficiency has signs and symptoms characteristic of the specific infections present. Because the immune system is not working properly, however, infections may produce uncharacteristic symptoms. Skin sores characteristic of viral herpes or chicken pox often develop uncharacteristically with bacterial infections. Infections often develop in areas not usually affected, such as the nail beds, the mouth, the liver, or the bones.

DIAGNOSIS

Childhood infections are obvious to parents. However, parents may suspect more than a normal childhood illness if their child suffers many or severe infections during the first 6 months of life, has recurrent or long-term infections, has no periods of good health between infections, never recovers fully from an infection even with treatment, or develops unexpected complications from a mild infection.

A physician bases diagnosis of an immune deficiency on signs and symptoms of infection, the child's medical history, and the results of a complete physical examination. Blood samples are analyzed to determine the numbers of T- and B-lymphocytes and immunoglobulins, as well as to identify infectious organisms. Mucus and stool are also examined for possible infectious organisms. X rays may be taken to detect underlying complications. Medical histories of family members may be helpful in making a diagnosis.

TREATMENT

If an immune disorder is present, treatment of infections is rarely (or only temporarily) successful unless the immune disorder is corrected or disappears on its own.

Treatment for transient hypogammaglobulinemia is usually unnecessary. Parents are simply assured that their child will outgrow the disorder. A physician can prescribe antibiotics if a child has a bacterial infection, and some children with severe problems resulting from transient hypogammaglobulinemia may be given injections of IgG from time to time.

Effective treatment of SCID and Wiskott-Aldrich syndrome can be accomplished only through a bone marrow transplant; the donor is usually a brother or sister with a matching marrow type. A child with a severe immunodeficiency often is isolated in a sterile hospital environment until the transplant can take place.

PREVENTION

Immune disorders cannot be prevented.

IMPERFORATE (OR ABSENT) ANUS

DESCRIPTION

Imperforate anus, also called absent anus, is a defect of the lower end of the large intestine (colon). Present at birth, an absent anus refers to the lack of an external rectal opening. It occurs about once in every 5,000 live births and must be corrected surgically. It appears in several forms, and those affected may have other malformations, especially in the urinary tract.

CAUSE

There is no known cause for imperforate anus, an abnormality in fetal development.

SIGNS AND SYMPTOMS

If a newborn has no bowel movements during the first 48 hours of life, it must be assumed that some type of *intestinal obstruction* exists. The problem may be either absence of an anus or a blockage at a higher level in the intestinal tract.

DIAGNOSIS

A physician or nurse usually identifies a baby born with an imperforate anus. If by chance the abnormality should go unnoticed initially, the lack of bowel movements calls attention to it. Narrowing of the anus or rectum or similar anatomical abnormalities can be detected by careful physical examination and the taking of X-ray films, if necessary.

TREATMENT

Imperforate anus occurs with varying degrees of severity. The abnormality can almost always be corrected surgically. The operation varies according to the specific abnormality, its complexity, its location, and the general physical condition of the infant.

Most, but not all, affected children develop acceptable bowel control, but this capability can take several years to accomplish.

PREVENTION

Imperforate anus at present cannot be prevented.

IMPETIGO

DESCRIPTION

Impetigo is a highly contagious skin infection usually caused by streptococcus (strep) bacteria, often occurring after a minor cut or insect bite has been scratched and becomes infected. Staphyloccocus (staph) bacteria may also cause impetigo, usually related to excessive humidity and a powerful strain of the bacterium.

Small children, because they play together, have more open cuts, and tend to get dirtier than adults, most often develop and spread impetigo. The infection sometimes occurs in epidemic outbreaks in camps, schools, and other places where children gather. Impetigo is prevalent in unsanitary and very warm conditions, but any child can develop it.

Although uncomfortable, impetigo is usually not a serious medical problem. With prompt and effective treatment a child can be cured of the infection in a week. There is no immunity to the infection, and it can recur if a child is reexposed to the infectious organisms.

CAUSE

Both strep and staph bacteria are found throughout the environment, including the air, water, feces, and soil. Most people can carry and spread the bacteria without becoming ill, but impetigo is usually spread by individuals who have visible signs of infection. Open cuts or sores, such as infected mosquito bites, offer a favorable environment for the bacteria to enter and multiply.

Impetigo   455

If a child scratches the first outbreak of sores, the bacteria are easily spread to other parts of the body.

The infection may be transmitted from one child to another through direct contact with the infected sores or contact with anything touched by the sores, including bicycles, the edges of swimming pools, toys, towels, bedsheets, and clothing.

SIGNS AND SYMPTOMS

Two to five days after a child has come in contact with the sores of infectious impetigo, small red bumps will break out on the skin, possibly resembling a cluster of insect bites or a scrape. The bumps rapidly form clear or pus-filled blisters which soon break, leaving round, oozing, honey-colored encrusted sores or dry erosions. Pus may ooze from the sides of the crusts that are attached at the center. Mild itching may occur.

Characteristic sores of impetigo may first appear on the face, especially near the nostrils and mouth, where small children often put their hands. Sores may also appear on the hands, arms, legs, and buttocks.

DIAGNOSIS

Impetigo is easily diagnosed by observation of its rapidly spreading crusty sores. A physician must be certain, however, that the sores are not caused by another childhood infection such as *chicken pox* or herpes simplex (see *oral herpes)*.

COMPLICATIONS

In rare cases, streptococcal impetigo can lead to glomerulonephritis, a severe kidney disease (see *nephritis)*. Streptococcal impetigo may lend a "scalded skin" appearance to the whole skin surface.

TREATMENT

If there are only a few sores, and there is no known epidemic, impetigo may be treated at home. The sores should be soaked with water to soften the crusts, then gently scrubbed with deodorant soap and water. The crusts must be entirely washed off the skin and the infected area washed 3 or 4 times a day. Antibiotic ointment should be applied to the area where the crusts have been removed and the whole area covered with gauze. An affected child should be told that impetigo spreads, and warned to wash the hands often, not to touch the infection, and to use only his or her own comb, hairbrush, washcloth, and towel.

If home treatment procedures are carefully followed, impetigo can be cleared up in a week. If sores do not show improvement within 4 to 5 days or seem to be spreading, a physician should be consulted. A physician should also be consulted if a newborn is infected. When impetigo is spreading, a physician may prescribe oral antibiotics.

PREVENTION

To prevent the spread of impetigo, an infected child should be kept home from school until the sores are no longer blistering, oozing, or crusting. Routine washing with deodorant soap and water is the best protection. While uncleanliness does not cause impetigo, washing will reduce the number and strength of potentially infectious bacteria on the skin. The child should be advised of the importance of cleanliness, including handwashing, and of the hazard of sharing combs, towels, and hairbrushes.

INFECTIONS, FREQUENT

DESCRIPTION AND CAUSE

The immune system is the body's defense against invading infectious organisms, including bacteria, viruses, fungi, and parasites. Each time an infectious agent enters the body, the immune system responds by creating organism-specific antibodies, special proteins that fight infectious agents. Antibodies work in the plasma (the clear, fluid portion of the blood), body secretions, and the fluids between cells. Even after an infectious agent is destroyed, these antibodies remain in the body and prevent future infection by the same organism.

Unlike adults, children have not been exposed to many infectious agents; as a result, their supply of antibodies and level of immunity are low, and they develop infections frequently. Because more than one type of infectious agent can cause the same type of infection, children may develop the same infection repeatedly. For example, about 200 different viruses each cause the common cold. (see *colds)*. *Influenza* and ear infections (see *earache and ear infections)* are also common during childhood.

SIGNS AND SYMPTOMS

Signs and symptoms vary according to the

particular infection. *Fever, headache,* runny nose, *sore throat,* listlessness, and loss of appetite are characteristic of many common childhood infectious diseases. See individual entries for specific information.

DIAGNOSIS

It may be fairly obvious to parents on the basis of a child's signs and symptoms that their child is ill with an infectious disease. However, if a parent is uncertain about whether to consult a physician regarding a child's illness, it is helpful to read first about degrees of severity in *fever, sore throat, headache,* and other symptom entries (such as *rash,* for example).

A physician should be consulted promptly

- if a parent is uncertain about the nature of the underlying problem,
- if a child fails to respond to the kinds of supportive treatment described below, or
- if the same type of illness seems to recur (see *immune disorders*).

TREATMENT

Most of the time, childhood infections are not cause for alarm. A combination of medication, rest, plenty of fluids, and the body's immune system usually eliminates infectious agents successfully. Since treatment of childhood infections varies, a physician's recommendations are needed in each case.

For more information about providing supportive care and comfort for children ill with common infectious diseases, see Chapter 7, "Caring for the Sick Child at Home."

PREVENTION

Many common childhood infectious diseases can be prevented by means of childhood immunizations. (See Chapter 6, "Going to the Doctor," for details and schedules of required and suggested immunizations.)

Childhood infections are always difficult to prevent, as infectious agents can rarely be detected or avoided. Whenever possible, children should avoid contact with an individual known to have an infection. Good hygiene, particularly after using the bathroom, playing outdoors, or handling pets, and before eating or preparing meals, helps reduce the risk of infection. For specific recommendations see the prevention sections of the various infectious-disease entries.

INFLUENZA

EMERGENCY ACTION

When a young child develops a high fever caused by influenza, a convulsion may occur. During a convulsion it is important to make certain that a child is lying down (preferably on the floor), breathing freely, and not in danger of injury from striking furniture or fixed objects. Consult a physician whenever a convulsion occurs, regardless of how brief the episode or how completely well a child may appear afterward (see *fever; seizures).*

If a child who is ill with influenza (or has recovered within the previous week) develops a stiff neck, extreme sleepiness or listlessness, and nausea or *vomiting,* consult a physician immediately. *Encephalitis* (brain inflammation) may come on suddenly and progress swiftly. Full recovery can depend upon prompt diagnosis and treatment. Some strains of influenza also cause *croup* during childhood.

DESCRIPTION

Influenza, or flu, is a highly contagious viral infection of the respiratory tract (nose, throat, and airways). The respiratory symptoms are accompanied by fever and often by pain in the head, eyes, and muscles. Small children often have symptoms in the gastrointestinal tract (esophagus, stomach, and intestines) as well.

A once deadly disease, influenza appears as two major types, A and B. Over time the viruses causing both types mutate (change slightly). As a result, an individual who once had type A influenza—and presumably acquired immunity as a result—may contract it again years later because the type A virus has changed slightly.

Both types of influenza most often affect children 5 to 14 years old; during an epidemic, between one quarter and one half the children in that age range without immunity are likely to contract the disease.

Severe type A influenza epidemics strike approximately every 10 to 15 years, while milder ones occur about once every 2 to 3 years. Type B epidemics occur approximately once every 4 to 7 years. In urban areas there is a substantial risk of an annual outbreak of some type of influenza. Widespread influenza illness almost always occurs in fall and winter.

"Flu" can refer to almost any illness characterized by *fever*, chills, *headache, cough, sore throat,* and muscle aches and pains; this combination of signs and symptoms accompanies many viruses, not exclusively the influenza virus. Large epidemics are characteristic of influenza, and adults as well as children usually become ill during such outbreaks.

One to three days after exposure to an influenza virus, a child without immunity begins to feel ill. Someone who has flu is most infectious from 1 day before to 1 day after the beginning of symptoms. The disease may last from 3 days in mild cases to as long as 2 weeks in severe ones.

Complications such as *pneumonia* can lengthen recovery time significantly. Children who suffer from long-term diseases often recover from influenza more slowly and are vulnerable to both relapse and complications. All children should recover fully from signs and symptoms before resuming normal activities.

CAUSE

A group of related viruses causes influenza; these viruses produce disease that is essentially identical in its effects. All types of influenza are highly contagious, especially because the virus is transmitted easily by direct person-to-person contact, often in droplets of mucus produced by coughing or sneezing. Clothing, bedding, personal possessions, and household articles contaminated by mucus droplets can also probably spread the virus.

SIGNS AND SYMPTOMS

Although all types of influenza virus produce similar illness, signs and symptoms of illness can vary somewhat according to a child's age. Children 5 years old and younger first usually have a sudden fever (102° to 105° F; 38.8° to 40.6° C) and many signs and symptoms of a common cold: runny nose, *cough, sore throat,* swollen glands, and loss of appetite (see *colds).* Earache, (see *earache and ear infections), vomiting,* and *diarrhea* commonly mark the illness during early childhood, but infrequently later on. Convulsions as a result of high fever may strike younger children without warning but usually have no aftereffects. Children 6 months to 5 years old may develop *croup.*

Older children and adolescents with influenza usually complain of chills or a cold sensation all over; *fever* (101° to 103° F; 38.3° to 39.4° C); sore throat; cough; *headache;* red, watery eyes; runny nose; and muscle aches and pains. Somewhat less often *dizziness,* eye pain, vomiting, swollen glands, and wheezing or raspy breathing occur. Coughing and sneezing do not seem to be as bothersome as fever, chills, headache, and red, watery, and painful eyes. Older children often tend to be overwhelmed by sickness because overall impact on the body is severe.

DIAGNOSIS

Influenza is usually diagnosed by a physician's examination of a child's signs and symptoms. If influenza is widespread in the community at the time of a child's illness, a physician usually does not order confirming tests. In fact, so common are signs, symptoms, and effects of influenza virus that in many cases health professionals are able to diagnose the illness and prescribe home treatment over the phone. Should a child's condition become worse, it is, of course, highly advisable that a physical examination be made. Laboratory cultures of secretions taken from a child's nose and throat can identify the influenza infection and isolate the specific virus, if necessary.

COMPLICATIONS

Occasionally severe cases of influenza lead to *encephalitis* and related nerve disorders. Several painful and potentially dangerous respiratory infections, including *pneumonia,* bronchitis, *bronchiolitis,* and *croup,* may arise if *sore throat* persists.

Rarely, very young children with influenza develop inflammation of the heart (see *cardiomyopathy)* or suffer *sudden infant death syndrome. Reye's syndrome,* a rare, severe disease affecting the liver and brain, may occur as a complication of influenza.

TREATMENT

Barring complications, influenza is usually treated at home. Severe cases may require hospitalization. Since influenza is a viral infection, antibiotics are not effective. Some antibiotics, however, may be necessary to combat bacterial infections such as *pneumonia,* which can develop after influenza has weakened a child. Certain antiviral medications may be prescribed for fighting infection caused by influenza A.

Bed rest helps conserve energy and prevent possible complications such as breathing and heart problems. As a child regains strength, physical activities should be resumed slowly to guard against relapses. It is important that a child get adequate nutrition, especially plenty of fluids.

Acetaminophen may be helpful in reducing fever and muscle aches and pains. Aspirin, however, should never be given to any child with influenza because of a possible connection between its use and the development of *Reye's syndrome* in the aftermath of influenza. (See discussion of medications and home care in Chapter 7, "Caring for the Sick Child at Home.") Children with chronic or immune-deficiency diseases often recuperate much more slowly than other children.

PREVENTION

Vaccination can be highly effective if the vaccine given matches the particular influenza virus being transmitted at any given time. Influenza vaccine, however, is usually given as a preventive measure only to infants and children with long-term diseases such as heart, lung, and kidney disorders. Healthy children do not ordinarily need influenza vaccine. During a particularly severe influenza outbreak, antiviral medications, prescribed by a physician, may also prevent illness if given before exposure to an influenza virus. In case of an anticipated epidemic, local public health officials may recommend vaccination of all young and school-age children.

INGROWN TOENAILS

DESCRIPTION, SIGNS AND SYMPTOMS, AND COMPLICATIONS

When a toenail becomes embedded in the surrounding skin, it is ingrown. This most often occurs on the big toe of an older child, but can occur among people of all ages.

An ingrown toenail develops when the upper corner of a toenail, or less frequently, both upper corners, grows into the skin surrounding the nail. As the nail becomes embedded, affected skin often hardens like callus tissue. If the problem is uncorrected, the entire side of the nail may become embedded as the nail continues to grow outward.

As a nail becomes ingrown, the toe becomes increasingly tender and infection usually develops. The toe may throb and be tender to the touch. It becomes red and inflamed, and a crust of dried pus may form on the skin surface. Pus may also form underneath the toenail, increasing discomfort. If infection is severe, it may spread from the toenail to the rest of the toe and into the foot. The toe turns red, and red streaks extend into the foot.

With proper treatment, toenails usually return to a normal growth pattern.

CAUSE

Ingrown toenails are usually caused by external pressure or stress on the toe that causes the nail to curve in at the edges. The structure of the foot, how the foot works while walking, and the effects of shoes upon the feet greatly influence development of an ingrown toenail. For example, a child with *flat feet* or high arches is more prone to developing an ingrown toenail than a child with normal feet. Shoes that do not fit properly aggravate an ingrown toenail by putting pressure on it and pushing it into the skin.

Improper nail clipping can also lead to an ingrown toenail. Nails that have sharp corners tend to grow into the surrounding skin and can become deeply embedded. Infants lying on their stomachs may dig their toes into surfaces such as soft crib mattresses, causing swelling of the skin surrounding the toenail and a resulting ingrown toenail.

Ingrown toenails may become chronic if they are not treated promptly and effectively when symptoms arise.

DIAGNOSIS

Characteristic redness and swelling around the nail indicate an ingrown nail.

TREATMENT

If an ingrown toenail can be trimmed easily, its edges should be rounded off. However, attempting to trim a deeply ingrown nail often does more harm than good. Generally it is not recommended to soak an affected toe, but it can be bathed repeatedly for 5 to 10 minutes in warm salt water, usually 1 tablespoon of table salt to 2 quarts of lukewarm water. Ointments should not be applied to the toe; if it is infected, the toe can be dressed with an iodine preparation and a sterile gauze dressing. A physician should be consulted.

An ingrown toenail that has caused severe infection may need to be removed. This usually involves surgical removal of the ingrown portion of the nail and some of the skin in which the nail is embedded. Once the infection has healed, the nail should grow back normally. Nail removal is also recommended if the area around an ingrown toenail repeatedly becomes infected despite preventive measures.

If foot structure contributes to development of an ingrown toenail, a child can be fitted for arch supports or custom-made orthotics (shoe inserts), prescribed by an orthopedist (a bone specialist).

PREVENTION

Wearing shoes that fit comfortably and have enough room for the toes will help reduce the chances of developing an ingrown toenail. Nails should be kept well trimmed or filed with slightly rounded edges.

INTESTINAL OBSTRUCTION

EMERGENCY ACTION

Total or partial intestinal obstruction is almost always an emergency. If any of the following extreme conditions exists, immediately notify a physician:

- severe pain, constant or recurring, anywhere in the abdomen from the bottom of the breastbone down to the groin
- severe stomachache (see *stomachache, stomach pain)* or nausea, with or without vomiting, which lasts two hours or longer
- absence of bowel movements for about 48 hours which affects any infant who seems irritable, lacks appetite, and normally has bowel movements daily or more often
- unexplained, persistent *vomiting,* usually associated with *abdominal pain* (vomit often contains bile in the form of green or yellow material)

Do not feed a child when any of these conditions exists; limit drinks to sips of water; avoid giving any medication, especially laxatives or sedatives.

DESCRIPTION

Intestinal obstruction is a blockage, either total or partial, that occurs at one or more points in the small or large intestine. Obstruction can occur at any age, although particular types are more common at one age than another, just as certain types affect one sex more frequently than the other.

Intestinal obstruction makes it difficult or impossible for solids and liquids to pass through the site of blockage. Bacteria in partially digested food multiply behind a blockage, threatening infection. It may be impossible for any gas or partially digested food to pass through an obstructed area and then along the usual route toward elimination.

Blood supply to an obstructed portion of intestine can be slowed, reduced, or blocked because of excessive swelling of a loop of bowel immediately above the obstruction. Obstructions almost never disappear without medical or surgical treatment.

Intestinal obstruction may cause cramping around the area of the obstruction. Sometimes, however, a child complains of a general stomachache (see *stomachache, stomach pain)* that "hurts all over." Pain may be continual or it may recur at regular or irregular intervals. Pain may be stabbing or steady, perhaps characterized by a burning or tearing sensation. Cramps may occur in waves, accompanied by nausea. *Vomiting* may occur suddenly or after a period of nausea. The vomit may resemble that from any minor stomach upset or it may be especially foul-smelling, dark-colored, and bad-tasting because of contamination by bacteria or fecal matter backing up through the intestine.

A portion of the abdomen near the obstruction may become especially tender, swollen, or bloated, making the abdomen even more sore and painful to examine. Fever sometimes occurs, especially if infection is present or if intestinal tissue is beginning to die because of reduced blood supply.

Medical or surgical treatment must be given promptly in order to relieve the obstruction and to prevent complications. Newborns and infants may experience complications rapidly, making more urgent the need for prompt, accurate diagnosis and treatment. Intestinal obstruction is fatal if it is not treated. If treated improperly, it can cause complications and unpredictable aftereffects. If treated correctly, a full, prompt recovery can be expected.

CAUSE

Intestinal obstruction has many causes; it may be congenital (present at birth) or acquired.

Congenital Causes

About one third of all congenital cases of

intestinal obstruction involve either <u>atresia</u> (complete blockage) or <u>stenosis</u> (partial blockage) at one or more locations in the intestinal tract (small and large intestines). In three quarters of all cases of intestinal atresia or stenosis, the obstruction lies in the small intestine, either just below the stomach in the duodenum or in the longest portion called the ileum.

The congenital causes are presented here in descending anatomical order, beginning at the upper end of the gastrointestinal tract (see Fig. 30, p. 437). *Pyloric stenosis* is the most common form of partial obstruction. The pylorus, the muscular valve located at the bottom of the stomach, becomes thickened and narrowed, making it difficult or impossible for food to be released into the intestinal tract for further digestion. Another congenital problem which appears early in life is <u>malrotation:</u> a portion of the intestines does not develop normally in the fetus. After birth, this abnormality may cause blockage in the upper small intestine. Occasionally the normal configuration of the intestinal tract in the abdomen becomes twisted or unbalanced.

Congenital duplication of a small portion of the intestines can also cause obstruction. Duplication occurs when an abnormal sac or tube which has branched off from the intestine during prenatal development becomes enlarged and blocks the passageway inside an adjoining loop of normal intestine. *Intussusception,* in which a section of intestine telescopes into an adjoining one, may cause obstruction. This occurs most often among children under 2 years old. Another one third of all congenital obstructions results from *Hirschsprung's disease,* ballooning of a portion of the large intestine caused by a nerve defect. <u>Hernia,</u> in which a loop of intestine bulges into the scrotum or labia, commonly causes pain and, rarely, obstruction (see *hernia, inguinal and umbilical).*

Acquired Causes

Acquired causes of intestinal obstruction are varied and often as unexpected as those that are congenital. Among children over 2 years old, the most common cause of acquired intestinal obstruction is <u>adhesions</u> resulting from previous surgery. (Adhesions are slender bands of fibrous tissue around which a loop of intestine can wrap itself.) <u>Peritonitis</u> (an inflammation in the abdominal cavity) can cause the intestines to function abnormally, yielding symptoms similar to those produced by a mechanical blockage.

Swallowed objects on very rare occasions pass through the esophagus and stomach only to become lodged in the narrow passageways of the intestines, causing partial or total obstruction. Some children habitually swallow their own hair or that of dolls, stuffed animals, or brushes; others pull fibers from blankets or clothing. On rare occasions a hairball accumulates in the stomach which can result in partial obstruction or marked bloating of the upper end of the small intestine.

DIAGNOSIS

Diagnosis of intestinal obstruction is made by a physician, who observes signs and symptoms, obtains a full history of the condition, and performs a careful examination. X-ray films are taken to confirm the diagnosis and, often, to locate the site of obstruction. A blood test may be necessary to identify possible infection.

COMPLICATIONS

Any obstruction which makes a child vomit and unable to eat or drink leads to *dehydration* (a condition characterized by cool, dry, pale skin; dry tongue; thirst; listlessness; rapid heartbeat; sunken eyes; and for an infant, sunken fontanel, the soft spot on top of the head). Children, especially infants, can be given intravenous fluids swiftly and effectively to replace lost fluids and essential body salts.

TREATMENT

Obstruction, both partial and total, from all causes, can usually be treated successfully if diagnosis is accurate and prompt. Surgery is necessary in most cases; the severity of the problem and the general health and strength of the child are carefully considered before surgery is elected as treatment. Surgical procedures vary according to the specific cause and location of obstruction. Recovery from successful surgery is usually rapid and complete, provided that neither extensive loss of intestine nor serious infection has occurred. (See entries on specific conditions mentioned under Cause, above, for descriptions of treatment.)

PREVENTION

Intestinal obstruction cannot be prevented. Severe complications can sometimes be avoided, however, by consulting a physician promptly whenever a child has severe abdominal distress, bloating, or nausea and/or *vomiting* lasting 2 hours or longer.

INTUSSUSCEPTION

DESCRIPTION

Intussusception is a condition in which a portion of intestine telescopes into an adjoining portion and becomes stuck. This problem occurs most commonly where the ileum (end of the small intestine; see Fig. 30, p. 437) joins the colon (beginning of the large intestine). The ileum, smaller in diameter, pushes up a short way into the colon and remains there. This bottleneck pinches the blood vessels of the colon, first reducing, then stopping, the blood flow (and therefore the oxygen supply) in that portion of the intestine. If the telescoping effect cannot be reduced (pushed back) by prompt hospital treatment, in a few hours the portion of intestine deprived of oxygen may develop gangrene, a serious problem. Gangrene can lead to a *bloodstream infection.* Pain, bloating, *vomiting,* and bloody stools often signal the presence of an intussusception.

Intestinal obstruction in children less than 2 years old is caused most often by intussusception. Its greatest frequency occurs between 4 and 12 months of age; 6-month-old infants seem to be affected most frequently. Males suffer from this condition more often than females by a 3 to 2 ratio. The typical individual with intussusception is a healthy, well-nourished 6-month-old with no history of abdominal distress. Hospital treatment is necessary, requiring from 2 to 7 days. Nearly all children recover without experiencing aftereffects.

CAUSE

A definite cause is identified in fewer than 10 percent of intussusception cases. Of the 10 percent, the most common cause is *Meckel's diverticulum,* a condition in which an abnormal outpouching of the small intestine becomes twisted and causes an obstruction. Less common causes include intestinal *polyps,* small abnormal tissue growths inside a loop of intestine; duplication, an extra, nonfunctional segment of intestine which is caused by a congenital (present at birth) abnormality; and a cancerous intestinal tumor

usually a result of *lymphoma,* a disease of the lymphatic system.

Any of these abnormalities can form a small lump, or "leading point," somewhere in the intestine. The leading point, for unknown reasons, starts the telescoping action into an adjoining segment of intestine. Some physicians believe that a viral infection may inflame lymph nodes located in the small intestine, causing them to become enlarged and serve as leading points for intussusception. Intussusception is not inherited nor does it result from a genetic abnormality.

SIGNS AND SYMPTOMS

A child who suffers from intussusception most often awakens from sleep with sharp *abdominal pain.* Unable to find comfort lying down or sitting up, the child cries, is restless, looks pale and sweaty, and may vomit. After this attack, which lasts about 5 to 10 minutes, the child usually falls back to sleep only to awaken soon with another attack. As the series of attacks progresses, the abdomen becomes swollen.

Vomiting may recur, followed by a bowel movement that contains dark or bright red blood, usually with mucus and clots (resembling currant jelly). Sometimes an abdominal mass or lump can be felt between attacks. *Fever* may develop. The child should be taken to a physician or emergency room immediately.

DIAGNOSIS

A physician carefully examines a child after recording details of the illness. An X-ray film of the intestine can reveal the exact location and extent of intussusception. A solution of barium sulfate is given by enema; the solution fills the colon and illuminates it for X-ray examination. A radiologist (a specialist in diagnosing disease by means of interpreting X-ray films and other visualizing techniques) uses a fluoroscope (an X-ray machine) to visualize the colon and to take films. This technique can locate an intussusception.

COMPLICATIONS

If intussusception is not reduced promptly, gangrene and perforation (a tiny puncture) of the colon can occur in a few hours. Unless corrected immediately, these problems can be life-threatening.

TREATMENT

In the hospital a barium enema used in diagnosis of the condition can also be used to push back the telescoped segment of intestine in about 85 percent of all cases. As the barium solution slowly fills the large and then the small intestine, the telescoped segment may be pushed back into normal position. When a radiologist sees on the fluoroscope screen that a telescoped segment is filled and no longer trapped, the enema is stopped and the barium solution allowed to flow out of the intestine through the rectum.

An X-ray film is taken to confirm that the intussusception is actually relieved. The problem can recur; such recurrence after a barium reduction develops about one in 20 cases. About 60 percent of children suffering from intussusception require no further treatment, and after 2 or 3 days they can be released from the hospital.

Although a barium enema is usually tried first, 2 out of 5 children with intussusception do not respond to this technique. Such children must undergo surgery. During surgery, once the intussusception is located in the abdomen, a surgeon can try manually to reduce the telescoped intestine by exerting gentle pressure. Such maneuvers usually succeed quickly. If they are not successful, the surgeon performs a resection, a procedure in which the trapped segment is cut out and the uninvolved, healthy ends of intestine are sewn together. In rare cases a child suffers recurrences of intussusception and requires treatment again.

PREVENTION

Intussusception cannot be prevented.

JAUNDICE

DESCRIPTION

Jaundice is a common symptom of abnormal functioning of the liver, and is characterized by yellow discoloration of the skin and whites of the eyes. Jaundice may occur at any age, but the newborn period is the most common time for children to be jaundiced. Approximately 15 percent of newborns have jaundice that requires treatment.

Jaundice is the result of excess bilirubin in the blood. Bilirubin is a yellow pigment that is a waste product of red blood cells. When red blood cells break down and are replaced by new ones, bilirubin is formed. Normally, the liver rapidly removes bilirubin from the blood, metabolizes it, and excretes it in bile. When the liver is immature, as in the newborn period, or is not functioning properly in older children, bilirubin accumulates in the bloodstream and stains the body fluids and tissues, including the mucous membranes (the membranes lining certain body cavities and canals). The child looks "jaundiced," or yellowish. This type of jaundice is a symptom of underlying disease.

Far more commonly, newborns develop a basically harmless and transient form of jaundice known as physiologic jaundice. Approximately 60 percent of all newborns, and 80 percent of premature infants, develop this form of jaundice 2 or 3 days after birth. The condition develops because a newborn baby does not need as many red blood cells in the blood as were necessary before birth. As a result, the extra red blood cells are broken down, forming excess bilirubin so that the infant may appear jaundiced. This harmless form of jaundice lasts only until the fifth to tenth day after birth. If jaundice appears during the first 24 to 36 hours after birth, with a high and rapidly rising bilirubin level, or persists beyond 8 to 10 days, the jaundice is probably a sign of underlying disease in the liver or in red blood cells.

Premature infants (see *prematurity),* because of immature livers, are more susceptible to jaundice and its more severe complications than are full-term infants. In a premature infant the liver and its enzymes, which are needed for excretion of bilirubin, are still underdeveloped; thus the excretion of bilirubin is delayed. Additionally, jaundice in premature infants may last longer and be more severe, especially in those infants who weigh the least.

In older children jaundice does not disappear until the underlying disease improves. In general, the duration and severity of jaundice and the outlook for a baby or child with the problem depend upon the cause.

CAUSE

Many diseases and conditions cause jaundice in the newborn infant. Excessive breakdown of red blood cells can lead to jaundice; a major cause used to be erythroblastosis, a serious blood disease caused by Rh incompatibility. Jaundice may also be caused by ABO incompatibility, when a mother with type O blood forms antibodies against her baby's type A or B blood. (See *Rh and ABO incompatibility.*)

Other causes of jaundice caused by rapid breakdown of red blood cells include some types of anemia, such as *sickle cell anemia, thalassemia,* and *hereditary spherocytosis.* Rarely, severe infections—including *typhoid fever, German measles,* cytomegalovirus, toxoplasmosis, congenital *syphilis,* and neonatal herpes simplex—cause blood poisoning (see *bloodstream infection),* damage the liver, or break down red blood cells, thereby causing jaundice. Jaundice caused by the inefficient excretion of bilirubin is associated with immaturity of the liver in premature infants (see *prematurity).*

Jaundice associated with obstruction of the flow of bile can be caused by any closure or narrowing of the bile ducts. Such conditions as gallstones (rare among infants) and infectious *hepatitis* (the most common cause of jaundice among children over 1 month of age) can block the flow of bile. When a child has *biliary atresia,* the bile ducts are defective. Any gastrointestinal obstruction, including *pyloric stenosis,* can obstruct the flow of bile.

Conditions that interfere with liver function can cause or increase jaundice in children. Such conditions include hypothyroidism and, rarely, *malnutrition* and *cystic fibrosis.* Among teenagers, *drug and alcohol abuse* or addiction can lead to infectious hepatitis, and alcoholism can cause cirrhosis of the liver. Rare metabolic disorders such as tyrosinemia and galactosemia also frequently cause jaundice in affected children.

SIGNS AND SYMPTOMS

In older children signs and symptoms of jaundice depend on the cause, but may include loss of appetite, a bitter taste in the mouth, belching, *constipation,* lethargy, *dehydration,* yellow tears, and sometimes itching, especially at night. The child may experience tenderness in the upper right portion of the abdomen (where the liver is located). The urine is discolored (dark orange, dark brown, or brownish yellow to brownish green, depending on the cause). The stools appear putty-colored, sometimes grayish white, when bile flow is blocked.

When bilirubin is not broken down, the resulting jaundice causes the skin to appear bright yellow or orange. When the bilirubin is broken down, but the bile ducts are obstructed, the skin appears muddy or greenish yellow. This difference is usually apparent only in severe jaundice.

DIAGNOSIS

Jaundice may be suspected by parents or a physician if a child's skin and whites of the eyes appear yellowish, even in natural lighting. A physician performs blood tests to check the level of bilirubin, and takes urine and stool specimens. In the newborn, if known causes of serious jaundice are excluded and the bilirubin level is not high, the infant probably has transient jaundice.

COMPLICATIONS

A substance in mother's milk may occasionally (though very rarely) cause a newborn baby's liver to work too hard. When this happens, the baby's normal case of transient jaundice may be prolonged by breastfeeding.

In premature infants especially, a high level of bilirubin in the bloodstream can cause bilirubin to be deposited in brain cells, a condition called kernicterus. Kernicterus may lead to severe permanent brain damage (and to such conditions as *cerebral palsy* or *deafness).* Kernicterus is rare now because erythroblastosis from Rh incompatibility is largely preventable, and high levels of bilirubin are treatable.

TREATMENT

No treatment is usually necessary for transient physiologic jaundice. If a baby has jaundice and suffers from poor nursing, excessive drowsiness, and *fever,* parents should consult a physician immediately.

Medical treatment for true jaundice varies, according to the underlying cause and the symptoms evident. Exchange transfusions are used for jaundice if bilirubin levels are markedly elevated, regardless of the cause. If exchange transfusions are performed, functioning of the heart and lungs, body temperature control, and acid-base balance must be monitored.

In phototherapy (light therapy) the baby is placed under a special white or blue fluorescent lamp. The light rays break down the bilirubin in tissues so that the liver can remove it, process it, and dispose of it in the bile. Side effects of light therapy may include *diarrhea, dehydration,* overheating, skin rashes, and a change in the skin's pigment. The change in pigmentation is not permanent, although it may last for several months. Jaundice related to infections requires that the specific infections be treated —with antibiotics, for example. Infants with underdeveloped livers (and without Rh incompatibility) may benefit from light therapy, thereby avoiding the need for exchange transfusions.

Narrowing or closure of the bile ducts requires surgical correction; in some cases of biliary atresia, liver transplantation may be attempted. No specific treatment exists for infectious *hepatitis* except supportive care (rest, proper medical supervision, and correct diet).

If a case of transient jaundice seems to be prolonged by breastfeeding, it may be necessary for a mother to cease breastfeeding for a number of days until the baby's liver matures and is able to break down bilirubin more efficiently.

Symptoms of jaundice that increase the risk of brain damage among newborns—especially premature ones—also need to be treated. In addition, symptoms such as *headache* and stomach problems may be relieved temporarily by medication, vitamin K, and a lowfat diet. Itching may be relieved with warm baths, lotions, antihistamines, and bile salts.

PREVENTION

Jaundice cannot often be prevented unless its underlying causes are prevented. Early treatment—light therapy—of an infant who is at high risk for developing kernicterus can prevent this serious complication.

JOINT PAIN

A joint is the flexible part of a limb, where two bones meet. Bones are held in place by ligaments (strong ropes of tissue) and are moved by muscles and tendons (which attach muscle to bone). Pain in any of these parts is regarded as joint pain.

Children of all ages may experience joint pain for a variety of reasons. It can result from a child's natural growth and development (see *growing pains),* and may be accompanied by stiffness and reduced motion. Pain may result from *sprains,* strains, *fractures,* or dislocation, or from such sports-

aggravated conditions as Osgood-Schlatter disease (see *knee injuries).* Mildly injured (twisted or overstretched) muscles, tendons, or ligaments retain much of their elasticity and ability to function and usually require only rest to heal. More severely damaged tissue may be partially or completely torn and may require surgery for full recovery.

Joint pain may also be caused by *arthritis* (inflammation of cartilage, tendons, and ligaments), muscle inflammation (myositis), bacterial infection of the bones (see *arthritis, acute; osteomyelitis),* and rarely, tumors (see *bone cancer).* With proper treatment most causes of joint pain heal or disappear without complications. See also *dislocation of joints.*

JUVENILE RHEUMATOID ARTHRITIS

DESCRIPTION

Arthritis is inflammation in one or more joints or in their tendons and ligaments (connective tissues). Signs of inflammation include swelling of the joint, limitation of motion, heat, pain, and redness. Arthritis can occur in over 100 different conditions, including infections and blood disorders. (See also *arthritis, acute.*)

Chronic arthritis is arthritis that persists for at least 6 weeks. The most common form of chronic childhood arthritis is juvenile rheumatoid arthritis (JRA), but there are as many as 50 less common forms, including those associated with systemic *lupus erythematosus* (inflammatory disease of joints, skin, and internal organs) and juvenile ankylosing spondylitis (inflammatory arthritis of the spine).

About 200,000 children in the United States under the age of 16 suffer from one of the three main forms of JRA. While the peak incidence occurs between 2 and 5 years of age, it can begin during the first year of life up until the age of 16. Approximately 2½ times as many girls as boys develop JRA.

The knees, wrists, ankles, and elbows are the joints most frequently affected early in the disease, but any joint may be affected, including the toes, fingers, jaw, and Achilles tendon. Depending on the particular form of JRA present, other organs and systems may be involved, including the eyes, skin, and heart. Although untreated JRA can become progressively disabling, modern management—combining careful medical supervision, the use of medication, physical therapy, and occasionally surgery—can give the majority of children a relatively normal life. Nonetheless, even with the best of therapy, not all symptoms can be controlled, and the disease may become more active without warning.

JRA includes three distinct subgroups, which are identified according to characteristic signs and symptoms. These forms are systemic (involving the entire system), polyarticular ("many joints," involving five or more joints), and pauciarticular ("few joints," involving fewer than five joints).

(1) JRA was once generally referred to as Still's disease, in honor of the physician who first clearly described it in 1896. The term "Still's disease" is now used to refer to the systemic form of JRA, which affects about 20 percent of all children with arthritis. Often the most difficult form to diagnose, systemic JRA may begin with a *fever* or *rash,* and enlargement of the liver, spleen, and lymph nodes. Many months may pass before inflammation and arthritis of a joint occurs, even though associated muscular and skeletal aches and pains are present.

(2) The polyarticular form of JRA affects 35 percent of children with arthritis and often involves the small joints in the hands and feet as well as ankles, knees, and hips. Involvement of the joints is usually symmetrical, so that if a joint on the left side of the body is affected, the corresponding joint on the right side is also affected.

(3) Pauciarticular JRA affects 45 percent of children with JRA. Onset is frequently gradual: a knee or ankle swells initially and is only noticed by the parents when a child begins to limp. Especially among younger children, joint pain is rarely present. Uveitis (persistent inflammation of the uvea, the iris and surrounding tissue with its network of tiny blood vessels in the middle of the eye) may also develop and can threaten vision if not treated adequately. Children with uveitis generally need to be seen by an opthalmologist (an eye specialist) at regular intervals to check that there is no eye inflammation. This inflammation can often occur without symptoms and not be associated with redness or other obvious sign.

In many cases of JRA the disease goes into spontaneous and sustained remission (inactivity) after months or years of activity, in some cases symptoms flare up from time to time, and in a minority of cases the child suffers persistent, long-term JRA.

CAUSE

Although the cause of chronic childhood arthritis is unknown, many factors may be involved, including developmental changes; agents of infection; *stress,* both physical and emotional; change of climate, weather, or season; genetic predisposition; and changes of diet or eating patterns.

SIGNS AND SYMPTOMS

The sequence of pain, stiffness, warmth, redness, swelling, and finally some loss of function in one or more joints is typical of arthritis. Limited motion of an affected joint may be caused by muscle spasms and accumulation of fluid around the particular joint. In the systemic variety of JRA, generalized illness, including *fever, rash,* listlessness, and loss of appetite, precedes joint involvement by as much as six months.

If JRA progresses unchecked, weakening and destruction of the joint can occur, severely limiting freedom and ease of movement. When such destruction involves the ankle and foot, a child often develops a waddling, flat-footed walk. Limping and shuffling occur when knees and hips become inflamed and swollen. A variety of other symptoms may accompany joint involvement.

Fever is frequently present, either low-grade and persistent or high and spiking, reaching peaks once or twice daily above 102° F (38.8° C). A pale red or pink, usually nonitching rash is often made more noticeable by fever. Lymph nodes, liver, and spleen may become enlarged. Loss of appetite and weight can sometimes occur.

DIAGNOSIS

JRA is diagnosed on the basis of a careful history and physical examination by a physician who notes the signs and symptoms, especially the degree of any joint involvement lasting at least 6 weeks in a child under 16 years old. A physician may order X-ray films of the affected joints. Sometimes a definite diagnosis is postponed until other known causes of arthritislike signs and symptoms have been eliminated as possibilities.

Even with tests, diagnosis of JRA may not be possible until a child has been observed carefully for a period of time and tests to exclude other diseases have been performed.

COMPLICATIONS

Slowing of a child's overall growth (or failure to grow altogether) is perhaps the greatest long-term danger of JRA. The most frequent complication is restriction or loss of joint function, either temporarily or permanently. Abnormal bone growth often accompanies these joint problems. Permanent or recurrent impairment of vision, caused by chronic uveitis, may occasionally occur in JRA.

A rare complication of JRA in North America is amyloidosis, a biochemical imbalance which leads, in turn, to either *nephrosis,* a kidney disease, or to chronic internal bleeding. Other potentially severe complications are liver disease, pleuritis, (inflammation of the lining of the lungs), and pericarditis (inflammation of the heart) caused by arthritis itself and by the anti-inflammatory medications used in its treatment.

TREATMENT

Because no cure exists as yet for JRA, treatment is geared toward preserving and, if possible, improving joint function and easing pain. Sufficient rest is essential. Carefully coordinated exercise, physical therapy, and diet can strengthen arthritic children and allow them to lead their lives as normally as possible.

All children who suffer from JRA should have a regular physical-therapy program designed to meet the varying activity of their disease. A regular program of exercise to maintain muscle strength and a full range of motion around inflamed joints is important in trying to avoid long-term side effects from inflammation of a joint. Failure to maintain adequately the range of movement in a joint can lead to muscle contractions and severe limitation of movements. If diagnosed early and treated vigorously with physical therapy and occasionally with splints to wear at night, these contractions are reversible. If they have persisted for a long period of time, surgical correction may be required.

Medication for treatment of JRA is intended to reduce inflammation and lessen the severity of disease. Aspirin is used most often, in dosages prescribed by a physician according to each patient's specific needs. Even if taken for years, aspirin is not addictive, although in large dosages it may affect liver function and irritate the stomach. For children who have severe JRA, stronger anti-inflammatory medications may be prescribed, including synthetic hormonelike medications called corticosteroids. Although corticosteroids are effective in reducing inflammation, long-term side effects (such as causing bones to become brittle) may make it necessary to try other medications.

Of the disease-modifying medications, three drugs are commonly used. Gold, currently given by injection, is initially prescribed on a weekly basis. If the disease goes into remission, injections may be spaced a month apart. Penicillamine, another medication, has effects similar to gold, although it may take longer to develop full benefit. Hydroxychloroquine, a third disease-modifying medication, was developed for the treatment of malaria, but has beneficial effects for children with JRA. Although all these medications may alter the long-term course of the disease, many weeks or months may pass before it is possible to determine their effectiveness. While these medications are more powerful than anti-inflammatory medications, more significant and frequent side effects may be associated with their use. Children taking these medications require medical evaluation with frequent blood, urine, and eye tests to monitor their progress. To avoid permanent vision impairment, an ophthalmologist may prescribe medication to control eye inflammation.

In some particularly severe cases, surgery may be required to correct, limit, or replace joint deformities.

Most children with JRA respond to a multiple-treatment approach focusing on medication and exercise. Joint problems and accompanying symptoms often subside when just the right combination of treatments is employed consistently. Sudden recurrence of one or more symptoms is possible, however, without warning.

The persistent pain and loss of mobility characteristic of JRA cause frustration, irritability, and depression among children and adolescents who are severely hampered by the disease. When a child suffers the multiple physical difficulties of chronic arthritis and must cope with its often unpredictable course of flare-up and remission, the entire family feels the impact.

The effects of special physical problems become a shared concern when parents of a child suffering from JRA begin to consider alternatives for education and recreation. Certain questions almost always arise: how to deal with possible extended absences from school; how to deal with social isolation if much of a child's day must be spent indoors; how to provide diversion if only certain physical activities are possible.

Patient and family need to learn as much as possible about chronic arthritis and how to manage its treatment. No two patterns of management prove to be identical, as the disease affects each child differently. Psychological support and counsel from health care professionals should be supplemented by support from relatives and friends. The child needs to feel that it is possible to lead a nearly normal life with chronic arthritis.

Arthritis and *cancer* attract more promoters with "quick cure" remedies than most other diseases. Patients and parents should be wary of any promotions offering a cure or permanent or instant relief from the symptoms and complications of arthritis. Consistent, flexible, and clinically sound treatments may not always be instantly satisfying, but in the long run they do provide the safest, most reliable relief.

PREVENTION

Prevention of JRA is not yet possible.

Information for parents and children with JRA about the disease and about local support services is available from the Arthritis Foundation, 1314 Spring Street, N.W., Atlanta, GA 30309 (Phone: 404-872-7100).

KAWASAKI DISEASE

DESCRIPTION

Kawasaki disease is an unusual illness characterized by *fever, rash,* swelling of hands and feet, irritation and reddening of the eyes, irritation and inflammation of the mucous membranes of the mouth, lips, and throat, and swollen lymph nodes in the neck.

Kawasaki disease affects children almost exclusively; most patients are under 5 years old. Males acquire the illness almost twice as often as females.

In the United States the disease occurs proportionally more often among children of Asian-American background. Kawasaki disease is not a common illness, and its exact incidence in the United States has not been determined. In recent years the disease has occurred in localized outbreaks, usually in the winter and spring.

Fever, swollen lymph nodes (usually called *swollen glands)* in the neck, rash, and mucous membrane irritation can be extremely uncomfortable and last for several weeks. About 20 percent of children who are affected by the disease develop heart problems in the later stages. Damage to large blood vessels supplying the heart muscle and to the heart itself can sometimes occur. A weakening of the coronary arteries (large vessels in the heart) can result in an aneurysm (enlargement or ballooning of the blood vessel wall).

Illness lasts for 2 to 3 weeks or more; complications may prolong recuperation. Full recovery can be expected in most cases, but the possibilities of blood vessel and heart disease in later life remain subjects of medical investigation.

Infants less than 1 year old usually become most seriously ill and are at greatest risk. Between .5 and 1 percent of the American children who contract the disease die.

CAUSE

Research suggests that a virus may play a role in causing Kawasaki disease. There is no evidence that the disease is contagious.

SIGNS AND SYMPTOMS

Fever and irritability often occur first. Fever fluctuates from moderate (101° to 104° F; 38.3° to 40.0° C) to high (above 104° F; 40.0° C). The throat and lymph nodes in the neck may become swollen.

A *rash* usually appears early in the illness and covers much of the body, sometimes even the face. Often vivid red in appearance, the rash is composed of either poorly defined spots of various sizes or larger masses of merging spots. Fever continues to rise and fall, possibly for up to 3 weeks. *Conjunctivitis* (eye inflammation) may develop. Also, a child may become sensitive to direct light.

A child's tongue may be coated, slightly swollen, and sore and show papillae (small, raised prominences), a condition called "strawberry tongue." The lips become dry and cracked, and often take on a bright red color. Mucous membranes of the mouth turn a darker red than usual. The palms of the hands and soles of the feet often begin to turn red. Hands and feet can swell. The child usually has great difficulty getting comfortable and remains very irritable. The joints may be stiff, so a child may refuse to walk.

When the fever subsides, the rash and the swollen lymph nodes usually disappear. Skin starts to peel around the toenails and fingernails, often beginning during the third week of illness. The skin on a hand or foot may peel off in large pieces (much as a snake sheds its skin). Knees, hips, and ankles can become more inflamed and painful (see *arthritis, acute)*.

Joint pain and inflammation occasionally persist after other symptoms have disappeared. Transverse (horizontal) depressed lines on fingernails and toenails, etched during the illness, may be visible for months afterward until they grow out.

DIAGNOSIS

A physician makes a diagnosis of Kawasaki disease after carefully examining the child and observing signs and symptoms, and after carefully ruling out the possibility of other diseases that can cause similar problems. Blood tests are used to detect mild *anemia,* above-normal white blood cell count, indications of inflammation, and a rise in the number of platelets, the major clotting element in the blood. Urine tests may reveal protein and white blood cells. Eye examination often shows inflammation behind the cornea. *Arrhythmias* (irregular heart rhythms) and evidence of heart muscle strain, indicating involvement of the heart, can be detected by an electrocardiogram (EKG). Echocardiography or cardiac catheterization (diagnostic tests of heart and blood vessel structure and function) may be necessary to evaluate possible damage to the heart or large blood vessels.

COMPLICATIONS

Aneurysms of coronary or other large arteries can be serious, and some require medical or surgical treatment. Severe blood vessel and heart complications may prove fatal, especially if a very young child is involved. Heart muscle inflammation (see *cardiomyopathy)* and congestive heart failure (see *heart failure, congestive)* may accompany fever. An abnormal and painful accumulation of fluid in the gallbladder resulting in severe *abdominal pain* sometimes occurs during the period of fever.

TREATMENT

Recent studies indicate that large doses of gamma globulin, a blood product, given intravenously (into the bloodstream through a tube in a vein) can reduce the chances of irreversible damage to the heart and blood vessels. Most physicians agree that gamma globulin should be given to children with Kawasaki disease during the early, severe phase of illness, preferably before the 10th day of fever. A child must be hospitalized to receive gamma globulin. There are no known risks of treatment with gamma globulin.

Aspirin is often prescribed to reduce fever, joint inflammation, and pain, as well as to prevent possible formation of a blood clot. If a child's platelet count is abnormally high, medication stronger than aspirin may be prescribed. Making a child as comfortable as possible while the illness runs its course is a major goal of home care.

If diagnostic tests reveal the presence of an aneurysm or any other heart or blood vessel abnormality, medical or surgical treatment may be needed. A cardiologist (a physician who specializes in heart problems) may monitor a heart or blood vessel problem for several years following recovery.

PREVENTION

Kawasaki disease, as yet, cannot be prevented.

KIDNEY FAILURE, ACUTE

EMERGENCY ACTION

Seek medical attention immediately if a child experiences any of the following signs and symptoms: a marked decrease in or cessation of urination; convulsions (see *seizures); dehydration* (signs and symptoms: cool, dry, pale skin; dry tongue; thirst; listlessness; rapid pulse; sunken eyes); or *shock* (signs and symptoms: cool, clammy, pale skin; weak, rapid pulse; thirst; dizziness or faintness; and increased breathing rate). Any of these conditions may indicate acute kidney failure.

DESCRIPTION

The kidneys are two fist-sized, bean-shaped organs that lie at the back of the abdominal cavity, one on each side of the spinal column (see Figs. 37 and 38, p. 698). One of the crucial functions of the kidneys is filtering certain wastes such as excess water, salts, and acids out of the blood into the urine. By producing urine, the kidneys maintain a balance of fluids (mostly water) in the body. Because the kidneys possess considerable reserve capacity, it is possible to live a normal life with only one functioning kidney.

Two types of kidney failure, acute and chronic, can affect children. Acute kidney failure (AKF) is an unusual, short-term problem that may result in severe illness and can be fatal if not treated promptly. By contrast, chronic kidney failure (CKF) (see *kidney failure, chronic*) is gradual, progressive, and long-term in its effects. It can be fatal unless treated effectively.

AKF stems from a sudden decrease in or loss of kidney function. The problem is characterized by inability or diminished ability to urinate, irregularities in mineral and acid-base balances in the blood and tissues, and impaired excretion of some of the waste products of metabolism. (Metabolism involves the chemical and physical breakdown of sugars, fats, and proteins and the use, storage, and elimination of the resulting materials.) Reduction in the volume of urine, however, is not an essential sign of AKF; other signs and symptoms of kidney failure can exist even if urine output continues at about normal volume.

AKF can occur at any age, although it is more common among adults than among children and adolescents. Because normal kidney function is essential for the entire body, AKF, if not diagnosed and treated promptly, can affect virtually every organ and system.

AKF does not usually recur unless the underlying causes arise again or, in the event of structural defects or abnormalities of the urinary tract, if they are not repaired correctly. The effects of AKF are usually reversible, leaving no long-term complications. Repeated episodes of AKF, however, may impair normal kidney function.

Initially the symptoms of AKF may be masked by the more obvious effects of the underlying cause. Medical attention is often directed first toward diagnosing and treating these more evident problems.

The specific signs and symptoms that comprise AKF can include a marked decrease in or cessation of urination; tissue swelling, especially in the joints and the abdomen; listlessness and drowsiness; and rapid, shallow breathing. Convulsions may occur. *Shock, dehydration,* and bleeding are obvious complications that can stem from the underlying cause.

AKF can last from two or three days to as long as two weeks, especially for those children for whom the underlying cause may be difficult to diagnose or treat successfully. The outlook for children with AKF depends on the nature and severity of the underlying cause and on the promptness and effectiveness of treatment. Although as many as 60 percent of adults with AKF die of the problem and its complications, the mortality rate for children is less than 20 percent.

CAUSE

The causes of AKF may be divided into three general types, each of which depends upon the physical location of the problem.

1. Prerenal kidney failure is any problem whose origin is above the kidney and genitourinary system. Such problems account for 40 percent of all AKF. Most of the failures are the result of decreased fluid content in the blood or of decreased heart output. The kidneys then fail to receive a sufficiently large volume of fluid in the blood to filter for impurities and from which to remove water. The most common causes of this kind of prerenal failure are *dehydration, shock, burns,* blood poisoning, drug poisoning, congestive heart failure (see *heart failure, congestive),* peritonitis (infection of the membrane lining the abdominal cavity), and postoperative complications of surgery, such as cardiac bypass surgery for congenital heart disease (see *heart disease, congenital)* in infants.

2. Intrinsic kidney failure is any problem whose origin is in the kidney itself. The most common specific causes are the following:

- blood-vessel-related disorders such as a blood clot in an artery or vein in the kidney
- high blood pressure *(hypertension)*
- bacterial infections of the blood and kidney tissue, especially pyelonephritis
- kidney tissue damage resulting from oxygen deprivation
- chemical poisoning, such as from mercury or carbon tetrachloride (a powerful hydrocarbon often used in cleaning fluid)
- tissue destruction resulting from exces-

sive quantities of uric acid in the urine
- the use of certain powerful medications, such as sulfa, for the treatment of some childhood diseases
- *nephritis,* especially that caused by the use of certain powerful antibacterial medications
- infiltration of the kidney by cancerous cells in *leukemia*

3. Postrenal kidney failure is any problem whose origin is in the lower genitourinary system, most often as a result of obstruction of urine flow in the urine-carrying tubes (ureters). Kidney stones (see *urinary tract defects and obstruction*) and blood clots resulting from injury are among the most common causes of postrenal failure.

DIAGNOSIS

In diagnosing AKF, a physician takes a history of all signs and symptoms of illness and performs a careful physical examination, which includes a blood pressure reading and a check for signs of dehydration. Blood tests, urinalysis, and urine cultures are performed to determine the composition of the blood and urine and to determine if any infection is present. X-ray films are taken of the chest and abdomen. An electrocardiogram (EKG) may be used to check the function of the heart muscle. These examinations and tests are performed to evaluate the severity of the problem and, if possible, to identify which of the 3 types of AKF is present.

Diagnosis of the underlying cause of AKF often requires further specialized tests and evaluation.

COMPLICATIONS

A number of complications may develop for children with AKF:

- excessive amounts of potassium in the blood
- excessive amounts of sodium and water, leading to swelling of and fluid in the lungs and other body tissues, *hypertension,* and excessive fluid volume in the blood
- acidosis (excessive amounts of acid in the blood and tissues)
- high blood pressure in the aftermath of streptococcal glomerulonephritis, a severe bacterial infection
- problems of blood chemistry, including *anemia* (reduced levels of red blood cells), thrombocytopenia (reduced levels of platelets), and hyperlipidemia (increased levels of fat molecules in the blood. See *cholesterol and triglyceride problems.*)

About half of all children who experience one or more episodes of AKF encounter long-term problems, including difficulties with filtration of wastes and production of insufficiently concentrated urine. In many instances these long-term problems prove to be quite mild and go unnoticed by the child so affected.

Complications improve when AKF is treated effectively.

TREATMENT

AKF can be treated in a number of ways, depending upon the type and severity of kidney failure, its underlying cause, and the likelihood that complications may develop.

If an infection is involved, antibiotics may be given even before the results of blood tests are received. If fluid volume overload is present, a diuretic (medication to stimulate fluid excretion and urination) may be given intravenously. If a child is dehydrated (see *dehydration*) or in *shock,* oral or intravenous fluids and salts are given. Acidosis can be corrected by treating shock, infection, and lack of oxygen and by providing an adequate diet with sufficient calories, especially carbohydrates. Sugar in the form of a glucose solution may be fed intravenously.

If a child is suffering from excessive amounts of potassium in the blood, excessive fluid volume in the blood, persistent *hypertension,* or acidosis, hemodialysis or peritoneal dialysis may be necessary. In both these processes excessively high fluid volume and large amounts of wastes are gradually reduced by treatments that may continue periodically for several days in a hospital. (See *kidney failure, chronic* for descriptions of dialysis.)

PREVENTION

Acute kidney failure can be prevented only if its underlying causes are preventable.

KIDNEY FAILURE, CHRONIC

DESCRIPTION

For a description of kidney function, see *kidney failure, acute.*

The functional unit of kidney tissue is the nephron; each kidney contains about a million tiny nephrons. The total blood of the body is filtered once every 5 minutes by the nephrons in the kidney. When kidney disease occurs, it often produces rather general, seemingly mild signs and symptoms, sometimes even when the problem has progressed quite far. The child who is ill with such "silent" kidney disease is able to continue a seemingly normal life because the filtering functions of the disabled nephrons are taken over by the remaining unaffected nephrons.

Over a period of months or even years, if the nephrons are unable to filter enough of the body's wastes, a number of severe signs and symptoms, collectively called chronic kidney failure (CKF), begin to affect the body.

Children of any age can experience chronic kidney failure, but characteristically, certain problems of the kidneys and urinary tract affect children under 5 years old. Children between 5 and 15 experience different problems when rapid growth and accompanying hormonal changes make heavy demands upon the kidneys.

Depending upon the particular underlying causes, CKF can affect physical growth and development, including bone and muscle development; the urinary tract; the heart, circulatory system, and blood chemistries; the gastrointestinal (GI) tract; and the central nervous system (brain, spinal cord, and their protective covering, the meninges).

CKF appears quite gradually. The first indications are general and mild: listlessness, fatigue, and headache. The child may look pale and slightly yellow and have a slightly puffy face and dry, itchy skin. Sometimes, the child may begin to urinate much more frequently than usual; sometimes nighttime accidents occur even though bladder control has been achieved. The child becomes unusually thirsty.

Bone or joint pains may develop and make sleeping difficult; joints may appear enlarged and unusually bony. Muscle cramps may become persistent, and muscles weaken. Coordination may be impaired, and the legs and feet begin to burn, tingle, or twitch. The tongue may be coated with a white film, the breath smell sour.

Loss of appetite and nausea develop, sometimes accompanied by *diarrhea.* Growth is usually slowed or may stop completely. Sexual development is also often delayed or halted.

When CKF has progressed far enough to produce obvious signs and symptoms, a condition known as <u>uremia</u> exists. Uremia is the presence of excessive amounts of urea, the body's nitrogen waste component, in the blood.

As illness grows worse, the volume of urine produced by the kidneys may begin to decrease. Failure of the blood to clot properly may cause the skin to bruise easily. A child may appear to be confused and disoriented at times. Headaches can persist, and occasionally convulsions may occur. Because the nephrons are damaged, *hypertension* (high blood pressure), acidosis (excessive acid in the tissues), and *anemia* (low levels of red blood cells) can develop. A severe complication of this cluster of problems can be congestive heart failure (see *heart failure, congestive),* marked by fatigue, shortness of breath, rapid breathing, coughing, and abdominal pain.

Managing the various signs and symptoms can be difficult for physician, parents, and child. Medication and diet may bring adequate relief for months, or sometimes even years, but eventually almost all children with CKF must undergo dialysis and a kidney transplantation to survive.

<u>End-stage renal (kidney) disease (ESRD)</u> is the term given to the final, severe phase of kidney failure. ESRD is a rare condition: in the United States each year about 25 new cases of ESRD in children under 16 years of age are reported for each 10 million people in the population, or about 650 new cases altogether.

Dialysis is a process by which an artificial kidney or the peritoneal membrane in the abdominal cavity is used to maintain fluid balance and purify the blood by elminating impurities. Dialysis is neither a completely adequate replacement for a living kidney nor a cure for ESRD, but it enables affected children to overcome many of the signs and symptoms of ESRD and to regain body weight. Children on dialysis can then wait for a suitable kidney to be found for transplantation. A successfully transplanted kidney can provide long-term relief from symptoms and afford many recipients a normal life.

CAUSE

CKF can be caused by one of a variety of kidney problems. Wasting and narrowing of the glomeruli (specialized microscopic blood vessels in the kidney) can occur in nephrosis and anaphylactoid purpura, a rare inflammatory disease of the skin and blood vessels (see *nephritis; nephrosis*). Systemic *lupus erythematosus* can also lead to CKF.

Abnormalities of the kidneys and urinary tract that become apparent or develop among older children constitute 20 percent of the causes of CKF (see *urinary tract defects and obstruction*). Another 15 percent of all causes stem from hereditary kidney diseases. Infections of the kidney, called pyelonephritis (see *urinary tract infections),* account for an additional 15 percent of the causes of CKF. The remaining 10 percent of causes are miscellaneous problems, including diseases of the blood vessels in the kidneys, hemolytic uremic syndrome, rare kidney and blood abnormalities, *spina bifida, Wilms' tumor* of both kidneys, and reactions to radiation and kidney-damaging medications or chemicals. *Hypertension* and *diabetes,* which are common causes of CKF among adults, do not often cause this condition among children.

Defects and abnormalities of the kidneys and urinary tract, often present at birth, cause signs and symptoms of CKF before children are 5 years old. Diseases of the glomeruli and hereditary kidney diseases often appear as causes of CKF later in childhood, usually between the ages of 5 and 15. During adolescence growth spurts and hormonal changes relating to sexual maturation make heavy demands upon the kidneys, and that is when most of these problems develop.

DIAGNOSIS

A child should be taken to a physician when unusual thirst and decreased volume of urination occur or when general health and strength seem to be declining. If a physician suspects the presence of CKF, the child may be referred to a pediatric nephrologist (a specialist in childhood kidney diseases).

Diagnosis of CKF can be made with specific blood tests. Urinalysis and urine culture are helpful in determining the extent of uremia and damage. These diagnostic tests can confirm the existence of CKF and determine the extent of damage to other organs. The physician will then order whatever tests seem appropriate to help diagnose the underlying cause.

COMPLICATIONS

The complications of CKF can be life-threatening. They are intensifications of some of the most damaging signs and symptoms of illness. Excessive calcium in the blood and tissues can lead to dangerous *arrhythmias* and to abnormal enlargement of bone and resulting joint pain (called renal osteodystrophy). Severe high blood pressure can lead to brain, heart, and blood vessel damage or even to heart failure or *stroke.* Fluid overload, usually caused by intake of excessive fluids, may bring on congestive heart failure, severe swelling of the joints and abdomen, and slowing of blood circulation. Infections of the urinary tract, especially the bladder and kidneys, can be life-threatening because of the generally weakened condition of a child with CKF and the danger of a bloodstream infection.

CKF can lead to delays in a child's growth and development. If severe, such a delay can cause a child to withdraw and experience difficulties in making friends and maintaining close relationships.

Abnormal kidney function brings about biochemical imbalances that can lead to listlessness, moodiness, or quarrelsome, excessively demanding behavior. A school-aged child may withdraw and lose interest in schoolwork and friends. Loneliness can develop, leading to poor grades and making learning and even regular school attendance problematic. With such a condition, the child can feel cut off from family and peers.

TREATMENT
Chronic Kidney Failure

Treating a child with CKF is almost always a long, slow process. First a physician attempts to control or reduce the most debilitating signs and symptoms of illness while attempting to identify the underlying cause. Much of this preliminary work is carried out in a hospital under a nephrologist's supervision.

Some of the medications used to combat underlying causes of CKF, paradoxically, may be harmful because these medications cannot be excreted quickly enough to prevent damage to the nephrons of the kidney and in other organs of the body. In such cases it is possible to give the smallest effective dosages of the medications or to use alternative treatment. Other medications have undesirable side effects. For example, some children with CKF are treated for high blood pressure with medication that may produce lethargy and depression.

For many children with CKF fluid intake must be measured carefully. Even slightly excessive amounts of fluids can overload the blood vessels, leading to increased blood pressure, swelling of tissues, and occasionally heart failure. Any of these conditions can make the kidneys work harder and thereby complicate the course of recovery. Children with CKF may have excessive levels of potassium in their blood, making it necessary to limit potassium-rich foods such as bananas, oranges, tomatoes, and chocolate.

Children with CKF retain abnormal quantities of phosphorus. Intake of phosphorus-rich foods, such as milk and milk products, must therefore be restricted so that bone damage can be minimized. Because of a defect in the absorption of vitamin D, bones are damaged as calcium slowly dissolves. For children who are deprived of large amounts of calcium because of milk restriction, calcium supplements in tablet or syrup form can be substituted along with a specially activated form of vitamin D. Additional sources of protein are essential for growth, especially if intake of dairy products must be limited. High-quality protein, which contains the essential amino acids in the correct proportions, can be found in eggs, chicken, fish, and meat. Children with CKF need moderate amounts of these foods in order to continue to grow.

If swelling of joints or the abdomen is present, it may be necessary to restrict the child's intake of sodium, specifically salt. (Salt permits body tissues to retain water.)

If untreated, high blood pressure can lead to heart failure or stroke. It may become necessary to control high blood pressure with antihypertensive medications and sometimes by restricting salt intake. Slowing of blood circulation because of excessive fluid can be treated by strictly controlling the intake of salt and fluids and the administration of special medications.

To compensate for *anemia* and improve the oxygen-carrying capacity of the blood, it may be necessary to give transfusions of packed red blood cells.

When kidney function is severely impaired, a child loses appetite, often feels nauseated, and may have *diarrhea*. It is difficult to get a child in this condition interested in eating any kind of food. A suitable, healthful diet can usually be arranged, compromising between the ideal and what a child is able—or willing—to eat. A registered dietitian or a qualified nutritionist can be helpful in working out a specially designed plan for eating and drinking and for the timing of food supplements, vitamins, and medications.

CKF is often difficult for a child and the entire family to live with. Children may be uncooperative or rebellious from time to time about following their treatment regimes, especially diet restrictions and medication schedules. Care by experienced, knowledgeable nurses is often essential in getting a child with CKF to cooperate with a plan of medication, diet, and activity.

Establishing a working alliance with a professional counselor—a psychiatrist, psychologist, or social worker—can be helpful for the child and for the well-being of the entire family. A counselor can serve as a reliable sounding board for the accumulated frustrations and conflicts caused by a serious chronic illness.

A skillful teacher can be extremely helpful in keeping the child motivated to attend school regularly or, when hospitalized, to keep up with assignments. A child with a chronic illness can be discouraged simply by failing to keep up with class assignments or by school failure. In addition, the child's friends should know about the illness and the problems it involves.

End-Stage Renal Disease

The major forms of treatment for ESRD are dialysis and transplantation.

Dialysis Dialysis does the kidney's work by eliminating blood impurities and the wastes of metabolism and ensuring fluid balance. Peritoneal dialysis and hemodialysis are the two kinds of dialysis. Peritoneal dialysis involves washing away impurities and wastes through the peritoneum, the membrane that lines the abdominal cavity. Hemodialysis involves filtering the blood through an artificial kidney, which is part of a mechanical kidney machine. Dialysis must be monitored carefully; with proper supervision it is not too uncomfortable. Both forms of dialysis initially involve surgery to gain access to blood vessels of the peritoneum for treatment. Dialysis may go on anywhere from 2 or 3 months to many years, depending upon a child's improvement and the availability of a kidney for transplantation.

Peritoneal dialysis involves surgical implantation of a small tube in the abdominal wall so that a solution called dialysate can be injected and withdrawn for the elimination of wastes and impurities. For young children, hemodialysis involves implanting small plastic tubes in a vein and an artery, creating a shunt. Each time the child is dialyzed, the dialysis machine is connected to the shunt. For older children, a small vein and artery of either the wrist or the thigh are surgically joined, creating a fistula (or loop). Each time the child is dialyzed, a needle at the end of a tube connected to the dialysis machine is inserted into the fistula, forming an intravenous circuit.

Peritoneal dialysis can be performed at home, in a hospital, or in a community dialysis center. Home peritoneal dialysis can be preferable for a child who prefers to be at home for treatment or who lives far from a pediatric dialysis center and needs dialysis while waiting for a kidney transplantation. Continuous ambulatory peritoneal dialysis (CAPD) involves injecting and withdrawing the dialysate about 4 to 6 times every 24 hours. While in the child's abdomen, the dialysate absorbs impurities in the bloodstream through the peritoneal membrane and withdraws excessive water as well. A child receiving this kind of dialysis does not need to be connected to a kidney machine.

The major complication of CAPD is peritonitis, a severe inflammation of the peritoneal membrane, which involves pain, swelling, and fever, and which can affect all abdominal organs. Peritonitis is fairly common among those children receiving CAPD, but it can most often be treated successfully with antibiotics. A child who has recovered from peritonitis may be able to resume CAPD when the inflammation has cleared, or it may be necessary to switch to hemodialysis.

A child on hemodialysis must receive a 3- to-5-hour treatment 3 times a week in a pediatric dialysis center. While dialysis is going on, a child can relax in bed and read, do homework, watch TV, or listen to tapes or the radio. Both forms of dialysis must be carefully monitored. Neither form usually requires medications or a recovery period afterward. While undergoing dialysis treatment, a child must follow a nutritious high-calorie diet that avoids foods high in potassium and phosphorus and emphasizes high-quality protein.

Short-term complications of hemodialysis —those that may occur during any treatment period—can include cramps, nausea, and headache. Long-term complications of hemodialysis include *anemia, hypertension,* growth retardation, and bone deterioration. Dialysis cannot correct delays in growth and sexual development associated with CKF.

Kidney Transplantation In almost all cases of ESRD the best long-term treatment is kidney transplantation. Kidneys can be procured from either live donors or from a cadaver. Physicians believe there is some advantage in having a kidney donated from a living related donor rather than one from an unrelated cadaver, even one with a very close tissue match. Studies show that a kidney donated from a living relative is less often rejected by the recipient's immune system and survives longer in the recipient. Cadaver-donated kidneys continue to be transplanted successfully, however, and function well for many children. Cadaver-donor-kidney waiting lists are maintained by about 20 to 30 regional centers in the United States.

Rejection remains the greatest obstacle to successful transplantation. If the transplanted kidney tissue is significantly different from the recipient's tissues, the child's immune system will attack and try to destroy the transplanted kidney. A sister or brother is often the closest tissue match for a kidney, but as a matter of public health policy, no one under 18 years old may donate a kidney. Therefore, even when a sibling's tissues match the recipient's most closely, it is usually a parent (whose tissue match may be somewhat less exact) who is chosen to donate a kidney. Living with just a single kidney involves a slight physical risk, which an older person often feels more ready to assume.

An acceptable kidney for transplantation can be matched with approximately 90 to 95 percent of all children with ESRD. A small number of children remain on dialysis for extended periods of time because of the difficulty of finding a suitably matched kidney or because the first transplanted kidney fails. In some cases a transplantation operation must be repeated one or more times before a kidney is found that functions properly.

Since kidney transplantation for children was introduced in the 1960s the results have been highly encouraging. As many as 85 to

90 percent of the children who receive transplanted kidneys live at least 5 years. Most individuals with transplanted kidneys continue to lead normal lives free of signs or symptoms of impaired or declining kidney function. Even though there is no known limit to the life of a functional transplanted kidney, physicians consider transplantation a temporary measure, not a cure for ESRD. They expect that the transplanted kidney may have to be replaced at some future time; if that happens, a second transplantation will be needed.

The possible complications of a kidney transplantation operation include short-term and long-term rejection of the transplanted kidney by the body's immune system, growth retardation, infections, *hypertension,* and psychological problems of adjustment. In order to minimize rejection, an individual with a transplanted kidney must take special medications to neutralize the immune response and potential rejection of the transplanted kidney. Because rejection may occur soon after a transplantation operation or gradually over months or even years, every individual with a transplanted kidney must be checked regularly by a physician. General health, strength, and weight are indications of how well a new kidney is functioning.

PREVENTION

Several causes of chronic kidney failure can be prevented. Notably, some kidney infections are preventable or can be treated successfully before kidney failure occurs. By avoiding kidney-damaging medications and certain toxic chemicals, chronic kidney failure can usually be prevented. Information about kidney disease and support services is available from local chapters of the National Kidney Foundation or its headquarters, 2233 Wisconsin Avenue, NW, Washington, DC 20007 (phone: 202-337-6600). Information and financial aid for persons with kidney disease is available from the American Kidney Fund, 7315 Wisconsin Ave., Bethesda, MD 20814 (phone: 800-638-8299).

KNEE INJURIES

EMERGENCY ACTION

If a fracture or dislocation is suspected, the knee should be immobilized immediately with a splint (anything sturdy to cushion and prevent movement). Ice packs should be applied to reduce swelling, and medical attention should be sought immediately.

DESCRIPTION

The knee is the point where the femur (thighbone), tibia (shinbone), and patella (kneecap) meet. These bones are held together by ligaments and moved by tendons and muscles. Injury of any of these parts is regarded as a knee injury.

The most common knee injuries during childhood are *sprains,* strains, torn ligaments, dislocations (see *dislocation of joints),* and *fractures.* These injuries most often occur among children active in sports (particularly skiing, football, basketball, gymnastics, wrestling, and running) but can occur at any age. Torn cartilage, a rare knee injury among children, often occurs in adolescents.

Sprains occur when knee ligaments are stretched or partially torn. Complete tearing of tissue results in a torn ligament or torn cartilage. A strain occurs when a tendon or muscle is stretched or partially torn; a "pulled muscle" is actually a muscle strain. When a child's knee is dislocated, either the shinbone or the kneecap has been moved forcibly from its normal position. Among growing children a fracture may damage the growth plate of a bone.

Knee injuries range in severity. Mild injuries of ligaments, tendons, or muscles involve a small amount of tearing; tissues are injured but retain their elasticity and ability to function. More severe injuries involve excessive tearing of tissue and require several weeks rest to regain normal functioning. Dislocations and fractures, mild or severe, usually require a physician's care to ensure proper healing.

With prompt treatment, most injured knees return to their normal strength and functioning without complications.

Knee conditions other than injuries may also develop from prolonged knee stress, particularly stress due to forceful running and jumping.

Osgood-Schlatter disease (not actually a disease) is an inflammation of the knee area that often severely restricts knee movement. It most often occurs among children ages 9 to 14, appearing as a tender lump just below the knee, and occurs in both knees in about 20 percent of cases. Osgood-Schlatter disease occurs because of stress in the growth plate at the top of the shinbone (see *joint pain*).

Chondromalacia, a condition in which cartilage on the underside of the kneecap wears down, occurs because the kneecap slips from its normal position. When the leg is bent, the kneecap slides repeatedly over the bottom of the thighbone. Repeated sliding results in a wearing down of cartilage. This condition most often develops during the adolescent growth spurt, and may recur. If chondromalacia is discovered early and treated promptly with muscle strengthening and stretching exercises, permanent knee damage can be avoided.

Excessive rolling in of a child's foot is often a stage of natural bone growth and development, but can be due to malformation of a child's shinbone or anklebone. This rolling in puts stress on the involved knee. A child with such a malformation who runs regularly may develop runner's knee, a form of chondromalacia. When the knee bends, the kneecap rubs vigorously against the thighbone, causing pain to develop behind the kneecap. Runner's knee occurs in approximately 25 percent of serious runners of all age groups.

CAUSE

Knee injuries most often occur when a child participates in vigorous activity that requires either abrupt stopping and starting, rapid changes in direction, twisting, or jumping. Physical contact can also injure a child's knee. *Sprains,* torn ligaments, torn cartilage, and strains usually occur when a child forcefully twists or overextends a knee, perhaps when jumping in basketball or soccer. *Fractures* and dislocations (see *dislocation of joints*) usually occur when a child's leg is stationary and receives a blow to the side of the knee. Such forceful blows are most common in contact sports such as football and hockey.

Knee injuries may also result from accidents unrelated to sports, such as automobile accidents.

Osgood-Schlatter disease, chondromalacia of the kneecap, and runner's knee often develop when a knee repeatedly receives stress, particularly during vigorous physical activity.

SIGNS AND SYMPTOMS

Signs and symptoms of a knee injury or knee condition include inflammation, swelling (due to bleeding in and around the knee), tenderness in the surrounding area, often severe pain, and decreased joint movement. Swelling due to accumulation of blood reaches its peak 24 to 48 hours after injury and the skin turns blue-black as a bruise forms. A knee almost always looks unusual and functions abnormally if it is severely fractured or dislocated or if connecting ligaments are severely torn.

Pain just below the knee is a sign of Osgood-Schlatter disease. A buckling sensation in the knee may occur if chondromalacia of the kneecap is present. In these conditions and in runner's knee, pain becomes worse whenever a knee is flexed.

DIAGNOSIS

A knee injury is identified by the presence of characteristic signs and symptoms. If an injured knee can bear weight and is only mildly painful, a minor sprain or strain has probably occurred. Any knee that is quite painful and cannot bear weight is often severely injured. The diagnosis of a ligament sprain is made by a physician only after it has been determined that bone growth plates are not infected. Abnormal appearance and impaired knee movement accompanied by severe pain also indicate torn ligaments, a fracture, or dislocation. An arthroscopy (an examination of the interior of a joint using a special flexible, lighted instrument) may be necessary to identify a knee injury.

A physician usually diagnoses Osgood-Schlatter disease, chondromalacia of the kneecap, and runner's knee after taking a medical history and performing an examination of the foot, knee, and leg. X-ray films may be taken to exclude rare diseases that occasionally affect the knee.

COMPLICATIONS

Even with treatment a severe knee injury may result in pain, limited motion, disruption of normal bone growth due to injury of a growth plate, bone deformities, failure of a bone to heal, and bone infection. Deformities can also occur if a fractured bone is not positioned properly during casting.

TREATMENT

The first step in home treatment of minor knee injuries is to reduce swelling. To slow the flow of blood through damaged blood vessels, an injured knee should be raised and cushioned. A knee should be moved as little as possible, and ice packs (ice wrapped in a towel or ice bag) should be applied for 10 minutes. Ice packs or cold compresses should be applied at 20-minute intervals, 10 minutes apart, over the next few hours until swelling begins to subside. A pain-relieving medication may be helpful. Consult the physician for specific recommendations and read the discussion of nonprescription medications beginning on p. 102.

In addition, an elastic bandage can be wrapped around the knee to provide support and ease pain. (An ideal combination is an elastic bandage soaked in ice water.) The bandage should not be stretched too tightly or it may interfere with blood circulation. When applying a bandage, it is wise to consult a person trained in first aid about correct wrapping techniques. The bandage should be comfortably wrapped so that each turn partly overlaps the preceding one. After the end of the bandage is fastened, the lower leg should be checked periodically to make certain that there is healthy color, no swelling, and a strong pulse (detectable in the ankle).

Knee pain lessens as swelling decreases. When pain is less severe, the child should bend the knee slowly several times a day to increase mobility. Soaking the knee in warm water may help relax injured ligaments, muscles, and tendons and ease movement. If movement is painful, the child should not bend the knee.

Once swelling and pain subside, the child should strengthen thigh muscles and tendons with exercises recommended by a physician or physical therapist. Stiffness and aching are expected during these exercises. If a particular movement is painful, however, the child should not exercise the knee. In the case of chondromalacia, strengthening exercises may help reposition the kneecap on the thighbone. If repositioning is not successful and knee cartilage continues to wear down, surgery may be necessary.

A child should use crutches to walk with an injured knee. The top of the crutch should reach just below the child's armpit when he or she stands upright. This ensures that the child's weight rests on the hands, not on the easily damaged nerves and blood vessels of the armpit. The child should continue to use crutches until able to put weight on the injured knee comfortably. The knee should remain wrapped in an elastic bandage for support, although bandaging does not prevent reinjury.

With home treatment, pain should subside significantly 24 to 48 hours after injury. If pain does not subside and the child cannot put any pressure on the affected knee, a physician should be consulted. Severe knee injuries must be treated promptly to prevent permanent weakness. Surgery may be required to restore severely stretched or torn ligaments, severely strained muscles or tendons, or torn cartilage to their original elasticity and strength.

Fractures require a physician's treatment to ensure proper healing. Since a fractured bone begins to mend shortly after injury, prompt action is needed to prevent the knee from healing incorrectly. A physician moves the ends of the bone into place and aligns, or "sets," them. The bones are then immobilized with a cast made either of plaster or of a lightweight casting material. The child should use crutches to move about. When a cast is removed, the child should strengthen the knee with exercises recommended by an orthopedist or physical therapist.

To prevent permanent pain and reduced functioning of the knee caused by Osgood-Schlatter disease and chondromalacia, the child must initially rest the knee to reduce inflammation. Once inflammation is reduced, the child should perform specific exercises, recommended by a physician, to strengthen and stretch the involved leg muscles.

To treat runner's knee, an orthopedist usually recommends the use of shoe inserts (orthotics) and exercises. These support the child's heel and prevent rolling in of the foot. Inserts can be rigid or flexible; rigid inserts provide better control of rolling, but flexible inserts are more comfortable. A child always needs shoe inserts unless foot rolling is outgrown or the bone malformation is corrected through bracing or surgery.

With proper treatment an injured or affected knee slowly regains its original strength and functioning. The child can slowly begin to use the knee when pain is almost gone. The child should not resume vigorous activity for at least a week, however, even if pain has disappeared. Complete healing of mild knee injuries or conditions requires approximately 7 to 10 days, and severe injuries may take 2 to 6 weeks to heal fully.

PREVENTION

Knee injuries and conditions are almost impossible to prevent. Twisting, straining, or tearing of ligaments, tendons, and muscles is less likely, however, if a child thoroughly stretches and limbers the knee area before vigorous activity. In addition, training programs can be used to tone and strengthen muscles to prevent injury. If a knee condition flares up, vigorous activity should be limited. Supporting a previously injured knee with an elastic bandage may occasionally reduce chances of reinjury. Children should not wear cleated athletic shoes: they anchor feet to the ground and thereby expose stationary knees to severe blows.

KNOCK-KNEES

DESCRIPTION

A standing child whose knees touch but ankles do not usually has knock-knees. During childhood, knock-knees are a part of normal growth and development; they usually become apparent when a child is 2 to 3 years old. If this condition does not appear until a child is 6 years of age or older, however, an underlying bone disease may be present.

During childhood, knock-knees usually develop as an effort to maintain balance, particularly when the child begins to walk or if the child's foot rolls inward or turns outward. When a child has knock-knees, both knees usually lean inward to an equal degree. One knee, however, may "knock" less than the other, or may even remain straight.

Overweight children are often knock-kneed. Their developing bones and joints cannot adequately support their weight and they tend to lean inward.

Knock-knees usually restrict a child's physical activities. The child cannot run easily and may not want to participate in sports or other physical activities. If knock-knees persist into adolescence, problems of appearance as well as physical activity may arise.

Knock-knees usually correct themselves by the time a child is 5 years old. Occasionally, however, they persist into adolescence.

CAUSE

Knock-knees most often develop as a part of natural growth. Diseases, such as *osteomyelitis* and *rickets,* may cause permanent knock-knees. Injury to the growth area of the tibia (shinbone) often impairs bone growth and may cause knock-knees. This injury usually occurs only in one leg, resulting in one "knocked" knee.

DIAGNOSIS

Knock-knees are obvious when a child stands with the legs straight and the toes pointed forward.

A physician can determine the severity of knock-knees by observing the position of the child's legs, knees, and ankles, and by measuring the distance between the child's inner ankle bones: the greater the distance between the ankles, the more severe the condition. X-ray films are usually taken to determine the severity of bone deformity.

COMPLICATIONS

Knock-knees place excessive stress on a child's leg bones and joints. They may cause foot or leg pain and muscle fatigue. Stress to the knee can lead to a softening or early breakdown of cartilage (a condition called chondromalacia; see *knee injuries).* A knock-kneed child also may tend to be pigeon-toed (see *pigeon toes)* in an effort to maintain balance.

TREATMENT

A mild case of knock-knees usually requires no treatment, since it often corrects itself.

More severe knock-knees may require the use of orthopedic appliances. A physician may prescribe a night brace, particularly if a family history of knock-knees exists. A night brace has no knee joint. It is attached to a shoe and works by pulling the knee up into a straight position. Orthopedic shoes, usually equipped with a heel wedge and occasionally an arch pad, may also be recommended.

If braces and shoes do not correct knock-knees, surgery may be recommended. Before suggesting surgery, however, a physician must be certain that a large space between ankle bones is not due to larger-than-normal thighs. For the best results, surgery should be performed when a girl is about 10 years old and a boy about 11. Waiting until a child reaches this age allows time for the bones to straighten naturally.

PREVENTION

In most cases, knock-knees cannot be prevented. A case caused by an underlying disease can be prevented if the disease itself can be prevented.

LANGUAGE DISORDERS

DESCRIPTION AND SIGNS AND SYMPTOMS

Language is the principal means through which people communicate their thoughts, exchange information, and make their needs known. It is one of the primary means through which people learn about the world around them. Obviously, learning to communicate with language is one of the most important achievements of childhood. While adults wishing to learn a language usually follow a course of study, children learn their first language through interactions with the family and social contacts. This process begins from the moment a child is born and continues throughout life.

Understanding what other people say precedes oral communication. By listening to the words and noting the actions of others, children begin to develop their own sense of words and how they fit together. Between birth and about age 3½, children develop the thinking skills necessary to comprehend language and the coordination skills necessary to produce it. During this time a child virtually acts as a creator of language, progressing from single words like "cookie" to simple word combinations like "want cookie" to complete sentences like "I want a cookie, Mommy." A child also learns the social conventions of language, such as how to engage in conversation and what certain inflections in the voice mean.

Each child progresses in learning language skills at his or her own rate. While most children learn language skills without difficulty, others are unable to come to an adequate understanding or production of language without extra language stimulation. A child may have difficulty understanding, remembering, or recognizing words, building meaningful sentences, or learning the subtleties of conversation, tone of voice, and other social conventions.

In many cases language disorders are accompanied by other communication problems such as *speech problems* or *stuttering.* Language disorders are also associated with *hearing loss, mental retardation,* and *autism.* About 10 percent of all children suffer from a communication disorder; those who suffer from such a disorder are usually boys. Since a certain minimum level of communication mastery is expected by the time a child enters school, communication disorders are considered basic to later *learning problems.*

Language disorders may be grouped into three broad categories based on signs and symptoms:

Receptive disorders involve impairment of a child's ability to understand language. In the most extreme cases children with receptive disorders cannot understand the literal meaning of most or all words. In milder cases they cannot comprehend the subtleties of language. A child with a receptive disorder may not understand, for example, that the remark "You forgot your lunch," uttered by a parent as a child leaves for school, contains an implicit message to get the lunch before walking out the door. Because a child with a receptive disorder might seem to ignore such a comment, the child may be labeled incorrectly by parents as disobedient, hearing-impaired, or mentally retarded.

Expressive disorders involve problems with communicating meaning or with using appropriate language and types of speech within certain contexts. Children with expressive disorders often use gestures to get their meaning across. Because of their communication problems, children with expressive language disorders may become frustrated and refuse to speak or become panicked about speaking.

Two variations of expressive disorders are especially common:

- Oral-language-formation deficits. These problems involve difficulty producing sentences appropriately. Affected children usually do not have an impaired learning capacity but may have additional speech problems. For many of these children, telling a clear story is a challenge. They will have problems in making themselves understood.
- Word-finding deficits. Children with this problem know and understand the meanings of the words they want to use but have difficulty recalling them, especially when put on the spot (as when answering a teacher's question). Some children with this problem learn to use definitions or descriptive replacements (such as "hump horse" for "camel")

when they can't think of a word. Others substitute related words or combinations of letters that simply sound the same. Some children mix up the order of letters in words, saying, for example, "aminal" instead of "animal." children with word-finding deficits often have difficulty telling stories and using written language. Anxiety stemming from such pressure situations may lead to stuttering.

Auditory-processing disorders involve an inability to distinguish, focus on, or remember certain sounds. A child with an auditory-processing disorder may be distracted by irrelevant background noise, such as the hum of a heating system. A child may respond to a certain sound in a different way every time it is heard. Shifting attention from one sound to another may be difficult. Some children with this problem are unable to remember sounds even for a short time. Because of these symptoms, a child with an auditory-processing problem may also appear to have an attention-deficit disorder (see *hyperactivity).*

For a child with a language disorder, the prognosis for improvement before adulthood is often excellent when no serious additional disorder exists. In general, the outlook is likely to be best if a conscientious language stimulation program is pursued by both parents and professionals.

CAUSE

Language disorders are sometimes associated with one or more of the following conditions: *hearing loss;* central nervous system damage, such as that associated with *cerebral palsy;* developmental disorders such as *mental retardation* or *autism;* and emotional difficulties. In other cases a child seems to have a specific developmental disorder of language.

Sometimes no cause at all can be discerned. Experts believe that certain children may be biologically more likely than others to develop them and that these tendencies are reinforced by emotional difficulties, poor role models, or associated communication disorders. Negative response to a child's speaking attempts is thought by experts at least to heighten if not to cause language disorders.

DIAGNOSIS

Since all children use language incorrectly during the first few years of life, it is often difficult for parents to detect a language disorder when no obvious related problem exists. Many children with receptive language disorders learn to pretend they understand other people by nodding, smiling, and following crystal-clear requests. Children who do not appear so attentive may be wrongly labeled as hearing-impaired or mentally retarded.

Despite the difficulty in recognizing language disorders, it is important to seek professional help as soon as any sign of a problem appears. Early diagnosis may help prevent associated problems with learning, self-esteem, and social interactions. In general, a physician—preferably the one most familiar with a child's medical history—should be consulted if any of the following circumstances exists:

- A child is 18 months old and does not use any true single words or expressive jargon, understand common words, or indicate what he or she wants through gestures or vocalization.
- A child is 2 years old and uses no single words other than parental nicknames such as "mama" and "dada".
- A child is 2½ years old and does not use at least several 2-word combinations such as "want cookie" or cannot make communication efforts understood.
- A child is 3 years old and does not use simple sentences or cannot understand simple explanations or the concept of past and future.

In an attempt to find an underlying cause, a physician reviews a child's medical history and performs a complete physical examination. Sometimes a neurologist (a nervous-system specialist) is consulted to interpret certain test results. In the absence of an obvious cause, referral is made to a speech and language pathologist, an expert at diagnosing and treating speech and language problems. Diagnosis is a complex process which may take months. During this time the pathologist carefully evaluates the child's hearing and speech capacities, intellectual and social abilities, and family circumstances.

In evaluating a child's language capabilities, a speech and language pathologist tries to answer the following questions:

- What does the child understand?
- What is the primary means through which the child communicates—signs, gestures, jargon, words, phrases, sentences, or a combination of several methods?
- How well does the child use words to specify objects and events and relationships between them?
- How well developed are the child's overall sentence-building and word-finding skills relative to his or her age?
- How appropriate are the child's word choices?
- How well does the child organize and tell a story?

During the process of diagnosis a speech and language pathologist often begins testing certain treatment methods, partly because some variations of language disorders can be diagnosed according to how a child responds to treatment.

COMPLICATIONS

Aside from learning problems, the obvious complications of speech and language disorders are social and emotional problems. Some children with speech or language disorders become overdependent on their parents and other family members, who learn better than others to understand special gestures or other subtle efforts at communication. These complications are especially likely to develop if language problems are not diagnosed until after the child begins school.

TREATMENT AND PREVENTION

Although it is not clear exactly what role parents play in a child's language development, there are steps parents can take to encourage language acquisition. Perhaps most important is an acceptance of the fact that children master language at different rates. Ridicule, chiding, and punishment only reinforce development of language problems. Attention, interest, and love can foster self-confidence and pride in this newfound skill. Here are a few general suggestions:

- Letting children know what parents are thinking, seeing, hearing, and doing is a natural way of teaching through example. If a child hears a parent ask "What is that noise?" and then answer with "I think I hear a bird singing," a small, practical lesson has been shared and is likely to be remembered.
- Providing children an opportunity to explain what they are doing stimulates conversation. Asking, for example, "What are you drawing?" gives the child a chance to answer or to listen to a parent's comment, "It looks like a house."
- Pictures in books are a natural catalyst for conversation. While reading to a child, a parent can point out a picture and gently stimulate conversation.

It is important, however, not to make questions too challenging or confining. Questions that can be answered yes or no challenge a child to guess rather than stimulate conversation and language skills. Children should not be pressured so that conversations with their parents become work or tests. Parents' enthusiasm can show children the richness and variety of language.

- Keeping children verbally informed about what is going on is a way of stimulating interest in daily routines and connecting words with actions (for example, saying "Now I am going to brush my teeth").
- Listening to a child's speech and responding encouragingly helps a child's language development. Specific suggestions:
  1. Guessing at the child's meaning and testing the guess. If, for example, a child says "gir," a parent can say "Girl? Yes, that is a girl."
  2. Adding new information to a child's comments. If, for example, a child says "doggie sleep," a parent can say "Yes, the doggie is sleeping. He must be tired, so he is taking a nap."
  3. Explaining "no" answers and providing alternatives. For example, when a child says "eat cookie," a parent can ask "Do you want a cookie? I'm sorry, you can't eat a cookie right now. We will be eating dinner very soon, after Mommy gets home. I have an idea! Here are your blocks. Let's build a castle and surprise Mommy!"

4. Providing words to explain a child's gestures. If for example a child in a high chair stretches downward, a parent can say "Down? Do you want to get down?" Regardless of the child's response, affection and approval are good ways of rewarding the attempt. Children should not be denied reasonable requests solely because they do not use words, even if a parent is sure the child knows the words.

■ Parents can be good language models for their children. A child's experience with language needs to be consistently pleasurable. Parents can help create such an environment by choosing warm, articulate, intelligent baby-sitters, home caretakers, and daycare teachers.

■ It is not helpful to encourage children to imitate language models. Urging a child, for example, to "say doggie" can be especially inhibiting if the child is already self-conscious about his or her speaking efforts. If a child wants to show off newly acquired language skills to an appreciative audience, it should be the child's choice and not the result of parental pressure.

If a child is suffering psychologically or emotionally as a result of a language problem, a speech and language pathologist may recommend that a child or family also consult a counselor, such as a psychiatrist, psychologist, or social worker.

During any treatment program, a child is made aware of language problems and shown ways of eliminating or getting around them. In some cases all the child may need are one or two good language models. In other cases games and exercises can stimulate better understanding of language.

Of the more than 1 million Americans who have never developed the communication skills necessary to make themselves understood, most are believed to suffer from an underlying developmental disorder. Speech and language professionals believe that many of these people could learn to communicate by using alternative methods, including sign language, communication boards, and assisted computer displays.

LARYNGITIS

DESCRIPTION
Laryngitis is an inflammation of the larynx (voice box) and windpipe. This common illness is rarely serious and occurs most often during the winter or spring. Laryngitis is more prevalent in males, and children between the ages of 3 months and 5 years are most often affected. The disease is generally accompanied by a mild cold (see *colds*) or *sore throat*.

Laryngitis has a tendency to recur, with each bout lasting up to 2 weeks.

CAUSE
Laryngitis is most often caused by respiratory viruses similar to cold viruses. For unknown reasons, some children are susceptible to laryngitis.

SIGNS AND SYMPTOMS
A child with laryngitis will sound hoarse and may be unable to speak above a whisper. An infant with laryngitis will have a hoarse cry. A scratchy throat and dry cough are common symptoms, although the child generally feels well. However, he or she may experience slight discomfort while swallowing, due to the *sore throat*. The child also may have a *fever*, though it will rarely exceed 101° F (38.3° C).

DIAGNOSIS
Laryngitis is diagnosed by a physician, who checks for hoarseness and a dry cough. The child will not have difficulty breathing.

COMPLICATIONS
A parent who suspects that a child has laryngitis should watch and listen for any signs of difficulty in breathing and should be alert for high *fever*. If these signs are present, a parent should call a physician immediately, as the physician will want to make sure that the child does not have *croup* or *epiglottitis*.

TREATMENT
Home treatment for laryngitis includes warm drinks and possibly a fever-reducing medication to lower the child's temperature. Consult the physician for specific recommendations and read the discussion of nonprescription medications beginning on p. 000. The parent should try to keep the child

from talking, perhaps by reading to the child, allowing television, and keeping other children away. A cool-mist vaporizer in the child's bedroom can help relieve most symptoms.

See also *croup; epiglottitis.*

PREVENTION
Laryngitis cannot be prevented.

LEAD POISONING

DESCRIPTION
Lead is found everywhere—in the air, on the ground, in objects in and around the home—and at least a little bit finds its way into everyone. It is a substance that has no biological value to the human body, but rather causes adverse biological and chemical responses.

Lead poisoning most often occurs among children 6 months to 6 years old who live in homes built before the 1960s and who tend to chew on things or put things in their mouths. Young children living in heavily industrialized and urban areas are also at risk to develop lead poisoning from unintentional swallowing of contaminated dust and soil. Susceptibility to lead poisoning seems to increase during the summer months.

Children take lead into their bodies by eating or swallowing inhaled lead dust. Conversely, lead leaves the body in urine, stool, sweat, saliva, and in hair and nail tissue. Little if any lead is lost through respiration. Approximately 10 percent of lead taken into the body is absorbed. However, in iron-deficient children as much as 50 percent of ingested lead may be absorbed.

Severity of lead poisoning is determined by the amount of lead a child's body absorbs and the length of time over which absorption occurs. Other factors determining the severity of lead poisoning include a child's nutritional status (especially iron deficiency), age, presence of an underlying illness (such as *sickle cell anemia*), and the speed with which treatment is received.

Lead poisoning interferes with body functioning. For example, it inhibits production of heme (the iron-carrying component of hemoglobin) by the bone marrow. *Anemia* may develop as a result. It also interferes with activity of brain and other organ cells. If cell activity is severely impaired, organ failure

may occur. Exposure to lead during early childhood may permanently impair growth and development of the brain, leading to such problems as *learning disabilities*. In severe cases the brain becomes inflamed and swells, a condition known as lead encephalopathy. This in turn can cause *seizures* or, if untreated, death. Kidney malfunction may occur, leading to loss of large amounts of amino acids, carbohydrates, and salts in the urine, and ultimately *kidney failure*.

The outlook for children with lead poisoning depends on the severity of the problem and the speed with which they receive proper treatment. Although the incidence of severe lead poisoning and lead encephalopathy has decreased dramatically since the 1940s, many cases of mild, undetected lead poisoning still occur and harm children.

CAUSE
The most dangerous cause of lead poisoning is frequent consumption of lead paint and putty found in homes built before the 1960s. This most often occurs when children chew on windowsills or doors that are painted with leaded paint, or when they put flakes of paint or paint-laden plaster in their mouths. Children may also chew on furniture or toys painted with leaded paint. If chips of lead paint are swallowed and remain in a child's stomach for any length of time, the lead is dissolved and absorbed into the bloodstream. The most common type of lead poisoning can occur if a child is exposed to industrial or automobile pollution, either through breathing lead-polluted air or by eating contaminated dirt and dust.

If children swallow anything kept in lead-soldered food cans, improperly lead-glazed pottery, lead-sealed storage containers or cooking vessels, or pewter vessels, lead poisoning can occur. Swallowing objects such as lead shot, lead fishing weights, and leaded jewelry sometimes causes lead poisoning.

SIGNS AND SYMPTOMS
If the exposure is mild, signs and symptoms of lead poisoning may not appear or may be delayed. Symptoms of lead poisoning include fatigue, paleness, *constipation, loss of appetite, irritability, anemia,* sudden behavioral changes, loss of short-term memory, slowing of mental development, and *sleep disorders*. More severe lead poisoning is indicated by persistent *vomiting, abdominal*

pain (called lead colic), *headache,* clumsiness, and weakness. These symptoms usually appear shortly before the onset of lead encephalopathy.

Lead encephalopathy is a life-threatening situation that indicates major involvement of the brain. Its onset is marked by sudden, forceful vomiting and headache. Symptoms include poor muscle coordination, staggering gait, confusion, erratic behavior, visual disturbances, *seizures,* loss of consciousness, and, if severe, *coma.*

DIAGNOSIS

A physician bases diagnosis of lead poisoning on a child's medical and behavioral history, nutritional status, and signs and symptoms, as well as the results of blood and urine tests, the occurrence of lead poisoning among other family members, and the environmental conditions at home. Samples of household paint and dust, soil found around the house, and other potentially contaminated materials are tested.

X-ray films are needed to determine the extent of lead deposits in bone tissue, as well as the involvement of organs such as the kidneys, heart, and brain. A physician may administer a special test to determine how much lead can be removed from the child's body through chelation therapy.

COMPLICATIONS

Severe lead poisoning and lead encephalopathy can cause permanent problems such as *seizures, mental retardation,* behavioral disorders (see *hyperactivity and attention problems),* and *cerebral palsy.* It can also cause *blindness* and slight paralysis of one side of the body; severe kidney involvement may limit kidney function. Liver malfunctioning may occur.

If a child suffers severe lead encephalopathy and resulting complications, death may follow.

TREATMENT

The most important aspect of treatment of lead poisoning is to prevent further exposure to lead. Even when a child has only mild symptoms of lead poisoning, an increase in lead levels of any amount can lead to brain injury, damage to kidneys and bone marrow, and in severe cases to encephalopathy.

For treatment to be successful, it should begin before encephalopathy develops. A physician chooses the appropriate action according to a child's age and the duration and severity of exposure to lead. In mild cases treatment may simply involve preventing further lead intake and allowing elimination of lead from a child's body. Unfortunately, this can be a slow process. An affected child should be examined by a physician every 1 or 2 months until most lead in the body is gone. Treatment of any underlying nutritional problem is begun, sometimes with the help of a nutritionist.

In more severe cases of lead poisoning, chelation therapy is required. If lead poisoning is moderate, this therapy can be administered in a physician's office on an outpatient basis. Chelation therapy works by binding lead to tiny particles which are filtered out of the bloodstream by the kidneys and passed out of the body in urine. Unfortunately, chelation therapy cannot release lead that is stored in bone tissue. However, as lead in body tissue and the blood is excreted, lead in bone tissue moves into the bloodstream for removal by the kidneys. As long as additional lead is not swallowed, most lead is excreted from the body over time.

A child with severe lead poisoning requires hospitalization. Usually the first form of treatment establishes urine flow to ensure passage of lead out of the body. Two to three hours later, chelating agents are administered by a physician either intravenously or intramuscularly. Chelation therapy can last from 3 days to several months, depending on the severity of the lead poisoning. Vitamin supplements are sometimes prescribed to restore needed metals often lost during treatment. Side effects of chelation therapy can include nausea, *vomiting,* irregular heartbeat, *rash,* and bruising; however, these conditions are reversible and less severe than symptoms of lead poisoning.

If encephalopathy is present, chelation therapy is started immediately while fluid levels are reduced to ease pressure within the skull. Swelling of blood vessels and brain cells lessens as excess fluid in the brain decreases and pressure in the skull is reduced. Surgery cannot relieve the pressure in the skull. In severe cases, long-term medication may be required.

Children recovering from severe lead poisoning and lead encephalopathy require close observation and long-term care. They may exhibit bizarre behavior during the first 3 to 6 months of healing. To ensure appropriate care during this time, a physician may recommend that a child be sent to a pediatric convalescent center to recover. If this is not possible, the child's parents and physician should discuss in detail the type of care the child needs, including a program of mental stimulation to strengthen mental faculties. Strong family support is essential. The child's physician usually recommends frequent follow-up examinations to monitor the child's progress.

Even after successful removal of lead from the body, affected children are still at high risk for recurrent lead poisoning. A child's home must be cleared of leaded paint BEFORE he or she returns to it. Affected children should have blood tests frequently to ensure that lead levels do not increase.

PREVENTION

Children in high-risk areas—those living in or near older houses or in heavily industrialized or urban areas—should be screened at least once a year for lead levels. If a test result is positive, screenings should be performed more frequently. After receiving three consecutive negative test results, screening programs should be individualized. Screening is done through a blood test. It is particularly important to screen children between the ages of 1 and 5 years every 6 months, since lead poisoning occurs most frequently in this age group. Children in lower-risk areas should be screened at least once before the age of 2, and perhaps once afterwards.

Any child who has suffered lead poisoning should have a complete neuropsychological assessment at about 5 years of age and should be monitored carefully by a physician throughout childhood and adolescence.

Precautions should be taken at home. Lead or pewter cooking utensils, lead-glazed pottery, and lead-lined storage containers should not be used. In addition, all small leaded objects should be kept out of a child's reach.

Inside the home, all lead-based paint should be removed. During the entire paint-stripping process, children must be kept out of the home, far from leaded dust and dirt. Before paint removal begins, floors should be covered with drop cloths or plastic to catch all lead paint chips and dust. If paint is being removed from exterior surfaces, the ground in the area should be covered to avoid soil contamination. Painted surfaces

should be patched, sealed, and repainted with lead-free paint. Precautions should be taken when removing paint by scraping or sanding because the resulting particles are very small and easily inhaled or swallowed.

Walls can be covered with wallpaper, wallboard, or paneling. Paint can be removed from small areas, such as windowsills or doors, with liquid paint removers. After surfaces are repainted or covered, the floors should be thoroughly swept and wet-mopped to remove leaded dust. Drop cloths should be disposed of properly. All furniture and toys painted with lead-based paint either should be refinished with lead-free paint or replaced.

LEARNING PROBLEMS

DESCRIPTION

Childhood is the time when people gain the intellectual tools necessary to learn about their environment and communicate with others. These tools include specific skills, such as the ability to identify letters and numbers, as well as the complex skills of reading and writing. Acquiring these skills involves development and refinement of basic abilities, such as perceiving and processing sights and sounds, concentrating, controlling body movement, and remembering. If one or more of these basic abilities is weak, then acquiring and using specific and complex tools—learning—can be difficult.

No two children have exactly the same abilities. Despite their differences, most children have relatively similar basic skills, and they are expected to be able to learn to use them. Indeed, that is a premise of the nation's educational system.

There may be a learning problem when a child's strengths and weaknesses do not match society's expectations. "Learning problem" is shorthand for indicating that a child so affected has difficulty acquiring knowledge and developing the complex skills necessary for learning in the way that most other children do.

Problems Maintaining Attention

In general, attention problems involve difficulty concentrating on those tasks that help the child develop more complex skills. Such difficulties are the most common causes of school failure. Signs of attention problems often appear when a child is 3 to 5 years old. Affected children may have trouble discerning the relative importance of sounds, and may focus, for example, on background noises instead of a teacher's voice.

In addition, a child with an attention problem may be uninhibited or impulsive, undertaking activities without considering their potential consequences. A child may also have difficulty continuing with a specific task for a necessary length of time. Children with attention problems are often hyperactive (see *hyperactivity and attention problems*). Sometimes, however, a child simply seems to be constantly daydreaming.

Children with attention problems commonly have associated behavior problems that interfere with their learning as well as their social relationships. It may be hard for a child to fall asleep at night, and drowsiness and related problems may ensue the next day. Even when *sleep disorders* are not a problem, a child's mood and behavior may change dramatically without warning and without apparent provocation. School performance may fluctuate greatly. A child may have difficulty understanding other peoples' feelings and may appear insensitive to them.

Problems Understanding and Interpreting Visual Stimuli

Some children, regardless of their eyesight, have difficulty perceiving things correctly or understanding their meaning. A child may have trouble understanding that different things have different positions, sizes, and shapes. He or she may not perceive the visual detail that distinguishes two similar objects; it may be difficult, for example, to understand the difference between a square drawn on a piece of paper and a three-dimensional cube. Likewise, a child may confuse things going on in the foreground with those taking place in the background and may be unable to distinguish between right and left. (Most children can tell right from left at about age 5.) Some children have difficulty relating sights and sounds.

Problems with visual perception make learning to read extremely laborious. A child may have great difficulty recognizing letters and numbers. He or she may be unable to recognize letter patterns such as "ing" and may be forced to slowly sound out words that other children spot quickly. If reading becomes a matter of sounding out words, a child may have a tendency to spell

phonetically. "Laugh," for example, may be written as "laf." In addition, similar letters may be confused: "dog" may be perceived or written as "bog." Such problems typically do not become evident until a child is in school and is trying to learn to read.

Problems Understanding Time and Other Sequences

Some children have difficulty understanding the concept of time or learning to tell time. They also tend to have trouble with days of the week, months, and years. In addition, a child may have difficulty with number manipulation, especially multiplication. Such problems usually become evident during the first few years of school.

As a child grows older, problems understanding time and sequence may affect organizational abilities. It may be hard, for example, to remember the order and content of a series of directions. Similar problems tend to pose even greater obstacles in late elementary school, when the emphasis traditionally shifts from reading to writing. It may be burdensome for a child to organize thoughts, remember which class follows which, write a well-ordered essay, and plan the steps required to complete a project.

Language and Speech Problems

Language problems can involve difficulty understanding language, using it, or both. In addition, some children have specific speaking difficulties (see *language disorders* and *speech problems*).

Problems With Memory

The capacity to remember things is multifaceted. Some children have difficulty remembering things they see, such as letters; others cannot recall sounds. It is also possible to forget how to perform mechanical tasks, such as writing, for some, grammar rules or math concepts may be difficult to retain. In addition, some children understand what sequences are and can learn them but later cannot recall them.

Problems With Coordination and Body Movements

A child can have problems with gross motor functions (large-scale body movements), such as maintaining balance, sensing body position, and controlling overall coordination. A child can also have problems with fine motor functions, such as writing, tying shoelaces, and using silverware. A child may have difficulty learning to execute such tasks because of an inability to imitate someone else's illustration or to recall it.

Motor function problems usually become evident when a child plays physical games, especially those requiring hand-eye coordination, such as baseball. Such problems may also appear during the first few years of school, when a child is learning fine motor skills.

Problems With Complex Thinking

Some children have difficulty performing tasks that require complex thinking, such as reasoning, generalizing, and classifying information. These difficulties often become apparent late in elementary school.

Problems Producing Schoolwork

Some children seem to have few problems learning things but great difficulties producing their own work. When the emphasis in school changes from learning complex skills to using them, they begin to have difficulty. They may have organizational problems: difficulty using time effectively, inability or reluctance to complete homework, progressive loss of interest in school, and trouble with writing. Such problems can be signs that a child has an underlying learning problem.

Approximately 15 percent of all children have one or more of the learning difficulties discussed above. About four times more boys than girls appear to have learning problems.

Unfortunately, certain labels for children with learning problems have been adopted, and many of them continue to be applied by both experts and the lay public. They include "minimal cerebral (or brain) dysfunction," "dyslexia," and "learning disabilities." These labels are misleading because they tend to emphasize the similarities among affected children instead of their individual strengths and weaknesses.

The term "minimal brain dysfunction," for example, purports to explain why children develop learning problems. Experts, however, have few clues as to precisely how the brain (or any other physical or mental faculty) is involved. Similarly, "dyslexia" has been used to denote many kinds of visual-perception or reading problems. Although many types of "dyslexia" exist, almost no children are solely "dyslexic." Using that label, obviously, can divert attention from a child's other learning problems —as well as his or her strengths.

The widely used term falsely implies that all children with learning problems have some sort of syndrome that leaves them "learning disabled." In addition, the severity of a learning problem can depend to a great extent on such factors as the quality of teaching, a child's language experience at home, lack of quality learning experiences, and emotional health. The term "learning disabilities" overemphasizes a child's weaknesses while neglecting significant strengths. For example, "distractibility" is often listed as a common "learning disability." Such a term ignores the positive side—imagination. Many "distractible" children eventually achieve success in fields that place a premium on creative thinking, such as art or architecture.

Some children find that their learning problems ease with time. Others find considerable success as adults because they can bypass their disabilities and refine their strengths. The outlook may depend, however, on how learning problems are handled during childhood. If handled poorly, a child may develop complications such as problems with emotional health and social relationships.

In general, the outlook is best if a child understands his or her strengths and weaknesses, has strong family support, receives sensitive professional assistance, is in an environment where small but encouraging successes are possible, receives individually planned education, is given appropriate incentives to overcome difficulties, has a positive self-image, and remains in good mental health.

CAUSE

Learning problems can develop as complications of an identifiable physical or developmental disability or disorder. Such conditions include *blindness* and other vision problems; *hearing loss; cerebral palsy; juvenile rheumatoid arthritis; autism; schizophrenia;* and conditions characterized by *mental retardation,* including *Down syndrome* and *Turner's syndrome.*

Learning difficulties can also result indirectly from long-term physical conditions that cause extended periods of absence from school. Such conditions include epilepsy (see *seizures), diabetes, cancer,* kidney disease, and liver disease. Extended periods of absence from school can also result from nonmedical circumstances, such as frequent family moves that entail changing schools. Switching schools repeatedly can trigger learning problems because a child is constantly forced to adjust to new teachers, new teaching methods, and new social situations.

The school environment may also be so different from the one at home that a child has difficulty adjusting. A child who is used to being active, for example, may have trouble sitting still at a desk for most of the day. Similar factors that can play a role in the development of a learning problem include overcrowded classrooms, poor teachers or curricula, and friendship problems, including shyness. Learning problems occur more often in financially pressed school districts, presumably because teaching conditions in such areas tend to be more difficult.

In some cases a problem at home causes or aggravates a learning problem. Some children receive inadequate language stimulation. Other children may be subjected to a tumultuous family life or other stresses, and they may develop emotional troubles that trigger learning difficulties (see *stress*).

For many children, however, the primary cause of a learning problem is not physical, emotional, social, or economic. These are the children who seem to have variations, deviations, or delays in usual intellectual development and who have been labeled "learning disabled." As yet, their problems are inexplicable. It is true, however, that learning problems tend to run in families and occur more often among children born prematurely or whose births were difficult.

SIGNS AND SYMPTOMS

Sometimes the signs and symptoms of learning problems are obvious. A child may, for example, have great difficulty reading or doing arithmetic. Sometimes, however, the signs and symptoms are less obvious. A child may develop behavior problems, such as resisting going to school or playing the class clown or bully, to compensate for a reputation among peers as "a dummy." Sometimes behavior problems such as hyperactivity (see *hyperactivity and attention problems)* are components (as opposed to results) of learning problems and appear even before a child begins school.

Another indicator of a learning problem can be repeated poor results on standardized tests. Parents should take low scores seriously, even though these measurements may not be too helpful per se in illuminating the specific nature of a child's problems. Similarly, repeated comments from teachers about a child's poor performance or difficult behavior sometimes indicate a learning problem, although teachers may misidentify learning problems as behavior or personality problems.

In general, parents are quite successful at sensing their own children's difficulties. Although a parent's description of a child's problem may simply be that "something is not quite right," such an observation can be the crucial first step toward obtaining needed help.

DIAGNOSIS

When it is suspected that a child has a learning problem in the absence of an obvious underlying cause, various tests and procedures are used to obtain a profile. The word "profile" is used instead of "diagnosis" because the goal is to understand the full picture—a child's strengths as well as weaknesses. The earlier a child's weaknesses are identified, the earlier his or her identifiable strengths can be developed to help bypass problems. If a child is of school age, parents should seek an in-school evaluation if they suspect their child has a learning problem. If test results suggest a problem or if parents are dissatisfied with test results, they should consult their child's pediatrician.

The pediatrician takes (or reevaluates) a detailed history of the child's physical health and mental health, as well as a history of medical care and a family history. The physician evaluates a child's current state of general physical health, then tests hearing and vision, and may perform a neurological exam.

A physician refers a child to specialists if the cause of a learning problem remains unclear after preliminary information is collected and evaluated. Sometimes such specialists work together in a "learning disabilities clinic" or a similar arrangement, which may include most if not all of the following:

- an educational psychologist to evaluate a child's learning potential through IQ and similar tests
- a psychologist, psychiatrist, social worker, or other mental-health professional for a psychological assessment
- a speech and language "pathologist" (expert) to evaluate language and speech development

- a neurologist or specially trained developmental pediatrician to look for evidence of subtle brain abnormalities
- an ophthalmologist (a physician who specializes in eye and vision problems) to evaluate vision
- an otolaryngologist (ear, nose, and throat specialist) to evaluate hearing

Developing a profile of a child's strengths and weaknesses takes time, perhaps weeks. A child and his or her parents should ask about any tests they do not understand. Parents should be especially skeptical of pronouncements that a child is "slow," "dyslexic," "learning disabled," "neurologically impaired," "emotionally disturbed," or "brain damaged." In addition, parents should be wary of diagnosticians whose goal is to determine the exact <u>cause</u> instead of the exact <u>manifestations</u> of a learning problem. Parents may want to consult with the nearest university-affiliated diagnostic center for further tests and advice.

Once a reliable profile of a child's strengths and weaknesses is developed, the child should be reevaluated annually.

COMPLICATIONS

Having a learning problem can lead to serious difficulties in other areas of life, including mental health, social relationships, and occupational pursuits. School, after all, is a child's first job. The general quality of a child's life can suffer substantially because of a learning problem. Specific possible complications include low self-esteem, gaps in skills and general knowledge, friendship problems, and school refusal (see *phobias*).

In the absence of obvious underlying emotional difficulties, such problems are most likely to develop when an adequate profile of a child's strengths and weaknesses is not developed or when "management approaches" by the child, parents, or professionals repeatedly do not help. A child who is misdiagnosed may begin to behave accordingly: a "stubborn" boy may try to fill that role.

TREATMENT

A unified treatment program should be tailored to a child's particular strengths and weaknesses. This process entails experimentation and depends upon cooperation and trust among the child, his or her parents, and professionals. Everyone involved should know as much about a child's strengths as his or her problems.

Several general treatment options exist. Some focus on attempting to cultivate basic skills through intensive therapy. If, for example, a child has great difficulty learning the alphabet, a therapist may teach each letter individually and slowly, introducing it in many forms.

Another strategy is to provide practical assistance by helping a child directly with school work—tutoring, for example, in reading, writing, and spelling. For older children, help is extended in such tasks as organizing and scheduling work, as well as taking notes and performing other in-class responsibilities.

One of the goals of treatment is to identify a child's strengths and capitalize on them: almost all children benefit from strategies that employ strengths to bypass weaknesses. A child who has difficulty with words, for example, may be given visual instead of written demonstrations of a concept. Children with fine motor control problems sometimes have more success learning to type than learning to write. If a child's mind wanders while listening to the teacher, he or she may benefit from sitting in the front row of the class, where there are fewer distractions.

Some children are helped by being in a regular classroom for most of the day and receiving extra help in a special-education classroom or resource room as needed. Others benefit from being in a special group all day. Regardless of the schooling arrangement, it is essential that a child's teacher be sensitive to individual needs and be willing to innovate and experiment. Classroom size should be small to obtain the best results.

In addition, counseling by a pediatrician or other professional is often helpful for a child with learning problems. The child can talk about frustrations and victories, and the counselor can offer support and specific suggestions.

In some cases, using medication as a supplement to other forms of therapy is of great help. For reasons that are unclear, stimulant medications are sometimes effective in controlling hyperactivity, distractibility, and other attention problems. Medication is never the only tool of therapy, however, and is discontinued if its results are not of obvious benefit.

Whatever techniques are used, parents should always look for opportunities to express praise. All children should feel that their parents are proud of them and speak highly of them.

Finding effective care can be difficult and frustrating. Although federal law mandates that the public school system provide adequate education for all children, regardless of their special needs, some schools have inadequate facilities, limited resources, or insufficiently trained teachers for children with learning problems. Parents must seek out other parents of children with learning problems and work for positive changes in the school system.

No matter how excellent the conditions, some children simply cannot overcome their weaknesses and achieve the successes in school that many other children are capable of achieving. Children, however, should be given the opportunity to try to improve any skills they feel are important. Succeeding at games, sports, and hobbies is often very satisfying, and the confidence children gain in such extracurricular activities may carry over and prove helpful as they pursue other tasks.

PREVENTION

Because the causes of most learning problems are complex, absolute prevention is impossible. Prevention of complications and problems in adulthood, however, is most likely when an effective program tailored to a child's individual strengths and weaknesses is planned and carried out cooperatively.

LEGG-CALVE-PERTHES DISEASE

DESCRIPTION

Legg-Calve-Perthes disease (named for three physicians who identified it) is a noninfectious, temporary disturbance in the blood supply to the ball in the hip socket. When this condition occurs, blood stops flowing into the rounded upper end of the thighbone, called the femoral head. Growth of the femoral head can become disturbed, and then the bone becomes misshapen.

The disease affects children between 3 and 11 years old, most often those from 4 to 8. Approximately 85 percent of the children affected are boys. In the United States the incidence of the problem for all children is 1 case in 2,200 (for boys, 1 in 750; for girls, 1 in 3,700). For 9 out of 10 children only 1 hip is involved.

The disease takes 1 to 5 years to run its cycle, depending on the age at onset (more rapid cycles occur among younger children). This cycle includes a short acute onset, followed by a lengthy period in which the bone tissue can soften and collapse without its blood supply, and finally a phase in which the bone repairs, rebuilds, and becomes solid once again.

Symptoms in the acute phase can last anywhere from 1 week to several months, and the bone-softening stage may last from 6 to 12 months. The third phase can take several years for the bone to regenerate and the acetabulum (socket) to modify, if necessary, to accommodate the new shape of the femoral head.

The severity of Legg-Calve-Perthes disease depends on the child's age, the stage in which the disease is diagnosed, the treatment used, and the extent of disturbance in growth of the hip as the bone rebuilds. Involvement can range anywhere from just the front third of the femoral head, in which case healing usually occurs quickly and independently, to situations where the entire femoral head deforms, often resulting in a severely arthritic joint in middle age.

Complete healing is likely for children younger than 4 years old because the femoral head has more time to reshape before maturity. For most children who receive proper treatment, prospects for complete recovery are excellent, but again, much depends on how far the disease has progressed when diagnosed and the extent of bone degeneration. The disease is never fatal.

CAUSE

The cause of the disease is unknown. Some physicians believe that excess fluid accumulates inside the joint, and the increased pressure cuts off or greatly reduces blood supply to the femoral head.

Other factors are suspected of playing a role in the onset of the disease. Male infants who weighed less than 5 pounds at birth, for example, are 5 times more susceptible to the disease than male infants whose birthweight was more than 8 pounds. Legg-Calve-Perthes disease also seems to run in some families.

SIGNS AND SYMPTOMS

Legg-Calve-Perthes disease often begins with pain in the thigh or knee and a persistent limp that grows worse immediately after periods of activity and improves with periods of rest. The child may attempt to hold the hip as stationary as possible in the most relaxed, comfortable position. There may be some limitation of hip motion, as well as soreness or tenderness when pressure is applied to the hip.

DIAGNOSIS

Diagnosing Legg-Calve-Perthes disease is difficult in the early stages because the limp and pain can easily be mistaken for muscle strain or bruises and swelling inside the joint. An orthopedist (a physician specializing in diseases of bone and muscle) is often consulted. X-ray films are necessary for a proper diagnosis; however, even X rays may reveal a normal joint at the onset of the disease.

In most cases an X ray or bone scan (an X ray using tiny amounts of injected radioactive material to visualize the bone) taken during the first phase show a widened space between the femoral head and the acetabulum. In the phase where the bony center of the head collapses, an apparent change in shape of the femoral head may be visible in X rays. If the child is examined in the third phase, the X-ray film may show increased density or bulges in the femoral head caused by the addition of new bone in the joint. X rays may also reveal a distorted acetabulum, which has reshaped itself to better contain the femoral head.

COMPLICATIONS

If a child does not receive proper treatment, a permanently deformed hip joint may result. Complications associated with a misshapen joint include a permanent limp, a shorter leg, wasting of muscle, reduced hip movement, and a greater probability of *arthritis* in later life. Children who have had Legg-Calve-Perthes disease may experience delayed skeletal development and may be as much as 1 to 3 inches shorter than their peers.

TREATMENT

Opinion varies as to the best way to treat this disease. Currently, physicians allow the child to continue weightbearing on the joint as long as the involved part of the femoral head is firmly contained within the acetabulum. Braces are often used to maintain the desired position of the joint, usually to hold the legs apart at least 60 degrees.

If the disease involves just a small portion of the femoral head and the child is younger than 4 years, no treatment is usually necessary. Physicians, however, examine the child periodically to ensure that the joint is healing properly. For older children the hip may be placed in traction for a number of days to relieve the symptoms and achieve proper placement of the femoral head. After this the joint may be held in place with some type of brace, usually for a period of 4 to 8 months. For older children and those children whose conditions are diagnosed in advanced stages of the disease, surgery is probable.

PREVENTION

No specific preventive measures are yet known. Permanent deformity of the hip, however, can be prevented by prompt diagnosis and treatment. Any child who complains of persistent hip pains or who limps for several days should be evaluated by a physician.

LEUKEMIA

DESCRIPTION

The leukemias of childhood are a group of severe disorders of blood cell production. Leukemias are considered to be forms of cancer for two reasons: they involve uncontrolled multiplication of abnormal blood cells, which interfere with normal organ function, and they can spread throughout the body with harmful effects. Cancer is a general term for more than 100 diseases characterized by uncontrolled growth of abnormal cells and the capacity to spread (see *cancer*).

As is true of all childhood cancers, leukemia is a rare disease; only about 2,500 new cases of childhood leukemia appear each year in the United States (or approximately about 40 new cases per million children each year). Many can be treated successfully because of continually improving medications and management methods.

To understand leukemia it is necessary to know what human blood normally contains. A fluid called plasma carries a complex substance composed of 3 types of blood cells. Red cells, white cells, and platelets are formed in the marrow, the spongelike tissue that fills the inner core of bones. Normally, as they mature, these blood cells are released from the marrow in blood vessels of the bone into the circulating blood. Red blood cells carry oxygen to body tissues, and white blood cells fight infections. Platelets are necessary to help clot the blood.

Two major types of white blood cells (leukocytes) are called granulocytes and lymphocytes. Granulocytes, produced in the bone marrow, fight infection by surrounding and destroying invading bacteria. Lymphocytes, produced mainly in lymphatic tissue, are involved in producing antibodies, protein particles that attack any foreign material (bacteria, viruses, fungi, or chemicals) that get into the body.

Immature white blood cells, called blast cells, normally found in small numbers in the bone marrow, begin to accumulate there without maturing into functional cells and spill over into the circulating blood as well. These blast cells multiply so rapidly that they slow the development of normal red blood cells, granulocytes, and platelets in the bone marrow.

As the blood circulates, great numbers of blast cells begin to clog healthy body tissues and organs. Organs severely affected include the brain, lymph nodes (numerous small bean- or pea-shaped lumps of infection-fighting lymphoid tissue, located just under the skin or deep in the body), spleen (a large lymphoid organ, lying in the upper left side of the abdomen, which is also important in combating infection), and liver.

As the accumulation of blast cells continues, body tissues and organs swell. They are damaged when microorganisms cause infection—which progresses unchecked because of the insufficiency of mature white cells—or when spontaneous bleeding (hemorrhage) occurs—the result of too few platelets. Anemia occurs when too few red blood cells are available to carry oxygen to body tissues.

A key characteristic of immature white blood cells is that they prove ineffective in combating infection. The white cell count, increasingly dominated by blast cells, grows abnormally high, the red cell count declines, and in time the number of platelets dips dangerously low. Bacterial and viral infections, such as *pneumonia,* are a constant threat because the disease prevents the development of granulocytes that ordinarily combat infection in the body. Sudden bleeding (hemorrhage) is also possible, because blast cells can clump inside blood vessels anywhere in the body. Once a blood vessel is blocked, pressure inside builds, often leading to a leak or a burst vessel; few platelets are available to control bleeding if it begins. Tiny hemorrhages are not unusual just under the surface of the skin. Much more serious is the risk of bleeding caused by blockage of small blood vessels in the brain.

Leukemia and the anticancer medications used to control it can cause severe imbalances of the metabolism. When levels of uric acid, calcium, and phosphate in the blood increase as a result of metabolic imbalance, kidney and heart problems can become additional threats to a child's health.

Other problems arise when leukemic cells circulate through the body. The central nervous system can be affected. In rare cases the eyes are invaded, threatening vision.

Out of 12 different types of childhood leukemias, the two most prevalent are acute lymphoblastic leukemia (ALL) and acute myeloblastic leukemia (AML). (These two are sometimes referred to as acute lymphocytic and acute myelocytic leukemia.) About 4 times as many cases of ALL occur annually in the United States as do cases of AML. Immature lymphoctyes called lymphoblasts are produced in excessive numbers in ALL, and abnormal granulocytes called myeloblasts are produced in excessive numbers in AML.

Nearly all childhood leukemias—about 95 percent—are classified as acute. Originally that meant that they developed suddenly and ran a single, rapid, fatal course in any patient who did not receive treatment. Since the development of chemotherapy (treatment with a combination of powerful anticancer medications), survival time for childhood leukemias has increased substantially; it probably would be more accurate now to describe these diseases as "chronic" or "long-term."

The outlook for children with leukemia depends upon several factors: the type of disease, the treatment, the speed with which a remission (elimination of all signs and symptoms of disease) is achieved, and whether a relapse occurs after treatment is ended. ALL is more easily controlled by chemotherapy than is AML. Accurate, skillful management of chemotherapy can often prevent sudden changes in the severity of disease or its site in the body.

The more swiftly a remission can be brought about, the stronger the chances for survival. Relapse into illness after treatment has stopped indicates that chances for long-term survival are less hopeful. About half of all children suffering from ALL can look forward to successful treatment and a disease-free life. The prospects for children suffering from AML are less hopeful, because treatment often is not as effective and relapses are more common. It should be remembered, however, that each additional year a child lives in remission lends strength to an assumption that leukemia may be in lasting remission.

CAUSE

Although intensive research continues, no cause of leukemia has yet been identified. It appears likely that a number of factors cause leukemia. It has been suggested that environmental factors such as excessive radiation and toxic chemicals (including medications) can increase the risk of a child's contracting leukemia and other types of cancer. Exactly how these factors may be linked to leukemia, however, has not yet been determined. But since human leukemia virus (HLV) has been implicated as a cause of an adult leukemia, further discoveries in research may be near.

SIGNS AND SYMPTOMS

The signs and symptoms of childhood leukemias are extremely variable. Generalized signs and symptoms may include a low-grade fever, sore throat, swollen lymph nodes in the neck and armpits, irritability, listlessness, lack of appetite, loss of weight, weakness, paleness, bone or joint aches and pains, or a combination of any of these. Because a child's normal infection-fighting abilities are diminished, the body is more likely to be invaded by bacteria, viruses, and fungi.

A tendency to bruise easily or to suffer spontaneous bleeding (appearing as tiny bruises just under the surface of the skin) are other possible early signs of leukemia. An enlarged spleen or liver or swollen lymph nodes (sometimes called "swollen glands") in the neck, armpits, or groin may be signs of clogging caused by blast cells (see *swollen glands*). What appears to be a cold (see *colds*) or a mild case of *influenza* may develop and persist.

None of these indications of illness may be considered serious until one or more grow noticeably worse and are brought to a physi-cian's attention. It is not unusual for such minor complaints to persist for a week or more before a physician is consulted. Family members sometimes blame themselves unnecessarily later on for not taking a leukemic child to a physician as soon as the first sign of illness appeared. It is worth observing, however, that sometimes not even a physician can identify the general signs and symptoms of illness as forerunners of leukemia. But once diagnosis is confirmed, the crucial step is to begin treatment immediately. That may make a difference in the long run.

Infrequently, the first signs and symptoms of leukemia are sudden or severe, involving such problems as a limp, breathing difficulty, bleeding from the small or large intestine, or sudden *vomiting, headache,* and lethargy, which may indicate bleeding from the brain.

DIAGNOSIS

Leukemia is diagnosed by a physician, who considers the child's medical history and then performs a physical examination. Diagnosis of leukemia is determined by laboratory tests of blood and bone marrow. Special blood tests can show the presence of high numbers of the specific abnormal cells characteristic of each kind of leukemia.

Blood tests that yield such abnormal results usually lead a physician to take (or "aspirate") a small bone marrow sample from one of the large bones, usually the hipbone. This procedure, called an aspiration or biopsy, is performed using a needle and syringe. Discomfort is reduced with local anesthesia. The sample is studied under a microscope by a physician who can identify the specific type of leukemia and its severity, information essential in choosing the specific course of treatment to begin. After treatment is under way, the findings of the biopsy are used to measure the effectiveness of treatment. The blood and the bone marrow must both be examined—the blood more frequently than the marrow—to check on the course of the disease and to select the proper combination and dosages of medications.

TREATMENT

Treatment, often in a cancer center, can begin the same day that a diagnosis is confirmed. The main goals of treatment are elimination of invading leukemic blast cells and, as much as possible, avoidance of damage to healthy cells and tissue.

Chemotherapy is administered in dosages that vary according to the type of leukemia and a child's age, weight, and physical condition. Using combinations of medications, physicians can achieve remission—elimination of all signs and symptoms of disease, especially in the blood and the bone marrow —in about 95 percent of cases of acute lymphoblastic leukemia (ALL). A somewhat smaller proportion of children—about 80 percent—suffering from acute myeloblastic leukemia (AML) experience remission after receiving chemotherapy. Even after remission has been achieved, sometimes in a matter of weeks, chemotherapy continues for several months or years before a child is taken off medication and the body is given a chance to function without intervention.

One of the causes of treatment failure in childhood leukemias is accumulation of blast cells in the brain. The central nervous system can serve as a kind of sanctuary for these cells, protecting them from the effects of chemotherapy. Because of special qualities in the blood vessel walls of the brain, some chemical substances cannot penetrate into brain tissues themselves. Among such substances are many of the medications used in chemotherapy. To overcome this so-called "blood-brain barrier," anticancer medications can be injected directly into the spinal fluid of leukemic children, even before any symptoms of central nervous system involvement occur. This preventive step is taken because statistics show that without such treatment about 3 out of 4 children suffering from ALL eventually develop signs and symptoms of disease of the central nervous system. Some children receive radiation therapy (precise exposure to certain high-energy X rays or to radiation emitted by radioactive substances such as cobalt) of the brain as another preventive measure.

Both leukemia and, paradoxically, the powerful medications used to combat it damage bone marrow and interfere with the production of platelets and granulocytes. On balance, the long-term benefits of medication usually outweigh the short-term risks. In addition, cancer specialists have found that certain secondary treatments can also be helpful, even life-preserving. For example, transfusions of red blood cells can combat *anemia*, and transfusions of packed blood platelets can prevent or halt a hemorrhage. A similar transfusion process is used to supply large quantities of infection-fighting granulocytes to leukemia patients who are suffering from severe infections.

Infection constantly threatens children undergoing treatment for leukemia. New antibiotics continue to be developed through the ongoing process of research, and special efforts are being made to develop new antiviral and antifungal medications.

A promising development is bone marrow transplantation, a technique that removes all leukemia-infested marrow from large bones and replaces it with healthy marrow from a donor. The new marrow is carefully screened and selected on the basis of a histocompatibility system, a highly refined version of blood-typing that screens the antigens in each child's lymphoctyes. Healthy marrow from a compatible donor, often a sibling or other family member, can function as if it were a child's own blood-producing tissue. The initial successes of bone marrow transplants may hold promise for many leukemic children in the future.

In the laboratory specially treated proteins called monoclonal antibodies have shown an ability to seek out and destroy cancerous blast cells in the bone marrow and blood while leaving healthy cells unharmed. Further development of this innovation of "biotechnology" may be especially important in the search for a leukemia cure.

The Leukemia Society of America offers counseling and limited financial assistance to families of children with leukemia. Consult the nearest chapter of LSA by checking the telephone directory, or write to the national headquarters: 733 Third Avenue, New York, NY 10017 (phone: 212-573-8484).

PREVENTION

No form of leukemia can as yet be prevented.

Environmental factors such as radiation and toxic chemicals (including some medications) are believed to increase a child's chances of developing leukemia. Research continues on determining whether casual relationships exist between these factors and the development of childhood leukemia. Parents should try to be alert to the appearance or existence of any environmental hazard to human health (see Prevention section of *cancer*).

LICE

DESCRIPTION

Lice are tiny parasitic insects that attach themselves to human skin and hair. Lice suck the blood of their hosts for nourishment, injecting their own salivary juices and digestive matter into the skin as they feed. This feeding process is responsible for the intense itching often characteristic of lice infestation. Their wingless bodies, flat and almost translucent, become dark brown when engorged with blood. Lice are visible to the naked eye, but move quickly and are difficult to locate. Adult female lice have lifespans of about 1 month and each lays up to 4 or 5 eggs daily.

Three kinds of lice infest humans: head lice, body lice, and pubic lice.

Head lice most often infest children and can become epidemic in schools, camps, and other places where children congregate. Nits, which are the eggs, are found cemented firmly to the hair shaft, anywhere along the length of each strand. Girls seem to acquire head lice more often than boys, but hair length has not been proved to be a significant factor. Nor are the presence of head lice, by themselves, evidence of a child's (or adult's) poor hygiene or lack of cleanliness. Because they are so easy to acquire from even brief contact with other children or their belongings, head lice can infest a child whose hair is shampooed daily and trimmed regularly.

Body lice are not found among children except under highly unsanitary conditions. Nits stick as if glued to the seams and fibers of clothing, where the eggs hatch as a result of the host's body warmth. Anyone who changes clothing regularly is not bothered by body lice.

Pubic lice, shorter in length than head or body lice, resemble tiny crabs. These lice, which are found most often on adolescents and adults, attach firmly to pubic hair. Occasionally pubic lice infest other hairy parts of the body such as the chest, thighs, beard, or even eyelashes.

CAUSE

Head lice are acquired primarily by coming in direct contact with an infested person. (Head lice are incapable of hopping, jumping, or flying.) Children also unwittingly spread head lice by sharing their hats, cloth-

ing, towels, combs, and hair brushes. Head lice may be transmitted when children lie on infested furniture, carpeting, or bedding. Body and pubic lice are transmitted primarily by skin-to-skin contact, but also by contaminated clothing, bedding, and towels. Unlike fleas, lice do not live or breed on environmental surfaces. If lice are there, they have fallen off or left one host in search of another.

SIGNS AND SYMPTOMS

Intense itching is the major symptom of lice infestation, but not everyone who is infested experiences itching. Head lice nits, which resemble tiny, tear-shaped specks, may be seen attached to the child's hair shafts, especially above the ears, at the nape of the neck, and on the crown of the head. They can be found, however, anywhere on the head. The lice may be visible on the skin near the scalp. Sometimes there will be what appear to be red pimples (actually bite marks) near the base of the hair shaft or scratch marks on the scalp. Examining the hair in natural light is often the only sure means of finding the nits. Using a strong incandescent lamp or a flashlight at close range can be effective.

DIAGNOSIS

Infestation with head lice is usually obvious because of a child's intense itching and scratching.

COMPLICATIONS

Prolonged scratching of areas infested by lice may contribute to the development of *swollen glands* or lead to an infection such as *impetigo* (either streptococcal or staphylococcal).

TREATMENT

Individual treatment for head lice is a two-step process involving the use of a louse-killing shampoo or lotion and a combing tool made especially for nit removal. Most adult head lice and not more than 70 to 80 percent of the nits can be killed by shampooing a child's hair with an insecticide shampoo. These shampoos include a solution of 1 percent gamma benzene hexachloride (available by prescription) and synergized pyrethrins (over-the-counter). Such products must be used very carefully, observing all the safety guidelines contained in the package insert. Parents should pay special attention to the restrictions regarding use of gamma benzene hexachloride. Second applications may be necessary to eliminate all of the egg-laying females, but thorough nit removal can eliminate the need for further use of insecticide shampoos. A physician should always be consulted about repeat applications of shampoo for children under 6 years old.

Because louse shampoos and lotions never kill all the nits, survivors hatch into crawling lice within 7 to 10 days, thereby producing a cycle of reinfestation. The nits must be removed, using the special combing tool, tweezers, or fingernails. It is usually necessary to use natural daylight or a bright light, such as a reading lamp or a flashlight, to illuminate the hair so that each strand can be separated and carefully examined. Nit-picking is a laborious, time-consuming procedure, but it is the only way to eliminate all nits, and prevent reinfestation.

A daily nit check is advisable for at least 10 days following a treatment. Retreatment may be needed within 7 to 10 days if there is evidence of new nits or newly hatched lice. Regardless of precautions taken at home, reinfestation from others remains a problem.

Combs and hairbrushes can be soaked in louse shampoo for an hour or in water heated to 150° F (66° C) for 5 to 10 minutes. Clothing and bed linen should be laundered in soapy hot water or dry-cleaned. Placing nonwashable clothing in an airtight plastic bag for about two weeks usually kills all the eggs. Rugs, upholstered furniture, and mattresses should be vacuumed to dispose of any living lice or nits attached to fallen hairs.

Anyone who may have had close physical contact with an infected child or adolescent should also be examined and treated if lice or lice eggs are found. (As a preventive measure for such people, physicians often recommend treatment with an insecticide shampoo even if there is no evidence of lice or nits.) Parents should be aware that symptoms, especially itching, may take as long as 4 to 6 weeks to appear.

Treatment for body and pubic lice includes the practice of personal cleanliness and frequent changes and laundering of clothing and bedding.

PREVENTION

General cleanliness and prompt, thorough treatment of individuals who have lice are the best ways to prevent outbreaks of lice infestation. Avoiding close contact with anyone who may have an untreated or recurrent case of lice can prevent infestation.

It is important to notify the child's school at once so that other families can be alerted to a possible outbreak of head lice. Families of playmates should also be informed promptly. Cooperation can help protect everyone concerned. Information about prevention is available from the National Pediculosis Association, P.O. Box 149, Newton, MA 02161 (phone: 617-449-NITS).

LUNG RUPTURE

EMERGENCY ACTION

If a child has sustained a severe chest injury, a lung or the chest wall may be ruptured. Seek immediate medical attention. (An open chest wound should be covered with an occlusive dressing.) Spontaneous rupture of the lung can also occur in normal adolescents, asthmatics, and patients with cystic fibrosis. The individual usually experiences sharp chest pain and some shortness of breath.

DESCRIPTION

A lung rupture allows air from a lung to leak into the thoracic (chest) cavity and become trapped between the lungs and the rib cage and diaphragm, causing a condition called pneumothorax (literally meaning air in the thoracic cavity). Pneumothorax can compress the lung and thus decrease the volume of lung available for respiration (breathing). *Shortness of breath* and, in severe cases, *cyanosis* (blueness of skin resulting from oxygen-deprived blood) can result. A continuing accumulation of trapped air in the pleural space (the space between the lung and the chest wall), may displace the heart and great blood vessels, interfering with their functions and threatening life.

CAUSE

During infancy, lung rupture can be caused by a number of respiratory disorders including *pneumonia,* hyaline membrane disease (see *respiratory distress syndrome),* and pulmonary hypoplasia (small lungs). Later in childhood it can occur with disorders such as *asthma* and *cystic fibrosis,* which can cause some lung units to become overdistended and rupture.

DIAGNOSIS

Pneumothorax is usually discovered by a physician (and not by parents) when he or she is investigating symptoms of a respiratory disorder, particularly the sudden onset of chest pain and shortness of breath. Often the diagnosis is made after X-ray examination.

TREATMENT

Excessive accumulation of air may be relieved by inserting a small tube between the ribs into the pocket of air and removing the air from the pleural space. The air leak in the lung usually seals in time. Some individuals experience a pneumothorax more than once. Surgery or chemical treatment of the pleural space to prevent the lung from falling away from the chest wall is sometimes recommended.

PREVENTION

Lung rupture can be prevented only if its causes are prevented.

LUPUS ERYTHEMATOSUS

DESCRIPTION

Lupus erythematosus is a lifelong disorder characterized by inflammation of the body's connective tissues (the tendons and ligaments), a low-grade *fever, rash,* and *joint pain.* The disease usually follows a pattern of flare-ups and remissions (disease-free periods).

Approximately 1 million Americans have been diagnosed with lupus; 50,000 new cases are identified each year. Lupus can occur at any age but is extremely rare among children under 5 years old. About one fourth of cases occur for the first time during adolescence; most victims develop the disorder during their 20s and 30s.

Approximately 1 out of every 500 American females develops lupus; it appears only about one tenth as often among males. Lupus affects all races and ethnic groups, although blacks are affected more often and more severely than whites.

Two types of lupus exist: discoid and systemic. Discoid lupus affects only the skin, particularly the face, neck, upper chest, back, and upper arms. Overall, this type is more common than systemic lupus. Occa-

sionally discoid lupus progresses to systemic lupus. Systemic lupus is more serious than discoid lupus because it can affect any body system or internal organ, individually or in combination. The joints, skin, blood, and kidneys are most often affected, although the heart, lungs, spleen, liver, other abdominal organs, and central nervous system may also be involved. Occasionally, however, symptoms of systemic lupus are so mild that the affected individual may not be aware of the disease.

No cure exists for lupus erythematosus, and the outlook depends on the severity of the disorder and the extent of organ involvement. Given proper treatment, 90 to 95 percent of lupus victims are alive 5 years after the initial diagnosis, and 70 to 85 percent survive for 15 years.

CAUSE

The exact cause of lupus erythematosus is unknown. It is known, however, that this disorder stems from the abnormal functioning of the body's immune system. Normally, the body produces white blood cells that control antibody-producing cells involved in fighting infection. (Antibodies are proteins that fight invading foreign organisms.) When lupus is present, these controlling cells are missing and antibodies attack the body's connective tissues.

Medical experts believe that development of lupus may be influenced by sex hormones. Female hormones appear to accelerate lupus-related tissue degeneration.

SIGNS AND SYMPTOMS

Discoid lupus is characterized by a *rash* of red, raised, scaly, disk-shaped lesions that enlarge gradually over time and become worse with exposure to the sun. The rash on the face typically appears across the bridge of the nose and on the cheeks and is called a butterfly rash.

Other signs and symptoms of systemic lupus vary, depending on which body systems or organs are involved. Symptoms of lupus usually include a low-grade *fever,* a general feeling of physical discomfort, sensitivity to the sun, and constant weakness and tiredness. Joints, particularly the knuckles, wrists, and knees, may be swollen and painful, but walking is seldom impaired.

If the kidneys are affected (as they are in 3 of 4 affected children), urine may be cloudy. Involvement of the gastrointestinal tract (the esophagus, stomach, and intestines) causes *abdominal pain,* nausea, *vomiting,* and rarely, bleeding, as well as loss of weight and appetite. If the central nervous system is involved, an adolescent may become dizzy and suffer *seizures.* If the eyes are affected, persistent *conjunctivitis,* inflammation of the iris (the colored portion of the eye), blurred vision, or occasional *blindness* may occur. Other symptoms may include *anemia,* hair loss, sores in the mouth or nose, and spasms, pain, and loss of color in the fingertips and toes. In fact, any organ may be affected.

DIAGNOSIS

A physician may suspect lupus if an adolescent has 4 or more of the above symptoms, especially the *rash,* sun sensitivity, and hair loss. A complete medical history, a thorough physical examination, and the results of urine and blood tests can confirm a diagnosis. In severe cases kidney trouble may develop.

Discoid lupus is diagnosed through observation of the *rash* and through a biopsy (analysis of a tiny sample of skin tissue).

COMPLICATIONS

Some complications can be fatal. Severe kidney disease, severe infection (often resulting from immune system malfunctioning), or central nervous system involvement are the most common causes of death associated with lupus.

Other complications of lupus erythematosus include inflammation of the membrane around the heart, of the membrane lining the abdominal cavity, or of the membrane surrounding the lungs.

TREATMENT

Treatment focuses on relieving and controlling symptoms. Treatment varies according to the severity of the disorder. In general, treatment of lupus includes plenty of rest, good nutrition, and avoidance of *stress* and exposure to sunlight.

If no symptoms are present, treatment is usually not required. Treatment of mild cases of systemic lupus often includes only over-the-counter medications to reduce inflammation and pain, and sunscreen (containing PABA) to limit exposure to the sun's rays.

Discoid lupus sometimes disappears spontaneously. Treatment for persistent cases includes the application of cortisone ointment (an anti-inflammatory steroid) to the skin to control the rash, and the use of mild soaps and body lotions to avoid further irritation of the skin.

Treatment of more severe cases of lupus involving the kidneys, heart, or central nervous system may include anti-inflammatory medications, such as steroids. A physician may also recommend blood transfusion and immunosuppressant medications to control the most serious lupus crisis.

Spasms of the fingertips and toes can be prevented by avoiding exposure to extreme cold or heat. Women who are severely affected by lupus often decide against pregnancy because lupus may become worse after childbirth.

PREVENTION

As yet, neither type of lupus can be prevented. For information, write to the Lupus Foundation of America, P.O. Box 12897, St. Louis, MO 63141 (phone 800-558-0121), or call a local chapter.

LYME DISEASE

DESCRIPTION

Lyme disease is an infectious disease that can be complicated by arthritis (see *arthritis, acute)* and other problems if not properly treated at an early stage. Named for the town in Connecticut—Old Lyme—where several children became ill with the infection in 1975, the disease was recognized in Europe much earlier.

The illness begins as a red *rash* that may be accompanied by *headache, fever,* fatigue, muscle pains, and other symptoms. Lyme disease can attack the joints, heart, and central nervous system (brain, spinal cord, and their protective covering, the meninges). Symptoms of the disease, particularly arthritis, may recur. Individuals who are treated during the initial stage of illness generally recover within a week or so. People usually become ill with Lyme disease during the spring and summer, most often from mid-April to mid-August; it affects individuals of all ages.

CAUSE

Lyme disease is caused by the bite of a species of tick which is no bigger than a pinhead and often sucks the blood of white-tailed deer. This deer tick transmits a spirochete (a specialized, spiral-form bacterium) which first invades the skin of humans, causing a distinctive *rash*. The bacteria later enters the bloodstream, causing other characteristic signs and symptoms of infection. If untreated, the infection can progress to affect one or more joints, the heart, and the central nervous system.

SIGNS AND SYMPTOMS

The illness usually begins as a red *rash* at the site of the tick bite. The rash is characterized by large, doughnut-shaped welts, sometimes as large as 1½ inches across. As many as 25 percent of those children affected show a red, raised bump, which develops into an red ring that can expand to a diameter of 5 inches or more. The rash is usually accompanied by listlessness, *headache,* chills, mild *fever,* swollen lymph nodes (see *swollen glands),* and bone and muscle pain. Some individuals also develop a stiff neck. If the illness is not diagnosed and treated while the initial signs and symptoms are present, some children develop arthritis (see *arthritis, acute)* in one or more joints within about 1 month, although the time interval can be either shorter or considerably longer. An affected joint is usually inflamed: warm, swollen, sore, and difficult to move. Arthritis has a tendency to recur, and different joints may be involved at various times. Joint disease may become disabling if bone and connective tissue become eroded. Still later, heart problems (including *cardiomyopathy)* can occur. Inflammation of the lining of the brain and spinal cord *(meningitis)* and other nerve problems also develop occasionally.

DIAGNOSIS

A physician should be consulted if the characteristic *rash* of Lyme disease is accompanied by its typical signs and symptoms. After recording the history of the illness, the physician examines the child, paying particular attention to the rash and its pattern. Since infected ticks are most often found in certain parts of the United States (coastal areas of New England, Middle Atlantic states, Minnesota, Wisconsin, and the West Coast), the physician may ask if the child has been in any of these areas recently.

The presence of Lyme disease sometimes can be diagnosed by analysis of a blood sample or some fluid extracted from the rash. If the disease has developed into *meningitis,* a diagnosis can be made in some cases by specialized laboratory analysis of a sample of cerebrospinal fluid.

TREATMENT

Lyme disease can be treated successfully at home with antibiotics prescribed by a physician. Typical signs and symptoms can be treated at home, as necessary, until the antibiotics eliminate the spirochete and end the infection. The period of convalescence for a very sick child can last 2 to 3 weeks. If complications such as arthritis (see *arthritis, acute), cardiomyopathy,* or *meningitis* develop, they must be treated promptly by the physician, often in a hospital. Treatment is not completely effective for every child, particularly if arthritis has developed.

PREVENTION

The most effective prevention against acquiring tick bites in brush or woodlands during the summer tick season is wearing protective clothing (long-sleeved shirts, turtleneck jerseys, long trousers, hats, and gloves) and using insect repellent. If a tick is discovered on any skin surface, it should be removed slowly and carefully, preferably with gloves and tweezers. The tick should be grasped as close to the head as possible and pulled straight out with tweezers. The tick should not be crushed because infection through unbroken skin is possible. After washing the wound, the parent should wash his or her hands with soap and water. Since deer ticks are so tiny, it is important for parents to search for them with care, perhaps using a flashlight to aid in detection. Because pets often pick up ticks, their coats should be examined after they have been outdoors during tick seasons.

LYMPHOMA

DESCRIPTION

The body's lymphatic system is composed of lymphoid vessels (the circulatory network of small vessels that transport lymph, a clear, pale yellow fluid that bathes cells in the body), specialized lymphoid tissue (the lymphoid organs, such as lymph nodes, spleen, and thymus, each of which produces or stores infection-fighting white blood cells called lymphocytes), and scattered patches of lymphoid tissue located in organs such as the tonsils, stomach, small intestines, and skin (see Fig. 31, p. 501).

Lymphoid tissue, rich in lymphocytes, is essential to the body's defense against infection. Lymphocytes combat disease by manufacturing antibodies, protein particles that seek out and destroy invading bacteria, viruses, and fungi. Whenever a cancerous tumor begins in lymphoid tissue, a condition called lymphoma exists (see *cancer*).

Although each variety of lymphoma looks different under the microscope, diagnostic tests and treatments for most lymphomas resemble one another. Forms of the disease are usually divided into two categories: the most common form of lymphoma, called Hodgkin's disease (HD), and non-Hodgkin's lymphoma (NHL).

Lymphocytic lymphoma (sometimes called lymphoblastic lymphoma), histiocytic lymphoma (previously called reticulum cell sarcoma), and undifferentiated Burkitt-type lymphomas are the major forms of non-Hodgkin's lymphoma; each has its own original site and behaves quite differently from the others.

Lymphoma is unusual during childhood; among children under 15 years old, only about 7 cases of NHL per million children can be expected in any given year in the United States. The incidence rate for HD is about 6 cases per million children each year. Altogether, about 800 cases of HD and NHL in children occur annually. The incidence rises with age, however, especially after the fifteenth birthday. Young adults are especially prone to acquiring the disease. More males than females become ill with HD, especially after the age of 12 years. It is more prevalent in white than nonwhite children. Children suffering from immunodeficiency diseases, such as severe combined immunodeficiency disease (SCID) and Wiskott-Aldrich syndrome, run a much greater risk of developing NHL (see *immune disorders*).

HD treatment has improved so that 80 to 95 percent of those children who are promptly treated survive for at least 5 years. Each additional year of life beyond 5 years is another significant step toward what may be considered a cure for an individual. Given proper treatment, children whose disease is confined to a single group of lymph nodes have a good chance of recovery. Those chil-

FIG. 31. LYMPHATIC SYSTEM
(showing principal lymph node clusters and lymphatic channels)

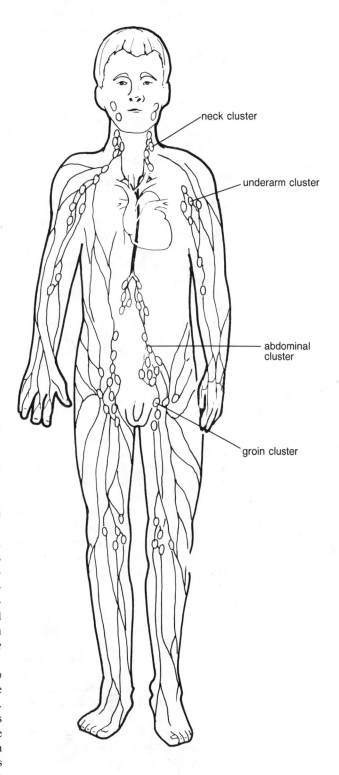

neck cluster

underarm cluster

abdominal cluster

groin cluster

dren whose disease is widespread when discovered face a much more difficult and unpredictable path to eventual recovery, because the chances of relapse and spread of disease remain high.

The outlook for children suffering from NHL is often less positive. The prospects for long-term survival of 5 years or more depend upon the type and stage when NHL is diagnosed and treatment begins. The probability of recovery is improving for children with each of the major types of NHL. The percentage estimates of those who survive at least as long as five years: lymphoblastic—60 percent; histiocytic—75 percent; undifferentiated Burkitt-type—50 percent.

CAUSE

The cause of HD is unknown, although some research indicates that it results from an infectious disease, especially a viral infection. In addition, HD sufferers often exhibit immune deficiency (inability of white blood cells to fight off infections), which may play a role in the origin of the disease.

A viral infection is strongly associated with Burkitt-type lymphoma, a type of NHL. The virus under investigation is Epstein-Barr virus, although a causal link has not been proved (see *mononucleosis, infectious*). Immunodeficiency (inability to fight infection) or immunosuppression (reduced ability to fight infection) is also suspected of playing a role in the origin of some types of NHL. Certain medications, such as steroids (synthetic, hormonelike drugs), can cause immunosuppression; immunodeficiency is a genetic characteristic, present from birth. Investigation is under way to determine if either problem is actually involved and, if so, whether the immune defect is genetic in origin or can be acquired by an individual. As yet, neither NHL or HD has been shown to be contagious.

SIGNS AND SYMPTOMS

The first sign of HD is often a painless, progressive swelling of a lymph node or group of lymph nodes (sometimes called *swollen glands*) in the neck, armpits, or groin. The most likely site is the neck, where more than three fourths of the childhood cases begin. Swollen lymph nodes, a common sign of infection, do not indicate serious illness in and of themselves; they should not cause undue concern unless they persist longer than 3 weeks.

Other symptoms of HD that may recur as the illness progresses include loss of appetite, weight loss, fatigue, persistent or recurrent *fever,* and night sweats that can vary in intensity from moist to drenching. A dry, hacking *cough* or wheezing may be annoying symptoms stemming from an HD tumor mass in the chest. *Abdominal pain* or *back pain* may be caused by swollen lymph nodes in the groin or in the abdominal cavity.

NHL may begin in a number of ways: a painless enlargement or swelling of lymph nodes in the region of the head and neck with a cough or wheezing; pain and swelling in the abdomen resembling that of appendicitis; or a variety of signs and symptoms including enlarged tonsils, pain somewhere in the back, and small lumps and bumps under the skin or groin. (Again, in the overwhelming majority of cases swollen lymph nodes do not indicate a malignant condition.) Persistent or recurrent fever, a feeling of general weakness, bone pain, and loss of appetite or weight are other signs and symptoms of NHL, but occur less frequently than in HD.

DIAGNOSIS
HD Diagnosis

A child who is suffering from persistent swollen lymph nodes and related signs and symptoms should see a physician. If the swollen lymph nodes and other problems do not disappear in 2 to 3 weeks after medical examination (and perhaps the use of antibiotics), further medical attention is indicated (see *swollen glands*). A physician, often an oncologist (one who specializes in the diagnosis and treatment of cancer and diseases of the blood) performs another physical examination and records all details of signs and symptoms associated with the illness.

The examination concentrates on areas of lymph node enlargement, checking for nodes that are located close to the body's surface—in the neck, armpits, groin, arms, and legs. Many lymph nodes, however, lie so deep that they are not easily located by the examiner's fingers. During this examination a physician may be able to locate a lymph node enlargement or a mass in an organ by knowing just where and how to feel for an abnormality. HD is diagnosed by biopsy of a lymph node (removal and analysis of the tissue). In addition, the entire lymphatic system can be visualized, using a special dye, in an X-ray procedure called a lymphangiogram.

If the finding is HD, a physician may require further tests to evaluate the spleen, liver, and abdominal lymph nodes. Such a procedure can be done as a laparotomy (operation on the abdomen) while a child is under general anesthesia. The spleen may be invaded by cancerous cells or masses, in which case the spleen is removed surgically. During the laparatomy, other biopsies of the liver, abdominal lymph nodes, and bone marrow may be performed.

Specialized X rays of suspected areas of lymphoid tissue involvement can also help identify disease. Any test specifically designed to identify the extent of disease is part of an overall diagnostic process called staging.

Staging can be crucial in selecting the most effective treatment for an individual, especially the best kind of radiation therapy. There are four major stages of HD: stage I—localized (confined to original lymph region); stage II—spread to adjacent lymph regions but confined either above or below the diaphragm; stage III—spread to lymph regions above and below the diaphragm; stage IV—spread to lungs, liver, bone marrow, or other tissues beyond the lymph node system. Each of these stages is further categorized as either group A or group B—clusters of related signs and symptoms characteristic of major disease variations. Group B, for example, is characterized by *fever,* weight loss, and night sweats. Following diagnosis of specific staging, treatment for HD often begins immediately, usually in a *cancer* center.

NHL Diagnosis

NHL usually starts to spread before being detected; it is usually diagnosed within the first 4 to 6 weeks of the appearance of signs and symptoms of illness. The diagnostic procedure for NHL is much the same as that for HD. Just as is done in suspected cases of HD, a physician usually orders blood studies, X rays, and aspirations of bone marrow, lymph nodes, and tissue masses that may be tumors. Kidney- and liver-function tests also may be helpful. A lumbar puncture (spinal tap) may be needed to check for abnormal cells in the cerebrospinal fluid, which bathes and protects the brain and spinal cord.

If any of these diagnostic tests indicates the spread of disease to the spleen, liver, or bones, a nuclear medicine scan may be employed to investigate further. In such an exam, a tiny amount of radioactive material is injected into a vein. A scanning device repeatedly sweeps over the body to detect possibly abnormal portions of the spleen, liver, or bones.

Precise staging to determine the best possible applications of radiation in NHL is not necessary, as these diseases are usually widespread at diagnosis and all children need chemotherapy for successful treatment.

COMPLICATIONS

Balancing the possible side effects of combined treatments—chemotherapy and radiation—is an ongoing challenge for a team of specialists. Complications can result from treatment, although they can be reversed if the disease has not progressed too far. Because treatment can depress a child's immune response (natural infection-fighting capabilities), infections often begin during or after treatment. Normal, healthy, disease-engulfing granulocytes (white blood cells) and antibodies produced by lymphocytes are not available in sufficient numbers to combat infections. Infections are a persistent problem as long as treatment continues, and this period can extend from 18 to 24 months. Inflammations of the lungs, small intestine, and heart muscle can also occur if medications and radiation cause reactions in the tissues.

TREATMENT

The most effective results in treatment of HD and NHL often occur in a *cancer* center, where a multidisciplinary team can pool its experience and expertise. Team members include oncologists, diagnostic and therapeutic X-ray specialists (radiologists and radiotherapists), pathologists, and surgeons. The difficulties involved in adequately treating a highly complex illness whose treatments are changing so swiftly make such a combined approach most effective.

The goal of treatment is to bring about a remission—a total absence of signs and symptoms detectable through physical examination and laboratory tests of blood, bone marrow, and involved organs. Treatment may continue for as long as 18 to 24 months following a remission to try to assure continued freedom from all signs and symptoms of disease. Relapse following treatment is much more common in children with NHL than in those with HD. The outlook for survival following relapse is difficult to predict.

HD Treatment

Treatment of early stage I and II is usually with radiation therapy. Regions where lymph nodes are involved are given radiation over several weeks or months. Radiation is also administered to the lymph node groups in the body that are likely to be involved next by the spread of HD. Chemotherapy, the administration of a combination of powerful anticancer medications, is useful in advanced stages of HD when disease has spread; it often continues for 6 to 12 months, during which a physician continually adjusts dosages to fit a patient's changing needs.

NHL Treatment

Treatment for NHL is designed for each child, depending upon the location and extent of disease. Radiation with high energy X rays can be helpful where lymph node or organ involvement is confined to one site. Radiation therapy is designed to destroy cancerous cells and tissues while avoiding harm to healthy cells and tissues.

Because NHL is likely to be widespread at diagnosis, regardless of treatment, radiation is never the only method prescribed. Chemotherapy is often prescribed because of the likelihood that the disease has spread to several other locations in the body, especially the spleen, liver, small intestine, skin, or bone marrow. In some cases, where tumors have invaded a specific organ or region, such as the abdominal cavity, surgery may be necessary in an attempt to remove the entire tumor mass. A combined approach using radiation, chemotherapy, and surgery often proves the most effective when dealing with NHL. Since the disease can invade the central nervous system (brain, spinal cord, and their protective covering, the meninges), oncologists often try to shield a child by administering anticancer medication before any signs or symptoms of central nervous system involvement appear. The sequence of treatment usually depends on how far the disease has advanced.

Side effects of treatment are common for most children, regardless of the kind of cancer being treated. Listlessness, loss of appetite, nausea, *vomiting,* and weight loss are common. Most children, especially adolescents, find hair loss the most disturbing side effect. It usually occurs during the course of chemotherapy. Hair may fall out in patches or all at once; a child may want to wear a hat, cap, scarf, or wig. (For a more complete discussion of side effects of treatment, see *cancer.*) Virtually all side effects are temporary and disappear after treatment is concluded.

Metabolic imbalances are common as a result of combined therapies. For example, increased or decreased amounts of salts (calcium, phosphate, or potassium) in the blood may interfere with heart and kidney function.

PREVENTION

Lymphoma—Hodgkin's disease and the various types of non-Hodgkin's lymphoma —cannot be prevented.

MALABSORPTION

DESCRIPTION AND CAUSE

Malabsorption (also known as intolerance) is a condition in which the body cannot break down and/or absorb sugars, proteins, or fats. Primary malabsorption is present at birth because of a specific defect in normal absorption, although symptoms may not develop until later during infancy. Secondary malabsorption usually develops when the enzyme production sites of the intestine, pancreas, or liver are damaged by disease, and enzyme production is hindered. Primary malabsorption is a lifelong condition; secondary malabsorption usually disappears when organ damage heals.

Symptoms of malabsorption do not appear until certain foods are introduced into a child's diet. If malabsorption is severe, symptoms can last from a few days to several weeks. Poor nutrition lengthens the duration of intolerance and may lead to intolerance of additional substances.

Among children, the most common forms of malabsorption involve intolerance of lactose (sugar found in milk) and sucrose (sugar found in fruits and vegetables). In addition, malabsorption is a component of certain diseases or infections.

Parasitic infections of the intestines are another cause of malabsorption. *Giardia lamblia,* a parasite that causes a disease called giardiasis, is transferred easily, most often by contact with stool that contains the parasite. This contact commonly occurs in families and institutions (such as schools) where children are in close contact with carriers. Exactly how giardiasis affects intestinal absorption of nutrients is unknown, but some medical experts believe that it causes changes in the structure of the intestinal mucous membrane, competes with the intestine for nutrients, irritates the intestine, and interferes with proper intestinal functioning.

Sugar Malabsorption

Lactose intolerance occurs when either little or no lactase, the enzyme that breaks down lactose, is in the intestine. Genetic lactose intolerance is very common, but by the ages of 3 to 5 years, the lactase enzyme decreases in concentration for about 75 percent of the children in the world. Children of Northern European heritage are an exception, and their lactose intolerance can continue to be a problem. Secondary intolerance is usually a result of diseases such as gastroenteritis, (a gastrointestinal-tract infection; see *diarrhea),* enterocolitis (severe inflammation of the mucous membrane of the intestine), and *cystic fibrosis.*

Sucrose intolerance is the most common form of primary malabsorption and results from lack of the enzyme sucrase. Symptoms usually do not appear, however, until foods containing sucrose are introduced into the infant's diet, usually several months after birth. The same diseases that cause secondary lactose intolerance cause secondary sucrose intolerance; the two intolerances often occur together.

Protein Malabsorption

Celiac disease is a disorder that prevents intestinal breakdown of wheat or rye protein. This disorder may be inherited, but how it is transferred is unclear. Because these proteins cannot be broken down, affected children suffer symptoms of protein malabsorption.

Fat Malabsorption

Fat malabsorption is often a component of diseases that cause the body's level of fat enzymes (which break down fats) to rise so drastically that tissue is damaged. Less often, fat malabsorption is present at birth because of an inherited lack of fat enzymes. Fat malabsorption usually occurs when the pancreas or liver is affected by one of the following:

- Cystic fibrosis. An inherited, incurable disease that not only causes malabsorption but also impairs a child's breathing and digestion and affects the lungs, pancreas, and sometimes the liver.
- Pancreatic insufficiency. A lack of enzymes to break down fats and protein most often found with cystic fibrosis, but also occurring with malnutrition and inflammation of the pancreas.
- Pancreatitis. A problem that occurs with several childhood illnesses, including *mumps* and mononucleosis (see *mononucleosis, infectious),* it also may develop when the pancreas is injured by a blow to the abdomen with a blunt object. In both cases, fat enzyme levels increase and cause pancreatic tissue damage. If tissue damage is severe, fat malabsorption may cause major complications.
- Liver disorders. These problems can cause both fat and sugar malabsorption. Liver problems causing fat malabsorption most often include cystic fibrosis, *hepatitis* (a viral infection of the liver), *biliary atresia* (a severe defect, present at birth, in the network of small tubes that carry bile through and away from the liver), and cirrhosis (progressive breakdown of liver tissue). In addition, sugar malabsorption may occur with liver-related disorders such as galactosemia (inability to break down galactose, a natural sugar), fructosemia (inability to break down fructose, also a natural sugar), and glycogen-storage disease (marked by a lack of enzymes needed to metabolize glycogen, one of the forms in which sugar is stored in the liver).

The severity of malabsorption varies according to the size of the enzyme deficiency and the extent of organ damage. Many children with enzyme deficiencies can tolerate a small amount of foods requiring those enzymes for digestion without producing malabsorption symptoms. For example, a child with lactose intolerance often does not develop symptoms until he or she drinks more than one glass of milk.

With proper treatment and diet management, a child suffering lactose intolerance, sucrose intolerance, and celiac disease has no symptoms of malabsorption. Parasitic infestations usually disappear completely with effective treatment. The outlook for children with cystic fibrosis, liver disease, and disorders of the pancreas is determined by the effectiveness of treatment and the progression of the disease.

SIGNS AND SYMPTOMS

Signs and symptoms of malabsorption

usually develop within eight hours of eating specific foods and last anywhere from a few days to several weeks. Stools are loose, watery, and foul-smelling. *Diarrhea, abdominal pain,* and abdominal bloating are usually present; intestinal gas, gurgling, nausea, *vomiting,* and *constipation* may also develop. In severe cases the child's growth may be stunted.

DIAGNOSIS

Diagnosis of malabsorption is made by a physician. A history of recent weight loss, unusual behavior, presence of characteristic stools, *abdominal pain* following ingestion of certain foods, and a history of long-term illness help identify the type of malabsorption. Information about a child's growth rate and feeding habits is also helpful.

A physical examination is performed in an effort to detect specific types of malabsorption. The child is given foods that contain fats, sugars, or proteins, following which a stool sample is collected and analyzed for the presence of unabsorbed substances. Stool samples should be fresh for accurate analysis, although a physician may request samples taken over a three-day period to determine the average amount of unabsorbed substances excreted daily.

The presence of excess fats in a child's stool indicates liver or pancreas problems, while excess sugar usually indicates intestinal problems. Natural acids may also be present as a result of bacterial breakdown of unabsorbed lactose or sucrose. Stool samples are also examined for the presence of parasites. If parasites are found both in stool and intestinal fluid, infection is confirmed.

Problems of the pancreas are identified by the presence of unabsorbed fats or proteins in pancreatic secretions and stool. In addition, sweat is analyzed for elevated salt content, which indicates *cystic fibrosis.*

Other diagnostic tests for malabsorption include blood tests to check for excess amounts of fats or sugars, presence of hepatitis virus, high levels of bilirubin (yellow pigment formed when red blood cells are broken down, indicating liver malfunction), and high levels of ammonia (also indicating liver malfunction). If necessary, X-ray films are taken to check for organ abnormalities or mucous membrane damage. X rays can also detect stunting of growth. A hydrogen breath test is used to determine the presence of unabsorbed lactose and sucrose. (As normal intestinal bacteria feed on sugar, hydrogen is given off and high levels in a child's breath indicate unabsorbed sugars.)

If the specific form of malabsorption cannot be identified through these procedures, a liver or intestinal biopsy (nonsurgical removal of a small tissue sample for analysis) may be performed to determine the extent of membrane injury and the type of enzyme missing. In rare cases intestinal biopsy is performed to determine parasitic infestation that cannot be detected through stool examination.

COMPLICATIONS

One of the most serious complications of malabsorption is *malnutrition,* the inadequate intake or absorption of nutrients and calories.

Acidosis (dangerous increase in the blood's acidity) may develop if large amounts of unabsorbed sugars and fats are broken down by bacteria. (Acid is a by-product of bacterial breakdown.)

If sucrose is introduced during the first few weeks of life into the diet of a child born with sucrose intolerance, dehydration and stunting of growth (see *height problems)* may occur.

Diaper rash is common because the stools of a child with malabsorption are characteristically acidic. Toilet training may be difficult for toddlers because of the discomfort caused by diarrhea.

TREATMENT

Although not always necessary, treatment of malabsorption may involve removing offending foods from a child's diet. Any diet modifications should be determined with the help of a physician or registered dietician. A child with primary malabsorption may initially become constipated on a restricted diet, but bowel movements usually become normal within a few days.

Lactose is easily removed from a child's diet by eliminating milk (not only cow's milk but also goat's or sheep's milk) and foods containing milk, such as prepared meats, breads, and some canned foods. For the most part, children with lactose intolerance can tolerate lactose in fermented forms such as yogurt or cheese. If milk is essential to a child's diet (particularly for infants and small children), a yeast lactase enzyme (available without prescription) can be added to milk to break down lactose.

Ingestion of sucrose can be avoided by eliminating certain infant formulas, juices, fruits, and vegetables from a child's diet. Dextrose, another sugar, is easily substituted for sucrose in home food preparation.

If lactose or sucrose intolerance is secondary, treatment of the underlying illness heals the intestine and restores enzyme production and sugar absorption. A sucrose- or lactose-free diet should be followed during treatment.

Disorders of the pancreas other than cystic fibrosis are usually treated with diet modification. A child's diet should be low in fats but high in protein and vitamins. In addition, supplemental enzymes may be given to compensate for pancreatic insufficiency and to help break down fats and proteins.

Treatment of liver disease usually focuses on preventing a child from becoming seriously ill and easing symptoms until disease is controlled. A child's diet should be low in fats and high in proteins, and should include vitamin supplements. Hospitalization is often required if liver disease is severe. Intravenous fluids may be given if danger of *dehydration* exists from frequent vomiting and diarrhea.

See also *celiac disease; cystic fibrosis; parasitic infections.*

PREVENTION

Most causes of malabsorption cannot be prevented. Symptoms, however, can be eliminated if the child carefully follows a restricted diet, and, when needed, a treatment program.

See also *hepatitis; parasitic infections.*

MALNUTRITION

EMERGENCY ACTION

Seek immediate medical attention if a child has signs and symptoms of any of the following:

- *dehydration* (cool, dry, pale skin; dry tongue; thirst; listlessness; rapid pulse; and sunken eyes)
- *shock* (cool, clammy, pale skin; weak, rapid pulse; thirst; and increased breathing rate)
- hypothermia (body temperature well below 98.6° F; 37.0° C)

Encourage a dehydrated child to drink water or other fluids. A child with any of these conditions should be kept warm with blankets.

DESCRIPTION

Malnutrition is the result of inadequate intake or absorption of food. It can be mild (first degree), moderate (second degree), or severe (third degree). Third-degree malnutrition can be further described as marasmus (severe starvation) or kwashiorkor (severe starvation with swelling caused by fluid accumulation). Worldwide, malnutrition is one of the leading causes of sickness and death in children, but it can affect people of all ages. The degree of malnutrition varies with duration of inadequate intake, specific nutrients missing from the diet, and increased nutritional requirements (such as those occurring with an underlying disease or stress).

In the developing world, severe heat or cold, drought, or floods can result in crop failure and decreased availability of food. In developed countries such as the United States, malnutrition is often secondary to an underlying disease.

A child with malnutrition does not get enough protein and/or calories, and the diet is often deficient in vitamins and minerals. Body processes do not function normally, and inadequate growth results. In addition, insufficient food intake causes the body to use existing muscle and fat to supply energy and protein.

With treatment, most malnourished children recover fully. A child with first- or second-degree malnutrition does not usually suffer permanent organ damage, although long-term *learning problems* may occur. Children with third-degree malnutrition may require longer treatment and may never reach normal growth levels.

CAUSE

Malnutrition results from decreased nutritional intake, decreased absorption of nutrients, increased nutrient losses, or increased nutritional requirements.

On a worldwide scale, poverty, with the inability to purchase or grow food, results in a decreased intake of needed nutrients. This is the most common cause of malnutrition. In more affluent areas, malnutrition may stem from a child's poor eating habits, including vigorous dieting or diets of food with little nutritional value. However, any underlying disease (even a cold) causes a loss of appetite and voluntary restriction of food intake. If a child does not meet his or her nutritional requirements, malnutrition may occur.

Decreased absorption occurs anytime the lining of the intestine is damaged (such as with infection or nutrient intolerance; see *malabsorption)* or nutrients move rapidly through the intestines (such as with *diarrhea).* Increased nutrient losses are associated with diarrhea. Increased nutritional requirements are present during *stress,* such as an infection or injury. If not treated, long-term disorders, including *cystic fibrosis, ulcerative colitis,* and *cancer* may cause malnutrition.

SIGNS AND SYMPTOMS

Inadequate weight gain is often the only sign of first-degree malnutrition among infants and children. If mild malnutrition is long-term (such as may occur with *cystic fibrosis)* a child's rate of growth, including head growth, decreases. Children become less active and may show some developmental delays, as well as changes in temperament and behavior. The cumulative effect of mild malnutrition may cause severe symptoms, such as *dehydration* or *shock* (see Emergency Action, above).

In addition to the initial symptoms above, signs and symptoms of a marasmic child include sunken cheeks and severe loss of tissue, muscle, and fat. The child is usually extremely apathetic. Loss of tissue and fat is not as apparent in a child with kwashiorkor, since fluid accumulation often gives the appearance of fat or muscle. (This fluid may account for as much as 20 percent of a child's total body weight.) Severe malnutrition (especially kwashiorkor) produces many skin changes, such as development of dark or light areas, peeling, and sores. (Some skin changes are associated with specific nutrient deficiencies.)

Other symptoms of severe malnutrition include a smooth red tongue, dry cracked lips, and dry cracked skin at the corners of the eyes and mouth. Hair is frequently sparse and brittle, may lose its shine, and may change color from dark to light.

DIAGNOSIS

Malnutrition is usually suspected by a physician when a child's rate of growth, specifically weight gain, slows or is reduced when compared with normal rates for age. (Failure to gain height occurs only when a child has been malnourished for a longer period of time.) In addition, histories of inadequate nutrition and of a child's previous growth rate help a physician determine the severity of malnutrition. Other indicators include decreased head circumference, loss of body fat (detected by measuring skin fold thickness) and loss of muscle (detected by measuring arm circumference).

Blood tests may show a decreased level of protein, including albumin. However, these measurements may be normal, or almost normal, in the presence of severe malnutrition, particularly if *stress* (such as infection) has not occurred and a child's diet has been deficient in all nutrients equally. Blood proteins are always low when a child suffers kwashiorkor.

Since malnourished children are more susceptible to infection, and infection makes malnutrition worse, malnourished children are very carefully examined for signs and symptoms of infection. A thorough physical examination, blood tests, and cultures of the throat, blood, urine, stool, and sometimes spinal fluid are performed. Tests for parasites (see *parasitic infections)* and *tuberculosis* are also performed.

COMPLICATIONS

Severe malnutrition may be accompanied by *dehydration* and an imbalance of electrolytes (substances in the blood needed to keep a fluid balance within the body) because of fluid loss resulting from *diarrhea* and *vomiting.* In addition, severe malnutrition affects the body's ability to use nutrients, resulting in further *malabsorption. Anemia* develops because the intestines do not absorb sufficient protein, vitamins, and minerals. A child's liver often becomes enlarged and malfunctions.

Because a malnourished child's immune system does not work properly, malnutrition is often accompanied by infections, particularly *pneumonia. Parasitic infections* (such as ascaris or hookworm) may also be present. Cardiovascular problems may lead to low blood pressure and poor circulation. *Jaundice* (a condition in which bilirubin, a yellow pigment that is a waste product of red blood cells, turns the skin yellow) may be present because of liver malfunctioning. Malfunctioning of the kidneys, gastrointestinal tract, (stomach, esophagus, and large and small intestines), pancreas, and heart may also occur. A severely malnourished child may develop *hypoglycemia* (low blood sugar).

Severely malnourished children have a mortality rate 4 to 7 times higher than moderately or mildly malnourished children. (Increased mortality is also associated with infection.)

TREATMENT

Depending on the cause of malnutrition, children suffering mild to moderate malnutrition can usually be treated without hospitalization. A physician and a nutritionist can design a diet plan that includes appropriate nutritional education and incorporation of accessible, affordable foods that ensure adequate nutrition. It is important that the diet is acceptable and realistic to both child and parents. Dietary changes should include sufficient amounts of protein, vitamins, minerals, carbohydrates, and fats.

Treatment of severe malnutrition may require hospitalization. Before dietary treatment is begun, life-threatening conditions such as *shock, dehydration, hypoglycemia,* hypothermia, and severe infection must be treated. A dehydrated child must receive fluids, electrolytes, and salts as needed. Once fluid levels are restored, nutrients are slowly replaced.

Sugar solution supplements are given to correct hypoglycemia. If a bacterial infection is suspected, antibiotics are administered. Treatment of parasitic infestation can be postponed until dietary therapy begins.

Once life-threatening conditions are under control, a child with third-degree malnutrition can begin dietary therapy. Initially a diet consists of small, frequent feedings of milk or infant formula. After a few days of treatment, signs of improvement (weight gain, return of appetite) are apparent. Once improvement is detected, cereal and other solid foods are added to the diet. If accumulated fluid is present, it begins to disappear during the initial days of dietary therapy and is usually gone completely by the tenth day of treatment.

With appropriate treatment most malnourished children begin to improve in 3 to 4 days. Indifference and irritability associated with moderate to severe malnutrition give way to cheerfulness, a longer attention span, a desire to play, and increased activity. Skin sores heal rapidly.

PREVENTION

Malnutrition can be prevented by a child's consuming nutritious food in adequate amounts. If a child is unable to eat, or if a child eats but is unable to absorb necessary nutrients from food, malnutrition is prevented by treating the underlying disorder. Such disorders can range from anorexia (see *eating disorders*) to *malabsorption.* As soon as treatment for the underlying disease is started, proper nutrition for the malnutrition begins as well.

MEASLES

EMERGENCY ACTION

If a child who is ill with measles develops a stiff neck, extreme sleepiness or listlessness, and nausea or *vomiting,* consult a physician immediately. *Encephalitis* (brain inflammation) may come on suddenly and progress swiftly. Full recovery often depends upon prompt diagnosis and treatment.

DESCRIPTION

Measles is a serious infectious disease that each year used to affect tens of thousands of American children between 5 and 10 years old. Today, as a result of a highly successful immunization program, the incidence of measles has been reduced dramatically. The disease still afflicts a small number of children, adolescents, and young adults who have not been vaccinated, who may have received defective vaccine, or who were vaccinated before their first birthday.

Before an effective vaccine became available, measles epidemics occurred almost every other year in the United States, most often in the winter and early spring. Even now, measles remains a major health threat in other parts of the world.

The disease makes children quite uncomfortable. It is characterized by rising *fever, cough,* runny nose, *sore throat,* red, watery eyes, and a *rash* that usually first appears on the forehead and behind the ears and then spreads to cover the entire body. Initial symptoms commonly appear 9 to 12 days after exposure to the disease. Symptoms occasionally develop as early as 6 days after exposure.

Measles usually lasts from 7 to 9 days or until fever has subsided and the rash has faded. This disease is rarely life-threatening, although younger children can develop several serious complications.

CAUSE

Measles is caused by a virus that is spread by direct contact with infected saliva, usually through droplets produced by a child's forceful *cough* or sneezing. Highly contagious, measles affects 9 of every 10 unvaccinated individuals who are exposed to the measles virus.

SIGNS AND SYMPTOMS

Measles is marked by two stages. The first, lasting 4 or 5 days, resembles a bad cold. A moderate *fever* (usually under 102° F; 38.8° C) is accompanied by a mild, hacking cough that grows worse day by day. Red, watery eyes, a runny nose, and mild *sore throat* also develop. Often a child begins to complain that direct light, whether natural or artificial, is annoying or even painful to the eyes.

Small, painless gray or white dots appear inside both cheeks, usually beside the lower molars. Less frequently, these dots (called Koplik spots) appear on the roof of the mouth and upper throat.

The second stage of measles begins on the fourth or fifth day of symptoms. Fever increases to 104° or 105° F (40.0° or 40.6° C). The cough noticeably worsens and may sound as if the child has developed *bronchiolitis* or *pneumonia*. A *rash* of faint red spots begins on the sides of the upper neck, along the upper forehead, and behind and in front of the ears, just at the back edge of the cheeks. Within hours the rash, which may itch slightly, spreads to the entire neck and face.

The rash begins as faint red spots and progresses to a bright red rash which may include raised areas. As the rash progresses, these raised bumps may overlap on some parts of the body until solid masses of angry-looking red skin are visible, giving a swollen appearance to face, palms, and soles of the feet. This rash may bleed if scratched.

During the sixth or seventh day of the illness, the rash spreads to the chest, back, abdomen, and thighs. On the eighth day, as the rash reaches both feet, it begins to fade from the head and face. When this occurs, redness fades to a brownish color and the skin slowly peels off in small flakes that resemble bran. This peeling process may go on for a week or more.

When the rash begins to fade, the fever drops. A child who has been miserable with rash, cough, runny nose, and red, watery eyes may feel better so rapidly as the rash fades that staying in bed no longer seems necessary. Fever often disappears within 24 hours and the child's strength returns quickly.

DIAGNOSIS

Measles can be diagnosed by the presence of characteristic signs and symptoms, especially sensitivity to light, Koplik spots, and the appearance of a head-to-toe rash. Public health authorities now request that physicians attempt to confirm a diagnosis of measles with special laboratory tests.

COMPLICATIONS

The 3 most common complications of measles are *pneumonia,* middle ear infections (see *earache and ear infections),* and *encephalitis.* Pneumonia may arise because of infection of the lungs by the measles virus or because of bacteria that invade the lungs after a child is weakened by measles infection. Middle ear infections are often caused by the measles infection finding another site in an ear already inflamed by fever and irritated by coughing and sneezing. Encephalitis is usually signaled by stiff neck, *headache,* nausea, and *vomiting.* It tends to occur at the time a child is beginning to improve from the *rash* and *fever.* Encephalitis can be severe, causing long-term aftereffects.

TREATMENT

Home treatment of measles focuses on relieving symptoms. Bed rest and plenty of fluids are helpful during the *fever.* A mild fever-reducing medication may be helpful. Consult the physician for specific recommendations and read the general discussion of nonprescription medications beginning on p. 102. A mild sedative or cough medication can soothe a hacking *cough.*

Antibiotics are not prescribed except in combating bacterial infections that occur as complications of measles. A warm room, humidified if the atmosphere is dry, can make a child comfortable, particularly if a child is weak from persistent coughing. Indirect or dim lighting may comfort a child who finds direct light painful. Some children are relieved by wearing sunglasses while indoors.

Although measles and several of its complications can severely affect children under

2 years old, deaths are rare in the United States.

PREVENTION

Measles can be prevented by vaccination. at 15 months of age, children routinely receive measles vaccine as part of a measles-rubella-mumps inoculation. Until 3 to 6 months of age a child is usually protected by immunity passed on by the mother. If a child under 15 months is exposed to measles, a dose of immunoglobulin may be given by a physician as a protective measure to ensure that infection does not occur. To be fully protected against measles, a child should be at least 15 months of age before receiving measles vaccination. Some children develop a slight reaction to the vaccination (a mild *rash* resembling measles and *fever* as high as 103° F [39.4° C], beginning on the sixth day following vaccination but lasting no longer than a day or two).

Any unvaccinated child who is exposed to measles during its contagious period (from the beginning of signs and symptoms through the fifth day of rash) should be vaccinated as soon as possible. If the vaccination occurs within 48 hours after exposure to measles, the vaccine is probably about 70 percent effective in preventing the disease itself.

Some teenagers (born before 1968) may have received killed virus vaccine when they were babies. This type of vaccine does not provide protection against measles. Individuals who received killed virus vaccine may develop particularly severe disease if exposed to measles. They should be reimmunized with live (attenuated) measles virus vaccine. This vaccine, however, should not be given to a female who is pregnant or might be pregnant.

(See Chapter 6, "Going to the Doctor," for further immunization information.)

MECKEL'S DIVERTICULUM

DESCRIPTION

A diverticulum is a small outpouching from a tubular organ such as the bladder or intestine. Meckel's diverticulum is a finger-like outpouching of intestine and often requires treatment. It can become inflamed, bleed, and cause an intestinal obstruction or *intussusception* (telescoping of one segment of the intestine into an adjoining segment). Complications associated with Meckel's diverticulum require surgery, usually as an emergency.

Meckel's diverticulum is a common congenital (present at birth) abnormality, present in about 1 percent of all individuals. Few children with this condition develop complications from it. This abnormality is neither hereditary nor due to a genetic defect. Meckel's diverticulum comes about when a duct necessary only during the first month of fetal development persists throughout prenatal life. Sometimes Meckel's diverticulum remains attached to the navel as it was during prenatal life, forming a small, somewhat flexible tissue bridge between the abdominal wall and the intestine.

Meckel's diverticulum may become a problem at any age, but about half of all cases occur among children under 2 years old. About 4 out of 5 children who undergo surgery for Meckel's diverticulum are under 10 years old; slightly more boys than girls have such an abnormality that requires treatment. Complications often arise when an infant has an inflamed or bleeding Meckel's diverticulum. Prompt treatment can be lifesaving.

CAUSE

If Meckel's diverticulum is lined with a mucous membrane that secretes stomach acid fluids, as occurs in the lining of the stomach, the diverticulum can develop an ulcer which may bleed. The ulcer is located at the point where the diverticulum arises from the loop of intestine.

SIGNS AND SYMPTOMS

A common sign of Meckel's diverticulum is sudden, painless rectal bleeding or a bloody bowel movement. Bleeding may start and stop; hemorrhage (heavy bleeding) occasionally occurs. Inflammation often develops, followed by nausea and *vomiting*. Initially the signs and symptoms of Meckel's diverticulum often resemble those of *appendicitis*.

COMPLICATIONS

Obstruction of the intestine can develop if Meckel's diverticulum turns inside out (points toward the interior of the segment of intestine), causing *intussusception*. As blood flow to the trapped segment of intestine is pinched off, the tissue is deprived of oxygen and gangrene can develop. Gangrene occurs when tissue dies and infection sets in. Obstruction can also develop if a loop of intestine becomes twisted around the tissue bridge to the navel. Pain caused by obstruction differs from pain from ulceration of the small intestine or stomach in that it cannot be relieved by antacids, food, or drink. In addition, pain caused by obstruction is usually confined to a specific region of the abdomen.

It is possible, also, for food or foreign objects to become trapped in Meckel's diverticulum, causing inflammation and, occasionally, perforation. If a child less than 2 years old has a perforation, the outlook for successful surgery and recovery is less certain than for an older child.

DIAGNOSIS

Any child who suffers a bloody bowel movement or bright or dark red bleeding from the rectum should be examined promptly by a physician. The physician performs a careful physical examination after taking note of the signs and symptoms of illness. Blood tests are performed to check for the possible presence of infection. Sometimes an abdominal scan can help to locate the source of bleeding. For this examination a tiny, harmless amount of radioactive material is injected into a vein. A scanning device is then passed over the child's abdomen to pick up the radioactivity. A bleeding Meckel's diverticulum can often be identified by the image which radioactivity conveys to a television monitor.

TREATMENT

Once diagnosis is made, surgery follows as soon as a child can be prepared, sometimes with the aid of blood transfusion. Surgery is occasionally performed as an emergency because bleeding cannot be stopped. Surgery consists of removing the diverticulum and, occasionally, part of the adjacent segment of intestine. The two healthy ends of the intestine are then sewn together. Recovery is almost always complete and uncomplicated. If surgery does not occur until complications have set in, however, the chances of survival and recovery depend upon the severity of complications and how healthy the child was before becoming ill.

PREVENTION

Meckel's diverticulum cannot be prevented.

MENINGITIS

EMERGENCY ACTION

If a child who is *vomiting* suddenly develops a high fever (101° to 106° F; 38.3° to 41.1° C), stiff neck, and extreme lethargy or sleepiness, seek medical attention immediately. Meningitis can begin suddenly and progress quickly, and full recovery often depends upon prompt diagnosis and treatment.

DESCRIPTION

Meningitis is inflammation of the 3 meninges (tissues enclosing and protecting the brain and spinal cord; (see Fig. 00, p. 000). Although inflammation is usually confined to those protective tissues, the brain can be affected as well.

Although meningitis can strike at any age, infants and young children are generally more likely to be affected. Male infants appear to be at higher risk of developing meningitis than female infants. Peak incidence often occurs during the summer months. Severity and duration of illness depend upon the child's age, general health before illness begins, the underlying cause of illness, and how promptly treatment is begun. If untreated, treated incorrectly, or treated too late, meningitis can rapidly grow worse and become life-threatening.

Meningitis occurs in 2 major forms: aseptic and bacterial. Aseptic meningitis is the more common viral form; bacterial is more severe, and can cause long-term complications. Bacterial meningitis is potentially one of the fastest-acting, most damaging of all infections.

Aseptic meningitis is usually associated with a previous viral infection that appears first as a nose and throat infection, a stomach or intestinal problem, or some other uncomfortable but usually brief viral illness. Aseptic meningitis usually lasts less than 2 weeks; in mild cases, recovery can begin as early as the third or fourth day. Children with viral meningitis almost always make a complete recovery, although temporary muscle weakness and decreased coordination may develop.

Bacterial meningitis is especially dangerous for infants less than 6 months old. Babies less than 1 month old run an especially high risk of life-threatening illness if they contract the disease. The fatality rate associated with bacterial meningitis has decreased dramatically over the past half century. As children grow older, the number of meningitis-caused deaths decreases.

CAUSE

At least 20 viruses, particularly a group called enteroviruses, cause aseptic meningitis; these include Coxsackie A and B viruses, Echo viruses, and *mumps* virus. These viruses are transferred in several ways, including through contact with infected nose and throat secretions or stool. Those children who have been vaccinated against specific viral diseases, such as *poliomyelitis* and mumps, do not develop meningitis caused by those viruses.

Among the bacteria which cause meningitis are streptococcal, staphylococcal, gram negative, pneumococcal, meningococcal, hemophilus and influenza bacteria (unrelated to the viruses which cause influenza). Hemophilus influenza and meningococcal bacteria can be transferred from infected children to their contacts.

Meningitis can also be caused by unusual infectious agents; for example, fungi (which particularly affect immunosuppressed individuals), rickettsiae, and the mycobacterium causing *tuberculosis.*

SIGNS AND SYMPTOMS

Signs and symptoms common to all forms of meningitis include nausea, *vomiting, headache, back pain,* stiff neck, loss of appetite, sensitivity to light, listlessness, and irritability. Moderate *fever* (101° to 104° F; 38.3° to 40.0° C) is usually present.

In cases of aseptic meningitis affecting children over the age of 10, symptoms may appear quite suddenly. Children between 2 and 10 years often develop fever first and then become quite lethargic and irritable. Infants may only be irritable and reveal a tight or bulging rather than flexible fontanel (soft spot on top of the head). Children of any age may develop a *rash* before or with other signs of aseptic meningitis.

In cases of bacterial meningitis, fever develops first, followed by other characteristic signs and symptoms. Muscle pain and respiratory and digestive disturbances may also be present. *Headache* is common among older children with bacterial meningitis, as are bulging fontanels. *Seizures,* sleepiness, and unconsciousness (see *coma)* may develop.

DIAGNOSIS

Meningitis is diagnosed by a physician. After observing characteristic signs and symptoms and examining the child, a physician can confirm a diagnosis by a lumbar puncture, sometimes called a spinal tap. A small sterile needle is inserted into the spinal canal containing spinal fluid. This is always done in the lower back, below the lower end of the spinal cord, to avoid possible nerve damage. A small sample of spinal fluid is removed and analyzed for the presence of blood cells and infectious organisms, and to measure protein and blood sugar content.

COMPLICATIONS

Bacterial meningitis can produce a range of unusual, sometimes permanent complications. Among the more common and severe are *seizures,* paralysis, *blindness,* deafness (see *hearing loss),* and *mental retardation. Learning problems* often occur in the aftermath of bacterial meningitis, but they usually prove to be mild. Many complications improve markedly over time, depending upon both the initial severity of infection and the kinds of long-term treatment and care that the child receives. A child with bacterial meningitis who does not receive a full course of the correct medication may suffer a relapse.

TREATMENT

Many children with aseptic meningitis are treated at home after a physician has diagnosed the problem. The child should rest in bed and drink plenty of fluids. If urination decreases noticeably, however, a hormonal irregularity may be present that reduces kidney function. If this occurs, a physician should be notified, because fluids may need to be temporarily restricted. A fever- and pain-relieving medication may be helpful. Consult the physician for specific recommendations and read the discussion of nonprescription medications beginning on p. 102. A child with the signs and symptoms of meningitis may be hospitalized until the possibility of bacterial meningitis is ruled out and until severe illness has passed.

Any infant or child with bacterial meningitis must be hospitalized. Antibiotics are prescribed according to the specific bacteria involved, and are administered for a minimum of 10 days and until *fever* is gone for at least a few days. Vital signs (pulse rate, blood pressure, breathing rate, and temperature) must be checked often. Fluid intake and urine output must be monitored to guard against fluid retention. If *seizures* occur, anticonvulsant medication is given.

PREVENTION

Effective vaccines for *poliomyelitis, measles,* and *mumps* have sharply reduced the incidence of those diseases. Viral meningitis as a complication of these diseases has declined correspondingly. As yet, other forms of viral meningitis cannot be prevented, but research continues toward developing effective vaccines to prevent specific viral illnesses.

An effective vaccine against infections stemming from hemophilus influenza bacteria is available. All children should be immunized against *H. influenza* (type B) disease at 2 years of age. (See Chapter 6, "Going to the Doctor," for immunization schedules.)

Some forms of bacterial meningitis (meningococcal and *H. influenza)* may be prevented by taking antibiotics. Members of the family of a child with bacterial meningitis and others who have frequent close contact may take particular antibiotics prescribed by a physician as a preventive measure against the spread of infection.

MENSTRUAL IRREGULARITIES

EMERGENCY ACTION

If menstrual (or other vaginal) bleeding is unusually profuse, or if bleeding lasts for more than 10 days, and is accompanied by signs and symptoms of excess blood loss (such as *dizziness, fainting,* and nausea), consult a physician promptly.

DESCRIPTION

Menstruation is the periodic (approximately monthly) shedding of uterine tissue, consisting of blood, degenerated cells from the uterine lining, mucus from the vagina and glands of the cervix, and bacteria (see Figs. 3A and B, p. 39).

Most girls have menarche (the start of menstrual cycles) between the ages of 9 and 16. The average age is around 12½ or 13 years. For the first year or two after menarche, a girl often has anovulatory cycles (i.e., she does not ovulate—release an egg—but her uterus responds to rising and falling levels of the hormone estrogen, which is produced by her ovaries). These menstrual periods may be regular or quite irregular (either close together or widely spaced). Later, as the pituitary gland and the ovaries mature, the adolescent begins to have ovulatory menstrual periods. The ovary produces an egg (in the middle of the cycle), which travels down the fallopian tube to the uterus. The ovary also produces a hormone called progesterone, which matures the lining of the uterus to make it ready for a fertilized egg.

If conception occurs, the lining of the uterus supports the fertilized egg. If conception does not occur (the egg that is released from an ovary is not fertilized), menstruation occurs about 2 weeks after the release of the egg because of falling estrogen and progesterone levels.

On the average, a menstrual cycle is 28 days long from the first day of one period to the first day of the next period. An average menstrual period lasts 4 to 6 days, an average menstrual flow is about 60 milliliters (about ¼ cup). The normal range varies, however, from a 21- to a 35-day cycle, from a 3- to a 7-day period, and from 20 to 100 milliliters of menstrual flow.

Irregular menstrual cycles may persist for a year or two after menarche or even continue into adulthood. Short, light menstrual periods and infrequent periods during the first years of menstruation are not generally cause for concern. If periods stop for more than 3 months or do not start by the time a young woman is 16, she should be seen by a physician. This condition, called amenorrhea, appears as either the absence, suppression (temporary), or cessation (permanent) of menstruation. Amenorrhea is not an illness but always represents a symptom of some underlying problem. A very thin or active girl may experience delay in reaching puberty and starting to menstruate. Most disorders causing amenorrhea can be cured or controlled so that menstruation begins or resumes.

Prolonged periods (more than 10 days) with heavy flow or periods that occur frequently (such as every 2 weeks) are usually signs of anovulatory cycles but occasionally indicate disorders of the reproductive system. In these cases medical evaluation is necessary. Most menstrual irregularities disappear as an adolescent's body matures and produces sufficient amounts of reproductive hormones.

Typically, anovulatory periods are painless. Uncomfortable symptoms before or during a period (such as backache, slight bloating, and cramps) usually indicate ovulation. (For more information about painful periods, see *menstrual pain*.)

For a girl who has not yet reached puberty (signaled by a growth spurt, broadening of the hips, breast budding, and the development of underarm and pubic hair), bleeding from the vagina is abnormal and requires prompt medical attention (see *vaginal bleeding*).

CAUSE

Failure to begin menstruating by the age of 18 is usually caused by a problem with the production of reproductive hormones (such as estrogen or progesterone) or in the glands (such as the ovaries and pituitary, thyroid, and adrenal glands) that produce those hormones.

A girl may cease having periods if she suffers from *stress* or anxiety. Even slight tension or worry can cause a period to be late. Jet lag, prolonged travel, or changes in environment (such as going away to school, camp, or college) can also cause a period to be delayed, as can illness or *fever*. Serious diseases—including *Crohn's disease,* congenital heart disease (see *heart disease, congenital*), and *cystic fibrosis*—that cause growth and development delays can lead to amenorrhea. Radiation therapy to the ovaries for the treatment of *cancer* can cause periods to stop permanently. If a young woman reaches late adolescence (approximately age 18) and has not begun to menstruate, a 2 in 5 chance exists that she has a congenital abnormality.

A girl's reproductive system may be completely normal except for an imperforate hymen (closed hymen), which blocks menstrual flow, resulting in amenorrhea. A completely closed hymen can cause menstrual blood to accumulate and back up as far as the fallopian tubes; outwardly the disorder may be indicated by a swollen abdomen.

Frequent periods with normal menstrual flow or periods with prolonged and profuse bleeding usually indicate that a teenage girl is not ovulating during her menstrual cycle.

Causes of irregular vaginal bleeding:

- stress or illness
- weight change (particularly if it is abrupt, such as that caused by crash dieting) or anorexia nervosa (see *eating disorders)*
- strenuous endurance activities (such as ballet, gymnastics, and track)
- infection of or injury to part of the reproductive system, such as the cervix or uterus
- ovarian cysts, benign (not cancerous) tumors, and rarely, cancerous tumors (see *ovarian tumors and cysts)*
- birth defects of the reproductive system
- overgrowth of the lining of the uterus
- exposure to drugs before birth (see *DES exposure)*
- diseases such as *tuberculosis, cystic fibrosis,* and *diabetes*
- a foreign object in the vagina (such as a forgotten tampon)
- a hormonal imbalance resulting from disorders such as *adrenal problems* and *thyroid problems*
- *blood disorders* such as clotting problems and *leukemia*
- the use of birth control pills (which may make menstrual flow lighter than normal or irregular)
- the use of an IUD (intrauterine device), which may cause heavy menstrual flow
- hormonal imbalances such as polycystic ovary syndrome (numerous cysts in the ovaries associated with an imbalance in the pituitary hormone levels and sometimes excess body hair growth)

Rarely, development of a fertilized egg outside of the uterus in a fallopian tube (tubal or ectopic pregnancy) causes persistent bleeding and severe pain. Miscarriages also produce cramping and vaginal bleeding. In addition, vaginal bleeding may occur during the course of a normal pregnancy. Light bleeding at midcycle may be a harmless sign that ovulation is occurring. Such "spotting" is rare among teenagers. A blood-stained vaginal discharge can be a sign of a vaginal infection (see *vaginitis and vaginal discharge*).

DIAGNOSIS

If a young woman is 14 years old and no signs of puberty are present, she should consult a physician for a physical examination. If a routine examination and laboratory tests reveal no cause for amenorrhea, she will probably begin to menstruate sometime between her sixteenth and eighteenth birthdays (particularly if she attains an appropriate weight).

If a sexually active teenager is overdue for a period by 1 to 2 weeks, a physician should be consulted. The physician generally begins by giving a test to rule out the possibility of pregnancy.

Women who have persistent menstrual irregularities or profuse bleeding should consult a physician. Once a young woman's menstrual cycles have established a pattern, a significant change in that pattern is reason for consulting a physician.

To determine the extent and cause of menstrual irregularities, a physician takes a history of growth and development, including the adolescent's age of menarche and her record of menstrual cycles. The physician may suggest keeping a menstrual calendar, so that the frequency, duration, and amount of flow off the periods can be charted. A physician also asks about prior medical problems and may review the family's medical history (particularly the reproductive histories of female members). A physician also performs a physical examination, including a pelvic exam (to check the vagina, cervix, and uterus), and may take a Pap smear or vaginal smear and blood tests (to check for levels of reproductive hormones). A cervical culture for *gonorrhea* may be taken if a young woman is sexually active. A *tuberculosis* skin test and a urine test may be performed.

Depending on the history and examination, a physician may gently scrape the lining of the uterus and have those cells analyzed for abnormalities, a procedure called an endometrial biopsy.

If the young woman has a mild case of irregular bleeding, the physician may observe the pattern for an additional few weeks or months. If the cycles are moderately irregular, simple hormone therapy may be started. If a physician suspects that a teenager has infrequent periods because she is not ovulating, a form of progesterone may be prescribed for certain days of her cycle. If her ovaries are making estrogen, she should have a period (withdrawal bleeding) when she stops taking the progesterone. If she does not have a period or has had a long history of infrequent periods, tests are usually performed to determine whether the problem lies in the pituitary gland, the thyroid gland, the ovaries, or the uterus.

Any woman who experiences bleeding during pregnancy should consult her physician.

COMPLICATIONS

Short-term complications of heavy or prolonged periods include excess blood loss and *anemia.*

Women who continue to have anovulatory cycles and untreated irregular periods into their twenties and thirties, particularly those who have polycystic ovary syndrome, often have difficulty with fertility and have an increased risk of developing cancerous growths of the uterine lining. Fertility problems caused by hormonal imbalances, however, usually respond to hormone therapies.

TREATMENT

Since amenorrhea is a symptom, not an illness, any underlying disorder must be treated for menstruation to begin. If a girl with amenorrhea has very little body fat, a physician may suggest weight gain.

If menstrual flow is slightly more than usual, a young woman might want to see a physician to obtain a prescription for iron supplements to prevent *anemia.* Moderately heavy blood flow is more likely to cause mild anemia and other side effects of excess blood loss. A young woman may need to take folic acid supplements as well as iron supplements to correct anemia. Oral contraceptives or a form of progesterone may be prescribed to stop heavy bleeding during anovulatory cycles and start a pattern of regular periods. (If bleeding does not stop, a gynecologist should be consulted for further tests and treatment.)

If blood flow is severe and/or cannot be stopped within 24 to 36 hours with hormones, hospitalization may be required. If bleeding continues, further tests and treatment are required. Anemia must be corrected, and if blood loss is significant, a blood transfusion may be needed. Blood tests may be taken to determine whether or not the blood is clotting properly. A procedure called a D & C (dilation and curettage, or scraping the lining of the uterus) may be necessary.

Once a young woman starts having regular ovulatory cycles, the problem of too frequent or profuse, prolonged periods should disappear.

If a woman in her twenties continues to have anovulatory cycles and heavy bleeding, hormone therapy may be prescribed to stimulate regular periods and, for some, to correct hormonal imbalances which may occur with polycystic ovary syndrome.

PREVENTION

Amenorrhea can be prevented if it is caused by weight loss (or gain) resulting from diet or exercise. Young female dancers and athletes should be sure to eat adequately. They may need to cut back on their physical activity if they cannot maintain a weight considered safe by a physician.

Menstrual irregularity caused by foreign objects in the vagina or by use of an IUD can be prevented. Most other causes cannot. Before puberty all girls should receive education in how their reproductive organs work in order to help judge for themselves what is normal and abnormal (see Sex Education section Chapter 2, "Promoting Physical Health").

MENSTRUAL PAIN

DESCRIPTION

Menstruation is a normal process that is not necessarily painful. However, some females do experience pain during menstruation.

Painful menstruation, or dysmenorrhea, is characterized by abdominal cramps and may be accompanied by *diarrhea,* nausea and *dizziness* during menstruation. The smooth (involuntary) muscles of the uterus and gastrointestinal (GI) tract (esophagus, stomach, small and large intestines) are usually involved in an episode of dysmenorrhea.

Adolescent girls and young women most often suffer dysmenorrhea, but women in their 30s and 40s may also be affected. It is estimated that two thirds of all adolescent females experience some degree of painful menstruation; about 30 percent of those have severe dysmenorrhea. In about 5 percent of these cases, however, abdominal pain may be caused by an underlying problem of the reproductive system, such as a pelvic disease.

The first episode of dysmenorrhea does not usually occur until a young woman begins to ovulate (release an egg), which happens anywhere from a few months to 1 to 2 years after she begins menstruating. Once ovulation occurs each month on a regular basis, a woman may experience dysmenorrhea, which starts just before the beginning of each menstrual flow. Episodes usually last about 24 hours, although they occasionally may last 4 days or more.

After a woman's first pregnancy, dysmenorrhea often disappears.

Abdominal cramps of dysmenorrhea vary in intensity. Mild to moderate cramps usually last a few hours and do not interfere with normal activity. Moderate to severe *abdominal pain* can interfere with daily activity and may cause an adolescent to double over in pain. Other characteristics of dysmenorrhea can include lower *back pain,* pain in the thighs, nausea, *vomiting,* dizziness, *headache,* hot flashes, and chills.

CAUSE

Small amounts of the hormonelike chemical prostaglandin are normally secreted in the uterus by the endometrium (uterus lining). During ovulation and menstruation, changing hormone levels may increase the production of prostaglandin, and strong contractions of the uterus and organs of the GI tract may result. If severe, these contractions can cause abdominal cramps, pain, and *diarrhea.*

DIAGNOSIS

Dysmenorrhea is usually diagnosed by elimination of other possible causes of abdominal cramps and pain, such as endometriosis (tissue growth in the uterus and pelvic cavity) or pelvic infection. An intrauterine device (IUD) may cause cramping, even if it has been correctly inserted and remains in place.

TREATMENT

Treatment focuses on relieving abdominal cramps and other characteristics of dysmenorrhea. For most cases of dysmenorrhea involving mild to moderate discomfort, heat (from a heating pad), exercise, and a bit of rest should help relax muscles and provide relief. A relaxed attitude toward menstruation is also a step in the right direction.

Certain medications are suitable for moderate to severe discomfort. A medication that inhibits the production of prostaglandin is often helpful. A pain-relieving medication may be helpful. Consult the physician for specific recommendations and read the discussion of nonprescription medications beginning on p. 102. If severe pain occurs, the physician may prescribe a prostaglandin inhibitor. This medication may produce occasional side effects, such as *constipation,* nausea, or *dizziness.* Such medications should not be used by a female who suffers from *asthma* or peptic ulcers or is allergic to aspirin.

If prostaglandin inhibitors do not sufficiently lessen *abdominal pain* caused by dysmenorrhea, a physician may recommend the administration of hormones. Hormones such as those found in birth control pills prevent ovulation, thereby reducing the production of prostaglandins.

PREVENTION

Dysmenorrhea cannot be prevented.

MENTAL RETARDATION

DESCRIPTION

The term "mental retardation" generally refers to a disability in the area of perception, thought, and memory. This disability in turn slows a child's development in motor, learning, and language skills. It can also hinder social development, although this depends a great deal on the kind of guidance and support a retarded child receives. Mental retardation is caused by brain abnormality that can result from hundreds of diseases, *genetic disorders,* brain damage from accidents, or physical deprivation. Brain function can be impaired before birth, during birth, during the newborn period, or during childhood.

About 2 to 3 percent of the population, or 6 million Americans, are classified as having mental retardation. More than 100,000 babies are born each year into this category; 1 out of every 10 Americans has a family member who has some mental retardation.

Mental retardation is often associated with other developmental disabilities, such as *cerebral palsy* or a seizure disorder (see *seizures).* Sometimes it is associated with *autism,* a pervasive developmental disorder.

A child with mental retardation moves through the same stages as a child who is not developmentally delayed, but more slowly. The growth and development of a child who is mentally retarded may stop before these stages are completed, limiting the child's ability to adapt and become self-sufficient.

Like children of normal intelligence, those with mental retardation develop faster in some areas than in others. For instance, a child who is mentally retarded may develop gross motor skills at a nearly normal rate, yet be severely delayed in language development.

No dividing line exists at which people can be classified as mentally retarded. For purposes of appropriate educational placement, however, an IQ score of 100 on standardized tests is generally considered average, and a score of 70 to 85 is regarded as the lower limit of normal intelligence. About 85 percent of affected people are defined as mildly retarded; they usually score between 55 and 70 on standardized IQ tests. They attain a mental age between 8 and 11 as adults, and can achieve a good deal of overall independence. They usually work at unskilled or semiskilled jobs. More than 80 percent of this group marry, usually to a spouse who is of normal intelligence. People who function at the lower end of this range, however, need some supervision and guidance all their lives.

Moderately mentally retarded people, about 10 percent of the retarded population, have an IQ score between 35 and 55. These people have more difficulty adapting to the world than do mildly retarded individuals and require special education to enhance self-help skills. With some assistance they may live in community residences or supervised apartment settings and may be employed at unskilled labor or within a sheltered workshop. As adults their mental age ranges between 5 and 7 years.

About 5 percent of the mentally retarded are severely or profoundly retarded. People with severe retardation have an IQ score between 20 and 35. Their ability to learn and care for themselves is limited; language skills are minimal. They may achieve some independence in supervised environments and as adults may live in community group homes or apartments, although they may require some nursing care. Adult mental age is usually under 5. Profoundly retarded persons have IQ scores under 20. They may not develop speech or the ability to walk, but may participate in day activity centers and learn rudimentary self-help skills.

CAUSE AND PREVENTION

Most mental retardation is irreversible. Depending upon the cause, however, some can be prevented.

Causes of mental retardation classified according to their possible sequence in a child's development include genetic factors, early influences on prenatal development, other pregnancy problems, birth difficulties, acquired childhood diseases, and environmental and behavioral problems.

Rarely, mental retardation is caused directly by genetic factors. Biochemical imbalances affect brain development in genetic diseases such as *PKU* (phenylketonuria), *Tay-Sachs disease,* galactosemia (also characterized by *jaundice,* liver enlargement, cataracts, and increased risk of infection), and Hurler syndrome (also characterized by growth retardation and heart disease). Couples who have family histories of *genetic disorders,* such as Tay-Sachs disease, that cause mental retardation may want to be tested to see if they carry the trait for the disorder. If they do, they should seek genetic counseling so they will know in advance their chances of conceiving affected children.

For children born with PKU or galactosemia, special diets can prevent mental retardation. Other genetic disorders that may cause mental retardation in a child include *neurofibromatosis,* tuberous sclerosis, and some forms of *muscular dystrophy.* (See Cause and Genetic Counseling sections of *genetic disorders.*)

Certain children may have a developmental handicap associated with unexplained spontaneous changes in their chromosomes. An example of this is *Down syndrome,* which can be diagnosed during pregnancy by amniocentesis.

Medical histories of infants who are mentally retarded may reveal disabling events or influences that occurred early in the mother's pregnancy. Changes in patterns of early prenatal development can be important sources of disabilities. A mother's excessive drinking of alcohol during pregnancy may cause the fetal alcohol syndrome, marked by mental retardation, heart disease (see *heart disease, congenital*) and altered facial characteristics (see *facial deformities, congenital*). A mother's infections during pregnancy, including *German measles* (rubella), toxoplasmosis (see *pets, diseases caused by*), and cytomegaloviral infection are also causes of mental retardation in children. Immunization against rubella has almost completely eliminated the incidence of congenital rubella and resulting mental retardation.

Excessive radiation from X-ray examinations during pregnancy has been linked to mental retardation and other birth defects. Certain medications taken by the mother during pregnancy are sometimes associated with mental retardation in infants.

Difficulties in fetal nutrition caused by abnormalities of the placenta may cause mental retardation. *Prematurity* and its complications, such as *respiratory distress syndrome,* may also be associated with developmental delays.

Good prenatal care, including improved nutrition and management of *diabetes* during pregnancy, reduces the risk of prematurity and of a child's being born with developmental problems. Prenatal care is especially important in teenage pregnancies, which often are at higher risk. Reduction of teenage pregnancies would lessen the risk of babies being born prematurely and having developmental disabilities. Reducing alcohol consumption during pregnancy lessens the risk of fetal alcohol syndrome; abstaining from drinking eliminates the risk. Women should consult their physicians before taking any medication during pregnancy. In addition, women should not receive X rays of any kind—unless absolutely necessary for a serious medical condition—if there is any chance that they could be pregnant.

Birth injuries or difficulties, including breech birth or prolonged labor leading to a cesarean section, may contribute to development delays. Other preventable factors early in an infant's life that may result in some degree of disability include complications of Rh incompatibility (see *RH and ABO incompatibility*) and *hypoglycemia* (a condition in which the blood contains an abnormally low concentration of sugar).

Internal bleeding in the brain, caused either by a difficult delivery or lack of oxygen to the brain, may be a cause of mental retardation. Congenital hypothyroidism (see *thyroid problems*) that is not treated can also be associated with mental retardation.

During childhood, mental retardation may occasionally be caused by brain injuries resulting from accidents and/or *child abuse.* Parents should make sure that children are in approved car seats or use seat belts whenever traveling in moving vehicles. Children participating in contact sports should wear protective helmets. (See Chapter 4, "Accident Prevention.")

Other preventive techniques to lower the incidence of mental retardation include efforts to decrease child neglect and abuse as well as health and nutrition education to promote health in young children.

Brain tumor is a rare cause of mental retardation. If the tumor can be removed or eradicated before spreading too far, however, developmental disabilities may be reversed or lessened. Severe childhood infections, such as *meningitis* (inflammation of the protective membranes covering the brain and spinal cord) or *encephalitis* (inflammation of the brain), may damage a child's nervous system. Premature infants are especially vulnerable to meningitis.

Lead poisoning, in combination with other factors, such as *malnutrition,* can cause developmental disabilities including mental retardation and *cerebral palsy.* Mental retardation caused by severe lead poisoning is not reversible; however, mental retardation caused by mild cases of lead poisoning can often be reversed.

SIGNS AND SYMPTOMS

Some syndromes characterized in part by mental retardation can be identified by the presence of a number of physical symptoms present at birth. Physical signs range from obvious to subtle, and may identify the particular disability and, to some extent, its degree of severity. The infant with birth defects is likely to be low in birthweight and short in length, and may have an unusually small or large head. Such children are often born with a heart defect, and may experience breathing difficulties and frequent respiratory infections during infancy. Gastrointestinal abnormalities may cause feeding and digestive difficulties.

Parents are often aware that a young infant is not developing like other infants. The two most common problems causing parental concerns are a child's slowness in sitting or walking and a failure to talk by 2 or 3 years of age. Many children experience slight delays in certain areas of development; children who are mentally retarded show a pattern of general delay within each area of development, although they too have stronger and weaker areas.

Moderately to severely retarded infants— like some normal babies—may have poor sucking and grasping responses. Their cry may be weak and high-pitched. As time progresses, they may not respond to family members as other infants their age usually do. Children who also have associated birth defects often continue to be small and underweight for their age and may not develop appropriate physical or social skills, such as taking their first steps or smiling, laughing, and making faces. They may not babble, or make "baby talk." This general pattern of delay continues throughout their development.

In school a child's inability to function as well as other children stands out immediately to an experienced teacher. A child with an undiagnosed developmental delay may be unable to join in group activities and may instead engage in solitary play. Such a child may have limited communication and self-help skills, and may be unable to concentrate for any length of time on class activities.

DIAGNOSIS

Diagnosis of mental retardation is a complex process involving a team of health professionals who evaluate a child's physical growth, development of gross and fine motor skills, development of language and cognitive skills, and development of social adaptability. If there is evidence of brain damage, a neurologist (nervous-system specialist) may be consulted to further evaluate a child's nervous system.

Diagnosis involves a physical examination and careful taking of prenatal, postnatal, developmental, and family histories. Tests may include a chromosomal study (see *genetic disorders).* If a child has experienced *seizures* (which, like mental retardation, can be caused by brain damage), an EEG (electroencephalogram) may be used to examine a child's brain waves. Vision and hearing are tested.

A physical therapist measures a child's muscle strength and control, flexibility balance, and agility, thereby identifying variations in development of gross and fine motor skills. A speech and language pathologist tests language and speech development, and an audiologist tests hearing ability.

A psychologist uses a variety of tests to measure a child's intellectual and emotional development. A special educator tests for specific learning abilities and academic achievement.

COMPLICATIONS

Having a child with mental retardation poses many challenges for parents. Children with associated birth defects may require extensive, consistent, and complex medical care. If a physical disability is involved, or if a child is severely retarded, parents may have trouble finding people to stay with their child to provide respite care, an interval of temporary relief or rest for the parents. Brothers and sisters of a developmentally delayed child may adjust slowly to this family member who is so "different" from them and their friends and who requires so much of their parents' time and attention. Parents need to explain to their other children—and, possibly, to classmates of their child who is mentally retarded—how to relate to people with developmental disabilities.

TREATMENT

Mental retardation cannot be cured. However, a child's level of disability can sometimes be significantly reduced if diagnosis is made early and if an appropriate educational program is begun as soon as possible after diagnosis.

Treatment and services for a child with mental retardation differ according to age, level of development, and health. If special problems are present at birth, there may be medical needs then and during the first few months of life, later decreasing. At the same time, educational and vocational needs increase. A child with developmental disabilities needs social support consistently throughout life.

Treatment and supportive services for mentally retarded people within their own communities can be invaluable. Federal and state laws passed in the 1970s require all school systems to provide children, no matter what their disability, with appropriate educational opportunities. With new developments in special education and support services, children and adults can be moved out of large institutions into their own homes and communities. Most children with mental retardation now live at home until they reach adulthood, when they may move into special supervised housing.

An educational plan designed to encourage optimal growth in all areas of development requires participation by a variety of educators, health professionals, and a child's parents. Parents should be involved in educational planning to assure that the program truly focuses on their child's special needs and abilities. Parents may need advice regarding home training for their child in the areas of physical development, language skills, and diet, along with toilet training, personal grooming, and other self-help skills. Child development workers, physical therapists, nurses, and special education and nursery school teachers can offer useful advice and can work with parents in a clinic, home, or school. Such professionals may offer special techniques, equipment, and furniture suitable for an individual child's development.

An educational program includes appropriate academic goals, training in self-help skills and socialization, and eventually, vocational training. During infancy a baby with special needs may take part in infant stimulation ("early intervention") programs. Special preschools can provide an important advantage to a child with mental retardation.

Children with mental retardation attend public schools. Depending on their level of academic ability, they may participate in certain classes—such as physical education, art, and perhaps social studies—with children of normal intelligence. Or they may work in separate rooms but eat in the school cafeteria and take part in school activities. For more severely disabled children, special programs of care and training in public or private schools are available until they reach 21 years of age.

A mentally retarded child who is nearing puberty should have a sex education program and information about birth control geared to his or her understanding. Children who are mildly retarded especially need such information since they are likely to date and be involved with members of the opposite sex.

The fundamental emotional needs of a child with mental retardation are the same as any other child's. A child with mental retardation needs extra attention to help deal with the frustration of his or her disability. He or she needs to feel like a valued member of the family, not an outsider. A child who is mentally retarded, like a child of normal intelligence, also needs to develop a good self-image and to know the feeling of success and fulfillment. Like other children, mentally retarded children need to know that their parents are proud of them.

All children need social contact. For mentally retarded children, it can be provided, for example, through volunteer organizations such as the Special Olympics, recreation programs sponsored by the local city or town, or church or parent groups. Children with mental retardation need physical activity. They may, however, need assistance and support in becoming involved in activities such as sports.

A serious concern of parents of children with developmental disabilities is their child's future as an adult. The ability of a person with mental retardation to be self-sufficient will always be limited to some degree, depending on the level of disability, so it is important that a child be encouraged to achieve his or her highest potential. Parents often find it difficult to encourage their child to be independent because of their concerns regarding their child's limitations.

In some situations, when a retarded child is one of many children needing care in a family, parents must give special consideration so that the energy of attending to a retarded child will not seriously affect the quality of the care they are able to give their other children. Working parents may need to find a good plan of daycare for the involved child.

Parents should become acquainted with the many local and national organizations and support groups that offer information about mental retardation and programs to enhance the lives of developmentally handicapped individuals. Parents can begin by communicating with one or both of the following:

- Association for Retarded Citizens/ U.S., 2501 Avenue J, Arlington, TX 76011 (phone: 817-640-0204)
- Joseph P. Kennedy, Jr., Foundation, 1350 New York Avenue NW, Washington, DC 20005 (phone: 202-393-1250)

MOLES

DESCRIPTION

Moles are collections of pigment cells that appear as raised brown spots on the skin. Rarely present at birth (only 1 newborn in 100 has one), moles begin to develop after a child is 1 or 2 years old, and continue to appear throughout adolescence. More than half of the children in the United States have at least one mole; some children have dozens.

Moles can appear anywhere on the body, and are usually slightly raised or dome-shaped. Although color usually ranges from tan to brown, a mole can also be flesh-colored. A mole called the blue nevus (nevus is another name for mole) is gray-blue in color.

Moles usually begin as brown specks during early childhood, enlarging to slightly smaller than the size of a pencil eraser when fully developed. Most pigmented moles are smooth, light to medium brown in appearance, with a well-defined and regular border. A giant nevus (also called a giant hairy nevus or bathing trunk nevus is a rare, large mole that may appear at birth. At least several inches in diameter, it is tan, medium brown, or dark brown, often covered with coarse hair, and usually distorts the skin surface.

Moles increase in number during the teens and twenties, and many disappear by age 60 or 70. Most moles are harmless, but some moles have a high risk of developing into a *cancer* called melanoma.

CAUSE

Moles are caused by an accumulation of pigment cells; frequency of development is often an inherited trait.

DIAGNOSIS

A physician can identify different types of moles by carefully examining a child's skin.

COMPLICATIONS

A mole rarely becomes cancerous. This can occur, however, if the mole is a giant birth mole, a small birth mole, or a very dark and irregularly pigmented acquired mole called dysplastic nevus. A physician who recognizes a giant pigmented nevus at birth may recommend its complete removal. The operation is often performed before the third year of a child's life to reduce the risk of *cancer.*

If a small congenital mole is typical in appearance and does not change significantly over time, immediate removal is not necessary. Many physicians recommend removal of small birth moles before a child reaches 13 years of age.

A dysplastic nevus may also become cancerous. This mole does not usually appear until a child reaches puberty or adolescence, and is very dark and/or irregularly colored with irregular and/or poorly marked outlines. Dysplastic nevus commonly runs in families.

Giant nevi of the head or neck area may be associated with *hydrocephalus* and *seizures.*

TREATMENT

Since most moles are harmless and usually do not change, treatment is usually not necessary. Congenital moles, small and large, should be evaluated for removal before 12 years of age.

A physician should examine any mole that has been partially removed, bleeds, forms a crust, changes color, grows in height rapidly, or begins to spread pigment into the surrounding skin. If any of these conditions is present, the mole usually is surgically removed by a physician. The operation is performed with either local or general anesthesia. A scar is left after surgery.

Moles may also be removed for cosmetic reasons.

PREVENTION

Moles cannot be prevented.

MOLLUSCUM CONTAGIOSUM

DESCRIPTION

Molluscum contagiosum is a common viral infection which appears as pearly pimples on the skin. It is most common among children, but it also affects adolescents and adults. Other skin disorders such as atopic *eczema* may be associated with molluscum. If associated with other rashes, molluscum can spread rapidly on the body.

Once a child is infected, it takes 2 to 7 weeks for the first pimples to appear. Molluscum contagiosum is self-limiting (it will not last indefinitely), and will usually disappear without treatment within about 18 months, though it may persist for longer periods.

CAUSE

A virus causes molluscum contagiosum. Mildly contagious, this virus is passed through direct skin-to-skin contact with an infected person or infected personal belongings. During adolescence and adulthood molluscum contagiosum is also contracted by sexual contact.

SIGNS AND SYMPTOMS

Below the skin surface, cells infected by the virus collect in condensed, pearllike clusters. Pushing through to the skin surface, the clusters erupt as firm, waxy, flesh-colored pimples with sunken centers. Most frequently, pimples will appear on the face, arms, eyelids, neck, thighs, and genital areas. These pimples may be barely visible when they first appear, about one sixteenth of an inch across, but then can grow to one quarter of an inch or more. Molluscum pimples may spread to number in the hundreds.

DIAGNOSIS

Parents can often identify molluscum contagiosum based on the appearance of the pimplelike eruptions. The characteristic indentation in the center of each pimple is easily seen on close inspection under good light. If there is doubt as to the diagnosis, a physician can be consulted for positive identification.

TREATMENT

Since molluscum contagiosum eventually disappears by itself, and treatment may be worse than the disease, treatment often is not recommended for small children. If the condition is severe, however, the child should see a physician.

Treatment by a physician usually consists of cutting each molluscum pimple with a pointed scalpel and scraping out the hard, white, pearllike center. The pimples may also be treated by light freezing with liquid nitrogen.

PREVENTION

Although only mildly contagious, molluscum contagiosum is spread easily by close contact with an infected person. Contaminated clothes, linens, and towels should be avoided, as should direct contact with the skin of an infected person. The virus is usually killed by ordinary dry cleaning or hot-water laundering.

Mononucleosis, Infectious

DESCRIPTION

Infectious mononucleosis is a relatively common viral disease that is prolonged but rarely dangerous among adolescents and young adults. More than 8 out of 10 American children contract the disease between the ages of 4 and 15, but many have only a mild illness. Mononucleosis before adolescence is often not recognized because it takes the form of *fever* accompanied by mild fatigue but usually is not a prolonged illness. When it strikes in adolescence or adulthood, it can take the form of a prolonged, exhausting illness.

Recurrences of mononucleosis are rare, but relapses sometimes occur just as the patient is recovering. The incubation period for the disease can be long, perhaps several weeks. Severe symptoms usually last 2 to 4 weeks, followed by a gradual recovery. Generally no serious complications occur, and those who contract mononucleosis usually recover completely.

CAUSE

Mononucleosis is caused by the Epstein-Barr virus. The virus is transmitted in saliva through coughing, sneezing, or kissing. An infected person's saliva contains the virus for 6 months or longer after recovery.

Not all people who have direct contact with an infected person will become ill. The Epstein-Barr virus appears to be only slightly contagious, and close contact with saliva is required for spread of the virus to occur.

SIGNS AND SYMPTOMS

During adolescence and young adulthood mononucleosis is characterized by the slow onset of *fever, swollen glands, sore throat,* vague physical discomfort, and tiredness. The sore throat is due to tonsillitis (see *tonsillitis and adenoiditis*). Other symptoms may include *headache,* congestion, runny nose, nausea or *abdominal pain,* aching joints, difficulty swallowing, bleeding gums, lack of appetite, and extreme fatigue. Infrequently, a red, spotty *rash* appears. The symptoms usually last for several weeks, and often low-grade fever, sore throat, poor appetite, and extreme fatigue persist for weeks or even months. Individuals with the disease require more sleep than usual and seem to feel tired all the time.

DIAGNOSIS

Mononucleosis is difficult for a lay person to diagnose since its symptoms are not specific and mimic many other illnesses. The persistence of the disease offers the first clue and, along with observable signs and symptoms, aids the physician in establishing the diagnosis. Two blood tests are usually very helpful. One is a test for heterophile agglutinins—the Monospot test, or some variation of it. This test is positive in about 90 percent of adolescents or adults with mononucleosis and a lower proportion of younger children. The other test is an identification and counting of unusual lymphocytes (infection-fighting white blood cells) in the blood smear. These are almost always present and numerous, particularly in early convalescence.

COMPLICATIONS

Complications are unusual. A mild form of hepatitis causing *jaundice* (yellowing of body tissues and darkening of urine) is the most common complication. Rarely, other problems may occur, such as marked swelling of the tonsils and throat leading to *breathing difficulty, encephalitis,* or most serious of all, rupture of the spleen.

TREATMENT

Home treatment for mononucleosis should include rest, until the *fever* decreases to normal or near normal. Gargling salt water may help to relieve the sore throat. Liquids are recommended, and a fever-reducing medication may be helpful. Consult the physician for specific recommendations and read the discussion of nonprescription medications beginning on p. 102. Activity should be limited until fatigue disappears, and vigorous activity should be avoided for several weeks because of the danger of rupturing an enlarged spleen.

PREVENTION

Mononucleosis cannot be prevented. Because of the low contagiousness of the infection, isolation of children or adolescents with the disease is not necessary.

MOTION SICKNESS

DESCRIPTION

Motion sickness is the sensation of nausea and dizziness that often affects people riding in moving vehicles such as cars, boats, buses, trains, and planes. Children are more likely than adults to become motion sick, because adults have usually learned how to prevent the illness. Also, as the nervous system matures and becomes better able to deal with the effects of movement, a child may outgrow motion sickness.

Some children are more susceptible than others to motion sickness. Susceptible children usually become motion sick each time they travel in a moving vehicle. Infants apparently are immune to motion sickness.

CAUSE

Motion sickness is caused by a disturbance of the body's balance fluids, located in the inner ear. Certain movements, such as the rolling of a boat or bouncing of a car, can set these fluids in motion. Continuous focusing of the eyes on rapidly moving objects, such as passing cars or scenery, aggravates this balance disturbance. Nerves affected by this imbalance send a message to the brain; the brain then sends another message to the stomach resulting in nausea and *vomiting*.

SIGNS AND SYMPTOMS

A child will become nauseated, pale or "green," and anxious. Sweating, *dizziness*, weakness, and *vomiting* can follow.

DIAGNOSIS

A parent can identify motion sickness by observing a child's appearance, symptoms, and behavior.

COMPLICATIONS

Prolonged unrelieved motion sickness can occasionally lead to excessive *vomiting* and *dehydration*.

TREATMENT

Unless a susceptible child outgrows motion sickness, he or she will frequently become ill when traveling. Treatment therefore focuses on prevention. If a child becomes motion sick, the best treatment includes rest and slow replacement of fluids (usually flat carbonated beverages that help settle the stomach).

PREVENTION

When traveling, several things can be done to keep a child "in balance." A child's attention can be occupied with games or songs. It may be helpful to supply plenty of cool air and to suggest that a child lie down, eyes open. Crackers, flat carbonated beverages, and gum may help settle a queasy stomach. A child should sit near the most stable part of a moving vehicle (over the wings of a plane, in the center of a boat or car), where disturbing motions will be at a minimum.

Before a journey begins, a child can be given antihistamines that may help prevent motion sickness. Such medication is available over the counter, can be given to children 1 hour before a trip begins, and once every 4 hours during the trip. These medications should be used carefully, however, as they can cause drowsiness.

Another medication, scopolamine, is very effective for control of motion sickness. The FDA, however, has approved scopolamine for use only by older children and adults. Originally used by astronauts while in space, this medication is administered as a small, flexible, self-adhesive patch placed behind the ear. This medication is transdermal (absorbed through the skin) and should be applied 2 to 4 hours before a trip begins. Scopolamine should be used carefully, since occasional side effects (such as disorientation and blurred vision) may occur.

MOVEMENT DISORDERS

DESCRIPTION

When a child persistently repeats a meaningless motion for no apparent purpose, the child is said to have a movement disorder.

Some of the more common movements:

- tics—sudden, uncontrollable, rapidly repeated movements of a muscle or group of muscles (see *tics and Tourette's syndrome*)
- *head-banging*—rhythmic hitting of the head against a solid object, such as a crib headboard
- rocking (see *head-banging*)—swaying back and forth on the hands and knees in a rhythmical fashion
- spasms—prolonged cramps (muscle

contractions), which can be painful or violent; if generalized can be a convulsion (see *seizures*)

- facial spasms—irregular, repetitive jerks of a facial muscle
- dancing in a random, irregular fashion
- dystonia and athetosis—slow twisting, interspersed with prolonged periods of muscle tension, often of the fingers and toes
- sudden, brief muscle contractions affecting one muscle or part of one muscle
- chorea—jumping and other movements involving a leg or an arm
- moving a corner of the mouth while closing an eye
- exaggerated chewing motions
- movement resulting from a lack of control of one or more groups of muscles

The prevalence, duration and severity of any movement symptom and the outlook for an affected child depend on the underlying cause.

CAUSE

A movement disorder is said to exist when movement appears to be an outlet for expressing everyday *stress* and tension. Experts believe that some young children release tension using motion (rocking, for example) because they have difficulty expressing feelings using more purposeful actions or words.

Another cause of movement disorders appears to be a need for self-stimulation. Experts believe this need is especially acute among children who have temporary or long-term difficulties sensing and responding to stimuli. These difficulties can be caused by such conditions as *failure to thrive,* developmental disabilities (such as *mental retardation),* or *psychosis.* In some cases movement symptoms become more pronounced during times of stress or excitement.

DIAGNOSIS

If a child appears to have any of the movements described above, parents should consult the physician most familiar with the child's medical history. The physician conducts a physical examination, notes any current signs or symptoms, and asks for a thorough description of the unusual movements. The goal of these steps is to determine the nature of the movements and a possible cause. Further procedures may be necessary if a physician suspects the cause to be anything more serious than a development-related tendency to deal with everyday tension using motion. The physician may consult a neurologist or psychiatrist to conduct special tests or interpret their results.

TREATMENT

If a very young child with abnormal movements appears to have no underlying problem, treatment is generally unnecessary. Such disorders are typically outgrown while the child is a toddler.

Treatment for movement disorders resulting from more serious problems depends on the causes. When the cause cannot be eliminated, treatment focuses on teaching the child to control the movements; in other cases treating the cause results in disappearance of the movements. In many instances treatment centers on both.

When a need for self-stimulation appears to exist, a physician or consultant may be able to help the child find other sources of stimulation. If *stress* is implicated, a physician may refer the child to a psychiatrist or other counselor, who can help the family identify sources of tension and explore ways of reducing them. A counselor can also try to teach the child ways of coping with tension more constructively.

PREVENTION

Movement disorders can be prevented only if the cause is preventable.

MUMPS

EMERGENCY ACTION

If a child who is ill with mumps develops a stiff neck, extreme sleepiness or listlessness, or *vomiting,* consult a physician immediately. *Encephalitis* (brain inflammation) may develop suddenly and progress swiftly. Full recovery can depend upon prompt diagnosis and treatment.

DESCRIPTION

Mumps is a highly contagious infection which causes *fever, headache,* loss of appetite, irritability, and painful swelling of the salivary glands below the ears and, less commonly, those under the lower jaw. The swelling temporarily alters a child's facial appearance, sometimes dramatically so.

Swelling may also extend into the pharynx (throat) and larynx (voice box) area, making swallowing uncomfortable and difficult. Both right and left salivary glands are usually affected, but swelling sometimes occurs on only one side.

Although mumps is not usually a serious illness, it can lead to a variety of other problems, the most severe of which is *encephalitis*. Complications are unusual, and the outlook for nearly all children is excellent. A single mumps virus infection, even one so mild as to produce no signs or symptoms, provides lifelong immunity against subsequent infection.

The virus probably cannot be transferred from an infected person to someone who is uninfected earlier than 1 day before swelling or other symptoms first appear or later than 3 days after swelling disappears. The incubation period in an individual varies from 2 to 3 weeks, with 17 or 18 days being the most likely duration.

Children under 15 years old account for 85 percent of all cases of mumps. Experts believe that mumps is continuously present in urban communities, where epidemics can occur at any time, particularly from January through May.

CAUSE

Mumps is caused by a virus. The virus is found in mucus and may be transmitted by person-to-person contact or by airborne droplets produced by sneezing and coughing. Household objects and personal possessions may be contaminated by a sick child's saliva. The urine of an infected child may also carry the virus.

SIGNS AND SYMPTOMS

Mumps usually begins with low *fever, headache,* stomachache (see *stomachache, stomach pain),* loss of appetite, and listlessness. Within a day, an earache (see *earache and ear infections)* begins around the earlobe of one ear. Chewing becomes painful and the area just below and in front of that ear swells noticeably over the next day or two. Occasionally all of the swelling occurs within the first 24 hours.

One of the parotids (a pair of large salivary glands located just under the ear) is infected by the mumps virus. Often the gland swells so extensively that it pushes the earlobe up and out. In most cases the parotid gland located under the opposite ear becomes infected as well and begins to swell in a day or so.

Swelling may be so extensive that the jawline is hidden completely, giving a child a moon-faced appearance. Other glands under the jaw may also become infected and swollen. Pain and fever may last as long as 6 or 7 days, although some children may not have any fever. Swelling usually begins to subside after a week or so. Complete recovery from swelling and other symptoms may require as long as 2 weeks.

COMPLICATIONS

Mumps virus may travel through the body, involving various organs and systems.

Occasionally *encephalitis* develops after the glands become swollen. The illness is marked by *fever, vomiting, headache,* irritability, stiff neck, and occasionally *seizures.* In some cases the child experiences weakness of the neck, shoulders, and one or both legs. All these difficulties associated with encephalitis may subside completely within a week to 10 days, leaving no aftereffects. In some cases mumps virus produces only the signs and symptoms of encephalitis without causing any of the swollen glands typically associated with mumps.

Occasionally males past puberty develop a painful inflammation of one testicle within a week or so of developing mumps. This inflammation usually lasts 3 or 4 days and rarely affects both testicles. In less than 10 percent of cases, sterility occurs.

Some girls (fewer than one in 10) who have passed puberty develop pelvic pain and tenderness caused by inflammation of an ovary. Such inflammation usually subsides within a week without affecting fertility.

Infrequently, mild nephritis (kidney inflammation) occurs, which disappears within a week. The child's eyes may be affected by swelling of the tear glands, sensitivity to light, and partial loss or blurring of vision. Full recovery requires between 10 and 20 days.

In rare cases deafness can be caused by nerve inflammation in the ear. This usually occurs in only one ear and can be total and permanent (see *earache and ear infections).* Other rare complications are arthritis (see *arthritis, acute),* pancreatitis (inflammation of the pancreas), and thyroiditis (inflammation of the thyroid; see *thyroid problems).*

DIAGNOSIS

A physician diagnoses mumps by observing a child's swollen glands and associated signs and symptoms. Diagnosis can be confirmed easily if the child has been exposed to mumps during the 2 to 3 weeks prior to onset of signs and symptoms.

TREATMENT

Mumps is usually treated at home. In those cases where complications such as *meningitis* or *encephalitis* require specialized diagnostic procedures or life support equipment, hospitalization is necessary.

Home treatment should make an ill child as comfortable as possible. Some children stay in bed with a *fever.* Even at the height of infection, however, some feel well enough to be up and around. The child should be encouraged to drink plenty of liquids and eat soft foods. Since drinking acidic liquids can be painful when salivary glands are swollen, citrus juices should be well diluted. Apple juice and flat carbonated beverages (such as ginger ale) are soothing.

Most signs and symptoms of mumps subside without use of any medication. Mild fever-reducing and pain-relieving medications, however, may be helpful for fever and *headache.* Consult the physician for specific recommendations and read the discussion of nonprescription medications beginning on p. 102.

PREVENTION

A mumps vaccine is one of the standard inoculations. At the age of 15 months a mumps, measles, rubella (MMR) vaccination is given to all children. Although the vaccination does not provide 100 percent immunity from the mumps, its effectiveness is rated above 90 percent. To be protected against mumps (or any infectious disease), a child must be vaccinated before being exposed to someone carrying the virus.

MUSCLE PAIN

DESCRIPTION

Pain can develop in any muscle because of injury, cramping, or inflammation. Pain may be present in a small part of a muscle, such as at the point of injury, or may extend throughout a muscle. Muscle pain itself is a symptom of an underlying condition or illness.

Severity of muscle injury ranges from mild to quite severe. Mildly injured muscles retain their elasticity and ability to function, usually healing with rest. More severely damaged muscles are partially or completely torn and may require surgery for full recovery.

Cramps, which are painful contractions of muscle fibers, frequently occur in growing and physically active children. Cramps may last from a few seconds to a few hours and may occur in any muscle of the body. They may vary from mild to strong enough to wake a child during the night (such as a charley horse). Cramps can be severe and violent enough to break a bone.

Myositis (muscle inflammation), frequently associated with common illnesses such as *colds* and *influenza,* may affect children of all ages. Myositis-induced pain frequently occurs as a dull ache in the large muscles of the body, such as those of the neck, back, shoulders, and arms.

CAUSE

The most common injuries causing muscle pain are muscle strain (stretching or partial tearing of muscle) or damage to muscle nerves and blood vessels (usually resulting in formation of a bruise) caused by a forceful blow. These injuries frequently occur during participation in contact sports or other vigorous physical activity. Such pain may be confused with pain caused by injuries such as *sprains* and mild *fractures.*

Pain due to cramps often occurs as a child's muscles grow and develop. These cramps (see *growing pains)* usually develop when a growing child is at rest, often during the night. Cramps may also develop when a child participates in vigorous physical activity involving previously inactive muscles.

Vigorous movement can also result in cramps if large amounts of the body's salts and minerals, such as potassium and magnesium, are lost through heavy sweating (see *dehydration).* Hyperventilating (fast, shallow breathing) and restriction of blood flow to muscles may also result in cramps. Because of their size and the frequency with which they are used, large muscles such as those of the calf and upper arm tend to cramp more frequently than others.

Muscle inflammation most often results from viral infections such as *influenza.*

Other, less common, causes of inflammation are infestation by parasites (such as those found in uncooked pork; see *parasitic infections)* and bacterial infection of muscle tissue. These organisms most often enter muscle tissue after injury.

DIAGNOSIS

Muscle pain is obvious; an underlying cause must be identified for proper treatment. Obvious causes such as cramps and inflammation can be diagnosed at home.

If the cause of muscle pain is not apparent, a physician can usually identify an underlying condition or disease on the basis of a child's medical history, a review of recent physical activity, and a physical examination.

COMPLICATIONS

If a muscle is injured repeatedly and inflammation is extensive, tiny pieces of bone may form in the injured tissue (a process known as ossification). If ossification is not stopped, normal muscle functioning will be difficult and painful.

TREATMENT

Relief from muscle pain requires treatment of underlying causes.

Minor muscle injuries usually heal with home treatment. Rest is essential, because the more an injured muscle is exercised, the more slowly it heals.

The first step in home treatment is to reduce swelling. An injured muscle should be raised to slow the flow of blood through damaged blood vessels. The muscle should be used as little as possible. An ice pack (ice wrapped in a towel or placed in an ice bag) should be applied immediately after injury for 30 minutes. If swelling does not decrease, ice packs should be applied at 30 minute intervals, 15 minutes apart, over the next few hours until swelling subsides.

Pain from injury lessens as swelling decreases. When pain has decreased, the child should begin to exercise the injured muscle several times a day, gently rotating it in all directions to increase mobility. Soaking in warm water helps relax injured muscles and ease movement. If exercise is painful, a child should not use the injured muscle.

If a leg muscle is hurt and cannot support pressure, the child can use crutches to walk. The top of the crutch should reach just below the armpit when the child stands up-right. This ensures that the child's weight rests on the hands, not on the nerves and blood vessels of the armpit, which are easily damaged. The child should continue to use crutches until able to put weight on the injured leg comfortably.

Treatment of inflammation also should begin with reduction of swelling. Rest is essential, as it helps reduce or prevent muscle contractions that can interfere with healing. Once swelling is significantly reduced, an affected muscle should be relaxed by applying heat, either through warm water soaks or warm compresses. Muscles should then be gently massaged and exercised to prevent stiffening during healing.

Muscle cramps are best treated by stretching and squeezing the involved muscle. Cramped calf muscles should be squeezed gently while the front of the foot is pushed upward; a cramped arm muscle should be squeezed while the elbow is straightened slowly. Stretching and squeezing should be repeated until the cramp is gone. Soothing liniments (medicated liquids or sprays) may relieve some muscle pain. A pain-relieving medication may be helpful. Consult the physician for specific recommendations, and read the discussion of nonprescription medications beginning on p. 000.

If muscle pain is not reduced significantly within 24 to 48 hours and a muscle cannot be used, medical attention is required. A physician's care or, in some cases, surgery may be recommended to avoid permanent muscle weakness.

The child can begin slowly to use a muscle when pain is almost gone. vigorous activity should not be resumed, however, for at least a week after a muscle injury occurs, even if pain disappears fairly quickly. Approximately 7 to 10 days are required for complete healing of a mild muscle injury; 2 to 6 weeks are required for more severe injuries.

PREVENTION

In general, muscle pain cannot be prevented. Some muscle injuries are less likely to occur, however, if a child thoroughly stretches and limbers muscles before participating in vigorous activity. Cramps caused by loss of minerals can often be prevented if a child eats or drinks something rich in potassium before participating in vigorous physical activity. Potassium is available in vegetables and fruits (such as potatoes, bananas, and cranberries).

MUSCULAR DYSTROPHY

DESCRIPTION, CAUSE, AND SIGNS AND SYMPTOMS

"Muscular dystrophy" is the term applied to any inherited muscle disorder that is characterized by progressive degeneration of muscles without apparent involvement of the nervous system. The heart and the respiratory system may be affected. In general, these muscle disorders are uncommon.

Duchenne

Duchenne muscular dystrophy is the most devastating of all muscular dystrophies. It is a progressive disease that usually ends in death before age 20, although a few individuals survive into their 20s. Children do not die because of the muscle disorder itself but because of complications caused by it. In most cases death results from respiratory infection, which initially may be mild but progresses rapidly; death may also be caused by heart failure.

Only male children develop Duchenne muscular dystrophy. It is usually inherited and occurs in 1 of every 3,500 live male births. The genetic factor, a defective gene, involved is passed on to children by mothers who carry it but do not develop the disorder themselves. There is a 50 percent chance that each male child of a woman who carries the genetic factor will develop the disease and a 50 percent chance that each female child will carry the factor (see *genetic disorders*).

In most cases signs and symptoms of Duchenne muscular dystrophy do not appear until a child begins to walk. Half of the children with the disease begin to walk after 18 months of age. Onset of symptoms usually occurs between ages 2 and 5, with muscles of the lower body areas and the spine affected first. Slowed intellectual development and borderline *mental retardation* can accompany muscular dystrophy.

Symptoms of Duchenne muscular dystrophy include a reluctance to walk or a delay in walking; an abnormal walk, most often a waddling or swaying gait; walking on the toes; inability to hop or run normally; difficulty climbing stairs, curbs, or getting in and out of cars; and frequent falls. Affected children have difficulty getting up off the floor; they must get on their hands and knees, bring their legs close to their arms, and fi-

nally "walk up" their legs into a standing position. Because of toe-walking, these children develop a forward tilt of the pelvis and subsequently a hollowing of the back, called lordosis.

A child with Duchenne muscular dystrophy tires easily and has difficulty supporting total body weight on one leg. Muscle enlargement is usually present, particularly in the calves; the legs are usually affected symmetrically. The arms are not usually affected until the disease is advanced. Dental problems, including widening of the jaw and widening of the spaces between the teeth, often develop.

Bone deformities do not usually occur until a child with Duchenne muscular dystrophy can no longer walk, usually about age 10 to 13. As the disease progresses, the muscles become thin and muscle reflexes disappear. Poor posture from constant sitting causes contractions of muscles and tendons of the hips, knees, and elbows. These contractions lead to abnormal positioning of the arms, legs, and feet (such as *clubfoot;* also see *foot abnormalities). Scoliosis* (curvature of the spine) often develops.

Children with Duchenne muscular dystrophy often become constipated because of continuous sitting. The diaphragm (the muscular partition between the chest and abdominal cavities) is still functional, but other respiratory muscles begin to deteriorate. As a result, a child's ability to breathe decreases. Changes in the functioning of heart muscle occur in 60 to 90 percent of all patients, and heart problems may result.

Limb-girdle

Limb-girdle muscular dystrophy predominantly affects the muscles of the pelvic area. The genetic factor for limb-girdle muscular dystrophy can be passed on to children of both sexes from either parent; a child must receive one gene from each parent in order to develop the disorder. Therefore, when both parents carry the factor, a child has a 25 percent chance of developing limb-girdle muscular dystrophy (see *genetic disorders).*

Limb-girdle muscular dystrophy ranges in severity from quite mild to very debilitating. When onset is early, this disorder may be quite severe and may closely resemble Duchenne muscular dystrophy. Other cases of early-onset limb-girdle muscular dystrophy are much less severe and progress slowly; an affected child continues to be able to walk into adulthood. Like those of Duchenne, symptoms of limb-girdle muscular dystrophy can include muscle enlargement and toe-walking. If disease begins early, deterioration is often rapid, and respiratory problems and severe *scoliosis* usually develop.

The outlook for children with limb-girdle muscular dystrophy depends on the extent of muscle weakness and the speed of muscle deterioration. Heart involvement is not common with this disorder, nor is mental development impaired. Death occurs less frequently with this problem than with Duchenne muscular dystrophy but can result because of complications.

Facioscapulohumeral

A far more mild form of muscular dystrophy, facioscapulohumeral (FSH) muscular dystrophy primarily involves the muscles of the shoulders, the upper back, and the face. Facial muscles tend to weaken before shoulder muscles do. In some cases muscles of the lower limbs are also affected. Both male and female children can develop this type of muscular dystrophy; the genetic factor responsible can be passed on by a parent who also has the disorder. Their children have a 50 percent chance of developing FSH muscular dystrophy (see *genetic disorders*).

FSH muscular dystrophy is usually mild and progresses slowly. Symptoms usually do not appear until adolescence or adulthood, although occasionally they appear during childhood. Weakness is usually slight and located only in one area. In rare cases, especially those with onset in childhood, weakness is so severe as to be debilitating.

Characteristically, individuals with FSH muscular dystrophy cannot close their eyes tightly, purse their lips, puff out their cheeks, or pucker their lips to blow or whistle. A double dimple usually appears at the corner of the mouth when an individual with FSH muscular dystrophy tries to smile.

When shoulder and upper back weakness is present, an individual has difficulty raising the arms or lifting objects. The scapulae (shoulder blades) push upwards toward the head, giving the shoulders a characteristic terraced appearance.

Mild cases of FSH muscular dystrophy do not usually become worse, and individuals usually live normal, active lives. When the disorder is more severe, movement of the arms and shoulders may be limited permanently, restricting some activities. Neither heart nor lung involvement occurs with this disorder, and intellectual development is not affected.

Becker

Becker muscular dystrophy is similar to Duchenne muscular dystrophy, but is much less common and less severe. As in cases of Duchenne, male children of mothers carrying the responsible gene have a 50 percent chance of developing this disorder, and female children have a 50 percent chance of becoming carriers of the genetic factor (see *genetic disorders)*. Individuals with this disorder usually die between 30 and 50 years of age; death rarely occurs before 20.

Symptoms of Becker muscular dystrophy resemble mild symptoms of both Duchenne and limb-girdle muscular dystrophies. Initial symptoms usually appear at a later age than those of Duchenne, but some cases are obvious during early childhood. Affected individuals do not lose the ability to walk until well into adulthood, and heart involvement is less common than in cases of Duchenne muscular dystrophy.

DIAGNOSIS

Many factors are involved in a physician's diagnosis of muscular dystrophy. These include the age at onset of signs and symptoms, the age at which the child loses the ability to walk, the results of blood tests, and if relevant, the age at death. Blood tests are used to measure levels of specific muscle enzymes (chemical messengers), which usually become elevated when muscular dystrophy is present; levels of these enzymes vary with each type of muscle disorder. Tests of heart and lung function are extremely important so that any functional muscle abnormalities can be detected.

Muscle biopsies, in which tissue samples are removed and analyzed, are performed by a physician to detect structural changes in muscle fibers. Such biopsies may also differentiate variations of limb-girdle muscular dystrophy among affected individuals. Electromyographies—tests that measure the electrical currents traveling through active muscle tissue—are performed to determine the effect changes in muscle fiber have on muscle functioning.

It is important for a physician to differentiate among the types of muscular dystrophy so that an accurate forecast of the course of the condition can be made. FSH muscular dystrophy can often be diagnosed from the presence of facial muscle weakness alone, or weakness of facial, shoulder, and upper back muscles. Limb-girdle and Becker muscular dystrophies are usually difficult to tell apart;

differentiation is based on the pattern of inheritance involved. Severe cases of limb-girdle often resemble Duchenne muscular dystrophy but can be differentiated according to the sex and age of affected children at the time of onset of symptoms.

TREATMENT

Because no cure exists for muscular dystrophy, treatment focuses on maintaining the child's ability to walk and use affected muscles as long as possible. Children should be encouraged to use involved muscles as much as possible to delay stiffening and deterioration. Even during periods of illness, children should be encouraged to move. Mild cases of FSH and Becker muscular dystrophy generally do not require further treatment, because disability is mild and does not interfere with an individual's daily routine.

In addition to using their muscles, children with Duchenne or limb-girdle muscular dystrophy should perform stretching exercises recommended by a physician or physical therapist. These exercises are designed to take the joints through a full range of movement and to prevent muscle and tendon contractions that may reduce walking ability. When not moving about or exercising, the child should be encouraged to lie on his or her stomach in an effort to extend the hips and reduce muscle contractions.

If leg muscles begin to deteriorate, braces can be used to prolong walking. These braces are made of lightweight plastic and are molded to the child's legs. Night splints can be used to support the ankles and reduce the chances of developing clubfoot.

In addition to exercising and wearing braces, walking may be prolonged through surgical release of contracted muscles and tendons. For example, release of a contracted Achilles tendon (located at the heel) and transplantation of tendons temporarily delays development of *clubfoot*. Individuals with FSH muscular dystrophy may require fixation of the shoulder blades to increase arm and shoulder mobility. After any orthopedic surgery the child must be encouraged to become mobile again as quickly as possible to avoid muscle deterioration. In many cases this means moving the involved areas of the body within 24 hours of surgery.

Once the child loses the ability to walk, posture supports are essential to control bone deformities. The child can be fitted with a vertical back brace or molded plastic jacket to keep the spine erect and help control *scoliosis*. If the child is using a wheelchair, the backrest should be soft but supportive enough to keep the child's spine erect. Scoliosis surgery for spinal fixation may be indicated for some patients. Clubfoot can be controlled by keeping the child's feet in a straight position with supportive boots and proper positioning of the footrests of the wheelchair.

No matter what type of muscular dystrophy is present, affected individuals need constant encouragement and emotional support from family and friends. Muscular dystrophy can be a devastating disease for all concerned and an especially difficult battle for a child to fight, even with all kinds of help.

PREVENTION

Muscular dystrophies cannot be prevented. Women can be screened for elevated enzyme levels which may indicate the presence of a genetic factor for muscular dystrophy. Genetic counseling can alert parents to the chances of having children with a severe, fatal muscle disorder (see *genetic disorders*).

At this time, prenatal detection of muscular dystrophy is not possible. The sex of the fetus can be determined, however, and if the mother is an identified carrier for severe, fatal muscular dystrophy, a fetus at risk can be identified.

Information about all types of muscular dystrophy and local sources of assistance and support is available from the Muscular Dystrophy Association, 810 Seventh Avenue, New York, NY 10017 (phone: 212-586-0808).

NAIL-BITING

DESCRIPTION

Nail-biting is one of the most common habits of both childhood and adulthood. More than 40 percent of all children bite their nails or engage in related practices, such as biting their cuticles or picking their toenails. About half of all children who bite their nails continue to do so as adults. The other half tend to replace nail-biting with another habit, such as gum-chewing, cigarette-smoking, or doodling.

Like *thumb-sucking,* nail-biting is considered a mechanism for discharging everyday tension. Some experts believe nail-biting is an extension or variation of thumb-sucking, especially among older children. A child is most likely to engage in nail-biting when fearful, sad, nervous, tense, or distressed.

Nail-biting once was considered a sign of psychological disturbance, partially because it involves self-destruction of nails and surrounding skin. Although some experts continue to believe that nail-biting may function as a form of self-punishment or guilt-release, no evidence exists that it is associated with any disorder—physical, psychological, emotional, or social. Nail-biting may be one sign that a child is troubled, but it is never the only one.

Because it is cosmetically unattractive and can temporarily damage nails and surrounding skin, nail-biting is generally considered an undesirable habit. Most nail-biters can be taught to stop biting their nails and to release tension in a different way.

CAUSE

The reason that some children bite their nails while others release tension in different ways is unclear.

DIAGNOSIS

Nail-biting is usually obvious to parents. It can be assumed that the underlying cause of the habit is everyday tension—unless a child has signs and symptoms of a deeper problem, such as poor appetite, unhappiness, or unusual academic trouble. If parents cannot determine the nature of a deeper problem after talking with their child in a concerned, understanding way, the help of a physician or counselor should be sought.

COMPLICATIONS

Surrounding skin can become infected if a nail is bitten too far down or if cuticles are torn. Signs and symptoms of infection include pain in the affected area, redness, swelling, and pus. If a child picks at or bites toenails, they can become ingrown (see *ingrown toenails).*

TREATMENT AND PREVENTION

Parents should not scold a child about nail-biting. In general, lavishing attention on negative behavior serves as a source of tension for a child and tends to reinforce habits. Accordingly, trying to stop nail-biting with mechanical restraints or bad-tasting nail-coating substances is usually unsuccessful.

To prevent complications and to avoid social embarrassment for a child, however, parents should not ignore nail-biting. The best way to put an end to the habit is to provide a child with an incentive to avoid it. One effective approach is to teach a child to take pride in nail-grooming and, perhaps, to reinforce this lesson by providing a nail file, clippers, scissors, or other manicure aids.

If a child is too young to appreciate this approach or is otherwise uninterested in it, parents can try engaging him or her in more constructive activities whenever nail-biting begins. Another effective technique is to offer a child small symbolic rewards, such as a star on a calendar, every day that he or she refrains from nail-biting. On days that nail-biting does occur, the family should avoid criticism, praise the child for trying, and look ahead to the next day.

Minor skin infections can usually be treated at home by washing the affected area with soap and warm water and covering it with a bandage. If signs and symptoms of infection become more pronounced or do not disappear after 3 days, a physician should be consulted.

The only other reason to seek the help of a physician or counselor is the possibility that a child is emotionally troubled. In this case the main goal of treatment is not to modify the child's behavior but to determine the source of difficulty and help the child cope with it.

NECK LUMPS

DESCRIPTION

Children sometimes develop lumps under the skin. Lumps can vary in size, location, shape, color, consistency, capacity for movement, and location. In the great majority of cases—about 90 percent—these lumps are benign (harmless).

When lumps appear on the neck, they may be composed of excessive numbers of a variety of normal skin, fat, or vascular (blood vessel) cells, for example. They may represent swelling of lymph nodes, special infection-fighting lymphoid tissues, often called *swollen glands.* A small percentage of lumps result from a serious underlying cause. Nevertheless, all lumps, no matter how small and seemingly trivial, should be evaluated by a physician.

A neck lump may be present at birth, or may develop at any age, either slowly or quickly. Although several lumps can appear simultaneously, a single lump is typical. A lump may be soft and easily moved by pressure of any kind or it may be firm and immovable. It may feel tender or painless to the touch. Lumps can vary in size and shape from one that is round and pea-sized to ones that are irregularly shaped or as large as a golf ball or a lemon. They may be skin-colored, red, blue, or almost black.

A neck lump may be located anywhere from the top of the neck, in front of or behind an ear, to the bottom of the neck, just above the collarbone. Some lumps feel warm to the touch; others maintain the same temperature as the surrounding skin. If a lump is part of a blood vessel malformation, it pulsates. Some lumps become briefly enlarged when the child strains or moves vigorously; most remain the same size, regardless of the child's activities.

It is difficult to generalize about the rate of growth of a neck lump and whether the rate of growth is an accurate indication of the seriousness of the underlying condition. If not treated, the majority of lumps slowly grow in size.

Most lumps are superficial; that is, they do not arise from or go down into structures deep in the neck, such as muscle, bone, connective tissue, nerves, or blood vessels. More than 95 percent of superficial lumps are composed of some type of harmless tissue growth or swelling.

Most superficial lumps that require treatment can be healed. Those that do not respond to medical treatment must be diagnosed with specialized tests and may require surgical treatment. Excluding those that are found to be cancerous, most neck masses can be treated successfully either medically or surgically.

CAUSE

Neck lumps can be caused by various types of problems. The most common cause is inflammation of a particular structure in the neck (lymphoid tissue, muscle, or a gland, for example), usually produced by invading bacteria or viruses. Inflammation is a common disease condition characterized by heat, swelling, pain, and occasionally redness.

Lymphadenitis is an inflammation of one or more lymph nodes (small pea-sized knots of tissue that produce lymphocytes—a type of white blood cell—and that filter infectious agents carried in the blood). Lymphadenitis, produced by bacteria or viruses, is a leading cause of inflammatory masses in the neck (see *swollen glands*). Mononucleosis (see *mononucleosis, infectious)* and toxoplasmosis (an infection commonly transmitted by infected cats, caused by a parasite; see *pets, diseases caused by)* also can produce inflammatory neck lumps. Less common inflammatory causes include salivary gland inflammation, *tuberculosis,* and abscess, a collection of pus in lymph nodes in the neck resulting from infection in the throat (see *strep throat)*. Among rare causes of inflammatory lumps are *syphilis,* cat scratch fever, and cytomegaloviral infection.

Some neck lumps are considered normal; they represent extensions or enlargements of such bones as the jawbone, the mastoid tip of the skull (in back of the ear), and certain cervical vertebrae (located in the back of the neck).

Other lumps result from malformations or abnormalities present at birth. These include cystic hygroma, an overgrowth of lymph channels of the neck, which forms a cyst (a fluid-filled capsule), and hemangioma, an enlarged mass of blood vessel tissue (see *birthmarks)*.

Superficial noninflammatory lumps can be composed of mature fat cells, fibrous connective tissue, or a type of fibrous scar tissue. (The last type, which forms a linear band, frequently follows an injury, a burn, or surgery.) Deep noninflammatory lumps include those in the salivary glands, hematomas (collections of blood under the skin often caused by injury), or abnormalities in the muscle at the side of the neck (see *wry neck, neck pain)*.

The least common cause of neck lumps is a malignancy—*cancer*. Of this rare type of mass, rhabdomyosarcoma and Hodgkin's disease are the most common (see *lymphoma*. Less common cancerous lumps are those caused by *neuroblastoma, leukemia,* and tumors of the thyroid gland (see *thyroid problems)*.

DIAGNOSIS

Methods of diagnosing a lump in the neck

vary according to the kind of mass, its exact location, its physical characteristics, its associated signs and symptoms, and the age of the child. Many neck malformations are obvious at birth and are detected during the early physical examinations. Others become apparent only as the child grows—sometimes during adolescence or even adulthood—when underlying structures become more clearly defined.

Diagnostic tests may include blood and urine tests, X rays, analysis of skin scrapings to identify cell types, or if the mass, or cyst, is filled with fluid, removal of a sample of fluid (a procedure called aspiration) for analysis. If tests fail to identify the nature of a solid tumor, biopsy is necessary. Biopsy involves removal and analysis of a tissue sample. If the lump is small, it may be removed entirely for analysis. Any lump that is removed is often analyzed immediately so that a surgeon can decide whether additional tissue needs to be removed.

COMPLICATIONS

Other than complications of treatment, or of various underlying causes, neck lumps of themselves rarely cause complications. Aftereffects of treatment are rare, except perhaps for scars following certain surgical procedures.

TREATMENT

Treatment of neck lumps varies according to the underlying cause. Most inflammatory lumps can be treated successfully with appropriate antibiotics. Most congenital abnormalities and noninflammatory benign lumps (the majority of which are superficial) can be corrected successfully by surgical removal.

Cancerous lumps can be treated with a combination of surgery, chemotherapy, and radiation. The success of any treatment for a malignant neck lump varies according to the specific kind of cancer involved and how advanced the disease is at the time of diagnosis (see *cancer).

Because the majority of neck masses are either inflammatory or noninflammatory and superficial, most treatment with medications or surgery is successful.

PREVENTION

Neck lumps cannot be prevented except for problems caused by infections. If infection is treated promptly, it can often be controlled or cured before a neck lump develops.

NEPHRITIS

EMERGENCY ACTION

Seek immediate medical attention if a child has decreased urine output in addition to one or more of the following symptoms: cola- or coffee-colored urine, puffiness around the eyes, blurred vision, *fever,* weakness, *vomiting, headache,* convulsions (see *seizures),* or severe chest pain. The child may be suffering from complications of a type of kidney disease called nephritis. Severe forms of this disease commonly involve high blood pressure *(hypertension)* or even encephalopathy, a form of reversible brain dysfunction. Such problems can be life-threatening, and emergency treatment in a hospital may be necessary.

DESCRIPTION AND CAUSE

Nephritis is a disease characterized by inflammation (especially swelling) of the kidneys. (The prefix "nephr-" denotes the kidneys, as does the word "renal." See Description section in *kidney failure, acute.)*

The first step in producing urine is removing water and salts from the blood. Each kidney contains about a million tiny structures called glomeruli, which are essentially microscopic tufts of blood vessels surrounded by sacs. Excess water and salts enter the sacs from the tufts of blood vessels and, after being processed by other structures in the kidneys, are eventually converted into urine.

If the glomeruli become inflamed—if glomerulonephritis develops—then excess water and salts remain in the blood. In mild cases of glomerulonephritis, only a little excess remains in the blood, and a child may not even appear to be sick. If the condition is severe, however, the retention of excess water and salts in the body can eventually have life-threatening consequences. A child's body may become swollen with fluid, blood pressure may rise to the point that it interferes with brain function, and excess waste products may poison body tissues. If glomerulonephritis progresses to the point at which kidneys cannot perform sufficiently, kidney failure results. In general, kidney failure occurs when excess salts and fluids in the blood and body tissues rise to levels that are life-threatening.

In most cases of childhood glomerulonephritis, such consequences never develop and inflammation disappears naturally in a matter of weeks. If kidney failure does develop, it is usually short-term and disappears spontaneously. This type of kidney failure is called acute kidney failure, and a self-limited bout of glomerulonephritis is called <u>acute glomerulonephritis, or AGN</u>. There are five major causes of AGN, none of which is particularly common:

- <u>Hemolytic uremic syndrome</u>. This rare syndrome, which tends to affect children less than 1 year old, is characterized by glomerulonephritis, acute kidney failure, hemolytic anemia (see *anemia, hemolytic),* thrombocytopenia, and bruises. Bloody *diarrhea* usually precedes kidney failure by several days. The cause of most episodes of hemolytic uremic syndrome among children is unknown.
- <u>Anaphylactoid purpura</u>. This rare condition, which most often occurs among children, involves a characteristic *rash* that is most prominent on the buttocks and lower extremities. The rash initially may appear to be *hives,* but it rarely itches. It may eventually become purple and appear to be a bruise. The cause of the rash is probably some sort of blood vessel inflammation. In addition to glomerulonephritis, anaphylactoid purpura usually produces a red tinge to the skin, inflammation of the joints (see *arthritis, acute),* and colicky *abdominal pain* (see *colic),* sometimes associated with blood in the stools and *intussusception.*
- <u>Bacterial infection</u>. Bacterial infections that can be followed by AGN usually involve streptoccocus bacteria and include *strep throat* and *impetigo.* Such infections are far more common among children than are hemolytic uremic syndrome and anaphylactoid purpura. However, it is unusual for nephritis to follow an infection. For every 100 children with strep infections, for example, only 3 to 5 eventually develop AGN; most of these children are under 5 years of age. In most cases, AGN develops 1 to 3 weeks after a strep infection sets in, regardless of whether the infection has been treated or has even disappeared before this point. The reason that AGN sometimes follows strep infections is not completely clear, but it appears that such infections can set off an immunologic reaction that affects the kidneys. While strep infections are contagious, AGN is not; a child who contracts a strep infection from someone with poststrep AGN does not necessarily develop short-term kidney problems.
- <u>Membranoproliferative glomerulonephritis</u>. This syndrome mimics AGN associated with bacterial infections, except that infection is very rarely involved and its cause is almost always unknown. About half of all children with this form of glomerulonephritis eventually develop chronic kidney failure.

See also *lupus erythematosus,* a disorder of the connective tissue that rarely surfaces during childhood. When it does, it can produce AGN in addition to arthritis, a characteristic rash, and other symptoms.

In general the severity of AGN does not depend on the condition that triggers it. The severity of symptoms is a good indication of the severity of AGN; a child who is very ill appears that way. Therefore, in most cases medical attention is sought before complications set in or at least become life-threatening; more than 90 percent of all children with AGN recover fully, either spontaneously or because of treatment. Of the remaining 10 percent, a small number die from lack of medical care for complications of AGN. It is rare for children with AGN eventually to develop a "chronic" form of nephritis; those that do usually have the membranoproliferative or the lupus form.

Most cases of "chronic" nephritis, however, are not preceded by AGN. In fact, by definition "chronic nephritis" is long-term, progressive kidney inflammation whose exact origin defies explanation by physicians. Physicians tend to use the term "chronic nephritis" to label any inexplicable, long-term, progressive, inflammatory disease of the kidneys. It is estimated that chronic nephritis affects about 1 out of every 500,000 children.

Chronic nephritis always leads slowly—usually over a matter of years—to chronic kidney failure. Eventually, a child has to undergo dialysis and kidney transplantation (see *kidney failure, chronic).*

Bacterial infection of the kidney, sometimes called <u>pyelonephritis,</u> is usually a complication of some other infection in the urinary tract (kidneys, urine-carrying tubes called ureters, bladder, and urethra), and is quite different from the forms of nephritis discussed here (see *urinary tract infections).*

SIGNS AND SYMPTOMS

Many cases of acute glomerulonephritis—especially those associated with strep infections—are very mild, and no signs and symptoms are evident.

When signs and symptoms are present, the one that usually appears first is *blood in the urine,* or hematuria. The blood leaks into urine from the inflamed glomeruli blood vessels and causes urine to appear rust-colored. Sometimes, however, hematuria is not obvious, and blood cells can be detected in the urine only by examining a sample through a microscope. Blood proteins can also escape with the blood cells. Depending on the degree of severity of AGN, a child's urine output may be mildly to severely reduced.

In addition, a child with symptomatic AGN typically develops puffiness around the eyes, especially in the morning. This puffiness results from retention of excess fluids in the body, a condition known as *edema.* Edema may eventually affect other parts of the body and cause them to swell. A child who is suffering from edema often is lethargic, loses his or her appetite, and generally feels ill. The child may also develop a fever or complain of abdominal or lower back pain.

In addition to these signs and symptoms, about 60 percent of all children with AGN develop high blood pressure *(hypertension)* within days or weeks of the onset of kidney inflammation. Although an excess of fluids in the blood would logically seem to be the cause of high blood pressure, experts believe the actual cause is more complicated—which could explain why not all children with AGN have hypertension. Signs that a child with AGN may be hypertensive include *headache,* blurred vision, *vomiting,* and convulsions.

A small minority of children with AGN—about 2 to 10 percent—eventually develop a form of reversible brain dysfunction called encephalopathy, which is usually related to the hypertension and can include symptoms such as headache, sleepiness, convulsions (see *seizures),* vomiting, confusion, visual disturbances, memory loss, and *coma.* In a few cases severe hypertension and encephalopathy are among the first signs of AGN. Another sign is *anemia,* a deficiency of oxygen-carrying components in the blood, which can occur because the kidney fails to make the hormone that tells the bone marrow to produce these components, or, as in the case of hemolytic uremic syndrome, because the blood cells are damaged.

The signs and symptoms of chronic nephritis often begin more gradually—well after the onset of the condition—and are somewhat more subtle (see *kidney failure, chronic).*

DIAGNOSIS

Whenever a child has decreased urine output, *blood in the urine,* or edema, a medical evaluation should be sought promptly. In addition, all children with strep infections should be checked for AGN about two weeks after the onset of the infection.

Diagnosis of AGN is made by a physician, who may consult a nephrologist (kidney specialist) to review the child's medical history and to help evaluate the results of a thorough physical examination and various laboratory tests. Tests are chosen according to the signs and symptoms of both AGN and its apparent underlying cause. Typically, urine is tested for blood, protein, and other signs of kidney inflammation; skin or throat cells are tested for strep infection; and blood tests are performed to determine whether excess salts and wastes are present. In addition, a child's blood pressure is taken to determine whether *hypertension* exists.

The goals of diagnosis are to determine whether AGN exists and, if so, what has caused it and how severe it is. Once the presence and cause of AGN are verified, examinations and lab tests are repeated at various intervals to monitor the course of the disease and determine whether complications are developing. In many cases physicians perform periodic follow-up checks for as long as a year or more after all tests become normal.

For chronic nephritis the diagnostic procedure is essentially the same, although more tests may be conducted in an attempt to understand the nature or cause of the disease (see *kidney failure, chronic).* Occasionally a biopsy of the kidney is necessary in order to define precisely the types of nephritis and the severity.

COMPLICATIONS

The most significant complication of nephritis is kidney failure. In most cases of acute glomerulonephritis, kidney failure is temporary, and in many cases the disease never progresses to the point of kidney failure (see *kidney failure, chronic*).

TREATMENT

The vast majority of children with acute glomerulonephritis recover spontaneously: even if kidney failure develops, it is acute and disappears without complications. Therefore, the goal of a physician's treatment is to control the signs, symptoms, and complications of the disease while the kidney recovers. When a particular sign, symptom, or complication disappears, treatment for that component of nephritis ends. Even though chronic nephritis inevitably progresses to chronic kidney failure, its signs, symptoms, and complications can be treated.

Edema, for example, can be controlled by restricting a child's intake of table salt and fluids. It remains important, however, to maintain adequate nutrition. To control mild *hypertension, anemia,* and other blood-related problems, special prescription medications are quite effective. To help increase the volume of urination, a physician may prescribe a type of medication called a diuretic.

If AGN produces no symptoms but evidence of the disease shows up in precautionary lab tests taken after a child has a bout with strep infection, a physician may continue antibiotics for several weeks to ensure that all strep bacteria are killed. Unless signs and symptoms develop, no other treatment is necessary, although the child's condition must be monitored carefully to detect signs and symptoms in case AGN grows worse. In mild cases of AGN that produce fatigue and a feeling of illness, bed rest is usually advised.

In typical cases of AGN, edema tends to disappear 5 to 10 days after it develops, blood pressure returns to normal in 2 to 6 weeks, and urine appears normal in color after 1 to 3 weeks. Lab tests, however, may detect microscopic traces of blood in the urine for a year or longer. For reasons that remain unclear, poststrep AGN almost never recurs; in other forms, AGN recurs infrequently (see also *heart failure, congestive; hypertension; kidney failure, chronic; seizures*).

During the initial stages of chronic nephritis, very little treatment is necessary. A child usually does not have to restrict activities or diet. As the disease progresses, signs and symptoms must be treated as they appear. Typically, restriction of salt and fluid intake eventually becomes necessary, as does medication to control hypertension. It is also important to obtain treatment promptly for any infection that a child with chronic nephritis may develop; for reasons that, again, remain unclear, infection anywhere in the body tends to aggravate chronic kidney problems.

When acute or chronic nephritis is severe —when a child has severe edema, very low urine output, pronounced hypertension, encephalopathy, or signs of kidney failure— the child is usually hospitalized so that his or her condition can be monitored continuously. Hospitalization lasts until complications disappear or are otherwise controlled. If complications cannot be controlled, dialysis becomes necessary.

If kidney failure is acute, dialysis must be used to help take over the kidneys' function until they recover. If, however, kidney failure is chronic or if kidneys are permanently damaged during a bout of acute kidney failure, transplantation is desirable.

Kidney disease of any sort—acute or chronic—can be an emotionally difficult experience for an affected child and his or her family. Parents should make sure they understand the treatment, and see that their child has adequate emotional as well as physical support. A physician can counsel a child and family or can suggest a mental health professional (see Chapter 3, "Promoting Mental Health"). Emotional support can ease the burden of living with kidney disease, especially since the outcome is rarely clear at the onset of nephritis.

PREVENTION

No form of nephritis can be prevented.

NEPHROSIS

DESCRIPTION

Nephrosis is not a single disease, but a collection of related diseases that have in common a defect of one of the kidney's primary functions—filtering products from the blood. Nephrosis is rare but persistent (in the United States, just 2 cases occur annually per 100,000 population). Among children, nephrosis appears most often between 1 and 6 years of age, with the largest number of children (mostly male) becoming ill between ages 2 and 5. Nephrosis usually occurs independently, but it is occasionally associated with other diseases such as *diabetes, lupus erythematosus, cancer, hepatitis,* and malaria.

Nephrosis results in excretion of large amounts of albumin (a protein) into the urine; at the same time, the disease lowers the protein and increases cholesterol in the blood. The disease affects both kidneys equally. Most children with nephrosis experience relapses even after successful medical treatment, but usually do not require hospitalization after the diagnosis has been made. For about half of all children who are diagnosed and treated promptly, nephrosis clears up within 5 years; for another 30 percent, within 10 years. Permanent kidney damage is rare, occurring among less than 2 percent of nephrotic children.

CAUSE

Nephrosis is caused by a malfunction of that portion of the kidney that filters the blood as the first step in the manufacture of urine. The origin of the malfunction remains unknown. Nephrosis is not contagious nor are the usual forms of the disease inherited.

SIGNS AND SYMPTOMS

Nephrosis is usually marked first by a swelling around the eyes, which most often appears early in the morning and then subsides as the day progresses. Later the legs and ankles swell; often the skin becomes puffy all over the body. A potbelly frequently appears, because fluid collects in the abdomen. Moderate to pronounced weight gain is common because of fluid retention, even though children with nephrosis tend to eat and drink less than normal.

DIAGNOSIS

Urinalysis and various blood tests identify nephrosis. Biopsy (removal and analysis of a tissue sample) of the kidney, however, may be necessary for some children in order to define precisely the type of nephrosis and its severity, and to direct further treatment.

COMPLICATIONS

Nephrotic children, if they do not receive proper treatment, can become malnourished and may fail to grow (see *failure to thrive; malnutrition*). Because of their weakened condition, these children often run a higher risk of infection. Without treatment, nephrosis may be fatal. With treatment, less than 2 percent of nephrotic children die.

TREATMENT

Treatment with medication controls episodes of swelling and loss of appetite by eliminating protein loss in the urine and returning blood chemistry to normal. Steroids (synthetic hormonelike medications) are commonly prescribed. For children who do not respond to steroids, other medications may be prescribed. Although hospitalization is often needed for diagnosis and treatment of nephrosis, children can get along quite well at home afterward, as long as parents follow their child's condition closely, see that medication is given, and provide a balanced diet adequate in protein and low in salt. Even if a child's treatment goes smoothly, supervision by a pediatric kidney specialist is best so that amounts and type of medication can be adjusted as the child grows. Moderate exercise is usually helpful to keep joints flexible and whet children's appetites.

Nephrosis commonly recurs, even among those children who respond to steroid treatment. The number of recurrences, however, does not affect a child's ability to recover. Once children respond to steroids, subsequent resistance to therapy is unusual. Children who have been successfully treated with medication rarely suffer permanent kidney damage.

Steroid-induced side effects, including sharply increased appetite, weight gain, *acne*, moon-faced appearance, and mood changes, can be controlled or even completely eliminated if monitored carefully. A program of treatment—medication, diet, and exercise, plus periodic checkups by a specialist—can be designed for each child. Surgery is not helpful.

PREVENTION

Nephrosis cannot as yet be prevented.

NEUROBLASTOMA

DESCRIPTION

Neuroblastoma is a *cancer* of the nerve tissue that occurs when immature nerve cells (neuroblasts) begin to multiply abnormally, clump together forming a tumor, and spread to adjoining healthy tissue and often to other parts of the body.

Neuroblastoma is second only to *brain tumor* as the most common solid tumor found in infants and children. It represents about 10 percent of all childhood cancers and about 15 to 30 percent of all newborn cancers. About 500 cases are reported annually in the United States, nearly half in children under 2 years old. Almost 90 percent occur in children under 10.

Neuroblastoma usually begins in the nerves of the neck, chest, abdomen, or pelvis. The abdomen is the most common site: over half of all neuroblastomas develop there.

If cells from the tumor spread through the blood or lymph to other regions of the body, they may "seed" additional or secondary tumors in sites such as the liver, lymph nodes, skeleton, spinal cord, brain, and even skin. Quite often these secondary tumors are discovered first because they produce noticeable signs and symptoms.

In about 3 of every 5 children with neuroblastoma, the disease begins as a "silent tumor," entirely without signs or symptoms until it is quite advanced or begins to spread. When signs and symptoms do appear, they may be in the form of an abdominal mass, lumps in the neck, swelling of an eye, loss of bladder control, or partial paralysis of the legs. If a tumor is discovered, diagnosed, and treated by an effective combination of surgery, radiation, and chemotherapy, a young child's chances of survival may be good.

In contrast to most other cancers, neuroblastoma may shrink and signs and symptoms may fade without any treatment in newborns and infants. It is not known why this occurs, but cancer researchers point to the possibility that a natural immune response (one of the body's biochemical defense systems that combats foreign organisms or tissue) attacks and destroys cancerous cells.

CAUSE
The cause of neuroblastoma is unknown.

SIGNS AND SYMPTOMS AND COMPLICATIONS
Abdominal swelling is the most frequent initial sign of neuroblastoma, but it may not be noticed until a routine physical examination is performed by a physician.

When neuroblastoma appears in the head, swelling can occur around an eye or the eye may bulge or protrude. Eye difficulties may be accompanied by a dark red or purplish mark—a black eye—caused by bleeding beneath the skin. Swelling of lymph nodes in the neck can occur. Dime-sized, blue-tinted lumps beneath the skin may arise, particularly among newborns. As disease advances and spreads, a child usually becomes irritable, loses appetite and weight, grows pale, may develop a *fever* and bone pain, and rapidly grows worse. Partial paralysis of the legs as well as loss of bladder control may occur if a tumor exerts pressure upon the child's spinal cord. A few children with neuroblastoma develop *hypertension* (high blood pressure).

DIAGNOSIS
A child who has any of the signs and symptoms of neuroblastoma should be examined by his or her physician and referred to an oncologist, a cancer specialist. After recording the history of illness, a physician carefully examines the child, noting any characteristic signs of neuroblastoma. X-ray films of the chest and specialized X rays such as ultrasound, CT scan, and intravenous pyelogram (IVP) are used to locate tumors (see *cancer*).

A bone marrow biopsy (tissue sample) is usually performed. Blood cells from the bone marrow (the spongy blood-cell-forming tissue in the core of large bones) can be removed by a needle and syringe (a technique called aspiration). Cell samples of bone marrow are usually aspirated from the hipbone with local anesthesia. A pathologist examines this tissue sample to determine whether cancerous cells are present. The biopsy can confirm a diagnosis of neuroblastoma.

The most specific confirmation of neuroblastoma is a urine sample that contains excessive waste products of complex chemicals called neurotransmitters. Neurotransmitters stimulate various nerve cell functions. When neurotransmitters are metabolized (utilized and broken) down during nerve cell activity, waste products form, which are excreted in the urine. By measuring the presence in the urine of excessive amounts of one or more of these waste products, a pathologist can identify 60 to 80 percent of children who have neuroblastoma.

These diagnostic tests are all part of an overall diagnostic process called staging, a procedure that defines and categorizes the extent of disease. Staging for neuroblastoma takes into account all test results and estimates how an organ is functioning, how much disease is present, and how the disease should be treated.

These are the five stages of neuroblastoma:

I. Tumor is confined to the organ or structure of origin.

II. Tumor has grown in limited ways beyond the organ or structure of origin; adjacent lymph nodes may be involved.

III. Tumor has grown more extensively and regional lymph nodes may be involved.

IV. Disease has expanded to involve skeleton, soft tissues, other organs, or distant lymph node groups.

IV-S. Stage I or II with expanded disease confined to one or more of the following locations: liver, skin, or bone marrow; no X-ray evidence of spread to distant parts of the skeleton.

TREATMENT

Neuroblastoma is treated most effectively in a cancer center by a threefold multidisciplinary approach. A team of medical specialists treats the child through a program that combines surgery, radiation therapy, and chemotherapy (see *cancer).*

If the tumor is confined (stage I, II, or III), surgery can often remove the entire growth and, if necessary, adjacent lymph nodes. If the tumor is in a life-threatening or vital-organ-threatening location, partial or total removal of the tumor may be delayed until chemotherapy has reduced the size of the mass. A second or even third operation may be required until the surgeon judges that partial or total removal of the reduced tumor mass can be achieved with diminished hazard for the child. Radiation therapy and chemotherapy may still be needed to reduce the risk of recurrence for children with stage II or III neuroblastomas.

If the neuroblastoma has spread, extensive surgery may not be performed. A brief operation for the purpose of obtaining biopsies, however, is usually required. (During biopsy surgery, metal clips may be inserted as future guides for radiation therapy.) If neuroblastoma has invaded the spinal cord or vertebrae, neurosurgery may be required to prevent permanent nerve damage.

Radiation is most useful if (1) treatment after surgery has removed most of a tumor; (2) a single secondary tumor requires treatment because it threatens to damage vital organs; (3) an infant has difficulty breathing because of pressure by the tumor on the trachea (windpipe) or air passages; (4) the child has great difficulty walking or urinating because of disease near the spinal cord or urinary tract.

As is true for the other treatment methods, chemotherapy tends to be less successful with children who suffer from more advanced stages of disease. However, chemotherapy can result in a cure, with or without extensive surgery or radiation therapy. Frequently used in conjunction with surgery for stages II, III, and IV disease, chemotherapy may go on for as long as 1 year.

Other kinds of treatment are being investigated. For example, research continues on the apparent immune reaction that neuroblastoma involves. Whether a specific medication or vaccine can be developed to induce an immune reaction to neuroblastoma remains a challenge for further research.

Another new treatment developed in several cancer centers is the use of very high-dosage chemotherapy for children with the most advanced stage IV disease. This involves total body irradiation with drug therapy in an effort to kill all remaining neuroblastoma cells. Then, in an effort to have his or her normal blood-forming cells regrow, the child receives a reinfusion of his or her own bone marrow (bone marrow transplantation), which has been stored. In some cases bone marrow from a sibling is used if special genetic blood tests show the children to be closely matched.

If treatment is successful and the child experiences a 2-year remission (absence of all signs and symptoms as demonstrated by physical examination and laboratory tests), the chances of cure are good. Statistics show, moreover, that children less than 1 year old are frequently cured—about 90 percent remain free of disease. However, only about 40 percent of those over 1 year of age remain disease-free.

PREVENTION

No form of *cancer,* including neuroblastoma, can as yet be prevented.

NEUROFIBROMATOSIS

DESCRIPTION

Neurofibromatosis (sometimes called Von Recklinghausen disease) is a disorder that affects many systems of the body, especially the skin, bones, and nervous system. The disorder is congenital (present at birth), although the only indication in infants may be café-au-lait spots (flat, light brown spots) that resemble large freckles. The incidence of the disorder is approximately 1 in 3,000 births. Individuals of any ethnic background and of either sex can be affected. Neurofibromatosis (NF) is one of the most common inheritable disorders that affects the nervous system.

Extreme variations of neurofibromatosis occur. Many people with mild cases are unaware that they have the disorder. Café-au-lait spots, benign (not cancerous) tumors, or freckles usually develop on the skin. Damage to the bones may be apparent in bowing of the leg bones, cysts or overgrowths on long bones, or defects of the skull. *Scoliosis* (curvature of the spine) may occur. Other parts of the body, including the eyes, ears, blood vessels, and gastrointestinal tract, may be affected as well. Severe *mental retardation* occurs rarely, but *learning problems* are common. Less than 5 percent of children affected by NF later develop cancerous tumors. The vast majority of children who are affected have a life expectancy near normal. The course of the disorder, however, is unpredictable.

CAUSE

Half of all NF cases are inherited from one of the parents. A baby who inherits one gene for the disorder develops NF; if a parent has NF and passes along the gene for the disorder to the baby, the baby is affected. Each child of an affected parent has a 50 percent chance of inheriting the gene for the disorder. However, although nearly all people with that defective gene show some signs of the disorder, the severity of NF varies, even within a family (see discussion of dominant inheritance in *genetic disorders).*

The remaining half of the children with NF also have one gene for the disorder. That gene, in either the sperm or egg cell prior to conception, underwent mutation (spontaneous alteration) for no known reason.

SIGNS AND SYMPTOMS

Aside from café-au-lait spots, signs and symptoms of neurofibromatosis may develop anytime in life. Usually about the time of puberty, skin-colored, firm or soft, benign tumors commonly form. They may vary in number from a few to perhaps hundreds. They are located anywhere on the skin (or just below its surface). These tumors may multiply and enlarge with age; they can become painful. There also may be freckling of the armpits or groin. Pregnancy may stimulate tumor growth.

Rarely, people with NF are born with enlargement of one or more fingers, toes, or extremities. A child with NF may grow at an abnormally slow or fast rate and may reach puberty abnormally late or early. High blood pressure (see *hypertension)* may develop due to the narrowing of certain blood vessels.

DIAGNOSIS

Diagnosis of NF can be very difficult. As a result, a physician may consult specialists in the fields of dermatology, orthopedics, neurology, and ophthalmology. Prenatal diagnosis is not possible. In a child, the diagnosis is suspected if more than 5 café-au-lait spots, each larger than half a centimeter in diameter, are present. Infants and small children, however, usually have fewer and smaller spots and require examination. Some individuals with NF have no café-au-lait spots (and some people with café-au-lait spots, of course, do not have NF).

A physician examines a child thoroughly, paying particular attention to the skin, hearing, and eyes. In late childhood or early adolescence 9 out of 10 people with NF develop distinctive tiny markings on the iris—the colored part—of the eye which often requires an ophthalmologist to detect. If skin tumors are present, a biopsy (removal and analysis of a tissue sample) may be performed. The physician may also want to examine immediate family members and take a careful family history to determine whether or not anyone else in the family is affected.

Large tumors on nerves can be detected with the use of CT (computed tomography) scans, a series of highly detailed X-ray films of very small cross sections of the body.

COMPLICATIONS

Tumors located in the brain, on the spinal cord, or along the course of certain nerves can cause serious complications. Signs and symptoms of brain involvement include impairment of balance, hearing, vision, or eye movement; unexplained *headache* or dizziness; changes in behavior or speech; or changes in the ability to feel. In rare cases affected children suffer convulsions (see *seizures).*

If a tumor is present on the acoustic (hearing) nerve, the affected individual may hear ringing in the ears and may experience vertigo (an illusion of movement), failure of muscular coordination, loss of reflex of the cornea, and deafness (caused by damage to a nerve in the ear). One or both ears may eventually be affected. A tumor on an optic (vision) nerve can cause *blindness,* usually in only one eye.

TREATMENT

At present, NF cannot be cured. Individuals with NF should have checkups once a year so that tumor growth and all other NF-caused problems can be monitored. Tumors that cause pain, impair functioning, or grow rapidly may be removed surgically, although some may grow back. Chemotherapy or radiation therapy or both may be needed for treatment of the rare cancerous tumors (see *cancer).* Plastic surgery may be highly desirable to repair disfigurement.

Getting help as soon as possible is highly recommended for children with learning problems. A psychologist, psychiatrist, or social worker can be invaluable in counseling individuals with NF and their families.

Several major medical centers sponsor neurofibromatosis clinics, which offer follow-up examinations and care to children with NF and, if necessary, to their families. Clinics can coordinate the care of a child who must be seen by several specialists.

PREVENTION

NF cannot be prevented. An individual who has the disorder or who has given birth to a child with the disorder may want to receive genetic counseling so that he or she can learn about the chances of having (other) affected children (see *genetic disorders).*

The National Neurofibromatosis Foundation and its chapters provide educational materials about the disorder and a support network for children with NF and their families. Address: 70 West 40th Street, 4th floor, New York, NY 10018 (phone: 212 869-9034).

NEUROTIC DISORDERS

DESCRIPTION

"Neuroses" is a term that once was commonly used by mental health experts to categorize emotional problems that were less severe than major psychiatric illnesses (such as *psychotic disorders)* and were related to the way a person dealt with anxiety. Anxiety is an irrational, but very real, feeling of fear, tension, or uneasiness. By definition, the anxiety associated with a neurosis could be expressed in a direct way—with physical signs and symptoms such as trembling—or it might be hidden—emerging, for instance, in the form of a conduct disorder, behavioral problem, or habit. A child diagnosed as neurotic may or may not have perceived the anxiety. The term "neurotic disorders" is appropriate in referring to the symptoms of a problem that is related to how a child handles anxiety.

The most common neurotic disorders affecting children are described in detail in individual entries:

- panic attacks (see *breathing difficulty; choking; dizziness; fainting; phobias)*
- *phobias*
- sleepwalking (see *sleep disorders)*
- depressive anxiety (see *depression)*
- somatoform disorders (see *psychosomatic disease and symptoms)*

Other neurotic disorders found among children:

Hypochondria, a disorder marked by a tendency to misinterpret physical signs and symptoms as abnormal and indicative of a serious health problem. Signs and symptoms frequently misinterpreted may involve bodily functions, such as sweating, or minor health problems, such as a slight *sore throat.* The belief that a serious disease exists is real and is not dispelled by a physician's reassurance that nothing is truly, or at least seriously, wrong. In mild forms hypochondria is common. It usually does not begin until adolescence.

Psychogenic amnesia, a sudden inability to remember significant things about one's life for reasons that are not physical. (The word "psychogenic" means "originating in the mind or feelings.") Before adulthood, psychogenic amnesia is most common among adolescents who experience a sudden shock, such as the violent death of a family member. The child's reaction to the shock may be to forget all the events surrounding the awful event, or to forget all or part of his or her own history. The amnesia is usually brief (no more than a few days), ends abruptly, and does not recur.

Depersonalization, a sense of unreality—a feeling that things are not as they should be. The feeling, which tends to come and go, is marked by a change in self-perception. A child may feel, for example, that he or she is viewing his or her body from a distance. Or there may be a feeling of living in a dream and moving mechanically, with little control. Depersonalization may be accompanied by *dizziness,* depression, a fear of becoming insane, obsessive thoughts, loss of a true sense of time, and hypochondria. In severe cases depersonalization interferes significantly with a child's life. In most cases, however, the feeling is mild and disappears quickly. It is estimated that about half of all teenagers sometimes experience mild depersonalization.

Hypochondria, psychogenic amnesia, and depersonalization may be related; some experts view them all as hysterical symptoms.

TREATMENT AND PREVENTION

With treatment, the outlook for neurotic disorders is usually good, unless complications exist or anxiety is extremely severe. Children with neurotic disorders usually have a good understanding of reality, accept that some sort of disorder exists, and are receptive to treatment. Diagnosis and treatment focus on identifying the sources of anxiety, alleviating them if possible, and helping the child cope with them. Specific forms of treatment vary greatly. For more information on both therapeutic measures and prevention of anxiety-related disorders, see Chapter 3, "Promoting Mental Health."

NOSE, INJURY TO AND FOREIGN OBJECTS IN

EMERGENCY ACTION

Seek immediate medical attention if a child's nose is obviously disfigured by a blow or other harsh contact. The child may have a broken nose, which should be treated immediately to prevent breathing problems and disfigurement. Tell the child to breathe through his or her mouth while waiting for medical help.

Medical attention should also be sought immediately if a child has a foreign object in his or her nose. Signs and symptoms may include nasal discomfort, sneezing, and a discharge that is characteristically foul-smelling and may contain pus (which looks like thick, milky mucus) and blood. Do not try to remove an object from a child's nose unless it is protruding from a nostril; attempts to remove the object are likely to force it farther into the nasal passage and may obstruct breathing.

DESCRIPTION

A child's nose can be injured through either harsh contact or irritation by a foreign object inserted in a nostril.

The most common nose injuries resulting from harsh contact involve only swelling, *bruises,* and sometimes *nosebleeds.* Sometimes, however, harsh contact can cause a fracture of the bony, upper part of the bridge of the nose (see *fractures)* or more rarely, a tear in the lower, cartilaginous part. Both of these parts help give the nose its shape. Harsh contact can also cause the cartilaginous part or the septum (wall dividing the nostrils) to become displaced. All of these injuries are fairly common during childhood, especially among those who play contact sports. They all are easily treated, usually without any complications.

Nose injuries can also occur if a child inserts or inhales a foreign object into a nostril. Such injuries are most common among children under 5, who tend, out of curiosity, to insert small objects into body openings. Objects commonly inserted in nostrils include food, crayon pieces, small toys, pieces of large toys (especially plastic ones), erasers, paper wads, dried beans, and pebbles.

If allowed to remain in the nasal passage, a foreign object can cause *breathing difficulty.* It can also lead to infection, by blocking the nasal passage and thereby providing a moist environment for bacteria to breed. Since a child can breathe through the mouth, however, a foreign object rarely leads to cessation of breathing. In addition, infection usually clears up rapidly once an object is removed.

Nonetheless, an inhaled object can lead to a potentially life-threatening situation if it travels from the nasal passages to the back of the throat and causes *choking*. As a precaution, prompt medical attention should be sought.

SIGNS AND SYMPTOMS

Swelling, redness, and pain are common symptoms of nose injuries caused by rough contact. If the nose is dislocated or broken, it is likely to be deformed. An affected child may have difficulty breathing and the nose may bleed. The nose contains many small blood vessels that break easily upon contact, and *bruises*—masses of escaped blood that collect below the surface of the skin—are likely to form. Sometimes blood does not rise to the surface of the skin until hours or even days after an injury occurs. It also may not rise to the area directly above the injury. Therefore, a few days after sustaining a nose injury a child may develop extensive bruises under the eyes as well as around and on the nose.

Initially a child with a foreign object in his or her nose is likely to experience mild discomfort (often involving breathing difficulty) but not pain. Periodic sneezing is also common. As the object remains in a nasal passage, these symptoms usually become worse, and the nose may become painful. Discomfort can be quite severe if the object is absorbent, because it is likely to soak up nasal secretions and expand. If the object remains in the nose for a day or so, infection may develop. Infection produces a foul-smelling discharge which often contains pus and sometimes contains blood. Usually the discharge hinders breathing and runs only from the affected nostril.

DIAGNOSIS

Because the nose area bruises so easily, nose injuries caused by rough contact usually look worse than they actually are. A physician need only be consulted if an obvious deformity exists or if pain, redness, or swelling develops or persists for more than 3 days after the injury.

If signs and symptoms indicate that a child may have a foreign object in his or her nose, parents should calmly ask the child whether the child remembers putting anything there. If a child does not remember doing so or is too young to say, parents should try to remember whether the child was playing with any small objects in the recent past. Any information parents can give a physician about the object is of great help, since small, absorbent objects often do not show up on X-ray films. If, for example, parents suspect the object is a felt eye from a stuffed animal, they should bring the physician the other eye.

A physician usually asks for a description of the child's recent activities and examines one or both nostrils by gently separating them with a special instrument. If the physician cannot spot the object and parents have no idea what it could be, X-ray films may be ordered. In addition, a physician makes an examination to rule out the possibility that the child's symptoms are being caused by an alternative problem, such as *sinusitis*.

COMPLICATIONS

If a fracture does not heal properly, a child may consider the nose cosmetically unattractive. In rare cases an improperly healed septum leads to long-term breathing difficulty. (See *deviated nasal septum.*)

Complications of foreign objects in the nose usually occur only if the condition is not detected for several days. The most serious potential complication is *choking*. In very rare cases severe bacterial infections develop. Sometimes complications develop only after an object is removed. Such complications include *sinusitis,* build-up of mucus near the former site of the foreign object, and the adherence of one side of a nostril wall to the other at the site.

TREATMENT

To reduce swelling and minimize bleeding, an ice pack should be applied immediately to an injured nose. Ice should never touch the skin directly; if need be, an ice pack can be made by wrapping a plastic bag full of ice cubes in a towel.

A physician consulted about a minor nose fracture or torn cartilage in the nose may simply warn the child to be careful of reinjury as the area heals. In some cases, however, a physician may reposition and tape the nose to help it heal properly. This simple procedure, performed under general anesthesia, is most successful when carried out within 10 days of injury. If a child has difficulty breathing after an injured septum heals, a physician may recommend corrective plastic surgery. Such surgery is optional when a cosmetic deformity results from a nose injury.

If parents know or suspect that a child has a foreign object in his or her nose, they should not try to remove the object unless it is protruding from a nostril and absolute certainty exists that removal will not damage the nasal passage. If the object cannot be removed at home—or is not sneezed out—parents should consult a physician immediately.

To remove a foreign object from a child's nasal passage, a physician first applies medication to numb the area or puts the child to sleep with general anesthesia. Removing the object is usually a relatively simple, painless procedure, but numbing the nose is necessary because it is essential that a child remain absolutely still. If the object is in an especially awkward place, a physician may refer a child to an otolaryngologist (ear, nose, and throat specialist).

Once an object has been removed, any infection usually clears up immediately, although antibiotic medication may be prescribed by a physician. A child should have a follow-up visit with a physician to ensure that no complications develop.

PREVENTION

Although not all nose injuries can be prevented, parents should teach their children safety measures, such as wearing protective headgear while playing contact sports and wearing seat belts in cars. If an athletic child has experienced several nose fractures, a physician may prescribe a protective brace to be worn while playing contact sports.

Whenever possible, small objects should be kept out of a child's reach, and children should be discouraged from putting things in their noses.

NOSEBLEEDS

EMERGENCY ACTION

Children who develop nosebleeds while sleeping may awake with bloody pajamas, pillows, and bedclothes. The actual amount of blood from the nose is usually much less than linens seem to indicate. To help stop the bleeding, firmly press both sides of the nose together and toward the face, and maintain pressure. Unless bleeding persists, consultation with a physician is not usually necessary.

DESCRIPTION

A nosebleed occurs when a very small blood vessel in the lining of the nose breaks. This lining is extremely thin and contains many small blood vessels that can break easily, especially when inflamed because of infection or when irritated by picking, scratching, rubbing, or forceful nose blowing.

Nosebleeds are common during childhood both because nasal infections, such as *colds,* are common during childhood and because children tend to pick and scratch the inside of their noses to alleviate itchiness and other causes of nasal discomfort. Childhood nosebleeds often develop at night, when children are asleep and unaware of their own scratching.

Nosebleeds usually involve breakage of blood vessels on the septum, the wall dividing the two nostrils, and they usually develop much closer to the opening of the nostrils than to the back of the nose. This part of the septum contains many blood vessels and is easily accessible for picking and scratching. The typical nosebleed lasts no more than 10 minutes and is easily treated at home.

Like any minor cut, the tear in the nasal lining that results in a nosebleed may close quickly but takes a week to 10 days to heal completely. During that time a scab forms at the bleeding point; if the scab is dislodged, another nosebleed can begin. Recurring nosebleeds are common during childhood and can be caused by such routine movements as rolling over during sleep. Often one nosebleed leads to several more in subsequent weeks.

CAUSE

The cause of simple nosebleeds is almost always a condition that causes nasal passages to become inflamed. When inflammation occurs, blood vessels expand and can rupture spontaneously. Conditions characterized by nasal inflammation include *colds, hay fever* and similar *allergies,* and *strep throat.*

A nosebleed can also result from physical irritation of the nasal lining through picking or rubbing. Most children who get nosebleeds in this way pick at their nasal lining not because they have bad manners or habits, but because their noses itch or feel uncomfortable. A common cause of itchiness is overly dry air, which can cause crusting of mucus inside the nose. Indoor air is often too dry during the winter months, when nosebleeds are most common.

A nasal blood vessel can also break from contact with a foreign object in the nose. Very young children, who are naturally curious about their bodies, are more apt than others to place objects in their noses. A blow to the nose can also cause a nosebleed. (See *nose, injury to and foreign objects in.*)

Finally, a nosebleed can result from a condition directly affecting the blood or blood vessels. Such conditions include *bleeding disorders* involving low platelet levels, low clotting-factor levels, or blood-vessel weakness. Bleeding disorders that can lead to nosebleeds include *hemophilia* and thrombocytopenia. Conditions that can cause thrombocytopenia include *leukemia* and certain viral infections. Another problem that can interfere with the blood-clotting mechanism is the use of aspirin. Other conditions affecting the blood or blood vessels include *hypertension* and blockage of blood vessels by an inflamed nodule or growth (see *polyps*).

SIGNS AND SYMPTOMS

When a child's nose begins to bleed, blood is likely to run slowly and freely only from the affected nostril. If a child holds his or her head back or lies down, blood may back up inside the nose and flow out of both nostrils or may travel through the nasal passage into the throat and be swallowed. Swallowed blood is often vomited up, but sometimes it enters the digestive tract and is passed out of the body in stools, which may appear tarry and black.

DIAGNOSIS

Although nosebleeds are obvious, their cause may not be. If anything more serious than inflammation or irritation is suspected as the cause of a nosebleed, medical attention should be sought. A physician also should be consulted if nosebleeds recur persistently for no apparent reason.

Diagnosis involves consideration of a child's medical history, a physical examination, and occasionally blood tests. In the rare event that a physician suspects something may be blocking a blood vessel or nasal passage, X-ray films may be helpful.

COMPLICATIONS

When the cause of a nosebleed is a nasal infection or a foreign object in the nose, a slight chance exists that the bleeding point can become infected, especially if blood clots remain in the nose.

TREATMENT

Most nosebleeds can be treated at home. Children with recurring nosebleeds should be taught how to treat the condition themselves. A child with a nosebleed should sit or stand with the back erect and with the head slightly forward. This position lowers blood pressure in the head and prevents blood from backing up in the nose. The sides of the nostrils should be pressed firmly against the septum and toward the face. Pressure allows for clotting by preventing the flow of blood through the broken vessel, and holding the whole nose helps prevent escaped blood from backing up and flowing into the unaffected nostril.

After 10 minutes of constant, firm pressure the nose should be released and examined to ensure that bleeding has stopped. If it has not, a large clot may be irritating the broken part of the blood vessel. The nose should be blown gently in an attempt to release the clot. The treatment process should then be repeated.

When bleeding stops, the child should avoid sniffling or any other forceful motion for as long as possible. If bleeding does not stop after 20 minutes of *constant* pressure, a physician should be consulted. Prompt medical attention is also necessary if a child is vomiting or coughing up blood and no bleeding point can be seen using a flashlight or mirror. Bleeding may originate internally. (see *blood in the stools, vomiting of blood*).

To examine the inside of a child's nostril, a physician carefully stretches it with a small, mirrored instrument and uses a gentle suction tube to remove all blood clots. This procedure is usually painless, but the physician may spray the inside of the nose with a mild anesthetic just in case probing irritates the nasal lining. Once the source of bleeding is found, the physician usually repeats the home treatment procedure.

If bleeding does not stop or if the bleeding point appears highly subject to reinjury, a physician may pack the nose with gauze (sometimes covered with petroleum jelly), a relatively painless although uncomfortable procedure. The gauze is usually left in place for 24 to 48 hours. This form of treatment is rarely used for younger children, as they are likely to pull at the gauze and cause reinjury.

If applying pressure or gauze to the nose is unsuccessful, a physician may suggest cauterizing the tissue at the bleeding point with a mild electric current or a chemical. This procedure causes all liquid at the bleeding point to solidify.

In the rare event that the source of bleeding is far back in the nose, a physician is likely to refer a child to an otolaryngologist (ear, nose, and throat specialist). The specialist sprays the nose with an anesthetic and then packs it tightly with gauze from the point where the nasal passages meet the back of the throat. The packing remains in place from a few hours to several days. During this time the child is usually hospitalized for observation. Antibiotics may be given to prevent infection, because the combination of mucus and drying blood may attract microorganisms from air inhaled through the mouth.

In cases of severe, recurrent nosebleeds, a physician may suggest a surgical procedure called ligation, which involves sealing off a vein or artery to control bleeding in a smaller blood vessel. In rare cases, having a *deviated nasal septum* predisposes a child to getting persistent nosebleeds, and surgical correction of the irregularity may be recommended.

When a nosebleed is caused by harsh contact, it can usually be stopped using the standard home method. If other injuries seem associated, however, a physician should be consulted. Treatment of other injuries usually stops a nosebleed.

When a nosebleed is caused by an underlying disease, a physician treats the disease or refers the child to a specialist.

PREVENTION

Children should be taught that picking or scratching the lining of the nose can easily cause nosebleeds.

The best way to discourage picking is to prevent drying and crusting within a child's nose. Keeping indoor air moist is important; a vaporizer or humidifier can help. If a child's bedroom contains a radiator, the air in the room can be kept moist by keeping a metal pan of water on top. Coating the inside of a child's nose with a small amount of petroleum jelly can help prevent dryness and protect the nasal lining. After a nosebleed

stops, petroleum jelly or an over-the-counter antibiotic cream should be applied for several days to the affected nostril to help prevent reinjury.

ORAL HERPES

DESCRIPTION

Oral herpes (commonly called cold sores or fever blisters) are small blisters that appear on the edge of the lip. Eight out of every ten people become infected with an oral herpes virus by age 15, but fewer than half of those infected ever get lip blisters.

Infection with an oral herpes virus commonly occurs before age 4, usually without symptoms. In a small percentage of cases painful sores appear inside the mouth and may be confused with an attack of *canker sores*.

After the oral herpes virus causes infection, it becomes dormant. The virus can become reactivated at any time, causing lip blisters to break out. Within 7 to 10 days the blisters dry and form scabs, which heal within a week or two.

Oral herpes can be a nuisance but is not serious unless rare complications develop.

CAUSE

Oral herpes is usually caused by the herpes simplex virus type 1. (This virus is related to, but is not the same as, herpes simplex virus type 2, which causes about 80 percent of *genital herpes* cases; herpes simplex virus type 1 causes the other 20 percent. The type 1 virus is transmitted from the oral herpes blisters to the genitals through direct contact, typically during oral-genital sex. Fingers can also carry the virus from the lips to the genitals.)

Reactivations of oral herpes can be triggered by many factors including sunburn, *fever,* general ill health, emotional *stress, colds,* and menstruation.

The virus is transmitted in saliva. Children usually get the virus through direct contact with siblings, parents, or other adults. The virus in oral herpes sores is contagious.

SIGNS AND SYMPTOMS

When a child first becomes infected with an oral herpes virus, painful sores may appear inside the child's mouth and on the lips. The sores will blister at first, then become small hollows with white centers and red edges. The gums will be red and swollen. The child may also have a *fever,* be irritable, and have difficulty eating and drinking.

Reactivations produce tiny, oozing blisters on the lip, which break, form scabs, and heal within 7 to 10 days. Before blisters appear, a spot on the lip will tingle and swell. Before the blisters form scabs, they may itch or burn.

Oral herpes blisters may also appear near the nostrils.

DIAGNOSIS

A parent can suspect oral herpes when lip blisters recur in the same location.

COMPLICATIONS

The oral herpes virus sometimes infects parts of the eye, including the conjunctiva and cornea. Untreated corneal infection (called herpes keratitis) may interfere permanently with vision.

TREATMENT

Lip blisters heal by themselves. The child should be warned not to touch the blisters nor pick at the scabs. Phenol and camphor preparations may give some relief, especially if they are applied at the very first sign of stinging; they may also prevent cracking or bleeding of the scabs.

A pain- or fever-reducing medication may be helpful. Consult the physician for specific recommendations, and read the discussion of nonprescription medications beginning on p. 102. Parents should be careful that infants who refuse to drink because of sores inside the mouth do not become dehydrated.

PREVENTION

Infection with an oral herpes virus cannot be prevented, although its acquisition may be delayed by discouraging children and adults with reactivated oral herpes from kissing infants and small children. Reactivations cannot be prevented either, although avoiding any triggering causes may help.

OSTEOMYELITIS

EMERGENCY ACTION

If a child complains of severe or inexplicable joint or bone pain, seek medical help immediately.

DESCRIPTION

Osteomyelitis is an infection of bone. Almost always painful, the infection always poses the threat of causing permanent problems. Osteomyelitis can affect any bone. Among children it develops most often in the bones around the knee or hip, because blood tends to flow sluggishly through the twisting vessels in this area.

Osteomyelitis typically begins in the end of a bone, where infectious agents—usually bacteria—lodge and multiply. As the body's systems for fighting infection attack the bacteria, a collection of pus (liquid produced by infection) may form. Pressure in the pus increases as bacteria multiply, and the pus may spread up or down the bone or rupture into soft tissues, forming an abscess. As the infection spreads in the bone, it kills bone cells. Like skin, bones can usually heal themselves, but osteomyelitis can be so severe that permanent bone damage is possible, particularly if the part of the bone that controls growth is severely affected.

Before antibiotics were developed to combat infection, osteomyelitis occasionally caused death. More frequently, it lingered for many months, producing slow bone degeneration. Some patients had lifelong draining wounds from permanently infected bones. Today the symptoms of osteomyelitis usually last only a few days once antibiotics have been introduced. Therapy, however, typically lasts at least a month; prolonged therapy is critical to eradicate the last vestiges of infection and prevent a relapse with further damage to the bone. Chances for full recovery now depend largely on the severity of osteomyelitis, when diagnosed, and how much time elapses before the start of treatment, which involves antibiotics and, in some cases, surgery. Even today a rare case of osteomyelitis becomes so severe that amputation of the infected part may be necessary to achieve a cure.

CAUSE

In about 85 percent of cases, osteomyelitis is caused by a common bacterium called Staphylococcus aureus. Less frequently, it is caused by other types of bacteria and, rarely, by fungi.

In general, bacteria can reach a bone and cause osteomyelitis in one of two ways: they can be carried by the bloodstream and deposited in the bone, or they can enter the bone directly from a deep, infected wound or burn. When bloodborne, the bacteria tend to lodge near the growth plate at the end of a bone, where new bone cells are being produced.

In general, active infection from any part of the body may spread through the bloodstream to reach a bone and cause osteomyelitis. Most bloodborne cases of osteomyelitis, however, have no obvious source of infection. (Sometimes a boil (see *boils)* or infected *acne* is identified as the source.) A previous injury is often reported in the area affected by osteomyelitis; it is possible that an injury to a bone increases the likelihood that bloodborne bacteria will gain a foothold in the area. This theory might explain why children with *sickle cell anemia,* which often produces bone damage, have an increased risk of developing osteomyelitis.

SIGNS AND SYMPTOMS

The first symptoms of osteomyelitis are pain and tenderness in the area surrounding the infection. Since osteomyelitis originates near the end of a bone, pain may seem to be coming from the nearby joint.

As osteomyelitis develops, the surrounding area becomes red and swollen. Movement becomes extremely painful, and the child is likely to stop using the affected part. The temperature of the skin directly above the affected area usually rises, and the child eventually develops a *fever* and an overall feeling of illness. Symptoms at this time may also include irritability and poor appetite. Occasionally osteomyelitis is present for a relatively long period (days to weeks) with only mild pain and little fever.

DIAGNOSIS

If a physician suspects that a child has osteomyelitis, the child is usually hospitalized during diagnosis so that treatment can begin as soon as possible. A physician may consult an orthopedist (bone, muscle, and connective tissue specialist) for diagnosis or treatment.

To diagnose osteomyelitis a physician conducts a series of blood tests and usually takes a sample of the bone or pus from the affected area for analysis. The infectious agent causing osteomyelitis must be identified through these tests so that proper treatment can be given. Occasionally cultures do not reveal the infectious agent, and treatment proceeds as though the most common agent is involved.

In addition, X-ray films and bone scans are usually ordered; at least one of these tests is likely to help reveal the disease (except, perhaps, in its very earliest stages). These tests are also helpful in ruling out other possible causes of the child's symptoms, including *bone cancer.*

COMPLICATIONS

Particularly among young children, pus from osteomyelitis may rupture into a nearby joint space, producing septic arthritis (see *arthritis, acute).* This complication most commonly develops when osteomyelitis is adjacent to the hip.

In general, permanent bone damage is most likely to occur if diagnosis and therapy are delayed or the hip joint is involved. Late diagnosis is most common among newborns with osteomyelitis, because signs of the problem can be difficult to detect.

TREATMENT

The first step a physician takes to treat osteomyelitis is to decide whether drainage of any pus or surgical removal of any dead bone are necessary. This treatment may be necessary to clean up the badly infected area of bone so that antibiotics can penetrate well enough to destroy the infection completely. Initially, dosages of antibiotics are administered intravenously in a hospital, where dosage and response can be monitored carefully. The exact dosage and type of medication depends on the cause of osteomyelitis and the severity of the disease. The use of intravenous antibiotics may be accompanied by immobilization of the affected area and may be followed by the use of oral medication.

Antibiotic treatment continues in some form for a total of at least 4 weeks. If an affected child is discharged from the hospital to continue oral administration of antibiotics at home, it is essential to follow the physician's instructions exactly. The physician may conduct blood tests to make sure the medication level in the blood is high enough to kill the infectious agents causing osteomyelitis.

PREVENTION

Steps can be taken to prevent some of the diseases and injuries that can lead to osteomyelitis. If a disease or injury that can lead to osteomyelitis does develop, bone infection is less likely to result as a complication when proper treatment for the initial problem is given promptly and, in the case of open wounds, when good hygiene is maintained.

OVARIAN TUMORS AND CYSTS

EMERGENCY ACTION

An ovarian cyst may rupture and cause pain and bleeding within the abdomen. A young woman experiencing severe pain, *nausea,* and *vomiting* should seek immediate medical attention.

DESCRIPTION

Tumors typically are masses of new tissue growth. Their severity varies greatly. Malignant tumors, the most severe, are cancerous and may recur. Their cells are abnormal, multiply uncontrollably, and can spread from one organ to other parts of the body (see *cancer*).

Tumors of the ovaries (see Fig. 3B, p. 39) develop relatively rarely during childhood and adolescence. Ovarian tumors are associated with many other disorders; for example, they can cause amenorrhea and *menstrual irregularities.*

From one fifth to one half of so called tumors of the ovaries are not really tumors but cysts. Unlike tumors, cysts—typically sacs containing liquid or semisolid material—are usually benign. Tumors and cysts can appear on one or both ovaries, singly or in clusters. Ovarian cysts tend to disappear by themselves after one or two months.

Chances for recovery from a malignant tumor are best if the tumor is diagnosed and treated early. Treatment of ovarian tumors during childhood and adolescence is complex, requiring that a delicate balance be achieved between eliminating the tumor and, if possible, preserving the female's capacity to conceive and bear children.

CAUSE

The cause of ovarian tumors is unknown. Ovarian cysts apparently develop in response to fluctuating levels of female sex hormones during the menstrual cycle.

SIGNS AND SYMPTOMS

A young child with an ovarian tumor may have no symptoms or may have a noticeable mass or lump within the abdomen. Sometimes no other symptoms appear; at other times a young female experiences persistent abdominal aches, nausea, *vomiting,* bloating of the abdomen, and frequent urination or retention of urine. A mass may be tender to the touch. Sometimes pain is sudden and sharp (as in pain caused by *appendicitis),* because the tumor twists.

Ovarian cysts may cause no symptoms or may cause menstrual irregularities, frequent urination, *constipation,* bloating of the abdomen, or pain. If a cyst twists, a young woman feels cramps or sudden, sharp *abdominal pain* accompanied by nausea and vomiting. If a cyst actually ruptures, pain and bleeding result, and an emergency exists. Certain cysts and tumors can cause either amenorrhea or heavy menstrual bleeding (see *menstrual irregularities).*

Among girls younger than 8 years of age an ovarian tumor or cyst may cause secretion of estrogen, a female hormone, which produces signs such as breast enlargement, pubic hair, and vaginal discharge or bleeding. These are signs of precocious puberty (onset of puberty before the age of 8). Among adolescents, such tumors can cause irregular menstrual periods.

DIAGNOSIS

Ovarian tumors and cysts are usually detected by a physician or gynecologist (a specialist in diseases of the female genital tract) during a routine physical examination.

Accurate diagnosis and classification of an ovarian tumor is important so that malignant tumors can be treated early. Ovarian tumors can be very difficult to diagnose, however, because symptoms of the disorder can mimic symptoms of other disorders such as *appendicitis.*

A girl may be referred to a specialized hospital treatment center for diagnosis and treatment. For all growths other than simple, small cysts, laparoscopy (examination of the interior of the abdomen using a special instrument) and laparotomy (surgical opening and exploration of the abdominal cavity) are used to determine the size, grade, and stage of a tumor. A biopsy (removal and laboratory analysis of a small portion of tissue) may be performed. Other diagnostic procedures include ultrasound exams, X rays, and urine and blood tests. If a tumor is suspected, further tests may be needed, such as a CT (computed tomography) scan.

COMPLICATIONS

A malignant ovarian tumor can result in a reduction of fertility. Any organ that is affected by *cancer* may cease to function or may have to be removed.

TREATMENT

Simple, small ovarian cysts that produce no abnormal symptoms and do not interfere with ovarian functioning require no treatment except follow-up examinations. Sometimes synthetic hormones (estrogen and progestin) are prescribed to hasten the disappearance of a simple cyst.

If a cyst ruptures and causes pain and bleeding within the abdomen, an emergency operation may be necessary. If there is no bleeding, treatment may consist of synthetic hormones and follow-up observation. Other cysts that may need to be removed include very large cysts and cysts that twist. In severe cases removal of the ovary or adjoining fallopian tube may be necessary.

Benign ovarian tumors require surgical removal. Successful treatment of malignant tumors may involve surgery, radiation therapy, or chemotherapy (see *cancer*).

If malignant cells have spread, chemotherapy and radiation are usually given. If a tumor recurs in or near a previously affected ovary, radiation therapy is generally used.

PREVENTION

Ovarian tumors and cysts cannot be prevented.

PARASITIC INFECTIONS

DESCRIPTION AND SIGNS AND SYMPTOMS

Parasites are organisms (in this case, worms and microorganisms) that live in and feed off of other organisms (the hosts). They are found worldwide and can cause infections in people of all ages. Parasitic infections are very common among children, who tend to put their unwashed fingers and hands in or near their mouths.

In the United States the most common parasitic infections are caused by adult worms and include pinworm, ascaris, whipworm, and hookworm infestations. Less common worm infections include infestation by beef, pork, and fish tapeworms, and trichinosis, a rare childhood parasitic infection. In addition, hookworm larvae can infest the skin, causing cutaneous larval migrans. Parasitic infections caused by tiny parasitic organisms (microorganisms) include giardiasis, amebiasis, babesiosis, and malaria. (See *pets, diseases caused by* for discussion of an uncommon microorganism infection, toxoplasmosis, and of another worm infestation, visceral larval migrans.)

The severity of any parasitic infection depends on the child's general health, the number of infective organisms inhabiting the child's body, the child's sensitivity to the parasite, and the presence of other parasites. Although parasitic infections are huge problems in tropical and underdeveloped countries, most cases in the United States clear up with proper treatment within a few days to a week. A child rarely suffers permanent complications.

Common Worm Infections

Pinworm Pinworm, a roundworm that inhabits the large intestine of humans, is the most common parasite infesting people in the United States. Nearly 30 percent of all children worldwide are estimated to be infested with pinworm, regardless of their social or economic status. An entire family may be infested. Because of their resemblance to short pieces of white sewing thread, pinworms are also called threadworms.

Pinworms are extremely hardy and may survive for weeks in dirt, house dust, furniture, bed sheets, clothing, toys, and even in the fur of house pets. Children become infected with pinworms after being exposed to contaminated objects. The eggs may be transmitted via food or a contaminated object that is placed in the mouth. Poor handwashing and other careless hygiene habits rapidly spread pinworm eggs. At night, as a child sleeps, female pinworms crawl out of the intestine to the anus, deposit their eggs on the skin near the anal opening, and then die.

Once children are infected, they easily transfer pinworms to uninfected children through close contact or by sharing food or clothing. Children continually reinfest themselves by scratching the irritated rectal area where the eggs have been deposited, then later touching or holding something they put in their mouths.

Pinworm infestation produces few symptoms. The most obvious sign is a child's severe anal itching and discomfort. Sometimes female worms that crawl out of the anus at night end up in pajamas or bed sheets and are found in the morning.

Hookworm Hookworm eggs hatch in soil contaminated with human or animal excrement containing the parasite. When a child walks barefoot on contaminated soil, a hookworm can enter the child's skin. The hookworm then enters the child's bloodstream and is transported to the lungs, where it is coughed up in the throat and swallowed. It eventually ends up in the child's small intestine, where it uses hook-like appendages to grasp the intestinal wall. A hookworm survives in the intestine by sucking the blood of its host. Once a child is infected, he or she can transfer hookworms to uninfected children through close contact or by contaminating shared food.

In some cases the first sign of hookworm infection is itching and inflammation near the point of entry. If intestinal infestation is moderate to heavy, a child may experience *fever, diarrhea,* and *abdominal pain.* The liver may become enlarged and tender. Mild *anemia* (low levels of iron in the blood) may develop, and the airways may become inflamed as the worm passes through the lungs.

Hookworm larvae causing cutaneous larval migrans enter a child's skin and aimlessly wander through it. This leads to intense itching and the appearance of raised, inflamed lines on the skin. If infestation is extensive, weight loss, irritability, and sleeplessness can occur.

Ascaris Ascaris is a parasite resembling the earthworm. It is spread by contact with soil contaminated by human or animal excrement where adult worms have laid eggs. In those areas where careless or improper sewage treatment and disposal are common, 60 to 100 percent of children are likely to be infested with ascaris. Once a child is infected, he or she can transfer ascaris to uninfected children through close contact or by contaminating shared food.

Ascaris infestation occurs in 2 phases. In the first phase, ascaris larvae migrate through the bloodstream to the lungs. The second phase occurs after an infested child coughs up and then swallows the larvae. The larvae then pass through the digestive system to the small intestine, where they hatch and mature. The adult worms curl up in knots and burrow into the walls of the child's intestines.

Most infested children do not have noticeable symptoms. However, a child may develop a *cough,* a slight *fever,* and symptoms of *pneumonia* during the migration of ascaris larvae through the lungs. A child may occasionally feel vague *abdominal pain.*

Less Common Worm Infections

Whipworm Like most other worm infestations, whipworm is spread through contact with soil or water contaminated by human or animal excrement containing the parasite, or through close contact with infected individuals. Most cases of whipworm do not produce symptoms, but occasionally a child may experience *diarrhea* and *abdominal pain.*

Tapeworm Tapeworms can be found in contaminated pigs, cattle, or fish. If pork, beef, or fish is incompletely cooked, tapeworm eggs do not die and are ingested when the food is eaten. Eventually they hatch and nest in the child's intestines, where they compete with the child's body for needed nutrients.

Mild tapeworm infestation rarely produces symptoms. Severe infestation causes increased appetite, weight loss, and weakness.

Trichinosis Trichinosis is caused by trichinella spiralis, a worm found in contaminated animals, especially pigs. If contaminated meat is incompletely cooked, trichinella eggs do not die. They are ingested when the meat is eaten, eventually hatching into adults, which live in the intestines for about 6 weeks. New eggs are laid deep in the intestinal mucous membranes and are carried in the bloodstream through the liver to the lungs, heart, and throughout the body. Trichinella larvae eventually burrow into muscle fibers.

Mild cases of trichinosis may not cause symptoms. More severe, prolonged infestations (2 to 3 weeks without treatment) produce *fever,* tenderness, *headache,* muscle pain, abdominal swelling, loss of appetite, nausea, and *vomiting.*

Parasitic Infections Caused by Microorganisms

Giardiasis At any given time approximately 7 percent of all Americans have giardiasis, infestation of the intestinal tract by the microorganism *Giardia lamblia.* Some medical experts believe that *Giardia* changes the structure of the intestinal mucous membrane, competes with the intestine for nutrients, irritates the intestine, and interferes with proper intestinal functioning.

Giardiasis may produce no symptoms, or a child may suffer *malabsorption,* specifically lactose intolerance, indicated by *abdominal pain, diarrhea,* and weight loss. Symptoms usually appear about 2 weeks after infestation and can last for about 2 months if the infestation is not treated.

Giardia lamblia is transferred easily, most often by contact with stool that contains the parasite. This contact most often occurs in families and institutions, particularly daycare centers and schools, where children have close contact with carriers. Once a child is infected, he or she can transfer giardia to uninfected children through close contact or by contaminating shared food.

Malaria Malaria is caused by the microorganism *Plasmodium,* acquired through the bite of a mosquito carrying the organism. Plasmodia enter the bloodstream and travel throughout the body, producing *fever,* malaise, *headache,* chills, and muscle and *joint pain.* In addition, spleen enlargement, loss of appetite, *vomiting,* or *diarrhea* may occur. An affected infant may have *jaundice* and be quite pale. If malaria is advanced and severe, a child may suffer *anemia,* thrombocytopenia (see *blood disorders),* and *delirium,* and may go into *shock* or *coma.* Death may occur. Mosquitos carrying malaria are not found in the United States, but world travelers must be careful to take antimalarial medication when traveling in endemic areas.

Babesiosis Babesiosis is a parasitic infection caused by the microorganism babesia. Babesia is transferred in the bite of a tick and travels throughout the body in the bloodstream. Children generally do not develop babesiosis unless their resistance to infection is low because their spleens have been removed.

Occasionally an infected child may not have symptoms, but more often symptoms resembling those of malaria develop, including *fever,* malaise, listlessness, and hemolytic anemia (see *anemia, hemolytic).*

Amebiasis Amebiasis, an infection caused by microscopic organisms called amoebas, can develop in the intestines alone or can involve additional organs, most often the liver. A child picks up amoebas by ingesting soil or water contaminated by human or animal excrement carrying the organism. Once infected, a child can transfer amoebas to uninfected children through close contact.

Symptoms of intestinal infestation may not be present, or a child may suffer *abdominal pain,* bloody *diarrhea,* a low-grade *fever,* and weakness. Symptoms of liver infestation include those of intestinal infestation as well as *fever,* chills, and an enlarged, tender, malfunctioning liver.

DIAGNOSIS

A physician determines the presence of a parasite by observing characteristic signs and symptoms and by isolating parasites from stool, body fluids, or body tissue. Knowledge of a child's activities and medical history and the presence of pets in the home or neighborhood sometimes helps identify the parasite. A history of travel outside the United States, especially to tropical countries, can also be an important clue.

Three fresh stool samples are usually required to confirm the presence of parasites. Stool is also examined for white blood cells. Blood tests measure white-cell levels, and help determine whether parasites, particularly those causing trichinosis, are present in the blood. If muscle pain is present, a muscle biopsy (removal of a tiny tissue sample for microscopic examination) is performed to determine whether trichinosis is present.

Pinworm infestation may be confirmed by examining the child's buttocks and rectal area. Upon close observation, parents can often discover tiny threadlike worms. Deposits of eggs near the anus can be collected with cellophane tape. Once the eggs have been collected the tape should be folded over so only the smooth sides are exposed. A physician can attach the tape to a microscope slide and examine it for the presence of pinworm eggs.

If stool, fluid, or tissue examinations cannot detect the presence of parasites, more involved tests such as liver X rays may be performed.

COMPLICATIONS

Heavy worm infestations can cause intestinal blockage. Long-term hookworm infestation can slow a child's growth and development.

If a child scratches the skin because of cutaneous larval migrans, a bacterial infection may develop. The parasite causing this eruption can also enter the bloodstream and travel to the eyes, brain, and heart, resulting in sudden vision loss, *seizures,* or myocarditis (inflammation of the heart muscle; see *cardiomyopathy).* Constant scratching because of pinworm infestation may spread the infection, possibly causing *vaginitis* in girls.

Rarely, tapeworm infection may form cysts (small sacs filled with semisolid material) in the brain, eye, heart, or spinal cord. Cysts can impair organ functioning and result in *seizures,* nervous system problems, *headaches,* and vision problems.

Untreated *malabsorption* caused by giardiasis may lead to *failure to thrive* and delayed growth and development.

Although rare, advanced trichinosis may cause inflammation of the brain, heart, kidneys, and lungs. If untreated, death can result.

TREATMENT

Parasitic infections do not always require treatment. For example, hookworm larvae causing cutaneous larval migrans usually die spontaneously within a week or two of infestation. However, a child suffering trichinosis and malaria must receive immediate treatment to prevent complications. Cases of amebiasis or pinworm, giardia, or tapeworm infestation must be treated promptly to prevent spread of infection to others.

In general, a physician must determine whether treatment of parasitic infections is needed. This is based on the severity of infestation, the type of treatment methods available, and whether severe side effects are likely to result from treatment. Side effects may include *rash,* loss of appetite, *diarrhea,* nausea, *vomiting,* increased heart rate, and *dizziness.*

If a physician decides that treatment is needed, an oral antiparasite medication is usually prescribed. Duration of treatment depends on the parasite involved and the severity of infection. After treatment a child's stool and blood are usually reexamined for evidence of remaining parasites.

An entire family is usually treated for pinworm infestation no matter how many members show symptoms. Treatment also includes taking extra care in the cleaning and trimming of nails and washing of hands. Daily showering is advisable.

If a bacterial infection has developed, antibiotics are prescribed. If a child has developed *anemia* from a hookworm infestation, iron supplements are recommended.

Severe cases of trichinosis, malaria, amebiasis, and babesiosis require hospitalization. Children are sometimes isolated during treatment to prevent contamination of others.

In most cases treatment of mild parasitic infections is successful within a few days to a week. Follow-up visits to a physician are always advised to determine whether treatment has been effective. In some cases no treatment can completely eliminate parasites from a child's system. In such instances a parasitic infection may clear up by itself, although it may take months to several years.

PREVENTION

Children should be encouraged to wash their hands immediately after playing outdoors, and to avoid putting their fingers in or near their mouths. They should wear shoes at all times when walking in unfamiliar areas or areas where there is even a slight possibility of contamination by untreated sewage.

Soil can be tested by public health officials if parasitic infestation is suspected. Cleanup procedures should begin if parasites are found. If soil is contaminated, children should play in other areas. Parasite-carrying insects such as ticks should be killed immediately.

It is impossible to completely prevent pinworm infestation among children. Keeping a child's hands and fingernails trimmed and clean, however, will help prevent the spread of pinworm, as will proper handwashing before meals and after urination and defecation.

Meats and fish should be completely cooked before eating (the temperature at the center of the meat or fish should reach at least 150° F; 66° C).

Before traveling outside the United States, it is wise to consult a physician so that appropriate preventive measures can be taken to avoid parasitic infection. When traveling abroad where sanitary practices are unreliable, individuals should drink only bottled or boiled water and should not eat uncooked foods such as salads. Fruit should be washed carefully.

PETS, DISEASES CAUSED BY

EMERGENCY ACTION

Wash all animal bites and scratches thoroughly with soap and warm water as soon as possible. Bite wounds should generally be seen by a physician, because additional treatment, such as antibiotics, may be necessary.

DESCRIPTION, SIGNS AND SYMPTOMS, AND TREATMENT

For a time in the lives of many children, a pet becomes an addition to the family. Pets become friends and companions, and supply hours of happiness.

Pets, however, can carry diseases that are easily passed on to children. Children under 12 years old are most often affected, but people of all ages may develop pet-related diseases. Most of these diseases interfere with normal functioning of the gastrointestinal tract (esophagus, stomach, and intestines), although other organs of the body can also be affected.

Visceral Larval Migrans (Roundworm)

A child develops visceral larval migrans when roundworm *(Toxocara)* larvae enter the body. These larvae, which are the immature stage of the worms, are transferred to soil in the feces of roundworm-infested puppies or kittens. When a child eats contaminated dirt or puts contaminated objects or fingers in his or her mouth, the larvae enter the body and make their way to the child's intestines. From there the larvae migrate throughout the body for several weeks or months. The child suffers an allergic reaction to the larvae as they travel.

Signs and symptoms of visceral larval migrans resemble those of other allergic reactions, including wheezing, *rash, cough,* and *fever.* A blood test may reveal eosinophilia, a rise in the levels of one type of white blood cell. Severe symptoms develop if the larvae enter the retina of the eye (which happens infrequently).

Complications can occur when the larvae travel through the body, causing small lumps to form in organ tissues, most often in the liver, but also in the lungs, kidneys, lymph nodes, eyes, brain, heart, and muscles.

Visceral larval migrans is usually self-limiting, and treatment may not be prescribed. If the retina or other organs are involved, however, a specialist may need to treat the problem.

Toxoplasmosis

Toxoplasmosis is one of the most dangerous diseases transmitted by pets. It is caused by a parasite, *Toxoplasma,* which is usually found in the intestines of cats that eat contaminated wild birds or rodents. Less frequently, toxoplasma may be found in uncooked meat. When a cat defecates, toxoplasma eggs are secreted; they hatch and become infectious in 1 to 3 days.

Toxoplasmosis can be either acquired or congenital. Acquired toxoplasmosis, which is usually mild, is spread when a child handles infectious stool, usually while cleaning a cat's litter box, and fails to properly wash his or her hands immediately afterwards. The parasite is transferred from the animal stool to the skin. Food and other surfaces can also become contaminated if they are touched. The parasite enters children's bodies when the children put contaminated fingers into their mouths or eat contaminated foods.

Symptoms of acquired toxoplasmosis resemble those of *mononucleosis* and include *fever,* muscle pain, swelling of the lymph nodes (a network of small lumps of tissue that filter bacteria and other infectious agents from body tissues and produce infection-fighting white blood cells; see *swollen glands),* and occasionally, generalized *rash,* which may persist for 3 days and then disappear spontaneously. Acquired toxoplasmosis may persist for weeks or longer as a nonspecific illness until accurately diagnosed by a physician.

In rare cases severe toxoplasmosis may develop during childhood, affecting young children who are unable to fight infection because of immune deficiencies.

Congenital toxoplasmosis, a more severe form of the disease, occurs when a pregnant woman ingests *Toxoplasma* and the parasite enters her bloodstream and is carried to the fetus. The infection is especially dangerous to the fetus during the early months of pregnancy. Even though the mother may have a mild or asymptomatic condition, the fetus may develop a life-threatening infection.

Symptoms of congenital toxoplasmosis include *seizures* and *encephalitis* (brain tissue inflammation) if the nervous system is affected. If a fetus develops toxoplasmosis, minor to severe birth defects are possible. Liver enlargement and involvement of other organs may also occur. The brain may be affected, leading to *hydrocephalus* (collection of fluid in the skull, causing brain enlargement and permanent malfunction), *seizures* and retardation. Chorioretinitis (a severe vision problem) may also be associated with congenital toxoplasmosis.

Mild cases of congenital toxoplasmosis may occur, and the disease often goes undetected at birth. In such cases the *Toxoplasma* organism may be deposited in the eye of the fetus, causing no problems for years, and then producing severe eye disease later in life.

Congenital defects associated with severe fetal toxoplasmosis cannot be reversed, but antibiotics are available that may limit ongoing damage. If a pregnant woman becomes infected with the parasite, a physician may recommend abortion to prevent birth of a severely brain-damaged infant.

In general, cats that are kept indoors, are maintained on diets of prepared cat food, and are not fed fresh, uncooked meat do not carry infectious *Toxoplasma.* To prevent possible infection of a fetus by *Toxoplasma,* pregnant women should not handle outdoor cats or cat litter.

Salmonellosis

Salmonellosis is caused by *Salmonella* bacteria, most often carried by turtles and other domestic pets. A child acquires the bacteria by putting his or her fingers into the mouth after handling a pet, especially a turtle or the water in which the turtle swims.

Symptoms of salmonellosis include *fever* and *abdominal* pain (see *food poisoning* and *diarrhea* for information on other diarrheal illnesses). Antibiotics are not usually prescribed to treat salmonellosis, which is a self-limited infection. Antibiotics are prescribed for children younger than 1 year old who are at risk for more serious disease.

Pasteurella

Pasteurella infection is caused by a bacteria that lives in the saliva of dogs and cats. When a child is bitten, the bacteria enters the wound. Inflammation or abscess may occur. Rarely, *Pasteurella* infection is associated with *osteomyelitis* (a severe bone infection) and *meningitis* (inflammation of the meninges, the protective membranes covering the brain and spinal cord).

A physician usually prescribes an antibiotic to treat a *Pasteurella* infection. *Pasteurella* infections, however, can often be prevented by immediate, thorough washing of an animal bite.

Psittacosis

Psittacosis is a disease caused by an organism that is carried in the droppings of infected birds, usually imported tropical birds. A child develops psittacosis through contact with contaminated bird droppings or by inhaling airborne chlamydia, a microscopic disease organism.

Psittacosis is a rare cause of *pneumonia,* and symptoms of the disease develop abruptly. They include *fever* (as high as 105° F; 40.6° C), *sore throat,* muscle pain, *cough,* shortness of breath, and occasionally, blood-streaked sputum.

Physicians prescribe antibiotics to treat psittacosis. Treatment usually lasts 7 to 10 days. Psittacosis can cause a serious, sometimes fatal pneumonia. As psittacosis is rare and mimics other diseases, it is difficult to diagnose. Parents should inform physicians about contact with pet birds.

Cat-Scratch Fever

Cat-scratch fever is an infection that develops following a cat scratch or bite. Its exact cause is unknown.

Symptoms of cat-scratch fever may not appear until days or weeks after a child is scratched. The scratch may be healed completely, or a sore may still be present when the child becomes ill. The sore swells, and *fever, rash,* and an overall feeling of illness may be present. The lymph node near the scratch becomes tender and quite large, and lymph nodes on other parts of the body may swell (see *swollen glands*). If the infection is prolonged, lymph nodes may break down and form pus-filled lumps resembling *boils* that drain through the skin. In rare cases *encephalitis* may develop.

Because the exact cause of cat-scratch fever is unknown, no specific treatment is recommended other than thorough cleaning of the wound with soap and water. Although cat-scratch fever does not always develop when a child is scratched or bitten, it is often not possible to prevent infection if the infecting organism is present. Diagnosis of the cat-scratch fever may require biopsy of a lymph node, although a thorough medical history and signs and symptoms usually indicate the disease's presence.

Rabies

Rabies is a dangerous disease that affects a child's nervous system. (See *rabies* for details, especially about prevention.)

Leptospirosis

Leptospirosis is a disease caused by a microscopic spiral-shaped organism that is often found in the urine of dogs. Dogs generally pick up the organism from the feces of wild rodents, and the infection can spread to humans when they come into contact with contaminated dogs' urine, either directly or through contaminated soil or water. The organism may be present in the urine several months after the initial infection.

Symptoms of leptospirosis may include *fever, headache,* muscular aches, nausea and *vomiting,* cramps, chills, and redness in the white part of the eye *(conjunctivitis)*. The disease is usually mild, with symptoms lasting from 2 to 20 days. In some cases, however, the disease may cause *jaundice,* hemorrhages of the skin, *meningitis,* and even death.

Treatment usually involves antibiotics, which may be used to reduce the fever and shorten the length of the illness. Prevention of the disease is difficult, as dogs who are allowed to run outside often come into contact with rodents. A vaccine given to dogs can prevent the animals from developing severe infections; however, the vaccine will not prevent the spread of the infection to humans.

Lymphocytic Choriomeningitis

A child develops lymphocytic choriomeningitis, an uncommon viral infection, primarily from infected house mice, although on rare occasions guinea pigs and pet hamsters have been found to be the source of the virus. The rodents excrete the virus in urine and feces, and through oral and nasal secretions.

Symptoms in the first stage of lymphocytic choriomeningitis are similar to those associated with *influenza*—high *fever,* chills, *headaches, cough,* and *vomiting*—which last from a few days to a few weeks. *Pneumonia* may develop in some cases. In the second stage of the disease a mild form of *meningitis* may occur, causing severe headaches, nausea, vomiting, lethargy, and stiff neck.

Treatment usually consists of alleviating the uncomfortable symptoms associated with the disease. Serious complications are unlikely, and complete recovery occurs in almost all cases.

Tick-borne diseases such as *Rocky Mountain spotted fever* and *Lyme disease,* and *scabies* can also be transmitted to children from pets. Flea and tick collars should be used on dogs and cats to help prevent the spread of these insects and the diseases they cause.

Also, children who are allergic to fur or feathers may develop *asthma* or *hay fever* when they come into contact with some kinds of pets.

With prompt treatment, children usually recover completely from diseases caused by pets. In every case a physician should be consulted without delay.

DIAGNOSIS

A physician diagnoses specific pet-transmitted diseases based on a child's recent activities, a history of contact with pets and other animals, presence of scratches or cuts, and development of signs and symptoms characteristic of certain infections. Blood tests are performed to isolate causes of infections or to indicate the need for other tests for identification.

PREVENTION

Virtually all pet-transmitted diseases can be prevented. Children should wash their hands immediately after playing outdoors, after playing with a pet, or after cleaning the pet's cage or living environment. Parents should teach their children to be careful with strange dogs and cats to avoid animal bites.

Pets should be taken regularly to a veteranarian for a complete examination, immunization shots, deworming, and treatment of any infections or illnesses.

PHOBIAS

DESCRIPTION

A phobia is an unfounded, irrational, and powerful fear. Young children are especially vulnerable to phobias, but their fears differ according to their age.

A toddler's phobias tend to focus on real things and events in the child's world. For example, the most common phobia of 2-year-olds is the fear of dogs.

As children's imaginative and intellectual powers expand, so do their fears, and 4- and 5-year olds are usually most afraid of the imaginary. Monsters, the dark, dreams, robbers, and being alone are among the phobias older preschool children experience.

School-age children sometimes develop a persistent fear of going to school, which is called school phobia.

CAUSE

A child's phobias may be caused by the mingling of the real and imaginary in the child's mind. Or a situation in the child's life may be causing anxiety, which becomes focused on the object of the phobia.

School phobia may be triggered by an actual illness, an unpleasant incident at school, or a school problem. The cause of the school phobia, however, may have to do with anxiety the child feels about a situation at home. The child may be experiencing separation anxiety about leaving a parent. Family problems such as a parent's illness or intense fighting between parents can lead to school phobia. Children who are perceived as fragile or children who are chronically ill may be especially vulnerable to the development of school phobias.

TREATMENT AND PREVENTION

Reassurance by parents, making it clear to the child that no one is actually threatened, can be very beneficial. Parents can also offer the child the opportunity to confront the feared object in a nonthreatening way, such as introducing a child who fears dogs to a friendly little puppy. Allowing the child to observe other children coping successfully with the feared object, such as the dog, may help the child overcome unrealistic fears. In addition, parents should look for sources of anxiety that might be causing the phobia.

The first step in dealing with the child who has a school phobia is to get the child to return to school. Parents may want to consult with the child's teacher and other school personnel and may also consider seeking advice about family situations that could have fostered the school phobia.

If little progress is made in overcoming the phobia, or if the phobia affects the child's ability to enjoy everyday life, parents should seek professional help. A phobia that persists beyond early childhood or becomes a disabling force in the child's life could be the symptom of a deeper emotional problem. If parents suspect that their child's fears have developed to this stage, a physician should be consulted (see Chapter 3, "Promoting Mental Health").

PIGEON TOES

DESCRIPTION

Toeing-in, or pigeon toes, is the turning in of part or all of the foot. This condition occurs when the bone of the thigh, lower leg, ankle, or foot turns inward. Although most common among infants and young children (affecting approximately 70 percent of infants at birth), toeing-in occurs frequently in all age groups. Toeing-in is usually outgrown; in some cases, however, it may be necessary to correct this condition with the use of special shoes, appliances, or surgery. Toeing-in does not usually result in walking difficulty, although severely pigeon-toed children may initially trip over their own feet.

Toeing-in may be a normal part of a child's development. Until 3 months of age an infant usually sleeps with his or her feet turned inward. In addition, as a child grows, the feet turn in to compensate for temporary physical changes such as *knock-knees* and *bowed legs*. Once a child begins to stand and walk, toeing-in usually disappears. By 4 or 5 years of age, most children's feet no longer turn in.

CAUSE

Several factors cause toeing-in. Most often, pigeon toes are the result of a child's position in the uterus. Congenital (present at birth) bone malformations and certain serious diseases (such as *cerebral palsy)* may also cause toeing-in.

As a child develops, toeing-in can occur. *Knock-knees* may cause body weight to shift inward, and a child may turn the feet in to maintain balance and reduce pressure on the arch of the foot. Crawling with feet turned inward or sitting in the W position (sitting directly on the legs and feet) rotates the hip inward and may contribute to the persistence of toeing-in.

Pigeon toes present at birth may result from fetal position or be the result of excessive inward rotation of the hip, shinbone, or foot.

Toeing-in can also be caused by such problems as *cerebral palsy.* Nerve spasms associated with this condition may cause certain hip muscles to overpower others and force the leg—and toes—to turn inward.

DIAGNOSIS

Toeing-in is obvious. Identification of the exact cause can be made by a physician. The physician observes a child's standing and walking patterns; particular attention is to be paid to the movement and position of the legs, feet, ankles, and hips. X-ray films may be ordered if a bone malformation is suspected.

TREATMENT

Since toeing-in often corrects itself, special treatment is not always required. A child should be encouraged to sit and sleep with toes pointed outward. Sitting cross-legged ("Indian-style") instead of W-style will also be helpful. Physical activities that help strengthen leg and thigh muscles should be encouraged. A program of exercises to stretch and strengthen a child's leg muscles may be recommended by a physician or physical therapist.

If toeing-in is severe and does not correct itself, a physician may recommend corrective orthopedic appliances. The most common appliance is a pair of turned-out shoes separated by a bar (approximately the width of a child's pelvis). Worn at night or when the child is resting, this appliance gently forces the child's joints to turn outward.

For structural malformations of the foot, application of a plaster cast in a corrected position is an effective form of treatment. Orthopedic shoes that turn the feet out are usually worn for several months after the casting treatment is completed.

If bone deformities cannot be corrected with exercises or corrective casts, a physician may recommend surgery. Bones are broken or ligaments released, repositioned, and held in place. Except for malformations of the foot that need early correction, surgical treatment is not usually recommended for a child under the age of 9.

PREVENTION

Toeing-in present at birth cannot be prevented. In some instances, teaching children to sit cross-legged and to sleep with legs and feet straight or turned slightly outward can help correct or prevent the development of pigeon toes.

PITUITARY PROBLEMS

DESCRIPTION AND SIGNS AND SYMPTOMS

The endocrine system is a network of organs and tissues in the body that controls growth, sexual development, and certain body processes. Each organ secretes substances called hormones into the circulating blood, and each hormone has a specific function in the body (see Fig. 18, p. 154).

Major components of the endocrine system are the hypothalamus and pituitary, thyroid, adrenal, and sex glands. The pituitary is called the master gland, because its hormones regulate the functioning of the thyroid, adrenals, and sex glands. Functioning of the pituitary gland is controlled by the hypothalamus through a complex system of stimulation and inhibition. In turn, the hypothalamus is controlled by other parts of the brain and through feedback from pituitary secretions. The pituitary gland and the hypothalamus cannot function independently of one another.

As a result of stimulation by the hypothalamus, the pituitary gland secretes several hormones. During childhood, growth hormone (GH) is produced, which promotes the growth of the skeleton and other tissues through its metabolic effects. Other pituitary hormones include thyroid-stimulating hormone (TSH), which stimulates production and secretion of thyroid gland hormones; adrenocorticotropin hormone (ACTH), which regulates adrenal gland secretion of steroid hormones; and leutenizing hormone (LH) and follicle-stimulating hormone (FSH), which regulate the function of the sex organs and induce sexual maturation. The amount of each hormone released by the pituitary gland is controlled by a variety of factors, including input from the central nervous system (including signals, for example, from emotional *stress* or the stress of illness or injury); activity of the hypothalamus; levels of circulating hormones, and levels of other circulating substances such as nutrients (including blood sugars, amino acids, and fatty acids).

Abnormal functioning of the pituitary gland not only affects the amount of each hormone secreted by the pituitary gland but also affects the organs controlled by the pituitary. Pituitary problems of childhood are often recognized by their effect on physical growth (height, weight, and sexual development); the effect may be either a decrease or increase in growth rate. These problems are usually accompanied by altered levels and patterns of pituitary hormones, which often lead to problems in thyroid, adrenal, and sex gland function.

Hypopituitarism

Hypopituitarism may be marked by decreased output of single or multiple pituitary hormones. It can have its onset at any age but often begins during the first years of life, presumably as a result of a developmental or prenatal accident. Boys are affected more often than girls.

Characteristically, a child with hypopituitarism appears young for his or her age. Slowing of growth results in short stature (see *height problems),* and the child is chubby with increased body fat and decreased muscle development for age. Parents may suspect a growth problem if a child seems unusually small or large for his or her age. A change in growth rate, however, is more significant. Hypopituitarism should be suspected if a child grows less than 2 inches per year after the age of 3. In addition, skin pigment cells are often diminished and a child cannot develop a suntan. Tooth eruption is delayed (see *teeth, developmental problems of).* A child may reach puberty later than normal, or puberty may not occur at all, and adult height is not attained unless he or she receives appropriate treatment.

Excess Production of Pituitary Hormones

This condition is usually the result of the development of a pituitary tumor, which usually produces only one of the pituitary hormones (prolactin, GH, or ACTH, for example). In addition, there may be stimulation of sexual development.

The increased GH production is marked by abnormally fast growth during early childhood (called <u>gigantism)</u> and overgrowth of certain tissues. Affected children may be obese and have weak muscles. Sexual development may occur at a normal rate or may be delayed. During the adult years overproduction of GH usually leads to <u>acromegaly,</u> a condition marked by coarsening of the skin and facial features, projection forward of one or both jaws, and development of a humped back.

Even with treatment, children with GH excess may grow to heights well above normal. If treated, these children can fully develop sexually, as long as gonadotropins (hormones that promote sexual development and maturation) are produced normally. Excess production of pituitary hormone, prolactin, also causes delay in pubertal development or loss of sexual function if development has occurred. When the prolactin levels are reduced by appropriate treatment, sexual development and function return. (The effect of excess ACTH production is discussed in *adrenal problems.)*

CAUSE

Hypopituitarism is caused by malfunctioning of either the hypothalamus and the pituitary gland, or by malfunctioning of the pituitary gland alone. Organ malfunctioning occurs if a child is born with structural organ defects, such as an absent or abnormally small pituitary gland or hypothalamus. Pituitary problems may also result from structural organ damage caused by a head injury received before, during, or after birth. An insufficient supply of oxygen to the brain resulting from impaired blood circulation can cause organ malfunctioning, as can development of tumors or severe illness, such as *meningitis* (inflammation of the protective membranes covering the brain and spinal cord).

Excess production of pituitary hormones is most often caused by hypothalamic or pituitary tumors, but may also result from injury or illness involving the hypothalamus. Early stimulation of sexual development is caused by early onset of the secretion of gonadotropic-releasing hormone by hypothalamic nerve cells. This can be caused by tumors of the hypothalamus that disturb its function but do not themselves produce hormones. A tumor can develop at any time but more commonly appears after infancy and may reduce or increase pituitary hormone production. These tumors seldom spread, but because of their location they are difficult to remove.

DIAGNOSIS

A medical history with past growth data and a complete physical examination performed by a physician often define the problem. CT (computed tomography) scans, highly detailed X-ray films, are required to detect tumors and structural abnormalities of the pituitary gland and the hypothalamus. Special laboratory tests are performed to evaluate pituitary function by measuring hormonal levels in the blood.

COMPLICATIONS

Tumors in the region of the hypothalamus or pituitary may cause an increase in pressure within the skull. As a result, a child experiences *headaches,* nausea, and *vomiting.* If the tumor is extensive, a child may have difficulty sleeping, become obese (see *weight problems),* have problems of body temperature regulation, and develop epilepsy (see *seizures)* or, rarely, *hydrocephalus.* Such tumors may also press on the nerves of the eye and cause visual problems. This complication is treated as a surgical emergency so that vision is not lost permanently. If a tumor in this area causes a marked increase in pressure within the skull, a life-threatening situation can develop unless treated promptly.

Because the pituitary gland controls other glandular and metabolic functions that are required to maintain blood pressure, normal blood sugar levels, and water balance, pituitary problems may lead to *shock, hypoglycemia,* and *dehydration.*

TREATMENT

If hypopituitarism is suspected, a physician may refer a child to an endocrinologist (a physician who specializes in the functions of the endocrine system) for evaluation and treatment. With treatment early in life, a child with hypopituitarism may reach full adult height. With appropriate treatment at a pubertal age, a child may have normal sexual development.

Treatment of tumors is required to prevent life-threatening complications. While prompt, successful treatment of the tumor may restore normal pituitary function, it may also cause pituitary deficiencies to grow worse because of the difficulty of treating the tumor without injuring normal brain tissue.

When a tumor is not involved, treatment focuses on the replacement of the hormonal deficiencies. In the case of growth failure, growth and thyroid hormones can be given before puberty, followed by sex hormones at adolescence. An endocrinologist administers and monitors treatment carefully to be sure that the dosage and schedule of hormone(s) provide optimal improvement in growth and development. The child and parents must be taught how to use hormones to prevent serious problems that can occur under stressful conditions such as illness, accidents, and necessary surgery. If thyroid hormone is needed, it is given by mouth.

Growth hormone is administered by injection 3 times a day under a physician's supervision. Children almost always show an immediate increase in growth with these hormones. Growth hormone treatment is given as long as a child continues to grow until a normal height for age is reached. At adolescence the child may need treatment with gonadotropins.

Treatment of pituitary problems caused by tumors involves surgery or radiation therapy (destruction of the growth through precise exposure to certain radioactive substances; see *cancer).* If a physician determines that a child is at low risk for surgical complications, surgery is recommended to remove a tumor completely. Following surgery or radiation, the child receives hormone therapy to correct delayed growth and development.

PREVENTION

Pituitary problems caused by tumors, illness, and structural defects cannot be prevented. Lifelong problems can be prevented, however, with early, effective treatment.

Pituitary problems caused by head injuries, can be avoided. To reduce the chances of injury, parents should make sure that their children ride in car seats when traveling in motor vehicles and wear safety helmets when riding on bicycles or motorcycles. Head injury occurring before or during the birth process cannot usually be prevented.

PITYRIASIS ROSEA

DESCRIPTION

Pityriasis rosea is a common, harmless skin eruption. Often unrecognized by parents because of its mild symptoms, this eruption is found most frequently in older children and young adults, but can affect anyone.

In 70 percent of cases pityriasis rosea begins with the appearance of a "herald" patch, a slightly raised, oval, reddish spot, usually 1 to 2 inches in length. This patch may be accompanied by *headache,* tiredness, *joint pain,* and *sore throat.* Five to ten days after the appearance of the herald patch, 10 to 100 smaller patches will break out on the body, most frequently on the trunk and torso. Among younger children patches may appear on the face, forearms, and lower legs. If an eruption is widespread and severe, the scalp may also be affected.

An eruption of pityriasis rosea usually lasts from 2 to 8 weeks. If an eruption lasts longer, it may not be pityriasis rosea. Patches usually heal without medication, though itching and scaling may require treatment.

CAUSE
The cause of pityriasis rosea is unknown, although a viral infection is suspected. Pityriasis rosea is not contagious or transmittable.

SIGNS AND SYMPTOMS
Eruptions usually follow the creases of the skin. A common appearance is the "Christmas tree" pattern, a distribution that occurs on the back along the skin creases that follow the shape of the rib cage.

Patches of pityriasis rosea are usually less than 1 inch in length, slightly raised, and vary from round to oval in shape and brown to pink in color. Well-developed patches have a covering of fine scales that result in a crinkled appearance. Patches often heal first in the center, resulting in a ring of scales attached at the outer edge.

Mild to moderate itching may accompany both herald and pityriasis patches.

DIAGNOSIS
Diagnosis is based on the characteristic appearance of eruptions. Pityriasis is easily confused with ringworm, eczema, impetigo, or the rash of secondary syphilis. Presence of a herald patch or a Christmas tree pattern helps to differentiate pityriasis from other skin disorders.

TREATMENT
Pityriasis rosea usually subsides without treatment. Exposure to ultraviolet light may help shorten duration of the eruption. To reduce itching, drying lotions that contain menthol may be helpful. Baths followed by mineral oil can help soften pityriasis scales. If itching is severe, a physician may prescribe oral antihistamines or a steroid ointment.

PREVENTION
Pityriasis rosea cannot be prevented.

PKU

DESCRIPTION
PKU (Phenylketonuria) is an inherited metabolic disorder that leads to mental retardation soon after birth if a special diet is not followed. In the United States 1 out of every 10,000 babies is born with PKU, and 1 out of every 50 people is a carrier, though unaffected by the disorder (see genetic disorders).

PKU afflicts boys and girls equally with an incidence higher among people of northern European descent and very low among blacks.

Babies with PKU appear normal at birth but, if the disorder goes untreated, show signs of intellectual delay by the sixth or seventh month. At least 90 percent of untreated children will be mentally retarded when they grow up. Untreated PKU becomes progressively worse until about age 6, when the brain seems to reach almost full growth.

CAUSE
A baby develops PKU only by inheriting 1 recessive defective gene from each parent. This defective gene causes an abnormality in the body's metabolism (the sum of all complex chemical and physical processes of matter and energy that occur within living cells). Babies born with PKU are deficient in an enzyme that normally metabolizes phenylalanine, an amino acid normally found in all food proteins. If phenylalanine accumulates in the blood and the brain, it can cause brain damage.

SIGNS AND SYMPTOMS
If PKU is not detected and treated swiftly, a child becomes mentally retarded (see mental retardation). Walking and talking may be delayed or may never occur. An affected child may suffer behavioral disorders, including irritability, hyperactivity, and destructive tendencies. The child may have eczema and a musty odor as well as a lighter color of eyes and hair than siblings or parents. About one third of children with PKU suffer seizures.

DIAGNOSIS
State programs routinely screen for PKU (not mental retardation) at birth with a simple test of blood taken from a newborn's heel. Urine tests are not reliable for de-

tecting PKU among newborns, but are used to test for other metabolic conditions that may be present.

COMPLICATIONS

If an infant with PKU is given a diet too low in protein, or is not given the special milk substitute described below, low blood sugar, *anemia,* lethargy, rash, *diarrhea,* and brain damage may develop.

Both the child and parents may become frustrated by the necessity of a strict diet, which must be followed at least through childhood. As the child starts school, he or she may resent feeling different from siblings and peers. As a result, the child may be tempted to ignore the prescribed diet, risking the consequences of possible brain damage.

Even with treatment, children with PKU have a somewhat higher risk of *learning problems* than their peers.

As females with PKU reach childbearing age, the danger of PKU again surfaces. Babies born to women with PKU are at high risk for birth defects because of the mother's high level of phenylalanine. Although babies born to PKU mothers usually do not inherit the disease, they may suffer from the effects of PKU on the mother. Birth defects common among children of PKU mothers include *mental retardation,* microcephaly (an abnormally small head), low birth weight, and congenital heart disease (see *heart disease, congenital).* These birth defects can probably be prevented if the woman resumes a low-phenylalanine diet before becoming pregnant.

TREATMENT

The goal of treatment for PKU is to lower the amount of phenylalanine in the diet while making sure the child receives enough nourishment for normal growth and development. Infants with PKU should be fed a special milk substitute, which is high in protein but low in phenylalanine, as soon as the diagnosis is made. Toddlers and older children must not eat meat, fish, poultry, eggs, or cheese. They can eat measured quantities of fruits and vegetables. To be on the safe side, many physicians recommend that the diet be continued through adulthood.

If PKU goes undetected until age 2 or 3, the special diet should be started immediately, but its effectiveness will be reduced.

The child should visit a PKU clinic every 2 to 4 months for a physical examination, blood tests, and if necessary, adjustment of the diet. During these visits children and parents should meet with the physician to discuss any questions or concerns they might have.

PREVENTION

Parents who have a family history of PKU should be tested to see if they carry the trait for the disorder. If they do, they may want to consider genetic counseling (see *genetic disorders).* Through genetic counseling and laboratory tests (effective on a limited basis), most carriers can now be detected and can be informed of their chances of passing on the gene for PKU. It is not yet possible to determine the presence of PKU in a fetus.

Screening of newborns is required by law in most states, but perhaps 10 percent of infants with PKU are still not detected in this manner. During pregnancy every parent should ask the attending obstetrician or hospital staff whether PKU screening is done routinely and, if not, how such screening can be arranged.

Though neither screening nor the subsequent special diet can prevent PKU, they can prevent the resulting *mental retardation.*

PNEUMONIA

DESCRIPTION

Pneumonia is an inflammation of one or more areas of the lungs. It can be mild, affecting only a small portion of one lung, or severe, affecting large areas of both lungs. Pneumonia is usually caused by viruses or bacteria, but may also be caused by other infectious agents or an inhaled foreign substance. Approximately 40 out of every 1,000 children under the age of 5 develop pneumonia each year. Children of all ages can be affected.

Pneumonia almost always appears abruptly. It usually develops as part of another disease, such as a cold (see *colds),* ear infection, or bronchitis. However, a healthy child may suddenly develop pneumonia without evidence of prior infection.

Microorganisms such as bacteria and viruses often enter the body through the mouth or nose, where they may or may not cause infection. If these microorganisms enter the bloodstream and spread throughout the body, they may settle in the lung and cause pneumonia. Bacterial pneumonia can occur at any time of the year, though it occurs most frequently during the winter months. Viral pneumonia appears chiefly in wintertime. During these colder months people tend to congregate indoors, where bacteria and viruses spread more easily.

Typically, viral pneumonia starts in one area and spreads, affecting other areas of the lung, rather than a whole lobe of one lung (see Fig. 19, p. 182). The bronchial tubes (the two main branches of the trachea, or windpipe, and the tubes branching from them) often become inflamed. Viral pneumonia may be severe, but is often mild and occasionally may go undetected. A child with a mild case seems to have a prolonged cold and feels very tired, but not sick enough to require bed rest. (As a result, viral pneumonia is sometimes called "walking pneumonia.") Symptoms such as *cough* may persist for several weeks. Once viral pneumonia is detected, a child is often confined to bed.

Bacterial pneumonia is more serious than viral pneumonia: whole lobes of the lungs can be affected. It begins when bacteria settle in the alveoli (air sacs) of the lung. Inflammation occurs, causing cough, *fever,* and rapid breathing. White blood cells are drawn into the lung in an effort to fight the infective bacteria. White cells and dead bacteria combine to form pus (liquid produced by infection). If bacterial pneumonia is treated with antibiotics, the child's condition begins to improve within 2 to 4 days. The bloodstream begins to absorb pus, slowly emptying the alveoli of fluid and leaving room for air. The cough eases and breathing becomes less difficult. Recovery is gradual.

A few children develop pneumonia because lowered resistance (from chronic illness) makes them susceptible. Children who are particularly susceptible to pneumonia include those with congenital heart disease, (see *heart disease, congenital),* asthma, malnutrition, and *cancer.* Children with impaired immune systems are also vulnerable. Infants of parents who smoke are more likely to develop pneumonia than are infants of nonsmokers. Alcoholic teenagers are at high risk of developing pneumonia. Weak, sick babies are at risk of inhaling food, and of subsequent pneumonia.

Infants and young children who never have been exposed to a particular strain of a virus or bacterium are more susceptible to pneumonia than others. Pneumonia is most dangerous for infants and the elderly because they have less effective defenses against illness.

Recurrent pneumonia generally suggests the presence of a foreign object, an abnormality in one part of the lung, an immune deficiency, or a chronic illness such as *cystic fibrosis.* Pneumonia from infection is not generally recurrent because during the first attack the child develops antibodies that prevent infection by the virus or bacterium thereafter.

There used to be a high mortality rate among children with bacterial pneumonia. Today, when treated properly and early, bacterial pneumonia rarely causes death in infants and children who are otherwise healthy.

CAUSE

Approximately three fourths of pneumonia cases are caused by viruses; most of the remaining cases are caused by bacteria. A small minority of pneumonia cases are caused by other infectious agents, such as chlamydia, mycoplasmas, yeasts, fungi, or rickettsia. Pneumonia is occasionally caused by inhalation of an irritating substance that affects the bronchial tubes and alveoli; these cases are called aspiration pneumonia. Irritating substances include food, small objects, and chemicals (such as kerosene, benzine, lighter fluid, or oily nose drops). If a child vomits while under anesthesia and inhales the vomit, aspiration pneumonia can result.

Two viruses that cause pneumonia frequently are respiratory syncytial (the most common cause of pneumonia among children under 5) and *influenza.* Infrequently, *measles,* varicella (which can cause *chicken pox),* rubella (see *German measles),* cytomegalovirus, Epstein-Barr (which can cause mononucleosis; see *mononucleosis, infectious),* and herpes simplex viruses may cause pneumonia.

Though the incidence of bacterial pneumonia caused by the pneumococcus has declined, pneumococcus is still the leading cause of bacterial pneumonia. Cases can be caused by staphylococcus, hemophilus influenza, and streptococcus. Pneumonia caused by staph bacteria is particularly serious and may progress rapidly. It is more common in infants than in children.

Mycoplasma is a common cause of pneumonia in children over the age of 5. Due to the highly contagious nature of mycoplasmas, multiple cases frequently occur in one family. This type of pneumonia is often mild, but may linger for weeks.

Most healthy people have bacteria and viruses in their mouths and noses and spread the microorganisms through coughing or sneezing. In fact, healthy people transmit the microorganisms that cause pneumonia more often than do people ill with pneumonia.

Any person exposed to a pneumonia-causing virus or bacteria may develop an infection as a result of such exposure. Whether infection occurs (and the type of illness that occurs) depends upon an individual's immunity, general health, and age. It is possible for a single virus or bacteria to cause several different infections. For example, the same virus that causes pneumonia in one child may cause nothing more than a cold or sore throat in another.

SIGNS AND SYMPTOMS

The first symptoms of bacterial pneumonia in older children occur suddenly and include repetitive coughing; rapid, sometimes painful breathing, at times accompanied by grunting; *wheezing;* chills; and a temperature from 100° to 105° F (37.8° to 40.6° C). Skin may be hot and dry, and the child may feel weak. *Abdominal pain* may be present, causing the child to lie on one side with knees drawn up to the chest. The child may feel drowsy or restless and anxious.

As the disease progresses, older children may cough up thick, yellow sputum occasionally tinged with blood; young children may not cough up much sputum because they often swallow what they cough up. Less common symptoms include nausea, *vomiting, diarrhea, headache,* and bluish lips or nails.

An infant or young child with bacterial pneumonia may have a stuffy nose, be fretful, and show little appetite. Then, along with an abrupt onset of *fever,* a child may become restless, have a rapid pulse, and begin breathing rapidly. These symptoms are accompanied by a *cough.* Symptoms more common in young children and infants include flaring of the nostrils, grunting sounds when exhaling, and indentations of the soft areas of the chest.

Symptoms of viral or mycoplasma pneumonia may include headache, fatigue, fever from 100° to 105° F (37.8° to 40.8° C—usually on the lower side), *sore throat,* chills, and severe, dry cough.

The symptoms of aspiration pneumonia are similar to those of bacterial pneumonia.

DIAGNOSIS

Pneumonia is diagnosed by a physician, who carefully examines the child's chest, listens with a stethoscope, and if necessary takes X-ray films. The physician obtains a full medical history and a complete blood count. If a child has bacterial pneumonia, the white blood cell count will be abnormally high. Cultures of blood and sputum may be taken to confirm a diagnosis.

COMPLICATIONS

Complications rarely arise in cases of viral pneumonia and are unusual in cases of bacterial pneumonia that have been treated. Complications of bacterial pneumonia are most common among infants.

In severe cases of pneumonia, breathing may be seriously impaired. Infection may spread outside a lung into the chest cavity, causing pneumothorax (development of a pocket of air), or empyema (accumulation of pus), and possibly leading to collapse of the lung (see *lung rupture).* These complications are uncommon in viral pneumonia and are seen occasionally with bacterial pneumonia. Other complications include pleurisy (inflammation of the membrane covering the lung), pericarditis (inflammation of the sac surrounding the heart), acute bacterial endocarditis (inflammation of the valves of the heart), and respiratory failure.

TREATMENT

Early treatment of pneumonia is essential to prevent complications. The type of antibiotic treatment of pneumonia is based on the responsible organism and the age and general health of the child. If an infant or chronically ill child has symptoms of pneumonia, or if a child coughs up sputum tinged with blood, a physician should be consulted immediately.

No medication has been developed to help the body fight most viral infections; only the body's own disease-fighting mechanisms cure viral pneumonia. Most cases of viral pneumonia are mild and can be treated at home with rest, fluids, and a light diet. A fever- or pain-reducing medication may be helpful. Consult the physician for specific recommendations and read the discussion of nonprescription medications beginning on p. 000. Cough expectorants liquefy sputum and may make it easier to cough up. A child should remain at home, often in bed, until the *fever* is gone (usually 2 or 3 days). If fever persists beyond 48 hours or the child's condition appears to be worse (rapid, difficult breathing), parents should consult a physician. The degree of fever is not necessarily indicative of the severity of the pneumonia. A slight fever can accompany a severe case of viral pneumonia.

In most cases only the youngest and most severely ill children with bacterial pneumonia (those having severe breathing difficulty or appearing ill) require hospitalization, although all children with bacterial pneumonia require a physician's care. For all cases of bacterial pneumonia, antibiotics are prescribed to reduce the severity of the disease and speed recovery. Antibiotics are also given to prevent the spread of infection both inside and outside the lung. Antibiotics must be taken for the full period of time prescribed, even if a child begins to feel well.

A physician may recommend that children with bacterial pneumonia be isolated from siblings for the first days of the illness.

Pneumonia caused by mycoplasmas may be treated with antibiotics such as erythromycin.

PREVENTION

A vaccine is now available that protects against the more common strains of pneumococcus bacteria. Its use is recommended only for the elderly and for children who have chronic diseases or immune deficiency or who do not have a spleen. It has limited effectiveness in children under the age of 2.

Children with chronic diseases should receive a flu vaccine each fall.

Parents who smoke should avoid doing so around their children.

POISON IVY, OAK, AND SUMAC

DESCRIPTION

Poison ivy dermatitis is an allergic reaction to the oils of the poison ivy plant. Poison oak and poison sumac can cause the same condition. This skin disorder can occur any time of the year, but most frequently arises in the spring, when plant oils are plentiful and exposure is greatest. Poison ivy dermatitis is the most common skin disorder among children of all ages.

Once contact is made, the first signs of poison ivy dermatitis, intense redness and itching, usually appear within 18 to 72 hours. The *rash,* however, may appear for the first time as long as 21 days after contact. Most often the rash erupts on exposed portions of the arms, legs, and face, but it can appear on other parts of the body that have come in contact with the oil.

After initial contact with poison ivy, each new exposure to the plant results in a rash in 12 hours to 3 days. The worst stage of the eruption occurs 4 to 7 days after contact. Even with prompt treatment, poison ivy dermatitis may take up to 1 to 2 weeks to disappear.

CAUSE

Sensitivity to a chemical contained in the oils of the plant causes poison ivy dermatitis. The degree of sensitivity varies: some children react only slightly to the oil while others remain highly allergic their entire lives. Contact with the leaves and stems of poison ivy, oak, or sumac, or the smoke from the burning of those plants, exposes a child to the oils. Shoes and pets may also carry the oils, which can be transferred to a child's skin.

Poison ivy dermatitis does not spread except when oil is transferred from the source to parts of the body. Poison ivy is not usually spread when a child touches or scratches an affected area and then touches unaffected areas of skin.

SIGNS AND SYMPTOMS

The first sign of poison ivy dermatitis is the appearance of red pimples accompanied by itching. Pinhead size blisters may form on these pimples if the *rash* is more advanced, and can merge to form blisters one-half inch or more in diameter. The blisters may ooze but are not contagious. The clear fluid that oozes from them is made of plasma and white blood cells, the body's response to the poison ivy oil.

The kind of contact made with the plant determines the pattern of the rash. Direct contact with the straight edge of a leaf results in a linear rash. A scattered pattern usually appears on the face or genitals due to occasional touching with "oily" hands. The palms of the hands are not usually affected, because of the thickness of the skin.

DIAGNOSIS

A blistered, red, itchy *rash* in a straight line (from the straight edge of the leaf) is usually diagnosed as poison ivy dermatitis. This eruption, however, can resemble other rashes. A detailed history of the child's activities can be helpful in determining the cause of the skin irritation.

COMPLICATIONS

Constant scratching of dermatitis may result in infection. Secondary infection is common, appearing as oozing blisters or crusting on previously affected patches of skin (see *impetigo).*

TREATMENT

A child who has developed poison ivy dermatitis should be kept cool, because sweating and heat make itching worse. Cold compresses on the affected areas, or cool, colloidal oatmeal baths if the rash is extensive, may be effective in soothing the irritation. Nonprescription drying lotions of calamine and oral antihistamines may also be helpful. An oral antibiotic may be necessary if infection develops after the poison ivy *rash.*

If the poison ivy rash is severe, the child should be seen by a physician. Symptoms may include swelling and pain around the eyes, nose, and genitals. Cortisone tablets may be prescribed. Response to this treatment is usually rapid. However, some children may experience recurrence of dermatitis symptoms following cortisone treatment (called the "rebound effect") if treatment is stopped too soon. This medication may have side effects and should be used only for severe cases. Cortisone creams have fewer side effects, but are not very effective.

PREVENTION

Avoiding contact with plants containing irritating oils is the most effective prevention. Learning to identify poison ivy, oak, and sumac will help older children avoid them. When walking in areas where poison ivy is often found, a child should wear shoes, socks, long pants, long-sleeved shirts, and perhaps even gloves. Young children should be watched when playing in areas where poison ivy may be present. Contaminated clothes should washed with soapy water.

Poison ivy plants growing around the outside of the house should be removed. Immediate washing (within 10 minutes of contact) with warm, soapy water of a child's skin may prevent the *rash.*

If contact with poison ivy is suspected, the skin needs to be washed with soap and warm water within 10 minutes of exposure. The oil penetrates the skin in 10 minutes and cannot be washed off after that time. Fingernails should be well scrubbed with a nail brush to make sure all oil is removed. The oil usually washes off with the first soaping. Clothing and shoes that have come in contact with the plant oils should be washed with soapy water. Dogs and cats may also be coated with poison ivy oils that are the source of the dermatitis. A warm, soapy bath usually removes the oil from an animal's fur.

POLIOMYELITIS

DESCRIPTION AND SIGNS AND SYMPTOMS

Poliomyelitis (also called polio or infantile paralysis) is a viral disease that in its very severe form affects the central nervous system (the brain, spinal cord, and their protective covering, the meninges). In the United States and other developed nations, immunization has all but eradicated the disease.

Polio is characterized primarily by high *fever, headache,* and an overall achy feeling. Additional signs include stiffness of the neck and back, *vomiting,* and irritability. These signs and symptoms may last for 3 to 4 days and then disappear. In most cases the disease progresses no further.

In paralytic poliomyelitis, a second phase of illness occurs in which symptoms recur, the brain and spinal cord are generally involved, and paralysis appears, involving any or all of the voluntary muscles. In the majority of diagnosed polio cases, paralysis appears by the third or fourth day of the illness if it occurs at all. Among children less than 1 year of age, parents often do not notice any signs of illness before the onset of paralysis. Paralysis from polio occurs when the nerve cells within the spinal cord are killed by the virus, thus interrupting nerve communication from the spinal cord to muscles.

The affected child loses, sometimes permanently, the ability to move those muscles controlled by the affected nerve cells. When poliomyelitis attacks the nerve cells that contol the muscles of the diaphragm (the partition between the chest and abdominal cavities) or attacks the center in the brain that controls respiration, breathing becomes virtually impossible and death may result unless artificial respiration is used.

By and large, children are more prone to involvement of the arms and legs than of the respiratory center. The outlook for a child who develops paralytic poliomyelitis depends on the number and location of damaged nerve cells and, to some extent, the quality of therapy the child receives.

CAUSE

Poliomyelitis is caused by the highly contagious poliovirus. The poliovirus is most contagious immediately before and during the onset of symptoms in a case of polio.

DIAGNOSIS

If a child has a high fever, *headache,* and stiff neck, parents should consult a physician.

No immediate method of diagnosing poliomyelitis exists. A physician is likely to suspect paralytic polio if, in taking a detailed medical history, the previously mentioned symptoms are noted and if, in examining the child, paralysis and/or muscle spasms are found. Tests can be performed for white blood cells (indicative of infection) in spinal fluid, and cultures can be taken from nose or stool to identify the virus. Finally, the rigidity of the spinal column is measured.

TREATMENT

Although there is no cure for the disease, a child with nonparalytic polio can be treated at home. Treatment is aimed at relieving *fever* and *headache.*

If examination reveals or symptoms suggest any form of paralysis, a child should be hospitalized. Paralysis can spread very rapidly. In those instances in which limbs are paralyzed or muscle spasms occur, applications of hot packs and careful evaluation by a physical therapist is important. The patient's spine must always be kept in a straight position to prevent *scoliosis* (inward curvature of the spine). The iron lung has provided lifesaving support for many victims of polio epidemics. Since the early 1960s more efficient types of respirators have been developed, but if long-term assistance is needed, the iron lung may still be used today.

Some muscles may recover completely if examination reveals that they have retained a fair to good degree of strength. Those muscles which are completely paralyzed or have only a slight degree of strength probably cannot recover. In subsequent rehabilitative orthopedic surgery, however, the surgeon may be able to transplant unaffected neighboring muscles to overcome the effects of paralysis in affected muscles.

It is important that the patient and family receive strong psychological support.

PREVENTION

Immunization is the only protection against the poliovirus. In the United States oral vaccine is most often used.

The law requires that children be immunized against polio before entering public school, and public health officials have estimated that nearly 99 percent of United States school children have been immunized. Full protection requires that children be immunized first at approximately 2 months of age and then again at 4 months, followed by a booster at 15 months. (See Chapter 6, "Going to the Physician," for vaccination schedules.)

POLYPS

DESCRIPTION

Typically, a polyp is a small, smooth, mushroom-shaped growth. Polyps most often grow in the intestines, especially in the colon (the last part of the large intestine) and the rectum (the lowest part of the colon). They may also be found in the nasal passages (including the sinuses), the respiratory tract (including the vocal cords), the urinary tract (including the bladder), and on the cervix of the uterus. Polyps can occur singly or in clusters and can vary in shape (ovoid or spherical, with or without stems) and size. Most polyps are harmless and disappear without treatment. In some cases, however, polyps may become cancers (masses of abnormal cells that grow uncontrollably). All polyps, no matter what the underlying cause, require a physician's examination.

Juvenile Polyps

Juvenile polyps grow in the intestines and account for approximately 90 percent of all childhood polyps. They are usually harmless and disappear without treatment; they never become cancers. These growths are rare before age 1 and after age 15; they most often appear among children ages 3 to 6 years old. Boys are affected much more often than girls.

The exact cause of juvenile polyps is unknown, but medical experts suspect that they may arise from long-term inflammation of mucous membranes, particularly in the intestine, colon, or rectum. Most of the time, juvenile polyps occur individually, but occasionally a child has many such growths.

In general, juvenile polyps cause few problems and are painless. The most frequent symptom is rectal bleeding, but only small amounts of blood are seen. The blood is usually pink (if mixed with mucus) or bright red. A child may bleed each time a stool is passed or only occasionally. Older children with polyps may suffer recurrent lower *abdominal pain* and *diarrhea.*

The outlook for a child with juvenile polyps is excellent. These growths usually disappear spontaneously by the time a child reaches puberty. Occasionally juvenile polyps recur during childhood.

Lymphoid Polyposis

Lymphoid polyps are made of large clumps of lymphoid tissue, the special infection-fighting tissue that is essential to the immune system. Children 1 to 3 years old are most often affected, but any child from 6 months to puberty can develop this condition. In most cases more than one polyp is present and the colon and small intestine are involved. This disorder often occurs with juvenile polyps or polyp disorders related to cancer.

Medical experts are not certain whether or not lymphoid polyposis is inherited. Exactly why this disorder occurs is unknown, but it may be a temporary response to immune-system activity, such as when the body is fighting a viral infection. It may also result from intestinal inflammation, which can be caused by disorders such as *Hirschsprung's disease, Crohn's disease,* or *ulcerative colitis,* or by problems of the immune system.

Symptoms of lymphoid polyposis include rectal bleeding, abdominal cramping, and *diarrhea. Intussusception* (a condition in which a segment of the intestine telescopes into an adjacent section) and *rectal prolapse* (a condition in which the mucous membrane lining of the rectum sags out of the anus) may occur.

Children with lymphoid polyposis usually recover completely, unless the disorder occurs in association with potentially cancerous polyps.

Peutz-Jeghers Syndrome

Peutz-Jeghers syndrome is an inherited polyp disorder in which polyps develop during infancy and early childhood, usually in the rectum, and small intestine, the colon, and the stomach. Less often they appear in the nasal passages, respiratory pathway, and urinary tract. More polyps form as a child grows; they are separated from older polyps by segments of normal intestine. New polyp formation may continue for months or even years. Peutz-Jeghers polyps bleed easily but are usually harmless, although in rare cases they can evolve into cancerous tumors.

Symptoms of Peutz-Jeghers include scattered blotchy, brown spots or dark freckles on the lips and, occasionally, on the lining of the cheeks, the tongue, the forearms, the palms of the hands, and the soles of the feet. Well-defined, dark brown spots may be present at birth around the mouth, the eyes, and the nostrils. These pigmented spots tend to fade at puberty.

Other symptoms of Peutz-Jeghers syndrome include *rectal prolapse* and *intussusception.* About one third of cases pass blood in the stools. If blood loss is heavy, a child may develop *anemia.* Brief spells of abdominal pain, similar to *colic,* may occur after eating. Vomiting may occur. Less common symptoms include slowing of growth and development of bony tumors.

In general the outlook for infants and children with Peutz-Jeghers syndrome is good. Large polyps should be removed, both to prevent or correct obstruction and to lessen the risk of tumor development. Small polyps may disappear by themselves and often do not require treatment.

Nasal Polyps

In addition to those caused by Peutz-Jeghers syndrome, nasal polyps may arise because of abnormal nasal secretions—caused by *cystic fibrosis,* for example—or from inflammation of the nasal membranes caused by long-term *hay fever* or *asthma.* Nasal polyps most often appear after 10 years of age and are harmless, although they may cause nasal obstruction. If the underlying cause of polyps cannot be eliminated, they may recur.

Symptoms of nasal polyps can include nasal obstruction, inability to breath through the nose, and heavy mucus secretions. If polyps persist, the bridge of the nose may become wider. A child may also have polyps in the throat, which can cause *hoarseness.*

Polyp Disorders Leading to Cancer and Cancerous Tumor Formation

Polyp disorders that lead to cancer are rare, but they deserve mention because of their potentially fatal outcome if not treated successfully. They are caused by genetic factors that are passed on to children by their parents; in most cases there is a family history of such disorders (see *genetic disorders*).

Early treatment of these disorders is essential: affected children usually die from untreated cancer. Even with proper treatment, however, cancerous tumors may recur among children with one of these polyp disorders (see *cancer*).

Familial Adenomatous Polyposis of the Colon Familial adenomatous polyposis is characterized by the formation of many polyps (up to 3,000) of various sizes in the colon and the rectum. In rare cases polyps form in the stomach and small intestine. Many cancerous tumors evolve from the polyps of this disorder; affected individuals usually develop cancer of the colon before age 40. Approximately 10 percent of individuals with this disorder also develop tumors in the thyroid gland (see *thyroid problems*) or the brain (see *brain tumor*).

Symptoms usually develop during late childhood or adolescence but may appear as early as the fourth month of life. They include *diarrhea, abdominal pain,* blood loss, and *anemia;* older children may suffer from *intussusception* and *intestinal obstruction.*

Gardner's Syndrome Gardner's syndrome causes formation of many polyps in the intestines and stomach, as well as in the thyroid gland, the adrenal glands, and the gonads (ovaries and testes). As this disorder progresses, polyps evolve into cysts (abnormal sacs containing fluid or semisolid fluid) and tumors, which are found throughout the body tissues, including the bones. In general the disease does not develop fully until an individual is more than 20 years old, but some symptoms are present during childhood. Family histories of this disorder are always present, and it is twice as common

among males as among females.

Symptoms of Gardner's syndrome include *abdominal pain* and *diarrhea.* Cysts usually appear on the face and extremities. When the jawbones are affected, dental abnormalities, such as the absence of tooth eruption (see *teeth, developmental problems of*), may occur.

DIAGNOSIS

Occasionally a parent notices a polyp protruding from a child's anus. In most cases, however, polyps cannot be seen without special examining instruments. A physician should be consulted if a child has rectal bleeding or severe abdominal pain.

A physician may suspect the presence of a polyp disorder if a family history of such problems exists and characteristic signs and symptoms are present. If involvement of the intestines, colon, or rectum is suspected, a physician examines the rectum and lower colon with a flexible, lighted instrument called a sigmoidoscope. A barium enema is also helpful in detection of polyps. Other tests are used to detect polyps in the stomach, the intestines, the respiratory tract, and the urinary tract. Presence of skin and bone cysts or tumors may arouse a physician's suspicion of a polyp disorder.

When a child is suspected of having intestinal polyps, a physician must rule out other conditions that produce rectal bleeding and abdominal pain. For example, disorders such as *Meckel's diverticulum, ulcerative colitis,* and *Hirschsprung's disease* must be ruled out before positive diagnosis can be made.

TREATMENT

Harmless polyps and those that produce no symptoms do not require treatment, because they usually disappear spontaneously. A child with harmless polyps should be examined periodically by a physician to determine if the polyps have grown or have disappeared. If any polyps persist for more than a year with no visible change in size, they should be removed surgically. Polyps causing intestinal obstruction or rectal bleeding should also be removed.

Successful treatment of nasal polyps cannot be accomplished until the underlying cause is eliminated. Surgical removal of polyps, however, will relieve nasal obstruction.

Use of nasal decongestants containing steroids (a synthetic, anti-inflammatory medication) has no effect on polyps, but antihistamines may help ease nasal obstruction.

If a child has a family history of polyp-related cancer and develops polyps, the polyps must be removed completely. In many cases this involves removing some or all of the involved organ. When the colon is involved, it is often best to remove it completely to prevent development of cancer of the colon. Surgical removal can usually be delayed until late adolescence or adulthood because the risk of polyp-related childhood cancer is low. Once polyps have been removed, a child must be monitored closely by a physician in case polyps recur.

PREVENTION

Polyps cannot be prevented. However, in the rare case when a family history of polyp-related cancer exists, parents should seek genetic counseling to determine the chances of having a child who is at high risk for this disorder (see Prevention section of *genetic disorders*).

PREMATURITY

DESCRIPTION

Premature or preterm babies (often called "preemies") are born too soon—after less than 37 weeks of gestation. (Full-term infants are born between 37 and 42 weeks after conception.) Those babies born after less than 24 or 25 weeks of gestation have essentially no chance of survival even if liveborn. After 25 or 26 weeks the probability of survival steadily improves.

The growth and development of premature babies is normal before their birth, but because they have not had time to grow and develop fully they may be unable to function independently.

Babies who are born abnormally small, even though they may have been full-term, are called dysmature. Both dysmature and premature babies generally weigh less than 5½ pounds at birth. Dysmature infants, often called "small for gestational age" or "in utero growth-retarded," grow more slowly than normal before birth. Although these babies have not grown to normal weight and length, they are usually fully developed. Newborns can be both premature and dysmature.

Prematurity is common, occurring in 6 to 8 percent of all births in the United States. The incidence of prematurity closely correlates with socioeconomic, racial, and biological factors. More than 7 percent of the nation's white infants and nearly 18 percent of nonwhite infants are premature.

During the 1950s nearly three fourths of babies weighing less than 3.3 pounds at birth died as newborns. Of the infants who lived, nearly half were mentally retarded (see *mental retardation)* or had *cerebral palsy* or other developmental disabilities. By the early 1980s more than 80 percent of infants weighing less than 3.3 pounds at birth were surviving, and less than 15 percent were suffering developmental disabilities. The greater the birthweight, the more likely the baby is to survive and to have no permanent health problems.

Premature infants usually lag behind full-term infants in physical and intellectual development. A 4-month-old baby who was born 1 month prematurely, for example, is usually at the developmental level of a 2- to 3-month-old full-term baby. Dysmature infants, on the other hand, are usually more awake, alert, and active than premature babies. Both premature and dysmature babies may be irritable and poor feeders.

Health problems of newborn premature babies can slow their growth and development. Still, by 2 years of age most premature babies have not only achieved the same intellectual development levels as their full-term peers but have reached the same physical growth and development levels as well. Today 90 percent of premature infants grow up free of serious complications.

CAUSE

Most premature births result from unknown causes. However, national statistics reveal that women who have a history of difficult pregnancies, miscarriages, or stillbirths (fetal deaths), who have had multiple abortions, or who have had one or more previous premature babies are more likely than others to give birth to premature infants. In addition, close spacing of pregnancies, more than 4 pregnancies, and multiple births (twins or more) appear to increase the likelihood of prematurity.

The mother's age (especially if she is under 20 or over 40) also appears to be related to prematurity.

Aside from these circumstantial factors, there are medical factors that seem to increase the probability of premature delivery:

- alcoholism (see *drug and alcohol abuse)*
- drug addiction (see *drug and alcohol abuse)*
- cigarette smoking (see *drug and alcohol abuse)*
- the mother's exposure to the synthetic hormone DES (see *DES exposure)* before her own birth
- unusual physical or psychological *stress*
- long-term illness
- generally poor physical condition
- undernourishment (see *malnutrition)*
- *anemia*
- congenital heart conditions (see *heart disease, congenital)*
- kidney or liver disorders
- respiratory ailments
- irregular thyroid function (see *thyroid problems)*
- toxemia (a condition in which the mother experiences high blood pressure, fluid retention, and for unknown reasons, protein in her urine)
- high blood pressure (see *hypertension)*
- maternal infection (during the last three months of pregnancy), such as *urinary tract infection*
- uterine malformations or fibroids
- weak muscles of the cervix (sometimes caused by multiple abortions)
- placental abruption (the placenta separates from the wall of the uterus)
- placenta previa (the placenta develops too low in the uterus and may become partly detached and bleed)

Fetal malformations are also associated with some cases of prematurity.

When certain medical problems occur, physicians may decide to deliver the infant early in order to protect its life. For instance, if a pregnant woman is diabetic, her unborn infant runs a higher than normal risk of being stillborn. In another instance, *Rh and ABO incompatibility* between the mother and fetus commonly used to lead to a disease called erythroblastosis that, in turn, could cause stillbirth. Now, however, the disease can be prevented.

Premature delivery may also be made necessary or caused by external factors such as an early rupture of the amniotic sac (leading to a risk of infection) or rarely, by severe falls or accidents.

Dysmaturity is caused either when the fetus has a limited potential for growth or when the mother's body (including the placenta) provides limited nutrition support to the fetus.

Limited potential for growth may be caused by maternal infections, such as *German measles* (rubella), cytomegaloviral infection, and infections of the urinary tract. Dysmaturity can also be caused by chromosomal disorders, such as *Down syndrome,* or by inborn errors of metabolism, such as *PKU* or galactosemia.

Limited nutritional support for a fetus is most likely to occur among pregnant teenagers, women over 40, or malnourished women. Also, women who have had one dysmature baby are likely to have another. The probability of dysmaturity seems to increase if the mother has severe anemia, high blood pressure, congenital heart disease, kidney disorders, respiratory ailments, irregular thyroid function, or a long-term illness, such as *diabetes.*

Other factors that can cause nutritional deficiencies include smoking, drug and alcohol use, or relative lack of oxygen from living at a high altitude. Dysmaturity also can be caused by pregnancy complications, such as toxemia or placenta defects.

SIGNS AND SYMPTOMS

When a baby is premature, underdevelopment is marked by several external physical characteristics. The skin may be thin, with little fat underneath (raising the risk of low body temperature), reddish, and covered with fine body hair. The breast tissue and ear cartilage are less developed than in full-term babies. The creases in the soles of the feet are not very noticeable. Preemies may have poor muscle tone and reflexes. Bones may be overly flexible and soft. The testicles of the premature male infant are more likely to be undescended than those of full-term babies (see *undescended testicles).* The scrotal sac of the premature male infant lacks the rough appearance of the sac of the term infant.

DIAGNOSIS

Until a few years ago physicians tended to pay more attention to the weight of the newborn than to the baby's length of gestation (period of development as a fetus) when determining prematurity. Now a gestation of less than 37 weeks is considered the most reliable indicator of prematurity.

Efforts are usually made during early pregnancy to determine when conception occurred, using information based upon the date of the mother's last menstrual period and upon early examination. If necessary the fetus's growth at a particular stage of pregnancy can be determined using ultrasound (in which sound waves are directed through the mother's abdomen to obtain an image of the fetus) to make such measurements as fetal head size and leg length. When growth is less than the tenth percentile for gestational age, dysmaturity is suspected. Unfortunately, ultrasound sometimes gives inaccurate information.

After the baby is born, weight, size, and physical signs of development can aid in diagnosis of prematurity and dysmaturity.

COMPLICATIONS

More than 8 out of 10 newborns who die are premature. Both premature and dysmature infants are especially susceptible at birth to *asphyxia* (a life-threatening condition involving a critically low level of oxygen in the brain). At birth a baby's heart rate, breathing effort, muscle tone, reflex irritability, and skin color (from blue to pink) are checked. Premature babies are likely to have problems in one or more of these areas.

Because of their small size and low birthweight, premature and dysmature infants are susceptible to problems such as *jaundice* (yellowing of skin), *hypoglycemia* (low blood sugar), and hypothermia (see *exposure to temperature extremes).*

The more underdeveloped the baby, the greater the danger of serious or life-threatening complications caused by immature parts of the body such as the lungs, brain, liver, kidneys, gastrointestinal tract, and muscles.

Underdeveloped functions in the premature infant usually require the most urgent and immediate special care. While in the intensive care nursery, a premature infant, especially one who is very premature, is at increased risk of such disorders as the following:

- hyaline membrane disease (a lung disease that also is called *respiratory distress syndrome)*
- patent ductus arteriosus (see *heart diseas, congenital),* a heart defect that can cause congestive heart failure due to too much blood being recirculated through the lungs (see *heart failure, congestive)*
- periodic breathing (brief pauses in breathing) or *apnea* (temporary stopping of breathing and slowing of the heart rate)
- intracranial hemorrhage (bleeding within the brain) leading to *hydrocephalus* (excessive cerebrospinal fluid within the skull)
- necrotizing enterocolitis (a condition in which an impaired blood supply to the gastrointestinal tract could lead to small perforations of the intestines)

In addition, premature babies have a limited ability to fight infection, do not have antibodies to common bacteria, and are therefore more susceptible to bacterial infections.

The very smallest and sickest premature babies are also vulnerable to long-term problems:

- deafness (see *hearing loss),* which occurs in less than 2 percent of all "graduates" of neonatal intensive care units (NICUs)
- *blindness,* which occurs in less than 0.2 percent of all NICU graduates. About 5 percent of all NICU graduates have had retrolental fibroplasia (RLF), an eye problem which in its most severe form may lead to partial or complete detachment of the retina and subsequent blindness
- lung disease such as bronchopulmonary dysplasia (BPD), a chronic disease characterized by damage to the tissues of the lungs and to the larger air passages leading to them, which causes recurrent respiratory infections and may affect growth. BPD affects newborns who have received oxygen and artificial breathing support for a long period of time (see *respiratory distress syndrome)*
- *mental retardation* (relatively unusual)
- *cerebral palsy* (relatively unusual)
- *seizures* (relatively unusual)

Dysmature infants may experience nutritional disorders, such as poor feeding and ongoing slow growth. With proper diet, however, most children born with growth retardation catch up to normal children in physical growth and in intellectual and social development. When dysmaturity is caused by prenatal infection, such as *German measles,* or chromosomal abnormalities, such as *Down syndrome,* effects on growth and development may be lifelong.

TREATMENT

Neonatal intensive care units have increased the chances of survival of premature infants, even those born after only 25 or 26 weeks of gestation. In these specialized nurseries the heart and breathing rates, temperature, and blood pressure of premature babies are monitored continuously. To help them breathe, many preemies are put on respirators. Medications are administered in small-spaced doses.

Both premature and dysmature infants are often kept warm in incubators (and sometimes wear stocking caps for additional warmth) and may sleep on tiny water beds. Often they are fed intravenously or through stomach tubes, and they may be given vitamin and mineral supplements. Blood is tested for the proper levels of oxygen, sugar, acid, and other chemicals. Special lights can be used for the treatment of *jaundice.*

Premature infants need extra, but brief and gentle, stimulation of their senses. For instance, a mobile may hang over the incubator and parents or nursery staff may talk or sing softly. Premature babies can be overstimulated very easily; swaddling and pacifiers can help to soothe them.

Because premature babies must usually be separated from their parents, it is natural for parents to worry about how close attachments can form between them and their baby. However, if the infant's condition permits, parents can touch, stroke, and eventually hold and rock their premature baby. No evidence exists that there is a critical bonding period which, if missed because of prematurity or illness, leads to a disrupted or compromised parent-child relationship.

Once a premature baby's digestive system has matured enough, he or she can receive breast milk. At first the mother may not be able to feed her baby directly and may have to use a breast pump, but eventually she will be able to breast-feed her baby.

Usually at about the date when a premature baby originally was supposed to be born, if weight gain and health permit, he or she can go home. A baby must be able to eat by mouth, keep a normal temperature without an incubator, and have regular, stable breathing and heart rates before being discharged.

Home care for premature babies is somewhat different from home care for full-term infants. Parents should ask physicians and nurses for advice regarding feeding, preventing infections, and monitoring conditions such as *apnea.* It is unusual for apnea to continue to be a problem beyond the expected due date. Parents should also ask about encouraging their baby's motor skill development through exercise and other methods.

It is important for premature and dysmature babies to receive follow-up testing of their health, growth, and development.

PREVENTION

Although prematurity and dysmaturity often cannot be prevented, the chances of delivering a healthy, normal-sized baby increase with high-quality prenatal care, including proper diet and regular medical check-ups. During pregnancy a woman should avoid taking drugs—including over-the-counter medication and certain prescription medication—unless her obstetrician prescribes a medication. She also should eliminate cigarette smoking and alcohol.

Pregnant women considered to be at high risk of premature delivery can be referred to hospitals equipped with the highest level of neonatal intensive care. If pregnant women are taught to pay attention to early signs of premature labor, it may be possible to halt labor by the use of tocolytic (labor-inhibiting) drugs. Even if premature labor cannot be stopped, labor and delivery can be managed in a highly specialized obstetrical center where drugs may be given to aid the fetus's lung development. Such care will increase the baby's chances of survival and health.

To prevent dysmaturity caused by maternal infection, a woman who lacks immunity to *German measles* (shown by a blood test) should be immunized at least 3 months before conceiving a child.

PSORIASIS

DESCRIPTION

Psoriasis (literally "an itching condition"), a chronic skin disorder, occurs among children of all ages. This disorder affects girls more often than boys. There is scientific evidence that it is an inherited trait (see *genetic disorders*); 50 percent of children with psoriasis have family histories of the skin disorder. Persistent and severe psoriasis rarely occurs in infants. Psoriasis often appears in areas where the skin has been damaged. Scratch marks, surgical wounds, or sunburns may develop psoriasis as they heal. This skin disorder rarely disappears spontaneously, but unexplained improvement is common.

Psoriasis may be associated with *juvenile rheumatoid arthritis,* occurring among approximately 5 percent of children with the disease. Occasionally it is also associated with bacterial respiratory infections, and may also occur following a viral infection or sunburn.

Duration of individual cases of psoriasis varies and cannot be predicted. Psoriasis tends to recur throughout an individual's lifetime, although eruptions may be spaced years apart.

CAUSE

The actual cause of psoriasis is unknown, although it may appear as a reaction to a serious illness or medication.

SIGNS AND SYMPTOMS

Psoriasis appears on the skin as thick, silver-scaled, irregularly shaped though well-defined reddened sores known as plaques. These plaques may enlarge, crack, and bleed. Most frequently they appear on the elbows, knees, scalp, and genital area, but can be found anywhere on the body. Itching is often present.

A characteristic of psoriasis is the pitting and thickening of nail surfaces on fingers and toes. Scalp sores occur among 4 out of 5 children with psoriasis, and small raindroplike sores on the face are also common. Characteristic pinpoint bleeding occurs when a plaque is removed. If a child has psoriasis, plaques often arise at the site of a skin injury such as a cut.

In infants psoriasis frequently appears in the diaper area. The plaques in the diaper area may be confused with *seborrheic dermatitis, eczema,* or *diaper rash,* caused by irritation or a fungus.

DIAGNOSIS

Diagnosis of psoriasis is based on the presence of fixed, silver-scaled plaques. Identifying characteristics include the occurrence of plaques at the site of a new injury and the pitting and thickening of toenails and fingernails.

If visual examination is not sufficient for diagnosis, a physician may take a skin biopsy (microscopic examination of a small skin sample) for positive identification.

TREATMENT

Type and duration of treatment depends on the location of the eruption, the age of the child, the success of previous treatment, and how far the disorder has spread. Shampoos, ointments, gels, and bath oils containing tar are effective home treatments. Because tar has a distinctive odor and color and can stain clothes and skin, some patients choose other preparations.

A physician can prescribe creams and ointments containing medication such as salicylic acid, which help remove scales and crusts. Cortisone creams or lotions, available by prescription, are also effective. Severe cases of psoriasis may be treated with internal medications prescribed by a physician.

For treatment of scalp psoriasis, a physician can prescribe a medicated solution containing sulfur and salicylic acid, which is thoroughly rubbed into the scalp; the hair and scalp are then washed with a medicated shampoo. This is usually repeated 3 or 4 times a week. Once plaques begin to disappear, a cortisone lotion or gel can be applied to speed healing.

Ultraviolet light (sunlight) can effectively be used to treat psoriasis. A physician often gives light treatments at the office, particularly in winter, but may also recommend that patients sit in the sun for specified lengths of time.

Psoriasis of the nails generally resists all treatment. Nails may improve spontaneously. Psoriasis readily flares up with scratching or rubbing, and skin irritation should be avoided. Except in stubborn and resistent cases, psoriasis improves with consistent treatment.

PREVENTION
Psoriasis cannot be prevented.

PSYCHOSIS

DESCRIPTION, CAUSE AND SIGNS AND SYMPTOMS

Psychosis is a severe mental problem characterized by disturbance in the ability to distinguish fantasy from reality and to perceive reality accurately. More precisely, "psychosis" is a general term used to describe several types of severe mental health problems. Each type of psychosis interferes significantly with an affected child's life. Psychosis typically causes problems with organizing thinking, using language correctly, controlling impulses, behaving in accordance with society's norms, expressing emotions, and relating to other people.

"Typical" psychotic behavior is difficult to describe, because it can take so many forms. One of the most obvious signs of psychotic behavior is the hallucination, an experience during which an affected child sees, hears, touches, tastes, or smells something that does not exist. Another obvious sign is the delusion, a misinterpretation of the meaning or significance of something that truly exists. Similar (though less telltale) types of behavior include making up words, laughing at things that clearly are not funny or even pleasant, and becoming very angry for little or no reason.

Hallucinations, delusions, and similar types of behavior clearly distinguish psychotic children from others. After hearing the tale of Cinderella, for example, a nonpsychotic child may dream of being the heroine and feel disgust when thinking of the wicked stepmother. A psychotic child may believe that he or she *is* Cinderella and that the stepmother is actually present in the same room.

For years medical experts debated whether or not psychosis affected preadolescent children and, if so, how it was to be distinguished from adult psychosis and from other childhood disorders. Although these issues are still subject to dispute, most medical experts now agree that preadolescent children can suffer from psychoses once thought to be found only among adolescents and adults. Most experts also agree that explicit evidence of psychosis—namely, the ability to verbalize grossly distorted preceptions of reality—must exist before a diagnosis can be made. Thus it may be impossible to diagnose a specific psychosis unless a child can speak, although psychosis may be suspected because of grossly disturbed behavior.

Psychosis among children can arise from a variety of short- and long-term physical conditions, including the use of drugs (such as beginning or withdrawing from steroids), high *fever, meningitis,* and hormonal imbalances (such as hyperthyroidism or hypothyroidism—see *thyroid problems).* In most cases of psychosis caused by a temporary physical problem, the episode ends when the problem clears up or abates. Sometimes, however, full recovery is not possible until several weeks after the underlying problem is cured because the patient needs time to recover and readjust to reality.

Although many types of physical problems can lead to psychotic episodes, psychosis sometimes develops in the absence of such problems and lasts briefly or persists continuously or episodically for months or even years. Experts speculate that such psychoses involve biochemical abnormalities, which can be present at birth or acquired through problems such as *drug and alcohol abuse.*

It appears that some people's biochemical abnormalities lead only to temporary episodes of psychosis and only in the face of some sort of environmental trigger, such as a stressful situation. In rare cases, for example, older children develop psychotic symptoms such as hallucinations in response to stressful situations such as leaving home to go to college. Such "psychotic breaks" tend to be brief, lasting only a few days or weeks.

Other people seem to be born with such severe constitutional abnormalities that psychosis appears spontaneously at an early age and disabilities persist lifelong. The reason for this phenomenon is not clear. Experts are certain that environmental stress is never the sole factor, and no conclusive evidence exists that it plays any role at all when symptoms appear early in a child's life. Medical researchers continue to investigate the theory that genetic factors play a role in causing persistent psychosis.

DIAGNOSIS

A child may need to be seen several times over a period of weeks or even months by professionals such as a physician who specializes in developmental disorders, a child psychiatrist, as well as a neurologist (nervous system specialist), an otolaryngologist (ear, nose, and throat specialist), and a speech and language expert (speech and language "pathologist"). Diagnostic procedures are likely to include thorough physical and psychological examinations, lengthy observation of the child's behavior, intelligence testing, and hearing and language tests. The child may be hospitalized for various central nervous system tests.

If a psychotic child appears to have an underlying physical health problem, diagnostic procedures may focus on identification of the underlying cause. If parents have any doubts about a diagnosis—whether it is sufficiently accurate or thorough, for example—they should seek a second opinion. (See Chapter 3, "Promoting Mental Health.")

TREATMENT

Short-term episodes of psychosis caused by a physical health problem tend to disappear when the underlying problem does. Most affected children, however, need to talk with a mental health specialist—such as a psychiatrist, psychologist, or social worker —to sort through the psychotic episode. Usually only a few discussions are necessary, although some children may need weeks or months of therapy. Similarly, a child who experiences a psychotic break because of a stressful situation often requires short- or long-term psychotherapy. In some cases such children can also be helped by short- or long-term use of medications that compensate for suspected biochemical abnormalities.

PREVENTION

Short-term psychotic episodes related to underlying physical health problems can be prevented only insofar as the underlying problem can be prevented.

PSYCHOSOMATIC DISEASE AND SYMPTOMS

DESCRIPTION AND CAUSE

Diseases and symptoms are not caused simply by physical factors—bacterial or viral infection, for example—but can also be influenced by a person's thoughts, feelings, and environment. "Psychosomatic" refers simply to the influence of psychological and social factors on disease ("psycho-" is a prefix denoting the mind; "somatic" indicates a relationship with the body).

A common misperception is that the word "psychosomatic" means "faked" or "imaginary." For many, to say that a symptom is psychosomatic is the same as saying it is "all in Mary's head—she's not really sick." It is true that a few people persistently "fake" illness (a problem called <u>factitious illness,</u> which is extremely rare among children). It is also true that some people frequently interpret normal bodily functions or minor physical problems as signs of serious disease (called <u>hypochondriasis</u>; see *neurotic disorders).* Still others have symptoms of disease but no true underlying problem (<u>somatoform</u> disorders). However, these problems are not, per se, any more "psychosomatic" than other diseases. Even though the role of psychological factors in causing such problems may be high, "psychosomatic" does not mean "caused predominantly by psychological factors."

What are these factors? Why are some children virtually disease-free while others always seem to have *abdominal pain* or *headaches,* for example? Why do some children in stressful family situations seem to respond by becoming ill, while others do not? *Stress* on parents correlates with visits to the doctor by children. Factors such as death of close relatives, family moves, trouble at school, and poverty tend to increase both the number of illness episodes a child has and how often parents seek medical care for the child.

Some children seem unaffected by environmental stressors, while others are visibly affected. The reason for the difference is unclear, as are the consequences. There is some evidence that the child who shows little or no reaction is at risk for development of a conditon with a psychosomatic dimension.

Experts believe that the way people express feelings is influenced from a very early age by such things as the parent-child relationship, early childrearing practices, and general family harmony. Research also shows that some children are biologically more predisposed than others to experience physical problems as a result of psychological and social influences.

SIGNS AND SYMPTOMS AND TREATMENT

Because almost any illness can be affected by psychological and social factors, we can only give an example. Suppose a child has pains in the abdomen or frequent headaches. A physician concerned only with physical illness would take a history of the child's health and perform a physical examination. Appropriate laboratory tests, perhaps including X-ray studies, might be ordered and evaluated. The physician might then tell the parents that since the diagnostic tests proved negative, the child could resume ordinary activities. Any inquiry into the psychological dimensions of the child's—and the family's—life would be brief.

Using concepts from psychosomatic medicine, however, another physician might take a different tack. He or she would talk with the affected child or family members about how things are going at home and school. The physician would try to find out what each parent thinks about the child's problem. It is conceivable that the physician might find, for example, that an older sibling nearly died of acute appendicitis and that one or both parents are fearful that such a situation might happen again.

When a stressful situation as such is identified and seems to correlate strongly with the child's illness, the physician explores with the entire family ways of dealing and coping with the problem. Other sources of support, such as school officials, counselors, or community groups might also be identified.

PREVENTION

Symptoms that occur frequently need parents' prompt, sympathetic attention. If a child needs a symptom to express unexpressed feelings or to signal unmet needs, it may be an indication that parents have not paid adequate attention to the child's worries. Expressing sincere interest in a child's problems, listening to the child's own solutions, and offering suggestions can go a long way toward lessening a child's need to find more dramatic ways to ask for genuine care and loving attention.

A child who is hurting in either a physical or psychological sense needs and deserves to have care directed to his or her pain, in whatever form that pain is experienced. Parents who avoid opportunities to deal directly and compassionately with their child's underlying feelings are contributing to the problem.

The most effective way to prevent a child's psychosomatic illness is to create an atmosphere of trust so that the child feels free to talk about his or her concerns and fears with parents. All children have the right to expect their parents' attention and love. Children also deserve frequent chances to be heard and responded to. Deferring problems because parents are not an available or willing audience to a child's concerns can foster psychosomatic illness as well as make children unwilling to confide in parents regardless of the magnitude of the problem.

The child's pediatrician or a qualified counselor (psychologist, psychiatrist, or social worker) can often help parents by reviewing with them any of a child's problems that could have a significant psychosomatic dimension (see also Chapter 3, "Promoting Mental Health").

PUNCTURE WOUNDS AND SPLINTERS

EMERGENCY ACTION

Seek medical attention immediately for any wound deeper than it is long or wide—even a wound as small as the puncture made by a carpet tack or fishhook—if any doubt exists about a child's immunity against *tetanus*.

A physician also should be consulted immediately if

- a child is stabbed deeply or punctured in a vitally important area (such as an eye, the chest, a joint, the skull, or the abdomen) with a sharp object;
- a child has a deep wound or a foreign

object embedded in any part of the body where serious damage is possible;

- it is likely that dirt, bacteria, or any other potentially harmful material is lodged in the wound;
- a foreign object is embedded too deeply to be removed without significantly damaging surrounding tissue;
- a piece of metal or glass becomes partially or wholly embedded in the skin;
- any sign of infection, including redness, swelling, pus, fever, or *swollen glands,* accompanies a deep wound.

DESCRIPTION

When a foreign object pierces the skin and causes an injury deeper than it is long or wide, the injury is considered a puncture wound. The entry point of a puncture wound is usually relatively small, and the injury is deep and narrow. Diagnosis, treatment, and complications of puncture wounds vary greatly; the particulars of each case depend on the puncturing object and the extent of the injury.

A splinter injury occurs when foreign material becomes wholly or partially embedded in the flesh. If a splinter injury is deeper than it is long or wide, it is treated as a puncture wound after removal of the material. The same is true of a deeply embedded fishhook.

The main difference between puncture wounds and other broken-skin injuries (see *cuts and lacerations)* is that deep wounds are more difficult to clean thoroughly and therefore more likely to become infected. Tetanus-causing bacteria, for example, thrive in such dark, oxygen-deprived places as the depths of a puncture wound. Common folklore has it that tetanus is a possibility only if a puncture wound is caused by a dirty object found outdoors—such as a rusty nail, to give the most popular example. On the contrary, tetanus bacteria, which thrive almost universally in soil contaminated with animal feces, can find their way into a deep wound at any time before the injury heals.

CAUSE

Virtually anything that is capable of piercing the skin can cause a puncture wound. Most children's puncture wounds are caused by nails, needles, pins, knives, ice picks, animal fangs (see *animal bites; snake bites*), arrows, splinters (such as glass and wood slivers), and fishhooks.

DIAGNOSIS

Minor puncture wounds are distinguishable from other broken-skin injuries because of their relatively narrow surface openings and because they tend to bleed less than superficial wounds.

A puncture wound can almost always be identified on sight. For treatment purposes, however, it is helpful to gather as much information as possible about the puncturing object, any foreign material trapped inside the wound, and the extent of the injury.

Such details are useful to a physician consulted about a puncture wound. The physician may attempt to determine the extent of the wound by sight or touch, or with an X-ray film. Injuries to the joints, abdomen, chest, skull, eyes, connective tissue, and other vital areas may be explored surgically.

COMPLICATIONS

Punctures of any vital body part, including lungs, kidneys, and spinal cord, can be life-threatening. Puncture of joints such as the knee can lead to temporary or permanent loss of movement, such as an inability to extend a leg to a straight position.

Properly treated, less serious puncture wounds almost always heal without complication within days or weeks. Problems may arise, however, if an injury becomes infected (as with *tetanus).* Telltale signs and symptoms of an infected wound include swelling, pus, redness, and red streaks under the skin around the wound. Sometimes fever develops or nearby lymph nodes swell. If infection is not controlled, it can spread to other parts of the body and lead to complications such as *bloodstream infection. Osteomyelitis,* a painful bone infection, can develop if infection from a very deep puncture wound spreads.

TREATMENT

When a child gets a puncture wound, a physician should be consulted immediately if any doubt exists about the child's tetanus immunity, about the seriousness of the injury, or about the possibility of infection. If the child has not yet had 4 basic *tetanus* immunizations or has not had a tetanus booster in 5 years, tetanus vaccine is given immediately.

Minor-to-Serious Puncture Wounds

A minor puncture wound can be cleaned with soap and water, treated with an antiseptic, and covered with a bandage. Home treatment should not be employed, however, if medical attention is clearly necessary at the outset. Any wound to be seen by a physician should be covered with a clean (preferably sterile) cloth. If internal organs are punctured, as by a bullet or a knife, or if anesthesia may be needed before surgery for a deep wound, a child should not be given food, drink, or medication. Attempts should not be made to remove foreign material from the wound, because further damage could result.

Deeply embedded foreign material may be removed immediately—and possibly, surgically—by the physician. In some cases, though, the physician may want to wait and observe the wound for a few days to see if the material will work itself out. The physician may recommend that, in the meantime, the wound be soaked in a saltwater solution. A good saltwater solution can be made by dissolving 1 teaspoon of salt in 1 quart of boiling water and allowing the mixture to cool to body temperature (about 100° F; 38.1° C).

If the chances that a puncture wound will become infected seem high, a physician may prescribe antibiotics as a preventive measure.

Splinters

The classic splinter—a sliver of wood embedded just under the surface of the skin, for example—can be removed and treated at home. Whoever performs the procedure should have clean hands and should use sterile first aid materials only. After the injured area is washed with warm, soapy water, the splinter can be removed with sterilized tweezers or a sterilized sewing needle. A metal instrument can be sterilized by immersing it in boiling water for five minutes or by holding it in an open flame until red-hot. A sterilized instrument should be allowed to cool before use.

If a splinter is poking out from the skin, it should be pulled out with tweezers at the angle at which it is embedded. If a splinter is embedded just below the surface of the skin, the surrounding skin can be loosened gently with a needle and the splinter can then be removed with tweezers. After splinter removal, the wound should be washed again with soap and water, treated with an antiseptic, and covered with a bandage. If signs of infection appear, a physician should be consulted.

Some physicians believe it is safe to ignore certain splinters, allowing them to work their way out naturally. A minor wooden splinter that embeds itself in the thick skin of the foot, for example, may require no treatment. To guard against infection, however, it is probably best to consult a physician if any doubt exists about the cause or extent of a wound.

Fishhooks

Like minor splinters, minor fishhook injuries may not need medical attention. In general, a physician should be consulted if the barb (the jagged part ending in the point) of the hook is embedded anywhere in the child's body or if the fishhook seems to have caused significant damage. If a physician is not readily available, a fishhook injury should be treated as soon as possible by anyone knowledgeable about emergency first aid procedures or fishhook removal. If the hook is embedded in the face or an eye, however, it should NEVER be removed by anyone who is not a medical professional.

If only the point of a hook—and not the whole barb—has entered the skin, the hook can be removed by pulling it out slowly. If the barb is embedded just under the surface of the skin, it can be pushed through the skin by applying gentle pressure on the shank (straight part) of the hook. Once exposed, the barb should be cut off. The rest of the hook can then be pulled out carefully. The wound should be cleaned with soap and water, treated with an antiseptic, and covered with a bandage. If infection seems to be a possibility, a physician should be consulted as soon as possible.

PREVENTION

At one time or another most children receive minor puncture wounds or splinter injuries. Prompt and thorough treatment of these wounds often prevents the development of serious complications. The likelihood decreases that a child will receive a serious puncture wound if sharp objects such as knives, ice picks, and awls are kept out of reach. In addition, children should avoid going barefoot in areas that tend to have sharp objects littering the ground, such as construction sites or sanitary landfills.

Puncture Wounds and Splinters   **581**

PYLORIC STENOSIS

EMERGENCY ACTION

An infant may become dehydrated because of repeated vomiting. *Dehydration* is characterized by cool, pale, dry skin, dry tongue, thirst, listlessness, rapid pulse, decreased urine production, sunken eyes, and for an infant, sunken fontanel (the soft spot on top of a baby's head). Notify a physician or take the child to an emergency room. Intravenous fluids can correct dehydration by replacing essential body fluids and salts.

DESCRIPTION

The lower end of the stomach, where it joins and empties partially digested food into the small intestine, is called the pylorus (see Fig. 30, p. 437). Pyloric stenosis (severe narrowing of the pylorus) is a common disease of young infants that causes persistent, forceful *vomiting*, called "projectile vomiting."

Projectile vomiting seriously interferes with a baby's nutrition. Digestion and general health suffer. If not adequately and promptly treated, pyloric stenosis can develop into growth failure. If untreated, the problem can result in death.

Pyloric stenosis usually affects babies around the second or third week of life, although it can begin as early as the first week and as late as the second or third month. Males have the problem 5 times as often as females; about 1 out of every 150 males develops the problem. Pyloric stenosis can subside spontaneously, sometimes with the assistance of intravenous feedings and medications. Months of hospitalization may be required.

CAUSE

A band of smooth muscle, called the sphincter, surrounds the pylorus, controlling the flow of partially digested food from the bottom of the stomach into the beginning of the small intestine. Sometimes, for unknown reasons, the pyloric sphincter is much more powerful than normal.

As the infant feeds, the stomach slowly fills. Passage of partially digested food into the small intestine is slowed or blocked by the enlarged pyloric sphincter, which narrows the pylorus. Since food cannot move down, it is either spit up (regurgitated) or *vomited* forcefully by the infant. Vomiting

usually does not occur until the stomach is fairly full, and then it may happen suddenly. Since the sphincter is very strong, vomiting almost always occurs with great force. Projectile vomiting can travel 3 feet or more.

Vomiting usually occurs during or immediately after feeding, but sometimes it may occur as long as an hour afterward. If vomiting is prolonged, contents of the stomach may be tinged pink, light tan, or brown, indicating the presence of blood as a result of irritation of the esophagus, the passageway that connects the stomach to the throat.

Other signs include wavelike bulges moving across the upper abdomen from left to right (as the stomach pushes repeatedly against the pyloric muscle), weight loss, lethargy, decreased skin elasticity, and irritability. *Dehydration,* excessive loss of body fluids and salts, can occur after repeated vomiting.

DIAGNOSIS

Pyloric stenosis is diagnosed by a physician who listens to the history of projectile vomiting and observes a child's physical condition. The physician can usually feel an enlarged pyloric sphincter muscle in the upper abdomen. If the lump is difficult to locate, an X-ray film may be taken of the child's stomach.

COMPLICATIONS

Yellowing of the skin *(jaundice)* and other complications of abnormal liver function including decreased blood sugar *(hypoglycemia)* may develop if pyloric stenosis is not treated. Infants who vomit repeatedly lose weight and fail to grow properly.

TREATMENT

Surgical treatment is almost always successful in providing immediate and permanent cure of pyloric stenosis. A simple operation splits the enlarged sphincter, thereby freeing the pinched pylorus. The infant is then able to resume feeding as soon as 4 to 6 hours after surgery.

Complications following this surgery are rare. They may be related to *dehydration* or an infant's accidentally inhaling contents of the stomach. In special cases, when anesthesia or possible blood loss could prove life-threatening, a physician may try nonsurgical treatment. Medical approaches include giving small feedings, maintaining an upright position for an hour or more after feeding, checking for stomach bloating, using mild sedatives, and providing intravenous feedings (parenteral nutrition). These medical approaches may require from 2 to 8 months before vomiting subsides and food can pass easily out of the stomach.

Few American physicians prescribe a medical approach, as it is much slower, more difficult for parents, and less certain for the child. Surgery is swift and effective in restoring full health. There also are fewer deaths from surgery—less than 1 percent—than from the medical approaches just described.

PREVENTION
Pyloric stenosis cannot be prevented.

RABIES

EMERGENCY ACTION
Prompt treatment of a bite from a rabid animal (or one suspected of being rabid) and immunization through a series of injections can halt the development or spread of infection. It is a lifesaving measure. If a child is bitten by an animal that may be rabid, seek medical aid immediately and try to identify or capture the suspect animal.

DESCRIPTION
Rabies (its root means "to rage") is a severe infection of the central nervous system (the brain, spinal cord, and their tough covering membranes, the meninges). When an infected, or rabid, animal bites another animal, the wound is contaminated by infectious saliva. Any human bitten by a rabid, warm-blooded animal can become infected with rabies. It is one of the most feared infections in the world, because nearly every untreated victim dies.

Rabies vaccination of dogs is required nearly everywhere in the United States, so the disease does not often occur in humans. Just a few cases are confirmed in North America annually. Rabies remains a hazard, however, because of the large numbers of wild animals that are potential carriers of the disease in North America.

Rabies primarily affects the brain. In most cases the inflammatory process destroys brain cells, causing permanent damage. Death usually follows.

Illness may begin as early as 9 days following exposure to rabies virus, but 30 to 60 days usually elapse before symptoms become evident. The closer the bite is to the brain of the victim, the shorter the time until symptoms begin.

After a human has been bitten by an animal possibly infected by rabies, prompt treatment of the bite and immunization through a series of injections can halt the development or spread of the infection. Once signs and symptoms appear, however, nothing can be done to halt the progression of the disease. If the animal cannot be caught and its tissue tested for rabies, immunization is carried out on the bite victim, just to be on the safe side.

CAUSE
Rabies is caused by the rabies virus. Dogs are the principal carriers of this virus in Central and South America, Africa, and Asia, but in North America most rabies is carried and transmitted by common wild animals such as raccoons, skunks, foxes, and bats. Very few cases of bites from rabid bats, however, have been confirmed. On rare occasions droppings from infected bats might carry sufficient virus to cause infection, particularly when airborne in an enclosed place such as a cave. Rabies can also be carried by domestic cats, infected by wild animals while outdoors.

Rabies virus infects the salivary glands, and the saliva is thereby contaminated. As soon as a bite occurs, rabies virus is passed on in saliva. Rabies virus can also be conveyed by a rabid pet's licking or scratching a child, or from contact with the animal's feces. A dog, cat, raccoon, fox, or skunk almost always becomes ill and dies within 10 days of being infected. Outdoors, a wild animal that appears to be friendly may be rabid, since one of the first symptoms of animal rabies is the loss of fear of people. Because wild animal behavior is so difficult for non-experts to interpret accurately, unprovoked bites by wild animals must be assumed to contain rabies until proved otherwise.

Among dogs, rabid behavior is of two types: furious and paralytic (or dumb). The furious type is characterized by *fever,* great excitement, and aggressive behavior. Agitation is followed by restlessness, then snapping at imaginary objects, and biting other animals. In the depths of illness, a furiously rabid dog goes into a continuous snapping and biting fit until it finally collapses.

The paralytic type of rabies progresses much more quickly. Paralysis occurs, especially in the lower jaw. The dog's tongue then hangs out as it foams at the mouth, with infected saliva dripping continuously. General paralysis sets in swiftly, followed by death.

SIGNS AND SYMPTOMS

The preliminary phase of human rabies infection is marked by mild *fever,* listlessness, *headache,* loss of appetite, and *vomiting.* Pain, numbness, or tingling at the wound is typical. Brain inflammation progresses as the infection develops into either furious or paralytic rabies.

Rabies has been called hydrophobia ("fear of water"). One type of the disease can cause muscle spasms in the throat, which make it impossible for a rabies victim to swallow liquids of any kind, even saliva. Attempts to drink almost always end in choking, because liquids are inhaled unintentionally and forced into the windpipe by muscle spasms.

As *encephalitis* (inflammation of the brain) increases, bizarre, combative, or feverish activity alternates with intervals of rational behavior. Convulsions are common. Within 10 days of the start of brain inflammation, heart or breathing failure usually causes death. Victims who do not die of heart and breathing arrest usually lapse into an irreversible coma. Because of worsening complications, it is unlikely that rabies victims can recover after being in a coma for as long as 2 weeks.

DIAGNOSIS

A physician can usually make an accurate diagnosis on the basis of a patient's (1) having been bitten by a warm-blooded animal, (2) reporting pain, numbness, and tingling around the wound, and (3) developing *encephalitis.* If doubt still exists, specialized laboratory tests can isolate rabies virus from saliva, spinal fluid, or urine.

TREATMENT

Prompt treatment of a bite by a rabid animal and immunization through a series of injections can halt the development or spread of infection. The injections must be started <u>before</u> the first symptom appears. The site is first thoroughly cleaned, including irrigation of tooth puncture wounds. The wound is usually left open to the air after cleaning. Second, if the animal is found or suspected to be rabid, the child is given human rabies immune globulin, half injected at the site of the wound, half into the arm or buttocks. Third, injections of 1 or 2 active vaccines are given, 5, 6, or 7 times, over the next 2 to 8 weeks, depending upon the age of the victim. Allergic reactions to the vaccine are unusual, but side effects such as low fever, listlessness, and muscle pain affect about one third of all vaccine recipients.

If symptoms begin, treatment of rabies takes place in a hospital, usually in intensive care. The victim is made as comfortable and free of pain as possible. Although a few victims have recovered from rabies, generally successful treatment has not been developed.

PREVENTION

Vaccination of dogs has all but eliminated land-based rabies from most urban and suburban areas in the United States, but any warm-blooded animal—especially a raccoon, skunk, or fox—that bites a human should be checked. If a child is bitten by a dog, the animal's rabies vaccination record must be verified. Raccoons living in urban and suburban areas have been known to acquire rabies, and parents should warn children about this possible danger. Children should never play with any strange wild animal that appears tame or friendly. Wild animals, including wild dogs, that have bitten children must be caught and killed if possible so that a laboratory test of brain tissue can determine whether rabies is present.

RASH

DESCRIPTION AND CAUSE

A rash is a passing skin eruption. The eruption may consist of itchy or nonitchy red or purple spots, red or purple bumps, or fluid-filled blisters. Rashes affect children of all ages and may develop anywhere. Rashes may affect only the skin, or they may indicate underlying illness.

Skin rashes may be accompanied by sores inside the mouth or genitals. This may occur with bacterial and viral infections, and reactions to medicines.

Harmless Rashes of Childhood

Heat Rash Heat rash (also called prickly heat or summer rash) consists of tiny crystalline blisters or small red bumps. Heat rash occurs when there is excessive sweating after the sweat pores become blocked, often following sunburn or other rash. Heat rash is particularly common when children perspire excessively, such as during hot, humid weather or when suffering a fever. Heat rash most often develops on a child's chest, stomach, and back, and is usually accompanied by mild itching and stinging.

Diaper Rash A diaper rash is a skin irritation, infection, or skin disease in the diaper area. Common causes of diaper rash include yeast infection, irritation from stool or urine, *seborrheic dermatitis, psoriasis,* and *eczema.*

Toxic Erythema of the Newborn Toxic erythema of the newborn is a common, temporary rash that develops during the first several days after birth. Its cause is not known. In its early stages the rash is composed of flat red spots that soon become raised and yellow. Spots may be few or number in the dozens. The rash usually disappears in 10 to 14 days.

Rashes Associated with Underlying Conditions

Rashes Caused by Infections Congenital *German measles* (rubella), a viral infection, produces a "blueberry muffin" rash at birth which is composed of purple spots. Other viral infections such as *chicken pox* and *genital herpes* produce rashes that start as red spots and turn into blisters that may be filled with clear fluid or pus.

Other viral infections producing rashes include *measles;* infectious *mononucleosis;* and *hand, foot, and mouth disease.* These rashes are composed of colored spots, colored bumps, or tiny blisters.

Scarlet fever, bacterial endocarditis, *impetigo,* and *Rocky Mountain spotted fever* produce rashes of diffuse redness, blisters, colored spots, or colored bumps, which may be accompanied by bleeding under the skin and bruises. Congenital *syphilis* may produce erosions and blisters at birth, particularly on the palms of the hands and the soles of the feet and in the genital area. Acquired syphilis may produce red spots in the skin, particularly the palms and soles. Among adolescents, *toxic shock syndrome* may cause a rash, due to a toxin produced by staphylococcus.

Rashes can also be caused by parasitic infections, such as toxoplasmosis (see *pets, diseases caused by),* and fungal infections, such as *thrush* and *ringworm.* Toxoplasmosis produces a rash of flat, red spots. Thrush ap-

pears as yellowish white spots in the mouth of a nursing child. Ringworm produces a round, red area with raised edges and a scaling border.

Rashes Caused by Allergies Rashes may appear when a child has an allergic reaction to foods (see *food allergy),* medications, plants (see *poison ivy, oak, and sumac),* or insect venom (see *stinging insect reactions).* Allergic rashes may be composed of blisters, colored spots, or colored bumps (see *hives)* which may be accompanied by bruising. Rashes caused by reactions to ingested substances usually appear on many parts of the body, whereas those produced by contact with plants develop at the point of contact.

Rashes Caused by Insect Bites Rashes caused by insect bites can be composed of spots, blisters, or bumps; bleeding under the skin may be present. The bite or sting of *lice,* mosquitoes, fleas, bees, and wasps (see *stinging insect reactions)* may cause a rash. The rash associated with *scabies* develops as an "allergic" reaction to the mite burrowing in the skin.

DIAGNOSIS

Rashes are obvious. If the cause cannot be determined according to a child's recent activities or health, a physician should be consulted for diagnosis. Diagnosis is made on the basis of the type of rash present, a physical examination, a child's medical history, and laboratory tests.

COMPLICATIONS

If heat rash is extensive, sweat output may be decreased, reducing the body's ability to cool the skin through evaporation and causing body temperature to rise. Cooling the skin by gentle, lukewarm tap water, sponge baths, and a fan may be useful.

If a child scratches a rash, the skin may become broken, susceptible to infection by bacteria.

TREATMENT

A rash cannot be eliminated until the underlying cause is treated. Itching and stinging can be eased, however, with cool compresses, cool baths, or calamine lotion. A physician may prescribe an antibiotic if a child's skin has become infected from scratching.

Treatment of heat rash includes reducing environmental temperature and humidity, usually with a fan or air conditioner; lowering skin and body temperature with cool compresses or baths; using drying preparations; and lightweight (preferably cotton), absorbent clothing. When possible, a child should go without clothes to allow maximum exposure to air. Consult the physician for specific recommendations.

(See also *allergies; diaper rash;* and entries on specific infections and illnesses.)

PREVENTION

Rashes can be prevented only if underlying conditions and causes can be prevented.

RECTAL ITCHING

DESCRIPTION AND CAUSE

Rectal itching is common among people of all ages and is usually secondary to irritation and swelling of the rectum (the last segment of the large intestine) or the anus (the external opening of the rectum). A variety of injuries and conditions can cause rectal and anal irritation, including *pinworm* infestation, skin irritation (often from coarse underwear, underwear made of nonporous materials such as nylon, or wet diapers), and anal fissures (surface tears in the anal canal often caused by the passage of hard stool or diarrhea).

DIAGNOSIS

A child with rectal itching usually complains. If a cause is not obvious, a physician should be consulted for diagnosis. Diagnosis is based on examination of a child's anus and rectum and the child's medical history.

TREATMENT AND PREVENTION

Treatment and prevention of rectal itching involves removal of the source of irritation. The anal area should be washed regularly with mild soap and water, and dried with a soft towel. Drying preparations, such as mild, unscented powder, preferably cornstarch, can be applied to absorb moisture. An infant's diaper should be changed often to prevent accumulation of moisture. Young children should wear soft, white cotton underwear to allow air to reach the skin. When possible, an infant or young child should go without diapers or underpants to maximize exposure to air. Pinworm infestation is treated with antiparasite medications prescribed by a physician.

Treatment of anal fissures includes warm baths and application of drying preparations. If pain is severe, numbing ointments can be applied. A physician may recommend oral doses of mineral or olive oil to soften stool, ease bowel movements, and avoid increased pressure in the anus. If healing does not occur within several weeks, a child may have ulcerative *colitis* or *Crohn's disease* and a physician should be consulted for appropriate diagnosis and treatment.

RECTAL PROLAPSE

DESCRIPTION

Rectal prolapse is the sagging of the mucous membrane lining of the rectum, usually resulting in its protrusion out of the anus (partial prolapse). If prolapse is severe, all layers of the rectal lining may sag (complete prolapse). Partial prolapse is most common among children less than 3, particularly during the first year of life. It may be the first indication that the child has a problem in the gastrointestinal tract (esophagus, stomach, and intestines), most commonly a *malabsorption* syndrome in which the stools are large in size.

Rectal prolapse usually develops gradually; the rectal lining weakens a little each time a child passes stool. When prolapse first occurs, the membrane goes back up into the rectum spontaneously once stool is passed. After repeated cases of prolapse, however, the membrane must be pushed back by hand. If the cause of rectal prolapse is not corrected, recurrent episodes may result in loss of control of bowel movements.

CAUSE

Some children develop rectal prolapse when abdominal pressure increases suddenly, such as when a child strains to move the bowels when constipated. Children with long-term gastrointestinal problems, such as *celiac disease, parasitic infections, cystic fibrosis* (considered the most common cause of rectal prolapse), *diarrhea,* or *polyps* are prone to rectal prolapse because the pelvic muscles are weakened by constant straining during bowel movements.

SIGNS AND SYMPTOMS

Signs and symptoms of rectal prolapse include soreness around the anus, bleeding from the anus, and passage of mucus in stool. The protruding mucous membrane varies in color from bright to dark red, and may be up to 6 inches in length. It may also be swollen and painful.

DIAGNOSIS

Rectal prolapse is obvious. Underlying gastrointestinal conditions can usually be detected by a physician through a physical examination and laboratory tests. A child's medical history may be helpful in making a diagnosis.

TREATMENT AND PREVENTION

In most cases, rectal prolapse corrects itself as a child's muscles mature. While a young child's muscles are maturing, treatment focuses on preventing buildup of abdominal pressure. If a child is constipated, fiber (such as bran and other cereals) and roughage (such as fruits and vegetables) should be added to the diet. If necessary, a child can be given stool softeners to ease constipation. To avoid constipation, children should be encouraged to move their bowels whenever they feel the urge (see Chapter 2, "Promoting Physical Health"). If underlying gastrointestinal conditions are present, they must be corrected before rectal prolapse can be treated. If rectal prolapse is severe or long-term, surgery may be required to prevent sagging of the rectum.

RESPIRATORY DISTRESS SYNDROME

DESCRIPTION

Respiratory distress syndrome (RDS) is a condition that causes *breathing difficulty* in a newborn infant. Nearly always, RDS (also called hyaline membrane disease) is a complication of premature birth.

At birth, every infant must start functioning independently from his or her mother. No longer attached to the placenta, the infant must assume vital functions such as breathing.

Premature babies, however, may not be fully developed at birth, and may be unable to breathe effectively on their own, since their lungs are underdeveloped. Immature lungs expand incompletely and with difficulty and will not stay as fully open between breaths as will normal lungs. The alveoli (air sacks) of lungs that are immature have an insufficient amount of a normal chemical coating called surfactant. Without enough surfactant, the alveoli collapse at the end of each breath. Collapsed alveoli cannot adequately provide oxygen for the blood or rid the blood of carbon dioxide. Because of this lack of surfactant, an abnormal material enters the alveoli and appears as a hyaline (transparent) membrane under the microscope. Hence the name hyaline membrane disease. This condition causes the premature infant extreme breathing distress.

About 20 percent of all premature infants suffer from RDS; over 60 percent of babies born after less than 32 weeks of pregnancy are RDS victims. The more premature the infant, the greater the severity of RDS. Male babies suffer from RDS twice as often as female babies, and the second-born of twins is more vulnerable to RDS.

Prenatal *asphyxia* may contribute to a decrease in the production of surfactant. Infants of diabetic mothers, especially those babies born after less than 37 weeks of pregnancy, are more susceptible to RDS, as are babies delivered by cesarean section before the onset of labor.

In mild to moderate cases of RDS improvement is evident after 3 to 5 days, when the hyaline membrane may begin to disappear and the infant seems to be capable of producing enough surfactant. The outlook in these cases is good for complete recovery with little likelihood of developmental delays or long-term lung problems. Even in severe cases infants may recover completely. The turning point seems to come after the third day of life; if an infant can survive that long, the outlook for recovery is generally good.

Before 1970 nearly half of all premature babies with RDS died. Today approximately 90 percent survive, and less than 15 percent suffer severe developmental delays. Yet RDS is still the leading cause of death among newborns, especially premature infants, in the United States. Half of all deaths of newborn babies are due to RDS or its complications.

CAUSE

The chief cause of RDS is a deficiency of surfactant (due to underdeveloped lungs). Immature lungs are generally a result of prematurity. In those rare cases when the infant is full-term, the mode of delivery is vaginal, and the mother does not have *diabetes,* the cause of underdevelopment is often unknown.

SIGNS AND SYMPTOMS
AND DIAGNOSIS

Signs and symptoms of RDS include progressive *breathing difficulty* observable within a few hours of birth; rapid, shallow breathing; chest retractions; grunting when exhaling; flaring of the nostrils; and an increasingly bluish tint to the skin. Other signs may include low blood pressure, low body temperature, increasing fatigue leading to irregular breathing or *apnea* (prolonged pauses in breathing), and paleness. X-ray films of the chest will reveal a typical pattern of abnormality associated with RDS.

COMPLICATIONS

RDS causes serious biochemical imbalances. Acidosis (an accumulation of acid), an excess of carbon dioxide, and a reduction of oxygen supply to the bloodstream and body tissues are common complications of this condition. Other complications of RDS may include *pneumonia, apnea,* or cardiac arrest from lack of oxygen. Brain damage due to oxygen deficiency used to be a common complication of RDS in surviving infants; if severe enough, it still may lead to *cerebral palsy* or other developmental disabilities.

Severe cases of RDS may be complicated by patent ductus arteriosus (see *heart disease, congenital),* brain hemorrhage, or chronic lung disease.

TREATMENT

Ideally, treatment for RDS begins even before the birth of the baby. If a woman goes into labor prematurely, the fetus's lung maturity can be assessed. If necessary, the mother can be given medication to stop or slow labor while she also receives medication that stimulates the production of surfactant in the fetus. Within 1 to 3 days a surfactant-stimulating steroid speeds the unborn baby's development of surfactant. This treatment method has greatly improved premature infants' chances of survival. In cases where labor cannot be delayed, infants suffering from RDS are best treated in special intensive care units for newborns.

The first priority for a newborn with RDS is to stabilize breathing. Oxygen is administered. In severe cases a procedure called continuous positive airway pressure, which keeps the alveoli open at all times, is used. This pressure is administered via a tube placed into the trachea (main breathing tube). Circulatory insufficiency is corrected, and *acidosis* is treated with intravenous fluids that also provide nutrition and prevent dehydration. The infant is kept warm in an incubator and is monitored for heart and breathing rates, blood pressure, temperature, and oxygen level in the blood. Many infants require mechanical ventilation for a few days, and some for longer periods.

Infants' lungs have a remarkable capacity to heal, and full recovery of the lungs in babies with RDS can be expected unless complications of the disease or its treatment occur.

Prolonged administration of oxygen, along with other factors, sometimes causes retrolental fibroplasia (a retina problem of *prematurity),* which, if severe, can lead to *blindness* in very premature infants with RDS. Oxygen levels are carefully determined during oxygen administration in efforts to prevent retrolental fibroplasia. Before an infant who has been given oxygen leaves the hospital, an ophthalmologist (a physician who specializes in eye and vision problems) checks the baby's eyes for any signs of retrolental fibroplasia.

From 80 to 90 percent of premature infants over 3.3 pounds recover from RDS. The most premature or ill infants who have required oxygen and mechanical ventilation for a long period of time, however, may develop a chronic lung disease called bronchopulmonary dysplasia (BPD). BPD is characterized by damage to the tissues of the lungs and to the larger air passages leading to them. Unfortunately, as BPD progresses, affected infants need increased breathing support, which may compound lung damage. The earlier an infant is started on assisted ventilation, and the sooner he or she is weaned from breathing support, the better the chances of survival without complications. Special feedings, including calcium and vitamin E, are given, as well as medications to assist the heart and kidneys.

About 10 percent of infants with BPD die from cardiopulmonary disease within a year of birth (yet RDS is a more dangerous disease). For 1 to 3 years, children who have had BPD and who have survived may have an increased susceptibility to other lung diseases, which can cause rapid breathing and wheezing. Although most infants with BPD appear normal after the ages of 3 to 5, pulmonary function studies still reveal the presence of abnormalities. What this means through adulthood is unknown.

PREVENTION

The key to preventing RDS is to prevent *prematurity*. Not all cases of premature birth can as yet be prevented, but the risk can be decreased through adequate prenatal care and the elimination of cigarettes and drugs (including alcohol) during pregnancy. Careful monitoring of high-risk pregnancies can also help lower the likelihood of premature delivery. High-risk pregnancies include teenage pregnancies, those complicated by maternal medical problems, and those of women who already have had a baby affected by RDS. Avoidance of unnecessary or poorly timed cesarean sections can also help prevent cases of RDS.

Monitoring the fetus during childbirth can help prevent asphyxia; if fetal *asphyxia* does develop, physicians will deliver the baby promptly and administer oxygen.

Although great advances in the treatment of RDS babies have occurred in recent years, more improvements seem likely. Research is being done on the production of artificial surfactant, on the uses of high-frequency ventilation, and on the development of mechanisms for control of an infant's breathing.

RETINOBLASTOMA

DESCRIPTION

Retinoblastoma, a highly malignant tumor of the retina (the rear portion of the eye, which receives light rays; see Fig. 23, p. 362), is the most common eye *cancer* among children and young infants. The tumor, usually congenital (present at birth), almost always becomes apparent by the time the child is 18 months old. Retinoblastoma occurs once in 14,000 births. The disease affects males and females equally. The number of cases of retinoblastoma has increased since more victims of this hereditary cancer now survive and transmit the tumor to their children (see *genetic disorders*).

While nearly 65 percent of children with retinoblastoma have tumors in just one eye, the remaining 35 percent of cases have tumors in both eyes. The tumor originates in the retina, may spread inside the eyeball and, if untreated, to the brain and throughout the body.

Early diagnosis and treatment of retinoblastoma can save a child's life and vision. New cancer therapies have dramatically increased the survival and cure rates of children with retinoblastoma. The survival rate of treated children with useful vision in the United States and England now exceeds 85 percent. In developing countries, however, where early detection is not likely and modern treatments are not available, retinoblastoma is nearly always fatal.

CAUSE

Retinoblastoma appears most often without a prior family history of the tumor because of a spontaneous gene mutation. In other cases, the gene responsible for this disease can be passed on to children by their parents who usually also have the disorder. About half the children whose parents have survived retinoblastoma in both eyes and a smaller percentage of the children whose parents have a tumor in one eye inherit the defective gene. More than half of those children who suffer from the 13q minus syndrome, a very rare chromosomal disorder characterized by *mental retardation,* also develop retinoblastoma (see *genetic disorders*).

SIGNS AND SYMPTOMS

The most common sign of retinoblastoma during childhood is the development of a "cat's eye," in which the pupil takes on a whitish cast because of the presence of the tumor in the retina. Another indication may be the child's sudden development of cross-eyes (see *cross-eyes* and *walleyes*). Less frequently, the child may experience pain in the eye.

DIAGNOSIS

After observing a cat's eye and cross-eyes or learning of a family history of retinoblastoma, an ophthalmologist (eye specialist) carefully examines the back portion of the child's eyeball with a lighted instrument called an ophthalmoscope. If retinoblastoma is diagnosed, samples of the child's bone marrow and cerebrospinal fluid (the fluid that bathes the brain and spinal cord) are analyzed for the presence of cancerous cells (see *cancer*).

COMPLICATIONS

Carriers of the retinoblastoma gene are also vulnerable to the development of other cancers. A few of the survivors of hereditary retinoblastoma may develop osteosarcoma, a type of *bone cancer.*

TREATMENT

Treatment focuses on preserving life and saving as much vision as possible. Treatment usually involves the combined efforts of the ophthalmologist, an oncologist (cancer specialist), a radiation therapist, and the pediatrician.

Radiation therapy often proves highly effective in destroying tumor cells while preserving vision. It is still often necessary, unfortunately, to remove the affected eye with surgery. About 6 weeks after the operation, the child is fitted for an artificial eye. As the child grows, artificial eyes must be adjusted periodically.

PREVENTION

Parents and other individuals who have had retinoblastoma should receive genetic counseling to learn about the risks of their transmitting retinoblastoma to their offspring (see Genetic Counseling section of *genetic disorders).*

REYE'S SYNDROME

EMERGENCY ACTION

Seek immediate medical attention if a child with *chicken pox, influenza,* or other viral infection displays any of these symptoms 2 to 7 days after becoming ill:

- forceful *vomiting*
- drowsiness
- hallucinations
- *delirium*
- unusually aggressive, uncooperative behavior

A link may exist between a child's being given aspirin and the subsequent development of Reye's syndrome. Do not give aspirin to children who have chicken pox or influenza.

DESCRIPTION

Reye's syndrome is a serious, noncontagious illness characterized initially by rapid deterioration of liver function (and to a lesser extent, other organs) and encephalopathy (brain disease leading to bizarre behavior and *coma).* This syndrome is one of the most common causes of encephalopathy in children. Reye's seems to occur most frequently during the winter months, usually affecting children from the age of 1 year through adolescence. It develops as a child recovers from a viral infection such as *chicken pox* or *influenza* and rapidly becomes severe; it can be fatal.

When liver function deteriorates, the ammonia-processing capabilities of liver cells are damaged. As a result, ammonia accumulates and eventually passes into the bloodstream and the brain. Liver deterioration is accompanied by the accumulation of fat in liver cells, liver enlargement, and loss of normal function.

Reye's syndrome affects other organs besides the liver, including the heart (which develops an irregular beat—*arrhythmia)* and the kidneys (which excrete increased amounts of amino acids into the urine). In addition, muscles and the pancreas may be affected.

Eventually liver and other organ malfunctioning contribute to fluid imbalance. As a result, fluid accumulates in brain cells, leading to a pressure increase within the skull. This condition interferes with normal brain function, and deep coma results.

Because Reye's syndrome progresses quickly, early diagnosis and treatment are crucial. Children with mild cases of Reye's frequently recover fully—often within 5 to 7 days—although mild speech and learning disabilities may result. Often, however, severe cases cannot be successfully treated, and permanent brain damage can result. Approximately 20 to 30 percent of children with severe Reye's syndrome die as a result of extensive brain damage.

CAUSE

The cause of Reye's syndrome is unknown.

SIGNS AND SYMPTOMS

Forceful *vomiting* (lasting a few hours to a few days) beginning as a child recovers from a minor viral infection usually indicates the onset of Reye's syndrome. Vomiting is often accompanied by *fever* (101°–103° F; 38.3°–39.4° C) and *headache.*

Shortly after the onset of vomiting, the

first signs of encephalopathy appear. Initially, the child is drowsy or confused. The child usually has a rapid heartbeat and dilated pupils. Hyperventilation (fast, deep breathing) is also common.

As Reye's syndrome progresses, encephalopathy affects other parts of the brain and the child's behavior grows more extreme. Hallucinations, restlessness, irritability, sudden violent movements or outbursts, and combativeness are typical signs of extensive encephalopathy.

As encephalopathy continues to become worse, the child loses control of voluntary and involuntary responses (reflexes or reactions to pain, for example). The child goes into a *coma;* eventually all responses disappear and death may occur.

DIAGNOSIS

Early diagnosis of Reye's syndrome is crucial: it can save a child's life.

Reye's syndrome is usually suspected by a physician if characteristic symptoms of encephalopathy follow a viral infection and *vomiting.* Before Reye's syndrome can be diagnosed, however, other causes of encephalopathy, such as ingestion of household chemicals or overdoses of medication, must be ruled out.

Positive identification of Reye's syndrome is based on the presence of encephalopathy and liver function abnormalities. If a blood test shows increased levels of ammonia in the bloodstream, Reye's syndrome must be suspected. A liver biopsy (analysis of a liver tissue sample) will detect increased fat content and abnormalities of the liver cell. A physician also checks for enlargement of the child's liver. An electroencephalogram (EEG) is used to detect unusual brain wave patterns indicative of encephalopathy.

COMPLICATIONS

Many body processes malfunction as a result of Reye's syndrome and contribute to the severity of encephalopathy. These include *hypoglycemia,* increased fluid in the brain leading to increased pressure within the skull, very low blood pressure, and hypoxia.

TREATMENT

Because of the speed with which Reye's syndrome can progress, early treatment is crucial.

There is no known cure for Reye's syndrome. Treatment focuses on preventing the child from becoming dangerously ill while the syndrome runs its course. Even mild cases of Reye's require hospitalization. Intensive care, involving monitoring of all bodily functions and vital signs, is essential for treatment of severe cases.

Since the most severe and damaging effects of Reye's syndrome result from a drastic increase in pressure within the skull, intracranial pressure is generally monitored. A pressure gauge is surgically inserted into a child's skull; pressure in the skull can then be carefully watched.

The next step is to prevent sudden changes in or to relieve pressure in the skull. This is done by controlling fluid levels throughout the body. Tubes (catheters) are inserted into specific blood vessels to control the flow of fluids, particularly through the brain. As fluid volume is controlled, swelling of blood vessels and brain cells diminishes and pressure within the skull is controlled.

If pressure within the skull increases, a physician recommends other fluid-control methods. Large doses of medications or, in extreme cases, surgery may aid elimination of fluid from the brain.

Intensive care procedures may include exchange blood transfusions (exchanging a child's blood supply for an entirely new supply) to reduce ammonia levels. Efforts to restore liver function include giving increased amounts of sugar intravenously. Antacid medications are given to help prevent development of stomach ulcers.

Oral antibiotics may be given to reduce the number of ammonia-producing bacteria in the gastrointestinal tract. Since Reye's prevents the breakdown of ammonia in the liver, reduction of these bacteria is essential to lessen the amount of ammonia passing into the bloodstream.

PREVENTION

Reye's syndrome presently cannot be prevented.

RH AND ABO INCOMPATIBILITY

DESCRIPTION

Rh factor is an inherited substance commonly found on the red blood cell. People who have the Rh factor in their blood are referred to as "Rh positive." Those who lack this factor are called "Rh negative." Approximately 85 percent of Caucasians, 93 percent of blacks, and 99 percent of Asians are Rh positive.

When a pregnant woman has Rh-negative blood and her unborn baby has Rh-positive blood, the potential for Rh incompatibility exists. In the past, although 15 percent of Caucasian women were Rh negative, only 3 percent of them had an Rh problem with their infants. Until the 1960s such Rh incompatibility commonly led to erythroblastosis, a serious blood disease that leads to severe *anemia* and *jaundice* in newborns. Rh incompatibility is now detectable early in pregnancy, and severe erythroblastosis is generally preventable.

Erythroblastosis occurs only if large numbers of the fetus's red blood cells cross from the placenta to the mother, and this takes place most often during birth (or miscarriage or abortion). When enough of a fetus's Rh-positive red blood cells enter the mother's Rh-negative bloodstream, the mother's immune system recognizes the Rh factor in the fetus's blood as foreign to her system and begins building up antibodies, which can then cross the placenta and destroy the fetus's red blood cells in subsequent pregnancies. When a large number of red blood cells are destroyed, the fetus becomes anemic (see *anemia, hemolytic*). Immediately after birth, such an infant's blood will contain excessive concentrations of bilirubin (a yellow pigment that is a waste product of red blood cells), and *jaundice* becomes evident.

During a woman's first pregnancy it is very rare that enough antibody production will have been stimulated to harm her fetus (unless a mother inadvertently had a prior transfusion of Rh-positive blood). However, when a woman has been sensitized by her first pregnancy, unless preventive measures are taken, subsequent Rh-positive fetuses may encounter antibodies in harmful quantities. (Antibodies increase in number with each pregnancy). Usually a mother's first infant is unaffected by Rh incompatibility, but at the time of delivery a significant possibility exists that some of her baby's Rh-positive cells will leak across the placenta into her bloodstream, thereby triggering the potential for future incompatibility.

Severity of erythroblastosis varies with the number of red blood cells destroyed. A woman's immune system may react mildly or destructively to the red blood cells of all of her Rh-positive babies.

Erythroblastosis used to lead to many miscarriages (unintentional delivery of a fetus before 20 weeks of pregnancy) or stillbirths, and some of the surviving infants suffered severe illness. Today the incidence of the disease has decreased greatly because of new diagnostic tests and prevention. In 1962 amniocentesis (removal of some amniotic fluid for testing) was begun for the detection of Rh incompatibility. New treatments can prevent the disease or reduce its severity when it does occur. The trend toward fewer children per family has helped reduce both the incidence and severity of the disease.

A related, more common, but far less serious condition is ABO blood incompatibility, in which the mother most commonly has type O blood and the fetus has type A or B. It can occur with a mother's first pregnancy. Approximately 25 percent of pregnancies result in possible ABO incompatibility, but only 10 percent of these cases lead to recognizable, usually mild, erythroblastosis. The disease occurs only if an unusually large number of antibodies attack the baby's blood. Most cases of ABO incompatibility are mild with prolonged newborn *jaundice* as the most common complication.

CAUSE

Only an Rh-positive father and an Rh-negative mother with a resulting Rh-positive baby can result in Rh incompatibility. Only about 20 percent of all Rh-negative women form antibodies to the Rh factor, so only 5 to 10 percent of pregnancies in the United States lead to Rh incompatibility and the possibility of erythroblastosis (see *genetic disorders).*

SIGNS AND SYMPTOMS

Anemia and *jaundice* are the most common signs for a newborn who has erythroblastosis, whether from Rh or ABO incompatibility. Babies may be born with an accumulation of fluids in body tissues, a condition called hydrops. Signs and symptoms that may appear in serious cases of the disease depend upon the number of red blood cells destroyed but include severe anemia with accompanying paleness; an accumulation of acid in the blood and body tissues; enlarged liver and spleen; and tiny red bruises under the skin. The most serious form of erythroblastosis is marked by low blood sugar *(hypoglycemia),* low blood pressure, reduction of oxygen supply to blood and tissues, and severe anemia, with consequent *asphyxia* (a loss of consciousness due to insufficient oxygen and excess carbon dioxide in the blood).

DIAGNOSIS

During a pregnant woman's first visit to a physician for prenatal care, a blood test is performed. If she is Rh negative and the father is Rh positive, an antibody screen test is performed as early as the twenty-second week of pregnancy to check for any Rh incompatibility. If one is present, amniocentesis is usually performed. If erythroblastosis has affected a previous sibling of the unborn baby, then an amniocentesis will be performed during the twentieth to twenty-second week. Amniotic fluid is then analyzed for a high level of bilirubin.

Erythroblastosis or ABO incompatibility may be diagnosed in a newborn using special blood tests.

COMPLICATIONS

Complications of erythroblastosis have been reduced greatly due to prevention and early fetal treatment. Only in those cases of severe erythroblastosis that occasionally occur is there even the possibility that surviving infants may suffer any long-term effects. Although rare today, an extremely severe case of *jaundice* may cause brain damage if erythroblastosis is untreated (see *cerebral palsy).*

TREATMENT

The major goals of treatment of erythroblastosis after birth are to prevent death from severe *anemia* and its complications and to prevent possible brain damage from severe *jaundice.* If monitoring of hemoglobin (the pigment of red blood cells) for anemia and bilirubin levels for jaundice in a newborn's blood indicates an excessive breakdown of red blood cells, the baby may be given an immediate exchange transfusion of blood containing no antibodies to Rh factor. Additional exchange transfusions may be needed, and phototherapy (treatment under fluorescent lights to lower bilirubin levels) may supplement the transfusion process.

If a fetus is suffering from severe erythroblastosis, blood transfusions can be administered while the fetus is still in the mother's uterus; the first transfusion is given between the twenty-fourth and thirty-second week of pregnancy. Without such a transfusion, severe anemia may cause stillbirth or *prematurity.*

In mild cases of erythroblastosis, fetuses are generally carried to or near term and do not require transfusions. Mild jaundice is treated after birth with phototherapy. Jaundice in cases of ABO incompatibility is treated with phototherapy; rarely, exchange transfusions are needed.

PREVENTION

The best method of preventing erythroblastosis is injection of a drug commonly called RhoGAM. If given within 72 hours of delivery (or miscarriage or abortion) of a woman's first Rh-positive baby, RhoGAM blocks the formation of antibodies in the mother's bloodstream and ensures that her second baby will not suffer from erythroblastosis. RhoGAM must be given immediately after the birth (or miscarriage or abortion) of each Rh-positive baby. Obstetricians now give RhoGAM to certain women during their pregnancy to prevent the fetus from sensitizing the mother even before delivery.

RHEUMATIC FEVER

DESCRIPTION

Rheumatic fever is a serious inflammatory disease, characterized by *fever, joint pain,* and sometimes *swollen joints.* A complication of a *strep throat,* rheumatic fever primarily affects the heart and joints.

Because of the effectiveness of antibiotics and improved public health conditions, rheumatic fever now rarely occurs among American children. In developing countries, however, where poverty and overcrowding are common and medical attention scarce, rheumatic fever continues to be a problem. Worldwide it is the leading cause of acquired heart disease among children.

Like strep infections in general, rheumatic fever is most common among children between 5 and 15 years old. It is extremely rare before the age of 2.

The disease usually appears within 3 to 5 weeks after a child has had a strep infection of the upper respiratory tract (nose, throat, and airways) that is ineffectively treated or not treated at all. Rheumatic fever may last from several weeks to several months. A child may experience severe discomfort from joint pain, swelling, and fever, but those symptoms subside as the child recovers.

The critical damage from rheumatic fever occurs in the valves of the heart (see Fig. 28, p. 419). Inflammation from the infection causes the valves to narrow and fuse, resulting in a backflow or leaking valve. The more a valve leaks, the harder the heart must work. When a valve is damaged, a physician can hear a murmur in the hearts of about half of the children with the problem (see *heart murmurs)*. During healing, permanent deformity of heart valves occurs. Over the years a valve may gradually change, sometimes improving but more often becoming worse. For this reason it is necessary to have a cardiologist monitor the condition, since minor valve damage may become more significant over the next 20 to 30 years.

Occasionally a child develops an unusual variation of rheumatic fever known as cho-rea, sometimes known as St. Vitus' dance. The symptoms of chorea are involuntary jerking movements, clumsiness, and swings of emotions, which may last for days or weeks. Although the movements may become so violent that the child cannot eat and requires sedation, recovery is complete. Unaccountably, chorea most often occurs among preteen girls.

A seriously ill child sometimes experiences congestive heart failure (the inability of the heart to pump enough blood to meet the body's needs, see *heart failure, congestive)*. Sometimes a child suffers only a *fever* and slight swelling of the joints for a day or two, and experiences a minimal heart murmur as the only aftereffect.

The outlook for a child with rheumatic fever depends on how severely the heart is affected. Unless given antibiotics daily, children who develop rheumatic fever risk recurrence. Children unprotected by antibiotics are more likely to develop recurrent attacks with progressive valve damage. In many cases all symptoms of rheumatic fever subside, even if changes in heart valves have occurred.

CAUSE

Rheumatic fever is caused by a group A strep infection of the upper respiratory tract such as *strep throat,* tonsillitis (inflammation

of the tonsils; see *tonsillitis and adenoiditis),* and *scarlet fever.* Medical research suggests that some children—and some families—are more vulnerable than others to the development of rheumatic fever.

Rheumatic fever itself is not contagious, although the strep infections that precede it are usually highly contagious.

SIGNS AND SYMPTOMS

For more than half the children who develop rheumatic fever, it begins with a *sore throat.* It may also start with a *cough* and sneezing, tonsillitis (see *tonsillitis and adenoiditis),* or infections of nose and throat. The first signs and symptoms of rheumatic fever can appear as early as 10 days following the first signs and symptoms of strep infection.

A child with rheumatic fever may have red, swollen, painful joints. The pain and inflammation are likely to migrate from one joint to another but focus in the knees, ankles, wrists and elbows (see *arthritis, acute).* The child often has a low-grade fever and may complain of *abdominal pain.* During the early stages of the illness the child may develop a red, slightly raised *rash* with a curved latticelike pattern.

If the heart is involved, a heart murmur can be heard (see *heart murmurs).* In very severe cases the child is also likely to suffer from an enlarged heart, endocarditis (inflammation of the heart muscle), and congestive heart failure (see *heart failure, congestive).*

DIAGNOSIS

No single symptom or laboratory finding identifies rheumatic fever; rather, a constellation of signs and symptoms combine with test results to yield a diagnosis. Typically, a physician takes into account a child's condition, a recent history of strep infection, a family history of rheumatic fever, and abnormal laboratory test results. Development of a typical heart murmur (see *heart murmurs)* may be the only "specific" indication of rheumatic fever.

TREATMENT

Antibiotic treatment should be started as soon as possible after a case of *strep throat* is discovered. Antibiotics, especially penicillin, are highly effective against strep bacteria.

Treatment focuses next on relieving inflammation of the heart and joints. The physician usually prescribes aspirin or a prescription anti-inflammatory medication to relieve swelling and inflammation of the joints. For severe inflammations children may be given corticosteroids (synthetic, hormonelike medications) to relieve inflammation of the heart muscle and joints. Digitalis may be given to improve weakened heart function.

The child with mild to moderate rheumatic fever requires 2 to 12 weeks of bed rest. Daily penicillin tablets or monthly injections of long-lasting penicillin are required for many years to prevent reinfection with strep bacteria.

PREVENTION

Rheumatic fever may be prevented by early detection and effective antibiotic treatment of strep infections of the upper respiratory tract. If all strep infections of the throat could be detected promptly and treated adequately, rheumatic fever would be nonexistent. Recurrent attacks may be prevented by continual antibiotic treatment of children who are at risk.

RICKETS

DESCRIPTION

Rickets is a childhood disorder in which bones become soft and deformed because of a vitamin D deficiency. Rickets usually results from prolonged vitamin D deficiency (stemming from dietary problems or *malabsorption,* an inability to break down and absorb needed nutrients), or takes the form of vitamin D–resistant rickets, an inherited disorder characterized by very low levels of phosphates (phosphorus salts) and calcium.

Vitamin D–deficient rickets most often develops in premature or breastfed infants because breast milk often does not contain adequate vitamin D. Children whose diet is severely lacking in vitamin D are also susceptible to rickets. In the United States dietary rickets has almost disappeared because of the addition of vitamin D to all processed milk and dairy foods.

Vitamin D is needed for many body functions, particularly the intestinal absorption of calcium and phosphorus. In turn, calcium and phosphorus are involved in many body functions, including bone formation (particularly bone calcification, the process in which bone tissue forms and hardens because of calcium deposits). When the supply of vitamin D is insufficient, the body's ability to absorb calcium and phosphorus decreases. This results in decreased calcification of bone. Bones soften and become malformed. Muscle development is also poor, and affected children tend to stand and walk later than normal children. A child may experience muscle pain.

Vitamin D–deficient rickets occasionally resolves itself with sufficient exposure to sunshine or an adequate intake of vitamin D through diet. For the most part, however, rickets requires intensive treatment. Vitamin D–resistant rickets is a lifelong condition; with proper treatment and management, however, a child can lead a symptom-free life.

CAUSE

A common cause of rickets is an inadequate intake of vitamin D. Intake is further reduced when a child does not receive enough ultraviolet light, usually from the sun, to activate vitamin D in the body. A child's body may not receive enough vitamin D because of absorption problems caused by damage to the intestine, pancreas, or liver (see *malabsorption).* Intestinal problems that can lead to rickets include severe *diarrhea,* gastrointestinal tract infections, enterocolitis (inflammation of the mucous membrane of the intestine), and *celiac disease.*

Disorders of the pancreas that can produce rickets include pancreatitis (inflammation of the pancreas) and *cystic fibrosis.* In addition, liver diseases, such as *biliary atresia* and *hepatitis,* affect the body's ability to absorb vitamin D.

Vitamin D–resistant rickets, also called X-linked familial hypophosphatemia, does not stem from vitamin D deficiency but is caused by an inherited inability to reabsorb phosphates by the kidneys. This inability can be inherited from either parent, who may also have the disorder (see *genetic disorders).*

SIGNS AND SYMPTOMS

The first signs of vitamin D–deficient rickets usually appear after several months of a deficient diet or untreated *malabsorption.* Infants who are breastfed and do not receive supplemental vitamin D usually develop symptoms within 2 to 3 months after birth. A child with vitamin D–resistant rickets usually shows no symptoms until 8 to 10 months of age.

One of the earliest signs of rickets is craniotabes (thin, soft areas of bone that develop on the skull) and misshaping of the skull. The head may become permanently larger than normal and take on a boxlike appearance if bone thickening occurs. Other changes in a child's bone structure include thickening of the wrist and ankle bones, *bowed legs* or *knock-knees,* chest deformities, misshaping of the shoulder bones, *scoliosis,* kyphosis (a spinal hump), or lordosis (hollowing of the back).

A child with rickets usually develops a potbelly because of weakening of the abdominal muscles and intestinal wall. In addition, an infant with rickets is restless and sweats more than usual, particularly around the head. *Tooth problems* may occur.

DIAGNOSIS

A physician's diagnosis of vitamin D–deficient rickets is based on a history of dietary deficiency, long-term illness, unexplained weight loss, presence of characteristic signs and symptoms, a physical examination, and laboratory tests. Information concerning a child's growth rate and eating habits is also helpful. Vitamin D–resistant rickets is identified by a family history of the disease, presence of characteristic signs and symptoms, laboratory tests, and a physical examination. X rays can reveal decreased bone mass, bone deformities, and other changes in bone structure. Changes caused by continued production of uncalcified bone tissue can also be detected.

Before a physician can attribute bone changes to rickets, however, other possible causes must be ruled out. For example, *hydrocephalus* can also cause craniotabes.

COMPLICATIONS

As a result of bone deformities, a child may be shorter than normal (see *height problems).* Children with rickets are susceptible to respiratory infections such as *pneumonia* and *tuberculosis.*

TREATMENT

Treatment of rickets focuses on preventing bone malformations and promoting bone healing. The best treatment for vitamin D–deficient rickets is large daily oral doses of vitamin D, which should be monitored by a physician. Once healing is under way, doses of vitamin D are reduced to the daily recom-

mended amount. Children with rickets should sit in the sun frequently. Healing occurs slowly, perhaps over months or even years, until full correction of bone deformities is reached. If bone deformities are severe, complete correction may be impossible.

Healing of bone malformations caused by vitamin D–deficient rickets can be accomplished more rapidly if the child is given a massive dose of vitamin D instead of many smaller doses. Since large doses of vitamin D can cause side effects such as *headache, vomiting,* and increased blood pressure, a physician monitors the treatment carefully.

Vitamin D–resistant rickets cannot be treated with vitamin D alone. A combination of phosphates and vitamin D is needed.

PREVENTION

Vitamin D–deficient rickets can be prevented if a child receives adequate amounts of vitamin D daily through diet and sufficient exposure to ultraviolet light. Premature and breastfed infants should receive daily vitamin supplements to ensure that they receive enough vitamin D.

Vitamin D–resistant rickets cannot be prevented. However, parents who have a family history of resistant rickets should be tested to see if they carry the trait for the disorder (see *genetic disorders).*

RINGWORM

DESCRIPTION

Ringworm, a common fungus infection, derives its name from the circular or ringlike appearance of its sores. People of all ages can be affected.

The ringworm fungus affects different parts of the body. It can invade the hair shafts of the scalp, the skin of the arms, legs, face, and neck, or the fingernails. Jock itch, an infection of the groin area common in boys, and athlete's foot (the most common of all fungal infections), an infection of the skin between the toes and on the soles of the feet, are also caused by the ringworm fungus.

Ringworm, if treated, is not serious; most cases will clear in a few weeks. Fungal infection of the nails may take 3 to 6 months to clear with continuous treatment. Infection of the scalp will usually clear up within 6 to 12 weeks of treatment.

CAUSE

Inadequate nutrition, poor hygiene, illness, and humid climates increase the likelihood of infection. Ringworm is highly contagious and is spread by direct contact with the fungus. Contact with contaminated combs, brushes, barber's tools, hats, or seat backs spreads hair and scalp infections. Cats and dogs that are infected with ringworm fungus may transmit the infection to children. A child can get a fungal infection from walking barefoot on damp, contaminated surfaces (such as the floors of locker rooms, showers, and swimming pool areas), or walking in infested soil. The continual wearing of rubber and nylon shoes, which is associated with excessive heat and moisture, may make fungal infection more likely.

SIGNS AND SYMPTOMS

On the body, the ringworm infection first appears as small, round red spots that grow until they reach the size of a pea. The sores then begin to heal from the center outward, resulting in the characteristic rings. Occasionally the sores become reinfected once the centers have healed. Inflammation and itching are often present throughout the infection.

Sores in the groin area may appear like sores found on other parts of the body. In the groin area, however, the scaly rings enlarge at a much more rapid rate.

Because the feet are constantly moist, athlete's foot is usually persistent. The skin above and between the toes will be covered with scaling and cracking, and the infection can spread to the soles of the feet. Blisters may also develop.

Two types of infection involve the hair and scalp. In both, the hair shaft is directly invaded, causing it to become brittle and then break. In the milder form of infection the scalp is not affected. The more severe form of infection causes the scalp to become inflamed and pus to form at the base of the hair shafts. In both cases hair shafts break in clumps. In the more severe form, the scalp becomes covered with crusting and pus.

DIAGNOSIS

A physician uses one of several methods to make a positive identification of ringworm. Identification can be made by examination of scales or stubs of a child's hair under a microscope. In rare cases the use of ultraviolet light can determine the presence of the ringworm fungus in the hair shafts and scalp; certain varieties of fungi are identifiable because they appear greenish white when viewed under ultraviolet light. Culture of the scale, pus, or hair stubs may be required to establish the diagnosis.

COMPLICATIONS

Untreated or severe ringworm infection can lead to permanent hair loss or persistent, long-term inflammation and itching, *fever,* enlarged lymph nodes (see *swollen glands),* and body *rash.*

TREATMENT

Most cases of ringworm can be treated successfully at home. Since fungal infections grow well in warm, moist environments such as the groin and between the toes, the skin should be kept cool and dry. The child should wear cotton underwear (boxer shorts for boys, loose panties for girls) and socks to allow air to reach these areas. Socks should be changed frequently to keep the feet as dry as possible. Drying agents such as rubbing alcohol should be avoided because they may further irritate the child's skin.

For infections of the groin, legs, arms, neck, and face, antifungal creams or solutions (available without prescription), are very effective. The infection should begin to fade in about 7 days, but treatment should continue for another week or two to insure that all fungus is gone. Antifungal creams and solutions are also effective in treating athlete's foot and should be applied once or twice a day. If ringworm does not diminish with these treatments, an oral antifungal agent available by prescription may be required.

Oral antifungal medication such as griseofulvin is prescribed by a physician to treat hair and scalp ringworm. It is given twice a day for at least 2 to 3 months. Daily hairwashing with antifungal shampoos (such as those containing 2½ percent selenium sulfide) reduces chances of infection spreading to others.

If a fungal infection becomes severe, blistering and oozing may occur. Application of damp compresses helps clear out the crushed areas. Blisters should not be broken, since further infection can occur.

If the condition does not improve after home treatment, or if infection continues to spread, the child should be seen by a physician. Scalp infection requires a physician's care.

PREVENTION

Fungal infection and its recurrence can be prevented by avoiding contact with infected children or surfaces. Children should not borrow combs, brushes, hats, socks, or shoes. Shoes or shower sandals should be worn when walking on damp surfaces. Antifungal footbaths should be available in public showers and swimming pools.

ROCKY MOUNTAIN SPOTTED FEVER

DESCRIPTION

Rocky Mountain spotted fever (RM spotted fever) is a potentially severe infectious disease characterized by <u>fever</u> and <u>rash.</u> Although first identified in the Rocky Mountain range of the United States, this disease is more common in North Carolina, Virginia, Maryland, and Oklahoma. Children and adults who are outdoors in tick-infested areas, such as woods, brush, and high grass, run the risk of contracting RM spotted fever, especially in summer.

The skin, small blood vessels (especially in the hands and feet), the central nervous system (brain, spinal cord, and their protective covering, the meninges) and heart may be affected. The characteristic rash spreads to cover even the soles of the feet and the palms of the hands.

One to eight days after the bite of an infected tick, a child becomes ill with RM spotted fever. Illness can last 2 to 3 weeks. Although a single episode of RM spotted fever usually provides lifelong immunity, the disease can recur. Except in cases with severe central nervous system or heart complications, however, RM spotted fever does not cause long-term aftereffects. The disease does make victims extremely ill, uncomfortable, and irritable until fever breaks and the rash begins to subside.

CAUSE

RM spotted fever is caused by one of a group of microscopic organisms called rickettsiae. These organisms possess characteristics of both bacteria and viruses. The particular variety of rickettsiae that causes this disease often lives in wild rodents (including chipmunks, jackrabbits, meadow mice, weasels, and ground squirrels) and domesticated dogs. These animals themselves do not become ill, but they carry the disease-producing organism. Wood ticks and dog ticks transmit the rickettsia from animal carriers to humans in the blood they suck.

Adults and children who spend time in wooded country are often prey to the wood tick, which bites and clings to the skin of its host. Dog ticks can be passed along to anyone who pets or hugs a family dog that has picked them up while romping outdoors.

SIGNS AND SYMPTOMS

The first signs of RM spotted fever are *headache,* moderate *fever* (100° to 103° F; 37.8° to 39.4° C), loss of appetite, and restlessness. Within 1 to 5 days a *rash* of small, rose-red spots appears, usually on the chest, back, upper arms, and thighs. These spots, which may itch, are flat or slightly raised.

At first, when pressure is applied, the spots may momentarily fade. After a day or two they become purple (blood-filled) and resist all pressure to make them fade. Rash spreads next to wrists and hands, ankles and feet. Fever and headache persist as generalized muscle pain develops along with listlessness. The spleen may become enlarged and tender to the touch.

DIAGNOSIS

A physician diagnoses RM spotted fever by taking a careful history of the child's activities and performing a physical examination. It is important to report any recent tick bites, time spent in tick-infested woods, or contact with a dog or other animal that has been in the woods. Once the illness begins to reveal telltale signs and symptoms, the key indicator of the presence of RM spotted fever is the spread of a rose-red or purple *rash* from the body to the wrists and palms of the hands and to the ankles and soles of the feet.

COMPLICATIONS

Complications of RM spotted fever include low blood pressure, resulting in inadequate circulation to hands and feet, perhaps causing the collapse of all circulation to those parts of the body. Inflammation of the heart or lungs may occur. If the infection is not treated promptly, kidney difficulties may develop. *Meningitis* and *encephalitis,* severe inflammation of the central nervous system, are dangerous complications of RM spotted fever.

TREATMENT

A child with a moderate to severe case of

RM spotted fever is treated in a hospital. Several antibiotics are effective in combating the infection. Once begun, antibiotic therapy provides relief from symptoms of RM spotted fever within days; full recovery usually occurs within 2 to 3 weeks. A child with RM spotted fever should be kept as comfortable as possible and well supplied with fluids.

PREVENTION

The most effective prevention against acquiring tick bites in the woods is wearing protective clothing (long-sleeved shirts, turtleneck jerseys, long trousers, hats, and gloves) and using insect repellent. If a tick is discovered on any skin surface, it should be removed slowly and carefully.

When attempting to remove a tick, it is advisable to use a curved forceps or tweezers. If neither forceps nor tweezers is available, protect the fingers with a tissue, paper towel, or rubber glove. The tick should be grasped as close to the skin as possible and pulled away with slow, steady pressure. (Jerking or twisting movements usually break off the tick's feeding parts.) Once removed, the tick should not be crushed; fluid in its body may contain agents of infection.

Finding ticks requires patience and persistence, since the insects are difficult to locate; they often hide in the body's hairy regions. Parents should examine carefully the hair of children who have walked in tick-infested woods or brush or pet a dog that has roamed the woods.

ROSEOLA

EMERGENCY ACTION

A young child with roseola can have a convulsion (see *seizures*) if a high fever (above 104° F; 40° C) comes on quickly. It is important to make certain that a child having convulsions is lying down (preferably on the floor), is breathing freely, and is not in danger of injury from striking furniture or fixed objects. Consult a physician whenever a convulsion occurs, regardless of how brief the episode or how well the child may appear afterward. A physical examination to check for aftereffects is almost always required.

DESCRIPTION

Roseola is a short-term illness affecting infants and young children. It is marked by high *fever* followed by a body *rash,* which disappears after several days. Infants 6 to 18 months old are most susceptible, although older children sometimes contract the disease. Occasionally an epidemic of roseola occurs in a community.

Aside from fever and rash, roseola produces few noticeable symptoms. A single case provides lifelong immunity to the virus. Many children apparently contract such a mild case that it goes unnoticed, but they acquire immunity as a result.

CAUSE

Although roseola is contagious and probably caused by a virus, how it is transmitted remains uncertain.

SIGNS AND SYMPTOMS

The initial symptom of roseola is a *fever* of 103° to 106° F (39.4° to 41.1° C), which develops quickly. The fever may be accompanied by a convulsion. A physician should be consulted after any convulsion, regardless of how brief the episode.

After 3 or 4 days of fever, the child's temperature returns to normal in a matter of a few hours. Just as the temperature has reached normal, a pink, often itchy *rash* of flat or raised spots begins to appear on the child's chest, abdomen, or back. In severe cases it may also appear on the arms, legs, neck, and face. These spots may be surrounded by a white circle or halo. The rash usually disappears after 24 hours, but may last as long as 3 days.

Occasionally the child also has a runny nose and a slightly sore or inflamed throat. Puffiness around the eyes and *swollen glands]* (enlarged lymph nodes) in the neck may also develop. Generally, however, a child with roseola looks well, even when a fever is present. When the rash fades completely, all other symptoms also disappear.

DIAGNOSIS

Roseola is often difficult to diagnose, since the initial *fever* is not usually accompanied by other obvious signs and symptoms. By the time the illness is identified by the appearance of the *rash,* most cases of roseola have nearly run their course.

COMPLICATIONS

Roseola rarely produces complications other than a convulsion (see *seizures*).

TREATMENT

A mild fever-reducing medication may be helpful. Consult the physician for specific recommendations and read the discussion of nonprescription medications beginning on p. 102. For information about fever reduction, see *fever*. Roseola usually runs its course without any other treatment.

PREVENTION

Roseola cannot be prevented.

SCABIES

DESCRIPTION

Infestation of the skin by mites (very small, round, spiny, four-legged, crawling insects) often results in a condition known as scabies. This condition arises from skin irritation and hypersensitivity and is characterized by red, itchy, swollen lumps. Two varieties of mites lead to scabies: the itch mite and the dog mite (carried on dogs and associated with mange).

Infestations usually occur in soft skin areas such as at the wrist, armpit, webbing between the fingers and toes, genitals, and buttocks. Infants become infested on the palms of the hands, soles of the feet, face, and scalp.

Scabies is not harmful unless superinfected by bacteria, but can be extremely annoying. With proper treatment mites can be eliminated, and resulting irritation clears up in a matter of weeks.

CAUSE

The itch mite spreads easily through contact with infested individuals. Clothing and bedding can also be a source of infestation, but less so than skin-to-skin contact. Itch mites can also be picked up through contact with infested wild birds or animals. Once picked up, the female itch mite burrows into the skin to lay her eggs and dies shortly thereafter. Eggs mature and hatch in 7 days. The immature mites spend the next 2 weeks burrowing in the skin; when full-grown, they mate and lay eggs.

Children usually come in contact with the dog mite by cuddling or petting infested dogs. The dog mite does not burrow or lay eggs in the skin, but rather irritates the skin surface by biting.

SIGNS AND SYMPTOMS

Symptoms of scabies may not appear for up to a month after mite infestation. Usually symptoms of a dog-mite infestation appear more quickly than those caused by the itch mite. Initial symptoms of itch-mite infestation are barely visible tiny gray or black lines formed as mites burrow in the skin. Small red bumps mark the openings to these burrows. Characteristic red, swollen, itchy bumps develop; itching is usually worse at night. As the irritation becomes more severe, pimples and small sores filled with clear fluid or pus may arise. If a child scratches inflamed and irritated areas, patches of crusting skin usually develop, possibly masking characteristic burrows.

When a child is infested by the dog mite, irritation and scratching give rise to pimples and patches of crusting skin. Most frequently these eruptions occur on the chest, arms, and abdomen, areas that come in contact with a dog when it is hugged.

DIAGNOSIS

A physician can identify scabies by examining skin scrapings taken from around the burrows. In addition, diagnosis is based on characteristic signs and symptoms, a child's recent activities, and knowledge of other cases of scabies in the community. If a pet is known to be infested, such information also helps confirm a diagnosis of scabies.

COMPLICATIONS

Infection may occur if a child continuously scratches pimples, blisters, and burrows.

TREATMENT

The most effective treatment of scabies is a nonprescription antimite preparation that contains benzyl benzoate. This compound kills both adult mites and eggs and is applied to all affected areas according to a physician's recommendations. One treatment of benzyl benzoate is usually sufficient to kill adult mites and their eggs. If necessary, a second treatment can be applied 7 days after the first. Following treatment, the medication should be completely washed off and the child given clean, mite-free clothes.

If benzyl benzoate is unavailable, a physician may prescribe a lindane preparation instead. Only 1 application is required for greater than 95 percent chance of cure.

Adequate treatment usually eliminates infestation within 72 hours, although itching may persist for a week or two. Cool baths and drying lotions may further reduce skin irritation. A child should try to avoid scratching, since infection and injury to the skin can occur. If itching does not diminish, a physician may prescribe oral antihistamines. A steroid, a synthetic, hormonelike medication, can also be prescribed to reduce itching and inflammation. An antibiotic can be used to treat infection caused by scratching.

A physician should be consulted if inflammation persists for more than 2 weeks even after treatment or new red bumps appear.

PREVENTION

Scabies can be prevented by avoiding contact with the itch or dog mite. A child should not handle wild animals that may be infested or pets that have mange. All clothing and bedclothes should be thoroughly laundered in detergent and hot water to remove all adult mites and eggs. Clothing and linens that belong to a child known to have scabies should not be borrowed or shared. Any pets suspected of carrying mites should be washed thoroughly and sprayed with an antimite preparation.

SCARLET FEVER

DESCRIPTION

Scarlet fever is a bacterial infection characterized by *fever, rash,* and usually a *sore throat.* The disease and its complications were severe among children in the United States until the 1940s, when penicillin became widely available. Scarlet fever now occurs less often and has become considerably milder.

Scarlet fever is generally the same disease as *strep throat* with a rash added. The rash of scarlet fever is sometimes confused with that of *measles, German measles, toxic shock syndome,* heat rash, or *sunburn.*

Children from 3 to 12 years old are most susceptible to scarlet fever because their immunity is still developing. The disease occurs most often during the winter.

Scarlet fever and strep throat sometimes go untreated because they are unrecognized. When the infection is identified and treated early, complications rarely occur.

CAUSE

Scarlet fever, like *strep throat,* is caused by group A streptococcal bacteria. These bacteria produce a toxin that spreads throughout the body in the bloodstream (see *bloodstream infection)* and cause the *rash* of scarlet fever.

Group A streptococcal bacteria are present not only in people ill with scarlet fever or strep throat but in many healthy people. The bacteria are contagious and are usually transmitted by air through coughing and sneezing. Food may become contaminated with this bacteria. Up to half of the siblings of children with scarlet fever contract a streptococcal infection.

The severity of a strep infection depends upon the strain of streptococcus and the child's age and immunity. (Certain strains of group A streptococci are more likely to result in both scarlet fever and *nephritis* than are other strains.)

By having prior streptococcal infections, older children and adults usually have acquired immunity against the type and strain of bacteria causing scarlet fever and against the toxin produced by the bacteria.

SIGNS AND SYMPTOMS

Scarlet fever appears suddenly. The first signs and symptoms of the disease include high *fever* (103° F—39.4° C—and above) and usually, *sore throat,* weakness, *headache,* chills, general discomfort, stomachache (see *stomachache, stomach pain),* nausea, and *vomiting.* Sometimes *abdominal pain* occurs or a child's pulse is rapid. A very young child with a high fever may experience convulsions (see *seizures)* or *delirium.* High fever typically begins to subside by the end of the second day; in severe cases high fever may last longer. In mild cases fever may be slight (101° F; 38.3° C) or nonexistent.

Within 12 to 48 hours of the onset of fever a red, very fine <u>rash</u> that feels like sandpaper and looks like a sunburn with goose bumps appears in the armpits and on the neck, groin, and inner thighs, then on the chest, back, arms, and legs. Within 24 hours of its first appearance this nonitchy rash spreads over most of the body. Finger pressure on the rash produces a white spot (blanching) that lasts a few seconds on light complexions. Skin creases, such as in front of the elbow, under the knee, and in the armpit, are very red and will not blanch. On the face the skin is smooth and flushed, but the area around the mouth is pale.

While the rash is present, the roof of the mouth is usually covered with a similar fine, bright red rash and sometimes with a few tiny, bruiselike spots. The throat is also bright red. The tonsils are red and swollen and may ooze pus; in severe cases ulcers may appear on the tonsils. At first the tongue has a white, fuzzy coating and a red tip and edges; then small red bumps appear. Later the white coating goes away and the tongue looks bright red and swollen (strawberry tongue).

Typically, the rash lasts 2 to 3 days (up to 5 in very red areas). The rash may be mild and last just a few hours or be nonexistent. After 5 to 7 days all of the above symptoms disappear. The skin then begins to peel in flakes, scales, or sheets, first on the face, then the chest and back, then the arms and legs, and finally on the hands and feet. After the rash disappears, peeling may last for 3 weeks in a mild case, or up to 8 weeks in a severe case. Sometimes the occurrence of peeling following a sore throat and rash leads to the after-the-fact recognition of scarlet fever.

DIAGNOSIS

After noting signs and symptoms, a physician takes a throat culture to try to identify the microorganism. A blood test may also be necessary if the results of a throat culture are unclear.

COMPLICATIONS

Complications rarely occur if scarlet fever is diagnosed and treated promptly. Without treatment, fever is likely to recur after a few days or several weeks. Lymph nodes under the jaw may become tender and swollen (see *swollen glands*).

Early complications of an untreated streptococcal infection can include middle ear infection (see *earache and ear infections*), an abscess (pocket of infection) of the tonsils, and *sinusitis* (inflammation of sinus tissues). In rare instances *pneumonia,* mastoiditis (inflammation of the area of the bone behind the ear), blood poisoning (see *bloodstream infection),* or *osteomyelitis* (bone infection)

develop. Slight liver or heart damage or *arthritis* may occur.

Complications of a streptococcal infection untreated for 1 to 3 weeks can include *rheumatic fever* (a serious disease that is rare in the United States) and acute *nephritis,* a kidney inflammation. Nephritis may occur in spite of treatment. The untreated initial infection leading to such complications can be mild or severe. Rheumatic fever frequently recurs with subsequent strep infections, although nephritis rarely does.

TREATMENT

If a child develops a high *fever* and other typical symptoms of scarlet fever, a physician should be consulted. If the characteristic *rash* appears, a physician should see it the same day. The most important step is for the child to begin an antibiotic without delay. The antibiotic is given orally for at least 10 days, even if a child appears well before the medication is finished. Until the fever has subsided, a child also requires bed rest, fluids, and a fever-reducing medication. A child's temperature usually returns to normal within a day of the initial dose of antibiotic; most other symptoms also disappear rapidly.

Children ill with scarlet fever should be kept away from other children for at least 48 hours after they begin taking an antibiotic.

PREVENTION

Most complications are prevented by treating *strep throat.* In very rare circumstances, some physicians may advise removing a child's tonsils.

SCHIZOPHRENIA

DESCRIPTION, AND SIGNS AND SYMPTOMS

Most mental health specialists now agree that childhood schizophrenia is the same as adult schizophrenia but that it affects very few children—probably only 1 in 10,000. Inexplicably, schizophrenia is about 5 times more common among boys than girls, and those girls who have it rarely show any signs of abnormality before beginning school. The prefix "schizo-" means "split." The root "phrenia" refers to the mind. The word "schizophrenia" thus denotes a disorder characterized by disorganization of mind processes.

This disorganization is revealed in 4 ways. First, a schizophrenic child is more concerned with inner thoughts and feelings than with external stimuli. Second, the child harbors many conflicting thoughts and feelings at the same time. Third, the child has great difficulty keeping his or her mind and speech on one topic. And fourth, the child seems to have a severely limited range of emotions and expresses inappropriate emotions in certain situations. When these 4 characteristics are accompanied by hallucinations or delusions, a child is said to be "actively" psychotic.

The course of schizophrenia tends to fluctuate, with mild and moderate periods giving way to periods of active psychosis and remission (characterized by an absence or great alleviation of signs and symptoms). Even the most successfully functioning of schizophrenics—the ones most aware of external reality—usually need help with social relations and self-care during active episodes.

As a schizophrenic child grows, signs usually appear indicating persistent, disabling disturbances in several important areas of function:

Disorders of Thought, Language, and Learning

The earliest telltale signs of schizophrenia often are peculiar, characteristic *language disorders,* which reflect the disorganization of the affected child's thought processes. A schizophrenic child typically has severe problems putting words in context. He or she may have difficulty understanding that a word like "play" can have different definitions or nuances (in this case, examples include putting on a play, playing with friends, and playing the piano). In addition, a schizophrenic child may not recognize that vocabulary is part of an external, preexisting language; about 50 percent of schizophrenic children make up words.

Another common language disorder among 3- to 6-year-old schizophrenic children is called "word salad"; it is the phenomenon of saying words together that have little or no relation to each other. Many schizophrenic children seem to say words largely because their sounds are appealing. An example of word salad, therefore, might be "I need my hat, bat, hat, cat, it's a rat, like a mouse, house, I'm home." It is also common for schizophrenic children to echo what others say, immediately or days or even weeks later. In general their grammar tends to be poor.

A schizophrenic child may not understand that things having similar attributes are not necessarily identical. For example, a child may be confused by the difference between a baseball and an orange if told that both things are "round." A schizophrenic child's thought processes often seem illogical. Instead of recognizing their lack of logic, however, schizophrenic children tend to express explosive *anger* when their sense of reality is challenged by someone else. A child who asks for a "baseball lemon," for example, may fly into a rage if someone incorrectly interprets such a request and tries to explain that baseballs are not lemon-colored.

Schizophrenic children have the ability to learn, but overcoming their tendency to be illogical and to become oppositional (often called "negativism") requires constant effort. More than 75 percent of all schizophrenic children do not achieve normal language milestones by age 3, and many have severe *learning problems.* A child may be burned several times by touching a hot stove before learning to avoid it. Instead of appreciating dangerous situations, a schizophrenic child's fears are more likely to take the form of irrational anxiety and *phobias.* Such fears make toilet-training problems and *sleep disorders*—particularly insomnia—very common among schizophrenic children. Another outstanding learning problem characteristic of schizophrenic people at any age is a severe inability to derive motivation from external sources. A schizophrenic child may play with one toy for hours on end and may reject attempts from others to interest him or her in another activity.

Disorders of Perception

Schizophrenic children seem to have great difficulty figuring out the difference between what is relevant and what is not. A schizophrenic child may, for example, be unable to screen out background noises and may throw a temper tantrum because of a sound that other people barely notice. Most schizophrenic children also have ongoing difficulty judging the loudness of their own voices and may switch from a loud to a soft voice (or vice versa) for no apparent reason (see also *speech problems*). A schizophrenic child's voice often sounds flat and mechanical.

Disorders of Emotions and Social Relations

Many young schizophrenic children seem to prefer their own company (or, occasionally, the company of adults) to that of other children. A schizophrenic child may seem to perceive conventional toys, such as dolls, as being real and may show a preference for toy vehicles, construction sets, or even number and letter games.

Although language ability usually improves somewhat during the child's elementary school years, socialization problems commonly persist. For example, schizophrenic children typically have little or no awareness of the need for privacy—theirs or anyone else's. They may interrupt others' conversations, seem unable to understand that people have conversations that do not involve them personally, and place themselves physically too close or far away when communicating with others. Schizophrenic children rarely exhibit feelings of intense pleasure or pain. They also have a tendency to laugh at inappropriate times, such as when telling a story they know to be unhappy, or to giggle hysterically without mirth or apparent cause.

Disorders of Movement

For reasons unknown, many schizophrenic children have poor muscle tone and coordination. They tend to shun activities that interfere with their eyesight or upset their balance. Oddly, coordination problems are likely to interfere with gross motor functions, such as walking downstairs or throwing a ball, more than fine motor functions, such as drawing or playing a musical instrument. Coupled with a typically vivid imagination, fine-motor-function talents eventually may lead a schizophrenic child to outshine his or her peers in artistic pursuits. Schizophrenic children may also excel at mechanical activities, such as putting together jigsaw puzzles. These real achievements may provide false hope that a schizophrenic child is "normal." Unfortunately, the other developmental disturbances and delays experienced by schizophrenic children clearly separate them from their peers.

Some experts believe that the main characteristic of schizophrenia is an inability to form a sense of self. Specifically, schizophrenic children seem to lack an ability to understand that other people do not necessarily share their thoughts and feelings and that external standards sometimes conflict with their own desires. During school years the schizophrenic child is likely to suffer his or her first observable hallucinations and delusions. Delusions tend to involve exaggerated self-image and suspicions about other people. When delusions develop, the child sometimes is said to have a form of the disorder called paranoid schizophrenia. (This form rarely occurs before adolescence.) Paranoid schizophrenics tend to develop a system of delusions that goes beyond any efforts on the part of others to explain reality. For example, if a paranoid child is convinced that others are conspiring against him or her, it is likely to be impossible to convince the child that no such conspiracy exists.

During adolescence many schizophrenic children develop a keen appreciation of their disorder. Since this appreciation accompanies sexual development, some children decide that sexuality is the key to normality, and they seek to have sexual intercourse. At the same time, their innate horror over their own sexuality—and over close contact in general—makes this endeavor exceedingly difficult. Some boys respond to nocturnal emissions ("wet dreams") by deluding themselves into believing that they no longer can control any body excretions. Girls may develop similar beliefs when they begin to menstruate. The result is often extraordinary inner tension that intensifies psychotic behavior.

Ironically, the more capable a schizophrenic child is, the more difficult adolescence is likely to be. Less disabled schizophrenic teenagers frequently ask, "Why me?" In severe cases, resulting despair may prompt a schizophrenic child to attempt *suicide.* In rare cases a child blames others for his or her disabilities and becomes violent.

On the other hand, many adolescent schizophrenics also experience a dramatic increase in their capacity to learn and in their understanding of the external world. Although disabilities are likely to be lifelong, many children can be taught to overcome their most disabling handicaps.

CAUSE

What causes schizophrenia remains a matter of controversy and the subject of research. Many experts contend that severe biochemical abnormalities can predispose a child to schizophrenic behavior very early in life. Others say that environmental *stress* plays a crucial role in triggering the behavior among older children, but there is agreement that such stress is never the sole factor. It is generally believed that stress plays no role when symptoms appear early in a child's life. Recent research supports the theory that genetic factors play a role in causing severe, persistent psychosis. This hypothesis seems likely; psychotic disorders appear, at least to some extent, to run in families (see *genetic disorders).*

DIAGNOSIS

Until a child's language has developed sufficiently, signs and symptoms of schizophrenia can easily be confused with those of *autism, mental retardation,* developmental language disorders, and abnormally slow development because of environmental deprivation. Parents should question a diagnosis of schizophrenia made before a child is 3 years old. An accurate diagnosis cannot usually be made before a child is 4 or 5.

No matter how young a child is, he or she should be seen by a physician if parents suspect schizophrenia or any other kind of developmental problem. The most reliable place to obtain a thorough, reliable diagnosis for a child with a developmental disorder is a university-affiliated developmental evaluation clinic, which is more likely than other facilities to use an interdisciplinary approach to diagnosis. These facilities usually employ a team of specialists who are trained to recognize a wide variety of abnormal signs and symptoms. (For information on how to find a university-affiliated diagnostic program, consult the local medical society and see Chapter 3, "Promoting Mental Health.")

Diagnosis of schizophrenia can be a lengthy process, and usually involves the same procedures as those used to diagnose a short-term episode of *psychosis.* In addition, any child diagnosed as schizophrenic should be reevaluated frequently to ensure that the diagnosis is correct and that the child's needs have not outgrown his or her treatment program.

TREATMENT

The first step parents can take is to accept a competent diagnosis. Persistent efforts need to be made to obtain the best possible treatment, and parents should be psychologically prepared for the repeated frustrations they are likely to encounter. Both the general public and many professionals misunderstand what schizophrenia is and what causes it. The schizophrenic has been stereotyped as a person who is "crazy," is likely to harm others, and should be institutionalized. The extreme difficulty in dealing with seriously ill adult schizophrenics has caused some professionals to shy away from treating psychotic children, thereby creating a shortage of qualified, caring professionals. In addition, many families of schizophrenics have been reluctant to speak candidly about their child's disabilities. As a result, a unified effort to advocate better services for schizophrenic children does not yet exist.

Parents can begin home treatment as soon as schizophrenia is diagnosed. One of the most helpful things parents can do is to discourage their child from following internal motivations and concentrating endlessly on one activity. They should gently but firmly prohibit their child from disrupting other people's activities and conversations and should teach the child not to wake others when he or she cannot sleep. Parents should also try to teach their child the difference between fantasy and reality by encouraging him or her to play out delusions using toys.

Parents can ease a child's delusions by challenging or contradicting them. Similarly, repeatedly reminding a child that not all thoughts need to be verbalized can reinforce the difference between mind processes and external reality. It sometimes helps to compare thoughts with dreams; many schizophrenic children understand that dreams take place only in the mind. To remedy speech and language problems, parents can use a tape recorder and point out to a child how his or her voice differs from others'. They can also discourage their child from talking loudly in public and try to be good speaking models themselves. Patient, repeated explanations of the meaning of words by parents often results in a child's finally comprehending them.

Most school-aged schizophrenic children require a special education program. In the United States, federal law mandates that the public school system provide education for all handicapped children. Few communities, however, have adequate programs for schizophrenic and other severely developmentally disordered children. If parents of schizophrenic children seek each other out, they can work to organize support groups and seek help from authorities.

The goal of a professional treatment program for a school-aged schizophrenic child is to prepare the child for functioning well in society as an adult. Specifically, programs need to aim at endowing the schizophrenic child with as much motivation as possible to learn and to overcome disabilities. If such a goal is pursued systematically, the outlook for a schizophrenic child can be surprisingly encouraging. But if a schizophrenic child is placed in an environment with children who are less competent or have very different needs, he or she is likely either to become absorbed in fantasy or to become increasingly negative and illogical.

During any treatment program, parents and professionals learn to search for signs of improvement and remission and then capitalize on them. Schizophrenic children often learn much faster during these periods than during periods of more severe illness. A schizophrenic child's skills and strengths also need to be praised and cultivated. Typically, schizophrenic adolescents lose faith in themselves because of disabilities in handling the maturation process, but having the motivation to cultivate a skill can be an asset.

Psychotherapy is necessary for most schizophrenic children. Medication, however, is not. Most schizophrenic children do not need medication unless they are suffering from severe insomnia or episodes of active *psychosis*. Similarly, hospitalization for schizophrenic children is not always necessary; it is usually recommended only if a child is suicidal, violent, or extremely disorganized. Sometimes, however, an adolescent schizophrenic can benefit from being in a good residential treatment center with a program designed especially for adolescent schizophrenics. Such a program can relieve the pressures of adjusting to maturation.

Unfortunately, many schizophrenic children are institutionalized in inappropriate facilities solely because very few alternatives currently exist. This is further motivation for parents of schizophrenic children to work together on behalf of their children, seeking better care from officials and from professionals. Schizophrenic children are capable of learning and adjusting to society, and through cooperative efforts parents can have the satisfaction of watching them develop.

Families of schizophrenic children often benefit from supportive counseling. They also need to seek out sources of practical support to help with caring for their child. For example, competent respite care may provide them with enough physical and emotional relief so that they can work persistently on their child's behalf.

PREVENTION

Because the causes of schizophrenia remain unclear, experts are uncertain about whether the disorder can be prevented.

SCOLIOSIS

DESCRIPTION

Scoliosis is any curvature of the spine to the right or left side of the body. It may be present at birth or develop as the child grows, and may become worse with age. Two types of scoliosis exist: nonstructural, a curve that is not caused by changes in the formation of the spine; and structural, a curve caused by changes in the shape of vertebrae or in the position of the spine. Nonstructural scoliosis disappears when the child bends to one side or lies down. Structural scoliosis is always apparent, however, and may affect the spine in more than one location (see Figs. 32A and 32B, p. 607).

There are 4 types of structural scoliosis: idiopathic, which does not have a known cause; congenital (present at birth); neuromuscular (caused by disorders of the nerves and muscles of the body); and disease-associated. Idiopathic scoliosis is the most common form and usually develops during adolescence, although it may also appear during infancy and childhood. Girls develop this form of scoliosis slightly more often than boys; an idiopathic spinal curve tends to increase more often among girls.

Adolescent idiopathic scoliosis usually begins to develop as a right curve in the upper back when a child is 10 to 12 years old and may increase as hormones become more active at puberty. As a result of the spinal curve, the shoulder blade and rib cage are pushed out. Treatment is sometimes necessary to prevent the development of a more severe spinal curve.

Infantile idiopathic scoliosis is more common among male infants than female infants

FIG. 32 A AND B. SCOLIOSIS

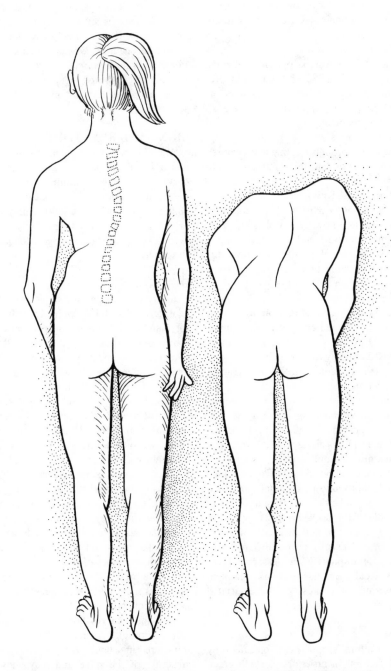

To determine the severity of a curve, a doctor instructs a child to bend forward and observes the back for the presence of a hump in the ribs. Shoulder and hip position are examined for unevenness.

and usually disappears without treatment during the first few years of life. In rare cases, however, a curve can increase and cause severe problems later during childhood if not treated. Juvenile idiopathic scoliosis may develop after age 3 and before puberty. This form of scoliosis may not correct itself and often increases over time. Without treatment, severe spinal malformation and complications may occur.

Congenital scoliosis is present and often detectable at birth. Severe and rapid progression may occur if the growth centers (areas of active growth) of the spine are affected. Approximately one half of congenital curves become worse as a child grows. Prompt and thorough treatment is required to prevent severe deformity and its complications.

Scoliosis caused by neuromuscular disorders such as *poliomyelitis* and *muscular dystrophy* involves an overly flexible spine, possibly bending at both ends to form a long C curve. When the child sits or stands, the curve may become more severe; the spine may even collapse, resulting in paralysis (called *paralytic scoliosis*). The child should wear a brace as soon as possible to prevent collapse or increased curvature of the spine. Bracing, however, is rarely the final solution and is used to delay the inevitable need for a surgical spinal fusion until the child reaches an appropriate age.

Scoliosis may be associated with diseases such as *neurofibromatosis, spina bifida,* and Marfan's syndrome (a disease of the connective tissue). These diseases affect vertebrae and back muscles and cause the spine to rotate into a curved position. When associated with neurofibromatosis, a spinal curve is a short sharp bend either to the right or left in the middle of the back. Scoliosis appears in 30 to 70 percent of children with Marfan's syndrome and usually occurs in more than one area of the spine. Disease-associated scoliosis is usually quite severe, and treatment may be difficult because of the associated problems.

CAUSE

Nonstructural scoliosis may be caused by several factors. In an effort to stand erect, the child will compensate for a difference in leg length or a muscle contraction around the hip or knee by curving the spine. Painful conditions such as a spinal tumor (see *bone cancer),* a spinal disk problem, or a spinal column infection may cause a child to curve the spine in an effort to ease discomfort.

Idiopathic scoliosis can usually be found in more than one member of a family, indicating that genetics plays a role in causing the curve (see *genetic disorders).* Exactly why a curve develops, however, is unknown.

Malformations of the developing vertebrae or spine occurring before birth result in congenital scoliosis. Diseases such as *rickets, tuberculosis,* and *muscular dystrophy* can affect the strength and structure of a child's bones and muscles, and may cause severe scoliosis.

SIGNS AND SYMPTOMS

A child with scoliosis has poor posture and a spinal curve to one side. The spinal curve usually causes a hump in one shoulder or an unevenness in the position of the child's hips. The child's clothes may not fit properly. A hem or waistband may be uneven or one pant leg may appear longer than the other.

DIAGNOSIS

A physician diagnosing scoliosis begins by considering the child's complete medical history, including age, presence of back pain, spine or bone problems, past severe illnesses or operations, and any family spinal problems. To determine the severity of a spinal curve, an orthopedist (bone specialist) instructs the child to bend forward and observes the back for the presence of a hump in the ribs. Shoulder and hip position are also examined for unevenness. (See p. 607.)

A thorough physical examination is made to check for possible underlying diseases such as syringomyelia (a disease of the spinal cord), spinal cord tumor, *poliomyelitis, muscular dystrophy, cerebral palsy,* or *spina bifida.* Certain *birthmarks* such as large café-au-lait spots and hemangiomas may indicate the presence of *neurofibromatosis.* At birth, the presence of heart or urinary tract problems may indicate the presence of congenital scoliosis.

Very mild curves now are routinely detected through screening clinics, often administered in schools. X-ray films reveal the structure of the spine and may show evidence of an underlying problem. Not all curves, however, require an X ray for diagnosis, and physical methods such as measuring spinal rotation are currently being developed and perfected for use.

COMPLICATIONS

Uncorrected structural scoliosis may lead to heart, respiratory, and neurological problems. Arthritis may develop in the back and cause severe pain.

TREATMENT

Careful observation of any spinal curve detected in a screening program or physical examination is required to assess its progression.

Treatment of scoliosis depends on the child's age and overall physical health, the cause and severity of the spinal curve, and the presence of underlying disorders. A spinal curve that does not progress or interfere with the child's normal functioning usually requires no treatment. A progressive curve, however, requires prompt treatment to prevent serious complications.

The first step in treating nonstructural scoliosis usually is correction of the underlying problem. Shoe lifts may be used to correct uneven leg length. Teaching the child to improve his or her posture may correct a nonstructural spinal curve. Reducing or eliminating pain caused by problems such as spinal tumors usually results in at least a partial correction of related scoliosis.

Mild to moderate adolescent and juvenile idiopathic scoliosis is often successfully treated with a spinal brace. A brace is most effective in treating growing children whose spines are flexible and can be straightened easily. Braces are fitted to each child by an orthopedist and worn nearly 24 hours a day for 1 to 3 years, usually until the child stops growing. Initially, a child may not be comfortable in a brace, but adjustment is usually made in a few weeks. The child usually sees a brace maker, a physicial therapist, and an orthopedist every 3 or 4 months to ensure that a brace fits correctly and that curve control is satisfactory.

The orthopedist will recommend an exercise program for a child wearing a brace. The combination of bracing and exercise is successful in managing most cases of mild to moderate idiopathic scoliosis. Under most conditions, the child is encouraged to lead a normal life and to participate in sports and other physical activities.

If scoliosis cannot be controlled through the use of a brace, an orthopedist may recommend surgery. Surgical correction is usually required if the child has severe idiopathic, congenital, or paralytic scoliosis, a rapidly increasing spinal curve, or a curve that interferes with daily activities. Surgery usually involves fusing vertebrae where the curve is located and permanent insertion of a rod or rods that are attached to the spine. If a child's spine has more than one curve, each curve is fused. Following surgery, the child may wear a cast or brace that covers the area from the armpits to the hips for approximately 6 months to protect the spine. The child should not participate in strenuous sports or physical activities for about 1 year after surgery.

PREVENTION

Scoliosis cannot be prevented. Severe curves or complications can be prevented, however, through prompt and effective treatment.

Information about scoliosis and its treatment is available from the National Scoliosis Foundation, 93 Concord Avenue, P.O. Box 547, Belmont, MA 02178 (phone: 617-489-0880).

SCROTAL AND TESTICULAR PROBLEMS

EMERGENCY ACTION

Seek a medical evaluation immediately if a boy experiences unexplained pain in his groin or if his genitals become swollen or discolored (bright pink or apparently bruised). These symptoms may be indications of a problem with the genital tract that could result in permanent damage to reproductive organs if not corrected IMMEDIATELY. If a boy has an *undescended testicle,* any unexplained *abdominal pain* could be a sign of a severe problem with the testicle; again, an immediate diagnosis is important.

If a boy experiences pain in the groin for an obvious reason, such as physical injury, monitor his symptoms carefully and seek immediate medical assistance if pain grows worse or if other symptoms develop. Although groin injuries almost never result in permanent damage, prompt action is a necessary precaution.

DESCRIPTION, SIGNS AND SYMPTOMS, TREATMENT, AND PREVENTION

The testicles are the two male organs that manufacture sperm (the male reproductive cells that fertilize female eggs) and semen (the fluid in which sperm are carried; see Fig. 3C and 3D, p. 39). Because the normal body temperature of 98.6° F (37.0° C) is too warm for the production of sperm, the testicles normally lie outside of the abdominal cavity. They are enclosed in and anchored to the scrotum, a thick-skinned protective pouch.

At one time or another virtually all boys experience scrotal or testicular problems such as jock itch (see *ringworm*). Other causes of scrotal and testicular problems are rare. Some of them, however, can be quite serious and may even necessitate emergency surgical removal of a testicle, which does not affect either fertility or sex characteristics. For this reason, parents should familiarize themselves with the signs and symptoms of various types of scrotal and testicular problems:

- *undescended testicles*
- inguinal hernia (see *hernia, inguinal and umbilical*)
- testicular tumors (see *genitourinary tumors*)

Injury to the Testicles from a Blow to the Groin

Although the testicles are among the most delicate of body structures, they are rarely injured severely because they are not buttressed against a hard surface. When a blow to the groin forces the testicles against another body structure, however, excruciating pain can result. If, for example, a boy falls forward from a bicycle seat and lands on the front bar, he may double up on the ground and cry or moan from the intense pain. The pain usually lessens within minutes, although soreness may persist for a day or so. Immediately after the injury, pain can be relieved by applying an ice pack to the groin. Ice should never be applied directly to the skin. If need be, an ice pack can be made by wrapping a plastic bag of ice cubes in a towel. Several hours after the injury, the boy can relieve soreness by taking a warm bath. The boy can resume physical activity as soon as he feels able to. Full recovery usually occurs within a couple of days.

A more severe blow to the groin, such as being hit by a hockey puck, usually causes more severe and persistent signs and symptoms. Immediately after the blow, a boy is likely to fall to the ground in agony. The intense pain can trigger spasms in the stomach, and the boy may retch or vomit repeatedly for minutes. Within a half hour or so the pain usually subsides, although the testicles may feel sore for days. The boy may even be unable to walk for a day or so. Treatment is the same as for a milder injury. Although more severe blows rarely cause permanent damage, a physician should be consulted if severe pain persists, if soreness worsens, if swelling or discoloration develops, or if doubt exists about the seriousness of the injury.

In very rare cases a sharp blow to the groin can cause a testicle to rupture or to dislocate into the abdomen or upper thigh. Dislocation usually occurs only after a very strong impact, such as being hit by a car. Surgery is necessary to repair both of these conditions. In some cases repair is not possible and surgical removal of the affected testicle or testicles is necessary.

Injury to the testicles cannot always be prevented, although a boy should always wear protective equipment when playing contact sports.

Hydrocele

Hydrocele is a common condition, characterized by swelling from accumulation of watery fluid in the scrotum. It usually affects only one side of the scrotum, causing it to become swollen, firm, and bright pink—but not painful. In some cases surrounding areas, including the penis, are also affected. In most cases hydrocele persists 2 days or less. Occasionally the scrotum remains discolored for several more days.

Hydrocele is usually caused by a minor problem, just as bumps involving fluid accumulation in other parts of the body—mosquito bites, for example—are usually not serious. The types of problems that tend to produce hydrocele among older boys include minor injury and *stinging insect reactions*. Among very young boys the cause may be an inguinal hernia with a communicating hydrocele (see *hernia, inguinal and umbilical*). When a teenage boy develops hydrocele, the cause is usually infection of the scrotum. In rare cases the cause of hydrocele is twisting of the spermatic cord (see below).

Hydrocele almost always subsides without complications or treatment. A physician should be consulted, however, in case treatment of the underlying cause is necessary. Hydrocele cannot be prevented.

Varicocele

Varicocele is enlargement of the veins surrounding one or both testicles. It almost always affects only the left testicle. It is usually caused by incompetency of valves in the veins that normally carry blood from the testicle to the heart. In rare cases it results from a tumor in the kidney (see *Wilms' tumor*), which can interfere with the drainage of veins.

An uncommon condition, varicocele tends to appear shortly after puberty. Although painless, the enlargement of the veins and the consequent pooling of blood cause swelling and raise the temperature within the testicle. This disruption of the delicate temperature balance between the abdomen and testicles can lower sperm count and, possibly, render a boy temporarily infertile. If varicocele is not corrected, it may interfere with sperm production. The condition can be fixed surgically by tying off the affected veins and forcing the blood to find different pathways to the heart. Varicocele cannot be prevented.

Torsion (Twisting) of the Spermatic Cord

Each testicle is connected to the internal reproductive organs by a spermatic cord, a structure that contains blood vessels, nerves, and muscles, as well as a tube for carrying semen. If this cord twists, the blood supply to the testicle is pinched off. Without blood, cells die. Blood is vital because it supplies cells with oxygen and vital nutrients and carries away cellular waste products. A testicle can be destroyed within as little as 12 hours after twisting occurs.

A boy of any age can suffer from a twisted spermatic cord. Less than 1 percent of all boys are affected. Specialists believe that having an unusually long spermatic cord may predispose to twisting. In the rare cases that an infant is born with a twisted spermatic cord, the condition seems to involve a loose connection between the scrotum and testicles.

Another condition that seems to increase a boy's chances of developing a twisted spermatic cord is *undescended testicles*.

Symptoms of spermatic cord twisting tend to come on gradually and often begin during sleep. An affected boy feels intense pain in the central abdomen or groin, a sensation that can be mistaken for a stomachache. In many cases similar but milder sensations have preceded this more intense episode. If the scrotum is examined by touch when intense pain begins, the affected testicle feels swollen, firm, and very tender. Within hours the scrotum becomes swollen and red, and the affected boy may develop a fever or begin to vomit. If the condition is not treated, pain may subside. In several days to weeks, the affected testicle will begin to feel smaller to the touch because the testicle disintegrates. This condition invites bacterial infection, which can cause an abscess (a collection of pus) to form in the testicle.

Parents who suspect that their son has a twisted spermatic cord should seek emergency medical assistance. Emergency room personnel usually consult a pediatric urologist (a specialist in diagnosing and treating problems of the urinary system and of the male reproductive system). Diagnosis involves highly sophisticated imaging techniques, including CT scans (highly detailed, three-dimensional X rays) and ultrasound, which produces pictures from sound waves. If necessary, the groin is explored surgically. During surgery the cord is untwisted and the testicle is fixed in place. The unaffected testicle is also fixed in place to prevent torsion on that side. If surgery reveals that a testicle is dead or dying, the testicle is removed. In most cases this drastic step is necessary only when the spermatic cord has been twisted more than 12 hours.

In rare cases the spermatic cord spontaneously untwists and emergency treatment is not required. Medical attention should be sought promptly, however, because surgery is required in the near future to prevent the cord from twisting again.

Among infants the diagnosis of torsion is often made too late to save the testicle because the symptoms of the twisting are slightly different. Instead of being tender, the affected testicle is simply enlarged and hard and the scrotum is bluish colored. These symptoms are not often evident unless suspicions are aroused while the baby is being diapered. Treatment for an infant is the same as that for an older boy.

Except for taking the surgical precaution of fixing a testicle in place, twisting of the spermatic cord cannot be prevented.

Torsion (Twisting) of the Testicular Appendix

In some cases it is not the spermatic cord

but a small appendix on the testicle itself that twists. Since vital blood vessels do not connect this appendage to the rest of the testicle, this type of twisting does not put a boy at risk of losing a testicle. The signs and symptoms of this condition can be the same as those of a twisted spermatic cord, although usually the only abnormality that can be detected through the scrotum is a small, hard, pea-sized lump. If physicians can determine by a testicular scan (an imaging technique) that twisting definitely involves only the appendix, surgical treatment is unnecessary; the appendix is allowed to die because it is unimportant to the functioning of the testicle. If, however, physicians cannot determine whether the spermatic cord or the appendix is twisted, they usually opt to explore the testicle surgically, and the affected appendix is removed during this clarifying process. The cause of a twisted appendix is usually unclear, and the condition cannot be prevented.

Structural Abnormalities

About 1 out of every 300 boys is born with a structural abnormality in the urinary or reproductive organs. Structural abnormalities tend to predispose a boy to infection and other problems involving the testicles and scrotum. They can be caused by a variety of problems, including drug abuse (see *drug and alcohol abuse)* by the boy's mother during pregnancy. Some structural abnormalities can be corrected surgically. In most cases they cannot be prevented (see also *urinary tract defects and obstruction).*

Mumps

Mumps is an infectious disease of childhood. It can cause testicles to become swollen and painful, although involvement of the testicles is rare among prepubertal boys. Since most boys never develop mumps or develop it before puberty, very few boys have testicular problems because of the disease. When mumps does affect a testicle, however, a slight chance exists that it will permanently lose its ability to produce sperm. No treatment for mumps or its possible testicular complications is possible. Mumps can be prevented by immunization.

Abdominoscrotal Disease

Any disease involving the abdominal cavity can produce signs and symptoms in the scrotum. If, for example, a baby is born with a hole in his intestines, fecal material can leak into the abdominal cavity and down into the scrotum; consequently the scrotum appears swollen and discolored. Treatment of abdominoscrotal disease varies. In a case of congenital (present at birth) intestinal perforation, for example, treatment involves surgical repair of the intestine and removal of fecal material from the abdomen. Abdominoscrotal disease typically cannot be prevented.

SEBORRHEIC DERMATITIS

DESCRIPTION

Seborrheic dermatitis is a chronic condition consisting of redness and scaling of the skin. This disorder commonly occurs in areas of the skin where oil glands are most active. Seborrheic dermatitis must be differentiated from dandruff, which is the simple accumulation of dead skin and scaling. During infancy, accumulation of dead skin and scaling appears as *cradle cap.* Seborrheic dermatitis may also occur during infancy. During later childhood and adolescence, seborrheic dermatitis is found most often on the scalp, on the face, and in the skin folds of the ear. The chest, genital area, and stomach can also be affected. Another form, seborrheic blepharitis, affects the edges of the eyelids and the eyelashes. It can be associated with mild *conjunctivitis.* Simple dandruff of the scalp is common in adolescence.

Even with proper and thorough treatment, seborrheic dermatitis and dandruff tend to recur when treatment is discontinued.

CAUSE

Hormonal activity causes the oil glands to secrete large amounts of oil and the skin to become inflamed. Seborrheic dermatitis develops when there is inflammation, scaling, and excess oil secretion. It is not known why this condition occurs.

Emotional or physical *stress* can aggravate seborrheic dermatitis. Heavy perspiration caused by physical activity or an emotional upset irritates this skin condition, as does accumulation of dirt and oil because of poor hygiene.

SIGNS AND SYMPTOMS

Seborrheic dermatitis appears as red, finely scaled patches. If scaling is severe, seborrhea may resemble *psoriasis.* The patches are irregularly shaped, and skin below the scales is thickened, yellowish, and greasy from oil buildup. Frequently the patches run together and cover large areas of a child's body. When the scalp is affected, inflammation of the hair follicle and hair loss are common; seborrheic dermatitis may also spread behind a child's ears. Intense itching may accompany seborrheic dermatitis.

DIAGNOSIS

Diagnosis of seborrheic dermatitis is based on the location and appearance of the redness and scaling. Because this skin problem often looks like *psoriasis,* careful diagnosis is needed. A physician may want to exclude fungus infection by examining scrapings under a microscope.

Seborrheic blepharitis is identified by redness and scaling of the eyelid margins and eyelashes.

COMPLICATIONS

Skin may become more susceptible to bacterial or yeast infections once affected by seborrheic dermatitis.

TREATMENT

Treatment of seborrheic dermatitis focuses on relieving itching and removing oils and crusts from the scalp and hair. Home treatment involves daily or twice daily use of a medicated shampoo, usually containing salicyclic acid, tar, or sulfur. These shampoos also contain detergents to break down oils and scale coating the hair and scalp. Each time the child's hair is washed, shampoo should remain on the scalp and hair for 2 to 3 minutes. Double shampoos are more effective than single shampoos. If seborrheic dermatitis is severe, a surface corticosteroid lotion, solution, or spray (available by prescription) may be applied after shampooing to control itching.

If thick crusts develop on the scalp, overnight soaking with mineral oil under plastic wrap can help soften them. These treatments should be followed by shampooing with a medicated preparation. To effectively control scalp seborrheic dermatitis, it may be necessary to continue treatment after symptoms disappear.

On other parts of the body, itching from seborrheic dermatitis usually responds quickly to corticosteroid or salicylic acid-sulfur creams. Prolonged use of strong corticosteroids, however, should be avoided, since they can cause the skin to become tissue-paper thin and accentuate tiny blood vessels. Seborrheic blepharitis can be treated with prescription corticosteroids and sulfur medications, but a daily regimen of cleansing is usually sufficient.

PREVENTION

Seborrheic dermatitis and seborrheic blepharitis cannot be prevented.

SEIZURES

EMERGENCY ACTION

Do not panic if a child experiences a convulsion—a series of uncontrollable muscle spasms in the head, truck, and limbs. A convulsion, the most dramatic form of seizure, is accompanied by loss of consciousness. Typically a child falls to the floor and thrashes or jerks in a way that can be very frightening to see. Contrary to appearances, however, a convulsion rarely leads to serious injury or complications. In fact, dramatic attempts to aid a child often result in more harm than good. Therefore:

- Do not place any object between a child's teeth. It is better to allow a child to bite his or her tongue than to risk having him or her break teeth by clamping down hard on an object or someone's finger.
- Do not restrain the child in any way, including putting the child in a tub of water.
- Do not pour liquid into the child's mouth; he or she may inhale the liquid and begin to choke.
- Do not attempt to ensure that the child does not swallow his or her tongue. It is physically impossible to swallow the tongue.

The few steps that witnesses of a seizure can take involve making the child's immediate environment as safe as possible and preventing the remote possibility of choking. Therefore:

- Do remove hard or dangerous objects —including furniture—from the area.
- Do ease the child to the ground, if possible.
- Do attempt to lay the child on his or

her side with the hips elevated and the head turned to the side. Such a position is most likely to prevent the possibility of choking by encouraging saliva to drain out of the mouth. However, do not worry about positioning the child's body if such a task seems difficult or impossible, since choking rarely occurs.

Although minutes may seem to pass like hours during a child's convulsion, the episode rarely lasts more than 5 minutes. If possible, time the length of the episode and note any movements the child makes. In the very rare cases—usually associated with severe birth defects—that a child's convulsion lasts for more than 10 minutes, take the child to a hospital emergency room immediately or call for emergency assistance. Medication can be given at the hospital to end the seizure. If a convulsion persists or recurs continually for an unusually long time (an hour or more), permanent brain damage can result. This complication is exceedingly rare.

When a convulsion ends, a child is usually very tired and falls into a deep sleep for several hours. Allow the child to rest. Meanwhile, call a physician and arrange for a consultation. On the basis of a parent's description of a convulsion, a physician may want to see a child as soon as he or she wakes up. If not, make an appointment for the near future so that the physician can evaluate the child and try to determine what prompted the seizure.

Sometimes convulsions are associated with rapidly rising fevers. In such a case attempt to bring down the child's fever as soon as a convulsion is over by sponging the child with tepid water, as described in the Treatment section of *fever*. Do not sponge the child with alcohol, which can be absorbed through the skin. Offer frequent sips of iced fluids, and keep the child uncovered.

DESCRIPTION

A seizure is a temporary problem within the brain that causes a person to do or perceive something involuntarily and without any external stimulus. This problem results from unusual electrical activity in the brain.

Electrical activity itself is normal in the brain. When a person decides to move his or her right thumb, for example, the brain cells that control that function generate an electrical impulse that travels from cell to cell via neurotransmitters (complex chemicals).

The impulse continues to travel in this fashion until it reaches the nerve cells of the spinal cord that control the muscles of the thumb and trigger them to move.

A seizure results when a group of nerve cells in the brain accidentally fire off an electrical impulse. A seizure can affect any function controlled by the brain—thoughts, sensations, or movements. The symptoms of a seizure can vary in intensity from a feeling of fear for a split second to a violent shaking of the entire body.

About 1 percent of all people have at least 1 seizure at some point during their lives. More than 50 percent of all seizures affect children. Many childhood seizures are isolated incidents—that is, they are associated with a short-term illness or injury and do not recur. Children who suffer from recurrent seizures associated with a long-term underlying condition or tendency are said to have epilepsy, a term that means, simply, "recurrent seizures." To say that a child is epileptic says nothing about the type, severity, or cause of a child's seizures and does not imply that the child has other brain-related problems such as paralysis or mental retardation.

In general, the following types of seizures are most common:

Grand Mal Seizures (Convulsions)

In French, *grand mal* means "great malady," and grand mal seizures are more incapacitating than any other type. A grand mal seizure, commonly called a convulsion, can begin suddenly, or the child can sense a warning signal that one is about to begin. During a classic grand mal seizure the child suddenly gives a startled cry as air involuntarily rushes from the lungs through the vocal cords. The child falls to the floor, unconscious, with all muscles tense. The eyes roll back in the head. Excess salivation begins, and the child may "foam at the mouth." Tensing the jaw muscles may cause the child to bite his or her tongue, resulting in red-tinted saliva. Within seconds after falling, the child's entire body begins to shake—or "convulse"—violently and rhythmically. The child has difficulty breathing and may begin to turn blue (see *cyanosis*). Because abdominal muscles are tensed against the bladder, the child may involuntarily urinate. Although the convulsion seems to observers to last for a long time, it is likely to be over in less than 5 minutes. Finally, the child's color returns to normal and, exhausted, he or she goes into a deep sleep for several hours. If sleep lasts less time, the child is likely to wake with a splitting headache that lasts for hours. Upon awakening, the child has no recollection of the seizure.

Not every grand mal seizure progresses in such a fashion, although they all involve a loss of consciousness and violent shaking of the body. The reason symptoms are so severe is that electrical abnormalities develop throughout the entire brain. The frequency with which an epileptic child has grand mal seizures varies from none or 1 a year to 5 or more a day. Grand mal is also the most common type of isolated seizure among children who are not epileptic.

Petit Mal Seizures

Petit mal, another French term, means "little malady," and petit mal seizures are far less obvious than grand mal seizures (even though both affect the entire brain). In general a petit mal seizure involves a momentary loss of consciousness, which observers may not even notice. During a petit mal seizure, a child's face may go blank for a second or two, or the child may appear to be staring into space. Because of this symptom, petit mal seizures are now called absence seizures. (The word "absence" is pronounced the French way—"ab-SAHNSE"—but it means the same thing in English. This term is also used to distinguish such seizures from others that are "little" but are not the same.) Sometimes the eyelids droop, and blinking or muscle twitching occur. In other cases arms and legs twitch slightly, and the child may drop what he or she is holding. Whatever the symptoms, the entire episode lasts only a few seconds, after which the child resumes what he or she was doing as though nothing ever happened.

About 5 percent of all children with epilepsy experience petit mal seizures, which are uncommon among children who do not have recurrent seizures. Most affected children are between the ages of 4 and 15. Many do not know they are having seizures, even though some children involuntarily "tune out" as many as 100 times a day. To an observer, a child who suffers from frequent petit mal seizures may seem to be an inattentive daydreamer.

Focal Seizures

Focal seizures are different from grand and petit mal because they affect only part of the brain. The symptoms of focal seizures vary according to what part of the brain is involved. Most often, a focal seizure affects a part of the brain called the temporal lobe, which is responsible for speech, perceiving smells, and storing feelings and memories. When a focal seizure occurs in the temporal lobe, a child may, for example, "smell" an unpleasant odor, become exceedingly anxious or confused, or have a strange feeling that something terrible is about to happen. When a focal seizure affects the memory, a child may have a vivid memory of some event from the past (usually the same one he or she remembers during other seizures) or may experience déjà vu (a sense of having been in the exact same situation before).

During a focal seizure a child interrupts what he or she is doing and seems to lose contact with the environment. The child may exhibit strange behavior, such as smacking the lips, turning the head to one side, stooping down, jerking arms and legs, or releasing objects from hands. The specific symptoms, which rarely last more than a minute, are a clue as to what part of the brain is being affected. Sometimes a focal seizure is the first stage of a grand mal seizure. In this case it is called an aura and can serve as a warning sign to a child that a grand mal seizure is about to begin. Focal seizures are rare among children who do not have epilepsy.

The following types of seizures are less common:

Minor Motor Seizures

Minor motor seizures involve movements that are less violent than those associated with grand mal seizures. However, unlike grand mal seizures (and other types), minor motor episodes tend to be associated with severe brain problems, usually ones that are congenital (present at birth) and involve *mental retardation.* A minor motor seizure tends to be characterized by a sudden fall or nodding of the head because of loss of muscle tone (atonic seizure); jerking movements in arms or legs (myoclonic seizure); or brief stiffening of the trunk or limbs (tonic seizure). These types of seizures may occur in the same child at different times.

Infantile Spasms

Infantile spasms are a type of minor motor seizure that affect babies less than 18 months old, often those who are born with severe brain disorders. Infantile spasms involve simultaneous spasms of all the muscles of the body. The spasms cause the thigh to bend so that the head and knees jerk together, and for this reason infantile spasms are also called jackknife seizures. The jackknifing motion is sometimes accompanied by breathing difficulty and a loss of consciousness. In some cases spasms resemble more subdued minor motor seizures; one or two extremities may simply shake, for example. A baby may experience 5 to 10 jackknife seizures in a row for 30 seconds. Bouts of spasms sometimes recur as often as every 10 minutes.

Before much was known about these seizure variations, epilepsy was a frightening disorder. Many epileptics suffered from discrimination, guilt, and feelings of low self-worth. Today, however, the mechanism that causes seizures is better understood. Almost every affected person can benefit from medical treatment, and some are candidates for surgery. Some children with epilepsy respond so well to treatment that seizures cease to occur. Many others experience seizures far less frequently. In addition, for reasons that remain unclear, some children without obvious, disabling underlying conditions outgrow epilepsy.

Because many seizure disorders can be controlled, most people with epilepsy are not restricted in their activities or occupational pursuits. Federal laws prohibit discrimination against epileptics by employers, and most employers realize that, statistically, people with epilepsy are no more likely than others to cause accidents or miss days at work.

CAUSE

The most common cause of an isolated seizure during childhood is a high, rapidly rising *fever.* The fever may rise so quickly that it is not detected until the onset of a seizure, which is usually of the grand mal variety. The way fever provokes seizures is not well understood. Febrile (fever-induced) seizures tend to run in families, and experts believe a genetic component is probably involved (see *genetic disorders).* For reasons that remain unclear, febrile seizures are most common among children between the ages of 6 months and 4 years.

Children who have 1 febrile seizure have a 20 percent chance of having another one. After 2 febrile seizures the risk of having more increases to 40 percent. Unless prolonged—lasting 20 minutes or longer—febrile seizures do not predispose to later epilepsy.

In addition to fever, certain short-term diseases, such as *nephritis* (kidney inflamma-

tion), can cause one or two seizures.

Congenital problems predisposing to epilepsy include brain malformation, malformation of blood vessels in the brain, or brain damage at birth. In addition, severe congenital disorders affecting the brain, such as *Tay-Sachs disease, cerebral palsy,* or tuberous sclerosis, are sometimes associated with recurrent seizures. Most children with seizures do not, however, have a severe congenital disorder, and epilepsy is not associated with *mental retardation.* People of all different levels of intelligence suffer from epilepsy.

Epilepsy can be caused by a severe, inborn (or sometimes, acquired) problem involving metabolism. Such problems can include *hypoglycemia* (lack of adequate sugar in the circulating blood), or drastically low levels in the blood of other needed chemicals.

After birth a severe infection of the central nervous system can produce scars on the brain that predispose to epilepsy. Such infections include *encephalitis* and *meningitis.* Other acquired problems that can lead to epilepsy include conditions that interfere with the flow of blood to the brain, such as clots in the blood vessels supplying the brain, heart problems, *brain tumor,* or *head injuries* (see also *stroke).*

Ingestion of large amounts of certain substances can also lead to seizures. Among children, the most common causes of seizures associated with ingestion of chemicals are use of drugs (such as antidepressants or stimulants) and *lead poisoning.*

Despite all of these known causes of epilepsy, about 40 percent of all childhood cases are idiopathic (of unknown cause). Since idiopathic epilepsy tends to run in families, experts believe that a complicated genetic process is involved. Children with idiopathic epilepsy appear to be more likely to outgrow the condition than those whose seizures have an identifiable cause.

Some children with idiopathic epilepsy find that certain stimuli can trigger a seizure. These include lack of sleep, fatigue, blinking lights, emotional *stress, colds* or other infections, sudden noises, or—among adolescent girls—menstrual periods.

DIAGNOSIS

Medical attention should be sought immediately after a child's first seizure. Even if parents are not sure that a child is having seizures—if, for example, they suspect that a child's "inattentiveness" may be due to petit mal seizures—a diagnosis should be sought promptly.

A physician examining a child with suspected seizures has three goals: to determine whether the child truly has had a seizure, to determine the cause of the seizure if there has been one, and to determine whether a child has, or is likely to develop, epilepsy. During the diagnostic procedure a physician may consult a neurologist (nervous system specialist) for assistance.

Before performing any examinations a physician asks the child and his or her parents to describe the suspected seizure (or seizures) and the circumstances under which it (they) occurred. The physician also takes the child's medical and family histories. These preliminary steps are followed by a thorough physical examination, with special attention to neurological functions such as reflexes and coordination.

The most reliable test for epilepsy is electroencephalography, a procedure that records electrical activity in the brain. For this test a child lies down on a testing couch. A technician uses special paste to apply metallic disks (electrodes) to various parts of the child's scalp. The electrodes detect electrical activity in the brain. They are connected by wires to a complex machine called an electroencephalograph, which records brain activity to produce an electroencephalogram (EEG). This entire procedure is painless and lasts about an hour.

If a child has epilepsy, abnormal electrical discharges are usually indicated on an EEG, even if the child is not having seizures during the test. Similarly, an EEG can be used to ensure that the child's treatment program is effectively suppressing the brain discharges. It is important to remember that a single EEG that fails to show electrical discharges does not disprove that a child has epilepsy; in a small percentage of cases an individual EEG does not show discharges when a child actually has epilepsy.

Other types of diagnostic tests ordered by a physician depend on the apparent cause of a seizure.

COMPLICATIONS

Children who have frequent, uncontrollable grand mal seizures may not be able to participate in as many activities as other children can. In many cases, however, seizures can be controlled and the only common complications are emotional difficulties stemming from negative feelings about epilepsy. All children think about who they are and what life has granted them. Epileptic children may have strong feelings of anger, sadness, or fear about their medical problem and the necessary diagnostic and treatment procedures. Emotional complications are most likely to ensue if an epileptic child fails to receive emotional support.

In very rare cases, usually associated with severe epilepsy and other serious brain disorders, a child may experience a grand mal seizure that continues far beyond the usual duration, resulting in brain damage, or even death (see Emergency Action, above).

TREATMENT AND PREVENTION

Nothing can be done to stop a seizure once it starts, except when a child is experiencing a life-threatening, prolonged grand mal seizure. In such cases emergency room personnel can administer medication to halt seizure activity (see Emergency Action, above). Other types of seizures tend to last only seconds or a few minutes, during which observers should remain calm and simply write down the details of the seizure—including its duration—for reporting to a physician later.

Treating epilepsy essentially means preventing seizures. To some extent the focus of a treatment program depends on the cause of the child's seizures.

In many cases the cause cannot be "cured" or is unknown. Fortunately, many children with epilepsy respond well to the use of special medications called anticonvulsants. These medications work by preventing nerve cells from accidentally firing off. Many different types of anticonvulsants exist. The type and dosage selected vary from child to child and must be carefully regulated for two reasons. First, an incorrect dosage of anticonvulsants can produce side effects such as sleepiness, dizziness, coordination problems, and nausea. In addition, a change in a child's condition can render his or her current medication ineffective. Anticonvulsant effectiveness can be monitored through periodic blood tests.

No matter how infrequent a child's seizures are, anticonvulsants are effective only when taken regularly, usually at least once a day. If a child abruptly stops taking an anticonvulsant, a great risk exists that many seizures will develop in the near future. Many children, however, can be gradually weaned from anticonvulsants because they stop having seizures for a significant period of time—usually 2 years or more—and improvement registers on their EEGs. In fact, about 50 to 60 percent of all children with idiopathic epilepsy or with certain types of partial seizures eventually stop taking medicine and never experience more seizures. Other epileptic children must continue taking anticonvulsants throughout their lives.

Some children who have experienced a febrile seizure also benefit from anticonvulsants, although a physician's decision to prescribe medication depends on many factors, including the results of the neurological examination and the EEG. If, for example, the child has a family history of febrile seizures that stopped in early childhood, medication is not likely to be prescribed.

Not all types of epilepsy respond to medication. Children with some types of focal epilepsy continue to have seizures while taking anticonvulsants. In some cases these types of epilepsy involve the presence of scar tissue on the surface of the temporal lobe of the brain. Surgical operations after thorough testing in a hospital are ordered for a small percentage of patients with focal epilepsies in an attempt to remove scar tissue and obtain a cure.

Sometimes seizures that cannot be controlled directly by medical or surgical means can be prevented by avoiding the circumstances that trigger them. If, for example, a teenage girl tends to develop seizures during menstrual periods, a physician may be able to suggest medication or other types of therapy to reduce the stressful effects of menstruation on the body. And since unusual changes in sleeping habits (such as staying up very late or all night) or in diet (such as skipping meals) can sometimes lead to extra seizures, good general health habits are important. If emotional factors seem to trigger seizures, psychotherapy may be useful.

Whether or not a child's epilepsy can be treated, steps can be taken to minimize the adverse effects of the condition on the child's life. Parents should come to a thorough understanding of a child's epilepsy and should come to grips with their own feelings about the condition. Parents sometimes worry too much about their child and are overly protective, preventing the child from enjoying the fullest possible range of activities. In other cases parents are afraid of their child's epilepsy and are unable to offer adequate emotional support. Many parents—as well as their children—benefit from discussing their feelings with a psychiatrist, psychologist, or social worker well acquainted with the problems of epilepsy.

In general, parents should encourage the child to be as active as he or she desires. Activities should be forcibly curtailed only if they are potentially dangerous for a child who is prone to have frequent seizures. For example, it may be inadvisable for a child who suffers frequent, uncontrollable grand mal seizures to swim alone, climb trees or poles, or ride a bike, or for a teenager to drive a car.

Even if a child's epilepsy is under control, the appropriate teachers and school authorities should be informed about the condition and should be told exactly what to do in case a seizure does occur. Speaking directly with a physician allows school personnel to obtain answers to any questions they may have.

If parents of a child with idiopathic epilepsy are concerned about the possibility that their future children will suffer from the condition, they may find genetic counseling helpful (see *genetic disorders*).

A good source of general information about seizures is the book *Does Your Child Have Epilepsy?* by J. Jan, R. Ziegler, and E. Erba (Baltimore: University Park Press, 1982). For more information write or call the Epilepsy Foundation of America, 4351 Garden City Drive, Landover, MD 20785 (phone: 800-332-1000).

SHOCK

EMERGENCY ACTION
Seek immediate medical attention if an injured or ill child has the following signs and symptoms:

- nausea, often *vomiting*
- weakness
- cool, clammy, pale skin
- weak, rapid pulse
- thirst
- *dizziness* or faintness
- increased breathing rate

These are signs of shock, a potentially life-threatening situation which requires immediate treatment.

Keep the child warm while waiting for transportation or help to arrive by covering the child with whatever is available. If the child is on the ground, place a blanket or coat underneath to insulate the body against dampness. Even leaves or newspapers can be used to protect the child from chilling.

Keep the child lying on his or her back with the feet raised about 12 to 18 inches off the ground. This can be done by placing a folded blanket or other suitable object underneath the child's heels. If the child has a head or chest injury or if breathing is labored, elevate only the head in the same manner. Elevate any injured limb so that it is higher than the heart in order to reduce circulation in that part of the body. See the Emergency Action section of *fractures* if appropriate. See Chapter 10, "Basic First Aid" for proper procedures to stop bleeding. If a child is not breathing, start artificial respiration immediately. If the child is unconscious and not breathing, start cardiopulmonary resuscitation (CPR). See instructions for giving artificial respiration and CPR in Chapter 10, "Basic First Aid."

If a child is bleeding from the mouth, is nauseated, or has vomited, have him or her lie on one side so that fluid of any kind may drain out of the mouth and not into the airways. Do not give the child food or water.

If a child in shock caused by insect venom has previously suffered a similar severe allergic reaction and has been treated with prescription antihistamines or hormones (epinephrine), administer these medications immediately.

DESCRIPTION

Shock is a serious disorder of blood circulation, caused by severe illness or injury. It is produced by slowed blood circulation and falling blood pressure, as well as the resulting strain on body organs. If untreated, shock becomes worse; vital body activities begin to fail, and death can occur if treatment is delayed. If both shock and the underlying cause, however, are treated promptly and effectively, an individual's chances of complete recovery are excellent.

The 3 major kinds of shock are traumatic, anaphylactic, and insulin. The most common is traumatic shock, resulting from serious injury. Severe reactions to certain substances can cause anaphylactic shock, while insulin shock occurs only when the level of insulin in a diabetic's body is too high. Anaphylactic shock is perhaps the most dangerous form, since sensitive individuals can begin to react violently within minutes after the offending substance enters the body.

CAUSE

Any of these general conditions may lead to shock:

- significant bleeding or *dehydration* (a condition characterized by cool, dry, pale skin, dry tongue, thirst, listlessness, rapid pulse, and sunken eyes), the loss of excessive amounts of body fluids
- insufficient oxygen supply to the lungs
- nerve damage and loss of control of bodily activities
- severe infection
- heart disease or injury to the heart and its blood vessels
- drug overdose

Falls, automobile accidents, and gunshot wounds often produce injuries among children that can lead to traumatic shock. Anaphylactic shock most often develops as a severe allergic reaction to the venom in certain insect stings (see *stinging insect reactions*). Much less common causes of anaphylactic shock are reactions to certain active medications (such as penicillin) and to some foods (see *food allergy*).

SIGNS AND SYMPTOMS

Traumatic shock is characterized by several of these signs and symptoms:

- extreme overall weakness, especially with faintness and tingling fingers and toes
- weak, rapid pulse—faster than 100 beats per minute among children or 140 beats per minute among infants
- pale skin ranging in color from ashen or "sick" white to bluish gray
- cool, clammy skin—perspiration or "cold sweat" appears most often on the upper lip, forehead, back of the neck, and palms of the hands
- a glassy or dull look to the eyes—pupils in one or both eyes may be dilated
- increased breathing rate, especially shallow, irregular breaths or long, sudden sighs
- nausea, often *vomiting*
- sudden, excessive thirst
- red or white blotches or streaks in the skin
- restless, anxious behavior and speech
- unresponsiveness or drowsiness
- in severe cases, loss of consciousness

Anaphylactic shock is characterized by several of these signs and symptoms:

- extreme overall weakness
- dizziness
- pale skin
- coughing, wheezing or both
- itching, hives, or both
- severe swelling at the location of an insect bite or possibly elsewhere on the body
- nausea, often vomiting
- anxious or restless behavior and speech
- *seizures*
- possibly, loss of consciousness

DIAGNOSIS

All types of shock are diagnosed by a physician or other health professional on the basis of signs and symptoms and the results of a physical examination that includes checking blood pressure, heart rate, and breathing rate.

Anaphylactic shock may be diagnosed by observing a child's signs and symptoms. All but the youngest children can report an insect sting, which usually is sufficient to diagnose anaphylactic shock. Parents should be alert to the statistically slim possibility of anaphylactic shock caused by reaction to a drug such as penicillin or to food, especially nuts. If a child shows any signs of a reaction, a physician should be notified immediately.

TREATMENT

In a hospital children with traumatic shock receive intravenous fluids and salts in order to restore blood volume and improve circulation. Whole blood and plasma transfusions may be given if necessary. If a child is unconscious, heart-lung resuscitation (CPR) may be necessary. Breathing assistance may be required. When shock is under control, diagnosis and treatment may be started for the underlying cause.

Hospital treatment of anaphylactic shock consists of epinephrine injection and, if necessary, CPR and breathing assistance. Recovery from anaphylactic shock is usually prompt, uneventful, and without complications.

For information about insulin reaction (insulin shock), see *diabetes.*

PREVENTION

Since traumatic shock usually results from an accident, parents and children should be alert at all times to the possibility of accidents. Many accidents at home, in school, and at play are preventable if care is exercised and precautions are taken in advance.

Shock that occasionally develops as a complication of *dehydration* in a serious illness or infection can usually be anticipated, prevented, or treated promptly by a child's physician.

Anaphylactic shock can often be prevented simply by avoiding those medications and foods to which a child is especially sensitive. Keeping a supply of appropriate antihistamines or epinephrine, a hormone, available for emergency use at home and in the car is helpful. It is difficult to prevent insect stings except by avoiding places where particular insects may be known to be a problem or where bees are swarming (see *stinging insect reactions).*

SICKLE CELL ANEMIA

DESCRIPTION

Sickle cell anemia is a serious hereditary blood disorder (see *blood disorders),* characterized by periods of relative health interrupted by crises (episodes of severe illness). Victims are always anemic (see *anemia)* and are susceptible to certain serious infections. (Anemia is the condition of not having enough oxygen-carrying components in the blood. It can cause fatigue and *jaundice.)*

Sickle cell anemia is seen only in individuals who inherit 2 genes—1 defective gene from each parent—for the production of an abnormal hemoglobin called sickle cell hemoglobin. Hemoglobin is the red pigment that gives color to red blood cells and that carries oxygen throughout the body. Hemoglobin picks up oxygen as the blood circulates through the lungs. As the oxygenated blood circulates through the body, hemoglobin becomes deoxygenated because oxygen is delivered to body cells. Although sickle cell hemoglobin functions normally in carrying oxygen, it has a tendency to congeal (sickle) as it loses oxygen. As a result, the normally round and puffy red blood cells become crescent- or sickle-shaped. Once the blood circulates through the lungs and picks up more oxygen, hemoglobin regains its normal shape.

Red blood cells containing sickle hemoglobin are particularly fragile. This fragility means that these red blood cells break down easily, causing persistent anemia (see *anemia, hemolytic*). Red blood cells containing sickle hemoglobin may also become distorted and stiffened and can actually block small capillaries (tiny blood vessels connecting the arteries with the veins), thereby depriving the surrounding tissues of essential nutrients and oxygen. On the positive side, sickle hemoglobin protects against infection with malaria.

The gene for sickle hemoglobin is seen most commonly in blacks, although it is also carried by rare individuals of Mediterranean, Indian, and Asian ancestry. In the United States approximately 1 out of every 10 blacks carries a single gene for sickle hemoglobin. These individuals are entirely healthy and have no symptoms of the disease; they merely carry the sickle cell trait. Approximately 1 in 500 American blacks carries two abnormal sickle hemoglobin genes and actually has the disease. Between 50,000 and 70,000 American blacks have sickle cell anemia.

By and large, individuals with sickle cell anemia lead productive lives and are able to hold good jobs, raise families, and participate fully in normal social, political, and educational activities. Many patients live into their forties and fifties, and rare patients have lived as long as 70 years.

CAUSE

If both parents carry the sickle cell trait, each of their potential children will have a 25 percent chance of having sickle cell anemia and a 50 percent chance of having the trait. If only 1 parent has the sickle cell trait, there is absolutely no risk of a child's having sickle cell anemia, although there is a 50 percent chance that the child will have the trait.

SIGNS AND SYMPTOMS AND COMPLICATIONS

The symptoms of sickle cell anemia fall into two major categories. Due to the fragility of the red blood cells, *anemia* is always present, leading to a tendency to become fatigued, to be less able to tolerate exercise, and to develop *jaundice* (which results from the breakdown of the hemoglobin pigment). In addition, due to the sporadic blockage of the small capillaries in any part of the body, a wide variety of symptoms can occur.

It is almost impossible to describe the "typical patient" with sickle cell anemia, since symptoms and their severity vary widely. Certain features, however, are common to almost all patients with sickle cell anemia. In general, newborns are entirely well with normal birthweights, normal developmental milestones, and no appearance of symptoms until about 3 months of age. The first sign of sickle cell anemia in a young baby is likely to be painful swelling of the hands or feet, crankiness, or somewhat later, refusal to walk. This symptom is due to sludging of the red blood cells in the capillaries of the small bones in the hands and feet, causing obstructed blood flow. Sludging means that red blood cells settle out of the liquid portion of blood and are deposited like sediment in capillaries. Sludging of the red blood cells gradually disappears by itself but, until it does, requires medical attention to alleviate pain and to identify any possible accompanying illness. The baby will probably appear pale, perhaps slightly jaundiced, but otherwise generally healthy.

The single most serious complication of sickle cell anemia in a child under 5 years of age is infection. Sludging and blockage of the capillaries in the spleen, an organ which normally filters out bacteria from the bloodstream, occurs during the first year of life, leaving the child particularly susceptible to a possibly fatal *bloodstream infection* called sepsis. Parents of young children with sickle cell anemia are therefore instructed to look for early symptoms of infection, including fussiness, irritability, *fever,* and poor feeding. Parents should seek immediate medical attention if their child has any of these symptoms. If bloodstream infections are treated early enough with antibiotics, affected children can be spared fatal complications. Over the age of 5, after the child has developed certain natural antibodies to these bacteria, the likelihood of a fatal bacterial infection is considerably less.

The problems of the school-age child with sickle cell anemia generally involve repeated episodes of sludging of red blood cells in the capillaries of large bones. In most cases these episodes are relatively mild, resulting in slight, aching bone pain.

As the child grows older, certain other organ systems may be involved in this capillary sludging process. If this happens in the lungs, for example, a serious respiratory illness develops. A very rare complication, which occurs in less than 10 percent of patients with sickle cell anemia, is sludging in the vessels of the brain, resulting in stroke.

Adolescents with sickle cell anemia experience considerable anxiety and concern because their physical development is usually delayed 2 to 3 years. These teenagers are usually smaller than their classmates and are frequently teased about their lack of sexual development. Puberty does occur, however, and studies have shown that women with sickle cell anemia are normally fertile. Women with sickle cell anemia are certainly capable of carrying and delivering normal children, but they have high-risk pregnancies with a high rate of complications that may result in miscarriages, premature deliveries, or increasing anemia in the mother. These pregnancies need to be followed by an obstetrician with particular experience in high-risk pregnancies, and blood transfusions may be required throughout the pregnancy.

Adults with sickle cell anemia may begin to show signs of chronic (persistent or long-term) sludging in the capillaries of the lungs and the kidneys and may go on to develop chronic lung failure and chronic kidney failure. These two complications contribute to the early death of some patients with sickle cell anemia.

Other individuals may experience sludging in the capillaries of the retina of the eye, a condition that ultimately may lead to *blindness.*

Although all of these complications (kidney failure, lung failure, blindness, serious infection, and repeated bone crisis) do occur in patients with sickle cell anemia, it is very rare for *all* of these complications to happen to a single individual.

DIAGNOSIS

Although the symptoms of sickle cell anemia rarely become apparent before an infant is 3 months old, the diagnosis of sickle cell anemia can be made at any time. Fetuses affected with sickle cell anemia can be identified by amniocentesis (withdrawal of amniotic fluid by a needle inserted into the uterus through the abdominal wall). Amniotic fluid contains fetal cells which in turn contain hemoglobin genes; as a result, the hemoglobin genes can be examined directly. Sickle cell trait can be identified by amniocentesis, but this is not done since the risk from amniocentesis is greater than the risk of sickle cell trait.

In many communities a simple blood test is performed on all black infants so that they can be diagnosed even before the first symptoms appear. This testing is very important to prevent some of the potentially fatal complications that are unique to the first 2 years of life.

The healthy carriers of sickle cell trait can also be easily identified by a simple blood test. It is particularly important that black couples who are planning a family be screened for sickle cell trait, so that they will be aware of the chances of having a child with sickle cell anemia.

TREATMENT

No cure exists for sickle cell anemia. However, improving general medical care has meant longer, healthier lives for children affected by the disorder. Current emphasis is on good nutrition, patient education, and control of infection. A close working relationship with a primary care physician who is acquainted with the early signs of complications of sickle cell anemia is of prime importance. Close follow-up of young children with sickle cell anemia is particularly important to prevent early life-threatening infectious complications. *Anemia* may worsen as a result of infection or sudden enlargement of the spleen; an affected child may need to be admitted to a hospital for treatment of infection or pain. Pregnancy and surgery, as well as eye disease, cause problems that should be treated by specialists who have particular experience with sickle cell anemia.

The use of pneumococcal vaccine and early antibiotic therapy has saved the lives of many young children with sickle cell anemia. Slight, aching bone pain can be handled easily at home with rest, fluids, and over-the-counter pain preparations. Occasionally these episodes can be severe enough to warrant hospitalization of the child for more thorough treatment of pain. Most children with sickle cell anemia have normal intelligence, function perfectly normally in school, and miss very few days because of these painful bone crises.

Serious respiratory illness requires hospitalization for the administration of oxygen and, possibly, blood transfusion therapy.

Newer techniques of laser therapy of the retina can be used to treat patients who experience sludging in the capillaries of the retina of the eye, and routine ophthalmologic care is advised to detect the early lesions before they lead to blindness.

PREVENTION

Sickle cell anemia cannot be prevented. However, couples with sickle cell trait should consider receiving genetic counseling (see *genetic disorders*).

The National Association for Sickle Cell Disease provides information and support services. Chapters are located in many cities. The headquarters' address is 3460 Wilshire Boulevard, Suite 1012, Los Angeles, CA 90010 (phone: 800-421-8453).

SINUSITIS

DESCRIPTION

Sinusitis is a disease that involves inflammation and infection of the mucous membrane that lines the sinuses. The sinuses are a group of air-filled hollows within the bones of the face and skull (see Fig. 36A, p. 679). These hollows are connected to the nasal passages through thin, strawlike passageways. The mucous membranes of both the nose and the sinuses secrete mucus to humidify inhaled air and to prevent the mucous membranes lining them from becoming dry. If inhaled air is too dry, the mucus produced is insufficient to keep the mucous membranes moist, and the mucus dries up.

Liquid mucus from the sinuses normally drains into the nasal passages. If the passageways connecting the sinuses and the nasal passages are blocked by dried mucus or by another obstruction, several problems arise: liquid mucus that is being secreted by the sinus membranes cannot drain from the sinuses, air cannot flow into the sinuses, the mucous membrane of the sinuses becomes inflamed, and pressure builds up within the sinuses, causing pain. Accumulated mucus allows growth of bacteria within the normally sterile sinuses, and infection results.

During infancy and early childhood, most cases of sinusitis are acute (occurring once or infrequently), self-limited, and uncomplicated. Acute sinusitis occurs more often after 2 years of age than before. An acute episode typically lasts for a week or 10 days. During middle childhood and adolescence, chronic (persistent or constantly recurring) sinusitis occurs more frequently.

The severity of sinusitis varies: it can be a mild, self-limited, temporary condition, one associated with other diseases, or one that can lead to serious complications.

CAUSE

Infection of sinus tissue is most often caused by bacteria.

Any condition that interferes with sinus drainage by blocking the passageways leading from the sinuses to the nose can result in sinusitis. The most common examples of such conditions are nasal congestion and inflammation of nasal membranes. These conditions can be caused by *colds* or other viral infections of the upper respiratory tract or by allergies (see *allergies*).

Other causes of obstruction include injury to the nose (see *facial fractures*) and *deviated nasal septum* (in which the partition dividing the nasal cavity is irregularly shaped). Infected or enlarged adenoids (see *tonsillitis and adenoiditis*) or growths, called *polyps,* in the nose can also impair sinus drainage. In addition, foreign objects in the nose (see *nose, injury to and foreign objects in*) can block the passageways to the sinuses.

Increased air pressure, such as that which occurs when an airplane is descending, can force infected nasal secretions into the sinuses, causing sinusitis. It can also be caused by contact with chlorinated water (which irritates the membranes lining the nose and sinuses), especially during diving, when water pressure can force bacteria present in the nasal passages into the sinuses. Less frequently, sinusitis develops when infection spreads from the decaying root of an upper tooth to the sinuses.

Children who are unable to clear their sinuses of secretions are particularly susceptible to sinusitis. For instance, sinusitis can appear in association with conditions such as *cystic fibrosis,* immune deficiency diseases (see *immune disorders*), and *asthma.*

Chronic sinusitis can be triggered by inhaling cigarette smoke. Contrary to popular belief, recurrent episodes of sinusitis can develop in virtually any climate—whether hot or cold, damp or dry.

SIGNS AND SYMPTOMS

The most prominent symptom of sinusitis is *headache* that is not relieved by lying down. The headache may be characterized by localized pain or a feeling of fullness in one side of the head. Pinpointing the region of the headache can help determine which sinuses are affected. For example, when frontal sinuses are involved, the headache centers in the lower forehead, above and between the eyes; the area may be painful when pressed or when the child bends over.

Other signs and symptoms of sinusitis include *fever;* nasal congestion; thick, profuse nasal discharge and resulting postnasal drip (a discharge of mucus from the back of the nose down into the throat); persistent breathing through the mouth and the bad breath that follows; *cough* in the early morning; paleness; and tiredness.

Children with persistent sinusitis may have a chronic cough.

DIAGNOSIS

If a child has a high *fever* and other signs of sinusitis, a physician should be consulted.

A physician diagnoses sinusitis by taking a child's medical history and performing a physical examination. The medical history of a child with sinusitis usually reveals persistent nasal congestion. The family or child may have a history of *allergies.* Physical examination involves looking inside the nose with an examining instrument. The first purpose of this examination is to detect persistent inflammation of the nasal and sinus membranes. The second purpose is to detect the presence of yellow, greenish, milky, or opaque discharge (pus).

As part of the diagnostic examination for older children, a physician may use a technique called transillumination: by holding a strong light source on one side of the nose and looking on the other side, the physician may be able to see cloudiness, an indication of inflammation. An X-ray film of the sinus may help a physician to confirm the diagnosis. Opaque, hazy, or cloudy spots on the X ray indicate the presence of pus, a key sign of infection.

Occasionally a physician takes a culture of the mucus to identify the specific organism causing sinusitis. In addition, if allergies are suspected, skin tests may be performed.

COMPLICATIONS

Complications of sinusitis are rare. When complications do occur, they indicate that the infection has spread beyond the sinuses. If a child has chills or a high fever with sinusitis, it is likely that complications have developed.

Infection from the sinuses can spread within facial and upper respiratory structures. Probable sites of secondary infection are the eyes, eye sockets, and brain. If infection spreads to the eyes, problems such as inflammation of the optic nerve can develop.

If infection spreads upward within the facial bones, one or both eye sockets may become inflamed. If inflammation is untreated, the eye sockets may even begin to decay, or an abscess (pocket of pus) or blood clot may form.

Infection from the sinuses can also spread in the bloodstream throughout the body. For instance, if the lungs are involved, bronchitis (inflammation of the breathing tubes) or *pneumonia* may develop. Kidney problems may also develop as a result of the spread of infection. An abscess in the brain can occur if pus from sinusitis collects in or near the brain. Because this is usually a complication of frontal sinusitis, it occurs most often among adolescents.

Sinusitis can also lead to a serious complication such as *meningitis* (an inflammation of the protective covering of the brain and spinal cord). Fortunately, only a very small number of children with sinusitis develop meningitis. The development of bacterial meningitis during infancy and early childhood usually follows a specific pattern: a viral upper respiratory infection leads to sinusitis, in turn leading to bacterial infection of the bloodstream, which eventually results in meningitis.

TREATMENT

The purpose of treatment is to clear the sinuses and the passageways to them so that accumulated fluid drains, air flows into the sinuses, inflammation can be diminished, pressure and resulting pain is relieved, and the infection is brought under control.

Many cases of sinusitis cannot be controlled or cured until obstructions such as septal defects (see *deviated nasal septum*), polyps, or foreign objects are removed or repaired. Treatment of underlying conditions such as *allergies* can also relieve sinusitis.

For acute sinusitis caused by nasal congestion due to an upper respiratory tract infection, a combination of decongestants and antibiotics is usually effective. Decongestants, either nasal or oral, help to clear the sinuses by reducing the swelling of nasal membranes. Antibiotics are prescribed to combat bacterial infection and prevent complications. Antibiotics are usually taken for 2 to 3 weeks for acute cases, 4 to 6 weeks for chronic ones.

For chronic sinusitis that does not respond to antibiotics, the physician may have to clean the sinuses and make an enlarged passageway into the nasal cavity to encourage better drainage of fluid. For some children a physician may drain the sinuses, using suction.

Application of heat, inhalation of steam, and a pain-reducing medication may help some children. Consult the physician for specific recommendations and read the discussion of nonprescription medications beginning on p. 102.

PREVENTION

It is helpful to try to maintain adequate levels of humidity indoors by placing pans of water on radiators and using cool-mist vaporizers in bedrooms. Children should drink plenty of fluids, which can keep their nasal membranes moist.

Goggles and nose plugs should be worn regularly by swimmers and divers so that chlorinated water does not get into their noses.

SLEEP DISORDERS

DESCRIPTION AND CAUSE

The amount of sleep a child needs depends on his or her age and varies to some extent among children. Almost as important as the amount of sleep a child gets is the quality of sleep; a child who fully awakens 6 or 7 times a night is not likely to function at his or her best the next day. For at least 15 percent of all children, a problem with the quality or quantity of sleep is serious enough to cause concern among parents.

Temporary or occasional sleep problems lasting a few nights to several weeks are common. Among young children they are often related to growth and normal stages of emotional development. A 1-year-old child may find separating from parents at night difficult and may have trouble settling down to sleep. As a toddler is toilet trained, he or she may resist going to sleep for fear of losing control over bladder and bowels. Preschoolers are subject to occasional nightmares as they learn to control their own urges and impulses. Such short-term problems tend to be outgrown. Unless these problems persist and interfere with the child's daytime functioning, parental com-

forting and reassurance are usually the only treatment necessary.

Some sleep disorders are more persistent and require more specific treatment. They may result primarily from emotional problems such as *depression* and anxiety (including *phobias)*, abnormal schedules, or inappropriate habits, or they can be triggered by physical or medical abnormalities. Most symptomatic sleep disorders can be treated successfully with professional counseling.

Nightmares

Nightmares are common among all age groups, but especially among preschoolers; they most often occur toward the middle or end of the night. The content of young children's nightmares is usually relatively simple; it tends to involve frightening creatures who cause the child to feel helpless. In many cases such fictitious monsters are based on things a child actually encountered during waking hours, such as a scary cartoon or an unpleasant encounter with a playmate.

A nightmare rarely provokes physical reactions as intense as in a sleep terror (see below), but a child scared by a bad dream may suddenly wake, begin crying, sit up, and even run to his or her parents for comforting. Young children have difficulty describing the dream and may in fact be confused, not really understanding what a dream is or that the monster they just "saw" was not really there.

Sleep Terrors, Sleepwalking, and Sleeptalking

Sleep terrors are characterized by behavior such as crying, thrashing, kicking, moaning, mumbling, and even running about. While often mistaken by parents for nightmares, sleep terrors are not dreams. Rather, they occur during partial arousal from a very deep, nondreaming sleep. Sleep terrors are most common among 2- to 5-year-old children and sometimes persist until adolescence or even adulthood. Boys suffer from them slightly more often than girls. Sleep terrors tend to occur at intervals of days, weeks, or months, but sometimes they occur every night.

When experiencing a sleep terror, a child usually appears to be very confused, perhaps terrified, and he or she may scream. The child is likely to breathe rapidly, sweat profusely, and show other signs usually associated with fear. During a sleep terror the child does not recognize parents and is likely to push them away if they offer comfort. The child is actually in an in-between state of consciousness, partially asleep and partially awake. Rousing the child into full wakefulness is impossible, and attempts to do so only lead to intensification and prolongation of the episode.

Sleep terrors can last from a few seconds to 30 or 40 minutes. They usually appear 1 to 3 hours after the onset of sleep. As soon as an episode ends, the child is likely to calm rapidly, wake briefly, and then go back to sleep, with no memory of the episode then or in the morning. Young children who suffer from sleep terrors are usually well adjusted, but ongoing sleep terrors beyond age 6 may be associated with subtle emotional factors.

In some cases, especially among older children (ages 6 to 12), partial waking from very deep, nondreaming sleep is associated with sleepwalking or sleeptalking. Sleepwalking (also called somnambulism) often involves semipurposeful acts such as dressing, opening doors, eating, urinating, and defecating. During these acts a child has a blank, staring face and either does not respond to others or does so with simple 1- or 2-word replies. The child is able to see and walk around most objects. Although uncommon, accidental injuries may occur during episodes of both sleepwalking and night terrors.

One or two incidents of sleepwalking or sleeptalking are common among all children, especially those who have other family members with a history of walking or talking in their sleep. Like sleep terrors, walking and talking are rarely remembered by the child in the morning.

Insomnia

Insomnia, or sleeplessness, includes difficulty falling asleep, staying asleep through the night, or remaining asleep late enough in the morning. Temporary insomnia is universal among children and adults. It is especially likely to occur when a person is exposed to a source of emotional or physical stress, such as loss of a loved one, a school examination, a move to a new home, or traveling across time zones.

The following variations of insomnia are also common:

- A child who has learned to fall asleep under a certain condition—being rocked by a parent, for example—cannot fall asleep under any other condition. When the child awakens at night, it is impossible for him or her to fall

back asleep. The child may also fight sleep at night, knowing parents will leave the bedside.
- A child who gets too much to drink during the night wakes up frequently. This problem is most common among children 6 months to 3 years old; wakings may be triggered by soaked diapers or learned expectations of nighttime feedings.
- A child does not fall asleep until late at night (10 or 11 P.M., for example) and does not wake up until midmorning (9 or 10 A.M.). The cause is a shifted sleep cycle, which makes it seem as if the child is operating in the wrong time zone. Sometimes the source of the problem is parents' attempt to have a child sleep when they do. Parents may not realize that a child whose cycle is shifted may be unable to fall asleep earlier until the shift is corrected.
- A child's napping schedule interferes significantly with his or her ability to sleep well at night. Naps taken late in the afternoon can cause difficulties at bedtime. Conversely, naps taken early in the morning can interfere with the time a child awakens on subsequent mornings.
- A child has fears that interfere with sleep. Although fear may seem to be focused on such things as the dark or sleeping alone, it often has deeper emotional roots.

Another cause of insomnia is medical illness. For example, one common medical problem leading to sleep disruption is chronic middle ear disease (see *earache and ear infections*).

Excessive Sleepiness

Excessive sleepiness during the day is called hypersomnia. A child may oversleep several hours in the morning or sleep much of the day as well as the night. Upon waking, the child may feel confused. Often the cause of excessive sleeping during the day is not getting enough regular night sleep or having an irregular sleeping schedule. In addition, a number of medical illnesses can cause children to sleep more than normal during the day. Finally, some children, especially adolescents, sleep excessively when they are suffering from *depression*.

Another cause of excessive sleepiness is narcolepsy, characterized by the periodic sudden onset of an overwhelming desire to sleep, which may be difficult to fight. An episode may last from several minutes to more than an hour, although short durations are most common. An affected child can generally be roused easily, feels refreshed upon awakening, and continues without impairment whatever activity he or she was performing before the episode. Narcolepsy is most common among older children, and it rarely begins before adolescence. Children with narcolepsy may become weak when showing a strong emotion, as when laughing or screaming, for example. This symptom, called cataplexy, often does not appear until at least several years after the onset of sleepiness episodes. Both sleepiness and cataplexy can often be treated fairly well with medication. Unfortunately, narcolepsy is a lifelong condition and is not outgrown.

Sleep Apnea

Sleep *apnea* is repetitive cessation of breathing during sleep. All infants have short breathing pauses during sleep; more prolonged episodes of sleep apnea are often experienced by premature infants.

A very different disorder that also involves respiratory pauses is obstructive sleep apnea. It is most common among children who have structural problems involving the nose and throat, such as enlarged tonsils or adenoids (see *tonsillitis and adenoiditis),* obesity (see *weight problems),* or a congenitally malformed jaw or other structure. Such conditions partially obstruct the breathing passage, and forceful breathing at night can actually cause the airway to collapse temporarily. Signs and symptoms of obstructive sleep apnea include loud snoring, struggles to breathe, and respiratory pauses. Daytime drowsiness, decreased performance in school, personality changes, and bed-wetting are also possible. A child's growth may even be delayed, although this happens rarely. Obstructive sleep apnea usually ceases when the underlying condition is detected and treated.

DIAGNOSIS

Parents who know or suspect that their child has a sleep disorder should try to define the disorder as precisely as possible on the basis of the child's signs and symptoms, age, and behavior at bedtime and during the day. If parents cannot decide whether a serious sleep disorder exists, they should mention their concern to a physician during a child's regular checkup.

A physician consulted for sleep terrors usually considers a child's medical history, performs a routine physical examination, and discusses signs and symptoms with parents and child. In many cases this simple procedure is enough for a diagnosis. If the physician suspects an underlying physical problem, appropriate tests are conducted to confirm the diagnosis. If an emotional problem is suspected, the physician may refer the child to a psychiatrist, psychologist, or social worker.

COMPLICATIONS

Certain persistent sleep disorders can interfere with the child's daytime functioning, lower the child's self-image, and create a stressful situation for the rest of the family. Medical complications are rare.

TREATMENT AND PREVENTION

Parents should be understanding and comforting when a child has a nightmare. Parents occasionally can allow a child to crawl into bed with them, if need be, but a child should not get used to sleeping with parents. In the long run a child will sleep better if he or she routinely sleeps alone, and it will be better for his or her psychological development.

Parents of a child who frequently sleepwalks should take accident-prevention measures such as locking doors and windows, removing potentially dangerous objects, and if possible, making any staircases inaccessible at night.

One of the best general guidelines to help a child's sleep is to be sure the child's sleep schedule is regular and appropriate. In general, the younger a child, the more sleep he or she needs; a 3-month-old baby, for example, requires about 18 hours of sleep per day. Preschool children generally feel sleepy during the day and want to take naps. Parents should follow their children's cues to help decide how much sleep and how many naps are needed, but the children should not simply set their own schedules. Parents should set a reasonable schedule that can be maintained consistently. Some flexibility is certainly all right, but not if the schedule interferes with sleep and daytime functioning. A child who naps from 1 P.M. to dinnertime and then sleeps from 11 P.M. until 6 A.M., for example, probably needs to have his or her nap schedule adjusted.

A child's bedtime should be based on the amount of sleep the child needs and what time the child should get up in the morning.

A 5-year-old child, who needs to be awake in time to get ready for school, might, for example, go to bed at 7 P.M. and wake up at 7 A.M. This pattern should be maintained, when possible, even on weekends and during vacations. Children should have a regular bedtime. In addition, prebedtime activities should not include strenuous physical games or exposure to potentially upsetting books, movies, or television shows, such as scary monster shows. Calming activities involving parent and child together, such as reading a pleasurable book, are more appropriate. Bedtime rituals should be time-limited and simple.

Whether or not a child is afraid of the dark or afraid of going to bed alone, it is useful to leave the child's bedroom door open. The child should know that if anything goes wrong during the night, he or she can call for help. A night-light should be left on in the child's bedroom, the hall, or the bathroom.

In the rare event that a child has a severe sleep disorder that does not respond to other forms of treatment, a physician or psychiatrist may prescribe medication to help the child sleep better. Medication is usually used sparingly and is discontinued as a child overcomes or outgrows the sleep disorder.

Information is available from the Association of Sleep Disorder Centers, 604 Second Street S.W., Rochester, MN 55905 (phone: 507-287-6006).

SNAKE BITES

EMERGENCY ACTION

Take a poisonous-snakebite victim to a physician or emergency room immediately. Even though life-threatening complications may not develop until approximately 12 hours after venom enters the body, immediate medical attention is necessary. If possible, telephone ahead so that antivenin treatment (which counteracts the effects of snake venom) can be available, if needed, upon arrival.

Before and during transport, keep the child warm and restrict movement as much as possible. If possible, place the bite area lower than the rest of the body to slow blood and venom flow to the heart. Do not give the child food, liquid, or medication. Watch

carefully for signs of *shock* (characterized by cool, clammy, pale skin, rapid pulse, thirst, dizziness or faintness, and increased breathing rate) and start treatment if necessary (see Chapter 10, "Basic First Aid").

DESCRIPTION

In the United States approximately 45,000 people are bitten by snakes each year. The majority of snakebites are from nonpoisonous varieties, and these bites present few problems. Approximately 8,000 snakebites are from poisonous snakes, resulting in fewer than 20 deaths a year. Ninety percent of all bites occur between April and October.

There are approximately 120 species of snakes in the United States, and only 20 of these are venomous. The 2 most common types of posionous snakes are coral snakes and pit vipers.

Coral snakes are identified by bright red, yellow, and black bands. Their short fangs and small mouths allow them to bite only small targets such as fingers and toes. Coral snakes rarely strike unless provoked. Their venom affects a victim's nervous system.

Pit vipers, including rattlesnakes, cottonmouths, and copperheads, are so named because of the small heat-sensitive pits located between their nostrils and eyes. These snakes strike without provocation, and their long fangs and large mouths allow them to bite deeply. A pit viper's venom affects a victim's circulatory system and may cause internal bleeding.

A rattlesnake is identified by the rattle located at the end of its tail, which emits a warning sound similar to escaping steam before it strikes. A northern copperhead is brown to copper red with darker bands. The southern copperhead is a lighter color, almost pink in some areas. A cottonmouth, also called a water moccasin, has olive, brown, or black skin on its back and a lighter underside. Dark-bordered bands encircle the cottonmouth's body.

The venom of coral snakes and pit vipers is extremely poisonous; victims may die without prompt treatment. With treatment, however, a person bitten by a poisonous snake usually recovers fully with no complications.

SIGNS AND SYMPTOMS

Nonpoisonous snakebites usually consist of 2 curved rows of tooth marks. Bites from nonpoisonous snakes infrequently cause swelling and itching around the bite area.

Venom from a poisonous snakebite usually travels rapidly through the body, and symptoms can appear within minutes.

On the skin surface, the bite of a coral snake appears as tiny puncture wounds resembling small, bloody scratches. Venom-induced symptoms include a slight burning around the bite, nausea or excessive salivation, paralysis of the eyeballs, speech slurring, breathing failure, and ultimately, *coma*.

The presence of 1 or 2 large, bloody puncture wounds on the skin surface followed by a strong burning sensation indicates the bite of a pit viper. Severe pain spreads outward from the bite area. Nausea, *vomiting, breathing difficulty,* generalized weakness, weak pulse, vision trouble, and *shock* usually follow as snake venom spreads throughout the body.

DIAGNOSIS

Diagnosis of a snakebite is based on the presence of imprints on the skin of rows of teeth or 1 or 2 puncture wounds and characteristic signs and symptoms of venom poisoning. Knowledge of a victim's recent whereabouts and activities may help determine the type of snake involved.

TREATMENT

Treatment of bites from harmless snakes involves cleansing of the wound and making sure the child's tetanus toxoid immunization is current (see immunization schedules in Chapter 6, "Going to the Doctor"). Antibiotics may be prescribed to prevent infection from bacteria contained in the snake's mouth. In some cases children have an allergic reaction to snake saliva, and antihistamines may relieve the symptoms.

Emergency action is needed for victims of poisonous snakebites. At the hospital the victim is first treated for *shock,* if necessary. An individual bitten by a poisonous snake may need an injection of antivenin.

PREVENTION

The surest way to prevent snakebites, of course, is to avoid snakes. This is not always possible, however, especially when walking through woods or fields. Wearing gloves, heavy boots, long-sleeved shirts, and heavy, long trousers, particularly when climbing over rocks or through brush, is recommended. Hikers should keep to marked trails, as they are usually well worn and do not provide good hiding places for snakes. In addition, children should learn to identify the most common poisonous snakes. Local libraries and science centers usually have books and pamphlets about snake identification.

Children should always be accompanied by at least one companion when hiking in the woods. A companion's quick action to seek help can mean the difference between life and death for a snakebite victim. (See also Chapter 10, "Basic First Aid.")

SORE THROAT

DESCRIPTION

A sore throat is a symptom of throat infection or irritation. Infection or irritation causes inflammation (swelling, redness, tenderness, and warmth) of throat tissues. The most obvious signs of sore throat are pain and swallowing difficulty. The pain may last for one or more days. Infants with sore throats may be unusually fussy, cry persistently, or refuse to eat or sleep. In general, an infant with a sore throat is difficult to diagnose.

If a sore throat is caused by an infection, the throat and mouth can be red, or have yellow or white spots. In general, sore throats caused by viruses come on gradually and appear with typical cold or flu symptoms (see *colds; influenza).* Sore throats caused by bacteria tend to appear abruptly along with more severe symptoms such as high *fever,* swollen lymph nodes in the neck (see *swollen glands),* and *headache.* It is difficult to distinguish viral from bacterial sore throats.

Frequent sore throats are common among school-aged children. Sore throat is a symptom of more than one third of all acute (occurring once or infrequently) respiratory illnesses of childhood. Children younger than 8 years old account for 60 percent of all sore throats; peak ages for sore throats are from 5 to 10 years.

CAUSE

Sore throat can be a symptom of pharyngitis (any inflammation of the pharynx, or throat) *laryngitis* (inflammation of the larynx, or windpipe), or tonsillitis, (see *tonsilli-*

tis and adenoiditis). Sore throat is frequently a symptom of viral infections—such as *colds*— of the upper respiratory tract (nose and throat). It can also be a symptom of other viral diseases such as mononucleosis (see *mononucleosis, infectious),* viral or mycoplasma *pneumonia,* or *influenza.* The major symptom of *strep throat* and certain other bacterial infections is sore throat.

Inhaling certain substances—such as dust, smoke, chemicals, or pollen—can irritate the mucous membranes of the throat. In addition, sleeping with the mouth open, particularly in a room with dry air, or breathing through the mouth can cause dryness and sore throat. Shouting and prolonged talking or singing can also irritate the throat.

DIAGNOSIS

A physician should be notified if a sore throat does not seem to be caused by a cold, brings severe pain, is accompanied by severe symptoms of a possible bacterial infection, is accompanied by a skin *rash* or by pus on the throat or tonsils, or appears after exposure to strep throat. Any child who has had *rheumatic fever* or kidney disease (see *nephritis)* should be seen by a physician if a sore throat develops.

The physician conducts a physical examination to try to determine the cause. The physician may discover, for instance, that a child has enlarged adenoids (see *tonsillitis and adenoiditis)* that cause breathing through the mouth and subsequent sore throat.

A physician also takes a family history for evidence of recent episodes of strep throat. The physician decides if a throat culture needs to be taken to determine if an infection is present and, if so, whether it is bacterial (see *strep throat).* Because bacteria—especially strep—respond to antibiotics, it is important to identify any infectious agent present.

TREATMENT

Parents can take some simple measures to make a child with a sore throat more comfortable. Fever- and pain-relieving medications may be helpful. Consult the physician for specific recommendations and read the discussion of nonprescription medications beginning on p. 102. A cool-mist vaporizer or humidifier in the child's bedroom adds moisture to the air and may soothe the throat. Sucking on hard candy or throat lozenges increases the production of saliva,

which can help to moisten a dry throat. A child should be encouraged to drink plenty of fluids—especially warm ones—to keep the mucous membranes of the throat and nose moist. A gargle (made by dissolving a teaspoon of molasses or corn syrup in one cup of warm water) can help relieve throat pain. Of course, rest is helpful.

Medical treatment of sore throat consists of treatment of the underlying condition.

PREVENTION

Because sore throat is a common symptom of upper respiratory tract infections, prevention is difficult. Parents, however, can try to limit their children's exposure to obvious irritants such as cigarette smoke.

SPEECH PROBLEMS

DESCRIPTION

Speech is the principal means through which people express their thoughts and ideas. It is a physical process that requires coordination of the lungs, trachea (windpipe), larynx (voice box), pharynx (throat), mouth, tongue, teeth, lips, and palate. (See Figs. 36A and B, p. 679.) Like all acts of coordination, speech is a learned process; mastery requires years of practice, which begins in infancy. During these years all children occasionally mispronounce words, have difficulty maintaining the rhythm and flow of speech, and speak too loudly or softly.

Speech performance may vary in different situations, and children may have difficulty speaking in different situations. Some children have trouble only when they feel nervous or under pressure. Others have speech problems—subtle or pronounced—at all times. In general, a problem exists if speech production draws more attention than the content of a child's speech, interferes with the child's ability to be understood, or disrupts the child's daily activities, learning, relationships, or self-image.

Speech problems are sometimes accompanied by *language disorders* and hearing problems (see *hearing loss).* About 10 percent of all children have one or more of these communication problems; most of the children with these problems are boys. Communication problems are associated with *learning problems* and can interfere with a child's educational and social progress.

Some children have speech problems because of disorders affecting muscle coordination, such as *cerebral palsy.* Other associated problems include developmental disorders and disabilitites, such as *mental retardation* and *autism.* Many children with speech problems show no signs of any associated problem, and research has shown that speech disorders can be associated with and caused by a number of different physical, emotional, and environmental factors. Speech and language pathologists have been quite successful at helping children overcome speech problems unrelated to obvious neurological (nervous system) or severe physical disorders.

Speech problems may be grouped into four broad categories:

Fluency disorders involve disruptions in the natural rhythm and flow of speech. The most common of these disorders is *stuttering.*

Articulation disorders involve difficulty producing speech sounds clearly. They are the most common childhood speech problems, accounting for about 75 percent of all communication disorders. Three common variations exist: substitution of one sound for another ("light" may be pronounced "wight"), omission of a sound ("book" may be pronounced "boo"), and slight distortion of a sound, as in lisping ("this" may be pronounced "thith"). Any of these variations can be present separately or in combination with other articulation disorders or speech problems.

Voice disorders exist when either loudness, pitch, or quality—most often quality—is so unusual that it distracts listeners. Unlike some other speech problems, voice disorders are sometimes temporary. Variations include *hoarseness,* harshness, breathiness, and shrillness. Other variations include speaking too loudly or softly or at a pitch higher or lower than is standard for age and sex.

Resonance disorders involve an overwhelming or insufficient nasal quality to the voice, which results from too much or too little air passing through the nose during speech. A child with resonance problems may sound like he or she is speaking through the nose or has a perpetually stuffy nose.

CAUSE

Speech problems can be caused by a variety of factors, including faulty structure or function of body parts involved in speech;

hearing impairment; the state of a child's brain and central nervous system; problems with physical, intellectual, and psychological development; and emotional problems. In the absence of an obvious cause or associated disorder, speech problems are usually thought to involve more than one underlying factor. A child who stutters, for example, may have a slight problem with speech mechanism coordination as well as emotional difficulties.

Articulation disorders are commonly associated with faulty structure or function of speech mechanism parts. In some instances articulation disorders are associated with a tongue of abnormal shape or size, with tongue-tie—the condition of having the tongue attached to the base of the mouth at a point unusually close to the front.

Children with cerebral palsy and other neuromuscular disorders often suffer from weakness, paralysis, or severe lack of coordination of speaking-mechanism muscles. These problems almost always lead to articulation disorders. For some children production of voice also is difficult.

Articulation problems sometimes result from inaccurate learning of sounds. The cause of this inaccurate learning is unknown. It may involve hearing or perceptual problems that interfere with a child's understanding of certain sounds. Or it may result from an absence of good speech models.

Voice disorders are often caused by abuse, including, for example, prolonged yelling. Misusing the voice (as, for example, purposely speaking in a very high or low pitch for a prolonged period) can also result in a voice disorder. Certain allergic reactions, upper respiratory infections, damage to the larynx, and growths such as *polyps* may cause voice disorders.

Resonance disorders are usually caused by structural defects. During pronounciation of most sounds, the soft palate is raised and meets the back of the throat. As a result, the air stream coming through the larynx is allowed to pass into the mouth. If there is damage to the soft palate, the air passes through the nose and mouth, breath pressure does not build up in the mouth, and consonants are difficult to pronounce. When the palate does not function properly, a condition called hypernasality (characterized by a very nasal quality to the voice) results.

A number of difficulties can cause problems in airstream direction. Among these are an abnormally formed palate (see *cleft lip and cleft palate)*, weakness or paralysis of palate muscles (as from *cerebral palsy)*, long-term *allergies*, injuries (such as a puncture of the soft palate from a lollipop stick), *breathing difficulty*, and blockage of the airway by adenoids or tonsils (see *tonsillitis and adenoiditis)*. If blockage is total—if no air at all passes into the nose—then a condition called hyponasality (characterized by a voice markedly lacking in nasal quality and sounding congested) results.

DIAGNOSIS

If what appears to be a speech problem is clearly associated with another disorder, the physician monitoring that disorder should be consulted for referral to a qualified speech and language pathologist.

Speech problems unaccompanied by other obvious disorders are usually recognized initially by a family member or, if the child is a family's first, by a friend or relative who has observed the speech development of other children. Suspicions that a child might have a speech problem usually do not arise until the child is at least 2 to 2½ years old; most children do not speak much until about this age. Whenever suspicions arise, however, a physician—preferably one familiar with the child's medical history—should be consulted. Early diagnosis and treatment are crucial in preventing development of learning problems and other complications.

See *language disorders* for a list of indications that a child may have a speech or language problem.

If a physician suspects that a child has a speech problem (or language or auditory-perception disorder), a referral is made to a speech and language pathologist, an expert at diagnosing and treating speech and language problems. Diagnosis is often a complex procedure. A speech and language pathologist meets with the child regularly and evaluates fluency, articulation, voice, and resonance, as well as vocabulary (the number of words understood and used) and grammar (how words are combined). Tests are performed to determine how well the child understands and responds to other people's speech and language. The nose, mouth, and throat are examined to detect any physical problems. Hearing is tested.

During the diagnostic period, a speech and language pathologist may begin trying certain treatment methods in an effort to begin planning a treatment program.

COMPLICATIONS

If a speech problem is not diagnosed or if treatment is delayed, speech problems are usually reinforced and become more difficult to correct (see also *language disorders)*.

TREATMENT AND PREVENTION

Although it is not clear exactly what role parents play in a child's speech development, it is crucial not to discourage a child's efforts at speaking. Ridicule, chiding, and punishment do not promote the development of speech. Parents should remember that children master speech at different rates. They should listen to their child's efforts with attention, interest, and love. Speech errors should not be pointed out except in an encouraging way. If a child says, for example, "big houze," a helpful response would be "Yes, that is a big house." This response overtly encourages a child's speech while subtly correcting the error. (For more information on promoting a child's speech and language development, see *language disorders.)*

Some speech problems work themselves out naturally, especially if a child is exposed to good speech models. A young child who says "wabbit" may begin to say "rabbit" after learning from example.

For more persistent speech problems, professional help from a qualified speech therapist should be sought. Treatment depends on the cause or, when the exact cause is unknown, symptoms. The physician consulted initially or the speech and language pathologist who diagnoses the speech problem and begins treating it may recommend one or more of the following:

- a plastic surgeon to restructure misshapen tissue
- a dentist or an orthodontist to correct tooth problems
- a prosthodontist to replace missing teeth
- an otolaryngologist to treat ear, nose, and throat problems
- a neurologist to evaluate motor (movement) abilities and brain function
- an audiologist to test for and treat hearing problems
- a psychologist or psychiatrist to treat complications
- a counselor to help family members provide a supportive and helpful environment

Articulation disorders are usually treated by a speech and language pathologist, who teaches the child to produce appropriate speech sounds by example. In the absence of an underlying physical problem, this therapy is usually highly successful over time.

When a voice disorder is suspected, an otolaryngologist examines the child's larynx and vocal folds before voice therapy begins, to determine whether physical damage exists. If vocal abuse has resulted in nodules or if a benign growth is the cause of the problem, surgery may be required. A speech and language pathologist is then needed to evaluate the child's vocal performance and to teach the child how to control voice loudness, pitch, and quality. This is often done by using a behavior-modification program that shows a child how to control voice in safe environments and then transfer that behavior to everyday situations.

Treatment of resonance disorders involves diagnosing and correcting the underlying problem. Sometimes surgical treatment is necessary to provide a better structural basis for speech. After the operation, continued speech therapy may be necessary.

More than 1 million Americans have never developed sufficient speech to communicate orally. Most of these people suffer from a significant neuromuscular or developmental problem. Speech professionals believe that many of these people can learn to communicate through the use of alternative methods, including sign language, communication boards, and assisted computer displays.

SPINA BIFIDA

DESCRIPTION

The spinal cord, part of the central nervous system, extends from the lower brain to the lower back. Composed of nerve cells and fibers, the spinal cord conducts impulses to and from the brain and controls many reflexes (muscle responses); 31 spinal nerves originate from the spinal cord. Three meninges (protective membranes) form a covering for the spinal cord. The spine, a series of small irregularly shaped bones called vertebrae, is the final protective layer enclosing the spinal cord (see Figs. 33–35, p. 634).

Spina bifida (literally, "2-part spine") occurs when 1 or more of the vertebrae in a fetus's spine fail to fuse (join) properly during the first month of prenatal development. Since the spinal rings of the vertebrae do not entirely close, the baby is born with an opening in the spine that may involve from 1 to 5 or 6 vertebrae. The severity of spina bifida is determined by the degree of associated damage to the spinal cord.

Spina bifida is one of the most common abnormalities of the nervous system present at birth; its incidence is about 4 per 1,000 live births. Highest incidence is among families of Welsh or Irish descent.

The mildest form of spina bifida is as spina bifida occulta. Skin covers the portion of the spine that has not properly fused so that the defect is hidden from view. Usually nerve tissues are intact. A small percentage of infants with spina bifida occulta have developmental defects of the underlying spinal cord and nerves.

A more severe form of spina bifida is meningomyelocele, in which the spinal cord and its nerves are exposed. Spinal nerves cannot develop past the opening of the spine. Nerve circuits needed for walking and bowel and bladder functions may be interrupted and remain incomplete. As a result, a child may be unable to walk and may have malfunctioning bowels and no or poor bladder control.

Some degree of *hydrocephalus* occurs in 85 percent of all cases of spina bifida. The open spine is associated with displacement of the lower brain into the spinal column cavity or other anatomical defects that block the circulation of the cerebrospinal fluid (CSF). (CSF, produced in the brain and absorbed at the base of the spine, circulates through the brain and spinal cavities, acting as a protective cushion for the brain and spinal cord while supplying vital nutrients.) If the circulation of cerebrospinal fluid is blocked, hydrocephalus occurs (the fluid accumulates in the brain, causing enlargement of the infant's head).

The outlook is good for infants with spina bifida who do not have serious complications from hydrocephalus or urinary tract involvement. Such children are not mentally retarded but may have learning problems and *developmental disabilities* and require special education and various forms of physical or occupational therapy.

Infants who are severely affected have ex-

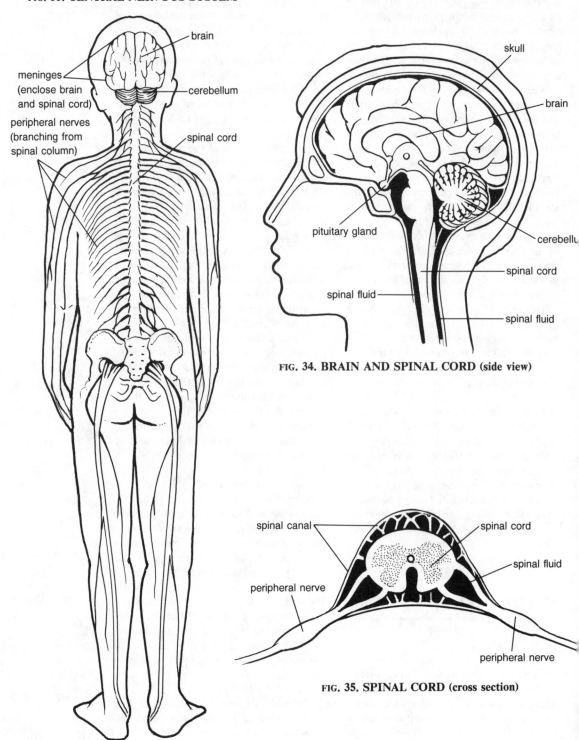

FIG. 33. CENTRAL NERVOUS SYSTEM

brain

meninges
(enclose brain
and spinal cord)

cerebellum

peripheral nerves
(branching from
spinal column)

spinal cord

skull

brain

pituitary gland

cerebellu

spinal cord

spinal fluid

spinal fluid

FIG. 34. BRAIN AND SPINAL CORD (side view)

spinal canal

spinal cord

spinal fluid

peripheral nerve

peripheral nerve

FIG. 35. SPINAL CORD (cross section)

634   Spina Bifida

treme difficulties; most deaths result from severe neurological problems, from complications of hydrocephalus or from failure of the shunt (tube) inserted to carry CFS away from the brain. The remainder are profoundly physically disabled, and about half experience *mental retardation.*

CAUSE

The cause of spina bifida and meningomyelocele is not known. Appearance of spina bifida among several family members suggests a genetic origin or influence, but familial trends are not always consistent (see *genetic disorders).*

SIGNS AND SYMPTOMS

The only symptoms of spina bifida occulta may be a small dimple or birthmark on the skin of the lower back at the site of the defect.

Meningomyelocele is evident at birth as a skin defect on the back. The gray and white matter of the spinal cord and its nerves may be exposed. CSF may leak from the protective membrane surrounding the exposed spinal cord.

COMPLICATIONS

Newborns with spina bifida are vulnerable to *meningitis,* an infection of the meninges. Exposed nerve tissue offers bacteria a direct route to the brain. Meningitis may be prevented by surgical repair of the opening of the spine as soon as possible after birth.

Parents of severely affected infants face a difficult ethical dilemma at their child's birth. If surgery is not performed, 90 percent of these children will die during the first year of life; even with surgery, some children with spina bifida will be severely disabled throughout their lives. Some parents have requested that treatment be withheld. The legal and ethical implications of such actions remain difficult and controversial.

DIAGNOSIS

Spina bifida with meningomyelocele may be detected during pregnancy through amniocentesis (withdrawal of amniotic fluid by a needle inserted into the uterus through the abdominal wall).

Meningomyelocele is diagnosed by the physician present at birth. An infant's spontaneous activity is watched closely to determine the degree of neurological damage. The potential ability of an infant's legs and

urinary system is evaluated. A full assessment of movement potential of each major muscle group is performed to evaluate damage to motor nerve pathways in the spinal cord and brain. The rectal and urinary areas are carefully examined to determine whether the child will have control of bladder and bowel movements.

TREATMENT

Immediate treatment is crucial in many cases of spina bifida, making a difference not only in whether a child lives but in the quality of life.

A newborn with spina bifida whose spinal cord and nerves are exposed requires surgical closure of the spine within 24 hours. If the opening is covered with skin, surgery may be delayed. Closure is necessary to avoid infections that could permanently damage the central nervous system. Later treatment focuses on correcting or compensating for neurological defects at the site of the opening of the spine.

If the fluid does not drain from around the brain (see *hydrocephalus),* a shunt operation may be performed to remove excess fluid. This involves surgical implantation of a plastic tube that enables fluid to drain from the brain into some other part of the body, such as the bloodstream or the abdominal cavity. Infants whose heads are growing rapidly around the ages of 2 and 3 months usually receive shunt operations.

Treatment of the urinary system may be required. If a child's bladder seriously malfunctions, catheterization may be required. This involves inserting a plastic or rubber tube through the urethra (the tube from the bladder to the outside of the body) into the bladder to drain urine. The procedure can take place 4 or 5 times a day and is accomplished by the parent or child. If necessary, a plastic cuff called an artificial sphincter can be surgically inserted around the urethra at the bottom of the bladder to prevent urine from leaking.

Malfunctioning bowels may also require treatment. Incontinence (inability to control bowel movements) and *constipation* are managed by a high-fiber diet to keep the stools soft, and by a consistent toileting schedule. If necessary, medication is prescribed in the form of suppositories or enemas to empty the bowel completely on a daily basis.

A strict routine of follow-up visits is required to check shunt functioning, the condition of urinary tract problems, and motor development.

Foot and knee deformities caused by interruption of spinal nerve circuits may require orthopedic surgery. Many children with spina bifida require short or long leg braces, forearm crutches, and other walking supports. Some manage with orthopedic shoes; others cannot walk at all. Some deformities can be corrected by surgical methods, including tendon transplants, fusion of bones to stabilize joints, muscle transplants, and cutting of certain tendons or bones.

Children who have *learning disabilities* or *mental retardation* require special education; children who suffer from physical disabilities need physical therapy, vocational counseling, and occupational therapy.

PREVENTION

Spina bifida with meningomyelocele may be detected during pregnancy by amniocentesis. In addition, a blood-screening test called the maternal serum alpha feta protein (MSAFP) can detect neural tube defects between the sixteenth and eighteenth week of pregnancy. If the test result is abnormal, ultrasound and amniocentesis are performed to confirm the diagnosis (see descriptions of diagnostic tests in *genetic disorders*).

Since women who have had a child with spina bifida may expect a higher than average incidence of neural tube defects in subsequent pregnancies, couples of affected families may wish to seek genetic counseling before conceiving children (see Prevention section of *genetic disorders*).

SPRAINS

DESCRIPTION

A ligament is a strong rope of tissue that connects the bones in the body and gives strength and stability to the body's joints. When twisted or stretched too far, a ligament can be damaged and may even tear. A stretched or partially torn ligament is called a sprain.

Sprains range from mild to severe. A mild sprain usually does not permanently damage a ligament and requires only minimal treatment. A more severe sprain can result in permanent loss of ligament elasticity and subsequent weakness of the involved joint. The most severe form of sprain results in partial tearing of the ligament, which sometimes requires surgery.

People of all age groups can suffer sprains; they are particularly common among people active in sports. Sprains most often involve ligaments of the ankle (see *ankle injuries*), but may also involve ligaments of other joints.

With proper treatment, most mild sprains heal fully within several weeks.

CAUSE

Sprains often occur when a child lands forcefully on a joint, perhaps after falling. As the child lands, a ligament of the involved joint twists and may stretch or tear. Knuckles can be sprained when a finger is forcefully pushed back by a thrown object such as a baseball. Sudden, forceful twisting of other parts of the body, such as the neck and shoulder, may also result in a sprain.

SIGNS AND SYMPTOMS

Signs and symptoms of a sprain include swelling (caused by accumulation of fluids and blood in and around the involved joint); tenderness of the surrounding area; often severe pain; and decreased joint movement. Swelling is greatest 24 to 48 hours after injury. Skin turns blue-black in the injured area as a bruise forms.

DIAGNOSIS

When a child's joint hurts after forceful twisting, a ligament may have been sprained. If the child can move the affected joint without difficulty or pain, the sprain is usually mild and may not require a physician's examination.

A painful joint that does not bear up under pressure usually means that a ligament has been moderately to severely sprained or that a fracture has occurred. A painful joint should be examined by a physician to ensure that there is no fracture (see *fractures*), an injury often mistaken for a sprain during childhood. A child's bones are more likely than ligaments to break because they are not as fully formed and strengthened. A physician will take X-ray films to determine whether a fracture is present.

COMPLICATIONS

Repeated sprains of the same ligament can result in permanent loss of elasticity. To regain normal functioning, surgery may be required.

TREATMENT

Most mild to moderate sprains heal with prompt home treatment. Severe sprains require prompt medical treatment to prevent permanent ligament weakness. For all sprains, rest is essential: the more an injured ligament is used, the more slowly it heals.

To reduce swelling, an affected joint should be raised and rested. An ice pack (ice wrapped in a towel or ice bag) should be applied immediately and left on for 10 to 12 minutes. If swelling does not decrease, ice packs should be applied at 30-minute intervals, 10 minutes at a time, over the next few hours (until swelling goes down). A pain-relieving medication may be helpful. Consult the physician for specific recommendations and read the discussion of nonprescription medications beginning on p. 102.

With home treatment, pain and swelling should be reduced 24 to 48 hours after injury. After pain becomes less severe, the child should begin to move the injured joint several times a day, gently rotating it in all directions, to increase mobility. If movement is painful, however, the child should not exercise the affected joint.

Supports such as slings should be used to minimize motion of the injured joint when the child moves about. Sprained wrists remain fairly stable and are less painful when carried in a sling. To support a shoulder sprain, the arm can be held close to the body with a sling or strap.

A child can use crutches to walk with a sprained ankle. The top of the crutch should reach just below the armpit when the child stands upright. This ensures that the child's weight rests on the hands, not on the nerves and blood vessels of the armpit, which are easily damaged. The child should continue to use crutches until able to put weight on the injured ankle comfortably.

If a sprained joint remains painful after home treatment, or if the child cannot apply any pressure to it, a physician should be consulted. A physician also should be consulted if a sprain is severe.

Severely sprained ligaments should be treated as soon as possible. Early surgery is sometimes necessary to ensure retention of ligament elasticity. Recommendation of surgery is made by an orthopedist (a bone and muscle specialist) following examination of the affected joint.

The child can slowly begin to use a sprained ligament when pain is almost gone. He or she should not resume vigorous activity, however, even if pain disappears fairly quickly. Approximately 7 to 10 days are required for complete healing of a mild sprain. A severe sprain usually heals in 4 to 6 weeks.

PREVENTION

Since most children are quite active, preventing sprains is almost impossible. Sprains are less likely, however, if a child thoroughly limbers and stretches ligaments before vigorous activity.

STINGING INSECT REACTIONS

EMERGENCY ACTION

A severe allergic reaction to insect stings can cause *asthma, breathing difficulty, hives,* and *shock* (characterized by cool, clammy, pale skin, weak, rapid pulse, thirst, dizziness or faintness, and increased breathing rate). Take a child with these symptoms to a hospital emergency room for immediate medical attention.

DESCRIPTION

An estimated 1 to 2 million people in the United States are severely allergic to stinging insect venom. Children are stung more often than adults because they frequently play outdoors where stinging insects may be found. Honeybees, bumblebees, yellow jackets, wasps, and similar insects sting when provoked or disturbed.

A honeybee's stinger is equipped with a barb that catches in the skin and pulls out of the bee's body. A honeybee dies shortly after stinging its victim. The stinger of every other insect remains attached to the insect's body and can be used to sting again.

Stinging insect reactions range from mild to severe. Mild symptoms last from a few minutes to hours. The point where a stinger has entered the skin becomes painful and red. Swelling and itching are usually present both at the site of the sting and in surrounding skin areas.

Severe reactions to insect stings may be quite painful or itchy and may affect the entire body. Such reactions can begin immediately after the child is stung. Symptoms include *dizziness,* nausea, weakness, *diarrhea,* and stomach cramps; widespread *hives* may develop. The child may have trouble breathing; blood pressure may drop sharply. Extremely severe stinging insect reactions may cause shock and unconsciousness; in rare cases, death may occur.

With prompt treatment pain and swelling from a mild reaction can be minimized. A severe reaction requires extensive treatment and, occasionally, hospitalization.

CAUSE

Honeybees, hornets, wasps, yellow jackets, and certain ants inject venom when stinging a victim. Stinging insect reactions are caused by allergic responses to this venom.

The immune system produces an antibody, made of the protein immunoglobulin, each time a foreign organism or substance enters the body. Immunoglobulin E (IgE) is the antibody that reacts with insect venom. In some cases the initial sting causes the level of IgE in the body to increase. It is not known exactly why this occurs, but when an individual is stung again, increased levels of IgE cause the body's defense system to overreact. This overreaction is the first step in a chain of events which together create a severe allergic response.

DIAGNOSIS

Parents can usually identify an insect sting. In severe cases, a physician diagnoses a stinging insect reaction on the basis of the child's symptoms and activities.

COMPLICATIONS

Impetigo, a bacterial infection, may develop if a child constantly scratches the area of the skin where the sting occurred.

TREATMENT

If a child has been stung by a honeybee, the stinger should be removed immediately to prevent injection of venom into the skin by the venom sac, a very small bag attached to the stinger. The stinger and sac can be removed with one quick scrape of the fingernail. The sac should not be squeezed, since this may inject more venom into the skin. Prompt removal of the stinger and the venom sac prevents more than a tiny amount of venom from entering the skin,

and the allergic reaction will be minimized.

Other stinging insects should be brushed off a child's skin to prevent them from stinging again. An insect usually becomes angry when brushed away; the child should leave the area immediately to avoid being re-stung.

After a child is stung, cool compresses applied to the sting area help control swelling. Oral antihistamines will help reduce swelling and itching.

As with many other allergies, a child can be desensitized against stinging insect reactions. Solutions containing the venom of honeybees, yellow jackets, hornets, or wasps are administered by a physician in gradually stronger doses. This stimulates a child's immune system to become more and more resistant to the effects of the venom.

If a child is severely allergic to insect venom, he or she should carry some form of identification indicating the allergy. An older child may want to carry an emergency self-treatment kit as well. The kit contains epinephrine, a medication that counteracts symptoms of a stinging insect reaction. A nurse or physician should instruct the parent—and when appropriate, the child—in the proper techniques for use of this kit.

PREVENTION

Stinging insects are attracted to certain odors and colors. Food odors from outdoor cooking, garbage cans, and fallen fruit are particularly attractive. Food should be kept covered outdoors and the garbage can area carefully cleaned. Fallen fruit should be swept up and removed. Outdoor use of insecticides will help keep stinging insects away. When outdoors, a sensitive child should not use perfumes, suntan lotions, or other sweet-smelling preparations that attract stinging insects.

Bright colors and flowery prints are thought to attact stinging insects because of their resemblance to garden flowers. During stinging insect season, very sensitive children should not wear clothing made of such fabrics. Light colors such as green, tan, and khaki do not attract insects and can be worn instead. A very sensitive child should wear shoes outdoors at all times to avoid stings on the feet.

Children sensitive to stinging insect venom should use caution when gardening or playing outdoors. Bushes, eaves of a house, low tree branches, or other possible nesting areas should be avoided. Disturbing a nest will anger stinging insects and cause them to swarm. Hives and nests found around the house and yard should be destroyed by someone who is not allergic to insect venom.

Children hypersensitive to insect stings should <u>always</u> be accompanied by others when in isolated outdoor areas.

STOMACHACHE, STOMACH PAIN

EMERGENCY ACTION

Any pain in the area of the stomach or lower abdomen that persists for more than a half an hour should not be dismissed as "just a stomachache." A child who experiences a stomachache affecting normal activities for an entire day should receive medical attention.

DESCRIPTION

Stomachache is one of the most common complaints children bring to parents, and parents then bring to pediatricians. Almost every child under 12 suffers a stomachache at least once a year.

Stomachaches may be a symptom of a wide variety of illnesses, mild or serious. They may signal nothing more serious than overeating, indigestion, physical or emotional stress, or a minor muscle strain in the abdominal region. Stomachaches are often associated with nausea and *vomiting* or *diarrhea*. Rarely, stomachache may signal a serious disease.

A stomachache may involve more than the stomach alone, since any of the organs in the gastrointestinal (GI) tract—esophagus, stomach, and intestines—or abdomen may be involved (see Fig. 30, p. 437). In addition, the liver, gallbladder, pancreas, urinary tract (kidneys and bladder), or reproductive system can cause pain in the general area beneath the breastbone and above the pubic region.

Stomachaches often are associated with <u>cramps,</u> wavelike pain that comes and goes, lasting a minute or less. Pain may also be localized around the navel, or the upper or lower abdomen on the right or left side. Occasionally a stomachache radiates (travels) back and forth across the abdomen or all the way through to the back. Pressure at that

spot can sometimes cause a child to wince, cry, or even double over in pain. Such pain, if it is continuous (regular and unrelenting) for more than half an hour, may require immediate medical attention (see *abdominal pain*). Steady, dull pain that does not have a single focus and does not cause extreme tenderness may throb like a headache or toothache.

Stomachaches that persist longer than a day or occur repeatedly during a week or longer may signal an underlying condition that requires further medical investigation. Parents should not hesitate to consult a physician about a stomachache, regardless of intensity, that lasts longer than 24 hours or recurs within a week or a month.

CAUSE

Stomachaches may be caused by overeating, indigestion, *constipation,* physical fatigue, or even a slight muscle strain in the abdominal region. They also may be caused by disease or infection; by accident or injury; by allergy, environmental factors, or emotions; or by unknown factors that resist diagnosis.

Stomachache associated with cramps, nausea, *vomiting,* or *diarrhea* can be caused by a viral infection or, occasionally, by a bacterial infection that runs its course in 24 to 72 hours. *Food poisoning* often results in a stomachache and infectious diarrhea. *Pneumonia* and *strep throat,* both common infections, may be associated with stomachaches.

Occasionally a stomachache progresses to constant pain and tenderness on the lower right side of the abdomen. Such a symptom can be caused by acute *appendicitis.* A physician should be consulted without delay.

Any of the organs in the GI tract may become infected, as may the liver, gallbladder, pancreas, urinary tract (the kidneys, ureters, and bladder), or reproductive system. Trauma (injury) to an abdominal organ may produce a stomachache that subsides gradually as healing proceeds.

Some children cannot tolerate milk, specifically its sugar (lactose). When they drink milk, a stomachache can occur which may be followed by diarrhea (see *malabsorption*). Food allergies of many kinds can cause stomachaches when a specific food or drink is consumed (see *food allergy*).

Children sometimes try to avoid going to school by complaining strenuously, "My stomach hurts." Such a complaint may have physical or emotional origins or both. "School phobia," fear of school or of something a child associates with school, is often blamed for such a stomachache, but then no further investigation is made to identify the root of that rear. A stomachache with a probable emotional cause—fears, troubles with friends, family conflicts, and the like— truly hurts. It deserves consideration, appropriate investigation, and possibly treatment (see *phobias).*

DIAGNOSIS

Diagnosis varies according to the location of the pain, the kind of pain, when the pain begins and how long its lasts, and the age of the patient. The overall physical and emotional health of the patient is also important. A physician needs to know whether *fever, nausea, vomiting,* or changes in defecation or urination have occurred. Other significant factors include any prior abdominal accident, surgery, or chronic disease.

A physician takes a history, noting especially how long the pain has lasted, and performs a thorough physical examination, focusing upon the painful region. It may be helpful to perform blood and urine tests. Further diagnostic studies may be necessary.

COMPLICATIONS

Complications and their severity often depend upon which organ or system is involved, the cause of pain, and the speed with which diagnosis can be made and treatment begun. The possibility of serious complications is reduced significantly if a child is in the care of experienced medical personnel.

TREATMENT

Medication may be required for a stomachache caused by overeating, indigestion, or physical fatigue. For a stomachache that accompanies or is followed by nausea, *vomiting,* and *diarrhea,* common-sense steps are often the most helpful. Resting the GI tract (clear liquids only; no food or milk) and providing warmth and reassurance are sensible first steps while waiting for the stomachache to run its course. A warm bottle or heating pad may be soothing. (See also Chapter 7, "Caring for the Sick Child at Home.")

No medicines should be given by mouth to try to relieve pain. Aspirin, aspirin substitute, and narcotics such as paregoric should be avoided. If a child is *constipated,* laxatives

and enemas should be avoided unless recommended by a physician.

If examination by a physician is required, treatment varies according to identification of the underlying cause of the stomachache.

PREVENTION

Stomachaches cannot be prevented except when caused by food sensitivity or by eating or drinking to excess.

STREP THROAT

DESCRIPTION

Strep throat is an infection and inflammation of throat tissues caused by a bacterium called streptococcus. The disease is characterized by a severe *sore throat.* Strep throat is the most common of the diseases caused by group A strep bacteria (another of which is *impetigo).* People of all ages are affected by strep throat, although it occurs most frequently among school-age children. Strep throat develops most often during cold weather, when people gather indoors and bacteria can be spread more easily. Occasionally epidemics of strep throat occur among people who live, work, play, or attend school together.

With antibiotic therapy, a case of strep throat generally disappears within a few days. If strep throat is untreated, it will last about 2 weeks. The disease itself is not serious, but if it is not treated, dangerous complications can develop.

CAUSE

The bacteria are usually spread by coughing, sneezing, or close contact. Occasionally the bacteria are spread by contaminated, poorly refrigerated food that is served in public places such as school cafeterias. In such cases, epidemics of strep throat may result. Usually strep bacteria are spread only by people with active or convalescent cases, not by carriers. Streptococcal bacteria can be carried in the upper respiratory tract (particularly the throat) for months and not cause detectable infection or inflammation. Indeed, it is not uncommon for people who have been adequately treated for strep throat to continue to carry streptococci in their throats without further symptoms.

SIGNS AND SYMPTOMS

In about 20 percent of strep throat cases

an affected child suffers a severe *sore throat* and *fever* and has a noticeably bright red throat. In the remaining cases a child may have only a fever and sore throat (or if a child is under 4 years old, only a runny nose); general symptoms of illness (such as *headache,* listlessness, nausea, *vomiting,* or rapid heart rate); or no symptoms at all. The lymph nodes on the sides of the neck may become swollen and painful (see *swollen glands*).

After several days fever lessens, and recovery occurs rapidly.

DIAGNOSIS

A physician performs a physical examination of a child with a *sore throat* and takes a family history for evidence of recent episodes of strep throat or of past occurrences of complications. The physician looks for typical signs of strep throat, such as a bright red throat and a discharge of pus (an indication of inflammation) from the tonsil area. Swollen lymph nodes of the neck (see *swollen glands)* always cause a physician to suspect strep throat. Even the best physicians, however, cannot be certain that a patient has strep throat without taking a throat culture to determine if an infection is present and, if so, whether it is bacterial. Because bacteria respond to treatment with antibiotics, it is important to identify the infectious agent present. Some physicians may have a rapid strep screening test available that can yield results the same day. Results of culture tests are not usually available until 2 days after the specimen is obtained. The physician may also take a blood test to count white blood cells, which fight infection, and look for strep antibodies.

If a child has a confirmed case of strep throat, a physician may recommend that throat cultures be taken of his or her siblings. If strep bacteria are found in the siblings' cultures, the siblings will receive treatment. Throat cultures are particularly important if siblings have symptoms of strep throat or if there is a family history of complications of strep infections.

COMPLICATIONS

Serious complications can develop if strep throat is untreated and if strep bacteria spread through the blood and lymphatic vessels to other parts of the body. In addition, streptococci may cause collections of pus (abscesses) in the lymph nodes of the neck or in adjacent tissues. Other complications are caused by the body's immune response to the infection, not by spread of the strep themselves. *Scarlet fever* is caused by a toxin released by strep in the throat. If complications are going to appear, they usually do so within 2 weeks of the appearance of a strep throat infection. However, if the infection causes no symptoms, a parent has no way of knowing that treatment is necessary.

The immune complications of strep throat include inflammation of the kidney *(nephritis),* which can cause kidney failure. Antibiotics do not prevent nephritis, but fortunately only a few strains of strep produce this disease. The most serious complication of strep throat is *rheumatic fever,* which causes *joint pain* and heart damage. If an individual comes down with strep throat, other family members should be particularly careful. Early antibiotic therapy prevents rheumatic fever.

TREATMENT

Symptoms of a strep throat infection can be treated at home. Fever-reducing and pain-relieving medications may be helpful to reduce fever and ease a headache or sore throat. Consult the physician for specific recommendations and read the discussion of nonprescription medications in Chapter 7, "Caring for the Sick Child at Home." A child may be given aspirin or aspirin substitute. Bed rest is not necessary unless a child wants it. However, a child with strep throat should be kept at home and away from other children until at least 24 hours after beginning antibiotic therapy.

Antibiotics, which are prescribed by a physician, are important not only in killing strep bacteria but in preventing most complications. A physician may decide to begin antibiotic treatment before results of a throat culture are available if there is a family history of rheumatic fever or if a child has *scarlet fever* in addition to a sore throat. If antibiotics are given, the entire dosage must be taken for the time prescribed (at least 10 days), even if a child begins to feel better sooner.

PREVENTION

Children with a history of *rheumatic fever* are often given penicillin, either monthly by injection or daily by mouth, to prevent recurrent strep infections and new attacks of rheumatic fever. During outbreaks it may be necessary to treat all members of the family, school group, or daycare center to stop the spread of infection.

STRESS

DESCRIPTION

Stress is a disruption of a person's mental or physical state of well-being or "balance." Everyone is subject to stress in daily life, but people handle it differently. The way people manage emotions is the result both of inborn factors (such as constitution and temperament) and environmental ones (such as parents' emotional style, early childrearing practices, and general family harmony). Some responses, such as overeating or working long hours, increase the likelihood that physical or psychological complications will develop. The key to avoiding such complications is learning how to handle stress.

Children encounter stress in their daily lives just as adults do, although the causes of stress during childhood are often different. Children also can learn to handle stress (see *psychosomatic disease and symptoms*).

CAUSE

Situations stressful for children include the birth of a sibling; being the oldest and always expected to set an example; being chosen last for a team sport or game; publicly performing on a musical instrument; wearing tooth braces; having *acne;* and being too short, tall, chubby, or skinny.

Children have less control over events in their lives than adults do and can consequently experience more frustration. Because adults think they have "bigger" problems, they tend to underestimate how powerless and helpless a child can feel.

Short-term stress tends to be less disruptive to children than long-term stress. Having to walk to school through an unfriendly neighborhood can cause temporary butterflies in the stomach, whereas experiencing a bitter parental divorce can cause chronic stomach pain.

Stress, however, can produce positive effects. For instance, the anger that arises when a child perceives that a classmate is cheating on a test can prompt him or her to speak to the teacher instead of being passive and submissive. Likewise, a surge of adrenaline can help a child over the last hurdle or obstacle during many kinds of races.

For children, causes of stress may include death of a family member; divorce or separation of parents; moving; loss of a friend; inability to achieve in school; being involved in too many activities; a feeling of inadequacy in sports; a change of school; loss of a pet; or failure to meet parental expectations regarding accomplishments and behavior. Additional causes may include serious illness, either of the child or of a family member; being hospitalized, especially if it involves being separated from parents; a natural disaster such as a fire or flood; or the threat of nuclear war.

Parents under stress affect children too. How parents deal with marital discord or a parent's alcoholism, unemployment, depression, or disability, for example, may cause children to feel stress, even if they do not appear aware of the parents' problems.

SIGNS AND SYMPTOMS

Physical signs and symptoms of short-term stress can include increased heart rate, rising blood pressure, rapid breathing or hyperventilation (see shortness of breath), stomachache (see *stomachache, stomach pain*), vomiting, abdominal pain, back pain, bowel or urinary changes, *headache, rash, acne,* or increased muscle tension. Psychological signs of short-term stress can include fear, anxiety, or anger. Signs and symptoms of long-term stress include irritability, diminished school performance, and recurrent problems with friends.

DIAGNOSIS

Children often do not bring up—or even recognize—their state of stress. In such cases parents may hear only about symptoms such as *headache* or *back pain.* Failure to recognize the cause of such symptoms can aggravate and prolong them. It is helpful for parents, teachers, and school counselors to pay attention to a child's early warning signs. Parents should seek professional help if any of these conditions exists:

- The cause of stress cannot be identified even after parents talk with their child, teachers, and siblings.
- School performance changes dramatically.
- Family life is upset or disrupted.
- Stress persists for more than a month or so.

Medically, stress is diagnosed by a physician who observes physical signs and symptoms and who records a history of the child's illnesses and behavior. A psychologist, psychiatrist, or social worker might also be consulted.

COMPLICATIONS

If a child has obvious difficulty handling stress, or if stress is persistent or recurrent, physical or psychological problems are likely to develop. Common physical complications may include a delayed or missed menstrual period, chronic tiredness or weakness, and frequent infections. More serious physical problems that can be aggravated by unrelieved stress include *asthma,* migraine headaches (see *headache*), allergies, peptic *ulcers, ulcerative colitis, eczema,* and epilepsy (see *seizures*).

Psychological complications may include refusal to eat (with subsequent weight loss); overeating (with subsequent weight gain); nightmares, night terrors, inability to fall asleep, or excessive sleeping (see *sleep disorders*); teeth grinding (see *bruxism*); bed-wetting by a child who previously has been dry; *encopresis* (uncontrolled bowel movements); frequently missing school; problems at school; friendship problems; excessive irritability; frequent crying; difficulty concentrating; unusual aggression; temper tantrums; and constant sadness. Serious psychological problems caused by unrelieved stress may include *depression, drug abuse,* and *suicide,* particularly among teenagers.

TREATMENT

Children deal best with stress if they know that they have the support of their families. Discussing difficult or traumatic events with children is a way to help, even if such ventilation cannot change the events. Sharing personal experiences that posed similar stress is a way of reassuring children that they are not alone in their problems. In addition, stress can often be reduced if parents encourage their children to work out difficulties that can be resolved—either independently or with parents' involvement. Children gain a sense of accomplishment when they have the experience of mastering complex problems.

In addition to receiving support from parents, children need to provide themselves with comfort. *Thumb-sucking* is a form of self-comfort that tends to be practiced most often when a young child is separated from others (as at bedtime) or is feeling a strong negative emotion (such as jealousy). Sometimes children who long ago stopped sucking their thumbs revert to the behavior during stressful times, such as during illness or after a family fight. At these times thumb-sucking can be especially self-comforting and indicates a need for a little extra attention and understanding from parents.

Young children may cope constructively with stress by holding tight to "security" blankets or favorite toys. For example, if a child is hospitalized, bringing along a favorite teddy bear and a treasured blanket can be enormously comforting. These possessions serve to remind a child in a stressful situation that he or she still maintains a grip on familiar parts of his or her life. Or if a child is separated from a parent for a few days or longer, writing letters to the parent or keeping a diary to share later may afford a reassuring sense of contact.

In addition, play and exercise help relieve children's stress. Children need the physical release that exercise of all kinds can provide. Play, especially engaging in imaginative games ("pretending"), affords children chances to express their strongest feelings, including joys and fears.

Parents should not hesitate to turn to their child's pediatrician for guidance if their child is experiencing unusual stress. The pediatrician may be able to provide a helpful solution for the problem, or suggest that the child be evaluated by a psychologist or psychiatrist.

PREVENTION

Most causes of stress cannot be prevented, but if children can learn to cope with particular causes of stress, some problems can be prevented. From the time they are very young, children need to be encouraged—especially by example—to express their feelings and vent frustration. Constructive ways to do this often include talking to family members or friends, especially on a one-to-one basis. "Private time" with a parent can be invaluable in giving a child the space and privacy necessary for sharing strong positive and negative feelings. Parents often become preoccupied and, as a result, may be uncertain or unaware when their children need "private time" and attention. To complicate matters, a child who knows that parents are busy may hesitate to bring up concerns. So parents should try carefully to set aside a specific period each day for each child.

Children gain deep satisfaction in developing their physical skills and capabilities. Participating in sports or other physical activities, actively building a fort or a playhouse, and caring for pets can give children a short-term lift and long-term confidence in their own abilities.

Some research indicates that children are pressured into growing up too fast. For example, parents who dress their children in "grown-up" clothes, overschedule their free time, push them into showing off their talents, expect them to be superachievers, or demand that they be perfectly well-behaved are increasing the probability of stress in their children's lives. Children who feel loved only for their accomplishments are likely to feel insecure. In addition, comparing a child to siblings or peers can be a source of stress. Parents of school-aged children may find that deemphasizing grades and emphasizing learning, including the importance of learning through experimentation—trial and error—can reduce stress for their children.

Parents should avoid making confidants of their children so that they are not given more responsibility or "worries" than they can handle. On the other hand, children, like adults, need to hear how they are doing from the people whose opinions they value most. By responding openly and constructively to their children's activities and questions, parents confirm children's gowing self-awareness and build their self-esteem. Likewise, when children have been unsuccessful or have made a mistake, they benefit from hearing specific constructive "feedback"—criticism and suggestions. If criticism is in order, disapproval of a child's specific activity or behavior can reduce a child's fear of punishment and relieve the child of the worry that he or she is "bad." No child should have to live with the stress that accompanies being labeled "bad." (See also Chapter 3, "Promoting Mental Health.")

STUTTERING

DESCRIPTION

Stuttering is a communication disorder characterized by a disruption in the natural rhythm and flow of speech. The disruption of speech production may be heard as a repetition of sounds or syllables, prolongation of sound, or blockage of speech (see also *speech problems*).

Although the cause of stuttering has been debated for thousands of years, a single theory of why people stutter is not available. What is known is that stuttering is a complex disorder that involves psychological as well as physical disturbances in producing speech. In all likelihood, stuttering has different specific causes.

All small children stutter occasionally. They may pause during production of a sentence or before responding to a question. They may also repeat or prolong certain sounds or revise sentences aloud. These "dysfluencies" are commonly found among children between ages 3 and 4. At this age children are expanding their use of language and developing more complex sentences and stories.

As a child becomes increasingly capable of using words and sentences to communicate, stuttering is likely to diminish. For all speakers, however, certain kinds of disruptions in speech are normal and occur periodically throughout life. For example, many people pepper their speech with meaningless words and phrases, such as "and uh," "like," "sort of," and "I mean." It is also common for a speaker to revise a sentence in midstream. The following sentence exemplifies these types of disruptions: "I said to her, I had said, uh, 'Don't go to the store without me,' and, you know, I was really angry when she went."

Although most children develop relatively fluent speech before beginning school, about 1 percent of all children continue to have significant problems with stuttering. For these children, the persistence of stuttering can interfere with self-image, social and family relationships, feelings about speaking ability, and learning.

More than 2.5 million people in the United States stutter. Stuttering is found among males 4 times more frequently than among females. There is a tendency for stuttering to run in families. For some people stuttering is little more than an occasional annoyance; for others it interferes with school performance, job opportunities, social interaction, self-esteem, and enjoyment of life.

The speech of a person who stutters seems to be less fluent when he or she is self-conscious about the problem. Many people who stutter avoid speaking before large groups, to strangers, on the telephone, or in unfamiliar stituations. They may also avoid words they have learned to fear. A person who stutters may dread ordering in a restaurant or answering a teacher's question in a classroom. Some people who stutter live in fear of having to answer the telephone. To avoid responding to questions and comments in difficult speaking situations, a person who stutters may appear not to hear or may ignore a question rather than risk the humiliation of stuttering.

The verbal communication of all people who stutter is fluent part of the time, especially when they are relaxed or speaking without self-consciousness. Most are able to whisper, speak or read in unison, sing, and talk to pets or children younger than themselves.

The incidence of stuttering seems to be higher for people with developmental problems such as *mental retardation*. Some people begin to stutter after an injury or illness affecting the central nervous system, but the exact relationship between these problems and stuttering is unclear. Most other people who stutter show no signs of any underlying physical disorder.

In the absence of severe underlying problems, most people who stutter achieve at least some control over their speech by developing insight into those factors that perpetuate stuttering and by using techniques provided by one or more modern therapies.

CAUSE

Hypotheses about the causes of stuttering may be divided into four categories: physical problems, learning problems, emotional problems, and heredity.

For centuries stuttering was believed to result from physical problems involving the tongue. The tongues of people who stuttered were believed to be too dry, large, stiff, or thick for proper pronunciation. In recent years some medical experts have proposed that stuttering involves a malfunction of the muscles of the larynx (voice box). No conclusive evidence exists supporting any hypotheses about physical cause.

Evidence does exist that overreaction to a young child's stuttering reinforces the problem. If other people constantly correct a child's speech, the child may become self-conscious about speaking and eventually de-

velop a fear of speaking and a self-image as a poor, ineffective speaker. No evidence exists, however, that stuttering results from imitating someone else who stutters.

Children learning to speak may begin to stutter because of *language disorders*. Anxiety about the content of what he or she is trying to say may cause a child to pause or otherwise delay the continuation of speech.

Evidence exists that certain children begin to stutter after sudden exposure to a situation producing extreme anxiety or *stress*. Examples of situations that can arouse such emotions include coming into contact with large numbers of people for the first time when beginning school, the birth of a sibling, or sudden changes in family structure or living situation. Little evidence exists that anxiety or stress alone is responsible for the onset of stuttering, but these conditions may aggravate stuttering in certain situations.

More boys than girls stutter, and stuttering tends to run in families, indicating to some observers that a hereditary factor plays a role in causing stuttering. Others believe, however, that the tendency to stutter has more to do with social than genetic phenomena. Traditionally, society's expectations have been higher for boys than for girls, and families have tended to pass such expectations on to succeeding generations.

Despite evidence that early language difficulty, overreacting parents, sudden onset of anxiety, and family history of speech dysfluency may all have something to do with stuttering, 50 percent of children who speak dysfluently have no history of such situations. The cause of stuttering in such cases is presumed to be complex.

SIGNS AND SYMPTOMS

Many children first show signs of stuttering by repeating sounds, syllables, or words (as opposed to pausing between or prolonging them). Such repetitions should not be cause for concern unless they involve many words in many situations.

Repetition of the schwa sound ("uh") is also a type of stuttering. This sound is the vowel found in the word "the," the first syllable of "suggest," and the second syllable of "normal." Saying "reh-reh-red" may not be a sign of stuttering, while saying "ruh-ruh-red" probably is, especially if the stuttering occurs between syllables of a word.

Other signs of stuttering include persistent prolongation of sounds, trembling of the lower jaw, and a rise in pitch and loudness of the voice.

In their struggle to break a stuttering block, some children contort their faces, blink, jerk their heads, or move some other part of their body. These accessory movements may be preceded by a look of fear on the child's face. Accessory movements rarely accompany the stuttering of very young children, presumably because these children do not feel pressured to pronounce a troublesome word.

While some people struggle physically in an effort to break a stuttering block, others substitute words they can pronounce for ones they are apt to get stuck on. Many people who stutter race ahead in their thoughts, trying to pinpoint troublesome words and avoid them.

DIAGNOSIS

If parents suspect that a child more than 2½ years old has a stuttering problem, the physician most familiar with the child's medical history should be consulted for referral to a speech and language pathologist, an expert in diagnosing and treating speech and language problems. If any doubt exists about whether to consult a professional, it is best to err on the side of safety; early diagnosis could well prevent future complications. Parents should take pains to avoid alarming a child who may have a stuttering problem. Anxiety only makes stuttering worse.

A speech and language pathologist usually listens to a child's speech and performs tests, including a language assessment, and examination of the mouth and throat and a thorough hearing test. A speech and language pathologist may then make an immediate diagnosis or may advise postponing the diagnosis until a child's speech develops more fully.

COMPLICATIONS

A child who stutters may have difficulties participating in the classroom. While reading aloud, for example, some children who stutter attempt to avoid embarrassment by automatically substituting incorrect words for words they tend to get stuck on. They may not respond to questions even though they know the answers. When stuttering interferes significantly with a child's progress in school, a learning problem exists (see *learning problems*).

A person who stutters may experience fear, embarrassment, loneliness, self-pity, and other emotions that interfere with social and occupational pursuits. A person who stutters may, for example, avoid seeking jobs requiring frequent speaking.

These complications are far less likely to develop if stuttering is diagnosed and treatment is begun before a child enters school.

TREATMENT

The best thing parents can do at home for a child who stutters is to control their own reaction to it. Remarks should not be made about how slowly or quickly a child speaks; words should not be filled in; pity should not be expressed; and speech problems should not be pointed out to other people. Such negative reactions usually intensify a child's anxiety and humiliation. Parents instead should appear relaxed, attentive, interested, and loving while listening to a child speak.

To encourage a young child to speak more fluently, parents might try reading, singing, or rephrasing what the child has said. Parents should speak clearly and slowly, talking *with* rather than *at* the child. If a child asks what is wrong with his or her speech, parents should explain the problem simply— with concern but not pity—and should avoid labeling the child a stutterer.

Different treatment techniques exist for control of stuttering, none of which helps every person affected. The appropriate professional treatment method depends on the child's age and symptoms. Working with the family, a speech and language pathologist may try a number of techniques before finding one that helps the child speak more fluently. The goal of treatment should be to eliminate self-consciousness about stuttering, to help the child develop a positive self-image, and to develop effective speech controls. Patience is essential.

Before initiating any treatment, parents should investigate a program thoroughly, asking questions about what is involved, how many children have been helped, and roughly how much time is required to achieve gains. If possible, parents should speak to families of children who have participated in the treatment program. Parents should be wary of any program relying on muscle-relaxing drugs or guaranteeing universal success.

Some children who stutter work with speech and language pathologists only on an individual basis. Others participate in both individual meetings and group sessions. Some families find counseling helpful in establishing the most supportive environment possible for a child who stutters. All families should be aware that experts are constantly at work on new therapies for stuttering.

Following are some of the most popular methods of professional treatment:

- teaching the child to relax and give in to the stuttering and then working toward "better" stuttering: "ruh-ruh-red" gradually becomes "r-r-red" and finally turns into "red"
- asking the child to speak at such a slow rate that stuttering disappears, and then gradually bringing speech back to a normal pace
- sounding a rhythm and having the child pace speech by the beat
- using special devices that prevent the child from hearing his or her own speech or that play back the child's speech a fraction of a second later, prompting the child to speak more slowly
- helping the child achieve more control of the speaking muscles through a self-awareness procedure known as biofeedback

Using one or more of these techniques, almost every person who stutters can improve speech fluency. Studies show, however, that initial gains tend to be lost if therapy is not continued. Some people revert to stuttering, retaining only an affectation from therapy such as a rhythmic way of stuttering. Therapy should continue over the long term, and new therapies should be tested if old ones lose their effectiveness.

STYES

DESCRIPTION

Styes are bacterial infections of the glands in the upper and lower eyelids, occurring where the eyelash enters the lid. Children often have styes that appear in groups because their pus contains bacteria that infect other glands in the eyelids.

With proper treatment, styes heal without complications. Recurrent styes may indicate an unusual susceptibility to infections.

CAUSE

Styes are caused by infection from staphylococci bacteria. Recurrence is common, often caused by the child's repeated rubbing of the eyes with unclean hands.

SIGNS AND SYMPTOMS

The child's eyelid appears red and swollen and feels painful. The eyes often water; small bumps may erupt on the upper or lower eyelid. Within a few days the stye usually forms a tiny pus-filled head on the edge of the lid near the base of the lash.

DIAGNOSIS

Styes are obvious through observation of swelling, redness, and the subsequent whitehead on the rim of the eyelid.

COMPLICATIONS

Untreated styes can lead to diffuse inflammation of the eyelids and surrounding tissues.

TREATMENT

Styes can usually be treated successfully at home. Within a day the head of the stye usually breaks, drains, and heals. Hot compresses (usually cotton balls or a clean washcloth) applied to the eyelids for 10 or 15 minutes several times a day bring the stye to a head and promote healing.

If styes persist, a physician should be consulted. The physician may prescribe antibiotic drops or ointment to be administered several times a day. It is rarely necessary for a physician to open and drain a stye. A stye should never be opened by anyone except a physician.

PREVENTION

Frequent handwashing and keeping an infected child's towel and washcloth separate from others can curb the spread of styes within a household.

SUDDEN INFANT DEATH SYNDROME

DESCRIPTION

When an apparently healthy baby dies suddenly and unexpectedly, most often during sleep, the death may be attributed to sudden infant death syndrome (SIDS). Nearly 8,000 babies (2 to 3 per 1,000 live births) die each year in the United States from SIDS (commonly called crib death).

SIDS is the major cause of death in the

first year of life after the first week. Approximately 9 out of 10 SIDS victims die between the ages of 2 and 6 months, with the peak incidence occurring at about 10 weeks of age. Another 9 percent of SIDS infants die between the ages of 6 and 12 months. Occasionally infants may die before 2 months or after 12 months.

SIDS tends to strike most often in winter months, at least in those areas of the country where distinct seasons exist. Male infants are victims of the syndrome more often than are females. The incidence is highest among Native Americans, followed by blacks, Caucasians, and Orientals. No socioeconomic conditions guarantee protection from SIDS. An increased incidence of SIDS exists among low birthweight or premature infants.

In a typical case of SIDS, a well-cared-for, apparently healthy baby is put to bed in the evening and is found dead during the night or the next morning. The death occurs very rapidly; typically, the baby does not struggle, cry out, or suffer. In many instances another person is sleeping in the same room but hears nothing. In some cases infants have died silently in car seats or even in a parent's arms.

SIDS is not a recent phenomenon; sudden, unexpected deaths of infants have been chronicled throughout history. In the past these unexplained deaths have been attributed to suffocation, sleeping positions, pneumonia, inhalation of fluid or food, choking on vomit, type of food eaten, allergy to cow's milk, and bottle-feeding. No evidence links SIDS deaths directly to any of these causes. Breastfed babies are victims of SIDS just as bottle-fed babies are.

CAUSE

The exact cause of SIDS is unknown; as many as 100 different theories have been offered. None of these theories has fully explained the mechanism of death in the vast majority of cases. Experts generally agree that some SIDS babies unexpectedly stop breathing, as many babies temporarily do, but unlike most babies these victims do not begin to breathe again. Other scientists have suggested that the upper breathing passages are closed off somehow, but they do not understand the cause of this closure. Still others have suggested that the baby is unable to respond normally—by coughing or breathing more deeply—to what should be a temporary pause or blockage. Some researchers

now believe that this dangerously abnormal respiratory control mechanism (or the susceptibility to respond abnormally) may develop prenatally.

Much research has centered on the theory that recurrent *apnea* (temporary cessation of breathing) causes death in SIDS babies. However, it has been found that only about 5 percent of SIDS victims have a previous history of persistent apena.

In all likelihood SIDS is due to a number of causes, one or more of which may be involved in each case.

SIGNS AND SYMPTOMS

Since SIDS strikes unexpectedly, no specific signs and symptoms point to its occurrence. Some infants have had previous mild infections, such as a slight cold with sniffles, but many have been completely well before death. Some have passed a physical examination by physicians just days or hours before death. Some SIDS babies have had feeding difficulties, but again, not all.

DIAGNOSIS

SIDS is diagnosed at death by excluding other possible causes of death. If a seemingly healthy baby between the ages of 1 week and 1 year is found dead during apparent sleep, SIDS is suspected. If, in additon to that, the death is unexplainable even after an autopsy, then the diagnosis is confirmed.

Most parents want autopsies to be performed, because they want to know why their babies died. Physicians agree that very few parents regret agreeing to an autopsy, but that many parents later regret not having had an autopsy performed.

COMPLICATIONS

When a baby dies so suddenly, unexpectedly, and inexplicably, parents are left in a state of shock and denial. They have had no time to prepare for the death of their baby, and in needing to know why it happened, they cannot help wondering if they were somehow at fault. Parents keep thinking "if only": if only I had been home, or checked on her again, or fed him differently, or not let her sleep on her stomach, or not covered him with a blanket. Parents (or baby-sitters or daycare personnel) are not responsible for SIDS deaths.

Siblings may also feel they are to blame. Young children quite often wish that their new brothers or sisters would go away, so that they could have their parents to themselves again. If the baby then dies, young children, who tend to believe strongly in the power of their own thoughts, may feel that their wish has come true and may blame themselves.

Young children need to express these feeling but are unable to verbalize them. They may act out their emotions in play instead. A parent who is paying close attention may discover that the child feels guilty or that the child does not understand the concept of death. To 3- to 5-year-olds, death is often understood to be nothing more than a form of sleep. They do not realize that death is permanent. The belief that death means sleep, combined with the knowledge that the baby died while asleep, may lead young siblings of SIDS victims to be afraid of going to sleep. They may resist falling asleep, fearing a loss of control, and may suffer nightmares. Not telling the truth, such as saying that the baby went away or is being cared for, often leads a child to believe that he or she can do something to make the baby come back or wake up. Euphemisms may also increase the child's guilt and may make the child fear that something will take him or her away. Parents should point out to the surviving children that the baby's death was unavoidable, and that the same thing is not likely to happen to them or to the surviving child. Still, parents should be prepared for repeated questions and possible changes in behavior as young siblings adjust to this new reality.

Grieving parents who have other children may develop an even stronger attachment to their surviving child or children. The child, in turn, may either try to comfort his or her parents or rebel and test their limits. Or the opposite may happen: parents may idealize the dead child and unknowingly neglect the emotional needs of the surviving child.

After the period of shock and denial has passed, parents may feel angry and powerless or depressed and lonely. They may have difficulty concentrating or sleeping. Parents typically are not prepared to deal with the death of a child, especially death for reasons that are not concrete. Though they may need to talk about the death, some parents control and suppress their emotions. Parents who have no verbal or emotional outlet tend to keep extra busy to keep from being reminded of the death. They may feel as if they have lost control over their lives; their self-worth may lessen. Many will not ask for help, however, feeling that death is a private matter. Couples who cannot bring themselves to confront the death and to talk about it may never recover fully.

Sometimes one parent is able or ready to talk about feelings but may be frustrated by a spouse's inability to confront emotions. Eventually the spouse's hidden grief, plus worry about any surviving children, may surface, enabling the couple finally to talk together about their feelings surrounding the death. Sometimes that hidden grief remains buried.

Some parents may find that their marriage becomes troubled after the death of their baby, particularly if they cannot overcome feelings of blame or guilt. In our society a taboo seems to exist against talking about young children who die. Yet part of grieving is sharing and reminiscing. When infants die, there is little opportunity to share or reminisce, making it harder for parents to work through grief. Friends and family members often avoid the bereaved family or do not mention the dead baby. Their actions are understandable, but they usually make parents feel more isolated.

Parents may have difficulty deciding when or if to have subsequent children. Some parents want another child right away as a way of regaining the lost child. Others are reluctant to have another baby so soon. Many couples find it best to wait until they feel emotionally stronger, and until they realize that their dead child cannot be replaced, before they have a subsequent child.

TREATMENT

By definition, SIDS is an irreversible process. Since nothing can be done for the SIDS infants, their families become the patients. Parents and siblings need support to deal with the suddenness of the death and information to enable them to understand the nature of SIDS and their absence of responsibility.

The best form of treatment may be referring parents to professionals who are able to help and to SIDS parents' groups, where parents can talk about their baby's death with people who have gone through the same experience.

The ultimate goal of treatment is to enable parents to accept their baby's death and to help each other and their surviving children in the years ahead.

PREVENTION

Research about determining the cause of SIDS is supported by the National SIDS Foundation, 2 Metro Plaza, Suite 205, 8240 Professional Place, Landover, Maryland 20785 (phone: 800-221-SIDS). This organization also provides referrals to local chapters, which organize support groups and offer counseling.

SUICIDE

EMERGENCY ACTION

All suicide threats or attempts—no matter how seemingly flippant or manipulative—must be taken seriously and dealt with immediately. It is easy to underestimate the seriousness of a suicide statement. At the very least, a suicide threat is a sign that something important is troubling the person who made the threat. Constructive action taken in response to a suicide threat is never superfluous or damaging; ignoring a suicide threat can passively encourage a suicidal individual to act out his or her intentions.

In an emergency—when parents feel certain that a child is contemplating suicide, for example—they should call their family physician or pediatrician at once for advice. Some families might choose to call a mental health specialist, such as a psychologist or psychiatrist. Many communities have suicide hotlines that provide emergency advice and assistance. If parents do not have a family physician or access to a hotline, they should call a hospital emergency room and explain their concerns. If an actual suicide attempt occurs, take the child immediately to a hospital emergency room.

If poisoning may be involved, phone the nearest poison information center.

WARNING SIGNS AND SYMPTOMS

Most adolescents who attempt suicide give some indication of their intent. Even when an attempt is impulsive, it is usually preceded by signs that the child is troubled. In some cases the signs are indirect and involve changes in the child's behavior. The child may, for example, appear sadder or quieter than usual, withdraw from formerly pleasurable activities, begin having trouble at school, stop planning for the future, experience sleep problems (especially hyper-somnia—see *sleep disorders),* or lose his or her appetite. More direct behavioral signs that a child may be considering suicide include putting affairs in order—giving away possessions, for example; writing long notes or letters filled with references to suicide or death in general; and, of course, actually attempting suicide.

Other direct signs that a child may be contemplating suicide include remarks such as "I wish I were dead" or "Pretty soon you won't have to put up with me." Less obvious remarks can include revelations of morbid dreams, threats of revenge, expressions of despair about a terminal disease, comments suggesting indifference to death—or life— and verbalized feelings of low self-esteem.

DESCRIPTION

Suicide is the third leading cause of death among adolescents. The other two leading causes are auto accidents and homicides, and experts suspect that a significant number of auto accidents resulting in teenage fatalities involve suicidal youths. Each year in the United States about 5,000 teenagers commit suicide and about 500,000 others attempt it. All the incidence figures in this essay are likely to be too low, however, since they are based only on statistics from hospital emergency rooms.

In general, the number of suicide attempts among children rises with age. Suicide is virtually nonexistent among children less than 4 years old. Among children 5 to 11 years old, threats of suicide are relatively common and are often meant to express anger and to "punish" parents. Many children in this age group talk of suicide without meaning to carry out their threats, and actual suicide attempts are rare. On some occasions, however, school-aged children who may not appreciate the danger of suicide attempts succeed accidentally in carrying them out.

The suicide rate among children 12 to 15 years old is significantly higher than that for younger children. (About 2 out of every 1,000 children in this age group during any given year commit suicide.) Whatever the reason, the suicide rate for adolescents and young adults aged 15 to 24 is higher than for any other group except middle-aged men.

In the 3 decades following 1955, the suicide rate among 15- to 24-year-olds tripled. This rise paralleled an increase in the sale of firearms, particularly handguns, and their use as a means of suicide. Between 1966 and

1975 alone, suicides by firearms doubled among 15- to 24-year-olds. Studies of differences in suicide rates among states show a correlation with the strictness of state gun control laws.

Because more boys than girls use firearms as a suicidal means, boys who attempt suicide are 4 times as successful as girls, but there are 3 times as many suicide attempts among girls as there are among boys. Studies show that teenage boys who want to commit suicide most often overdose on drugs, shoot themselves, hang themselves, or poison themselves with gas (usually carbon monoxide from automobile exhaust). Adolescent girls most commonly ingest overdoses of substances, such as prescription antidepressant pills. The number of adolescent girls who shoot themselves, however, is increasing.

Some Misconceptions About Suicide

When a child commits suicide, adult notions about the idyllic nature of childhood are shattered. Perhaps because the subject of suicide is so disturbing, studies show that the majority of people in the United States are misinformed about the prevalence of suicide among youth. The following misconceptions seem to be widespread:

"People who talk about suicide don't go through with it." Studies show that about three quarters of all people who commit suicide have communicated their intent beforehand. Often a direct indication of intent is given.

"Everyone who attempts suicide wants to die. It's an accident if a suicide attempt fails." Many people who fail in attempting suicide do not use decisive means, such as a loaded handgun. Studies show that most people who attempt suicide do not want to die but are desperately seeking help. In most cases people who fail in suicide attempts are ambivalent afterwards about wanting to die.

"Only poor, oppressed, desperate people kill themselves. People who are well to do don't commit suicide." Suicide occurs among every socioeconomic, racial, religious, and political group in the country. The suicide rate among teens in rapidly growing, affluent communities in the Sunbelt states (from California to Florida) has escalated. Some teenagers in such communities report that although they do not want for material comforts, they suffer from a sense of isolation because of the constant flux of residents in their community and because of their parents' preoccupation with financial and social pursuits.

"All people who attempt suicide are depressed." It is true that many people who attempt suicide suffer from *depression*. However, a significant number of people who kill themselves show no signs of depression before the attempt. A person deeply in debt, for example, may not be depressed but may still attempt suicide.

"Only insane people kill themselves." The vast majority of people who commit suicide do not suffer from *psychosis,* the influence of mind-altering drugs (see *drug and alcohol abuse),* or any similar mental disturbance. Most people who attempt to kill themselves are rational and logical, and truly believe that attempting suicide is their best option.

"In retrospect, the reason for the suicide is always obvious." Even when a precipitating stressful situation can be discerned (which is not always the case), the motives are not always clear; the question of why the person felt unable to cope with the situation still remains.

"Most people plan out their suicide attempts." Impulsive suicides are more common among teenagers than among any other age group. The reason behind this phenomenon is unclear.

"Suicides are isolated events. After someone attempts suicide, everyone realizes how bad suicide is and people are more convinced than ever that they'll never do it." Double suicides are more common among teenagers than among any other age group. Two unhappy friends sometimes decide, for example, that nothing in the world is meaningful except their relationship, and they commit suicide together. For some teenagers the suicide of a friend is so painful or so revealing of the dark side of life that they commit suicide days, weeks, or months later. Multiple related teenage suicides seem to be occurring increasingly.

CAUSE

Many theories have been proposed to account for the current high rate of suicide among teenagers and young adults in the United States, but no theory is completely satisfying. Insofar as an understanding of the cause of suicide among teenagers and young adults may help prevent attempts, the following generalizations may prove informative.

While most young people who commit

suicide are not insane, psychotic individuals do seem more prone to suicide attempts. Teenagers and young adults who suffer from *psychosis* may not have a full appreciation of the danger of a suicide attempt.

Studies show that one characteristic that is prevalent among young people who attempt suicide is a lack of meaningful support relationships or a drastic change in an important relationship. Sometimes problems with relationships are generalized and constant. An adolescent may suffer from general social isolation, persistent friendship problems, a growing need for intimacy that is not met, or a sense of isolation precipitated by the changes of adolescence—specifically, the feeling of being on the margin between childhood and adulthood.

In many cases ongoing problems specifically involve the suicidal child's family. Examples of such problems include a continually troubled relationship with one or both parents and a feeling of alienation from the family, perhaps because of a severe communication problem.

In some cases a recent stressful situation can be identified as a possible cause of an adolescent suicide. Such situations sometimes involve a broken relationship; an unwanted pregnancy; a bitter fight with a parent or loved one; the death, illness, or suicide attempt of a close friend or family member; frequent family moves and a subsequently high number of school changes; school failure; and chronic illness.

Experts believe that the vast majority—about three fourths—of people who attempt suicide suffer from *depression*. Feelings of despondency and hopelessness are commonly accompanied by self-pity, anger directed against the self, and other manifestations of low self-esteem. These feelings sometimes increase the attractiveness of suicide to those who suffer from them. In about half of all suicides among teenagers and young adults, feelings of low self-esteem are associated with some form of substance abuse, such as alcohol dependency or regular use of mind-altering or addicting drugs.

TREATMENT FOR SUICIDE THREATS

Any indications that a child is contemplating suicide must be taken very seriously. Parents should not respond to a child who verbally threatens suicide "Don't say that!" because such a comment sounds judgmental

and unhelpful. It is a good idea, however, to ask a child in a concerned fashion if he or she is serious about the threat. If the child seems to mean what he or she says or otherwise appears troubled, parents should immediately allow a few minutes of time to begin to discuss the child's concern. The discussion should take top priority, preempting other activities, even ones that seem pressing. Talking about suicide does not precipitate the event; on the contrary, talking relieves a child's social isolation, which is often a key element of the problem.

The theme of a parent's verbal response to a child's thoughts about suicide should be that the child is loved deeply. During any discussion about suicide, parents should listen carefully and patiently to a child's concerns. They should say that they take the child's concerns seriously and very much want the child to feel better. They should treat all concerns with respect and refrain from becoming defensive or otherwise argumentative during the discussion. If the child asks questions, parents should attempt to answer them honestly, even if the answer is "I don't know." Most importantly, the child should get a sense that help is available. To this end, it often helps for a child and parents to call a suicide hotline or counselor right away.

A child who is contemplating suicide or who has already attempted it needs to develop the emotional resources to survive. A mental health specialist—such as a psychiatrist, psychologist, or social worker—can offer emotional support and practical advice. The specific type of help needed depends on the emotions of situations that are prompting suicidal feelings. Sometimes the child needs to sort through emotions and overcome depression. In other cases the child needs relief from a specific stressful situation, such as family turmoil. In addition to counseling, some children suffering from *depression* benefit from antidepressant medication prescribed by a psychiatrist or other physician. Whether or not parents sit in on some of the counseling is up to the child: some adolescents feel that the presence of parents disrupts the trust and intimacy between patient and professional.

Although sorting through suicidal feelings can take weeks, months, or even years, the probability that a child will attempt suicide often decreases greatly when he or she is given a sense of hope. Such a feeling must not, however, stem from hollow promises or trite reassurances, which can precipitate further disappointment and intensify suicidal urges. Instead, hope must come through feelings of attachment to others—parents, family members, friends, or if need be, counselors. Parents of a child who threatens suicide are likely to be best equipped to help the child if they talk with their own physician, their child's counselor, or another mental health specialist.

A frequent problem for parents of adolescents who seem suicidal is that the child resists seeing a counselor. Any discussion about seeing a counselor must be open and honest. Parents must persuade their child that they want to seek professional help because they love their child so much and truly want him or her to feel better. It should be explained to a resistant child that the child's suicidal feelings are a matter of concern for the whole family and that the whole family needs counseling. Seeing a counselor should be considered a positive step for the family and not a punishment for the child.

To a degree, parents should be flexible as they attempt to motivate their child to seek counseling. If, for example, the child wants to talk to the family physician instead of a counselor parents have selected, parents should readily agree. If, however, a child who seems suicidal persistently refuses any counseling, parents may need to force him or her to go for an evaluation. This action is likely to be extremely difficult and emotionally taxing in the short run, but it may be necessary for the child's long-term survival, and it does show that parents truly care.

TREATMENT FOR SUICIDE ATTEMPTS

Professional assistance should always be sought for a child who attempts suicide. In an emergency—when the child is physically hurt from a suicide attempt—immediate medical care should be sought at a hospital emergency room. If parents are unsure about how to proceed or if their child resists seeking emergency help, parents should call a physician, hospital emergency room, rescue squad, or local suicide hotline. If parents suspect that a child has taken an overdose of drugs or a similar substance, they should immediately seek advice from a poison control center.

If a child is not physically hurt from a suicide attempt, parents should still seek professional assistance promptly to avert another attempt. Again, a telephone consultation with a physician or suicide specialist can be valuable. Between the time of the attempt and the time the child sees a professional, parents should be profuse in their expressions of honest reassurance and general support. Although the shock of a child's attempted suicide is likely to be devastating, parental support immediately after the attempt can be a great source of strength for the child.

If parents feel unequipped to offer full support because they are baffled and hurt by the suicide attempt, counselors who specialize in talking with families of children who attempt suicide are available for help. Often, coming to an understanding of the child's suicide attempt takes time; the immediate need is to administer medical treatment and reduce any remaining desire on the part of the child to attempt suicide again.

Studies show that the danger is low that a child will attempt suicide again in the emergency room. Presumably, the child has not thought beyond the first attempt, is relieved it has failed, or is too seriously injured to act out any remaining suicidal desires. As a precaution, however, a child who has attempted suicide is watched constantly by a caregiver, usually a physician or nurse, until the likelihood of another suicide attempt seems low. Any necessary medical or surgical treatment is given for injuries sustained during the attempt.

Once a child's physical and emotional conditions are relatively stable, a physician leads a discussion among family members—including the child who has attempted suicide—in an effort to reassure the child that the family is supportive. Such a discussion can help decrease the child's sense of isolation and may help block another attempt.

After discussing the situation briefly with the family and child, a physician takes a history of the child's growth and development, including health problems. In addition, a mental health specialist, usually a psychiatrist, is consulted to conduct a thorough psychological evaluation. The original physician may continue to consult the psychiatrist, or the psychiatrist may take primary responsibility for the child's care.

Whichever professional continues the evaluation then talks at length with the child to formulate an impression of the seriousness of the child's intent to commit suicide. Primarily, the professional tries to assess the child's risk of dying given the type of attempt and the circumstances under which it was made. In general, a professional tries to determine whether the child took active precautions against being discovered after the attempt, whether a potential helper was notified, for how long the attempt was planned, whether the child believed the attempt would succeed, and whether he or she regrets that it failed.

In addition to discussing the child's feelings about the suicide attempt, the professional tries to talk to the child about future plans, both to offer practical advice and to explore any remaining suicidal feelings. In particular, a professional asks a child whether he or she feels supported by family and community leaders. If a child feels alienated from all the people in his or her environment, a professional may decide that the child should be admitted to the hospital until a dependable support network can be established.

One fifth of all children who attempt suicide are hospitalized, often in adolescent or pediatric wards. Hospitalization is mandatory for the protection of any child who almost died from a suicide attempt, appears to be psychotic, took precautions to avoid rescue, regrets survival, or completely shuns help or support. Parents are often concerned about hospitalizing their child for emotional, logistical, financial, and a variety of other reasons. It is encouraging to report, however, that virtually all children hospitalized after suicide attempts—more than 99 percent—are alive a year after being discharged from the facility. Parents may have to override a child's immediate objections if hospitalization seems necessary to ensure the best possible outcome.

When a decision is made to hospitalize a child who has attempted suicide, the antisuicide precautions taken in the hospital vary. Sometimes the child has no unusual restrictions. In other cases potentially dangerous objects are removed from the child's environment. If a teenager is seriously disturbed —if he or she is severely depressed, for example—a professional may recommend that the child be admitted temporarily to an adolescent psychiatric ward. Parents should feel comfortable with the quality, resources, and treatment methods of such a facility.

Whether or not a child is hospitalized after a suicide attempt, parents need to take time to understand their child's plea for help and deal with it. The child's family often needs help coping with conflicting feelings of guilt and anger, as well as feelings of helplessness or fear. Parents should not hesitate to ask the person who is treating their child to counsel the family or seek the help of another professional.

When a child successfully carries out a suicide attempt, feelings of guilt, anger, fear, and helplessness are heightened and are compounded by grief. A counselor well versed in the concerns and problems of such families can be an invaluable source of advice and support after such a tragedy occurs.

PREVENTION

Since the causes of suicide are complex, absolute prevention of suicide attempts is not possible. Evidence suggests that loving and open familial relationships can go far in decreasing the child's sense of isolation and hopelessness, but even the best family relationship sometimes cannot prevent tragedy. The most effective way to prevent suicide may be to be aware of possible warning signs and to deal with the situation immediately.

In addition, parents should keep lethal means out of the home, especially when a child seems suicidal or has already made a suicide attempt. Handguns—even unloaded ones—should never be available to children of any age. All medications—especially tranquilizers, sleeping pills, and sedatives— should be inaccessible to children. While an adolescent's environment cannot be "child-proofed," parents can keep the most commonly used means of suicide out of their homes.

The suicide rate in Great Britain declined significantly when the carbon monoxide content in domestic gas—the number one means of suicide in that country—was lowered. Some advocates contend that the suicide rate in the United States might decline if handgun ownership were more strictly regulated or curtailed and if the number of pills prescribed at one time for psychological ailments were limited.

(See also Chapter 3, "Promoting Mental Health.")

SUNBURN

EMERGENCY ACTION

Seek immediate medical attention if a sunburned child has symptoms of sun poisoning, including a *rash,* chills, *fever,* and nausea, or burning is extensive (see *burns.)* Also seek medical attention if signs of *shock* appear: cool, clammy, pale skin; rapid pulse; thirst; dizziness or faintness; and increased breathing rate.

DESCRIPTION

Sunburn is a common, painful skin condition that occurs when skin is overexposed to the sun or to a sunlamp (see *burns* for description of first-, second-, and third-degree burns). Overexposed areas become tender, red, and very warm. Anyone can become sunburned. Infants and young children and light-skinned, fair-haired people are particularly susceptible, but even dark-skinned people may be vulnerable after prolonged exposure. The pain of sunburn is most severe 6 to 48 hours following exposure.

As healing begins, the upper layer of skin starts to peel. This layer, which was injured by ultraviolet radiation in sunlight, falls off to make room for a new, healthy layer of skin. Peeling usually beings 3 to 10 days after a sunburn and ends when skin is fully healed, from a few days to a week later.

CAUSE

Sunburn results from overexposure to ultraviolet radiation from the sun or from sunlamps. Sensitivity to the sun is often heightened by environmental factors such as the time of day (the sun's rays are strongest between 11 A.M. and 1 P.M. standard time) and elevation (the higher the locale, the stronger the sun's intensity). In addition, reflection of sunlight on sand, snow, and water increases the amount of radiation that reaches the skin. Oils or creams applied to the skin also intensify the ultraviolet radiation reaching the skin.

SIGNS AND SYMPTOMS

Blisters appear if a second-degree burn has occurred. If burning is severe, sunburn-reddened skin may take on a bluish color. Swelling may hinder motion. Blistering may appear several days after exposure.

DIAGNOSIS

Sunburn is obvious—by red, tender, often blistered skin. History of a child's recent outdoor activities can be helpful in diagnosing a sunburn.

TREATMENT

Second- or third-degree sunburn should not be treated at home. A child should be taken immediately to a hospital emergency room or physician's office for treatment.

A mild sunburn can be treated easily at home. Soaking burned areas in tepid water and baking soda (a water softener) helps cool and soothe tender skin. Repeated applications of wet dressings to specific burned areas and soaking the whole body in a tepid bath also are effective. Bath water should be lukewarm to avoid chilling the child. Extensive use of wet dressings may also chill a small child. Between soakings, cold cream or petroleum jelly helps cool and protect the burned skin. A pain-relieving medication may be helpful. Consult the physician for specific recommendations and read the discussion of nonprescription medications beginning on p. 102. Antihistamines may reduce itching as the skin heals. To avoid infection, allow small blisters to heal by themselves without being opened. If blistered skin has opened, however, a physician should be consulted. If blisters become infected, a physician may prescribe an antibiotic.

Products containing benzocaine should be avoided for children's sunburn. These preparations may give temporary relief, but can cause hypersensitivity and *eczema,* which will delay healing.

PREVENTION

Avoiding overexposure is the best way to prevent sunburn. Sunscreens containing PABA (para-amino-benzoic acid) or sun blocks (such as zinc oxide ointment), reduce or bar the sun's burning rays; these preparations should be used during initial exposure to the sun. Sunscreens may wash off and must be reapplied. Children should be exposed to summer sun for short periods of time (starting at 3 to 5 minutes and doubling the time of exposure each day unless redness develops) until it is clear what their response is.

Certain medications (diuretics, anticancer drugs, and coal tar ointments, for example) increase the skin's sensitivity to sunlight. If a child is using one of these medications, a physician should be consulted before allowing the child to go out in the sun.

SWOLLEN GLANDS

DESCRIPTION

Enlarged or swollen lymph nodes are common among children and can be signs of a health problem. A general term for any abnormality or disease of the lymph nodes is lymphadenopathy (literally, "disease of the lymph gland"). Most often, however, swollen lymph nodes are referred to simply as swollen glands." This popular term overlooks the reality that most often it is not glands but lymph nodes which are enlarged. True glands do become swollen, however. When a child is ill with *mumps,* for example, the parotid glands under the jaw are enlarged and painful. Since the term lymphadenopathy is all-inclusive, it is the one used generally in this essay. However, calling the problem "swollen glands" is not a mistake; health professionals understand what is meant by the term and often use it themselves.

Lymph nodes are small bean- or pea-sized lumps or lymphoid tissue, a specialized infection-fighting material. Lymph nodes filter bacteria and other potential agents of infection from body tissues. They also produce lymphocytes, infection-fighting white blood cells. Lymph nodes are found either in clusters or singly in strategic locations throughout the body and represent part of the lymphatic system, which includes a circulatory network of vessels that carry a substance called lymph (see Fig. 31, p. 501).

Lymph is a transparent, slightly yellow fluid. It originates in, bathes, and protects many cells and tissues in the body. The fluid is collected in lymph vessels from all parts of the body and then channeled into the bloodstream. In addition to the lymph-carrying vessels, the lymphatic system consists of 2 varieties of lymphoid tissue: lymphoid organs, such as the lymph nodes, spleen, and thymus gland; and patches of lymphoid tissue, either prominent or hidden, located, for example, in the tonsils, stomach, small intestine, and skin. All lymphoid tissues play a role in the body's defense against infection.

Among the most physically prominent lymph node clusters—each one protecting or draining a different region of the body—are those in the neck, armpits, and groin (along the creases where the thighs join the pubic region). Other individual lymph nodes or lymph node clusters lie deep within the body—in the chest or abdominal cavity, for example—and usually cannot be seen by external physical inspection or felt on examination.

Depending upon how extensive the disease may be, lymphadenopathy is described as localized or generalized. It is localized when just one region or cluster of lymph nodes is affected; it is generalized when more than two nonadjacent regions of nodes are involved.

In most cases, lymphadenopathy is a response to a mild infection, localized or generalized, which may require medical treatment. It is possible, however, for a variety of serious disorders, including infection, to begin with swelling of a single lymph node or with a region or cluster of nodes. Accordingly, parents should pay attention to any swollen glands (degree of lymphadenopathy) which a child experiences.

Swollen lymph nodes can be indicative of many conditions, ranging from common (localized infection such as *colds* or a *sore throat)* to rare (an early sign of *cancer,* such as *leukemia* or *lymphoma).* It is often difficult at first for health professionals to determine the seriousness of the underlying cause of swollen lymph nodes because lymphoid tissue changes rapidly in character and extensiveness as children grow. Moreover, ill children develop swollen lymph nodes faster and more obviously than do adults, in part because children have relatively more lymphoid tissue in their developing bodies. Generally, then, children are more likely than adults to have swollen glands (enlarged lymph nodes) regardless of the severity of the cause.

Among some children, normal lymph nodes, especially those at the base of the skull and in front of the neck, are prominent and may even feel enlarged when examined. In the absence of other signs and symptoms of illness, a particular child's enlarged lymph nodes may not indicate the presence of disease or illness and, in fact, may be normal for that child. It is true, however, that a single very large lymph node—an inch or more in diameter—can be indicative of a serious condition.

Lymphadenopathy affects children of all ages, all year round. When numbers of colds or cases of *influenza* are rising, the incidence of lymphadenopathy, a typical sign of those diseases, usually rises as well. A child may complain sometimes of soreness in the neck or throat at the site of swollen lymph nodes, but more often enlarged lymph nodes are painless and easily felt with the tips of the fingers. Swollen nodes can range from the size of a small pea to that of a walnut. Following an infection that causes severely swollen lymph nodes, especially in the neck or behind the ears, it is possible for a node to remain somewhat enlarged and not be painful.

Swollen lymph nodes may appear as small, only slightly raised areas of skin on the neck, under the armpits, and in the groin. Others may be unmistakable lumps. They can be soft and movable to the touch or hard and immovable. They may fluctuate or remain constant in size.

Lymphadenopathy lasts until the underlying cause is cured or disappears spontaneously. More often than not, lymphadenopathy proves to be a short-term, readily curable condition. As long as lymphadenopathy persists, however, it should not be ignored. If lymphadenopathy does not respond to treatment, a swollen node is usually removed surgically and examined for evidence of disease—a procedure called a biopsy—by a pathologist (a diagnostic specialist who identifies the cause, course, and effects of disease).

CAUSE

The causes of lymphadenopathy can be divided into six categories: localized infections, generalized (widespread) infections, connective tissue disorders, hypersensitivity conditions, cancers, and granulomatous diseases.

Localized Infections

Bacterial: A single episode of lymphadenopathy is typically caused by a staphylococcus or streptococcus infection. Rare bacterial causes include diphtheria and plague. *Tuberculosis* is a cause of persistent localized infections.

Viral: Cat scratch disease (see *pets, diseases caused by)* and *German measles (rubella)* are typical causes.

Other infectious causes include one-celled organisms (protozoans), fungi, and spirochetes. One of the most common causes of localized lymphadenopathy is the temporary inflammation that occurs just after immunization for childhood diseases such as vaccination for diphtheria, pertussis *(whooping cough),* and *tetanus* (DPT).

Generalized Infections

Bacterial: General skin infections (such as *impetigo), tuberculosis,* blood poisoning (see *bloodstream infection),* and *typhoid fever* are typical causes of lymphadenopathy.

Viral: Infectious mononucleosis (see *mononucleosis infections),* cytomegaloviral infection, rubella, and *chicken pox* are typical causes. Some research suggests that AIDS (acquired immune deficiency syndrome) is a virus-triggered cause of lymphadenopathy.

Other causes of generalized infection include protozoans and spirochetes, microscopic organisms which can produce infection and swelling.

It is important to remember that a generalized infectious lymphadenopathy may first be localized and later become generalized (widespread).

Connective Tissue Disorders

Connective tissue disorders that may cause lymphadenopathy include *arthritis* and *lupus erythematosus.*

Hypersensitivity Conditions

Hypersensitivity conditions that commonly lead to lymphadenopathy include reactions to certain medications and to substances, such as horse serum, that are occasionally used in producing inoculations against certain diseases.

Cancers

Cancers that can cause lymphadenopathy include *leukemia,* Hodgkin's disease, and non-Hodgkin's lymphoma (see *lymphoma).*

Granulomatous Disease

Granulomatous diseases, characterized by formation of lumps in body tissue, causing lymphadenopathy are unusual. They include sarcoidosis, a rare disorder which produces small nodules in several organs in the body.

Lymphadenopathy itself is not contagious, although some of the causes producing it can be.

DIAGNOSIS

Diagnosis of an underlying cause of lymphadenopathy is made by a physician, who performs a careful physical examination and takes a history of all signs and symptoms of illness. Of special interest to a physician would be a history of inflamed tonsils (as indicated by swelling, redness, warmth, and pain); infections located near the affected group of lymph nodes; skin cuts or abrasions; or the occurrence of animal scratches or bites of rodents or ticks.

The location of swollen lymph nodes may be helpful in making a diagnosis. Swollen lymph nodes in the neck or the groin are not usually signs of serious disease, but severely swollen nodes in the armpits or directly above the collarbone can indicate a more serious underlying condition. As noted earlier, any node as large as an inch in diameter is cause for concern.

If the cause of enlarge lymph nodes is not clear after a week or so, a physician may decide to take a chest X ray and order blood tests of various types. A throat culture may prove helpful in confirming a bacterial cause for lymphadenopathy. A CT scan (computed tomography), which takes detailed X rays of very small cross-sections of the swollen lymph nodes and adjacent areas of the lymphatic system, may be useful in diagnosis. If a lymph node is swollen, tender, red, and pus-filled, fluid can be aspirated (removed with a needle) and analyzed for a specific infectious agent. An antibiotic can be prescribed if a bacterium or fungus is found.

If *cancer* is suspected, specialized X rays of the entire lymphatic system (using dye injected into the lymphatic vessels) may be required. A sample of bone marrow (usually aspirated from the hipbone or pelvis) can be analyzed. Finally, a biopsy (removal) of an entire swollen lymph node can be performed for analysis if earlier tests do not identify a cause.

TREATMENT
Treatment of lymphadenopathy depends upon its underlying cause. When the cause disappears spontaneously or is diagnosed and treated successfully, lymphadenopathy subsides. Taking the appropriate antibiotic for a strep infection, for example, can cure lymphadenopathy associated with a *sore throat* in a few days. Sometimes, when infection is strongly suspected as a cause, an antibiotic is given on a trial basis, until test results identify a specific agent of infection. If the underlying cause is difficult to treat, lymphadenopathy may improve slowly. In the case of Hodgkin's disease and non-Hodgkin's lymphoma, for example, radiation or chemotherapy may be effective in reducing the number of lymph nodes involved and the degree of swelling.

If lymphadenopathy fails to heal spontaneously or to respond to medical treatment, surgical removal and biopsy of the swollen node(s) is performed.

PREVENTION
Lymphadenopathy can be prevented if the cause of the particular swelling is itself preventable.

SYPHILIS

DESCRIPTION
Syphilis is a serious infectious disease. Two types exist. The more well-known type, acquired syphilis, is usually contracted by adolescents and adults through sexual contact. It is categorized as a venereal disease (VD) or sexually transmissible disease (STD). The other type, fetal or congenital (present at birth) syphilis, is contracted by babies from their mothers before or during birth.

In 1983, 32,575 cases of syphilis were reported in the United States. (Actual incidence of acquired syphilis could be higher. Before symptoms appear, some cases of syphilis are inadvertently cured—and thus never diagnosed—when concurrent cases of *gonorrhea* or other infectious diseases are treated.) The incidence of syphilis is especially high in urban areas. Males are infected 3 times as often as females. At least one third of all individuals with reported acquired syphilis are homosexual. Although acquired syphilis is usually contracted by adolescents and young adults, young children are sometimes infected.

Congenital syphilis is now rare.

Acquired Syphilis
Once a person is infected, acquired syphilis enters a period of incubation ranging from 3 to 90 days but most often lasting 21 days. During the incubation period the bacteria that cause syphilis invade the lymph (a protective fluid carried in a circulatory network of vessels) or blood (see *bloodstream infection)* and are transported throughout the body. No symptoms are present during the incubation period.

After incubation, acquired syphilis is characterized by 3 active stages alternating with 1 or 2 latent (present but inactive) ones.

The disease is curable during the latent as well as the first two—but not the third—active stages.

The first active stage is indicated by a chancre: a small, hard, open—but painless—sore characteristic of syphilis. The chancre appears at the site of infection, typically on the external genitals: on the penis or scrotum in males or on the vulva of females. Less often a chancre may appear inside the vagina or on the cervix in females, or in the mouth, on or near the lips, on the fingers, on the perianal area, or in the anal canal in either sex. (In rare cases more than one chancre appears. More commonly an atypical chancre or none at all appears. Before puberty, children rarely have a detectable chancre.) A woman may not notice the chancre on her genitals, and cannot see it if it is hidden inside the vagina or on the cervix. Even without treatment, the chancre generally heals within 3 to 6 weeks (as early as 2 weeks or as late as 12 weeks), usually leaving no scar.

Another sign of the first stage of syphilis is swollen but painless lymph nodes in the area of the chancre. This sign can linger after the chancre has healed.

Next, acquired syphilis may enter a latent stage (in which no signs and symptoms are present) before entering the second active stage. Sometimes, however, the second active stage begins while the chancre is still present.

The second active stage occurs as early as 2 weeks or as late as 3 months after the first active stage, although on the average it occurs about 6 weeks later. This stage of syphilis appears first as small, pinkish red, flat spots on the skin, which often become solid, elevated inflamed lumps (like pimples), and then, occasionally, become infected lumps containing pus. All 3 types of skin lesions may appear at the same time. The lesions may appear all over the body (especially the palms of the hands and soles of the feet) or in a limited area. Even if untreated, the skin lesions disappear by themselves after 4 to 8 weeks. The pimplelike lesions may become painless, moist, grayish or reddish plaques on parts of the body where creases or folds exist: under the breasts or on the vulva in females, on the scrotum in males, or on the inner thighs or the perianal area in either sex.

The skin lesions may be accompanied by other symptoms, since any part of the body may be invaded by the bacteria. Symptoms that may appear include listlessness, loss of appetite, weight loss, low-grade fever, scaly skin, painless mucous patches on any mucous membrane, severe pain in the joints, *sore throat, laryngitis,* spleen or lymph node enlargement, patchy hair loss, or inflammation of the iris in the eye. (The symptoms may resemble those of *meningitis.* In a very few cases meningitis may actually occur.) Rarely, the kidneys or liver are affected. In a few cases, *headache,* double vision, decreased vision, vertigo, or a ringing in the ears occurs.

If still untreated by the end of the second active stage, acquired syphilis becomes latent (again, with no signs or symptoms) for a period ranging from 2 to 50 years. However, the bacteria continue to attack the body and the disease progresses. During the first 4 years of the latent stage, especially during the first 1 or 2 years, "relapses" of the secondary stage can occur in which potentially infectious lesions appear on the skin and mucous membranes. Grayish or reddish plaques may also appear during a relapse.

The third active stage is fatal.

Congenital Syphilis

The severity of congenital syphilis depends on when the fetus is infected, the fetus's health, the mother's stage of syphilis, and whether and when her syphilis is treated. Severity varies: a fetus may be miscarried or stillborn, or a newborn may die, have active syphilis, or have latent syphilis. The risk of congenital syphilis is highest during the first year after the mother is infected.

Symptoms of congenital syphilis are first noticeable in newborns: *fever,* sniffles, failure to gain weight (see *failure to thrive),* restlessness, and a skin condition of discolored spots and pimplelike or blisterlike lumps or of mucous patches. Fine, scaly peeling of the skin may occur. No chancre appears in congenital syphilis.

The second stage, occurring within the first 6 weeks of life, may bring a nasal discharge of mucus, pus, and sometimes blood; continuation of the skin condition; inflammation of bones; and bleeding cracks and sores at the corners of the mouth and around the anus. Enlargement of the liver (causing *jaundice),* spleen, or lymph nodes may occur. *Anemia,* kidney problems, and lung damage are also common. The central nervous system may be affected, leading to *meningitis.* Any part of the body may be involved.

After 6 months or a year have passed, congenital syphilis usually becomes latent for an unpredictable length of time.

Three fourths of congenital syphilis cases go unrecognized in early infancy. However, to prevent complications, it is at this time that the disease should be treated. Later in life, if congenital syphilis was untreated, the child may suffer malformed teeth, serious bone inflammation, *blindness,* deafness (see *hearing loss*), heart problems, nervous-system damage, or *mental retardation.* A child may be 10 years old or more before physical damage is traced to fetal syphilis.

If either acquired or congenital syphilis is detected and treated early, the outlook for complete recovery is good. Acquired syphilis, however, can be contracted more than once.

CAUSE

Syphilis is caused by a bacterium. Acquired syphilis is most contagious when a chancre or other skin condition is present. The bacteria are usually transmitted by sexual contact with an infected person, especially a person in the first or second stage of syphilis. Any form of sexual contact, not just intercourse, can spread the bacteria into nearly any body opening (such as the vagina, rectum, or mouth) or break in the skin. Sexual abuse, including incest, also can transmit the bacteria (see *child abuse*). If a chancre forms on or near the lips (as a result of oral-genital sex), a simple kiss could spread the bacteria, although this is uncommon. Infants, children, and adolescents can acquire syphilis from an infected adult.

Typically, a fetus contracts syphilis when bacteria in the mother's blood (from acquired syphilis) are transferred through the placenta into the fetus's blood. The mother may have contracted syphilis during pregnancy. Or she may have had the disease weeks or even years before the pregnancy and never have been treated. The bacteria remain active in her bloodstream when the disease is latent. In other cases a pregnant woman may have very highly infectious, syphilitic lesions in her vagina (birth canal) that may infect her baby as it is born.

Any secretions from the nose or mouth or from a *rash* of an infected newborn are highly contagious.

DIAGNOSIS

Syphilis can be difficult to diagnose be-

cause it can resemble many other diseases, particularly during the second and third stages. During the first stage, acquired syphilis can sometimes be confused with a *genital herpes* infection or venereal warts.

Screening for both acquired and fetal syphilis involves a blood test. However, false positive reactions to this initial blood test are fairly common. For instance, pregnancy, rheumatoid *arthritis, lupus erythematosus, chicken pox, measles, tuberculosis, scarlet fever, hepatitis,* or mononucleosis (see *mononucleosis, infectious)* could cause a false positive reaction.

To confirm the diagnosis of syphilis, more definitive, specific blood tests can be used as a backup to initial blood tests. Or the diagnosis can be confirmed through a microscopic evaluation of skin lesions during the first or second stage of acquired syphilis or early congenital syphilis.

COMPLICATIONS

A chancre can become infected, particularly if it is in the mouth or anal canal. An infected chancre is painful and contains pus. Other skin lesions are also painful if they become infected. The serious disabilities of the third stage of syphilis can cause various, severe complications, resulting from permanent damage to nerves and blood vessels.

TREATMENT

If, during the first or second active stage, acquired syphilis is treated in a sufficient dosage for an adequate length of time with antibiotics such as penicillin, it can usually be cured.

Fetal syphilis can be cured if the mother's acquired syphilis is treated promptly, while she is still pregnant.

PREVENTION

The spread of syphilis can be prevented or at least reduced. The regular use of condoms by sexually active males is recommended. The pill, IUD, and diaphragm, however, offer no protection against syphilis.

Public health measures to curb the spread of syphilis include the notification and treatment (with preventive antibiotics) of the sexual contacts of infected persons.

Premarital blood tests are required in many states.

Additionally, blood tests for syphilis are given routinely to all pregnant women who receive prenatal medical care in most of the United States; ideally, the test should be performed twice, in the first and third trimesters, since transmission to the fetus is most likely to occur after 4 months of pregnancy. If the test is positive, the pregnant woman can receive treatment with penicillin. Fetal syphilis can be prevented if women with acquired syphilis are treated during the first 4 months of pregnancy.

A blood test for congenital syphilis should be given at birth. Infected newborns should be isolated and handled with sterile gloves until treatment has been given (treatment takes effect very quickly). Parents should instruct their children aged 10 or older about venereal diseases, including how they can be transmitted, identified, prevented, and treated. (See discussion of venereal diseases in Chapter 2, "Promoting Physical Health.")

TAY-SACHS DISEASE

DESCRIPTION

Tay-Sachs disease is a hereditary condition that affects the central nervous system (the brain and spinal cord and their protective covering, the meninges). Children with Tay-Sachs disease appear normal for about the first 6 months of life, but brain function then begins to deteriorate rapidly and death occurs by 3 to 4 years of age.

An early sign of Tay-Sachs disease can be an infant's extreme sensitivity and startled reaction to loud noises. Other than that, the first indication of the disease is a slowed rate of growth and development. The infant also becomes less attentive to surroundings and family members and begins to regress until he or she loses learned skills, such as sitting up. Over time, a child with Tay-Sachs disease loses the ability to perceive any stimulation, becomes blind and severely mentally retarded, and loses all muscular functions, including the ability to move, respond, make sounds, eat, or drink. *Seizures* may occur in the later stages of the disease.

The final phase of the disease is a debilitated state in which a child with Tay-Sachs disease may require tube feeding. At this point, little can be done for an affected child other than to provide supportive physical care and treatment of recurrent infections, which can weaken a child with already low resistance. Often, *pneumonia* or another infection is the ultimate cause of death.

The highest incidence of Tay-Sachs disease is among Ashkenazic Jews, whose ancestors formerly lived in eastern and central Europe. Tay-Sachs disease first appeared in Ashkenazic families living in eastern Poland in the early nineteenth century; the trait (carrier state) has been inherited for generations. Among couples of this ethnic background, the incidence of Tay-Sachs is about one in 2,500 live births; in the non-Jewish United States population, it is approximately one in 250,000. The disease is cause for concern among American Jews, many of whom are Ashkenazic. In the United States about 1 in 25 Jews is a carrier of the gene involved with Tay-Sachs disease (carriers do not develop the disease). It has been confirmed that some families of French-Canadian Catholic ancestry may also have an increased carrier rate, although this is more rare.

CAUSE

Tay-Sachs disease is caused by a genetic defect that prevents the body from producing hexosaminidase A, an enzyme (chemical messenger) necessary for the metabolism of certain substances within the central nervous system. (Metabolism is the body's conversion, use, and storage of substances and disposal of resulting waste products.) In the absence of hexosaminidase A, these substances accumulate in the nerve cells of the brain, interfering with the cells' function and eventually destroying them.

Carriers of the gene for Tay-Sachs disease have diminished amounts of the enzyme—although enough for metabolic purposes.

Tay-Sachs disease is transmitted from parent to child by a recessive abnormal gene. If two carriers of the gene have children together, there exists with each pregnancy a 25 percent risk that their child will inherit a defective gene from each parent and develop Tay-Sachs disease, a 50 percent chance that the child will inherit only 1 defective gene and be a carrier, and a 25 percent chance that a child will inherit no defective genes and be neither a carrier nor affected. The gene for Tay-Sachs disease, in fact, is usually passed down recessively from generation to generation without any child being affected by the disease (see *genetic disorders*).

DIAGNOSIS

A physician or ophthalmologist (a physician who specializes in eye and vision problems) may be able to make an initial diagnosis of Tay-Sachs disease by observation of a "cherry red spot" at the back of a child's eye.

All testing to confirm the diagnosis of Tay-Sachs disease or the carrier state involves analyzing the amount of the enzyme present in body fluids or tissues. Blood tests can detect the disease and the carrier state. Diagnosis of the disease itself can be confirmed further by a skin biopsy (removal and analysis of a tiny tissue sample). Prenatal diagnosis of the disease is possible through amniocentesis (aspiration of a sample of amniotic fluid through a needle inserted into the uterus through the abdominal wall and analysis of the fluid).

TREATMENT

There is currently no cure for Tay-Sachs disease. The progressive effects of the disease on affected children can be an agonizing process for family members who must care for an affected child. Counseling and emotional support services are helpful.

PREVENTION

Ashkenazic Jews planning to have children should be screened (tested) for the presence of the enzyme. Genetic counseling can be invaluable (see *genetic disorders*). Even if both partners are carriers of the defective gene, they still may wish to have children. Such a couple can use prenatal diagnosis to determine whether a fetus is affected by Tay-Sachs disease.

Parents of affected children and others can receive information about the condition and learn about local support services from the National Tay-Sachs and Allied Diseases Association, 92 Washington Avenue, Cedarhurst, NY 11516 (phone: 516-569-4300).

TEETH, DEVELOPMENTAL PROBLEMS OF

DESCRIPTION

Development of primary (baby) teeth begins before birth and continues through the first years of life. A child normally acquires 20 primary teeth: incisors, sharp front teeth used for cutting; first- and second-year molars used for chewing and grinding; and canines, pointed teeth located between the

incisors and the first-year molars. The eruption process for primary teeth usually begins when a child is about 7 months old and is completed by 3 years of age, although the order and rate of eruption vary from child to child (see *teething*). Eruption of permanent teeth usually begins when a child is 6 years old and continues through age 13. Third molars (wisdom teeth) usually erupt between the ages of 19 and 25.

Any major deviation from normal tooth development or eruption is considered a developmental problem of the teeth. Most children suffer at least one tooth problem, and some experience more than one at a time.

Imperfect Enamel

Imperfections of the enamel (the hard, white substance covering the exposed portion of the tooth) may be mild (such as pitting and slight discoloration of the enamel surface) or severe (such as large areas of irregularly formed enamel). Enamel may also be thin, smooth, and brownish yellow in color. Rarely, enamel thickness may be abnormal, ranging from a thin coating to being completely absent. Imperfections are particularly common among children who were premature or who had serious illnesses before birth or during infancy. Severe injury occurring before birth can also interfere with enamel formation.

Defective Dentin

Defects involving dentin, the ivory that forms the body of a tooth, are found more often among primary than permanent teeth. These defects may be the result of diseases of the dentin itself or may be associated with disorders that affect other body tissues. Dentin may be very thin, causing the affected tooth to appear opalescent (resembling an opal in color) or blue. Sometimes an otherwise normal tooth with thin dentin is a direct result of the absence of a tooth root. The affected tooth is misplaced or mispositioned and can easily fall out.

Defective dentin may also be associated with a bone condition that inhibits calcification (the process by which bone forms and hardens), in which enamel breaks away from the tooth soon after dentin is formed. Teeth take on a reddish brown or gray-blue opalescent color, and exposed dentin wears down quickly, possibly to the level of the gum.

Structural Problems

Structural tooth problems include poorly or incorrectly shaped teeth (such as those that are tapered or very thin), bent or curved teeth, shell teeth (in which the inner pulp, the living tissue, is missing), and unusually small or large teeth. In rare cases small or large teeth occur with *pituitary problems.* Two teeth may be joined at the base, a result of incomplete division of a tooth bud. Structural problems are often accompanied by enamel imperfections. Unless an underlying disorder is present, structural problems are present in only a few teeth.

Discoloration

Teeth may become mottled, opaque, blue, or brown as a result of a serious illness during infancy, use of certain medications (such as tetracycline), or injuries or death of tooth pulp (the inner living tissues of a tooth). This type of tooth discoloration is not caused by staining from mouth bacteria.

Early or Delayed Eruption

Primary teeth that erupt early are classified as natal, neonatal, or premature. Natal teeth are present at birth and are the most common type of early-eruption teeth; they are usually primary incisors that have erupted prematurely but may be immature. Neonatal teeth are teeth that erupt during the first 30 days of life; they too are usually primary incisors. Premature teeth are those that appear during the first 3 months. Premature teeth (most often lower incisors) are very loose because of insufficient root development. Permanent teeth rarely erupt early.

Delay or prevention of permanent tooth eruption may occur if primary teeth are lost prematurely, for example because of an accident. Eruption can also be delayed or prevented if a child has an underlying disorder such as *Down syndrome.* In this case the first primary teeth may be delayed until the child is 2 years old, and primary tooth eruption may not be completed until age 4 or 5. In some cases primary teeth do not fall out until a child is 14 or 15 years old. Permanent teeth may be crowded, and resulting tooth impaction may further delay tooth eruption.

Tooth impaction is caused by the presence of a physical barrier that prevents eruption. Such barriers include lack of space between teeth because of crowding or because of misplaced teeth. In addition, tooth buds that become twisted in the dental arch may try to erupt in the wrong direction. Another tooth is usually in the way, and these impacted teeth cannot erupt. Impaction most often involves the molars and canines.

Eruption may also be delayed if a tooth remains in the dental arch because it is unable to erupt. This may result from insufficient developmental activity or from ankylosis (the embedding of the tooth in the dental arch). When this occurs, space between teeth progressively increases. Enamel defects may be present in teeth adjacent to the embedded tooth.

Minor Eruption Problems

A harmless eruption problem is the presence of a tiny piece of bone on the gum tissue above the erupting tooth. Another harmless problem involves the development of bubble as a tooth erupts. This bubble can be clear, called an eruption cyst, or filled with blood, called an eruption hematoma.

Extra Teeth

Extra teeth (also called supernumerary teeth) are teeth that erupt in addition to the normal number of primary or permanent teeth. They are usually small. These teeth most often develop in the upper incisor area and are usually permanent rather than primary teeth. The presence of extra permanent teeth is a common condition (affecting as many as 1 in every 100 children), particularly among children who have cleft lip (see *cleft lip and cleft palate)* or underlying inherited disorders. Extra teeth can cause eruption problems by presenting a physical barrier to eruption of adjacent teeth (possibly for several years) or causing ectopic eruption (rotation or out-of-place eruption) of adjacent teeth. Extra teeth may also cause impaction of permanent teeth.

Malocclusion

Any deviation from the normal fit between top and bottom teeth or between adjacent teeth is called malocclusion (or "bad bite"). Every child experiences temporary tooth malocclusion as primary teeth fall out and permanent teeth come in. When permanent tooth eruption is complete, this temporary malocclusion usually disappears. However, children often develop some type of permanent tooth malocclusion, such as an underbite (in which the bottom front teeth fit in front of the top front teeth) or an overbite (in which the top front teeth lap too far over or beyond the bottom front teeth). Other types of malocclusion include crowding or wide-spacing of teeth or an open bite (in which the teeth do not meet), or problems involving the position of the upper or lower jaw. The degree of malocclusion varies from minor (involving only a few teeth) to severe (involving, for example, all the front teeth).

With proper treatment, most developmental tooth problems can be corrected. If they result from an underlying disorder, however, treatment may be unsuccessful or may produce only temporary correction.

CAUSE

Many tooth problems are passed on genetically from parents to children. Inherited problems include enamel or dentin imperfections, premature teeth, unusually large teeth, shell teeth, extra teeth, and malocclusion.

Enamel imperfections can also be caused by interference with normal tooth formation. For example, enamel imperfections may develop if a fetus is exposed to *German measles* or *syphilis,* or develops hemolytic anemia (see *anemia, hemolytic*). Imperfections may also develop because of a severe nutritional deficiency before or after birth.

Other factors producing imperfect enamel include tooth infection or injury (see *tooth problems*); long-term childhood illness such as kidney disease; frequent exposure to therapeutic radiation; use of certain medications, particularly the antibiotic tetracycline or those involved in chemotherapy; ingestion of excessive fluoride; and neurological problems (particularly in children with *mental retardation*).

Structural tooth problems can be caused by external factors as well as inherited traits. Some of these external factors include frequent radiation therapy and dislocation of primary teeth (which can interrupt the calcification and formation of underlying permanent teeth).

Several factors can cause tooth discoloration. Use of excess fluoride and certain medications (such as tetracycline) can discolor teeth, as can pigment carried in the blood. Tooth injury may also cause tooth discoloration. Erythroblastosis (a serious blood disease resulting from Rh incompatibility; see *Rh and ABO incompatibility*) may discolor an infant's teeth.

Overactivity of hormones, such as in the case of hyperpituitarism (see *pituitary problems*), may cause premature tooth eruption. Delayed tooth eruption may be caused by poor nutrition and hygiene, low birthweight, or underlying disorders such as hypothyroidism (see *thyroid problems*), or hypopituitarism (see *pituitary problems*).

If a developing tooth continues to bud or excessive dental tissue cells are produced, extra teeth may develop.

Cases of malocclusion that are not inherited may be caused by premature loss of primary teeth; abnormal or delayed tooth eruption; prolonged sucking on pacifiers, fingers, or thumbs; tongue thrusting; gum disease (see *gum problems*); reduced contact with adjacent teeth because of damaged enamel, usually resulting from cavities; and tooth injury. Premature loss of primary teeth allows adjacent primary or permanent teeth to move into improper positions. Movement of these teeth not only interferes with proper bite but may hinder normal eruption of permanent teeth.

Other factors that cause or contribute to dental malocclusion include excessive tooth pressure from the muscle that moves the jaw up and down, which can be caused, for example, by excessive muscle tension associated with *cerebral palsy.*

DIAGNOSIS

For most developmental problems of the teeth, early diagnosis by a dentist is important to ensure successful correction. Diagnostic procedures include an oral examination and X-ray films. X rays are also used to determine the amount of root development present in any tooth that is unusual in its eruption, and the position of unerupted adjacent teeth.

COMPLICATIONS

Cavities and resulting abcesses often develop in teeth with enamel imperfections, exposed dentin, or structural problems (see *tooth problems*). Misplaced or delayed eruption of teeth may cause malocclusion (problems of spacing or bite). Malocclusion in turn can contribute to tooth decay, gum disease, or loss of teeth, and can cause *headache,* earache (see *earache and ear infections),* or facial pain.

TREATMENT

Tooth problems are most often treated by a dentist. If teeth need complicated alignment, the child may be referred to an orthodontist (a dentist who specializes in straightening and moving teeth).

If permanent teeth have enamel imperfections, treatment usually involves restoring enamel with a variety of materials. A dentist restores the enamel of front teeth with bonded resin or with caps of porcelain, metal, or acrylic. Imperfections of back teeth are capped in metal and may be coated with a white porcelain for cosmetic value. Primary teeth with enamel imperfections are not generally treated.

When a front primary tooth has both severe structural and enamel problems, a dentist usually applies a resin cap to prevent enamel erosion and potential infection of inner tissue. If a back primary tooth is severely affected, a stainless-steel cap can be applied. Structural problems of permanent teeth are usually treated with fitted caps made of chrome, gold, porcelain, or acrylic.

Discolored teeth resulting from injury can be bleached internally by a dentist with a hydrogen peroxide solution. If discoloration is severe and bleaching is ineffective, a dentist may decide to mask the tooth surface by bonding a white resin veneer to the surface.

A dentist may have to remove very loose early-eruption teeth. However, securely rooted teeth should not be removed because they help guide other primary teeth into their proper positions and ensure normal eruption of permanent teeth.

If a permanent tooth is impacted or embedded in the dental arch, a dentist may expose the crown by removing surrounding tissue and bone. If necessary, orthodontic appliances are used to ensure that the tooth will erupt properly (see below). Delay in treatment may result in permanent eruption problems of primary or permanent teeth. A tooth that has erupted out of place should be treated to prevent impaction of underlying teeth.

If primary teeth are lost prematurely, the resulting space must be maintained to ensure correct permanent tooth eruption. If permanent tooth eruption has been prevented, the space must be maintained to avoid movement of adjacent permanent or primary teeth until eruption of the permanent tooth can occur.

Extra teeth are usually removed if they are likely to interfere with the development and eruption of adjacent teeth, unless a dentist believes they are going to fall out by themselves when adjacent permanent teeth erupt. Space is closed with orthodontic appliances.

A variety of orthodontic appliances are used to correct dental malocclusion. They work by moving teeth gently into a correct position or by holding teeth firmly in place to prevent movement. All of them are adjusted periodically. Teeth can sometimes be realigned with a removable appliance commonly called a retainer or bite plate, a plastic plate that rests against the gums, cheeks, and roof of the mouth and is often equipped with wires to hold or move teeth into place. Recently a new type of removable appliance, called a functional appliance, has been introduced for use in correcting improper jaw positions by influencing jaw growth.

Nonremovable appliances can also be used to correct dental malocclusion. These include braces, which are combinations of plastic or metal brackets that are bonded or cemented to teeth. Wires are placed through these brackets to hold or move teeth into place. Other fitted appliances are used as space maintainers, anchoring appliances (to hold teeth in place), or as a combination of both.

Appliances that are worn outside the mouth include face bows, which are large wires that curve around the face and attach to braces (usually on the back teeth). Adjustable elastic straps, which fit around the back of the head, are worn to apply tension to the face bow. The tension is then transferred to the teeth to move them in the appropriate direction.

Unless a primary tooth is abscessed or injured, premature removal is not generally recommended because the resulting space may interfere with permanent tooth eruption. If teeth are removed, remaining teeth must be held in place to prevent movement and malocclusion. This is usually done with a fixed space maintainer made of metal wire.

If permanent teeth are missing, a dentist may use braces or other appliances to move teeth into and close the resulting gaps in an effort to maintain proper spacing between teeth. If the jaw is in an abnormal position, the child may be referred to an orthodontist for early treatment that influences jaw growth or realigns jaw position. In severe cases surgery to correct an abnormal jaw may be performed once a child has stopped growing.

Teeth can usually be realigned successfully in one to two years if no complications are present. Malocclusion associated with structural jaw or tooth problems usually takes longer to correct. If malocclusion is caused by muscle spasms, such as with *cerebral palsy,* ideal tooth realignment may not be possible.

PREVENTION

Developmental problems of the teeth cannot be prevented, although treatment can keep the problems from becoming worse. Good nutrition, oral hygiene, and regular professional cleanings may prevent some enamel imperfections from decaying. Children should be encouraged to stop thumb sucking or finger-sucking by 5 years of age; pacifiers should not be used after age 2.

TEETHING

DESCRIPTION

The process of tooth eruption is known as teething. Teeth begin to form before birth; after birth, the teeth continue to develop and begin to move through the overlying bone and gums. Several months before teeth actually appear (erupt), an infant usually starts the normal developmental process of chewing and salivation. The entire teething process usually begins at the age of 4 months and is completed by the age of 3 years.

A total of 20 primary teeth (also called baby teeth or milk teeth) normally appear during a child's first 3 years of life. A child will have 3 types of teeth: incisors (sharp front teeth used for cutting); first- and second-year molars (used for chewing and grinding), and canines (pointed "dog" teeth located between the incisors and the first-year molars). The order and speed of eruption varies from child to child.

The 8 incisors come in first. The 2 bottom center incisors usually push through the gums by the time an infant is 9 months old, but can erupt anytime from ages 6 to 9 months. The top 4 incisors usually come in next, when a child is 7 to 14 months old, followed by the 2 lateral (side) bottom incisors at 11 to 15 months of age. All incisors are usually in place shortly after a child's first 12 to 14 months of life.

Over the next 4 months the 2 upper and 2 lower 1-year molars, located near the back of a child's mouth, push through the gums. Within a few months these are followed by the 2 upper and 2 lower canines. The final 4 teeth (2 upper and 2 lower 2-year molars) come in behind the first-year molars sometime between a child's second and third birthday.

Chewing motions are an infant's way of dealing with the new, often uncomfortable mouth sensations that occur as teeth move through the gums. As teeth push through the gums, the tissue becomes tender, sore, and often inflamed. Gum pads are moved away by the teeth. Frequently a blue blood-blister forms just before the eruption of a first- or second-year molar.

Swallowing is often avoided, and drooling is common. Drooling overnight can cause chafed, red, "cherry cheeks." A teething child may be uncomfortable, cranky, fretful, and unwilling to eat, and may sleep poorly. Because rubbing and stimulating the gums helps ease discomfort, a teething child frequently chews on fingers and other objects.

CAUSE

Teething is part of a child's normal developmental process.

DIAGNOSIS

Red, tender, swollen gum pads, usually accompanied by drooling and crankiness, generally indicate that teething is taking place.

COMPLICATIONS

An eruption cyst or hematoma (a collection of blood under the skin) may form as a tooth is pushing through the gum. The area around the new tooth becomes swollen, red, and very tender. Eruption cysts or hematomas usually rupture by themselves and do not require treatment by a physician or dentist.

TREATMENT

The only treatment necessary involves easing a child's pain and discomfort and stimulating gums.

Chewing on teething rings that have been frozen can numb a child's gums and relieve pain. A surface application of a local anesthetic, available by prescription, will also numb tender gums. A pain-relieving medication may be helpful. Consult the physician for specific recommendations and read the discussion of nonprescription medications beginning on p. 102. Firmly rubbing a child's gums with clean fingers also helps lessen teething discomfort.

Stimulating the gums can be done with any hard (usually rubber) object. Children will usually chew on anything within reach. Biting on hard teething biscuits or rings helps relieve pain. Plastic toys should be avoided because they splinter and crack easily. Any furniture or toys painted with lead paint (or painted first with lead paint and repainted with lead-free paint) should be put out of an infant's reach (see *lead poisoning).*

Unless a long-lasting cyst or hematoma forms or a child experiences great pain during teething, it is not necessary to consult a dentist, except to check the progress of the child's teeth.

PREVENTION

Teething is a natural process of development.

TETANUS

EMERGENCY ACTION

Seek medical assistance for any child who suffers a puncture or deep flesh wound. Tetanus is a threat to anyone who does not possess active immunity conferred by tetanus toxoid injection. If doubt exists about a child's tetanus immunity, inform the physician who cares for the child.

DESCRIPTION

Tetanus is an infectious disease with a well-deserved reputation for being painful and life-threatening to unimmunized children and adults. If it develops to the point of producing spasms, tetanus can cause lockjaw (paralysis of the jaw muscle that forces the mouth shut), which has become synonymous with tetanus.

Since the disease attacks nerve tissue, many different muscles may be affected, including those of the head, neck, back, arms, and legs. Breathing, digestion, and bowel and bladder functions may be impaired or blocked completely.

Such a crisis does not occur in every case, but tetanus is feared because of the possibility of severe illness. Although an effective immunization program has sharply reduced the number of cases of tetanus each year in the United States to an average of 250, as many as 60 percent of those people die.

The period of greatest incidence occurs annually from May to October with more cases developing in the southern United States than elsewhere. It affects males more often than females by a 3-to-2 ratio. Signs and symptoms of infection begin from 1 day to 3 weeks following exposure to the tetanus organisms. The greater the degree of con-

tamination, the sooner signs and symptoms usually appear, the worse the illness may be, and the more uncertain are the chances of uncomplicated recovery.

Tetanus can last for 1 week in mild cases, but recovery often requires 2 to 6 weeks. Fatal cases of tetanus last no more than 3 or 4 days. Infants and young children are most seriously affected; children over 10 years old have the best chances of swift recuperation.

CAUSE

Tetanus bacteria are found almost everywhere in soil contaminated by animal feces. When the bacteria find their way into human flesh, often by means of a puncture wound, they begin to produce a strong toxin (poison), which then circulates and affects nerve tissue.

A typical accident story concerns a child who steps on a rusty nail and then develops tetanus. The rusty nail does not cause tetanus. The tetanus bacteria must first contaminate a penetrating object for infection to develop. Or bacteria may be introduced later into the wound, usually by unclean hands or bandages. Infection is acquired only if the individual has not received immunization against tetanus.

Tetanus bacteria flourish where little oxygen is available. Puncture wounds (see *puncture wounds and splinters),* even if seemingly superficial, are likely sites for such infection to develop, as are *burns* and deep flesh wounds. Among infants not born in a hospital, the umbilical stump can be a site for tetanus if the bacteria are present on a nonsterilized scissors or knife. The incubation period for tetanus varies from 3 to 4 days following an injury, but it can be as brief as a single day or as long as a month before signs and symptoms of tetanus appear.

SIGNS AND SYMPTOMS

Muscle stiffness, rigidity, and spasms are typical signs of tetanus. Stiff neck and stiff jaw develop within 24 hours of the first appearance of a symptom. Swallowing becomes difficult. Difficulties with muscle control develop into spasms, muscle contractions that last for several seconds or longer. The best-known spasm that can occur is lockjaw.

In the most severe cases the body grows rigid, head and neck are drawn back, and the entire back is arched. The legs and arms stiffen, the fists clench. Spasms of facial muscles can raise the eyebrows and pull the corners of the mouth down and out, producing a grotesque grin of pain. Breathing and rest become problematic because muscle spasms recur so frequently.

During the most severe stage of illness, spasms can be triggered by nearly anything the child feels, sees, or hears. Spasms produce great pain and provoke fear and anxiety. If spasms affect the throat and breathing muscles, breathing capability can be reduced or paralyzed. Children who experience difficulty breathing may turn blue from lack of oxygen. Low *fever,* sweating, rapid and irregular heartbeat, and increased blood pressure usually accompany the spasms.

DIAGNOSIS

In almost all cases a physician can diagnose tetanus on the basis of muscle spasms and other signs and symptoms and a report of a recent puncture or flesh wound. Early diagnosis is essential so that treatment can begin promptly. The infection can be confirmed by laboratory cultures of material taken from the wound.

COMPLICATIONS

Breathing difficulties may lead to *pneumonia.* Muscle spasms in the face, neck, and throat may lead to cuts in the tongue or cheek. Black and blue marks caused by hematomas (blood-filled tumors) may appear in muscle tissue. Severe spasms of the back and chest may cause compression fractures of vertebrae (see *fractures).* If treatment and recuperation are lengthy, the dangers of weight loss and *dehydration* may arise because of problems involving eating and drinking.

TREATMENT

Treatment of tetanus infection almost always takes place in a hospital. The child receives tetanus immune globulin in order to combat any tetanus toxin freely circulating in the body. The wound is thoroughly cleaned and, if possible, left open to the air. An antibiotic is often given to fight possible infection in the wound.

A vital ingredient in treatment is expert medical care so that a child can be made as comfortable and spasm-free as possible. Constant monitoring of vital signs, particularly breathing, is necessary, as is protection against anything that might trigger a spasm. Sedatives and muscle relaxants are often

helpful. Reassurance and encouragement should be offered by anyone who visits a child fighting a tetanus infection.

If any doubts exists regarding the immunity of a child who has sustained a puncture or deep flesh wound, inform the physician.

PREVENTION

Active immunization is the most effective prevention against tetanus. Tetanus toxoid, a compound derived from the toxin itself, is routinely given to infants as part of the DPT (diphtheria, pertussis, tetanus) series of 3 injections when a child is 2, 4, and 6 months old. A booster is given at 15 months. Another booster follows when the child begins kindergarten or first grade. Thereafter 1 dose of combined tetanus and diphtheria toxoid is recommended every 10 years. (See immunization schedule in Chapter 6, "Going to the Doctor.")

Any child who is 6 years old and has not received the DPT series should be given a series of 3 injections of the adult toxoid, spread out over a year. This series is essential for a child's future health.

Any child who suffers a puncture or flesh wound should have the wound carefully cleaned. If the wound proves difficult to clean with soap, water, and a clean cloth or sterile pad, medical assistance should be sought.

THALASSEMIA

DESCRIPTION

Thalassemia (sometimes called Cooley's anemia or Mediterranean anemia) is a hereditary blood disorder (see *blood disorders* in which the production of hemoglobin A, a substance found in red blood cells, is reduced or never occurs. Without sufficient hemoglobin, red blood cells cannot function. Also, the membranes (cell walls) of the red blood cells may be defective, further limiting each cell's ability either to leave the bone marrow (where the cells are produced) or to circulate and recirculate within the bloodstream. All red blood cells are broken down after a period of time, but these damaged cells break down too soon; the bone marrow responds by producing greater than usual numbers of new red blood cells, but its production cannot compensate for this tremendous rate of destruction. The result is *ane-*

mia. Since red blood cells carry oxygen and nutrients, the deficiency in production of these cells results in the body tissues receiving an adequate amount of oxygen and nutrients.

Though relatively uncommon in North America, thalassemia is the second most common cause of anemia in children worldwide. The leading (and much more common) cause is iron deficiency (see *anemia, nutritional*).

Thalassemia most often affects children of Mediterranean descent; about 3 to 10 percent of Americans of Italian or Greek ancestry are carriers of thalassemia. It occurs more frequently among children of Middle Eastern and Oriental descent than among other racial groups. About one half of one percent of American blacks carry the trait for thalassemia. Like *sickle cell anemia,* the disorder is associated with a high resistance to malaria.

Thalassemia becomes evident within the first year and is a lifelong condition. The disorder varies widely in severity, depending on the amount of hemoglobin A missing. Thalassemia trait, in which hemoglobin A production is reduced only slightly, produces very mild anemia and rarely causes symptoms. Children with it are not significantly affected. Often it is confused with iron deficiency anemia.

In thalassemia intermedia, a more serious condition, hemoglobin A production is reduced moderately to severely. Anemia, an enlarged spleen, and thin bones caused by expansion of the bone marrow result from this production decrease. In severity, thalassemia intermedia can lie anywhere between asymptomatic (without symptoms) disease and severe disease. Most often it more closely resembles severe disease.

In thalassemia major, the most serious form of the disorder, hemoglobin A production is reduced drastically or never occurs at all. Thalassemia major is characterized by severe anemia; an enlarged liver, spleen, or heart; overgrowth of the jawbone; a rounded protrusion on the surface of the skull; thin bones; stunted growth; and frequent infections. Infants with thalassemia major typically are pale and fussy, and they are usually picky eaters. Older children are frequently pale, jaundiced, listless, breathless, and fatigued and have no appetite.

Without treatment, the life expectancy of a child with thalassemia major is only a few years. Even those who receive treatment usually die in their teens. Individuals with less severe thalassemia (intermedia), however, have survived until their seventies.

CAUSE

The amount of hemoglobin A missing and the resulting severity of thalassemia depends in part on the number of genes for the disorder that the child inherits and in part on the degree to which each gene depresses hemoglobin production. A baby can inherit thalassemia major (or intermedia) only by acquiring 2 defective genes: if each parent carries 1 defective gene (thalassemia trait), a 1-in-4 chance exists that both will pass along a defective gene to the baby. Thalassemia intermedia results from the inheritance of 2 less severely abnormal genes (see *genetic disorders*).

DIAGNOSIS

Thalassemia major and intermedia are diagnosed by a physician, who observes signs and symptoms, examines the child, and performs laboratory studies, including a complete blood count, a hemoglobin test, and several specialized blood tests. Thalassemia trait often goes undetected until thalassemia major appears in a family member and a family history is taken.

Carriers may be detected through a blood test, and prenatal diagnosis is now possible using amniocentesis or occasionally fetal blood samples.

COMPLICATIONS

Possible complications of thalassemia major include *diabetes,* cirrhosis of the liver, and bone and joint changes. In older children growth is impaired and puberty does not occur due to multiple hormonal abnormalities. Other complications can include pericarditis (inflammation of the membrane surrounding the heart) or congestive heart failure (see *heart failure, congestive*) caused by deposits of excess iron in the heart, both of which can lead to death.

If thalassemia intermedia resembles thalassemia major, regular blood transfusions are needed. Liver problems, congestive heart failure, and possibly death can occur. If thalassemia intermedia causes only mild anemia, no transfusions are required.

TREATMENT

No cure exists for thalassemia. Regular

blood transfusions, however, can supply the body with hemoglobin A, necessary to prevent severe *anemia,* an enlarged spleen, and bone deformities in children with thalassemia major. Unfortunately, frequent transfusions cause toxic levels of iron to accumulate in the blood and subsequently in body tissues, especially in the kidneys, heart, liver, and pancreas. Eventually, those organs function poorly because the iron level becomes excessive.

Certain drugs cause iron to be excreted from the body, but injections of these drugs are only marginally effective because of the speed with which the drugs pass out of the body. However, a special pump called an autosyringe allows very slow administration of those drugs. In effect, iron is chelated (attached to these drugs) in the blood and eliminated through the urine; it is hoped that this treatment method will reduce damage to organs affected by iron.

Children with thalassemia intermedia may also need regular blood transfusions, not to prevent severe anemia but to prevent bone abnormalities or spleen enlargement. The body can develop antibodies against transfused red blood cells, so blood types must be very carefully matched. Regular care includes prompt treatment of infections and prevention of *dehydration* (excessive loss of body fluids and salts).

Studies are now under way to determine whether thalassemia can be safely cured by bone marrow transplantation.

PREVENTION

Parents with a family history of thalassemia should be tested to see if they carry the trait for the disorder. If they do, they should seek genetic counseling to learn their risk of having children with the disorder. Prenatal diagnosis is available. (See discussion of genetic counseling in *genetic disorders.*)

When two people of Mediterranean descent marry, they should consider genetic counseling in an effort to determine whether either family has a history of thalassemia.

THRUSH

DESCRIPTION

Thrush is an infection characterized by white, filmy spots inside the mouth. It is caused by a fungus. This oral infection is common among healthy babies under 6 months old; later in life it is rare except among children in poor health or who have been taking certain antibiotics.

The same fungus can also appear as a *rash* on babies' diaper areas, in vaginas of adolescent girls and women, and very rarely, in skin folds of children who perspire excessively.

If treated promptly, oral thrush is not serious and lasts only a few days, although some cases persist in spite of treatment.

CAUSE

Thrush is caused by the fungus *Candida.* An otherwise healthy newborn usually contracts the fungus from the mother's vagina during birth. Occasionally, poorly sterilized nursery supplies, such as nipples on bottles, spread the fungus, as can contaminated hands or infected breast nipples. Children who have been taking antibiotics are susceptible to thrush because antibiotics eliminate normally present bacteria, allowing a fungus to grow in their place.

SIGNS AND SYMPTOMS

An outbreak of white spots on the tongue, gums, and roof of the mouth, in the throat, and inside the lips and cheeks is usually the only symptom of thrush. These spots look like milk curds, but cannot be wiped away easily; attempts to do so reveal inflamed sores underneath that may bleed. Rarely, small, hollow sores appear. If untreated, the white spots spread into thick, flaky patches.

In severe cases of thrush, the sores are so painful that the baby is irritable and unable to nurse adequately. Immune-compromised babies suffering from the disease sometimes develop *fever, cough,* and digestive problems.

White spots that appear only on the tongue are not usually caused by thrush; they simply may be partially digested regurgitated milk.

DIAGNOSIS

Simple cases of thrush can be diagnosed at home from the appearance and persistence of the white spots. A child with extremely painful sores or *fever, cough,* and digestive problems should be seen by a physician who examines the mouth or examines a scraping of the white spots under the microscope. Usually the diagnosis is made simply by physical examination.

TREATMENT

Thrush sometimes disappears by itself, but medical treatment is advisable. A physician may prescribe an antibiotic. Fever-reducing and pain-relieving medications may be helpful. Consult the physician for specific recommendations and read the discussion of nonprescription medications beginning on p. 102. Plenty of fluids are helpful.

PREVENTION

If recurrent thrush becomes a problem, further recurrence can be prevented by sterilizing objects that may be placed in the baby's mouth. A nursing mother may need to use a medicated cream on her breasts to avoid reinfecting her baby.

THUMB-SUCKING

DESCRIPTION

Thumb-sucking is the most common childhood habit. More than half of all children suck their thumbs (or, less often, other fingers) during infancy, and many continue to engage in this harmless habit at least until they start school. Thumb-sucking should not be considered a problem unless it appears to be associated with a more serious underlying condition or causes a child unhappiness.

The possibility that thumb-sucking might be a harmful habit was not seriously considered until the nineteenth and early twentieth centuries. Without evidence, certain physicians and psychologists of that era decided that thumb-sucking had its origin in mental problems and that it would permanently damage the personality and moral character (not to mention dental alignment) of children who were not cured of the habit by any means. It was also feared that thumb-suckers were far more prone than other children to develop terrible diseases from sticking germ-laden thumbs in their mouths.

It is now believed that children suck their thumbs (or substitute objects, such as pacifiers) for the simple reason that sucking is a natural, soothing activity. All babies instinctively suck during feedings, times that provide comfort as well as nourishment. In addition, one of the ways babies first learn about their environment is by putting objects in their mouths. As babies grow, they develop other ways of receiving emotional satisfaction and learning, and thumb-sucking usually stops before or during the first few years of school. The number of children who develop any complications—physical or psychological—because of thumb-sucking is minuscule.

The majority of all children begin thumb-sucking during the first few months of life. The peak incidence of thumb-sucking occurs between 18 and 21 months of age. One quarter of all children continue sucking their thumbs beyond their third year, but most stop by the onset of the fourth. Certain other habits are close relatives of thumb-sucking. They include tongue-sucking, pacifier-sucking, and blanket-sucking. Some toddlers supplement thumb-sucking with other movements; they may, for example, twist their hair (see *hair-pulling*) or stroke a favorite blanket or toy. Such associated motions also tend to cease as a child grows and develops.

Since thumb-sucking is a form of self-comfort, it tends to be practiced most often when a child is separated from others (as at bedtime) or is feeling a strong negative emotion (such as jealousy). Sometimes children who long ago stopped sucking their thumbs regularly revert to the behavior during stressful times, such as during illness or after a family fight. In these cases thumb-sucking is especially self-comforting and indicates a need for a little extra attention and understanding from parents.

CAUSE

The reason some children suck their thumbs while others do not is unclear. Many children who do not suck their thumbs suck on other things or engage in other harmless habits.

DIAGNOSIS

There is no reason to suspect that thumb-sucking is a sign of a more serious underlying physical or emotional condition unless other signs or symptoms—such as failure to respond to voice or touch stimulation—are also present. In the absence of such signs or symptoms, a physician need only be consulted if a child who is ashamed of thumb-sucking cannot stop engaging in the habit alone or with family help.

COMPLICATIONS

The only common complication of thumb-sucking is the development of calluses on the thumb.

In rare cases thumb-sucking causes baby teeth to become slightly misaligned. Misalignment of permanent teeth is extremely rare; when it does occur, it usually reverses itself unless a child continues to suck his or her thumb frequently well beyond age 6 or 7. Other rare complications of thumb-sucking include the development of an abnormal way of swallowing or speech impediments. Both of these correctable problems can be detected by a physician at a child's regular check-up.

TREATMENT AND PREVENTION

There is no harmless, reliable way to prevent habits like thumb-sucking, and there is no reason for parents to try to do so. The best way for parents to deal with the thumb-sucking of a preschool-aged child is to ignore it. The child is likely to outgrow the habit naturally before starting school. Because this is also true of many other kinds of behavior, it is good general practice for parents to reinforce the positive aspects of a young child's behavior while ignoring the negative ones. Providing other sources of comfort and interesting a child in learning activities can be helpful in diverting the child's attention from thumb-sucking.

Thumb-sucking can become a source of embarrassment for a school-aged child. Parents can help an older child stop the habit by offering rewards, such as stars on a calendar for every day that the child does not suck his or her thumb. On days that thumb-sucking does occur, a child's family should praise the child for trying and should look ahead to the next day.

If there is any indication that thumb-sucking is a sign of an emotional problem, parents should try to pinpoint the source of unhappiness and help the child deal with it, perhaps with the help of a physician or counselor.

Parents should not expect a physician to recommend or prescribe any physical form of treatment, such as mechanical restraints or bad-tasting substances to coat the thumb. These treatment methods were developed when old theories about the cause and effects of thumb-sucking were popular. They are largely ineffective in stopping the habit and tend to promote nothing but unhappiness for parents and child—and, in turn, the prolongation of thumb-sucking. Parents should be prepared to hear praise for old-fashioned treatment methods from relatives or friends—and should gently but firmly resist.

If a child continuously engages in thumb-sucking after the age of 4, parents may wish to ensure that dental misalignment is not a problem by bringing up the matter at a child's regular dental checkup. In rare cases a dentist recommends using orthodontic devices to prevent or correct misalignment and help prevent further thumb-sucking.

THYROID PROBLEMS

DESCRIPTION AND SIGNS AND SYMPTOMS

The thyroid gland (see Fig. 18, p. 154), located in the lower neck, is controlled by the pituitary hormone TSH (see *pituitary problems*). The function of the gland is to absorb iodine from the blood and concentrate it into hormones that are used by the body. Triiodothyronine (T3) and thyroxine (T4), the 2 major thyroid hormones, influence bodily growth and development; oxygen consumption; nerve function; metabolism of fats, carbohydrates, proteins, and vitamins; and the actions of other endocrine hormones.

Thyroid problems are usually lifelong but can be controlled with treatment. The two major types of thyroid problems are hypothyroidism, in which the output of thyroid hormones is abnormally low, and hyperthyroidism, in which excess hormones are produced.

Thyroid problems are frequently accompanied by a goiter—an enlargement of the thyroid gland. Enlargement occurs when excess TSH overstimulates the thyroid gland because of a deficit of thyroid hormones and when the gland is affected by an autoimmune disease (condition in which tissues are attacked by the body's own immune system). Thyroid enlargement also occurs when a thyroid tumor develops. If a goiter is small, a child may experience a slight enlargement of the neck with no, or almost no, throat discomfort. A large goiter can produce pressure on the trachea (windpipe) and cause breathing difficulty which on rare occasions can be life-threatening. With prompt treatment, however, this threat to life can be resolved.

Hypothyroidism, one of the most frequent endocrine problems of childhood, is much more common among children than hyperthyroidism.

Congenital Hypothyroidism

Congenital hypothyroidism results from abnormal functioning or development of the thyroid gland during fetal growth. An affected infant's family may occasionally have a history of thyroid disorders.

Symptoms of congenital hypothyroidism appear 6 to 12 weeks after birth. Facial features include a generally dull appearance with an underdeveloped nasal bridge (flat nose), eyes that appear widely spaced, and a large, protruding tongue that prevents closing of the lips. The neck appears short and thick, and the hands are broad and fat. *Seborrheic dermatitis* (a harmless scaling of the skin) of the scalp and forehead is often present.

The skin is usually mottled (with a pattern of prominent veins) and cool to the touch. If the problem has been present for some time, the skin becomes dry and coarse, often developing a yellowish tinge reflecting an increase of an orange pigment, carotene, present in the blood. Perspiration is reduced. Nails and hair grow very slowly and are coarse, dry, and brittle.

A child's heart rate and circulation are slowed; blood pressure is low. Poor circulation partially accounts for mottled, cool, sometimes grayish-appearing skin. *Anemia* may develop.

Appetite is usually reduced, and feeding of infants tends to be slow because of occasional difficulty in swallowing. Affected children, however, tend to be moderately overweight. A hoarse cry may be present because of swelling of the vocal cords. *Constipation* develops because of reduced intestinal activity. Babies with congenital hypothyroidism may have associated *hearing loss.*

The deposit of calcium in centers of bone formation is delayed, and bone growth is retarded. Body proportions are immature. As a result, the child's legs and arms in relation to the size of the trunk are much shorter than normal. The child's movements are usually slow, and if hypothyroidism remains untreated, motor development (sitting and walking, for example) may be delayed. Muscles may be underdeveloped and weak, and

nerve reflexes are slowed. Muscle strength, however, is usually normal. Tooth development and eruption are usually delayed.

Because thyroid hormone is essential to the development of the central nervous system (brain, spinal cord, and their protective covering, the meninges), any deficiency during fetal development or early life causes slowed mental activity and responsiveness and, if untreated, may be associated with *mental retardation.*

Children with untreated hypothyroidism usually have delayed puberty. Occasionally, however, such children can show premature sexual development (a situation called precocious puberty) because of pituitary overactivity, but this condition is usually incomplete and does not result in normal sexual function.

Acquired Hypothyroidism

Acquired hypothyroidism (also called juvenile hypothyroidism) most often develops among children 11 to 14 years of age because of autoimmune damage to the thyroid gland with suppression of thyroid hormone secretion. These children are born with normal thyroid glands but may have a family history of acquired thyroid disorders due to autoimmune disease (see *immune disorders).*

Signs and symptoms of acquired hypothyroidism resemble those of congenital hypothyroidism, although since the disease occurs later in childhood, as a rule, there are few or no long-term complications. Growth is slowed, and if the disease is untreated, the child may not reach a normal adult height. Sexual development and the onset of puberty are delayed, although occasionally children have precocious but incomplete puberty. If a child has already reached puberty, sexual function may be affected.

With prompt treatment, characteristics of acquired hypothyroidism disappear and the child's original facial features return. *Mental retardation* does not develop, although a child's mental reactions may be temporarily slowed.

Hyperthyroidism

A toxic goiter is usually caused by the presence of a substance (immunoglobulin resulting from an autoimmune disorder) that stimulates thyroid gland enlargement. In turn, toxic goiter is the most common cause of overproduction of thyroid hormone and hyperthyroidism (thyrotoxicosis).

The most common form of hyperthyroidism is Graves' disease, a condition that occurs much more often among girls than boys. Onset is slow and may not be suspected until a child becomes persistently restless and irritable. Other symptoms include emotional swings—crying easily, impatience, becoming easily upset—as well as intolerance of heat, an increased appetite without weight gain (and sometimes even with weight loss). The child usually has trouble concentrating, particularly during school, and is restless during sleep. He or she does not tolerate exercise well and tires easily. If hyperthyroidism is severe, the child may develop peculiar *movement disorders* associated with muscle weakness.

A hyperthyroid child usually grows much faster than normal and attains tall stature (see *height problems*). Weight loss may occur; heart rate is increased, and circulation time is deceased. The skin becomes flushed and warm; body temperature and perspiration increase. More frequent bowel movements may occur, but *diarrhea* is uncommon.

Hyperthyroidism may be accompanied by prominence of the eyes (staring) or bulging of the eyes due to swollen tissue behind the eye. When the child looks up, the skin on the forehead does not wrinkle. The child's eyes may appear unusually prominent and may become irritated, inflamed, and painful.

Without treatment, symptoms of hyperthyroidism persist and often grow worse. If treated, however, signs and symptoms of the hyperthyroidism usually disappear once thyroid function returns to normal. The enlarged thyroid and bulging of the eyes, however, may persist for some years.

CAUSE

Thyroid problems can be caused by a number of factors. In some areas of the world the most common cause of congenital and acquired hypothyroidism is a dietary deficiency of iodine. Insufficient iodine leads to inadequate secretion of thyroid hormones, which in turn causes excessive TSH secretion and development of a goiter.

Excess TSH secretion also occurs when problems with thyroid metabolism or enzyme activity develop during fetal growth and prevent thyroid hormone synthesis. (Enzymes trigger biochemical changes.) The tendency to develop such problems is inherited by children from their parents (see *genetic disorders*). Pituitary or hypothalamic problems, such as pituitary tumors, absence of the pituitary gland or hypothalamus, and tissue damage from illness or injury—all of which result in decreased production of TSH—cause secondary hypothyroidism.

Other causes of hypothyroidism include the absence or incorrect positioning of the thyroid gland or a mother's taking hormone-suppressing medications. Incorrectly positioned thyroid glands are usually found high in the neck or at the base of the tongue, rather than in the base of the neck. Insufficient amounts of hormones are produced by these misplaced thyroid glands. A newborn infant may also have disturbed thyroid function if the mother's body produces antithyroid antibodies (proteins produced by the body's immune system to combat foreign substances) during pregnancy that cross the placenta.

Another cause of hypothyroidism is autoimmune thyroiditis, an immunological reaction to antigenic components of the thyroid gland. This problem occurs especially among children older than 6 years of age. There seems to be a genetic predisposition, with more females than males affected. Other illnesses that can be associated with autoimmune hypothyroidism include *diabetes,* Hodgkin's disease (see *lymphoma),* hypoadrenocorticism (see *adrenal problems),* or hypopituitarism (see *pituitary problems).* Hypothyroidism also develops when radiation therapy or surgery results in destruction of the thyroid gland.

If a woman takes antithyroid medications, given to suppress hyperthyroidism, they will interfere with fetal production of thyroid hormone during pregnancy and can produce a fetal goiter that is present at birth. The goiter usually disappears within a few weeks of birth if the thyroid gland is not greatly enlarged.

Hyperthyroidism usually results from toxic goiter caused by an autoimmune disorder. Rarely, among children and adolescents, hyperthyroidism may result from a benign thyroid tumor. Very few thyroid cancers are associated with either hypothyroidism or hyperthyroidism. Thyroid cancers may be caused by prior exposure to radiation, usually administered for an enlarged thymus (an organ involved in development of the immune system) or for tonsil problems.

DIAGNOSIS

Diagnosis and treatment of thyroid problems should begin as early as possible to prevent permanent problems. Screening of newborns with measurement of blood thyroid hormone levels and TSH can diagnose the problem even before symptoms are evident.

The history of a child's medical problems and the record of past growth, development, and physical changes can help a physician make a diagnosis. Of special importance in the physical examination are measurements of height and weight for comparison with normal standards and past measurements of the child. Enlargement of the thyroid gland requires further evaluation to define its function. Altered thyroid function affects pulse and blood pressure.

A physician orders blood tests to determine levels of thyroid hormones, antibodies against thyroid antigens, and TSH. Radioiodine tests are used to define the location and structure of the thyroid (especially absent or abnormally placed glands, nodules or tumors, and cysts) and in special cases to study iodine metabolism (how the gland uses iodine). Occasionally thyroid hormone, TSH, and TRH (thyrotropin-releasing hormone) are given to test thyroid gland function and regulatory control.

COMPLICATIONS

If congenital hypothyroidism is not treated soon after symptoms appear, the infant may suffer permanent brain damage with *mental retardation.*

Long-term hypothyroidism can cause growth failure, with resulting failure to reach normal height.

Large goiters may cause pressure on the windpipe and throat, impairing the child's ability to swallow or breathe. If such complications are not treated promptly, a life-threatening situation could develop.

Thyrotoxicosis can lead to thyrotoxic crisis, which is characterized by *vomiting, fever, diarrhea,* nervousness, loss of strength and, if severe and prolonged, death.

TREATMENT

Treatment of a child with congenital hypothyroidism should begin as soon as possible (4 to 6 years of age) to avoid permanent mental, nerve, and muscle problems. Infants with the condition should be treated as early as possible; older children should be treated as soon as a positive diagnosis is made. Initial treatment of hypothyroidism consists of daily doses of thyroid hormones, which are increased to age-appropriate amounts as rapidly as the child can tolerate them. When the cause of goiter is mild thyroiditis without hypothyroidism, a physician may decide against treatment, as associated goiters frequently are small and do not cause problems.

With treatment, signs and symptoms of hypothyroidism usually disappear within 2 to 4 months. Children begin to grow and develop and become active and energetic, both physically and mentally. Blood circulation and pulse improve dramatically, and the skin becomes pink and warm. Children may require vitamin supplements to meet bodily needs during rapid growth.

A physician usually recommends follow-up visits to ensure that hormone therapy is working properly. If hormone dosage is too large, symptoms of hyperthyroidism may develop. If dosage is too small, a child's growth will not catch up although he or she may appear well.

If a child with hypothyroidism is older than 3 years of age when treatment begins, marked changes in personality may occur as he or she adjusts to the effects of thyroid hormone. A previously quiet, good-natured child may become highly active, have a shorter attention span, and sleep less. Such behavior persists until a child has fully adjusted to the hormones, a process which may take from 6 to 12 months.

Treatment of hyperthyroidism focuses on suppression of hormone secretion and reduction of its adverse effects. Possible treatment methods include giving medication to block secretion of hormones, surgery on the thyroid gland to reduce its output, and giving radioactive iodine to destroy thyroid tissue and decrease hormone secretion. If the method chosen is surgery, total or partial removal of the thyroid gland is performed to prevent recurrence of hyperthyroidism. Surgery is performed for removal of thyroid tumors and locally involved lymph nodes. Radioactive iodine therapy may be used for treatment of spread of *cancer* to the lungs.

Unless a tumor is present, most medical experts treat hyperthyroidism with hormone-suppressing medication, although 3 to 5 years of treatment and careful monitoring are usually required for successful resolution of the problem. The child is initially given large doses of this medication for several weeks to reduce thyroid activity to a normal level. Once a normal level is reached, medication is continued at a lower dose until the thyroid gland reaches a normal size and functions normally on its own. Follow-up visits at 6-week and 4-month intervals are recommended by a physician to ensure that adequate control of hyperthyroidism is accomplished. If side effects such as *hives, rash, fever, sore throat,* and mouth sores occur with drug therapy, the medication must be stopped.

A physician usually recommends surgical removal of part of the thyroid gland only when medication does not effectively control the hyperthyroidism. Surgery is required if a thyroid nodular tumor is present, even if the tumor is not cancerous. Before surgery for hyperthyroidism, a child is given medication to suppress thyroid overactivity so that hormone levels remain normal during the operation. Often a child develops hypothyroidism after surgery and requires lifelong treatment with thyroid hormone. As a result of surgery, damage may occur to a laryngeal nerve, causing alterations to the voice, but such a development is rare. Parathyroid glands may also be removed or their function altered, resulting in parathyroid deficiency. Lifelong vitamin D treatment can compensate for the parathyroid hormone deficiency.

Treatment with radioactive iodine is effective in controlling hyperthyroidism, but often causes hypothyroidism later. The risk of cancer formation as a result of radioactive treatment appears negligible, but it is still too early to evaluate long-term effects (20 years or longer). Radioactive iodine, therefore, is used only to treat children and adolescents for whom other therapies cannot be used because of associated problems.

With appropriate treatment, thyroid functioning becomes normal and most signs and symptoms disappear. In addition to treatment of the physical problems associated with thyroid disorders, children and their families often require counseling for guidance in dealing with problems that may be associated with hypothyroidism or hyperthyroidism (see Chapter 3, "Promoting Mental Health").

PREVENTION

Cases of congenital hypothyroidism caused by maternal use of thyroid-suppressing medications can be prevented if the mother receives careful medical supervision during her pregnancy. Congenital hypothyroidism resulting from other causes cannot be prevented. Early diagnosis of congenital hypothyroidism by newborn screening followed by early treatment has reduced markedly the long-term complications associated with this disease. (See discussion of genetic counseling in *genetic disorders.*)

Hyperthyroidism cannot be prevented.

TICS AND TOURETTE'S SYNDROME

DESCRIPTION

Tics are sudden, uncontrollable, rapidly repeated movements of a muscle or group of muscles. They often appear to be distorted repetitions of common movements, such as blinking, throat-clearing, head-shaking, shoulder-shrugging, and flexing of the arms and legs.

Almost everyone gets a minor tic, such as involuntary eye-twitching, for a few minutes or so every once in a while. Some children—about 15 percent—have occasional or frequent episodes of minor tics. Episodic tics can affect children as young as 2 years old. Studies show that 3 times as many boys as girls are affected.

Episodic tics typically involve eye or face muscles, although the whole head or parts of the torso and limbs can be affected. A child may have only 1 tic; if 2 or more tics are present, they may appear at the same time, in a pattern, or randomly. Tics sometimes appear more frequently or with greater intensity when the child feels excitement, anxiety, or *stress,* or when the child is engaged in strenuous physical activity. They may seem less exaggerated when the child's attention is captured. They always disappear during sleep. In most cases of episodic tics, the frequency and intensity of the tics wax and wane, and then the condition disappears without treatment. Very few adults have episodic tics.

In very rare cases (involving approximately 1 out of every 4,000 to 10,000 children), tics are part of a long-term disabling disorder known as Tourette's syndrome. (A syndrome is a cluster of signs and symptoms that appear to be connected although no exact cause for the connection can be found.) Tourette's syndrome is a condition which is characterized by multiple tics, usually involving many parts of the body, as well as bizarre vocalizations.

Tourette's syndrome typically begins when a child is between ages 4 and 10. It tends to start with a single tic, usually involving the face, upper body, or arms. Common first tics include eye-blinking; meaningless, involuntary "smiling"; chewing; tongue-thrusting; and tightening and relaxing the neck muscles. Within the next few months or years tics usually appear in progressively lower parts of the body. Lower-body tics may involve kicking, bending, and jumping. Sometimes tics involve complicated movements such as squatting, skipping, hitting, repetitive touching of objects or other people, and startle reactions. Many children with Tourette's syndrome report that tics are preceded by irresistible impulses and can be halted voluntarily only with great difficulty.

As more tics appear, a child with Tourette's syndrome is likely to begin producing involuntary vocal noises or words. The noises may resemble throat-clearing, coughs, grunts, shrieks, yelps, squeals, guttural sounds, lip-smacking, or humming. Words may be blurted out involuntarily or pronounced oddly. By or during the teenage years a child with Tourette's syndrome typically has periods of severe tics, with violent body-shaking. Less commonly, children with Tourette's syndrome suffer from overwhelming compulsions to utter obscene language or from echolalia (a tendency to echo others' words) or echopraxia (a tendency to imitate others' actions).

The symptoms of Tourette's syndrome tend to fluctuate greatly in intensity. Sometimes an affected child has no symptoms whatsoever for several months and then develops severe tics for a time. In many cases Tourette's syndrome begins to abate during late adolescence or early adulthood, but it usually persists in at least a mild form throughout life. About one half of all children with Tourette's syndrome eventually stop having tics. Why the others do not is unclear.

Although Tourette's syndrome is not caused by emotional problems or *mental retardation,* affected children suffer emotionally and experience *learning problems.* A high proportion of these children also have *language disorders.* A treatment program involving medication, supportive therapy, and education custom-made for a child with Tourette's syndrome can reduce the interference created by the syndrome. In addition, some affected children will not be handicapped as adults by the condition or its complications.

CAUSE

The mechanism that causes tics to develop is unknown. It appears, however, that occasional or episodic tics can develop as a result of one or more of many predisposing conditions. Some children, for example, may be constitutionally prone to develop tics at times of *stress* or at certain stages in development. Studies indicate that certain children seem likely to develop tics, just as some children are likely to develop allergies.

In certain cases tics appear to be linked to a more serious cause than normal development or simple stress. They are sometimes a response to living in an extremely stressful environment. In addition, certain children develop tics as a result of brain damage, a long-term brain disorder, or an episode of brain disease, such as *meningitis* or *encephalitis.* Some children who suffer from such a disease do not develop tics until months or even years after the infection has disappeared.

There is much controversy among experts about what causes Tourette's syndrome. Most believe that it involves a disturbance in some part of the central nervous system (the brain and spinal cord and their protective covering, the meninges). It seems likely that most cases of Tourette's syndrome involve multiple causes, including, perhaps, problems with brain chemistry, damage to the brain at birth, or some other sort of brain dysfunction.

Evidence exists that Tourette's syndrome runs in families. One theory is that Tourette's is an inherited metabolic disorder involving the chemicals that transmit messages from nerve cell to nerve cell (see *genetic disorders).*

It is possible that elements of a child's environment—school or home life, for example—may have something to do with the appearance or severity of the syndrome. Experts suspect that the combination of causes varies from case to case, which helps explain why it is difficult to pinpoint the cause of Tourette's syndrome.

DIAGNOSIS

Tics are distinguishable from other uncontrollable movements (see *movement disorders)* because they repeatedly involve a specific muscle or muscles. In most cases tics are first noticed by a parent or teacher, especially if they tend to interfere with routine tasks as, for example, finger-flexing or shoulder-lifting might. If parents suspect a child has tics, they should consult the physician most familiar with the child's medical history.

The goal of a physician consulted in such a case is to identify the child's movements as tics and to determine whether Tourette's syndrome exists. Diagnosis is based on observation of the movements, physical and psychological tests, and physical and psychological histories. The specific tests used vary according to a physician's suspicions about the cause of the movements. If a physician suspects Tourette's syndrome, referrals may be made to a neurologist (nervous-system specialist) or psychiatrist.

Once the diagnosis of tics or Tourette's syndrome is confirmed, a physician may order further evaluations to determine whether any associated complications of the disorder—learning disabilities or speech and language problems, for example—exist. Again, the specific tests used vary (see entries mentioned in Complications, below).

COMPLICATIONS

Occasional or episodic tics usually disappear before complications develop. It is not clear whether emotional problems are, strictly speaking, complications of Tourette's, or whether they arise from the same fundamental problem that causes the tics. Children with Tourette's syndrome, in addition, frequently suffer from one or more of the following difficulties: *learning problems, speech problems, language disorders,* behavioral problems. Specifically, a child with Tourette's syndrome may have problems with memory, perception, finding words pacing speech, speaking clearly, comprehending the meaning of sounds and spoken words, maintaining attention, sitting still, respecting the "space" of others, concentrating, controlling impulses, exercising coordination, and tolerating frustration.

What is clear is that these secondary problems are often of more concern to parents, teachers, and even the affected child than are the tics themselves. If not ad-

dressed, they can lead to even graver problems, such as great trouble making friends, low self-esteem, extreme difficulty controlling anger, other debilitating emotional problems, or even, in the worst cases, *suicide.* But if diagnosis is made early, the problem understood as not being the child's "fault," and sympathetic attention immediately paid to any secondary problems, complications are likely not to progress further and can often be overcome with time and patient effort.

TREATMENT

There is no cure for tics or Tourette's syndrome, except in those few cases of less complex tics for which a cause—such as emotional *stress*—can be identified and eliminated. Many tics do disappear with time. Even if tics persist, steps can be taken that may alleviate their severity and frequency.

Most physicians counsel parents to ignore the actual tics. Imitating or scolding a child or otherwise drawing attention to a tic is likely to be stressful for the child and, consequently, to aggravate the problem. Parents can try to find other ways to reduce stress in a child's life. In this endeavor it can be extremely helpful to work with a physician or a recommended counselor. Sometimes a child benefits directly from discussions with such a person. A counselor's explaining the phenomenon of tics and helping the family identify sources of stress may be of enormous relief to the child from the start.

For children with Tourette's syndrome there are medications that are often extremely effective in suppressing the most obvious symptoms of the condition—tics and vocalizations. Estimates of the effectiveness of these medications range from 60 to 90 percent; in other words, well over half of all children with Tourette's syndrome improve significantly on medication. Some studies show that medication is most successful among children with a family history of chronic tics.

Medication does not, however, affect any secondary problems or complications of Tourette's syndrome, and may aggravate them because it can cause side effects such as sleepiness. Therefore, medication rarely serves as the sole form of treatment for Tourette's. Other possibilities include remedial education, speech and language therapy, supportive psychotherapy, and family counseling, depending on the specific problem.

PREVENTION

Unless the cause of tics is known, prevention is impossible.

TONSILLITIS AND ADENOIDITIS

DESCRIPTION

Tonsils and adenoids are components of the body's immune system. Tonsils are located in the throat near the base of the tongue. Adenoids are located at the upper back part of the throat, opposite the nasal passages and near the eustachian tubes, which are connected to the middle ear (see illustration).

Both tonsils and adenoids are small masses of lymphoid tissue, which serves as a defense against infection. Tonsils and adenoids help to filter bacteria and other infectious agents that are in the mouth. They also aid in the formation of lymphocytes (a type of white blood cell) and antibodies, both of which combat infection.

Tonsils and adenoids naturally become enlarged when they are fighting infections of the throat, nose, and mouth. (Tonsils and adenoids may also become enlarged as a result of an allergy; see *allergies*.) Tonsils and adenoids reach their largest size when children are from 2 to 6 years old. Tonsils may shrink after age 8 and adenoids may decrease in size at puberty.

Despite their protective functions, tonsils and adenoids are less significant when fighting local infections than when they themselves become infected. Infection and subse-

FIG. 36A. UPPER RESPIRATORY TRACT

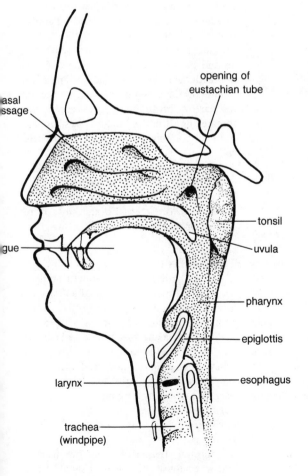

nasal passage

opening of eustachian tube

tongue

tonsil

uvula

pharynx

epiglottis

esophagus

larynx

trachea (windpipe)

FIG. 36B. MOUTH AND THROAT

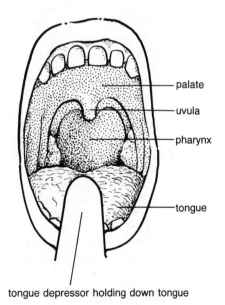

palate

uvula

pharynx

tongue

tongue depressor holding down tongue

quent inflammation (swelling, redness, tenderness, warmth, and impairment of function) of the tonsils or adenoids typically occur when bacteria or viruses present in the mouth or nose attack the tonsils or adenoids. The bacteria that most often infect tonsils, for example, are commonly present in a child's mouth and nose without causing harm.

When tonsils are infected and inflamed, the condition is called tonsillitis; with adenoids, the condition is known as adenoiditis. The conditions can occur separately or together. When adenoiditis is severe, it interferes only with breathing; severe tonsillitis impairs both breathing and swallowing.

Tonsillitis or adenoiditis can occur at any age, although they are most common among young children. Children usually outgrow the susceptibility to tonsillitis and adenoiditis. As children become older, they develop increased resistance to infection.

Tonsillitis and adenoiditis can be acute (occurring once or infrequently) or chronic (persistent or recurring frequently). An acute episode of either tonsillitis or adenoiditis typically lasts 4 or 5 days.

CAUSE

Tonsillitis is most often caused by a virus. It can also be caused by group A streptococcus ("strep") bacteria. Adenoiditis usually results from a viral infection.

SIGNS AND SYMPTOMS

Acute tonsillitis usually develops suddenly. Swallowing becomes painful, and the child may have a *headache, fever,* aching arms and legs, and lack of energy. A 2- or 3-year-old child may have a high fever, accompanied by drowsiness, *vomiting,* and stomachache (see *stomachaches, stomach pain).* A young child may also refuse to eat.

Signs of chronic tonsillitis include persistent *sore throat* and bad breath.

Acute adenoiditis may be indicative by fever, headache, and vomiting.

Symptoms of chronic adenoiditis include breathing through the mouth instead of the nose (which occurs when the nasal passages are blocked by enlarged adenoids), bad breath, impaired taste and smell, snoring and night coughing, and a nasal-sounding or muffled voice.

DIAGNOSIS

A physician observes signs and symptoms during a physical examination.

Acute tonsillitis is indicated by swelling of the tonsils themselves and often accompanied by swelling of the lymph nodes of the neck and jaw. A discharge of pus from the tonsils may be evident. After two or three days of tonsillitis, tonsils may be covered with a whitish coating.

Chronic tonsillitis is marked by enlargement and scarring of the tonsils. If enlargement is severe, obstruction of the swallowing and breathing mechanisms may be evident.

Acute adenoiditis is indicated by streaks of mucus and pus inside the nose. In addition, the mucous membranes of the inner nose appear inflamed.

Chronic adenoiditis is marked by persistent inflammation of the mucous membrane of the nose and chronic nasal obstruction.

The physician is likely to take a throat culture for analysis to see if group A strep is causing the infection.

COMPLICATIONS

Following an untreated group A strep infection, serious complications can result, including inflammation of the heart valves and muscle (see *rheumatic fever)* and inflammation of the kidneys (see *nephritis).*

Sometimes abscesses (pus-filled sacs) form around the tonsils; they can cause difficulty in breathing, swallowing, and opening of the mouth. If the respiratory passages become too narrow, breathing difficulty can be life-threatening. If untreated, abscesses can lead to blood poisoning through spread of bacteria.

Adenoid enlargement may cause swelling and blockage of the eustachian tubes, which leads to chronic middle ear infections (see *earache and ear infections)* and, in turn, recurrent or persistent *hearing loss.*

TREATMENT

Bacterial infection is treated with antibiotics, usually for about 10 days. If an infection is viral, antibiotics are not effective. Treatment then is aimed at relieving symptoms.

Pain from acute tonsillitis or adenoiditis may be relieved by a nonprescription pain-relieving medication, and read the discussion of these drugs on p. 102. A dry throat may be soothed by gargling.

Abscesses on the tonsils may need to be punctured by a physician to extract accumulated pus.

Important treatment issues are whether and when tonsils or adenoids should be removed. Little evidence exists to show that removing these tissues helps to prevent or lessen the severity of other illnesses, such as frequent *colds.* In recent years, therefore, fewer tonsillectomies (surgical removal of tonsils) and adenoidectomies (surgical removal of adenoids) have been performed in the United States. In general, surgery should be considered only when tonsils or adenoids cause persistent or recurrent problems (such as repeated cases of *strep throat),* particularly pronounced difficulty in breathing or swallowing.

Although tonsillectomy and adenoidectomy traditionally have been performed at the same time, physicians today are more likely to make independent decisions about removing tonsils and adenoids. It is probably best not to have both tonsils and adenoids removed when there is a persistent problem with only one.

PREVENTION

It is not possible to prevent occasional tonsillitis or adenoiditis in the normal course of childhood.

TOOTHACHES AND INJURY TO TEETH

EMERGENCY ACTION

Tooth pain as a result of decay or trauma (injury) must be treated by a dentist as soon as possible.

DESCRIPTION

Toothaches from decayed or damaged teeth occur commonly in all age groups. Pain varies from mild to quite intense and may occur quite suddenly when an injured or decayed tooth is tapped, used in chewing, or stimulated by hot, cold, or sweet substances. The gum surrounding a painful and damaged tooth may be red, swollen, and tender. The tooth may be discolored and may be associated with a swelling of the face, cheek, eye, or neck.

If the cause of a toothache is not treated, the pain almost always grows worse, and eventually the tooth may have to be extracted.

CAUSE

The most common cause of toothache in children is tooth decay. Even a small cavity can cause pain on stimulation from hot or cold or sweet substances. If tooth decay reaches the pulp (the inner core) of blood vessels and nerves of a tooth, an infection known as an abscess may occur, indicating irreversible damage to the pulp. The tooth is usually sensitive to hot substances at this time.

A blow or other injury to the jaw can damage teeth in 2 ways: fracture and displacement. Pain caused by a fractured tooth crown may be mild or severe, depending how close the fracture is to the pulp. Displacement of a tooth occurs if the crown is fractured from the root or the entire tooth (along with the root) is moved within the bone. The tooth must be treated immediately; otherwise it may not heal properly, resulting in eventual loss.

DIAGNOSIS

The decayed or damaged tooth causing the toothache may be hard to locate, since the child may feel pain throughout the jaw. Redness, swelling, tenderness, or bleeding of the gum may indicate an injured or decayed tooth. Gently tapping the child's teeth can help locate the affected tooth. A sore and damaged tooth can be extremely sensitive to touch. Teeth that are gray, loose, or very sensitive generally indicate previous damage to the tooth or root.

Children often complain to parents of toothaches resulting from canker sores or oral viruses, thereby aiding in diagnosis.

COMPLICATIONS

Severe infection or abscess of a tooth may be accompanied by *fever,* swelling of the jaw, face, cheek, eye, or neck, or by redness of the gums around the tooth.

TREATMENT

Home treatment focuses on reducing tooth pain. Fever-reducing and pain-relieving medications can be helpful if an abscess is present. Consult the dentist for specific recommendations and read the discussion of nonprescription medications beginning on p. 102. (Some over-the-counter preparations for relief of pain, such as mouthwashes, contain mild numbing preparations that should not be used for temporary pain relief.) An ice pack applied to the jaw or near the damaged tooth often helps ease the pain. Appli-

cation of heat is not advisable, since that inflames rather than soothes tender areas.

Toothaches resulting from tooth decay or
injury should be treated by a dentist immediately. If a tooth is decayed, the decayed
portion is usually removed (drilled out) and
replaced initially with a temporary filling,
which helps to decrease pain. At a later time
a permanent restoration can be made. When
the tooth is abscessed, the pulp is usually
removed through a procedure known as a
root canal. Antibiotics may also be prescribed to fight infection in an abscess.

A dentist usually treats a tooth crown
fracture by covering, or bonding, the damaged tooth with a white plastic material. At
a later time the dentist can make a permanent restoration to approximate the size and
shape of the tooth. If the fracture is severe
and has affected the pulp or root of the
tooth, the tooth may need to be splinted and
a root canal may be required. If damage is so
severe that repairs cannot be made, the dentist may decide to remove the tooth, eventually replacing it with a fixed bridge or partial
denture, depending on the age of the patient.

Displaced or loosened teeth should be
treated immediately. If the tooth is loosened,
a splint may be required to allow for proper
healing. When a tooth is displaced, it must
be repositioned immediately by a dentist and
temporarily splinted in its original position
for approximately 3 weeks. A root canal is
often necessary once the tooth is firmly reat-
tached to the bone.

PREVENTION

Most children's toothaches are caused by
tooth decay.

One of the most important steps in
preventing tooth decay is the use of fluoride,
a substance that helps strengthen tooth
enamel. To be certain children are getting
sufficient fluoride, most cities in the United
States fluoridate their water. In areas where
water has not been fluoridated, a supplementary supply, in vitamin form, is needed. This
type of fluoride (systemic) is only effective
for teeth still developing in the jaw. Topical
application of fluoride benefits teeth already
present in the oral cavity. One such source
of topical fluoride is toothpaste; most brands
on the market now contain fluoride. At least
one application of fluoride every day is necessary for effective tooth decay prevention.
Topical fluoride rinses or gels used daily can

also help reduce tooth decay. Semiannual
professionally applied fluoride treatments
can reduce tooth decay by as much as 30
percent.

Application of sealants on the grooves
(pits and fissures) of permanent molars is
highly beneficial in decreasing decay.

In addition, regular brushing and rinsing
of teeth after meals and avoiding sugary
foods that may stick to and between teeth
will help prevent tooth decay. Small children should not go to bed with bottles that
contain juices or milk. Bacteria feed on juice
and milk sugars; they also may invade a
child's tooth enamel, causing nursing-bottle
cavities (see *tooth problems*). Frequent
snacking on sugary foods has a direct effect
on tooth decay and should be minimized.

Face masks and other protective equipment should be worn when playing rough
sports to help protect a child's face and jaw,
especially if a child's front teeth protrude
(see Chapter 2, "Promoting Physical
Health").

TOOTH PROBLEMS

EMERGENCY ACTION

Immediate emergency action is necessary
if a child's tooth has been dislocated, fractured, or completely knocked out of the
socket. Apply ice to the injured area of slow
bleeding and reduce swelling. Put the
knocked-out tooth back into the socket, or if
that is not possible, into milk (to keep it
from deteriorating) and take it with the
child to the nearest emergency room for immediate reimplantation. Dislocated teeth
must be repositioned and splinted by a dentist or properly trained physician immediately.

DESCRIPTION

Children have a variety of dental problems, the most common of which are tooth
decay (including cavities), tooth dislocation,
tooth fracture, and toothaches. These problems affect children of all ages, and range in
severity from mild, requiring minimal treatment, to serious problems that require immediate dental attention.

Tooth decay is the most common tooth
problem among children. Cavities, also

called caries, occur when tooth enamel, the outer shell of a tooth, is broken down by acids found in the mouth. This breakdown exposes the soft, living parts of a tooth (pulp and nerve) to decay and damage. If decay goes far into a tooth, inflammation of the pulp and nerve usually occurs. Untreated inflammation may become infected, a condition known as a dental abscess.

A form of tooth decay occasionally found in infants and young children is nursing-bottle cavities. These cavities appear in children who fall asleep while nursing either at a bottle of milk or sweet liquid or a mother's breast. With nursing-bottle cavities, decay usually affects the top front incisors, the top upper primary molars, and the canines (see *teething*). A child's bottom teeth are initially protected from decay because the tongue covers most of the teeth and they are constantly washed by saliva from active salivary glands. If a child is continually allowed to fall asleep with a bottle or at a mother's breast, decay can reach the bottom teeth as well.

A severe form of tooth decay, known as rampant tooth decay, results in the development of 10 or more cavities a year. This occurs most often in young adolescents, particularly those who do not practice good dental care, but can affect all age groups. Rampant cavities occur suddenly in any part of a child's mouth, rapidly break down tooth enamel, and enter the pulp. Teeth considered immune to ordinary decay are often affected by rampant cavities.

Injury of a child's teeth can result in loosening, dislocation, or fracture. An injury severe enough to affect the inner pulp may cause a tooth to lose blood, thereby becoming grayish in color. When a tooth becomes dislocated, supporting bone and gum tissue are involved and teeth become loose in their sockets. The tooth nerve or pulp may eventually die if appropriate treatment is delayed.

Tooth fractures may affect only surface enamel, or may be severe enough to damage tooth pulp. The tooth is often sensitive to air or hot and cold temperatures. Surrounding gum tissue usually becomes red, swollen, and tender. Tooth and then jaw pain usually accompany injured teeth.

Toothaches most often arise from tooth decay or abscess, but may also be caused by damaged teeth. Pain may be a constant, dull ache or may not be present until pressure is applied to a tooth or a tooth comes in contact with hot, cold, or sweet substances.

CAUSE

The most common cause of tooth decay in children is poor dental care. Tooth decay begins when bacteria (usually streptococci) that live in tooth plaque begin to digest sugars and other carbohydrates found in a child's mouth. This breakdown creates acids which remove calcium from tooth enamel, thereby weakening a tooth's protective outer covering. Other enamel minerals and tooth tissue are exposed to these acids and breakdown and decay continue. If not treated, decay can progress to the pulp (the nerves and root) of a tooth, often producing inflammation, pain, and abscess.

Certain teeth may be more susceptible to decay than others, regardless of preventive dental care. Teeth with structural irregularities, such as an incompletely closed pit (the depression in the top of the tooth formed by the points of the crown), enamel defects, and irregularly shaped teeth, tend to decay more easily than normal teeth. Crowded, irregularly spaced teeth or teeth covered with dental appliances (e.g., braces) are difficult to clean (see *teeth, developmental problems of*). If not cleaned properly, these teeth are especially susceptible to decay.

Rampant cavities often develop when a child's mouth has numerous sugar deposits, a result of poor dental care and a diet high in sugary foods. Rampant cavities form through the same decay process as other cavities.

A blow or other injury to a tooth or surrounding bone often causes loosening, dislocation, or a fracture.

DIAGNOSIS

A severe cavity appears as a yellow-brown or black crater in a tooth's surface. A dentist will take X-ray films of the child's teeth to check for tooth problems that cannot easily be seen (including cavities in between teeth).

Redness, swelling, and tenderness of the gum usually indicate an injured or abscessed tooth. Affected teeth may be loose and extremely sensitive to touch. Loose and painful teeth usually indicate abscess, dislocation, or fracture. Gray teeth may indicate pulp death from a previous injury. Jaw pain may help locate and identify damaged teeth.

A toothache is often hard to locate, since a child may not be able to identify the exact source. Gently tapping a child's teeth can sometimes help locate an affected tooth.

COMPLICATIONS

A severe tooth abscess may be accompanied by *fever,* pus formation, swelling of the jaw, and redness of the gums. Abscess or injury of baby teeth may affect developing permanent teeth.

TREATMENT

Tooth decay should be treated by a dentist. The decayed portion of a tooth is usually removed (drilled out) and replaced with a filling. If decay results in an abscess, tooth pulp is removed and the root canals are filled in a process known as a root canal. If tooth abscess is quite severe or a large portion of surrounding bone is involved, tooth extraction may be necessary. If there is fever and obvious swelling, antibiotics and a fever- or inflammation-reducing medication may be helpful. Consult the dentist for specific recommendations and read the discussion of nonprescription medications beginning on p. 102.

A dentist may treat a minor tooth crown fracture by covering, or capping, the affected tooth. If a fracture is severe and affects the tooth root, a root canal may be necessary. A tooth that is too severely damaged to repair may be removed and replaced with a false one.

Dislocated, fractured, or knocked-out teeth should be treated immediately (see Emergency Action, above).

Until the underlying cause of a toothache is corrected, treatment focuses on lessening tooth pain. Cotton swabs dipped in essence of clove and rubbed on the gum surrounding the tooth may temporarily relieve a toothache; a pain-reducing medication, prescribed by the dentist, may be helpful. Some over-the-counter mouthwashes, often used for home treatment of colds and sore throats, contain mild numbing preparations and can be used for temporary pain relief. An ice pack applied to the jaw may help ease an aching tooth. Application of heat is not advisable, since it inflames rather than soothes tender areas.

PREVENTION

One of the most important steps in preventing tooth decay is the use of fluoride, a substance that helps strengthen tooth enamel. To be certain children are getting sufficient fluoride, check to see if your water is fluoridated. Most major cities in the United States fluoridate their water. In areas where water has not been fluoridated, a supplementary supply is needed. Surface applications by brushing with fluoridated toothpaste at least once a day are necessary for effective tooth decay prevention.

After age 2 or 3 a child should see a dentist regularly for an examination of all teeth through X ray and a dentist's inspection, a thorough cleaning of the teeth, instruction in preventive measures against tooth decay, and a fluoride treatment. A dentist may also apply a sealant, a protective covering over the susceptible surfaces of the teeth, in an effort to reduce tooth decay. In addition, regular brushing and rinsing of teeth after meals and avoiding sugary foods that may stick to and between teeth help prevent tooth decay.

Nursing-bottle cavities can be prevented if small children are not allowed to fall asleep while nursing. This is not always preventable, however, since many children fall asleep while nursing. If a child is put to bed with a bottle, it can be filled with water instead of liquids that contain sugar.

Face masks, mouthpieces, and other protective equipment should be worn when playing rough sports to help protect the teeth.

TOXIC SHOCK SYNDROME

EMERGENCY ACTION

An actively menstruating female should see a physician immediately if most of these signs and symptoms develop: fever above 102° F (38.8° C), *diarrhea* or *vomiting* or nausea; shaking chills; fainting or *dizziness* when standing; and sunburnlike *rash.* If the woman is using a tampon, it should be removed immediately.

A female who is not menstruating but who is using a diaphragm or contraceptive sponge should also see a physician immediately if most of the above symptoms appear suddenly. The diaphragm or contraceptive sponge should be removed immediately.

DESCRIPTION

Toxic shock syndrome (TSS) is an uncommon but serious disease that occurs suddenly and eventually affects systems throughout the entire body. Almost all of those affected by the disease are female, most of whom are actively menstruating and using tampons continuously. They are usually under the age of 30 and in good health when the disease strikes. Occasionally, men develop TSS, and their illness may be the most difficult to diagnose since toxic shock is so rare in men.

Typically, TSS strikes suddenly on the second to fourth day of a menstrual period, though occasionally it does occur just after the end of the period. Within hours, the woman may become critically ill. In the case of males or nonmenstruating females it may strike at any time (see Causes, below).

TSS recurs in about 1 of every 3 women who received treatment but continue to use tampons. Among untreated women who continue to use tampons, the recurrence rate is twice as high. A recurrent episode is usually less severe than the first.

TSS generally lasts 7 to 10 days. Its severity varies; mild cases are often undiagnosed. Of those individuals diagnosed as having TSS, less than 5 percent die. Fatalities occur usually within one week of the onset of illness. Some TSS victims suffer long-term disabilities (see Complications, below). Most, however, make a complete recovery, especially if TSS is diagnosed and treated promptly and properly.

CAUSE

All females with TSS are infected with *Staphylococcus aureus* bacteria in the cervix and vagina; apparently, these bacteria are able to grow rapidly and produce toxins that may spread throughout the body through the bloodstream. However, since the bacteria can also be found in the nose and throat and on the skin of many people (both women and men) who do not have TSS, it is still unclear what causes such a serious disease as TSS to develop in certain people. It is theorized that most people are immune to the toxins produced by the bacteria. Why some people are not immune is unknown. Apparently, those females with TSS who have partial immunity against the toxins have mild cases of the disease.

The bacterial infection seems to be aggravated by the use of tampons during menstruation, especially of "supers" (high absorbency tampons introduced in 1977). Certain fibers formerly used in some tampons unfor-

tunately promoted the growth of bacteria. The offending fibers have been removed from all tampons, thereby greatly reducing the risk of tampon-associated TSS.

Tampons left in place more than 8 hours help create a warm, moist environment ideal for the rapid growth of bacteria. In the rare cases when the disease strikes males or nonmenstruating females, a staph infection such as an infected wound or burn, an abscess, or pneumonia may be the cause.

SIGNS AND SYMPTOMS

The first signs and symptoms of TSS usually include *fever* above 102° F (38.8° C), *diarrhea* or *vomiting* or nausea, shaking chills, fainting or *dizziness* when standing, and sunburnlike *rash.* Many other symptoms may appear, either immediately or within hours or days, depending on the severity of the case: feeling weak or fatigued; *cough; sore throat; headache;* red eyes; disorientation; severe muscle pain; *abdominal pain;* painful urination or decrease in urine flow; sore lymph nodes; lethargy; and *shock.* During the recovery period (1 to 2 weeks after onset of the disease), peeling of scaly skin on the palms of the hands and soles of the feet may occur.

Victims of recurrent TSS generally experience fever, low blood pressure, and rash followed by skin peeling. The gastrointestinal (GI) tract is usually affected as well.

DIAGNOSIS

TSS is diagnosed by a physician, who observes signs and symptoms, measures blood pressure and pulse rate, checks for unusual redness of the throat or vagina, and for a woman, takes a culture of secretions from the vagina or cervix. Secretions from the throat, nose, or rectum may also be used to identify the bacteria. Urine and blood tests may be performed to see whether kidney or liver function is impaired. A physician might also discover impaired heart and lung function, decrease in number of blood platelets, and decreased levels of calcium and phosphate in the blood.

COMPLICATIONS

Uncommon complications include temporary hair or nail loss and partial or total loss of use of fingers and toes (which results from impaired blood circulation). Restoration of full use of fingers and toes depends on how quickly full circulation can be restored; impairment is usually temporary. In many cases complications include liver abnormalities or kidney failure, due to severe loss of fluids and impaired circulation (see *kidney failure, acute*).

TREATMENT

In severe cases victims of TSS are treated in hospital intensive care units. TSS infection is treated with antibiotics. A crucial part of treatment is replacement of fluids lost from *vomiting* and *diarrhea*, in order to keep kidneys functioning and blood circulating. The vagina may be irrigated (flushed out) with a salt solution or antibiotic solution to wash out staph bacteria and the toxins they produce.

PREVENTION

Physicians recommend that tampons should be changed every 4 to 6 hours.

Women who have had TSS should check with a physician before resuming use of tampons. At least 3 months must pass before the vagina can be completely free of the bacteria after treatment with antibiotics. Research indicates that certain antibiotics may help prevent recurrences of TSS.

TRACHEOESOPHAGEAL FISTULA

DESCRIPTION

Tracheoesophageal fistula (TEF) is a rare abnormal connection between the trachea (windpipe) and the esophagus, the tube that carries food and liquids from the back of the throat to the stomach (see Fig. 30, p. 437). Its incidence is about 1 in every 4,000 births.

TEF is usually detected during or after the first feeding when an infant will regurgitate (spit up) any liquid swallowed. In those babies with TEF, digestive juices will also flow up from the stomach through the lower end of the esophagus into the trachea. Those fluids may pass into the lungs, setting off a severe reaction that results in *pneumonia*.

In normal babies the esophagus and trachea are separate. In babies with TEF the esophagus is divided into upper and lower parts that are unconnected. The upper portion ends in a blind pouch in the chest and the lower one joins the bottom of the trachea at the point where the 2 bronchi usually branch off.

Since the upper portion of the esophagus comes to a dead end, nothing swallowed—food, drink, or saliva—can reach the stomach. Any child with this problem is likely to develop serious lung complications if material in the mouth finds its way into the lungs, since it cannot go down into the stomach. If surgery is performed promptly, most children with this problem can expect to have a fairly normal life with only minor alterations in the swallowing mechanism.

CAUSE

TEF is caused by a defect in prenatal development of the esophagus. It is not hereditary. It is almost always associated with a blockage of the esophagus and with a number of other abnormalities that are congenital (present at birth), especially congenital heart disease (see *heart disease, congenital*).

SIGNS AND SYMPTOMS

If a mother has accumulated excessive amniotic fluid during pregnancy, a physician will look for an abnormality of the esophagus immediately after a baby's birth. (It is possible for a baby to have esophageal difficulty even if its mother has not experienced excessive amniotic fluid.)

Excessive drooling can be an indication of a closed esophagus. Newborns with this abnormality will choke, cough, and spit up when first attempting to feed. These newborns may have poor color or even *cyanosis* (blue color resulting from lack of oxygen) because lung congestion and choking on the aspirated (inhaled) fluids interfere with breathing. If a mother tries to continue feeding, lung infection can occur because the infant aspirates milk or formula and gastric juices into the lungs.

DIAGNOSIS

Diagnosis is made by X rays and by a physician's determination that a catheter (a thin plastic tube) cannot be passed into the baby's stomach. These diagnostic procedures are swift and accurate.

COMPLICATIONS

Lung inflammation and *pneumonia* are the most common complications. Both can be avoided or eliminated by prompt surgical treatment.

TREATMENT

Surgery is always required. The operation

involves separating the lower end of the esophagus from the trachea and then connecting it to the upper, closed end. In order to allow the esophagus to heal, the infant is fed through a plastic tube leading directly into the stomach for a week or so.

Almost all full-term infants respond well to surgery and survive. Others may require further treatment to assure a well-functioning esophagus.

Even after surgery, these children do not have normal swallowing function. By chewing thoroughly and swallowing slowly, however, most children can learn to manage quite well and lead virtually normal lives.

PREVENTION
TEF presently cannot be prevented.

TUBERCULOSIS

DESCRIPTION
Tuberculosis (TB) is a chronic infectious disease that nearly always involves the lungs, although almost any part of the body can be affected (see Fig. 19, p. 182). TB can cause permanent damage in affected parts of the body. Because of improved sanitation, medical care, and nutrition, TB occurs much less frequently in the United States than it did a century ago. Only 1 or 2 cases occur for every 10,000 American children. The younger a child, the greater the susceptibility not only to infection but also to spread of TB bacteria within the lungs and, possibly, to other parts of the body.

Once the infection becomes dormant (present but inactive), TB does not appear again in most people. Inactive bacteria are nearly always left behind, however, and may become reactivated when resistance is low, months or (more often) years later in adolescence or adulthood. This reactivation TB can be more serious than initial TB.

More than 90 percent of all cases of initial TB involve infection of the lung (called pulmonary TB). Usually only a small area becomes infected at first. If the child's resistance to initial TB is low, a larger area of infection results, and the infected area dies and becomes dry and cheeselike. This process is called caseation. Nearby lymph nodes also caseate. In time, all that is left of the area is a small scar that hardens after about 6 months.

If the child's resistance is low, bacteria may spread into other parts of the lung, producing other patches of infection in one or both lungs. Symptoms of respiratory difficulty appear. These infected areas are likely to become caseated. If areas of caseation are extensive, cavities of destroyed lung tissue are formed. Bacteria may also escape from the lungs, entering the chest cavity and causing effusions (accumulations of infected fluid).

The second most common site of initial invasion by TB bacteria is the lymph nodes of the neck. These lymph nodes enlarge and sometimes poke through the skin, where ulcers form and may caseate.

The severity of TB varies, depending upon which parts of the body are affected. The disease is most severe when the blood, meninges (membranes surrounding the brain and spinal cord), or kidneys are infected.

Initial TB is most dangerous if the disease spreads quickly through the lungs or through the body via the bloodstream (the latter condition is called miliary TB). Miliary TB is the most severe form of the disease. If infection from the lung invades a blood vessel, bacteria are discharged into the bloodstream, then spread quickly through the body. Tubercles (hard, irregular lumps) can form in various organs throughout the body. The spleen and bone marrow are likely to be involved at first; later the kidney, adrenal glands, liver, bones, and joints may be affected.

If the central nervous system is invaded by bacilli, the infection can lead to *meningitis,* especially among children aged 6 to 24 months. Meningitis is very serious and must be diagnosed early; it is the chief cause of death from TB among children. Involvement of the kidney is also serious, although rare in childhood.

Intestinal TB, also rare, can occur if a child swallows infected sputum from his or her own lungs or if TB bacteria spread through the bloodstream.

Reactivation TB may start from any previous site of infection, although the top of the lung is most common. Once reactivation begins, these points of infection may increase in size and rapidly become enclosed within tubercles. Then the infected areas caseate and abscesses form. When these abscesses involve large areas, treatment is slow and difficult.

In both initial and reactivation TB, infected bacteria can enter the bronchi (breathing tubes) of the lung and be released into the air through coughing, thereby increasing the likelihood of infection of other individuals.

The severity of TB depends not only upon which parts of the body are affected but upon the number and strength of bacteria and upon the resistance of the infected person. Infants, adolescents, and the elderly are most susceptible, particularly if they suffer from another disease (such as *diabetes*), *malnutrition*, or generalized infectious diseases (such as *measles, whooping cough,* or *influenza*). Pregnancy, steroids, and immunosuppressant therapy also increase a person's vulnerability to TB.

CAUSE

TB is caused by the tubercle bacillus, a type of bacteria that is unusually resistant to ordinary antibiotics. Tubercle bacilli are carried by humans and cattle, as well as by other animals.

These bacilli are usually spread when a person with active TB coughs them up. The bacilli in mucus are carried by air currents and are inhaled into the lungs. They are almost never spread by kissing or other physical contact. Occasionally bacilli enter the body through the skin, tonsils, or mucous membranes of the mouth, throat, or eyes. In rare cases bacilli are transmitted from mother to fetus through the placenta.

Children with TB have nearly always been infected through the droplets of an infected adult. Brief exposure by chance outside the home is much less likely to cause TB.

SIGNS AND SYMPTOMS

The early symptoms of initial TB are slight, but may include tiredness, loss of appetite, weight loss, *headache,* slight *fever, cough,* and irritability. Especially at night, a child may sweat and may cough up blood. In its early stages TB may be mistaken for *pneumonia.* If the infection spreads within the lungs and worsens, typical symptoms include a persistent cough, breathlessness, and fever.

DIAGNOSIS

If none of the above symptoms is present, initial TB usually goes unnoticed unless it is known that a child has been exposed to someone with active TB. Diagnosis is made by a physician based on 6 factors: exposure to TB, characteristic symptoms, physical examination, chest X ray, tuberculin skin testing, and lab tests isolating the infective bacteria from sputum (coughed-up mucus secretions).

About 5 or 6 weeks after first exposure to TB, the child's skin reacts to a tuberculin skin test. This test involves the injection into the skin of the forearm of a small amount of protein derived from the tubercle bacillus. Individuals who have been infected will show a raised red area at the side of the injection.

Early diagnosis of reactivated TB is important because it is most effectively treated before long-term abscesses and cavities develop in the lungs.

COMPLICATIONS

Although most cases of initial TB become dormant even without treatment, untreated initial TB can lead to death in severe cases, especially in the first 2 to 4 years of life. If reactivation TB is untreated, it may disappear spontaneously or develop into progressive lung disease with serious complications.

TREATMENT

Months or even years of treatment are necessary to control TB. Although initial TB usually becomes dormant even without treatment, medication prescribed by a physician is necessary to keep the infection from spreading within the lung or to sites outside the lung, particularly the central nervous system. It may also help prevent reactivation. Children with initial TB lead normal lives except that they must take medication for at least 6 months to 1 year. A child with initial TB who is taking proper medication is not contagious and does not need to be isolated. Since TB can be most serious among young infants, these children are generally hospitalized.

A child with lung abscesses must be isolated until antibiotics are given for at least 2 weeks, lab tests show an absence of bacteria in sputum, and coughing has decreased. A child with TB involvement of a kidney may also be isolated.

PREVENTION

The most effective preventive measure is to protect a child from exposure to adults with active TB. Adults who work with children should be screened regularly. When a case of TB occurs, it is imperative that everyone who has been exposed to the infected person be identified and screened. If infection is not found, testing should be repeated 6 to 10 weeks later, since incubation of bacteria within the body takes time. If the results of any screening indicate infection, even if a child has no symptoms, a physician may recommend antibiotic treatment for 6 months to 1 year. A child who cannot avoid exposure to an adult with an active infection is also given antibiotics for at least 1 year.

A vaccine called the BCG vaccine offers some protection to TB and is used routinely in areas where the disease is common.

Most physicians recommend screening for TB around a child's first birthday and at 1- to 3-year intervals thereafter in areas where TB is known to exist in the population.

Screening remains important because the incidence of TB in the United States can rise owing to the increased mobility of people who unknowingly have been exposed to TB and as a result of an increase in emigration from areas of the world where TB occurs more often.

Information is available from local chapters of the American Lung Association or from its headquarters: 1740 Broadway, New York, NY 10019 (phone: 212-315-8700).

TURNER'S SYNDROME

DESCRIPTION

Turner's syndrome occurs in females who are born with an abnormal chromosome pattern that affects sexual development. They lack 1 of the 2 sex chromosomes. The syndrome is the fourth most common sex chromosome abnormality; approximately 1 out of every 3,000 female infants born each year has the syndrome.

In addition to having an abnormality in their sexual development, girls with Turner's syndrome usually are abnormally short, have a "webbed neck" (see Signs and Symptoms, below), and are affected with congenital heart disease (see *heart disease, congenital*). While they appear to be normal females, their gonads (reproductive organs) either fail to develop or develop abnormally. Although some of these children may have sufficient ovarian tissue to experience normal puberty with fertility, most do not possess gonadal tissue and consequently are

sterile. Without treatment, therefore, most girls born with 1 sex chromosome do not develop breasts or menstruate, although other secondary sexual characteristics do develop spontaneously, such as pubic hair (which results from adrenal hormones).

Since most girls with Turner's syndrome have no ovaries, even with hormone treatment they cannot produce eggs (and therefore remain sterile). However, females who begin hormone treatment in their early teens usually develop secondary sex characteristics and can lead normal sex lives.

CAUSE

Most female babies with Turner's syndrome are born with 45 rather than 46 chromosomes, and have only one X chromosome instead of two. In the process of fertilization, either an X chromosome from the egg of the mother or from the sperm of the father is lost. Recent research indicates that the paternal X is the missing chromosome in two thirds of females with Turner's syndrome. The problem may recur in some families. (See *genetic disorders*.)

SIGNS AND SYMPTOMS

Many females with Turner's syndrome are low birthweight babies. A girl born with the syndrome has skin and bone abnormalities, such as a "webbed neck" (one with loose skin folds, especially at the base). She may have swollen hands and feet at birth. Other characteristics include a broad, shieldlike chest and a low hairline at the nape of the neck. Many of these females have congenital heart disease; the most common abnormality is coarctation of the aorta (see *heart disease, congenital*).

Later in childhood and adolescence, absence of breast development and of menstruation may indicate the presence of this condition. A girl's pattern of skeletal growth, which appears to be determined genetically, results in short stature (see *height problems*), with a usual adult height of 54 to 57 inches.

The majority of girls with Turner's syndrome are of normal intelligence, although they may suffer from hearing problems and subsequently experience learning difficulties.

DIAGNOSIS

In the past, the sexual consequences of Turner's syndrome were not usually diagnosed until a girl reached her midteens and had not begun to develop breasts or to menstruate. Now the disorder may be suspected at birth by the presence of other skin, skeletal, and cardiac abnormalities that are part of this condition. They are verified by chromosomal and hormonal analyses (see *genetic disorders*). An abnormal sex chromosome pattern (most often a cell line with a missing X chromosome) and elevation of a special hormone in the blood indicate Turner's syndrome, with the absence of ovaries.

TREATMENT

Treatment with female sex hormones for children with Turner's syndrome is usually quite effective at producing sexual maturation. Hormonal treatment is customarily begun between 13 and 15 years of age, when growth in height begins to slow. It should not be initiated too early, since prolonged use is associated with fusion of the growth plates of bones and limitation in achievement of normal height. Since absent or abnormal ovaries cannot produce estrogen, the hormone estrogen is given daily at low dosage for 6 months or more to start breast and genital development. After sexual development has progressed for a year or more, cyclic therapy (21 to 25 days each month) is begun, with estrogen and progesterone given to initiate menstrual cycles. This treatment is required until the normal age of menopause.

Surgery is required for congenital heart abnormalities and at times may be helpful in correcting marked webbing of the neck. If heart problems are treated promptly, life expectancy is normal.

PREVENTION

Turner's syndrome cannot be prevented. Parents who have a daughter with Turner's syndrome should seek genetic counseling to learn their risk of having another daughter similarly affected. (See discussion of genetic counseling in *genetic disorders.*)

TYPHOID FEVER

DESCRIPTION

Typhoid fever is a severe infectious disease that usually begins by attacking the large intestine and then spreads through the bloodstream to involve other organs. Once a major American health problem, typhoid fever now affects only about 500 people in the United States annually, most of them children and adolescents. Since typhoid fever is often transmitted in water contaminated by human waste, the disease appears mainly in rural areas or where regular supplies of clean water have been interrupted. The average incubation period varies from 10 to 20 days.

Bacteria lodge initially in the intestine, where an inflammatory reaction occurs leading to *diarrhea.* Diarrhea may be so mild that a patient may not recall it later. After a day or two, diarrhea usually subsides and the bacteria begin to enter the lymphatic system (a network of organs and tissue involved in fighting infection in the body), where they multiply and eventually reach the bloodstream. They find their way to distant organs, particularly the bile ducts of the liver and the gallbladder, which serve as a reservoir for the bacteria. The bacteria continually find their way back to the intestine in the bile, thereby completing the cycle. Bloodstream infection often develops quickly and can be life-threatening. Persistent *fever,* often higher than 103° F (39.4° C), is characteristic and may be accompanied by *headache, abdominal pain,* and curiously enough, *constipation* rather than diarrhea.

Typhoid fever may last 4 weeks or more, with a patient's strength returning slowly after a month or so of recuperation. Relapses can occur even after appropriate treatment but are especially common among individuals not treated with antibiotics, who begin to feel better within 2 weeks.

Even for those children treated promptly with the correct medication, typhoid fever is an uncomfortable experience that may require hospitalization for up to a month. The major long-term consideration is whether some bacteria remain in a child who has made a complete recovery. Such an individual is known as a carrier of typhoid fever.

The outlook for a child suffering from typhoid fever depends upon the child's age, health before the illness, and the number and seriousness of any complications. About 10 percent of infants not treated with antibiotics die from the illness. Among untreated older children, the fatality rate is somewhat lower. Fatalities among treated individuals are rare in the United States.

CAUSE

Typhoid fever is caused by a specific type of *Salmonella* bacteria that only affects humans. (Other types of *Salmonella,* found in contaminated food and water, cause *food poisoning* and *diarrhea.*) These bacteria are spread by human carriers, who may be completely free of any symptoms of the disease. The bacteria may be transmitted by person-to-person contact or in food or water contaminated by the stool of carriers.

SIGNS AND SYMPTOMS

Typhoid fever produces many different signs and symptoms. The same signs and symptoms may occur during infancy and childhood, but they often vary in sequence and intensity.

During infancy the disease often begins with *vomiting,* abdominal cramps, bloating, and *diarrhea.* A period of relative calm may follow, marked only by lack of appetite, *constipation,* and *fever.* Convulsions may occur if the fever rises above 103° F (39.4° C; see *seizures).* Enlarged spleen and liver may be accompanied by yellowing of the skin *(jaundice).*

Among children older than 3 years, a fever that varies from 100° to 102° F (37.8° to 38.8° C) is often accompanied by *headache,* listlessness, and abdominal cramps or pain. Diarrhea affects over half of these older children.

A second, more severe stage of illness usually comes on 5 or 6 days after the initial symptoms. As bloodstream-carried infection develops, fever rises and stays above 102° F (38.8° C). Symptoms of the first stage grow noticeably worse, and overall alertness decreases. Headache is persistent. Sleepiness and *depression* often make it difficult for a child to communicate. Rose spots, a *rash* of small red dots, can appear on the lower chest and abdomen and then fade within two or three days.

DIAGNOSIS

Positive identification of typhoid fever is sometimes difficult until stool and blood samples can be analyzed. A laboratory culture of stool can identify the specific *Salmonella* bacteria, but the finding is most often confirmed by blood cultures.

COMPLICATIONS

Bleeding, usually from the ileum (lower end of the small intestine), sometimes occurs even after medication is begun. A severely irritated and ulcerated segment of intestine may bleed and perforate. Both bleeding and perforation are accompanied by increased cramping, bloating, and pain in the abdomen.

Pneumonia occasionally develops during the second stage among older children because of the child's generally weakened condition.

In rare cases, *meningitis* (an inflammation of the brain, spinal cord, and their protective coverings, the meninges) or pericarditis (an inflammation of the sac surrounding the heart) may develop. Antibiotics are usually effective against these complications.

TREATMENT

Almost all children suspected of having typhoid fever are hospitalized for diagnosis. Treatment includes a 2- to 3-week course of antibiotics. Once antibiotic medication is started, a week may pass before fever subsides; then other signs and symptoms begin to fade. Almost all children respond to antibiotics.

A few children may recover spontaneously from mild infection without medications. Many typhoid fever victims unknowingly become carriers of the disease because their systems continue to contain the bacteria even though they suffer no symptoms. Bacteria continue to be excreted in their stools and occasionally in their urine. Carriers can be identified by stool culture; individuals identified as carriers should be particularly careful to wash their hands after defecation and urination. It is best for carriers not to work at public food service jobs.

PREVENTION

No lifelong preventive medical measure against typhoid fever now exists. However, a vaccine of moderate effectiveness can provide limited protection. Vaccine may be appropriate for a child who is exposed to a family member shown to be a long-term carrier (one without symptoms), for a child exposed to an outbreak of typhoid fever in the community or in a local institution, or for a child about to travel in a country where typhoid fever is a constant problem. Vaccination produces sore arms and muscle aches for about 2 days.

The best general prevention against any illness caused by *Salmonella* bacteria is effective sanitation, including clean drinking water, modern toilet facilities, and sanitary waste disposal. Parents should remind children to wash their hands with soap and water after using the toilet.

ULCERATIVE COLITIS

EMERGENCY ACTION

An attack of ulcerative colitis can produce *diarrhea* with mucus, pus, blood, or any combination of the three. Emergency treatment for ulcerative colitis may be necessary if severe rectal bleeding occurs or if the individual's colon is in danger of perforation. Any child who is losing bright red blood from the rectum should see a physician. Blood transfusions may be needed; if blood loss continues, surgery to correct the condition may be necessary.

In case of a severe attack, *dehydration* (a condition characterized by cool, dry, pale skin; dry mouth and tongue; thirst; listlessness; rapid pulse; sunken eyes, and for an infant, sunken fontanel—the soft spot on top of the head) must be corrected with intravenous fluids to replace essential body fluids and salts.

DESCRIPTION

Ulcerative colitis is an inflammatory disease of the colon (large intestine), which often recurs unpredictably throughout life (see Fig. 30, p. 437). It most often strikes children after the age of 10. Symptoms at the onset of ulcerative colitis vary. It may first become noticeable following viral or bacterial *diarrhea.* Occasionally a child first becomes ill with an attack of ulcerative colitis after a family has returned from a trip to a country where traveler's diarrhea (usually caused by impure water) is common. More often, however, the onset of ulcerative colitis cannot be related to other preceding illnesses or events.

The colon becomes irritated as its mucous membrane lining begins to swell and pain results from swelling and occasional spasms. Inflammation can develop producing swelling, pain, partial loss of absorptive function, and sometimes *fever.* If untreated, inflammation leads to ulceration (erosion of the mucous membrane lining and formation of tiny, open sores) of sections of the mucous membrane of the colon. Eventually some tissue in the colon wall is damaged, scarred, or destroyed.

Attacks of ulcerative colitis can produce diarrhea marked by mucus, pus, blood, or any combination of the three. A severe episode can involve hemorrhaging from an ulcerated area. Rarely, a perforation (tiny puncture) can occur where ulceration has broken through the colon wall. This condition may threaten life as a result of blood loss, contamination, peritonitis (inflammation of the lining of the abdominal cavity) caused by bacteria and microscopic food particles that have passed through the perforation.

Ulcerative colitis, which often causes weight loss, can impair growth. It sometimes produces signs or symptoms similar to those typical of *arthritis, anorexia nervosa, rheumatic fever,* or *lupus erythematosus.* Ulcerative colitis is sometimes confused with *Crohn's disease;* sometimes a disease believed at first to be ulcerative colitis is identified later as Crohn's disease.

Ulcerative colitis is an unpredictable illness; it may respond to treatment only to flare up again months or years later. The medical history of a child who suffers from ulcerative colitis is important, as treatment of the disease can be affected by how the disease began and how often—and with what degree of severity—it has recurred.

Most victims of ulcerative colitis require lifelong medical supervision. Care of inflammatory bowel disease, including ulcerative colitis, has become more effective with the development of new medications and improved nutritional techniques.

Children with ulcerative colitis run an increased risk of colon *cancer* later in life. If the disease is treated surgically, the risk of cancer is reduced. Life expectancy for individuals whose disease is successfully controlled is the same as that for children who do not have colitis.

CAUSE

The cause of ulcerative colitis is unknown. Nutritional, emotional, and allergic factors have erroneously been suggested as possible causes. No scientific evidence exists that they can give rise to ulcerative colitis, but these factors may influence the later course of the disease. Although ulcerative colitis does not seem to be genetic in origin, chronic inflammatory bowel disease in one form or another afflicts some families in several generations.

SIGNS AND SYMPTOMS

Diarrhea is the most common sign of ulcerative colitis. It may vary from alternately loose and formed bowel movements to multiple watery ones, resembling those accompanying a viral or bacterial intestinal infection. Mucus, pus, or blood, in any combination, can mark the diarrhea in flare-ups of ulcerative colitis.

Other intestinal signs may include abdominal cramping and pain, gas and bloating, and loud "growling" bowel noises from the intestinal tract. Nausea, *vomiting,* and *fever* sometimes develop. Loss of appetite, weight loss, and failure to grow occur often in children and teenagers. Among likely blood irregularities, *anemia* and loss of blood protein are the most common.

Although episodes of ulcerative colitis differ from child to child, the disease is characterized by several degrees of severity.

A minor episode may involve pain and cramps in the abdomen; diarrhea, sometimes marked by mucus, but little pus or blood; and weight loss.

A moderate episode may involve more prolonged *abdominal pain* and cramps; diarrhea, with mucus, pus, or blood and marked by urgency of bowel movements; loss of appetite; weight loss; listlessness; low fever; and anemia.

A severe episode may involve severe pain and cramping; diarrhea with blood or blood with little stool at all; a spiking fever, often reaching 103° F (38.8° C) or more; anemia; loss of appetite; weight loss; *dehydration;* and abdominal bloating. Accompanying signs may also be more severe: *joint pain* with heat and swelling (see *arthritis),* muscle wasting, swollen lymph nodes (see *swollen glands),* and a red, blisterlike *rash.*

A severe episode is a medical emergency requiring prompt hospital care. Because ulcerative colitis is so variable, few victims of the disease experience exactly the same signs and symptoms. The suddenness with which an episode may come on, however, or the emergence of new and unexpected symptoms, can be alarming to both child and parents.

DIAGNOSIS

Ulcerative colitis is diagnosed by a physician, often a pediatric gastroenterologist (a specialist in diseases of the digestive system), who takes a detailed history of the illness and performs a careful physical examination. Special attention is given to a child's abdomen and overall physical development. Blood tests and stool specimens are evaluated.

An internal examination is made of the lining of the lowest end of the intestine (sigmoid colon and rectum), using a slender, illuminated, plastic or metal instrument called a sigmoidoscope. A similar, longer, flexible instrument called a colonoscope is often used to view the interior of the entire colon. During examinations, in some cases, a physician may also take a biopsy (tiny bits of tissue) from the inner wall of the colon to determine the kind of changes that have occurred. During acute flare-ups, X-ray films of the abdomen may be helpful. Barium enema is usually reserved for later, when the acute attack has quieted down.

COMPLICATIONS

Childhood ulcerative colitis and some medications used in its treatment can interfere with growth.

Arthritis, with *joint pain,* stiffness, and swelling, which can interfere with walking and vigorous physical activities, may affect children who have ulcerative colitis. This problem usually subsides when GI tract signs and symptoms are successfully treated. Other problems include changes in the eyes, blurring of vision, *rash,* and changes in liver function.

With blood loss and sometimes *fever, dehydration* can become a problem which must be dealt with promptly.

TREATMENT

Treatment varies according to the severity of the ulcerative colitis attack, and may take place at home or in a hospital. In general the most frequently prescribed medications for chronic intestinal inflammation are sulfa drugs, corticosteroids (synthetic anti-inflammatory drugs), and several other nonsteroid anti-inflammatory agents. Diet must be nutritious, high in protein and carbohydrates, and initially low in bulk (fiber from fruits, vegetables, and nuts). Medical treatments are often tried in an effort to control the disease and to promote growth.

A minor episode of ulcerative colitis is usually treated at home with rest, proper nutrition, and medication prescribed by a physician.

A moderate episode of ulcerative colitis may be treated in a hospital with bed rest, medication, and suitable nutrition. Parenteral nutrition (intravenous feeding with a special fluid diet through a small plastic tube in the vein) is sometimes helpful in nourishing an underweight, ill child who has little appetite. The fluid contains all necessary nutrients, including vitamins.

A severe episode requires hospitalization. Intravenous fluids, blood transfusions, medication, and X-ray films of the GI tract are usually needed. If bleeding cannot be controlled, surgery may be necessary to remove all or a portion of the colon.

Removal of the entire colon is called a colectomy. It may also be necessary for the surgeon to create an ileostomy (an artificial abdominal opening). After such an operation, fecal matter is collected in a small, inconspicuous plastic or rubber pouch which is attached to the stoma (the outlet of the artificial opening). This treatment of bowel function is quite effective. Alternative methods now exist to avoid the use of an external appliance or even to preserve normal rectal function. Extensive discussions with the individual and parents are necessary before a surgical approach is chosen.

No two children with ulcerative colitis have exactly the same pattern of illness, nor is treatment identical. Working cooperatively with their physician, each child and family can usually find the right combination of care, activity, diet, and medication. Counseling may be helpful.

PREVENTION

Ulcerative colitis presently cannot be prevented. If a child develops *diarrhea* with *fever* after traveling abroad, it is wise to consult a physician.

The National Foundation for Ileitis and Colitis can provide helpful information and referrals for a family with a child who has ulcerative colitis. Chapters are located in many cities; the address of the national headquarters is 444 Park Avenue South, New York, NY 10016 (phone: 212-685-3440).

ULCERS

EMERGENCY ACTION

Call a physician or hospital emergency room if a child has any signs or symptoms of stomach or intestinal bleeding, such as bloody vomit or tarry, black stools. If the cause of bleeding is a peptic ulcer, the most serious potential complication is severe blood loss, which can lead to life-threatening problems. Severe blood loss may be signaled by *shock*, a condition characterized by cool, clammy, pale skin; weak, rapid pulse; thirst; dizziness or faintness; and increased breathing rate. Although peptic ulcers tend to bleed slowly, if at all, and rarely lead to severe blood loss, bleeding must be stopped to prevent complications.

DESCRIPTION

An ulcer is an open sore on the surface of the skin or an internal lining. The word "peptic" is used to describe anything related to digestion to food in the stomach; a peptic ulcer is an open sore inside the stomach or the first part of the small intestine. That part, called the duodenum, is connected to the stomach by a valve. The duodenum and the stomach are lined with a mucous membrane that secretes lubricating mucus and other substances important for digestion. When a sore develops on this membrane, it is usually irritated by the secretion of acid from the stomach. In most cases the exact cause for the formation of such a sore cannot be discerned.

A person of any age can get a peptic ulcer. During childhood 3 basic types of peptic ulcers are possible. The first is the acute ulcer, which appears suddenly for no apparent reason, runs its course, heals, and does not recur. The second is the secondary ulcer, which results as a complication of an underlying disease or from ingestion of substances that damage the stomach lining. Secondary ulcers also tend to run their course, heal, and not recur. The third type is the chronic ulcer, which is essentially the same as the typical adult ulcer. "Chronic" means "long-lasting or recurring"; a chronic ulcer is likely to persist or recur, especially if it is not monitored carefully by a physician.

Acute and secondary ulcers are most common among preschool children. Chronic ulcers are found among children of all ages; about 50 percent of all childhood ulcers seem to persist or recur. For reasons that are unclear, boys tend to get ulcers about one and a half times as often as girls. The total incidence of all types of ulcers among all children is difficult to estimate, however, because they have not always been diagnosed accurately.

Among children under 6, ulcers are found with equal frequency in the stomach and the duodenum. Stomach ulcers are also called gastric ulcers; "gastric" means "related to the stomach." Among children over 6, at least 80 percent of ulcers are found in the duodenum. Regardless of the location or type, 90 percent of ulcers clear up within 3 months after appropriate therapy has begun. For ulcers that persist or recur, treatment is available to reduce discomfort and minimize flare-ups.

CAUSE

Certain people seem more prone to develop ulcers than others. More than half of all people with ulcers have a family history of the problem; a person whose father has had an ulcer seems particularly susceptible. Slightly less than half of all people with chronic ulcers seem to have higher levels of anxiety and emotional and physical *stress* than other people. The incidence of acute ulcers among newborn babies, especially premature ones (see *prematurity),* is somewhat higher than that for older children.

Secondary ulcers seem to be associated with the following conditions: chronic use of alcohol or heroin (see *drug and alcohol abuse);* aspirin use; severe blood loss; severe *burns;* severe systemic infections; *cancer;* certain disorders of the central nervous system (the brain and spinal cord and their protective covering, the meninges); chronic lung disease; alkali or acid ingestions; *hypoglycemia; pyloric stenosis;* use of certain types of therapy for treating kidney disease.

The relationship between each of these conditions and the development of ulcers is unclear. Most likely, an ulcer results when something goes wrong with a small portion of the gastric or duodenal lining and when secretion of digestive substances is excessive. In general, problems with the lining seem predominant in cases of gastric ulcers, while excessive secretion of digestive chemicals seems to play a greater role in causing duodenal ulcers.

SIGNS AND SYMPTOMS

The most common signs and symptoms of peptic ulcers are pain and *vomiting,* although specific manifestations vary according to the type of ulcer and the age of the affected child.

For a child who is less than 2 years old, the predominant signs of an ulcer are likely to be vomiting, irritability, *failure to thrive,*

and tarry, black stools. Such stools are indicative of bleeding in the upper abdomen; as the blood passes through the intestinal tract, digestive chemicals change its composition and cause it to appear thick and black. Bleeding occurs when the ulceration process erodes tiny blood vessels in the affected portion of the gastric or duodenal lining, causing them to break. In some cases a child vomits blood in addition to passing it out of the body through stools. In rare cases ingesting a toxic substance perforates the entire wall of the stomach or duodenum in addition to producing ulceration. Severe bleeding occurs, and bloody *diarrhea* may result, because large amounts of blood in the intestines stimulate frequent bowel movements.

A child who develops an acute or secondary ulcer between the ages of 2 and 6 is also likely to vomit, and the ulcer is likely to bleed. In some cases a child of this age complains of pain in the abdomen.

For children 6 years old and up, pain is usually the predominant symptom of any type of ulcer, and bleeding and vomiting are far less common than among younger children. A typical ulcer for a child of this age group is not painful all the time. Instead, an affected child has several attacks of pain per day. In about half of all ulcer cases affecting children—especially those involving chronic ulcers—the child feels a burning or gnawing sensation in the mid-stomach area. The pain most typically develops 2 to 3 hours after meals, is relieved by food, and can awake the child in the middle of the night. In the other cases pain is atypical; the child may complain, for example, that his or her navel hurts. Food may relieve pain, or it may provoke vomiting, thereby aggravating discomfort. Bleeding occurs in about a quarter of all cases of chronic ulcers.

DIAGNOSIS

A child who has any signs of internal bleeding should be seen at once by a physician to prevent possible complications from severe blood loss. Although a nonbleeding ulcer does not require emergency action, a child who seems to have such a condition should receive medical attention promptly.

The goal of a physician diagnosing an ulcer is to rule out other causes of signs and symptoms, pinpoint the location of the sore, and identify any precipitating factors. Conditions that must be ruled out include inflammation of the lower part of the esophagus, the tube that carries food into the stomach; inflammation of the pancreas, a gland located in back of the stomach; disease of the gallbladder, an organ located near the duodenum; *Crohn's disease;* and other causes of stomachache and stomach pain (see *stomachache, stomach pain*). A physician performs a complete physical examination, including chemical testing of stools for blood. A detailed accounting of signs and symptoms by the child and his or her parents is also important.

The location of an ulcer can be pinpointed in 1 of 2 ways. The first is called a barium study. The child drinks a sweet-tasting liquid containing barium, which illuminates the upper gastrointestinal tract (esophagus, stomach, and duodenum) for X-ray studies. In 80 percent of ulcer cases, the sore shows up on X-ray film.

If a barium study fails to illuminate the ulcer, the physician may use a technique called endoscopy. And endoscope is a thin hollow tube which can be inserted easily from the mouth to the stomach or duodenum. The physician looks through the tube to get a direct view of those areas. Endoscopy, which is performed after the child's throat is sprayed with a mild anesthetic, is not painful, but it can be uncomfortable. It often reveals the location of an ulcer and any complicating conditions. Endoscopy can also be helpful in revealing the cause of the ulcer; drug-induced ulcers, for example, tend to be less inflamed than others.

In an attempt to discern a precipitating factor in an ulcer case, a physician performs blood tests to measure the level of the hormone gastrin that stimulates secretion of gastric acid. The physician also considers any family history of ulcers.

COMPLICATIONS

Severe internal bleeding can be life-threatening, but it is rarely a complication. More often, sporadic bleeding from an ulcer leads to iron-deficiency anemia (see *anemia, nutritional*). This complication seems to be relatively common among children with chronic ulcers, perhaps because they are not diagnosed early enough. Late diagnosis may be a consequence of a misconception that "children don't get ulcers." For those children who live with undiagnosed chronic ulcers, pain can interfere with routine activities. Similarly, misunderstanding on the part of other people an lead to emotional difficulties and problems with social relationships.

TREATMENT

In an emergency, an ice-cold saltwater solution is administered via a tube in the stomach by a physician in a hospital emergency room to slow blood flow and give broken blood vessels time to heal. If necessary, a child is given a special hormone to control bleeding, or in serious cases, surgery is performed. Gastric secretions may be suctioned from the stomach or duodenum to minimize irritation. In addition, transfusions of blood and essential body fluids and salts are administered to prevent *shock* and *dehydration.*

Most cases do not involve emergencies. The goal of treatment is to relieve pain, promote healing of the sore, and prevent new ulcers from appearing. In almost all cases the treatment program involves administration of antacids, substances that neutralize the acidity of stomach and duodenal secretions. Antacids are used because reducing gastrointestinal acid seems to promote healing of ulcers and because antacids seem to prevent some ulcers from forming. Their only drawback is that they sometimes promote *diarrhea,* but then a physician can recommend another form of antacid. In most cases any pain or *vomiting* is minimized soon after antacid therapy begins, although healing may take months.

Diet generally seems to have little effect on an ulcer, although ulcers can be irritated by drinks that contain caffeine—coffee, tea, and colas—as well as alcohol and spicy foods. Parents should make sure that the child maintains adequate nutrition while avoiding foods and drinks that aggravate the ulcer. Most doctors advise against eating at bedtime; eating promotes increased gastric-acid secretion, which 2 or 3 hours later can lead to pain that interferes with sleep.

In addition to antacids, some physicians prescribe a medication that prevents gastric-acid secretion instead of simply neutralizing it. Another medication is available that coats the surface of the ulcer, protecting it from digestive substances and permitting it to heal.

PREVENTION

If a child has a recurring ulcer, a physician usually recommends antacids for several months after an ulcer heals—in some cases for as long as a year.

Some types of secondary ulcers can be prevented. Parents can give their children other pain- and fever-reducing medication instead of aspirin or aspirin-containing products. See discussion of nonprescription medications on p. 102. In addition, all toxic drugs and chemicals should be kept out of reach of young children. For information about childproofing, see Chapter 4, "Accident Prevention."

UNDESCENDED TESTICLES

DESCRIPTION

The male reproductive glands, called the testicles, form early in the development of the fetus. During normal development they remain high in the fetus's abdominal cavity until the thirty-second to thirty-sixth week of pregnancy and then descend into the scrotum. A testicle that does not reach the scrotum is known as an undescended testicle.

In about 20 percent of male premature births (see *prematurity)*, the testicles have not yet descended. This condition generally corrects itself as the infant develops. In about 98 percent of full-term baby boys, the process of descent has been completed by the time of birth; in nearly all cases the testicles have descended by the baby's first birthday. Only about 0.6 percent of boys older than a year still have a testicle that has not descended into the scrotum. After that age descent is unlikely to occur naturally.

Some undescended testicles remain high in the abdominal cavity; others have progressed downward but have stopped short of the scrotum. Rarely, a testicle lodges in the upper thigh. In about three fourths of cases, only one testicle is undescended, and the right testicle is involved more often than the left. The affected testicle is generally smaller than the normal testicle.

Sometimes a testicle will reach the scrotum but may retract periodically toward or into the abdominal cavity. This condition is known as a retractile testicle and is not an undescended testicle. It follows an active reflex of protecting the testicles.

CAUSE

The cause of undescended testicles is not understood completely. Some researchers suspect that a mechanical blockage is responsible. Other researchers theorize that delayed or abnormal hormonal production by the affected testicle could cause failure to descend. Neither theory is proven; in addition, there may be other, as yet undetermined, causes.

SIGNS AND SYMPTOMS

If only one testicle is felt (or no testicles are felt) in the scrotal sac, then the baby has an undescended testicle (or testicles).

DIAGNOSIS

Examination to establish the location of the testicles is a routine part of the complete physical checkup of the infant and child. An undescended testicle can be felt in the groin but cannot be pushed or pulled down into the scrotum. It addition, it does not descend spontaneously into the scrotum when the boy is in a warm bath or when he is placed in a squatting position.

COMPLICATIONS

It is important for parents to recognize the risks involved if undescended testicles are not corrected at the appropriate time (usually when the boy is around 1 to 2 years old). The farther the undescended testicle is from the scrotum, the greater the likelihood that the higher temperature in the abdominal cavity will eventually cause abnormal or incomplete development of the testicle, with consequent failure of sperm production. In most cases the testicle that remains in the abdominal cavity after puberty will not produce sperm even if brought down by surgery at that time. Usually one undescended testicle will not affect the child's development or reproductive capacity. If both testicles remain in the abdominal cavity after puberty, sterility is likely, with or without surgery.

TREATMENT

For a retractile testicle, no treatment is necessary.

When surgery is necessary to free an undescended testicle, it is nearly always successful. The timing of surgery depends in large part upon the boy's physical and psychological development, but the preferred age is around 1 to 2 years, whether one or both testicles are involved.

PREVENTION

Undescended testicles cannot be prevented.

Urinary Tract Defects and Obstruction

DESCRIPTION

The urinary tract is the system that produces urine and conducts it to the outside of the body. Tubes called ureters conduct urine from its production sites in the kidneys to the bladder, where it is stored until it passes out of the body via a tube called the urethra. When any urinary tract structure is not properly formed at birth (congenital abnormality), the production or flow of urine can be impaired, possibly damaging the system.

Urinary tract defects range in severity from undetectable to life-threatening. The majority of defects are serious—requiring surgery—but at least correctable. Other urinary tract defects do not cause problems with internal functioning but are cosmetically unattractive or prevent the achievement of bladder control. It is difficult to estimate the incidence of urinary tract defects because so many different types are possible.

The main complication of most urinary tract defects occurs when the flow of urine from its production site in the kidneys to the outside of the body is partially or totally blocked, creating a urinary tract obstruction. When the normal flow of urine is blocked, urine can stagnate in the urinary tract or back up into the upper structures of the tract (see *urinary tract infections*). The structures above the obstruction can swell beyond their normal range, causing permanent damage. The greatest danger when a child has a urinary tract obstruction is permanent damage to the kidneys, with resulting kidney failure (see *kidney failure, acute; kidney failure, chronic*).

Obstruction is a relatively uncommon urinary tract problem. In general, more males than females are affected. Most often, obstruction occurs in girls at a junction between the kidney and ureter or ureter and bladder; in boys, between the bladder and

FIG. 37. URINARY TRACT

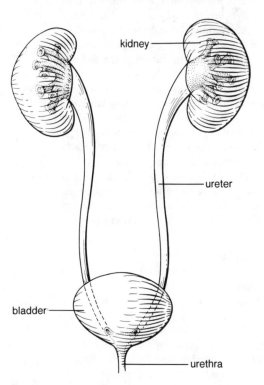

kidney

ureter

bladder

urethra

FIG. 38. URINARY TRACT (position of)

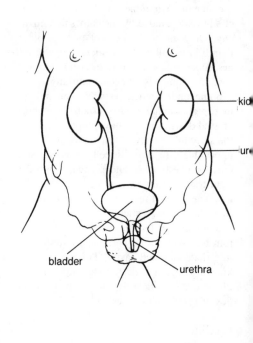

kid

ur

bladder

urethra

the end of the penis. Obstructions in the upper portion of the urinary tract tend to affect the left side more often than the right.

Whenever obstruction interferes with the function of the urinary tract, surgery—minor or major, depending on the case—is necessary to prevent complications. The most common complications, urinary tract infection and kidney stones (tiny lumps of crystallized salts and minerals), are both related to stagnation of large volumes of urine in the urinary tract. The incidence of the most serious complications, kidney damage and potential loss of kidney function, varies according to the completeness and duration of urinary tract obstruction. In general, the longer obstruction is present, the greater the chance of permanent impairment of kidney function.

When urinary tract obstruction is caused by a congenital structural abnormality, it is essential that surgical correction of the defect take place during infancy. When a child is less than 1 year old, the prospects are excellent that surgery will prevent long-term complications. If surgery is not performed until a child is 2 or 3, it is likely that kidney damage and loss of kidney function has already occurred. In most cases, however, prompt treatment at this time will minimize the long-term effect of the obstruction.

Other urinary tract defects generally involve absence or duplication of one or more structures. They can also involve improper placement of urinary tract structures or abnormal openings in the structures. The 2 most common such problems are exstrophy (a defect involving the bladder, abdominal wall, umbilical cord, pubic area, genitalia, or intestines) and epispadias (a defect of the penis and urethra).

Cloacal Exstrophy

Cloacal exstrophy is a defect in development of the lower abdominal wall structures. (The cloaca is the part of an embryo that eventually develops into these structures.) A child with cloacal exstrophy is born with many inner-abdomen structures exposed. A portion of the large intestine lies outside of the body, and on either side of it are the two halves of the bladder. In males the penis is usually flat and short; in females, the clitoris is split. The incidence of this devastating condition is only about 1 out of every 200,000 live births.

Despite the severity of cloacal exstrophy, most babies born with the defect survive. The bladder can be surgically reconstructed. The lower colon and rectum are deficient so that surgery is performed to bring the fecal material into a small, disposable bag outside the body.

Bladder Exstrophy

Bladder exstrophy is a congenital urinary tract defect characterized by exposure of the bladder outside of the body. It affects about 1 out of every 25,000 children. About twice as many boys as girls have this defect.

In all cases of bladder exstrophy, the external genitalia are unusual. Among boys, epispadias (see below) exists. About 40 percent of all boys with bladder exstrophy have *undescended testicles.* In addition, the penis tends to be short and flat. The penis is likely to be broader than normal, attached in an unusual way to the pubic area, and angled upward.

Among girls, the clitoris tends to be split, the labia (protective folds of skin around the vaginal and urethral openings) may be widely separated, and the vaginal opening is often exceedingly small or nonexistent. Most girls with these abnormalities are capable of becoming pregnant, and vaginal delivery of a baby may be possible.

For both boys and girls, bladder exstrophy is usually associated with positioning of the anus and rectum too close to the front of the body. *Rectal prolapse,* a condition in which the lining of the rectum tends to slip in and out of the anus, can result. Other associated defects include a low-set navel and absence of the cartilaginous connection between the two pubic bones. The latter problem does not affect the way children tend to walk.

Advanced surgical techniques allow for relatively safe treatment of most cases of bladder exstrophy.

Epispadias

Epispadias is a defect of the urethra characterized by an abnormal urethral opening. Among boys, epispadias involves an abnormal opening on the upper side of the penis, where it meets the body wall. Among girls, the abnormal opening is in the correct location, but the urethra is wide open. Epispadias is commonly associated with bladder exstrophy. As an isolated defect, its incidence is about 1 in 95,000. Males are affected 4 times as often as females.

CAUSE

Most children who develop obstructions are born with a structural abnormality of the urinary tract. Such abnormalities include unusual growths in the tract, such as folds in the urethra or sacs in the bladder, and malfunctioning structures, such as a segment of ureter that fails to propel urine into the bladder. The urethra can also become obstructed if a child pushes an object into the opening or suffers a pelvic fracture or straddle injury.

Defects of the urinary tract are caused by unusual or arrested development of structures during the early stages of embryologic development (the first 6 weeks after conception). The exact mechanism that produces urinary tract defects remains unclear. It appears, however, that certain environmental conditions are likely to impede embryologic development. For example, the incidence of structural defects is significantly higher among mothers who abuse drugs (see *drug abuse and alcohol).*

Kidney stones, which can occur as a result of urinary tract obstruction, also arise from other causes. However formed, they can create obstructions if they lodge in the urinary tract.

SIGNS AND SYMPTOMS

Urinary tract defects—even certain external ones—are not immediately evident to most obstetricians or pediatricians. The baby's physician consults a urologist, a specialist in disorders of the male and female urinary tract as well as the male genital system.

When a child is born with an upper urinary tract obstruction, the most common sign is an abdominal mass. A physician can detect such a mass during a routine newborn examination. More rare signs and symptoms during infancy include those associated with related *bloodstream infection* or *failure to thrive.*

During later childhood it is common for obstruction to cause urinary tract infection; signs and symptoms may include *blood in the urine, abdominal pain,* difficulty urinating, or other voiding disturbances. There may also be signs of vesicoureteral reflux, including lack of bladder control, vague *back pain,* and high *fever.* In rare cases a child with urinary tract obstruction feels nauseated, vomits, and complains of *headache,* perhaps because of associated high blood pressure *(hypertension).*

DIAGNOSIS

A urologist can often make a preliminary diagnosis of a urinary tract defect after physical examination of the baby. A more specific diagnosis can be achieved through imaging techniques (such as special types of X-ray films and ultrasound), endoscopy (direct observation of internal structures through a special lighted tube), or surgery.

If a physician suspects that a child has a urinary tract obstruction, he or she refers the child to a urologist. A urologist attempts to get a good picture of the obstruction, largely through X ray or ultrasound. Often a urologist orders an IVP (intravenous pyelogram), a special X-ray procedure that involves injecting a substance into a vein and taking special pictures of the urinary tract as the child excretes the substance. In addition, a urologist may order blood tests to check the function of the kidneys. Cystoscopy, which involves passing a small lighted tube into the urinary tract via the urethra using general anesthetic, is also used as a method of diagnosing obstruction. Using this tube, a urologist can sometimes view an area of obstruction directly.

COMPLICATIONS

Children with urinary tract defects are at high risk for all disorders of the urinary tract, including urinary tract infection, urinary tract obstruction, and vesicoureteral reflux. This last problem, if left untreated, can lead to hydronephrosis—dilation (stretching) of kidney structures (see *nephrosis)*—and eventually chronic kidney failure (see *kidney failure, chronic).*

A urinary tract obstruction can be complicated by infection and kidney stones. Infection is difficult to control, as a stagnant pool of urine is such an excellent breeding ground for bacteria. In addition, medication may have difficulty reaching the tract because of decreased kidney function. If a kidney stone forms, it can aggravate the existing blockage of the urinary tract and increase the possibility of kidney damage.

TREATMENT

The goals of treatment for a child with a urinary tract defect are to correct or prevent obstruction of the tract, achieve adequate function of as many structures as possible, and modify at least the most severe cosmetic abnormalities. Almost all urinary tract defects eventually require surgery.

The type of surgery necessary to relieve a urinary tract obstruction depends on the nature of the problem and the presence of any complications. In most cases it is possible to stretch a constricted area of the urinary tract in a relatively simple surgical procedure that involves insertion of tubes into the tract through the urethra. In other cases kidney stones must be surgically removed. In the most severe instances—when kidneys are irreparably damaged—kidney dialysis or transplantation become necessary (see *kidney failure, chronic*).

Alteration of the system may be necessary. For example, bladder exstrophy may necessitate removal of the bladder and diversion of the ureters into the large intestine.

Correction of epispadias involves surgical closure of the abnormal opening and cosmetic repair of the penis. When epispadias is severe, a child is likely to be incontinent (unable to control the bladder), regardless of the success of an operation. Most cases of epispadias, however, can be markedly improved through surgery, and a child can be helped to live with any remaining cosmetic defects. In still other instances, the altered urinary tract will end at an artificial opening on the outside of the body, which may or may not require a urine-collecting device.

With advanced surgical techniques available, most pediatric urologists elect to try repairing a urinary tract defect as soon as possible after an affected child's birth. Almost all children born with urinary tract defects can be helped significantly by surgery.

All children born with urinary tract defects need help in dealing with the emotional aspects of their disabilities. A sensitive urologist can help provide support and recommend other health professionals and further resources, if needed.

PREVENTION

Most cases of urinary tract obstruction cannot be prevented. Only rarely, as when a child has a tendency to form kidney stones, can a potential problem of urinary tract obstruction sometimes be avoided.

Urinary tract defects cannot be prevented.

URINARY TRACT INFECTIONS

DESCRIPTION

Urinary tract infections (UTIs) occur when bacteria multiply to an excessive degree in all or part of the body's liquid waste system: the urethra, the canal which transports urine from the bladder out of the body; the bladder, which stores urine for excretion; the ureters, which carry urine from the kidneys to the bladder; and the kidneys, which extract liquid wastes from the bloodstream. The most common type of infection is cystitis (inflammation of the bladder). Infection that reaches the kidneys is called pyelonephritis (see *nephritis*). Cystitis is less severe than pyelonephritis, which produces very painful symptoms and can cause permanent kidney damage.

UTIs occur in approximately 1 to 2 percent of infants. Among infant males UTIs are often associated with urologic abnormalities. Beyond the newborn period UTIs occur more often in females, and usually result from contamination of the urinary tract. UTIs are rare among boys and young men; young women acquire them more often. UTIs recur often: among one third of females UTIs recur within a year of the first infection, and may require treatment for a number of years. Untreated infections may lead to serious physical or functional abnormalities of the body's liquid waste system, eventually requiring surgery.

UTIs can be associated with other urologic disorders and defects, such as vesicoureteral reflux. They are sometimes linked with metabolic disorders, such as *malnutrition* or *diabetes*.

Vesicoureteral reflux is a condition characterized by urine backing up from the bladder into one or both ureters and sometimes into the kidneys, instead of passing out of the body. This retention of urine causes pressure and stretching of the urinary structures and connections. Reflux, or reverse flow, can result from a physical abnormality somewhere in the urinary system—particularly the ureters—or from a UTI. Vesicoureteral reflux occurs in 30 to 70 percent of children with recurrent UTIs; the condition is 5 times more common among females than among males, affects more children than adults, and seems to run in families.

Vesicoureteral reflux can be present at birth or develop later for a variety of reasons (see *urinary tract defects*). It can also result from surgical injury or the presence of a foreign body in the urinary system. The degree of reflux varies greatly; the more severe the degree of reflux, the more likely the chances of kidney damage. Generally, however, reflux that occurs without accompanying infection usually does not cause kidney damage.

While vesicoureteral reflux is more severe during infancy then during childhood, it often disappears as the ureters mature or infection is controlled. Spontaneous disappearance of reflux is very common before age 5, and prior to adolescence nearly 70 percent of cases of persistent reflux resolve without treatment.

CAUSE

Bacteria are normally present in the urethra and sometimes in the bladder. Ordinarily, most bacteria are washed away by urination and do not have an opportunity to multiply in the urinary tract. Should they multiply, however, an infection can result.

In addition to physical abnormalities (see *urinary tract defects*), conditions that may cause a UTI during infancy and childhood include incomplete drainage of the urinary system, frequent *constipation,* and *malnutrition.* Girls are more susceptible to UTIs because the urethra is much shorter in the female body than in the male body and allows migration of bacteria to the bladder. Also, the female urethral opening is close to the vagina and rectum, where infectious organisms may be present. Contamination by these bacteria is the most common cause of a UTI among girls.

Among young women conditions that contribute to a UTI include irritation and swelling of the urethra or bladder as a result of sexual intercourse, pregnancy, or irritants such as bubble baths. Although UTIs are neither contagious nor sexually transmitted, sexual activity is a common cause in young women, particularly when they have become sexually active for the first time, acquired a new partner, or recently resumed activity.

Vesicoureteral reflux may be inherited. It may also be caused by a variety of physical abnormalities and blockages in the urinary system (see *urinary tract defects*). UTIs can also cause reflux, just as the reflux itself can cause a UTI.

SIGNS AND SYMPTOMS

A UTI may be present with no symptoms at all, with symptoms that direct attention to the urinary system, or with symptoms that suggest disorders in other organ systems.

Among infants, symptoms usually do not involve the urinary tract, and may include feeding difficulties, *jaundice, fever, vomiting, diarrhea,* lethargy, and irritability. Specific urinary symptoms may easily be overlooked.

Among older children, symptoms include painful urination, urinary frequency or urgency, burning with urination, foul-smelling urine, pain in the abdomen or back, and *bedwetting.* UTIs may be present without signs or symptoms, particularly among children over 5 years old or children with recurrent urinary tract infections.

Signs and symptoms of vesicoureteral reflux may range from no symptoms at all to complete lack of bladder control. During infancy a difference in kidney size is often a sign of reflux. Since some degree of reflux may be revealed when children are examined for UTIs, signs and symptoms may be similar. A high fever and abdominal or back pain may also be present.

Because it is not unusual for vesicoureteral reflux to remain unnoticed for a long time, extensive kidney damage may occur before symptoms appear.

DIAGNOSIS

Analysis and culture of the urine are necessary to diagnose A UTI. A physician can check the specimen under the microscope for the presence of bacteria or white cells (indicating infection); the specimen also can be sent to a laboratory, where the bacteria can be cultured so that the number and type of contaminating organisms can be identified. Although the urinalysis may suggest infection, cultures are helpful for accurate diagnosis and treatment.

Since recurrent UTIs in infants occasionally signal a physical abnormality, X-ray films may be taken to identify the problem (see *urinary tract defects*).

Vesicoureteral reflux is usually detected when a child is examined because of a suspected UTI. Positive diagnosis is based on the result of a voiding cystourethrogram, a special urinary tract X ray that shows bladder function.

Reflux and other urinary problems can be diagnosed through a variety of techniques, including ultrasound, CT (computed tomography) scan, and nuclear medicine. Cystoscopy—a direct visual examination of the urinary tract using an instrument called a cystoscope—may also be necessary.

Since this condition often runs in families, brothers and sisters of children with vesicoureteral reflux should be checked.

COMPLICATIONS

Obstruction in one part of the urinary system strains other parts, increasing the risk of organ damage. Because the increasing pressure of retained urine stretches the kidneys, vesicoureteral reflux can lead to long-term kidney disease (see *kidney failure, chronic*).

TREATMENT

Treatment of a UTI is intended to eliminate infection, correct physical abnormalities, and prevent recurrences. Elimination of infection requires the use of an appropriate drug, usually an antibiotic prescribed by a physician. Among patients with symptoms of acute infections, treatment may begin before results of a urine culture are available. A second culture may be obtained to confirm the effectiveness of antibiotics. Even though symptoms may disappear in a day or two, it is important to complete the full course of medication prescribed because it may take that long to eliminate all infecting organisms. If the infection recurs, a new culture is necessary, and the results may suggest that a different drug is needed.

In addition to taking antibiotics, a child should drink plenty of fluids to increase urination. When taking some drugs, the urine should be kept highly acidic, so a physician may advise drinking cranberry juice or other fluids containing vitamin C.

Treatment of vesicoureteral reflux depends on a child's age at onset, duration of the problem, and the number and severity of UTIs the child has had. Nearly all children with vesicoureteral reflux recover fully without complications. Children with mild cases usually do not require surgery; they are treated with antibiotics to prevent infection. A physician usually asks that the child return for a follow-up visit every 2 months to check the progress of the reflux.

Surgery is required to correct vesicoureteral reflux if UTIs recur despite antibiotic treatment, if reflux is quite severe, if kidney growth does not occur, or if reflux persists after the child reaches puberty. Approximately 10 to 30 percent of children develop UTIs after surgical correction of vesicoureteral reflux; this problem occurs more often among girls than boys.

PREVENTION

Recurrent UTIs can be prevented by maintaining a high fluid intake every day (6 or more 8-ounce glasses of water) and urinating frequently. A daily glass of cranberry juice may help ward off infection. Girls should keep the genital area clean by using mild soap and water, and, after urinating, wiping from front to back to prevent contamination of the urethra from the vagina or rectum. Sexually active young women often find it helpful to empty their bladders before and after intercourse.

Vesicoureteral reflux cannot be prevented.

VAGINAL BLEEDING

DESCRIPTION

Bleeding from the vagina (birth canal) is normal for adolescent and adult women during menstruation. Newborn baby girls sometimes bleed slightly from the vagina as a result of withdrawal from the influence of the hormone estrogen in their mother's bodies. Any bleeding—no matter how slight in intensity or brief in duration—from the vagina after 3 weeks of age and before a girl is well into her pubertal development is abnormal. Puberty in females is signaled by a growth spurt, broadening of the hips, development of underarm and pubic hair, and breast budding. Vaginal bleeding in childhood can be a sign of the presence of a foreign object in the vagina, a tumor, trauma (injury), or an infection. For a discussion of abnormal vaginal bleeding among adolescent females, see *menstrual irregularities.*

The outlook in any case of vaginal bleeding depends upon the cause.

CAUSE

Causes of vaginal bleeding in young girls include vaginitis (inflammation of the vulva and vagina, usually resulting in a discharge of infectious pus that may be blood-tinged; see *vaginitis and vaginal discharge*), pinworms (see *parasitic infections*), and the presence of foreign objects (such as toilet paper, pins, buttons, crayons, or wads of paper). Less common causes include abnormal blood conditions, *polyps* (growths that protrude from the cervix), noncancerous tumors made up of blood vessels, and other benign and cancerous tumors (see *DES exposure*). Urethral prolapse (protrusion of urethral tissue through the urethral opening) may also cause a bloody discharge. The urethra is the canal through which urine is discharged from the bladder. In rare cases a girl may have precocious puberty (onset of puberty before the age of 8). A girl's vulva may be injured on bicycles or playground equipment, and tissue damage may cause vaginal bleeding. Injury to the vagina (sometimes caused by sexual molestation or rape) can cause bleeding (see *child abuse*).

See also *gonorrhea; menstrual irregularities; syphilis.*

DIAGNOSIS

If a girl says nothing about abnormal bleeding, a parent may not become aware of it until blood is noticed on her underpants. A foreign body in the vagina causes a foul odor. A physician should be consulted promptly.

The first step in diagnosing the cause of vaginal bleeding is a physical examination, including a general checkup and a gynecological assessment. If sexual molestation is suspected, tests will be performed for *syphilis* and *gonorrhea* and for the presence of sperm. In addition, a physician considers a girl's growth patterns, development, and medical history. A family history (particularly the reproductive history of female members) may be requested in some cases. If a child has urethral prolapse, she may be referred to a urologist or pediatric surgeon.

TREATMENT AND PREVENTION

Abnormal bleeding undoubtedly will have alarmed a young girl; the first general step in treatment should be an explanation of the cause in terms understandable to the child, with time given to listen to and reply to her concerns. Specific treatment depends upon the source of the bleeding:

- Presence of a foreign object. Treatment begins with removal of the foreign body from the vagina. The girl should be asked how the object got into her vagina in order to rule out sexual abuse. If she has a history of putting objects in her vagina, professional counseling might be advised.
- Urethral prolapse. Treatment begins with observation. Surgical correction may be needed. Some mild cases may be corrected through warm baths and time.
- Precocious puberty. Depending upon the age of the child, hormone therapy may be recommended in an effort to delay further development until a more normal age.
- Tumors and *polyps* (very rare). Treatment consists of surgical intervention and referral to a children's cancer service for malignant tumors.
- Injuries to the vulva and vagina. Surgical repair may be needed. If injury is a result of sexual molestation, the child should receive professional counseling and should receive education in how to know what is "good and bad touching."

For treatment and prevention of pinworms see *parasitic infections.* See also *vaginitis and vaginal discharge.*

In addition, a young female should be taught to be aware of her body and its structure and functions and should be made familiar with proper hygiene methods.

VAGINITIS AND VAGINAL DISCHARGE

DESCRIPTION AND SIGNS AND SYMPTOMS

In females, the external genital region (called the vulva) and the vagina (the canal leading from the vulva to the uterus) are vulnerable to irritation, inflammation, and infection. Vulvovaginal problems are common among girls of all ages, although underlying causes tend to differ between younger and older age groups.

Normal Vaginal Discharge

All females have vaginal discharges; some types of discharge are normal. The vagina is kept moist and lubricated continuously by a mixture of mucus secreted by glands in the cervix (the narrow, lower end of the uterus), vaginal cells, and normal vaginal bacteria. This mixture forms a clear, whitish, odorless, normal discharge called leukorrhea in adolescents and newborns. This discharge causes no itching, burning, or other irritation.

As a result of certain types of stimulation, normal discharge can become temporarily heavier. During the first 1 to 3 weeks of life, for example, stimulation of an infant's vagina by high maternal levels of the hormone estrogen causes a discharge. After puberty, but before menarche (the onset of menstruation), estrogen levels are again high and a girl may begin to notice a vaginal discharge, which may continue for several years after menarche. By the time her menstrual cycles become regular, she may notice that certain situations cause the amount of discharge to increase. *Stress,* pregnancy, sexual excitement, and the use of oral contraceptives may stimulate increased production of normal vaginal discharge. In addition, use if IUDs (intrauterine devices used for birth control) may increase the amount of cervical mucus. When ovulation (release of an egg from an ovary) occurs, mucus from the cervix becomes very watery and elastic and may be noticed as a wet sensation by the adolescent.

Abnormal Vaginal Discharge

Vaginitis is an infection of the vagina. A girl may have symptoms of pain, itching, a burning sensation of the vulva, and/or an abnormal discharge, which can be yellow or white, watery or thick, and may smell unpleasant.

CAUSE

Prepubertal Girls

Before puberty, girls are susceptible to vulvovaginal problems in part because the mucous membranes of their vaginas are thin and undeveloped compared with postpubertal (after puberty) mucous membranes.

Generally the most common cause of vulvovaginitis among prepubertal (before puberty) girls is poor hygiene. Specifically, bathing and toilet habits are often inadequate. Because the vagina is close to the anus, young girls who wipe from back to front after bowel movements may spread bacteria from the rectal area to the vagina. As a result, organisms that normally live harmlessly in the intestines may cause vaginitis. One type of organism *(Monilia)* occasionally produces a form of vaginitis commonly called a <u>yeast infection</u>; yeast infections are most common among girls who have *diabetes* or who have been taking antibiotics, both of which can change the vaginal environment. If the girl—or a parent or a sibling—has an upper respiratory tract infection with streptococci or other bacteria, the bacteria may be spread to the vagina, perhaps through hand contact. Other organisms that may cause vaginitis can be transmitted through sexual contact.

Gonorrhea (and other sexually transmitted infections) may be contracted by a prepubertal girl; transmission may involve sexual abuse by a family member (adult or sibling), baby-sitter, playmate, or other person known to the child (see *child abuse).*

Inflammation of the vulva can be caused (or aggravated) by many factors other than infection (see Prevention, below.) Very young, curious children sometimes place foreign objects, such as pins, crayons, buttons, or wads of paper, in body openings; in the vagina, such objects can cause vaginitis. The vulva and vagina may become irritated when a child sits on sand (in a sandbox or on the beach, for example) or on the ground.

Pinworms (which can grow in a child's rectum) are common among young children, and scratching of the anus can easily contaminate the vaginal area. In rare cases, a worm actually crawls into a child's vagina (see *parasitic infections).*

In rare instances a tumor develops in the vagina and sometimes causes vaginal discharge. Frequent masturbation or scratching may cause irritation and redness of the vulva.

An abnormal vaginal discharge sometimes appears when a girl has an infection such as *measles, scarlet fever,* or *chicken pox.* An abscess within the pelvis rarely causes a discharge containing pus. An uncommon disorder called <u>precocious puberty</u> (onset of puberty before the age of 8) triggers estrogen production, resulting in a vaginal discharge that is normal in appearance but abnormal for such a young child.

Adolescent Girls

The vaginal environment can be changed not only by antibiotics and diabetes but by oral contraceptives, pregnancy, treatment with hormones, and douching (the use of liquid to flush out the vagina, in theory to cleanse it). These changes can cause certain organisms normally present in the vagina to multiply, leading to an imbalance of vaginal organisms and infection.

General signs of vaginitis among adolescents are inflammation of the vulva, vaginal discharge, and painful (or frequent) urination, sometimes accompanied by intense itching. A young woman may find sexual intercourse painful. Sometimes, however, certain infections cause no symptoms at all.

Specific signs among adolescents vary depending upon the source of infection. The discharge can be whitish, yellow-green, or gray. It can be heavy or light and the consistency may be watery, bubbly, or thick (like cottage cheese). The discharge may be foul-smelling, sweet-smelling, or odorless. It may or may not contain pus or blood.

Among adolescents, causes of vaginitis are usually specific. Yeast infections (mentioned above), which are itchy, are common among adolescents, both virginal and sexually active. If a female's sex partner is diabetic, is using antibiotics, or has a persistent yeast infection, a yeast infection may be sexually transmitted to the girl. Douching equipment can become unclean if used when a girl has a yeast infection; if the equipment is reused, the infection can recur.

Another common type of vaginitis involves a parasite *(Trichomonas)* that is usually transmitted through sexual relations, but may also be spread on wet towels, washcloths, and bathing suits. *Trichomonas* infections cause itching and sometimes a foul odor. Other organisms spread through sexual relations that may cause vulvar and cervical inflammation are herpes (herpes simplex virus type 2 or, sometimes, herpes simplex virus type 1—see *genital herpes)* and *gonorrhea* (which may cause inflammation of the cervix with vaginal discharge). Another bacteria, *Gardnerella vaginalis,* may combine with other types of bacteria, causing a foul odor and scant discharge.

Inflammation and infection of the cervix by *Chlamydia* and gonorrhea organisms also may cause a vaginal discharge.

Vaginal discharge during adolescence may also be caused by a foreign object in the vagina, such as a forgotten tampon or diaphragm; cuts or abrasions in the vagina; and exposure to DES before birth (see *DES exposure).* (See also Prevention, below.)

DIAGNOSIS

Diagnosis of vulvovaginitis is made by a physician, who takes a medical history and performs a physical examination.

If the girl is prepubertal, she (or her parent) is asked about the appearance, amount, and duration of any discharge; any itching of the anus, vulva, or vagina; any *bed-wetting* episodes; any recent infections that the girl, a sibling, or a parent has had; her hygiene practices (including her method of wiping after a bowel movement); and any use of bubble baths or medications.

A careful physical examination includes a general assessment plus a gynecologic assessment of the vulva and vagina. If a discharge appears to contain pus, a specimen is taken from the vagina for analysis. Because the majority of vaginitis cases among prepubertal girls are caused by poor hygiene, a physician may recommend improved hygiene measures before taking specimens. If the condition persists, then a specimen is taken.

If the girl is postpubertal, she is asked about her symptoms, the appearance of any discharge, any recent or long-term infections, use of medications (particularly antibiotics and oral contraceptives), recent sexual activity, and whether or not she was exposed to DES before birth.

She may need to have a pelvic exam (in which the vulva, vagina, cervix, uterus, and ovaries are checked) while the procedure is explained to her. In the case of a young adolescent the physician may take a specimen of the vaginal discharge to look for the infectious organisms without doing a full pelvic examination.

TREATMENT

Home treatment of vaginitis involves the same techniques as prevention (see Prevention, below).

A physician's treatment of vaginitis or vaginal discharge depends upon its cause and the age of the affected girl.

Prepubertal Girls

- Irritation of the vulva: removal of irritants, followed by sitz baths (in plain, warm water) 2 to 3 times per day for 10 minutes each time. (In cases of severe irritation of the vulva, pads soaked in witch hazel may be recommended as a temporary replacement for toilet paper.)
- Persistent vaginitis: application of an antibacterial cream or administration of oral antibiotics. (Occasionally, an estrogen-containing cream is prescribed in order to thicken the vaginal walls to

make the vagina more resistant to infection.)

- Specific bacterial infections such as strep: antibiotics.
- Yeast infection: application of an ointment or cream. (If the infection persists, medicated vaginal suppositories may be prescribed.)
- *Trichomonas* infections: administration of oral medications.
- Foreign object in the vagina: removal of the object. (If a physician suspects sexual abuse, he or she will try to speak to the girl alone and ask her who put the object in her vagina. If a girl older than 3 has a habit of putting objects in her vagina, professional counseling might be advised.)

Adolescent Girls

- Yeast infection: use of vaginal suppositories (or creams) containing antifungal medication.
- *Trichomonas* infections: use of an oral antibiotic. (A sexually active adolescent and her partner must avoid intercourse until both of them have been treated. If her infected partner is not treated, her infection may recur.)
- *Gardnerella* infection: use of oral antibiotics. (A sexual partner who is the source of infection may also need to be treated to prevent recurrence of the girl's infection.)
- Herpes: in first cases, an antiviral drug; in recurrent cases, oral medication, Burow's solution, or anesthetic ointments, depending on the recommendation of the physician. (Research is being done on new therapies with antiviral drugs; See *genital herpes.)*
- Foreign object (such as a tampon): removal.
- Irritation of the vulva: use of hydrocortisone cream.
- Allergic vulvovaginitis: removal of the source of allergy.
- Persistent vaginal discharge due to inflammation of the cervix: referral to a gynecologist (specialist in diseases of the female reproductive system) for further treatment.

PREVENTION

Every girl should be taught about her body's structure and functions and instructed in proper hygiene methods. Each age group needs to have certain areas emphasized; young girls need reminders about wiping methods and handwashing, and older girls need knowledge about sexual activity, normal versus abnormal discharges, changes in vaginal secretions, and the use of sanitary products. Following are basic measures to help prevent vaginitis and vaginal discharge:

For Girls of All Ages

- Practice good hygiene, including daily baths in clear, warm water (no bubble baths). (A physician may recommend that a girl who is susceptible to frequent vulvovaginal infections take baths more than once a day. The vulva should be washed gently with mild, nondeodorant, nonscented soap. After a girl uses the toilet, she should wash her hands thoroughly.)
- Wipe from front to back after a bowel movement.
- Avoid tight, nonabsorbent, synthetic clothing such as all-nylon underpants, tights, panty hose, leotards, and jeans.
- Wear white, all-cotton underpants (or at least nylon underpants with a cotton crotch), changed daily and panty hose with a cotton crotch. (If a girl is particularly vulnerable to infection, she might try wearing socks more often than tights and skirts more often than pants.)
- Be gentle with the delicate tissues of the genital region.
- Use white toilet paper. (Dyes can be irritating and, in some people, can cause allergies.)
- Never use unclean washcloths, towels, or bathing suits belonging to someone else.

Additional Measures for Adolescent Girls

- Be sure to change tampons and sanitary pads frequently and do not wear diaphragms more than 12 hours after intercourse.
- Avoid deodorant tampons and deodorant sanitary pads, which may cause irritation of the vulva and vagina.
- Never use vaginal ("feminine hygiene") sprays.
- Avoid douching, especially more often

than once a week, unless recommended by a physician. (Girls should avoid chemical irritants; if douche is recommended, use vinegar douche: 1 to 2 tablespoons of white vinegar per quart of warm water.)

Adolescent girls who are sexually active should urge their partners to use condoms to help prevent the spread of infections. If either partner may have a sexually transmitted disease, sexual activity should be avoided until treatment has eliminated the infection.

VITILIGO

DESCRIPTION

Vitiligo is a loss of pigment resulting in white patches of skin. This condition may occur anywhere, but commonly affects the eyelids, the hands, and the anal-genital area. If the scalp or brow is affected, the hair on the head may lose its color. People of all ages and colors can acquire vitiligo.

Vitiligo is associated with several diseases, including alopecia areata (spot baldness), a specific *anemia* (B-12 deficiency, or Addison's anemia,) *diabetes,* hyperthyroidism (an overactive thyroid gland; see *thyroid disorders),* and a malfunction of the adrenal gland (see *adrenal disorders).*

Duration and severity of vitiligo vary with each case. Though uncommon, depigmented areas may regain color spontaneously. This may occur even while other areas of the skin are losing pigment. Rarely, a persistent, widespread loss of pigment may occur. Treatment is difficult, and may not be possible on some areas of the body.

CAUSE

The cause of vitiligo is unknown. This condition seems to occur more frequently in some families than in others, but no clear genetic pattern has been identified. The appearance of the depigmented patches occurs often following trauma, but the mechanism is unknown.

SIGNS AND SYMPTOMS

Vitiligo is indicated by white, smooth, patches of skin. These patches vary greatly in size and shape, and may have darkly pigmented borders. Patches can expand in size and merge with other depigmented areas, creating a large, irregularly shaped white patch.

DIAGNOSIS

Diagnosis is based on the presence of smooth, white patches of skin. Laboratory studies, including a skin biopsy (removal and analysis of a small skin tissue sample) to examine the skin for the absence of pigment cells, can also be used to identify vitiligo.

COMPLICATIONS

Skin *cancer* may develop if depigmented areas are repeatedly exposed to the sun.

TREATMENT

In many cases of vitiligo, only cosmetic treatment is needed. Tinted waterproof makeup can mask the depigmented areas. Since depigmented areas do not tan, avoiding exposure to the sun may help reduce the visual difference between the pigmented and nonpigmented areas. Vitiligo patches should be protected with a sunscreen, since they can redden, burn, and become "sun-damaged."

A physician should be consulted if vitiligo is widespread.

PREVENTION

Vitiligo cannot be prevented.

VOMITING

EMERGENCY ACTION

Consult a physician promptly if any of these vomiting conditions exists:

- A child's vomit is red or brown in color. Blood may be present, although it is often difficult to estimate how much. If possible, take a sample of vomit to the physician.
- Vomiting is preceded, accompanied, or followed by steady or recurring *abdominal pain,* lasting longer than 1 hour.
- Vomiting occurs 4 times within 2 hours, possibly leading to *dehydration.* Signs of dehydration include listlessness, sunken eyes (and for an infant, sunken fontanel, the soft spot on top of the head), dry tongue, thirst, rapid pulse, cool, dry, pale skin, and decreased urine production.
- A newborn (under 3 months old) displays especially forceful vomiting,

called <u>projectile vomiting,</u> often a sign of *pyloric stenosis.* Repeated projectile vomiting can lead rapidly to dehydration.

- Vomiting occurs after any head injury or before or after a seizure. The central nervous system (brain, spinal cord, and their protective coverings, the meninges) is highly sensitive, and vomiting is sometimes a danger sign.
- A child has a high fever or headache, experiences painful or labored breathing, or seems unusually sleepy, listless, or confused after vomiting.
- An unconscious or semiconscious child vomits. A child in that condition can inhale vomit into an airway or the lungs and, possibly, choke or suffocate (see discussion of choking in Chapter 10, "Basic First Aid").
- An infant (under 1 year old) vomits at any time. True vomiting is not the same as regurgitating (spitting up). Spitting up usually results from an infant's not being burped after feeding. Swallowed air in the stomach propels food up past the undeveloped muscle located where the baby's esophagus and stomach come together.

DESCRIPTION

Vomiting is common during childhood. It occurs when part or all of the stomach contents are expelled by the vomiting reflex, a series of involuntary muscular contractions of the stomach. Sometimes even the contents of the duodenum, the first section of the small intestine, are forced up into the stomach and vomited. Vomit may contain mucus, bile, or blood, in addition to partially digested food and liquids.

Vomiting usually indicates that the body needs to rid itself of a foreign substance that it cannot tolerate. These substances include products of bacterial and viral infection, poisons, and foods or other substances that produce an allergic reaction or are highly irritating to the lining of the stomach. In situations such as these, vomiting is a natural response to a threat to the body's health.

Vomiting may also indicate an abnormality in the gastrointestinal (GI) tract (esophagus, stomach, and intestines) that interferes with or prevents digestion from proceeding in the stomach or on down through the GI tract. The severity of underlying conditions that cause vomiting can vary from mild to life-threatening.

Any of these signs and symptoms may be associated with an episode of vomiting:

- cold, moist skin
- sweating, especially noticeable on the forehead, upper lip, and back of the neck
- rapid heartbeat
- mild *fever*
- hiccups
- an aching feeling (especially around the ribs after vomiting)
- weakness
- *dizziness*
- sore or scratchy throat (sometimes caused by particularly forceful vomiting)

Coughing may trigger vomiting, especially when a child gags or chokes on mucus brought up by coughing.

Most episodes of vomiting run their course in a day or two without complications and require little treatment other than replacement fluids and emotional reassurance. Vomiting associated with a severe or complicated condition may recur, however, until the underlying cause is identified and treated.

CAUSE

The causes of vomiting originating in the GI tract can be divided into two groups, congenital (present at birth) and acquired.

Congenital GI causes are uncommon, but abnormalities of intestinal structures are capable of producing *intestinal obstruction.* Congenital causes of vomiting include *cystic fibrosis, hiatus hernia and gastroesophageal reflux, tracheoesophageal fistula, pyloric stenosis, Hirschsprung's disease,* duplication (in which an abnormal tube or sac branches out from any point in the intestines), and volvulus (in which any portion of the GI tract may be abnormally placed or twisted).

Acquired GI causes, which can occur throughout life, include inflammation of the GI tract producing *diarrhea,* vomiting, or both; dysentery—in which a bacterial infection, usually more severe than one of viral origin, causes a GI tract infection, producing diarrhea, intense vomiting, or both; *appendicitis;* any inflammation or *ulcer* of the stomach or duodenum; enterocolitis (severe inflammation of a newborn's large intestine); *intussusception; inguinal hernia;* injury to a part of the GI tract or to any organ in the abdominal cavity; pancreatitis (inflammation of the pancreas); severe *food allergy;* severe *malabsorption,* including intolerance to cow's-milk protein or lactose intolerance; *Crohn's disease;* and *ulcerative colitis.* Other causes of vomiting that do not originate in the GI tract include infections of the ear, upper respiratory tract, urinary tract, and blood, as well as *pneumonia.* Emotional factors such as anxiety, fear, and anger, or illnesses with a strong psychological component such as *eating disorders* (including anorexia nervosa and bulimia) can cause vomiting.

Motion sickness, especially car sickness, and excessive consumption of beverages or food, especially alcohol and highly seasoned or salted commercial snacks or fast foods, are also causes. Chemotherapy and, occasionally, radiation therapy for various types of cancer can cause nausea and vomiting. Accidental or deliberate consumption of an overdose of a medication (either prescription or over-the-counter) including, most commonly, aspirin and sleeping pills, often causes vomiting, as does accidental consumption of common household cleaning products (such as liquid dishwashing soap, laundry detergent, liquid bleach, furniture polish, floor wax, and toilet bowl cleaner).

DIAGNOSIS

The cause of most vomiting is obvious and does not require diagnosis. A physician should be consulted if it becomes necessary to identify the underlying cause. Diagnosis is based on a child's medical history, signs and symptoms, and results of a physical examination, with particular attention given to the abdominal area. Urine and blood tests may be performed. If vomiting persists or is accompanied by signs and symptoms of severe illness, a child may require hospitalization for further tests.

COMPLICATIONS

In addition to *dehydration,* persistent or prolonged vomiting can lead to loss of appetite, weight loss, and listlessness. Occasionally, loss of appetite persists even after all other signs and symptoms have disappeared.

TREATMENT

If a child who has vomited once or twice feels sick or weak, wants to stay in bed, has little or no fever, and first refuses food and water but later becomes thirsty, it is sensible to adopt a wait-and-see attitude. If the *fever* rises or vomiting recurs, a physician should be consulted. On the other hand, if an infant vomits, a physician should always be consulted.

It is best to allow a child's stomach to rest for several hours after vomiting. A child who has vomited needs comfort and reassurance during and after vomiting. Younger children may be alarmed by sudden or repeated vomiting; they should not be left alone until they feel better.

Gradual replacement of fluids is necessary to satisfy the body's water, salt, and sugar requirements. However, it is never advisable to force a sick child to drink. In all likelihood a child who is too ill to drink still feels nauseated; any liquid forced down is likely to be vomited immediately. If vomiting begins again, no further liquids should be given.

Fluid replacement should begin with sips of fluids containing sugar every 10 minutes or so, gradually increasing to 2 to 3 ounces every hour. Several commercially prepared electrolyte solutions (which include carefully proportioned body salts) are available for this purpose, or sugar water can be made easily by mixing 2½ tablespoons of sugar in a quart of water. For children older than 6 years, the following fluids or fluid substitutes can be given instead:

- Fruit-flavored syrup drinks (diluted with extra water for infants)
- fruit-flavored gelatin water, made by adding 1 small package of dry gelatin to 1 quart of water (Gelatin containing red food coloring may stain diarrheal stool and be mistaken for blood.)
- flat carbonated beverages, particularly ginger ale (shaken or left at room temperature for at least one half hour to allow most gas to escape to avoid further vomiting or stomachache)
- ice pops (made with fruit juice or fruit-flavored drinks)
- crushed ice chips

For children who are reluctant or unwilling to drink, fruit-flavored hard candy or lollipops may be helpful. Sugar stimulates thirst, which often causes a child to drink. (Children younger than 4 years should not be given hard candies because they may cause choking.)

Commercially prepared clear broth, consommé, and bouillon should be avoided because they contain too much salt.

It is wise to limit a child to clear liquids for about 6 hours. After that, a hungry child who is able to tolerate fluids can be given plain crackers. After about 8 hours, soft, easy-to-digest foods can be added, including rice cereal, pureed chicken, milk-free mashed potatoes, or sweet potatoes. Feedings should be small, and the child should be encouraged, but not forced, to drink liquids. (Pedialyte or Rehydralyte, available at drug stores, can be given to children, especially infants, who will not accept the fluids mentioned above.) Fruit juices should be given only in very small amounts. If the child continues to improve, a normal, well-balanced diet can be resumed gradually over the next 1 to 3 days.

When a child resumes drinking milk, it is often best to start with skim milk diluted with water, then switch to plain skim milk. A child should not be given whole milk until all signs and symptoms of illness have disappeared. A child should not be given fresh vegetables and fruits (except bananas) until recovery is complete.

If the specific cause of vomiting is identified, a physician may need to prescribe medication or other appropriate treatment. Antibiotics are prescribed for vomiting only if the underlying cause is a bacterial infection. Antivomiting medications (pills or suppositories) are not usually helpful and should not be given unless prescribed by a child's physician.

PREVENTION

With the exception of vomiting caused by overeating, *food poisoning, food allergy,* or *motion sickness,* vomiting cannot be prevented.

Children who vomit after repeated eating binges should see a physician if a parent's recommendations do not help (see *eating disorders*).

WARTS

DESCRIPTION AND COMPLICATIONS

A wart is an abnormal growth of skin cells, the visible result of a viral infection. Warts often appear at the site of an injury because broken skin is highly susceptible to infection. Warts are harmless but can be unsightly and cause some discomfort. Most frequently they arise on the hands and the feet, but they may also appear on the face and neck and in the genital area.

Viral warts are most common in children and adolescents but may appear in adults. If they bleed, become infected, or are annoying, they may be removed, they may also be removed for cosmetic reasons.

In most cases viral warts disappear in 2 to 3 years without medical treatment; nearly all infected children lose untreated warts within 10 years. With treatment, warts generally disappear in a few weeks to a few months. Warts are occasionally resistant to therapy and can recur even after thorough treatment.

Four varieties of warts are found in children: plantar, occurring on the soles of the feet; juvenile or plane, most often arising on the face; common, the most widespread variety; and genital, most frequently found on sexually active adolescents.

Plantar warts are usually small but may spread to one quarter inch or more in diameter. They often become surrounded by a horny callus with a mosaiclike appearance. Plantar warts are usually inbedded in the foot, making walking painful and treatment difficult. Sometimes, however, they exhibit no symptoms.

Plane warts are flat and flesh-colored. Occurring in great numbers, these warts are very small, about one sixteenth to one quarter of an inch in diameter. They tend to grow together into a large, flat mass.

Common warts are larger than the plane variety, ranging in size from one eighth inch to one inch across. Surface texture is rough and color varies from flesh tone to dirty yellow to dark brown. These warts may occur anywhere, particularly in areas where the surface of the skin is constantly being injured, such as around bitten fingernails and cuticles. Common warts can number in the hundreds and may last years.

Genital warts arise on skin or mucous membranes of the genital and rectal areas. Ranging in frequency from small and isolated to large masses of hundreds, these warts are quite contagious.

CAUSE

Warts are caused by at least 19 varieties of virus. The infection is passed by direct contact with the virus or by scratching the warts and then touching the skin surface. Shaving can spread the virus to other sites. Each time a razor removes the surface layer of a wart, the virus may be transmitted.

Plantar warts are usually contracted by walking barefoot on contaminated surfaces. Genital warts are spread through contact with a specific virus, most often through sexual contact (see *child abuse)*. An infant can contract genital warts at birth through contact with infectious warts in the mother's genital area. If an older child has genital warts, they may be the result of inappropriate sexual contact.

DIAGNOSIS

Warts are usually identified by their appearance. Frequently, however, they may resemble other kinds of lumps. A physician's examination may be needed to make a positive identification.

TREATMENT

Treatment is not generally recommended unless a wart is bothersome.

In areas of continued injury (nail biting, shaving), warts may recur even with constant treatment. Two methods are most effective. Painting the wart with salicylic-lactic acid solution once a day for 3 months or longer causes the wart to fall off. Freezing with liquid nitrogen (performed by a physician) causes the wart to fall off shortly after treatment. Other treatments include drying the tissue with an electrical current and performing surgery with a laser, both of which may cause scarring and recurrence.

A child with anal or genital warts should be seen by a physician. The possibility that inappropriate sexual contact has occurred should be considered. Treatment once a week for several weeks may be required. It is usually necessary for a physician rather than the parents to apply medication. Freezing with liquid nitrogen, chemical removal, use of a laser, or electrodessication may be effective. All of these therapies may cause some scarring.

Unless causing problems, plantar warts are best left untreated. These warts often occur on areas of the foot under pressure when walking, and a child should wear shoes that are roomy and comfortable.

If a plantar wart hinders a child's movement, treatment is advisable. A solution of salicylic acid and lactic acid causes the wart to shrink or disappear. Surgery and other forms of therapy may be required in more complicated cases.

PREVENTION

Warts are impossible to prevent.

WEIGHT PROBLEMS

DESCRIPTION AND CAUSE

Body fat constitutes 10 to 15 percent of a newborn's body weight, but this proportion varies according to sex, size, and physical activity. Normally, body fat increases with age; females tend to have more body fat than males.

An infant usually gains 1 to 2 pounds a month, usually doubling birthweight by the sixth month of life. By a child's second birthday, weight gain has slowed to one-half pound per month. It slows further between ages 2 and 3, resulting in a total yearly weight increase of 5 to 6 pounds, and between ages 3 and 5, resulting in total yearly gains of 4 to 5 pounds. Rate of weight gain increases after age 6; children gain about 7 pounds per year until age 10 or 12.

When a child's weight, and weight gain, deviate significantly from the normal range for height, a weight problem exists. A weight problem occurs when the intake of calories (furnished by proteins, carbohydrates, and fats) is persistently below or above the body's nutritional requirements. A child becomes underweight when body fat and muscle are reduced and overweight when they are increased.

Underweight

Children are considered underweight when their weight is persistently less than that of 97 percent of healthy children of the same height. This problem often occurs between 9 and 15 months of age, when children are weaned from bottle-feeding or breastfeeding to solid foods. The change in food types and eating habits often results in slowed weight gain, although this is rarely cause for concern. A child eventually regains weight as he or she increases milk intake from the cup and adjusts to solid food and new eating habits. Children may be slightly underweight during rapid growth or illness, but this corrects itself as growth slows or good health returns. Children with long-term illnesses are often slightly underweight.

In some areas of the world, *malnutrition* (the result of an inadequate intake of calories and protein) is the primary cause of prolonged low weight among infants and children. In more developed areas of the world, *failure to thrive* is a relatively common cause of low weight, affecting approximately 1 percent of all children. Failure to thrive is a persistent nutritional disorder in which a child loses or fails to gain weight and subsequently does not grow adequately. It can result from a combination of factors. Fussy infants, for example, may be difficult to feed, and parents may become frustrated and lose patience at feeding time. As a result, an infant may not receive adequate nutrition, and weight loss occurs.

A child may lose weight if the body cannot absorb and retain calories and nutrients. This problem occurs with *malabsorption* (particularly *celiac disease* and *cystic fibrosis*). Childhood weight loss can also occur with disorders that affect growth and development, such as congenital heart disease (see *heart disease, congenital)* kidney problems (see *kidney failure),* and endocrine problems, such as hyperthyroidism (see *thyroid problems).* Medications, such as large doses of vitamin D to prevent *rickets,* may also cause weight loss.

Psychological factors can diminish a child's desire to eat, contributing to or causing weight loss. Anorexia nervosa, an *eating disorder* that most often affects adolescent females, can 'result in severe, self-induced weight loss. Other psychological factors that can contribute to an underweight problem include friendship problems, *stress, depression,* anxiety, grief, and *phobias.*

As a result of weight loss a child may have little or no energy, feel weak and tired, and be dizzy and unable to concentrate. A child's body functions are affected. As a result, a child does not grow or develop adequately. The onset of puberty is often delayed; prolonged low weight may cause sterility.

With timely, effective treatment, underlying causes of weight loss can often be resolved, and a child reaches a normal weight for height.

Overweight

A child who weighs significantly more than average for height may not have a permanent weight problem. It may be a symptom of an endocrine problem, such as hypopituitarism (see *pituitary problems),* Cushing's disease (see *adrenal problems),* or hypothyroidism (see *thyroid problems),* that is correctable with appropriate therapy. Abnormal weight gain may also occur from prolonged muscle inactivity, such as *musuclar dystrophy, cerebral palsy,* paralysis, or long-term bed rest because of illness.

If these underlying conditions are ruled out, and a child's body weight persistently remains 20 percent or more above that considered normal for height, a serious weight problem—obesity—exists. Unfortunately, obesity is frequently a lifelong problem.

Contrary to popular belief, children usually do not become obese because of an endocrine problem or solely by overeating, although overeating is a major contributing factor. Obese children may be born with an increased number of fat cells and an increased ability to store fats. These differences result from a genetic trait passed on by a child's parents, and obesity usually affects other family members. Extra fat cells are present even after an obese child loses weight.

An increased number of fat cells also occurs with several rare disorders, including Prader-Willi syndrome and Pickwickian syndrome. Prader-Willi syndrome is a condition of unknown cause that is marked by an extremely large appetite, short stature, mental retardation, and sexual immaturity. Pickwickian syndrome is a condition, also of unknown cause, that is marked by extreme and deforming obesity, respiratory problems, and general physical debility. Disorders that contribute to obesity include problems of fat metabolism (the conversion, use, and storage of fats and disposal of resulting waste products; see *cholesterol and triglyceride problems)* and of hormonal function—especially of the hypothalamus, a part of the brain involved in regulating appetite as well as rates of hormonal secretion (see *pituitary problems).*

Obesity occasionally develops even when a susceptible child follows a healthy diet suitable to age and development. For the most part, however, a child born with too many fat cells becomes obese from persistent overeating. Many factors can aggravate a child's overeating patterns, including habitual overeating and copying the eating patterns of other family members. In addition, parents often have the misconception that a child must eat large, highly caloric meals to be healthy; children may overeat to please their parents.

Psychological factors, including friendship problems, *depression,* poor self-esteem, and poor self-image may also influence a child's eating patterns. Obesity itself has a serious, often permanent impact on a child's psychological state. These factors may also contribute to overeating in children who are not obese. For some children obesity is both the cause and result of unhappiness. When their peers do not accept them socially because of their weight and appearance, obese children often turn to food for comfort. The more food these children eat, the more obese they become, and their personal and social discomfort increases.

Obese infants are usually large at birth and gain weight very rapidly during their first 6 months of life. By 6 to 8 years of age these children may be quite overweight. They frequently have broad shoulders, chest, and hips; are taller than normal; and have advanced bone development. Obese children are often clumsy at a young age and much less physically active than children of normal weight.

An obese child feels the effects of excess weight in many ways. Respiratory problems are common, as are high blood pressure and heart problems. Frequent stomach upset and bloating can occur, and a child may develop gallstones (hard masses in the gallbladder or a bile duct) and varicose (enlarged) veins. Skin is likely to be flabby and to hang in loose folds that can harbor fungi and yeast; obese children tend to develop more surface infections than other children. Excess weight may damage the actively growing portions of bones, causing bone deformities.

As a result of obesity, a child may develop endocrine problems, including inhibition of growth hormone, impaired metabolism of carbohydrates, and reduced sensitivity to and use of insulin, causing *diabetes.* Premature onset of puberty may occur, especially among females, and menstrual cycles are usually irregular.

Obesity requires lifelong treatment. The success rate has not been heartening: less than 5 percent of treated individuals have reached or maintained a weight ideal for height and age. However, with newer treatment programs and determination on the part of the whole family, a child's chances may improve markedly.

DIAGNOSIS

A weight problem and its cause are diagnosed according to a child's weight for height, amount of body fat, eating habits, medical history of underlying conditions, and family history of weight problems. A physician performs a complete physical examination and usually orders blood and urine tests. Organ function tests and X rays may be needed to determine underlying causes of weight problems.

In order for the most effective treatment to be prescribed, a physician must determine the cause. Overweight children with underlying endocrine disorders usually have height problems as well, whereas obese children usually grow well and have normal body proportions for their age.

TREATMENT

Treatment of underweight children involves providing adequate nutrition and correcting underlying disorders. Parents of a child with *failure to thrive* should consult a physician as to ways to determine when a quiet child is hungry, and how to reduce feeding frustrations. A physician or nutritionist outlines a well-balanced, nutritional diet designed to help the child gain weight and ensure adequate calories and nutrients.

If weight loss is extensive, the child may require hospitalization for specialized medical care. If psychological problems contribute to or cause severe weight loss, a physician may refer the child for counseling to a mental health professional, such as a psychiatrist, a psychologist, or a social worker (see Chapter 3, "Promoting Mental Health").

Once an underlying cause for overweight is excluded, motivation, patience, and determination are constant requirements for successful treatment of obesity. Correction of obesity during childhood requires the development of good eating habits with a significantly reduced caloric intake as well as increased activity to use stored fats. In addition, a child must learn to modify his or her eating behavior.

A physician can recommend an appropriate behavior modification program which includes adopting new eating patterns, becoming aware of the types and quantities of food eaten, and learning to eat more slowly so that the body has time to feel full. If possible, parents should not keep highly caloric foods in the house and should discourage children from frequent snacking. A reward system may give a child incentive to lose weight; it can involve toys, weekly allowances, special television time, or going to special events. Neither drugs nor surgical techniques should be used to control childhood obesity unless closely supervised by a physician with special experience in the problem because they can interfere with growth and development.

With parents, a physician nutritionist works out a suitable diet for an obese child. If parents are also overweight, a physician may suggest that they follow the same diet to set an example for their child. In addition, a child should increase his or her daily physical activity in an effort to use stored fats. If dietary control is successful, a child's weight decreases as growth and development continue, and a child eventually "grows into" his or her weight.

It is important for an obese child to receive support and encouragement from family members and friends during weight reduction attempts. Successful weight loss takes time and determination, and children may become impatient and frustrated when loss is slow.

PREVENTION

Weight problems caused by underlying disorders can be prevented only if the disorders are controllable. Dealing successfully with the psychological and environmental influences that lead to weight problems is an important step in correcting weight loss or gain. Parents can help prevent some weight problems by encouraging a child's good eating habits and moderation of diet and by listening to and sharing contributing problems with their son or daughter.

WHEEZING

EMERGENCY ACTION

A previously healthy child who suddenly begins to wheeze may have inhaled a foreign object. A physician should be consulted immediately. If the child is turning blue or not breathing, attempt the Hiemlich maneuver (p. 138). Do not attempt to dislodge the object; the airway may become completely blocked. Do not slap the child on the back, as this may cause the foreign object to completely block the airway.

DESCRIPTION

Wheezing is a whistling sound made when a child is having difficulty breathing (see *breathing difficulty)*; it is particularly obvious upon exhalation. Wheezing is usually a symptom of airway obstruction, such as *asthma.* Occasionally its cause is an inhaled foreign object or a defect in the development of the lung.

Wheezing caused by asthma can occur at any age. Wheezing from other causes occurs most frequently among younger children; the breathing passages of young children are narrow and a small amount of mucus can occupy a considerable amount of room in the airway. Wheezing comes from the bronchial tubes, in contrast to whooping sounds (characteristic of *whooping cough)* or barking sounds (associated with *croup)*, which originate in the voice box.

Wheezing occasionally indicates serious disease. Wheezing caused by inhalation of foreign objects generally disappears when the cause is eliminated. Many children with asthma seem to outgrow wheezing, which may occur less frequently or less severely as the child grows and breathing passages widen.

CAUSE

Wheezing can be caused by anything that blocks or narrows the breathing passages from the lower trachea (windpipe) to the small and large bronchial tubes. The most common cause of wheezing is *asthma,* in which muscles of the bronchial tubes contract, causing narrowing. Allergies to substances such as pollen, certain foods, insect venom, and animal dander can trigger attacks of wheezing. In very rare cases a child allergic to aspirin or other medicines begins to wheeze after taking the medication.

Respiratory tract infections such as *colds, bronchiolitis, tuberculosis,* and *pneumonia* are common causes of isolated episodes of wheezing. Rarely, wheezing is caused by the inhalation of foreign objects (such as small toys), food, or vomitus. Birth defects of the respiratory tract or cardiovascular system (see *heart disease, congenital; heart failure, congestive)* occasionally cause wheezing. *Cystic fibrosis* and severe combined immune deficiencies (see *immune disorders)* are often associated with recurrent attacks of wheezing.

DIAGNOSIS

Wheezing is obvious, but the cause should be identified by a physician. Examination of the child's throat and lungs may be supplemented by chest X rays and breathing tests. A physician will want information on any history of allergies in the family.

COMPLICATIONS

In children who have *asthma,* wheezing may lead to severe respiratory distress.

TREATMENT

A child who is wheezing for the first time, or who has a fever along with wheezing, should always be seen by a physician. A physician may prescribe medication to widen the breathing passages. Some of these medications can be taken by inhalation and provide rapid improvement. A child who is wheezing should be given clear, room-temperature fluids. Sleeping in a room with a cool-mist vaporizer may help some children.

A child with severe *breathing difficulty* may require several days of hospitalization to receive intravenous fluids, medications, and humidified oxygen, and to be observed by medical personnel.

Wheezing caused by infection may not disappear until the infection is cured. Allergy-induced wheezing may require special medication to alleviate spasms of the bronchial tubes. In the case of *asthma* due to allergic substances, treatment may involve efforts to remove the irritant or to build up the child's tolerance of the irritant through desensitization therapy (injections of increasing amounts of irritants over a long period of time).

PREVENTION

As a general preventive measure, a child who is susceptible to wheezing should sleep in a dust-free room, especially during wintertime in cold, dry climates. Vulnerable children should be protected from obvious allergens or irritants and should avoid tobacco smoke, noxious fumes (such as from wet paint or disinfectants), ice-cold drinks (which may constrict the bronchial tubes), and rapid changes in temperature and humidity.

WHOOPING COUGH

EMERGENCY ACTION

If an infant or young child suddenly cannot breathe or has great difficulty breathing because of increasing congestion or persistent spasms of coughing, give artificial respiration (p. 124). After making certain that uninterrupted breathing has been restored, take the child at once to a hospital emergency room for examination and treatment.

DESCRIPTION

Whooping cough is a severe infection of the respiratory tract (nose, throat, windpipe, and lungs) that causes serious, prolonged breathing problems. Whooping cough gets its name from the loud whooping sound heard after a series of uncontrollable coughs. The person who is ill tries to take a full breath quickly after a coughing spasm and the whooping sound results.

Whooping cough is one of the most contagious diseases. The medical term for whooping cough is pertussis, which means "intensive cough." Infants and young children are most likely to develop whooping cough, and they run the highest risk of experiencing its disabling effects. Although whooping cough vaccine has greatly reduced the incidence of the disease in the United States, several thousand cases of whooping cough are reported annually. Whooping cough sometimes occurs in a milder form among older adolescents and young adults as their childhood immunity acquired through vaccination begins to wear off.

Because of its persistence, whooping cough weakens those children who contract the disease. Whooping cough, which an unimmunized child can develop within 5 to 10 days of exposure, may result in illness for as long as 2 months, especially among the very young. Children under 5 years old generally become more severely ill with whooping cough than do older ones. Moderate cases of the disease produce less severe symptoms, and the child may recover in less than 2 weeks.

CAUSE

Whooping cough is caused by infection with a particular bacterium. The bacteria are carried in mucus droplets produced when an infected person coughs or sneezes.

Inhaling these droplets is the typical way that the disease is contracted by individuals who are not immunized or who possess only partial immunity.

SIGNS AND SYMPTOMS

The typical case of whooping cough goes through 3 stages: inflammation, spasm, and recuperation.

During the inflammation stage (lasting 1 to 2 weeks), symptoms of nose and throat infection are obvious: sneezing and runny nose; sore throat; red, watery eyes; a mild *cough;* and mild *fever*—101° F (38.3° C) or less. Infants may develop thick mucus in their noses and throats, which makes eating and drinking difficult.

During the spasm stage (the next 2 to 4 weeks), the cough becomes dramatically worse, coming in spasms of several consecutive explosive coughs (as many as 5 to 10) in a single expiration of breath. Each spasm is usually followed by a sudden, massive whoop of inhaled air. The child's face typically reddens or even turns purple because of the effort and strain involved in both the cough out and the whoop back in. Painful, tiring, and frightening for a child, these symptoms always cause concern for members of the family as well.

The effort of coughing often produces bulging, watery eyes, a protruding tongue, enlarged veins in the neck, and increased salivation. *Vomiting* is common as a result of coughing; the coughing and vomiting can leave a child dazed and listless. Those children who experience prolonged coughing and vomiting often lose weight.

Attacks of coughing can be triggered by many actions: sneezing, physical exertion, or simply eating or drinking. It is important to remember that not all whooping cough victims whoop after they cough; this is particularly true of those less than 1 year old and those whose disease is mild. Between coughing spasms and after recovering from vomiting, most children appear only mildly ill. Fever may continue but does not usually become a major concern or cause of discomfort.

During the recuperation stage (the final 1 to 2 weeks), recovery is steady. Coughing episodes subside in number and intensity, but dry coughing may be a problem for several months afterward. Fits of coughing may return whenever the child comes down with infections of the nose and throat. Recovery of full strength and weight may take several months.

DIAGNOSIS

A physician diagnoses the disease by listening to the characteristic cough and whoop. Cultures of nose and throat taken during the inflammation stage can identify the bacteria and make earlier treatment possible. X-ray films of the lungs may be helpful in identifying lung complications.

COMPLICATIONS

Pneumonia is the major and most frequent complication of whooping cough. It often occurs because a child's resistance to infection is drastically lowered. Long-term lung problems may develop because of damage caused by whooping cough.

Ear infections (see *earache and ear infections*) often affect children who have whooping cough. Other complications include development of sores on the tongue; tiny eye hemorrhages; diaphragmatic hernia and inguinal hernia (see *hernia, diaphragmatic; hernia, inguinal and umbilical*), weakening of the wall of the rectum; *dehydration;* nutritional problems; and temporary growth failure because of feeding difficulties. If the brain is deprived of oxygen, the child may have a convulsion (see *seizures*).

TREATMENT

Severely ill infants and older children often require hospitalization for diagnosis and care. Infants in the inflammation stage may suddenly require emergency care if a thick mucus discharge blocks normal breathing. Older children with mild to moderate symptoms may be able to receive adequate care at home throughout the course of the disease.

At home, a child should be kept comfortable and as relaxed as possible in order to try to avoid coughing fits. Keeping an older child occupied may be a challenge, because someone who does not have a high *fever* may try to do too much. Attention to adequate nutrition is important, especially when *vomiting* is a problem. During the long course of the illness, children need continual encouragement and reassurance.

An antibiotic given very early in the illness to shorten the period of contagiousness may block further progress of whooping cough. Infants and young children suffering from whooping cough may require suctioning to clear the nose and airways in the lungs in addition to oxygen and, rarely, ventilation to assist their breathing.

Hospitalization may be necessary if an infant or child develops *pneumonia*. Although whooping cough is not often fatal any longer, severe, even life-threatening, illness can occur if pneumonia develops.

PREVENTION

Immunity to whooping cough can be acquired by a series of three inoculations, usually given during infancy, at 2, 4, and 6 months of age, as part of a series called DPT (diphtheria, pertussis, tetanus). The immunity should be reinforced with another injection at 15 months and again when the child enters kindergarten or first grade (see immunization chart, p. 96).

Immunity is neither permanent nor complete. As long as the vaccine remains effective in the body, however, it greatly reduces the chances of contracting whooping cough. If an immunized child contracts the disease, a milder form of illness occurs.

Because immunity is temporary, whooping cough can strike adolescents or adults who mistakenly consider themselves immune on the basis of childhood vaccination. For these people the illness generally is mild and difficult to distinguish from a severe viral upper respiratory infection such as a bad cold. Ill adults, however, can infect nonimmunized children, who may in turn develop full-blown whooping cough.

A variety of reactions to the pertussis portion of the DPT can occur. They include soreness, redness, and swelling in the area of the injection; fever lasting 24 to 48 hours; high-pitched screaming and persistent crying; collapse or shocklike episodes (turning blue or white); excessive sleepiness; and convulsions (with or without fever). It should be remembered that severe reactions are rare.

Most children experience either no reaction or a mild one, such as slight soreness and redness around the point of injection and a low-grade fever (99° to 101° F; 37.2° C). If a child experiences a more severe reaction, the physician should be notified immediately. An infant who has experienced a febrile *seizure* or any other type of seizure or who has a disorder of the central nervous system (brain, spinal cord, and their protective covering, the meninges), may run a higher risk of having an adverse reaction to the pertussis portion of the DPT inoculation. A physician should be consulted about the advisability of this particular immunization for such a child.

In Japan and in some European countries, when pertussis immunization for children was suspended, the incidence of the disease rose, causing considerable illness among children and even death. When weighing the risk of an adverse reaction to the pertussis immunization against allowing children to go unprotected against the disease, most United States pediatric health experts strongly advocate giving the pertussis immunization. Research continues on producing an improved pertussis vaccine, one less likely to cause adverse reactions.

WILMS' TUMOR

DESCRIPTION

Wilms' tumor, a potentially life-threatening disease of the kidney, is the most common abdominal *cancer* affecting children.

Wilms' tumors, abnormal growths that form solid masses in the kidney, grow rapidly, often causing the entire abdomen to become swollen. If not treated promptly, Wilms' tumor can destroy the entire kidney and metastasize (spread) to other parts of the body, such as the lungs, liver, or bone.

Wilms' tumor can affect either kidney, and approximately 10 percent of children with Wilms' develop the disease in both kidneys. It is sometimes possible to restore normal kidney function with only one healthy part of a single kidney. If both kidneys must be removed, a kidney transplantation or the use of an artificial kidney are life-sustaining alternatives.

Wilms' tumor appears most often when children are between 1 and 5 years of age but can occur from infancy to 15 years of age. More children contract the disease when they are 3 years old than at any other age.

Wilms' tumor is associated with a number of developmental abnormalities, including abnormal development of the genitals or urinary tract, enlargement of one part of the body, or the absence of the iris (the colored portion) of one or both eyes.

Even though Wilms' tumor is the sixth

most common kind of cancer among children, only approximately 450 cases are reported each year in the United States. If detected early, the disease can be treated successfully.

CAUSE

The cause of Wilms' tumor is unknown. Research continues on whether an inherited tendency to develop the disease exists in the families of Wilms' tumor patients (see *genetic disorders*).

SIGNS AND SYMPTOMS

A swollen or bloated abdomen is the most common sign of Wilms' tumor. Occasionally Wilms' tumor may cause acute *abdominal pain*. Approximately 1 of every 4 children suffering from Wilms' tumor shows microscopic *blood in the urine*. Occasionally children with Wilms' tumor have *hypertension* (high blood pressure).

Wilms' tumor may be accompanied by low-grade *fever* (99.4° to 101° F; 37.9° to 38.3 C), fatigue, loss of weight, and *anemia*.

DIAGNOSIS

Wilms' tumor is diagnosed by a physician, who examines the child and takes a medical history. Specialized tests are performed in a hospital to confirm the presence of a tumor in the kidney. A CT (computed tomography) scan may also be performed in order to obtain a highly detailed picture of cross sections of the kidney(s). Ultrasound can provide detailed images of the kidney. If a CT scan is not available, a kidney X ray, called an IVP (intravenous pyelogram), is performed. An IVP involves injecting dye into a vein to reveal the internal structure of a kidney. Because a kidney tumor may spread, chest and bone X rays and other tests may also be performed.

COMPLICATIONS

If cancer has spread, tumors may develop in lungs, liver, and bones.

TREATMENT

Wilms' tumor is one of approximately 20 cancers for which a threefold treatment program—surgery, radiation therapy, and chemotherapy—is used (see *cancer*).

Surgery is designed to remove the entire diseased kidney and any other tissue possibly affected by the tumor. Radiation is given to prevent recurrence of cancer. For Wilms'

tumor, radiation is used if the tumor extends beyond the kidney, if the tumor is ruptured during surgical removal, or if the tumor appears especially expansive when examined under a microscope after removal.

Radiation produces several side effects, such as temporary inflammation of a healthy kidney. Over time, radiation can affect growth and development of the spinal column among some children, especially younger ones whose bone growth is not complete. Radiation can slow the growth of any bone exposed to it and produce progressive curvature of the spine *(scoliosis)* later in childhood or adolescence.

Chemotherapy consists of use of anticancer drugs to destroy any remaining cancer cells following surgery and radiation therapy.

Success in treating Wilms' tumor is excellent. Many individuals go on to lead normal or near-normal lives, limited only by the precautions anyone with a single kidney would take. Approximately 4 out of every 5 children with Wilms' tumor recover completely after treatment.

PREVENTION

Wilms' tumor cannot be prevented.

WRYNECK, NECK PAIN

EMERGENCY ACTION

If a child suffering from a stiff neck seems listless or unusually sleepy, is feverish, or begins to vomit, seek medical attention promptly. These signs and symptoms can indicate the beginning of *meningitis* or *encephalitis*, severe inflammations of the central nervous system (brain, spinal cord, and their protective covering, the meninges).

DESCRIPTION

Wryneck, or torticollis (often called "stiff neck"), is a painful condition that causes a child's head to tilt or tip to one side. It is difficult or impossible to straighten the neck for more than a few seconds at a time because of the pain.

Congenital (present at birth) or neonatal wryneck affects some newborns. Physicians do not agree about whether this condition occurs during development of the fetus or very early in life. The outcome, whatever its origin, results in a shortened or contracted muscle in the side of the child's neck, which pulls the head to one side. In some cases the condition may not be obvious to a parent until the child is 3 or 4 years old and the neck has grown and lengthened considerably. For reasons that are not entirely clear, the condition occurs on the right side of the neck in 3 out of 4 cases. Wryneck is sometimes associated with a hip joint defect (see *dislocation of the hip, congenital),* resulting in difficult or delayed walking, or walking with a limp.

Congenital wryneck is occasionally associated with tenderness on one side of the neck. The head tilts down toward the sore side and the chin rotates out toward the opposite side, giving the child's head a lopsided appearance. Congenital wryneck is usually marked by a small knotty mass of scar tissue on the affected side.

If congenital wryneck is not treated by the time a child is about 10 years old, the child's face begins to look lopsided. The affected side becomes shorter than the opposite side, where facial muscles, under constant pressure, are stretched and elongated. The neck muscle may be permanently impaired, and progressive curvature of the neck can develop, with decreased turning ability. Given correct, prompt treatment (involving physical therapy), however, most forms of congenital or neonatal wryneck can be corrected, leaving little or no sign of the problem.

Other forms of wryneck and neck pain may develop during childhood and adolescence. Children may experience temporary neck stiffness and pain, for example, when suffering from common viral illnesses such as *colds, measles,* or *chicken pox.*

CAUSE

Congenital or neonatal wryneck is believed by some physicians to be caused by an injury at birth, resulting from difficult deliveries. These include a breech delivery (a fetus is so positioned in the mother's uterus that delivery occurs head last); a forceps delivery (the obstetrician uses instruments to assist a baby's passage through the birth canal); or a cesarean section (surgical delivery). Other physicians believe that wryneck is a prenatal defect of development.

When wryneck develops without warning among older children, it may be the result of muscle inflammation caused by disease, an injury to a spinal disk or vertebra (frequently sustained in an automobile or contact-sports accident), or very rarely, a spinal cord tumor (see *neuroblastoma).* Inflammation most often occurs when the lymph nodes (small lumps of special infection-fighting tissue) in the neck become swollen because of an infection (see *swollen glands).* Less often, inflammation occurs because of diseases such as *arthritis* and *tuberculosis.* Rarely, wryneck develops when a young child tries continually to compensate for strabismus (crossed eyes) by tilting the head to one side.

DIAGNOSIS

Diagnosis of the underlying cause of wryneck is made by a physician, who carefully examines the child's head and neck, as well as other areas of the body. Shortening of the neck muscle can almost always be identified by such external examination, especially because of the small knotted mass in the affected muscle. If the cause is not shortening of the neck muscle, X ray films may be needed to identify the underlying problem.

COMPLICATIONS

Occasionally, wryneck causes abnormal bone formation in the section of the spine located at the neck.

TREATMENT

Most children who suffer from wryneck caused by an injury around the time of birth can be treated successfully with a series of muscle-stretching exercises. Parents can gently bend the child's head to one side so that the ear opposite the affected side touches the infant's shoulder; they can also rotate the head toward the affected side. If these exercises are done twice daily with the child lying faceup, gradual improvement in flexibility may begin. At least 90 percent of children who suffer from congenital or neonatal wryneck recover without surgery. However, if a child reaches the age of 6 to 9 months without showing significant improvement, surgery may be necessary.

Wryneck brought about by common childhood diseases and swollen glands usually respond to rest, local gentle heat, and a pain-relieving medication. Consult the physician for specific recommendations and read the discussion of nonprescription medications beginning on p. 102. If wryneck is caused by an infection, medication prescribed by a physician usually reduces pain and swelling and restores movement.

If a rare spinal cord tumor is present, wryneck may require several kinds of treatment, including surgery and medication. An injury to a vertebra or spinal disk may require evaluation by an orthopedist. Rest, medication, and/or surgery may be necessary. If visual difficulties seem to be causing a child's head to tilt, an ophthalmologist should be consulted.

PREVENTION

Wryneck cannot be prevented. Neck pain cannot usually be prevented, unless inflammation can be relieved before pain develops.

Index

Lysergic acid diethylamide (LSD), 315–316

Rhabdomyosarcoma, 534
  of bladder, 387, 388
Rheumatic fever, 423, 593–595
  and strep throat, 641
Rheumatoid arthritis, juvenile, 465–468
Rh incompatibility, 240, 463–465, 591–593
Rhinitis, allergic, 161, 405–406
Rickets, 595–596
  and bowed legs, 212, 213
Rickettsiae, 598
Ringworm, 596–598
  and hair loss, 399
Rocking, 40, 413
Rocky Mountain spotted fever, 589
Roseola, 599–600
Roundworm, 556
Rubella, 95, 96, 388–391
  maternal, and blindness, 200
Rumination, 326–331
Runner's knee, 477

S Safety precautions
  in automobiles, 66–71
  for bathing children, 18, 21, 61
  bicycle safety, 71–72
  childproofing, 59–61, 228, 253, 372
  for eating, 253
  face and jaw protection, 37, 344, 682, 684
  fire safety, 62–66, 227–228
  fireworks, 76
  for food preparation and storage, 366, 367, 368
  furniture safety, 60, 74
  guns, 76
  ice-skating and sledding, 75
  and infant care, 18, 20
  kidnapping prevention, 78–79
  and lead poisoning, 486
  for medications, 60, 62, 103–104
  pet safety, 76–77
  poison prevention, 61–62
  street safety, 73
  toy safety, 73–74
  tricycle safety, 71
  water safety, 74–75
St. Vitus' dance, 594
Salmonella infections, 367–368, 557
Sanitary pads, 25, 707
Sarcoma, 210–212, 228
Scabies, 600–601
Scarlet fever, 601–602
  and strep throat, 641
Schizophrenia, 602–606
School. See Education
School-age children
  checkups for, 92
  development of, 7, 12
  and exercise, 37
  nutrition in, 33
  sleep patterns in, 36
School phobia, 559, 640
  and learning problems, 490
School screenings, 94–95
Scoliosis, 606–609
  and heart defects, 422
  and muscular dystrophy, 530, 532
Scrotum, disorders of, 609–612
Seat belts, 70

Seborrheic dermatitis, 612–613
  and hypothyroidism, 673
"Security" blankets, 643
Sedatives, 310–311
Seizures, 613–618
  and brain tumors, 214
  care during, 613–614
  and DPT vaccine, 95, 718
  due to fever, 355, 359, 599
  first aid for, 139
  in hypoglycemia, 450, 452
  and lead encephalopathy, 484
Self-esteem and self-image
  in adolescents, 15
  and depression, 283
  and learning problems, 490
  and mental retardation, 521
  promotion of positive, 48–49
  in school-age children, 7, 93
  and stress management, 643–644
  and weight problems, 714
Separation anxiety, 5, 35, 559
Septal defects, 419
Septicemia, 207
Severe combined immunodeficiency disease, 453, 455, 501
Sex education, 39–45
  and genital herpes, 387
  and gonorrhea, 394
  for mentally retarded children, 521
Sexual abuse, 248
  and genital warts, 712
  and gonococcal infection, 393
  and vaginal bleeding, 704
Sexual development
  in adolescence, 13–16
  reproductive systems, 39
Sexually explicit "entertainment," 57
Sexually transmitted diseases, 41–43, 708
  AIDS, 42, 43, 158–160
  chlamydial infection, 251–252
  genital herpes, 42, 384–391, 707
  gonorrhea, 42, 200, 391–394, 705
  syphilis, 42, 658–661
Shellfish, poisoning due to, 368–369
Shingles, 245
Shock, 144, 618–620
  and asphyxia, 179
  and dehydration, 279
  and heat stroke, 339
  and hypothermia, 341
  and ulcers, 694
Shoes, fitting of, 22
Short-bowel syndrome, 295
Shortness of breath. See Breathing difficulty or failure
Short stature, 425, 426
  and failure to thrive, 351, 353
  and malnutrition, 508
Shoulder injuries, 175–176
Sickle cell anemia, 150, 484, 620–623
Sickness. See Illness
Singer's nodes, 442
Sinusitis, 258, 623–625
Skin care
  in adolescents, 24–25
  bathing of babies, 17–18
Skin disorders. See also Rashes
  acne, 152–153

broken or dislocated, 682, 683
care of, 21, 22, 682, 684
damage or injury to, 681, 683
decay in, 681, 683
and sweets, 32
developmental disorders of, 662–666
grinding of (bruxism), 222–223
loosened or displaced, 682
problems of, 24, 189–190, 682–684
sealants for, 684
treatment of toothaches, 681–682, 684
Teething, 21, 666–667
Television, 56–57
Temperature, how to take, 105–107, 358–359
Temperature extremes, exposure to, 140, 339–342
Temper tantrums, 7
Testicles. *See also* Undescended testicles
disorders of, 609–612
injury to, 610
self-examination of, 27
tumors in, 387, 388
Tetanus, 95, 96, 143, 667–668
and puncture wounds, 580
Tetrology of Fallot, 420–421
Thalassemia, 167, 668–670
Thermometers, fever, 105–107, 358–359
13q minus syndrome, 589
Thought disorders, in schizophrenia, 603
Threadworm, 552–553
Throat, sore. *See* Sore throat
Thrombocytopenia, 197, 198
Thrush, 396, 670–671
Thumb, flexed, 401
Thumb-sucking, 40, 52, 643, 671–672
Thyroid problems, 672–676
and arrhythmias, 177
and short stature, 425, 426
Ticks and tick-borne disease, 131, 558
babesiosis, 554
and Lyme disease, 499–500
Rocky Mountain spotted fever, 589
Tics, 677–679. *See also* Habits
Tinnitus, 323
Tobacco
abuse of, 308–309
and cancer, 229, 234
and hoarseness, 442
Toddlers
body care of, 21–24
car safety seats for, 68–69
checkups for, 92
development of, 5–6
nutrition in, 31–32
sleep patterns in, 35
Toe, loss of, 142
Toeing-in, 559–560
Toenails
ingrown, 459–460
trimming of, 19
Toilet training, 22–24
and bed-wetting, 191
and encopresis, 337
in schizophrenia, 603
Tonsillitis, 679–681
Toothbrushing, 22. *See also* Teeth, care of
after sweets, 32
Tooth problems. *See* Teeth, problems of

Torsion
of spermatic cord, 611
of testicular appendix, 611–612
Torticollis, 719–721
Tourette's syndrome, 676–679
Toxemia, 573
Toxic erythema of newborn, 585
Toxic shock syndrome, 684–686
and tampon use, 25
Toxins, and food poisoning, 365
Toxoplasmosis, 534, 556–557
Toy safety, 73–74
Tracheoesophageal fistula, 686–687
Traction, 375
Tranquilizers, 310–311
Transplantation
bone marrow, 163–165, 495
kidney, 475–476
liver, 194
Transposition of great arteries, 420–421
Traumatic shock, 619
Treacher Collins syndrome, 347
Trichinosis, 553
Trichomonas infection, 706, 707
Tricycle safety, 71
Triglycerides, elevated, 253–255
Tuberculosis, 95, 687–689
Tuberous sclerosis, 195
Tumors. *See also* Cancer *and specific tumor, e.g.,* Brain tumor; Genitourinary tumors
diagnosis of, 230
types of, 228
Turner's syndrome, 689–690
and short stature, 425
Typhoid fever, 690–692

U Ulcerative colitis, 692–694
Ulcers, 694–697
Umbilical cord, care of in newborns, 19
Umbilical hernia, 434–436, 461
Unconsciousness, 123–124, 260–262
due to apnea or asphyxia, 172–174, 179–180
due to choking, 252, 371
fainting, 354–355
due to head injury, 410, 411
Underweight. *See* Weight problems
Undescended testicles, 697–698
and bladder exstrophy, 699
Uremia, 472
Urethral prolapse, 704
Urethritis, gonococcal, 391, 392
Urinary tract defects, 698–701
and bed-wetting, 191
and chronic kidney failure, 473
obstruction, 698–699, 701
Urinary tract infections, 95, 205, 701–703
and backache, 188
and bladder tumors, 388
and obstruction, 698
Urine, blood in, 205–206, 537
Urticaria, 440–441
Uveitis, 345, 466

V Vaccination. *See* Immunization
Vaginal bleeding, 515, 703–704

Index **739**

Vaginal contraceptive sponge, 44
  and toxic shock syndrome, 684
Vaginal discharge, 704–708
Vaginitis, 25, 704–708
Variocele, 611
Vascular birthmarks, 195, 196
Venereal disease. *See* Sexually transmitted
    diseases
Vertebra, fracture of, 411, 412
Vertical talus, 369, 370
Vertigo, 304
Vesicoureteral reflux, 700
  and urinary tract infection, 701–702
Visceral larval migrans, 556
Vision, testing of, 94
Visual disorders. *See also* Eye disorders
  blindness, 199–201, 342, 343, 390
  color blindness, 259–260
  perception problems, 487
Vitamin deficiencies
  and anemia, 168–169
  and bleeding disorders, 197, 198
  in rickets, 212, 213, 595–596
Vitamins, 28, 29
Vitiligo, 708
Voice disorders, 631, 633
Volvulus, 147, 148
Vomiting, 364, 708–711
  of blood, 203, 204
  care of child with, 105, 708–709
  and dehydration, 279–281
  in eating disorders, 325–326, 329
  fluid replacement after, 710–711
  in food poisoning, 364–365
  in gastroesophageal reflux, 437–438
  induction of, 61, 143
  and intestinal obstruction, 460

  and intussusception, 462
  in motion sickness, 525
  projectile, in pyloric stenosis, 708–709, 582
  in Reye's syndrome, 590–591
  in ulcers, 695, 696
Von Recklinghausen disease, 542–543
Von Willebrand's disease, 197, 198, 199
Vulvovaginitis, 705–708
  gonococcal, 392

W

Walleyes, 269–271
Warts, 711–712
Water safety, 74–75
Weight problems, 32, 33, 712–715
  and eating disorders, 325–332
  and height problems, 425, 426
  and hypertension, 448
Weights, mean, 33
Wheezing, 715–716
  in asthma, 182–183
  in bronchiolitis, 220, 221
Whipworm, 553
Whooping cough, 95, 96, 716–718
Wilms' tumor, 147, 148, 387, 718–719
Wiskott-Aldrich syndrome, 453, 455, 501
"Word salad," 603
Worms. *See* Parasitic infections
Wounds
  cuts and lacerations, 272–274
  puncture, 143, 579–581
Wrist injuries, 175–176
Wryneck, 719–721

Y

Yeast infection, 705, 707

ABOUT THE AUTHORS

Boston Children's Hospital

The Children's Hospital in Boston is the largest pediatric health care institution in the United States and the world's largest pediatric research center. Founded in 1869 as a 20-bed hospital for children, it is now an internationally renowned center for comprehensive pediatric health care. Its 344-bed inpatient clinics and ambulatory services handle more than 200,000 patient visits annually.

Children's offers a wide range of health care services, including medical and surgical services for patients from birth through age 21 (and older in special cases). Approximately one third of the hospital's patients are adolescents and young adults.

Children's is the primary pediatric teaching hospital of the Harvard Medical School, where most of its senior physicians hold faculty appointments. The staff includes more than 500 active physicians and dentists, 400 house staff members and fellows, and a nursing staff of nearly 800. The hospital employs approximately 3,300 people and is served by 700 volunteers.

Children's has pioneered many areas of child health care, including cardiovascular surgery, neonatal intensive care, kidney, liver, and heart transplantation, cystic fibrosis, cerebral palsy, adolescent medicine, child development research, sports medicine, and psychosomatic medicine.

The Health Information Department

Founded in 1981 under the auspices of the Office of Public Affairs, the department's major objective is to provide factual, easy-to-comprehend, and vital information about child health. Other publications include *Parents' Guide to Nutrition.*

Frederick H. Lovejoy, Jr., M.D.

Dr. Lovejoy, Professor of Pediatrics at Harvard Medical School, is Associate Physician-in-Chief at Children's Hospital and formerly Director of the Massachusetts Poison Control System. He is the associate editor of *Pediatrics,* second edition, and the author of over 100 scientific papers on many aspects of pediatric medicine, especially toxicology.